Paper I

Teaching & Research Aptitude

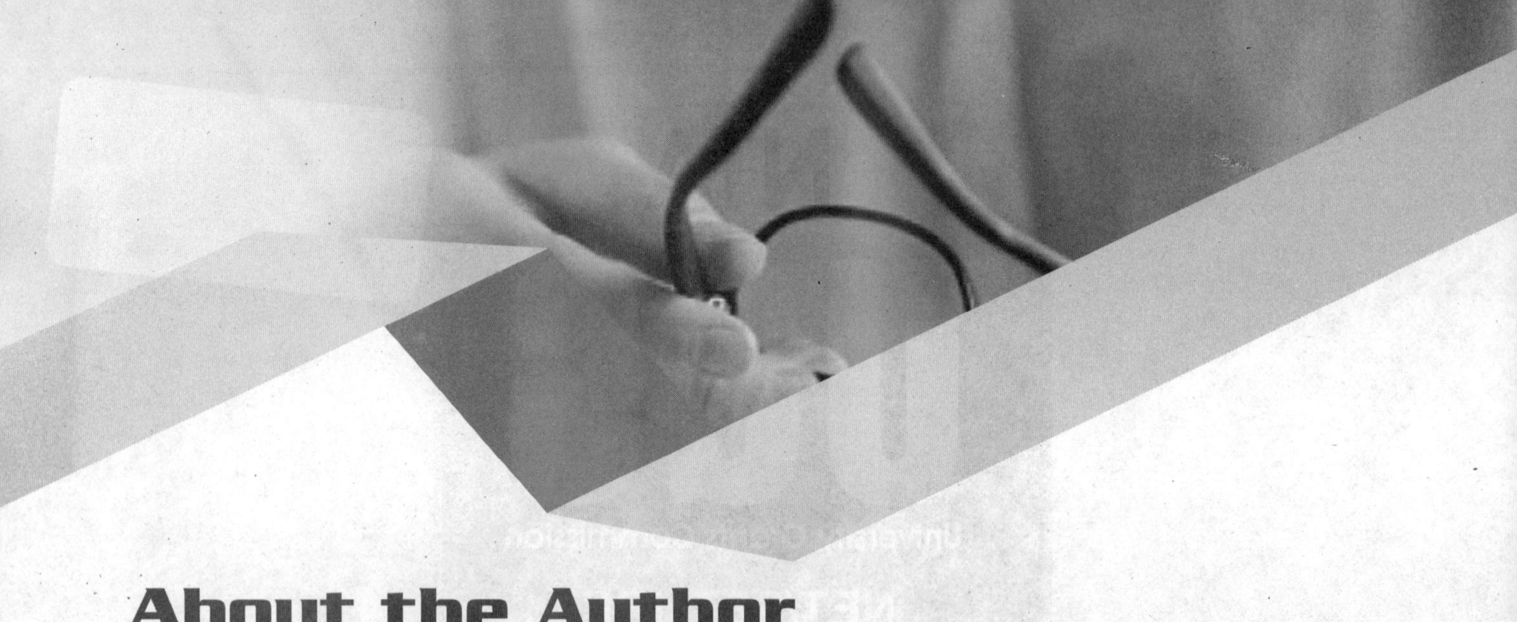

About the Author

Tejinder Singh Sodhi, a post-graduate in Economics, is founder of Prof. Sodhi's Academy of Competitions, at Amritsar. His passion for teaching made him to start the academy in 1987. He, along with his dexterous team has been rendering coaching for various competitive exams like UGC NET, IAS/PCS, Banking, SSC, Defence, Railways and other competitive exams. He switched over to coaching for UGC NET Paper 1 in 1992. Since then he has been imparting coaching to NET aspirants. So far hundreds of NET aspirants have prepared for NET paper 1 under his guidance and have qualified NET and JRF. He is popular as a connoisseur of NET paper 1 among teaching fraternity and NET aspirants. Even while serving as a Punjab Civil Services officer, he did not let his passion for teaching diluted and practised the most professional approach in rendering coaching to NET aspirants through oral lectures and thoroughly prepared sufficient and updated study material covering all the ten sections of NET paper 1 equipped with practice assignments and mock tests.

Besides imparting coaching to NET aspirants at his academy, he is also serving as guest faculty for NET paper 1 at following reputed institutions of higher learning:

1. D.A.V. College, Amritsar.
2. Khalsa College, Amritsar.

He has also been on the panel of guest faculty of following Central and State Government Training Institutes:

1. RICM, Chandigarh.
2. Mahatma Gandhi State Institute of Public Administration (Punjab Govt.), Chandigarh.
3. All India Institute of Co-operative Banking Management and Training, Bangalore.
4. ACSTI, (Punjab Govt.), Jalandhar.

NTA

4th Edition

UGC

University Grants Commission

NET/SET/JRF

Paper I

Teaching & Research Aptitude

T.S. Sodhi

Founder : Prof. Sodhi's Academy of Competitions, Amritsar

G. K. PUBLICATIONS (P) LTD.

Title : NTA-UGC : NET/JRF/SET - Paper 1 - Teaching & Research Aptitude - Guide (4ed)

Language : English

Author's Name : T.S. Sodhi

Typeset & Published by :

Career Launcher Infrastructure (P) Ltd.

A-45, Mohan Cooperative Industrial Area, Near Mohan Estate Metro Station, New Delhi - 110044

Marketed by :

G.K. Publications (P) Ltd.

Plot No. 9A, Sector-27A, Mathura Road, Faridabad, Haryana-121003

ISBN **: 978-93-56811-29-4**

Printer's Details : Printed in India, New Delhi.

For product information :

Visit ***www.gkpublications.com*** or email to ***gkp@gkpublications.com***

Contents

Unit-I Teaching Aptitude

Unit-II Research Aptitude

Unit-III Comprehension

Unit-IV Communication

Unit-V Mathematical Reasoning and Aptitude

Unit-X Higher Education System

Preface

Today teaching is the most secured, lucrative, progressive, creative, philanthropic, status oriented and stable career. All these traits of teaching career are found to be more established in teaching at tertiary level education. An appreciable number of assistant professors, associate professors and professors are enjoying their life while serving in various universities and colleges.

With diversification of higher education in India after independence, various universities and colleges have been established in public and private sector. This has resulted into creation of ample teaching jobs in colleges and universities. The post-independence era also witnessed establishment of University Grants Commission (UGC), an apex body to regulate higher education enabling it to meet international standards from every aspect. Along with. bringing excellence and competitiveness in college and university education through accreditation and other policies, UGC also channelized recruitment of quality faculty by introducing a common National Eligibility Test (NET) for Assistant Professor and Junior Research Fellow (JRF). NET is conducted twice a year (in June and December) by National Testing Agency (NTA) on behalf of UGC. NET Aspirants are to appear in two papers i.e. paper 1 of Teaching and Research Aptitude and paper 2 of that optional subject, which an aspirant has opted in his/her Master's degree.

Syllabus of NET paper 1 has been changed about more than a year ago. It is now more transparent and diversified. Further new topics viz. Traditional, Modern and ICT based Teaching support System, Positivism and Post-positivistic Approach to Research, Fallacies, Indian Logic, Mapping of Data, Data and Governance, Digital initiatives in Higher Education, ICT and Governance, Climate change, MDGs and SDGs, Institutions of Higher learning in Ancient India, Evolution of Higher Learning and Research in Post-independence India, Learning Programmes in India etc. have been added to the old syllabus. Today preparation for NET paper 1 demands equal weightage as for paper 2 due to diversified syllabus. Further marks of paper 1 are also counted in merit. Final merit is outcome of summing up of marks obtained in paper 1 and 2.

About 8 to 10 lakh aspirants appear each time in biannual NET exam to fulfil their ambition to clear Net and JRF. But only 6% find place in the merit list. These 6% are those who have maintained steadiness and consistency in their preparation. At preparation stage an aspirant looks that source of knowledge i.e either coaching or book, which helps them in concept clarity through effective content and confidence building. During my about 30 years of experience in training NET aspirants, I have noticed that NET aspirants prepare for NET paper 1 with a unique psychology. They do not want to run after different sources of knowledge, rather they want a compact source, either coaching or a book, which should comprehensively cover the whole, otherwise diversified, syllabus in an accessible language and effective presentation backed by practice MCQs and mock tests in the same style and language as are asked in NTA NET paper 1. In nutshell they want that they should consult that source which may not be coming up with superfluous and irrelevant content creating confusion or panic in them. They also want sufficient practice with MCQs of that difficulty level which is found in NTA NET paper 1.

Smelling this requirement of aspirants I started rendering coaching to NET aspirants. I have been rendering coaching with full study material along with practice assignments and mock tests. I have been preparing and updating study material with thorough research for about 30 years. Aspirants maintained trust in my coaching and study material and many of them qualified NET and JRF. Now they are serving as assistant/associate professors and research associates in various universities and colleges.

This book is a twin presentation of the study material I have been preparing since long. Utmost care has been taken to meet the latest requirements of NET paper1. Latest syllabus and previous years UGC/CBSE/NTA question papers have been meticulously scanned while writing this book. Priority has been given to lucid presentation in an accessible language. All the topics of theory and mathematical reasoning, logic and data interpretation in the current syllabus have been described from fundamentals to advance level required for preparation of paper 1 with sufficient number of relevant MCQs. There are certain topics of mathematical & logical reasoning, out of which asking questions has become tradition of paper setters. Extra care has been taken to describe such topics in depth in this book. These topics include:

1. Assertion-Reason
2. Coding-Decoding
3. Number Series
4. Letter Series
5. Relationship
6. Square of Opposition
7. Fallacies
8. One or Two Questions From Profit and Loss, SI/CI, Ratio Proportion etc.
9. Data Interpretation - Tables

Similarly in theory section also certain topics are popular with paper setters like

1. Effective Classroom Communication
2. Teaching Methods
3. Evaluation
4. Communication Terminology
5. Mass Communication & Media
6. Types and Methods of Research
7. Sources and Acquisition of Data
8. Sampling
9. ICT Terminology
10. Fundamentals of Computer
11. Natural Hazards
12. Pollutants and Their Impact
13. Energy Resources
14. Flora and Fauna
15. Climate Change
16. Sustainable Development
17. Institutions of Higher Learning in India
18. Growth of Higher Education in India
19. Various Schemes for Development of Higher Education in India

This aspect has been taken care of while writing this book. All the topics of current syllabus have been meticulously covered. Following important but unattended topics have also been exhaustively covered in this book:

1. Assertion-Reason
2. ICT Number System
3. Communication Terminology
4. Research and Statistics Terminology
5. Data and Governance
6. Mass Media and Society
7. Environmental Terminology

It has been observed that questions have been invariably asked from time to time on above topics in paper1.Each topic of the current syllabus along with topics mentioned above has been covered as an independent chapter in this book and each chapter is followed by sufficient number of MCQs. **Some Vital facts** at the end of some chapters of theory will help aspirants in a long way to solve MCQs as these facts are inspired from various questions asked in previous years question papers.

Practice

This book provides practice section at the end of each chapter with the aim to bring aspirants in a closer and stronger alliance with each topic from every aspect. Qualitative rather than quantitative approach has been followed to frame MCQs. In order to present practice section exactly in examination style, this section of MCQs is divided into three sections as follows:

1. General Questions Format
2. Assertion – Reason Format
3. Questions Asked in Previous NET Exams

There is a set of mock tests, to be solved online, available with this book. These tests have been set up strictly on current pattern conducted by NTA. Format, content and language are exactly on the pattern used in the actual tests to give aspirants a feeling as if they are appearing in actual exam. Exposure to these tests will certainly increase confidence among aspirants and I guarantee that solving these tests properly will help aspirants in achieving high acclaims in NET paper 1. They can easily bet on 80+ marks in paper 1 after consulting this book in a thorough manner.

In nutshell I state that this book has not been written like a book but it has been written like a thesis as my vast and long research work is in the background and it took about 1½ years to write this book and the book has been thoroughly updated in relevant sections. This book is a humble presentation from a well-wisher praying to see the readers in NET/JRF merit list. I hope my this research work will serve as a panacea for all NET paper 1 related problems and issues being faced by NET aspirants and its content will do full justice to the spirit behind it.

May this book transform aspirants' ambition into success.

All the best NET aspirants.

T.S. Sodhi
Author

Acknowledgement

It is said that every voluntary effort is the result of motivation. I am indebted to various sources of motivation i.e. my family, friends, students and many others who motivated me to pen this book.

I am thankful to my prime source of inspiration, my better half Harvinder Kaur Sodhi, who took extra care of my health and kept me fit during the course of writing this book. My affectionate thanks to my son Rajdeep and my daughter Gurleen, who gave tangible assistance in various tasks related to writing of this book.

I fully acknowledge all the aspirants who maintained trust in my coaching for NET Paper 1 and qualified NET and JRF and are working as professors or pursuing Ph.D in various colleges and universities. Naming some of them; Dr. Savita Saggar (Professor Khalsa College, Amritsar), Dr. Sawraj Kaur (Professor Khalsa College, Amritsar), Prof. Mandeep Sokhi (HOD, BBK DAV College), Prof. Pooja Chawla (Hindu College, Amritsar), Prof. Punit Dhillon (Khalsa College, Amritsar), Prof. Amanjyoti (Khalsa College, Amritsar), Gurpreet Singh (Research Associate GNDU Amritsar), Prof. Harmeet Kaur (Government College, Amitsar), Prof. Taman Walia (DAV College, Amritsar), Prof. Vikas Behal (DAV College, Amritsar), Mr. Satpal, Mr. Amritpal Singh, Mrs. Richa Saraf, Prof. Harpreet Uppal (SSSS College), Prof. Neha Bhatia (DAV College, Amritsar), Mrs. Shivani Narad, Prof. Ulhas Chopra (DAV College, Amritsar, Dr. Harman Deep Kaur, (Assistant Professor, Khalsa College Amritsar), Niti Anand (BBK DAV College, Amritsar) and many more who had been pursuing me to write this book since long.

I am grateful to Dr. Rajesh Kumar, Principal, DAV College Amritsar, who always supported and motivated me as a guest faculty for NET paper 1 and encouraged me to write this book.

I express my gratitude to my friends and well-wishers; Dr. Sunita H. Khurana, Former Director, ISTM, New Delhi, Dr. Sharanjeet Dhillon, Former Registrar GNDU Amritsar, Prof. H.S. Walia (former Vice – Principal DAV College, Amritsar), Prof. Rajneesh Popi (HOD, Commerce Department, DAV College Amritsar), Dr. Swant Singh (Director, Career Guidance Cell, Khalsa College, Amritsar) for their moral support.

Last but not the least, I am highly grateful to GK Publication and its team for dexterously publishing this book. I also acknowledge the support and guidance provided to me by Meenakshi Ramesh Product Head at GK Publication and my humble thanks to Mr. Sanjay Veer.

T.S. Sodhi
Author

Messages

1. It gives me immense pleasure to congratulate Mr. T.S. Sodhi on publication of his book on "Teaching and Research Aptitude" for NET paper-1. He has been rendering coaching to NET Paper-1 aspirants for the last about 30 years and has many successes to his credit. A good number of lecturers and research associates of this college have also been his students and they cleared NET exam. His wide spread popularity among aspirants of NET paper-1 has established him as a brand ambassador of success in NET. He is rendering services to this college also as guest faculty for NET Paper-1 and other competitions. I have always found him devoted and passionate about teaching. Determination, humility, hard work, commitment, transparency, mastery over the subject and dedication towards teaching are the defining traits of his personality.

   This book is the best possible outcome of his in-depth knowledge and vast experience of the last three decades in the teaching/coaching field. I am sure that his book will provide tangible help to aspirants of NET paper 1 and transform their ambition into success.

   I wish all the best to Mr. T.S. Sodhi for this new attempt as an author.

   Dr. Rajesh Kumar
   Principal
   D.A.V. College, Amritsar

2. It gives me immense pleasure to congratulate Mr. T S Sodhi on publication of his book on 'Teaching and Research Aptitude' for UGC NET paper. I know Mr. Sodhi from our student days. He has always believed in putting in hard work with lots of dedication. This has resulted in him now leading a prominent coaching centre to equip candidates preparing for various job-related examinations.

   This book is outcome of his knowledge and experience that he accumulated over last three decades of active work in the teaching/coaching field. I am sure this book will help aspiring candidates in achieving their goals.

   I wish Mr. T S Sodhi all the best in this new endeavour.

   Dr.Sunita H Khurana
   Former Director
   Institute of Secretariat Training and Management (ISTM),
   (Govt. of India) New Delhi

3. Heartiest congratulations to Mr. T.S. Sodhi on publishing a book "Teaching and Research Aptitude" for NET paper 1. This book will be very useful for students preparing for NET exam for college and university teachers and UGC junior research fellowship. He has been rendering coaching to NET aspirants for the last about three decades. He is very dedicated and passionate about his work. He is very committed and conscientious teacher. Large number of candidates are serving in colleges and universities after successfully clearing NET and JRF under his guidance.

   I have a long association with him since 1975, when we were undergraduate and masters students in GNDU. He is very creative person and then used to help other fellow students in solving their problems.

   This book is another milestone of his illustrious career of three decades. This book is the result of his hard work, vast knowledge and experience of seasoned teaching paper 1 of NET.

   I wish Mr. Sodhi best of luck for his new 'Avtar' as an author.

Prof. (Dr). Sharanjit Singh Dhillon,
Former Registrar
Guru Nanak Dev University (GNDU), Amritsar
Former Professor and Head
Punjab school of Economics GNDU, Amritsar.

4. Congratulations on your upcoming book entitled 'Teaching and Research Aptitude' pertaining to UGC-NET paper-1.It's really a painstaking effort to actualise the dreams of the aspirants who want to enter the domain of teaching /research in the institutions of higher learning.The book is not only a reservoir of information / knowledge but it has also been written in simple,clear and lucid way to make even an average student grasp the various facets of the subject. I am quite sure the book will soon be on the best seller list. Looking forward to your next endeavour in the realm of competitive exams.

Prof. H.S. Walia
Former : *1. Vice Principal and Head, Dept. of Economics DAV College Amritsar*
2. Research Officer , Reserve Bank of India,Bombay.

5. It gives me immense happiness and gratitude that Mr Sodhi is coming out with such a great book on a very important topic in UGC NET examination. It has been a long standing demand of the students that they cannot find a comprehensive book on the subjects covered in paper 1 of the NET exam. The students have been blessed with a gift by this great scholar. Sodhi sir, also serving as guest faculty for NET paper 1 and other competitions in this college, is a very diligent, assiduous and active person who has a passion to teach young minds, frame their careers and dreams under his guidance. Wish him best of luck for his efforts.

Dr Sawant Singh Manto
Director, Career Guidance Cell
Faculty PG Department of English
Incharge Department of Social Sciences
Khalsa College Amritsar

Words From Successful Aspirants

1. Professor Sodhi is indeed a pure and noble soul possessing the traits of a refined and well learned teacher. I owe my success in qualifying UGC exam with JRF to his worthy guidance and teaching. He has released a book on paper 1 of UGC NET which I hope that would definitely prove beneficial for the aspiring students .

Harmeet kaur

Assistant Professor Music vocal

Saroop Rani Govt College Amritsar

2. I am working as Associate professor of Commerce in Khalsa College Amritsar.To be in this profession the basic eligibility is to qualify UGC NET& I am thankful to S .Tejinder Singh Sodhi for the preparation of paper one in this exam. I congradulate Mr Sodhi on publication of his book "Teaching and Research Aptitude "for NET PAPER 1 and wish him all the best.

Dr Sawraj Kaur

Associate Professor of Commerce &Dean Students Welfare

Khalsa College Amritsar

3. Please accept my heart full congratulations and best wishes on the publication of your book on preparation of U.G.C- NET. I still remember when I took classes for the same from you which were instrumental in my success in cracking the Exam. I am sure this book will be of great help to anyone who wishes to pass the U.G.C exam.

Shelly Sharma,

Assistant Professor (Commerce)

Hindu College, Amritsar

4. I am delighted to learn that you are going to publish your book on guiding students towards success in passing the U.G.C Exam. After taking classes from you and clearing the U.G.C Paper, I am sure the book is a destination of your vast Knowledge and experience. It will prove to be invaluable for students. My heartiest congratulations and best wishes for all your endeavours

Pooja Chawla

Assistant professor in commerce

Hindu college, Amritsar

5. I congratulate Mr. Sodhi for his latest venture, which is wonderful outcome of dedication, hard work, and passion to impart quality education. This book is definitely going to be highly significant for the young aspirants, who are focussing towards their career. I am sure that this book will be preparing not only NET aspirants but also those, who are preparing for other competitive exams. Mine had a fruitful experience with his coaching style when I was preparing for UGC-NET. I owe my success to Mr. Sodhi. I wish him good luck and success in his new 'Avtaar.'

Mandeep Kaur Sokhi

Head, Department of Design,
BBK DAV College for Women,
Amritsar

6. I am working as assistant professor (Commérce) in DAV College, Amritsar. As a NET aspirant I got training from Mr. T.S. Sodhi and cracked NET twice. My heartiest congratulations to him on publication of his book 'Teaching and Research Aptitude' for NET aspirants. I wish him all the best. May this book be a lighthouse for NET aspiants.

Vikas Behal,

Assistant Professor (Commerce),
DAV College, Amritsar.

7. Sodhi sir, it is really wonderful to know that your book for NET paper 1 "Teaching and Research Aptitude" is going to be published. It will be a boon for prospective NET aspirants. I hope this book will be as comprehensive as your coaching due to which I could crack NET. All the best sir.

Gurdeep Singh

Research Associate

Department of Political Science.

GNDU, Amritsar

8. Congratulations on writing book for NET paper 1. I wish that my friends aspiring to crack NET should read the book and be successful as I cleared NET after getting coaching from you.

Amritpal Singh

9. Mr. Sodhi, you have really made cracking NET quite easier for the aspirants by writing a book on NET paper 1. I am confident that it is composition of your vast knowledge and experience. I thank you for preparing my daughter Kajole for NET and she cleared JRF. I congratulate you and wish all the best for your book.

Dr. (Mrs.) Paramjit Nanda
Former head & Professor,
Punjab School of Economics,
GNDU Amritsar.

10. Congratulations sir for your upcoming publication... so aspirants if u want to crack net in first attempt m sure this is the best book at its best place as I cleared NET after getting coaching from Sodhi Sir...thank u

Richa. Saraf

11. I feel immensely proud to have got the opportunity to say few words about such a wonderful and dedicated teacher ' S. Tajinder Sodhi' who has enlightened the future of many students with his valuable knowledge , hardwork and moral support. It is my great pride to thank him who has played a great role in making what I am. I congratulate him for his upcoming book " Teaching and Research Aptitude" for NET paper 1, which is going to be very fruitful for the UGC- NET aspirants to crack the exam in flying colours. Good luck for the future!

Dr. Harmandeep Kaur
Assistant Professor
Khalsa College
Amritsar.

12. Sodhi sir,your help and guidance to your students is very much appreciated. I look back to you as a brilliant teacher who is very kind and compassionate. I am always grateful to you for your guidance and support. .I hope that your book on Teaching and Research Aptitude for NET paper 1 would be of immense help to the students preparing for NET. All the best for your endeavour

Dr. Saveeta Saggar
Associate Professor
Department of Economics,
Khalsa College.
Amritsar

Tips To Score 80+ Marks In NET Paper 1

Dos:

1. **In-depth Understanding of Current Syllabus:** Aspirants should be thoroughly clear about all the 10 sections of the current syllabus. It will help the aspirants to choose the appropriate source of preparation.
2. **Choose Appropriate Source of Preparation:** Various books and coaching centres are claiming to be effective sources of preparation. Aspirants should choose that source which is compact and comprehensively covers full syllabus.
3. **Pursue Concept Clarity:** Make sure that basic concepts of every topic, you prepare, are clear to you. This will help you to understand advance level as well as solving concept based questions asked in the exam. Concept clarity results in building confidence.
4. **Prepare a Schedule of Preparation:** Prepare a schedule of preparation to ensure systematic preparation. Follow that schedule steadily and consistently.
5. **Target The Challenging Areas on Priority:** As current syllabus of NET paper is quite versatile, it has been generally observed that topics from Research Aptitude, Mathematical Reasoning, Logical Reasoning, ICT etc are challenging for aspirants. Priority should be given to conquer any such topic through reliable source of preparation.
6. **Go For 'On Track' Preparation:** If you plan to join a coaching institute or consult a book for paper 1, ensure that preparation offered by these sources is 'On Track' i.e. they dexterously cover all the 10 sections of current syllabus along with practice assignments and mock tests.

Don'ts:

1. **Never Underestimate or Overestimate Your Worth:** Your journey of preparation for NET paper 1 may be filled with technical and non-technical challenges. Do not get perturbed due to these challenges and have faith on your worth. Underestimating your worth will result in desperation and overestimating your worth will result in incomplete and inappropriate preparation. If you have made up your mind to prepare for paper 1 in an organised way, then maintain a consistent state of confidence as you can easily come up with flying colours in paper 1 with a uniform state of mind.

2. **Do Not Go For Imbalanced Preparation:** Do not prepare one paper at the cost of other paper. Go for parallel preparation of both paper 1 and paper 2. Prepare your study schedule in this way that there may not be imbalance in preparation approach i.e. fixed study hours should be allotted to study both the papers simultaneously.
3. **Do Not Go For Erratic Preparation:** Always go for ordered and organised preparation even if you are preparing voluntarily. Preparation should be steady and consistent. Follow the schedule of all the 10 sections of the whole syllabus which you have prepared.
4. **Do Not Start Late**: It has been observed that some aspirants start preparation after the closing date of registration and some start even pretty long after that. An ideal duration for the preparation for paper 1 is at least two months before the examination and this preparation should be finished at least one week before the date of actual examination. So that aspirants can revise their preparation.
5. **Do Not Take Paper 1 As Granted:** It has been also observed that aspirants seem to be more concerned about paper 2 and consider paper1 their cup of tea. In the light of diversified and highly technical syllabus, do not take paper 1 lightly. There may be certain areas in the syllabus, about which you may have superficial knowledge due to which you may be confidant to conquer paper 1 without any organised preparation. But mind it paper 1 is now equally decisive in making your merit as paper 2 is.
6. **Do Not Get Perplexed Due To A Large Number of Applicants:** It has been estimated that about 8 to 10 lakh aspirants appear in every attempt of NET, but it should neither baffle you nor affect your preparation in any way. If you are preparing sincerely, then your competition is only with those competitors who have also prepared sincerely like you and number of such candidates is very low and accessible for competition. Actually applicants travel in different orbits of preparation around success. We can see it though following sketch:

Following sketch reveals the percentage distribution of applicants of NET. Each orbit is the orbit of preparation.

Orbit C is the outermost orbit and is the farthest from success. This orbit consists of those aspirants who do not prepare at all and appear in the exam just to see the style of paper and appear just to avail a chance. They are already having this notion in mind that they will take next attempt seriously. They constitute the biggest percent of applicants i.e 60-65%.

Orbit B of preparation contains those applicants who even after preparing are confused and do not have faith on their preparation and worth. They are ailed by examination phobia. This orbit also contain those aspirants who prepare with a casual approach and are least bothered. Percentage of such applicants is 25-30%

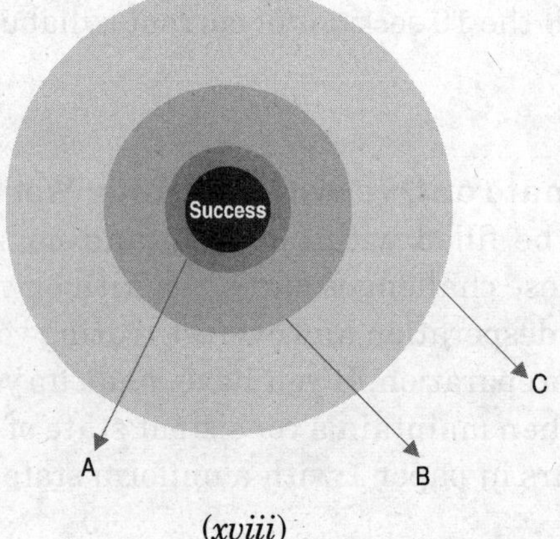

Orbit A consists those 10% aspirants, who prepare sincerely in an organised way and appear with confidence while having faith on their worth and preparation. So actual competition of sincere aspirants is with only 10% of total number of applicants A, which are the closest to success. Qualified candidates belong to orbit A only. So big number of applicants is not an issue. Your aim should be to reach orbit A.

7. **Do Not Ignore Previous Years Question Papers:** Previous years question papers are pathways to crack NET/JRF. Consult previous years question papers thoroughly, solve them as this practice will prevent you to make silly mistakes in the actual exam and boost your confidence. It will also acquaint you with the typical style of questions being asked in the exam and help you in shaping your preparation accordingly.
8. **Do Not Believe in Guesses in Covering Syllabus:** Cover all the sections of whole syllabus. Guessing does not yield desired result in preparation of a competitive exam. Prepare all the ten units of the current syllabus exhaustively. Don't get trapped in the game of important and unimportant topics. This will result in utter confusion and affect your preparation.
9. **Don't Study Up to Eleventh Hour:** Plan a steady and consistent preparation and give up studying 24 hours before examination and be relaxed.

Tips To Solve Paper 1 For Promising Result

1. Do not develop any anxiety in the examination hall while waiting for question paper to be displayed on your monitor.
2. Scroll down and read the whole paper in first round after getting questions on the monitor.
3. Solve those questions first which you find accessible and the easiest ones.
4. Try to finish the mathematical reasoning part first, if accessible.
5. In case you find answer choices to be very close, recollect the facts patiently and chose the appropriate answer choice
6. Be prepared that out of 50 questions 7-8 questions you will find beyond syllabus, even if you fall in Orbit A of preparation. In such situation read the questions thoroughly and use intelligent guessing to solve these questions as though they are beyond syllabus, they are related to topics of the syllabus.
7. If you find a question taking your much of time in solving it, leave it as it is there and scroll up or down to go other accessible question.
8. Solve time consuming questions like comprehension at the end.
9. Do not leave any question un attempted, as even a wrong attempt will not affect your merit due to no negative marking.
10. Maintain your cool and calm throughout the examination duration.

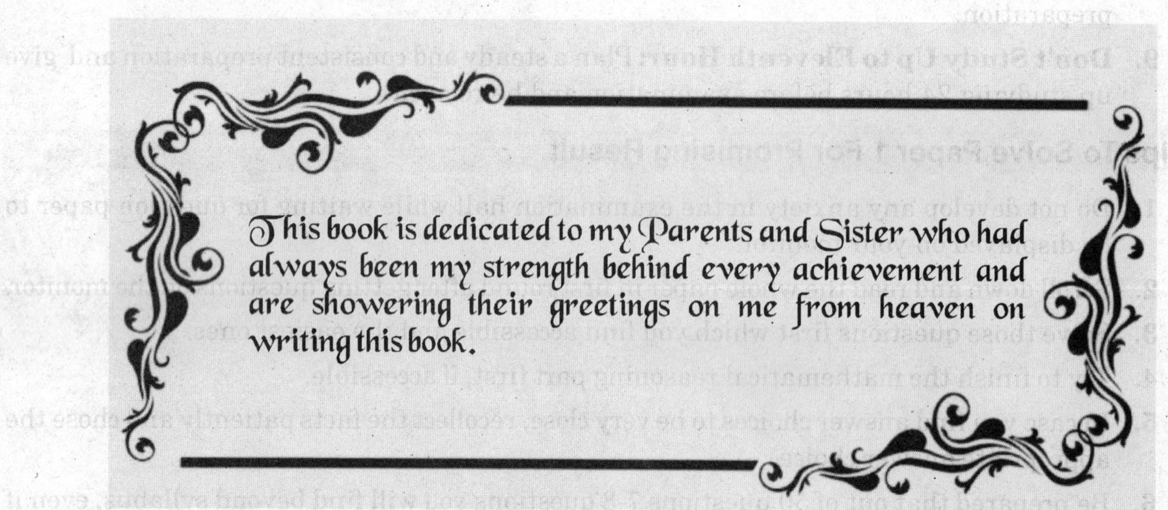

This book is dedicated to my Parents and Sister who had always been my strength behind every achievement and are showering their greetings on me from heaven on writing this book.

Unit I

Teaching Aptitude

Teaching
(Concept, Nature, Objectives, Characteristics, Basic Requirements & Levels)

INTRODUCTION

Teaching is an activity to impart knowledge of unknown facts with the motive of developing personality (developing power of reasoning and thinking) of the learner though effective communication.

American Scholar Edmund J. Amidon defined it as: " Teaching is an interactive process, primarily involving classroom talk which takes place between teacher and pupil and occurs during certain definable activity."

FORMS OF TEACHING

Before discussing nature of teaching, let us discuss forms of teaching. Teaching has three forms:

1) Formal Teaching
2) Non-Formal Teaching
3) Informal Teaching

1) **Formal Teaching:** Classroom teaching is called Formal Teaching. Teachers and students formally assemble in classrooms of colleges or universities and participate in the teaching-learning process. There is a face-to-face interaction between the teacher and the students in a class. The teacher is academically qualified in the subject he is teaching. The teacher teaches as per pre-prepared curriculum and syllabus. He is to finish the course within the time limit of a semester or any other time framework. He may be teaching as a fulfilment of a degree course of either graduation or post-graduation level.

2) **Non-Formal Teaching:** Non-formal teaching is also imparted to fulfil the requirements of a degree course, but there is no classroom teaching, i.e., there is no face-to-face interaction between a teacher and students. Teaching is imparted under distance education programme in non-formal teaching. It is also called teaching imparted through correspondence, satellite, newspaper, or any other medium.

3) **Informal Teaching:** This is the teaching imparted by the nature. Man does not learn only through formal and non-formal means, rather, the biggest chunk of learning is acquired through informal means. Whatever family, friends, strangers, enemies, and daily experiences teach him is called Informal Teaching. Actually, formal and non-formal teaching imparts literacy, whereas education is imparted by informal means. Teachers of informal means may not necessarily possess any academic degree; it is the experience which is the measure of qualification in informal teaching. There is no formal distinction between a teacher and a learner. A teacher may be a learner first and the next moment vice versa. Man keeps on learning throughout his life through this means of teaching.

Formal Teaching-Part of NET Syllabus

Though there are three forms of teaching as discussed above, yet majority of topics given in NET syllabus of Teaching Aptitude belongs to Formal Teaching. So this chapter and most of the other chapters will be discussed with respect to the concept of Formal Teaching. Following points explaining nature of teaching also belong to the discipline of formal teaching.

NATURE OF TEACHING

1) **Tripolarity:** Teaching is the only channel of imparting education. The ancient and medieval times advocate that imparting education is bipolar in nature as education is imparted by the teacher and acquired by the learner. But the modern scenario of education establishes its Tripolarity. American pioneer of Modern Education Theory, John Dewey advocated that education is a tripolar process. These three poles are teacher, learner, and social environment. Dewey asserts that in modern times when the society is making progress, education is effectively conducive in making its vital contribution in the society's overall development. A society, by and large, determines the purpose and goals of education for its political, social, economic, and cultural development. A

teacher as well as a student survives in the society. What a teacher is teaching and what a student is learning are influenced by the social ethics, atmosphere, and demand. Imparting of education as per the requirement of progressive society becomes subject matters which then are developed into syllabi and are taught to the classes.

2) **Interactivity:** Academically, there are two modes of teaching, i.e., formal and non-formal. Formal teaching is imparted in the classrooms and non-formal teaching is provided through non-formal means like correspondence, Internet, etc. Formal or classroom teaching-learning process demands a healthy interaction between a teacher and students to achieve effective teaching, learning, and feedback. Cordial interaction between the teacher and the students acts as a strong stimulant for teaching and learning. Both teacher and students are motivated to make the teaching-learning process successful.

3) **Planned Process:** Teaching is practiced with proper planning. A teacher prepares his/her lecture in advance which he/she is to deliver to the class the next day. The teacher not only plans his/her lecture in advance, but also prepares the reply to expected queries from the students.

4) **Multiple Phases:** Teaching has three phases: Pre-active, Inter-active, and Post-active phase.

   a) **Pre-Active Phase:** In the pre-active phase, the teacher plans his lecture, strategy of teaching, and all those activities which a teacher performs before going to the classroom.

   b) **Inter-Active Phase:** The activities a teacher performs in the classroom is the inter-active phase. In this phase, a teacher interacts face-to-face with the students. Here, the teacher delivers his/her lecture, explaining all the aspects of the topic being discussed in the class in his/her style by creating an amicable atmosphere in the classroom and concluding the lecture. The teacher also answers all the queries of the students to clear their doubts and inculcate confidence in them.

   c) **Post-Active Phase:** In this phase, the teacher evaluates the students' knowledge on the topic, either through oral or written tests. In this way, the teacher also gets feedback from the students. If they perform well in the test, it means they have clearly understood the topic/chapter, otherwise not.

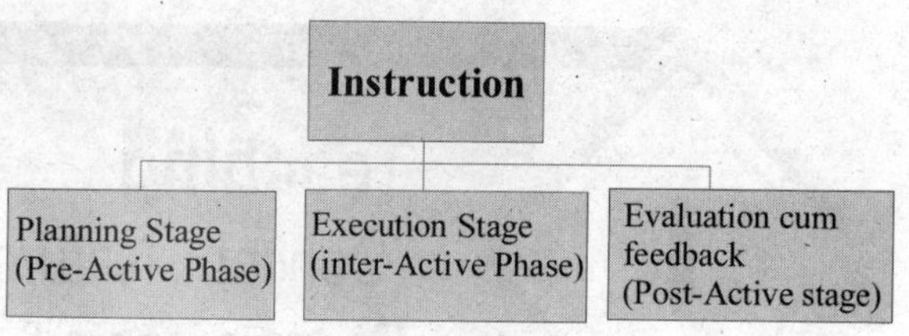

Phases of teaching

5) **Quality:** Teaching sustains a quality that aims to develop the overall personality of the learners through imparting knowledge of unknown facts to the learners. Teaching not only imparts knowledge of the subject matter, it also develops the desirable behaviour and personality traits in learners and refining their reasoning power.

6) **Motivating Stimulant:** Teaching acts as a motivating stimulant to learners. Learners are motivated to learn that subject in which teaching is offered. Effective teaching requires motivated teachers as well as learners.

7) **Guidance:** Teaching is guidance also. Teaching guides the learners about the role of studies or course they are doing in shaping their careers. Teaching also guides the students on behavioral and personality traits.

8) **Art as well as Science:** A teacher performs in the class in the way an actor performs on a stage. A teacher develops a teaching style which is enjoyed by the students. A teacher works like a fine artist to make teaching-learning simple and enjoyable which helps in better grasping and fine results. Teaching on the other hand is a science also as various experiments are performed to assess the understanding level of students. Moreover, it works on theories and hypothesis which are subject to research. A teacher experiments new methods of teaching in the class to make lecture accessible for students up to the maximum extent.

9) **Diagnostic and Therapeutic in nature:** In teaching, sometimes a teacher makes a pre-assessment of students' complexes on the topic to be discussed, their willingness to attend the lecture, extent of their familiarity with the topic, etc. This practice is called Diagnostic nature of teaching. Teaching is also therapeutic in nature when the lecture is delivered in an interesting and absorbing way which results in removing phobia among the students about the concerned topic.

CHARACTERISTICS OF TEACHING

The following characteristics of teaching can be summarized here:

1) **Matter of drawing out:** Teaching is two-way communication. A cycle of communication sets in between the teacher and the students. It is not only a matter of drawing out but also a matter of extracting feedback from the learners.

2) **Process that causes to learn:** Availability of teaching in different streams motivates students to learn and join a particular subject.

3) **Sympathetic and kind:** Teaching is open to learners from every caste and creed. Gaining education is a fundamental right of every citizen. While imparting education in different streams, it complies with the Right to Education and Directive Principles of State Policy.

4) **Only channel of learning:** Teacher and Teaching cannot be substituted by any other means. If one is to learn, one will have to join the teaching-learning process.

5) **Stimulating and progressive:** Teaching motivates learners to learn. There is teaching; that is why there are learners. Motivation is by and large done by the teacher.

   Teaching is also progressive as new means and styles of teaching are being invented and teaching goes on progressing by adopting these modern means.

BASIC REQUIREMENTS OF TEACHING

1) **Motivation:** Voluntary effort to do any work has motivation behind it. Similarly, teaching requires motivated teacher and motivated learners for success of the teaching-learning process. It is the teacher who motivates learners to learn with his aptitude and attitude.

2) **Support material:** Support material like classroom, board, chalk or marker, library, laboratory, etc. is required basically for effective and successful teaching.

4) **Objective:** Teaching always requires an objective to be fulfilled. Objective of teaching is to justify the service of teaching by making learners understand the lecture delivered in the class by the teacher while using traits of effective communication and other traits of a good teacher.

5) **Proper channelisation:** Teaching should be available in all those streams in which teaching is possible. It requires its proper channelisation so that maximum learners should avail opportunity of fulfilling their right to education.

OBJECTIVES OF TEACHING

1) **Facilitating learning:** Teaching is a service with a mission. Its sole objective is to facilitate learning so that teaching may justify its mission.

2) **Developing overall personality of the learner:** Teaching is not confined to the subject knowledge only, rather, it also teaches traits of general mannerism to the learners. Learners are to survive in the society. Teaching teaches them how to behave nicely with the members of the society. Teaching also teaches them about moral and social values. Reasoning power of the learners is also enhanced in learners through teaching. So teaching teaches learners how to develop and maintain an overall personality.

3) **Motivating learner to acquire right knowledge:** As teaching is the only channel of learning and acts as a learning stimulant, objective of teaching is to motivate learners to learn. .

4) **Creating awareness:** Teaching creates awareness in the society and also encourages one to raise his/her voice against various social evils. Its objective is to bring about various reforms through awareness.

5) **Maintaining healthy interactions:** Another leading objective of teaching is to maintain a healthy teacher-student, teacher-society, and student-society interactions.

6) **Materialising Universalisation of Education:** Objective of teaching is not to confine itself to a particular class of learners or particular region or religion; it works with the objective of Universalisation of Education. This objective of teaching can be effectively fulfilled by teachers, students, and citizens volunteering their services.

7) **Establishing itself a faithful and specialised channel:** Teaching always works for establishing itself as an effective channel of teaching-learning process through effective communication and healthy interaction.

8) **Updating the knowledge of learners:** Learners can update their knowledge regarding any subject through learning in the classroom. Teaching also removes the learners' various complexes.

TYPES OF TEACHING

1) **Team Teaching:** While taking into consideration learners' requirements and convenience in learning, team teaching is practiced. In this type of teaching, two or more teachers simultaneously teach a class.

They plan the strategy, schedule, and syllabus to be covered with the class. A teacher may start a lecture and the other teacher may perform the role of an observer to ensure that every learner is participating in the ongoing interaction. Team teaching sometimes involves an activity in which one teacher goes on writing on the black or white board and the other teacher elaborates and explains the concept. Team teaching is practiced for better understanding by learners and it involves the activity of narrating, explaining, illustrating, and evaluating by two or more teachers at the same time. Team teaching basically targeting the overall personality development of learners. Team teaching can be practiced at all levels of learning. The idea of team teaching was originated in the USA in 1954.

2) **Micro Teaching:** Technique of micro teaching was devised during the 1960s by an American scholar and teacher Dwight W. Allen. Micro teaching helps the novice teacher to learn teaching and get some experience in teaching. In this technique, a teacher is asked to teach a small number of students or peers (say 5 to 10) for a short period. When a teacher teaches a small group of learners, a video recording of his lecture is made. Video recording of his lecture is reviewed by the teacher himself, his experienced colleagues, and students who attended that lecture. The teacher gets feedback and suggestions to improve upon the lacunae in his teaching technique and resultantly, the teacher improves his technique of teaching. Micro teaching is considered to be the most effective technique of teacher training.
3) **Macro Teaching:** Teaching a large group of students at one time in a lecture hall is Macro Teaching. In this technique, a large chunk of a topic is covered at one time (taking time longer than the usual timing of 20-25 minutes). There is no one-to-one interaction in this technique due to the big group of students. The teacher delivers the lecture while addressing all the students attending that lecture. This technique is also used by a teacher while introducing a topic (when the aim is to complete the whole content in a single lecture).

PEERS

> *Word peer is derived from Latin word 'Par', which means Equal. In the education field, peers are the same level or grade students from different schools and colleges. For example, students studying in B. A. in different colleges are peers for one another.*

4) **Simulation Teaching:** It is a learner-centered technique of teaching. Simulation means imitation. In this technique of teaching, teachers and students depend on 'Role-Play' activity, i.e., participants of simulation teaching play a role of a character related to the subject of study. The role is played extempore. Teacher creates a situation like the real world and students are asked to adapt it as the real world. This arouses interest among the students and they learn more effectively. It is the platform to display aesthetic skills by students and teachers simultaneously. This teaching technique teaches the student the skill of handling and experience situations close to real life.

PRESCRIBED LEVELS OF TEACHING

It has been established that teaching aims at effective learning by the students and reformation of their behavioral and personality traits. A teacher comes across learners with different ages and psychology and the teacher adopts that approach of teaching which is required for a particular age group, so that all the learners should clearly understand his/her lecture irrespective of difference in psychology. Learning is a gradual process and it passes through different stages or levels with the progress of age of the learner. The level of teaching which is required for kids is not suitable for learners of a higher age. When students are exposed to learning for the first time, they take time to learn every aspect of the concept. Accordingly, teaching is practiced at the following different levels.

a) Memory level
b) Understanding level
c) Reflective level

Memory Level

It is the fundamental level of teaching. At this level learners learn about the concept at its face value, i.e., learners cram whatever is taught like definitions, explanations, illustrations, and formulae. This level of teaching is meant for kids whose thinking and understanding power has not fully developed. Students depend on rote learning. Students do not use their thinking power to understand the content being taught. The teacher plays the fundamental role at this level of teaching. While teaching at this level, the teacher considers the age of the students.

Merits of Memory Level Teaching

1) Knowledge attained through cramming becomes the base for understanding the same topic when required in a higher age group.

2) Teacher as a primary participant of this level of teaching makes students learn the concept through cramming in the class which they cannot learn independently.

3) While considering the tender age of students, teacher at this level of teaching selects that content for teaching which can be easily memorised by the students.

Demerits of Memory Level Teaching

1) Basic flaw in this level of teaching is that it promotes rote learning. Sometimes, students develop the habit of cramming and depend upon it even when they enter understanding level of learning. Resultantly, they cannot understand the concept and fail in many fields of life.

2) As rote learning is compulsory at this level of teaching, students gain the superficial knowledge of the concept. This leads to lack of confidence in students and they cannot improve upon it even after attaining a higher age.

3) As there is no room for learning with intelligence at this level of teaching, there is an apprehension that students may develop a learning phobia due to persistent and heavy cramming. They may lose interest in learning.

Understanding Level

Teaching at understanding level aims at teaching a concept at its depth. Students participating in this level of teaching-learning process have attained an age capable of understanding a concept being taught by the teacher. Teaching at this level widens the perception of the learners about the topic or the concept being taught. Formulae, definitions, principles, statutes, and phenomena are not learnt at the superficial level but learners understand these up to their depth. The teacher explains relationship of various concepts with the facts and how various norms and principles are applicable to real life.

Merits of Understanding Level Teaching

1) The knowledge gained by the students in the understanding level has practical relevance.

2) Learning at understanding level acts as a basis for reflective level of teaching.

3) There is no room for cramming at this level of teaching-learning process. Students go for understanding the concept and view its practical relevance.

4) The teacher teaches at this level in an organised manner.

5) With thorough understanding, students are able to relate it with the previous knowledge which they have attained through cramming and thus, gain confidence.

Demerits of Understanding Level Teaching

This level of teaching is subject-centered, thus it reduces teacher-student interaction. This demerit loses its relevance in the light of merits of the understanding level of teaching.

Reflective Level

Reflective level is the highest level of teaching which a student reaches after crossing memory level and understanding level. This level of teaching emphasises on an introspective approach to some topic, concept, or subject. Here, one thinks deeply about the concept being taught. The teacher puts a problem before the students and motivates them to find solution to that problem. Learning through this level enables students to face various challenges of life. Students also learn how to come out of a deadlock or crisis in life. Reflective level of teaching emphasises on identifying a problem, defining it, and finding a solution. At this level of teaching, students' creative abilities are exploited and refined.

Merits of Reflective level of Teaching

1) This level of teaching is problem-centered and by voluntarily solving it, they gain confidence and acquire the ability to face various challenges in life.

2) The teacher plays a democratic role as nothing is imposed on the students in the name of teaching and learning.

3) Reflective level teaching is highly conducive to students to solve various problems.

4) At this level, the subject matter so provided to students is quite close to reality.

5) This level of teaching strengthens the decision-making power of the students and they join the mainstream as mature and rational beings.

Demerits of Reflective Level of Teaching

The only demerit of reflective level teaching is that it is not suitable for kids.

Some Vital Facts

1) The quality of questions asked by students in classroomreflects best the quality of teaching in a classroom
2) Teaching means convincing others with effective communication and proper management and monitoring.
3) Instructional variety justifies teaching and increases students' success rate.
4) Teaching and learning are integrally related.
5) Concern of all teaching is to ensure some kind of transformation in students.
6) Teaching is a social act whereas learning is a personal act.
7) Teaching implies learning whereas learning does not imply teaching.
8) Teaching is an interaction and is triadic in nature whereas learning is an active engagement in a subject domain.
9) Teaching is a 'task' while learning is an 'achievement'.
10) Socio-economic background of teachers and students does not impact teaching
11) Students asking questions is a sign of motivated teaching
12) Effective teaching is a function of teacher's making students learn and understand.
13) Dynamic approach to teaching means The students should be required to learn through activities.
14) Micro teaching is most effective for the student and teacher during the practice-teaching
15) Punishing the students is not a sign of motivated and effective teaching.
16) One of the major objectives of teaching is to develop the capacity to take decisions.
17) Team teaching has the potential to develop cooperation.

Practice Exercise

General Questions Format

1. Teaching motivates a learner to

(A) learn and teach others

(B) bring reforms in the society

(C) use his knowledge for the development of his personality

(D) All of the above

2. Which of the following indicates that teaching is a planned process? It ______.

(A) is practiced for a year

(B) follows a set curriculum

(C) gets response after a certain time period

(D) None of the above

3. The ultimate objective of teaching is to ______.

(A) develop the overall personality of the learner

(B) popularise the teaching profession

(C) create maximum teaching opportunities in the society

(D) exploit the inner talent of teachers

4. Which of the following is NOT TRUE about teaching?

(A) Teaching promotes knowledge campaigns for learners.

(B) Teaching results in reforming the personality of the learner.

(C) Teaching is dynamic and progressive.

(D) No medium of instructions can replace teaching.

5. Which of the following justifies that teaching is a missionary activity?

(A) No other profession simultaneously imparts education and literacy.

(B) Teaching motivates one to learn not only for himself but also for others.

(C) One who really teaches never cheats.

(D) None of these

6. Teaching is not possible if there is no

(A) Learner (B) Opportunity

(C) Infrastructure (D) Motivation

7. Sincere and motivated learners ultimately become sincere and motivated

(A) citizens (B) teachers

(C) professionals (D) job seekers

8. An interactive teaching always demands
(A) reciprocity (B) regularity
(C) concentration (D) evaluation

9. Some of the basic requirements of teaching are:
I) infrastructure II) objectivity
III) motivation IV) channelisation
Arrange them in priority.
(A) III-IV-II-I (B) I-II-III-IV
(C) III-II-IV-I (D) III-I-II-IV

10. Tripolarity teaching involves
(A) Teacher, Learner, and Social environment
(B) Teacher, Teaching, and Learner
(C) Education, Knowledge, and Teacher
(D) None of the above

11. Professionalism in teaching activity is ______.
(A) sign of progress in teaching service
(B) against ethics of teaching
(C) necessary as per the current requirement and trend
(D) always part of it

12. Effective teaching always results in effective ______.
(A) learning (B) reforms
(C) implementation (D) education

13. Which of the following is NOT an objective of teaching?
(A) Awareness (B) Motivation
(C) Discrimination (D) Universalisation

14. A democratic teaching activity means teaching
(A) without discrimination
(B) about democracy
(C) by any teacher
(D) at any time

15. "Teaching is a service with mission"-which of the following best explains this notion that teaching is never..............mission?
(A) more than a (B) less than a
(C) over and above a (D) short of a

16. Teaching to an illiterate is always more .... than teaching a normal learner.
(A) enjoyable (B) cumbersome
(C) challenging (D) can't say

17. Interactivity in teaching makes teaching ______.
(A) practical (B) effective
(C) meaningful (D) none of these

18. A teacher's life should be the life of a/an
(A) instructor (B) man
(C) reformer (D) guide

19. Motivating stimulant in teaching benefits
(A) teachers (B) students
(C) both (D) society

20. Teaching poses certain challenges to a teacher:
I. Tolerance II. Commitment
III. Service IV. Results
If a teacher is successful in meeting all these challenges successfully, then this results in the teacher's
(A) satisfaction (B) goodwill
(C) justification (D) confirmation

21. What is the common requirement in the teaching of even subjects of altogether different nature?
(A) Teacher's teaching method
(B) Motivation of students
(C) Teaching schedule
(D) All of the above

22. Which of the following is/are TRUE about memory level teaching?
i) Rote learning is the basic task for the students.
ii) Teacher teaches that topic which can be easily understood by the students.
iii) There is hardly any feedback by the students due to unilateral teaching.
iv) This level of teaching becomes the foundation for higher levels of teaching.
(A) i, ii, and iv (B) ii and iv only
(C) i, iii, and iv (D) All of the above

23. Which of the following doctrine was developed by Dwight W. Allen ?
(A) Two or more teachers simultaneously teach in a class of students to justify the concept of teaching in letter and spirit.
(B) Novice teachers are allotted a class of 5-10 students to review their performance and gain teaching experience.
(C) A teacher creates a real world-like situation in the class and students are to solve a problem associated with that world.
(D) None of these

24. 'Teaching is sympathetic and kind' signifies that teaching ________.
(A) aims at catering to educational needs of all learners from any caste, creed, or religion
(B) motivates teachers to express sympathy with students poor in understanding to establish pedagogy in its true spirit
(C) is a service rendered to achieve Universalisation of Education
(D) educates the learners to come up as sympathetic and kind citizens

25. Basic requirements of teaching signify that teaching essentially ________.
(A) is not hassle-free without motivated learners
(B) justifies itself only if practiced by experienced teachers
(C) comes out as a mission if it is channelised with full equipment
(D) All of the above

KEY

1. D	2. B	3. A	4. A	5. B	6. D	7. A
8. A	9. C	10. A	11. A	12. A	13. C	14. A
15. D	16. D	17. B	18. C	19. C	20. B	21. B
22. C	23. B	24. C	25. C			

Assertion–Reason Format

1. **Assertion (A):** Teaching through 'Role-Play' takes both teachers and students close to reality
Reason (R): In simulation teaching, a real world-like situation is created in the class.
(A) Both A and R are true and R is the correct explanation of A
(B) Both A and R are true but R is not the correct explanation of A
(C) A is true but R is false
(D) Both A and R are false

2. **Assertion (A):** Multi-phased teaching ensures the full participation of teacher and learners in the teaching-learning process.
Reason (R): Success of formal teaching depends upon different phases of teaching.
(A) Both A and R are true and R is the correct explanation of A
(B) Both A and R are true but R is not the correct explanation of A
(C) A is false but R is true
(D) A is true but R is false

3. **Assertion (A):** Formal teaching fully justifies its mission.
Reason (R): Teaching in any form is an attempt for reformation.
(A) Both A and R are true and R is correct explanation of A
(B) Both A and R are true but R is not correct explanation of A
(C) Both A and R are false
(D) A is true but R is false

4. **Assertion (A):** Reflective level of teaching determines the introspective skills of the learners.
Reason (R): Rote learning is found at every level of teaching.
(A) Both And R are true and R is correct explanation of A
(B) Both A and R are true but R is not correct explanation of A
(C) A is true but R is false
(D) Both A and R are false

5. **Assertion (A):** Interactive phase of teaching does not necessarily require students' response.
Reason (R): The teacher is responsible for making interactive phase of teaching successful.
(A) Both A and R are true and R is correct explanation of A
(B) Both A and R are true but R is not correct explanation of A
(C) A is true but R is false
(D) A is false but R is true

6. **Assertion (A):** Role of effective teaching starts after getting motivated learners.
Reason (R): Motivated learners always look for macro teaching.
(A) A is true but R is false
(B) Both A and R are false
(C) Both A and R are true and R is correct explanation of A
(D) Both A and R are true but R is not correct explanation of A

7. **Assertion (A):** Simulation teaching is a learner-centred technique of teaching.
Reason (R): Learners play roles of characters related to the subject in simulation teaching.

(A) Both A and R are false
(B) A is true but R is false
(C) Both A and R are true and R is correct explanation of A
(D) Both A and R are true but R is not correct explanation of A

8. **Assertion (A):** Teaching overconfident students is challenging.
Reason (R): Overconfident students can be tamed through evaluation.
(A) Both A and R are true and R is correct explanation of A
(B) Both A and R are true but R is not correct explanation of A
(C) A is true but R is false
(D) A is false but R is true

9. **Assertion (A):** There is teaching because there are learners.
Reason (R): There are learners because there is teaching.
(A) Both A and R are false
(B) A is false but R is true
(C) Both A and R are true but R is not correct explanation of A
(D) Both A and R are true and R is correct explanation of A

10. **Assertion (A):** A novice teacher's teaching aptitude is determined in macro teaching.
Reason (R): Macro teaching covers a large chunk of a topic through a single lecture.
(A) Both A and R are true and R is correct explanation of A
(B) Both A and R are true but R is not correct explanation of A
(C) A is false but R is true
(D) A is true but R is false

11. **Assertion (A):** Formal and non-formal teaching are two sides of the same coin.
Reason (R): Informal teaching fills the gaps between formal and non-formal teaching.
(A) Both A and R are false
(B) A is true but R is false
(C) A is false but R is true
(D) Both A and R are true but R is not correct explanation of A

12. **Assertion (A):** Reflective level of teaching is the most suitable for degree-seeking students.
Reason (R): Memory and understanding levels are the basis of reflective level teaching.
(A) Both A and R are true and R is correct explanation of A
(B) Both A and R are true but R is not correct explanation of A
(C) A is true but R is false
(D) A is false but R is true

13. **Assertion (A):** Peer groups are found at every level of education.
Reason (R): Teaching peers at higher education level is more challenging than teaching them at primary or secondary level.
(A) Both A and R are true and R is correct explanation of A
(B) Both A and R are true but R is not correct explanation of A
(C) A is true but R is false
(D) A is false but R is true

14. **Assertion (A):** Two or three novice teachers gain experience at the same time in team teaching.
Reasoning (R): Team teaching is a teacher-centred teaching technique.
(A) Both A and R are true and R is correct explanation of A
(B) Both A and R are true but R is not correct explanation of A
(C) A is true but R is false
(D) Both A and R are false

15. **Assertion (A):** Teaching is that activity which aims to draw out.
Reason (R): Learners' feedback on teaching is important.
(A) Both A and R are true and R is correct explanation of A
(B) Both A and R are true but R is not correct explanation of A
(C) A is true but R is false
(D) A is false but R is true

16. **Assertion (A):** Teaching is an effective tool to universalise education.
Reason (R): Proper channelisation of teaching attracts learners from all around.

(A) Both A and R are true and R is correct explanation of A

(B) Both A and R are true but R is not correct explanation of A

(C) Both A and R are false

(D) A is true but R is false

KEY

1. A	**2.** A	**3.** B	**4.** D	**5.** D	**6.** B	**7.** A
8. B	**9.** B	**10.** C	**11.** A	**12.** B	**13.** C	**14.** D
15. A	**16.** A					

Questions Asked in Previous NET Exams

1. Which among the following reflects best the quality of teaching in a classroom?

(UGC NET JUNE 2019)

(A) Through the use of many teaching aids in the classroom

(B) Through the quality of questions asked by students in the classroom

(C) Through full attendance in the classroom

(D) Through observation of silence by the students in the classroom

2. In which level of teaching, lower level learning outcomes get focussed

(UGC NET DECEMBER 2019)

(A) Memory level

(B) Understanding level

(C) Reflective level

(D) Autonomous development level

3. From the following list of statements, select those which indicate the characteristics and basic requirements of teaching.

(UGC NET JULY 2018)

(i) Teaching implies communication.

(ii) Teaching is like selling goods.

(iii) Teaching means managing and monitoring.

(iv) Teaching implies influencing others.

(v) Teaching requires convincing others.

(vi) There can be no teaching without infrastructural support.

Choose the correct answer from the codes given below:

Codes:

(A) (i), (iii) and (iv) (B) (i), (ii) and (iii)

(C) (iv), (v) and (vi) (D) (ii), (v) and (vi)

4. In the list given below, identify those key teaching behaviours which have been observed to be contributive to effectiveness.

(UGC NET JULY 2018)

(i) Lesson clarity

(ii) Probing

(iii) Teacher-task orientation

(iv) Student success rate

(v) Instructional variety

(vi) Using student ideas

Choose the correct answer from the codes given below:

Codes:

(A) (i), (ii), (iii) and (iv)

(B) (iii), (iv), (v) and (vi)

(C) (i), (iii), (iv) and (v)

(D) (ii), (iii), (v) and (vi)

5. Which of the following set of statements best describes the nature and objectives of teaching?

(UGC NET JULY 2018)

(a) Teaching and learning are integrally related.

(b) There is no difference between teaching and training.

(c) Concern of all teaching is to ensure some kind of transformation in students.

(d) All good teaching is formal in nature.

(e) A teacher is a senior person.

(f) Teaching is a social act whereas learning is a personal act.

Codes:

(A) (a), (b), and (d) (B) (b), (c), and (e)

(C) (a), (c), and (f) (D) (d), (e), and (f)

6. Which of the following set of statements best represents the nature and objective of teaching and learning? **(UGC NET NOVEMBER 2017)**

(a) Teaching is like selling and learning is like buying.

(b) Teaching is a social act while learning is a personal act.

(c) Teaching implies learning whereas learning does not imply teaching.

(d) Teaching is a kind of delivery of knowledge while learning is like receiving it.

(e) Teaching is an interaction and is triadic in nature, whereas learning is an active engagement in a subject domain.

Codes:

(A) (b), (c), and (e) (B) (a), (b), and (c)

(C) (a), (b), and (d) (D) (a), (d), and (e)

7. Which of the following set of statements reflects the basic characteristics of teaching? Select the correct alternative from the codes: **(UGC NET AUGUST 2016)**

(i) Teaching is the same as training.

(ii) There is no difference between instruction and conditioning when we teach.

(iii) Teaching is related to learning.

(iv) Teaching is a 'task' word while learning is an 'achievement' word.

(v) Teaching means giving information.

(vi) One may teach without learning taking place.

Codes:

(A) (i), (ii), and (iii) (B) (iii), (iv), and (vi)

(C) (ii), (iii), and (v) (D) (i), (iv), and (vi)

8. A college level assistant professor has planned his/her lectures with an intent to develop cognitive dimensions of students centred on skills of analysis and synthesis. Below, given are two sets of items: Set I consisting of levels of cognitive interchange and Set II comprising basic requirements for promoting them. Match the two sets and indicate your answer by choosing the correct alternative from the codes: **(UGC NET JULY 2016)**

Set I (Levels of cognitive interchange)	**Set II** (Basic requirements for promoting cognitive interchange)
a. Memory level	i. Giving opportunity for discriminating examples and non-examples of a point.
b. Understanding level	ii. Recording the important points made during the presentations.
c. Reflective level	iii. Asking the students to discuss various items of information
	iv. Critically analyzing the points to be made and discussed.

Codes:

	a	b	c
(A)	ii	iv	i
(B)	iii	iv	ii
(C)	ii	i	iv
(D)	i	ii	iii

9. What is required for good teaching? **(UGC NET DECEMBER 2015)**

(a) Diagnosis (b) Remedy

(c) Direction (d) Feedback

Select the correct answer from the codes given below:

(A) (a), (b), (c), and (d)

(B) (a) and (b)

(C) (b), (c) and (d)

(D) (c) and (d)

10. Which of the following factors does not impact teaching? **(UGC NET JUNE 2015)**

(A) Learning through experience

(B) Teacher's knowledge

(C) Classroom activities that encourage learning

(D) Socio-economic background of teachers and students

11. Which of the following is not a prescribed level of teaching? **(UGC NET DECEMBER 2014)**

(A) Memory (B) Understanding

(C) Reflective (D) Differentiation

12. Which one of the following is considered a sign of motivated teaching? **(UGE NET JUNE 2014)**

(A) Students asking questions

(B) Maximum attendance of the students

(C) Pin drop silence in the classroom

(D) Students taking notes

13. Effective teaching is a function of **(UGC NET DECEMBER 2013)**

(A) Teachers' satisfaction

(B) Teachers' honesty and commitment

(C) Teachers making students learn and understand

(D) Teachers' liking for professional excellence

14. Arrange the following teaching process in order: **(UGC NET DECEMBER 2013)**
    (i) Relating the present knowledge with the previous one
    (ii) Evaluation
    (iii) Reteaching
    (iv) Formulating instructional objectives
    (v) Presentation of instructional materials
    (A) (i), (ii), (iii), (iv), (v)
    (B) (ii), (i), (iii), (iv), (v)
    (C) (v), (iv), (iii), (i), (ii)
    (D) (iv), (i), (v), (ii), (iii)
15. Which one of the following is a scaled-down teaching situation? **(UGC NET SEPTEMBER 2013)**
    (A) Macro teaching
    (B) Team teaching
    (C) Cooperative teaching
    (D) Micro teaching
16. Dynamic approach to teaching means **(UGC NET JUNE 2012)**
    (A) Teaching should be forceful and effective
    (B) Teachers should be energetic and dynamic
    (C) The topics of teaching should not be static, but dynamic
    (D) The students should be required to learn through activities
17. Micro teaching is more effective **(UGC NET DECEMBER 2009)**
    (A) during the preparation for teaching practice
    (B) during the teaching practice
    (C) after the teaching practice
    (D) always
18. Micro teaching is most effective for the student and teacher ________. **(UGC NET JUNE 2007)**
    (A) during the practice teaching
    (B) after the practice teaching
    (C) before the practice teaching
    (D) none of the above
19. Which is the least important factor in teaching? **(UGC NET JUNE 2007)**
    (A) Punishing the students
    (B) Maintaining discipline in the class
    (C) Lecturing in an impressive way
    (D) Drawing sketches and diagrams on the blackboard
20. The main objective of teaching at Higher Education Level is: **(UGC NET DECEMBER 2006)**
    (A) To prepare students to pass the examination
    (B) To develop the capacity to take decisions
    (C) To give new information
    (D) To motivate students to ask questions during lectures
21. Which of the following comprise teaching skill? **(UGC NET JUNE 2006)**
    (A) Blackboard writing
    (B) Questioning
    (C) Explaining
    (D) All of the above
22. Which of the two given options is of the level of understanding? **(UGC NET JUNE 2006)**
    (I) Define noun.
    (II) Define noun in your own words.
    (A) Only I (B) Only II
    (C) Both I and II (D) Neither I nor II
23. Which of the following statements is correct? **(UGC NET JUNE 2006)**
    (A) Syllabus is a part of curriculum.
    (B) Syllabus is an annexure to curriculum.
    (C) Curriculum is the same in all educational institutions affiliated to a particular university.
    (D) Syllabus is not the same in all educational institutions affiliated to a particular university.
24. Team teaching has the potential to develop **(UGC NET DECEMBER 2005)**
    (A) competitive spirit
    (B) cooperation
    (C) the habit of supplementing the teaching of each other
    (D) highlighting of the gaps in each other's teaching

KEY

1. B	2. A	3. A	4. C	5. C	6. A	7. B
8. C	9. A	10. D	11. D	12. A	13. C	14. D
15. D	16. D	17. B	18. A	19. A	20. B	21. D
22. B	23. A	24. B				

Learner's Characteristics
(Adolescent and Adult Learners)

CONCEPT

Present day teaching is learner-centred at all levels. This nature of teaching is more marked in the arena of higher education. A learner's characteristics play a decisive role in planning and executing teaching activity at higher education level. A learner's characteristics are those characteristics which play a conducive role to facilitate learning for learners. Such characteristics collectively reflect a learner's aptitude and attitude towards learning.

Learner: Anyone who learns any concept is a learner. In teaching aptitude, definition of a learner is someone who learns about a subject by becoming a part of the formal or non-formal education system. A learner also learns from his/her family, surroundings, circumstances, nature, experiences and social interactions.

Significance of Learner's Characteristics

1) **Facilitate teaching:** Learner's characteristics facilitate teaching. If a teacher is aware of the learner's academic, social, cognitive, or emotional characteristics, it becomes easier for a teacher to plan and execute teaching accordingly and thus, learning also becomes easy for learners.
2) **Conducive to plan curriculum:** Knowledge of various learners' characteristics help planners to draft and execute the syllabus and curriculum suitable for the learners' understanding level.
3) **Facilitate learning:** Learning become easier for a learner due to his/her characteristics. A learner is curious to learn about anything.
4) **Healthy interaction between teacher and learners:** Success of classroom teaching depends upon the perfect reciprocity between the teacher and students.

Learner's Characteristics

The force behind determining a learner's characteristics is cognition. Characteristics of a learner keep on changing as he/she experiences growth in age. As social scientists like Bloom and Piaget have defined, during different stages of learning in a person which he/she experiences along with growth in his/her age, characteristics of a learner also experience changes. It is not necessary that characteristics of an adolescent and an adult learner are the same. Characteristics of an adolescent and an adult learner can be studied separately with respect to academic, social, emotional, and cognitive traits. Before discussing these characteristics separately for adolescent and adult learners, let us study them in a general sense.

1) **Academic Characteristics of a Learner :** Academic characteristics of a learner reflect the academic needs of a learner (learner wants to join which stream in the formal or non-formal education system). Accordingly, such characteristics are visible in a learner's academic behaviour which reflects his/her inclination towards seeking knowledge of different subjects.
2) **Social Characteristics :** Social characteristics of learners are inspired by moral, cultural, ethical, political, and economic issues prevailing in the society. A learner surviving in the society wants to learn various such issues and also wants answers to various questions arising in his/her mind regarding all such issues of the society. When he joins the education stream, these quests to know answers to his questions appear as his/her characteristics.
3) **Emotional Characteristics :** Emotional characteristics of a learner are reflected in mood swings, self-awareness, and emotional aspects.
4) **Cognitive Characteristics :** These characteristics of a learner are concerned with his/her memory, intellect, cognitive development, stress level, retention potential of brain, and potential of understanding a concept.

CHARACTERISTICS OF AN ADOLESCENT LEARNER

> *"Adolescent students vary greatly in their development and readiness for learning and teachers play a critical role in judging the developmental stage of each student." Reys et al*

An adolescent learner is in the age group of 13-19. Characteristics of an adolescent who displays different traits are studied as follows:

Academic Characteristics

1) **Accepting challenges and win over them:** An adolescent learner accepts challenges in his/her academic life and does not surrender before them, but rather makes efforts to win over them. When an adolescent learner experiences learning in classroom teaching, he accepts the various obstacles in learning as a challenge and overcomes his weaknesses.
2) **Giving priority to active learning over passive learning:** As an adolescent learner accepts challenges, he/she prefers active learning over passive learning. He/she prefers to learn in the classroom through direct interaction between him/her and the teacher.
3) **Shifting interest in abstract thinking from concrete thinking:** in childhood, a learner is taught about various objects having physical existence. As he/she enters adolescent age, he/she develops a liking towards values and ethics.
4) **Developing urge for interacting with peers during learning activities:** The adolescent learner opens up at this age and looks for peers and initiates interaction with them during the phase of learning.
5) **Curiosity about new concepts:** When an adolescent learner is exposed to new concepts, he/she shows curiosity to learn basics from them. Further, he/she is curious about any new education stream.
6) **Investigative about subject matter:** An adolescent learner is investigative about relevance of learning and subject matter being taught, i.e., what the type of education is and what is the level of education.
7) **Use intellect for perennial learning:** Being investigative about relevant learning, an adolescent learner uses his/her intellect to learn concepts for long-term retention of the concept in mind.
8) **Develop capability of introspection:** An adolescent learner becomes able enough to examine his/her own thoughts and consciousness, enabling him/her to reform his/her personality.

Social Characteristics

1) **Adopting model behaviour:** An adolescent tries to adopt behavioural traits of old students. The motive is to bring reformation in his/her personality as a learner.
2) **Looking for social position:** An adolescent learner looks for his/her position and identity in the society. He/she is on an exploring spree for his/her position and identity viz-a-viz peers in the society.
3) **Looking for like-minded peers on the issue of racial and ethnic identity:** Adolescent learners develop faith in idealism, They make groups of like-minded peers and question discrimination on caste, creed, religion, and region basis.
4) **Initiating questions on gender identity issues:** Adolescent learners want that both male and female members of the society should enjoy their identity. He raises questions in the classroom on such issues, considering that it is also a part of learning.
5) **Believer of popular culture:** An adolescent learner is believer of common man's culture as he/she is of the opinion that popular culture teaches one a lot.
6) **Direction seeker:** An adolescent learner looks for independence as far as learning and surviving in the society is concerned. He seeks direction from his teachers or elders to choose a stream of education enabling him to secure an independent career in the society.
7) **Exhibiting reciprocity:** Being interrogative, a learner develops reciprocity with his/her teachers on various issues being discussed in the class.

Emotional Characteristics

1) **Overreactive:** An adolescent learner is overreactive to remarks made to him/her with a motive to ridicule or embarrass him/her. Such remarks may be from his teacher or any other person and he/she expresses his/her overreaction over it. He/she also overreacts on rejection of his idea or proposal by anyone.
2) **Seeker of independent identity like adults:** As an adolescent learner witnesses in family and society that adults enjoy an independent identity, so he/she also seeks that status. He does not want interference of anyone as far as his/her learning is concerned. He also seeks to be accepted like independent adults.
3) **Unpredictable and unstable mood:** An adolescent learner experiences extreme mood swings, due to which there are extremities in his expression. Resultantly, his nature becomes unpredictable.
4) **Possessor of misconceptions:** An adolescent learner usually possesses misconceptions that his personality traits are unique, i.e., any issue, problem, or development concerned with him/her are personal and widely different from those of children and adults.
5) **Sensitive:** A learner of adolescent age is sensitive to his criticism. He takes his criticism seriously as he/she is possessive about himself/herself.
6) **Conscious about physical growth:** As the learner enters adolescence, there are physical changes. He/she recognises these changes and changes his/her behaviour and gestures and he feels that he/she is heading towards maturity.
7) **Urge to release energy:** In adolescence, the learner is filled with energy. He needs to release this energy through various activities. Energy is released with sudden outburst of activity.

8) **Attention seeker:** He/she displays behaviour with the motive that others should pay attention to him. He shares this attitude with peers and also seeks their approval for such behaviour.

Cognitive Characteristics

1) **Concerned about social change:** An adolescent learner is impatient regarding the pace of changes around him, He is seriously concerned about changes. He/she develops a complex regarding these changes that bringing social change is a difficult task.
2) **Seeker of parents' advice:** In this age he/she seeks advice from parents or adults close to him but takes his own decisions.
3) **Investigative over moral issues:** He/she starts understanding moral issues. He feels that traditions and rituals are complex. He puts questions on values as he/she tries to understand rituals, cultural expressions, and religious teachings.
4) **Influenced by adult role models:** He/she is convinced of behaviour, gestures, and understanding level of adults. In this age he/she wants to share his/her feelings, observations, and queries. He feels that adults will listen to him and they are trustworthy.
5) **Confidant about participation in democracy:** He/she feels that he/she understands politics and is capable of participating in democracy as a responsible citizen.
6) **Advocates philanthropy:** He/she raises his voice for the welfare of the downtrodden and is concerned about environmental issues and preserving biodiversity.
7) **Maker of paradoxical judgements:** An adolescent learner quickly judges others and finds faults in them but is slow in confessing about faults in him/her.

CHARACTERISTICS OF ADULT LEARNERS

Adult learner: Adult learner is a person accepted as an adult by the society and he learns in the formal, non-formal, and informal stream of education. Learning of an adult starts in the higher education stream, i.e., an adult learner joins a college or university to acclaim knowledge. There is clear-cut diversity among adult learners as they belong to different castes, creeds, regions, religions, ethnicity, and majority or minority group. Learning needs of an adult learner are determined by the group to which he/she belongs. Characteristics of an adult learner are also studied with respect to their academic, social, emotional, and cognitive characteristics.

Academic Characteristics

1) **Join learning voluntarily:** An adult learner joins an education stream voluntarily. Unlike children, he/she is not enforced to join a particular stream of education. Due to this characteristic, he joins an education stream of his choice.
2) **Believer of magnified learning:** An adult learner wants to learn big. Whatever he/she learns is put into a magnifying view. Their interest is to apply what he/she has learnt from childhood to adolescence to a bigger and broader phenomenon.
3) **Result-oriented:** An adult learner does not confine himself/herself to gaining knowledge only. He wants to bring results as they have certain expectations from the teacher, for example, the teacher will give lecture in such a way that he/she will understand fully. While participating in the teaching-learning process, they have result of this process in his/her mind. If they learn and understand what was communicated by the teacher, they continue with that stream. On the other hand, if they do not see the desired result, they drop out of that stream.
4) **Examining relevance of education being imparted:** An adult learner examines the relevance of what is being taught to him/her. As adult learners are diverse in caste, creed, region, religion, etc., they have different academic needs. An adult learner is convinced about the relevance of education being imparted to him, if it is according to his academic needs.
5) **Inclined towards practical work rather than theory:** An adult learner does not want to confine his/her knowledge to theory only. He is inclined towards knowing the practical viability. So rather than listening to the lectures only, he wants to do practical work.
6) **Gaining vast knowledge and experience:** An adult learner while progressing, gains vast knowledge and experience. Teachers should realise this unique characteristic. His/her experience can be used as a resource in the teaching-learning process.

Social Characteristics

1) **Seeking a like-minded learner fraternity:** An adult learner is mature and understands the structure of the society around him. He does not want to be a silent spectator to various changes in the society. He wants to share his views with his like-minded learning community, with whom he/she can discuss various issues.
2) **Committed to family and society:** An adult learner realises his/her commitments to his/her family. On the other hand, he/she is committed to his learning and himself/herself. He/she fulfils these commitments at the cost of learning as he/she does not have enough time and space to maintain a balance between his/her learning and his/her commitments as far as sparing time is concerned. Curriculum of such learners should be designed in such a way that it has a flexible schedule so that he may learn comfortably while fulfilling his/her commitments.

3) **Respect seeker:** He/she wants that he/she should be treated with respect in the society. An adult learner gains knowledge and experience with age. At this age he/she should not be ignored, especially by teachers. He/should be given due respect when he/she becomes part of the teaching-learning process.

Emotional Characteristics

1) **Believes in self control and self-direction:** An adult learner is a mature person. He does not lose patience even in odd situations. Further, he/she chooses his/her learning stream and career himself/herself. Even if the self-directed stream gives anxiety to the learner, he/she observes control and appreciates his/her selection.
2) **Likes options in learning environment:** An adult learner feels comfortable if there are plenty of options of learning streams and careers, out of which he/she chooses one.
3) **Slow in developing psychomotor skills:** As in the adult age, mind is no more tender enough to learn basics (like alphabets, small fonts, and movement of limbs), development of such skills is slower as compared to kids.

PSYCHOMOTOR SKILLS

Psychomotor skills are those activities which are related to movement of hands, i.e., psychomotor skill is skill of performing those activities which involve movement of hands (dexterity), limbs, speed, strength, etc. Psychomotor skills are conducive in developing one's personality. A learner is exposed to progressive learning due to this skill. Psychomotor skills develop faster in kids as compared to adult learners.

4) **Apprehensive and scary:** An adult learner is always apprehensive about various changes in the society which result in politicisation, groupism in religions, regional disparities, etc. and this may affect his/her learning. Though he does not lose patience and self-control in challenging situations, yet , sometimes circumstances compel him/her to develop fear, anxiety, and anger on forced changes in jobs, religion, Policies, etc. He/she feels that when he/she will join a job, such developments may hamper his/her future. Such apprehensions let him/her make learning plans. From the teacher's side, such an environment of teaching should be created so that learner should feel safe and secure in learning and come out of apprehensions of the future.
5) **Developing competence:** An adult learner develops competence skill and become self-confident. Due to this, he learns with concentration and fares well in the exam.
6) **Seeking positive self-image:** With experience, an adult learner develops physical and mental maturity. When such learners are in stress, excited, or under tension, they need motivation from someone to realise their positive self-image. During teaching-learning process, teachers should try to motivate them to come out of that cover of tension and make them realise their self-image of a positive thinker.

Cognitive Characteristics

1) **Accepting self-responsibility:** An adult learner holds himself responsible for his successes and failures in learning.
2) **Self-motivated:** An adult learner voluntarily joins a steam as he himself is motivated to join that. They don't need directions or advise from elders unlike an adolescent learner. He/she is more stable in intellect than an adolescent learner. As the learning needs of an adult learner are determined by the activities in a group to which he/she belongs, there should be ample space in the teaching-learning process for him/her, thus enabling him/her to achieve his/her academic needs.
3) **Autonomous and self-directed:** An adult learner is independent to take his decisions and he/she is also well aware of his direction regarding learning. Teachers should understand this and teaching should be imparted when there is a requirement. Teachers should also assist adult learners to achieve their goals which they set before becoming part of the teaching-learning process
4) **Curious to apply new skills:** He/she wants to apply new skill and knowledge immediately to experience better results in learning.

INDIVIDUAL DIFFERENCE

Though learners are learning jointly in a class, yet each learner differs on various accounts. Individual differences are visible among learners as learners differ in terms of attributes, psychology, culture, way of learning, genetic factors, physical development, environment, cognitive abilities, prior knowledge, etc. The purpose of education is to develop overall personality of learners. Teaching pattern should be planned in such a way that every learner with his/her individual characteristics may achieve his/her learning goals. Knowledge of individual differences helps a teacher a lot and the teacher can be effective in the achievement of learning goals of each learner with individual differences. According to a British social scientist Rod Ellis, individual differences are governed by two factors:

1) Personal Factors 2) General Factors

Personal Factors

As far as learning is concerned, there is variation in personality of individual learners.

Personal factors are further divided into three classes:

1) Group dynamics
2) Attitude to teacher and learning material
3) Individual learning technique

1) **Group dynamics:** Learners can be divided into groups on the basis of their individual differences and accordingly, curriculum and teaching can be planned and executed for overall achievement of teaching-learning approach.
2) **Attitude to teacher and learning material:** Learners have different attitudes towards teachers. Some learners prefer a teacher who motivates them to follow and implement their own learning path. On the other hand, some other learners prefer a teacher who designs the learning path for them which they follow to achieve their learning goals. Further, some learners prefer a teacher who just guides them. Others want a teacher who delivers the lecture with logic and uses all traits of teaching in a systematic way. There are differences among learners with respect to their attitude towards teaching material. Adult learners do not prefer particular course books or notes given to them as a part of curriculum. They think notes and books are being imposed on them. They are of the opinion that various sources of knowledge, i.e., varied notes and books should be placed before them and they should be asked to choose the best among them.
3) **Individual learning techniques:** Learners have different learning techniques which mark individual differences. Some learners follow rote learning techniques (mugging up), whereas some follow technique of understanding. Still, others follow technique of frequent and maximum practice.

General Factors

Individual differences based on general factors include social and cognitive factors. General factors as a measure of individual differences include:

a) Age
b) Aptitude
c) Intelligence
d) Cognitive ability
e) Motivation
f) Attitude
g) Personality

a) **Age:** It is a common observation that children and adolescent learners are better learners as compared to adult learners. A tender-aged learner when exposed to learning for the first time grasps what is being taught as he/she never has been to learning in a formal mode. Here, the child totally depends upon the content delivered by the teacher and learns it in an effective way. Further, children learn many concepts from their family well before joining school. His/her previous knowledge helps him/her in further learning. On the other hand, an adult learner at a definite age considers himself self-directed and does not easily depend upon the content delivered by the teacher.

b) **Aptitude:** Learners differ individually with respect to the aptitude they possess. Learners with a higher aptitude learn faster than learners with a lower level of aptitude.

c) **Intelligence:** Intelligence is the capacity of brain to grasp content delivered by the teacher. Intelligence is reflected in the result of learning. For example, if a learner comes out with a bright performance in evaluation of his/her learning, he or she will be considered as an intelligent learner. Intelligence is also used as a measure of individual differences because a learner with a better performance in evaluation is considered to be more intelligent than a learner with a poorer performance.

d) **Cognitive style:** Learners also differ in terms of individual cognitive styles. Cognitive style means choosing the means of getting knowledge and the way to present it. This style is different between an adolescent learner and an adult learner. An adult learner is autonomous and takes his/her own decision for choosing a learning stream. On the other hand, an adolescent is directed by parents or any other family member to choose a particular learning stream.

e) **Motivation:** This factor also becomes an element of individual differences. An adolescent learner is not self-directed so does not get motivated voluntarily; he/she needs support from any one of his/her associates. On the other hand, an adult learner is autonomous and self-directed so he is inspired by a particular learning stream and joins that voluntarily.

f) **Attitude:** Attitude of a learner towards learning is one of the individual differences. Attitude is how a learner thinks about a subject or person. Adolescent learners also have attitude as they also think about their teachers, subject matter, and learning process. In spite of having an attitude, they cannot display them as for every action they are to consult their elders. Attitude of an adolescent learner may develop into a phobia against subject matter, teacher, or school or college. On the other hand, an adult learner due to his maturity factor, thinks rationally and displays his/her attitude confidently.

g) **Personality:** Personality means how does a person look, how does he/she think, how does he/she react in difficult and challenging situations, how he reacts with anxiety over an issue, etc. These traits mark the difference in an adolescent learner and an adult learner. Here also, adolescent personality traits are not as effective as these are in an adult learner.

INDIVIDUAL DIFFERENCE BETWEEN ADOLESCENT AND ADULT LEARNERS IN A NUTSHELL

ADOLESCENTS	ADULTS
• They are in search for personal identity. • They are in need of activities that meet their needs and learning expectations. • They become disruptive when they lose interest in the lesson or feel bored. • They need help and support from the teacher and need to be provided with constructive feedback. • They can draw upon a variety of resources in the learning environment, including personal experience, the local community, and the Internet. • They need the teacher to build bridges between the syllabus and their world of interests and experiences. • They can learn abstract issues and do challenging activities. • Their personal initiative and energy are moved into action through meaningful involvement with relevant and current content.	• Adults are more disciplined than adolescents. • They have a clear understanding of their learning objectives. • They need to be involved in choosing what and how to learn. • They prefer to rely on themselves and work at their own pace. • They come to the classroom with a wide range of knowledge, expectations, and experiences. • They are able to do a wide range of activities. • Adults learn at various rates and in different ways according to their intellectual ability, educational level, personality, and cognitive learning styles. • They come into the classroom with diverse experiences, opinions, thoughts, and beliefs which need be respected.

Some Vital Facts

1) Learner's commitment, prior knowledge and skill in the concerned area are some of effective characteristics of learner.
2) Curiosity about learning is a natural characteristic of a learner.
3) Modification of behavior is considered to be the most appropriate purpose of learning

Practice Exercise

General Questions Format

1. Which of the following is NOT a social characteristic of an adolescent learner?
   a) Questioning society over uncertain status leading to anxiety and anger
   b) Getting inspired from like-minded peers and adopting their behaviour to bring reformation in the society
   c) Seeking directions from the elders to adopt an independent career
   d) Preferring to remain at the receiving end during a classroom lecture due to underdeveloped psychomotor skills

   (A) b and d only (B) only c
   (C) a, c, and d only (D) b only

2. Which of the following best explains the reason of difference in adolescent learner and an adult learner characteristics?
   (A) Being matured in age, an adult learner possesses a sound cognition whereas an adolescent learner asks questions on cognition.
   (B) An adolescent learner is emotionally weak in the challenging phases of maintaining relationship other than peers, whereas an adult learner prefers to take emotional challenges on sound footings.
   (C) Autonomy enjoyed by an adult learner is conducive to be auto-motivated whereas an adolescent learner, though investigative, is not motivated until he gets an external support.

(D) An adolescent learner fully concentrates on the lecture in the class, even if it is monotonous, whereas an adult learner being matured, requests the teacher to deliver the lecture in an absorbing way.

3. A 14 year-old learner interacts with the teacher and says that he/she does not feel as comfortable while reading in the library as he/she feels during a classroom lecture on the same topic. Which characteristic is being displayed by learner in this situation?
(A) Cognitional (B) Social
(C) Emotional (D) Academic

4. Consider a statement given below followed by two arguments. One argument is strong due to its strong logic, whereas the other argument is weak its due to weak logic Read the statement and the arguments carefully and choose the right option from the given answer choices.

Statement: Should we motivate an adolescent learner to choose a career of his choice independently?

Argument I: Yes, such attempt will inject confidence in the learner as he/she is heading towards adulthood where one is free to take his/her own decision.

Argument II: No, this attempt will sabotage the natural growth of the learner's characteristics.

(A) Only argument I is strong
(B) Both the arguments are weak
(C) Only argument II is strong
(D) Both the arguments are strong

5. Which of the following is TRUE about emotional characteristics of adult learners?
a) Pace of psychomotor skill is faster than that in adolescent learners
b) Inability to choose among given options
c) Needing motivation by some external source in a challenging situation
d) Needing direction to choose a particular stream of learning
(A) a and d only (B) c only
(C) b and d only (D) a, b, c, and d

6. Some characteristics of adolescent learners is given under Column I and the category to which they belong is given under Column II. Match the characteristic with its category and choose the right answer among the codes given below:

	Column I (Characteristic)	Column II (Category)
a)	Urge for interacting with peers	i) Emotional
b)	Urge to release energy	ii) Cognitive
c)	Direction seeker	iii) Academic
d)	Advocating philanthropy	iv) Social

Codes:

	(a)	(b)	(c)	(d)
(A)	iii	i	iv	ii
(B)	ii	iii	i	iv
(C)	iii	ii	iv	i
(D)	i	ii	iii	iv

7. Consider a statement "Individual difference in the characteristics of adolescent and adult learners are natural". This statement is a/an
(A) natural fact (B) derived fact
(C) overdrawn fact (D) implied fact

8. Attitude of adult learners towards teachers differs from learner to learner because of ________.differences.
(A) biological (B) cognitive
(C) academic (D) All of them

9. Find the odd choice among the following with respect to a learner's characteristics
(A) Result-oriented
(B) Developing competence
(C) Attention seeker
(D) Apprehensive

10. Complete the analogy in terms of a learner's characteristics
Overreactive: Negative remarks:: Curiosity: ?
(A) New skills (B) Self-respect
(C) Autonomy (D) Energy

11. Which of the following characteristics is common between an adolescent and adult learner?
(A) Self-motivated (B) Identity seeker
(C) Autonomous (D) All of these

12. If an adolescent learner advocates philanthropy, it is display of which characteristic?
(A) Emotional
(B) Cognitive
(C) Social
(D) Academic

13. Which of the following is NOT TRUE about an adult learner's characteristics?
   a) He/she is committed to his/her family and society.
   b) He/she comes to the class with a vast knowledge of problems.
   c) He/she seeks respect from the society.
   d) He/she is free to choose his/her learning stream and career.
   (A) b only (B) None
   (C) a, c, and d only (D) None of these
14. Which of the following is not a ground on which basis differences among learners are visible?
   (A) Family background
   (B) Learning stream
   (C) Cognition
   (D) Prior knowledge
15. Arrange the following learner's characteristics of an adult learner in increasing order of effectiveness.
   (A) Social > Cognitive > Emotional > Academic
   (B) Cognitive > Academic > Emotional > Social
   (C) Academic > Social > Emotional > Cognitive
   (D) Cognitive > Academic > Social > Emotional
16. Which of the following actions by a class teacher would be in concurrence with learners' characteristics?
   (A) Informing the Principal to plan a rational style of teaching matching with learners' characteristics.
   (B) Asking the learners to share their characteristics with him/her so that he/she can plan teaching strategy accordingly.
   (C) Obtaining feedback from learners' parents and asking them to suggest the appropriate strategy.
   (D) None of these
17. An adolescent overreacts on certain remarks. Which of the following is exactly the purpose behind those remarks?
   a) person wants to ridicule him
   b) rejection of some idea floated by him
   (A) Only a (B) Only b
   (C) Both a and b (D) Neither a nor b
18. Which of the following is a cognitive characteristic of an adolescent learner?
   (A) Advice seeker
   (B) Investigative over moral issues
   (C) Concerned about social change
   (D) All of the above
19. Which of the following is correct about individual difference between adolescent and adult learners?
   a) Adults search for personal identity whereas adolescents remain in discipline.
   b) Adults are concerned with cognitive learning whereas adolescents are concerned with challenging activities.
   c) Adults rely on themselves whereas adolescents need support from the teacher.
   d) Adults are active in learning whereas adolescents are passive in learning.
   (A) b and c only (B) d only
   (C) b, c, and d only (D) a, b, c, and d
20. Shifting of a learner's interest from physical subjects to abstract subjects indicates transformation from
   (A) Childhood to adolescence
   (B) Adolescence to adulthood
   (C) Emotional adult to cognitive adult
   (D) Cognitive adolescent to emotional adolescent

KEY

1. A	2. C	3. D	4. B	5. C	6. A	7. B
8. B	9. C	10. A	11. B	12. B	13. A	14. B
15. D	16. D	17. C	18. D	19. C	20. A	

Assertion–Reason Format

1. **Assertion (A):** Knowledge of learner's characteristics helps a teacher to prepare questions to be asked to the learners during lecture in the class.

   Reason (R): While delivering a lecture in the class, a teacher notices some characteristics of learners which are contrary to the characteristics displayed in the previous lecture.
   (A) A is true but R is false
   (B) Both A and R are false
   (C) A is false but R is true
   (D) None of these

2. **Assertion (A):** An adolescent learner tries to be associated with like-minded peers.
   Reason (R): An adolescent learner wants to share various evils of the society.
   (A) A is true but R is false
   (B) Both A and R are true but R is not correct explanation of A
   (C) A is false but R is true
   (D) Both A and R are true and R is correct explanation of A
3. **Assertion (A):** Characteristics of adolescent and adult learners streamline the teaching-learning process.
   Reason (R): Adolescent learners' characteristics strengthen the base of teaching-learning process, whereas adult learners' characteristics strengthen the secondary part of it.
   (A) Both A and R are true and R is the correct explanation of A
   (B) A is false but R is true
   (C) Both A and R are true but R is not correct explanation of A
   (D) A is true but R as false
4. **Assertion (A):** Adults are better learners than adolescents.
   Reason (R): Age is not considered a characteristic of an adult learner.
   (A) Both A and R are true but R is not correct explanation of A
   (B) A is true but R is false
   (C) Both A and R are false
   (D) Both A and R are true and R is correct explanation of A
5. **Assertion (A):** Learners' characteristics vary from learner to learner.
   Reasoning (R): Variation in the characteristics make it difficult for a teacher to draft a suitable curriculum.
   (A) Both A and R are true and R is correct explanation of A
   (B) Both A and R are correct but R is not correct explanation of A
   (C) Both A and R are false
   (D) A is false but R is true
6. **Assertion (A):** Learners' characteristics should be considered by a teacher while planning his/her lecture.
   Reason (R): A teacher's teaching strategy is successful only when learners learn actively.
   (A) Both A and R are true and R is correct explanation of A
   (B) Both A and R are correct and R is not correct explanation of A
   (C) A is true but R is false
   (D) A is false but R is true
7. **Assertion (A):** An adolescent learner joins an academic stream as per parents' advice.
   Reason (R): Seeking parents' advice is one of the characteristics of an adolescent learner.
   (A) Both A and R are true and R is correct explanation of A
   (B) Both A and R are correct but R is not correct explanation of A
   (C) Both A and R are false
   (D) A true but R is false
8. **Assertion (A):** Adult learners develop psychomotor skills faster than adolescent learners.
   Reason (R): Psychomotor skills are activities involving the movement of limbs.
   (A) Both A and R are true and R is correct explanation of A
   (B) Both A and R are true but R is not correct explanation of A
   (C) A is true but R is false
   (D) A is false but R is true
9. **Assertion (A):** Learners' attitude towards teaching material varies with age.
   Reason (R): Adolescent learners prefer to make choice from varied teaching material of books and notes.
   (A) Both A and R are true and R is correct explanation of A
   (B) Both A and R are true but R is not correct explanation of A
   (C) A is true but R is false
   (D) A is false but R is true
10. **Assertion (A):** Group dynamics of learners helps in planning curriculum.
    Reason (R): Learners are divided into different groups according to individual differences.
    (A) Both A and R are true and R is correct explanation of A
    (B) Both A and R are true but R is not correct explanation of A
    (C) A is true but R is false
    (D) A is false but R is true

KEY

1. B	2. D	3. D	4. C	5. C	6. A	7. C
8. D	9. C	10. A				

Questions Asked in Previous NET Exams

1. Which of the learner characteristics will influence his/her perspective in a course of study? **(UGC NET JUNE 2019)**
   (i) Learner's commitment
   (ii) Parents' interest in the learner
   (iii) Prior knowledge of the learner
   (iv) Skill of the learner in the concerned area
   (v) Family size of the learner
   (vi) Socio-economic background of the family to which the learner belongs
   Choose the correct answer from the options given below:
   (A) (i), (iii), and (iv)
   (B) (i), (ii), and (Iii)
   (C) (iii), (iv), and (v)
   (D) (iv), (v), and (vi)
2. Which of the following learner characteristics is highly related to effectiveness of teaching? **(UGC NET JULY 2018)**
   (A) Prior experience of the learner
   (B) Educational status of the parents of the learner
   (C) Peer groups of the learner
   (D) Family size from which the learner comes
3. From the list given below, identify the learner characteristics which would facilitate the teaching-learning system to become effective. Choose the correct code to indicate your answer. **(UGC NET NOVEMBER 2017)**
   (a) Prior experience of learner
   (b) Learner's family lineage
   (c) Aptitude of the learner
   (d) Learner's stage of development
   (e) Learner's food habit and hobbies
   (f) Learner's religious affiliation
   Code:
   (A) (d), (e), and (f)
   (B) (a), (d), and (e)
   (C) (b), (c), and (f)
   (D) (a), (c), and (d)
4. Some students in a class exhibit great curiosity for learning. It may be because such children **(UGC NET DECEMBER 2016)**
   (A) Are gifted
   (B) Come from rich families
   (C) Show artificial behaviour
   (D) Create indiscipline in the class
5. Which set of learner characteristics may be considered helpful in designing effective teaching-learning systems? Select the correct alternative from the codes given below: **(UGC NET JULY 2016)**
   (i) Prior experience of learners in respect of the subject
   (ii) Interpersonal relationships of learner's family friends
   (iii) Ability of the learners in respect of the subject
   (iv) Student's language background
   (v) Interest of students in following the prescribed dress code
   (vi) Motivational orientation of the students
   Codes:
   (A) (i), (ii), (iii), and (iv)
   (B) (i), (iii), (iv), and (vi)
   (C) (ii), (iii), (iv), and (v)
   (D) (iii), (iv), (v), and (vi)
6. The most appropriate purpose of learning is: **(UGC NET DECEMBER 2007)**
   (A) personal adjustment
   (B) modification of behaviour
   (C) social and political awareness
   (D) preparing oneself for employment
7. The students who keep on asking questions in the class should be: **(UGC NET JUNE 2007)**
   (A) encouraged to find answer independently.
   (B) advised to meet the teacher after the class.
   (C) encouraged to continue questioning.
   (D) advised not to disturb during the lecture.

KEY

1. A	2. A	3. D	4. A	5. B	6. B	7. A

3 Factors Affecting Teaching

INTRODUCTION

A teacher is considered to be a lighthouse of education which is imparted by him/her through teaching with the aim of increasing the knowledge of learners and reforming their personality. There are various factors which contribute in affecting a teacher's teaching in formal and non-formal system of education. Factors affecting teaching are related to the following participants in the teaching-learning process:

1) Teacher
2) Learners
3) Support material
4) Instructional facilities
5) Learning environment
6) Institution

FACTORS RELATED TO TEACHER

Various aspects of a teacher's personality affect teaching as is clear from the following:

1) **Academic qualification:** A teacher's academic qualification is a decisive factor regarding the capability of a teacher to teach effectively in a formal or non-formal stream of teaching. As syllabus, subject matter, and curriculum are revised time to time under a policy framework, a teacher with a higher academic qualification can effectively handle any such change and teach effectively. Higher qualification means specialized qualification so he/she can teach effectively in any circumstances. On the other hand, a teacher with a lower qualification will not be effective due to academic handicaps.
2) **Experience:** A teacher is considered to be perfect in that subject which he/she is allotted for teaching. Perfection is attained by a teacher through experience. Experience, therefore becomes a dominating factor in affecting teaching. A novice teacher cannot teach with that confidence with which an experienced teacher can. A teacher while gaining experience learns many traits of teaching effectively, like how to motivate learners for learning, how to interact with learners to make the lecture interesting and absorbing, how to face and overcome various challenges related to the teaching-learning process, and how to yield results. As a teacher gains experience, his/her confidence level goes on rising, his way of teaching improves, and he also starts producing results. This earns him/her the goodwill of an effective teacher.
3) **Mastery over the subject matter:** If on one side a teacher's academic qualification becomes a strong factor affecting teaching, on the other hand, a teacher's concept clarity and mastery over the subject matter is an equally strong factor. If a teacher has mastery over his/her subject he/she can clear doubts of the learners on any concept. Further, he/she will be effective in making the concept clear to the learners.
4) **Motivating acumen:** Learning is a voluntary activity. No teacher can force a learner to learn or attend his/her lecture. Fundamental requirement of a teaching-learning process is that a learner must be ready to learn. If a teacher finds that a learner is indifferent towards learning, he/she can motivate him/her to learn. It is the motivating acumen of the teacher that creates an interest for studies in the learner's mind. It is generally observed that only those teachers are popular with the learners who have motivated them to learn. It becomes easier for the teacher to teach motivated learners and this also results in a healthy interaction between the teacher and the learners. So a teacher's motivating acumen helps a teacher to go ahead with a particular teaching approach.
5) **Communication skills:** A good communicator can become a good teacher. Communication skills of a teacher affect his/her teaching in an effective way. The way in which a teacher presents his lecture in a class or online, depends upon his/her communication skills. A teacher's communication skills are displayed through the language in which he/she delivers the lecture and his/her gestures.

6) **Method of teaching:** Which method of teaching a teacher adopts, affects teaching in a long way. The teacher should be capable enough to assess whether a teacher-centered or learner-centered method is to be adopted in a class. Teaching with a teacher-centered method is based on factors which are different from the factors which are required for adopting a learner-centered method. Learners' potential to learn and understand the concept determines a particular method which will be adopted by the teacher. It is the skill of the teacher to choose an appropriate method and teach accordingly.
7) **Personality traits:** A physically fit, mentally sound, punctual, committed, well-mannered, and motivated teacher teaches in a better way than a normal teacher. A teacher's job is not only to impart subject knowledge to learners but also inculcate personality traits in them. Such teachers become an ideal for the learners and they also follow his/her routine and guidance for developing similar personality traits.
8) **Economic factor:** A teacher's teaching is affected if he/she is to settle any financial issue like salary or perks with the management of the school or college where he/she is teaching. In such circumstances, the teacher is not able to concentrate on his teaching responsibilities and this hampers a sound teaching-learning process.
9) **Value teaching:** Factor of value teaching affects a teacher's teaching in a way that the teacher along with rendering subject knowledge to the learners also teaches learners about various moral values like truth, hospitality, honesty, punctuality, determination, respect, humbleness, and many others.

FACTORS RELATED TO LEARNERS

In formal and non-formal teaching-learning process, learners also become reasons for affecting teaching. Following are such learner related factors:

1) **Motivation level:** A learner's motivation level towards learning affects teaching. If a teacher finds that the learner is not motivated to learn, then the foremost target of the teacher will be to motivate him/her first and then start actual teaching. If the learner is already motivated to learn, then it becomes easier for a teacher to teach such a learner.
2) **Age group:** A learner may be an adolescent or an adult. Age group of a learner becomes a strong factor affecting teaching. Adolescent and adult learners require their respective classroom environments and different approaches towards teaching as they differ in their characteristics on social, academic, cognitive, and emotional grounds.
3) **Prior knowledge:** If a learner has prior knowledge of the topic which is to be discussed in the class, then the teacher can teach such a learner effectively. On the contrary, a different teaching discipline is required for that learner who does not have prior knowledge.
4) **Psychology:** Psychology of a learner also affects teaching in its own way. Learners do not possess a similar state of mind. Some learners are introvert and others are extrovert. Difference in their psychology demands different approaches of teaching.
5) **Promptness in feedback:** If a learner is prompt in giving feedback to what a teacher is teaching in class, it becomes easier for the teacher to understand about the status of the present teaching strategy. If there is positive feedback, then the teacher continues with the present strategy, but if there is negative feedback, then the teacher changes the teaching strategy accessible to the learners.

COMMON FACTORS RELATED TO BOTH TEACHER AND LEARNERS

Following are certain factors which affect teaching due to teacher's and learners' mutual or common traits.

1) **Environment in the class:** Environment in the class is the result of mutual efforts of the teacher and the learners. Congenial atmosphere will result in effective teaching to strengthen the teaching-learning process.
2) **Family background:** Family background of both the teacher and the learner affect teaching. A teacher hailing from a teacher's family will be highly effective in imparting quality teaching. On the other hand, a teacher from business or other family will take time to teach in the desired way, so a teacher's family background is a strong factor in affecting teaching. Similarly, if a learner hails from a teacher's family, he displays the nature of a sincere and motivated learner and the teacher can use an appropriate teaching strategy. Whereas, if a learner comes from a non-teacher family, he is tackled with a different teaching strategy.

3) **Physical and mental health:** It applies to both the teacher and the learner; a healthy teaching-learning process is possible if the teacher and learner both enjoy a sound mental and physical health.

FACTORS RELATED TO SUPPORT MATERIAL

In present day teaching, the teacher needs some material conducive to teaching and making teaching and learning interesting and absorbing. Support material is that material which helps in strengthening the teaching-learning process. Support material affects teaching according to its availability, variety, quality, and accuracy. If such material is readily available, it facilitates quality teaching and teaching yields promising results. The following material is included in support material:

1) Textbooks
2) e-books
3) Wall charts
4) Audio-visual teaching aids
5) Mic and sound system
6) Workbooks
7) Dictionaries
8) Laboratory equipment
9) Models
10) Diorama
11) Encyclopedias
12) Well-stocked library
13) Stationery
14) Equipment for powerpoint presentation

FACTORS RELATED TO INSTRUCTIONAL FACILITIES

A teacher may be well qualified, experienced, or possessing all traits of a good teacher. Similarly, a learner may be motivated and determined, but the teaching-learning process does not gain fillip if there is lack of instructional facilities. Following are the instructional facilities which should be available to the teacher for quality, perennial, and effective teaching:

1) Well-maintained classrooms
2) Well-equipped laboratories
3) Seminar rooms (Sufficient spaces to instruct a big strength of students)
4) Well-stocked libraries
5) Cyber cells
6) High-tech instruction equipment
7) Sufficient spaces to instruct a big strength of students

FACTORS RELATED TO LEARNING ENVIRONMENT

Learning environment is a big factor affecting teaching and learning. Following factors related to the learning environment affect teaching.

1) **Location of the educational institute:** Teaching is greatly affected by the location of school, college, or university. Location of the institute should be at a peaceful place. Further, such a location builds up a congenial learning environment. An effective teaching-learning process is possible in a peaceful, hassle-free, and serene environment as teaching and learning requires concentration and participation of both the teacher and the learners. On the other hand, if teaching is provided at a crowded or traffic-infested location, the teacher will not be able to teach properly due to the loud noise and this will badly affect teaching.
2) **Holding of seminars and quiz competitions:** Periodical holding of seminars and arranging quiz competitions on subject knowledge and general knowledge by a school, college, or university creates a learning environment which affects teaching. Teachers prepare the learners to participate in such competitions and teach accordingly. Such events not only increase the confidence level among learners but learners also develop a spirit to fight and win.
3) **Spacious and modern libraries:** Spacious and well-stocked libraries in the institutes also build up a learning environment both for the teacher and learners. Such libraries create interest in the learners' mind to study in the library and discuss problems with the teacher. While getting feedback from learners, a teacher plans and executes his/her teaching strategy.

INSTITUTION

Location, type, level, and goodwill of an educational institute become tangible factors affecting teaching. Following are institution related factors which affect teaching:

1) **Management and policies of the institution:** If the management of the institution has a policy to encourage its teachers to have a free hand in planning and executing teaching strategies in the interest of learners' welfare, then the teacher will have a sense of achievement and plan such teaching strategies which are conducive to learning by the learners. On the other hand, if the management of the institution frequently interferes in the teachers'

work and there is a policy to exploit the hardworking and sincere teachers, then his/her teaching is badly affected. The teacher then loses the spirit to teach.

2) **Politics of the institution:** Involvement of an education institute in politics also becomes an important factor which affects teaching. Frequent strikes, either by the teachers or the students, in an educational institute badly interrupt regular teaching and the teacher and the learners both suffer academic losses.

3) **Goodwill of the institution:** An institution with a sound goodwill maintains a minimum standard of teaching, as it is quality teaching which determines the goodwill of an institute. Such institutions engage the best possible teachers to impart education. Teachers of such institutions are directed to choose those teaching methods which strengthen the teaching-learning process and bring results. A teacher being a part of the institution, devises and applies effective teaching methods.

4) **State of general and academic infrastructure:** If an institution possesses a sound and complete general and academic infrastructure, including smart classrooms, e-libraries, hi-tech laboratories, teachers' independent cabins, student centers, refreshment joint, etc., a teacher can teach while using the infrastructural facility. He/she can then teach any topic while using the required infrastructure.

Some Vital Facts

1) Education system is one of the strongest factor in determining effectiveness of teaching.
2) Teacher's internal locus of control, learner's motivation, teacher's self-efficacy, teacher's skill in managing and monitoring and teacher's knowledge of the subject including general knowledge are some of the factors affecting teaching.
3) In affective domain of learning it is the attitude of the teacher which affects his/her teaching

Practice Exercise

General Questions Format

1. Which of the following is NOT TRUE about factors affecting teaching?

a) Varied nature of factors affecting teaching brings dynamism in teaching.
b) Teaching of formal and non-formal system is not necessarily affected by the same factors.
c) Statutory factors affecting teaching yield better results than voluntary factors affecting teaching.
d) Teaching is an exercise in futility unless it is challenged by factors affecting it.

(A) a and c only (B) b only
(C) a, b, c, and d (D) c and d only

2. Academic qualification of the teacher is ______ condition for teaching.

(A) necessary
(B) sufficient
(C) necessary and sufficient
(D) None of these

3. Where there are teachers there ______.

a) is support material
b) are learners
c) is learning environment
d) is motivation

(A) a and d only
(B) none of a, b, c and d
(C) all a, b, c, and d
(D) d only

4. Name of a factor affecting teaching has been given under Column I and source of that factor is given under Column II. Match the factors with their sources and choose the correct code among the given codes.

	Column - I (Name of factor)	Column - II (Source)
a)	Infrastructure	i) Instructional facility
b)	Seminar rooms	ii) Institution
c)	Age group	iii) Teacher
d)	Experience	iv) Learners

Codes:

	(a)	(b)	(c)	(d)
(A)	i	iv	ii	iii
(B)	iv	i	iii	ii
(C)	ii	i	iv	iii
(D)	iii	ii	i	iv

5. Institutional policies can become an effective factor affecting teaching if it is executed at ______ level.

(A) management (B) teacher

(C) student (D) people

6. Which of the following factor is not related to the learning environment which affects teaching?

(A) Location of the institution

(B) Well-stocked library

(C) Organising quiz competitions

(D) Cyber cell

7. Who needs motivation sufficient enough to ensure a successful teaching-learning process in the class?

a) learners b) teachers

c) management d) learners' parents

(A) a and b only (B) b, c, and d only

(C) a, b, and c only (D) a, b, c, and d

8. Which of the following factors related to instructional facilities least affect teaching?

a) Classrooms b) Laboratories

c) Cyber cells d) Libraries

(A) b only (B) none

(C) d only (D) a only

9. Here are certain teacher related factors which affect teaching:

I) Experience

II) Personality

III) Academic qualification

IV) Motivation skill

Arrange them in priority.

(A) IV-I-III-II (B) IV-III-I-II

(C) IV-II-I-III (D) IV-I-II-III

10. Which of the following best explains the significance of classroom environment as a factor affecting teaching?

(A) Teacher and learners take an open pledge in the class to make classroom environment teaching and learning-friendly.

(B) Teacher teaches that topic which the learners like the most and they get absorbed in the lecture.

(C) Teacher motivates learners to attend the lecture while complying with classroom ethics.

(D) Teacher delivers the concerned lecture in an interesting way to engage the learners and learners actively respond to make it a mutual effort.

11. Consider the statement, "A learner-centered method of teaching is a more effective factor affecting teaching than a teacher-centered method". The above statement is a

(A) Derived truth

(B) Statutory hypothesis

(C) Long-drawn truth

(D) Fallacy

12. Imagine you are an experienced teacher. You are allotted that class to teach where all learners are introvert. Which approach will you follow to establish an effective teaching-learning process? You will ______.

(A) try to know the reason behind their introvert behaviour and follow a teaching method accordingly

(B) follow micro teaching strategy and ensure their participation

(C) advise them to abandon this behaviour and teach them with discussion method.

(D) have separate dialogue with each of them and motivate them to participate in the teaching-learning process

13. What policy should the management of a college follow so that there is a positive effect on teaching?

(A) Teachers should be included in the committee responsible for drafting the curriculum.

(B) There should be separate committees for science and non-science subjects for drafting curriculum and senior teachers should be taken as active members.

(C) Representation in curriculum committee should be given to students also as their learning needs are to be realised to follow an appropriate method of teaching.

(D) None of these.

14. What is the nature of learners' related factors which affect teaching?

(A) Pervasive (B) Judicious

(C) Prospective (D) Sentimental

15. Various factors affecting teaching are actually affecting ______.

a) learners' spirit of taking learning initiatives

b) management's plans to draw curriculum

c) institution's academic goodwill

d) compilation of study material

(A) b, c, and d (B) a, b, and c

(C) a and d only (D) a only

16. Which is the strongest factor affecting teaching of an introvert teacher?

(A) Indifference from learners

(B) Interference of management

(C) Motivation from colleagues

(D) Ignorance from family

17. Which learner related factor puts the least impact on a teacher's teaching?

(A) Age group

(B) Prior knowledge

(C) Promptness in feedback

(D) Motivation level

18. Which of the instructional facilities plays the maximum role in affecting a teacher's teaching?

(A) Seminar room

(B) Classroom

(C) Laboratory

(D) Library

19. Various components of the learning environment affect a teacher's teaching. Which of the following is the best explanation of that?

a) Teaching in a peaceful and serene environment is enduring and pervasive.

b) Inspired by the environment, a teacher designs his/her strategy of teaching.

c) Learners' willingness to learn motivates the teacher to plan his teaching strategy.

d) A good teacher always looks for a learning environment whereas a sincere learner creates it.

(A) b and c (B) a and c

(C) b, c, and d (D) a, b, c, and d

20. Support material affects teaching according to its ______.

(A) availability

(B) variety

(C) quality and accuracy

(D) All of the above

21. Which of the following factor(s) really improve(s) a teacher's teaching?

a) Support material

b) Instructional facilities

c) Learning environment

d) Goodwill of a college or university

(A) a and c only (B) a and d only

(C) a, b, c, and d (D) d only

22. Some of the teacher related factors affecting teaching are given under Column I and their respective significance is given under Column II. Match the factor with its correct significance and choose the right code from the codes given below.

Column I (Factor)	Column II (Significance)
a) Value teaching	i) Control on the class
b) Academic qualification	ii) Hindrance in teaching process
c) Economic factors	iii) Morality
d) Experience	iv) Specialisation

Codes:

	(a)	(b)	(c)	(d)
(A)	ii	i	iii	iv
(B)	iii	ii	i	iv
(C)	iii	iv	ii	i
(D)	i	iii	ii	iv

KEY

1. D	2. C	3. B	4. C	5. B	6. D	7. C
8. B	9. A	10. D	11. A	12. D	13. C	14. B
15. B	16. C	17. B	18. B	19. A	20. D	21. D
22. C						

Assertion–Reason Format

1. **Assertion (A):** Most of the factors affecting teaching are determined by the learners' characteristics.

   Reason (R): Methods of teaching vary with the age group of learners.

   (A) Both A and R are true and R is the correct explanation of A

   (B) A is true but R is false

   (C) A is false but R is true

   (D) Both A and R are true but R is not correct explanation of A

2. **Assertion (A):** A teacher's experience is vital for teaching a large number of students.

   Reason (R): Number of students a teacher is to teach becomes another factor affecting teaching.

   (A) Both A and R are false

   (B) Both A and R are true and R is the correct explanation of A

   (C) A is true but R is false

   (D) A is false but R is true

3. **Assertion (A):** Some factors affecting teaching are related to the learning environment.

   Reason (R): Serene and peaceful location of a college motivates learners to learn.

   (A) Both A and R are false

   (B) A is true but R is false

   (C) A is false but R is true

   (D) Both A and R are true and R is the correct explanation of A

4. **Assertion (A):** While teaching with support material a teacher cannot show his teaching skill.

   Reason (R): Learners learn better when taught with support material.

   (A) Both A and R are true and R is the correct explanation of A

   (B) Both A and R are true but R is not correct explanation of A

   (C) A is false but R is true

   (D) A is true but R is false

5. **Assertion (A):** Instructional facilities prove to be a means of smooth running of teaching-learning process.

   Reasoning (R): Smart classrooms and cyber cells, teaching aids, etc. fulfil the present day requirement of teaching and learning.

   (A) Both A and R are true and R is the correct explanation of A

   (B) Both A and R are true but R is not correct explanation of A

   (C) A is true but R is false

   (D) Both A and R are false

6. **Assertion (A):** Family background of a teacher temporarily affects his/her teaching.

   Reason (R): There are other factors permanently affecting a teacher's teaching.

   (A) Both A and R are true and R is correct explanation of A

   (B) Both A and R are correct but R is not correct explanation of A

   (C) Both A and R are false

   (D) A is false but R is true

7. **Assertion (A):** A teacher with higher qualification is supposed to be more effective than a teacher with lower qualification.

   Reason (R): Higher education means specialisation and specialisation brings quality.

   (A) Both A and R are true and R is correct explanation of A

   (B) Both A and R are true but R is not correct explanation of A

   (C) A is true but R is false

   (D) A is false but R is true

8. **Assertion (A):** All factors affecting teaching hold true in learner-centred teaching.

   Reason (R): Learner-centred teaching methods are in high demand.

   (A) Both A and R are true and R is correct explanation of A

   (B) Both A and R are true but R is not correct explanation of A

   (C) A is true but R is false

   (D) A is false but R is true

9. **Assertion (A):** Age of a learner is a strong factor affecting teaching.

   Reason (R): Adolescent and adult learners learn differently from the same teacher.

   (A) Both A and R are true and R is correct explanation of A

   (B) Both A and R are true but R is not correct explanation of A

   (C) A is true but R is false

   (D) A is false but R is true

10. **Assertion (A):** Motivated learners are inspiring factors affecting a teacher's teaching in the interest of effective teaching.

    Reason (R): Motivating students is not a statutory job of a teacher, thus it does not affect a teacher's teaching.

    (A) Both A and R are true and R is correct explanation of A

    (B) Both A and R are true but R is not correct explanation of A

    (C) A is true but R is false

    (D) A is false but R is true

KEY

1. C 2. A 3. D 4. C 5. A 6. C 7. A 8. D 9. B 10. C

Questions Asked in Previous NET Exams

1. One of the most powerful factors affecting teaching effectiveness is related to the **(UGC NET JANUARY 2017)**

   (A) Social system of the country

   (B) Economic status of the society

   (C) Prevailing political system

   (D) Educational system

2. Which of the following factors affect teaching? **(UGC NET AUGUST 2016)**

   Choose the correct code to indicate your answer.

   (i) Teacher's internal locus of control

   (ii) Learner motivation

   (iii) Teacher's biographical data

   (iv) Teacher's self-efficacy

   (v) Learner's interest in co-curricular activities

   (vi) Teacher's skill in managing and monitoring

   (vii) Teacher's knowledge of the subject including general knowledge

   Codes:

   (A) (i), (ii), (iv), (vi), and (vii)

   (B) (i), (ii), (iii), (iv), and (v)

   (C) (iii), (iv), (v), (vi), and (vii)

   (D) (ii), (iii), (iv), (v), and (vi)

3. Select the alternative which consists of positive factors contributing to effectiveness of teaching: **(UGC NET JULY 2016)**

   List of factors:

   a. Teacher's knowledge of the subject

   b. Teacher's socio-economic background

   c. Communication skill of the teacher

   d. Teacher's ability to please the students

   e. Teacher's personal contact with the students

   f. Teacher's competence in managing and monitoring the classroom transactions

   Codes:

   (A) (b), (c), and (d)

   (B) (c), (d), and (f)

   (C) (b), (d), and (e)

   (D) (a), (c), and (f)

4. Attitude of the teacher that affects teaching pertains to **(UGC NET DECEMBER 2014)**

   (A) Affective domain

   (B) Cognitive domain

   (C) Conative domain

   (D) Psychomotor domain

KEY

1. D 2. A 3. D 4. A

Methods of Teaching in Institutions of Higher Learning and Government Initiatives

CONCEPT

Success of formal teaching depends upon the methods of teaching. Effective teaching does not depend upon what is delivered; rather it depends upon how it is delivered. An effective method of teaching makes a teacher popular among the learners as they can understand the lecture very well and can also give feedback to the teacher; thus it yields results. Though the basic format of classroom teaching is same at primary, secondary, and tertiary levels of education, yet learners of higher education stream require a bit different method of teaching due to their emotional, academic, cognitive, and social characteristics. As learners at higher education level are adolescents and adults, teaching methods in institutions of higher learning are planned and devised while keeping characteristics of the learners under consideration.

METHODS OF TEACHING

Following methods of teaching are practised in the institutions of higher learning:

1) Teacher-centred
2) Learner-centred
3) Offline
4) Online

TEACHER-CENTRED METHOD

This method is also known as 'Traditional Method of Teaching'. In this method the teacher devises the curriculum and teaching strategy according to his/own aptitude and attitude. This method has been in practice since long in colleges and universities. Only the teacher in the classroom is active. Learners are not allowed to discuss or ask questions. Learners' role is passive in the class. They are to listen and note down the information being given by the teacher. Learners take the teacher as an expert in the subject on which he/she is giving the lecture. Learners are not allowed to indulge in any classroom activity; rather they are asked to memorise or understand the topic of the lecture to be recited to the teacher later. Students or learners are to independently work on assignments and they can't share it with others or copy that from others. Example of this method is lecture method. However, this method has some advantages and disadvantages.

Characteristics of Teacher-Centred Method

i) **Centre of knowledge:** Teacher is the centre of knowledge in this method as he is to speak in the class.

ii) **Empty vessels:** Students are considered as empty vessels which are filled by the teacher by teaching and giving knowledge in the class.

iii) **Passive learning:** As students are not to react over the lecture or share a point with the classmates or the teacher, a process of passive learning is set in by the teacher in the class where students are to simply receive what the teacher delivers.

iv) **Unilateral flow of knowledge:** Information flows from the teacher to learners and not vice versa.

v) **Primary and ultimate communicator:** Teacher is the only communicator in the class. He is also the primary evaluator of knowledge of the students.

vi) **Structured lectures:** Teacher delivers structured lectures and learners listen to it and note down believing that whatever content the teacher is delivering is correct and complete.

vii) **Summative evaluation:** As teacher does not encourage interaction with the students during the lecture or whole course, there are neither doubt clearing sessions nor question/answer sessions during the progress of the course. Evaluation is done only at the end of the course.

Advantages

i) **Orderly and quiet classroom:** As students are not allowed to indulge in any discussion in the class, classroom remains quiet and in order.

ii) **Barrier-free lecture:** Teacher has full control on the classroom and there is no interruption, no barrier (noise), and no distortion in the delivery of lecture. On one hand, teacher's aim to deliver a barrier free lecture is achieved. On the other hand, students also receive and understand the lecture.

iii) **Increase in confidence among learners:** As students work independently to solve the assignments, they develop more confidence in the topic.

iv) **No apprehension of indifference by learners:** As the teacher is the primary and ultimate communicator in the class and learners are to listen to him with full concentration, there is no apprehension of learners missing the topic or showing their indifference from that.

Disadvantages

i) **Obsolete:** Teacher-centred method is a traditional method being practised since ancient times. But today it has become obsolete in comparison to modern methods of teaching which stand on equal teacher-learner active participation.

ii) **Boring:** As there are restrictions on students to listen the lecture, they can't relish it. Learning is a voluntary initiative. No one can be compelled to learn. Learners find the lecture boring amid restrictions. It appears that they are listening and learning but actually their mind wanders somewhere else as they are finding the lecture boring, so they do not understand the lecture fully. Such teaching does not yield positive results.

iii) **Affects learners' communication skills:** As students in the teacher-centred method are not allowed to interact with classmates or the teacher, their communication skills suffer.

iv) **Attack on learner's liberty:** Learning is imposed on learners in this method and further, they cannot share the lecture, assignments, etc. with class fellows and are also not allowed to ask the teacher. So this is an attack on learners' liberty which is an obstacle in the way of learning and understanding of the lecture.

v) **Promotes rote learning:** In this method students are to listen and learn what the teacher is delivering in the class. Learners are asked to cram the content and recite it to the teacher. So emphasis is on rote learning rather than understanding the concept. Understanding is a result of thorough discussion and interaction which learners are not allowed.

LEARNER-CENTRED METHOD

As the name indicates, this method of teaching is devised to teach according to the convenience and learning interest of the learners. This is also known as Modern Method of Teaching. It is currently practised in colleges and universities. Draft National Education Policy (NEP) 2019 recognises and recommends promotion and execution of learner-centred teaching methods in universities and colleges by the government of India. National Knowledge Commission was also established by the government of India to work for reviewing the scope of this method of teaching in Indian universities and colleges. Learners are not passive participants in the teaching-learning process in this method. Both teachers and students participate actively and equally in the classroom activity and debate or discussion among learners or between learners and the teacher. In this method there is effective teacher-student interaction. Knowledge of adolescent and adult learners' characteristics helps a lot to teachers and policy makers to devise student-centred methods of teaching. Constructivist theories of learning support this teaching method to be practised in the institutions of higher learning. Innovative ways of interaction between students and professors are devised in this method. This method emphasises learning through communication among learners and between teacher and the students. Teacher encourages feedback from students on his/her lecture. This is followed by doubt clearing, problem-solving, and critical appraisal sessions in the interest of effective teaching and proper understanding of the topic. Examples of this type of teaching method include Discussion method, Inquiry-based method, and Hills Model of Learning through Discussion (LTD).

Constructivist Theory of Learning

Constructivist Theory has its base in Epistemology. This theory also explains the source of attaining knowledge and then learning from the acquired knowledge. Constructivism believes that humans acquire knowledge and learn from their experience. Teacher plans and executes constructivism in his teaching method which aims at fulfilling the requirements of learners. Focussing on learners in a teaching method is Constructivism.

Characteristics of Learner-Centred Method

i) **Dual role of teacher:** Teacher plays the role of a teacher as well as a learner because there is bilateral interaction between the teacher and the learners. In this way teacher not only teaches but also learns in this method.

ii) **Teacher is a source:** As there is a bilateral discussion between the teacher and learners, teacher does not remain an authority anymore. Teacher becomes a source like other participants.

iii) **Active and deep learning:** At higher education level, learners are sufficiently wise and aware to accept content while verifying its authenticity. So learners, unlike in teacher-centred method, actively learn in this method through thorough inquiries and discussion. This also results in deep learning and understanding of the topic.

iv) **Accountability of the learners:** Due to teacher-learners active participation in exchanging and disseminating knowledge, students are equally accountable as the teacher regarding the authenticity of knowledge.

v) **Sense of autonomy:** Learners develop a sense of autonomy as far as their active participation in the teaching-learning process is concerned.

vi) **Healthy equation:** This method paves way for a healthy interaction and hence, equation between the teacher and the learners.

vii) **Motivated teacher as well as learners:** While following learner-centred method, both the student and the teacher are motivated to be part of the teaching-learning process. the The teacher uses his teaching skills and motivates the learners to actively participate in the lecture. The teacher himself/herself is also motivated to teach, as if teacher is not motivated, he/she cannot motivate learners. Motivation even makes introvert learners also to actively participate in bilateral communication.

> *"If the child is not learning the way you are teaching, then you must teach in the way the child learns."*
>
> **Dr. Rita Dunn**

Advantages

i) **Skill for life:** Learners learner various skills of effective communication in this method. They shed their hesitation and gain confidence. These skills stay with them throughout their life and are conducive to their success and achievements.

ii) **Independent learners:** As this method gives learner a chance and platform to interact independently, this sense develops in them skill of taking decisions independently.

iii) **Quality enhancement:** This method helps institutions of higher learning to enhance quality of higher education because teachers and learners both yield promising results.

iv) **Universal benefit:** This method of teaching provides overall benefit to colleges, universities, other institutions of higher learning, teachers, students, and the society.

Disadvantages

i) **Noisy classrooms:** As teacher has no control on the class, there are scenes of noisy and chaotic classrooms disturbing others in the name of discussion.

ii) **Loss of control:** Teacher loses control over classroom activities and sometimes discussion becomes unruly.

iii) **Clash of opinion:** There is always apprehension of discussion becoming aggressive or violent due to clash of opinion among students.

iv) **Problematic Group Working:** Some students want to learn alone. In this case, group work may be problematic.

One-to-one Differences Between Teacher-Centred and Learner-Centred Teaching

Teacher-Centred	Learner-Centred
Focus is on instructor	Focus is on both students and instructor
Focus is on language forms and structures (what the instructor knows about the language	Focus is on language use in typical situations (how students will use the language)
Instructor talks; students listen	Instructor (models), students interact with the instructor and one another
Students work alone	Students work in pairs, in groups, or alone depending on the purpose of the activity
Instructor monitors and corrects every student utterance	Students talk without constant instructor monitoring; instructor provides feedback/correction when questions arise
Instructor answers students' questions about language	Students answer each other's questions, using the instructor as an information resource
Instructor chooses topics	Students have some choice of topics
Instructor evaluates student learning	Students evaluate their own learning; instructor also evaluates
Classroom is quiet	Classroom is often noisy and busy

OFFLINE TEACHING METHODS

Delivery of a lecture by a teacher in a classroom is called Offline teaching method. This is termed as formal teaching in which teacher and learners come and assemble in a classroom of a college or university. There are different methods of classroom teaching which are explained as follows:

Lecture Method

This is the traditional method of teaching in which the teacher delivers an already prepared lecture to the students. It is also called **Expository method of teaching**. In spite of the advent of modern information technology, lecture method is still a pivotal method of teaching in the institutions of higher learning. A teacher uses his skill of teaching while delivering a lecture in the classroom with the motive of feedback from the students. The teacher defines and elaborates the topic with illustrations. The teacher is an expert in the concerned subject and clears doubts of the learners on the topic. Though it is a teacher-centred method, yet there is a scope of learners' participation in the form of feedback or asking questions. By and large, learners depend upon the knowledge provided by the teacher as they have little knowledge of the topic.

Characteristics of Lecture Method

a) **Formal teaching method:** Lecture method is a strong example of the formal teaching system. Teacher and students assemble in the classroom of a college or a university. In the class the teacher interacts with the students of the class. There is gap of decorum between the teacher and the students. It is a traditional but indispensable method of teaching in colleges and universities even today and will be in future also.

b) **Traits of a good teacher:** The teacher teaches in the class while using traits of a good teacher like making the delivery of lecture simple and interesting, never losing patience while teaching, or replying to the queries of learners, and ensuring feedback. These traits a teacher can use only in this method of teaching and not in any other method.

c) **Most reliable method:** As this method has been tested and found to be effective since ancient times, teachers, students of every type of college and universities, and curriculum and policy makers rely on this method even today.

d) **No impact of technology:** Lecture method is a primitive method to impart education. Its format is man-to-man direct interaction without any electronic medium between the teacher and the students. Even after advent of computer and communication technology, its format is the same. Even today there is dyadic communication between the teacher and students. A teacher can use electronic and computer technology in the class as a support material but no electronic or computer device can substitute a teacher.

Advantages

i) **Time saving for students:** In the lecture method, students get knowledge in compact form prepared by the teacher while consulting different sources. Students are not to waste time in running after different sources, thus lecture delivered to students give overall knowledge and saves their time.

ii) **Technically relevant material:** In the lecture method the teacher prepares material as an expert; thus provides relevant material on the topic in the class. Further, it is the lecture method in which teacher states how the material is technicality relevant and how it should be grasped.

iii) **Instant clarity of doubts:** At higher education level, students are well aware of the topic and subject. When teacher completes his lecture, students ask questions regarding the topic of the lecture. Teacher spontaneously answers them and students understand the topic after clarity of their doubts.

iv) **Basis of goodwill:** Though computer and electronic technology has entered in the education field and various technically advanced teaching methods are coming up, yet lecture method determines the goodwill of the teacher and the college or the university. Those colleges or universities become popular which enjoy the reputation of quality teaching which is due to quality teaching by the teacher using the lecture method.

v) **Confidence booster:** It is the lecture method in which learners get an opportunity to ask questions or raise their doubts about the topic of lecture and spontaneous solution to their doubts and questions boosts confidence in them. The teacher also injects confidence in introvert and underconfident learners by his/her skill of teaching. It is possible only in the lecture method.

vi) **No risk for students:** As lecture method is a teacher-centred method, learners are to be attentive to the teacher and concentrate on the contents being delivered in the lecture. Learners therefore have no risk of missing any point of the topic.

Disadvantages

i) **Boring:** As lecture method is a teacher-centric method, students feel bored during the course of lecture and their concentration is shaken and they do not properly grasp the lecture.

ii) **One-sided:** As the teacher dominates and asks learners to listen and note down the lecture, it becomes one-sided communication. Even if learners raise doubts, they are to be satisfied with the teacher's answer and there is virtually no bilateral communication.

iii) **Non-retention of content:** As learners are passive participants in this method, they can't retain the content of the lecture too long, hence they forget everything which is against the ethics of effective teaching and effective learning.

iv) **Risk of poor presentation:** Lecture method can be made successful only by a highly skilled and experienced teacher. A novice or underconfident teacher poses a risk of ineffective presentation which wastes the learners' time.

v) **Ignoring learners' psychology:** In lecture method the teacher dictates and explains the concept without considering the varying psychology of the learners. In this method it is assumed that all learners possess the same level of psychology so they are taught accordingly. Every student cannot learn with the same pace due to variation in their psychology. Some students who cannot keep pace with other students in learning, do not understand the lecture, hence their confidence is shaken.

vi) **No promotion of independent learning:** As it is a teacher-centred method of teaching, it does not promote independent learning, hence learners do not develop confidence.

Discussion Method

The word 'Discuss' is derived from a Latin word 'Discutere' which means to shake or strike. Discussion on a topic is also shaking the topic or striking in the course of discussion. This is a modern and learner-centred method. In this method, the teacher gives a subject to the learners and initiates discussion. After this, the teacher spends some time listening and the teacher spends some time speaking. There is bilateral interaction among the students or between the students and the teacher. After giving the topic, the teacher starts listening to the students. After some time the teacher gives a signal of discussion. Though at the start of discussion the teacher also participates in the discussion, yet he/she withdraws steadily handing over full charge of the discussion to the students. This method is practised in institutions of higher learning, as students at higher education level have potential for discussion and they are investigative also regarding the authenticity of the content of the topic. With discussion they learn many concepts and all their doubts about the topic become clear. Discussion may be led by the teacher or by a student; it may be in a small group or in whole class. Verbal exchange of ideas among participants gives an opportunity to them to know about different viewpoints. Such exposures clear many doubts of the students.

Stages of Discussion Method

Discussion method passes through three stages:

a) Orientation
b) Engagement
c) Debrief

a) **Orientation:** At this stage students are given topic of discussion. They are told the procedure of discussion and they are motivated to think about the topic for some time before starting discussion.

b) **Engagement:** A discussion environment is developed by the teacher. Then the teacher asks one student to start speaking on the fundamentals of the topic. All the students are given a fixed time to speak. During this stage teacher listens and if there is a need, helps the learners also. After that, the teacher also starts participating in the discussion and while complying with all norms, the discussion is concluded with a summary.

c) **Debrief:** This stage consists of allotting time to students to make notes on the topic and asking them to brief what they have learnt.

Characteristics of Discussion Method

i) **Bilateral communication:** Due to exchange of ideas among students or between students and the teacher, this method exercises bilateral communication.

ii) **Maximum participation:** All students, even introverts, are asked to participate and the teacher also participates in the discussion. This ensures maximum participation, hence clarity of the topic to maximum students.

iii) **Active learning:** Being a learner-centred method, it encourages active learning.

iv) **Uniform emphasis:** In this method, the teacher gives a topic to all the students and all are given equal opportunity and time for discussion. So there is no bias in this method of teaching.

v) **No monopoly in evaluation:** The teacher does not enjoy monopoly in evaluation. Here, the teacher consults leaders of different groups involved in discussion and evaluation is jointly completed and there is no chance of either discrimination or bias.

Advantages

i) **Developing leadership qualities:** These methods develop leadership qualities in students as they lead the discussion and try to win over when competing with other groups involved in discussion.

ii) **Perennial learning:** Students can retain content of the topic for a sufficiently long time because they have learnt it by exhaustive discussion and not just by cramming.

iii) **Developing communication skills:** This method develops communication skills in learners as they are given an exhaustive exposure to discussion.

iv) **Development of reflective thinking:** As students discuss the given topic exhaustively with their companions or the teacher and reach concrete conclusions, it helps in development of reflective thinking, i.e., ability to make judgement about something that has happened.

v) **Development of democratic spirit:** Learners develop democratic spirit through this method because they discuss the topic with everyone in the class without consideration of caste, creed, religion, or region. Further, every participant gets a chance to discuss.

vi) **Confidence builder:** This method proves to be a confidence builder of learners. Individual representation of the topic followed by discussion and defending strategy used by students inject confidence in the learners.

vii) **Learning stimulant:** Discussion method works as a learning stimulant because due to active participation of students, it makes learning interesting.

viii) **Problem-solving ability:** Learners develop ability to solve problems independently due to extensive nature of this method.

Disadvantages

I) **Cannot work extempore:** This method is successful only when the participants, i.e., students and teachers have already prepared the topic. Discussion cannot be successful if started extempore and it leads to confusion rather than clarification of a topic or concept.

II) **Uneven presentation:** There are chances that only dominant students get a chance to discuss. Remaining students or introverts may not get a chance so there are chances of uneven presentation and all students may not understand the topic too.

III) **Noise and chaos in the class:** The teacher has no control over the class as he/she himself/herself is party to discussion. Classroom becomes noisy and chaotic. Some discussions end with no conclusion due to participants creating noise.

IV) **Time consuming:** This method has three stages through which it is to pass to make discussion fruitful. It consumes a lot of time to pass these stages and fulfil other formalities. The teacher consumes separate time and learners consume their separate time. Lot of time is wasted in preparing the ground for discussion. This may lead to loss of interest in the participants.

V) **Not useful for introvert and shy learners:** This method requires the ability of taking initiative. This spirit is lacking in introvert and shy learners. So they gain nothing from this method of teaching.

VI) **Does not cover all topics:** There are certain topics which do not have scope of discussion but these are part of the syllabus, then these topics are to be covered through the lecture method. So discussion method is of no use in case of certain topics.

JIGSAW METHOD OF TEACHING

This method was devised by Elliot Aronson in 1971. It is based on the logic of Jigsaw puzzle. It is a strategy of cooperative learning in which students are divided into 4 to 6 groups of equal number of students. The content of the lecture is also divided into the same number of chunks. Each student in a group is given a separate chunk or task.

Each student of a group works independently. Each student is to memorise the content given to him/her. For example, if knowledge about different economic indicators is to be given to students, the whole content is divided into Prices, Money supply, Exports, Imports, Poverty, and GDP. As there are six chunks, students are divided into say 5 groups of six students in each group. Six chunks are given separately to six students of each group by giving one chunk to one student. No two students in a group get the same chunk. After studying the content of each chunk, students of all the groups join the students with the same chunk. These groups are called expert groups. There, each student exchange ideas with the others on the respective chunk and they clarify the topic through discussion. Now again they join their original groups in which each student has a different chunk. Now, knowledge of students is evaluated by the teacher. Every time one student of a group gives presentation, the other members listen and note down the content. Similarly, other students do the same on their turn. In this way each student gains knowledge of all the six chunks and hence, gains knowledge of the full topic.

Demonstration Method

It is the process of teaching through examples or experiments. It is also called Laboratory method. For example, a science teacher may teach an idea by performing an experiment for students. A demonstration may be used to prove a fact through a combination of visual evidence and associated reasoning. Teachers not only demonstrate specific learning concepts within the classroom, they can also participate in demonstration classrooms to help improve their own teaching strategies, which may or may not be demonstrative in nature. It is considered to be the best method of teaching. Every subject of higher education, whether science or non-science, is subject to rapid changes. Definitions, theories, and other norms are getting new terminology, new principles, norms, and significance, so colleges and universities need such a faculty who is well-versed with new concepts and is capable of explaining it to learners in such a way so that they understand it well. Certain perfect teachers believe in demonstration of their teaching. Such teachers demonstrate the concept in the form of pictures, charts, models, and explain that in full depth. This method is also useful for those learners who fail to understand practical significance of any concept or feel difficulty in applying theories to actual practice. This method is considered to be the most effective method of teaching. This method requires simple language, reasonable size of object being demonstrated, and answers to the enquiries from students to remove their doubts. Sometimes, according to the need of curriculum and syllabus, certain theoretical operations are performed by the teacher to show them when these are to be done, why these are done, and where these are done.

Characteristics of Demonstration Method

i) **Well-planned strategy:** Demonstration method is not practised without preparation. The object to be demonstrated along with content explaining every technical aspect is already planned and is executed in the class accordingly.

ii) **Learner-centred:** Demonstration method is devised and practised to fulfil the expectation and need of the learners. Learners actively learn whatever is taught. There are queries which are duly answered by the teacher.

iii) **Transparency:** There is complete transparency in teaching with this method. The goal of teaching with this method is already clear to students.

iv) **Easiest approach:** Simple language and objects of reasonable size is used to make things as clear as possible.

Advantages

i) **Perennial understanding:** As learners learn practically what they have learnt in theory, their understanding on this topic gains strength and they do not forget the topic for a very long time.

ii) **Deep understanding:** Demonstration helps the learners to learn and understand the topic in depth.

iii) **No wastage of time:** There is no wastage of time as in this method, learners watch the demonstration live.

iv) **Active participation:** As this is also a learner-centred method of teaching, students actively participate in the teaching-learning process.

v) **Development of reflective thinking:** As during experimentation or demonstration various judgements are to be made and decisions are to be taken, it develops reflective thinking in learners.

vi) **Absorbing method:** Due to its norm of demonstration or experimentation, this method creates interest in the mind of students to learn and they learn it while fully absorbing themselves in the demonstration.

Disadvantages

i) **One-way communication:** Though claimed to be learner-centred, students are not allowed to ask questions.

ii) **Limited method:** It is limited to particular teaching situations only.

iii) **Costly:** This method involves costly equipment. Colleges or universities charge extra fee from learners to attend demonstration classes.

iv) **Time Consuming:** Certain operations are highly technical, lengthy, and consume much time in completion. Learners start getting bored after some time and lose interest in learning.

Role Play Method or Simulation Teaching Method

It is a learner-centred technique of teaching. Simulation means imitation. In this technique of teaching, teachers and students depend on 'Role play' activity, i.e., participants of simulating teaching play a role of a character related to the subject of study. The role is played extempore. The teacher creates a situation like the real world and students are asked to adapt it as the real world. This arouses interest among the students and they learn more effectively. It is the platform to display aesthetic skills by student and teachers simultaneously. This teaching technique teaches the student the skill of handling and experience situations close to real life.

Characteristics of Role Play Method

i) **Universal participation:** In role play, as learners are to enact different characters of their studies, all the students take part in role play.

ii) **Debriefing:** Purpose of role play is not fulfilled without debriefing. Players are properly taken care of by the teacher and they are given sufficient time to prepare for their performance.

iii) **Person-to-person communication:** In role play method, simulation or enactment is possible when there is person-to-person interaction.

iv) **Source of practical knowledge:** Role play technique becomes source of practical knowledge by enacting a real life incident and characters.

v) **Enthusiastic approach:** As students are to play the role of certain characters, there is an enthusiasm among the participants. This is because this is a new venture for them.

vi) **Enactment closest to reality:** Those incidents are chosen for enactment which is closest to reality.

According to Confucius:

> *"I hear and I forget. I see and I remember. I do and I understand."*

Advantages

i) **Development of interpersonal skills:** Students enact different incidents and have interaction with different players. This develops interpersonal skills of communication in them.

ii) **Inclusive teaching strategy:** In role play method, every student is given a role to play. In this way the whole class is covered and the whole class learns at the same time.

iii) **Experience of real life incidents:** Students realise and experience incidents that can happen in real life. This makes them strong, confident, and risk-takers.

iv) **Promotion of lifelong learning:** While playing roles of different characters and incidents close to life, learners learn the concept very deeply and as they experience it through enactment, they retain this knowledge throughout their life.

v) **Development of emphatic understanding:** With role playing, students develop emotional understanding, i.e., they learn to feel like how others feel. They experience a feeling of others' emotions and sentiments which help in developing better human relationships and interaction.

vi) **Practical teaching method:** Learners play different roles and interact with other role players and observers. Whatever they enact is close to reality and role players also live the character and realise the realities, ups, and downs of life. All these things make this method a practical teaching method.

vii) **Kinaesthetic learning:** Role play provides learning which is not attained by listening to lectures or watching demonstrations. Kinaesthetic learning is practical and is useful for the whole life of the learners.

KINAESTHETIC LEARNING

> *This is also known as Tactile Learning. This term was used by Favre in 2009. Kinaesthetic learning is the mode in which learning takes place by students carrying out physical activities rather than listening to lectures in classrooms and watching demonstrations.*

viii) **Development of cognitive and psychomotor abilities:** As students are exposed to subject matter and role play, they develop cognitive and psychomotor abilities.

Disadvantages

i) **Hesitating participants:** All learners are not extroverts who are ready to play different roles. There are introvert learners also who hesitate to play a role. This totally disturbs the role play set-up and the purpose of role play is not met and justified.

ii) **Costly:** This method of teaching wastes much time in rehearsing, preparing students for enactment, and convincing shy students for role-playing. It is costly moneywise too and the cost is recovered from students by enhancing their fees.

iii) **Emotional imbalance:** As this method involves emotional traits also, there may be scenes of emotional imbalance and sometimes emotions of participants go out of control resulting in destructive outcomes.

iv) **Difficulty in evaluation:** As all the students play their role collectively, it becomes difficult to evaluate them individually.

v) **Requires like-minded participants only:** This method is successful only when there are like-minded participants as participants with different psychologies and mental states generally indulge in clashes and the role play method ends in a fiasco.

Case Study Method of Teaching

This method of teaching has been basically devised for laws and business studies, but institutions of higher learning are using this method in engineering, commerce, economics, and liberal and creative arts. Motive behind this method is to bring learners face-to-face with real life cases and to develop in them problem-solving skills and critical thinking. In this method students are given a circumstantial situation based on real life or imaginary events, personalities, or institutions close to reality and they are asked to identify the problem, provide panacea to the problem, and reasons for doing so.

Characteristics of Case Study Method

i) **Small units under study:** In case study, small units are picked for study which make study handy and convenient.

ii) **Particularistic:** Study is focussed on a particular situation or event or case.

iii) **Qualitative and quantitative techniques:** As case study is conducted for sciences and arts, both qualitative and quantitative techniques suitable to a particular case study are used.

iv) **Deep study:** A case under study is studied from all aspects and after a deep study, problem is identified and solution is suggested.

v) **Liberal time limit:** In the interest of accurate study with productive solutions, liberal time limit is allowed which makes study accurate and authentic.

vi) **Heuristic:** Case study confirms what is already known, gives experience to the learner for tackling practical problems, and new meanings and terms are discovered helping to present identification and solutions of the case in an effective way.

Advantages

i) **Simplifies complex concepts:** Certain concepts about any subjects are difficult to understand in classroom lectures. These become simple and easy to understand when practical work is done on the subject while taking it as a case for study.

ii) **Exposure to real life situation:** It is in the case study method of learning and studying a case that they are exposed to real life situations, which are otherwise difficult.

iii) **Value-adding phenomenon:** As study of a case requires meticulous coverage, it adds to the value of the learner conducting study.

iv) **Develops analytic thinking and reasoning power:** In case study, detailed analysis is conducted. This refines skill of analytical thinking in learners. Further, they can present their viewpoint with reasoning and logic.

v) **Holistic account of the case or phenomenon:** When a learner brings a case under study, he/she studies it from every angle. No part is left untouched. This makes the learner master of the case and concepts.

Disadvantages

i) **Time consuming:** A teacher makes the learner understand the subject to be covered under case study. Before actually starting case study, students are to understand its technical aspect, terms, etc. After that study is started. Further, process also takes much time due to which liberal time limit is allotted. So there is consumption, rather wastage of much time if the desired results are not achieved after completing the study.

ii) **Difficult to generalise:** It is not necessary that findings of a single case from a case study are applicable to all other cases. Such findings cannot be generalised.

iii) **Too subjective:** As case study involves a single subject at a time and is concerned about its characteristics only, further findings of a case study cannot be generalised. It is criticised for being too subjective.

iv) **Limited scope:** Different subjects are being taught in colleges and universities. It is not certain that cases will be found suitable to all subjects. So this method has limited scope.

v) **Difficulty in validation:** When a learner completes case study, he/she faces the difficulty to prove its validity as others may be viewing the same case from a different viewpoint.

vi) **Suitable for comparatively matured learners:** Though in higher education stream learners are matured, still all learners (say undergraduates) generally do not understand the concept and application of case study. Comparatively matured learners (say graduates and post graduates) may easily handle case studies.

Brainstorming

The term was given by an American educationist Alex F. Osborn. In a session (method) in a classroom, a discussion in structured form is initiated for learners to generate new ideas by giving full freedom to learners (participants) without making any unproductive analysis of participants like criticism, interference, etc. The learners generate and share ideas in groups in full autonomy. After all the generated ideas are presented, then evaluation is initiated.

Characteristics of Brainstorming

i) **Motivation of wild ideas:** Learners are encouraged to generate maximum ideas on the topic under discussion.

ii) **Quantitative approach:** There is emphasis on recording a greater quantity or number of ideas irrespective of their quality.

iii) **No instant evaluation:** Ideas are recorded without evaluation as the motive is to let the learners generate as many ideas as they can.

iv) **Equal participation:** All learners are asked to participate in generating ideas and then share these. Even introvert learners are also to participate.

v) **No criticism:** Participants are given a free hand to generate even the wildest possible ideas as the aim is to gather maximum ideas and then share these to understand a particular topic.

vi) **Small groups:** Learners are divided into smaller groups as generating and sharing ideas yield desired results in small groups.

Advantages

i) **Democratic in nature:** In brainstorming, every participant has the right to speak and the right to object. So it is purely democratic in nature.

ii) **Develops creative thinking:** When the learners are divided into small groups and they are to generate wild ideas, it is but natural that they develop creative thinking. Skill of creative thinking helps in solving various problems of life.

iii) **Useful technique of problem-solving:** The basic aim of brainstorming is problem-solving. Total effort by all the groups is to solve the problem on which the brainstorming session is being organised.

iv) **Fostering trust and friendship:** Brainstorming sessions give opportunity to learners to interact with one another on some neutral issue. Learners get a platform to know each other. As learners are working closely together and talk with one another, foundations of relationships at work is laid down.

v) **Promoting creativity:** Learners are asked to generate their own ideas by using their respective wild imagination. Learners try to come up with the best possible ideas to be noticed as the best solution provider. In this process they make optimum use of their imaginary skills and hence, experience promotion of creativity.

vi) **Skill of decision-making:** As learners are to generate ideas independently and decide to go with a particular idea or not while keeping its pros and cons in mind, they develop the skill of decision-making.

vii) **Energising:** The very idea of participation is quite energising. Even the introvert students become ready to participate.

viii) **Generation of new ideas:** When freedom of generating wild ideas is given, it is but natural that new and useful ideas will be generated.

Disadvantages

i) **Promoting clashes:** Learners develop ideas and compare their ideas with those of others. As they are on a spree of developing the best ideas, they often reject others' ideas. This leads to argumentation and clashes.

ii) **Not always effective:** Success of brainstorming depends upon collective existence of various factors, but if one member lacks in communication skills, brainstorming will end in a fiasco.

iii) **Not suitable to everyone:** There are certain learners who fumble in front of a group whereas they are excellent in presentation in one-to-one interaction. So for such learners, brainstorming is not comfortable.

iv) **Complex procedure:** Observing brainstorming in its statutory format is a complex procedure and any compromise with statute will make brainstorming ineffective.

v) **Intimidation of slow learners:** Some learners who are faster in discussion dominate the groups and in the mood of supremacy, they intimidate slow learners.

Inductive Method

In this method, the teacher gives certain situations or problems to students with examples and then students are asked to solve problems with the method they find convenient. Students solve the problem by applying various methods and consulting examples and submit it to the teacher. The teacher evaluates the performance and tells them a single principle or rule to solve that problem. In this way, learners understand that single principle.

For example: A teacher explains the concept of gravitational pull by giving related problems with examples of various products going down. Students are asked to submit their answers. After reviewing that the teacher tells them the Newton's Rule of Gravity which is applicable to all the problems and examples. So the single rule of gravity is applied to all the problems related to gravity and that is inductive method of teaching.

Characteristics of Inductive Method of Teaching

i) **New knowledge:** As students have no prior knowledge of the concept which they are given in the form of an example, they gain new knowledge when ultimately, the teacher reveals to them the single principle or rule applicable to all examples.

ii) **Discovery of a principle:** Learners discover new principles and rules in this method of teaching.

iii) **Gaining knowledge through observation:** Learners are given examples and cases. They observe them, understand them in their own way, and ultimately get knowledge of the principle behind the phenomenon.

iv) **Slow process:** The whole process of acquiring knowledge with this method is slow but acquired knowledge is enduring.

v) **Upward process:** Teaching in this method is proceeding from examples and ultimately ending in finding out a single principle which is generalised.

Advantages

i) **Full of activity:** This method is filled with activity and is a learner-centred method. Learners are active participants and learn about the principle with full participation.

ii) **Injects self-confidence:** The method injects self-confidence among learners as they solve the problems without knowing the principle behind that.

iii) **Developing HOTS:** This method, due to its nature and structure develop Higher Order Thinking Skills (HOTS) in students which strengthen their cognitive abilities.

Disadvantages

i) **Time consuming:** Giving problems and examples to learners at the first instance and after that giving knowledge of the single principle and again generalising its application is a lengthy process and a lot of time is wasted.

ii) **Causes irritation and frustration:** Sometimes, students want to know the principle only. They get irritated from the lengthy procedure of the method.

iii) **Possibility of wrong conclusions:** When students are asked to solve problems independently without telling them the formula or the principle, students with low IQ are likely to land with wrong conclusions.

iv) **Requires highly skilled teacher:** if teacher is not highly skilled, this method is not successful. Only a highly skilled teacher can review the performance of the learners and explain to them the rule or principle behind the examples. He should be skilled enough to make them aware of the concept of generalisation and its practical relevance.

Deductive Method of Teaching

This is a teacher-centred method. In this method a teacher introduces a norm or principle to students and then gives examples to make the rule clearer. Then students are given practice exercise after they understand the rule introduced by the teacher.

Characteristics of Deductive Method

i) **Teacher-centred:** As teacher starts the lecture by giving a principle or rule to the learners and learners listen and note down what teacher states, it is a teacher-centred method of teaching.

ii) **Already known facts:** Students work on already known facts because the teacher already explains the rule with examples before giving practice assignments to them.

iii) **Poor student activity:** As students are passive learners in this method, there is hardly any active learning.

iv) **Downward process:** Contrary to inductive method, there is a downward thought process starting from a rule or principle, then examples and solving exercises.

Advantages

i) **To the point and relevant knowledge:** As deductive method straightway introduces principle or rule in the lecture, students get straight to the point of knowledge.

ii) **Time-saving:** In this method there is great time-saving as students are not to find out the rule of law themselves; rather they get readymade knowledge which is a big time- saver.

iii) **Liberal time limit:** Students get liberal time limit for practising.

iv) **Scope of applying more rules:** As this is a time-saving method, there is a scope of covering more rules.

v) **Universal validity:** The inferences adopted and the conclusions made under this method have universal validity. The reason is that the inferences are based on certain principles.

Disadvantages

i) **Difficult for beginners:** This method is difficult for beginners as they may not understand the technicality of the rule. Learners must have some prior knowledge of the concept.

ii) **Promotes rote learning:** This method requires to keep many formulae in mind. So learners have no choice but cramming.

iii) **No scope of divergent thinking:** In this method learners are to rely on the given rule or concept and their total activity in teaching-learning process revolves around that formula. So there is no scope of divergent thinking.

Miscellaneous Methods of Teaching

In addition to the ones discussed above, there are some other methods of teaching which require attention:

1) **Laboratory method:** Practical demonstration of what students study in classroom, aiming at strengthening the understanding and retention power of students

2) **Problem-solving method:** Holding problem-solving sessions in the classroom, aiming at clarity of basics and fundamental concepts of a subject leading to increase in confidence level of students as students while coming up with their respective problems speak properly, view properly, listen properly, think properly and concentrate properly

3) **Self study method:** Students asked to develop habit of self study as in library, aiming at strengthening the power of concentration

4) **Textbook method:** Delivering the lecture from the textbook, aiming at a universal approach to teaching making learning handy for students. Students may be asked to read the lesson from a textbook one by one backed by explanation from the teacher.

5) **Investigative method:** It is a learner-centred method which is practised by science teachers for the learners in the science stream. Scientific methods are used to conduct experiments on various theories. Learners are active learners as they actively participate in every activity of this method. Techniques used for investigation in this method include laboratory technique, field study technique, problem-solving technique, and research technique. Every subject to be investigated is taken as a challenge.

6) **Personalised or individualised teaching method:** In this method, instructions from the teacher, pace of teaching, and content of the lecture so delivered are based on abilities and interest of each learner. As at one time only one learner is taught, aim is to strengthen the learner's knowledge and understanding resulting in confidence-building.

7) **Buzz group discussion:** This is a method in which small groups of 2-3 participants discuss a specific question or issue in order to come up with many ideas in a short time. Since the small groups produce a **buzzing** sound while discussing, this method is known as buzz group.

Teaching Aids

Various teaching aids are used by a teacher in the classroom to make the concepts clearer.

1) Audio Aids: Audio aids are concerned with hearing only. These aids include radio, tape recorder, audio CD player, microphone with amplifier, linguaphone, etc. These aids help in learning about the correct pronunciation of different words in the language which is spoken. They also make the lecture properly audible.

2) Visual Aids: Visual aids are concerned with viewing the objects. A teacher explains various theoretical concepts with the help of visual illustrations. These aids include black/white/electronic board, charts, pictures, specimens, working models, figures, hanging posters, maps, cinema slide projectors, diorama (a three-dimensional full-size or miniature model, sometimes enclosed in a glass showcase for a museum), and epidiascope (a type of magic lantern that projects the image of an opaque object onto a screen). These aids help the student to practically watch the concepts being studied in books.

3) Audio-Visual Aids: These are the most advanced type of medium of instructions. They include Computers with CD-ROM's, Internet, Cinema, and Film projectors, Television, etc. These aids help the students to understand properly what they have studied from books. They can enjoy while learning from any such source. They can supplement their classroom knowledge with the knowledge given by these aids. These aids create a long-time impact on the learner or student.

ONLINE TEACHING METHODS

Following online methods of teaching are being implemented in different colleges and universities on government initiative:

1) SWAYAM
2) SWAYAMPRABHA
3) MOOCs

SWAYAM

Study Webs of Active Learning for Young Aspiring Minds (SWAYAM) is a programme which has been initiated as MOOCs portal by Ministry of Human Resource Development (MHRD), Government of India and aims to achieve the three principles of Education Policy viz., access, equity, and quality. This initiative has an objective to make the best teaching-learning within the reach of all, including the most disadvantaged. SWAYAM seeks to bridge the digital divide for students who have remained untouched by the digital revolution and have not been able to join the mainstream of the knowledge economy. Centrally sponsored institutions like IITs and IIMs along with Central University of Haryana are providing online courses for students across the country. This is done through a platform that facilitates hosting of all the courses, taught in classrooms from Class 9 till post graduation to be accessed by anyone, anywhere, and at any time. All the courses are interactive, prepared by the best teachers in the country, and are available free of cost to any learner. More than 1,000 specially chosen faculty and teachers from across the country have participated in preparing these courses.

The courses hosted on SWAYAM are in 4 quadrants- (1) video lecture, (2) specially prepared reading material that can be downloaded/printed, (3) self-assessment tests through tests and quizzes, and (4) an online discussion forum for clearing the doubts. Steps have been taken to enrich the learning experience by using audio-video and multi-media and state of the art pedagogy/technology.

In order to ensure that best quality content is produced and delivered, nine National Coordinators have been appointed. They are:

1. AICTE (All India Council for Technical Education) for self-paced and international courses
2. NPTEL (National Programme on Technology Enhanced Learning) for Engineering)
3. UGC (University Grants Commission) for non-technical postgraduate education
4. CEC (Consortium for Educational Communication) for undergraduate education
5. NCERT (National Council of Educational Research and Training) for school education
6. NIOS (National Institute of Open Schooling) for school education
7. IGNOU (Indira Gandhi National Open University) for out-of-school students
8. IIMB (Indian Institute of Management, Bangalore) for management studies
9. NITTTR (National Institute of Technical Teachers Training and Research) for Teacher Training programme

Courses delivered through SWAYAM are available free of cost to the learners. However, learners wanting a SWAYAM certificate should register for the final proctored exams that come at a fee and attend in-person at designated centres on specified dates. Eligibility for the certificate will be announced on the course page and learners will get certificates only if these criteria are matched. Universities/colleges approving credit transfer for these courses can use the marks/certificate obtained in these courses for the same.

SAWAYAM PRABHA

The SWAYAM PRABHA is a group of 34 DTH channels devoted to telecasting of high-quality educational programmes on 24X7 basis using the GSAT-15 satellite. The DTH Channels shall cover the following:

- Higher education: Curriculum-based course contents at postgraduate and undergraduate level covering various disciplines such as arts, science, commerce, performing arts, social sciences and humanities, engineering, technology, law, medicine, agriculture, etc. Certificates are available in all courses through SWAYAM, the portal developed for offering MOOCs courses.
- School education (9-12 levels): Modules for teacher's training as well as teaching and learning aids for children of India to help them understand the subjects better and also help them in preparing for competitive examinations for admissions to professional degree programmes.
- Curriculum-based courses that can meet the needs of life-long learners of Indian citizens in India and abroad.
- Assist students (class 11th and 12th) prepare for competitive exams.

  Every day, there will be new content for at least (4) hours which would be repeated 5 more times in a day, allowing the students to choose the time of their convenience. The channels are uplinked from BISAG, Gandhinagar. The contents are provided by The National Program on Technology Enhanced Learning. (NPTEL), IITs, UGC, Consortium for Educational Communication (CEC), IGNOU, NCERT, and National Institute of Open Schooling (NIOS). The INFLIBNET Centre maintains the web portal.

MOOCs

A massive open online course (MOOC) is an online course and is a web-based platform to provide a chance to access distance education to numerous students across the world with the best institutes and universities in the world. It was established in 2008 and came up as a popular learning platform in 2012. The University Grants Commission (UGC) along with the HRD (Human Resource Development) Ministry has launched the MOOC program in India for higher secondary, bachelor's, and master's degrees. This will cover a wide range of subjects that may or may not be taught in regular campus studies. MOOCs provide participants with course materials that are normally used in a conventional education setting-such as examples, lectures, videos, study materials, and problem sets. Apart from this, MOOCs offer interactive user forums, which are extremely useful in building a community for students, Teaching Assistants (TAs), and professors. Generally, MOOCs do not charge tuition fees or provide academic credit.

Some Vital Facts

1) A method of teaching in which systematic, step-by-step presentation is made is called Expository method of teaching.
2) Freedom to choose a theme and scope for frank exchange of ideas is one of the characteristics of Discussion Method of teaching.
3) Trust and openness in relationship is found in Personalised method of teaching.
4) Maximum participation of students during teaching is possible through Inuctive method of teaching.
5) Initiating a discussion and participating in it is considered to be the best learner centred method of teaching.
6) Writing the important points as clearly as possible is the basic requirement for a successful blackboard teaching method.
7) Discussion method of teaching aims at giving freedom to learners to interact.
8) Lecture method, though develops knowledge yet is a teacher-centric method.

Practice Exercise

General Questions Format

1. A teacher's method of teaching depends on his/her ________.
   (A) knowledge about the subject
   (B) experience as a teacher
   (C) nature and behaviour
   (D) level of devotion in teaching
2. Audio aids of teaching are successful where
   (A) the number of students is enormous
   (B) teaching is imparted in an open ground
   (C) listening is more important than reading or writing
   (D) None of these
3. Which of the following is NOT a characteristic of teacher-centred method of teaching?
   (A) Empty vessels
   (B) Formative evaluation
   (C) Passive learning
   (D) Structured lectures
4. Which of the following is TRUE about Discussion method of teaching?
   a) Learners are given equal chances of evaluation.
   b) It is a teacher-learner method ensuring equal participation of teacher and students.
   c) Learners develop reflective thinking through active participation in discussion.
   d) Teacher participates as a primary and ultimate communicator.
   (A) c only (B) c and d only
   (C) a, b, and d (D) a, b, c, and d
5. Which method of teaching is called "Close-ended" method?
   (A) Teacher-centred method
   (B) Learner-centred method
   (C) Content-centred method
   (D) Expository method
6. Which of the following is NOT TRUE about learner-centred method of teaching?
   (A) Teaching technique motivates learners to plan and initiate active learning process.
   (B) Teaching is practised by encouraging learners to give feedback on the lecture and collaborate in doing the assigned task.
   (C) Teacher and learners are parties to bilateral communication in which not only learners but teachers also learn.
   (D) All of the above are true
7. Consider the statement, "A teacher was a learner one day so teacher knows which is the best method of teaching to benefit learners." This statement is ________.
   (A) an effective evidence of teaching ethics
   (B) a prejudice against the learning ethics
   (C) a hypothetical truth amid present teaching methods
   (D) an underestimated evaluation of various teaching plans which involve factors other than teaching also
8. Which of the following is NOT a feature of Discussion method of teaching?
   (A) Learners are motivated to actively participate in the discussion initiated by the teacher.
   (B) Learners are asked to choose a topic of their respective choice and then the teacher initiates discussion on that topic.
   (C) Each learner is given an opportunity to speak on a pre-decided topic before starting actual discussion.
   (D) Teacher withdraws after initiating the discussion and evaluates learners' performance at the conclusion of discussion.
9. What is the other name of Expository method of teaching?
   (A) Demonstration method
   (B) Discussion method
   (C) Library method
   (D) Lecture method
10. Following are the steps taken in Deductive method of teaching:
    a) Examples b) Practice
    c) Rule
    Arrange them in chronological order and choose the correct answer choice among the following:
    (A) b-c-a (B) a-c-b
    (C) c-a-b (D) c-b-a

11. Statement: Should traditional teacher-centred method of teaching still be preferred to modern learner-centred method?

Arguments:

I. Yes, old is gold.

II. No, effective learning is possible due to active learning only through learner-centred method of teaching.

(A) Only argument I is strong

(B) Only argument II is strong

(C) Both arguments I and II are strong

(D) Neither argument I nor II is strong

12. Teaching methods are given under Column I and their mode is given under Column II. Match the method of teaching with its correct mode and choose the correct code as given below:

Column I (Method)	Column II (Mode)
a) Demonstration	i) Enacting
b) Brainstorming	ii) Generalisation
c) Inductive	iii) New ideas
d) Role play	iv) Teaching aids

Codes:

	(a)	(b)	(c)	(d)
(A)	ii	i	iv	iii
(B)	iv	iii	ii	i
(C)	iii	ii	i	iv
(D)	iv	ii	iii	i

13. Statement: Should credit of a learner's success be given to the teaching method?

Arguments:

I. Yes, it is a teaching method which motivates learners to work hard and yield results.

II. No, it is learners' determination which pays irrespective of the teaching method.

(A) Only argument I is strong

(B) Only argument II is strong

(C) Both arguments I and II are strong

(D) Either argument I or II is strong

14. In which of the circumstances Lecture method of teaching is not applicable?

(A) Learners are not matured enough to take part in the discussion.

(B) Learners are to come across the topic for the first time in their life.

(C) Sole objective is to give learners complete knowledge of the topic.

(D) Learners are enthusiastic to effectively understand the whole topic.

15. Which method of teaching is useful for a novice teacher?

(A) Expository (B) Role play

(C) Deductive (D) Inductive

16. Is micro teaching a method of teaching?

a) Yes, there is an effective teacher-student interaction.

b) No, micro teaching is a type of teaching and not a method.

c) Yes, due to small size of class there is blend of teacher-centred and learner-centred approach to teaching.

d) No, micro teaching is not possible without adopting a suitable method of teaching.

(A) Only a and c (B) Only b

(C) Only d (D) Only b and d

17. Which method of teaching does not instantly evaluate students' performance during a session in the class?

(A) Deductive (B) Inductive

(C) Brainstorming (D) Discussion

18. Consider the statement, "Where there is learning there is a method of teaching." The statement signifies that

(A) Learning generates a method of teaching.

(B) A teaching method depends on demand for learning.

(C) A teaching method is planned as per learning needs.

(D) Learning governs teaching through a method of teaching.

19. In Role play method of teaching:

(A) Learners learn and teacher experiences

(B) Teacher learns and experiences both whereas learners only learn

(C) Learners learn and experience both but teacher only experiences

(D) Both teacher and learners learn as well as experience

20. Had there not been Brainstorming method of teaching, there would not have been ___.

(A) initiative for learning

(B) planning for teaching

(C) autonomous learning

(D) motivated teaching and learning

21. Which of the following is NOT TRUE about SWAYAM?

a) It aims at bridging the digital divide among students.

b) It is to achieve three principles of Education Policy viz. Access, Equality, and Quality.

c) This programme is a joint venture of Union Ministry of Human Resources and Union Ministry of Information Technology.

d) UGC is one of the coordinators of this programme.

(A) b and c only (B) d only

(C) b only (D) All are true

22. Which of the following is NOT the content provider for SWAYAM PRABHA?

(A) IGNOU (B) INFLIBNET

(C) NCERT (D) NPTEL

23. Interactive user forums of students and teachers are created through

(A) MOOCs

(B) SWAYAM

(C) SWAYAM PRABHA

(D) CEC

24. Which of the following is NOT provided to participants by MOOCs?

(A) Study material

(B) Video lectures

(C) Study schedule

(D) Problem sets

25. What is the full form of SWAYAM?

(A) Study Webs of Advanced Learning for Young Aspiring Minds

(B) Social Webs of Active Learning for Young Aspiring Minds

(C) Social Webs of Actual Learning for Young Aspiring Minds

(D) Study Webs of Active Learning for Young Aspiring Minds

KEY

1. C	2. C	3. B	4. A	5. A	6. A	7. C
8. B	9. D	10. C	11. B	12. B	13. C	14. D
15. A	16. D	17. C	18. C	19. D	20. C	21. A
22. B	23. A	24. C	25. D			

Assertion–Reason Format

1. Assertion (A): Teacher-centred methods are not beneficial for learners.

Reason (R): Learners cannot learn under restrictions.

(A) Both A and R are true and R is correct explanation of A

(B) Both A and R are true but R is not correct explanation of A

(C) Both A and R are false

(D) A is false but R is true

2. Assertion (A): No teaching aid can substitute lecture method of teaching.

Reason (R): Today, teaching aids have become an indispensable part of teaching.

(A) Both A and R are true and R is correct explanation of A

(B) Both A and R are true but R is not correct explanation of A

(C) A is true but R is false

(D) A is false but R is true

3. Assertion (A): Active participation of learners is not the only characteristics of learner-centred method of teaching.

Reason (R): Motivation plays its own role in preparing learners to actively participate in teaching-learning process, even in learner-centred method of teaching.

(A) Both A and R are true and R is correct explanation of A

(B) Both A and R are true but R is not correct explanation of A

(C) Both A and R are false

(D) A is false but R is true

4. Assertion (A): Teaching with teaching aids is part of demonstration method of teaching.

Reason (R): Teaching aids are useless if learners are tired of routine classroom studies.

(A) Both A and R are true and R is correct explanation of A

(B) A is true but R is false

(C) A is false but R is true

(D) Both A and R are true but R is not correct explanation of A

5. **Assertion (A):** MOOCs cover all those subjects which are taught in regular campus studies.

Reason (R): MOOCS provide an easy access to distance education.

(A) Both A and R are true but R is not correct explanation of A

(B) Both A and R are true and R is correct explanation of A

(C) A is true but R is false

(D) A is false but R is true

6. **Assertion (A):** Higher education courses completed under SWAYAM PRABHA are certified by MOOCs.

Reason (R): SWAYAM PRABHA is a group of 20 DTH channels for providing quality education.

(A) Both A and R are true and R is correct explanation of A

(B) Both A and R are true but R is not correct explanation of A

(C) Both A and R are false

(D) A is true but R is false

7. **Assertion (A):** In Discussion method of teaching discussion environment is made by the teacher.

Reason (R): Active participation of learners is a prerequisite of Discussion method.

(A) Both A and R are false

(B) Both A and R are true but R is not correct explanation of A

(C) Both A and R are true and R is correct explanation of A

(D) A is true but R is false

8. **Assertion (A):** Jigsaw method of teaching encourages individual learning.

Reason (R): Learners are divided into 4 to 6 groups of equal number of students.

(A) Both A and R are true and R is correct explanation of A

(B) Both A and R are true but R is not correct explanation of A

(C) A is true but R is false

(D) A is false but R is true

9. **Assertion (A):** Kinaesthetic learning emphasise learning through physical activity.

Reason (R): Learners learn more effectively through physical activities than classroom lectures.

(A) Both A and R are true and R is correct explanation of A

(B) Both A and R are true but R is not correct explanation of A

(C) A is true but R is false

(D) A is false but R is true

10. **Assertion (A):** Role play and Case study methods of teaching are two sides of the same coin.

Reason (R): Like Role play and Case study, many other methods of teaching aim at active learning through active participation of learners in teaching-learning process.

(A) Both A and R are true and R is correct explanation of A

(B) Both A and R are true but R is not correct explanation of A

(C) A is true but R is false

(D) A is false but R is true

KEY

1. C **2.** B **3.** A **4.** B **5.** D **6.** C **7.** C
8. C **9.** A **10.** B

Questions Asked in Previous NET Exams

1. In the spectrum of teaching methods which of the following will be called 'Dialogic'?

(UGC NET DECEMBER 2019)

(a) Demonstration Method

(b) Problem-solving Method

(C) Chalk and Talk Method

(d) Team Teaching based Method

(e) Interactive Presentation

(f) Tutorials

Select your answer from the options given below:

(A) (a), (b) and (c) (B) (b), (c) and (d)

(C) (c), (d) and (e) (D) (b) , (e) and (f)

2. In the two lists given below, List I provides the list of teaching methods, while List II indicates the factors helpful in rendering them effective. Match the two lists and choose the correct answer from the code given below. **(UGC NET JULY 2018)**

List I (Teaching methods)	List II (Factors helpful in making them effective)
(a) Expository method	(i) Trust and openness in relationship
(b) Investigative method	(ii) Freedom to choose a theme and scope for frank exchange of ideas
(c) Discussion method	(iii) Creating a challenge to address the problems
(d) Personalised method	(iv) Systematic, step-by-step presentation
	(v) Maximising infrastructural support

Codes:

	(a)	(b)	(c)	(d)
(A)	(iv)	(iii)	(ii)	(i)
(B)	(i)	(ii)	(iii)	(iv)
(C)	(ii)	(iii)	(iv)	(v)
(D)	(iii)	(i)	(ii)	(iv)

3. In the list given below, identify those key teaching behaviours which have been observed to be contributive to effectiveness. **(UGC NET JULY 2018)**

(i) Lesson clarity
(ii) Probing
(iii) Teacher-task orientation
(iv) Student success rate
(v) Instructional variety
(vi) Using student ideas

Choose the correct answer from the code given below:

Code:

(A) (i), (ii), (iii), and (iv)
(B) (iii), (iv), (v), and (vi)
(C) (i), (iii), (iv), and (v)
(D) (ii), (iii), (v), and (vi)

4. In the two sets given below Set-I indicates methods of teaching while Set-II provides the basic requirements for success/effectiveness. Match the two sets and indicate your answer by choosing from the code: **(UGC NET JULY 2018)**

Set–I (Method of teaching)	Set–II Instructional procedure (Basic requirements for success/effectiveness)
(a) Lecturing	(i) Small step presentation with feedback provided
(b) Discussion in groups	(ii) Production of large number of ideas
(c) Brainstorming	(iii) Content delivery in a lucid language
(d) Programmed	(iv) Use of teaching aids
	(v) Theme-based interaction among participants

Code:

	(a)	(b)	(c)	(d)
(A)	(i)	(ii)	(iii)	(iv)
(B)	(ii)	(iii)	(iv)	(v)
(C)	(iii)	(v)	(ii)	(i)
(D)	(iv)	(ii)	(i)	(iii)

5. Techniques used by a teacher to teach include: **(UGC NET JUNE 2015)**

(a) Lecture
(b) Interactive lecture
(c) Group work
(d) Self study

Select the correct answer from the codes given below:

(A) (a), (b), and (d)
(B) (a), (b) and (c)
(C) (a), (b), (c), and (d)
(D) (b), (c), and (d)

6. MOOC stands for **(UGC NET DECEMBER 2014)**

(A) Media Online Open Course
(B) Massachusetts Open Online Course
(C) Massive Open Online Course
(D) Myriad Open Online Course

7. Maximum participation of students during teaching is possible through **(UGC NET DECEMBER 2014)**

(A) Lecture method
(B) Demonstration method
(C) Inductive method
(D) Textbook method

8. Which one of the following is the best method of teaching? **(UGC NET JUNE 2014)**
   (A) Lecture
   (B) Discussion
   (C) Demonstration
   (D) Narration
9. Which one of the following is the best method of teaching? **(UGC NET SEPTEMBER 2013)**
   (A) Lecture method
   (B) Discussion method
   (C) Demonstration method
   (D) Question-Answer method
10. The best method of teaching is to ______. **(UGC NET DECEMBER 2012)**
   (A) impart information
   (B) ask students to read books
   (C) suggest good reference material
   (D) initiate a discussion and participate in it
11. For a teacher, which of the following methods would be correct for writing on the blackboard? **(UGC NET JUNE 2012)**
   (A) Writing fast and as clearly as possible
   (B) Writing the matter first and then asking students to read it
   (C) Asking a question to students and then writing the answer as stated by them
   (D) Writing the important points as clearly as possible
12. In a lively classroom situation, there is likely to be ____. **(UGC NET DECEMBER 2010)**
   (A) occasional roars of laughter
   (B) complete silence
   (C) frequent teacher-student dialogue
   (D) loud discussion among students
13. Which among the following gives more freedom to the learner to interact? **(UGC NET JUNE 2009)**
   (A) Use of film
   (B) Small group discussion
   (C) Lectures by experts
   (D) Viewing country-wide classroom programme on TV
14. Maximum participation of students is possible in teaching through: **(UGC NET DECEMBER 2007)**
   (A) Discussion method
   (B) Lecture method
   (C) Audio-visual aids
   (D) Textbook method
15. Which of the following statement is not correct? **(UGC NET DECEMBER 2006)**
   (A) Lecture method can develop reasoning
   (B) Lecture method can develop knowledge
   (C) Lecture method is a one-way process
   (D) During Lecture method students are passive

KEY

1. D 2. A 3. C 4. C 5. B 6. C 7. C
8. C 9. C 10. D 11. D 12. C 13. B 14. A
15. A

5 Teaching Support System
(Traditional, Modern and ICT-Based)

CONCEPT

Any teaching method or object which helps the teacher in building his/her capacity to teach learners effectively is Teaching support system or Teaching aid. Teaching support system is built up while taking learners' academic needs and characteristics into consideration. Methods practised by a teacher are generally learner-centred. Accordingly, teachers build up their capacity with the help of the teaching support system aiming at the effective teaching resulting in learners' participation in the teaching-learning process.

Traditional Teaching Support System

Traditional support system is required in the traditional method of teaching. Traditional methods of teaching include both teacher-centred and learner-centred methods. No teaching method is successful without teaching support system. Various traditional teaching methods like lecture method, discussion method, and demonstration method are practised with the teaching support system. Following items are included in the traditional teaching support system:

1) **Blackboard:** Traditional teaching is not successful without the blackboard. Blackboard is used to elaborate definitions and arithmetic and science formulae. The board may be the traditional blackboard which requires chalk of any colour which leaves a visible impression on the board. Tradition of using blackboard has been in practice since the advent of classroom teaching. Blackboard becomes the prime learning source for the learner. The teacher narrates the lecture and elaborates the concept on the blackboard. Blackboard is either of wood or painted with black paint on the wall.

OPERATION BLACKBOARD

While considering the importance of teaching support system and considering it a primary tool of learning, India's National Policy of Education 1986 recommended launching of Operation Blackboard.

In compliance to this Government of India launched Operation Black Board in 1989 with the aim of strengthening teaching through teaching support system and compulsory and free education up to 14 years of age. The scheme also contained teachers' orientation programmes at various levels. It was found that teachers were not fully acquainted with the teaching support material; there was a provision to train teachers in handling and utilising teaching support material in an effective manner.

2) **Chalk:** Chalk and blackboard have an inseparable relation with each other. Whatever the teacher wants to explain, he/she writes it on the board. Some important facts are highlighted by using chalks of different colours. Using board and chalk for teaching purpose requires a skill. Ultimate aim is to make learning easy and effective. That is why teachers are given training on how to effectively use chalk on the blackboard and that skill is termed as 'Chalk and Talk'.

3) **Textbooks:** Textbooks prescribed for different subjects for different levels of education have been time-tested teaching support material. As an effective traditional teaching support material, textbooks save time for both teacher and students in the teaching-learning process. As the teacher and the students are having the same book, the teacher asks students to open a particular chapter and then he starts reading it. After covering some portion of the chapter, the teacher explains that part of the chapter. Along with that, he/she explains the meaning of difficult terms and asks learners to note down the meaning of difficult terms. Textbooks have been used as a traditional teaching support material in the formal teaching system. This has also been the traditional practice to ask students to open the books on a certain chapter and read different stanzas of the chapter one by one. As and when a student finishes a stanza, the teacher explains the meaning of that stanza and after that, he/she asks the next student to read the next stanza and so on.

4) **Maps, atlases, and globes:** The lessons in geography and history become realistic when the teachers use wall maps, atlases, and globes to make the student understand and know various geographical and historical concepts and to know the locations of various places in the world and India. Historical maps help the students to understand the jurisdiction of different kings and the area annexed by them through wars. Teaching of geography in the classrooms will be meaningless without the use of these traditional teaching aids.

5) **Charts, pictures, and posters:** Since the advent of classroom teaching, the teachers use teaching aids like the charts, pictures, and posters for easy understanding of the lessons, which they display on the walls of the classrooms. These not only decorate the walls of the classrooms but are also an important tool for teaching in the classrooms. Colourful charts in the classrooms attract the students to get attracted to the classrooms. Further, it has been observed since long that maps and charts as traditional teaching-learning support material have been an effective learning stimulant and resultantly, students also volunteer to make colourful and attractive charts. After finding it an effective and absorbing tool of teaching and learning and keeping in view the students' interest, teacher arranges competitions of drawing charts, posters, and pictures. Even after introduction of various high-tech teaching support devices today, tradition of drawing and displaying colourful charts and posters has been still surviving with the same glory.

6) **Flashcards, flip cards, and worksheets:** Flashcards are cards bearing information on both sides, which is intended to be used as an aid in memorisation. Each flashcard bears a question on one side and an answer on the other. Flashcards are often used to memorise vocabulary, historical dates, formulae, or any subject matter that can be learned via a question-and-answer format. Flip cards are durable cards, usually created as sets, which convey printed information in a simple and convenient format. Used most often for reference or instructional purposes, flip card sets may consist of just a few cards or they may compile a thick deck. These are also useful teaching aids used especially in small classes to teach vocabulary and important concepts. Worksheets are an important aid to the students to work out the exercises given in them.

7) **Scientific apparatus, materials, and models used in classrooms and science labs:** No science lesson at any level of education is complete unless the learners are shown the practical examples by conducting the science experiments in the lab or class. Models of parts of the human body and many other models depicting the replica of the things taught in the class are very important teaching aids. Clay models are very prominently seen in the schools and colleges. And it has been observed these have been serving as an effective teaching support material since the beginning of science education.

8) **Study tours:** Visit to science museums, planetariums, zoological parks, botanical parks, places of geographical, historical, and places of scientific importance has been serving as very good teaching support material for teachers to teach the students.

9) **Use of Abacus in teaching:** The use of Abacus in learning numbers and small mathematical operations has been in use since times immemorial.

10) **Geometry kits:** The teacher uses a bigger version of the geometry kit to explain the geometrical concepts by drawing sketches and figures on the board. The learners learn how to draw these and they practise by following the pattern by drawing them on their note books with smaller geometric kits.

11) **Dictionaries and encyclopaedias:** Dictionaries and encyclopaedias have been helping the teacher as a support material since the inception of classroom teaching. Teachers have been consulting these teaching aids to clarify the meaning and basic phenomenon of any concept so that they can teach effectively.

Modern Teaching Support System

1) **Whiteboard and marker:** Blackboard and chalk have been replaced with whiteboard made of special material and markers of different colours in modern classroom teaching. In some cases where still chalk is used, there is use of green board in place of blackboard.

2) **Computers:** Computers are the fundamental teaching support system of the modern times. Today's education is considered incomplete without computers. This is the basic machine on which all other electronic media of learning depend. These can be bought in various forms like desktops, laptops, notebooks, and simply e-readers. The computers have been playing an important tool for teaching from the last few years of the 20th century and since then, it has brought about a revolution in the methods of teaching which will be used by future teachers also for many years to come. The computers make use of multimedia programmes which includes attractive colours, clear graphics, wonderful sounds, fascinating animations, and enjoyable videos discharging to the students the various elements of their subjects of study.

3) **Internet:** With the advent of Internet technology, the use of a computer as part of today's educational aids has become inevitable. Internet is such a teaching support tool that helps the teacher to obtain any information from any part of the world and he can also verify the authenticity of the obtained knowledge. So with the support of Internet, a teacher imparts relevant and authentic information to the students.
4) **E-reader:** E-reader is a mobile app on which material from books, magazines, and newspapers can be downloaded. A teacher suggests the students to download books and other course related material. E-reader facilitates handing of the downloaded material and the material becomes portable also. Even complete books are downloaded and learners can take that material from one place to the other very easily. Books and other text material which can be read on the computer are also known as e-books, e-text, etc.
5) **Podcast:** This is the digital audio file which is available on the Internet for downloading and listening at a later stage. That audio may be a song, poem, lesson content, etc. The teacher asks learners to go for podcasting to supplement their classroom lecture.
6) **Online encyclopaedia:** It is the collection of information which is accessible to students through Internet channels like Wikipedia. This makes a teacher's job easier as whatever teacher was to explain to them is available to students through Wikipedia. This channel has updated information about any topic in any language.
7) **Audio and audio-visual support material:** In modern times audio aids like audio recorders, CD players, lingua phone, public address system, radio, etc. makes the teacher's job convenient for both the teacher and the students. Teachers' message becomes interesting and effective. Similarly, audio-visual support material like television, cinema projector, and video CD player with the feature of giving message with audio and visual mode together makes it a direct hitting on the target, i.e., fulfilling the learning needs of the students in the most interesting and absorbing way.
8) **Visual support material:** Even though the traditional visual support material like blackboard, charts pictures, models, etc., continues to be much supportive for teachers even today, yet certain modern visual devices have further strengthened the support to the teacher. The devices used are Diorama (a three-dimensional full-size or miniature model, sometimes enclosed in a glass showcase for a museum) and Epidiascope (a type of magic lantern that projects the image of an opaque object onto a screen). Students learn while visualising and enjoying colourful real life-like characters and situations which they have studied in the books.
9) **PowerPoint Presentation (PPP):** The PowerPoint Presentation (PPP) in the form of slides is part of the lecture in the modern classrooms. PPP serves a very important role in the modern education. Any person with a basic knowledge of PowerPoint can learn to make slides and games on the relevant subjects of teaching with a very little training. If a teacher is really interested to use this media to teach his or her students, he/she can do it in a very short period of time.

ICT-Based Teaching Support System

With the advent of the 21st century, ICT-based teaching support system has taken over as an effective teaching support system. It opens a vast jurisdiction of knowledge for the learners and they can learn that with the help of the teacher. Major supporting tools are:

1) **Blended classroom:** This is the classroom where teacher blends the traditional teaching pattern with online teaching methods.
2) **Flipped classroom:** It is also called 'Inverted classroom'. In flipped classroom, teaching with traditional support material is inverted. Here, the teacher teaches students online while students can be sitting anywhere outside the classroom.
3) **Open Educational Resources (OER):** The term was created by UNESCO in 2002. Open Education Resources (OER) are freely available online licensed educational material accessible to all, i.e., teachers, learners, researchers, and any other person concerned with education without any cost. This material can be copied, adapted, shared, and reused. The material is instantly available so OER are time-savers also.

Features of OER:

a) **Legal resource:** Material available is available through OER centres and is licensed under a universal protocol.
b) **Variety in material:** There is plenty of variety of material offered by OER, for example, learning content (such as lesson plans, assignments, textbooks, exams, and videos) as well as tools for learning (like software for creating videos and websites, course management systems, word processing programs, etc.) and teaching materials.

c) **Availability in any medium:** OER material is available both in digital and non-digital medium.

d) **No discrimination and restriction on access:** OER material is freely available to all, irrespective of their status in the educational field and origin. OER gives right to every seeker to adapt and use material in any way.

e) **5R:** OER permits 5R which are

Retain: The right to make, own, and control copies of the content (e.g., download, duplicate, store, and manage)

Reuse: The right to use the content in a wide range of ways (e.g., in a class, in a study group, on a website, or in a video)

Revise: The right to adapt, adjust, modify, or alter the content itself (e.g., translate the content into another language)

Remix: The right to combine the original or revised content with other material to create something new (e.g., incorporate the content into a mashup)

Redistribute: The right to share copies of the original content, your revisions, or your remixes with others (e.g., give a copy of the content to a friend)

The 5Rs discussed above were proposed by David Wiley. Users of OER are allowed to engage in any of these 5R activities, permitted by the use of an open license. So OER material is the perfect ICT-based support material available to teachers.

4) **Virtual labs:** These labs provide access to remotely placed institutions and students who do not have access to experiments in various disciplines of science. These labs provide simulation-based experiments. Labs do not require any additional infrastructure for their setup. The labs are easily accessible to remotely placed lab seekers via the Internet.

VIRTUAL LABS (INDIA)

Virtual Labs project is an initiative of Ministry of Human Resource Development (MHRD), Government of India under the aegis of National Mission on Education through Information and Communication Technology (NMEICT). This project is a consortium activity of twelve participating institutes and IIT Delhi is coordinating institute. It is a paradigm shift in ICT-based education. For the first time, such an initiative has been taken-up in remote?experimentation. Under Virtual Labs project, over 100 Virtual Labs consisting of approximately 700+ web-enabled experiments were designed for remote-operation and viewing. The intended beneficiaries of the projects are all students and faculty Members of Science and Engineering Colleges who do not have access to good lab?facilities and/or instruments.

5) **Virtual reality:** It is a simulation training given by a teacher. The teacher creates an artificial environment/world/situation on a computer with a particular software and presents it to the student in such a way that the student accepts it as the real environment/world/situation. Virtual reality is used as an illustration for any concept explained by the teacher. Creation of an artificial environment/world/situation close to the actual one makes learning interesting and absorbing and the student gets motivated to learn and understand it.

EduSAT

Launched in August 2011, the first exclusive satellite for serving the educational sector in India, EduSAT (Education Satellite) is a collaborative project of Indian Space Research Organization (ISRO,) the Union Ministry of Human Resource Development, state departments of education, and the Indira Gandhi National Open University in response to the growing demand for an interactive satellite-based distance education system from school to higher education level. The satellite has multiple regional beams covering different parts of India-five Ku band transponders with spot beams covering northern, north-eastern, eastern, southern, and western regions of the country. It is serving as a strong ICT-based teaching support system.

Some Vital Facts

1) Edusat is an instructional software.
2) Optimising learning outcomes is the underlying purpose of teaching aids.
3) Virtual reality provides participatory experience.
4) Blended learning is considered to be the most effective mode of learning of modern times.
5) "A diagram speaks more than 1000 words." Signifies use of teaching aids in the class.
6) An effective teaching aid activates all faculties.

Practice Exercise

General Questions Format

1. Which of the following traditional teaching support material has been the most motivating material for the students to concentrate on learning in the classroom teaching?
   (A) Flip cards (B) Charts
   (C) Textbooks (D) Blackboard

2. Which of the following is NOT one of 5R of OER teaching support material?
   (A) Restore (B) Remix
   (C) Redistribute (D) Reuse

3. A sound teaching support system injects
   (A) Confidence in teacher and motivation in learners
   (B) Motivation in teacher and confidence in learners
   (C) Confidence and motivation in teacher and motivation in learners
   (D) Confidence and motivation in both teacher and learners

4. Teaching support systems are given under Column I and their tools are given under Column II. Match the system with its respective tool and choose the correct answer choice among the given answer choices given below:

Column I (Teaching support system)	Column II (Tool of teaching support system)
a) Modern support system	i) Abacus
b) Traditional support system	ii) Flipped classroom
c) ICT-based support system	iii) PowerPoint presentation

   (A) a-ii, b-iii, c-i (B) a-iii, b-ii, c-i
   (C) a-iii, b-i, c-ii (D) a-i, b-ii, c-iii

5. Combination of which of the following teaching support systems is the best for learners?
   (A) Traditional and Modern
   (B) Modern and ICT-based
   (C) Traditional and ICT-based
   (D) None of these

6. A teaching support system is always needed because ________.
   (A) a teacher alone cannot bear the burden of cumbersome teaching
   (B) teaching is to be made learner-centric
   (C) teacher-learners conflicts are to be minimised
   (D) it is part of the curriculum and fulfils statutory requirements

7. Find the odd choice:
   (A) Diorama (B) CD Player
   (C) Flip card (D) e-reader

8. Which of the following is NOT TRUE about Virtual Labs project of India?
   a) It is a joint initiative of Union Ministry of Information and Technology and Department of Higher Education though Union Ministry of Human Resource Development
   b) It is a paradigm shift in ICT-based education.
   c) The project aims at constructing 100 labs in those science colleges which are situated in remote areas and do not have laboratories.
   d) This project is a consortium activity of twelve participating institutes and IIT Delhi is the coordinating institute.

   (A) b and c only (B) a and c only
   (C) b and d only (D) a and d only

9. Which of the following ICT-based teaching support term has been created by UNESCO?
   (A) Open Education Resources
   (B) Blended classroom
   (C) Virtual Labs
   (D) Flipped classroom

10. Introduction of Internet as teaching support material has caused transformation of which support system to which other category of support system?
   (A) Modern to ICT-based
   (B) Traditional to ICT-based
   (C) Traditional to modern
   (D) Traditional as well as modern to ICT-based

11. **Statement:** Are whiteboard and marker more effective than blackboard and chalk?

Arguments:

I. Yes, whiteboard and marker are more attractive than blackboard and chalk.

II. No, it is a natural transition from traditional teaching support system to modern one.

(A) Only argument I is strong
(B) Only argument II is strong
(C) Both arguments I and II are strong
(D) Neither argument I nor II is strong

12. To strengthen traditional teaching support system, government of India launched 'Operation……'.

(A) Chalk & Talk
(B) Blackboard
(C) Classroom
(D) One Teacher One Class

13. How do textbooks help a teacher to teach effectively in the classroom?

(A) Textbooks guide a teacher to make appropriate notes for the class, thus saving much of his time and energy.
(B) Same textbooks are available with both teacher and students, so it become easier for the teacher to set tuning with the students.
(C) An advanced reading and understanding of the chapter from the textbook enables the teacher to give relevant information to the students in an easy language.
(D) Textbooks raise confidence in the teacher to teach better in the class as the teacher gets readymade material on the course chapters.

14. Which of the following is NOT TRUE about OER?

a) The term was created by UNICEF in 2002.
b) OER material is available in digital medium.
c) Material is available through OER centres which does not need any license.
d) OER material is freely available to all teachers and students of higher education.

(A) a, b, c, and d (B) b and d only
(C) a only (D) a and c only

15. Which of the teaching support material is also called 'Inverted classroom'?

(A) Virtual Labs
(B) Virtual reality
(C) Model classroom
(D) Flipped classroom

KEY

1. B	**2.** A	**3.** A	**4.** C	**5.** D	**6.** B	**7.** C
8. B	**9.** A	**10.** C	**11.** C	**12.** B	**13.** C	**14.** A
15. D						

Assertion–Reason Format

1. **Assertion (A):** Teaching support system plays a role of capacity builder in a teacher.

Reason (R): Learners expect a sound teaching system provided by the teaching support system.

(A) Both A and R are true and R is correct explanation of A
(B) Both A and R are correct but R is not correct explanation of A
(C) A is true but R is false
(D) A is false but R is true

2. **Assertion (A):** OER is an ICT-based transition in the teaching support system.

Reason (R): Any transition in a teaching support system is not easily adapted by learners.

(A) Both A and R are true but R is not correct explanation of A
(B) Both A and R are false
(C) A is false but R is true
(D) A is true but R is false

3. **Assertion (A):** Virtual Labs project in India will further deepen the digital divide among learners.

Reason (R): Virtual Labs project does not define the areas to be covered under this initiative.

(A) Both A ad R are true and R is correct explanation of A
(B) Both A and R are true but R is not correct explanation of A
(C) Both A and R are false
(D) A is true but R is false

4. **Assertion (A):** E-reader as a teaching support material has made learning handy for learners.

   Reason (R): Learners can download content of bulky books and notes on their mobile and learn that at any place as it becomes portable.

   (A) Both A and R are true and R is correct explanation of A

   (B) Both A and R are true but R is not correct explanation of A

   (C) A is true but R is false

   (D) A is false but R is true

5. **Assertion (A):** PowerPoint Presentation (PPP) is easy to learn both for the teacher as well as for learners.

   Reason (R): PPP is rarely used these days after the advent of ICT-based teaching support system.

   (A) Both A and R are true and R is correct explanation of A

   (B) Both A and R are true but R is not correct explanation of A

   (C) A is true but R is false

   (D) A is false but R is true

KEY

1. B **2.** D **3.** C **4.** A **5.** C

Questions Asked in Previous NET Exams

1. Among the following, which one is instructional software? **(UGC NET JUNE 2019)**

   (A) Audio podcast

   (B) Printed material or book

   (C) Radio talk

   (D) EduSAT

2. What is the purpose underlying the use of teaching aids? **(UGC NET JULY 2018)**

   (A) To make the lessons interesting

   (B) To capture the students' attention

   (C) To enhance access to technological resources

   (D) To optimise learning outcomes

3. **Assertion (A):** Teaching aids have to be considered as effective supplements to instruction.

   Reason (R): They keep the students in good humour. **(UGC NET AUG 2016)**

   Choose the correct answer from the codes given below:

   Codes:

   (A) Both (A) and (R) are true and (R) is the correct explanation of (A)

   (B) Both (A) and (R) are true, but (R) is not the correct explanation of (A)

   (C) (A) is true, but (R) is false

   (D) (A) is false, but (R) is true

4. The use of teaching aids is justified on the grounds of **(UGC NET JULY 2016)**

   (A) Attracting student's attention in the classroom

   (B) Minimising indiscipline problem in the classroom

   (C) Optimising learning outcomes of students

   (D) Effective engagement of students in learning tasks

5. Instructional aids are used by the teacher to **(UGC NET DECEMBER 2014)**

   (A) Glorify the class

   (B) Attract the students

   (C) Clarify the concepts

   (D) Ensure discipline

6. Virtual reality provides **(UGC NET DECEMBER 2013)**

   (A) Sharp pictures

   (B) Individual audio

   (C) Participatory experience

   (D) Preview of new films

7. The blackboard can be utilised best by a teacher for **(UGC NET JUNE 2013)**

   (A) Putting the matter of teaching in black and white

   (B) Making the students attentive

   (C) Writing the important and notable points

   (D) Highlighting the teacher himself

8. Nowadays, the most effective mode of learning is **(UGC NET JUNE 2013)**

   (A) Self study

   (B) Face-to-face learning

   (C) E-learning

   (D) Blended learning

9. "A diagram speaks more than 1000 words". The statement means that the teacher should ______. **(UGC NET JUNE 2013)**
   (A) use diagrams in teaching
   (B) speak more and more in the class
   (C) use teaching aids in the class
   (D) not speak too much in the class
10. For a teacher, which of the following methods would be correct for writing on the blackboard? **(UGC NET JUNE 2012)**
    (A) Writing fast and as clearly as possible
    (B) Writing the matter first and then asking students to read it
    (C) Asking a question to students and then writing the answer as stated by them
    (D) Writing the important points as clearly as possible
11. Which of the following does not belong to a projected aid? **(UGC NET JUNE 2012)**
    (A) Overhead projector
    (B) Blackboard
    (C) Epidiascope
    (D) Slide projector
12. Which of the following belongs to a projected aid? **(UGC NET DECEMBER 2011)**
    (A) Blackboard
    (B) Diorama
    (C) Epidiascope
    (D) Globe
13. An effective teaching aid is one which ______. **(UGC NET JUNE 2011)**
    (A) is colourful and good looking
    (B) activates all faculties
    (C) is visible to all students
    (D) is easy to prepare and use
14. Why do teachers use teaching aids? **(UGC NET JUNE 2009)**
    (A) To make teaching fun-filled
    (B) To teach within understanding level of students
    (C) For students' attention
    (D) To make students attentive
15. Teacher uses visual aids to make learning: **(UGC NET JUNE 2007)**
    (A) simple
    (B) more knowledgeable
    (C) quicker
    (D) interesting
16. Which of the following is not an instructional material? **(UGC NET DECEMBER 2006)**
    (A) Overhead projector
    (B) Audio cassette
    (C) Printed material
    (D) Transparency

KEY

1. D	**2.** D	**3.** B	**4.** C	**5.** C	**6.** C	**7.** C
8. D	**9.** C	**10.** D	**11.** B	**12.** C	**13.** B	**14.** B
15. D	**16.** D					

6 Evaluation Systems and Innovations

CONCEPT

Evaluation system has been an integral part of the teaching-learning process since the inception of teaching and learning. Whatever is imparted by the teacher and gained by the learner needs a review. This review is formally known as evaluation. Evaluation system is an organised way to assess the knowledge of the learners which has been given to them by their teachers in a set time framework. Evaluation is practised through oral and written tests at every level of education. It is a continuous appraisal of the performance of the students and becomes a scale of promotion to higher standards in education.

Significance of Evaluation

Evaluation in the education system is an exercise conducted by teachers or the concerned authority to review the performance of students in different oral and written tests given to them on the subjects which they are learning in the formal or non-formal stream. Evaluating the knowledge of the students on different subjects, in a way, also provides an opportunity to the teacher to review his work also. Evaluation in teaching is a process of collecting, analysing, and interpreting information about teaching and learning in order to make informed decisions that enhance student achievement and the success of educational programs.

Characteristics of Evaluation

1) **Overall assessment:** Evaluation does not assess the subject knowledge only; rather it is the assessment of a learner's ambition of achieving educational heights, behavioural changes, interest, attitude, and aptitude. Evaluation establishes the extent of overall personality of a learner in the academic field.
2) **Assessment of learning difficulties:** Evaluation also targets to assess the learning difficulties being faced by the learner in the teaching-learning process. If a learner does not fare well in evaluation, it is an indication about the learning difficulties. Evaluation therefore is a review of such problems of learners.
3) **Continuous process:** Evaluation is a continuous process. There is continuous interaction between the teacher and students in the teaching-learning process at every level of education. Teachers evaluate the students' learning performance and accordingly, grades are allotted and promotion to the next class is allowed. Evaluation continues throughout the academic life of a learner.
4) **Comprehensive:** Evaluation is not only the judgement of a learner's subject knowledge; rather it is the judgement of his overall growth in the academic arena.
5) **Use of all tools of evaluation:** Evaluation includes all tools, i.e., written test, interview, rating scale, observation, etc. Use of all the tools of evaluation ensures the overall assessment of the learners.

Types of Evaluation

Since evaluation is an integral part of the educative process, the teacher should guide every learning experience in relation to the needs and interest of the learners. Evaluation forms the basis for deciding what type of appraisal is needed to assess a particular learning situation.

- **Diagnostic evaluation:** This is the type of evaluation the teacher considers at the beginning of the unit or course to determine the different levels in terms of learning experience of children to serve as a basis for grouping them-slow, average, or fast. Diagnostic evaluation will also enable the teacher to ascertain or analyse the nature or cause of difficulties, and, in effect, help them plan remedial activities to meet their interests and needs.
- **Formative evaluation:** This type of evaluation consists of learning activities performed by the teacher to find out how well he is doing and what is needed during the next learning experience by the learners. This is important to give the learners adequate information for self-appraisal. This is one way of motivating them. Information from formative evaluations is not used to make decisions or judgments about the learners' work; but rather used on matters as learner's grouping, preparation of lesson plans, and execution of teaching strategy.

- **Summative evaluation:** Under this type, the teacher undertakes the evaluation of the learning outcomes of a unit in order to grade the learners and make his own personal judgment on the effectiveness of his methods of teaching at the end of a course. This evaluation process serves as a basis for deciding whether promotion or retention will be better for the learner. Besides, it can also serve as a guide in determining the effectiveness of instruction and be a gauge for planning future learning activities. Summative evaluations are those used by the teacher to determine grades and form the reports sent to the students and their parents.
- **Continuous and Comprehensive Evaluation (CCE):** This was a process of assessment, mandated by the Right to Education Act, of India. This approach to assessment had been introduced by state governments in India, as well as by the Central Board of Secondary Education in India, for students of sixth to tenth grades and twelfth in some schools. From this, the students of smaller classes can have a practice to face the Board exam in a younger age. The Karnataka government has introduced CCE for grades 1 through 9. Later, it was also introduced for 12th grade students. The main aim of CCE is to evaluate every aspect of the child during their presence at the school. This is believed to help reduce the pressure on the child during/before examinations as the student will have to sit for multiple tests throughout the year, of which no test or the syllabus covered will be repeated at the end of the year, whatsoever. The CCE method is claimed to bring enormous changes from the traditional chalk and talk method of teaching, provided it is implemented accurately.
- **Norm-referenced test:** This is a type of test, assessment, or evaluation which yields an estimate of the position of the tested individual in a predefined population, with respect to the trait being measured. Scores from norm-referenced tests are used to compare students' progress to others in their peer group. This group may contain students in the same grade across the nation, or other categories such as special education, disability status, English learners, gifted students, and more. Most commonly, norm-referenced tests use a national peer group.
- **Criterion-referenced test:** This is designed to measure a student's academic performance against some standard or criteria. This standard or criteria is predetermined before students begin the test. Authorities choose a standard, such as a percent of items answered correctly or a state test benchmark, as the criteria for the test. The student's score then shows the progress they have made toward the agreed-upon standard-if they fall short, they must continue to work toward the standard. It is a style of test which uses test scores to generate a statement about the behavior that can be expected of a person with that score. Most tests and quizzes that are written by teachers can be considered criterion-referenced tests. In this case, the objective is simply to see whether the student has learned the material.

ACHIEVEMENT TEST

An achievement test is a test of developed skill or knowledge. The most common type of achievement test is a standardised test developed to measure skills and knowledge learned in a given grade level, usually through planned instruction, such as training or classroom instruction.

THE CHOICE BASED CREDIT SYSTEM (CBCS)

Traditionally, there had been teacher-centric methods of teaching in the Indian teaching system. In such methods, learners are passive participants in the teaching-learning system. There has not been choice among the learners to choose subjects of their choice. With the passage of time, there have been trends in favour of the learner-centric system. One such approach is the Choice Based Credit System (CBCS). It is a student-centric course which allows students to choose their subjects. The subjects can be at a basic or advanced level. Instead of the conventional marking system, CBCS system uses credits.

This system provides flexibility in preparing the curriculum and granting credits based on the course intensity and teaching hours. This helps students to pursue courses of their choice, study at their own pace, learn extra courses, and acquire more than the required credits. CBCS emphasises on group discussions, assignments, class activities, and internal examinations, thus creating a beneficial education environment.

Origin of CBCS in India

In the year 2015-16, the UGC introduced Choice Based Credit System in Delhi University.

Types of Courses

Choice Based Credit System (CBCS) provides a learning platform wherein the student or knowledge seeker has the flexibility to choose their course from a list of elective, core, and soft skill courses. This is a student-centric approach to learning or acquiring higher education.

- Core course: Students need to choose a core subject to complete the credit requirement.

- Elective course: These subjects have more generic content and aim to increase the students' skill. They expose the student to subjects which are not in their curriculum.
- Foundation: They are value-based subjects that lead to knowledge enhancement.

Working of CBCS

CBCS works on the simple principle of the choice being in the students' hand. Colleges provide subject options to students. Students can choose subjects according to their interests and credits required for that particular semester. They will then attend classes and practicals and obtain credits. Once they acquire the required credits, they pass the semester. Choice Based Credit System not only opens pathways for learning opportunities but also manifests learning goals and objectives. CBCS follows a credit system which is attached to course components offered to students. A credit system for higher education measures various parameters like student performance, outcomes, entrepreneurship skills, contact hours, innovation and creativity talents, etc. This CBCS system is an initiative of University Grants Commission (UGC) which enhances and promotes educational liberalisation of existing conventional higher education models.

UGC Evaluation Criteria through CBCS

UGC has fixed a 10-point grading system by defining various CBCS concepts as follows:

- Choice based: Choice of multiple courses
- Grading: Marks secured is in letter grade format
- Semester: Learner-teacher engagement quotient can be measured/identified semester-wise
- Credit: Class hours per week carries additional importance in credit system
- Assessment: In the form of classroom attendance, mid-term tests etc; is continuous and wide-ranging.

UGC has introduced a 10-point grading system as follows:

O (Outstanding)	10
A+ (Excellent)	9
A (Very Good)	8
B+ (Good)	7
B (Above Average)	6
C (Average)	5
P (Pass)	4
F (Fail)	0
Ab (Absent)	0

Credits are calculated keeping in mind the following components:

- Lecture (L)
- Tutorial (T)
- Practical (P)

The course may have all components of evaluation or combination of any two listed above. Although CBCS system is tried and tested, it sometimes lacks accurate estimation of marks. Teachers are further challenged to keep pace with many courses. This system furthers confusion among students; as each student has a different timetable and course of study. Nonetheless, CBCS system is flexible and student-centric and this approach matches today's demands of the student/learner community.

Advantages of CBCS

1) **Freedom of choice:** CBCS allows students to choose subjects that they find interesting. Students perform better when they learn about things they like.
2) **Varied combination of subjects:** Students can take up varied subject combinations like Economics-Microbiology, Physics-Accounts, English-Chemistry, etc. With the conventional education system, this was not possible.
3) **Employment generation:** CBCS prepares students for the future. Industries want employees who are all-rounders with multidisciplinary knowledge and not students with knowledge about just one stream. Thus, CBCS imparts job-oriented skills.
4) **Freedom to change combination:** Students can change their subjects every semester. This helps them to learn about various fields and recognize where their talent lies.
5) **Self-reliance:** As students choose their own subjects, they learn to make decisions which are beneficial for them. This helps students to become self-reliant at an early age.
6) **Flexibility:** CBCS offers students to study at different times and at different institutes to complete a course.
7) **Transferable:** As the grading system is the same across all universities in India, a student can easily transfer from one university to the other.
8) **Credits compensation:** If a student falls sick or is unable to cope, they can choose fewer subjects and earn fewer credits in one semester. They can then compensate for the lost credits in the next semester.
9) **Achieving global standards:** CBCS takes Indian education on par with global standards.

Disadvantages of CBCS

1) **Teachers fail to keep pace with course:** Teachers are often criticised for not keeping pace with the courses due to their varied nature.
2) **Not yet acquainted with CBCS:** As this is a new system, evaluators are not fully acquainted with this yet, which results in wrong estimation of credits.
3) **Confusion among students:** As different students have different courses and different time spans, there exists confusion among students regarding acquiring credits.

In spite of the above, CBCS is a student-centric choice system of evaluation in higher education and it is the need of the day to carry evaluation system to global standards.

COMPUTER-BASED TEST (CBT)

Computers and technology have impacted almost every industry across the globe. One specific area that has experienced substantial change is the education industry. The pace at which the process of teaching, assessing, and learning has evolved is enough to signify the impact. Books have moved to e-books, physical classrooms have turned into online classrooms, and paper-based tests have become online tests.

For a very long time, until the arrival of computers, paper-based tests were the only method of assessment available to educators and instructors. It was only when technology-based assessment systems arrived that the idea of pen and paper assessments became redundant and slowly gave way to a better, more effective system of assessment, i.e., computer-based tests.

Computer-based assessment is the practice of assigning quizzes and tests to learners on a computer instead of paper. Computer-based assessment is already used widely in many e-learning environments. Online tests can be designed for diagnostic, formative, or summative evaluation.

Advantages of CBT

1) **More efficient:** CBTs are more efficient than paper-based tests as these are based on a well-defined and planned computer programme.
2) **Year-round Assessment:** CBT can be conducted around the year after short durations so that learners can give better performance by covering a smaller portion of their syllabus. It is not like conventional tests which are conducted after a long period, say six months at least, where students cannot perform well due to the burden of a bulky syllabus.
3) **Flexible schedule:** CBTs have flexible scheduling. All the students are not to appear in the exam in one shift or two shifts only. CBT gives a schedule of some days, i.e., a week during which a definite number of students appear in the exam turn-by-turn. For example, National Testing Agency (NTA) is conducting NET exam within a one week's schedule which gives sufficient time to students to prepare for the exam.
4) **Individual testing environment:** Each candidate is allotted a separate and independent testing compartment with an individual computer, on the screen of which questions are asked and he/she independently gives answers. This increases his/her efficiency as he can independently think and give answers. He/she is not influenced by whispering of other students as is found in conventional type of tests.
5) **Faster and accurate results:** It used to take very long time in declaring results of conventional types of tests. On the contrary, CBT gives accurate and faster results.

Disadvantages of CBT

1) **No scope of rectification of error:** In conventional evaluation, errors if any can be rectified, whereas in CBT, once an error is created, it becomes part of the programme that cannot be rectified. This will land learners in confusion.
2) **System breakdown:** A deadlock is created when the server or system breaks down. It wastes time of students who are appearing in CBT. Due to wastage of time students' efficiency is affected.
3) **Poor scope of creativity:** CBT is conducted under set IT instructions and learners are to give answers to questions in an electronic discipline. They cannot think on their own which affects their scope of being creative and thinking independently while solving questions.
4) **Computer glitches:** Even a minor fault in the computer system puts the whole CBT process to a halt and causes unnecessary delays in the smooth completion of CBT.
5) **Computer virus:** There is apprehension of the computer system being attacked by virus. This corrupts files dealing with the question paper and badly affects the conducting of CBT.
6) **Apprehension of deadlock in the wake of huge organisation:** Conducting of CBT involves hardware, software, and many technical and non-technical personnel. Due to this, there is apprehension that if there is a deadlock at any level, the whole process of CBT comes to a halt. Such a huge involvement of machines and people does not ensure smooth conduct of the exam.

7) **Wastage of time and money due to re-conduct:** It has been observed that in many places, due to power failure or any other snag developing in the system, CBT has to be cancelled and it is re-conducted after a certain time period. This on one hand involves wastage of time and money and on the other hand, it shakes the confidence of the candidates as they have to again prepare everything from the beginning.

8) **Poor handling of CBT due to lack of training:** CBT is installed in a hasty manner without giving training to candidates. Candidates are made to sit before the computer system with a brief introduction. Due to lack of training, candidates cannot understand the procedure and thus, cannot adjust in the sudden switching over from the conventional type test to computer-based test. This hampers their smooth solving of questions and affects their performance.

However, in spite of the above drawbacks, CBT is an integral part of the modern ICT-based evaluation system.

INNOVATIONS IN EVALUATION SYSTEM

Though evaluation system is becoming more and more hi-tech due to advancement in information technology, yet there is always a scope of innovations in the evaluation system.

Basis of Innovations in the Evaluation System

Need of innovations arise due to certain limitations in the current evaluation system. These limitations become the basis of further innovations in the evaluation system as explained below:

1) **Obsolete curriculum:** Curriculum in some courses does not contain flexibility and is not compatible to evaluation schedule and kind. For example, curriculum does not include detail of syllabus only, it also contains style of evaluation. Certain curricula have not been revised since long and these are to be revised while incorporating the new pattern of evaluation.

2) **Emphasis on rote learning:** Still there are various courses where there is emphasis on rote learning and accordingly, primitive method of evaluation is practised. So there is a need of innovation in the study pattern and evaluation pattern to discourage rote learning and promote a level of understanding. In such a pattern of studies, superficial knowledge of the subject is tested. So innovations are introduced with the aim of fundamental clarity of the subject and testing the fundamental knowledge of the subject through a hi-tech evaluation system.

3) **Internal versus external examination:** In some academic quarters, there is still a system of external and internal evaluation system which is totally subjective in nature and does not measure the actual intellect of the candidate. This becomes the basis to introduce a single uniform pattern of evaluation.

4) **Subject-wise grade and overall grade:** This type of grading system is superfluous and confusing and is again subjective in nature. Due to this, there always exists possibility of corruption and thus favouring some students, ignoring merit. There arises a need to bring innovations in this stream.

5) **Mismanagement of examinations:** Prevailing examination channels are mismanaged to benefit a certain few. Curriculum is so designed that some people may be given undue advantage in examinations. Exam pattern is quite suitable to a privileged few in which evaluation is made on the basis of influence and underhand connections and not on merit. So this becomes a strong basis to reform the evaluation system with a transparent and efficient evaluation technique.

6) **Examination Phobia:** Even after various reforms in the examination system, yet phobia of exam still exists today. So there is a need to bring student-friendly innovations in the evaluation system. Such exams should act as a stimulant for students so that they may appear in the exam without any fear.

Modifications in the Evaluation System

1) **Curriculum development and streamlining examination:** Under new national policy of education, a uniform curriculum is being brought in which is adopted by every university and accordingly, examination system is streamlined.

2) **Students' mobility:** The rigid structure of examinations used to hinder students' mobility but innovations like Choice Based Credit System (CBCS) has made students' mobility possible with system of obtaining credits with subject combination of their choice.

3) **Common national tests for institutions of higher learning:** Common national tests for admission to various national level openings like NET, CAT, CLAT, MAT, etc. are being conducted to select the best possible candidates for these openings.

4) **Semester system:** Introduction of semester system has made the preparation task easier for candidates as compared to the annual system. In the annual system of exams, candidates had to prepare the whole syllabus at a stretch which was difficult to retain in the mind, so there was a practice of guessing

and rote learning which was of no use to students as far as evaluation of their performance was concerned. Semester examination system has distributed the whole syllabus into four parts and candidates are to prepare one-fourth of the syllabus and they are to appear in the semester exam each time. This makes their preparation sound and effective and they perform better in semester exams.

5) **Question banks:** Question banks are prepared to give sufficient practice to students regarding the current pattern of evaluation. An item analysis of these questions is done and important questions are compiled and preserved in the form of question banks. These are kept in libraries of various universities, colleges, or other institutions of higher learning and candidates consult them and acquaint themselves with the latest innovations of the evaluation system and hence, gain confidence.
6) **Multiple sets of question papers:** Multiple sets of the same question paper are given to candidates to minimise the element of copying and other unfair means. No two candidates in connectivity get the same set of question paper. Further, recently NTA has introduced a system to conduct examination for six days with two shifts each day. In each shift and on every day, question paper with different series and sets are given to candidates in the computer mode.
7) **Internal assessment:** Regular teacher of the class observes learning habits and learning activities of his/her students. He/she gives certain percentage of marks to students on the basis of their academic performance, regularity, punctuality, and general progress in the class. This percentage is out of a certain fixed percentage allotted to the teacher and this is called internal assessment, i.e., formative evaluation.
8) **Grading system:** Giving grades like A, A+, B, B+, etc. has proved to be more yielding instead of percentage given to candidates.
9) **Continuous and Comprehensive Evaluation (CCE):** This innovation in evaluation system includes formative and summative evaluation and it is different for different students. The evaluation is according to an individual's own traits.
10) **Assessment for learning, Assessment of learning, and Assessment as learning:** Assessment for learning is formative assessment, assessment of learning is summative assessment, and assessment as learning is different from both. In assessment for learning and assessment of learning, assessment is made by the teacher, whereas assessment as learning is the self-assessment made by the learner in higher order of education and this is an innovation to judge the true evaluation skills in a student. This self-assessment is also called metacognition.

METACOGNITION

This term has been given by American psychologist John H. Flavell. This refers to "Thinking about one's own thinking". It is the knowledge one has about one's own cognitive process. It is an act of self-assessment and self-regulation. It is a tool of successful learning. It is self-assessment of one's own strengths and weaknesses. Metacognition is considered as an effective innovation in the evaluation system in studies of higher order.

11) **Learning experience is more than grades:** Latest innovations in the evaluation system believe that overall learning is more important than grades. So formative and summative innovations are given priority.
12) **Changes from Minimum Level of Learning (MLL) to Essential Level of Learning (ELL):** Innovative evaluation shifted from MLL, i.e., fixing a minimum level of learning, say matric or secondary education to ELL, that is, the candidate should essentially qualify a particular level of education, say graduation.
13) **Shifting from ELL to learning outcomes:** Recently, the concept of learning outcomes in evaluation has taken place of ELL. Learning outcomes is the evaluation of a learner's cognitive, affective, and psychomotor skills.

Some Classroom Innovations in Formative Evaluation

1) **Minute Papers:** At the end of the class, the teacher asks the students to highlight the important points they have learnt from that lesson within a minute or two. In this way the teacher can make an assessment.
2) **Just in Time:** It is another innovation in which after finishing a topic in the class, the teacher asks the students to state whether they have any knowledge of the topic which is going to be discussed next in the class. Students give information as per their level and extent of knowledge. From here, the teacher comes to know the level of students' knowledge and when he teaches that topic actually in the class, he tries to take the topic up to that level.

The pace with which scenario of higher education is changing, innovations in higher education are tools for its survival, due to which innovations in curriculum design, policy, and in evaluation have become tools of survival of higher education in this world of global access.

Some Vital Facts

1) Diagnostic Evaluation ascertains causes and remedies of persistent learning problems during instructions
2) Shift in focus from teacher-centric to student-centric educationisthe best advantage of choice based credit system.
3) Criterion-Referenced Testing (CRT) focuses on a delimited domain of learning tasks.
4) Norm-Referenced Testing (NRT) requires a clearly defined group.
5) Formative evaluation requires quizzes and discussions.
6) Summative evaluation involves grading the final learning outcomes.
7) Continuous and comprehensive evaluation works for evaluating cognitive aspects with regularity
8) Multiple choice questions are beneficial as they are more objective than any other form of objective type questions.
9) Assessing the amount of learning after teaching is considered as Achievement Test
10) Formative evaluation provides continuous feedback to both teachers and students during instruction?

Practice Exercise

General Questions Format

1. Which of the following is TRUE about evaluation?

a) Evaluation of a learner keeps him/her conscious about learning.

b) Evaluation establishes a healthy interaction between the learner and the teacher.

c) A teacher plans his/her lecture after assessing the performance of the students through evaluation.

d) Evaluation is a continuous and comprehensive assessment of students' knowledge at every level of education.

(A) d only (B) a, c, and d only
(C) b and d only (D) a, b, c, and d

2. Innovations in the evaluation system have become the need of the day mainly because ______.

(A) teachers and students have been demanding it for long

(B) objective is to optimise the understanding level of learners

(C) aim is to bring uniformity in the evaluation system to facilitate mobility of the students

(D) evaluation system is to be adopted in spirit and not in letter

3. In which of the following evaluation, scores of the test are used to compare student's progress to others in the peer group?

(A) Summative evaluation

(B) Norm-referenced evaluation

(C) Diagnostic evaluation

(D) Criterion-referenced evaluation

4. Which of the following is NOT a component considered to award credits in Choice Based Credit System?

(A) Lecture

(B) Practical

(C) Tutorial

(D) Course

5. Metacognition is ________.

(A) a process of obtaining cognition beyond a normal level of cognition

(B) an innovation in the evaluation system

(C) a level of thinking where one starts thinking like his opponent

(D) a stage in evaluation where the teacher makes an assessment of a student's performance in comparison to what he has delivered to the students.

6. Types of evaluation are given under Column I and the central theme of each is given under Column II. Match the evaluation with its theme and chose the correct code given below:

Column I (Evaluation)	Column II (Theme)
a) Diagnostic	i) Learning experience
b) Summative	ii) Multiple tests
c) Formative	iii) Treatment of difficulties
d) CCE	iv) Determination of grades

Codes:

	(a)	(b)	(c)	(d)
(A)	ii	iv	i	iii
(B)	iv	i	iii	ii
(C)	iii	iv	i	ii
(D)	i	iv	iii	ii

7. Choice Based Credit System was introduced in 2015-16 by the UGC in
   (A) Delhi University
   (B) Indian Institute of Science, Bangalore
   (C) IIT Roorkee
   (D) IIM Ahmedabad

8. Which innovation in the evaluation system helps the teacher to gather the level of knowledge of learners of the topic yet to be discussed in the class?
   (A) Minimum learning level
   (B) Learning outcomes
   (C) Minute Papers
   (D) Just in Time

9. Choice Based Credit System is successful due to its pivotal component of
   (A) Grading system (B) Flexibility
   (C) Innovations (D) Self-reliance

10. Which of the following is NOT a characteristic of evaluation?
   (A) Comprehensive (B) Continuous
   (C) Explorative (D) Uniform

11. Which of the following streams of education does not require evaluation?
   (A) Formal (B) Non-formal
   (C) Informal (D) None of these

12. Which of the following assessment is formative evaluation?
   (A) Assessment as learning
   (B) Assessment for learning
   (C) Assessment of learning
   (D) Assessment by learning

13. Innovations in the evaluation system ensure ____.
   (A) a highly technical evaluation where there is no apprehension of under-evaluation or over evaluation
   (B) replacement of number system with grading system
   (C) individual evaluation which is a break in the tradition of indiscriminate evaluation
   (D) keeping pace within the rapidly changing scenario of higher education not only at national level but at global level also

14. Computer-based test is conducted as ____.
   a) an extension to conduct online tests with OMR sheets
   b) an improvement over paper-based test
   c) a substitution to traditional tests in all its forms
   d) an advanced form of diagnostic, summative, and formative evaluation
   (A) b, c, and d only (B) d only
   (C) a and c only (D) a only

15. Computer-based test is popular with ____.
   (A) curriculum designing authority
   (B) examination conducting bodies
   (C) paper setters
   (D) students' organisations

KEY

1. A 2. C 3. B 4. D 5. B 6. C 7. A
8. D 9. B 10. C 11. C 12. B 13. D 14. A
15. B

Assertion–Reason Format

1. **Assertion (A):** Evaluation is the scale of measuring progress in the formal system of education.
   Reason (R): There has been a tradition of evaluation since education in ancient times.
   (A) Both A and R are true and R is correct explanation of A
   (B) Both A and R are true but R is not correct explanation of A
   (C) Both A and R are false
   (D) A is true but R is false

2. **Assertion (A):** Computer-based tests are successful in science exams.

   Reason (R): Institutions of higher learning are resorting to computer-based tests in order to keep pace with current global requirements.

   (A) Both A and R are true and R is correct explanation of A

   (B) Both A and R are true but R is not correct explanation of A

   (C) A is true but R is false

   (D) A is false but R is true

3. **Assertion (A):** Introduction of semester system has made evaluation easier and beneficial both for the teacher and the learners.

   Reason (R): Annual system of examination is used to measure learners' performance at superficial level only.

   (A) Both A and R are true and R is correct explanation of A

   (B) Both A and R are true but R is not correct explanation of A

   (C) A is true but R is false

   (D) Both A and R are false

4. **Assertion (A):** Choice Based Credit System is preparing students to effectively contribute in the socio-economic development of the country.

   Reason (R): Administrative bottlenecks are posing a great hindrance in the success of any innovation in the evaluation system.

   (A) Both A and R are true and R is correct explanation of A

   (B) Both A and R are true but R is not correct explanation of A

   (C) Both A and R are false

   (D) A is true but R is false

5. **Assertion (A):** Metacognition is a part of summative evaluation.

   Reason (R): Self-assessment of one's own cognitive abilities is an evaluation in fiasco.

   (A) Both A and R are true but R is not correct explanation of A

   (B) Both A and R are true and R is correct explanation of A

   (C) Both A and R are false

   (D) A is true but R is false.

6. **Assertion (A):** Choice Based Credit System is an initiative of Union Ministry of Human Resource Development.

   Reason (R): A credit system for higher education measures various parameters like student performance, outcomes, and entrepreneurship skills.

   (A) Both A and R are true and R is correct explanation of A

   (B) Both A and R are true but R is not correct explanation of A

   (C) A is true but R is false

   (D) A is false but R is true

7. **Assertion (A):** Internal assessment is a form of formative evaluation.

   Reason (R): Informative evaluation a teacher assesses the learning experience of a student during the progress of a course.

   (A) Both A and R are true and R is correct explanation of A

   (B) Both A and R are true but R is not correct explanation of A

   (C) A is true but R is false

   (D) A is false but R is true

8. **Assertion (A):** Decision regarding promoting or retaining a student is taken on the basis of summative evaluation.

   Reason (R): Summative evaluation helps in planning future strategies of the teaching-learning process.

   (A) Both A and R are true and R is correct explanation of A

   (B) Both A and R are true but R is not correct explanation of A

   (C) Both A and R are false

   (D) A is false but R is true

9. **Assertion (A):** Erratic power supply is the main reason of failure of computer-based test system in India.

   Reason (R): It has been too early to introduce computer-based tests in India.

   (A) Both A and R are true and R is correct explanation of A

   (B) Both A and R are true but R is not correct explanation of A

   (C) A is false but R is true

   (D) Both A and R are false

10. **Assertion (A):** Criterion-referenced evaluation is the traditional form of evaluation.

    Reason (R): Students' performance is evaluated against a predetermined standard fixed for qualification.

    (A) Both A and R are true and R is correct explanation of A

    (B) Both A and R are true but R is not correct explanation of A

    (C) A is true but R is false

    (D) A is false but R is true

KEY

1. B	2. D	3. B	4. B	5. C	6. D	7. A
8. B	9. D	10. A				

Questions Asked in Previous NET Exams

1. Diagnostic evaluation ascertains

   (UGC NET JUNE 2019)

   (A) Students' performance at the beginning of instructions

   (B) Causes and remedies of persistent learning problems during instructions

   (C) Degree of achievement of instructional objectives at the end

   (D) Learning progress and failures after instructions

2. The performance of a student is compared with another student in which type of testing?

   (UGC NET JUNE 2019)

   (A) Criterion-referenced testing

   (B) Diagnostic testing

   (C) Summative testing

   (D) Norm-referenced testing

3. Which of the following evaluation systems belongs to the category of innovative practice?

   (A) Semestarized Examination

   (B) Practice Evaluation

   (C) Portfolio Evaluation

   (D) Learning Outcome based Evaluation

4. Which among the following is the best advantage of Choice Based Credit System?

   (UGC NET DECEMBER 2018)

   (A) Shift in focus from teacher-centric to student-centric education

   (B) Improving classroom attendance

   (C) Helping teacher to complete syllabus on time

   (D) Reducing examination anxiety among students

5. Below are given statements pertaining to evaluation systems. Identify those which correctly explain them.

   (UGC NET JULY 2018)

   (i) Criterion-referenced Test (CRT) focuses on a delimited domain of learning tasks.

   (ii) Norm-referenced Test (NRT) requires a clearly defined group.

   (iii) Formative tests are given at the end of a course.

   (iv) Both Norm-referenced Test (NRT) and Criterion-referenced Test (CRT) use the same type of test items.

   (v) Summative tests are used regularly during teaching transactions.

   (vi) Mastery tests are examples of Norm-referenced Test.

   Choose the correct answer from the code given below:

   Code:

   (A) (i), (ii), and (iii)

   (B) (i), (ii), and (iv)

   (C) (iv), (v), and (vi)

   (D) (ii), (v), and (vi)

6. From the list of evaluation procedures given below, identify those which will be called 'formative evaluation'. Indicate your answer by choosing from the code:

   (UGC NET JULY 2018)

   (a) A teacher awards grades to students after having transacted the course work.

   (b) During interaction with students in the classroom, the teacher provides corrective feedback.

(c) The teacher gives marks to students on a unit test.

(d) The teacher clarifies the doubts of students in the class itself.

(e) The overall performance of a student is reported to parents at every three months interval.

(f) The learner's motivation is raised by the teacher through a question-answer session.

Codes:

(A) (a), (b), and (c)

(B) (b), (c), and (d)

(C) (a), (c), and (e)

(D) (b), (d), and (f)

7. On the basis of summative tests, a teacher is interpreting his/her students' performance in terms of their wellness and lifestyle evident in their behaviour. This will be called:

(UGC NET NOVEMBER 2017)

(A) Continuous and comprehensive evaluation

(B) Norm-referenced Test

(C) Criterion-referenced Test

(D) Formative testing

8. Match the items of the first set with that of the second set in respect of their evaluation system. Choose the correct code:

(UGC NET JULY 2016)

Set-I	Set-II
a. Formative evaluation	i. Evaluating cognitive and co-cognitive aspects with regularity
b. Summative evaluation	ii. Tests and their interpretations based on a group and certain yardsticks
c. Continuous and comprehensive evaluation	iii. Grading the final learning outcomes
d. Norm and criterion-referenced tests	iv. Quizzes and discussions

Codes:

	a	b	c	d
(A)	iv	iii	i	ii
(B)	i	ii	iii	iv
(C)	iii	iv	ii	i
(D)	i	iii	iv	ii

9. What are the characteristics of Continuous and Comprehensive Evaluation?

(UGC NET DECEMBER 2015)

(a) It increases the workload on students by taking multiple tests.

(b) It replaces marks with grades.

(c) It evaluates every aspect of the student.

(d) It helps in reducing examination phobia.

Select the correct answer from the codes given below:

(A) (a), (b), (c), and (d)

(B) (b) and (d)

(C) (a), (b), and (c)

(D) (b), (c), and (d)

10. Which one of the following statements is correct in the context of multiple-choice type questions? **(UGC NET DECEMBER 2015)**

(A) They are more objective than true-false type questions.

(B) They are less objective than essay type questions.

(C) They are more subjective than short-answer type questions.

(D) They are more subjective than true-false type questions.

11. Achievement tests are commonly used for the purpose of: **(UGC NET JUNE 2015)**

(A) Assessing the amount of learning after teaching

(B) Making selections for a specific job

(C) Selecting candidates for a course

(D) Identifying strengths and weaknesses of learners

12. Diagnostic evaluation ascertains

(UGC NET DECEMBER 2014)

(A) Students' performance at the beginning of instructions

(B) Learning progress and failures during instructions

(C) Degree of achievements of instructions at the end

(D) Causes and remedies of persistent learning problems during instructions

13. Identify the category of evaluation that assesses the learning progress to provide continuous feedback to the students during instruction.
(UGC NET JUNE 2014)
(A) Placement
(B) Diagnostic
(C) Formative
(D) Summative

14. Which one of the following types of evaluation assesses the learning progress to provide continuous feedback to both teachers and students during instruction?
(UGC NET SEPTEMBER 2013)
(A) Placement evaluation
(B) Formative evaluation
(C) Diagnostic evaluation
(D) Summative evaluation

15. Which of the following is not a characteristic of a good achievement test?
(UGC NET JUNE 2012)
(A) Reliability
(B) Objectivity
(C) Ambiguity
(D) Validity

16. By which of the following methods the true evaluation of the students is possible?
(UGC NET DECEMBER 2011)
(A) Evaluation at the end of the course
(B) Evaluation twice in a year
(C) Continuous evaluation
(D) Formative evaluation

17. The academic performance of students can be improved if parents are encouraged to
(UGC NET DECEMBER 2010)
(A) supervise the work of their wards
(B) arrange for extra tuition
(C) remain unconcerned about it
(D) interact with teachers frequently

18. Good evaluation of written material should not be based on: **(UGC NET JUNE 2009)**
(A) Linguistic expression
(B) Logical presentation
(C) Ability to reproduce whatever is read
(D) Comprehension of subject

19. Which of the following indicates evaluation?
(UGC NET DECEMBER 2006)
(A) Ram got 45 marks out of 200.
(B) Mohan got 38 percent marks in English.
(C) Shyam got First Division in the final examination.
(D) All of the above

KEY

1. B	**2.** D	**3.** D	**4.** A	**5.** B	**6.** D	**7.** C
8. A	**9.** D	**10.** A	**11.** A	**12.** D	**13.** C	**14.** B
15. C	**16.** C	**17.** A	**18.** D	**19.** D		

Unit II

Research Aptitude

1 Research Meaning, Characteristics and Types

MEANING OF RESEARCH

Research is an investigation into a hypothesis to establish the authenticity in the society by using specific methodology and collecting relevant data from the compatible source.

Constituents of Research

A research project comprises of

1) **Hypothesis:** The problem selected for research work is called hypothesis. It is a theory, doctrine, or phenomenon which is true in theory and it is subject to research, experimentation, and verification.
2) **Objective:** A research work is started by chalking out certain objectives. Fundamental objective of any research work is testing the hypothesis under investigation. Further, a research work is supposed to make a vital contribution in the development of a society while coming up with various suggestions. Studying and investigating a hypothesis related to any field of society and making the research work is a major contributor in the overall development which is a pivotal objective of research.
3) **Methodology:** A research work is never complete without acquiring data. Data to be acquired is either qualitative or quantitative from a primary or secondary source. An appropriate methodology is needed to analyse the data and test the hypothesis. So, appropriate methodology is an integral constituent of a research project.
4) **Database:** As data are required to complete any research work, an appropriate database that is primary or secondary is chosen according to the requirement of the research work.
5) **Findings:** These constitute conclusion and suggestions.

Participants of a Research Project

Though a research work is undertaken by a research scholar, it is not complete without participation of some other members also. So there are the following participants of a research project:

1) **Research Scholar:** Research scholar is the primary participant of a researcher project.
2) **Guide:** Research scholar always works under a guide. The guide is an expert in the field and has many established research works to his credit. The guide helps the research scholar to successfully complete his research work.
3) **Allied Helpers:** Other than the guide, senior research scientists, colleagues of the research scholar, librarian, laboratory technicians, and research scholar's family are allied helpers of the research scholar in completing his/her research work.
4) **Persons Acting as Data Source:** In case of a micro-level research, primary data is collected. In this case, persons become data source who are interviewed by the research scholar. So persons acting as data source become effective participants of a research project.

Objectives of Research

Conducting research is a highly technical and target-oriented activity. It cannot be initiated without objectives. Already chalked out objectives of a research work provide direction to the research scholar to investigate the variables properly. Following are the objectives of a research work:

1) **Gaining Familiarity:** Primary objective of the research worker for undertaking research is to gain familiarity with the problem under study while collecting data, use suitable methodology, and come up with findings fulfilling the objectives. Besides this, gaining familiarity with the research project is also an underlying objective of research.
2) **Accurate Results:** Accuracy of a research work is a measure of its credibility. Research is initiated with the objective of achieving accurate results by applying various methods of analyzing qualitative and quantitative data.
3) **Hypothesis Testing:** Testing the hypothesis is the ultimate objective of initiating research. Various statistical or other tools are applied during the research for analyzing data. This tests the hypothesis, i.e., whether hypothesis comes out to be null or alternative.

4) **Understanding Occurring and Reoccurring Phenomenon:** Various phenomena in human body are occurring and reoccurring like winking of eyes, heartbeat, etc. Similarly, many phenomena around us like occurring and reoccurring of seasons, day and night, etc. are governed by geographical norms. Objective of research is to understand the logic of these phenomena. Understanding of these phenomena enables a research scientist to come up with accurate, comprehensive, and credible research work.

Motivation for Research

Whenever someone works voluntarily, it indicates that he is motivated to do that work. As motivation is the force behind initiating and successful completion of a task, there are motivating forces behind undertaking a research project, given as follows:

1) **Desire to get Research Degree:** A research scientists well recognises the status of a research degree. Hence, there is a desire to get a research degree and its consequential benefits.
2) **Desire to Serve the Society:** A research work makes vital contribution to various developments in the society through its suggestions. A research scientist is motivated to serve the society through his/her research work.
3) **Intellectual Joy:** A research scholar gets motivated to undertake research as it gives him/her an intellectual joy of doing some creative work.
4) **Curiosity about New Things:** As a research scientist is curious to explore new facts, he/she is motivated to initiate research work.

Characteristics of Research

1. **Analytic:** Research is analytic in nature. It makes use of all the available data so that there is no ambiguity in inference.
2. **Systematic:** No research can be conducted haphazardly. Each step must follow the other. There are set of procedures that have been tested over a period of time and are thus, suitable to use in research. Each research follows a procedure. Rules and procedures are an integral part of the research process.
3. **Accuracy:** Accuracy is the fundamental characteristic of research. Qualitative or quantitative data collected during the research process is accurate and yield findings compatible to objectives.
4. **Based on Logical Reasoning:** Research uses logical reasoning as it involves both deductive and inductive methods of data analysis.
5. **Cyclic:** Research is cyclic in nature. It begins with a problem, sees the goal clearly, divides the problem, provides tentative solutions, gathers, organises, and interprets data, and it again creates scope for new questions or problems.
6. **Foundation of Knowledge:** Research is the foundation of knowledge as it is an important source for providing guidelines or norms for solving different social, business, or governmental problems.
7. **Controlled:** Research in physical sciences is conducted in controlled conditions as it is conducted in a laboratory in which factors except those are tested are kept constant. This is not possible in research on social sciences.
8. **Non-Anomalous:** Research requires in-depth analysis of obtained data, so there is no apprehension of any anomaly in analysis or findings.
9. **Empirical:** Research is empirical in nature, i.e., research has been conducted following rigorous scientific methods and procedures. Each step in the research has been tested for accuracy and is based on real-life experiences.
10. **Valid and Verifiable:** Research work completed with either qualitative or quantitative data is correct and can be verified also.
11. **Replicable:** Research is always having scope of revision and repetition but with new objectives. This further means that research on any completed research work can be again conducted with new objectives.
12. **Rigorous:** Research involves lot of labour and exertion of researcher and other participants. Whether qualitative or quantitative, data are collected through sampling techniques which need proper concentration and steadiness in work due to their highly technical nature. Further, analysing data and interpreting findings also require a rigorous approach to work.

Types of Research

Various types of research are undertaken as per the requirement of an investigation. Data acquired in different types of research is either qualitative or quantitative.

1) **Basic Research:** This research is an investigation on basic principles and reasons for occurrence of a particular event or process or phenomenon. It is also called theoretical research. Study or investigation of some natural phenomenon relating to pure science are termed as basic research. It is

the systematic study and investigation undertaken to discover new knowledge, facts, or principles. It is the pursuit of knowledge for the sake of knowledge. Its principles are used in applied research.

2) **Applied Research:** This research is the systematic study to gain knowledge or understanding necessary to determine how a recognised and specific need may be met. Applied research is designed to solve practical problems of the modern world, rather than to acquire knowledge for knowledge's sake. Evaluation research is a type of applied research. Most of the experimental research, case studies, and inter-disciplinary research are essentially applied research. Applied research is helpful for basic research.

3) **Qualitative Research:** It is research that produces findings not arrived at by means of statistical procedures or other means of quantification. Qualitative data can be collected through interviews, focus groups, observation, or review of documents.

4) **Quantitative Research:** It is research that produces data that can be statistically analysed and whose results can be expressed numerically. Surveys using structured questionnaires and IQ tests are both examples of quantitative research.

5) **Mixed Research:** There are research projects which require collecting qualitative and quantitative data. A research scholar undertaking research involving mathematical and statistical tools needs to review literature on the concerned hypothesis to make research viable, thus gathering qualitative data followed by collecting quantitative data. Such research is called Mixed Research. In such research variables are expressed in text, numerals, and images.

6) **Action Research:** This research is undertaken by practitioners or other researchers involved in providing services like doctors, lawyers, teachers, consultants, etc. to assess the impact of their services on the subjects. Practitioners examine their existing practices; form a question about their practice; collect, analyse, and interpret data, and use the research results to enhance and improve their professional practice. In this way this research becomes cyclic in nature.

7) **Descriptive Research:** This research systematically describes a phenomenon, situation, problem, or state of affairs of a society belonging to different fields. The description is provided as per the requirement of a particular research project. This further means that description research describes features of the targeted population for facilitating sampling and proper study of the problem under investigation.

8) **Relational or Correlational Research:** This research examines the relation or correlation between the two variables present in the targeted population or the two variables in the same set of population are compared in the interest of systematic investigation. This research is also known as Explanatory Research. For example, when studying the playing preference (cricket/hockey) of a proportion of male and female players, this will be a study of relationship between gender and games preference.

9) **Cross-Sectional Research:** This research involves obtaining data of a variable in a targeted population at a single point of time, i.e., it determines the prevailing characteristics of a population. Even relevant information of continuous data like population, age, income, temperature, etc. is obtained while assessing their current status. Their current values are not compared with their values in the past. Neither a future projection is given. This research is concerned with how the things look now without considering their history or future trend. For example, a cross-sectional study might be used to determine if current exposure to specific risk factors might correlate with particular outcomes.

10) **Longitudinal Research:** This research involves study that takes place over a certain period of time. First, data are collected at the start of the study and then may be repeatedly collected throughout the period of study comparing past and current figures defining some trend. Similarly, a future trend can also be depicted on the basis of current information. Some longitudinal studies may occur over a short period of time such as a few days and some may take even decades.

11) **Historical Research:** This research is a systematic study and examination of past events with the aim to interpret those events. It further explains the cause of those events and their effect even on today's events. It is a qualitative technique obtaining primary data of past events for study. Knowledge and proper interpretation of past events can influence present decisions also. For example, knowledge and interpretation of excellent civic engineering and sense of Indus valley civilisation may be instrumental in planning the present civic system.

12) **Exploratory Research:** This research is undertaken to explore areas which have not yet been brought under the jurisdiction of research or little investigation has been made so far.

13) **Formative Research:** Formative research is exploratory and is done at the beginning of the design project to guide the entire process. It is used to gain insight into the subject the project deals with and helps in problem identification and solving.

14) **Summative Research:** This research is also termed as conclusion research. It is done at the end of a project and is used to determine its success. It can also gauge customer satisfaction or aid in the development of future projects.

15) **Replication Research:** It is a term referring to the repetition of a research study, generally with different situations and different subjects while applying the same methods. Replication research also aims to determine the applicability of previous findings on different age groups, location, races, or cultures.

16) **Interdisciplinary Research:** It is a type of study or research that integrates information, data, techniques, tools, methodology, perspectives, concepts, and/or theories drawn from two or more disciplines in order to gain a broader and well-developed perspective, or discover something new. Interdisciplinary research is conducted in the field of political science, sociology, economy, geography, history, etc. which have various interdisciplinary factors paving way for such research.

17) **Philosophical Research:** It is a qualitative research. It is a study about values or other behavioural traits. It involves field study, interviews, and focus groups for obtaining primary data.

18) **Experimental Research:** This is quantitative research and is conducted in natural sciences. It is conducted in the laboratory to see cause and effect relationship of a phenomenon by manipulating one variable and keeping other variables constant. Thus, experimental research is conducted under controlled conditions.

19) **Ex Post Facto Research:** It is a research work in which the research scholar predicts the causes of an effect that has already occurred and investigation is started after occurring of the effect.

20) **Empirical Research:** It is based on observed and measured phenomena and derives knowledge from actual experience rather than from theory or belief.

21) **Evaluative Research:** It is the systematic assessment of the worth or merit of time, money, effort, and resources spent in order to achieve a goal.

22) **Ethnographic Research:** It is a qualitative method where researchers observe and/or interact with a study's participants in their real-life environment.

23) **Scientific Research:** This research is conducted in two stages. It involves basic and applied research. Basic research is signified in acquiring knowledge of scientific theories and principals. This stage is concerned with developing abstract concepts about a natural or social phenomenon and relationships between those concepts. On the other hand, the empirical or applied stage is concerned with testing the theoretical concepts and relationships to see how well they reflect our observations of reality, with the goal of ultimately building better theories. Scientific research aims at providing relevant and accurate findings while eliminating spurious ones.

24) **Developmental Research:** The purpose of developmental research is to assess changes over an extended period of time. For example, developmental research would be an ideal choice to assess the differences in academic and social development in low-income versus high-income neighbourhoods.

25) **Participatory Research:** This research integrates scientific investigation with education and political action. Researchers work with members of a community to understand and resolve community problems, to empower community members, and to democratise research. Participatory research can be identified by five characteristics: (1) participation by the people being studied; (2) inclusion of popular knowledge; (3) a focus on power and empowerment; (4) consciousness raising and education of the participants; and (5) political action.

26) **Objective Research:** This research is application of quantitative methods to analyse data and find conclusions. Research on natural sciences is an objective research. Objective research is carried through experiments and large-scale surveys. It is also called experimental research.

27) **Subjective Research:** This research is conducted while applying qualitative methods of research. It is concerned with facts of individuals gathered by a research scientist through semi-structured or unstructured interviews.

28) **Emancipatory Research:** This research is conducted on and with people from marginalised groups/communities, i.e., communities which remain disadvantaged in the society. The research is a philanthropic approach towards such communities. Data is collected through structured

interviews while taking the support of a senior member of the community under study. The research is conducted largely for the purpose of empowering members of that community and improving services for them. It also engages members of the community as co-constructors or validators of knowledge.

29) **Grounded Theory Research:** Grounded theory is a qualitative research method. It explains why a course of action developed a particular way of progress. For example if a college A wants to conduct a research on why students prefer to get admission in its rival college B, the college A will follow grounded theory research design. Data so collected will help concerned college to devise ways for students' satisfaction.

30) **Narrative Research:** This also a type of qualitative research.Narrative research is conducted while collecting data through written or spoken words or visual representation of individuals. These approaches typically focus on the lives of individuals as told through their own stories. The emphasis of research is on the stories i.ie. what and how is it being narrated. Narrative research is taken both as a concept and research method.

31) **Exegetic Research:** This research has its basis in the term 'Exegesis', which means critical interpretation of a religious text. Historically this term is associated with critical interpretation of the Bible. Exegetic research is the critical analysis over the interpretations out of text of a religious text.

32) **Phenomenological Research:** Phenomenological research is a qualitative research. This research is investigating how one experiences a phenomenon. This method utilizes interviews, observation and surveys to gather information from subjects. Phenomenology is highly concerned with how participants feel about things during an event or activity. For example if a researcher wants to investigate how do tourists coming from the USA to India feel about the changed climatic conditions, he will go for phenomenological research.

Some Vital Facts

1) Participant observation is a part ofEthnographic Research.
2) Some of the major operations in scientific research are: Demonstration of co-variance, Elimination of spurious relations, Sequencing in terms of time order and Theorization.
3) Fundamental research develops an effective explanation through theory building
4) Applied research explores the possibility of a theory for use in various situations
5) Action research improves an existing situation through use of interventions
6) Evaluative research finds out the extent of perceived impact of an intervention
7) Deductive and inductive methods get integrated in a research process.
8) Research is the use of scientific method to provide answers to meaningful questions
9) The answers provided by research can be empirically verified.
10) Action research focuses on ameliorating (improving) the prevailing situations
11) Asking a research question is an initial mandatory requirement for pursuing research
12) Research refers to a series of systematic activity or activities undertaken to find out the solution of a problem.
13) Research is a systematic, logical and an unbiased process wherein verification of hypothesis, data analysis, interpretation and formation of principles can be done.
14) Research is an intellectual enquiry or quest towards truth.
15) Research leads to enhancement of knowledge.
16) Jean Piaget gave a theory of cognitive development of humans on the basis of his fundamental research
17) Hypothesis testing is the main concept of experimental research.
18) To discover new facts or to make fresh interpretation of known facts is the main objective of research.
19) Controlled group condition is applied in experimental research.
20) The research that applies the laws at the time of field study to draw more and more clear ideas about the problem is Applied Research.
21) Research problem is selected from the stand point of social relevance.
22) Field-work based research is classified as Empirical research.
23) The main aim of inter disciplinary research is to create a new trend in research methodology.
24) The depth of any research can be judged by the objectives of research.

Practice Exercise

General Questions Format

1. A Research work has its roots in ______.
   (A) synopsis
   (B) objectives
   (C) interest and aptitude of the research scientist
   (D) database
2. Successful collection of primary data is possible only when the ______.
   (A) data source is a person
   (B) research scientist is cooperative
   (C) guide is interested in a particular source
   (D) problem under study requires primary data only
3. Which of the following is TRUE about Research? It......
   (A) is an investigation into an already accepted notion.
   (B) carries forward some objectives through an accessible methodology for the benefit of the society.
   (C) is an enquiry into a principle to establish its worth by exhausting all the required channels with findings that ultimately put the society further on the path of development.
   (D) brings out the solutions to the various social, political, economic, communicational, navigational, and transportation hurdles which a society is generally facing, by using appropriate methodology and database.
4. A research project is NOT successful if ......
   (A) findings are not compatible to objectives.
   (B) data source is inaccessible.
   (C) guide is not cooperative.
   (D) All of the above
5. The relationship of a research scientist with his guide is like that of
   (A) the earth with the sun
   (B) a UPS with computer
   (C) a poet with poetry
   (D) an airhostess with an aircraft
6. A research work based on secondary data is
   (A) more authentic than a research work based on primary data.
   (B) the most sought after by the upcoming research scholars
   (C) not an original work rather an improvement over an original work
   (D) a study on a problem involving wide coverage
7. Research is possible in that field which ______.
   (A) is full of hypothesis and theory
   (B) is the closest to practical life
   (C) is finalised by the guide
   (D) has maximum scope of productive and fruitful investigation
8. Objectives are chalked out in every research work because ______.
   (A) application of suitable methodology needs them
   (B) findings are not possible without them
   (C) they provide a base for data collection
   (D) All of the above
9. Who is the least helpful, among the following, in progressing a research work of a researcher?
   (A) Librarian (B) Data Source
   (C) Guide (D) Senior Researchers
10. A research project is undertaken because
    (A) one is to fulfill the requirement of a degree course
    (B) it helps in effecting various reforms in the society
    (C) there are fields which demand innovations and discoveries
    (D) it is part of the curriculum
11. A research work always comes out with
    (A) Innovation
    (B) Discovery
    (C) Both innovation and discovery
    (D) Either innovation or discovery
12. Which of the following is essential in qualitative research?
    (A) Observation (B) Interview
    (C) Description (D) All of the above

13. Quantitative research is successful in case of those variables which _____.

(A) are accepted by the methodology

(B) are easily measurable

(C) require knowledge of quantitative techniques

(D) none of the above

14. No research is successful until and unless the research scientist _____.

(A) makes it compatible to the chosen problem

(B) verifies its validity well before adopting it in the research

(C) adopts it and verifies its validity

(D) none of these

15. In the field, a research scholar collects a data which can be attributed to...... research.

(A) experimental (B) qualitative

(C) quantitative (D) any of these

16. 'Research is analytical in nature' implies that

(A) Research analyses every type of acquired data through various statistical techniques to establish its authenticity.

(B) Data so obtained in a research is analysed with the aim of leaving no chance of ambiguity in the findings.

(C) Research depicts its analytic nature where it does not compromise with the statistical technique to be chosen for analysis of data.

(D) All of the above

17. Which of the following is NOT TRUE about Applied research?

a) Applied research belongs to the category of empirical research.

b) Various practical problems can be effectively solved with Applied research.

c) Applied research is applicable to that hypothesis which seeks assimilation of data of varied nature becoming root cause of many practical problems of society.

d) Applied research allows the data so collected to become evidence of problematic issues currently dominating the society and create sufficient scope of right analysis.

(A) Only c and d (B) a, b, c, and d

(C) Only c (D) Only b

18. Which of the following research most effectively tests the hypothesis? .... research

(A) Experimental (B) Formative

(C) Action (D) Replication

19. Which of the following fully justifies the contribution of guide as a prime participant in a research process?

(A) It is the guide who helps the research scholar to choose that hypothesis which comes out to be either null or alternative hypothesis.

(B) As an expert on the subject of research, the guide helps research scholar to escape any deadlock in the research process.

(C) Guide motivates the research scholar to go ahead in research by adopting all ethics, steps, and methods of research for making research work accurate, credible, and authentic.

(D) All of the above

20. Type of research is given under Column I and its meaning/significance is given under Column II. Match Column I with Column II and choose the correct code among the codes given below:

Column I (Type of Research)	**Column II (Meaning/ Significance)**
a) Longitudinal research	i) Feedback
b) Formative research	ii) Beginning of a research project
c) Basic research	iii) Across time period
d) Action research	iv) Knowledge

Codes:	(a)	(b)	(c)	(d)
(A)	ii	iii	iv	i
(B)	iii	ii	iv	i
(C)	i	iv	ii	iii
(D)	iv	iii	ii	i

21. Which characteristic of research signifies analysis of quantitative data only?

(A) Controlled (B) Replicable

(C) Cyclic (D) Rigorous

22. Replication of a research is repeating a research work with

a) new guide and original research scholar

b) original guide and new research scholar

c) new guide and new researcher scholar

d) original guide and original research scholar

(A) Only c (B) Only a

(C) Only d (D) None of these

23. Where there is research, there is

(A) a systematic investigation aiming at making hypothesis under study practically viable

(B) sampling technique of data collection from primary or secondary source representing targeted population.

(C) application of compatible methodology yielding results compatible with objectives

(D) review of literature pertaining to hypothesis under study before initiating data collection

24. Which type of research is also known as Explanatory research?

(A) Summative research

(B) Ex post facto research

(C) Correlational research

(D) Cross-sectional research

25. For being non-anomalous, a research work requires

(A) chalking out viable objectives

(B) in-depth analysis of obtained data

(C) establishing compatibility between findings and objectives

(D) elaborating the methodology used to analyse data

KEY

1. B	**2.** A	**3.** C	**4.** D	**5.** A	**6.** D	**7.** D
8. D	**9.** A	**10.** C	**11.** D	**12.** D	**13.** A	**14.** A
15. D	**16.** B	**17.** A	**18.** A	**19.** C	**20.** B	**21.** A
22. D	**23.** A	**24.** C	**25.** B			

Assertion–Reason Format

1. Assertion (A): Quality of a research work establishes credibility of a research scholar.

Reason (R): A dedicated research scholar is effective in establishing credibility of a research work.

(A) Both A and R are false

(B) Both A and R are true but R is not correct explanation of A

(C) A is true but R is false

(D) Both A and R are true and R is correct explanation of A

2. Assertion (A): Ex post facto research is conducted in a laboratory.

Reason (R): There is study of cause and effect relationship in ex post facto research.

(A) Both A and R are true but R is not correct explanation of A

(B) Both A and R are false

(C) Both A and R are true and R is correct explanation of A

(D) A is true but R is false

3. Assertion (A): Qualitative research ends with some unanswered questions.

Reason (R): Quantitative research supplements the findings of qualitative research.

(A) Both A and R are true and R is correct explanation of A

(B) Both A and R are true but R is not correct explanation of A

(C) Both A and R are false

(D) A is true but R is false

4. Assertion (A): Formative research paves way for summative research.

Reason (R): Getting feedback from affected subjects at the beginning and end of a research project is a tradition of such research.

(A) A is true but R is false

(B) A is false but R is true

(C) Both A and R are true and R is correct explanation of A

(D) Both A and R are true but R is not correct explanation of A

5. Assertion (A): Hypothesis testing is the ultimate objective of a research.

Research (R): Testing of hypothesis involves application of many qualitative and quantitative. techniques of sampling.

(A) A is true but R is false

(B) A is false but R is true

(C) Both A and R are true but R is not correct explanation of A

(D) Both A and R are true and R is correct explanation of A

6. **Assertion (A):** Some of the participants in a research process are passive.

   Reason (R): Every research work needs a supportive team of participants for its successful completion.

   (A) Both A and R are true and R is correct explanation of A
   (B) A is true but R is false
   (C) A is false but R is true
   (D) Both A and R are true but R is not correct explanation of A

7. **Assertion (A):** A research work full of deadlocks does not see its successful completion.

   Reason (R): A motivated and determined research scholar can take a research work out of any deadlock.

   (A) Both A and R are true and R is correct explanation of A
   (B) Both A and R are true but R is not correct explanation of A
   (C) A is true but R is false
   (D) A is false but R is true

8. **Assertion (A):** Research on physical sciences is conducted under controlled conditions.

   Reason (R): Physical sciences involve experimentation in which the factor under investigation is manipulated while keeping other factors constant.

   (A) Both A and R are true and R is correct explanation of A
   (B) Both A and R are true but R is not correct explanation of A
   (C) A is true but R is false
   (D) A is false but R is true

9. **Assertion (A):** Status of a scientist fascinates one to obtain a degree in research.

   Reason (R): At present, research has become an effective measure of a scientist's status.

   (A) A is true but R is false
   (B) A is false but R is true
   (C) Both A and R are false
   (D) Both A and R are true and R is correct explanation of A

10. **Assertion (A):** Basic research is a prerequisite to applied research.

    Reason (R): Knowledge so acquired is taken as a hypothesis for testing it through experimentation.

    (A) Both A and R are true and R is correct explanation of A
    (B) Both A and R are true but R is not correct explanation of A
    (C) A is true but R is false
    (D) A is false but R is true

11. **Assertion (A):** Success of an empirical research rests on its accuracy.

    Reason (R): An accurate research work establishes that all ethics of conducting research have been sincerely followed.

    (A) Both A and R are true but R is not correct explanation of A
    (B) Both A and R are true but R is not correct explanation of A
    (C) A is true but R is false
    (D) A is false but R is true

12. **Assertion (A):** Various frequently occurring phenomena in practical life motivate a research scholar to undertake research.

    Reason (R): Study of natural sciences reveal about many frequently occurring phenomena in practical life.

    (A) A is true but R is false
    (B) A is false but R is true
    (C) Both A and R are true and R is correct explanation of A
    (D) Both A and R are true but R is not correct explanation of A

13. **Assertion (A):** Every research is an exploratory research.

    Reason (R): Replication research explores those areas which remained unexplored in previous research.

    (A) Both A and R are true and R is correct explanation of A
    (B) Both A and R are true but R is not correct explanation of A
    (C) A is true but R is false
    (D) A is false but R is true

14. Assertion (A): Many of the present day development projects are inspired from findings of historical research.

Reason (R): A research scholar working on history is often consulted for developing present day development projects.

(A) A is true but R is false

(B) A is false but R is true

(C) Both A and R are true and R is correct explanation of A

(D) Both A and R are true but R is not correct explanation of A

15. Assertion (A): Cross-sectional research is static in nature.

Reason (R): Only current state of continuous data is obtained for studies without comparing with its previous or projected trend.

(A) Both A and R are true and R is correct explanation of A

(B) Both A and R are true but R is not correct explanation of A

(C) A is true but R is false

(D) A is false but R is true

KEY

1. B	**2.** C	**3.** C	**4.** B	**5.** A	**6.** D	**7.** D
8. A	**9.** C	**10.** A	**11.** B	**12.** D	**13.** C	**14.** A
15. A						

Questions Asked in Previous NET Exams

1. Participant observation is a part of **(UGC NET JUNE 2019)**

(A) Philosophical research

(B) Mentalist theory language

(C) Mathematical research

(D) Ethnographic research

2. Hypothesis testing is the main concept of which type of research? **(UGC NET DEC. 2019)**

(A) Experimental Research

(B) Historical Research

(C) Survey Research

(D) Exegetic research

3. Which of the following provides the overreaching vision that provides vision that guides research into socially relevant areas? **(UGC NET DECEMBER 2019)**

(A) ARIIA (B) IMPRINT

(C) NIRF (D) SWAYAMPRABHA

4. The four major operations in scientific research are: **(UGC NET DECEMBER 2018)**

(a) Demonstration of co-variance

(b) Elimination of spurious relations

(c) Sequencing in terms of time order

(d) Self-education

(e) Operationalisation of personal choice

(f) Theorisation

Codes:

(A) (a), (b), (c), and (d)

(B) (c), (d), (e), and (f)

(C) (a), (b), (c), and (f)

(D) (b), (c), (d), and (e)

5. There are two sets given below. Set - I specifies the types of research, while Set - II indicates their characteristics. Match the two and give your answer by selecting the appropriate code. **(UGC NET JULY 2018)**

Set - I (Research types)	**Set - II Characteristics)**
(a) Fundamental research	(i) Finding out the extent of perceived impact of an intervention
(b) Applied research	(ii) Developing an effective explanation through theory building
(c) Action research	(iii) Improving an existing situation through use of interventions
(d) Evaluative research	(iv) Exploring the possibility of a theory for use in various situations
	(v) Enriching technological resources

Codes:

	(a)	(b)	(c)	(d)
(A)	(ii)	(iv)	(iii)	(i)
(B)	(v)	(iv)	(iii)	(ii)
(C)	(iii)	(ii)	(i)	(iv)
(D)	(ii)	(iii)	(iv)	(v)

6. In the list given below, identify those statements which correctly describe the meaning and characteristics of research.

(UGC NET JULY 2018)

(i) Research is a method of improving our common sense.

(ii) Deductive and inductive methods get integrated in a research process.

(iii) Research is creativity and charisma.

(iv) Research is the use of scientific method to provide answers to meaningful questions.

(v) Method of consulting and using experience is called research.

(vi) The answers provided by research can be empirically verified.

Choose the correct answer from the code given below:

Code:

(A) (ii), (iv), and (vi) (B) (i), (ii), and (iii)

(C) (iv), (v), and (vi) (D) (i), (iii), and (v)

7. Which of the following research types focuses on ameliorating the prevailing situations?

(UGC NET NOVEMBER 2017)

(A) Applied research

(B) Action research

(C) Experimental research

(D) Fundamental research

8. The principal of a school conducts an interview session of teachers and students with a view to explore the possibility of their enhanced participation in school programmes. This endeavour may be related to which type of research? **(UGC NET JANUARY 2017)**

(A) Evaluation research

(B) Fundamental research

(C) Action research

(D) Applied research

9. In qualitative research paradigm, which of the following features may be considered critical?

(UGC NET JULY 2016)

(A) Data collection with standardised research tools

(B) Sampling design with probability sample techniques

(C) Data collection with bottom-up empirical evidences

(D) Data gathering to take with top-down systematic evidences

10. Which of the following is an initial mandatory requirement for pursuing research?

(UGC NET JULY 2016)

(A) Developing a research design

(B) Formulating a research question

(C) Deciding about the data analysis procedure

(D) Formulating a research hypothesis

11. Which of the following statements is not true in the context of participatory research?

(UGC NET DECEMBER 2015)

(A) It recognises knowledge as power.

(B) It emphasises on people as experts.

(C) It is a collective process of enquiry.

(D) Its sole purpose is production of knowledge.

12. Which of the following statements regarding the meaning of research are correct?

(UGC NET JUNE 2015)

(a) Research refers to a series of systematic activity or activities undertaken to find out the solution of a problem.

(b) It is a systematic, logical, and an unbiased process wherein verification of hypothesis, data analysis, interpretation, and formation of principles can be done.

(c) It is an intellectual enquiry or quest towards truth.

(d) It leads to enhancement of knowledge.

Select the correct answer from the codes given below:

(A) (a), (b), (c), and (d)

(B) (a), (b), and (c)

(C) (b), (c), and (d)

(D) (a), (c), and (d)

13. Jean Piaget gave a theory of cognitive development of humans on the basis of his:

(UGC NET JUNE 2015)

(A) Evaluation research

(B) Fundamental research

(C) Applied research

(D) Action research

14. When planning to do a social research, it is better to **(UGC NET DECEMBER 2014)**
    (A) Approach the topic with an open mind
    (B) Do a pilot study before getting stuck into it
    (C) Be familiar with literature on the topic
    (D) Forget about theory because this is a very practical undertaking

15. The research stream of immediate application is **(UGC NET JUNE 2014, JUNE 2012)**
    (A) Conceptual research
    (B) Action research
    (C) Fundamental research
    (D) Empirical research

16. Which is the main objective of research? **(UGC NET DECEMBER 2013)**
    (A) To review the literature
    (B) To summarise what is already known
    (C) To get an academic degree
    (D) To discover new facts or to make fresh interpretation of known facts

17. The principles of fundamental research are used in____. **(UGC NET DECEMBER 2013)**
    (A) action research
    (B) applied research
    (C) philosophical research
    (D) historical research

18. Nine-year olds are taller than seven-year olds. This is an example of a reference drawn from **(UGC NET JUNE 2012)**
    (A) Vertical study (B) Cross-sectional study
    (C) Time series study (D) Experimental study

19. Controlled group condition is applied in **(UGC NET DECEMBER 2011)**
    (A) Survey research
    (B) Historical research
    (C) Experimental research
    (D) Descriptive research

20. Newton gave three basic laws of motion. This research is categorised as **(UGC NET JUNE 2011)**
    (A) Descriptive research
    (B) Sample survey
    (C) Fundamental research
    (D) Applied research

21. Research is conducted to **(UGC NET JUNE 2011)**
    I. Generate new knowledge
    II. Not to develop a theory
    III. Obtain research degree
    IV. Reinterpret existing knowledge
    Which of the above are correct?
    (A) I, III, & II (B) III, II, & IV
    (C) II, I, & III (D) I, III, & IV

22. Action research means **(UGC NET JUNE 2010)**
    (A) a longitudinal research
    (B) An applied research
    (C) A research initiated to solve an immediate problem
    (D) A research with socio-economic objective

23. Research is **(UGC NET JUNE 2010)**
    (A) Searching again and again
    (B) Finding solution to any problem
    (C) Working in a scientific way to search for truth of any problem
    (D) None of the above

24. If a researcher conducts a research on finding out which administrative style contributes more to institutional effectiveness, this will be an example of **(UGC NET JUNE 2010)**
    (A) Basic research
    (B) Action research
    (C) Applied research
    (D) None of the above

25. The research which is exploring new facts through the study of the past is called **(UGC NET DECEMBER 2009)**
    (A) Philosophical research
    (B) Historical research
    (C) Mythological research
    (D) Content analysis

26. Action Research is **(UGC NET DECEMBER 2009)**
    (A) An applied research
    (B) A research carried out to solve immediate problems
    (C) A longitudinal research
    (D) Simulative research

27. The process not needed in Experimental research is **(UGC NET DECEMBER 2009)**
(A) Observation (B) Manipulation
(C) Controlling (D) Content Analysis

28. Manipulation is always a part of **(UGC NET DECEMBER 2009)**
(A) Historical research
(B) Fundamental research
(C) Descriptive research
(D) Experimental research

29. The research is always **(UGC NET DECEMBER 2008)**
(A) verifying the old knowledge
(B) exploring new knowledge
(C) filling the gap between knowledge
(D) All of the above

30. The research that applies the laws at the time of field study to draw more and more clear ideas about the problem is **(UGC NET DECEMBER 2008)**
(A) Applied Research
(B) Action Research
(C) Experimental Research
(D) Summative Research

31. Research problem is selected from the standpoint of **(UGC NET JUNE 2008)**
(A) Researcher's interest
(B) Financial support
(C) Social relevance
(D) Availability of relevant literature

32. Field-work based research is classified as **(UGC NET JUNE 2008)**
(A) Empirical (B) Historical
(C) Experimental (D) Biographical

33. The experimental study is based on **(UGC NET DECEMBER 2007)**
(A) the manipulation of variables
(B) conceptual parameters
(C) replication research
(D) survey literature

34. A research problem is feasible only when **(UGC NET JUNE 2007)**
(A) it has utility and relevance
(B) it is researchable
(C) it is new and adds something to knowledge
(D) All of the above

35. Research can be classified as **(UGC NET DECEMBER 2006)**
(A) Basic, Applied, and Action research
(B) Qualitative and Quantitative research
(C) Philosophical, Survey, and Experimental research
(D) All of the above

36. Which of the following options are the main tasks of research in the modern society? **(UGC NET JUNE 2006)**
i) To keep pace with the advancement in knowledge
ii) to discover new things
iii) to write a critique on the earlier writings
iv) to systematically examine and critically analyze the investigations/sources with objectivity
(A) iv, ii, and i (B) i, ii, and iii
(C) i and iii (D) ii, iii, and iv

37. Match List I (Interviews) with the List II (Meaning) and select the correct answer from the code given below: **(UGC NET JUNE 2006)**

List I (Interviews)	**List II (Meaning)**
(a) Structured Interviews	(i) greater flexibility approach
(b) Unstructured Interviews	(ii) attention on the questions to be answered
(c) Focused Interviews	(iii) individual life experience
(d) Clinical Interviews	(iv) predetermined questions
	(v) non-directive

Codes:	(a)	(b)	(c)	(d)
(A)	(iv)	(i)	(ii)	(iii)
(B)	(ii)	(iv)	(i)	(iii)
(C)	(v)	(ii)	(iv)	(i)
(D)	(i)	(iii)	(v)	(iv)

38. What do you consider as the main aim of inter-disciplinary research? **(UGC NET JUNE 2006)**
   (A) To bring out a holistic approach to research
   (B) To reduce the emphasis of single subject in the research domain
   (C) To oversimplify the problem of research
   (D) To create a new trend in research methodology

39. The depth of any research can be judged by **(UGC NET JUNE 2006)**
   (A) title of the research
   (B) objectives of the research
   (C) total expenditure on the research
   (D) duration of the research

40. Which one of the following is NOT the characteristic of a research? **(UGC NET DECEMBER 2004)**
   (A) Research is systematic
   (B) Research is not a process
   (C) Research is problem-oriented
   (D) Research is not passive

41. Which of the following statements is correct? **(UGC NET DECEMBER 2004)**
   (A) Discoveries are researches
   (B) Researches lead to discovery
   (C) Invention and research are related
   (D) None of the above

42. Which of the following statements is correct? **(UGC NET DECEMBER 2004)**
   (A) In research, objectives can be worded in question form.
   (B) In research, objectives can be worded in statement form.
   (C) Objectives are to be stated in chapter I of the thesis.
   (D) All of the above.

43. Books and records are primary source of data in **(UGC NET DECEMBER 2005)**
   (A) historical research
   (B) participatory research
   (C) clinical research
   (D) laboratory research

44. Fundamental research reflects the ability to _____. **(UGC NET JUNE 2006)**
   (A) synthesise new ideals
   (B) expound new principles
   (C) evaluate the existing material concerning research
   (D) study the existing literature regarding various topics

45. The study in which investigators attempt to trace an effect is known as **(UGC NET JUNE 2006)**
   (A) Survey research
   (B) Ex post facto research
   (C) Historical research
   (D) Summative research

46. How can the objectivity of research can be enhanced? **(UGC NET DECEMBER 2009)**
   (A) Through its impartiality
   (B) Through its reliability
   (C) Through its validity
   (D) All of these

47. Which of the following is classified in the category of the Developmental research? **(UGC NET DECEMBER 2009)**
   (A) Philosophical research
   (B) Action research
   (C) Descriptive research
   (D) All of the above

48. Who among the following, propounded the concept of Paradigm? **(UGC NET JUNE 2014)**
   (A) Peter Haggett
   (B) Von Thunen
   (C) Thomas Kuhn
   (D) John K. Wright

KEY

1. D	**2.** A	**3.** B	**4.** C	**5.** A	**6.** A	**7.** B
8. C	**9.** C	**10.** B	**11.** D	**12.** A	**13.** B	**14.** A
15. B	**16.** D	**17.** B	**18.** B	**19** C	**20.** C	**21.** D
22. C	**23.** C	**24.** C	**25.** B	**26.** B	**27.** D	**28.** D
29. D	**30.** A	**31.** C	**32.** A	**33.** A	**34.** D	**35.** D
36. A	**37.** A	**38.** D	**39.** B	**40.** B	**41.** B	**42.** D
43. A	**44.** B	**45.** B	**46.** D	**47.** D	**48.** C	

2 Positivism and Post-Positivistic Approach to Research

POSITIVISM

The term **Positivism** was introduced to the world by French social thinker and research scientist **Auguste Comte** in his work *The Course in Positive Philosophy and A General View of Positivism*. Positivism is based on epistemology. It is the approach which believes that there must be scientific evidence to knowledge, i.e., only channel of true knowledge is science. The society observes some universal and scientific laws of nature for its survival and progress. Further, it believes that knowledge about what is existing in the society can be verified through experiments, observation, and mathematical and logical proofs. Obtaining knowledge of these laws and experimenting to verify the truth is positivism. Comte's doctrine of positivism advocates the role of natural sciences in developing social sciences. Like empiricism, positivism also advocates that human sensual experience is the source of true knowledge.

POSITIVISTIC APPROACH TO RESEARCH

Positivistic approach to research is fact-based investigation. It is also known as 'Positivist Paradigm.' The positivistic approach to research is explained as follows:

Characteristics of Positivist Research

1) **Application of Quantitative Methods in Research:** As positivism considers phenomenon of natural science as means of knowledge, it emphasises the application of quantitative methods for research. Factual knowledge so obtained is quantifiable, i.e., measurable.
2) **Scientific Approach to Research:** It suggests the social scientists to adopt a scientific approach to their research on attaining knowledge and experimenting over it. Positivism urges that as the research scientists investigating laws of natural sciences like Physics and Biology use the scientific methods to attain knowledge of those laws, social scientists should also adopt a scientific approach to attain knowledge of social laws prevailing in the society.
3) **Structured Investigation:** Positivistic approach to research suggests that investigation during research should be based on pre-drafted questionnaire, formulae, and focus group discussions, i.e., initiating structured investigation.
4) **Systematic Approach:** One aspect of positivism advocates empiricism, that is, knowledge is gained while observing human experience, particularly sensual experience. Positivism advocates that one should observe the human experience and record the events and phenomenon around people in a systematic way so that it may be exposed to quantitative techniques during experimentation and verification.
5) **Deductive Approach:** Positivistic study adopts deductive approach, i.e., developing a hypothesis from a prevailing theory or law, then testing the hypothesis by applying quantitative methods of research.
6) **Large Size of Population:** Positivist research is conducted on a large size of the targeted population and findings are obtained through observation and quantitative techniques.
7) **Measureable Concepts:** Concepts derived out by applying quantitative and scientific techniques are measurable.
8) **Experimental Approach:** Experiment is the base of positivist research. A positivist researcher observes cause and effect relationship by studying the effect of independent variables on the dependent variable.
9) **Objective in Nature:** Positivist approach to research is objective in nature as it seeks precise measurement and analysis of the targeted population by picking up a sample through a specific sampling technique.
10) **Researcher Independent:** In positivist research, researcher is independent of study and there is no room for human interests within the jurisdiction of study, i.e., research is not influenced by the researcher. Researcher is outside research and value-free.
11) **Full Knowledge of Reality:** Positivistic doctrine believes that knowledge of reality (each and every force, concepts, laws, and structures existing in the universe and causing various phenomena perceived by human beings through their senses) obtained through scientific and quantitative techniques is complete in all respects as it uncovers truth.

12) **Phenomenal Approach:** Knowledge obtained through scientific methods is treated as the right knowledge.

13) **Inductive Approach:** Researcher gathers facts and provides data for developing scientific laws and knowledge.

INDEPENDENT AND DEPENDENT VARIABLES

Independent Variable: *In an experiment, independent variable is that variable which is manipulated or controlled to observe its effect on the dependable variable. The change in independent variable is man-made or natural. Age and time are those independent variables which experience natural change.*

Dependent Variable: *Dependent variable is that variable in an experiment, which is affected by any change in the independent variable. This means that effect of any change in independent variable on the dependent variable is tested, measured, and recorded. Dependent variable is also known as responding variable.*

Example: *If a researcher conducts an experiment to observe effect of fodder on milk yield of cow, he/she changes the quantity of fodder to notice changes in the milk yield. Here, fodder is the independent variable and milk yield is the dependent variable.*

Advantages of Positivistic Approach to Research

1) **Accurate Results:** Positivist approach to research always end up with accurate results as it uses scientific and quantitative methodology to test the hypothesis.
2) **Non-ambiguous Approach:** Data are collected in a well-structured way under positivist research. Resultantly, results are specific and relevant to hypothesis, thus leaving no ground for ambiguity.
3) **Valid and Reliable Findings:** A positivist researcher collects data by applying statistical techniques to test a hypothesis. Findings so obtained are outcome of various quantitative techniques which work under set rules and are also yielded after group discussions and the findings are generalised. All this makes findings valid and reliable.
4) **Better Understanding of Humans and Society:** As findings of the research are authentic and can be generalised, the researcher can better understand humans and their problems which comprise a section or subsection of the targeted population in the social set-up.
5) **Time Saving:** As in the positivist approach a quantitative technique is used to test a hypothesis on targeted population, same technique can be used for a similar group or subgroup of the population even in a large number. This saves time for the researcher and he/she comes up with an authenticated research well within the stipulated time.
6) **Future Predictions:** Quantitative and scientific techniques in positivist research are used to make future predictions on the basis of results so obtained as results so obtained are precise and accurate. These results are established as logical principles for making future predictions.

Limitations of Positivistic Approach

1) **Deadlock in Research due to Human Emotions:** While positivist research advocates empiricists that human experiences with respect to its senses is considered source of true knowledge, on the other hand it does not accept abstract traits of human behaviour like emotions and sentiments as source of knowledge. But while undertaking research, a research scientist cannot escape from emotional aspect of human behaviour, while studying the human sensual experience. Human sensual experience is accompanied with emotions and sentiments. This creates a deadlock for the researcher and the research process comes to a standstill.
2) **Inflexible:** Positivist researcher goes with the belief that every result can be obtained through quantitative techniques, thus making the research approach and outcomes inflexible. It means results obtained once are suitable to a particular group.
3) **No Attention to Individual:** Individual opinion or response has a place in positivist research. As the research aims to cover a large size of the targeted population, an individual response is not given attention, however important it may be.
4) **Lack in Depth:** No in-depth study of the population is made as the approach is totally dependent on numerals which are obtained by applying a quantitative formula which yield information at a superficial level.
5) **Limiting Boundaries of Research:** The approach to the research is so highly structured that it does not allow the research to go beyond a limit of data collection. It also confines the research to the boundary of quantitative techniques, thus narrowing down the scope of research.
6) **No Room for Qualitative Research:** There is no room for qualitative research in positivist research even though many aspects of social development are connected with abstract human behaviour like values, emotions, sentiments, etc. These are also indicators of social development and can be proved

to be great contributors of social development through qualitative methods of research. By keeping no room for such research, positive research fails to present the complete picture of social development.

7) **Not Suitable for Small Population:** As positivist research has to cover a large size of the targeted population to generalise the results, it is not suitable for a small-sized targeted population.

POST-POSITIVISM

There had been a shift of paradigm from positivist to logical positivist paradigm in the 19th century. Philosophers from Vienna (Austria) circle were exponents of Logical Positivism. They believed that only that knowledge is valid which is obtained through science. Only such knowledge carries logic because such knowledge is verifiable through empirical observations. Other components of metaphysics were rejected. However, in the middle of the 20th century, the concept of post-positivism cropped up. An Austrian philosopher **Karl Popper** voiced against logical positivism. He asserted, ***"All knowledge is provisional, conjectural, hypothetical"***. It was the result of challenging positivism. Post-positivism was considered a contemporary school of thought as like positivists, post-positivists also believed in acquiring reality through science, but they believed that the knowledge of reality will not be fully known. Post-positivists assert that scientific methods used to know the single reality are limited due to sensory and intellectual limitations of humans.

Characteristics of Post-Positivistic Approach to Research

1) **Incomplete Knowledge of Reality:** Post-positivistic school of thought asserts that in spite of all efforts and experiments to explore reality and uncover the truth, full knowledge of reality is not possible due to some limitations. Research is confined to exploring the limited knowledge of reality.
2) **Fallible Observations:** In post-positivistic research, observations are fallible, i.e., a researcher is bound to commit error, thus making the theory so developed revisable. Post-positivists call it Critical Realism. Critical realism puts doubt on the human ability to know reality with certainty.
3) **Triangulation of Observations:** Post-positivists believe that observation of a single research scientist contains errors, thus it does not yield full knowledge of reality. Post-positive philosophers highlight the importance of conducting multi-observations and experiments from all angles by different scientists. They are of the opinion that though multi-observations will also carry errors, yet the best possible results about knowledge of reality can be obtained through triangulation of all observations by all the scientists.
4) **No Difference between Scientific Reasoning and Common Sense Reasoning:** Post-positivistic school of thought sees almost know difference in viewpoint of a scientist and a common man about reality. Both commit errors while undertaking research, but the degree of error varies. Scientists, even with scientific techniques in research, cannot obtain complete reality.
5) **Use of Quantitative and Qualitative Methods of Research:** As post-positivistic approach advocates triangulation of observations made by different research scientists, it goes for both quantitative and qualitative methods of research.

Advantages of Post-Positivistic Approach to Research

1) **Flexible Approach:** In contrast to positivistic approach, post-positivistic approach is flexible as it advocates to revise the observations to minimise the error factor to obtain maximum knowledge of reality.
2) **Practical Approach:** Positivistic approach ignores the practical aspect of human, sensual, and intellectual limitations whereas post-positivistic approach is very well aware of such limitations. That is why while conducting research, the post-positivist research scientist considers this practical aspect and records observations which are revisable due to these limitations. Hence, post-positivistic approach is practical.
3) **Best Results through Triangulation:** Triangulation technique of research yields the best possible results as when different scientists pool their findings (which contain errors also), it gives a chance to the society to pick up the best results, leading to accepting that theory which is carrying minimum errors.
4) **No Discrimination against Common Reasoning:** Positivistic research approach depends upon knowledge of reality obtained through scientific methods only. This notion does not accept the viewpoint of common subjects of the society. On the contrary, post-positivistic approach considers scientific and common reasoning together and comes out with the best possible results regarding knowledge of reality.
5) **No Imposition of Scientific Principles:** Positivist approach of research asks for imposing scientific principles on the social set-up of the society. It advocates that social research scientists apply the norms of natural sciences to achieve social

development. On the other hand, though post-positivism also believes in scientific approach to research, yet it does believe that norms developed by social researchers and science researchers should go parallel. In addition, as there are chances of errors in the findings, the best results should yield the best possible results about knowledge of reality through triangulation.

6) **No Monopoly of a Single Scientist:** Positivism believes that findings of a single scientist by applying scientific techniques should be generalised, thus establishing monopoly of that scientist in the society. On the other hand, post-positivistic approach advocates research by various scientists and accepts the best possible findings through triangulation.

Limitations of Post-positivistic Approach to Research

1) **Triangulation creates Confusion:** Triangulation creates confusion over getting the best level of knowledge of reality. In triangulation, there is an amalgamation of findings of various scientists and it thus creates confusion. There is no scope of a concrete and uniform result.
2) **Biased Research:** Post-positivism believes that every research scientist is influenced by his own culture and values, thus having a biased view. In triangulation even, the biased thinking of scientists prevail, so no uniform theory comes up.
3) **Subjective Approach:** In contrast to positivistic approach, post-positivistic approach to research becomes subjective as it follows qualitative methods of research also.
4) **Hypothetic Element:** Even though post-positivistic approach claims to yield practical doctrine, yet hypothetical element crops up in amalgamation of findings of different scientists due to biased opinion of individuals.

SOME RELATED CONCEPTS

1) ***Interpretivism:*** *Interpretivistic approach advocates social science as an instrument to know reality against the positivistic approach depending on natural science. Reality can be accessed through social construction human traits like communication, language, and awareness. Interpretivism advocates an unstructured approach to research. Researcher's beliefs influence researcher. For example, a research scientist may ask people why they read the newspaper while having their breakfast. The scientist records their responses and reaches a conclusion.*
2) ***Epistemology:*** *The term is derived from Greek words 'episteme' means 'knowledge' and 'logy' means 'science or study'. Thus, epistemology is study of nature, origin, and limits of knowledge. It examines what is the source of knowledge, what is the content of knowledge, and whether it is a justified belief. Its principles are 'Truth, Belief, and Justification'. In a nutshell, it is the study of valid knowledge and its source. This concept helps a researcher of social sciences by stating what is and what is not to be included in the knowledge about a particular field/subject under research.*
3) ***Metaphysics:*** *It is concerned with the study about origin of the universe, nature of being, and the world. Aristotle called it "First Philosophy'. It is the study of nature of reality and causes of its origin.*
4) ***Ontology:*** *Ontology is study of reality, i.e., what kind of things exists in the world. It is the study of reality which is actually existing in the world. Sometimes, ontology is said to be branch of Epistemology, but there is a minor difference. Ontology is the study of what is actually existing in the world while on the other hand, Epistemology is the study of constitution of knowledge and how it is obtained, i.e., description of reality on the basis of perception and paradigm.*
5) ***Phenomenology:*** *It is a method of research developed by German philosophers Edmund Husserl and Martin Heidegger. The method is based on the notion that reality exists in the objects and events which human beings experience in their consciousness. The main components of this method are experience and consciousness. An individual stating the first experience or view about an object or event in his consciousness is the fundamental aspect of this method. This is called 'first-person point of view' in Phenomenology.*
6) ***Paradigm:*** *Originally, the term was used by the US philosopher and scientist Thomas Kuhn in his book "The Structure of Scientific Revolution". According to him, it is the way an individual or society perceives the world, its systems, beliefs, scientific discipline, and principles prevailing in the society at a particular point of time. It also means to accept a model or example of research method a researcher holds about a particular sphere of knowledge. Perceiving any change in the set principles of society is Paradigm Shift.*
7) ***Axiology:*** *It is the study or judgement of values and ethics. This term was introduced by the French philosopher Paul Lapie in the twentieth century. For a researcher, Axiology is concerned with aims of research. Further, it is what a research scientist*

values in his research. Defining the objective which the researcher values will determine the way of conducting research. For example, if a researcher is conducting a research on the philosophy of a holy book, he will value religious sentiments of the community having faith in that holy book.

8) ***Constructivism:*** *It is a theory which is related to learning. It states that people learn and construct their own understanding of the world through their experience. A researcher follows qualitative methods to conduct research on constructivism.*

9) ***Pragmatism:*** *Pragmatic research believes that the world can be interpreted in different ways. There are various realities and no single point of view can give the entire knowledge about reality.*

10) ***Realism:*** *Philosophy of realism claims that human beings observe the natural and social world on the basis of various scientific process, beliefs, causes, structures, and principles. It works on the notion that there is a scientific approach which develops knowledge about reality. Direct realism presents that world for the humans which they perceive through their senses. While Critical Realism claims that sensual perception does not present the real world before humans, the real world is different. Qualitative methods of research are compatible to study on realism.*

Some Vital Facts

1) Post-positivistic approach to research emphasises on Phenomenological, Ethnographic and Action Research.,
2) In post-positivistic research, observations are fallible i.e a researcher is bound to commit error thus making theory so developed revisable.
3) Ontology is the study of what is actually existing in the world.
4) Term Positivismwas introduced to the world by French social thinker and research scientist Auguste Comte in his work The Course in Positive Philosophy and A General View of Positivism.
5) Pragmatic research believes that the world can be interpreted in different ways.
6) Philosophers from Vienna (Austria) circle were exponent of Logical positivism.
7) Principles of epistemology are 'Truth, Belief and Justification'
8) Metaphysics is also called "First Philosophy' as stated by Aristotle

Practice Exercise

General Questions Format

1. Which of the following rightly signifies/signify limitations of positivistic approach to research?

a) Limitations built basis for the development of not only post-positivism but also interpretivism.

b) Epistemology of positivism failed to appreciate overall human involvement while applying quantitative research methods to get knowledge of reality.

c) Post-positivistic approach to research emerged as a substitute of positivistic approach to research as a fallout of limitations of positivism.

d) But for its limitations, positivistic approach to research could not take post-positivism as its supplement approach to research.

(A) a and c only (B) b and d only
(C) a, b, c, and d (D) b and c only

2. Which of the following concept of research was termed as 'First Philosophy' by Aristotle?

(A) Metaphysics (B) Ontology
(C) Interpretivism (D) Axiology

3. Terms applicable in different research methods are given under Column I (Term) and their inventors are given under Column II (Inventor). Match the term with its inventor and chose right answer choice from codes below:

Column I	Column II
a) Phenomenology	i) Thomas Kuhn
b) Post-Positivism	ii) Paul Lapie
c) Paradigm	iii) Edmund Husserl
d) Axiology	iv) Karl Popper

Codes:	(a)	(b)	(c)	(d)
(A)	iii	iv	i	ii
(B)	ii	iv	iii	i
(C)	iv	iii	ii	i
(D)	ii	i	iv	iii

4. Which of the following is NOT a characteristics of Positivist approach to research?
   (A) Quantitative research methods
   (B) Large sized target population
   (C) Unstructured investigation
   (D) Generalisation of research findings
5. Consider the statement, "It does not accept abstract traits of human behaviour like emotions and sentiments as source of knowledge". This statement signifies which approach to research?
   (A) Postivistic (B) Post-postivistic
   (C) Interpretivistic (D) Constructivistic
6. Which of the following paradigms does not advocate quantitative method of research?
   (A) Positivism, Ontology, Axiology
   (B) Post-positivism, Phenomenology, Epistemology
   (C) Interpretivism, Constructivism, Realism
   (D) All of the above
7. In which of the following approaches to research, independent variable is manipulated to observe the effect on dependent variable?
   a) Post-positivistic b) Positivistic
   c) Intrepretivistic d) Phenomenological
   (A) a and c only (B) b only
   (C) a and b only (D) a and d only
8. If a research scholar is investigating whether gesture of present day hospitality really values the guests or it is just a demonstration, which research approach is he following?
   (A) Ontology (B) Phenomenology
   (C) Pragmatism (D) Axiology
9. Interpretivism is ___________ to positivism.
   (A) supplementary (B) contrast
   (C) prior (D) similar
10. Which of the following research paradigm is compatible to Positivism?
   (A) Realism (B) Interpretivism
   (C) Constructivism (D) None of these
11. While conducting a research on a customary ritual of a particular community, a researcher puts high value to objective of education and awareness. Which paradigm of research is he following?
   (A) Ontology (B) Pragmatism
   (C) Axiology (D) Constructivism
12. The interpretive approach to scientific research generates which of the following?
   (A) Knowledge which assists with personal liberation and freedom of constraints on one's rationale and independence
   (B) Knowledge which is dependent up on the process of discovery
   (C) Proven facts
   (D) Evidence of generalizable laws not affected by context
13. 'Critical realism' is the characteristic of which approach to research?
   (A) Post-positivism (B) Positivism
   (C) Realism (D) Phenomenology
14. A study exploring the economic impact of the Olympic Games would normally be related to which approach?
   (A) Positivistic (B) Interpretivistic
   (C) Post-positivistic (D) None of these
15. Which is NOT generally a characteristic of Postivist research?
   (A) Control by researcher
   (B) Hypothesis testing
   (C) Use of interview
   (D) Replication
16. Which one of the following statements characterises the difference in observation methods using the Interpretive approach versus Post-positivist approach?
   (A) Interpretive approach relies on a flexible set of rules, whereas the post-positivist approach relies on the social, linguistic, and cognitive skills of the researcher.
   (B) Interpretive approach relies on a firm and unchanging set of rules, whereas the post-positivist approach relies on the social, linguistic, and cognitive skills of the studied subjects.
   (C) Post-positivist approach relies on a flexible set of rules, whereas the interpretive approach relies on the social, linguistic, and cognitive skills of the researcher.
   (D) Post-positivist approach relies on firm and unchanging set of rules, whereas the interpretive approach relies on the social, linguistic, and cognitive skills of the researcher.

17. The interpretivist view of the social sciences is that:
    (A) Their subject matter is fundamentally different to that of the natural sciences
    (B) We should aim to achieve the interpretive understanding of social action
    (C) It is important to study the way people make sense of their everyday worlds
    (D) All of the above

18. Which of the following is TRUE about experiments conducted in Positivistic approach to research?
    (A) Any change in independent variable does not affect the dependent variable.
    (B) Dependent variable is affected by any change in independent variable.
    (C) Any change in dependent variable affects the independent variable.
    (D) Changing independent or dependent variable depends upon the nature of problem under investigation.

19. Which of the following approaches of research applies qualitative and quantitative methods of research together for obtaining knowledge of reality from all aspects?
    (A) Realism (B) Constructivism
    (C) Logical Positivism (D) None of these

20. Which of the following study titles reflects the use of a Phenomenological methodology?
    (A) Effect of poverty and unemployment on economy of a society
    (B) Factors governing psychology of watching a movie first day first show
    (C) Experience of foreign tourists visiting India
    (D) Investigation into reasons of increasing stress level in working class

KEY

1. B	2. A	3. A	4. C	5. A	6. C	7. C
8. D	9. B	10. D	11. C	12. B	13. A	14. A
15. C	16. D	17. D	18. B	19. D	20. B	

Assertion–Reason Format

1. **Assertion (A):** Positivist approach to research claims to acquire full knowledge of reality.

   Reason (R): Scientific methods are applied on social set-up in positivism.

   (A) Both A and R are true and R is the correct explanation of A
   (B) Both A and R are true but R is not correct explanation of A
   (C) A is true but R is false
   (D) A is false but R is true

2. **Assertion (A):** Triangulation of observations is a characteristic of Positivistic approach to research.

   Reason (R): Positivism considers the human experience as the source of knowledge of reality.

   (A) Both A and R are true and R is the correct explanation of A
   (B) Both A and R are true but R is not correct explanation of A
   (C) A is true but R is false
   (D) Both A and R are false

3. **Assertion (A):** Ontology is a research method used by the researcher to explore reality which actually exists in the world.

   Reason (R): A research scholar explores reality by applying quantitative methods of research.

   (A) Both A and R are true and R is the correct explanation of A
   (B) Both A and R are true but R is not correct explanation of A
   (C) A is false but R is true
   (D) A is true but R is false

4. **Assertion (A):** Interpretivistic approach to research advocates social science as an instrument to know reality.

   Reason (R): Reality can be accessed through social construction human traits like communication, language, and awareness.

   (A) Both A and R are false
   (B) A is true but R is false
   (C) Both A and R are true and R is correct explanation of A
   (D) Both A and R are true but R is not correct explanation of A

5. **Assertion (A):** Every approach to research works on its respective Epistemology.

   Reason (R): Truth, Belief, and Justification are three principles of Epistemology.

(A) Both A and R are true and R is correct explanation of A

(B) Both A and R are true but R is not correct explanation of A

(C) A is true but R is false

(D) A is false but R is true

6. **Assertion (A):** A research on origin of universe is covered under Metaphysics.

Reason (R): Seeking knowledge about origin of the universe is a valid approach to research.

(A) Both A and R are true and R is correct explanation of A

(B) Both A and R are true but R is not correct explanation of A

(C) A is true but R is false

(D) Both A and R are false

7. **Assertion (A):** A research on Paradigm shift helps in assessing the growth of a society.

Reason (R): Perceptible changes in the people's outlook towards life are appreciable.

(A) Both A and R are true and R is correct explanation of A

(B) Both A and R are true but R is not correct explanation of A

(C) Both A and R are false

(D) A is false but R is true

8. **Assertion (A):** Sensual perception is the central theme of Realism.

Reason (R): Qualitative methods of research are compatible to study on Realism.

(A) Both A and R are false

(B) Both A and R are true but R is not correct explanation of A

(C) A is true but R is false

(D) Both A and R are true and R is correct explanation of A

9. **Assertion (A):** The main components of Phenomenology are experience and consciousness.

Reason (R): Reality exists in the objects and events which human beings experience in their consciousness.

(A) Both A and R are true and R is correct explanation of A

(B) Both A and R are true but R is not correct explanation of A

(C) A is true but R is false

(D) A is false but R is true

10. **Assertion (A):** Post-positivism believes that human sensory and intellectual traits supplement the knowledge of reality obtained through scientific methods.

Reason (R): Theory of empirical observations of Post-positivism is an improvement over analytic theory of Positivism on knowledge of reality.

(A) Both A and R are true and R is correct explanation of A

(B) Both A and R are true but R is not correct explanation of A

(C) A is true but R is false

(D) Both A and R are false

KEY

1. A **2.** D **3.** A **4.** C **5.** D **6.** B **7.** C **8.** B **9.** A **10.** D

Questions Asked in Previous NET Exams

1. In the post-positivistic approach to research which of the following types of research got emphasised? **(UGC NET DECEMBER 2019)**

a) Experimental research

b) Phenomenological Research

c) Ethnographic Research

d) Ex-post Facto Research

e) Action Research

(A) (a), (b) and (c) (B) (b), (c) and (d)

(C) (b), (c) and (e) (D) (c), (d) and (e)

KEY

1. C

3 Methods, Steps and Ethics of Research

CONCEPT

There are various fields in which research is undertaken. Ultimate objective of a research is to test the hypothesis. Testing of hypothesis involves a highly technical procedure adopted throughout the research process. Data are collected from a compatible source, i.e., primary or secondary. Nature of data collected is either qualitative or quantitative. Collection and analysis of data involve various methods of research depending upon the nature of problem under study.

METHODS OF RESEARCH

Following are the leading methods of research:

1) **Experimental Method:** Experimental method of research is a systematic approach to research. This method aims to see cause and effect relationship among variables. This method is generally applied on natural sciences. In this method, a researcher manipulates the independent variable and keeps and observes effect of this manipulation on dependent variables, which are kept constant. Experimental research is conducted under controlled conditions.

RESEARCH DESIGN

> *Whatever research method is used to conduct research, is part of research design. Research design is a set of methods and procedures used in data collection and data analysis. Research design constitutes sampling technique of data collection, method of research, hypothesis under study, dependent and independent variables in case of experimentation, statistical tools, and findings after data analysis.*

2) **Historical Method:** Historical method is a systematic method of research in which events of the past are examined. Data regarding various civilisations, people, and socio-economic and cultural structure of past societies are obtained. Various other systems like judicial, educational, political, health, and trade of various civilisations are studied. The process involves investigating, recording, analysing, and interpreting the events of the past for the purpose of discovering generalisations that are helpful in understanding the past, understanding the present, and to a limited extent, in anticipating the future as study of past events help in making plans for present and future reforms in different spheres of present day society.

3) **Qualitative Method:** Qualitative research method is used to study various behavioural traits and other abstract phenomenon or variables which cannot be put into quantitative units. This research method uses technique of in-depth interview, participant's observation and focus groups, ethnographic search, content analysis, and case study to obtain data. Results of qualitative method of research are descriptive which can be compared but cannot be quantified.

4) **Quantitative Method:** Quantitative method of research goes for statistical or mathematical analysis of data collected of those variables which can be measured in numerical units. Data are collected through surveys, questionnaires, or by manipulating pre-existing statistical data using computational techniques. Quantitative research focuses on gathering numerical data and generalising it across groups of people or to explain a particular phenomenon. Goal in conducting quantitative research study is to determine the relationship between one thing [an independent variable] and another [a dependent or outcome variable] within a population.

5) **Descriptive Method:** Descriptive method is used to gather data regarding characteristics of population or phenomenon under study. Data are collected through observation (naturalistic or laboratory), case studies and surveys (structured or unstructured interviews).

Example: If a car manufacturing company wants to assess the car purchasing trend of prospective buyers, it will conduct a demographic survey of this region, gather population data, and then conduct descriptive research on this demographic segment. The research will then uncover details on "what is the purchasing pattern of buyers", but not cover any investigative details on "why" the pattern exists. So descriptive research method focuses on "What" of research subject and not "Why" of research subject.

INTERVIEWS IN RESEARCH

A researcher while collecting data from primary source collects data by conducting interviews from those members of the targeted population, who have been picked up as a sample. According to the nature and requirement of research projects, researchers conduct the following types of interviews:

1) ***Structured Interview:*** *In structured interview a researcher asks those questions which he/she has already planned and formed a questionnaire.*
2) ***Semi-structured Interview:*** *In such interview a researcher asks some questions he has already planned and some on the spot he thinks will be useful for his research.*
3) ***Unstructured Interview:*** *Here, the researcher is free to ask questions extempore. Such questions are also conducive in the research he undertakes.*
4) ***Focused Interview:*** *Here, a researcher asks questions while focussing on the main objective of the research project.*
5) ***Clinical Interview:*** *In this interview a subject shares his/her life experiences with the researcher. Further, such interviews demand sharing of an experience of a particular life trait. For example, interaction between a doctor and patient, lawyer and client, and teacher and student is clinical interview.*

6) **Ex post Facto Method:** Ex post facto method is a quasi-experimental method. In experimental method the cause and effect relationship between independent and dependent variable is examined. On the other hand, in ex post facto research method, it is examined how an independent variable, present before study, affects the dependent variable. Here, researcher cannot manipulate the independent variable as it has already been manipulated due to its presence before the study. Now researcher will examine how this manipulation has affected the dependent variable.

Example: A research scholar examines how a change in curriculum (independent variable) by education authorities have affected study habits of students (dependent variable). Here, independent variable (curriculum) has already been manipulated before the researcher starts a study to examine its effect on dependent variable (students). So it is a quasi-experimental method of research.

7) **Case Study Method:** Case study method studies a phenomenon in its real-life context through in-depth investigation of a single individual, group, or event to explore the causes of underlying principles. A case study is a descriptive and exploratory analysis of a person, group, or event. Case study method becomes prominent when real-life issues or phenomenon like poverty, unemployment, drug addiction, illiteracy, etc. are to be examined. This method is also used to examine business issues.

8) **Philosophical Method:** Philosophical method of research advocates the use of philosophy in research, i.e., categorical and comprehensive knowledge of fundamental notions. This method determines meaning of ideas and aims in clarifying them, i.e., achieving pragmatism. It aims at achieving sound reasoning and knowledge of basic principles of life.

STEPS OF RESEARCH

Various steps involved in the research process are not mutually exclusive; nor are they separate and distinct. They do not necessarily follow each other in any specific order. However, a uniform order of steps in research process can be studied as under:

1) **Identifying research problem:** Research scholar chooses a particular research problem from the subject in which he/she undertakes research.
2) **Formulating hypothesis:** After identifying the problem, a research scholar consults the guide and develops a hypothesis after considering the feasibility of the chosen hypothesis while chalking out objectives.
3) **Examining/reviewing the relevant literature:** After formulating hypothesis, a research scholar reviews and consults the relevant literature available on the problem under study.
4) **Rephrasing the problem:** A researcher rephrases the chosen hypothesis after reviewing the relevant literature, thus making it suitable for researchers for putting it in analytical and operational terms.
5) **Development of working hypothesis:** After above step, a researcher develops a working hypothesis which becomes a base of further research. Here, the hypothesis is to be put to empirical approach. A working hypothesis indicates the type of data to be collected and particular methodology to be used for proper analysis. The role of the hypothesis is to guide the researcher by delimiting the area of research and to keep him on the right track.
6) **Preparing the research design:** At this step, the researcher prepares the research design, i.e., he decides about the conceptual structure within which the research would be conducted. A research design carries the considerations like means of obtaining information, time availability for research, cost factor relating to research, etc.
7) **Determining sample design:** After above step, a researcher develops a sample design for collecting data. Sample design is a plan for obtaining sample from a given set of items, usually called 'Population'.
8) **Collecting the data:** Data are collected with a sampling technique already determined in the previous step. Source of data may be primary or secondary and nature of data may be qualitative or quantitative.
9) **Methodology:** After collecting data the research scholar selects the methodology to be used for analysis of collected data.
10) **Analysis of data:** Data is put to analysis while using quantitative or qualitative techniques.
11) **Hypothesis testing:** Results of data analysis test the hypothesis under study, i.e., whether hypothesis is a null hypothesis or alternative hypothesis.
12) **Generalisation and interpretation:** At this step the researcher gives a touch of generalisation to the hypothesis so tested and then he interprets it in his findings. Findings so obtained for the sample data are generalised and applied to the whole of the targeted population. Further, proper interpretation serves the purpose of establishing the authenticity.
13) **Preparation of the report or thesis:** This is the final step of research in which the research scholar puts the whole research work in black and white in the form of a report or thesis.

RESEARCH ETHICS

A research scientist is to observe the following ethics while undertaking research:

1) **Original Hypothesis:** Chosen hypothesis should be original and prospective.
2) **Unambiguous:** Purpose of research should be clearly defined.
3) **Detailed Description:** Research procedure should be described in detail.
4) **Planned Process:** Procedural design should be carefully planned.
5) **Ordered Approach:** Proper research order should be followed.
6) **Unbiased:** Formulation of hypothesis, collection of data, application, and findings should be free from any bias.
7) **Adequate Analysis:** Analysis of data should be sufficiently adequate to reveal its significance.

8) **Anonymity:** Research should maintain secrecy and anonymity of the respondent.

9) **Authenticity:** Research reporting should be evidence-based in the interest of authenticity.

10) **Plagiarism-free Interpretation:** When a research work is written in the form of a thesis, it should be free from plagiarism.

11) **Referencing and Citation Style:** Research scholar should cite references of those research scientists, whose original statements or theories have been used by him in his research.

Some Vital Facts

1) Comparison, control, manipulation and generalisation are components of a research design.
2) Identifying and defining a research problem, formulating a hypothesis, testing of hypothesis and reporting the results is the most logical sequence of doing research.
3) Ex-post facto research states the effect of a phenomenon as if a university teacher intends to study relationship between level of aspiration and achievement of rural children.
4) The conceptual framework in which a research is conducted is called a research design.
5) Formulation of a research problem can be compared to laying the foundation of a building.
6) Formulation of a research problem depends on object behind the researcher's choice, specific questions, what is the conceptual model and construction of hypotheses.
7) Scientific method of research follows the following sequence of research steps: Perceiving the problem situation, Locating the actual problem and its definition, Hypothesizing, Deducing the consequences of the suggested solution and Testing the hypothesis in action.
8) The problem of 'research ethics' is concerned with evidence based research reporting.
9) Ex-post facto method establishes causal comparison and correlational studies.
10) Case study method of research conducts in-depth study of a unit specified for the purpose.
11) Philosophical method of research gives interpretation of thoughts of a great thinker
12) Descriptive survey method finds out the status based on a study of a large sample
13) In Experimental method data are collected through standardized tests.
14) In Ex post-facto method of research data are collected through typical characteristics tests.
15) In Descriptive survey method data are collected through questionnaire.
16) Observing research ethics becomes important at the stage of data collection and interpretation
17) Deconstruction is a popular method of research in literature.
18) Conducting a review of the literature that acknowledges the contributions of other people in the relevant field or relevant prior work is considered a good research ethics.
19) Working hypothesis is a provisionally accepted hypothesis for further research.
20) Searching sources of information to locate problemis the first step in starting the research process

Practice Exercise

General Questions Format

1. A research work completed with a step-wise approach, is always
   (A) time consuming because while following various steps, a researcher is to fulfil various formalities
   (B) effective because various steps followed during research process fulfil the ethics of undertaking research, hereby increasing its chances of being accurate and unambiguous.
   (C) attractivebecause steps undertaken during research give the research work a beautiful shape
   (D) None of these

2. Which of the following is not considered during the step of Preparing the Research Design?
   (A) Source of information
   (B) Consulting empirical literature
   (C) Availability of time
   (D) Cost to be incurred

3. Following steps are generally followed in a research process:
   I) Preparation of Synopsis
   II) Collection of data
   III) Execution of the project
   IV) Hypothesis testing. *Arrange them in chronology.*
   (A) I-II-III-IV (B) II-I-III-IV
   (C) III-I-IV-II (D) IV-III-II-I

4. For understanding a research problem, the best way before a researcher is to consult his _____.
   (A) mind
   (B) colleagues
   (C) Head of the department
   (D) none of the above

5. In the research process the step of developing working hypothesis comes after the step of
   (A) Rephrasing of the problem
   (B) Preparing the research design
   (C) Preparing synopsis
   (D) Collection of data

6. Following different steps in the process of research is.........for the research scientist.
   (A) mandatory (B) optional
   (C) natural (D) headache

7. In the research terminology, term 'population' stands for
   (A) Set of units from where sample is obtained
   (B) Sum total of samples collected during a research project.
   (C) Total number of sources of samples so used in a particular research work.
   (D) None of these

8. A problem undertaken for research is formulated in general framework and then it is narrowed down for...............purpose.
   (A) economic (B) welfare
   (C) writing (D) operational

9. Out of different steps required to be followed during research, which of the following steps is superfluous?
   (A) Execution of the project
   (B) Generalisation and interpretation
   (C) Preparation of research design
   (D) None of the above

10. Under which step of research process, problem under research is to be developed on an exhaustive scale?
    (A) Research designing
    (B) Execution of project
    (C) Data analysis
    (D) None of these

11. Which of the following is essential in the qualitative method of research?
    (A) Observation (B) Interview
    (C) Description (D) all of the above

12. Which of the following is a fundamental ethics of research?
    (A) Planning
    (B) Accuracy
    (C) Originality
    (D) Investigation

13. Library plays an important part in one of the methods of research because ____.

(A) nature of hypothesis differs

(B) nature of data to be collected differs

(C) nature of research scholars differs

(D) none of these

14. Quantitative method of research is successful in case of those variables which

(A) are accepted by the methodology

(B) are easily measurable

(C) require knowledge of quantitative techniques

(D) none of the above

15. No method of research is successful until and unless research scientist ______.

(A) makes it compatible to the chosen problem

(B) verifies its validity well before adopting it in the research

(C) adopts it and verifies its validity

(D) none of these

16. Under which method research is undertaken under controlled conditions?

(A) Quantitative (B) Experimental

(C) Qualitative (D) Comparative

17. In the field, a research scholar collects a data which can be attributed to......method of research.

(A) Experimental (B) Field survey

(C) Quantitative (D) Any of these

18. Which of the following is NOT an ethics of research?

(A) Ordering (B) Planning

(C) Imitating (D) Indiscriminating

19. Which is the most popular method of conducting research?

(A) Quantitative (B) Experimental

(C) Field survey (D) Can't say

20. Adoption of research ethics makes a research work ______.

(A) practical (B) ideal

(C) ethical (D) popular

21. Which of the following is NOT TRUE about descriptive method of research?

a) Data are collected through case studies.

b) Demographic survey is the essential condition.

c) Priorities of people in looking for different professional commitments are studied.

d) Observations are gathered through laboratory technique.

(A) Only c and d (B) Only a, c, and d

(C) Only b (D) Only d

22. Consider the statements:

P: A research method provides autonomy to the research scholar for its optimum use.

Q: Establishing rational relationship among different variables is the optimal use of a research method.

(A) Both P and Q are true

(B) P is false but Q is true

(C) Both P and Q are false

(D) P is true but R is false

23. The ultimate objective of the quantitative method of research is

(A) Authenticity (B) Randomisation

(C) Optimisation (D) Generalisation

24. A research scholar is to gather data regarding difference in the spending habits of male and female employees of a company X after getting a hike in their pay. Which interview method should he use to collect data?

(A) Semi-structured

(B) Structured

(C) Unstructured

(D) Clinical

25. Which of the following research activity is not in the jurisdiction of ex post facto method of research?

(A) Analysis of dependent variable

(B) Examining relation between dependent and independent variable

(C) Manipulation of Independent variable

(D) Consideration of independent variable

KEY

1. B	2. B	3. A	4. D	5. A	6. C	7. A
8. D	9. D	10. D	11. D	12. A	13. D	14. B
15. A	16. B	17. B	18. C	19. C	20. B	21. A
22. C	23. D	24. B	25. C			

Assertion–Reason Format

1. **Assertion (A):** Research design is an index of the whole research process.

   Reason (R): It constitutes sampling technique of data collection, method of research, hypothesis under study, analysis, and findings.

   (A) Both A and R are true and R is correct explanation of A

   (B) Both A and R are true but R is not correct explanation of A

   (C) A is true but R is false

   (D) A is false but R is true

2. **Assertion (A):** Replication of a research is generally not supported by ethics of research.

   Reason (R): A research work becomes ethical if completed without interference of a guide.

   (A) Both A and R are true and R is correct explanation of A

   (B) Both A and R are true but R is not correct explanation of A

   (C) Both A and R are false

   (D) A is false but R is true

3. **Assertion (A):** Various reforms in present day research are inspired from historical method of research.

   Research (R): History reveals that research had been a means to progress even in the ancient times.

   (A) Both A and R are false

   (B) A is true but R is false

   (C) A is false but R is true

   (D) Both A and R are true and R is correct explanation of A

4. **Assertion (A):** Developing working hypothesis is a pivotal step of the research process.

   Reason (R): Various steps of research process minimise the chances of any bias in research.

   (A) Both A and R are true and R is correct explanation of A

   (B) A is true but R is false

   (C) A is false but R is true

   (D) Both A and R are true but R is not correct explanation of A

5. **Assertion (A):** Plagiarism found in any research presentation is against ethics of research.

   Reason (R): It involves incorporating some other person's creation in his research account without revealing it.

   (A) A is true but R ais false

   (B) Both A and R are true and R is correct explanation of A

   (C) A is false but R is true

   (D) Both A and R are true but R is not correct explanation of A

6. **Assertion (A):** Step of sampling design in research process immediately follows the step of working hypothesis.

   Reason (R): Findings of a research work are influenced by steps of research.

   (A) Both A and R are but R is not correct explanation of A

   (B) Both A and R are true and R is correct explanation of A

   (C) Both A and R are false

   (D) A is true but R is false

7. **Assertion (A):** An unstructured interview covers a broader area of investigation than a structured interview.

   Reason (R): Both the interviewer and respondent are not bound by exchanging a fixed number of questions and answers.

   (A) Both A and R are true and R is correct explanation of A

   (B) Both A and R are true but R is not correct explanation of A

   (C) A is true but R is false

   (D) A is false but R is true

8. **Assertion (A):** Ethics of research are too idealistic to work in a practical research process.

   Reason (R): Conducting of a research with ethics of research is a research on idealism.

   (A) Both A and R are true and R is correct explanation of A

   (B) Both A and R are true but R is not correct explanation of A

   (C) Both A and R are false

   (D) A is false but R is true

9. **Assertion (A):** Quantitative method of research houses experimental method of research.

Reason (R): Research on natural sciences involve quantitative and experimental methods of research.

(A) Both A and R are true and R is correct explanation of A

(B) A is true but R is false

(C) A is false but R is true

(D) Both A and R are true but R is not correct explanation of A

10. **Assertion (A):** Philosophical method of research aims at achieving pragmatism.

Reason (R): Meaning of ideas is determined in the research process and the aim is to clarify them.

(A) Both A and R are true but R is not correct explanation of A

(B) Both A and R are true and R is correct explanation of A

(C) A is true but R is false

(D) A is false but R is true

KEY

1. A **2.** C **3.** C **4.** D **5.** B **6.** C **7.** A **8.** C **9.** D **10.** B

Questions Asked in Previous NET Exams

1. The components of a research design are: **(UGC NET JUNE 2019)**

(a) Comparison

(b) Control

(c) Reactivity

(d) Manipulation

(e) Non-representativeness

(f) Generalisation

(A) (c), (d), (e), and (f)

(B) (a), (c), (e), and (f)

(C) (b), (c), (d), and (e)

(D) (a), (b), (d), and (f)

2. The conceptual framework in which a research is conducted is called a **(UGC NET JUNE 2019)**

(A) Synopsis of research

(B) Research design

(C) Research hypothesis

(D) Research paradigm

3. A university teacher intends to study relationship between level of aspiration and achievement of rural children. Which design of research will be the most appropriate in the context? **(UGC NET DECEMBER 2019)**

1) Experimental research design

2) Ex Post facto research design

3) Historical research design

4) Survey research design

4. Which o the following sequences of represents the most logical sequence of doing research? **(UGC NET DECEMBER 2019)**

(A) Identifying and defining a research problem, formulating a hypothesis, testing of hypothesis and reporting the results.

(B) Identify a research problem, defining the population and sample, collecting data and analysis of data

(C) Survey of research, defining the research problem, collecting data and presenting the outcomes.

(D) Defining research variables, hypothesizing, testing of research and reporting of research outcomes

5. Formulation of a research problem can be compared to **(UGC NET JUNE 2019)**

(A) Laying the foundation of a building

(B) Building the walls of a home

(C) Polishing the doors of a building

(D) Constructing the ceiling of a house

6. Formulation of a research problem depends on: **(UGC NET DECEMBER 2018)**

(a) What is the object behind the researcher's choice?

(b) What are the specific questions?

(c) What is the conceptual model?

(d) What negative factors to research upon?

(e) Reasons for unlimiting the study.

(f) Construction of hypotheses.

(A) (a), (c), (e), and (f)

(B) (c), (d), (e), and (f)

(C) (b), (c), (d), and (e)

(D) (a), (b), (c), and (f)

7. Identify the correct order of the following components which are interrelated in research.

(UGC NET JULY 2018)

(i) Observation

(ii) Hypothesis making

(iii) Developing concepts

(iv) Deducing the consequences of theories

(v) Methods employed to obtain them

Choose the correct answer from the code given below:

Code:

(A) (v), (iv), (iii), (ii), and (i)

(B) (i), (iii), (ii), (iv), and (v)

(C) (ii), (iii), (i), (iv), and (v)

(D) (iv), (v), (iii), (ii), and (i)

8. Which of the following sequence of research steps is nearer to the scientific method?

(UGC NET JULY 2018)

(A) Suggested solution of the problem, Deducing the consequences of the solution, Perceiving the problem situation, Location of the difficulty, and Testing the solutions

(B) Perceiving the problem situation, Locating the actual problem and its definition, Hypothesising, Deducing the consequences of the suggested solution, and Testing the hypothesis in action

(C) Defining a problem, Identifying the causes of the problem, Defining a population, Drawing a sample, Collecting data, and Analysing results

(D) Identifying the causal factors, Defining the problem, Developing a hypothesis, Selecting a sample, Collecting data and arriving at generalisation, and Conclusions

9. The problem of 'research ethics' is concerned with which aspect of research activities?

(UGC NET JULY 2018)

(A) Following the prescribed format of a thesis

(B) Data analysis through qualitative or quantitative technique

(C) Defining the population of research

(D) Evidence-based research reporting

10. In the two lists given below, List I provides the types of research methods, while List II indicates the critical features associated with them. Match the two lists and choose the correct answer from the code given below.

(UGC NET JULY 2018)

List I **(Research methods)**	**List II** **(Critical features)**
(a) Ex post facto method	(i) Finding out the status based on a study of a large sample
(b) Case study method	(ii) Interpretation of thoughts of a great thinker
(c) Philosophical method	(iii) Intervention based ameliorative approach
(d) Descriptive survey method	(iv) Causal comparison and correlational studies
	(v) In-depth study of a unit specified for the purpose

Codes:	(a)	(b)	(c)	(d)
(A)	(i)	(ii)	(iii)	(iv)
(B)	(ii)	(iii)	(iv)	(v)
(C)	(i)	(iii)	(ii)	(v)
(D)	(iv)	(v)	(ii)	(i)

11. A researcher attempts to evaluate the effect of method of feeding on anxiety-proneness of children. Which method of research would be appropriate for this?

(UGC NET NOVEMBER 2017)

(A) Experimental method

(B) Ex post facto method

(C) Survey method

(D) Case study method

12. Which of the following is susceptible to the issue of research ethics?

(UGC NET NOVEMBER 2017)

(A) Faulty research design

(B) Choice of sampling technique

(C) Reporting of research findings

(D) Inaccurate application of statistical techniques

13. Which sequence of research steps is logical in the list given below?

(UGC NET JANUARY 2017)

(A) Problem formulation, Analysis, Development of Research design, Hypothesis making, Collection of data, Arriving at generalisations and conclusions

(B) Development of Research design, Hypothesis making, Problem formulation, Data analysis, Arriving at conclusions and data collection

(C) Problem formulation, Hypothesis making, Development of a research design, Collection of data, Data analysis, and Formulation of generalisations and conclusions

(D) Problem formulation, Deciding about the sample and data collection tools, Formulation of hypothesis, Collection and interpretation of research evidence

14. Below are given two sets-Research methods (Set-I) and Data collection tools (Set-II). Match the two sets and indicate your answer by selecting the correct code:

(UGC NET JANUARY 2017)

Set-I (Research Methods)	**Set-II (Data Collection Tools)**
a. Experimental method	i. Using primary and secondary sources
b. Ex post facto x method	ii. Questionnaire
c. Descriptive survey method	iii. Standardised tests
d. Historical method	iv. Typical characteristic tests

Codes:	(a)	(b)	(c)	(d)
(A)	ii	i	iii	iv
(B)	iii	iv	ii	i
(C)	ii	iii	i	iv
(D)	ii	iv	iii	i

15. The issue of 'research ethics' may be considered pertinent at which stage of research?

(UGC NET JANUARY 2017)

(A) At the stage of problem formulation and its definition

(B) At the stage of defining the population of research

(C) At the stage of data collection and interpretation

(D) At the stage of reporting the findings.

16. Research ethics has a direct connection more often with which stages of research?

(UGC NET AUGUST 2016)

(A) Defining and delimiting the scope of research

(B) Problem formulation and reporting of research findings

(C) Defining the population and deciding the sampling technique for research

(D) Deciding about statistical techniques and data analysis

17. A research intends to explore the effect of possible factors for the organisation of effective mid-day meal interventions. Which research method will be most appropriate for this study?

(UGC NET JULY 2016)

(A) Historical method

(B) Descriptive survey method

(C) Experimental method

(D) Ex post facto method

18. From the following list of statements identify the set which has negative implications for 'research ethics'. **(UGC NET JULY 2016)**

i. A researcher critically looks at the findings of another research.

ii. Related studies are cited without proper references.

iii. Research findings are made the basis for policymaking.

iv. Conduct of practitioner is screened in terms of reported research evidences.

v. A research study is replicated with a view to verify the evidences from other researches.

vi. Both policy making and policy implementing processes are regulated in terms of preliminary studies.

(A) i, ii, and iii (B) ii, iii, and iv

(C) ii, iv, and vi (D) i, iii, and v

19. Ethical norms in research do not involve guidelines for: **(UGC NET DECEMBER 2015)**
(A) Thesis format
(B) Copyright
(C) Patenting policy
(D) Data sharing policies

20. What is a Research design?
(UGC NET DECEMBER 2014)
(A) A way of conducting research that is not grounded in theory
(B) The choice between using qualitative or quantitative methods
(C) The style in which you present your research findings, e.g., a graph
(D) A framework for every stage of the collection and analysis of data

21. When planning to do a social research, it is better to **(UGC NET DECEMBER 2014)**
(A) Approach the topic with an open mind
(B) Do a pilot study before getting stuck into it
(C) Be familiar with literature on the topic
(D) Forget about theory because this is a very practical undertaking

22. The sequential operations in scientific research are **(UGC NET DECEMBER 2013)**
(A) Co-vaiation, Elimination of spurious relations, Generalisation, Theorisation
(B) Generalisation, Co-variation, Theorisation, Elimination of spurious relations
(C) Theorisation, Generalisation, Elimination of spurious relations, Co-variation
(D) Elimination of spurious relations, Theorisation, Generalisation, Co-variation

23. Deconstruction is a popular method of research in **(UGC NET SEPTEMBER 2013)**
(A) Basic Science (B) Applied Science
(C) Social Science (D) Literature

24. Which one of the following belongs to the category of good 'research ethics'?
(UGC NET JUNE 2013)
(A) Publishing the same paper in two research journals without telling the editors.
(B) Conducting a review of the literature that acknowledges the contributions of other people in the relevant field or relevant prior work.
(C) Trimming outliers from a data set without discussing your reasons in a research paper.
(D) Including a colleague as an author on a research paper in return for a favour even though the colleague did not make a serious contribution to the paper.

25. A working hypothesis is
(UGC NET JUNE 2013)
(A) a proven hypothesis for an argument.
(B) not required to be tested.
(C) a provisionally accepted hypothesis for further research.
(D) a scientific theory.

26. Good 'research ethics' means
(UGC NET DECEMBER 2012)
(A) Not disclosing the holdings of shares/ stocks in a company that sponsors your research.
(B) Assigning a particular research problem to one Ph.D./research student only.
(C) Discussing with your colleagues confidential data from a research paper that you are reviewing for an academic journal.
(D) Submitting the same research manuscript for publishing in more than one journal.

27. Arrange the following steps of research in correct sequence:
(UGC NET DECEMBER 2012)
1. Identification of research problem
2. Listing of research objectives
3. Collection of data
4. Methodology
5. Data analysis
6. Results and discussion

(A) 1 - 2 - 3 - 4 - 5 - 6
(B) 1 - 2 - 4 - 3 - 5 - 6
(C) 2 - 1 - 3 - 4 - 5 - 6
(D) 2 - 1 - 4 - 3 - 5 - 6

28. Research ethics do not include
(UGC NET JUNE 2012)
(A) Honesty (B) Subjectivity
(C) Integrity (D) Objectivity

29. Research is not considered ethical if it **(UGC NET DECEMBER 2011)**
(A) tries to prove a particular point.
(B) does not ensure privacy and anonymity of the respondent.
(C) does not investigate the data scientifically.
(D) is not of a very high standard.

30. In the process of conducting research "Formulation of Hypothesis" is followed by **(UGC NET JUNE 2011)**
(A) Statement of objectives
(B) Analysis of data
(C) Selection of research tools
(D) Collection of data

31. Which of the following is the first step in starting the research process? **(UGC NET JUNE 2010)**
(A) Searching sources of information to locate problem.
(B) Survey of related literature
(C) Identification of problem
(D) Searching for solutions to the problem

32. Formulation of hypothesis may NOT be required in: **(UGC NET JUNE 2008)**
(A) Survey method
(B) Historical studies
(C) Experimental studies
(D) Normative studies

33. Which of the following is not a method of research? **(UGC NET DECEMBER 2006)**
(A) Observation
(B) Historical
(C) Survey
(D) Philosophical

34. The first step of research is: **(UGC NET DECEMBER 2006)**
(A) Selecting a problem
(B) Searching a problem
(C) Finding a problem
(D) Identifying a problem

35. One of the aims of the scientific method in research is to: **(UGC NET JUNE 2006)**
(A) improve data interpretation.
(B) eliminate spurious relations.
(C) confirm triangulation.
(D) introduce new variables.

36. Match List-I (Interviews) with List-II (Meaning) and select the correct answer from the code given below: **(UGC NET JUNE 2006)**

List-I (Interviews)	**List-II (Meaning)**
(a) Structured interviews	(i) Greater flexibility approach
(b) Unstructured interviews	(ii) Attention on the questions to be answered
(c) Focused interviews	(iii) Individual life experience
(d) Clinical interviews	(iv) Predetermined questions
	(v) Non-directive

Codes:	(a)	(b)	(c)	(d)
(A)	(iv)	(i)	(ii)	(iii)
(B)	(ii)	(iv)	(i)	(iii)
(C)	(v)	(ii)	(iv)	(i)
(D)	(i)	(iii)	(v)	(iv)

KEY

1. D	**2.** B	**3.** B	**4.** A	**5.** A	**6.** D	**7.** B
8. B	**9.** D	**10.** D	**11.** B	**12.** C	**13.** C	**14.** B
15. C	**16.** B	**17.** D	**18.** C	**19.** A	**20.** D	**21.** A
22. A	**23.** D	**24.** B	**25.** C	**26.** B	**27.** A	**28.** B
29. B	**30.** D	**31.** A	**32.** B	**33.** A	**34.** D	**35.** B
36. A						

4 Thesis and Article Writing

THESIS WRITING

In a layman's language, thesis is a research work, which is written and compiled by a research scholar, published and submitted to the respective authority, which evaluates it and grants a certain degree or certificate to the research scholar. Technically, a thesis represents the culmination of a substantial piece of original work over a period of at least one year. It is an evidence of independent writing. However, some research works, called thesis, replicate the previous research with the object of testing the reported findings of that research or testing the relevance of findings of research completed in different fields. In any case, a thesis is expected to make original contribution to knowledge.

Characteristics of a Thesis

A thesis being a research-based way of presenting a problem with findings and suggestions, possesses the following characteristics:

1) **Original work:** A thesis is black and white form of a research conducted by the research scholar and that work is original, so thesis becomes an original work.
2) **Scholarly style:** A thesis is written in scholarly style, i.e., sound reasoning and intellectual honesty is used in thesis writing.
3) **Compatible write-up:** A write-up is compatible to the nature of the problem and objectives.
4) **Standardized format:** Thesis is compiled in a standardized format, i.e., referencing, footnoting, presenting tables, etc.
5) **Precise and to the point expression:** Thesis is written with careful selection of words and clear definition of terms.
6) **Written in third person pronoun:** While complying with the ethics of a general writing, a thesis is always written in third person. Terms like I, we, you, me, etc. should not appear in the thesis write-up except in quotations.
7) **Critical analysis of the problem:** As detailed analysis of collected data is done by using appropriate methodology, account of analysis becomes part of thesis.
8) **High level of readability:** Thesis aims at high level of readability; that is why it is written in a scholarly style. Further, it uses simple language and unambiguous words.
9) **Correct spellings, grammar, and punctuation:** Author does not compromise with grammar, sentence structure, spellings, and standard of language used in the thesis.
10) **Consistency and universal distribution of emphasis:** A thesis is written while maintaining consistency and balance in the presentation. A thesis aims at universal distribution of emphasis, i.e., all chapters of the thesis share equal emphasis.

Motivation Behind Thesis Writing

Ultimate destination of a research work is a thesis which presents the whole research work in a proper order. Whatever factors motivate a research scholar to undertake a research are also behind writing a thesis. Following factors motivate a research scholar to write a thesis:

1) **Desire to get a research degree:** Ultimate evaluation of a researcher's research work is done by the concerned authority from the thesis submitted by the research scholar. After qualifying viva on the thesis, a research scholar gets a research degree.
2) **Intellectual joy of own creation:** As a thesis presents an original research work, a research scholar rejoices in the experience of his own creation put into black and white in the form of a thesis.
3) **Exposure of research work:** A thesis introduces a researcher's research work to the society. Objective of giving suitable exposure of his research work to the society for the benefit of the society motivates him/her to write a thesis.
4) **Guide to the future researchers:** A research scholar earnestly wants that his/her research work should serve as a guide to the future researchers who will replicate his research. This feeling motivates him to write a thesis as he can preserve his work in libraries for studies for consultation by future researchers.

FORMAT OF A THESIS

A thesis is written in the following format:

General Format

Preliminary Format

This includes the following sequence:

a) **Title page:** This page contains Title of thesis, Designation of Faculty (Optional), Name of the institution to which thesis is being submitted, Degree for which the thesis is presented, Name of candidate submitting the thesis, and Date of submission, respectively.

b) **Preface, including Acknowledgements:** It is also called Foreword. It includes the writer's purpose in conducting the study, a brief resume of the background, scope, purpose, and general nature of the research. Acknowledgement recognizes that person(s), institutions, etc. to whom the writer is indebted for valuable guidance and assistance during the study.

c) **Table of Contents:** Table of contents includes the major divisions of the thesis; introduction, chapters with their subsections, bibliography, and index respectively, along with page numbers.

d) **List of Tables:** List of tables is mentioned after the contents. This list is mentioned on a separate page, where List of Tables is centered.

e) **List of Figures or Illustrations:** List of illustrations or figures is given in the same way as the list of tables.

Text Format

After preliminary format, a writer is to develop text format in the following order:

a) **Introduction:** Introduction is written very meticulously as it is not only to introduce the problem in a suitable context but also to arouse and stimulate the reader's interest. Introduction mainly includes general purpose of study, importance of the study, etc. In a thesis, it runs into a chapter's length.

b) **Main Body:** Though main body format of a thesis depends upon the nature and dimension of the problem, yet some general format specifications include presentation of arguments and findings in a logical and orderly way, accurate documentation, forceful writing, and division of material into chapters. Main body contains the following chapters in a set order:

i) **Objectives:** This chapter illustrates the objectives of the study. Major part of research work rests on the objectives chalked out according to the nature and scope of a research work. Objectives act as guidelines for further proceedings of the research project throughout its journey.

ii) **Nature of Data and Source:** This chapter reveals whether data acquired during the research is of qualitative or quantitative or mixed nature and whether source of data has been primary or secondary. All the required details of nature and source of data so acquired are discussed exhaustively in this chapter.

iii) **Sampling Technique:** This chapter explains about the sampling technique followed in collecting data. Size of the targeted population and size of the sample feasible for research is discussed in this chapter. It is also stated whether data was picked up with probability or non-probability sampling method.

iv) **Methodology:** This chapter explains about a particular methodology compatible to the nature of data which has been used to analyse the collected data. Conceptual and technical aspects and scope of methodology is discussed in this chapter to justify the selection of that particular methodology used to analyse data collected for the research problem under study. Methodology may be involving quantitative or qualitative techniques or both.

v) **Analysis:** This chapter highlights the process of analysing data and the results. It is also mentioned in the chapter whether results are compatible with the objectives of study.

vi) **Findings:** This chapter comes out with the verdict regarding hypothesis testing, i.e., whether hypothesis has proved to be null or alternative.

c) **Conclusion:** Conclusion needs a separate chapter with separate heading, which performs the important function of tying together the whole thesis. Conclusion is an effective summary of the whole thesis along with practical and reformatory suggestions on various drawbacks and problems found during the study. The writer may enlist the unanswered questions which have occurred during research work on the concerned problem and which require further research beyond the limit of the present research work being presented in the form of thesis. In a nutshell, conclusion should leave the reader with the impression of completeness and positive gain.

Reference Material

After conclusion, there is the turn of Bibliography, Appendix, and/or Index. Bibliography follows the main body of text and is a separate but integral part of the thesis. Bibliography is the list of books, journals, dissertations, and other reference with their names, author name, name of publisher, year of publishing, etc. However, this part and the main text has a division sheet between them. Appendix gives a list of supporting evidences like some certificates, format of certain forms, etc. If there are more than one appendices, then each appendix should be separately developed. An index in a thesis follows the bibliography and appendix. Index is the list of various terms used in thesis given in alphabetical order along with page number where that term appears in the thesis. Further, if a thesis is published as a book, etc. then index is definitely required.

Page and Chapter Format

a) **Numbers and Headings:** In the interest of readability and ease of reference, the chapters of thesis are usually divided into sections and subsections. Such divisions are made through centered headings, side headings, paragraph headings, etc. Further, each chapter has a chapter number and chapter heading. Traditionally, centered headings are used for major divisions and side and paragraph headings are used for subdivisions. Each heading should be a caption and not a sentence. In addition to it, every page in a thesis is given a number.

b) **Margins:** A margin recommended at the left end of pages is 1.50 inches.

c) **Footnotes:** Use of footnotes in a thesis is conventional. These are references of various books consulted during the research work, given at the foot of a page of the thesis. In some cases they are given at the end of a chapter or end of a paper.

A checklist of the above formats is also prepared with the preparation of the final draft.

Common Abbreviations Used in Footnotes

anon.: anonymous

bk., bks.: book(s)

c., ca.: circa ('about'), used with approximate dates

cf. ante: confer ante ('compare above')

cf. post: confer post ('compare after')

cf.: confer, compare

ch., chs.: chapter(s)

col., cols.: column(s)

comp., comps.: compiled by, compiler(s)

diss.: dissertation

ed., eds.: edited by, edition(s), editor(s)

et al.: et alia ('and others')

ibid.: ibidem ('in the same place')

illus.: illustrated by, illustrator, illustration(s)

infra: below

l., ll.: line(s)

loc. cit.: loco citato ('in the place cited'), used when several footnotes intervene between two citations not only to the same work, but also to the same place in that work

ms.,mss.: manuscript(s)

n. pag.: no pagination

n., nn.: note(s), as in p. 24, n. 2

n.d.: no date (of publication)

n.p.: no place (of publication), no publisher

no., nos.: number(s)

op. cit.: opere citato ('in the work cited'), used when several footnotes intervene between two citations to the same work, in the same chapter

p., pp.: page(s)

q.v.: quod vide ('which see')

rev.: revised, revision, revised by, review

rpt.: reprint, reprinted

sec.: section

supp., supps.: supplement(s)

supra: above

trans.: translator, translated by

univ., U: university

vid.: vide ('see')

viz: videlicet ('namely')

vol., vols.: volume(s)

ARTICLE WRITING

An article is that piece of writing which is written for a large number of readers. The article is published in either newspaper or magazines or journals with the motive of reaching the masses.

Objectives of Article Writing

1) **Topic of Common Interest:** As an article is written with the aim to reach maximum readers, it is written on the topic of common interest. Topic may be belonging to the political, social, economic, sports, or cultural field. In every case issues of common interest are highlighted in an article

2) **Influencing Readers:** An article very easily influences the readers as it is written on a topic of their interest.

3) **Floating Message:** One of the objectives of writing an article is to float message through the write-up. An article is generally written on common issues of the community for floating reformatory messages.

4) **Complete Information:** Another major objective of writing an article is to provide complete information on the topic of the article to readers, so that readers may relish the content.

Format of an Article

Format of an article contains the following components in the following order:

1. **Heading /Title:** Heading of an article should reflect the spirit of the whole issue on which article is to be written, thus heading should be an eye-catcher for readers.
2. **A line having the writer's name:** Writer's name with short introduction is given at this slot.
3. **Body (the main part of the article):** Main body contains the following components
   a) **Introduction:** Introduction starts with a general overview of the topic of article and then converging on the topic in an accessible and absorbing language.
   b) **Description:** Description part of an article contains the complete knowledge of the topic of the article. In this slot an account of all the basic and advanced level concepts, present state of affairs, practical relevance, and future development is given by the writer. The language and expression is simple and absorbing for a common reader.
4. **Conclusion:** Article ends with suggestions for reformation to improve the present state of issue discussed in the article in a simple and tempting style. An effective conclusion strengthens the credibility aspect of the article.

Types of Articles

Following types of articles are published in newspaper and journals:

1) **News Story:** A news report of any length, usually presented in a straightforward style and without editorial comment.
2) **Feature story:** Story that is written not only to inform, but also to entertain, i.e., such articles provide 'Infotainment.'. This includes the story behind the story, describing atmosphere, personalities, locations, general awareness, etc.
3) **Editorial:** An article in a newspaper or other periodical presenting the opinion of the publisher, editor, or editors.
4) **Review:** An article critically studying movie, concert, recording, television program, book, art, restaurant, etc.
5) **Sports Story:** An article written about a sport. Could be an advance story, featuring an upcoming game or event; a coverage story, which tells the story of a just completed game, tournament or event; or a feature story about an athlete or athletes. Uses elements of both features and news writing.
6) **Column:** A signed article containing the writer's opinion.
7) **Press release:** Written or recorded communication directed at members of the news media for the purpose of announcing something ostensibly newsworthy. Typically, they are mailed, faxed, or e-mailed to assignment editors at newspapers, magazines, radio stations, television stations, or television networks.

Format and Style of References or Citation

While writing a thesis or article, author or researcher sometimes borrows some ideas or knowledge from the works done by other authors, scientists, and researchers and includes that knowledge in his write-up to provide strength to his account. As this knowledge is not his/her creation, researcher or author gives reference or citation of that source from where the information has been borrowed, mentioning name and other details of the original author as an acknowledgement to his/her work which has provided strength to a researcher's or author's write-up. So in a way, referencing or citation is a way of giving credit to individuals for their creative and intellectual works that a researcher or author utilizes to support his/her research. It can also be used to locate particular sources and combat plagiarism. Another purpose of giving references is to make readers aware about that source. Such references or citations are given in different styles established and acknowledged worldwide. Some popular referencing styles are discussed below:

1) **APA Style:** APA (American Psychological Association) style originated in 1929. APA format and style of references is used by Education, Psychology, and Sciences. This style is also known as author-date reference style. The style of references is given in the following order:

   Author's last name, initial(s). (Year of Publication). Article title. Name of Book/Journal in italics form, Place of Publication: Publisher.

   Example: Manav, T.K., A.D. (2012). Biodiversity in Peril. *Ecotimes*, Dehradun, India: Mudra.

2) **Harvard Style:** Harvard is a style of referencing, primarily used by university students, to cite information sources. This is also an author-date reference style. Its format and style is as follows:

   Last name, First initial. (Year published). *Title*. City published: Publisher, Page(s).

Example: Manav, T.K. (2012). *Biodiversity in Peril*. Dehradun, India: Mudra, p. 123.

When there is more than Single Author;

Style of reference will be in following order:

Last name, First initial. and Last name, First initial. (Year published). Title. City: Publisher, Page(s).

Example: Manav, T.K. and Riar, J.S. (2014). *Anthropogenic Activities and Climate Change*. Dehradun, India: Mudra, p. 64.

Imp: Except first edition, number of a particular edition is also mentioned after title of the article.

Example: Manav, T.K.and Riar, J.S. (2014). *Anthropogenic Activities and Climate Change*. 4th ed. Dehradun, India: Mudra, p.64.

3) **MLA (Modern Language Association) Style:** This style is used in Humanities including Languages, Arts, and Literature. This style of referencing is given in the following order:

   Author's last Name, Author's First name/ Initials. *Title*, Publisher, Year. Page(s).

   Example: Manav, T.K. *Biodiversity in Peril*, Mudra, 2012. p.114.

4) **Chicago/Turabian Style:** This style is generally used in Business, History, and the Fine Arts. This style was adopted by Chicago University in 1906. Turabian style is the simpler version of Chicago style This style is expressed in the following order:

   Name of author, Article title in inverted commas Name of journal in italics, Year of publication: Pages

   Example: Manav, T.K., "Biodiversity in Peril" *Ecotimes*, 2012: 220

Some Vital Facts

1) "Research Abstract" is a must for Research Article, Seminar Paper and Thesis
2) In finalizing a thesis writing formatBibliography and Appendicesform part of supplementary pages.
3) The format of thesis writing is the same as in research dissertation.
4) A good thesis writing should involve reduction of punctuation and grammatical errors to a minimum, careful checking of references, consistency in the way the thesis is written and a clear and well written abstract.
5) A thesis statement is an assertion.
6) In a thesis, figures and tables are included in the text itself.
7) Bibliography given in a research report helps those interested in future research

Practice Exercise

General Questions Format

1. For a layman, a thesis is a

(A) book
(B) journal
(C) piece of work undertaken to fulfill a formality
(D) none of the above

2. A research scholar writes a thesis because he is to

(A) secure a status-oriented degree
(B) establish his acumen for research
(C) serve the society
(D) all of the above

3. Which of the following is NOT a characteristic of a thesis?

(A) Originality (B) Formality
(C) Vitality (D) Totality

4. If a research scholar takes up a project with the objective of modifying a previous research work, then he has ______.

(A) taken research in a sportsman spirit
(B) shown that research on a particular problem never ends and is not confined to the boundaries of a thesis
(C) challenged the concerned research work
(D) initiated a reformatory step in the field of research and thesis writing

5. For giving his thesis a high level of readability, a research scholar

a) takes care of grammar and spellings
b) follows the instructions of his guide
c) puts the thesis in proper format
d) consults senior researchers

Which of the above is the least important one?

(A) d (B) a
(C) c (D) b

6. During the past few years thesis writing has become a/an
(A) ambition (B) tradition
(C) fashion (D) passion

7. Different stages in the course of thesis writing are more or less
(A) self-created by the thesis writer himself
(B) fulfilling the norms of thesis writing
(C) depending upon the nature of hypothesis
(D) none of the above

8. Standardized format of a thesis does not include ______.
(A) footnoting (B) referencing
(C) table presentation (D) none of the above

9. Thesis writing gives a research scholar a ____.
(A) limelight
(B) much needed destination
(C) coveted way to satisfaction of an academic career
(D) promising future

10. A thesis is written in third person because it is
(A) evaluated by a third person
(B) mainly confined to three persons, i.e., research scholar, the guide, and the examiner
(C) based on data collected from a third person
(D) none of the above

11. Thesis writing is possible in every field because ______.
(A) research workers are available in every field
(B) there is a potential and possibility of investigation in every field
(C) rapid and abrupt changes in every field are posing new challenges paving way for research and investigation
(D) all of the above

12. Thesis writing is a/an.........form of research.
(A) critical (B) analytical
(C) typical (D) cyclical

13. Had there not been tradition of thesis writing, there would not have been ______.
a) research scholarsb) guides
c) hypothesis
d) research projects
Which of the above is the most important?
(A) c (B) a
(C) d (D) b

14. Some abbreviations used in footnotes of a thesis are given under Column I and their expansion/meaning is given under Column II. Compare the abbreviation with its expansion/meaning and choose the correct code among the codes given below:

Column I (Abbreviation)	Column II (Expansion/Meaning)
b) et al	i) below
c) ibid	ii) in the work cited
d) infra	iii) and others
e) op. cit	iv) in the same place

Codes:	(a)	(b)	(c)	(d)
(A)	ii	iii	iv	i
(B)	iii	iv	i	ii
(C)	iii	i	iv	ii
(D)	i	ii	iv	iii

15. Which of the following is NOT an objective of writing an article?
a) Influencing readers regarding present status of various issues of minimum common interest
b) Presenting topics of common interest to make common readers to launch awareness campaigns regarding issues needing reformation
c) Giving complete and in-depth information on the topic to make readers fully equipped withupdated facts motivating them to express their independent opinion over it
d) Presenting the content in the easiest possible language ensuring maximum readability to make common readers attentive to various issues of common interest
(A) Only c (B) Only a and d
(C) a, b, c and d (D) Only a and b

16. Following reference belongs to which style of referencing?
Seth Mahindru, "Traits of Effective Communication" *Messaging Today*, 2010: 65
(A) Chicago (B) MLA
(C) Harvard (D) APA

KEY

1. C **2.** D **3.** B **4.** B **5.** A **6.** A **7.** B
8. D **9.** D **10.** D **11.** B **12.** B **13.** C **14.** B
15. D **16.** A

Assertion–Reason Format

1. **Assertion (A):** A researcher writes a thesis to acquire a research degree.

   Reason (R): Factors motivating a researcher to write a thesis vary from researcher to researcher.

   (A) Both A and R are false
   (B) A is true but R is false
   (C) Both A and R are true and R is correct explanation of A
   (D) Both A and R are true but R is not correct explanation of A

2. **Assertion (A):** Article writing has exhaustive research at its base.

   Reason (R): Objective of writing an article is to influence the common readers.

   (A) Both A and R ae true but R is not correct explanation of A
   (B) Both A and R are false
   (C) Both A and R are true and R is correct explanation of A
   (D) A is true but R is false

3. **Assertion (A):** Format of an article is a miniature of format of a thesis.

   Reason (R): Both article and thesis have a targeted population.

   (A) Both A and R are true and R is correct explanation of A
   (B) Both A and R are true but R is not correct explanation of A
   (C) A is true but R is false
   (D) A is false but R is true

4. **Assertion (A):** A thesis can be published as an article in a newspaper.

   Reason (R): An article can be presented as a thesis for review.

   (A) Both A and R are true and R is correct explanation of A
   (B) Both A and R are true but R is not correct explanation of A
   (C) A is true but R is false
   (D) Both A and R are false

5. **Assertion (A):** Text format of a thesis does not include bibliography.

   Reason (R): Bibliography is part of references section of a thesis.

   (A) A is true but R is false
   (B) A is false but R is true
   (C) Both A and R are true and R is correct explanation of A
   (D) Both A and R are true but R is not correct explanation of A

KEY

1. B **2.** A **3.** C **4.** D **5.** B

Questions Asked in Previous NET Exams

1. In which h of the following formats, "Research Abstract" is a must?

   a) Research Article
   b) Seminar Paper presented
   c) Thesis
   d) Research Synopsis

   Choose the most appropriate choice from those given below:

   (A) (a), (c), (d) (B) (a), (b), (d)
   (C) (a), (b), (c) (D) (b), (c), (d)

2. In finalizing a thesis writing format, which of the following would form part of supplementary pages? **(UGC NET NOVEMBER 2017)**

   (A) Table of contents
   (B) Conclusions of the study
   (C) Bibliography and Appendices
   (D) List of tables and figures

3. In a Ph.D. thesis, which one is the correct sequence for showing scheme of Chaptalization? **(UGC NET AUGUST 2016)**

   (A) Survey of related studies, Introduction, Design of the study, Data analysis and interpretation, Conclusions and generalisations, Suggested further study, References, Appendix
   (B) Introduction, Design of study, Data analysis and interpretation, Generalizations, Conclusions and survey of related studies and suggestions for further research, References and Appendix
   (C) Introduction, Survey of related studies, Design of study, Data presentation, analysis, and interpretation, Formulation of generalization and conclusions, Suggestions for further research, References and Appendix
   (D) Survey of related studies, References, Introduction, Design of study, Data analysis and interpretation, Conclusions and generalizations, Suggestions for further research, Appendix

4. The format of thesis writing is the same as in

(UGC NET JULY 2016)

(A) Preparation of a research paper/article

(B) Writing of seminar presentation

(C) A research dissertation

(D) Presenting a workshop/conference paper

5. Which of the following are the basic rules of APA style of referencing format?

(UGC NET DECEMBER 2015)

(a) Italicize titles of shorter works such as journal articles or essays

(b) Invert authors' names (last name first)

(c) Italicize titles of longer works such as books and journals

(d) Alphabetically index reference list

Select the correct answer from the codes given below:

(A) (a) and (b) (B) (b), (c), and (d)

(C) (c) and (d) (D) (a), (b), (c) and (d)

6. A good thesis writing should involve:

(UGC NET JUNE 2015)

(a) Reduction of punctuation and grammatical errors to a minimum

(b) Careful checking of references

(c) Consistency in the way the thesis is written

(d) A clear and well written abstract

Select the correct answer from the codes given below:

(A) (b), (c), and (d)

(B) (a), (b), (c) and (d)

(C) (a), (b), and (c)

(D) (a), (b), and (d)

7. The core elements of dissertation are

(UGC NET DECEMBER 2014)

(A) Introduction; Data Collection; Data Analysis; Conclusions and Recommendations

(B) Executive Summary; Literature review; Data gathered; Conclusions; Bibliography

(C) Research Plan; Research Data; Analysis; References

(D) Introduction; Literature Review; Research Methodology; Results; Discussion and Conclusion

8. A thesis statement is _____.

(UGC NET EXAM JUNE 2014)

(A) an observation (B) a fact

(C) an assertion (D) a discussion

9. In a thesis, figures and tables are included in

(UGC NET JUNE 2014)

(A) The appendix

(B) A separate chapter

(C) The concluding chapter

(D) The text itself

10. Which one of the following references is written according to American Psychological Association (APA) format?

(UGC NET DECEMBER 2012)

(A) Sharma, V. (2010). Fundamentals of Computer Science. New Delhi : Tata McGraw Hill

(B) Sharma, V. 2010. Fundamentals of Computer Science. New Delhi : Tata McGraw Hill

(C) Sharma. V. – 2010. Fundamentals of Computer Science, New Delhi : Tata McGraw Hill

(D) Sharma, V. (2010), Fundamentals of Computer Science, New Delhi : Tata McGraw Hill

11. When two or more successive footnotes refer to the same work which one of the following expressions is used?

(UGC NET JUNE 2012)

(A) ibid (B) et.al

(C) op.cit (D) loc.cit.

12. Bibliography given in a research report ____.

(UGC NET JUNE 2007)

(A) shows vast knowledge of the researcher

(B) helps those interested in future research

(C) has no relevance to research

(D) all of the above

KEY

1. C **2.** C **3.** C **4.** C **5.** B **6.** B **7.** D
8. C **9.** D **10.** A **11.** A **12.** B

5 Application of ICT in Research

CONCEPT

While pursuing a research work a researcher looks for using those tools which make research work original, authentic, and accurate. A researcher also wants a tool easing the knowledge-gathering process and enhancing resource development. Application of ICT in research helps a research scholar to accomplish all the above targets. ICT helps a research scholar to identify the research problems and skilfully solve them.

Significance of ICT Application in Research

1) **Providing relevant information:** ICT does not accumulate information for the research scholar, it rather helps him/her to discriminate, analyse, and create information.
2) **Precise information:** Generally, a research scholar has to consult various references to gather information. In this process, he/she sometimes gathers excess information and it becomes difficult to encapsulate it. ICT helps a research scholar to give him/her precise information which saves time, cost, and energy which otherwise would have been spent in gathering information through traditional means.
3) **Making analysis easier:** A research work involves highly complex information, the analysis of which is not easy with the traditional approach. ICT makes this analysis easier and accurate.
4) **Convenience for research scholar:** A research scholar comes across vivid stages of research and he/she is to follow certain steps to undertake research. Further, research requires various situations to be tackled accurately. Application of ICT creates convenience for the research scholar to tackle the following research related tasks:
   a) Identifying appropriate information sources
   b) Critically analysing information
   c) Using the information to extend and communicate knowledge across subject fields
   d) Searching up to ten databases and electronic resources simultaneously
   e) Making research effective
   f) Managing information obtained for research
   g) Receiving results in a common format
   h) Linking to individual databases for more specialised searching
   i) Selecting favourite resources and e-journals, saving searches and records, and setting up email alerts

ICT APPLICATION IN DIFFERENT CATEGORIES OF RESEARCH

Applications of ICT have many effects on research. They can be classified into three categories which include:

1. Applications of ICT in Pre-data Analysis
2. Applications of ICT in Data Analysis
3. Applications of ICT in Post-data Analysis

Applications of ICT in Pre-Data Analysis

Applications of ICT in pre-data analysis refers to the activities of how ICTs are applied on activities of social science research before reaching the stage of data analysis.

ICT application in pre-data analysis includes:

1. Literature Search, Article Availability, Thesis and Dissertation Availability
2. Content Search
3. Literature Tracking
4. Data Collection

Literature Search

1. Traditionally, researchers needed to perform a manual search on hard copies of literature in libraries whereby this is a tedious effort and the search results were limited. On the contrary, with ICT application, a lot of research materials, literature, and artefacts can be searched using Internet search engines and databases. Following are some sources:

- **Shodhganga:** The Shodhganga@INFLIBNET Centre provides a platform for research students to deposit their Ph.D. theses and make it available to the entire scholarly community in open access. The repository has the ability to capture, index, store, disseminate, and preserve thesis submitted by the researchers. It is an Indian theses repository where one can search and download the theses.
- **Google Scholar:** Google Scholar provides a simple way to broadly search for scholarly literature. From one place, one can search across many disciplines and sources-articles, theses, books, abstracts and court opinions, from academic publishers, professional societies, online repositories, universities, and other websites. Google Scholar helps you find relevant work across the world of scholarly research.
- **Microsoft Academic Search:** This is a search engine through which one can find information about academic papers, authors, conferences, journals, and organisations from multiple sources.
- **Mendeley:** Mendeley is a free reference manager and academic social network that can help a researcher to organise his/her research, collaborate with others online, and discover the latest research.
- **SSRN:** The SSRN, formerly known as Social Science Research Network, is a repository and international journal devoted to the rapid dissemination of scholarly research in the social sciences and humanities and more.
- **Elsevier:** It is a Dutch information and analytics company and one of the world's major providers of scientific, technical, and medical information.
- **Project MUSE:** This project is a non-profit collaboration between libraries and publishers. It is an online database of peer-reviewed academic journals and electronic books. Project MUSE contains digital humanities and social science content from over 250 university presses and scholarly societies around the world. A researcher can obtain information concerned with research from this source.
- **JSTOR:** It is a digital library founded in 1995. Originally containing digitised back issues of academic journals, it now also includes books and other primary sources, and current issues of journals. It provides full-text searches of almost 2,000 journals.
- **Indian Citation Index (ICI):** ICI is developed by "The Knowledge Foundation" (a registered society) and is one of the pioneers in India to develop, preserve, disseminate, and serve customised knowledge products and services to the scholarly world. Currently, ICI is publishing ~170 journals from India with one of the specific motives to promote knowledge content published in local national journals and bridge the gap between the content sources and content users via World Wide Web. Full text online access of its journals is available to the users.

Content Search

When applying ICT applications to research, researchers can utilise the softcopy literature's search or find function (also called content search) to search for specific keywords or phrases in which this is more effective and productive. Further, online search using technology is inexpensive and can improve the identification of relevant sources of literature. Such content search also enables a researcher to evaluate quickly whether a particular article or thesis is worthy for his or her deeper review. Moreover, the content search also helps a qualitative researcher to count the frequency of certain keywords that appear in an interviewed transcript more effectively.

Literature Tracking

Traditionally, researchers had to sort, classify, and store all their literature or artefacts that they had reviewed into computer folders or physical folders/place holders. Researchers also need to create their own tracking mechanism, e.g., in a word document or spreadsheet format to track and manage their reviewed literature so that they can reuse or refer to in the future. Doing these manually can be a daunting task. With the advancement of ICT, researchers can still use the old approaches but more and more researchers now are using software like Mendeley which can help manage, share, and discover the literature contents and contacts that they had reviewed. Using software like Mendeley to track a researcher's literature saves time and effort and makes it capable to manage lots of literature that was not possible without ICT application.

Data Collection

With the help of application of ICT, Data collection can be done via online, web-based, or Internet survey. Using this purpose-built software and Internet technology (which is a green technology in data collection) can reduce the time and cost to collect surveyed responses from the respondents. Not only can an online survey be administered more effectively, but the data collected in its original format can also be input directly into the statistical software.

Important Data Collection Applications of ICT

1. ***Google Forms:*** *Google Forms is a tool that allows collecting information from users via a personalised survey or quiz.*
2. ***SurveyMonkey:*** *SurveyMonkey is an online survey development cloud-based software as a service company. The company provides free, customizable surveys, as well as a suite of paid back-end programs that include data analysis, sample selection, bias elimination, and data representation tools.*

Applications of ICT in Data Analysis

Application of ICT in data analysis includes the ICTs which are applied on activities during the stage of data analysis and can be divided into:

1. Quantitative Data Analysis
2. Qualitative Data Analysis

Quantitative Data Analysis

The exploratory factor analysis, multiple regression, t-test, and Analysis of Variance (ANOVA) are some common data analysis techniques used among researchers conducting quantitative research. There are also some advanced and popular data analysis techniques like path analysis, covariance-based Structural Equation Modeling (SEM), Partial Least Squares Structural Equation Modeling (PLS-SEM), hierarchical regression analysis, and hierarchical linear modelling. Following are ICT applications for analysing quantitative data:

- **Statistical Package for Social Science (SPSS):** SPSS Statistics is a software package used for interactive or batched, statistical analysis. it was acquired by IBM in 2009. The current versions (2015) are named IBM SPSS Statistics. SPSS is a widely used program for statistical analysis in social science. It is also used by market researchers, health researchers, survey companies, government, education researchers, marketing organisations, and data miners. The current version is more advanced and rich with a lot of features and functionalities.
- **R:** R is a language and environment for statistical computing and graphics. 'R Foundation for Statistical Computing' provides support for the R project and other innovations in statistical computing. This foundation works for development of future innovations in software for statistical and computational research.
- **Matrix Laboratory (MATLAB):** MATLAB is a multi-paradigm numerical computing environment and proprietary programming language developed by MathWorks.
- **Microsoft Excel:** Microsoft Excel is a spreadsheet developed by Microsoft for Windows, macOS, Android, and iOS. It features calculation, graphing tools, pivot tables, and a macro programming language called Visual Basic for Applications.
- **SAS Statistical Analysis Software (SAS):** SAS is used all over the world in approximately 118 countries to solve complex business problems. SAS is so powerful that it can understand any type of data and it can access data from any software and any format.
- **GraphPad Prism:** GraphPad Prism is a commercial scientific 2D graphing and statistics software available for both Windows and Macintosh computers. It provides statistical guidance for novices. It also reviews whether appropriate data analysis has been made.
- **Minitab:** Minitab is a leading provider of software and services for quality improvement and statistics education.

Qualitative Data Analysis

The following statistical software packages are for qualitative data analysis:

- **NVivo:** NVivo is a qualitative data analysis computer software package produced by QSR International. It has been designed for qualitative researchers working with very rich text-based and/or multimedia information, where deep levels of analysis on small or large volumes of data are required.
- **ATLAS.ti:** ATLAS.ti is a powerful workbench for the qualitative analysis of large bodies of textual, graphical, audio, and video data.
- **MAXQDA:** MAXQDA is a world-leading software package for qualitative and mixed methods research and the only leading QDA (Qualitative Data Analysis) software to offer identical features on Windows and Mac. It is one of the most comprehensive programs in the field and is used by thousands of researchers in more than 150 countries around the world.
- **SPSS Text Analytics:** IBM® SPSS® Text Analytics for Surveys uses powerful natural language

processing (NLP) technologies specifically designed for survey text. It leads the way in unlocking open-ended responses for better insight and statistical analysis.

- **Transana:** Transana is a software package used to analyze digital video or audio data in certain qualitative research.
- **Aquad:** Aquad is a free computer-assisted qualitative data analysis software that supports content analysis of open data in qualitative research in psychology, education, sociology, philosophy, medicine, ethnography, politics, etc.

Application of ICT in Post-Data Analysis

Application of ICT in post-data analysis refers to the ICTs that are applied on activities of research after completing the stage of data analysis which covers:

1. References and Bibliography Compilation
2. Article and Thesis/Dissertation's Discussion among Researchers, Supervisors, Supervisees, etc.
3. Plagiarism Detection
4. Journal Manuscripts Submission

References and Bibliography Compilation

Traditionally, before the advent of ICT, researchers used to compile references and bibliography manually. They literally resorted to typing in to build the entire section of the references or bibliography, and then followed by sorting them in ascending order. After the application of ICT in research, while researchers are writing, they can use citation or reference management software to help select citations and populate the references or bibliography automatically. This type of software can improve researchers' efficiency and accuracy while preparing their articles or theses.

The following software is used for referencing and bibliography compilation:

- **EndNote:** EndNote is a commercial reference management software package, used to manage bibliographies and references when writing essays and articles. It is produced by Clarivate Analytics.
- **Zotero:** Zotero is a free and open-source reference management software to manage bibliographic data and related research materials (such as PDF files). Notable features include web browser integration, online syncing, and generation of in-text citations, footnotes, and bibliographies.

Article and Thesis/Dissertation's Discussion

In the course of producing an article, thesis, or dissertation, there are needs for discussions or communications among researchers, supervisors, and supervisees or during the viva voce in the traditional approaches. Now due to the advanced application of ICT to facilitate sharing of research materials, seeking comments from subject matter experts enable analytics to monitor papers published, as well as following some scholarly works.

There are online platforms or websites which can be used for such discussion:

- **Academia.edu:** Academia.edu is a commercial social networking website for academics. The website allows its users to create a profile, upload their work, and select areas of interests. After that the user can browse the networks of people with similar interests. The platform can be used to share papers, monitor their impact, and follow the research in a particular field.
- **ResearchGate:** ResearchGate is the professional network for scientists and researchers. It helps researchers to connect and makes it easy for them to share and access scientific output, knowledge, and expertise. ResearchGate adds a researcher's research to his/her profile to make it discoverable by other researchers. It also asks research related questions to experts and gets answers for the benefit of researchers.

Plagiarism Detection

Traditionally, plagiarism acts were slow and hard to detect as the authority of universities or journals were dependent on readers to identify them manually while they were reading through the submitted articles or theses/dissertations. With the advancement of ICT, readers or researchers can use a plagiarism checker software available in the market. Some examples are provided here:

- **Grammarly:** Grammarly is a technology company that develops a digital writing tool using artificial intelligence and natural language processing. Grammarly's product offers grammar checking, spell checking, and plagiarism detection services along with suggestions about writing clarity, concision, vocabulary, delivery style, and tone.
- **Article Checker:** Article Checker is another plagiarism checking software. Article Checker is a free product and is used to secure articles from being copied or duplicated.

- **Turnitin:** Turnitin is an American commercial, Internet-based plagiarism detection service launched in 1997.
- **Duplichecker:** Duplichecker is an entirely free plagiarism checker tool.
- **Unplag:** Unplag is an online based plagiarism and grammar detection tool.

Journal Manuscripts Submission

Before the advent of ICT, journal manuscript submission used to be via email communications between researchers/authors and journal's editors/coordinators. With ICT application in research, web-based journal manuscript management and peer-review software, electronic manuscript submission, or management systems are commonly used among the community of researchers and journals/publishers. Using such systems can reduce their time of submission and checking the status of publishing. Moreover, using such systems can greatly improve the productivity and quality of work to administer the submission as well as the peer-review management in which miscommunications, loss, or delay of communication can be minimised.

The following are the applications of ICT for manuscripts' submission and publicising:

- **Elsevier:** It is a publishing company publishing journals and manuscripts submitted by researchers.
- **Wiley:** It is a journal and manuscript publishing company with a huge library housing journals from all over the world.

4 **Sage Publishing:** This is a US-based publishing company publishing journals submitted by researchers from all over the world.

PLAGIARISM

A lot of material in text, audio, and video forms is available on the Internet. This material covers all subjects belonging to different streams. This material is conceived by specialists. Some people download this material, copy it word by word, and paste it in toto. They claim this material as their own. This is called Plagiarism. Plagiarism is an illegal activity and the person practising plagiarism is liable to legal action as he violates copyright norms.

Types of Plagiarism:

1) ***Direct or Verbatim Plagiarism*** *occurs when an author copies the text of another author, word for word, without the use of quotation marks or attribution, thus passing it as his or her own.*
2) ***Auto-Plagiarism****, also known as* ***Self-Plagiarism*** *or* ***Duplication****, happens when an author reuses significant portions of his or her previously published work without attribution. Thus, this type of plagiarism is most likely to involve published researchers.*
3) ***Paraphrasing Plagiarism*** *involves the use of someone else's writing with some minor changes in the sentences and using it as one's own. Even if the words differ, the original idea remains the same and plagiarism occurs.*
4) ***Accidental Plagiarism*** *refers to plagiarism which has occurred because of neglect, mistake, or unintentional paraphrasing.*
5) ***Mosaic plagiarism*** *refers to the process of a user using synonyms to replace the words of existing authors in an attempt to pass off the work as their own. Typically, this act of plagiarism often involves the user retaining the author's main, central idea or argument and simply replacing a few words to pass off the work as their own.*

Some Vital Facts

1) Duplichecker is entirely a free plagiarism checker tool.
2) With ICT application, a lot of research materials, literature and artefacts can be searched using Internet search engines and databases.
3) MAXQDA is one of the most comprehensive programs in the field and is used by thousands of researchers in more than 150 countries around the world.
4) ICT tools help a research scholar in searching up to ten databases and electronic resources simultaneously.
5) Elsevier is a publishing company publishing journals and manuscripts submitted by researchers

Practice Exercise

General Questions Format

1. Which of the following signifies the contribution of ICT in research?
   a) Relevant information
   b) Easier analysis
   c) Precise information
   d) Convenience for research scholar
   (A) Only c and d (B) Only b
   (C) a, b, c, and d (D) Only a

2. Which of the following software is used to analyse qualitative data?
   (A) SPSS (B) ATLAS.ti
   (C) Transana (D) All of these

3. Plagiarism detection is initiated in ________ analysis.
   (A) Data (B) Pre-Data
   (C) Post-Data (D) Mega-Data

4. Names of software are given under Column I and its nature of research activity is given under Column II. Match the software with nature of research activity and choose the correct code among the codes given below:

Column I (Software)	Column II (Research Activity)
a) Turnitin	i) Journal submission
b) Wiley	ii) Plagiarism detection
c) ResearchGate	iii) Bibliographic compilation
d) Zotero	iv) Discussion on article

Codes:	(a)	(b)	(c)	(d)
(A)	ii	i	iv	iii
(B)	iii	iv	i	ii
(C)	i	iv	ii	iii
(D)	ii	iii	iv	i

5. Which of the following is NOT covered by ICT application in pre-data analysis?
   a) Article availability
   b) Journal submission
   c) Literature tracking
   d) Theses discussion
   (A) Only b and d (B) Both a and b
   (C) Only d (D) a, b, c, and d

6. Shodhganga is managed by
   (A) SPARC (B) INFLIBNET
   (C) IMPRESS (D) RISE

7. A research scholar collaborates his research work with another researcher online through
   (A) SSRN (B) Shodhganga
   (C) Mendeley (D) Elsevier

8. Which of the following is the most comprehensive software to analyse qualitative data?
   (A) Aquad (B) NVivo
   (C) ATLAS.ti (D) MAXQDA

9. Consider the statement, "The repository has the ability to capture, index, store, disseminate, and preserve theses submitted by the researchers". Which repository is being referred in the statement?
   (A) Google scholar (B) Shodhganga
   (C) Elsevier (D) SSRN

10. Which plagiarism refers to the process of a user using synonyms to replace the original words of a text?
    (A) Mosaic (B) Accidental
    (C) Paraphrasing (D) Self

11. Ultimate objective of applying ICT tools in the research is to make research ________.
    (A) acceptable (B) verifiable
    (C) effective (D) autonomous

12. Which software helps research scholars by asking research related questions to experts and obtain answers for researchers?
    (A) ResearchGate (B) Academia.edu
    (C) EndNote (D) Zotero

13. Which ICT software helps a researcher in sample selection?
    (A) SurveyMonkey (B) Google Forms
    (C) Minitab (D) MATLAB

14. Which ICT software provides statistical guidance to novice researchers?

(A) Microsoft Excel

(B) SPSS

(C) R Foundation

(D) GraphPad Prism

KEY

1. C	**2.** D	**3.** C	**4.** A	**5.** A	**6.** B	**7.** C
8. D	**9.** B	**10.** A	**11.** C	**12.** A	**13.** A	**14.** D

Assertion–Reason Format

1. Assertion (A): Plagiarism is an undesirable activity of ICT application in research.

Reason (R): Misutilisation of ICT is found in the field of research also.

(A) Both A and R are true and R is correct explanation of A

(B) Both A and R are true but R is not correct explanation of A

(C) Both A and R are false

(D) A is true but R is false

2. Assertion (A): Application of ICT in research has helped even novice research scholars to excel in research.

Reason (R): Traditional approach to research did not yield much even for experienced researchers.

(A) Both A and R are true and R is correct explanation of A

(B) Both A and R are true but R is not correct explanation of A

(C) A is true but R is false

(D) A is false but R is true

3. Assertion (A): Shodhganga is a repository inviting research scholars to write theses.

Reason (R): Thesis written through Shodhganga enjoy creditability status.

(A) Both A and R are false

(B) Both A and R are true but R is not correct explanation of A

(C) A is true but R is false

(D) Both A and R are true and R is correct explanation of A

4. Assertion (A): JSTOR is a big source of literature search for a research scholar.

Reason (R): It is a huge library housing thousands of journals helping in search of literature.

(A) Both A and R are false

(B) Both A and R are true but R is not correct explanation of A

(C) A is true but R is false

(D) Both A and R are true and R is correct explanation of A

5. Assertion (A): Analysis of quantitative data through ICT software is demand of today's research ethics.

Reason (R): ICT-based analysis of quantitative data provide autonomy to research scholar regarding its interpretation and generalisation.

(A) A is true but R is false

(B) Both A and R are false

(C) Both A and R are true but R is not correct explanation of A

(D) Both A and R are true and R is correct explanation of A

6. Assertion (A): Plagiarism detection is the responsibility of the research scholar before submitting thesis to Shodhganga.

Reason (R): Shodhganga does not own responsibility of plagiarism detection afterwards.

(A) Both A and R are true and R is correct explanation of A

(B) Both A and R are true but R is not correct explanation of A

(C) Both A and R are false

(D) A is false but R is true

7. Assertion (A): Managing bibliography in a thesis requires skill.

Reason (R): EndNote is a software package to manage bibliographies.

(A) Both A and R are true and R is correct explanation of a

(B) Both A and R are true but R is not correct explanation of A

(C) A is true but R is false

(D) A is false but R is true

8. **Assertion (A):** Application of ICT in research does not diminish the significance of traditional approach to research.

Reason (R): Even during non-ICT era, researchers used to acquire research degrees at different levels.

(A) Both A and R are true and R is correct explanation of A

(B) A is true but R is false

(C) A is false but R is true

(D) Both A and R are true but R is not correct explanation of A

9. **Assertion (A):** Indian Citation Index (ICI) has been developed by 'Knowledge Commission'.

Research (R): ICI is an effective means of helping a research scholar in literature search.

(A) A is true but R is false

(B) A is false but R is true

(C) Both A and R are true and R is correct explanation of A

(D) Both A and R are true but R is not correct explanation of A

10. **Assertion (A):** ICT tools have introduced the concept of literature tracking in research.

Reason (R): Literature tracking by software like Transana saves a lot of time and effort of the researcher.

(A) Both A and R are false

(B) Both A and R are true but R is not correct explanation of A

(C) A is true but R is false

(D) A is false but R is true

KEY

1. B **2.** C **3.** A **4.** D **5.** A **6.** C **7.** B **8.** C **9.** B **10.** A

Questions Asked in Previous NET Exams

1. Plagiarism in research is _______.

(UGC NET JUNE 2019)

(A) creative use of previous data

(B) copying unscrupulously and making use of it

(C) quoting someone and citing him/her

(D) referring to previous data and working over it with new objectives

KEY

1. B

6 Research and Statistics Terminology

Credibility: A researcher's ability to demonstrate that the object of a study is accurately identified and described, based on the way in which the study was conducted

Data: Recorded observations, usually in numeric or textual form

Generalizability: The extent to which research findings and conclusions from a study conducted on a sample population can be applied to the population at large.

Hypothesis: A tentative explanation based on theory to predict a causal relationship between variables.

Population: The target group under investigation, as in all students enrolled in first-year composition courses taught in traditional classrooms. The population is the entire set under consideration. Samples are drawn from populations.

Random sampling: Process used in research to draw a sample of a population strictly by chance, yielding no discernible pattern beyond chance.

Response Rate: In survey research, the actual percentage of questionnaires completed and returned.

Rigor: Degree to which research methods are scrupulously and meticulously carried out in order to recognize important influences occurring in a experiment.

Sampling Frame: A listing that should include all those in the population to be sampled and exclude all those who are not in the population

Sample: The population researched in a particular study. Usually, attempts are made to select a "sample population" that is considered representative of groups of people to whom results will be generalized or transferred.

T-Test: A statistical test used to determine if the scores of two groups differ on a single variable. For instance, to determine whether writing ability differs among students in two classrooms, a t-test could be used.

Triangulation: The use of a combination of research methods in a study. An example of triangulation would be a study that incorporated surveys, interviews, and observations. Also called multi-modal methods

Unique case orientation: A perspective adopted by many researchers conducting qualitative observational studies; researchers adopting this orientation remember every study is special and deserves in-depth attention. This is especially necessary for doing cultural comparisons.

Validity: The degree to which a study accurately reflects or assesses the specific concept that the researcher is attempting to measure.

Verisimilitude: Having the resemblance of truth; in research, it refers to the probability that the research findings are consistent with occurrences in the "real world." A work of art, or any part of a work of art, has verisimilitude if it seems realistic. The word verisimilitude is derived from the Latin words *verum* and *similis* meaning "truth" and "similar." A verisimilitudinous narration or account has details, subjects, and characters that seem similar or true to real life.

Bias: is a loss of balance and accuracy in the use of research methods. It can creep into research via the sampling frame, random sampling, or non-response. It can also occur at other stages in research, such as while interviewing, in the design of questions, or in the way data are analysed and presented. Bias means that the research findings will not be representative of, or generalisable to, a wider population.

Coded Data: refers to a way of recording material at data collection, either manually or on computer, for analysis. The data are put into groups or categories, such as age groups, and each category is given a code number. Data are usually coded for convenience, speed, computer storage space and to permit statistical analysis.

Hard Data: Precise data, like dates of birth or income levels, which can reasonably be subjected to precise forms of analysis, such as statistical testing.

Pilot-Study: A trial, both to examine the effectiveness of various aspects of the proposed research, such as procedures for data gathering, and to aid the completion of detailed project plans.

Questionnaire: A questionnaire comprises the questions to be asked of respondents. There are three main types questionnaires to be used in face to face or telephone interviews; self completion questionnaires, which are read, completed and returned by respondents; and computer administered questionnaires, which allow more complex question patterns than paper questionnaires.

Soft Data: Data such as people's ideas and opinions. A characteristic of qualitative research.

Co-operative Studies: Surveys sponsored by a number of organisations, mostly sharing the same agreed data.

Filter: When only a section of the total sample are required to answer the question, e.g. if the question asks why people are dissatisfied with a particular service, only those who are dissatisfied should answer the question. Those who are satisfied will skip to the next question that is to be asked of all respondents.

Key Informants: They are people who are known to have knowledge, experience, expertise and/or opinions specific to the subject of the research, and who are selected as data sources for this reason.

Grey Documents: It is literature which is not 'published' in the conventional sense, but is usually available on request.

Extraneous Variables: When an experiment is seeking to monitor the impact of one variable on another (like counselling on stress level), attention has to be paid to other variables which could have an impact (that is, other factors which could affect a person's stress level). These other variables are called 'extraneous'.

Method/Methodology: While 'method' describes what you as a researcher have done, methodology is about your reasons for doing it.

Narrative or biographical approaches: They are used to research are primarily qualitative, and include gathering/ using data in the form of diaries, stories and life histories.

Predictive Research: It is concerned with identifying indicators of future behaviour or demand in a population on the basis of the current behaviour and demands of a sample.

Replicability/Replication: As the name suggests, replication is the process of repeating a study undertaken by someone else, in the sense of using the same methodology. Commonly the location and research subjects will be different.

Standard Variables: In social science research, especially in survey analysis, there are a range of variables which are usually considered 'standard' or 'key', in the sense that some analysis is undertaken in relation to each of them. The list will change according to the specific research project, but may well include such items as age, gender, socio-economic group, ethnicity, employment, family background, housing.

Symposium: Symposium is a public meeting or conference to discuss a topic in which participants make presentations. A symposium can be a one-time conference or a regular meeting, but it will probably include some amount of discussion or public speeches on a particular subject. Many people who attend symposiums will be part of the audience for many of the presentations, but during the course of the event, give their own presentation or be part of a panel discussion. The participants of symposium have full knowledge of the topic which is discussed in symposium.

Seminar: A seminar is a meeting of small group of students/participants in which certain topic is discussed while complying with academic instructions. Seminar is held in an academic institution, if organised by a college or university and in a meeting hall if organised by an organisation. There is a focus on some particular subject or topic which is discussed by the participants under the supervision and guidance of a seminar leader, generally teacher, who is an expert on the subject/topic under discussion.

Conference: Conference is a formal meeting of people with a shared interest over an agenda, typically one that takes place over several days.

Workshop: It is a meeting at which a group of people engage in intensive discussion and activity on a particular subject or project. A workshop is also organised by an institution, government department or private organisation to impart training in certain skill or launching awareness campaign for general public over various social, safety and health issues.

Research Paper: A research paper is a piece of academic writing based on its author's original research on a particular topic, and the analysis and interpretation of the research findings. It can also be taken as miniature of thesis. Research paper can be read in a seminar, conference or symposium in. A researcher is free to expresses his creative abilities in compiling a research paper

Research Journal: A research journal is a systematic record, usually written, that is kept by a researcher for the purpose of observing and reflecting on phenomena relevant to a particular research study. .

The impact factor (IF) of a Research Journal: It is a measure of the frequency with which the average article in a journal has been cited in a particular year. It is used to measure the importance or rank of a journal by calculating the times it's articles are cited.

The g-index: The g-index is a measure of quality of a research journal and is also for quantifying productivity in research, based on publication record. It was suggested in 2006 by Leo Egghe. It is calculated by considering number of citations received by research articles published in the journal.

The h-index: It is a quality of a resrach journal which to measures both the productivity and citation impact of the publications of a research scientist or scholar. The index is based on the set of the scientist's most cited papers and the number of citations received in other publications.

i10 index: I10-Index has been a measure design and develop by Google Scholar and used in Google's My Citations feature. It measures the quality of a research journal on the ground of the number of publications with at least 10 citations.

STATISTICS TERMINOLOGY

Continuous Data: A set of data is said to be continuous. The values / observations belonging to it may take on any value within a finite or infinite interval. One can count, order and measure continuous data. For example height, weight, temperature.

Dispersion: The data values in a sample are not all the same. This variation between values is called dispersion.

Sample: A sample is a group of units selected from a larger group (the population). By studying the sample it is hoped to draw valid conclusions about the larger group.

Mean: The mean is an estimator available for estimating the population mean. It is a measure of location, commonly called the average. Mean is calculated by taking the sum of all the data values and dividing by the total number of data values:

$$\bar{x} = \frac{5+3+54+93+83+22+17+19}{8} = 37$$

Imp. In mean sum of deviations is zero

Median: The median is the value halfway through the ordered data set, below and above which there lies an equal number of data values.

Ordered Data: 4 6 7 13 27 28 34 36 39 42 48 54 65 68 69 70 72 74 95 96 99

Median: 48, leaving ten values below and ten values above

With an even number of data values, for example 20, we have:

Ordered Data: 2 6 7 8 24 30 33 41 43 47 49 50 51 55 57 65 71 85 91 94

Median: Halfway between the two 'middle' data points - in this case halfway between 47 and 49, and so the median is 48

Mode: The mode is the most frequently occurring value in a set of data. There can be more than one mode if two or more values are equally common. Suppose the results of an end of term Statistics exam were distributed as follows:

Student:	Score:
1	94
2	81
3	56
4	90
5	70
6	65
7	90
8	90
9	30

Then the **mode** (most common score) is 90, and the **median** (middle score) is 81.

Nominal Data: A set of data is said to be nominal if the values / observations belonging to it can be assigned a code in the form of a number where the numbers are simply labels. One can count but not order or measure nominal data. For example, in a data set males could be coded as 0, females as 1; marital status of an individual could be coded as Y if married, N if single.

Ordinal Data: A set of data is said to be ordinal if the values / observations belonging to it can be ranked (put in order). one can count and order, but not measure, ordinal data.

Null Hypothesis: The null hypothesis, H0, represents a theory that has been put forward, either because it is believed to be true or because it is to be used as a basis for argument, but has not been proved. For example, in a clinical trial of a new drug, the null hypothesis might be that the new drug is no better, on average, than the current drug. We would write H0: there is no difference between the two drugs on average.

Alternative Hypothesis: The alternative hypothesis, H1, is a statement of what a statistical hypothesis test is set up to establish. For example, in a clinical trial of a new drug, the alternative hypothesis might be that the new drug has a different effect, on average, compared to that of the current drug. We would write H1: the two drugs have different effects, on average.

Outlier: An outlier is an observation in a data set which is far removed in value from the others in the data set. It is an unusually large or an unusually small value compared to the others. An outlier might be the result of an error in measurement, in which case it will distort the interpretation of the data. For example referring to following set of ordered data

32, 35, 39, 41, 4300, 46, 51, 56

In above case 4300 is outlier noted down inadvertently.

Skewness: Skewness is defined as asymmetry in the distribution of the sample data values. It is just like outlier

Statistical Inference: Statistical Inference makes use of information from a sample to draw conclusions (inferences) about the population from which the sample was taken.

Chi square (X^2) test: is used to investigate whether distributions of categorical variables differ from one another i.e. to test null hypothesis or alternative hypothesis.

Analysis of Variance (ANOVA): is a statistical method for making simultaneous comparisons between two or more means; a statistical method that yields values that can be tested to determine whether a significant relation exists between variables.

Factor analysis: It summarizes information contained in a large number of variables and condenses it into a smaller number of factors containing variables that are interrelated. For example: In a study about a group of players, their characteristics of height, weight, hobbies, activities, and interests might be summarized, using factor analysis, as size (height and weight) and lifestyles (the combination of hobbies, activities, and interests). In so doing, five variables have been condensed into two separate factors.

Combined Mean: When total figures of two sets are given along with their respective means.

A combined mean is calculated as follows:

$$\bar{z} = \frac{n_x\bar{X} + n_y\bar{y}}{n_x + n_y}$$

In above formula n_x and n_y are two sets depicting total number number of people in them and $\bar{X}, \bar{y}$ are their respective means. Example: In set n_x the number of people = 35 and mean = 75. In set n_y, the number of people = 55 and mean = 95.

Then combined mean is:

$$Z = \frac{(35 \times 75) + (55 \times 95)}{35 + 55} = 71.36$$

Meta-analysis: A statistical procedure for combining the results of several studies on the same topic.

Correlation: It is a statistical measurement of the relationship between two variables. Possible correlations range from +1 to –1. A zero correlation indicates that there is no relationship between the variables. A correlation of –1 indicates a perfect negative correlation, meaning that as one variable goes up, the other goes down. A correlation of +1 indicates a perfect positive correlation, meaning that both variables move in the same direction together.

Correlation coefficient: A statistic representing how closely two variables co-vary; it can vary from –1 (perfect negative correlation) through 0 (no correlation) to +1 (perfect positive correlation).

Correlation analysis: It is a method of statistical evaluation used to study the strength of a relationship between two, numerically measured, continuous variables (e.g. height and weight)

Population parameter: It is a numerical summary of a population.

Sample statistic: Any numerical measure computed from a subset of the population (typically a sample) is a statistic.

Scatter Diagram: A scatter diagram is a tool for analyzing relationships between two variables. One variable is plotted on the horizontal axis and the other is plotted on the vertical axis. The pattern of their intersecting points can graphically show relationship patterns. Most often a scatter diagram is used to prove or disprove cause-and-effect relationships.

Frequency distribution: It is an arrangement of the values that one or more variables take in a sample. Each entry in the table contains the frequency or count of the occurrences of values within a particular group or interval, and in this way, the table summarizes the distribution of values in the sample.

Categorical Data: Categorical variables represent types of data which may be divided into groups. Examples of categorical variables are race, sex, age group, and educational level.

Two-Way Tables: When analysis of categorical data is concerned with more than one variable, **two-way table** (also known as contingency tables) are employed. These tables provide a foundation for statistical inference, where statistical tests question the relationship between the variables on the basis of the data observed. A **two-way table** presents categorical data by counting the number of observations that fall into each group for two variables, one divided into rows and the other divided into columns. For example, suppose a survey was conducted of a group of 20 individuals, who were asked to identify their hair and eye color. A two-way table presenting the results might appear as follows:

Eye Colour

Hair Colour	Blue	Green	Brown	Black	Total
Blonde	2	1	2	1	6
Red	1	1	2	0	4
Brown	1	0	4	2	7
Black	1	0	2	0	3
Total	5	2	10	3	20

Rank correlation: It is the relationship between different rankings of the same set of items. A rank correlation coefficient measures the degree of similarity between two rankings, and can be used to assess its significance.

Sampling error: It is incurred when the statistical characteristics of a population are estimated from a subset, or sample, of that population. Since the sample does not include all members of the population, statistics on the sample, such as means and quantiles, generally differ from parameters on the entire population. For example, if one measures the height of a thousand individuals from a country of one million, the average height of the thousand is typically not the same as the average height of all one million people in the country. Since sampling is typically done to determine the characteristics of a whole population, the difference between the sample and population values is considered a sampling error. Sampling error decreases with increase in the sample size as it increases the proportion of representation of the population.

Statistical Probability: Being able to draw a conclusion from a sample and generalising it to a wider population

Hypothesis Testing: it is always null hypothesis which is tested. Alternative hypothesis is also called Research Hypothesis. While testing Null Hypothesis, some error is committed which is explained as follows:

Null Hypothesis	Accepted	Rejected
Not True	✓ α error	×
True	×	✓ β error

Normal Distribution Curve:

NORMAL DISTRIBUTION CURVE

The normal distribution is a continuous probability distribution that is symmetrical on both sides of the mean, so the right side of the center is a mirror image of the left side.

The area under the normal distribution curve represents probability and the total area under the curve sums to one.

Most of the continuous data values in a normal distribution tend to cluster around the mean, and the further a value is from the mean, the less likely it is to occur. The tails are asymptotic, which means that they approach but never quite meet the horizon (i.e. x-axis).

For a perfectly normal distribution the mean, median and mode will be the same value , visually represented by the peak (center) of the curve.

The normal distribution is often called the bell curve because the graph of its probability density looks like a bell. It is also known as called Gaussian distribution, after the German mathematician Carl Gauss who first described it.

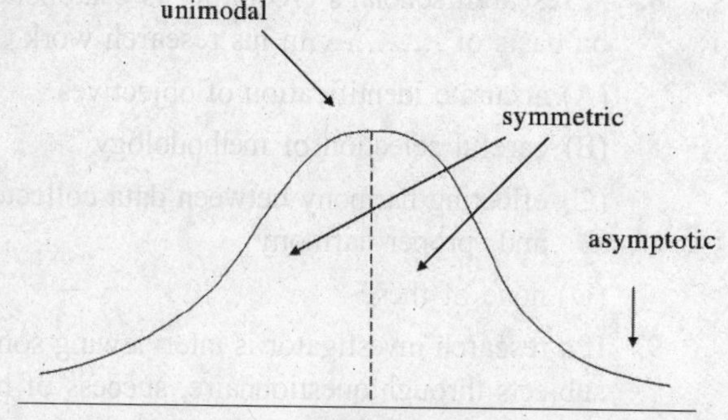

Practice Exercise

General Questions Format

1. Soft data is a characteristics of .... research.
(A) quantitative (B) empirical
(C) qualitative (D) None of these

2. A target group under investigation is called
(A) population (B) sample
(C) core group (D) quota

3. Data capable of statistical testing is called ...... data.
(A) soft (B) hard
(C) copied (D) primary

4. Degree of influence of a research method in an experiment is called
(A) pilot (B) creditability
(C) rigor (D) none of these

5. Research conducted on marginalised communities is called...........Research.
(A) Emancipatory (B) Co-operative
(C) Communal (D) Hypothetic

6. Combining various research methods in a study is called
(A) Bilingual (B) Triangulation
(C) Speculation (D) Accumulation

7. Data are recorded observations in ...... form
(A) numerical (B) textual
(C) both (D) neither

8. A research scholar's credibility is established on basis of ....in his research work
(A) accurate identification of objectives
(B) careful selection of methodology
(C) effecting harmony between data collected and proper harmony
(D) none of these

9. If a research investigator is interviewing some subjects through questionnaire, success of his exercise depends on
(A) Number of subjects covered
(B) Response Rate
(C) Nature of questions asked
(D) Time devoted to the job

10. Random sampling is exclusively depending on...............factor.
(A) survey (B) collection
(C) chance (D) relevance

11. A research work found to be unfit for generalisation, is said to contain
(A) snag (B) deadlock
(C) overestimation (D) bias

12. Versimilitude establishes a research work findings applicable to
(A) real world
(B) objectives
(C) supernatural forces
(D) None of these

13. A methodology used in a research process justifies the reason of
(A) doing a particular research
(B) chalking out the objects
(C) collecting a particular type of data
(D) All of above

14. Replicability is found in............Research.
(A) Pre-project (B) Longitudinal
(C) Predictive (D) All of above

15. A Narrative Research is basically of .... nature.
(A) quantitative (B) periodical
(C) repetitive (D) qualitative

16. Average value of a sample population is calculated by taking
(A) mode (B) mean
(C) mode (D) None of above

17. Data so collected to assess values of variations in temperature is termed as........data
(A) alternative (B) stratified
(C) ordered (D) None of these

18. An unusually small or large value in a data so collected is termed as
(A) Outlier (B) Skewness
(C) Dispersion (D) None of these

19. Dispersion indicates that data values in a sample are
(A) different (B) same
(C) repeated (D) None of above

20. Null Hypothesis puts forward a theory that serves as........of an argument.

(A) inference (B) basis

(C) structure (D) None of these

21. Find out Mode in the following set of data.

42, 98,76,42,21, 78, 42, 65, 42, 57.

(A) 21 (B) 65

(C) 42 (D) 98

22. Which of the following is NOT possible in case of an ordinal data?

(A) measurement (B) counting

(C) ordering (D) All of above

23. A statement put to hypothesis testing is taken under...........hypothesis.

(A) working (B) alternative

(C) null (D) None of these

24. Head department of Commerce calls a meeting of incumbents under the supervision of a lecturer of Public Finance to discuss a topic on Public Finance to assess the level of understanding of the participants on that topic. This meeting will be known as

(A) Symposium (B) Workshop

(C) Seminar (D) Conference

25. Public awareness campaigns are launched through

(A) Workshop (B) Seminar

(C) Symposium (D) None of these

KEY

1. C	2. A	3. B	4. C	5. A	6. B	7. C
8. A	9. B	10. C	11. D	12. A	13. A	14. B
15. D	16. B	17. D	18. A	19. A	20. B	21. C
22. A	23. B	24. C	25. A			

Assertion–Reason Format

1. **Assertion (A):** Difference between sample value and population value yields sampling error

Reason (R): Statistical characteristics of a sample are estimated from entire population.

(A) Both A and R are true and R is correct explanation of A

(B) Both A and R are true but R is not correct explanation of A

(C) A is true but R is false

(D) A is false but R is true

2. **Assertion (A):** Categorical data are analysed through two-way table

Reason (R): Two-way table is also known as contingency table

(A) Both A and R are true and R is correct explanation of A

(B) Both A and R are true but R is not correct explanation of A

(C) Both A and R are false

(D) A is false but R is true

3. **Assertion (A):** Age and gender are taken as independent variables in a research analysis

Reason (R): A Research analysis is not successful without including independent variable.

(A) Both A and R are false

(B) A is true but R is false

(C) Both A and R are true and R is correct explanation of A

(D) Both A and R are true but R is not correct explanation of A

4. **Assertion (A):** Replicability in research is the process of repeating a research

Reason (R): A research work is repeated by different research scholar using same methodology analysing new aspects not touched in the original research

(A) A is true but R is false

(B) Both A and R are true and R is correct explanation of A

(C) A is false but R is true

(D) Both A and R are true but R is not correct explanation of A

5. **Assertion (A):** Common feature between a seminar and symposium is discussion on a topic by the participants.

Reason (R): In spite of common feature seminar and symposium are put in separate brackets.

(A) Both A and R are true but R is not correct explanation of A

(B) Both A and R are false

(C) A is true but R is false

(D) A is false but R is true

6. **Assertion (A):** A research paper presents a researcher's original idea regarding that research.
   Reason (R): No research work is feasible until a research paper is released.
   (A) Both A and R are true and R is correct explanation of A
   (B) Both A and R are false
   (C) A is true but R is false
   (D) A is false but R is true
7. **Assertion (A):** Audience of a symposium comprises of research scholars.
   Reason (R): Only research related problems are discussed in a symposium.
   (A) Both A and R are false
   (B) A is false but R is true
   (C) A is true but R is false
   (D) Both A and R are true but R is not correct explanation of A
8. **Assertion (A):** A biased research work can also be service to society
   Reason (R): An outlier makes a research work biased one.
   (A) A is false but R is true
   (B) A is true but R is false
   (C) Both A and R are true and R is correct explanation of A
   (D) Both A and R are true but R is not correct explanation of A
9. **Assertion (A):** Null hypothesis necessitates replication of research
   Reason (R): Chi square test determines whether a hypothesis is null or alternative
   (A) A is true but R is false
   (B) A is false but R is true
   (C) Both A and R are true and R is correct explanation of A
   (D) Both A and R are true but R is not correct explanation of A
10. **Assertion (A):** Ordinal data are of representative nature.
   Reason (R): Qualitative research is conducted by obtaining ordinal data
   (A) Both A and R are true and R is correct explanation of A
   (B) Both A and R are true but R is not correct explanation of A
   (C) A is true but R is false
   (D) Both A and R are false

KEY

1. C **2.** B **3.** A **4.** B **5.** A **6.** C **7.** A **8.** A **9.** B **10.** D

Questions Asked in Previous NET Exams

1. The major characteristic of correlation analysis is to seek out **(UGC NET JUNE 2019)**
   (A) Differences among variables
   (B) Variations among variables
   (C) Association among variables
   (D) Regression among variables
2. The sum of deviations taken from which of the descriptive statistical measure is always equal
   (A) Mean (B) Median
   (C) Mode (D) Percentile
3. Which of the following provides more latitude to the researcher for creative expression ?
   (UGC NET JULT 2018)
   (A) Thesis writing
   (B) Writing of a research article
   (C) Presentation of a conference paper
   (D) Preparing a research synopsis
4. In which of the following activities, potential for nurturing creative and critical thinking is relatively greater? **(UGC NET JULY 2018)**
   (A) Preparing research summary
   (B) Presenting a seminar paper
   (C) Participation in research conference
   (D) Participation in a workshop
5. In which of the following arrangements a wider spectrum of ideas and issues may be made possible? **(UGC NET NOVEMBER 2017)**
   (A) Workshop mode
   (B) Conference
   (C) Symposium
   (D) Research Article

6. In a research on the effect of child-rearing practices on stress -proneness of children in competing school projects, the hypothesis formulated is that 'child rearing practices do influence stress- proneness'. At the data-analysis stage a null hypothesis is advanced to find out the tenability of research hypothesis. On the basis of the evidence available, the null hypothesis is rejected at 0.01 level of significance. What decision may be warranted in respect of the research hypothesis? **(UGC NET JULY 2016)**
   (A) The research hypothesis will also be rejected.
   (B) The research hypothesis will be accepted.
   (C) Both the research hypothesis and the null hypothesis will be rejected.
   (D) No decision can be taken in respect of the research hypothesis.
7. Which of the following are the characteristics of a seminar? **(UGC NET DECEMBER 2015)**
   (a) It is a form of academic instruction.
   (b) It involves questioning, discussion and debates.
   (c) It involves large groups of individuals.
   (d) It needs involvement of skilled persons.
   Select the correct answer from the codes given below
   (A) (b) and (c) (B) (b) and (d)
   (C) (b), (c) and (d) (D) (a), (b) and (d)
8. Which of the following statements is true in the context of the testing of a hypothesis? **(UGC NET EXAM DECEMBER 2015)**
   (A) It is only the alternative hypothesis that can be tested.
   (B) It is only the null hypothesis that can be tested.
   (C) Both, the alternative and the null hypotheses can be tested.
   (D) Both, the alternative and the null hypotheses cannot be tested.
9. A researcher is interested in studying the prospects of a particular political party in an urban area. What tool should he prefer for the study? **(UGC NET DECEMBER 2015)**
   (A) Rating scale (B) Interview
   (C) Questionnaire (D) Schedule
10. "Male and female students perform equally well in a numerical aptitude test." This statement indicates a: **(UGC NET JUNE 2015)**
    (A) Statistical hypothesis
    (B) Research hypothesis
    (C) Null hypothesis
    (D) Directional hypothesis
11. "Sampling Cases" means **(UGC NET EXAM DECEMBER 2014)**
    (A) Sampling using a sampling frame
    (B) Identifying people who are suitable for research
    (C) Literally the researcher's brief case
    (D) Sampling of people, newspapers, television programmes etc.
12. The population information is called parameter while the corresponding sample information is known as **(UGC NET DECEMBER 2013)**
    (A) Universe (B) Inference
    (C) Sampling design (D) Statistics
13. Sampling error decreases with the **(UGC NET DECEMBER 2013)**
    (A) decrease in sample size
    (B) increase in sample size
    (C) process of randomization
    (D) process of analysis
14. With which one of the following techniques communality is associated ? **(UGC NET SEPTEMBER 2013)**
    (A) Univariate analysis
    (B) Factor analysis
    (C) Case studies
    (D) SWOT analysis
15. The population information is called parameter while the corresponding sample information is known as **(UGC NET DECEMBER 2013)**
    (A) Universe (B) Inference
    (C) Sampling design (D) Statistics
16. A research paper **(UGC NET JUNE 2013)**
    (A) is a compilation of information on a topic.
    (B) contains original research as deemed by the author.
    (C) contains peer-reviewed original research or evaluation of research conducted by others.
    (D) can be published in more than one journal.

17. A workshop is **(UGC NET JUNE 2013)**
(A) a conference for discussion on a topic.
(B) a meeting for discussion on a topic.
(C) a class at a college or a university in which a teacher and the students discuss a topic.
(D) a brief intensive course for a small group emphasizing the development of a skill or technique for solving a specific problem.

18. Which one of the following is an indication of the quality of a research journal? **(UGC NET DECEMBER 2012)**
(A) Impact factor (B) h-index
(C) g-index (D) i10-index

19. Identify the incorrect statement: **(UGC NET DECEMBER 2012)**
(A) A hypothesis is made on the basis of limited evidence as a starting point for further investigations.
(B) A hypothesis is a basis for reasoning without any assumption of its truth.
(C) Hypothesis is a proposed explanation for a phenomenon.
(D) Scientific hypothesis is a scientific theory.

20. Conferences are meant for **(UGC NET JUNE 2012)**
(A) Multiple target groups
(B) Group discussions
(C) Show-casing new Research
(D) All the above

21. A hypothesis is a **(UGC NET DECEMBER 2011)**
(A) law (B) canon
(C) postulate (D) supposition

22. Workshops are meant for **(UGC NET DECEMBER 2011)**
(A) giving lectures
(B) multiple target groups
(C) showcase new theories
(D) hands on training/experience

23. A research paper is a brief report of research work based on **(UGC NET JUNE 2011)**
(A) Primary Data only
(B) Secondary Data only
(C) Both Primary and Secondary Data
(D) None of the above

24. A group of experts in a specific area of knowledge assembled at a place and prepared a syllabus for a new course. The process may be termed as **(UGC NET JUNE 2011)**
(A) Seminar (B) Workshop
(C) Conference (D) Symposium

25. A null hypothesis is **(UGC NET DECEMBER 2009)**
(A) when there is no difference between the variables
(B) the same as research hypothesis
(C) subjective in nature
(D) when there is difference between the variables

26. Which one of the following methods serve to measure correlation between two variables? **(UGC NET DECEMBER 2010)**
(A) Scatter Diagram
(B) Frequency Distribution
(C) Two-way table
(D) Coefficient of Rank Correlation

27. Which of the four data sets have more dispersion? **(UGC NET DECEMBER 2009)**
(A) 88 91 90 92 89 91
(B) 0 1 1 0 –1 –2
(C) 3 5 2 4 1 5
(D) 0 5 8 10 –2 –8

28. A null hypothesis is **(UGC NET DECEMBER 2009)**
(A) when there is no difference between the variables
(B) the same as research hypothesis
(C) subjective in nature
(D) when there is difference between the variables

29. We use Factorial Analysis: **(JUNE 2009)**
(A) To know the relationship between two variables
(B) To test the Hypothesis
(C) To know the difference between two variables
(D) To know the difference among the many variables

30. A statistical measure based on entire population is called parameter while measure based upon sample is known as **(UGC NET JUNE 2008)**
   (A) Sample parameter
   (B) Inference
   (C) Statistics
   (D) None of these

31. The importance of correlation co-efficient lies in the fact that **(UGC NET JUNE 2008)**
   (A) There is a linear relationship between the correlated variables.
   (B) It is one of the most valid measures of statistics.
   (C) It allows one to determine the degree or strength of association between two variables.
   (D) It is a non-parametric method of statistical analysis.

32. To test null hypothesis, a researcher uses **(UGC NET JUNE 2007)**
   (A) t test (B) ANOVA
   (C) x^2 (D) All of above

33. The number of students in four classes A,B,C,D, and their respective mean marks obtained by each of the class are given below:
   The combined mean of the marks of four classes together will be
   (UGC NET DECEMBER 2006)

	Class A	**Class B**	**Class C**	**Class D**
Number of Students	10	40	30	20
Arithmatic Mean	20	30	50	15

   (A) 32 (B) 50
   (C) 20 (D) 15

KEY

1. 3	**2.** 1	**3.** 3	**4.** 3	**5.** 2	**6.** B	**7.** D
8. B	**9.** C	**10.** C	**11.** D	**12.** D	**13.** B	**14.** B
15. D	**16.** C	**17.** D	**18.** A	**19.** D	**20.** D	**21.** D
22. C	**23.** B	**24.** A	**25.** A	**26.** A	**27.** D	**28.** A
29. C	**30.** C	**31.** C	**32.** C	**33.** A		

Unit III

Comprehension

1 Comprehension

CONCEPT

Comprehension means to solve MCQs given along with an unseen passage on any issue. Comprehension passage generally carries social, economic, political, cultural, sports, and scientific issues. In various competitive exams like IAS/PCS, IBPS, SBI, SSC, Railways, CDS, NDA, and many other competitions, a paragraph is given along with MCQs. MCQs are based on the content of the passage. Similarly, comprehension passage is given along with MCQs in NET Paper 1. Paragraphs in NET are generally from theory topics of syllabus of Paper 1. If a candidate is well prepared in theory topics, he/she can solve comprehension very easily.

Why Comprehension in Syllabus of NET Paper 1?

Solving comprehension is not new to NET aspirants. UGC has put it in NET syllabus with a purpose to test an aspirant's skill to comprehend, i.e., ability to understand. As NET aspirants are going to join teaching and research streams, it is essential that they should possess the skill to read content and understand it. Such skill helps teachers and research scientists to resolve various academic and non-academic issues during their career.

Steps to Solve Comprehension Passage

Solving comprehension is a time-consuming task. Following steps can help an aspirant to solve it in a minimum possible time.

1) Aspirants should have complete knowledge of theory topics as generally comprehension contains the content from theory topics, particularly environment, communication, and higher education.
2) In the first round, read the paragraph along with the questions.
3) In the second round, read the paragraph again while keeping the questions in mind and try to locate that part of the given paragraph where answer to a question is enveloped.
4) Try to catch the theme of the passage as there are questions on the message conveyed by the paragraph.
5) Practice maximum passages to build confidence and sharpen time management skill.
6) In the exam comprehension should be solved after solving all other questions. If one starts solving it in the early moments of the exam, there is apprehension of trapping, confusion, and wastage of time which will consume time to be given to other questions.
7) An aspirant should not panic over length and language of the paragraph.
8) One should possess reasonable vocabulary.
9) Aspirant should be relaxed while solving comprehension.

Practice Exercise

General Questions Format

PARAGRAPH – 1

Directions: *Read the following passage carefully and choose the appropriate answer to the questions which follow the passage.*

Monsoon has always been bountiful for the people of Bundi in the relatively water-scanty state of Rajasthan. After a short span of scorching summer, rain brings hope and joy.

About 30 kms from Bundi on way to Menal lies a waterfall called Bhimlat, spread in an area of six kms away from the effects of human invasions. The water falls from about 60 m. making it a fine tourist spot. The sound of splashing water is audible from a distance. The zigzag roads and the green countryside view, along with the flocks of cattle, present a natural kaleidoscope. The beautiful lakes of Jait Sagar, Dhoondaleshwar, near Talwas, Dugari overflow and flood the surrounding region.

Rameshwar, around 20 kms from Bundi, has a waterfall falling on the Shivalingam from the top. At Rameshwar Mahadev, the cave temple of Shiva is surrounded by Aravalli ranges. Interestingly, all these falls have temples relating to Shiva and his deities. There are a few rock painting sites around.

As raindrops fall on the parched land and aroma of wet soil rises into the air, swings or jhoolas are hung from trees and decorated with flowers. Young women dress up in green and sing to celebrate and welcome the advent of the monsoon. Teej, essentially a women's festival, is dedicated to the goddess Parvati, commemorating her union with Lord Shiva.

During the monsoon, the local Kajli Teej festival is uniquely celebrated. In Bundi, it is celebrated on the third day of Bhadra whereas it is celebrated on the third day of Shravana in other parts of the state. The festival begins with the traditional procession of Teejmata in a decorated palanquin passing through the main bazaar. Though the main function lasts for two days, the celebrations continue till Janmashtmi.

A drive in the countryside finds all streams overflowing with water. Reservoirs like the Bharda dam, 15 kms from the district headquarters, and Guda Dam, 22 kms From the nearby Hindoliki Paal overflow, converting it into a fine picnic spot. A taste of the local Bhutta roasted in the coal oven and served with salt and lemon is delightful. A local recipe Kutta Baati made up of roasted wheat balls soaked in oil is also quite popular in the season. It is served with a special curry and garlic sauce.

1. Surroundings of Bundi become picnic spots during monsoon because
   (A) monsoon makes various dams overflow leading to creation of waterfalls which attract tourists.
   (B) excess water due to rains attract tourists from water-scanty Bundi to the surrounding spots.
   (C) lakes like Jait Sagar become an ideal spot for boating.
   (D) monsoon creates an ideal environment for roaming, strolling, eating, and enjoying local stuff.

2. Young women of Bundi region dress up in green, which signifies their gesture of
   (A) celebrating reunion of lord Shiva and Parvati.
   (B) welcoming advent of monsoon.
   (C) displaying rituals of Bundi to the tourists.
   (D) swaying jhoolas.

3. Which of the following is NOT true according to the passage?
   (A) During monsoon Bundi becomes the best bet for the tourists from all over India.
   (B) Majority of the temples in Bundi belong to Shiva and his deities.
   (C) Different lakes and water bodies surrounding Bundi are the basic source of attraction for tourists.
   (D) Teej Mata festival is celebrated in Bundi with full peoples' participation.

4. The author, in the passage, has portrayed Bundi a............tourist spot.
   (A) promising (B) well-established
   (C) seasonal (D) water-scanty

5. Author points out which common feature of different waterfalls around Bundi? All....
   (A) have zigzag approach
   (B) have temples relating to lord Shiva and his deities
   (C) make the surrounding lakes overflow
   (D) are surrounded by Aravalli hills

6. Author's experience at Bundi and around seems to be full of
   (A) adventure (B) exploration
   (C) research (D) rejoicing

7. Which of the following is NOT part of celebrations of advent of monsoons at Bundi?
   (A) Boat festival at Dhoondaleshwar Mahadev
   (B) Traditional procession of Teej Mata
   (C) Swaying of jhoolas by women
   (D) Preparation of seasonal foodstuff

8. "....effects of human invasions", as mentioned in the paragraph, signifies the effects of
   (A) wars (B) encroachments
   (C) pollution (D) vested interests

KEY

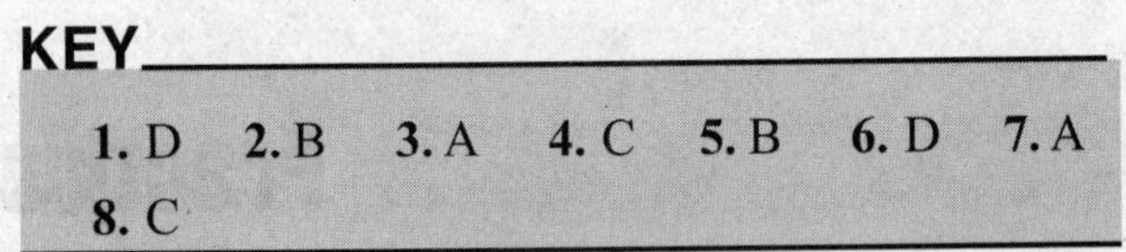

1. D 2. B 3. A 4. C 5. B 6. D 7. A 8. C

PARAGRAPH – 2

Directions: *Read the following passage carefully and choose the appropriate answer to the questions which follow the passage.*

The Constitution guarantees every citizen the fundamental right to equality. Yet, after 50 years of independence, just one perusal of the female infant mortality figures, the literacy rates, and the employment opportunities for women is sufficient evidence that discrimination exists. Almost predictably, this gender, bias is evident in our political system as well. In the 13th Lok Sabha, there were only 43 women MPs out of total of 543; it is not a surprising figure, for never has women's representation in Parliament been more than 12 per cent.

Historically, the manifestos of major political parties have always encouraged women's participation. It has been merely a charade. So, women's organizations, denied a place on merit, opted for the last resort; a reservation of seats for women in Parliament and State Assemblies. Parties, which look at everything with a vote bank in mind, seemed to endorse this. Alas, this too was a mirage.

But there is another aspect also. At a time when caste is the trump card, some politicians want the bill to include further quotas for women from among minorities and backward castes. There is more to it. A survey shows that there is a general antipathy towards the bill.

It is actually a classic case of doublespeak: in public, politicians were endorsing women's reservation but in the backrooms of parliament, they were busy sabotaging it. The reasons are clear: Men just don't want to vacate their seats of power.

1. The problem raised in the passage reflects badly on our:

(A) Political system

(B) Social behaviour

(C) Individual behaviour

(D) Behaviour of a group of people

2. According to the passage, political parties have mostly in mind:

(A) Economic prosperity

(B) Vote bank

(C) People' welfare

(D) Patriotism

3. "Trump Card" means:

(A) Trying to move a dead horse

(B) Playing the card cautiously

(C) Sabotaging all the moves by others

(D) Making the final jolt for success

4. The sentence "Men just don't want to vacate their seats of power" implies:

(A) Lust for power

(B) Desire to serve the nation

(C) Conviction in one's own political abilities

(D) Political corruption

5. What is the percentage of women in the Lok Sabha?

(A) 10 (B) 7.91

(C) 43 (D) 9.1

KEY

1. B **2.** B **3.** D **4.** A **5.** B

PARAGRAPH – 3

Directions: *Read the following passage carefully and choose the appropriate answer to the questions which follow the passage.*

At the turn of this century, when the country was poised for major social and political reforms, a new entertainment form dawned in India-the Cinema. The 7th of July 1896 is a landmark in the history of Indian cinema when the Lumiere Brothers' Cinematography unveiled six soundless short films at Watson Hotel, Esplanade Mansion, Bombay. This was the first time a movie was shown in India. And the first exposing of celluloid in camera by an Indian and its consequent screening took place in 1899, when Harishchandra Bhatavdekar (Save Dada) shot two short films and exhibited them in Bombay. Then in 1913, Dadasaheb Phalke made Raja Harishchandra which was the first Indian movie to be made. The movies were black and white with no sound in the beginning. Then came the movies with sounds. Alam Ara was the first movie with sound and it was released in 1931.

Then emerged the films in colours. This happened only in the late 1950s. Colours brought in tremendous growth in this industry. This was a time when the musicals and a melodrama were seen everywhere. Stars like Raj Kapoor, Dilip Kumar, and Dev Anand each created a mark for themselves. 1960s and 1970s brought in action movies and stars like Dharmendra, Jeetendra, and Rajesh Khanna who were known as action heroes. Another landmark in the Indian film industry took place in 1975 and that was the launch of the 70 mm movies. Sholay, the first movie to be released as a 70 mm movie, didn't do good business in the first week. The movie became a major blockbuster later as slowly slowly people went in to see the movie.

1. Which of the following is NOT TRUE according to the paragraph?

(A) Raja Harishchandra was the first movie that was shown in India.

(B) Indian cinema emerged in the era of various socio-political reform movements.

(C) Action heroes gave a turning point to Indian cinema.

(D) Indian film producers had been producing movies according to taste of the viewers.

2. Which field of Indian cinema is highlighted the most by the author?

(A) Direction (B) Acting

(C) Photography (D) Can't say

3. Paragraph projects Dev Anand as a/an
   (A) Director (B) Actor
   (C) Musician (D) Cameraman

KEY

1. A 2. D 3. B

PARAGRAPH – 4

***Directions:** Read the following passage carefully and choose the appropriate answer to the questions which follow the passage.*

A successful teacher is one who is able to foster creative thinking, develop skills, as well as instill a desire for lifelong learning among students. Teaching is a noble profession. It is considered to be a pursuit that has the potentials to make or mar the destiny of the people. The administrators, scientists, doctors, engineers, and all other professionals are the proud products of a sound teaching order. Job of teaching is self-rewarding so far as experience, knowledge, and emotional satisfaction is concerned. In this profession you may work, earn, and remain youthful as all the time you are among the youth. The teaching community includes pre-primary and primary teachers, school teachers, subject teachers, general teachers, teachers of physical education, science, commerce, medicine, engineering and technology, and language; lecturers and readers in colleges and universities.

With ever increasing growth in population and awakening among the populace, there has been a substantial increase in the number of school teachers, particularly female teachers. Although a large number of teachers are available in humanities, yet shortage is generally felt in finding suitable hands to take up teaching jobs in engineering, medicine, technology, etc. To attract persons of the right caliber to the teaching profession, a lot has already been done to improve the working conditions of the teaching community at all levels. Teachers are permitted to appear as private candidates for various university examinations to improve their qualifications. They may also add to their income by writing books, evaluating answer sheets, or acting as invigilators, examiners, or paper setters. Private tuition work may also be a source of their additional income, particularly in big cities.

The profession demands cheerful, cool, and friendly temperament and immense patience and energy, since working with students-whether children or grown-up youth-can cause considerable strain. Persons with physical defects, such as impediment of speech, poor hearing, nervous disorders, etc. are likely to be handicapped in this profession. Teaching profession should be adopted by persons who regard it as a service to the society and are prepared to inspire and guide the youth by contributing to their success and building up their character.

1. Teaching profession demands a cool and friendly temperament as a teacher is to
   (A) work for increasing the lot of teaching community
   (B) tackle with the possible strain caused by students
   (C) reform the whole society
   (D) none of the above

2. Which of the following is NOT TRUE about the paragraph?
   (A) Teaching profession is adopted by those persons who are healthy and cheerful.
   (B) A teacher is very effective in determining the destiny of the students.
   (C) Working conditions of teaching community are effective in attracting more persons to teaching.
   (D) Population growth has paved the way for female teachers in the education field.

3. According to the author, teaching profession should be adopted by those persons who believe in
   (A) character building of the students
   (B) serving the society
   (C) motivating the students to work hard and achieve success
   (D) All of the above

4. There has been appreciable increase in the number of school teachers mainly because of
   (A) opening of more and more schools
   (B) awareness about merits of the teaching job
   (C) increase in the number of students in schools
   (D) revision in pay packets of school teachers

5. Various steps have been taken to attract persons of the right................ for appointing them as teachers.
   (A) family (B) status
   (C) caliber (D) approach

KEY

1. B 2. A 3. D 4. B 5. C

PARAGRAPH – 5

Directions: *Read the following passage carefully and choose the appropriate answer to the questions which follow the passage.*

India's first truly educational TV channel Gyan Darshan (GD) was launched on January 26, 2000. It is the solitary 24-hour satellite based education and developmental channel, by the Ministry of Human Resource Development, Govt. of India and Prasar Bharti, with Indira Gandhi National Open University (IGNOU) as a nodal agency. GD free-to-air transmission can be accessed all over the country throughout the year and round the clock without any break. GD signals can be conveniently received without any special equipment anywhere in the country. Gyan Darshan, as it entered its fourth year, went completely digital and expanded into a bouquet of channels namely GD-1, GD-2, GD-3 'Eklavya', and GD-4 'Vyas'.

In collaboration with various agencies, Gyan Darshan offers interesting and informative programmes of relevance value to specialized categories: pre-school kids, primary and secondary school children, college/ university students, youth seeking career opportunities, housewives, and many others. Major educational institutions like IGNOU, Central Institute of Educational Technology (CIET), National Council of Educational Research and Training (NCERT), Directorate of Adult Education, IITs, and other educational/developmental organizations of the country, contribute these programmes. The time slots are convenient and the programmes are reared with the help of experts in the field and experienced production teams as per international standards of production and technical quality. In addition, programmes from abroad are also telecast to offer the viewers a window to the world.

In the chain of GD channels, GD-2 is entirely devoted to interactive distance education. Its signals are available anywhere across the country through INSAT-3 C. Live interaction and teleconferencing, the latest intervention in the distance education system, etc., are available through this channel. 'Eklavya', the third GD channel, brings quality education to the students pursuing engineering education throughout the country. The lectures and course material are of IIT level. It is a 24-hour channel and is running eight courses in parallel.

Keeping the priorities of reaching out to a large number of youth, the UGC launched in August 1984, Country Wide Classroom (CWCR) for enrichment education programmes for students, teachers, and general public. In persual of the objective of providing quality education to all, a separate channel 'Vyas' was launched on 26th January, 2004. Vyas is fourth in GD channel series. The channel is student-friendly. The programmes on this 24-hour channel can be seen as a high value supplement to the students registered in various universities.

1. Gyan Darshan channel has been launched to provide education to

(A) school going kids (B) housewives

(C) job seekers (D) All of the above

2. Which of the following is NOT TRUE in the passage?

(A) Eklavya is the third in the bouquet of TV channels providing service to the students pursuing engineering education.

(B) GD channel is providing hi-tech quality education through formal and informal channels of education.

(C) Prasar Bharti is one of the governing bodies of GD channel beaming.

(D) GD channel also telecasts programmes from abroad with a view to increase general knowledge of the viewers

3. Another name of GD-4 is

(A) Eklavya

(B) Vyas

(C) Prasar Bharti

(D) Country Wide Classroom

4. Which of the following is NOT clearly revealed by the paragraph?

(A) Gyan Darshan programmes are being transmitted in colour.

(B) There was a need to launch a hi-tech educational TV channel.

(C) Gyan Darshan is imparting education with entertainment.

(D) Gyan Darshan is helping the students to prepare for competitive exams.

5. "The channel is student-friendly", as used in passage, means that

(A) Students can make friends all over the country through this channel.

(B) Programmes are prepared by keeping interests of the students in mind.

(C) Programmes are so prepared that these are easily understood and enjoyed by the students.

(D) The channel is helping the students like a friend.

6. Which of the following is NOT mentioned about Vyas in the paragraph?
   (A) It is a separate GD channel launched to provide quality higher education.
   (B) It is a completely digital channel.
   (C) The channel has been launched because institutions of higher education have failed to provide higher education.
   (D) The channel is providing 24-hour service to the students.

KEY

1. D 2. B 3. B 4. A 5. C 6. C

PARAGRAPH – 6

Directions: *Read the following passage carefully and choose the appropriate answer to the questions which follow the passage.*

Everybody wants to go to the Sariska wild life sanctuary. It is green, serene, and so close to home. But what many happy troopers don't know is that Sariska used to dance to a very different beat not too long ago. The beat of the royal drums, to be precise, heralding the arrival of Maharajas and their hunting dogs. For Sariska was the hunting preserve of the royal family of Alwar.

Early morning and evening are the best times to make trips into Sariska National Park, a project tiger reserve, though chances of spotting the big cat are few and far between. That's not just on account of diminishing tiger population, but more on account of the terrain-undulating low hills, steep escarpments, wide valleys, and hill plateaus. What you will in all likelihood see, though, are herds of deer-nilgai, chital, and sambar. Birdwatchers can spot the white-breasted kingfisher, golden-backed woodpecker, serpent eagle, grey partridge, great Indian horned owl, and other avifaunal species quite easily.

It is the drive through the park that is the most enjoyable part, though; as the paths dip down to the valley level and sinister shadows move across the silent jungle. When you are done with the animals, drive deep into the forests and into history, to the ruined fortress atop a solitary hillock at Kankwari. Here, emperor Aurangzeb imprisoned his elder brother Dara Shikoh, widely held to be the legitimate successor to the throne. On to Neelkanth, a temple town built by the Gurjara-Pratiharas, which was mysteriously submerged under a deluge of sand and rocks centuries ago. What remains is over 300 Hindu, Buddhist, and Jain temples in a spectacularly secular complex. The shrine at Naldeshwar nearby attracts hordes of pilgrims to a natural Shiva lingam formed within an old tree trunk and the little brook and seasonal waterfall below the 364 steps you climb to reach it.

1. As conveyed by the passage, Sariska National Park is situated in the state of
   (A) Madhya Pradesh (B) Karnataka
   (C) Maharashtra (D) Rajasthan
2. Author has portrayed Sariska as a place of..................importance.
   (A) religious (B) historical
   (C) faunal (D) all of the above
3. Which of the following is NOT TRUE about Sariska, according to the passage?
   (A) Project Tiger is not well established here.
   (B) History of Sariska has its roots into the Mughal emperors of Medieval India.
   (C) It is much more than merely a national park.
   (D) Its greenery and serene atmosphere leaves nothing strange and alien for the visitors.
4. Which feature of Sariska National Park has been highlighted the most by the author?
   (A) Temples (B) Habitat
   (C) Legend (D) Can't say
5. According to the author, what had been undesirable in Sariska?
   (A) Terrain topography
   (B) 364 climbing steps to Shiva lingam
   (C) Diminishing tiger population
   (D) Imprisoning of Dara Shikoh by Aurangzeb
6. The paragraph..........the reader about Sariska National Park.
   (A) informs (B) teaches
   (C) guides (D) encourages
7. The sentence "Sariska used to dance to a very different beat not too long ago" means that
   (A) Sariska was inhabited by dancers in the recent past.
   (B) Sariska was not a wild life sanctuary few years ago.
   (C) It is not very long ago when it was not easy to travel through the dense forest of Sariska as it is today.
   (D) Sariska was a reserve for hunting by an erstwhile royal family in the recent past.

KEY

1. D 2. D 3. A 4. D 5. D 6. C 7. B

PARAGRAPH – 7

Directions: *Read the following passage carefully and choose the appropriate answer to the questions which follow the passage.*

Kos Minars, that is, Mile Stones, or say Mile Pillars were erected by the Mughal Emperors on the main highways across the empire to delineate the route or mark the distance. They played a significant role in the system of governance during the Mughal period. But over the years, these significant road monuments have gone into a state of despair and are almost lost in obscurity. The geographic span of the Mughal Empire in India had about 3000 kms of roads, accounting for nearly 1000 Kos Minars, erected by Mughal monarchs (1556-1707). "Kos", a medieval measurement of distance, denoted approximately three kilometers or two miles. Thus, the distance two Kos Minars covered between them was approximately four miles.

However, no systematic study has been undertaken so far to find out as to how many Kos Minars still survive. Perhaps the reason for this apathy is that Kos Minars were always seen singly as architecturally insignificant structures. But when one looks at them as part of a much larger design, their real significance emerges. For instance, some of major cities of historical significance, monuments, and battlefields are situated on the route marked by Kos Minars. One discovers a network of caravan sarais (travelers' resting places) and baolis (stepped drinking water wells)-though some of them are extinct now-built close to Kos Minars for the comfort and benefit of travellers. Nearly 400 years later, modern highways have come up much along the same route as one delineated by Kos Minars.

Historical evidences have it that Kos Minars played an important role in day-to-day administration of the Mughal Empire. Each Kos Minar was equipped with a horse, a rider, and a drummer to relay back and forth royal messages with speed. Historians maintain that their principal function was to facilitate transport and communication. Enquiries made from the Archaeological Survey of India (ASI) reveal that so far no systematic study or census has been done to identify and count the surviving Kos Minars. Nor are all the Kos Minars protected monuments, though some of them are. Some of the Kos Minars have become victims of development, industrialization, and land encroachment. Others are on the verge of collapse and are crumbling and peeling off.So far no efforts have been made for the maintenance and upkeep of Kos Minars. Verily, Kos Minars present a great travel story, and need an immediate exercise to check their status and retrieve them from oblivion.

1. As per the passage, so far no systematic study has been conducted on Kos Minars because

(A) Minars are in such a shabby condition that no study is possible on them.

(B) Mughal Empire did not assign them the status of architecturally significant structures.

(C) No reason is given in the passage.

(D) None of these.

2. Which of the following is NOT TRUE according to the passage?

(A) Kos Minars were equipped with horses for helping tourists to facilitate their journey.

(B) Modernization and industrialization have created hurdles in the survival of Kos Minars.

(C) Mughals erected Kos Minars according to the geographical span of their empire.

(D) Kos Minars served as mile pillars throughout the whole Mughal Empire.

3. Author seems to be........about Kos Minars

(A) thrilled (B) pessimistic

(C) analytic (D) none of these

4. Which of the roles, as highlighted in the passage was significantly played by the Kos Minars during the Mughal era?

a) Bureaucratic b) Educational

c) Historical d) Philanthropic

e) All of the above

(A) All (B) Only a and c

(C) Only a, b, and d (D) Only b and d

KEY

1. D **2.** A **3.** D **4.** D

PARAGRAPH – 8

Directions: *Read the following passage carefully and choose the appropriate answer to the questions which follow the passage.*

Few would have dreamt in their wildest dreams before the fateful May 11 and May 13, 1998 that the trundling elephant that India had all along been compared to in the Western media would and could metamorphose overnight into a ferocious lion that could not only roar but charge and kill anyone daring to cast an evil eye. Few could have foretold that the five underground nuclear tests at the Pokhran range in Rajasthan in May 1998, catapulting this nation of 950 million people overnight into a superpower on its own, would send shock waves across Beijing, Islamabad, Washington, the European capitals, and even Tokyo.

The Buddha smiled once way back in 1974 and he smiled five times on May 11, 1998 on the Buddha Poornima day and May 13 when Indian's Prime Minister, Mr. Atal Bihari Vajpayee proudly announced to the nation and the rest of the world about India venturing into the exclusive club of nuclear weapon states as part of the national security shield even as he congratulated the top scientists of India over their great achievement.

India is a country wedded to peace and non-violence and her great sons like Lord Buddha, Ashoka, and Gandhiji had been living examples to prove this gospel. But India as a self-respecting nation would not propagate the peace of the graveyard or the non-violence of the weak; it is a pity that our non-violence has been mistaken by many as our weakness and many assume that India is a nation of weak-willed people. Time and again our leaders have reminded the world community that India has an inalienable right to defend its freedom, sovereignty, and its ancient heritage and that it would take appropriate measures at the appropriate time to make its defensive preparedness as strong as it could. No nation need be apologetic, if it tries its best to defend its freedom. And a nation like India that has suffered centuries of foreign subjection has every right-more than any other nation-to strengthen its defence. Moreover, India cannot take any chances when it lives in a hostile nuclear environment, with Pakistan receiving all sorts of smuggled nuclear and missile material from North Korea, China, and other sources and China itself having conducted several nuclear tests and armed herself to the teeth.

In times of crises, India has to fall back upon its resources to defend itself, its hard won freedom, its economic gains, and its own ancient cultural legacy. It has had three wars with Pakistan and another disastrous war with China and both the countries are still in illegal occupation of Indian territory. India hopes that the smiling Buddha on May 11, 1998 would have conveyed the right message to the right quarters that evil designs on this country would not be tolerated. It was this logic, too, that prevented India from signing both NPT and CTBT- treaties that are discriminatory in nature. When the BJP government came to power, they had announced that India would go nuclear. The decision of the Vajpayee government to go nuclear does not emanate from any kind of jingoism or sabre-rattling mentality; it arises from the supreme concern to preserve the integrity of a nation described by many of its detractors as a 'functioning anarchy'. Far from it, India has conveyed to the rest of the world that it has the best brains that can excel the best in the world.

1. As per the paragraph, "Buddha smiled five times" on
   (A) May 11, 1998 (B) May 13, 1998
   (C) Both (D) NOA
2. According to the author our non-violence has been mistaken as
   (A) Others' weakness
   (B) Lack of willingness to fight
   (C) Our weakness
   (D) Trying to prove a gospel
3. How many wars India has fought with Pakistan?
   (A) One (B) Two
   (C) Three (D) Four
4. Decision by the government to go nuclear is because of
   (A) Sabre-rattling mentality
   (B) Concern to preserve the integrity
   (C) Some kind of jingoism
   (D) Functioning anarchy
5. According to the passage, India has the right to
   (A) Strengthen its offence
   (B) Fight with neighbours
   (C) Strengthen its defence
   (D) Be hostile

KEY

1. C 2. C 3. C 4. B 5. C

PARAGRAPH – 9

Directions: *Read the following passage carefully and choose the appropriate answer to the questions which follow the passage.*

A recent report in Newsweek says that in American colleges, students of Asian origin outperform not only the minority group students but the majority whites as well. Many of these students must be of Indian origin, and their achievement is something we can be proud of. It is unlikely that these talented youngsters will come back to India, and that is the familiar brain drain problem. However, recent statements by the nation's policy-makers indicate that the perception of this issue is changing. 'Brain bank' and not 'brain drain' is the more appropriate idea, they suggest since the expertise of Indians abroad is only deposited in other places and not lost.

This may be so, but this brain bank, like most other banks, is one that primarily serves customers in its neighbourhood. The skills of the Asians now excelling in America's colleges will mainly help the USA. No matter how significant, what non-resident Indians do for India and what their counterparts do for other Asian lands is only a by-product.

But it is also necessary to ask, or be reminded, why Indians study fruitfully when abroad. The Asians whose accomplishments Newsweek records would have probably had a very different tale if they had studied in India. In America they found elbow room, books, and facilities not available and not likely to be available here. The need to prove themselves in their new country and the competition of an international standard they faced there must have cured mental and physical laziness. But other things helping them in America can be obtained here if we achieve a change in social attitudes, specially towards the youth.

We need to learn to value individuals and their unique qualities more than conformity and respectability. We need to learn the language of encouragement to add to our skill in flattery. We might also learn to be less liberal with blame and less tight-fisted with appreciation, especially.

1. Among the many groups of students in American colleges, Asian students:
(A) are often written about in magazines like Newsweek.
(B) are most successful academically.
(C) have proved that they are as good as the whites.
(D) have only a minority status like the blacks.

2. The student of Asian origin in America include:
(A) a fair number from India.
(B) a small group from India.
(C) persons from India who are very proud.
(D) Indians who are the most hard working of all.

3. In general, the talented young Indians studying in America:
(A) have a reputation for being hard working.
(B) have the opportunity to contribute to India's development.
(C) can solve the brain drain problem because of recent changes in policy.
(D) will not return to pursue their careers in India.

4. There is talk now of the 'brain bank'. This idea:
(A) is a solution to the brain drain problem.
(B) is a new problem caused partly by the brain drain.
(C) is a new way of looking at the role of qualified Indians living abroad.
(D) is based on a plan to utilize foreign exchange remittances to stimulate research and development.

5. The brain bank has limitations like all banks in the sense that:
(A) a bank's services go mainly to those near it.
(B) small neighbourhood banks are not visible in this age of multinationals.
(C) only what is deposited can be withdrawn and utilized.
(D) no one can be forced to put his assets in a bank.

6. The author feels that what non-resident Indians do for India:
(A) will have many useful side effects.
(B) will not be their main interest and concern.
(C) can benefit other Asian countries, as a by-product.
(D) will be of service to the world community.

7. The performance of Indians when they go to study in the West:
(A) shows the fruits of hard work done by school teachers in India.
(B) should remind us that knowledge and wisdom are not limited by the boundaries of race and nation.
(C) is better than what people in the West expect of non-whites.
(D) is better than what it would have been if they had studied in India.

8. The high level of competition faced by Asian students in America:
(A) helps them overcome their lazy habits.
(B) makes them lazy since the facilities there are good.
(C) makes them worried about failing.
(D) helps them prove that they are as good as the whites.

9. The author feels that some of the conditions other than the level of facilities that make the West attractive:
(A) are available in India but young people do not appreciate them.
(B) can never be found here because we believe in conformity.
(C) can be created if our attitudes and values change.
(D) can also give respectability to our traditions and customs.

10. One of the ways of making the situation in India better would be:
   (A) to eliminate flattery from public life.
   (B) to distinguish between conformity and respectability.
   (C) to give appreciation and not be tight-fisted.
   (D) to encourage people and not merely flatter them.

KEY

1. C **2.** A **3.** D **4.** C **5.** A **6.** B **7.** D
8. D **9.** C **10.** C

PARAGRAPH – 10

Directions: *Read the following passage carefully and choose the appropriate answer to the questions which follow the passage.*

As we enter the new millennium, the challenge for humankind is to transform the existing economy into one that does not threaten or destroy the environment. This Environmental Revolution can be compared to the Agricultural Revolution and the Industrial Revolution of the past.

Archaeological findings reveal that the great civilizations at the dawn of history pursued economies that were fairly destructive to the environment. However, the people then were unable to change what they were doing because they did not understand what was happening. Either that or they could not persuade their governments to bring about the necessary changes.

Today, however, we have the power to bring about changes to stop the destruction of the environment because we are becoming more aware of how our lives are shaped by the environment. Even when events do not directly affect us, reports in the mass media expose us to the extensive damage caused by such events. Fishery collapses, water shortages, rainforests burning uncontrollably, sudden deaths of birds, dolphins, and fish, record heat waves, and raging storms that cause widespread destruction only serve to increase our awareness that our survival depends on the weather which in turn depends on our ability to maintain the ecological balance.

Decades before, it was mainly environmental activists who played a dominant role in drawing attention to the gradual destruction of the environment. Today, directors of large corporations, government ministers, prominent scientists, and intelligence agencies are speaking out on the need to change. They have a clear sense of what has to be done for they know that the current economy cannot take us as far as we want to go under the present circumstances.

People can now make decisions that will help restructure economies. For example, companies who want to buy timber products can decide whether to buy from companies that are managing forests in a responsible manner or from companies suspected of illegal logging practices. Consumers in the United States, for example, can choose to buy power from 'green' sources as consumers become more aware of different energy sources available. Governments can also decide to become a 'green consumer' by opting for sources of electricity that are climate-friendly and buy paper that has a high recycled content.

Time is of the essence and the new economic practices must be accepted quickly. The only way this can be done is to spread accurate information quickly and on a regular basis. For example, information on climatic changes and of how the inefficient use of water can lead to food shortages must be shared. Media coverage of environmental trends and events must also be stepped up. Can the global economy be restructured in time before environmental deterioration in turn, leads to economic decline?

1. Why do you think the author compared the Environmental Revolution to the Agricultural Revolution and the Industrial Revolution?
   (A) These Revolutions had a great impact on the lives of people.
   (B) These Revolutions took place a long time ago.
   (C) These Revolutions took place over many, many years.
   (D) These Revolutions brought about bloodshed.

2. Why couldn't people in the past stop the destruction of the environment?
   (A) They were ignorant, simple, peaceful people.
   (B) They did not realize that their actions were slowly destroying the environment.
   (C) They did not know people in the governments.
   (D) Their governments did not believe that the environment was being destroyed.

3. The people of today have become more aware of the relationship between the weather, environment, and global economies because of
   (A) the havoc caused by storms and heat waves
   (B) the efforts of governments
   (C) extensive media coverage
   (D) collapsed fisheries

4. Who is paying more attention to preserving the environment today?

(A) Environmental activists as opposed to big companies

(B) Strong individuals as opposed to weak individuals

(C) Public corporations as opposed to individuals

(D) Ecologists as opposed to economists

5. How can business decisions affect economies and consequently, the environment?

(A) If a country buys paper from only one company, the other paper-producing companies will have no market and so their revenue will decrease.

(B) If countries decide to buy paper with a high recycled content, then paper-producing countries must heed to this demand, otherwise there will be no demand for their products.

(C) Paper-producing countries must plant more trees to meet the demand for paper, otherwise they may not have any more trees to produce paper.

(D) Companies wishing to buy paper often scrutinize the type of paper because they only want to buy paper with a high recycled content.

6. What is the writer trying to convey in the expression 'Time is of the essence'?

(A) The very essence of life is time

(B) It is important

(C) We must not delay

(D) Time is life

7. The writer emphasizes two elements in the last paragraph: time and

(A) climatic changes

(B) environmental trends

(C) the sharing of information

(D) food shortages

KEY

1. A **2.** B **3.** C **4.** C **5.** B **6.** C **7.** C

Questions Asked in Previous NET Exams

PARAGRAPH – 1

(UGC NET DECEMBER 2004)

Directions: *Read the following passage carefully and choose the appropriate answer to the questions which follow the passage.*

Each day at the Shantiniketan school starts with the Sarswati Vandana. When painting competitions are held in the school, images of Hindu god and goddesses are the most common. Sanskrit is a favourite subject of many a student. Nothing new about it, except that the 1200-odd students studying in the Hindu-run school are Muslims.

In 1983 when Ranchodbhai Kiri started Shantiniketan in the all-Muslim Juhapura area of Ahmedabad in Gujarat, only 20% students were Muslims. But when riots involving the Muslims of Juhapura and the Hindus of nearby jivrajpark -vejalpur affected the locality, Hindus started migrating. Today, all the students are Muslims and the school is an unparalled example of harmony. In the 2002, when a section of inflamed Muslims wanted the school closed, parents of the students stood like a wall behind it.

Shantiniketan's principal says, "We never thought of moving the school out of the area because of the love and affection of the local Muslims. Indeed, they value the high standard of education which we have set". Such is the reputation of the school that some of the local Muslim strongmen accused of involvement in the communal riots are willing to protect the school during the riots.

The parents of Shantiniketan's students believe that it's the best school when it comes to the quality of teaching. A large number of students have gone both for graduation and post-graduation studies. Significantly, the only Muslim teacher in the 40-member teaching staff, Husena Mansuri, teaches Sanskrit. In fact, she is so happy at the school that she recently declined the principalship of another Muslim-run school.

Some of the students' entries in the recent school painting competition were truly moving. One drew a picture of Bharat Mata with a mosque and a temple, while another portrayed a boy tying a Rakhi to his sister. Truly, Shantiniketan is a beacon of hope that, despite the provocation from both communities, Hindus and Muslims can live side-by-side with mutual respect.

1. How does the Shantiniketan school start the day?

(A) National Anthem (B) Prayer

(C) Sarswati Vandana (D) Puja

2. Write the subject which is preferred by most of the students.

(A) Hindi (B) English

(C) Sanskrit (D) Gujarati

3. Who protects the school during riot times?

(A) Local muslims (B) Hindus

(C) Politicians (D) Christians

4. Who is the teacher of Sanskrit?
   (A) Ranchodbhai Kiri (B) Manisha Vakil
   (C) Husena Mansuri (D) Husena Khatoon
5. What is the hope despite the communal riots?
   (A) Hindus and Muslims cannot live side-by-side
   (B) Hindus and Muslims can live side-by-side
   (C) Only Hindus can live
   (D) Only Muslims can live

KEY

1. C 2. C 3. A 4. C 5. B

PARAGRAPH – 2

(UGC NET DECEMBER 2005)

Directions: *Read the following passage carefully and choose the appropriate answer to the questions which follow the passage.*

Knowledge creation in many cases requires creativity and idea generation. This is especially important in generating alternative decision support solutions. Some people believe that an individual's creative ability stems primarily from personality traits such as inventiveness, independence, individuality, enthusiasm, and flexibility. However, several studies have found that creativity is not so much a function of individual traits as was once believed, and that individual creativity can be learnt and improved. This understanding has led innovative companies to recognise that the key to fostering creativity may be the development of an idea-nurturing work environment. Idea generation methods and techniques, to be used by an individual or groups, are consequently being developed. Manual methods for supporting idea generation such as brainstorming in groups can be very successful in certain situations. However, in other situations, such an approach is either not economically feasible or not possible. For example, manual methods in group creativity sessions will not work or will not be effective when: (1) there is no time to conduct a proper idea generation session; (2) there is a poor facilitator (or no facilitator at all); (3) it is too expensive to conduct an idea generation session; (4) the subject matter is too sensitive for a face-to-face session; or (5) there are not enough participants, the mix of participants is not optimal, or there is no climate for idea generation. In such cases, computerised idea-generation methods have been tried with frequent success. Idea-generation software is designed to help stimulate a single user or group to produce new ideas, options, and choices. The user does all the work, but the software encourages and pushes something like a personal trainer. Although idea-generation software is still relatively new, there are several packages in the market. Various approaches are used by the idea-generation software to increase the flow of ideas to the user. IdeaFisher for example, has an associate lexicon of English language that cross references words and phrases. These associative links based on analogies and metaphors; make it easy for the user to be fed words related to a given theme. Some software packages use questions to prompt the user towards new, unexplored patterns of thought. This helps a user to break out of cyclical thinking patterns, conquer mental blocks, and is ideal with bouts of procrastination.

1. The author in this passage has focussed on
   (A) knowledge creation
   (B) idea generation
   (C) creativity
   (D) individual traits
2. Fostering creativity needs an environment of
   (A) decision support system
   (B) idea-nurturing
   (C) decision support solutions
   (D) alternative individual factors
3. Manual methods for support of idea generation, in certain occasions:
   (A) are alternatively effective
   (B) can be less expensive
   (C) do not need a facilitator
   (D) require a mix of optimal participants
4. Idea-generation software works as if it is a
   (A) stimulant
   (B) knowledge package
   (C) user-friendly trainer
   (D) climate creator
5. Mental blocks, bouts of procrastination, and cyclical thinking patterns can be won when
   (A) innovative companies employ electronic thinking methods
   (B) idea-generation software prompts questions
   (C) manual methods are removed
   (D) individuals acquire a neutral attitude towards the software

KEY

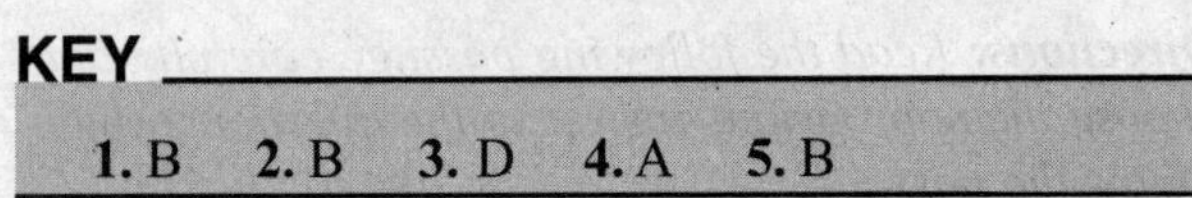

1. B 2. B 3. D 4. A 5. B

PARAGRAPH – 3

(UGC NET DECEMBER 2006)

Directions: *Read the following passage carefully and choose the appropriate answer to the questions which follow the passage.*

After almost three decades of contemplating Swarovski-encrusted navels on increasing flat abs, the Mumbai film industry is on a discovery of India and itself. With budgets of over 30 crore each, four soon to be released movies by premier producers are exploring the idea of who we are and redefining who the other is. It is a fundamental question which the bling-bling, glam-sham, and disham-disham tends to avoid. It is also a question which binds an audience when the lights go dim and the projector rolls: as a nation, who are we? As a people where are we going?

The Germans coined a word for it, zeitgeist, which perhaps Yash Chopra would not care to pronounce. But at 72, he is the person who can best capture it. After being the first to project the diasporic Indian on screen in Lamhe in 1991, he has returned to his roots in a new movie Veer Zara, set in 1986, where Pakistan, the traditional other, the part that got away, is the lover and the saviour. In Subhash Ghai's Kisna, set in 1947, the other is the English woman. She is not a memsahib, but a mehbooba. In Ketan Mehta's Mangal Pandey? The Rising, the East India Englishman is not the evil oppressor of countless cardboard characterisations, which span the spectrum from Jewels in the Crown to Kranti, but an honourable friend.

This is Manoj Kumar's Upkar with a difference: there is culture, not contentious politics, balle balle, not bombs: no dooriyan (distance), only nazdeekiyan (closeness).

All four films are herald in a new hero and heroine. The new hero is fallible and vulnerable, committed to his dharma, but also not afraid of failure?less of a boy and more of a man. He even has a grown up name: Veer Partap Singh in Veer Zara and Mohan Bhargava in Swades. The new heroine is not a bebe, dressed in traditional Punjabi clothes, often with the stereotypical body type as well, as in Bride and Prejudice of Gurinder Chadha.

1. Which word Yash Chopra would not like to pronounce?
   (A) Bling-bling (B) Zeitgeist
   (C) Montaz (D) Dooriyan
2. Who made Lamhe in 1991?
   (A) Subhash Ghai (B) Yash Chopra
   (C) Aditya Chopra (D) Shakti Samanta
3. Which movie is associated with Manoj Kumar?
   (A) Jewel in the Crown
   (B) Kisna
   (C) Zaara
   (D) Upkar
4. Which is the latest film by Yash Chopra?
   (A) Deewar
   (B) Kabhi Kabhi
   (C) Dilwale Dulhaniya Le Jayenge
   (D) Jab Tak Hain Jaan
5. Which is the dress of the heroine in Veer Zara?
   (A) Traditional Gujarati clothes
   (B) Traditional Bengali clothes
   (C) Traditional Punjabi clothes
   (D) Traditional Madrasi clothes

KEY

1. B **2.** B **3.** D **4.** D **5.** C

PARAGRAPH – 4

(UGC NET JUNE 2007)

Directions: *Read the following passage carefully and choose the appropriate answer to the questions which follow the passage.*

All political systems need to mediate the relationship between the private wealth and public power. Those that fail risk a dysfunctional government captured by wealthy interests. Corruption is one symptom of such failure with private willingness to pay trumping public goals. Private individuals and business firms pay to get routine services and to get to the head of the bureaucratic queue. They pay to limit their taxes, avoid costly regulations, obtain contracts at inflated prices, and get concessions and privatised firms at low prices. If corruption is endemic, public officials-both bureaucrats and elected officials-may redesign programmes and purpose public projects with few public benefits and many opportunities for private profit. Of course, corruption, in the sense of bribes, pay-offs, and kickbacks, is only one type of government failure. Efforts to permute 'good governance' must be broader than anti-corruption campaigns. Governments may be honest but inefficient because no one has an incentive to work productively, and narrow elites may capture the state and exert excess influence on policy. Bribery may induce the lazy to work hard and permit those not in the inner circle of cronies to obtain benefits. However, even in such cases, corruption cannot be confined to 'functional' areas. It will be a temptation whenever private benefits are positive. It may be a reasonable response to a harsh reality but, over time, it can facilitate a spiral into an even worse situation.

1. The governments which fail to focus on the relationship between private wealth and public power are likely to become
   (A) Functional
   (B) Dysfunctional
   (C) Normal functioning
   (D) Good governance
2. One important symptom of bad governance is
   (A) Corruption
   (B) High taxes
   (C) Complicated rules and regulations
   (D) High prices
3. When corruption is rampant, public officials always aim at many opportunities for:
   (A) Public benefits (B) Public profit
   (C) Private profit (D) Corporate gains
4. Productivity-linked incentives to public/private officials is one of the indicatives for
   (A) Efficient government
   (B) Bad governance
   (C) Inefficient government
   (D) Corruption
5. The spiralling corruption can only be contained by promoting
   (A) Private profit
   (B) Anti-corruption campaign
   (C) Good governance
   (D) Pay-offs and kickbacks

KEY

1. B **2.** A **3.** C **4.** A **5.** C

PARAGRAPH – 5
(UGC NET DECEMBER 2009)

Directions: *Read the following passage carefully and choose the appropriate answer to the questions which follow the passage.*

The decisive shift in British Policy really came about under mass pressure in the autumn and winter of 1945 to 46-the months which Perderel Moon while editing Wavell's Journal has perceptively described as 'The Edge of a Volcano'. Very foolishly, the British initially decided to hold public trials of several hundreds of the 20,000 INA prisoners (as well as dismissing from service and detaining without trial no less than 7,000). They compounded the folly by holding the first trial in the Red Fort, Delhi in November 1945, and putting on the dock together a Hindu, a Muslim, and a Sikh (P.K. Sehgal, Shah Nawaz Khan, and Gurbaksh Singh Dhillon). Bhulabhai Desai, Tejbahadur Sapru, and Nehru appeared for the defence (the latter putting on his barrister's gown after 25 years), and the Muslim League also joined the countrywide protest. On 20 November, an Intelligence Bureau note admitted that "there has seldom been a matter which has attracted so much Indian public interest and, it is safe to say, sympathy … this particular brand of sympathy cuts across communal barriers.' A journalist (B. Shiva Rao) visiting the Red Fort prisoners on the same day reported that 'There is not the slightest feeling among them of Hindu and Muslim … A majority of the men now awaiting trial in the Red Fort is Muslim. Some of these men are bitter that Mr. Jinnah is keeping alive a controversy about Pakistan.' The British became extremely nervous about the INA spirit spreading to the Indian Army, and in January, the Punjab Governor reported that a Lahore reception for released INA prisoners had been attended by Indian soldiers in uniform.

1. Which heading is more appropriate to assign to the above passage?
   (A) Wavell's Journal
   (B) Role of Muslim League
   (C) INA Trials
   (D) Red Fort Prisoners
2. The trial of P.K. Sehgal, Shah Nawaz Khan, and Gurbaksh Singh Dhillon symbolises
   (A) communal harmony
   (B) threat to all religious persons
   (C) threat to persons fighting for the freedom
   (D) British reaction against the natives
3. INA stands for
   (A) Indian National Assembly
   (B) Indian National Association
   (C) Inter-national Association
   (D) Indian National Army
4. 'There has seldom been a matter which has attracted so much Indian Public Interest and, it is safe to say, sympathy … this particular brand of sympathy cuts across communal barriers.'

   Who sympathises with whom and against whom?
   (A) Muslims sympathised with Shah Nawaz against the British
   (B) Hindus sympathised with P.K. Sehgal against the British

(C) Sikhs sympathised with Gurbaksh Singh Dhillon against the British

(D) Indians sympathised with the persons who were to be trialled

5. The majority of people waiting for trial outside the Red Fort and criticising Jinnah were the

(A) Hindus (B) Muslims

(C) Sikhs (D) (A) and (B) both

6. The sympathy of Indian soldiers in uniform with the released INA prisoners at Lahore indicates

(A) Feeling of nationalism and fraternity

(B) Rebellious nature of Indian soldiers

(C) Participative spirit in the reception party

(D) None of the above

KEY

1. C **2.** D **3.** D **4.** D **5.** D **6.** A

PARAGRAPH – 6
(UGC NET JUNE 2012)

Directions: *Read the following passage carefully and choose the appropriate answer to the questions which follow the passage.*

James Madison said, "A people who mean to be their own governors must arm themselves with power that knowledge gives." In India, the Official Secrets Act, 1923 was a convenient smokescreen to deny members of the public access to information. Public functioning has traditionally been shrouded in secrecy. But in a democracy in which people govern themselves, it is necessary to have more openness. In the maturing of our democracy, right to information is a major step forward; it enables citizens to participate fully in the decision-making process that affects their lives so profoundly. It is in this context that the address of the Prime Minister in the Lok Sabha is significant. He said, "I would only like to see that everyone, particularly our civil servants, should see the Bill in a positive spirit; not as a Draconian law for paralyzing Government, but as an instrument for improving Government-Citizen interface resulting in a friendly, caring, and effective Government functioning for the good of our People." He further said, "This is an innovative Bill, where there will be scope to review its functioning as we gain experience. Therefore, this is a piece of legislation, whose working will be kept under constant reviews." The Commission, in its Report, has dealt with the application of the Right to Information in Executive, Legislature, and Judiciary. The judiciary could be a pioneer in implementing the Act in letter and spirit because much of the work that the Judiciary does is open to public scrutiny. Government of India has sanctioned an e-governance project in the Judiciary for about Rs. 700crores which would bring about systematic classification, standardization, and categorization of records. This would help the judiciary to fulfil its mandate under the Act. Similar capacity-building would be required in all other public authorities. The transformation from non-transparency to transparency and public accountability is the responsibility of all three organs of the State.

1. A person gets power

(A) by acquiring knowledge

(B) from the Official Secrets Act, 1923

(C) through openings

(D) by denying public information

2. Right to Information is a major step forward to

(A) enable citizens to participate fully in the decision-making process

(B) to make the people aware of the Act

(C) to gain knowledge of administration

(D) to make the people Government-friendly

3. The Prime Minister considered the Bill

(A) to provide power to the civil servants

(B) as an instrument for improving Government-Citizen interface

(C) a Draconian law against the officials

(D) as an instrument to check the harassment of the people

4. The Commission made the Bill effective by

(A) extending power to the executive authorities

(B) combining the executive and legislative power

(C) recognizing Judiciary a pioneer in implementing the Act in letter and spirit

(D) educating the people before its implementation

5. The Prime Minister considered the Bill innovative and hoped that

(A) It could be reviewed based on the experience gained on its functioning.

(B) The civil servants would see the Bill in a positive spirit.

(C) It would not be considered as a Draconian law for paralyzing Government.

(D) All of the above

6. The transparency and public accountability is the responsibility of the three organs of the State. These three organs are
   (A) Lok Sabha, Rajya Sabha, and Judiciary
   (B) Lok Sabha, Rajya Sabha, and Executive
   (C) Judiciary, Legislature, and the Commission
   (D) Legislature, Executive, and Judiciary

KEY

1. A **2.** A **3.** B **4.** C **5.** D **6.** D

PARAGRAPH – 7
(UGC NET DECEMBER 2014)

Directions: *Read the following passage carefully and choose the appropriate answer to the questions which follow the passage.*

The literary distaste for politics, however, seems to be focussed not so much on the largely murky practice of politics in itself as a subject of literary representation but rather, more on how it is often depicted in literature, i.e., on the very politics of such representation. A political novel often turns out to be not merely a novel about politics but a novel with a politics of its own, for it seeks not merely to show us how things are but has fairly definite ideas about how things should be, and precisely what one should think and do in order to make things move in that desired direction. In short, it seeks to convert and enlist the reader to a particular cause or ideology; it often is (in an only too familiar phrase) not literature but propaganda. This is said to violate the very spirit of literature which is to broaden our understanding of the world and the range of our sympathies, rather than to narrow them down through partisan commitment. As John Keats said, 'We hate poetry that has a palpable design upon us'.

Another reason why politics does not seem amenable to the highest kind of literary representation seems to arise from the fact that politics by its very nature is constituted of ideas and ideologies. If political situations do not lend themselves to happy literary treatment, political ideas present perhaps an even greater problem in this regard. Literature, it is argued, is about human experiences rather than about intellectual abstractions; it deals in what is called the 'felt reality' of human flesh and blood, and in sap and savour (rasa) rather than in lifeless ideas. In an extensive discussion of the matter in her book 'Ideas and the Novel', the American novelist Mary McCarthy observed that 'ideas are still today felt to be unsightly in the novel' though that was not so in 'former days', i.e., in the 18th and 19th centuries. Her formulation of the precise nature of the incompatibility between ideas on the one hand and the novel on the other betrays perhaps a divided conscience in the matter and a sense of dilemma shared by many writers and readers: 'An idea cannot have loose ends, but a novel, I almost think, needs them. Nevertheless, there is enough in common for the novelists to feel... the attraction of ideas while taking up arms against them-most often with weapons of mockery.'

1. The constructs of politics by its nature is
   (A) Prevalent political situation
   (B) Ideas and Ideologies
   (C) Political propaganda
   (D) Understanding of human nature
2. Literature deals with
   (A) Human experiences in politics
   (B) Intellectual abstractions
   (C) Dry and empty ideas
   (D) Felt reality of human life
3. The observation of the novelist, Mary McCarthy reveals
   (A) Unseen felt ideas of today in the novel
   (B) Dichotomy of conscience on political ideas and novels
   (C) Compatibility between ideas and novels
   (D) Endless ideas and novels
4. According to the passage, a political novel often turns out to be a
   (A) Literary distaste for politics
   (B) Literary representation of politics
   (C) Novels with its own politics
   (D) Depiction of murky practice of politics
5. A political novel reveals
   (A) Reality of the things
   (B) Writer's perception
   (C) Particular ideology of the readers
   (D) The spirit of literature

KEY

1. C **2.** D **3.** B **4.** C **5.** B

PARAGRAPH – 8
(UGC NET DECEMBER 2015)

Directions: *Read the following passage carefully and choose the appropriate answer to the questions which follow the passage.*

I did that thing recently where you have to sign a big card?which is a horror unto itself, especially as the keeper of the Big Card was leaning over me at the time. Suddenly I was on the spot, a rabbit in the headlights, torn between doing a fun message or some sort of a joke or a drawing. Instead, overwhelmed by the myriad options available to me, I decide to just write: "Good luck, best, Joel". It was then that I realized, to my horror, that I had forgotten how to write. My entire existence is "tap letters into computer". My shopping lists are hidden in the notes function of my phone. If I need to remember something I send an e-mail to myself. A pen is something I chew when I'm struggling to think. Paper is something I pile beneath my laptop to make it a more comfortable height for me to type on. A poll of 1, 000 teens by the stationers, BIC found that one in 10 don't own a pen, a third have never written a letter, and half of 13 to 19 years-olds have never been forced to sit down and write a thank you letter. More than 80% have never written a love letter, 56% don't have letter paper at home. And a quarter have never known the unique torture of writing a birthday card. The most a teen ever has to use a pen is on an exam paper. BIC, have you heard of mobile phone? Have you heard of e-mail, Facebook, and snap chatting? This is the future. Pens are dead. Paper is dead. Handwriting is a relic. "Handwriting is one of the most creative outlets we have and should be given the same importance as other art forms such as sketching, painting or photography."

1. According to the author, which one is not the most creative outlet of pursuit?

   (A) Reading (B) Handwriting

   (C) Photography (D) Sketching

2. When confronted with signing a big card, the author felt like "a rabbit in the headlight". What does this phrase mean?

   (A) A state of pain (B) A state of confusion

   (C) A state of pleasure(D) A state of anxiety

3. How many teens, as per the BIC survey, do not own a pen?

   (A) 100 (B) 800

   (C) 560 (D) 500

4. The entire existence of the author revolves round:

   (a) Computer (b) Mobile phone

   (c) Typewriter

   Identify the correct answer from the codes given below:

   (A) (b) and (c) only (B) (b) only

   (C) (a) and (b) only (D) (a), (b), and (c)

5. What is the main concern of the author?

   (A) That the teens have forgotten the art of handwriting

   (B) That the teens use social networks for communication

   (C) That the teens use mobile phones

   (D) That the teens use computer

KEY

1. B **2.** D **3.** A **4.** C **5.** A

PARAGRAPH – 9

(UGC NET JULY 2016)

Directions: *Read the following passage carefully and choose the appropriate answer to the questions which follow the passage.*

In terms of labour, for decades the relatively low cost and high quality of Japanese workers conferred considerable competitive advantage across numerous durable goods and consumer electronics industries (e.g., machinery, automobiles, televisions, and radios). Then labour-based advantages shifted to South Korea, then to Malaysia, Mexico, and other nations. Today, China appears to be capitalizing best on the basis of labour. Japanese firms still remain competitive in markets for such durable goods, electronics, and other products, but the labour force is no longer sufficient for competitive advantage over manufacturers in other industrializing nations. Such shifting of labour-based advantage is clearly not limited to manufacturing industries. Today, a huge number of IT and service jobs are moving from Europe and North America to India, Singapore, and like countries with relatively well-educated, low-cost workforces possessing technical skills. However, as educational levels and technical skills continue to rise in other countries, India, Singapore, and like nations enjoying labour-based competitive advantage today are likely to find that such advantage cannot be sustained through emergence of new competitors. In terms of capital, for centuries the days of gold coins and later even paper money restricted financial flows. Subsequently, regional concentrations were formed where large banks, industries, and markets coalesced. But today, capital flows internationally at rapid speed. Global commerce no longer requires regional interactions among business players. Regional capital concentrations in places such as New York, London, and Tokyo still persist, of course, but the capital concentrated there is no longer sufficient for competitive advantage over other capitalists distributed worldwide. Only if an organization is able to combine, integrate, and apply its resources (eg. land, labour, capital, IT) in an effective manner that is not readily imitable by competitors, can such an organization enjoy competitive advantage sustainable over time. In a knowledge-based theory of the firm, this idea is extended to view organizational knowledge as a resource with at least the same level of power and importance as the traditional economic inputs. An organization with superior knowledge can achieve competitive advantage in markets that appreciate the application of such knowledge. Semiconductors, genetic engineering, pharmaceuticals, software, military warfare, and like knowledge-intensive competitive arenas provide both time-proven and current examples. Consider semiconductors (e.g. computer chips), which are made principally of sand and common metals. These ubiquitous and powerful electronic devices are designed within common office buildings, using commercially available tools, and fabricated within factories in many industrialized nations. Hence, land is not the key competitive resource in the semiconductor industry.

1. Which country enjoyed competitive advantages in automobile industry for decades?
   (A) South Korea (B) Japan
   (C) Mexico (D) Malaysia
2. Why labour-based competitive advantages of India and Singapore cannot be sustained in IT and service sectors ?
   (A) Due to diminishing levels of skill
   (B) Due to capital-intensive technology making inroads
   (C) Because of new competitors
   (D) Because of shifting of labour-based advantage in manufacturing industries
3. How can an organisation enjoy competitive advantage sustainable over time?
   (A) Through regional capital flows
   (B) Through regional interactions among business players
   (C) By making large banks, industries, and markets coalesced
   (D) By effective use of various instrumentalities
4. What is required to ensure competitive advantages in specific markets?
   (A) Access to capital
   (B) Common office buildings
   (C) Superior knowledge
   (D) Common metals
5. The passage also mentions about the trend of
   (A) Global financial flow
   (B) Absence of competition in the manufacturing industry
   (C) Regionalisation of capitalists
   (D) Organizational incompatibility
6. What does the author lay stress on in the passage?
   (A) International commerce
   (B) Labour-intensive industries
   (C) Capital resource management
   (D) Knowledge-driven competitive advantage

KEY

1. B	2. C	3. D	4. C	5. A	6. D

PARAGRAPH – 10
(UGC NET JANUARY 2017)

Directions: *Read the following passage carefully and choose the appropriate answer to the questions which follow the passage.*

The last great war, which nearly shook the foundations of the modern world, had little impact on Indian literature beyond aggravating the popular revulsion against violence and adding to the growing disillusionment with the 'humane pretensions' of the Western World. This was eloquently voiced in Tagore's later poems and his last testament, Crisis in Civilisation. The Indian intelligentsia was in a state of moral dilemma. On the one hand, it could not help sympathising with England's dogged courage in the hour of peril, with the Russians fighting with their backs to the wall against the ruthless Nazi hordes, and with China groaning under the heel of Japanese militarism; on the other hand, their own country was practically under military occupation of their own soil, and an Indian army under Subhas Bose was trying from the opposite camp to liberate their country. No creative impulse could issue from such confusion of loyalties. One would imagine that the achievement of Indian independence in 1947, which came in the wake of the Allies' victory and was followed by the collapse of colonialism in the neighbouring countries of South-East Asia, would have released an upsurge of creative energy. No doubt it did, but unfortunately it was soon submerged in the great agony of partition, with its inhuman slaughter of the innocents and the uprooting of millions of people from their homeland, followed by the martyrdom of Mahatma Gandhi. These tragedies, along with Pakistan's invasion of Kashmir and its later atrocities in Bangladesh, did indeed provoke a poignant writing, particularly in the languages of the regions most affected- Bengali, Hindi, Kashmiri, Punjabi, Sindhi, and Urdu. But poignant or passionate writing does not by itself make great literature. What reserves of enthusiasm and confidence survived these disasters have been mainly absorbed in the task of national reconstruction and economic development. Great literature has always emerged out of chains of convulsions. Indian literature is richer today in volume, range, and variety than it ever was in the past.

1. What was the impact of the last great war on Indian literature?
   (A) It had no impact.
   (B) It aggravated popular revulsion against violence.
   (C) It shook the foundations of literature.
   (D) It offered eloquent support to the Western World.
2. What did Tagore articulate in his last testament?
   (A) Offered support to Subhas Bose
   (B) Exposed the humane pretensions of the Western World
   (C) Expressed loyalty to England
   (D) Encouraged the liberation of countries
3. What was the stance of Indian intelligentsia during the period of the great war?
   (A) Indifference to Russia's plight
   (B) Favoured Japanese militarism
   (C) Prompted creativity out of confused loyalties
   (D) Expressed sympathy for England's dogged courage
4. Identify the factor responsible for the submergence of creative energy in Indian literature.
   (A) Military occupation of one's own soil
   (B) Resistance to colonial occupation
   (C) Great agony of partition
   (D) Victory of Allies
5. What was the aftermath that survived tragedies in Kashmir and Bangladesh?
   (A) Suspicion of other countries
   (B) Continuance of rivalry
   (C) Menace of war
   (D) National reconstruction
6. The passage has the message that
   (A) Disasters are inevitable.
   (B) Great literature emerges out of chains of convulsions.
   (C) Indian literature does not have a marked landscape.
   (D) Literature has no relation with war and independence.

KEY

1. B **2.** B **3.** D **4.** C **5.** D **6.** B

PARAGRAPH – 11
(UGC NET NOVEMBER 2017)

Directions: *Read the following passage carefully and choose the appropriate answer to the questions which follow the passage.*

Climate change is considered to be one of the most serious threats to sustainable development, with adverse impacts on the environment, human health, food security, economic activity, natural resources, and physical infrastructure. Global climate varies naturally. According to the Inter- governmental Panel on Climate Change (IPCC), the effects of climate change have already been observed, and scientific findings indicate that precautionary and prompt action is necessary. Vulnerability to climate change is not just a function of geography or dependence on natural resources; it also has social, economic, and political dimensions which influence how climate change affects different groups. Poor people rarely have insurance to cover loss of property due to natural calamities, i.e., drought, floods, super cyclones, etc. The poor communities are already struggling to cope with the existing challenges of poverty and climate variability and climate change could push many beyond their ability to cope or even survive. It is vital that these communities are helped to adapt to the changing dynamics of nature. Adaptation is a process through which societies make themselves better able to cope with an uncertain future. Adapting to climate change entails taking the right measures to reduce the negative effects of climate change (or exploit the positive ones) by making the appropriate adjustments and changes. These range from technological options such as increased sea defences or flood- proof houses on stilts to behavioural change at the individual level, such as reducing water use in times of drought. Other strategies include early warning systems for extreme events, better water management, improved risk management, various insurance options, and biodiversity conservation. Because of the speed at which climate change is happening due to global temperature rise, it is urgent that the vulnerability of developing countries to climate change is reduced and their capacity to adapt is increased and national adaptation plans are implemented. Adapting to climate change will entail adjustments and changes at every level from community to national and international. Communities must build their resilience, including adopting appropriate technologies while making the most of traditional knowledge, and diversifying their livelihoods to cope with current and future climate stress. Local coping strategies and knowledge need to be used in synergy with government and local interventions. The need of adaptation interventions depends on national circumstances. There is a large body of knowledge and experience within local communities on coping with climatic variability and extreme weather events. Local communities have always aimed to adapt to variations in their climate. To do so, they have made preparations based on their resources and their knowledge accumulated through experience of past weather patterns. This includes times when they have also been forced to react to and recover from extreme events, such as floods, drought, and hurricanes. Local coping strategies are an important element of planning for adaptation. Climate change is leading communities to experience climatic extremes more frequently, as well as new climate conditions and extremes. Traditional knowledge can help to provide efficient, appropriate and time-tested ways of advising and enabling adaptation to climate change in communities who are feeling the effects of climate changes due to global warming.

1. Given below are the factors of vulnerability of poor people to climate change. Select the code that contains the correct answer.
   (a) Their dependence on natural resources
   (b) Geographical attributes
   (c) Lack of financial resources
   (d) Lack of traditional knowledge
   Code :
   (A) (a), (b), and (c)
   (B) (b), (c), and (d)
   (C) (a), (b), (c), and (d)
   (D) (c) only
2. Adaptation as a process enables societies to cope with:
   (a) An uncertain future
   (b) Adjustments and changes
   (c) Negative impact of climate change
   (d) Positive impact of climate change
   Select the most appropriate answer from the following code:
   (A) (a), (b), (c), and (d)
   (B) (a) and (c)
   (C) (b), (c), and (d)
   (D) (c) only
3. To address the challenge of climate change, developing countries urgently require:
   (A) Imposition of climate change tax
   (B) Implementation of national adaptation policy at their level
   (C) Adoption of short-term plans
   (D) Adoption of technological solutions
4. The traditional knowledge should be used through:
   (A) Its dissemination
   (B) Improvement in national circumstances
   (C) Synergy between government and local interventions
   (D) Modern technology

KEY

1. B **2.** C **3.** B **4.** C

PARAGRAPH – 12

(UGC NET DECEMBER 2018)

Directions: *Read the following passage carefully and choose the appropriate answer to the questions which follow the passage.*

Singapore has long advocated for India to take up its role as an integral part of the region. It is gratifying to see how Asean-India relations have grown during the past 25 years. In 1991, when the Cold War ended and India began its economic liberalization, Singapore saw an opportunity to deepen ties and build on its historical and cultural links with the Asian region. Singapore pushed for India to become a full Asean dialogue partner in 1995 and join the EAS in 2005 and since then, Asean-India ties have strengthened. All in all, around 30 platforms for co-operation exist, including seven ministerial dialogues and the Annual Leaders' Summit. However, there is scope for more and it is a must. For instance, there are tremendous opportunities in enhancing physical and digital connectivity between India and Asean. Asean is committed to strengthening land, air, and sea linkages with India. These linkages will enhance people-to-people flows, as well as boost business, investment, and tourism. The India-Myanmar-Thailand trilateral highway will connect India's Northeast to mainland Southeast Asia. While one can fly directly between India and several Asean countries, there is still much room to expand air links to support growing business and tourism. Beyond physical linkages, digital connectivity is the new frontier in the Fourth Industrial Revolution. India has made great progress in innovation, start-ups, and digital inclusion. There are opportunities to apply initiatives such as Aadhaar in our region. E-commerce and Fintech are two other areas potential collaboration. As an economic hub, Singapore can serve as a springboard to launch these ideas to Southeast Asia and beyond. India's role in Asean should be anchored by growing economic ties with Singapore. The economic integration involving 16 countries with one-third of global GDP and trade will create an integrated Asian market.

1. Who can be India's launchpad for an integrated Asian market as per the passage?

   (A) Southwest Asia (B) Thailand

   (C) Singapore (D) Myanmar

2. The areas of collaboration between India and Asian are:

   (a) Fintech

   (b) Aadhaar

   (c) e-commerce

   (d) Digital backwardness

   (e) Trilateral highways

   (f) Fourth industrial revolution

   (A) (b), (c), (d), and (e)

   (B) (a), (b), (c), and (d)

   (C) (a), (c), (e), and (f)

   (D) (c), (d), (e), and (f)

3. The commitment of Asean with India is:

   (A) Offer political platforms

   (B) More and more dialogues

   (C) Improve transport links

   (D) Hold leadership summits

4. What is needed to encourage tourism between India and Asean?

   (A) Waterways (B) Innovation

   (C) Air links (D) Start-ups

5. What prompted Singapore to opt for stronger ties with India?

   (A) Historical past

   (B) End of cold war

   (C) Geo-political equations

   (D) Economic liberalization in India

KEY

1. C **2.** B **3.** C **4.** C **5.** D

PARAGRAPH – 13
(UGC NET JUNE 2019)

Directions: *Read the following passage carefully and choose the appropriate answer to the questions which follow the passage.*

Geography seeks to understand the physical and human organization of the surface of the Earth. In the field of geography, inter-related themes are frequently seen. These are scale, pattern, and process. Scale is defined as the level of structure of organisation at which a phenomenon is studied. Pattern is defined as the variation observed in a phenomenon studied at a particular scale. The third theme, process, further connects the first two. Process is defined as the description of how the factors that affect a phenomenon act to product a pattern at a particular scale. For instance, when a passenger on an aircraft looks out of the window, the view changes according to the scale. At the global scale when the aircraft maintains its height, he can see the chunks of clouds in all their patterns, the sun, or the moon, as per the time. When the aircraft loses a little height, passengers can see the land and water masses in their different colours and the shape of land masses. At the continental scale, the passengers can see the shapes of the land features and how they are distributed. The pattern emerges as the variation of land and water and the proportion of each. Looking carefully, passengers can note how each land mass aligns with the others and how each mountain bears the signs of the process through which it emerged.

The processes in a geography change in a regular and repetitive manner. One instance of this is the annual solar cycle of the sun and the earth. Most systems in nature display time cycles that are organised in a rhythm of their own as these time cycles and natural processes are always active. The environment of the earth is always in a state of dynamism. This environmental change is not only the result of natural processes but also the result of human activity. Physical geography works towards understanding the interaction between man and nature and also the results of this interaction in order to manage global climate change better.

1. The time cycles of the system of nature follow their own
   (A) Path (B) Rhythm
   (C) Process (D) Cycle
2. The view seen by a passenger looking out of the window of an aircraft will be affected by the
   (A) Process (B) Pattern
   (C) Scale (D) Rhythm
3. Physical geography studies the results of the interaction between man and nature in order to
   (A) Understand global climate change
   (B) Study the impact of man's activities on nature
   (C) Address the issue of global climate change
   (D) Reduce man-animal conflict
4. In geography, pattern studies the variation observed in a phenomenon at
   (A) A particular scale
   (B) Any scale
   (C) Every scale
   (D) Most scales
5. The alignment of landmass with other elements can be seen by a passenger on a flight on a
   (A) Global scale (B) Continental scale
   (C) Local scale (D) Time scale

KEY

1. B **2.** C **3.** C **4.** A **5.** B

COMPREHENSION

(UGC NET DECEMBER 2019)

The pre-first world war era is really in a way is well suited for an in-depth evaluation of popular movements, as they were spontaneous and no more than marginally affected intelligentsia ideologies, objectives or techniques. The limitations of such spontaneity are fairly clear. Popular movements were directed usually against the immediate Indian oppressor rather than the distant white superior and so were often not consciously or subjectively anti-imperialist. They tended to be fairly widely scattered in both space and time and were extremely volatile with different social forms of articulation interpenetrating and passing oversee each other with bewildering case. All this makes it rather difficult to accept without some qualification the concept of 'Peasant Nationalism' as a coherent alternative to elite patriotic ideologies and movements. Popular initiative and autonomy were undoubted even remarkable at times, but, unlike middle class nationalism which does not have certain continuity, at the level of ideology at least., from the formulation of drain of wealth theory in the 1870s onward, the movements that have been considered were clearly fragmented. Yet despite such limitations and crudities, popular unrest did anticipate much of middle class nationalism in terms of issues and forms of struggle, while its specific gains were at times not inconsiderable. Forest rights, the burden of rent, usury and land revenue, planter exploitation and labour grievances were all themes taken over by middle class nationalism later.

1. The pre-war popular movements were of
   (A) uniform social form
   (B) insignificant value
   (C) middle class nationalism
   (D) specific gains at times
2. What is the author's assessment of popular movement?
   (A) Some of the popular issues were taken over by the middle class nationalism
   (B) It was bewildering and amusing
   (C) It was remarkable and time tested
   (D) Pre-war popular unrest was ant-imperialist
3. What does the analysis of pre-first world war popular movements reveal?
   (A) Intelligentsia's on popular movement was less
   (B) The movements were ideological
   (C) The movements had clear objectives
   (D) Limited spontaneity
4. According to the passage, the issue with peasant nationalism was
   (A) a viable alternative to elite nationalism
   (B) coherence and control
   (C) lack of continuity
   (D) quite timely

KEY

1. D **2.** A **3.** A **4.** C

Unit IV

Communication

1 Communication Meaning and Characteristics

MEANING

The Latin noun **'Communis'** means common and Latin verb **'Communicare'** means 'make something common'. These are the words from which word 'Communication' has been derived. Communication in its true sense is based on contact between two persons or more. The persons contact with one another to share their successes, failures, sorrows, joys, happiness, grievances, emotions, sentiments, and every type of state of mind prevailing at the time of contact. Communication is a flow like flow of water, air, sound, or electricity. In every communication there is a sender and a recipient.

Nature of Communication Process

Unilateral Communication Process: When a message sent by the sender is received by the recipient but recipient does not respond, such communication process is Unilateral or One-way process. There are certain communication processes which are unilateral where there is no binding on the recipient to respond to the sender even after receiving it. Communication by media is by and large a one-way process.

Bilateral Communication Process: In this process the recipient responds to the sender after receiving it. Official, organised, and formal communication process is bilateral.

Stages of Communication

1) **Thought:** Thought is the message which a sender wants to communicate, i.e., emotions, sentiments, and any feeling in the mind of the sender.

2) **Encoding:** When sender communicates his/her thoughts in written or oral form, it is called Encoding. Encoding is the message communicated from the point of view of the sender.

3) **Decoding:** When recipient of the message interprets or translate the message for better understanding, then it is called Decoding. Decoding is done from the point of view of the recipient.

Sequence of Communication

Communication is a flow which follows a sequence of source, message, channel, and receiver. It can be shown as follows:

SOURCE → MESSAGE → CHANNEL → RECEIVER

HISTORICAL FACTS OF COMMUNICATION

1) *Writing was invented in Iraq in 3300 BC.*
2) *In 3100 BC, Hieroglyphic Writing (Pictorial Writing) was developed in Egypt.*
3) *Greeks developed Phonetic Style of writing (Writing from left to right).*
4) *First ever Encyclopaedia was developed in Syria in 1250 BC.*
5) *First ever postal system was established by China.*
6) *Printing was invented by China in 1500 BC.*
7) *The idea of printing newspaper was first floated by German printer Gutenberg.*
8) *Telephone was invented by Scottish scientist Alexander Graham Bell in 1876.*
9) *The first ever communication satellite 'Echo' was launched by NASA in1960.*
10) *First fax machine was invented by Scottish Alexander Bain in 1843.*
11) *BBC was established in 1922.*

NATURE OF COMMUNICATION

Nature of communication is by and large determined by circumstances, environment, means, and ways of sharing. Nature of communication is seen through the following shades:

A) **Nonverbal communication**

B) **Verbal communication**

Nonverbal Communication

It is a communication in which there is no use of words, sentences, and grammar. Communicator communicates with the receiver while using certain wordless cues and the receiver also receives them and interprets accordingly. According to Dr. Albert Mehrabian, 93% of routine communication is nonverbal. Following are various forms of nonverbal communication:

1) **Haptic Communication:** It is that form of nonverbal communication in which message is exchanged via touching. For example, handshake, slapping, patting, and embracing are the usual haptic gestures. Touching yields sense of pleasure, pain, motivation, greetings, anger, etc.
2) **Silent Communication:** Silence plays its own role in the communication process. Silence conveys pause in the communication, protest, patience, trust, observation, agreement, disagreement, etc. Silence is an effective tool in the communication process as silence speaks more than words. Though silence is a tool of nonverbal communication, yet it is used as a communication tool in verbal communication process.
3) **Sensory Communication:** Senses in humans and animals communicate information quite effectively. External senses like smelling, taste, vision, and hearing convey the information which is good or bad smell and taste. Visionary sense conveys how different colours, places, persons, geographical structures, and other vision related subjects look. Hearing sense conveys various sound related verbal and nonverbal cues. Similarly, internal sensory system (somatosensory system) catches information from surroundings through touching skin. Skin as a sensory organ can feel temperature if touched. It is the sense of itching, pain, and relief, which is felt on skin.
4) **Audio Communication:** This communication covers the field of paralanguage. This comprises vocal qualities such as tone of voice, pitch, rhythm, and rate of speech. Though this is taken as nonverbal communication, yet various aspects of paralanguage are expressed with verbal communication. For instance, if a word or sentence is spoken in an appropriate pitch and tone, it reflects confidence of the speaker who also has mastery over the concept that word or sentence is related to. Appropriate tone of voice and pitch from the speaker leave a positive impression on recipients or listeners about the capability of the speaker. On the other hand, if the same word or sentence is spoken in a weak tone and pitch of voice, it leaves a weak and unhealthy impression on the recipients.
5) **Kinesics or Gestured Communication:** Movement of limbs, body language, facial expressions, and eye contact convey a lot without speaking or writing any word or sentence. One's facial expressions convey whether one is happy, dejected, relaxed, pensive, fatigued, or energetic. Similarly, body language also conveys one's physical or mental state. Eye contact conveys the level of confidence of the communicator or the recipient of communication. Further, different body postures, facial expressions, and movement of eyes in various dances convey different moods.
6) **Visual Communication:** A very first sight of a person conveys many messages. It is popularly said that first impression is the last impression. One's appearance, clothing, and dressing sense conveys one's mood, status, culture, age, level of confidence, economic status, and gender. Similarly, one's lifestyle, hairstyle, objects worn on body like ornaments, footwear, watch, etc. (artefacts), and possession of movable and immovable property also convey similar information about a person.
7) **Proxemics:** A space or distance is generally maintained by the people as a nonverbal communication tool to define their relationship with various groups of persons around them in terms of maintaining verbal communication with them. For communicating with most intimate persons like family members and close friends, a distance from touch to eighteen inches is maintained. For communicating with casual friends and associates, a space from eighteen inches to four feet is maintained. Further, for communicating with a small group of persons around the communicator, a social space is maintained measuring from four feet to twelve feet. For communicating with general public, communicator maintains a space beyond twelve feet.
8) **Chronemics:** It is a nonverbal communication tool which is used according to importance given to time. Punctuality or getting late conveys someone's status, habit, attitude towards work, and sense of responsibility. A punctual person is always praised and acts as a source of motivation for others. On the other hand, at a workplace, it is the general impression that a boss can come late as being a boss it is his prerogative, but a subordinate must be punctual.

Characteristics of Nonverbal Communication

1) **Ambiguous:** Nonverbal messages are sometimes misunderstood due to ambiguity factor.
2) **Variety:** Messages are conveyed either deliberately or unintentionally.
3) **More trustworthy:** In case of a conflict with verbal message, nonverbal message comes out to be more reliable than the verbal one.
4) **Supportive:** Nonverbal codes like haptic and kinesics support the verbal communication and add strength to it.

5) **Demonstrative:** Nonverbal code haptic demonstrates the intensity of relationship. For example, hugging demonstrates intimacy.

Verbal Communication

Verbal communication refers to the use of words and language to relay a message. It serves as a vehicle for expressing desires, ideas, and concepts and is vital to the processes of learning and teaching. In combination with nonverbal forms of communication, verbal communication acts as the primary tool for expression between two or more people. Verbal communication involves an exchange or presentation of ideas, information, feelings, or views. A sender composes a message and sends it to a recipient. The recipient interprets the message and has the option of sending a response. It has the following forms:

1) **Oral Communication:** Oral communication consists of all spoken exchanges. Casual as well as formal conversations among friends and with others fall into this category. In oral communication, verbal feedback typically follows the initial message, whether in the form of a question or comment.
2) **Written Communication:** Written communication commonly falls under the umbrella of verbal communication for the use of words to convey ideas. Books, letters, email, texts, memos, magazines, newspapers, and personal journals are all examples of verbal communication.
3) **High-Tech Communication:** Its major means are computer, Internet, satellite television, mobile phones, digital radio, etc.

Characteristics of Verbal Communication

1) **Contact:** Contact is the basic characteristic of verbal as well as nonverbal communication. Any idea or feeling can be shared between then communicator and the recipient when they have a contact.
2) **Feedback:** Communication is an exercise in futility if there is no feedback from the receiver of the message. When a recipient receives a message, he/she is to respond to the communicator whether he/she has understood the message or not. Feedback is expected by every communicator indulged in formal or informal communication. Teaching of a teacher is effective only if learners respond to the teacher whether they have understood the content delivered by the teacher or not. Feedback helps the teacher to assess the psychology and IQ level of students and accordingly proceed further.
3) **Language:** A communication becomes effective only when the language being used by the communicator to deliver the message is known to the recipient of the message.
4) **Encoding and Decoding:** Encoding is related to the actual message sent by the communicator. When the recipient receives the message and understands it, it is called decoding.
5) **Clarity of Expression:** Clarity of expression in the message of the communicator plays a pivotal role in making communication effective and fruitful. In case of oral communication, correct pronunciation of words measures clarity. On the other hand, in written communication, communicator's handwriting measures the clarity of expression.
6) **Purpose:** Communication without purpose is no communication. Communication between a teacher and students, a doctor and patients, lawyer and the judge, and vice versa carries a purpose which is fulfilled with effective communication.

LEVELS OF COMMUNICATION

American author John Powell describes following levels of communication:

Phatic Communication: *This refers to words used before communicating actual message and words used after completing the delivery of message. Initially, the words like 'hello, good morning, good evening, and how are you' are used as ice-breakers. At the end words like' thanks, good bye, good night, good day, and see you' are used at the end of the message. Phatic communication is used on all formal or informal occasions but on formal occasions use of phatic communication becomes a measure of the communicator's personality. Use of such words at the beginning and end of any conversation helps to establish a rapport between the communicator and the recipient. This communication is also known as cliché conversation or small talk.*

Factual Communication: *Sharing information on the basis of statistics, pictures, and other factual evidences is factual communication. Such communication is used to prove a point.*

Evaluative Communication: *Offering suggestions or opinion on some issue after evaluating it is evaluative communication. But such communication may create a conflict if the recipient responds with his/her own evaluation and opinion. Offering any suggestion or opinion voluntarily is always risky.*

Gut-Level Communication: *This is sharing of emotions with others. Sharing of emotions also demand self-control on the part of the communicator and the recipient.*

Peak Level Communication: *This is the ultimate level of communication. This is the communication between two like-minded persons. In this communication two souls merge into one while experiencing gut-level communication.*

FLOWS OF COMMUNICATION

In an organization, communication flows in 5 main directions:

1) **Downward Flow of Communication:** Communication flowing from a superior to subordinate or junior in an organisation is Downward flow of communication. In organisational hierarchy, downward flow of communication is statutory and part of duty for smooth working of the organisation. This communication is oral as well as written under statutory commitments.

2) **Upward Flow of Communication:** Communication flowing from subordinates or juniors to their seniors is an Upward flow of communication. Subordinates report to their seniors about the compliance of orders from seniors. There is upward communication by the subordinates to their seniors as part of routine duty in an organisation. This communication is oral or written.

3) **Horizontal or Lateral Communication:** Communication flow among the same level of hierarchy in an organisation is Lateral or Horizontal Communication. Manager-manager communication and clerk-clerk communication of an organisation is Lateral or Horizontal communication. This communication can also be oral or written.

4) **Diagonal Communication :** This communication flows between superiors of an organisation and subordinates of another organisation. Such communication generally flows in training courses, workshops, and other such events.

5) **External Communication:** This is a communication between an organisation with external players like bankers, raw material suppliers, and government offices.

Sketch of Flows of Communication

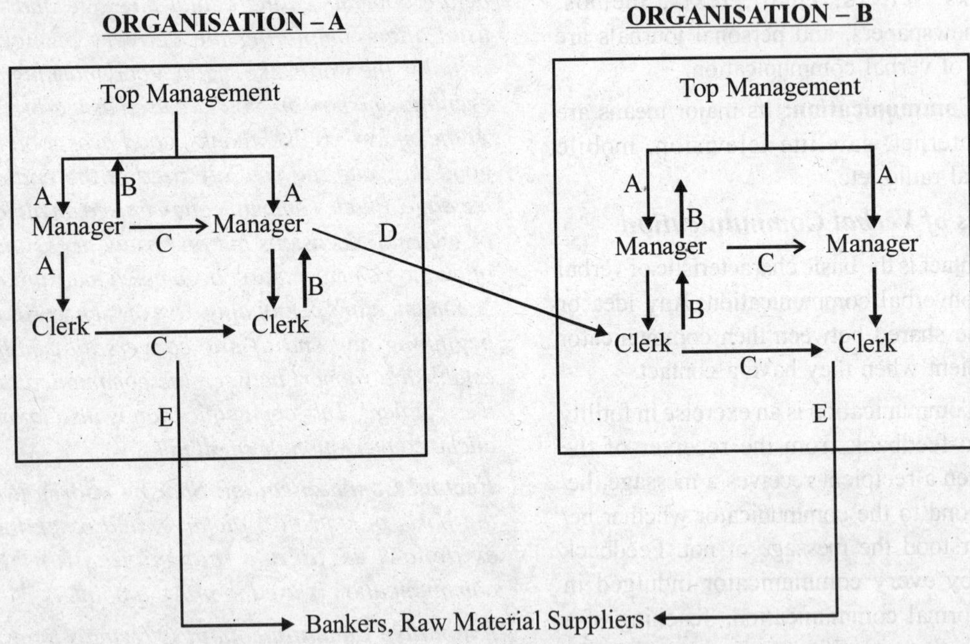

In above sketch:

A is Downward Communication

B is Upward Communication

C is Horizontal/Lateral Communication

D is Diagonal Communication

E is External Communication

FIVE Ws MODEL

American sociologist and psychologist Harod Lasswell developed a linear model of communication, which contains Five Ws for successfully completing a communication process.

1) ***Who:*** *It is referring the communicator who initiates the communication. In the communication process it matters the most that who is the communicator. It is the style of the communicator which makes a message effective.*
2) ***What:*** *It refers to the content of the message. It is the content of the message which yields feedback.*
3) ***Which Channel:*** *Communicator chooses a relevant channel to deliver his message. Various channels including mass media, social media, or any other communication channel, which is relevant to deliver the message effectively is chosen.*
4) ***To Whom:*** *Here recipient of the message is being referred to. Communicator sends his message while considering the convenience of the recipient. Who is receiving the message matters a lot. Sometimes, a message is meant for a target group of recipients conducive in research works and surveys.*
5) ***What Effect:*** *Every message leaves an impact. Communicator delivers a message to achieve a desired effect. Fetching the desired effect depends on the style of delivery of the message and the relevant content of the message. For example, a teacher wants that his/her lecture so delivered by him to students, should be clearly understood by them. This effect can be achieved by his technique of teaching while considering the convenience of the students in terms of listening and understanding the message.*

THEORIES OF COMMUNICATION

INFORMATION THEORY: An American mathematician Claude E. Shannon propounded theory of information. Shannon stated that when an information is transmitted though electronic signals through an electronic device, say telephone, what is the impact of noise on transmission of the message and what measures then receiver takes to receive perfect signal. Information is transmitted under rules of coding the information. Information is encoded through a communication channel and then received and decoded. Concern of Shannon was the uncertainty in perfect transmission of message due to noise and that has been termed as Entropy. Other media of transmitting quick information are telegraph, television, radio, and Internet.

TECHNOLOGY THEORY: This theory illustrates the flow of communication and information through electronic media and newspapers. Such channels facilitate the flow of communication.

MAGIC-BULLET THEORY: This theory believes that message released by mass media directly reaches the recipient and recipient directly and wholly receives the message. This theory is also called Hypodermic Needle Theory. Hypodermic Theory also believes that media injects an injection of information directly to the recipient.

MINIMAL EFFECTS THEORY: This theory states that during election days, various contestants in the fray go door-to-door and request for votes in their favour. Such canvassing has hardly any effect on voters. Voters according to their choice and canvassing have minimum effect on them.

HUMAN COMMUNICATION

Human communication system is an advanced one as compared to all other natural communication systems. There are two modes of communication, verbal and non-verbal. Human communication is the skill in learning and understanding and sending the message through any mode of communication. Humans communicate better than animals. Human communication comprises organised messages which have a source, language, symbol, sign, transmitting channel, media, and recipient. As social animals, humans have their professional and personal lives where they are to communicate. A particular skill is required to effectively communicate in the society in which there is human interaction round the clock. Various studies conducted on human communication endorse the importance of skills of oral and written communication acquired by the human being.

Characteristics of Human Communication

1) **Individual Initiative:** Human communication is initiated by an individual. Starting of communication also requires a skill and that skill leads the communication to success. The skill of taking initiative is found in human beings.
2) **Bilateral Communication:** Human communication is bilateral; that means there must be exchange of ideas between the communicator and the recipient. A communicator is to communicate with a recipient who in turn gives feed back to the communicator. Feedback acts as a rectifier of communicator's communication.
3) **Irreversible:** Human communication is irreversible. Once a communicator makes a written or oral communication, it cannot be taken back. An undesirable and unwanted communication made due to mistake can be rectified later or corrigendum over it is issued, but once it is made, it is irreversible like a bullet shot from pistol. Using misinterpreted messages may yield misunderstandings.

4) **Direct or indirect Interaction:** Human communication progresses in direct or indirect interaction. In direct interaction, communicator and recipient are face-to-face and direct communication is being exchanged, On the other hand, in indirect interaction, communicator is communicating with the recipient through some means. Communication in the direct interaction is only oral. On the other hand, communication in indirect interaction can be oral or written. If there is oral communication means of indirect communication, it can be through telephone and audio or video conferencing through Internet. In case indirect communication is written, then means of communication can be letter, e-mail, SMS, etc.

5) **Use of Words as well as Symbols:** Human communication is a blend of verbal and nonverbal communication. For effective communication, communicator uses words as well as symbol and gestures in the process of communication.

6) **Context Based:** Human communication is not without context or setting. This has also been propounded by Dr. Sue Devine and James McCroskey. According to them, setting or context is there in interpersonal communication, group communication, organisational communication, and communication through mass media.

7) **Social and Cognitive:** Human communication is basically related with learning skill of communication while surviving in the society. The way humans communicate with one another is influenced by their psychology and cognitive abilities. Survival in the society and dependence on one another makes communication social.

CODES OF COMMUNICATION

There has been a tradition to code or decode messages so communicated due to various reasons. Reasons may be maintaining secrecy or creating a short icon for convenience. In any case, codes have been the pivotal part of every type of communication process. There are different codes of communication: Verbal, Nonverbal, and Iconic.

Verbal Code

Whether spoken or written, verbal communication is governed by certain rules. The codes of communication are set by a society's traditions, customs, and culture. The set codes are understood to be conducive in expressing emotions, norms, relationship, and all aspects of communication. Verbal codes are also taken as meaning of some concepts, actions, and thoughts surviving in the cultural sphere of a society. Certain liberties and taboos present in a society also act as codes and there is universal understanding that these are to be complied with by the members of the society. So there is symbolic representation by codes for general understanding and compliance. Language is spoken under two norms:

a) **Constitutive Norms:** These norms teach the way to recognise parts of speech, i.e., learning language.

b) **Regulatory Norms:** These norms teach to differentiate appropriate speech of one context from the other.

Verbal codes are formed with the combination of the following rules:

i) **Phonology:** Fundamental components of language are phonemes. There are particular phonemes for different cultures.

ii) **Morphology:** It is the study of morphemes.

iii) **Semantic:** It is the study of meaning of words and their relationship with one another. There are two types of meanings, i.e., Denotative and Connotative. Denotative meaning is the dictionary and legal meaning, whereas connotative meaning is the meaning with respect to a person's emotions.

iv) **Syntactics:** It is the study of sentence structure as per grammatical norms.

Phonemes: *A phoneme is the smallest unit of sound in speech. It is how an individual letter of the alphabet sounds or how it is pronounced. For example, in a word 'ink', there are three phonemes: 'i'-'n'-'k'.*

Morphemes: *A morpheme is a smallest unit of grammar in a language. It is a word which cannot be divided further. Example: word 'portable' has two morphemes; 'port' and 'able'. Phonemes and morphemes jointly convey sound and meaning of a word containing one or more than one morpheme. Morphemes are either free words or bound words. For example, in a word 'Unbelievable' there are three morphemes, i.e., 'Un', 'believe', and 'able'. In this word 'Un' is a bound morpheme as it cannot stand alone, whereas other words 'believe' and 'able' are free morphemes as they stand free for communication and convey respective meanings independently. Morphemes are often used as prefixes and suffixes while using language in communication.*

v) **Pragmatics:** It is the study how a single word is used with different meanings in different situations or settings. Effect of language on human perception and thinking is also studied in Pragmatics.

Nonverbal Code

Nonverbal codes are governed by the rules of communication without words or language. Various nonverbal codes are:

i) Kinesics ii) Haptic
iii) Paralanguage iv) Proxemics
v) Environment vi) Artifacts
vii) Appearance viii) Chronemics

(All of the above have already been explained earlier in this chapter)

Iconic Code

Iconic code or icon indicates resemblance, i.e., it physically resembles with what it stands for. For example, someone's picture is an icon for him/her. On the computer screen, a small image of the printer is an icon for the actual printer connected with the computer.

Some Vital Facts

1) Sequence of communication is Communication ⇒ Language ⇒ Society ⇒ Civilization
2) Non-verbal communication is considered as informal communication
3) Human communication process stimulates ideas, it is a learnt ability and cannot breakdown.
4) A good communicator begins his/her presentation with an ice breaker.
5) When verbal and non-verbal messages are contradictory, it is said that most people believe in non-verbal communication.
6) Facial expression, kinesics and personal space are the components of non-verbal communication in the classroom.
7) Acknowledgement of thoughts, reflection, and asking open-ended questions are basic factors of effective listening
8) Communication involves exchange of ideas, facts and opinions.
9) Transforming thoughts, ideas and messages into verbal and non-verbal signs is referred to as encoding.
10) In communication chatting in internet is verbal communication.
11) The Telephone Model of Communication was first developed in the area of Information Theory
12) Communicator, message, medium, receiver and effect is the chronological order of communication process.
13) In communication, the language is the symbolic code.
14) Sequence of communication flow is source, message, channel and receiver.
15) Feedback of a massage comes from the audience.

Practice Exercise

General Questions Format

1. Which of the following does not define Communication?
   (A) Exchange (B) Contact
   (C) Sharing (D) None of the above
2. Nature of Communication is
   (A) wonderful (B) awful
   (C) fruitful (D) useful
3. When A communicates with B then
   (A) A has a purpose and B fulfills it.
   (B) B has a purpose and A fulfills it.
   (C) Both have a purpose and fulfill each other's purpose.
   (D) Both find the purpose during the course of communication and then fulfil it with proper communication.
4. A communication goes futile when
   (A) sender does not recognize the receiver
   (B) there is use of foreign language in the communication
   (C) receiver does not want the message from the sender
   (D) None of the above
5. Newspaper is an example of .... communication.
   (A) sensory (B) gestured
   (C) verbal (D) hi-tech
6. Nature's communication is
   (A) mandatory (B) perennial
   (C) reformatory (D) All of the above
7. Which of the following is NOT TRUE about communication?
   (A) Word communication has been derived from a Greek word 'Communicare'.
   (B) Communication process survives under certain codes of conduct.
   (C) Communication is distorted if either of the sender or receiver is not attentive.
   (D) Every living organism communicates in its own way.

8. Communication is a bilateral process means that
(A) Communication is confined to two persons
(B) There are two ways to communicate
(C) Communication involves bi-media approach for its application
(D) None of these

9. Which of the following is a Purposive Communication? Communication of
(A) a defeated political leader with the victorious one
(B) a failed student with one who has passed
(C) an unsuccessful lover with the successful one
(D) All of the above

10. Communication technology has brought revolution in every type of communication except............ communication.
(A) silent (B) gestured
(C) purposive (D) All of the above

11. Sharing of ....fully justifies the purpose of communication.
(A) sorrows (B) affections
(C) grievances (D) All of the above

12. There are certain ways to improve the distorted media communication for want of clarity of expression
I) Changing the medium
II) Changing the language
III) Changing the sound
IV) Changing the communicator
Arrange them in priority.
(A) II-I-IV-III (B) III-II-IV-I
(C) III-IV-II-I (D) II-IV-III-I

13. Feedback in the communication makes it
(A) evaluative (B) complex
(C) common (D) personal

14. Communication of whom among following becomes a headache for the listener? Communication of.........
a) an irritating boss b) a suspicious wife
c) a fussy friend d) an uninvited guest
(A) a and b (B) Only c
(C) a, b, and d (D) All of the above

15. Here are some characteristics of communication. *Arrange them in priority.*
a) Purpose b) Clarity of expression
c) Feedback d) Contact
(A) a-d-b-c (B) b-a-d-c
(C) d-a-b-c (D) a-b-d-c

16. Technology and innovations have............ present day communication.
(A) widened (B) refined
(C) facilitated (D) All of the above

17. If a communicator gets a negative feedback of his communication, it means his communication did not have
(A) purpose (B) contact
(C) language (D) None of the above

18. Communication between the two countries on a common problem is a/an ...... communication.
(A) symbolic (B) verbal
(C) hi-tech (D) none of these

19. Reception and understanding of communication is essential because it provides .... to the message so communicated.
(A) meaning (B) reciprocity
(C) language (D) none of these

20. Mixture of which of the following communications provides the best and result-oriented communication?
(A) Symbolic & Visual
(B) Auditory & Visual
(C) Gestured & Verbal
(D) Gestured & Sensory

21. Hi-tech communication has refined the ...... of communication.
(A) medium (B) concept
(C) purpose (D) feedback

22. Which of the following is NOT shared in the communication?
(A) Joy (B) Experiences
(C) Affections (D) None of these

23. It is the...........which makes communication between two aliens the most meaningful.
(A) understanding of each other's language
(B) purpose
(C) feedback
(D) expression

24. Communication by...........does not always need contact.
(A) nature (B) animals
(C) human beings (D) any of the above

25. Match the List-I with the List-II and select the correct answer using the codes given below:

List - I	List - II
a) Redundancy	i) movement of speech organs
b) Entropy	ii) pronunciation & translation
c) Articulation	iii) superfluousness in communication
d) Verbalization	iv) Breakdown in communication

Codes:	(a)	(b)	(c)	(d)
(A)	iii	i	iv	ii
(B)	iii	iv	i	ii
(C)	i	iv	iii	ii
(D)	ii	iii	i	iv

KEY

1. D	**2.** C	**3.** A	**4.** C	**5.** C	**6.** B	**7.** A
8. D	**9.** D	**10.** A	**11.** D	**12.** B	**13.** A	**14.** B
15. A	**16.** D	**17.** D	**18.** B	**19.** A	**20.** C	**21.** B
22. D	**23.** A	**24.** D	**25.** B			

Assertion–Reason Format

1. **Assertion (A):** Feedback is not binding in unilateral communication process.

Reasoning (R): Communication without feedback is autonomous.

(A) Both A and R are true and R is correct explanation of A

(B) Both A and R are true but R is not correct explanation of A

(C) A is true but R is false

(D) A is false but R is true

2. **Assertion (A):** Downward communication is universal in nature.

Reason (R): Organisational hierarchy necessitates to practise different levels of communication.

(A) Both A and R are true and R is correct explanation of A

(B) Both A and R are true but R is not correct explanation of A

(C) A is true but R is false

(D) Both A and R are false

3. **Assertion (A):** A message to be delivered needs an ice-breaker.

Reason (R): Greetings before and after the delivery of a message establish rapport between communicator and the recipient.

(A) Both A and R are true and R is correct explanation of A

(B) Both A and R are true but R is not correct explanation of A

(C) A is true but R is false

(D) A is false but R is true

4. **Assertion (A):** Human communication is irreversible.

Reason (R): Element of irreversibility enables man to communicate in any mode.

(A) Both A and R are true and R is correct explanation of A

(B) Both A and R are true but R is not correct explanation of A

(C) A is true but R is false

(D) A is false but R is true

5. **Assertion (A):** Upward communication in an organisation is a statutory communication.

Reason (R): A subordinate communicates with his/her senior to fulfil official commitment.

(A) Both A and R are true and R is correct explanation of A

(B) Both A and R are true but R is not correct explanation of A

(C) Both A and R are false

(D) A is false but R is true

6. **Assertion (A):** Like-minded people do not experience gut-level communication.

Reason (R): Sharing of emotions with restraints prevent communication ending with catastrophic outcomes.

(A) Both A and R are true and R is correct explanation of A

(B) Both A and R are true but R is not correct explanation of A

(C) A is false but R is true

(D) A is false but R is true

7. **Assertion (A):** Communication is binding on encoder and is an option for decoder.

Reason (R): Encoder is to follow statutes of communication whereas decoder is not.

(A) Both A and R are true and is correct explanation of A

(B) Both A and R are true but R is not correct explanation of A

(C) Both A and R are false

(D) A is true but R is false

8. **Assertion (A):** Paralanguage is an aesthetic form of nonverbal communication.

   Reason (R): Communication skills are required both for verbal and nonverbal communication.

   (A) Both A and R are true and R is correct explanation of A
   (B) Both A and R are true but R is not correct explanation of A
   (C) A is true but R is false
   (D) A is false but R is true

9. **Assertion (A):** Haptic communication is demonstrative in nature.

   Reason (R): Conveying message through touching demonstrates the intensity of relationship between communicator and recipient.

   (A) Both A and R are true and R is correct explanation of A
   (B) Both A and R are true but R is not correct explanation of A
   (C) A is true but R is false
   (D) A is false but R is true

10. **Assertion (A):** Information theory of communication apprehends entropy in transmission of message due to noise.

    Reason (R): Electronic devices of communication like telephone are likely to develop entropy.

    (A) Both A and R are true and R is correct explanation of A
    (B) Both A and R are true but R is not correct explanation of A
    (C) A is false but R is true
    (D) A is false but R is true

11. **Assertion (A):** Verbal codes of communication denote taboos in the society.

    Reason (R): Society is empowered to decide the fate of a verbal code of communication.

    (A) Both A and R are true and R is correct explanation of A
    (B) Both A and R are true but R is not correct explanation of A
    (C) Both A and R are false
    (D) A is true but R is false

12. **Assertion (A):** Connotative approach to communication is literally sound.

    Reason (R): Semantic communication carries dictionary and emotional meaning of words.

    (A) Both A and R are true and R is correct explanation of A
    (B) Both A and R are true but R is not correct explanation of A
    (C) A is true but R us false
    (D) A is false but R is true

13. **Assertion (A):** Evaluative communication carries the risk of retaliation from the recipient.

    Reason (R): Evaluating by communicator may not always be appreciated by the recipient.

    (A) Both A and R are true and R is correct explanation of A
    (B) Both A and R are true but R is not correct explanation of A
    (C) Both A and R are false
    (D) A is true but R is false

14. **Assertion (A):** Communication without purpose is an exercise in futility.

    Reason (R): Communicator has a purpose and recipient has execution.

    (A) Both A and R are true and R is correct explanation of A
    (B) Both A and R are true but R is not correct explanation of A
    (C) A is true but R is false
    (D) A is false but R is true

15. **Assertion (A):** Nonverbal communication serves the dual purpose of saving time and accurate delivery of message.

    Reason (R): Precise but complete delivery of message is always desirable.

    (A) Both A and R are true and R is correct explanation of A
    (B) Both A and R are true but R is not correct explanation of A
    (C) A is true but R is false
    (D) A is false but R is true

KEY

1. C **2.** B **3.** A **4.** C **5.** A **6.** A **7.** C
8. D **9.** A **10.** B **11.** C **12.** D **13.** A **14.** C
15. D

Questions Asked in Previous NET Exams

1. In the context of communication, usual sequence is **(UGC NET JUNE 2019)**
   (A) Language > Communication > Society > Civilization
   (B) Communication > Society > Language > Civilization
   (C) Communication > Language > Society > Civilization
   (D) Language > Society > Communication > Civilization
2. Identify values specially related to organisational ethos from the list given below: **(UGC NET DECEMBER 2019)**
   (i) Team work in the approach
   (ii) Productivity of the tasks
   (iii) Changes in the global contents
   (iv) Financial security
   (v) Humility in dealing with others' concern
   (vi) Technological Resources
   Choose your answer from the following options:
   (A) (i), (ii) and (vi) (B) (iii), (iv) and (v)
   (C) (ii), (iii) and (iv) (D) ((i), (ii) and (v)
3. Nonverbal communication is considered: **(UGC NET DECEMBER 2018)**
   (A) Formal (B) Culture-free
   (C) Informal (D) Precise
4. Which of the following set of statements is correct for describing the human communication process? **(UGC NET JULY 2018)**
   (a) Nonverbal communication can stimulate ideas.
   (b) Communication is a learnt ability.
   (c) Communication is not a universal panacea.
   (d) Communication cannot break down.
   (e) More communication means more effective learning by students.
   (f) Value of what is learnt through classroom communication is not an issue for students.
   Code:
   (A) (a), (c), (e), and (f)
   (B) (b), (d), (e), and (f)
   (C) (a), (b), (c), and (d)
   (D) (a), (d), (e), and (f)
5. A good communicator begins his/her presentation with a/an: **(UGC NET NOVEMBER 2017)**
   (A) Complex question (B) Non-sequitur
   (C) Repetitive phrase (D) Ice-breaker
6. When verbal and nonverbal messages are contradictory, it is said that most people believe in **(UGC NET JANUARY 20017)**
   (A) indeterminate messages
   (B) verbal messages
   (C) nonverbal messages
   (D) aggressive messages
7. Figure out the components of nonverbal communication in a classroom from the following: **(UGC NET AUGUST 2016)**
   (A) Facial expression, cultural space, and seating arrangement
   (B) Speed of utterance, feel good factor, and acoustics
   (C) High sound, physical ambience, and teacher-learner distance
   (D) Facial expression, kinesics, and personal space
8. Which of the following are the basic factors of effective listening? **(UGC NET AUGUST 2016)**
   (A) Opinionation, stare and glare, and interruptions
   (B) Aggressive questioning, continuous cues, and frequent movement
   (C) Me-too-ism, glancing sideways, and offering advice
   (D) Acknowledgement of thoughts, reflection, and asking open-ended questions
9. Imagine you are working in an educational institution where people are of equal status. Which method of communication is best suited and normally employed in such a context? **(UGC NET JULY 2016)**
   (A) Horizontal communication
   (B) Vertical communication
   (C) Corporate communication
   (D) Cross communication
10. The choice of communication partners is influenced by factors of **(UGC NET JULY 2016)**
   (A) Proximity, utility, loneliness
   (B) Utility, secrecy, dissonance
   (C) Secrecy, dissonance, deception
   (D) Dissimilarity, dissonance, deviance

11. Every communicator has to experience **(UGC NET JULY 2016)**
(A) Manipulated emotions
(B) Anticipatory excitement
(C) The issue of homophiles
(D) Status dislocation

12. Which of the following are the characteristic features of communication? **(UGC NET JUNE 2015)**
(a) Communication involves exchange of ideas, facts, and opinions.
(b) Communication involves both information and understanding.
(c) Communication is a continuous process.
(d) Communication is a circular process.
Select the correct answer from the codes given below:
(A) (a), (b), (c) and (d)
(B) (a), (b), and (c)
(C) (a), (b), and (d)
(D) (b), (c), and (d)

13. In communication, chatting in Internet is
(A) Verbal Communication
(B) Nonverbal Communication
(C) Parallel Communication
(D) Grapevine Communication

14. Breakdown in verbal communication is described as **(UGC NET JUNE 2014)**
(A) Short circuit (B) Contradiction
(C) Uneven D) Entropy

15. The Telephone Model of Communication was first developed in the area of **(UGC NET JUNE 2014)**
(A) Technological theory
(B) Dispersion theory
(C) Minimal effects theory
(D) Information theory

16. In the process of communication, which one of the following is in the chronological order? **(UGC NET JUNE 2013)**
(A) Communicator, Medium, Receiver, Effect, Message
(B) Medium, Communicator, Message, Receiver, Effect
(C) Communicator, Message, Medium, Receiver, Effect
(D) Message, Communicator, Medium, Receiver, Effect

17. The English word 'Communication' is derived from the words **(UGC NET DECEMBER 2012)**
(A) Communis and Communicare
(B) Communist and Commune
(C) Communism and Communalism
(D) Communion and Common Sense

18. Transforming thoughts, ideas, and messages into verbal and nonverbal signs is referred to as **(UGC NET JUNE 2011)**
(A) channelisation (B) mediation
(C) encoding (D) decoding

19. In communication, the language is **(UGC NET JUNE 2010)**
(A) the nonverbal code
(B) the verbal code
(C) the symbolic code
(D) the iconic code

20. Identify the correct sequence of the following: **(UGC NET JUNE 2010)**
(A) Source, channel, message, receiver
(B) Source, receiver, channel, message
(C) Source, message, receiver, channel
(D) Source, message, channel, receiver

21. Which of the following statements is not connected with communication? **(UGC NET DECEMBER 2009)**
(A) Medium is the message.
(B) The world is an electronic cocoon.
(C) Information is power.
(D) Telepathy is technological.

22. Feedback of a message comes from **(UGC NET JUNE 2007)**
(A) Satellite (B) Media
(C) Audience (D) Communicator

23. Which of the following can be termed as verbal communication? **(UGC NET DECEMBER 2006)**
(A) Professor Sharma delivered the lecture in the classroom.
(B) Signal at the crossroad changed from green to orange.
(C) The child was crying to attract the attention of the mother.
(D) Deepak wrote a letter for leave application.

KEY

1. C	**2.** D	**3.** C	**4.** C	**5.** D	**6.** C	**7.** D
8. D	**9.** A	**10.** A	**11.** B	**12.** A	**13.** A	**14.** D
15. D	**16.** C	**17.** A	**18.** C	**19.** C	**20.** D	**21.** B
22. C	**23.** A					

2 Mass Media and Society

CONCEPT

Today, that society survives which is well-informed, well-entertained, and well- educated. In the age of communication technology, members of the society get information, entertainment, and education from different individual or collective sources. No source can inform, entertain, and educate members of the society individually. That source is considered to be the best which smells the uniform need of the society as far as providing information, entertainment, and education is concerned and the source is to provide these services to all members of the society collectively at the same time. In this way the source is communicating with the masses and this is mass communication.

MASS COMMUNICATION

> *Mass communication is a process in which messages are sent spontaneously to a large number of people, generally running into lakhs, scattered over a very large area. As it is not possible to convey the message individually, a medium or media is required to convey the message to the masses. The media covering masses are known as mass media. Mass media includes newspapers, journals, radio, TV, cinema and social media like Facebook, Twitter, etc.*

MASS MEDIA

Background: The term 'Mass Media' began to be used in 1920's in Europe. Only newspaper was considered to be the channel of mass media until post Second World War period. After that, the term mass media was widened to radio, television, cinema, videos, etc. as these ware invented around this period.

Mass media include various channels of media which are capable of giving message to the masses or audience at a single point of time. There has been a tradition of communicating with masses or audience since ancient times. There had been media communicating to the audience even during those days when there was no newspaper, radio, TV, cinema, and other channels of satellite communication technology. Such media is known as traditional media and this media is surviving even today and it has an effective education, information, and entertainment appeal which is establishing its individual identity even in the presence of communication technology. On the basis of this, mass media include all the channels of media communicating with the masses.

Functions of Mass Media

Basically, mass media provide information, entertainment, and education to the society. In the present day scenario, functions of mass media are viewed as under:

1) **Infotainment:** When mass media provides information along with entertainment
2) **Edutainment:** When mass media provides education with entertainment

While providing information or education, the ultimate objective of mass media is to provide these messages effectively and effective delivery of message becomes possible through entertainment. So mass media has dual objective of delivering the message, i.e., massage with entertainment.

Types of Mass Media

1) **Traditional Media:** Every society has its respective folk and cultural heritage. Folk and classical arts like dances, songs, plays, songs, paintings, drama, poetry, etc. carry messages and these are conveyed spontaneously to a large number of the audience. This media also fulfils the commitment of infotainment or edutainment.
2) **Print Media:** Print media is the production of modern times. This includes newspapers, journals, magazines, books, and periodicals.
3) **Electronic Media:** Electronic media is a sort of revolution in mass media services. Electronic media include radio, television, and cinema.

4) **Social Media or Web Media:** Internet communication technology has given birth to social and web media. It has brought revolution in mass communication. In web or social media, mass communication is effected through e-mail, podcasts, websites, e-books, e-newspapers, blogs and social networking sites, Internet radio, Internet television, etc. Social media include Facebook, WhatsApp, Instagram, Twitter, LinkedIn, Google+, etc.

Significance of Mass Media for Society

Mass media has a big significance for a society as it becomes the basis of its survival. Its significance is discussed as follows:

1) **Indispensable Source of Information:** Today, mass media has become an indispensable source of information. Members of the society needing information on day-to-day activities, education, health, commerce, politics, sports, business, ethics, culture, government policies, climate changes, weather forecasts, national and international news, and entertainment resort to newspapers, radio, television, cinema, and social media. Society, thus fully depends upon mass media to be well-informed and updated.
2) **Generator of Employment:** Popularity of mass media is necessitating its continuous expansion so mass media creates ample employment opportunities and absorbs thousands of aspirants. Leading newspapers, TV channels, radio channels, film companies, and social media channels are involved in composition of news and events, editing, shooting, processing, advertising, broadcasting, reporting, etc. and they need technical personnel in a good number. A great number of the workforce is absorbed in these departments, hence making a dent on the problem of unemployment.
3) **Opening of Professional Courses and Self-Occupation:** Members of the society are benefitted by the expansion phase of mass media as institutes of higher education are coming up with various courses in mass communication, web designing, software designing, data entry, journalism, acting, dancing, and many skill-based courses. Various media houses enter into contract with such diploma or degree holders for acquiring their various services, hence creating avenues for self-occupation.
4) **Education Provider:** Mass media provide non-formal education for the benefit of students pursuing academic diplomas or degrees. Radio and television arrange online audio and video classes. Expert faculty of various universities and research institutes prepare lectures which are delivered online. Thus, mass media plays an effective role in meeting out the objective of universalisation of education.
5) **Helping Career Aspirants:** Lakhs of aspirants preparing for various competitive exams to fetch their coveted careers consult general awareness content provided by newspapers, radio, TV, Internet sites, and social media. Aspirants prepare from these channels and get successful.
6) **Entertainment Providers:** In the present life full of tension and pressure, one gets relief and respite while enjoying various entertainment programmes including reality shows, stand-up performances, music, songs, and serials aired by TV and radio. Newspapers, books, and magazines are coming with various stories, narrations, and features which prove as a good time pass. Similarly, cinema, social media, various websites, e-books, etc. provide entertaining content, thus rejuvenating the audience.
7) **Social Reformer:** Mass media make society aware about the dangerous impacts of various social, economic, cultural, and environmental evils being committed by the society. All channels of mass media appeal to the people to voluntarily initiate efforts to make society economically, politically, economically, and environmentally sound and safe. Mass media appeal is very effective in changing the outlook of the general public.
8) **Ambassadors of a Society's Culture, History, and Values:** All mass media channels cover various features and reports on diverse customs, traditions, values, culture, history, and heritage of a society and other societies, thus making members aware about various cultures, history, and values. Such knowledge helps the society to bring various reforms,

undertake research works, and work for cultural exchanges leading to peace and harmony. These channels serve the society as ambassadors of these traits.

9) **Messenger of Society's Problems:** Mass media covers various problems faced by the society due to indifference and non-cooperation of local, state level, or national level administration. Every channel of media acts as a messenger of society's civic, health, education, and law and order problems and pressurise the authorities to resolve the problems.

10) **Political Awareness:** Mass media is very effective in making society politically aware. Newspapers, TV, radio, cinema, and social media provide knowledge to citizens about their rights, duties, and power of voting. Media also provide analysis of various welfare policies of the government enabling citizens to assess the pros and cons of the policies. Media also play an effective role in creating awareness of women empowerment. Mass media also expose various scandals of politicians and officials making society cautious against such elements. Thus, mass media make society politically aware.

Influence of Mass Media on Society

Due to its indispensable nature or society, mass media strongly influences society. However, there is a negative influence also along with positive influence.

Positive Influence

a) **Trustworthy:** Mass media has such a magnetic effect on masses that masses start showing trust in mass media as they believe the information given by mass media regarding any field to be authentic.

b) **Influencing Shopping Habits:** Various online shopping offers on mass media make audience and masses to shift their shopping priorities to online destinations from traditional shopping joints as they are offered various benefits by online shopping companies.

Negative Influence

a) **Hypnotising Young Generation:** Mass media hold the audience spellbound, particularly the young generation through magnificent advertisements. Sometimes, they advertise those products which are not suitable health-wise to humans, like lavish ads of junk food. But young generation under the influence of those advertisements become inclined to go for eating junk food which is a big health hazard.

b) **Intoxicating Young Generation:** In this age of liberalisation, various TV channels and social media channels are showing obscene content which badly influences the young generation and contaminates its character. Such obscene display provokes many to follow the same path and under its influence, crimes like abductions and rapes are committed.

c) **Inclination towards Violence:** Various crime-related programmes are aired by mass media. Such displays promote incidents of violence in the society. Some members of the society under the influence of mass media content resort to violence and other crimes.

HISTORICAL GLIMPSES OF MASS MEDIA

*1) **Newspaper:***

- *First handwritten newspaper was circulated in Italy in 1566.*
- *The first ever printed newspaper was published in Germany in 1609.*
- *The first English newspaper, the Weekly News, was published in 1622 in England.*
- *Journalism began in 1883 with the starting of Charted Institute of Journalists in England.*

*2) **Radio:***

- *Radio waves were first identified and studied by German physicist Heinrich Hertz in 1886. That is why radio waves frequency is measured in Hertz.*
- *Radio was invented by Guglielmo Marconi of Italy in 1895.*
- *Radio became an effective channel of mass media during and after World War II as it used to transmit news faster than the newspaper.*
- *Radio began to be used commercially around 1900.*

3) ***Television:***

Mechanical television was invented by John Logie Baird of Scotland and Charles Francis Jenkins of the USA in early 1920s.

- *Electronic television was invented by Philo Taylor Farnsworth of USA in 1927.*
- *The first colour TV broadcast was done in USA in 1951.*
- *During 1950s television became a household name*

4) ***Cinema:***

- *Cinema has its roots in the first screening of short films to the audience by Lumiere Brothers in Paris in 1895.*
- *The first colour movie was shot in 1902 in England.*

5) ***Social Media:***

* *Tom Truscott and Jim Ellis of USA are considered to be creators of social media when they created 'Usernet' in 1979.*

* *However the first recognizable social media site, Six Degrees, was created in 1997.*

* *Facebook and Twitter were available to users by 2006.*

* *WhatsApp was founded in 2009 by Brian Acton and Jan Koum of USA, former employees of Yahoo!*

Theories of Influence

Following theories have been developed regarding influence of mass media on society. These theories depict a lot of variation regarding influence of mass media on society:

1) **Limited Effects Theory:** This theory was developed in 1940s. The theory argues that because people generally choose what to watch or read based on what they already believe, media exerts a negligible influence.
2) **Class-Dominant Theory:** This theory states that mass media projects the viewpoint of that elite class who owns various TV channels, newspapers, and other means of mass media. That content is presented to the society which is in the interest of that elite class which owns mass media channels. Hence, accordingly they try to influence the audience and so opinion of that elite class dominates.
3) **The Culturalist Theory:** The culturalist theory, developed in the 1980s and 1990s, combines the other two theories and claims that people interact with media to create their own meanings out of the images and messages they receive. This theory sees audiences as playing an active rather than passive role in relation to mass media. This theory believes that on one hand it should be assessed how the audience interacts with media and on the other hand, content that is produced and presented by mass media should be focussed.
4) **Gratification Theory:** It states that people select a particular media to fulfil their particular need.

MASS COMMUNICATION IN INDIA

India could hold a free hand on media of mass communication only after independence. Before that, during British period, means of mass communication were restricted. After independence there was a need to revive past glory of India which was not possible without involving the masses. There was a need to communicate with the masses regarding initiatives required for the overall development of India. Thus, the country needed a strong and free mass media. Resultantly, all the mass communication media like print and electronic media, viz radio and television were established and through various legislatures, mass media have been made autonomous to justify the motto of freedom of press and electronic media. With the passage of time there was a continuous improvement in communication technology, thus making channels of mass media the most efficient, authentic, and comfortable means of communication with the masses. The purpose of communicating masses had been to inform and educate masses through entertainment. There have been establishment of various means of communication through print and electronic media. Today, social networking is another strong media to disseminate information among masses and getting their feedback. Besides print and electronic media, there have been certain agencies working for communication with the masses. These can be explained as follows:

1) **Directorate of Advertising and Visual Publicity (DAVP):** It is a nodal agency of the government of India which undertakes multimedia advertising of various policies and programmes of the government through print and electronic media.

2) **Film industry:** Various documentary and feature films in Hindi and other regional languages convey very strong messages to the masses for various reforms. Film industry has produced such personalities like Shyam Benegal, Raj Kapoor, Dadasaheb Phalke, K. Asif, Dev Anand, and Basu Chatterjee who have conveyed very effective messages to the people of India through their films.
3) **Children Film Society:** It is responsible for organising children film festivals.
4) **National Film Development Corporation (NFDC):** It works in financing and producing films.

MEDIA IN INDIA

Background: Indian media is one of the oldest and largest media of the world. It consists of newspapers, magazines, radio, cinema, and television. Today's media also comprises of Internet-based websites and portals. Indian media has its roots in late 18th century with the start of print media in 1780. Radio broadcasting was started in 1927.

GLIMPSES OF MEDIA HISTORY IN INDIA

1) ***Bengal Gazette*** *was the first English daily published in India in 1780 by James Augustus Hicky.*
2) ***Samachar Sudha Varshan*** *was the first Hindi daily published in India in 1854.*
3) ***Samachar Darpan*** *was the first vernacular daily in India published in Bengali in 1818.*
4) ***Oriental Magazine or Calcutta Amusement*** *was the first magazine published in India in 1785.*
5) ***Associated Press of India (API)*** *was the first news agency in India established by K.C. Roy in 1905.*
6) ***Vyarawalla*** *was India's first woman photo journalist. She was popularly called 'Dalda13'*
7) ***Radio Club of Bombay*** *broadcasted first radio programme of India in 1923.*
8) ***First television programme*** *was telecasted in India in 1959 on behalf of All India Radio.*
9) ***First colour TV transmission*** *was started in India by Doordarshan in 1982.*
10) ***Raja Harishchandra*** *was the first full length film produced in India by Dadasaheb Phalke, 'The Pioneer of Indian Cinema'.*
11) ***Raja Harishchandra*** *was the first silent film of India.*
12) ***Marathi film industry*** *is the oldest in Indian film industry.*
13) ***Alam Ara*** *was the first movie with soundtrack released in 1931.*
14) ***Kisan Kanya*** *was India's first colour feature film released in 1937.*
15) ***B. Dattaram and Co.*** *was the first advertising agency of India which was established in 1902.*

Media in India is studied under:

1) Print Media
2) Electronic Media
3) Social Media
4) Aesthetic Media

PRINT MEDIA

Hicky's 'Bengal Gazette' laid the foundation of newspaper industry in India in 1780. This newspaper and newspapers that followed its path made a tangible contribution in the freedom struggle. Bengal virtually became the seat of Indian journalism. Later half of 19th century witnessed the introduction of today's prominent English newspapers like The Pioneer (1861), The Times of India (1861), The Statesman (1875) and The Hindu (1878).

> *"A newspaper is a tool of national reconstruction and social reformation."*
>
> ***Jawaharlal Nehru***

News Agencies In India

1) **Press Trust of India (PTI)**

   PTI is India's largest news agency of India. It was founded in 1947. It started functioning in 1949. It is collectively owned by 500 newspapers working as a co-operative and non-profit concern. It has its Hindi service BHASHA. Correspondents of PTI are based on leading centres all over the world. Having tie-ups with various foreign news agencies, it has attained the status of India's premier new agency. PTI is the only news agency in South Asia, which operates its own communication satellite INSAT. It is run by a Board of Directors and the Chairman is appointed in rotation at each annual General Meeting. Its routine administrative work is taken care of by CEO, an Editor-in-Chief.

Headquarter: New Delhi

2) **United News of India (UNI)**

India's another leading new agency, UNI was established in 1959, under the Company's Act in 1956. It started its commercial operations in 1961. UNI was the first news agency to start a multi-language news service UNIVARTA in 1982 and started providing news service to Hindi newspapers. In the year 1992 it also became the first news agency in the world to supply news in Urdu. Its subscribers include Doordarshan, All India Radio (AIR), State & Central governments, and news dailies of 14 languages. It also became the first new agency to start national news photo service. It has a tie-up with Chinese news agency Xinhua to supply international news photographs. At present it is providing news service in English, Hindi, and Urdu. It has also pioneered in providing service to foreign subscribers in collaboration with the British news agency Reuters.

Headquarter: New Delhi

3) **Indo-Asia News Service (IANS)**

It was established in 1986. It is providing 24-hours seven days service and covering news events of India and South Asia. IANS clientage is spread over to leading publishing houses, news channels, central and state government departments, and overseas Indian missions. IANS is headed by Editor-in-Chief and CEO.

Headquarter: Noida (UP)

4) **Asian News International (ANI)**

ANI is South Asia's leading multi-media news agency. It provides text, picture, and video content to various TV channels, print, mobile, and online media. It also extends services to foreign and domestic channels to prepare their reports in India and send them through satellite.

Headquarter: New Delhi

5) **Hindustan Samachar**

Hindustan Samachar was established in 1948. It is a multi-lingual news agency providing service to All India Radio (since 1968), Nepal Radio (since 1953), and Nepal TV and Doordarshan (since 1964). Hindustan Samachar shaped the goodwill of regional newspapers. It is providing services in Indian regional languages besides Nepali language.

Headquarter: Noida, India

6) **Samachar**

Samachar was created by merging four leading news agencies viz. PTI, UNI, Samachar Bharati, and Hindustan Samachar during emergency in 1976. Kuldip Nayar Committee was constituted to conduct a review over this step. The committee came up with the suggestions of creating two news agencies, i.e., Sandesh for English news and Varta for Hindi news. However, these agencies never saw the light of day due to clash of opinion among members of the committee. Resultantly, in 1978, those four merged news agencies were revived.

7) **Samachar Bharati**

Samachar Bharati is India's first bi-lingual news agency providing news services in Hindi and English simultaneously. It became operational in 1967. It has dedicated its services to take up issues which are neglected by mainstream media. It is covering national and international issues with full photo coverage.

Headquarter: Bhopal

8) **Non-Aligned News Agencies Pool (NANAP):**

It is an organization to exchange news among news agencies of non-aligned countries. The pool was established in 1976. It was created with initial support of Yugoslavia's national news agency Tanjug. India took over it as its first chairman for the duration from 1976-79. Arrangement of exchanging news covers four continents Asia, Europe, Africa, and Latin America. News is provided in English, Arabic, Spanish, and French.

Working Headquarter: Belgrade (Yugoslavia)

Newspapers-Vital Statistics

- Newspaper with maximum circulation: Dainik Bhasker (HQ: Bhopal)
- Hindi Newspaper with maximum circulation: Dainik Bhaskar (HQ: Bhopal)
- English newspaper with maximum circulation: The Times of India (HQ: Mumbai)

- Uttar Pradesh publishes maximum number of newspapers in India followed by Maharashtra.
- Maximum newspapers in India are published in Hindi followed by English.
- Besides Hindi and English, newspapers in India are published in 21 states' official languages.

Leading International News Agencies

News Agency	*Country*
Xinhua	*China*
Reuters	*United Kingdom*
Antara	*Indonesia*
MENA	*Egypt*
Associated Press	*USA*
Tanjug	*Yugoslavia*
Kyodo News	*Japan*

PRESS REGULATORY AGENCIES IN INDIA

First Press Commission of India: *The commission was constituted in 1952 under the chairmanship of J.S. Rajadhyaksa to streamline the state of print media in India. The commission recommended establishment of Registrar of Newspapers of India and the Press Council of India. The commission recommended various measures to ensure freedom of press and smoothening the working and lot of journalists.*

Second Press Commission: *The commission was set up in 1978 under the chairmanship of Justice P.C. Goswami and was reconstituted in 1980 under the chairmanship of Justice K.K. Mathew. The commission recommended setting up of Newspaper Development Commission (NDC) and amendment in the press law to widen the area of press in terms of accessibility.*

Registrar of Newspapers for India (RNI): *It was constituted in 1956 on the recommendation of first Press Commission. RNI was assigned the task of streamlining the discipline of newspapers in India.*

Press Council of India (PCI): *PCI was established in 1966 by the Parliament on the recommendation of the first Press Commission to raise standard of the press and ensure freedom of the press. The council is headed by a retired Supreme Court judge and 28 other members out of which 20 members are from the field of press and remaining are representatives of Rajya Sabha, Lok Sabha, UGC, legal, cultural, and literature field. It acts as a watchdog of the press and addresses grievances and free working of the press.*

HQ: New Delhi

Press Information Bureau (PIB): *PIB is working as a nodal agency of Government of India. It furnishes information about government plans, policies, and achievements to print electronic and new wave media. PIB was established in 1919. Started as Bureau of Public Information, it attained its present name in 1946. PIB serves as a channel of communication with the government. PIB provides authentic information of government policies and programmes through media to public and provide feedback from media to the government. Its HQ is in New Delhi.*

ELECTRONIC MEDIA IN INDIA

Electronic media is studied under two heads:

1. Electronic media in public sector
2. Electronic media in private sector

Electronic Media in Public Sector

All India Radio (AIR):

All India Radio came into existence in 1936 after converting Indian State Broadcasting Service of 1927 into All India Radio and it was placed under Ministry of Labour and Industries. In 1941, AIR came under Ministry of Information and Broadcasting. Commercial broadcasting was started in 1957 by launching Vividh Bharati.

At present AIR is providing the following services:

1) **Livestreaming:** 17 channels of AIR are livestreamed, viz. Vividh Bharati, FM Gold, FM Rainbow, and AIR in various state official languages.
2) **News Services:** AIR is broadcasting more than 510 bulletins daily in 82 languages in national, regional, and external services.
3) **Vividh Bharati:** It is the wholesome entertainment service of AIR.
4) **FM Radio:** FM radio service was introduced in India by AIR in 1977 in Chennai. Presently, FM Rainbow and FM Gold are AIR's leading FM radios.

5) **Direct-to-Home:** Various channels of AIR are available on Doordarshan Direct-to-Home service.
6) **Primary Channel:** This service primarily covers rural masses. The aim is to provide information through entertainment, i.e., 'Infotainment.'
7) **External Services:** External Services Division of AIR broadcasts 57 transmissions daily covering 108 countries in 27 languages out of which 15 are foreign languages and 12 are Indian.

PRASAR BHARATI

Prasar Bharati was created in 1997 as a public broadcaster. All India Radio and Doordarshan are its two constituents. Prasar Bharati is supervising broadcast and telecast of AIR and Doordarshan respectively. Major aim of Prasar Bharati is to provide information, education, and entertainment to people under two heads, i.e., 'Edutainment' and 'Infotainment.' Prasar Bharati also ensures balance in broadcasting and telecasting. It plans and approves programmes on national integration, women's' rights, freedom of press, spreading literacy, agricultural and rural development, health and family welfare, science & technology, and citizens' rights. Prasar Bharati has introduced Digital Terrestrial TV transmission in Doordarshan replacing analogue transmission while adopting Digital Video broadcasting (DVB) standard for more coverage and better viewing.
HQ: New Delhi

Community Radio: Community radio usually is a short-range, not-for-profit radio station or channel that caters for the information needs of people living in a particular locality, in the languages and formats that are most adapted to the local context.

Doordarshan (DD):

Doordarshan started its services in 1959. Initially, it was put under All India Radio and telecast was made from Akashvani Bhawan, New Delhi. Satellite technology was introduced in Doordarshan in 1975. Colour transmission was introduced in Asian Games of 1982 which were hosted by India. In 1976, it was put under Ministry of Information and Broadcasting. Ultimately in 1997, Prasar Bharati was created and Doordarshan and All India Radio were put under Prasar Bharati. Major national channels of Doordarshan are DD National, DD Metro, DD Sports, DD India, DD Gyan Darshan, DD Bharati, and DD Kisan. It is presently operating with 34 satellite channels. Doordarshan is providing services at national, regional, and local level.

National Level: At this level the subject of the programmes are issues or events of national interest. These include current affairs, news, documentaries on environment, science, art, culture, social issues, music, songs from Hindi films, feature films, dance, and drama.

Regional Level: Regional programmes are telecast on DD national at a particular day and time. These are also beamed on regional channel of Doordarshan. Here, programmes and issues of the interest of a particular region or state are transmitted including features and news.

Local Level: Such programmes are for a specific area at the local level. Here, local issues are taken up by involving local people.

HISTORIC PROGRAMS ON DOORDARSHAN

1) ***Krishi Darshan*** *was the first program telecast and it is being telecast even today, thus becoming the longest program.*
2) ***Bharat Ek Khoj (Documentary)*** *since 1988*
3) ***Hum Log (First Soap Opera)****:1984-85*
4) ***Ramayan (Mythological)****:1987-88*
5) ***Mungeri Lal ke Haseen Sapne (Comedy)****: 1989-90*
6) ***Buniyaad (Soap opera)****:1986-87*
7) ***Malgudi Days (Fiction)****: 1988*
8) ***Yeh Jo Hai Zindagi (Comedy)****: 1984*
9) ***Wagle ki Dunya (Satire)****: 1989-90*
10) ***Surabhi (Cultural Magazine Show)****: 1993-2001*
11) ***Rajani (Fiction)****: 1985*

Electronic Media in Private Sector

Radio:

Various FM radio stations are operating in India. These are given as under:

1) Radio Mirchi
2) Big FM
3) My FM

4) Fever 104 F,M,
5) Red FM
6) Radio Mango
7) Club FM
8) Radio City

Television Channels:

After introduction of satellite technology and due to liberalised broadcasting policy, there has been a mushrooming growth in private TV channels on various concepts of life. Some of the leading channels are listed below:

Entertainment Channels:

Sr. No	Name of Channel	Name of Group
1.	Life O.K.	Star India
2.	Channel V	Star India
3.	Zee TV	Zee Entertainment Enterprises
4.	&TV	Zee Entertainment Enterprises
5.	Sony Pictures TV	Sony Pictures Networks
6.	Sony Sab	Sony Pictures Networks
7.	Colors	Viacom 18
8.	Rishtey	Viacom 18
9.	MTV	Viacom 18
10.	Bindass	UTV
11.	EPIC	EPIC Television Network

Movie Channels

1.	Sony Max	Sony Pictures Networks India
2.	Sony Pal	Sony Pictures Networks India
3.	&Pictures	Zee Entertainment Enterprises
4.	Movies OK	Star
5.	B4U Movies	B4U
6.	UTV Movies	UTV
7.	Filmy	Sahara One
8.	Cinema TV	Softline Creations
9.	Manoranjan TV	Manoranjan Group
10.	R T Movies	Royal Television
11.	Rishtey Cineplex	Viacom 18
12.	AXN	Sony Pictures Networks India

Music and Bollywood

1.	Zing	Zee Entertainment Enterprises
2.	Music India	Media Worldwide
3.	9XM	9X Media
4.	B4U Music	B4U Television Network
5.	Sony MIX	Sony Pictures Networks
6.	Mastiii	Sri Adhikari Brothers Television
7.	MTV India	Viacom 18
8.	Sun Music	Sun TV network
9.	Bindass Play	Walt Disney Company (India)
10.	M Tunes	Pioneer
11.	Zoom	Times Group
12.	VH1	Viacom 18

News Channels

1.	Zee News	Zee Media (Essel Group)
2.	Republic TV	Arnab Goswami, Asianet News, and ARG Outlier Media
	(Sister channel is R. Bharat	Arnab Goswami and Asianet News)
3.	Sahara Samay	Sahara India Parivar
4.	News18 India (Formerly IBN7)	Network 18
5.	News Nation	News Nation Network
6.	India News	ITV Network
7.	DD News	Prasar Bharati
8.	India TV	Rajat Sharma and Ritu Dhawan
9.	NDTV India	New Delhi Television Limited
10.	ABP News	ABP Group
11.	Aaj Tak	Living Media
12.	News 24	B.A.G. Films and Media Limited
13.	CNBC Awaaz	TV18 and CNBC
14.	ET Now (English)	Times Group
15.	Times Now (English)	Times Group

16.	India Today (English)	Living Media
17.	CNN-News 18 (English)	Network 18
18.	BloombergQuint (English)	Raghav Behl, Ritu Kapur
19.	TV9 Bharatvarsh	Associated Broadcasting Company Private Limited
20.	World is One News (WION)	Zee Media

Sports Channels

1)	Fox Sports (Former ESPN)	Walt Disney Company
2)	Sony Ten (1-3)	Sony Pictures Network
3)	Neo Prime	Nimbus Communications
4)	Star Sports (1-3)	Walt Disney Company India
5)	DSport	Discovery Asia-Pacific

Information Channels

1)	National Geographic	National Geographic Partners
2)	Discovery	Discovery
3)	Animal Planet	Discovery
4)	Travelxp	Celebrities Management Private Limited
5)	History	A + E Networks

Taglines of Different TV Channels

Sr. No	TV Channel	Tagline
1)	Star Plus	Rishta Wahi Soch Nayi
2)	Zee TV	Ummeed Se Saje Zindagi
3)	Sahara One	Moh Le Aapka Man
4)	Colors	Jasbaat Ke Rang
5)	SAB TV	Asli Maza SAB Ke Sath Aata Hai
6)	Channel V	Bloody Cool
7)	MTV	Stay Raw
8)	9XM	Haq Se
9)	Set MAX	Deewana Bana De
10)	UTV Bindass	Rest Less
11)	Life OK	Kal Ki Mat Fikar Karo, Aaj Ka Jashn Manao
12)	Star GOLD	Karo Dil Ki
13)	UTV Movies	Jeeyo Bollywood
14)	B4U	The Digital Entertainment Channel
15)	Filmy	Maa Kasam Filmy Hai
16)	DD National	Satyam, Shivam, Sunderam
17)	E24	Bollywood Ka Pehla News Channel
18)	Zoom	Isko Dekho
19)	Zee News	Zara Sochiye
20)	R. Bharat	You are Republic, we are your Voice
21)	News 18 India	Hausla Hai
22)	India News	Desh ki Dharkan
23)	DD News	Only news complete news (English), Bharosa Bharat Ka (Hindi)
24)	India TV	Aap Ki Awaaz
25)	ABP News	Aapko Rakhe Aage
26)	Aaj Tak	Sabse Tez
27)	News 24	Nazar Har Khabar Par
28)	CNBC Awaaz	India's No. 1 Business Channel
29)	ET Now	Rise with India
30)	Times Now	Action begins here always with the news
31)	World is One News	(WION) World is One
32)	Sony Ten	Go beyond Sports inspires life
33)	Discovery	"Let's All Discover..."

34)	Animal Planet	Surprisingly Human
35)	Travelxp	See more. Xplore more.
36)	History	And the rest is history

Taglines of Radio Stations in India

Sr. No.	Name of Radio Station	Tagline
1.	All India Radio	'Bahujan Hitaya : Bahujan Sukhaya'
2.	Red FM	Bajate Raho
3.	Big FM	Suno Sunao Life Banao
4.	Radio Mirchi	Mirchi Sunnewale Always Khush, Its Hot
5.	My FM	Jiyo Dil se
6.	Radio City	Whatte Fun
7.	Dhamaal 24	Dhinchak

Renowned Journalists/Reporters of Print and Electronic Media

Sr. No	Name	Associated Group
1.	Prannoy Roy	NDTV
2.	Barkha Dutt	NDTV, Freelancer
3.	Ravish Kumar	NDTV
4.	Arnab Goswami	R. Bharat
5.	Gauri Lankesh	Freelancer
6.	Rajat Sharma	India TV
7.	Sweta Singh	Aaj Tak
8.	Boria Majumdar	Freelancer
9.	Farid Zakaria	CNN
10.	Shoma Chaudhury	Tehelka
11.	Aroon Purie	TV Today, Reader's Digest
12.	Arun Shourie	Indian Express, Times of India
13.	Bobby Ghosh	Times magazine, Hindustan Times
14.	Chandan Mitra	The Pioneer
15.	Rajdeep Sardesai	India Today Group
16.	Sagarika Ghose	Times of India, Indian Express, Outlook, CNN-IBN
17.	Vinod Dua	HW News
18.	Abhisar Sharma	HW News
19.	Harsha Bhogle	Freelancer
20.	Vir Sanghvi	HT Media
21.	Khalid Mohamed	Hindustan times, Filmfare
22.	Narsimhan Ram (N. Ram)	The Hindu
23.	M.J. Akbar	India Today
24.	Shekhar Gupta	India Today
25.	Dibang	ABP News
26.	Mark Tully	BBC India
27.	Kuldip Nayar	The Statesman
28.	Prabhu Chawla	India Today
29.	Swapan Dasgupta	Daily Telegraph, The Times of India, India Today, Indian Express
30.	Tarun Tejpal	Tehelka

CELEBRATING DAYS ON MEDIA, PRESS, AND JOURNALISM

1) *World Press Freedom Day - May 3*
2) *National Press day - November 16*
3) *National Journalism Day - November 17*
4) *World Social Media Day - June 30*
5) *World Television Day - November 21*
6) *World Radio Day - February 13*

DIRECT-TO-HOME (DTH) SERVICES IN INDIA

Direct to Home (DTH) is a service in which TV services are received directly at home through satellite. A small dish antenna is to be installed. There is no need of cable connection. The first DTH service in India was started by Dish TV in 2003. However, Prasar Bharti started the first free DTH service in 2004. Presently, following DTH service providers are operating in India:

1) DD Free Dish
2) Airtel Digital TV(Slogan-TV saath saath Dekhne Mein Maza Aata Hai Na)
3) Dish TV (Launched by Zee Media, Slogan-Dish Nahi Dishkiyaon)

4) Reliance Digital TV (Slogan-TV Ho Toh Big Ho) (Now its name is Independent TV)
5) Tata Sky (Slogan-Isko Laga Dala toh Family Jhingalala)
6) Videocon D2H (Slogan-Direct Hai Correct Hai)
7) Sun Direct (Slogan-Har Ghar Mein Sun Tan Tana Tan)

SOCIAL MEDIA (NETWORKING & CHAT) SITES

1) Facebook
2) WhatsApp
3) QQ
4) QZone
5) Instagram
6) Twitter
7) Baidu Tieba
8) Skype
9) Viber
10) Bing (Search engine by Microsoft)
11) Tumblr
12) LINE
13) Snapchat
14) Pinterest
15) LinkedIn
16) Foursquare
17) Badoo
18) Tagged
19) Myspace

Some Vital Facts

1) A characteristic of modern mass media is capital intensive.
2) The mode of communication that involves a single source transmitting information to a large number of receivers simultaneously is called mass communication.
3) The first multi-lingual news agency of India was Hindustan Samachar.
4) Referential framing used by TV audience connects media with reality
5) Bengal Gazette, the first Newspaper in India was started in 1780 by James Augustus Hicky
6) The largest circulated daily newspaper is The Times of India.
7) The pioneer of the silent feature film in India was Dada SahebPhalke.
8) All India Radio (A.I.R.) for broadcasting was named in the year 1936
9) Term 'DAVP' stands for Directorate of Advertising & Visual Publicity
10) In mass communication, selective perception is dependent on the receiver's receptivity
11) Media that exist in an interconnected series of communication - points are referred to as Network Media.
12) The information function of mass communication is described as surveillance.
13) Newspaper is an example of asynchronous medium.
14) In analog mass communication (Analog mass communication is the one way process of transferring message to the receiver, or audience), stories are static.
15) The main objective of F.M. station in radio is Entertainment, Information and Interaction
16) Community Radio is a type of radio service that caters to the interest of local residents
17) All India Radio before 1936 was known as State (Indian) Broadcasting Service.
18) The biggest news agency of India is PTI.

Practice Exercise

General Questions Format

1. Which of the following is wrongly paired?
(A) Bimillah Khan - Shehnai
(B) Rehman Bakhs - Sitar
(C) Panna Lal Ghosh - Flute
(D) L. Subramaniam - Violin

2. Which journalist has been popularly called 'Dalda 13'?
(A) Vyarawalla (B) K.C. Roy
(C) J.A. Hicky (D) B. Dattaram

3. Which of the following is NOT a Direct-to-Home (DTH) service provider?
(A) Sun Direct (B) Tata Sky
(C) Flash TV (D) Free Dish

4. Names of journalists are given under Column I and names of their associated groups are given under Column II. Match the name of the journalist with group and choose the correct code among the codes given below:

Column I (Name of the journalist)	Column II (Name of news channel)
a) Bobby Ghosh	i) Freelancer
b) Abhisar Sharma	ii) Daily Telegraph
c) Swapan Dasgupta	iii) Pioneer
d) Gauri Lankesh	iv) HT Media
	v) Times
	vi) HW News

Codes:	(a)	(b)	(c)	(d)
(A)	vi	v	iii	iv
(B)	iv	ii	i	iii
(C)	v	vi	iii	iv
(D)	v	vi	ii	i

5. Class Dominant Theory on influence of mass media on society depicts that
(A) Mass media influences elite class of society which has an easy access to mass media
(B) That class of society dominates which is fully influenced by mass media
(C) Elite class of owners of mass media channels dominate in influencing the society
(D) The most affluent class of society establishes its dominance in the society though mass media

6. TV channel Movies OK is owned by
(A) Star (B) Viacom
(C) Sahara (D) Multi Screen Media

7. Which of the following justifies the relationship between mass communication and mass media?
(A) Mass communication and mass media are two sides of the same coin.
(B) Mass communication justifies the existence of mass media.
(C) Mass media justifies the existence of mass communication.
(D) Mass media and mass communication are contemporary to each other.

8. Which is India's first bi-lingual news agency?
(A) UNI
(B) Hindustan Samachar
(C) Samachar
(D) Samachar Bharati

9. Which of the following is NOT TRUE?
a) First printed newspaper was published in France.
b) The first coloured movie was shot in England.
c) Radio began to be used commercially around 1900.
d) First English newspaper was published in Germany.
(A) Only b and d (B) Only c
(C) Only a and d (D) Only a, c and d

10. *"A newspaper is a tool of national reconstruction and social reformation."* It was stated by
(A) Jawahar Lal Nehru
(B) Dr. Radhakrishnan
(C) Mahatama Gandhi
(D) Dr. Zakir Hussain

11. 'Bajate Raho' is the tagline of which FM Radio?
(A) Mirchi (B) Red FM
(C) Big FM (D) Radio City

12. Which of the following is a negative influence of mass media?
(A) Hypnotising children
(B) Intoxicating young generation
(C) Inclination towards violence
(D) All of these

13. AXN is an associate channel of...........TV.
(A) Sony (B) Zee
(C) Doordarshan (D) Star Plus

14. Which of the following truly justifies the relation between society and mass media?
(A) Mass media presents the content after feeling the pulse of the society.
(B) Society is not easily influenced by mass media.
(C) Pervasiveness of mass media determines its influence on the society.
(D) Society needs inputs from mass media for every activity.

15. Which channel of mass media was the most popular during the days of World War II?
(A) Television
(B) Radio
(C) Newspaper
(D) Cinema

16. What is full form of DAVP?
(A) Directorate of Advertising-Visual Publicity
(B) Department of Audio-Visual Publicity
(C) Directorate of Audio-Visual Publications
(D) Directorate of Advanced-Visual Publicity

17. Which of the following is/are NOT TRUE?
a) Hindustan Samachar was first news agency of India.
b) Raja Harishchandra was the first silent film of India.
c) Calcutta Amusement was the first magazine published in India.
d) Samachar Darpan was the first vernacular daily in India.
(A) Only c and d
(B) a, b, c, and d
(C) Only a
(D) Only d

18. Which was the first soap opera of Doordarshan?
(A) Buniyaad (B) Hum Log
(C) Malgudi Days (D) Wagle ki Duniya

19. Hindi news service 'Bhasha' has been started by which news agency of India?
(A) PTI (B) UNI
(C) IANS (D) ANI

20. ANTARA is news agency of
(A) Egypt (B) Afghanistan
(C) Russia (D) Indonesia

KEY

1. B	2. A	3. C	4. D	5. C	6. A	7. B
8. D	9. C	10. A	11. B	12. D	13. A	14. C
15. B	16. A	17. C	18. B	19. A	20. D	

Assertion–Reason Format

1. **Assertion (A):** Mass media depicts the real picture of society.
Reason (R): Society considers mass media an authentic source of information.
(A) Both A and R are true and R is correct explanation of A
(B) Both A and R are true but R is not correct explanation of A
(C) A is true but R is false
(D) A is false but R is true

2. **Assertion (A):** Print media is in tough competition with electronic media.
Reason (R): Even today people relish reading the newspaper.
(A) Both A and R are true and R is correct explanation of A
(B) Both A and R are true but R is not correct explanation of A
(C) Both A and R are false
(D) A is true but R is false

3. **Assertion (A):** Prasar Bharati was created to give Doordarshan and AIR a single identity.

Reason (R): Programmes aired by Doordarshan and AIR needed a single platform.

(A) Both A and R are true and R is correct explanation of A

(B) Both A and R are true but R is not correct explanation of A

(C) A is true but R is false

(D) Both A and R are false

4. **Assertion (A):** Survival of mass communication depends upon mass media.

Reason (R): Mass media address masses with aims of infotainment and edutainment.

(A) Both A and R are true and R is correct explanation of A

(B) Both A and R are true but R is not correct explanation of A

(C) A is false but R is true

(D) A is true but R is false

5. **Assertion (A):** Radio became more popular than newspaper during post World War II period.

Reason (R): People found radio faster than newspaper in transmitting news.

(A) Both A and R are true and R is correct explanation of A

(B) Both A and R are true but R is not correct explanation of A

(C) A is true but R is false

(D) A is false but R is true

6. **Assertion (A):** Masses find aesthetic media more pervasive than electronic media.

Reason (R): Direct interaction carries stronger feedback than interactive interaction.

(A) Both A and R are true but R is not correct explanation of A

(B) Both A and R are true and R is correct explanation of A

(C) A is false but R is true

(D) A is true but R is false

7. **Assertion (A):** Mass media channels are hurting society's sentiments through their content.

Reason (R): Channels claim in the disclaimer that the content does not belong to them.

(A) Both A and R are true and R is correct explanation of A

(B) Both A and R are true but R is not correct explanation of A

(C) Both A and R are false

(D) A is true but R is false

8. **Assertion (R):** First Press Commission of India recommended ensuring freedom of press.

Reason (R): Press Council of India was established to ensure freedom of press.

(A) Both A and R are true and R is correct explanation of A

(B) Both A and R are true but R is not correct explanation of A

(C) A is true but R is false

(D) A is false but R is true

9. **Assertion (A):** Vernacular newspapers hinder universalisation of mass communication.

Reason (R): Mass media in regional language is mandatory to cover diverse cultures uniformly.

(A) Both A and R are correct and R is correct explanation of A

(B) Both A and R are true but R is not correct explanation of A

(C) Both A and R are false

(D) A is true but R is false

10. **Assertion (A):** Influence of mass media on society is reflected in people's routine behaviour.

Reason (R): Society takes mass media as an indispensable source of information on every issue of routine life.

(A) Both A and R are true and R is correct explanation of A

(B) Both A and R are true but R is not correct explanation of A

(C) A is true but R is false

(D) A is false but R is true

11. **Assertion (A):** Mass media promote a culture of violence in the society.

Reason (R): Violence sells in the market as people themselves are violent in character.

(A) Both A and R are true and R is the correct explanation of A

(B) Both A and R are true, but R is not the correct explanation of A

(C) A is true but R is false

(D) Both A and R are false

KEY

1. D **2.** B **3.** D **4.** A **5.** A **6.** C **7.** B **8.** B **9.** C **10.** A **11.** C

Questions Asked in Previous NET Exams

1. Which of the following is a characteristic of modern mass media? **(UGC NET JUNE 2019)**

(A) Capital intensive

(B) labour Intensive

(C) Sustainable

(D) Developmental

2. Mass media do not have predetermined functions for everyone and people use them the way they like. This is suggestive of the fact that, **(UGC NET JUNE 2019)**

(A) Audiences are active

(B) Content is of little significance

(C) Content lacks plurality

(D) Audiences are homogeneous

3. The mode of communication that involves a single source transmitting information to a large number of receivers simultaneously, is called **(UGC NET DECEMBER 2014)**

(A) Group Communication

(B) Mass Communication

(C) Intrapersonal Communication

(D) Interpersonal Communication

4. The first multi-lingual news agency of India was **(UGC NET DECEMBER 2013)**

(A) Samachar

(B) API

(C) Hindustan Samachar

(D) Samachar Bharati

5. Referential framing used by TV audience connects media with **(UGC NET SEPTEMBER 2013)**

(A) reality (B) falsity

(C) negativity (D) passivity

6. Bengal Gazette, the first Newspaper in India was started in 1780 by **(UGC NET JUNE 2013)**

(A) Dr. Annie Besant

(B) James Augustus Hicky

(C) Lord Cripps

(D) A.O. Hume

7. The largest circulated daily newspaper among the following is **(UGC NET DECEMBER 2012)**

(A) The Times of India

(B) The Indian Express

(C) The Hindu

(D) The Deccan Herald

8. The pioneer of the silent feature film in India was **(UGC NET DECEMBER 2012)**

(A) K.A. Abbas

(B) Satyajit Ray

(C) B.R. Chopra

(D) Dadasaheb Phalke

9. All India Radio (AIR) for broadcasting was named in the year **(UGC NET JUNE 2012)**

(A) 1926 (B) 1936

(C) 1946 (D) 1956

10. The term 'DAVP' stands for **(UGC NET JUNE 2012)**

(A) Directorate of Advertising & Vocal Publicity

(B) Division of Audio-Visual Publicity

(C) Department of Audio-Visual Publicity

(D) Directorate of Advertising and Visual Publicity

11. In which language the newspapers have highest circulation? **(UGC NET DECEMBER 2011)**

(A) English (B) Hindi

(C) Bengali (D) Tamil

12. In mass communication, selective perception is dependent on the receiver's

(UGC NET JUNE 2011)

(A) competence (B) predisposition
(C) receptivity (D) ethnicity

13. Media that exist in an interconnected series of communication points are referred to as

(UGC NET DECEMBER 2010)

(A) Networked media
(B) Connective media
(C) Nodal media
(D) Multimedia

14. The information function of mass communication is described as

(UGC NET DECEMBER 2010)

(A) diffusion (B) publicity
(C) surveillance (D) diversion

15. An example of asynchronous medium is

(UGC NET DECEMBER 2010)

(A) Radio
(B) Television
(C) Film
(D) Newspaper

16. Analogue mass communication stories are

(UGC NET DECEMBER 2010)

(A) static
(B) dynamic
(C) interactive
(D) exploratory

17. Which is not a 24-hours news channel?

(UGC NET JUNE 2009)

(A) NDTV 24x7
(B) ZEE News
(C) Aaj Tak
(D) Lok Sabha channel

18. The main objective of FM station in radio is:

(UGC NET JUNE 2009)

(A) Information, Entertainment, and Tourism
(B) Entertainment, Information, and Interaction
(C) Tourism, Interaction, and Entertainment
(D) Entertainment only

19. Community Radio is a type of radio service that caters to the interest of:

(UGC NET DECEMBER 2008)

(A) Local audience
(B) Education
(C) Entertainment
(D) News

20. Match List I with List II and select the correct answer using the codes given below:

(UGC NET DEC.2008)

List I (Artists)	**List II (Art)**
(a) Amrita Sher-Gil	(i) Flute
(b) T. Swaminathan Pillai	(ii) Classical Singing
(c) Bhimsen Joshi	(iii) Painting
(d) Padma Subramaniyam	(iv) Bharatanatyam

Codes:	(a)	(b)	(c)	(d)
(A)	(iii)	(i)	(ii)	(iv)
(B)	(ii)	(iii)	(i)	(iv)
(C)	(iv)	(ii)	(iii)	(i)
(D)	(i)	(iv)	(ii)	(iii)

21. All India Radio before 1936 was known as:

(UGC NET JUNE 2008)

(A) Indian Radio Broadcasting
(B) Broadcasting Service of India
(C) Indian Broadcasting Service
(D) All India Broadcasting Service

22. The biggest news agency of India is:

(UGC NET JUNE 2008)

(A) PTI
(B) UNI
(C) NANAP
(D) Samachar Bharati

23. Prasar Bharati was launched in the year:

(UGC NET JUNE 2008)

(A) 1995
(B) 1997
(C) 1999
(D) 2001

24. First free DTH service was started in the year: **(UGC NET DECEMBER 2007)**
(A) 2000 (B) 2002
(C) 2004 (D) 2006

25. National Press day is celebrated on: **(UGC NET DECEMBER 2007)**
(A) 16th November
(B) 19th November
(C) 21th November
(D) 30th November

26. The total number of members in the Press Council of India are: **(UGC NET DECEMBER 2007)**
(A) 28 (B) 14
(C) 17 (D) 20

27. Press Council of India is located at: **(UGC NET JUNE 2007)**
(A) Chennai
(B) Mumbai
(C) Kolkata
(D) New Delhi

28. Which of the following pair is not correctly matched? **(UGC NET DECEMBER 2006)**
(A) N. Ram: The Hindu
(B) Barkha Dutt: Zee News
(C) Prannoy Roy: NDTV 24×7
(D) Prabhu Chawla: Aaj Tak

29. Which is the 24-hours English Business news channel in India? **(UGC NET DECEMBER 2006)**
(A) Zee News (B) NDTV 24×7
(C) CNBC (D) India News

30. The function of mass communication of supplying information regarding the processes, issues, events, and societal developments is known as: **(UGC NET JUNE 2006)**
(A) content supply (B) surveillance
(C) gratification (D) correlation

KEY

1. A	**2.** A	**3.** B	**4.** C	**5.** A	**6.** B	**7.** A
8. D	**9.** B	**10.** D	**11.** B	**12.** C	**13.** A	**14.** C
15. D	**16.** A	**17.** D	**18.** B	**19.** A	**20.** A	**21.** C
22. A	**23.** B	**24.** C	**25.** A	**26.** A	**27.** D	**28.** B
29. C	**30.** A					

3 Effective Communication

CONCEPT

Today, the concept of communication is no more confined to its original meaning. It is going beyond that as today mere sharing of the message does not complete the communication process. Today is the age of effective communication which aims at not merely sharing the message; rather it is to make the recipient understand the message and getting the feedback and this is considered as ***Effective Communication***. Whatever field of life we pick up, there is a need to communicate effectively, if we want to achieve breakthroughs in that field. In the present day life 'How we say' is more important than 'What we say'.

Importance of Effective Communication

While going by the concept of effective communication, it is clear that neither the communicator nor the recipient is satisfied by mere sharing of the message. The aim of present day communication is to yield an effective impact on both the participants. So it becomes desirable to realize the importance of effective communication.

1) **Trust Builder:** As communication is initiated by the communicator, it is the communicator who has the purpose of communication. That is, communicator is the primary participant in communication process, though recipient is also a party to the communication process. Effective communication builds the trust regarding the communicator in the mind of the recipient. Due to this, recipient participates in every communication process in future while observing all ethics of effective communication. And this gesture also justifies the notion that first impression is the last impression. In the case of classroom teaching, students prefer to trust that teacher who is sincerely involved in the teaching-learning process. So effective communication is a major trust builder.
2) **Healthy Interaction:** Effective communication process yields healthy interaction between the communicator and the recipient as communication is recipient-centered. Similarly, practising learner-centered methods of teaching by a teacher gives an opportunity to actively participate in the teaching-learning process.
3) **No Communication Gap:** There is apprehension of communication gap in normal sharing of the message due to assumptions and over-assumptions. On the other hand, in effective communication, there is no such apprehension. In such communication process, both the communicator and recipient are actively participating with full concentration, thus nothing is missed or misunderstood.
4) **Widens Social Circle:** With effective communication, a communicator can widen his/her social circle as people have trust in him/her as far as dissemination of any information is concerned. It is believed that information provided through an effective communication process is authentic and accurate.

Essentials of Effective Communication

It is the communicator who has a purpose of communication. He/she may be a teacher, doctor, lawyer, or any other person but purpose of communication is always with him. In spite of belonging to different professions, the common aim is to deliver the message effectively. For this, communicator and sometimes the recipient are to follow certain essentials, given as follows:

1) **Positive and Pleasant Approach:** A communicator with a positive approach and pleasant personality makes every communication effective. With this objective in mind, various industrial and business houses in public and private sectors employ staff with a pleasant personality along with being optimistic about their duty.
2) **Appropriate Tone, Pitch, Quality, Force, and Intensity of Voice:** Oral communication can be made effective by the communicator while maintaining an appropriate tone, pitch, quality, force, and intensity of voice. These traits are found in a good teacher, who aims to be audible to every student in the class to achieve the aim of effective communication.

3) **Clarity of Purpose and Objective of Communication:** A communication becomes effective if the communicator clears the purpose and objective of communication. This is true both for oral and written communication.

4) **Clarity of Thought and Expression:** A communicator makes his communication effective while clearly revealing his viewpoint on the subject or matter to be communicated. Further, he/she must be able to express his thoughts clearly. In written communication, legibility is a measure of expression and in oral communication, correct pronunciation of the words and sentences become the expression. It has been found that a communicator with illegible handwriting does not leave an effective impact on the recipient as if he/she is not able to read the message so delivered, then he/she cannot give feedback. Similarly, if a communicator does not know how to pronounce a word or has some speaking disorder, then recipient will not be able to listen and understand the message and again, there will be no feedback. It is generally suggested by experts that those personnel including teachers, whose duty is to address public or students, should be outstanding orators and the concerned authorities should consider this factor while employing them.

5) **Adequate Knowledge of the Subject:** A communicator must possess sufficient knowledge of the subject he/she is going to share with the recipient to ensure effective communication. A teacher must have an authority on his subject which he teaches in the class as his/her purpose in the true sense is not merely to impart knowledge to students but also make them understand the content. For this, the teacher chooses that style of teaching which will leave the students spellbound.

6) **Objective and Realistic Approach:** A good communicator communicates with an objective in mind. He/she also follows the practical and feasible approach for delivering his/her message so that the recipient may easily understand the content and gives due feedback to establish effective communication.

7) **Self-Confidence and Conviction:** It is generally observed that only those communicators, including teachers make their communication effective, if they make their presentation with confidence and conviction.

8) **Adequate Knowledge of the Communication Receiver:** It is essential for the communicator that he/she must have the knowledge of the recipient with whom he/she is going to share information. For example, it is advised by experts that education planners and teachers should have sufficient knowledge of learners' characteristics and prepare education policies and teaching strategies accordingly. Such teaching methods will be effective as these are learner-centered methods.

9) **Organisation of Message:** A well-organized message, when delivered, leaves the desired impact on the recipient. If a teacher delivers an organized lecture, learners concentrate on it and the teacher's aim to achieve the desired feedback is met.

10) **Proper Selection and Use of Media:** Selecting and using an appropriate medium makes a communication effective as the recipient decodes the message, understands it, and gives the desired feedback. A teacher makes his classroom communication effective by resorting to that medium of instruction which is easily accessible by learners. Further, if a communicator is to address a large gathering, he uses the medium of public address system. To address masses, appropriate mass media can be used and feedback can be invited.

11) **Proper Selection and Use of Channel:** Effective communication is achieved by selecting appropriate channels of communication. Communicator is to select whether he should practise oral or written communication. Channel of formal or official communication is generally written communication and informal communication resorts to oral communication. Other channels to be chosen for effective communication in an organisation or otherwise include interpersonal communication channel, group communication channel, interactive communication channel, and electronic or social media communication channels. Any of these chosen channels will be appropriate if it helps in making communication effective.

12) **Appropriate Formality:** Whether communication is formal/ informal or written/oral, it requires an icebreaker before delivery of a message and vote of thanks after delivery in the interest of effective communication. A communicator follows appropriate formality by resorting to phatic cues in the communication process to make communication effective. Even nonverbal cues are also used to express such formality conducive in making communication effective. Embracing and handshaking before and after delivery of the message makes delivery of the message effective.

13) **Active Participation of Recipient:** A communicator's every effort to make his/her communication effective will result in futility if recipient does not actively participate in the communication process. The role of the recipient in making a communication effective includes proper attention, concentration, decoding, understanding, giving feedback, patience in listening in case of oral communication, etc. The central idea behind defining the role of a recipient is to ensure his/her attention towards the message. In case of classroom teaching, learners can make teacher's communication effective by concentrating on the lecture while endorsing the teacher's efforts to make delivery of the lecture convenient for them.

14) **Adaptability:** If a communicator and the recipient continue communication while adapting to even the odd circumstances prevailing around them, communication will definitely be effective.

15) **Courtesy:** While practicing oral communication, communicator should exhibit courtesy towards the recipient before sharing the message with him/her. Courtesy shown by the communicator will make the recipient feel noticed and he mentally prepares to listen to the communicator with full attention. Communicator's courtesy gesture makes communication effective.

16) **Time Consciousness:** A communication is effective if it is made within the requisite time limit. It means that the message must be shared in time. Content of time-bound occasions and situations must be shared within their prescribed time limit. If such content is shared after the lapse of the time limit, that message does not carry any relevance for the recipient.

17) **Conciseness and Relevance:** Message to be shared should be brief, to the point, and relevant to the subject of discussion. Lengthy messages always carry irrelevant and superfluous content which is not appreciated by the recipient and hence, communication goes ineffective.

18) **Correctness:** The shared message must be grammatically and conceptually correct. In case of written communication, even spellings should also be correct. Only then, the message leaves an impact on the recipient making him to respond and give feedback.

19) **Completeness:** Sharing of incomplete message leaves the recipient in limbo and such communication is never effective.

20) **Blending Nonverbal Cues with Verbal Message:** In case of oral communication, if the communicator blends nonverbal cues like making gestures, facial expression, use of limbs, eye contact, nodding, etc., the message being delivered earns extra strength and the recipient easily gets convinced about the authenticity and validity of the message and motivates him/her to feedback. When a teacher delivers a lecture in the classroom while using nonverbal gestures, it is established that the teacher is fully absorbed in delivering the lecture. Learners are also convinced as the nonverbal gestures used by the teacher make learning and understanding easy for them.

21) **'You Attitude':** To make communication effective, the communicator gives due recognition to the recipient. Recipient is made to realize that he/she is the only one who can understand this message and give the due feedback. This motivates the recipient to actively participate in the communication process.

INTERCULTURAL COMMUNICATION

Intercultural communication is sharing messages or communication through verbal and nonverbal cues among people belonging to different cultures and social groups.

Edward T. Hall

> *The term 'Intercultural Communication' was propounded by an American anthropologist Edward. T. Hall in his book* ***"The Silent Language"*** *in 1959.*

Purpose

For a researcher, purpose of intercultural communication is to understand the process on three grounds:

1) **Culture-Specific:** Here, researcher concentrates on studying the communication behaviour of members of a specific culture, i.e., intracultural communication.
2) **Culture General:** Here, the study focusses on communication across different cultures.
3) **Intercultural Interaction:** Here, study concentrates on communication involving combination of both culture-specific and culture general traits.

Significance of Intercultural Communication

1) **Useful for achieving Academic Excellence:** Intercultural communication is useful for achieving academic excellence in social sciences like Anthropology, Psychology, Linguistics, Cultural Studies, etc.

2) **Basis for International Trade:** Intercultural communication becomes the base for international trade and business. Every culture has its heritage industries, handicrafts, garments, toys, and artefacts which become popular internationally. Intercultural communication enables traders from different cultures to exchange their heritage products.
3) **Avenues for Developing Intercultural Skills:** Various service providers are imparting intercultural communication skills resulting in vital pacts and agreements of cultural exchange at an international level.
4) **Awarding Identity to Different Cultures:** Intercultural communication enables members of different cultures to speak to one another and respect the identity of each culture. Learning intercultural communication skills help each culture to establish its identity at an international level.
5) **Research and Cultural Exchanges:** Intercultural communication skills facilitate research on different cultures and there becomes an ample scope of cultural exchanges. Various research and academic institutes have started various courses on intercultural communication.

GROUP COMMUNICATION

Group communication is an extended form of interpersonal communication where more than two individuals are involved in exchange of ideas, skills, and interests. A group is a number of people with a common goal who interact with one another to accomplish their goals, recognize one another's existence, and see themselves as part of the group. In the group communication, participants get an opportunity to discuss and exchange views of common interest. Group may comprise family members, friends, colleagues, various sports teams, defence personnel regiments, etc. Group communication may be direct in face-to-face interaction in meetings or interactive through phone, email, WhatsApp, social media, etc.

Group communication is considered as an effective communication as participants are indirectly effective in changing ideas and beliefs. On the contrary, time-consuming feature of group communication makes it inefficient. Further, there arise barriers in the group communication due to clash of status, skills, and individual goals of members. Further, communication in a large group is no more effective as it leaves a weak impact due to almost no feedback.

Advantages of Group Communication

1) **Promotes Team Work Culture:** Group communication promotes a culture of teamwork. Today, various projects require teamwork for their successful completion.
2) **Polishing Communication Skills:** Group communication polishes communication skills of participants as people of different status, attitude, and aptitude share some common idea. Hence, each member learns from the experience and skills of the other.
3) **A Platform of Effective Communication:** A group is a promising platform of effective communication as it provides an opportunity to members of different disciplines to interact with more resources, knowledge, and ideas which yield unanimous decisions useful for various developments.
4) **Promotes Creativity:** Group communication promotes creativity as persons with specialised skills interact with each other.
5) **Contributor in Research and Development:** Various academic and research groups become effective in bringing research and development in various fields which is the result of the unanimous decision of the group.

Limitations of Group Communication

1) **Weak Impact:** Communication of a large group leaves a weak impact as feedback is lost in large-scale multiple interaction, i.e., there is no personal interaction due to a large number of participants, so group communication remains no more effective.
2) **Time-Consuming:** Group communication process is a time-consuming process as a discussion is initiated and arriving at any decision consumes lot of time. Due to this, group communication becomes inefficient.
3) **Clash of Opinion:** In group communication, sometimes clash of opinion among participants arises as each participant comes with his/her own viewpoint which may not be acceptable to others. This clash of opinion creates a barrier in the group communication.

Part – I

EFFECTIVE COMMUNICATION
(Types and Barriers)

Types of Communication

1) **Intrapersonal Communication:** This communication is talking to oneself. It is also known as Transcendental communication, i.e., something supernatural and abstract like meditation.
2 **Interpersonal Communication:** This is communication directly between two persons, without any medium like telephone, etc., and has instant feedback.

3) **Group Communication:** This is communication by many persons talking to one another in a social function or public gathering, organisation, etc. with weak impact without instant feedback.
4) **Mass Communication:** This refers to large-scale communication with masses through various media like newspaper, TV, Radio, Internet, etc.
5) **Interactive Communication:** This is communication via cable, teleshopping, pager, cell phone, etc.
6) **Grapevine Communication:** This refers to informal communication network, spreading gossips, rumours, with no direction, no plan, spreading like grapevine.
7) **Dyadic Communication:** It is a sort of Interpersonal communication mostly between a teacher and a student, a doctor and a patient, a lawyer and a client, or a priest and a follower under direct interaction.
8) **Analogous communication:** It is a typical symbolic communication (e.g., intentional use of speech and signs with conventional semantic) in human interaction or respectively, interaction between humans and computers.
9) **Transpersonal communication:** This refers to conversing with spirits and ancestors.
10) **Mass Line Communication:** This type of communication was used by Chinese Cultural Revolution leader Mao Zedong to talk to the masses.
11) **Public Communication:** This type of communication takes place when one individual addresses a large gathering of people. Election campaigns and public speeches are example of this type of communication. In such cases, there is usually a single sender of information and several receivers who are being addressed.
12) **Aesthetic communication:** This refers to creative expressions such as dancing, painting, and the like.
13) **Organizational Communication:** It is a process by which activities of a society are collected and coordinated to reach the goals of both individuals and the collective group. It is a sub-field of general communications studies and is often a component of effective management in a workplace environment.
14) **Circular Communication:** The three stages of circular communication are listening, learning, and leveraging (taking maximum advantage of communication). Circular communication is also someone narrating an incident without coming to the main point; rather making narration to revolve around the main point.
15) **Expressive Communication:** This refers to the communication when one communicates with verbal and nonverbal cues. Expressive communication requires use of language along with movement of limbs, eye contact, and face expression.
16) **Utilitarian Communication:** This is a type of communication which advocates morality. Such communication is found between a teacher and student, preacher and a follower, etc.
17) **Polylogical Communication:** It is a communication between people and media.
18) **Metacommunication:** It is a form of narrating some original message due to which it is also called Secondary Communication. Metacommunication occurs when a communicator narrates an original message in his own way along with his usual gestures. Such narration sometimes distorts the meaning of the original message.
19) **Linear communication:** It is a model of **communication** in which the **communication** process does not include feedback, or the feedback is quite delayed.
20) **Analog Communication:** It is a data transmitting technique in a format that utilizes continuous signals to transmit data including voice, image, video, electrons, etc.
21) **Digital communication:** This mean transferring data from one place to another with digital means. It is done by using the physical path or physical connection. In digital communication, digital values are taken as the discrete set (individually separate set). For example, communications done over the Internet is a form of digital communication.

MODELS OF COMMUNICATION

Aristotle's Model: *Around 300 BC, Aristotle developed a linear model of oral communication. It is taken as the first model of communication and is the most widely accepted among all communication models. This model states that there is one-way communication. The communicator sends the message and it goes straight to the recipient who listens to it. There is no feedback from the recipient. This model is speaker-centered. The speaker's motive is to influence the audience or listener. The basic flow of communication according to Aristotle is:*

Speaker → Speech → Occasion → Audience → Effect

Barnlund's Model: *American thinker Dean Barnlund developed the transactional model of communication in 1970. This model advocates that communication is a two-way process. There is a true interpersonal communication, where the process of sending the message and feedback simultaneously take place.*

Helical Model: *The model was developed in 1967 by Frank Dance. Dance was inspired by the helix (a curve of the shape of a cone). Helican model states that communication is a dynamic process and it widens with the passage of time. The model works on the fact that in the beginning, communication is narrow between the two persons like bottom of a cone, as the two are meeting for the first time, and as time passes and they regularly meet, communication between them widens like the upper surface of a cone. The belief of this model is that with age, people learn the techniques of effective communication which strengthens and widens the communication.*

Schramm's Model: *Wilber Schramm developed this model in 1954. The model states that the message to be communicated must be encoded and decoded. If a communicator thinks to deliver a message but does not deliver it, there is no relevance of this thought. One must convey one's thought in the form of content (Encoding). Recipient should receive the message and understand it (Decoding). Communication is not complete until it is practised between the sender and the recipient and it is channelized through encoding and decoding. Further, there must be a feedback from the recipient of the message to the sender. This model advocates 'Interactive Communication' and considers means of mass media like Internet, Radio, TV, etc. as senders of the message on which recipients can give feedback.*

BARRIERS TO EFFECTIVE COMMUNICATION

Barriers are obstacles or difficulties that come in the way of communication. These barriers are physical, sociological, and psychological obstacles. These barriers interfere with the planning, organization, transmission, and understanding of the message. Technically, a barrier is termed as 'noise'. These barriers may be in any form of communication, i.e., formal or informal, and due to these barriers, communication no more remains effective.

Language Barriers

1) **Lack of Common Language:** Such barrier arise when both sender and receiver do not know each other's language. They need an interpreter if they want to communicate with each other and make their communication.
2) **Poor Vocabulary:** Sometimes, poor vocabulary creates a barrier in the communication. If a communicator or receiver does not know the meaning of a word, the communication is not complete and effective. It makes the communicator difficult to deliver the message and for the receiver to receive the message properly. Such a barrier may arise in oral and written communication.
3) **Poor Knowledge of Grammar and Punctuation:** Communication does not become complete and effective if the communicator or receiver or both do not have proper knowledge of grammar and punctuation. For a barrier-free communication, both must have knowledge of proper sentence structure. Correct use of different parts of speech like noun, pronoun, article, verb, adjective, preposition, conjunction, etc. is important and for written communication, incorrect use of signs of punctuation like full stop, comma, etc. will create barriers in the effective communication.
4) **Roundabout Verbiage:** When a communicator or sender does not know the exact meaning of a word (rather, they assume the meaning of the word), then also message is distorted and communication barrier is created as either sender or receiver or both are confused over the meaning of the word and depend upon their respective assumptions.

Physical Barriers

1) **Noise:** Unwanted noise, i.e., of traffic, etc. interrupts communication between a sender and the receiver. Such barrier is created in oral interpersonal communication, intrapersonal communication, group communication, and organizational communication.
2) **Environmental Stress:** If extremities of climate are not suitable, even then barrier is created in effective communication. Environmental barriers include extremities of winter, summer, and uncongenial environment in an organisation due to which effective communication is hindered.
3) **Time:** If a communication is effected within suitable and conducive time, only then communication becomes effective and complete. Time should be convenient both for communicator and receiver to make communication barrier-free.

4) **Subjective Stress:** Barrier to a communication is also created if any of the party is ill, fatigued, or in tension. It is true both for a communicator and receiver of the message. If communicator experiences any of such state, he does not want to communicate the message and if it is true for the receiver, he cannot receive the message.
5) **Ignorance of the Medium:** In informal communication, generally oral communication is practiced and in formal or organizational communication, written communication is used. Ignorance of such medium on the part of the communicator or receiver creates barrier to the communication.
6) **Distance:** If the distance between the sender and the receiver is long enough to take a long time in receiving the message and response, then distance becomes a very big barrier. But in today's life of mobile phones, Internet, etc. distance is no more a barrier.
7) **Age:** Every generation has its own viewpoints. Barriers to communication are created among two or more generations due to clash of opinion.

Socio-Psychological Barriers

1) **Status Barriers:** In an organization, barriers to communication between a superior and a subordinate is created as there is a concept of downward and upward communication. A subordinate hesitates to share something with his superior whereas a superior does not like to share anything with his subordinate. Similar barrier is found in the society as well, even on occasions of informal communication.
2) **Self-Defence Attitude:** Some arrogant persons create barrier in the communication by defending themselves even when they are wrong in communication. This is applicable both on the communicator and receiver of the message.
3) **Negative Emotions:** If there is a feeling of hatred, jealousy, etc. between the sender and the receiver, or either of them, even then the communication is not possible.
4) **Resistance to Change:** If a communicator or sender or both resist change, even then the barrier is created.

Cultural Barriers

Such barriers are things like misunderstanding the meaning of the message (usually phrases are interpreted differently), taboos or forbidden subjects, assumptions, and prejudices.

Some Vital Facts

1) Effective communication presupposes understanding.
2) Attitude, performance records and selection of appropriate channel are determiners of effective communication
3) Effective communication needs a supportive social environment.
4) Communicator should have good personality
5) A good communicator is the one who offers to his audience plentiful of information.

Part – I

Some Vital Facts

1) Semantic barrier of communication is implied when the receiver does not understand meaning of the message.
2) Semantic noise, physical noise and psychological noise are barriers to effective communication.
3) Transcendental communication (communication with spirits) is intrapersonal communication
4) Every type of communication is affected by its context.
5) Term 'Grapevine' is also known as Informal Communication.
6) The mode of communication that involves a single source transmitting information to a large number of receivers simultaneously is called Mass Communication.
7) In circular communication, the encoder becomes a decoder when there is feedback.
8) Organisational communication can also be equated with group communication.
9) Video-Conferencing is classified as audio-visual two-way communication.
10) Audience attitude is a major barrier to reception of messages in communication.
11) The function of mass communication of supplying information regarding the processes, issues, events and social developments is known as content supply

Practice Exercise

General Questions Format

1. 'You Attitude' makes a communication effective as it demands
(A) conversation in second person
(B) communicator to be humble
(C) listener to be patient
(D) None of these

2. Effectiveness of communication is NOT necessary in case
(A) a ticket checker asks for ticket
(B) a traffic policeman asks for a driving license
(C) a landlord asks for rent
(D) All of the above

3. Effective communication is always effective for those who........for it.
(A) aspire (B) think
(C) try (D) plan

4. Proper selection of media makes a communication effective on the basis of its
(A) clarity (B) relevance
(C) availability (D) range

5. Effective communication in a nutshell requires
(A) formality (B) gesture
(C) participation (D) all of the above

6. Completeness is required in an effective communication as it makes communication
(A) effective (B) complete
(C) brief (D) useful

7. Effective communication means that communication in which the people
(A) listen, think, and communicate
(B) understand, realize, and propagate
(C) listen, understand, and realize
(D) listen, understand, and appreciate

8. Which of the following is the least important in making a communication effective?
(A) audibility (B) attention
(C) appearance (D) adaptability

9. In the field of communication, the gesture of 'How we say' indicates that communication is a/an
(A) expression (B) style
(C) obligation (D) none of the above

10. Communication by which of the mass media is the most effective?
(A) Newspaper (B) Radio
(C) Computer (D) None of these

11. Difference between a normal communication and an effective communication can be communicated by stating that former is a/an.............whereas latter is a/an..........
(A) exercise in futility, expression in utility
(B) subjective gesture, objective approach
(C) delivery, reciprocity
(D) all of the above

12. Patience in listening is required in effective communication because an impatient listener
(A) is always in a hurry
(B) never gives desired feedback
(C) leaks out even the secret information
(D) None of the above

13. The most effective expression making a communication effective is
(A) writing (B) signalling
(C) observing (D) speaking

14. Which of the following does not contribute in making communication an effective one?
(A) status consciousness in the communicator
(B) inadequate knowledge of the listener
(C) humid climate
(D) all of the above

15. Effective communication lies in the
(A) subject of communication
(B) style of the communicator
(C) attention of the listener
(D) environmental conditions

16. Which of the following fields of life essentially needs effective communication?
(A) Business (B) Government job
(C) Crime (D) All of the above

17. An incomplete communication is not effective because
(A) receiver of the message is unable to cooperate
(B) communicator is unable to convince the receiver
(C) communication is misunderstood by the receiver
(D) both communicator and receiver are in a fix

18. A time-barred communication is not effective as it leaves a communicator in the state of
(A) humiliation (B) desperation
(C) frustration (D) none of these

19. A receiver can make a communicator's communication effective only if he
(A) knows the purpose of communication, receives the communicator, and recognizes him
(B) receives the communication, understands it, and reciprocates
(C) receives message of communicator, reaches the venue of communication, and spares time for the communicator
(D) all of the above

20. Which of the following communication is NOT likely to result into effective communication?
(A) A leader addressing a press conference
(B) An employee requesting his boss for leave
(C) A candidate appearing for an interview
(D) A tourist guide communicating with a tourist at some site

21. Which of the following is NOT TRUE about intercultural communication?
a) Participants of intercultural communication possess professional qualification of cultural skills.
b) Intercultural communication becomes the base of international trade.
c) Culture-specific communication is the primary stage of intercultural communication.
d) Cultural exchanges among different countries carry hidden proliferation of ethnicity.
(A) Only d (B) Only a and d
(C) Only b and c (D) Only b

22. Essentials of effective communication are given under Column I and their hidden significance is given under Column II. Match the essentials with its hidden significance and choose the correct code among the given codes:

Column I (Essentials)	Column II (Hidden significance)
a) Appropriate formality	i) Determination
b) Adaptability	ii) Motivation
c) Pleasant approach	iii) Phatic
d) 'You Attitude'	iv) Stimulation
	v) Patience

Codes:	(a)	(b)	(c)	(d)
(A)	iii	i	iv	ii
(B)	i	v	iv	ii
(C)	iv	i	ii	iii
(D)	v	i	ii	iii

23. An organized message
(A) establishes that it is an essential element of effective communication
(B) motivates the communicator to communicate with confidence
(C) motivates the recipient to accept the message without knowing its details
(D) creates an atmosphere of amicability between the communicator and the receiver

24. Group communication is
(A) an indicator of unanimity in decision-making among members
(B) a representative of different status and skills of the participants
(C) an opportunity for the participants to exhibit their status and skills
(D) all of the above

25. Which of the following traits of intercultural communication becomes a ground for research?
(A) Culture-specific
(B) Culture general
(C) Intercultural interaction
(D) All of these

KEY

1. D	2. D	3. C	4. B	5. D	6. D	7. D
8. C	9. B	10. A	11. C	12. B	13. D	14. D
15. B	16. A	17. B	18. D	19. B	20. B	21. B
22. A	23. B	24. A	25. D			

Part – I

1. Which of the communication styles possesses the strongest impact?
   (A) Group (B) Intrapersonal
   (C) Interpersonal (D) None of these

2. Following are some evidences of interpersonal communication:
   (A) A teacher teaching a student
   (B) A patient explaining his problem to a doctor
   (C) A stranger asking a way from a native
   (D) A rickshaw puller quarrelling with client.

   Which of the features of interpersonal communication is definitely present in A, B, C, and D above?
   (A) Local language (B) Gesture
   (C) Direct interaction (D) None of these

3. Teleshopping is an evidence of .... communication.
   (A) interactive (B) interpersonal
   (C) group (D) grapevine

4. Feedback is quite poor in the case of group communication for want of
   (A) Language (B) Closeness
   (C) Interaction (D) All of the above

5. A communication becomes noise when
   (A) a sender speaks in a louder voice
   (B) when the listener is hard of hearing
   (C) it is sabotaged by any barrier
   (D) a lot of people are communicating together at the same place and at the same time

6. There are barriers to communication because these are
   (A) natural
   (B) deliberate
   (C) both natural and deliberate
   (D) neither natural nor deliberate

7. Grapevine communication mainly depends on the gesture of
   (A) informality (B) intrigue
   (C) planning (D) none of the above

8. Which of the following communication failure is due to barrier of time?
   (A) A watchman making an enquiry from a stranger at 1 AM
   (B) A host is asking for lunch at 7 PM
   (C) One is proposing for marriage at the age of 45
   (D) None of the above

9. Language becomes barrier to a communication when
   (A) the sender does not know it
   (B) the receiver does not know it
   (C) both of them don't know it
   (D) when no interpreter is available

10. It is prohibited to create noise near the hospitals because it sabotages the communication between
    (A) a doctor and patient
    (B) two patients
    (C) two doctors
    (D) none of these

11. Communication is not possible when there is humidity and poor ventilation because one does not want to
    (A) talk
    (B) listen
    (C) both listen and talk
    (D) either listen or talk

12. An officer does not properly communicate with his subordinate because he
    (A) is trained like this
    (B) wants to maintain a bureaucratic distance
    (C) is status conscious
    (D) hesitates to talk to the subordinate

13. Mass communication, by and large, is ...... communication.
    (A) effective (B) one-way
    (C) big level (D) all of the above

14. Which component of communication is not always found in case of mass communication?
(A) addressing (B) receiving
(C) feedback (D) language

15. Which media of mass communication attracts the fastest feedback?
(A) radio (B) newspaper
(C) television (D) can't say

16. There is a need to promote mass media communication mainly because
(A) communication cannot be confined to few persons or regions only
(B) wider the communicational coverage, more is the awareness
(C) communication with masses guarantees them their right to communicate
(D) mass communication ensures indiscrimination, equality, and secularism in the communication process

17. Traffic police in a city wants to educate general public about traffic rules with a motive to create general awareness about road safety. Which type of communication will best serve the purpose? ....communication.
(A) Group (B) Mass
(C) Interpersonal (D) Interactive

18. Employees of a concern are expecting a higher pay package from the management. However, due to certain unavoidable circumstances, the management has to take austerity measures resulting in delaying the hike in the pay of employees. In reaction, employees openly start alleging foul play on the part of the management. The type of communication they adopt is.......................communication.
(A) group (B) interpersonal
(C) mass (D) grapevine

19. A barrier to communication is
(A) but natural (B) avoidable
(C) desirable (D) none of these

20. There are different types of communication as there are different types of
(A) communicators (B) purposes
(C) languages (D) masses

KEY

1. C	2. C	3. A	4. B	5. C	6. C	7. B
8. B	9. C	10. D	11. D	12. C	13. B	14. C
15. D	16. B	17. B	18. D	19. D	20. B	

Assertion–Reason Format

1. **Assertion (A):** Intercultural communication helps in developing international trade.
Reason (R): Pressure groups in each culture pursue governments to initiate culture-based trade across the countries.
(A) Both A and R are true and R is correct explanation of A
(B) A is true but R is false
(C) A is false but R is true
(D) Both A and R are true but R is not correct explanation of A

2. **Assertion (A):** Effective communication is the result of effective subject under communication.
Reason (R): Participants of a communication process make a subject effective with their communication skills.
(A) Both A and R are true and R is correct explanation of A
(B) Both A and R are true but R is not correct explanation of A
(C) A is true but R is false
(D) Both A and R are false

3. **Assertion (A):** Group communication is considered to be an effective communication.
Reason (R): Meticulously taken unanimous decisions of the group leave an impact on society.
(A) Both A and R are true and R is correct explanation of A
(B) Both A and R are true but R is not correct explanation of A
(C) Both A and R are false
(D) A is false but R is true

4. **Assertion (A):** Sharing of messages is common between an effective and an ineffective communication.
Reason (R): No communication skill is required for sharing a message.

(A) Both A and R are true and R is correct explanation of A

(B) Both A and R are true but R is not correct explanation of A

(C) Both A and R are false

(D) A is true but R is false

5. **Assertion (A):** Gesture of 'You attitude' motivates a recipient to make communication effective.

Reason (R): An indifferent recipient sabotages communication even after experiencing 'You attitude'.

(A) Both A and R are true and R is correct explanation of A

(B) Both A and R are true but R is not correct explanation of A

(C) A is true but R is false

(D) A is false but R is true

6. **Assertion (A):** Group communication leaves a weak impact when the group leader is weak.

Reason (R): Participants of a group communication are empowered to change the group leader.

(A) Both A and R are false

(B) A is true but R is false

(C) A is false bur R is true

(D) Both A and R are true but R is not correct explanation of A

7. **Assertion (A):** Only verbal cues are used in intercultural communication.

Reason (R): Intercultural communication does not depend upon verbal or nonverbal cues.

(A) Both A and R are true and R is correct explanation of A

(B) Both A and R are true but R is not correct explanation of A

(C) Both A and R are false

(D) A is true but R is false

8. **Assertion (A):** Delivering a precise and relevant message is the communication skill of the communicator.

Reason (R): Effective communication involves use of various communication skills by the communicator.

(A) Both A and R are true and R is correct explanation of A

(B) Both A and R are true but R is not correct explanation of A

(C) A is true but R is false

(D) A is false but R is true

9. **Assertion (A):** A recipient is a passive partner in an effective communication process.

Reason (R): Making communication effective is the responsibility of the communicator.

(A) Both A and R are true and R is correct explanation of A

(B) Both A and R are true but R is not correct explanation of A

(C) A is true but R is false

(D) A is false but R is true

10. **Assertion (A):** Intracultural communication is an interpersonal communication.

Reason (R): Culture of various societies need to be exchanged in the interest of peace and prosperity.

(A) Both A and R are true and R is correct explanation of A

(B) Both A and R are true but R is not correct explanation of A

(C) A is true but R is false

(D) A is false but R is true

KEY

1. B **2.** D **3.** A **4.** C **5.** B **6.** A **7.** C **8.** A **9.** D **10.** B

Part – I

1. **Assertion (A):** A barrier to effective communication is undesirable.

Reason (R): Barriers to effective communication is either natural or man-made or both.

(A) Both A and R are true and R is correct explanation of A

(B) Both A and R are true but R is not correct explanation of A

(C) A is true but R is false

(D) A is false but R is true

2. **Assertion (A):** Grapevine communication travels through directions opposite to the system.

   Reason (R): A directionless communication is likely to yield catastrophic results.

   (A) Both A and R are true and R is correct explanation of A

   (B) Both A and R are true but R is not correct explanation of A

   (C) A is true but R is false

   (D) A is false but R is true

3. **Assertion (A):** Dyadic communication has a strong impact.

   Reason (R): it is an Interpersonal communication between the two with instant feedback.

   (A) Both A and R are true and R is correct explanation of A

   (B) Both A and R are true but R is not correct explanation of A

   (C) A is true but R is false

   (D) A is false but R is true

4. **Assertion (A):** Schramm's model of communication states that communication is a dynamic process.

   Reason (R): The model advocates interactive communication.

   (A) Both A and R are true and R is correct explanation of A

   (B) Both A and R are true but R is not correct explanation of A

   (C) A is true but R is false

   (D) A is false but R is true

5. **Assertion (A):** Transpersonal communication creates superstitions in the society.

   Reason (R): Mass media is proliferating superstitions by showing transpersonal communication in its various programmes.

   (A) Both A and R are true and R is correct explanation of A

   (B) Both A and R are true but R is not correct explanation of A

   (C) A is true but R is false

   (D) Both A and R are false

6. **Assertion (A):** Status conscious people cannot experience barrier-free communication.

   Reason (R): Social status of someone should not dominate the effective communication process.

   (A) Both A and R are true and R is correct explanation of A

   (B) Both A and R are true but R is not correct explanation of A

   (C) Both A and R are false

   (D) A is true but R is false

7. **Assertion (A):** No barrier affects the flow of intrapersonal communication.

   Reason (R): Communicating with self is an abstract concept.

   (A) Both A and R are true and R is correct explanation of A

   (B) Both A and R are true but R is not correct explanation of A

   (C) A is true but R is false

   (D) A is false but R is true

8. **Assertion (A):** Linear communication is incomplete without feedback.

   Reason (R): No feedback is yielded after the message is received through TV or radio.

   (A) Both A and R are false

   (B) Both A and R are true and R is correct explanation of A

   (C) Both A and R are true but R is not correct explanation of A

   (D) A is false but R is true

9. **Assertion (A):** Time is no more a barrier to communication today.

   Reason (R): Some barriers to communication are temporary.

   (A) Both A and R are true and R is correct explanation of A

   (B) Both A and R are true but R is not correct explanation of A

   (C) Both A and R are false

   (D) A is true but R is false

10. **Assertion (A):** Metacommunication involves simultaneous use of verbal and nonverbal cues.

Reason (R): Verbal and nonverbal cues are used together to resolve a deadlock in the communication process.

(A) Both A and R are true and R is correct explanation of A

(B) Both A and R are true but R is not correct explanation of A

(C) Both A and R are false

(D) A is false but R is true

11. **Assertion (A):** Mass media promote a culture of violence in the society.

Reason (R): Violence sells in the market as people themselves are violent in character.

(A) Both A and R are true and R is the correct explanation of A.

(B) Both A and R are true, but R is not the correct explanation of A.

(C) A is true, but R is false.

(D) Both A and R are false.

KEY

1. B	**2.** D	**3.** A	**4.** D	**5.** B	**6.** B	**7.** A
8. A	**9.** B	**10.** C	**11.** C			

Questions Asked in Previous NET Exams

1. A good communicator begins his/her presentation with a/an: **(UGC NET NOVEMBER 2017)**

(A) Complex question

(B) Non sequitur

(C) Repetitive phrase

(D) Icebreaker

2. Effective communication presupposes

(UGC NETJANUARY 2017)

(A) Non-alignment (B) Domination

(C) Passivity (D) Understanding

3. Effectiveness of communication can be traced from which of the following?

(a) Attitude **(UGC NET JUNE 2015)**

(b) Performance records

(c) Students' attendance

(d) Selection of communication channel

Select the correct answer from the codes given below:

(A) (b), (c), and (d)

(B) (a), (b), and (d)

(C) (a), (b), (c), and (d)

(D) (a), (b), and (c)

4. Effective communication needs a supportive

(UGC NET JUNE 2011)

(A) economic environment

(B) political environment

(C) social environment

(D) multicultural environment

5. Which of the following is correct?

(UGC NET DECEMBER 2005)

(A) Communicator should have fine senses

(B) Communicator should have tolerance power

(C) Communicator should be soft-spoken

(D) Communicator should have good personality

6. A good communicator is the one who offers to his audience

(UGC NET DECEMBER 2005)

(A) plentiful information

(B) a good number of statistics

(C) concise proof

(D) repetition of facts

KEY

1. D	**2.** D	**3.** B	**4.** C	**5.** D	**6.** A

Part – I

1. Semantic barrier of communication is implied when the **(UGC NET JUNE 2019)**

(A) signal is lost before reaching the recipient

(B) message transmitted by the source is unclear

(C) receiver's attention is diverted

(D) receiver does not understand the meaning of the message

2. Which of the following are barriers to effective communication? **(UGC NET JUNE 2019)**

(A) Physical noise

(B) Semantic noise

(C) Psychological noise

(D) Non-semantic noise

Choose the correct answer from the choices given below:

(A) A, B, and D (B) A, B, and C

(C) A, C, and D (D) Aand D only

3. In analog communication, contents are considered to be **(UGC NET JUNE 2019)**

(A) Convergent (B) Static

(C) Physical (D) Ethereal

4. Which of the following is a stage of intrapersonal communication?

(UGC NET JUNE 2019)

(A) Phatic stage (B) Intimate stage

(C) Personal stage (D) Transcendental stage

5. Expressive communication is driven by

(UGC NET JANUARY 2017)

(A) Passive aggression

(B) Encoder's personality characteristics

(C) External clues

(D) Encoder-decoder contract

6. What are the barriers to effective communication? **(UGC NET JULY 2016)**

(A) Moralising, being judgemental, and comments of consolation

(B) Dialogue, summary, and self-review

(C) Use of simple words, cool reaction, and defensive attitude

(D) Personal statements, eye contact, and simple narration

7. Every type of communication is affected by its: **(UGC NET DECEMBER 2015)**

(A) Reception (B) Transmission

(C) Non-regulation (D) Context

8. The term 'grapevine' is also known as

(UGC NET JUNE 2015)

(A) Upward communication

(B) Horizontal communication

(C) Downward communication

(D) Informal communication

9. The mode of communication that involves a single source transmitting information to a large number of receivers simultaneously, is called

(UGC NET DECEMBER 2014)

(A) Group communication

(B) Mass communication

(C) Intrapersonal communication

(D) Interpersonal communication

10. In circular communication, the encoder becomes a decoder when there is

(UGC NET JUNE 2014)

(A) noise (B) audience

(C) criticality (D) feedback

11. Organisational communication can also be equated with **(UGC NET DECEMBER 2013)**

(A) intrapersonal communication

(B) Interpersonal communication

(C) group communication

(D) mass communication

12. Means of Grapevine communication are

(UGC NET SEPTEMBER 2013)

(A) formal (B) informal

(C) critical (D) corporate

13. Communication via new media such as computers, teleshopping, Internet, and mobile telephony is termed as

(UGC NET JUNE 2013)

(A) Entertainment

(B) Interactive communication

(C) Developmental communication

(D) Communitarian

14. Conversing with the spirits and ancestors is termed as **(UGC NET DECEMBER 2012)**

(A) Transpersonal communication

(B) Intrapersonal communication

(C) Interpersonal communication

(D) Face-to-face communication

15. Chinese Cultural Revolution leader Mao Zedong used a type of communication to talk to the masses known as **(UGC NET DECEMBER 2012)**

(A) Mass line communication

(B) Group communication

(C) Participatory communication

(D) Dialogue communication

16. Video conferencing can be classified as one of the following types of communication: **(UGC NET JUNE 2012)**
    (A) Visual one-way
    (B) Audio-Visual one-way
    (C) Audio-Visual two-way
    (D) Visual two-way
17. A major barrier in the transmission of cognitive data in the process of communication is an individual's **(UGC NET JUNE 2011)**
    (A) personality
    (B) expectation
    (C) social status
    (D) coding ability
18. In communication, a major barrier to reception of messages is **(UGC NET JUNE 2010)**
    (A) audience attitude
    (B) audience knowledge
    (C) audience education
    (D) audience income
19. Didactic communication is **(UGC NET JUNE 2010)**
    (A) intra-personal
    (B) Interpersonal
    (C) organisational
    (D) relational
20. Postmodernism is associated with **(UGC NET JUNE 2010)**
    (A) newspapers (B) magazines
    (C) radio (D) television
21. Orkut is a part of **(UGC NET DECEMBER 2008)**
    (A) Intrapersonal communication
    (B) Mass communication
    (C) Group communication
    (D) Interpersonal communication
22. Communication with oneself is known as **(UGC NET JUNE 2008)**
    (A) Group communication
    (B) Grapevine communication
    (C) Interpersonal communication
    (D) Intrapersonal communication
23. The function of mass communication of supplying information regarding the processes, issues, events, and social developments is known as: **(UGC NET JUNE 2006)**
    (A) content supply (B) surveillance
    (C) gratification (D) correlation

KEY

1. D	**2.** B	**3.** B	**4.** D	**5.** B	**6.** A	**7.** D
8. D	**9.** B	**10.** D	**11.** C	**12.** B	**13.** B	**14.** A
15. A	**16.** C	**17.** A	**18.** A	**19.** B	**20.** A	**21.** B
22. D	**23.** A					

4 Communication Terminology

TERMS RELATED TO COMMUNICATION

Pragmatic Effect: A communicator always desires that the recipient must get, understand his massage, and give a feedback on it. This desire is fulfilled when he communicates with pragmatics, i.e., local language and gestures. Communicator's such desire is pragmatic effect.

Brainstorming: In case of a deadlock in the process of communication, participants are given the liberty to come up with various ideas to come out of the deadlock and this free flow of ideas is called Brainstorming.

Whistleblowing: It is a practice of highlighting unethical and corrupt practices of a system by the person who himself is part of that system.

Artefact: It is a trait of nonverbal communication. It is believed that whatever one possesses in the form of property, ornaments, clothing, cars, etc. convey a message. While viewing these possessions, the observer comes to know about the level of affluence of the person possessing various assets.

Cultural Capital: It is the knowledge communicated in the classroom.

Gangplank: It is another name of Horizontal Communication.

Paralanguage: It refers to any voice other than speech. It also includes movement of limbs and various gestures during communication.

Monologue: It is the situation when a single communicator gives a speech or plays a role in any drama, film, etc.

Charisma: A communicator's main motive is to convince the recipient or listener and getting feedback. A communicator's attractive personality, command on the subject, and stimulating style of communication is known as Charisma.

Interactivity: It occurs when there is interactive means like a computer with which humans communicate. For example, giving instructions to a particular software and getting the desired work done on computer.

Ethos: It is the trustworthiness of the speaker or communicator in the mind of the recipient or audience.

Entropy: It refers to the breaking down of communication flow.

MUM effect: It is the hesitation of people to share bad news with anyone.

Surveillance: It refers to the observation and monitoring of people's activities through (Closed Circuit Television (CCTV) camera.

Differentiation: It is an effort to develop and refine certain skills during a communication session.

Redundancy: It is the superfluous information in a communication session.

Feedback: It is the reaction or response of a recipient of a communication to the communicator.

Reverse Speech: It is said that when one is engaged in forward speech, one's unconscious mind starts generating thoughts, ideas, and words in the reverse direction. It is a natural phenomenon occurring in the brain. This theory was propounded by an Australian scholar David John Oats.

Gatekeeping: It is a process through which mass media filters any type of information meant for the audience.

Steady State and Dynamic Homeostasis: It is contrary to entropy. It is an attempt to make a barrier-free communication until its completion.

Negative Feedback: Feedback to a communication is negative when someone points out drawbacks and lacunae in a system with the suggestion of improving upon them.

Positive Feedback: Positive feedback is appreciating someone's efforts and motivating him/her to continue the same.

The Hawthorne Effect: This occurs when people change their behaviour as a reaction to the awareness that they are being observed by someone.

Diffusion: It refers to communicating any innovation to the general public through various channels.

Active Listening: It is the process of concentrating fully on the communicator in case of oral communication.

Non-linguistic Communication: As the name suggests, it is communication with gestures. This communication is a nonverbal communication. It is also called Extralinguistic Communication.

Articulation: It is the communication with the movement of articulators (speech organs).

Province: It refers to the field in which one is working like mass media, films, etc.

Acculturation: When transformation of cultures of different societies take place through various contacts, that is termed as acculturation. With growth of a society, modernisation sets in and acculturation is imminent in every section of the society.

Cybernetics: It is the study of control and communication in machines, animals, and men.

Signposts: Signposts or verbal signposts are different verbal statements a communicator makes during his/her presentation to spell bound the audience.

Cliche: It is an overused expression which loses its original meaning. Cliche are expressions which were fresh and were liked when these were used for these first time, but now these have lost their charm and thus become irritating to hear due to their overuse. For example narrating story of a greedy dog at present will be a cliche.

TERMS RELATED TO JOURNALISM & MEDIA

Op-ed page: An abbreviation for the page opposite to the editorial page of a newspaper

Libel: Any material published to tarnish the image of someone

Framing: Certain events which are under the focus of attention of media, which are related to different fields of life, and after that those events are reported with a particular meaning

Yellow journalism: Publishing sensational news in the newspaper which attracts maximum attention of readers, thus increasing circulation

Flag: Title of a newspaper

TRP (Television Rating Point): It is the tool that tells us which channel and the programme is viewed most or it indicates the popularity of a TV channel or a programme. It shows how many times people are watching a channel or a particular programme. TRP enables the advertisers and investors to understand the mood of the people. According to the TRP of a TV channel or programme, advertisers decide where to display their advertisements and investors will decide about the investment of the money.

Cultivation: Television viewers cultivate a belief in their mind that what facts about the social set-up of the society TV is showing, that is true.

Morgue: Newspaper library

Wire services: It is the other name of press associations

Cool media: Media cannot work without human intervention. That media which always require human involvement is Cool Media. This term was coined by a Canadian Professor McLuhan.

Fourth Estate: This term is used for press and electronic media. It also advocates freedom of press in a democratic society.

Jump: Continuing a news item, article, story, etc. to the next available page

Guild: An international union of journalists, reporters, and all those concerned with the newspaper field

Bulldog: First edition of a newspaper

Hot Media: Opposite to cool media

Inverted Pyramid: Arrangement of news items in descending order of importance

Soft News: Any account or story depicting changing trends and lifestyles in the society

Deck: A headline actually reflecting the summary version of the main article, story, account in a newspaper or journal, etc.

Cub: A nóvice reporter who has just entered in the field of journalism

Cutline: In any newspaper or journal, what is explained below a picture is called Cutline

Stringer: A part-time reporter or correspondent

Ear: Any corner at the top of the front page of a newspaper

Public Journalism: Reporting style of a stuff which targets unity and harmony among the communities

Fifth Estate: Term for bloggers

Hard News: Reporting some tragic event like accident or murder and action taken by the government in maintaining law and order

Modernism: In late 19th and early 20th century, there was a movement of reformation in different fields like social set-up, music, and literature. Modernism developed on the basis of logical thinking and application of various inventions in the field of science. This era advocated the rationality of life as it has an optimistic view about the world. Telephone and telegraph are the evidence of the modern era.

Postmodernism: After II World War, movement of this era developed those doctrines, which put a question mark on the rationality of modernism. Postmodern era brought transformation in art, culture, and architecture. This era is also known as era of enlightenment. This era is known for witnessing advent of radio and television.

Masthead: The published matter stating the basic details of a newspaper illustrating name of Editor and other management officials

Pagination: Paging of a newspaper with a computer

Green Proof: Proof of any news item, article, or story which yet to be corrected

Gutter: Margin between the pages of a newspaper where there is a fold in it

Press Run: Total number of copies printed

Deck: A headline actually reflecting the summary version of the main article, story, or account in a newspaper or journal, etc.

Integrated media: This refers to a combination of various aesthetic forms, in which a message is communicated under due compliance of the required technology. Advertising and other forms of communication are included in it.

Banner: The headline which is on the top of a newspaper

Fluff: News that has a poor scope of becoming popular

Churnalism: Publishing news provided by news agencies. The main motive of the newspaper is to save cost of framing news itself.

NIB: News in brief

Tease: During the commercial break of a television or radio programme, it is the hint regarding the upcoming programme or news after the current programme

Indicia: Publishing the statutory information about newspaper depicting price, number of copies printed, address of publication office, etc.

Ezine: Specialised online magazines

Beat: Area and subject allotted to a reporter

New Media: Digital media

VHF(Very high frequency): Frequencies from 30 MHz (wavelength 10 m) to 300 MHz (wavelength 1 m), used for radio and television broadcasting

NTSC: National Television System Committee

Byline: That line which describes the name of the author in an article

Pitch: Idea of a story or article which a reporter sends to the editor of a newspaper

Scoop: Any account which is published first in a newspaper

Hegemony: It is a paradoxical state of affairs in media where people controlling media use it for their vested interests and exploit it, and on the other hand, same media is inviting the views of critics.

Blurb: Short version of a story, article, etc.

Recto: Right-hand page of a newspaper, journal, etc.

Hammerhead : It is the main headline of two or three words, in a newspaper, followed by smaller headlines under it.

Protagonist: A pivotal character of a narration in media presentation

Bumper: A filler during a commercial break in a TV or radio programme

Splash: Any account which is published on the front page of a newspaper

Clutter: An army of commercials appearing spontaneously during a TV and radio programme

Bug: Permanent logo of a TV channel kept hanging at one corner of the screen. It looks like an insect hanging, thus term so named.

PAL (Phase Alternating Line): It is a television broadcasting system prevalent in Europe, New Zealand, and parts of Asia including India.

Jingle: Signature tune or verse of a particular TV channel or radio

Lead: Starting paragraph of any article or news item acting as a gist of the main news or article

DOG: Digital on-screen graphic

Pilot: An experimental episode of a TV or radio programme broadcasted to assess the reaction of viewers/listeners

Indent: A symbol, logo, or jingle of a TV appearing on screen

Sting: A musical break between two programmes to be broadcasted

Genre: The type or category of a media text, according to its form, style, and content

Balloon: A caricature or cartoon shown to deliver dialogues

TERMS RELATED TO PHOTOGRAPHY

Dilation: A photographic technique to increase the size of an object

Scrim: A semi-transparent device, which is used to soften or diffuse light in order to get best result while shooting an object

Crop: Shelving unwanted parts of a photograph

Graf: Acronym for the word photograph

Depth of Field (DOF): Distance between the closest and farthest objects considered while focussing a camera

Bitmap Image: An image which is composed of black and white pixels

Erosion: Opposite to term Dilation

Bokeh: This term is used when the image of a subject or its background to be captured goes out of focus or it yields blurred images.

Gobo: Blocking a wild or unwanted light falling on the main object to be captured

Digital Combine: This refers to the combination of different devices of digital photography for making advertising films or other programmes for the companies. Operation here is with multimedia approach.

Scaling: A process that changes the size of an image

Photoshop: Manipulating any image size-wise, colour-wise, or through cropping. Such software is developed by Adobe system.

Practice Exercise

General Questions Format

1. Continuation of a story from one page to another in a newspaper or magazine is termed as
   (A) Flag (B) Jump
   (C) Morgue (D) Graf
2. Gutter is related to Newspaper as Mainstreaming is related to
   (A) Radio (B) TV
   (C) Cinema (D) Photography
3. Tick-tock is a communication
   (A) theory (B) method
   (C) channel (D) style
4. First edition of a newspaper is known as
   (A) Bulldog
   (B) Pointer
   (C) Gutter
   (D) Flag
5. Find the odd choice
   (A) Libel (B) Masthead
   (C) Proxemics (D) Gutter
6. Find the WRONG pair
   (A) Articulation–Printing
   (B) Spamming–Mail
   (C) Cub–Reporter
   (D) Gatekeeper–Media

7-10. Match the term given under Column I with their field/meaning given under Column II.

Column I (Term)	Column II (Field/Meaning)
7) Ethos	A) Latitude
8) Throughput	B) Photography
9) Equifinality	C) Persuasion
10) Crop	D) Conceptualisation

11. Consider the following statements:

a) Telephone and telegraph were the main means of communication in modernism.

b) Splash is a front page story in a newspaper or magazine.

c) Pragmatic effect is a superfluous effect that a sender gets by his/her communication activity.

d) Chronemics is the study of how people perceive, structure, and use distance as communication.

Which of the above statement(s) is/are NOT true?

(A) a, c, and d (B) d only

(C) c and d only (D) a, b, and d only

12. In media communication DOG stands for

(A) Digital on-screen graphic

(B) Digital on-screen graph

(C) Digital over-screen graphic

(D) Digital over-screen graph

13. A process that changes the size of an image is termed as

(A) Bokeh (B) Cropping

(C) Gobo (D) Scaling

14. PAL is a communication system of____ media.

(A) print (B) electronic

(C) cool (D) None of these

15. An image composed of black and white pixels is called __________ image.

(A) Deck (B) Fluff

(C) Dope (D) None of these

16. What is the full form of NTSC?

(A) National Television System Commission

(B) National Television Systematic Committee

(C) National Television System Company

(D) National Television System Committee

17. Match the term given under Column I with its field given under Column II.

Column I	Column II
a) Bulldog	i) TV
b) Encryption	ii) Newspaper
c) Sting	iii) Photography
d) Scrim	iv) Music

Codes:	(a)	(b)	(c)	(d)
(A)	ii	i	iii	iv
(B)	ii	i	iv	iii
(C)	iv	ii	i	iii
(D)	iii	i	ii	iv

18. Artefact conveys that message through ______ communication.

(A) utilitarian

(B) expressive

(C) visual

(D) dyadic

19. Which of the following term is NOT used in photography?

(A) Clutter (B) Bracketing

(C) Erosion (D) Dilation

20. Whistleblowing is initiated by ________ of a system.

(A) outsider

(B) insider

(C) either outsider or insider

(D) both outsider and insider

21. Yellow Journalism is also known as __________ Journalism.

(A) Red (B) Cool

(C) Public (D) None of these

22. A transition to or from commercial breaks in TV or Radio is termed as

(A) Ident (B) Jingle

(C) Clutter (D) Bumper

23. Consider the following statements:

a) Enigma is a question in a text that is not immediately answered and creates interest for the audience.

b) Tease is a brief news item in a commercial break which hints of an upcoming story.

c) Paralanguage includes eye gaze and head nod in face-to-face encounter.

Which of the above statement(s) is/are TRUE?

(A) a and c only

(B) b and c only

(C) a only

(D) All of the above

24. Latent Public is a group of people who is
(A) aware of future problems and not of existing problems
(B) neither aware of future nor of present problems
(C) not aware of existing problems
(D) None of the above

25. Consider the following statements
a) Negative feedback means that partners reciprocally monitor their reactions and accordingly adjust their communicative behaviour.
b) Entropy is a tendency towards generation of order within systems.
c) Medium is a language in which a message is conveyed.
d) Information does not necessarily need a particular channel.

Which of the above statement(s) is/are TRUE?
(A) Only b and d (B) Only a
(C) All a, b, c and d (D) Only c and d

26. In a communication process, Hawthorne effect is the result of
(A) adjustment of gestures both by the communicator and the recipient
(B) change in the communication channel to make communication more effective
(C) improvement in the behaviour and approach by the participants in the process
(D) glorifying the communication process by adding ice-breaking phrases

27. Term 'Bracketing' is used in______
(A) Photography
(B) Journalism
(C) Dancing
(D) Mass Communication

28. Shelving unwanted parts of a photograph is known as photo
(A) shopping (B) bleeding
(C) doctoring (D) cropping

KEY

1. B	2. B	3. D	4. A	5. C	6. A	7. C
8. D	9. A	10. B	11. C	12. A	13. D	14. B
15. D	16. D	17. B	18. C	19. A	20. B	21. A
22. D	23. D	24. C	25. B	26. C	27. B	28. D

Assertion–Reason Format

1. Assertion (A): Acculturation is a process of cultural transformation initiated by contacts between different cultures.

Reason (R): The global trend towards modern economic organization and developed market economies has been accompanied by a process of cultural transformation.

(A) Both A and R are true and R is the correct explanation of A
(B) Both A and R are true but R is not correct explanation of A
(C) A is true but R is false
(D) Both A and R are false

2. Assertion (A): Postmodernism believed that there is a strong connection between the past and the present and that past events are relevant in the present.

Reason (R): Television was the major media of communication in postmodern society.

(A) Both A and R are true and R is the correct explanation of A
(B) Both A and R are true but R is not correct explanation of A
(C) A is false but R is true
(D) A is true but R is false

3. Assertion (A): Paralanguage is a tool of nonverbal communication.

Reason (R): Various nonverbal cues are effective in establishing the charisma of the communicator.

(A) Both A and R are true and R is correct explanation of A
(B) Both A and R are true but R is not correct explanation of A
(C) A is true but R is false
(D) A is false but R is true

4. Assertion (A): Advertisement films are produced with digital combine technique.

Reason (R): A multimedia approach is used to combine various devices of digital photography.

(A) Both A and R are true and R is correct explanation of A
(B) Both A and R are true but R is not correct explanation of A
(C) Both A and R are false
(D) A is true but R is false

5. **Assertion (A):** Achieving pragmatism is the ambition of every communicator.

Reason (R): Pragmatic effect is the ultimate destination of every communication.

(A) Both A and R are true and R is correct explanation of A

(B) Both A and R are true but R is not correct explanation of A

(C) Both A and R are false

(D) A is true but R is false

6. **Assertion (A):** Hegemony is a paradoxical state of affairs in media.

Reason (R): Controllers of media using it for vested interests, invite views of critics.

(A) Both A and R are true but R is not correct explanation of A

(B) Both A and R are true and R is correct explanation of A

(C) A is true but R is false

(D) A is false but R is true

7. **Assertion (A):** Bug provides identity to a TV channel.

Reasoning (R): It is a signature tune of a TV channel.

(A) Both A and R are true and R is correct explanation of A

(B) Both A and R are true but R is not correct explanation of A

(C) A is true but R is false

(D) A is false but R is true

8. **Assertion (A):** Element of redundancy makes communication monotonous for the audience.

Reason (R): It is the communicator's style of presentation which makes a communication monotonous or interesting.

(A) Both A and R are true and R is correct explanation of A

(B) Both A and R are true but R is not correct explanation of A

(C) A is true but R is false

(D) A is false but R is true

9. **Assertion (A):** Post-modern era is known as an era of enlightenment.

Reason (R): Scientific inventions in the modern era did not bring desired enlightenment.

(A) Both A and R are true and R is correct explanation of A

(B) Both A and R are true but R is not correct explanation of A

(C) A is false but R is true

(D) A is true but R is false

10. **Assertion (A):** Whistleblowers can be effective in reforming a system.

Reason (R): Highlighting malpractices of a system are ethical and a caution for the system holders.

(A) Both A and R are true and R is correct explanation of A

(B) Both A and R are true but R is not correct explanation of A

(C) Both A and R are false

(D) A is true but R is false

11. **Assertion (A):** Formal communication tends to be fast and flexible.

Reason (R): Formal communication is a systematic and orderly flow of information.

(A) A is false but R is true

(B) Both A and R are correct and R is correct explanation of A

(C) Both A and R are correct, but R is not correct explanation of A

(D) A is true but (R) is false

KEY

1. A **2.** C **3.** B **4.** A **5.** C **6.** A **7.** C
8. B **9.** D **10.** B **11.** A

Questions Asked in Previous NET Exams

1. Postmodernism is associated with

(UGC NET JUNE 2010)

(A) newspapers (B) magazines

(C) radio (D) television

2. Breakdown in verbal communication is described as **(UGC NET JUNE 2014)**

(A) Short circuit

(B) Contradiction

(C) Unevenness

(D) Entropy

3. Media is known as

(UGC NET DECEMBER 2014)

(A) First Estate (B) Second Estate

(C) Third Estate (D) Fourth Estate

4. The term "Yellow Journalism" refers to

(UGC NET DECEMBER 2014)

(A) Sensational news about terrorism and violence

(B) Sensationalism and exaggeration to attract readers/viewers.

(C) Sensational news about arts and culture

(D) Sensational news prints in yellow paper

5. Aspects of the voice, other than the speech are known as: **(UGC NET DECEMBER 2015)**

(A) Physical language

(B) Personal language

(C) Paralanguage

(D) Delivery language

6. In communication, the language is:

(UGC NET JUNE 2015)

(A) The nonverbal code

(B) The verbal code

(C) Intrapersonal

(D) The symbolic code

7. Referential framing used by TV audience connects media with

(UGC NET SEPTEMBER 2013)

(A) reality (B) falsity

(C) negativity (D) passivity

8. The science of the study of feedback systems in humans, animals, and machines is known as: **(UGC NET JUNE 2006)**

(A) cybernetics

(B) reverse communication

(C) selectivity study

(D) response analysis

9. A dialogue between a human being and a computer programme that occurs simultaneously in various forms is described as: **(UGC NET JUNE 2006)**

(A) man-machine speak

(B) binary chat

(C) digital talk

(D) interactivity

KEY

1. D **2.** D **3.** D **4.** B **5.** C **6.** D **7.** A **8.** A **9.** D

5 Effective Classroom Communication

CONCEPT

Classroom communication, generally considered a cultural capital, becomes effective when it is cognitive, i.e., backed with reasoning and logic and is like a discourse. The place of effective communication is quite central and indispensable in the classroom teaching and learning process. The teacher in the classroom requires effective communication skills in delivering his/her lecture to make learners understand and give feedback over the delivered lecture.

Teaching-learning situation in the classroom requires skillful and effective communication. In the formal education system, quite a number of students fail not because they have low mental ability to cope academically or lack readiness for learning, but because of ineffective communication of some teachers in the classrooms. As the teacher's communication is pivotal for the class, it is the teacher who can make classroom communication effective while practicing teaching skills.

TYPES OF CLASSROOM COMMUNICATION

1) Verbal Communication
2) Nonverbal Communication

Verbal Communication in the Classroom

This is the most common and traditional form of communication; it involves talking to one another and face-to-face interaction between the teacher and the students as well as between and among the students. This type of style of communication is the most significant and effective means of classroom interaction between the teacher and the students as far as imparting and gaining knowledge is concerned. It attracts an immediate feedback. This communication is both oral and written.

Nonverbal Communication in the Classroom

A teacher's intention is to make his classroom lecture as interesting and absorbing for the learners as he can. For achieving this objective he practices some effective nonverbal communication cues along with verbal communication. Various body gestures as the eye contact, facial expression, postures, dress, and even physical setting of the classroom provide strength to a teacher's lecture and he/she is successful in making learners spellbound. In teaching-learning process, the teacher in most cases ensures that learning is effectively imparted by complementing both oral and written communication with eye contact with the students, facial expression, postures, and even touching or patting them at the back for a good response to the teacher's teaching or question.

TEACHING SKILLS FOR EFFECTIVE CLASSROOM COMMUNICATION

Teaching skills are complex behaviours that are used in facilitating teaching-learning in the classroom. These skills can only be effective if they are well complemented and conveyed through appropriate communication methods. These are as follows:

(i) **Set induction:** This skill, otherwise called pre-instructional orientation, is concerned with the skills required by the teacher while introducing the lesson. This skill is required by the teacher while introducing the intended lesson in such a way that the learners' attention will be captured and their anxiety to learn will be aroused. In doing this, the teacher must use the appropriate channel, language, and style of communication, putting into consideration the learners' age, environment, and even time in doing so.

(ii) **Stimulus variation:** This is another skill required by the teacher to inculcate knowledge in the learners in a better way. This skill is needed in the classroom to prevent boredom and make learning more interesting. The teacher needs to change from time to time the stimuli or the mode being used in passing across his message to learners in the classroom. In doing this, the teacher requires a good sense of humour and appropriate communication skills to prevent or remove boredom from the pupils.

(iii) **Use of instructional materials and illustrations:** Another teaching skill that requires the use of effective communication in the classroom is the use of instructional materials and illustrations which are the carrier of relevant information in facilitating the learners' understanding of a particular fact and concepts. The teacher in the application of this skill needs a contribution of both nonverbal and visual communication techniques.

(iv) **Reinforcement skill:** Reinforcement skill is another vital skill the classroom teacher needs in ensuring effective learning among the students. They are gestural skills from the teachers to either encourage or discourage certain responses from the students in the classroom teaching-learning situation. More often than not, the teacher makes use of this skill to motivate the learners to be active and be well involved in the classroom activities. An effective communication system is required in the teacher's efforts to reinforce learners' attempts to answer his/her questions in the class. The teacher makes use of verbal words as: good, excellent, that is good enough, etc. to motivate learners to actively participate in the teaching-learning process. Similarly, other body gestural skills can still be used to reinforce learners' response politely. The teacher can ask the pupils to clap their hands for a learner's correct response to the question just asked, nod the head, or even smile as a sign of appreciating the correct answer given by the learner to the question asked. Facial expressions or head nod can be used to approve or disapprove the answer given by the learner.

(v) **Questioning skill:** This skill is otherwise known as the Socratic Method. It is very important to be understood by every teacher. The teacher puts questions at every stage of his lesson. Questions are useful at the beginning, middle, and at the end of the lesson. The teacher needs to have good communication skills in asking his questions at different levels and stages of his lesson to facilitate effective learning among the learners. One of the right ways of doing this is to ask a question, pause for a while, and then call a learner's name to answer it.

(vi) **Recognising attending behaviour:** Quite a number of learners in the class have a lot of behaviours that the teacher needs to attend to; among such behaviours are noise-making, emotional instability, loss of attention, and even problem of indiscipline. These forms or behaviours, if not properly managed by the teachers will hinder the attainment of the aims and objectives of leaning in the classroom. In solving the problem, the teacher needs to make use of a combination of communication skills. Teacher's direct eye contact with any learner whose mind wants to stray from the lesson is required to command the attention of such an erring student. Also, the teacher's mere pat on any learner's back goes a long way to tell such a child that he/she is being appreciated. This will especially prevent such a learner from becoming indifferent from the classroom lecture.

BARRIERS TO EFFECTIVE CLASSROOM COMMUNICATION

There are certain obstacles in the way of effective classroom communication which when not adequately considered and avoided, may impede learning in the classroom. Some of these obstacles are:

(a) **Lapse in Communication Skill:** If a teacher fails to display adequate communication skill in the classroom, it sabotages the purpose of effective classroom communication and leaves learners in a state of limbo and this proves to be a big barrier to effective classroom communication.

(b) **Incompatibility between Verbal and Nonverbal Message:** Classroom communication becomes effective when the teacher knows the skill of getting support of nonverbal communication while delivering a lecture. But if the teacher does not know this skill and there is incompatibility between the verbal and nonverbal codes, communication does not leave any favourable impact on learners and hence, a barrier to effective classroom communication is created.

c) **Noise Around:** Classroom communication becomes ineffective if there is a noise of any kind around or in the classroom. Unwanted noise interrupts the flow of communication and learners are not able to receive the content being delivered by the teacher, they are not able to understand it instantly and hence, fail to give any spontaneous feedback which is a primary component of effective communication. Delayed feedback due to noise is suicidal for effective classroom communication.

d) **Perception Problems:** If the teacher is not audible to the learners, learners do not get the message properly and such delivery of message ends in futility as far as effective communication is concerned. Similarly, if a teacher is delivering a lecture with the help of a visual aid, and is not accessible to even some students, communication becomes no more effective.

e) **Learners' Psychological Issues:** A teacher comes across different psychological traits of students in the class. Some students are introvert and underconfident. Due to this trait, they do not actively participate in teaching-learning process. Such traits of students become a big barrier in the way of effective communication.

f) **Overloaded Message:** Delivery of superfluous or overloaded content or message also acts as a barrier in the way of effective communication. The learners start feeling monotonous and their attention from the lecture is diverted.

Prevention of Barriers

The teacher in the classroom can prevent this problem through the following measures:

a) The teacher should speak at the levels of the learners using clear, simple, and concise words that will be meaningful to them.

b) The teacher can use an appropriate channel in impacting the needed knowledge, i.e., in case there is a big number of students, teacher can use a mic and speaker to make him audible to each student. Further, teaching aids can be used where and when needed.

c) The teacher can prevent barrier to classroom communication by encouraging quick feedback.

d) The teacher can present an appropriate blend of verbal and nonverbal communication.

e) The teacher can practice face-to-face communication which will motivate even introvert and underconfident students to be part of the active teaching-learning process, thus ensuring barrier-free effective classroom communication.

f) Teaching with relevant instructional material and compatible teaching style will help preventing barriers in the way of effective classroom communication.

Some Vital Facts

1) In a classroom, delayed feedback happens due tosemantic noise

2) The rhetorical approach in classroom communication considers teachers as influencing agents of students.

3) In a classroom, teachers and students use self-interest issues to judge their acceptability.

4) Perception levels, learned habits, attitudes, beliefs, values and selectivity factor are variables that affect the information processing in a classroom.

5) Differentiation between acceptance and non-acceptance of certain stimuli in classroom communication is the basis of selective attention.

6) In classroom communication possibility of receiving a message is increased by establishing a viewpoint.

7) Cognitive load in understanding is reduced while using teaching aid in classroom communication.

8) Factual information is the typical feature of information-rich classroom communication.

9) Internal and external factors that affect message reception by the students in the classroom are referred to as noise.

10) Semantic classroom communication carries power in the form of content and authority over message, structure of the message and tradition of delivering the message.

11) A good classroom communicator uses justified pauses while delivering the lecture

12) Facial expression, kinesics and personal space are components of non-verbal communication in a classroom.

13) Repetitive pause is the important element a teacher has to take cognizance of while addressing students in a classroom.

14) Mind mapping is the pivotal point, which a teacher uses, in classroom communication when he is to begin his communication with dynamic pattern of ideas.

15) Eye contact determines a communicator's trust level in the classroom.

16) Teacher is encoder of the message he sends in the classroom and students are decoders of that message who receive it.

17) Classroom communication is described as a discourse.

18) The knowledge provided in the class room communication is described as cultural capital.

19) Classroom communication is always considered as cognitive.

20) A teacher's purpose of communication in the classroom is to provide edutainment.

21) Classroom communication must be learners' centric.

22) Classroom communication is a type of interpersonal communication.

Practice Exercise

General Questions Format

1. Which of the following is/are TRUE about effective classroom communication?

   a) It is a mutual effort of the teacher and students in the classroom.

   b) Effective communication is a subjective concept and varies from class to class.

   c) Classroom communication is always effective if the teacher develops a rapport with the students in the initial phase of the lecture.

   d) Classroom communication is effective only in the learner-centered methods of teaching.

   (A) Only b and c (B) Only c

   (C) Only a and d (D) Only d

2. Any distortion in classroom communication can be rectified if

   (A) teacher is convinced that it is a routine part of classroom teaching.

   (B) learners request the teacher to try for rectification in the interest of effective learning.

   (C) authorities direct the teacher and the students to rectify it with collective effort.

   (D) None of these

3. Which of the following fully justifies the contribution of nonverbal communication in making classroom communication effective?

   (A) Nonverbal communication strengthens the verbal message enabling learners to fully understand the concept.

   (B) Nonverbal communication naturally blends with verbal communication if a teacher is to effectively deliver a lecture.

   (C) Nonverbal cues are exchanged between the teacher and students along with verbal communication.

   (D) Statutes of classroom communication require mandatory support of nonverbal communication to the verbal communication to ensure effective classroom communication.

4. A teacher's efforts to make classroom communication effective go in vain if learners are

   (A) overconfident (B) underconfident

   (C) indifferent (D) stubborn

5. Essential components of effective classroom communication are

   (A) Assembly, Knowledge, Logic

   (B) Reasoning, Logic, Discourse

   (C) Discourse, Knowledge, Application

   (D) Logic, Discourse, Style

6. Which of the following is NOT TRUE?

   (A) A novice teacher cannot make classroom communication effective.

   (B) Fussy students in a class act as a motivation for the teacher to secure effective communication.

   (C) A classroom communication is naturally effective as it involves the participation of teacher and students.

   (D) All of these

7. Efforts to make a classroom communication effective are started in the ________ phase of the lecture.

   (A) introductory (B) middle

   (C) concluding (D) interactive

8. Here are certain components helping the teacher to make classroom communication effective:

   a) instructional material

   b) stimulus variation

   c) Reinforcement skill

   Arrange them in priority of effectiveness.

   (A) a-c-b (B) c-a-b

   (C) b-c-a (D) c-b-a

9. What is the role of management of a college in making classroom communication effective?

   (A) Passive

   (B) Authoritative

   (C) Active

   (D) Conducive

10. What do the barriers to effective classroom communication establish?
   a) Classroom communication is not as smooth as it looks to be.
   b) Efforts to achieve a desired objective are full of challenges.
   c) Achieving effective classroom communication is the test of a teacher's communication skill.
   d) Teacher has not made skillful use of his teaching skills.

   (A) Only b and d (B) Only a, c, and d
   (C) Only b (D) a, b, c, and d

11. Consider these statements:
   P: Effective classroom communication has long-lasting impact on learners' cognitive abilities.
   Q: Ensuring effective classroom communication is a statutory duty of a teacher.

   (A) Both P and Q are true
   (B) P is true but Q is false
   (C) Both P and Q are false
   (D) P is false but Q is true

12. **Statement:** Should a teacher alone try to achieve effective communication in the class?

   Argument:
   I. Yes, effective communication is the sole outcome of teaching style.
   II. No, teacher's lone efforts keep no meaning when the management and learners are indifferent.

   (A) Only argument I is strong
   (B) only argument II is strong
   (C) Both arguments I and II are strong
   (D) Neither argument I nor II is strong

13. Teaching skills required to make classroom communication effective are given under Column I and their nature is given under Column II. Match the teaching skill with its nature and choose the correct code among the codes given below:

Column I (Teaching skill)	Column II (Nature)
(a) Induction	i) Endorsement
(b) Stimulus variation	ii) Introduction
(c) Reinforcement	iii) Motivation

Codes:

	(a)	(b)	(c)
(A)	iii	ii	i
(B)	ii	iii	i
(C)	i	ii	iii
(D)	ii	i	iii

14. Teaching skills do not secure effective classroom communication until these are
   (A) comprehensive (B) motivating
   (C) philanthropic (D) all of these

15. Which of the following teaching skill securing effective classroom communication is not influenced by introduction of communication technology in the teaching-learning process?
   (A) Presentation of instructional material
   (B) Style of delivering lecture
   (C) Use of nonverbal cues
   (D) Use of appropriate channel

KEY

1. C 2. D 3. A 4. D 5. B 6. D 7. A
8. C 9. A 10. C 11. A 12. A 13. B 14. D
15. C

Assertion–Reason Format

1. **Assertion (A):** Effective classroom communication is always desirable.

   Reason (R): Dearth of teachers with required skill create hindrance in the way of effective classroom communication.

   (A) Both A and R are true and R is correct explanation of A
   (B) Both A and R are true but R is not correct explanation of A
   (C) A is true but R is false
   (D) A is false but R is true

2. **Assertion (A):** Attitude of learners play a stronger role than attitude of teacher in making classroom communication effective.

   Reason (R): Learner-centered methods of teaching are gaining popularity for securing effective communication.

   (A) Both A and R are true but R is not correct explanation of A
   (B) Both A and R are true and R is correct explanation of A
   (C) Both A and R are false
   (D) A is false but R is true

3. **Assertion (A):** Nonverbal cues can alone make a classroom communication effective.

   Reason (R): A teacher resorts to nonverbal cues in the class to attract attention of indifferent Learners.

   (A) Both A and R are false

   (B) Both A and R are true and R is correct explanation of A

   (C) Both A and R are true but R is not correct explanation of A

   (D) A is false but R is true

4. **Assertion (A):** An overloaded lecture in the class acts as a barrier to effective classroom communication.

   Reason (R): Superfluous content of the lecture creates monotony in the class and students fail to give required feedback.

   (A) A is false but R is true

   (B) Both A and R are true and R is correct explanation of A

   (C) A is true but R is false

   (D) Both A and R are true but R is not correct explanation of A

5. **Assertion (A):** Perception plays an important role in making classroom communication effective.

   Reason (R): Classroom communication nurtures the teacher with experience and learners with knowledge.

   (A) Both A and R are true and R is correct explanation of A

   (B) A is true but R is false

   (C) Both A and R are true but R is not correct explanation of A

   (D) Both A and R are false

6. **Assertion (A):** Teacher communication is central to classroom management.

   Reason (R): Teacher communication behaviours should not be used to regulate the classroom behaviour of students.

   (A) A is false but R is true

   (B) Both A and R are true

   (C) Both A and R are true but R is not the correct explanation of A

   (D) A is true but R is false

7. **Assertion (A):** Meanings of messages used in the classroom are arbitrary in nature.

   Reason (R): Meanings are learnt as a result of one's prior experiences.

   (A) Both A and R are true and R is the correct explanation of A

   (B) Both A and R are true but R is not the correct explanation of A

   (C) A is true but R is false

   (D) A is false but R is true

8. **Assertion (A):** Classroom communication has a cultural dimension.

   Reason (R): Beliefs, habits, customs, and languages are the cultural characteristics of communication.

   (A) Both A and R are true and R is the correct explanation of A

   (B) Both A and R are true, but R is not the correct explanation of A

   (C) A is true but R is false

   (D) A is false but R is true

9. **Assertion (A):** Selective exposure in the classroom is dependent upon students' perceptions and knowledge about the source of information.

   Reason (R): The effectiveness of the communication source determines the selective exposure of students to information.

   (A) Both A and R are true and R is the correct explanation of A

   (B) Both A and R are true but R is not the correct explanation of A

   (C) A is true but R is false

   (D) A is false but R is true

10. **Assertion (A):** The initial messages to students in the classroom by a teacher need not be critical to establish interactions later.

    Reason (R): More control over the communication process means more control over what the students are learning.

    (A) Both A and R are true and R is the correct explanation of A

    (B) Both A and R are true but R is not the correct explanation of A

    (C) A is true but R is false

    (D) A is false but R is true

11. **Assertion (A):** To communicate well in the classroom is a natural ability.

Reason (R): Effective teaching in the classroom demands knowledge of the communication process.

(A) Both A and R are true and R is the correct explanation of A

(B) Both A and R are true but R is not the correct explanation of A

(C) A is true but R is false

(D) A is false but R is true

12. **Assertion (A):** Classroom communication is a transactional process.

Reason (R): A teacher does not operate under the assumption that students' responses are purposive.

(A) Both A and R are true and R is the correct explanation of A

(B) Both A and R are true but R is not the correct explanation of A

(C) A is true but R is false

(D) A is false but R is true

13. **Assertion (A):** For an effective classroom communication, at times it is desirable to use the projection technology.

Reason (R): Using the projection technology facilitates extensive coverage of course contents.

(A) Both A and R are true and R is the correct explanation of A

(B) Both A and (R) are true but R is not the correct explanation of A

(C) A is true but R is false

(D) A is false but R is true

KEY

1. C	2. D	3. A	4. B	5. C	6. D	7. A
8. A	9. A	10. D	11. D	12. C	13. B	

Questions Asked in Previous NET Exams

1. In a classroom, delayed feedback can happen due to **(UGC NET JUNE 2019)**

(A) Use of technology

(B) Expanded communication

(C) Semantic noise

(D) Participatory environment

2. Communication in classroom takes place in which of the following levels?

(UGC NET DECEMBER 2019)

(A) Opportunistic meaning

(B) Surfacial meaning

(C) Noise level meaning

(D) Non coded meaning.

3. Which of the following are rhetorical techniques for structuring classroom communication?

(UGC NET DECEMBER 2019)

a) Relating the day's topic to the students' interest.

b) Providing scattered information to the target audience.

c) Smooth transition from one idea to another.

d) Avoiding the use of Artefacts.

e) Using media to improve the quality aspect of reception of message.

f) Opting for one-way communication.

Choose the correct option from choices given below:

(A) (a), (b) and (c) (B) (b), (c) and (f)

(C) (a), (c) and (e) (D) (d), (e) and (f)

4. Learner communication has relatively high potential of challenging

(UGC NET DECEMBER 2019)

(A) Teaching as profession

(B) Innovative and creative ideas.

(C) Methods of evaluation

(D) Long-held attitudes

5. Given below are two statements - One is labelled as Assertion (A) and other is labelled as Reason (R)

(UGC NET DECEMBER 2019)

Assertion (A): Defining the objectives of the topicof discussion is not necessarily the first step in classroom communication.

Reason (R): Clear definition of objectives makes students understand the topic well

(A) Both A and R are true but R is correct explanation of A

(B) Both A and R are true but R is not correct explanation of A

(C) A is true but R is false

(D) A is false but R is true

6. Effective classroom communication can transform **(UGC NET DECEMBER 2019)**
   (A) academic administration
   (B) academic marketing
   (C) teaching-learning process
   (D) management strategies

7. In the digital era, there is a fear that classroom communication may result in: **(UGC NET DECEMBER 2018)**
   (A) Passive adaptation
   (B) Quick adaptation
   (C) Stimulation
   (D) Over-stimulation

8. Negative criticism as an element of classroom communication will lead to: **(UGC NET DECEMBER 2018)**
   (a) External sympathy
   (b) Justification
   (c) Defensiveness
   (d) Demotivation
   (e) Supportive listening
   (f) Confrontational empathy
   (A) (b), (c), and (d) (B) (d), (e), and (f)
   (C) (a), (b), and (c) (D) (c), (d), and (e)

9. The rhetorical approach in classroom communication considers teachers as _____ agents of students. **(UGC NET DECEMBER 2018)**
   (A) Influencing (B) Non-official
   (C) Academic (D) Official

10. In a classroom, teachers and students use self-interest issues to judge **(UGC NET JULY 2018)**
   (A) Their acceptability
   (B) Uncritical dispositions
   (C) Negative reinforcement of ideas
   (D) External nonverbal cues

11. Variables that affect the information processing in a classroom are **(UGC NET JULY 2018)**
   (i) Perception levels
   (ii) Learned habits
   (iii) Attitudes, beliefs, and values
   (iv) Selectivity factor
   (v) Market expectations
   (vi) Institutional intervention
   Choose the correct answer from the code given below:
   Code:
   (A) (i), (ii), (v), and (vi)
   (B) (ii), (iii), (iv), and (v)
   (C) (iii), (iv), (v), and (vi)
   (D) (i), (ii), (iii), and (iv)

12. Differentiation between acceptance and non-acceptance of certain stimuli in classroom communication is the basis of: **(UGC NET JULY 2018)**
   (A) Selective expectation of performance
   (B) Selective affiliation to peer groups
   (C) Selective attention
   (D) Selective morality

13. In a classroom, probability of message reception can be enhanced by: **(UGC NET NOVEMBER 2017)**
   (A) Exposing the ignorance of students
   (B) Increasing the information load
   (C) Using high decibel audio tools
   (D) Establishing a viewpoint

14. The spatial audio reproduction in a classroom can reduce the students': **(UGC NET NOVEMBER 2017)**
   (A) Respect for the teacher
   (B) Motivation for excellence
   (C) Interest in technology-orientation
   (D) Cognitive load in understanding

15. The typical feature of an information-rich classroom lecture is in the nature of being **(UGC NET JANUARY 2017)**
   (A) Sedentary (B) Staggered
   (C) Factual (D) Sectoral

16. Internal and external factors that affect message reception by the students in the classroom are referred to as **(UGC NET JANUARY 2017)**
   (A) Feedback (B) Fragmentation
   (C) Channelization (D) Noise

17. A teacher in a classroom has immediate control over **(UGC NET AUGUST 2016)**
    (A) The self, selected methods of communication, and the message
    (B) The audience, the noise, and the reception
    (C) The feedback, the technology, and the audience experience
    (D) The communication channel, other communicators, and external factors
18. What do communicated words carry in a classroom situation? **(UGC NET AUGUST. 2016)**
    (A) Inspiration, controversy, and introspection
    (B) Diversion, criticism, and irrationality
    (C) Insipidity, irrationality, and non-acceptance
    (D) Power, structure, and tradition
19. As a good classroom communicator, you are supposed to know your **(UGC NET AUGUST 2016)**
    (A) Audience emotions
    (B) Silent cues
    (C) Artful pauses
    (D) Counter arguments
20. Figure out the components of nonverbal communication in a classroom from the following: **(UGC NET AUGUST 2016)**
    (A) Facial expression, cultural space, and seating arrangement
    (B) Speed of utterance, feel-good factor, and acoustics
    (C) High sound, physical ambience, and teacher-learner distance
    (D) Facial expression, kinesics, and personal space
21. As a teacher, select the best option to ensure your effective presence in the classroom. **(UGC NET JULY 2016)**
    (A) Use of peer command
    (B) Making aggressive statements
    (C) Adoption of well-established posture
    (D) Being authoritarian
22. Identify the important element a teacher has to take cognizance of while addressing students in a classroom. **(UGC NET JULY 2016)**
    (A) Avoidance of proximity
    (B) Voice modulation
    (C) Repetitive pause
    (D) Fixed posture
23. Using the central point of the classroom communication as the beginning of a dynamic pattern of ideas is referred to as: **(UGC NET DECEMBER 2015)**
    (A) Systemisation
    (B) Problem-orientation
    (C) Idea protocol
    (D) Mind mapping
24. Attitudes, actions, and appearances in the context of classroom communication are considered as: **(UGC NET DECEMBER 2015)**
    (A) Verbal (B) Nonverbal
    (C) Impersonal (D) Irrational
25. In a classroom, a communicator's trust level is determined by: **(UGC NET DECEMBER 2015)**
    (A) The use of hyperbole
    (B) The change of voice level
    (C) The use of abstract concepts
    (D) Eye contact
26. In the classroom, the teacher sends the message either as words or images. The students are really **(UGC NET DECEMBER 2014)**
    (A) Encoders (B) Decoders
    (C) Agitators (D) Propagators
27. Classroom communication can be described as **(UGC NET DECEMBER 2013)**
    (A) Exploration
    (B) Institutionalisation
    (C) Unsignified narration
    (D) Discourse

28. The communicated knowledge in a classroom is considered as **(UGC NET SEPTEMBER 2013)**
    (A) non-pervasive treasure
    (B) limited judgement
    (C) autonomous virtue
    (D) cultural capital

29. Classroom communication is normally considered as **(UGC NET SEPTEMBER 2013)**
    (A) effective (B) affective
    (C) cognitive (D) non-selective

30. Classroom communication of a teacher rests on the principle of **(UGC NET JUNE 2013)**
    (A) Infotainment (B) Edutainment
    (C) Entertainment (D) Enlightenment

31. Classroom communication must be **(UGC NET DECEMBER 2012)**
    (A) Teacher-centric (B) Student-centric
    (C) General-centric (D) Textbook-centric

32. Interaction inside the classroom should generate **(UGC NET DECEMBER 2012)**
    (A) Argument
    (B) Information
    (C) Ideas
    (D) Controversy

33. The type of communication that the teacher has in the classroom, is termed as **(UGC NET DECEMBER 2012)**
    (A) Interpersonal
    (B) Mass communication
    (C) Group communication
    (D) Face-to-face communication

KEY

1. C	**2.** B	**3.** C	**4.** D	**5.** D	**6.** C	**7.** D
8. A	**9.** A	**10.** A	**11.** D	**12.** C	**13.** D	**14.** D
15. C	**16.** D	**17.** A	**18.** D	**19.** C	**20.** D	**21.** C
22. C	**23.** D	**24.** B	**25.** D	**26.** B	**27.** D	**28.** D
29. C	**30.** B	**31.** B	**32.** C	**33.** C		

Unit V

Mathematical Reasoning and Aptitude

1 Types and Pre-requisites of Reasoning

REASONING

Reasoning means thinking about some subject rationally and logically.

Types of Reasoning

With respect to questions asked in various competitive exams, there are two types of reasoning:

1) **Verbal Reasoning:** Language-based questions are asked in this type of reasoning. Nature of questions include series, analogies, classification, relationship, coding-decoding, directions, sitting arrangement, logical reasoning, mathematical reasoning, problem solving, analytical reasoning, puzzles, and all other topics mentioned in the verbal reasoning syllabus of a particular competitive exam.

2) **Non-Verbal Reasoning:** This type of reasoning carries figure and picture based questions. Here, questions on series, classification, analogies, paper folding, paper cutting, images, and all other questions mentioned in the syllabus of non-verbal reasoning of various competitive exams are included.

Imp: NET Paper 1 Syllabus of Mathematical Reasoning and Logical Reasoning contains topics of Verbal Reasoning only. This book therefore discusses topics of Verbal Reasoning.

PREREQUISITES FOR VERBAL REASONING

Many pivotal topics of verbal reasoning like Letter series, Number Series, Analogy of Letters, Classification of Letters, Analogy of numbers, Classification of numbers, Number series, Coding-Decoding, Analytical Reasoning, Directions, Sitting Arrangements, and Mathematical reasoning involving value of X are frequently asked in NET Paper 1. Questions on all these topics can be solved quickly with confidence if there is mastery on these prerequisites discussed below:

1) **Arrangement of Letters in English Alphabet**

26	25	24	23	22	21	20	19	18	17	16	15	14	13	12	11	10	9	8	7	6	5	4	3	2	1
A	B	C	D	E	F	G	H	I	J	K	L	M	N	O	P	Q	R	S	T	U	V	W	X	Y	Z
1	2	3	4	5	6	7	8	9	10	11	12	13	14	15	16	17	18	19	20	21	22	23	24	25	26

$A \rightarrow Z =$ Succeeding order

$Z \rightarrow A =$ Preceding order

Position of each letter in both the above orders is shown above.

2) **Pairs of Corresponding Letters**

Two letters are corresponding to each other when each of them is at same position from its respective extreme letter, as it is shown below:

1	2	3	4	5	6	7	8	9	10	11	12	13
A	B	C	D	E	F	G	H	I	J	K	L	M
Z	Y	X	W	V	U	T	S	R	Q	P	O	N

In the above table, A is starting letter in A to Z order and Z is starting letter from Z to A order, so A & Z are corresponding to each other. Similarly, B is second from A and on the other hand Y is second from Z, so B & Y are corresponding to each other and so on. In this way we find that following pairs of letters are corresponding to each other. However, pair A-Z and M-N are not only corresponding to each other but also consecutive to each other.

A-Z, B-Y, C-X, D-W, E-V, F-U, G-T, H-S,
I-R, J-Q, K-P, L-O, M-N

3) **Sequence of Prime Numbers**

A prime number is that number which is divisible by 1 or by itself only.

Prime Numbers

1–10	11–20	21–30	31–40	41–50	51–60	61–70	71–80	81–90	91–100
2	11	23	31	41	53	61	71	83	97
3	13	29	37	43	59	67	73	89	
5	17			47			79		
7	19								

Sequence in the ascending & descending order should be on finger tips.

4) **Squares and Cubes**

Squares from 1-30

1–10	11–20	21–30
$1^2 = 1$	$11^2 = 121$	$21^2 = 441$
$2^2 = 4$	$12^2 = 144$	$22^2 = 484$
$3^2 = 9$	$13^2 = 169$	$23^2 = 529$
$4^2 = 16$	$14^2 = 196$	$24^2 = 576$
$5^2 = 25$	$15^2 = 225$	$25^2 = 625$
$6^2 = 36$	$16^2 = 256$	$26^2 = 676$
$7^2 = 49$	$17^2 = 289$	$27^2 = 729$
$8^2 = 64$	$18^2 = 324$	$28^2 = 784$
$9^2 = 81$	$19^2 = 361$	$29^2 = 841$
$10^2 = 100$	$20^2 = 400$	$30^2 = 900$

Cubes from 1- 0

1–5	6–10
$1^3 = 1$	$6^3 = 216$
$2^3 = 8$	$7^3 = 343$
$3^3 = 27$	$8^3 = 512$
$4^3 = 64$	$9^3 = 729$
$5^3 = 125$	$10^3 = 1000$

Directions

We have the following directions around us:

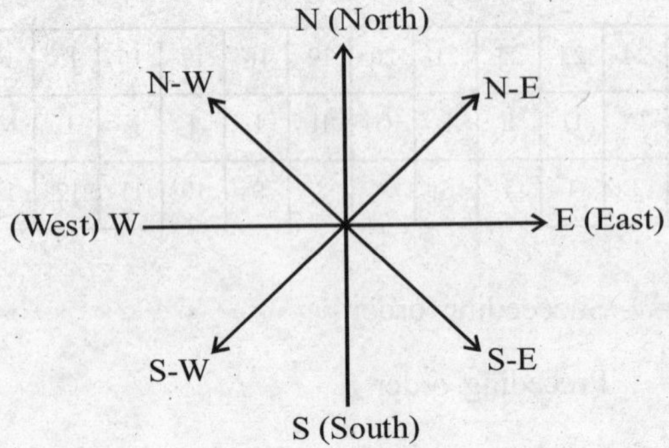

The questions on directions can be tackled with the knowledge of TURNS which one takes after proceeding towards a particular direction. A NORMAL TURN IS ALWAYS TAKEN AT RIGHT ANGLE (90º), i.e., if a person is proceeding towards say North and if he takes a turn to his left or right side he will always turn by 90º. Whether one is following horizontal, vertical, or diagonal direction, he will take a turn at right angle in the following course:

Turn After

a) Vertical Directions:

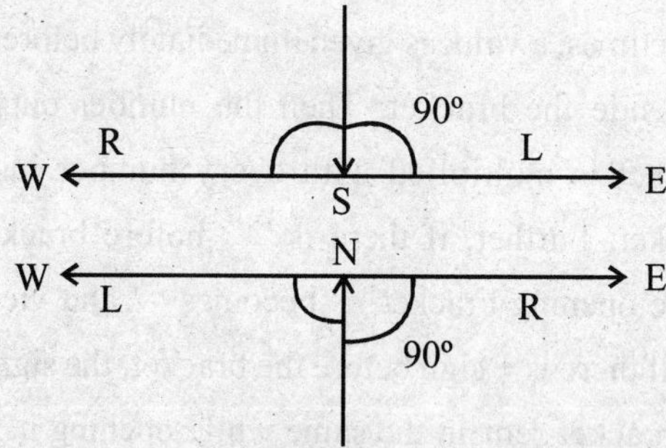

b) Horizontal Directions:

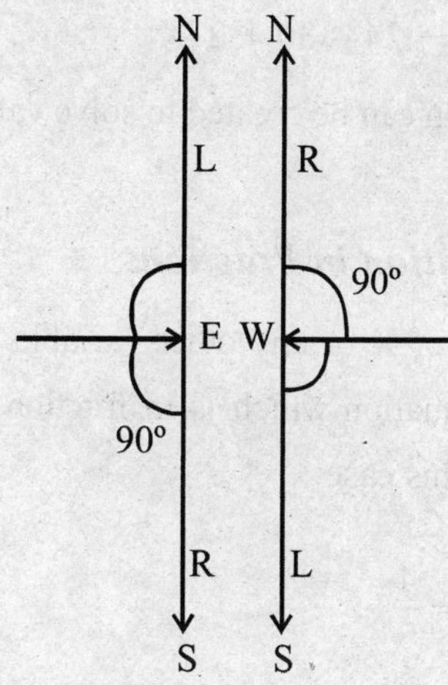

c) Diagonal Directions:

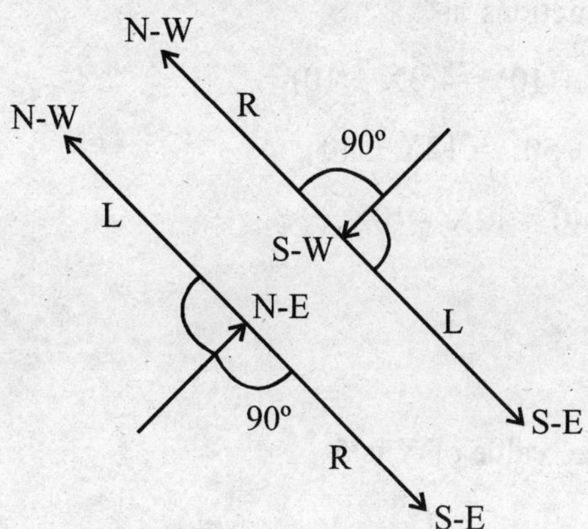

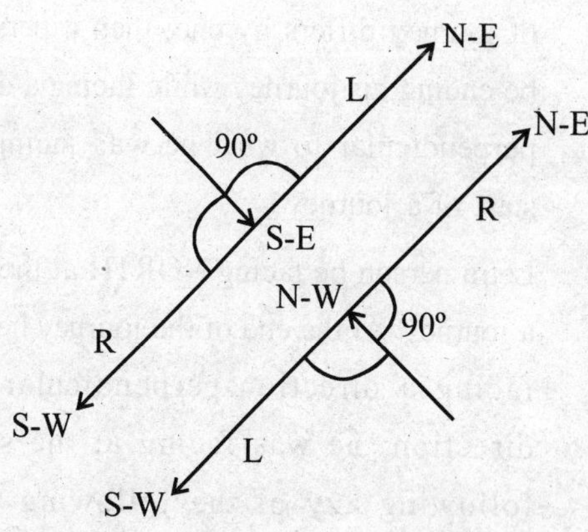

Here R: Right L: Left

Fundamentals of Sequential Turns in Directions

1. If sequences of turns during a journey contain same number of Left (L) and Right (R) turns, then a person at the end of his journey faces the SAME direction what he was facing at the start of journey, whatever is the ordering of L and R turns.

   Suppose a person is facing WEST at the start of a journey. He will again face WEST at the end of his journey while following any of the following sequences of turns:

   a) L-R-R-L-R-L-R-L
   b) L-L-L-L-R-R-R-R
   c) R-L-R-L-R-L-R-L
   d) R-L-L-R-L-L-R-R

2. If the number of L and R turns during a journey differs by two, then the person at the end of the journey faces OPPOSITE direction to what he was facing at the start of the journey.

   Let a person be facing SOUTH at the start of a journey. He will face NORTH at the end of his journey while following any of the sequences given below:

   a) L-R-L-L-R-R-L-L
   b) R-L-R-L-R-R-L-R
   c) L-L-R-R-L-R-R-R
   d) R-R-R-L-L-L-R-R

3. If the number of L and R turns in a sequence of journey differs by one, then a person will be ending his journey while facing a direction perpendicular to what he was facing at the start of a journey.

   Let a person be facing NORTH at the start of a journey. At the end of the journey he will be facing a direction perpendicular to the direction; he was facing at the start by following any of the following turning sequences:

   a) L-R-R-L-L-R-L

   b) R-L-L-R-R-L-R

   c) R-L-R-L-R-L-R

   d) L-L-R-R-L-L-R

Above rules are applicable on DIAGONAL turns also.

Solving Value of X

In some questions of Reasoning and Quantitative Aptitude, value of X is to be calculated through an equation which has two sides, viz. left hand side and a right hand side. Both these sides carry a mixture of values with X and without X with '+', '–', 'x', or '÷'. Some values are without these signs. To calculate the value of X, all the values are picked up and segregated on either side. Now values with X are on one side and values without X are on the other side. Now to calculate value X, values without X are picked up and taken to that side, where other values without X are already placed. Similar action is done with values with X. Now on one side there are values without X and on the other side, values are with X. In this process four fundamental signs like ÷, ×, –, +, i.e., any of the above signs is between the two digits. While taking one digit to the other side, the original sign is converted into its opposite sign, e.g., plus becomes negative and vice versa, and multiplication becomes division and vice versa. Then the equation is solved with the rule of BODMAS.

E.g.: Solve the value X in the following equation:

$$30X + 9 - 24 = 10X + 7 - 5X + 28$$

Sol: $30X - 10X + 5X = 24 - 9 + 28 + 7$

$25X = 50$ (By applying rule of BODMAS)

$$x = \frac{50}{25} = 2$$

Solving a Value Outside or Inside the Bracket

Sometimes, a value is given immediately before bracket or inside the bracket. Then the number outside the bracket is multiplied with every number inside the bracket. Further, if there is '–' before bracket, then while opening bracket '+' becomes '–' and vice versa. But if there is + sign before the bracket, the signs inside the bracket remain the same while opening it.

e.g. .... $- 3(5X - 8 + 10 - 9X)$

Sol. .... $- 5X + 24 - 30 + 27X$

Further, an equation can be created to solve value of X as stated above.

Solving an Equation in Fractions

Sometimes, value of X or any other variable is to be solved from an equation which is in fraction in both sides as given in this case:

$$\frac{2X + 10}{3X + 10} = \frac{4}{5}$$

Here, Value of X can be calculated by cross-multiplying the fractions as

$5(2X + 10) = 4(3X + 10)$

$10X + 50 = 12X + 40$

$50 - 40 = 12X - 10X$

$\frac{10}{2} = X$

Hence, value of X is 5

2 Analogy and Classification of Words

ANALOGY OF WORDS

Analogy means balancing the two sides. Each side contains two groups. The two sides become analogous to each other only when the nature of relationship existing between the two groups of one side is exactly similar to the nature of relationship existing between the two groups on the other side. This rule of analogy is applicable to all forms of analogies asked in reasoning, i.e., analogy of words, letters, numbers (in verbal reasoning), and analogy of figures (in non-verbal reasoning).

Analogy of words in particular requires some additional skills also from a candidate, which include possessing **reasonable vocabulary, analytical observation, correlating acumen, and a little general knowledge**.

Structure

The usual structure of a question on analogy can be in any one of the following forms:

1) A : B : : C : ?
2) A : B : : ? : D
3) A : ? : : C : D
4) ? : B : : C : D
5) ? : ? : : C : D
6) A : B : : ? : ?

In the above forms of analogy, sign : means 'is to' and sign :: is the sign of equality which separates the two sides of the equation or analogy, i.e., it puts the two given sides opposite to each other. It is further clear from the above forms of analogy that each side either to the sign of equality has two groups (A, B & C, D). The side before : : is called the Left Hand Side (LHS) and the side after : : is called Right Hand Side (RHS). It is further observed that in each of the above forms there is a ? on one or the other side. This signifies the actual question, the answer of which is to be found from the answer choices. Another form of asking above question is:

1) A is to B as C is to ___
2) A is to B as ___ is to D
3) A is to ___ as C is to D

However, the strategy of solving questions is same in above forms also.

Example 1: Food : Hunger : : Water : ? OR Food is to Hunger as Water is to ___

a) Lust
b) Thirst
c) Desire
d) Appetite

Answer: b

Explanation: Thirst. Thirst establishes the same relation with Water traditionally and practically, as Hunger has with food, so Thirst is the correct answer.

Example 2: Bird : Fish :: Aeroplane : ?

a) Boat
b) Ship
c) Submarine
d) Crocodile

Answer: c

Explanation: Bird flies in sky and fish floats on water and can go inside water. The relationship of Aeroplane and Submarine also has similar relationship.

Example 3: Culprit : Crime :: Judge : ?

a) Case
b) Court
c) Law
d) Verdict

Answer: d

Explanation: Culprit commits Crime and Judge gives Verdict.

Example 4: Shoes: Cobbler :: Clothes : ?

a) Darner
b) Shopkeeper
c) Merchant
d) Tailor

Answer: a

Explanation: Cobbler mends Shoes. Similarly, Darner repairs Clothes.

Example 5: Horse : Jockey :: Car : ?

a) Mechanic

b) Dealer

c) Chauffeur

d) Owner

Answer: c

Explanation: Jockey takes care of Horse. Similarly, Chauffeur takes care of Car.

Example 6: Bull : Horns

a) Elephant : Wings

b) Paper : Pen

c) Car : Wheeld) Money : Purse

Answer: c

Explanation: As Horns are fixed on the body of a Bull, similarly Wheels are fixed on the body of a Car.

Example 7: Whole : Fraction

a) Plus : Minus

b) Star : Planet

c) Rain : Water

d) Ocean : Drop

Answer: d

Explanation: As Fraction leads to Whole, similarly Drop leads to Ocean.

Example 8: Dune : Sand

a) Flower : Rose

b) Doctor : Nurse

c) Book : Magazine

d) House : Brick

Answer: d

Explanation: Dune is a structure made of Sand. Similarly, House is a structure built of Bricks.

Example 9: Bridge: Cards

a) Glass : Mirror

b) Fencing : Sword

c) Swim : River

d) Table : Furniture

Answer: b

Explanation: Bridge is a game of Cards, similarly Fencing is a game of Sword.

Example 10: 'Moon' is related to 'Earth' in the same way as 'Earth' is related to?

a) Moon

b) Mars

c) Venus

d) Sun

Answer: d

Explanation: As the Moon revolves around the Earth, similarly the Earth revolves around the Sun.

Practice Exercise

General Questions Format

Analogy of Words

1. King is to Rule as Lawyer is to?
(A) Defend (B) Advocate
(C) Plead (D) Appeal

2. Library : Books :: Hospital : ?
(A) Doctors (B) Patients
(C) Beds (D) Nurses

3. Train : Platform : : Aeroplane : ?
(A) Airport (B) Airline
(C) Aircraft (D) None of these

4. Faith : Devotion : : ? : Hard work
(A) Initiative (B) Determination
(C) Success (D) Reward

5. Tourism is to Hospitality as Insurance is to?
(A) Assurance
(B) Premium
(C) Security
(D) Future

6. Office is to Staff as Film is to?
(A) Musicians (B) Editors
(C) Artists (D) Writers

7. India is to Asia as Egypt is to?
(A) Europe (B) N. America
(C) Australia (D) Africa

8. Aroma : Fragrance : : ? : Shortage
(A) Abundance (B) Crisis
(C) Hoarding (D) Paucity

9. Education is to Literacy as ? is to Publicity
(A) Advertisement
(B) Communication
(C) Newspaper
(D) Popularity

10. Desire : Satisfaction : : ? : ?
(A) Journey: Destination
(B) Light: Sun
(C) Land: House
(D) Youth: Old age

11. Flower is to Fragrance as....... is to.........
(A) Sun-Light
(B) Hard work-Reward
(C) Wood-Furniture
(D) Fan-Air

12. ? : ? :: Sin: Crime
A) Shortage: Paucity
(B) Sincerity: Loyalty
(C) Kindness: Generosity
(D) Love: Devotion

13. Month is related to Week in the same way as ? is related to?
(A) School-Children
(B) Auditorium-Visitor
(C) Doctor-Treatment
(D) Bouquet-Flower

14. Lawyer : Teacher : : ? : ?
(A) Temple : Mosque
(B) Car : Petrol
(C) Drama : Film
(D) Shoe : Sox

15. What is related to Train in the same way as School is related to College
(A) Passenger (B) Bus
(C) Ticket (D) Journey

16. TV is to Telecasting as - is to -
(A) Cloth-Stitching
(B) Food-Cooking
(C) Cake-Baking
(D) Teacher-Teaching

17. Summer is to Winter as - is to -
(A) Bunch-Keys (B) Success-Failure
(C) Day-Sun (D) Job-Business

18. Black: ?: : Top : ?
(A) Cloud-Mountain
(B) Negro-Building
(C) White-Bottom
(D) Dog-Camel

19. Computer is to Processor as Man is to?
(A) Life (B) Heart
(C) Blood (D) Brain

20. Jahangir : Mughals : : Changez Khan : ?
A) Mongols (B) Chinese
(C) Tatars (D) Tzars

Classification of words

Find the odd choice in the following:

1. (A) Flat (B) House
(C) Bungalow (D) Home
2. (A) Crisis (B) Shortage
(C) Paucity (D) Scarcity
3. (A) Laugh (B) Joker
(C) Clown (D) Cartoon
4. (A) Pair (B) Sox
(C) Pigeon (D) Goggles
5. (A) Bull (B) Chair
(C) Cake (D) Bake
6. (A) Doctorate (B) Matriculate
(C) Graduate (D) Directorate
7. (A) Buffer (B) Load
(C) Burden (D) Stress
8. (A) Camera (B) Photography
(C) Flash (D) Lens
9. (A) Furniture (B) People
(C) Rickshaw (D) Crew
10. (A) River (B) Stream
(C) Canal (D) Ditch
11. (A) Physician (B) Surgeon
(C) Neurologist (D) Doctor
12. (A) Coincide (B) Suicide
(C) Matricide (D) Pesticide
13. (A) Cricket (B) Hockey
(C) Volleyball (D) Kabbaddi
14. (A) Plankton (B) Kiwi
(C) Coral (D) Octopus
15. (A) Island (B) England
(C) Ireland (D) Finland
16. (A) Research (B) Investigation
(C) Enquiry (D) Resumption
17. (A) Ointment (B) Comb
(C) Paste (D) Gel
18. (A) Quick (B) Brisk
(C) Quiet (D) Rapid
19. (A) Rome (B) Tashkent
(C) Ontario (D) Uruguay
20. (A) Trouble (B) Mend
(C) Repair (D) Correct

KEY

Analogy of Words

1. **B** As King's basic gesture is to Rule the subjects, similarly a Lawyer's basic gesture to Advocate.
2. **C** Books are the basic constituents of Library. Similarly, Beds are basic constituents of a Hospital.
3. **D** Just like Train reaches a particular Platform allotted to a particular train, in the same way an Aeroplane reaches a Hanger meant for a particular aeroplane.
4. **B** As Faith in any subject is the basis of Devotion towards any subject, Determination becomes basis of Hard work.
5. **A** Tourism survives on the gesture of Hospitality. Similarly, Insurance survives on the gesture of Assurance.
6. **C** An Office comprises of Staff. Film comprises of Artists.
7. **D** Asia is a continent and India belongs to it. Similarly, Egypt is a country which belongs to Africa, which is a continent.
8. **D** As Aroma and Fragrance are synonymous to each other, similarly Paucity and Shortage are also synonymous to each other.
9. **A** Literacy is part of Education. Similarly, Publicity is part of Advertisement.
10. **A** Satisfaction is the end point of Desire. In the same way Destination is the end point of Journey.
11. **A** Flower emits Fragrance, so in the same way Sun emits Light.
12. **D** Every Devotion is Love but every Love is not Devotion. Similarly every Crime is a Sin but every Sin is not a Crime.

13. A Weeks make a Month, similarly Flowers make a Bouquet.

14. A Both Lawyer and Teacher guide and provide education in their respective framework.

Similarly, Temple and Mosque also impart preaching in the way their ethics permit.

15. B Schools and Colleges are two different modes of imparting education; similarly Bus and Train are two different modes of transportation.

16. D TV is a medium of Telecasting; similarly Teacher is medium of Teaching.

17. B Success and Failure are antonyms just like Summer and Winter.

18. C Black is opposite White and Top is opposite Bottom.

19. D Processor is the brain for the Computer just as the human Brain is for Man.

20. A As Jahangir belonged to Mughal clan, Changez Khan belonged to Mongol clan.

Classification of Words

1. D Home is the odd choice as Home is a qualitative concept and is made with family whereas rest of the others are physical structures providing shelter.

2. A Crisis is a general term meaning any type of man-made or natural disaster where as other three terms are synonyms meaning shortage.

3. A Laugh is an activity whereas others are means of yielding this activity.

4. A Pair is a numeral whereas others are tangible objects.

5. D Bake is an activity while others are nouns.

6. D Directorate is a department whereas others are different academic level of or degrees.

7. A Buffer is a provision of amenities which are kept as reserve to be used in emergency and is used as a mitigation measure against man-made or natural crisis, whereas others are synonyms of pressure.

8. B Photography is a field of activity and rest of others are its components.

9. C Rickshaw is a single entity while rest of others are collective names of various individuals taken together.

10. D Ditch a small narrow channel dug for water drainage whereas others are full water bodies serving the community.

11. D Doctor is a general term while others are specialists.

12. A Coincide indicates things which happen at the same time, whereas others are different forms of killings.

13. D Except Kabbadi, all other games mentioned in the question use a ball.

14. B Kiwi is a bird and rest of others are part of sea life.

15. A Island is the name of geographical structure while others are names of countries.

16. D Resumption is restarting any action after a break while others are different names of investigation.

17. C Comb is for setting hair whereas all others are applied on body.

18. C Except Quiet all others indicate speed.

19. D Uruguay is a country while others are cities of different countries.

20. A Trouble is a botheration while rest of others indicate repeated activity of reformation.

Questions Asked in Previous NET Exams

Analogy of Words

1. Choose the proper alternative given in the code to replace the question mark.

   Cow - Milk **(UGC NET JULY 2018)**

   Bee - Honey

   Teacher - ?

   Code:

   (A) Marks (B) Discipline

   (C) Wisdom (D) Lesson

2. Warrior is related to Sword, Carpenter is related to Saw, and Farmer is related to Plough. In the same way, the Author is related to

   (UGC NET DECEMBER 2014)

   (A) Book

   (B) Fame

   (C) Reader

   (D) Pen

3. Choose the appropriate alternative given in the codes to replace the question mark.

   Examiner - Examinee, Pleader - Client, Preceptor -?

   (UGC NET DECEMBER 2012)

   (A) Customer
   (B) Pathfinder
   (C) Perceiver
   (D) Disciple

4. Determine the relationship between the pair of words Numerator : Denominator and then select the pair of words from the following which have a similar relationship:

   (UGC NET JUNE 2011)

   (A) Fraction : Decimal
   (B) Divisor : Quotient
   (C) Top : Bottom
   (D) Dividend : Divisor

5. Determine the relationship between the pair of words

   (UGC NET DECEMBER 2010)

   Always : Never and then select from the following pair of words which have a similar relationship:

   (A) Often : Rarely
   (B) Frequently : Occasionally
   (C) Constantly : Frequently
   (D) Intermittently : Casually

Classification of words

1. Choose the odd word:

   (UGC NET DECEMBER 2007)

   (A) Nun (B) Knight
   (C) Monk (D) Priest

2. Out of four cities given below three are alike in some manner while the fourth one is different. Identify the odd one.

   (UGC NET JANUARY 2017)

   (A) Lucknow (B) Rishikesh
   (C) Allahabad (D) Patna

KEY

Analogy of Words

1. **C** As Cow yields Milk, Bee yields Honey, similarly Teacher yields wisdom.
2. **D** Instrument of Warrior is Sword, that of Carpenter is Saw and that of Farmer is Plough, Similarly, instrument of Author is Pen.
3. **D** Examinee is there as there is Examiner, Client is there as there is Pleader, similarly Disciple is there as there is Preceptor.
4. **C** Numerator and Denominator are antonyms and so are Top and Bottom.
5. **A** Always and Never are antonyms, similarly Often and Rarely are antonyms.

Classification of Words

1. **B** Knight is a king enjoying all the worldly pleasures while others have renounced such pleasures and are leading the life of saints.
2. **A** Lucknow is situated along river Gomti while other cities are situated over Ganga.

Directions

CONCEPT

Following types of questions on Directions are asked in various exams:

1) Journey 2) Positioning 3) Turning sequences

Journey

In this question an account of a traveller's journey is given in which he/she starts from a particular point while facing a particular direction, makes various turns, covers various distances before each turn, and ultimately reaches the destination. Question is on measuring the straight distance covered by the traveller from the starting point to the end point and the direction of the destination point with respect to the starting point. Knowledge of prerequisites of directions helps in solving these questions. Further following tips will help in finding out a particular straight horizontal, vertical, or diagonal distance and direction with respect to the starting point.

For solving any question on direction, a sketch of the total account of the journey is to be drawn. It helps in the following way:

I) If the end point (E) of a journey comes just above the starting point, then the E is towards North of S.

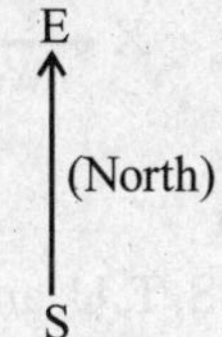

II) If E comes just below S, then E is in the south of S.

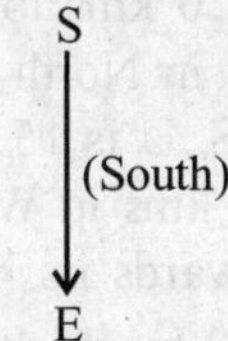

III) If E is just to the right of S, then E is towards East of S.

S ——→ E
(East)

IV) If E is just in line of S towards left, then E is towards of West of S.

E ←—— S
(West)

V) E is towards South-East of S, if E is diagonally below right of S.

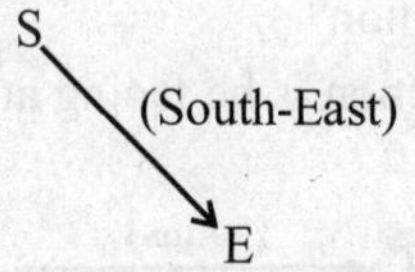

VI) If E is above right of S, then E is towards North-East of S

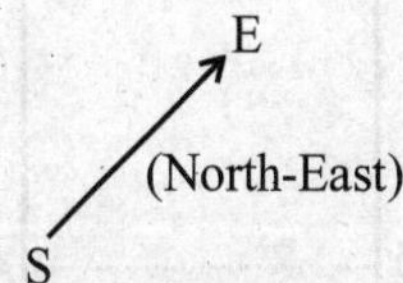

VII) If E is diagonally below left of S, then E is towards South-West of S.

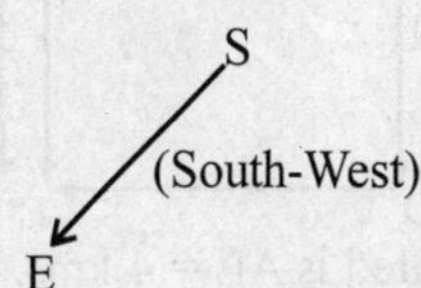

VIII) E is towards North-West of S, when E comes to be diagonally above left of S.

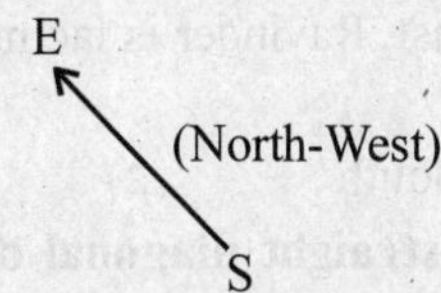

Format:

a) **Calculating straight horizontal distance:**

Swaran starts moving towards East. He covers a distance of 15 kms and turns to his left. He further turns to his right after covering 8 kms. He covers 6 kms. Finally he turns towards right and covers 8 kms. How far is he from the starting point and in which direction?

Strategy: Drawing the sketch of the journey:

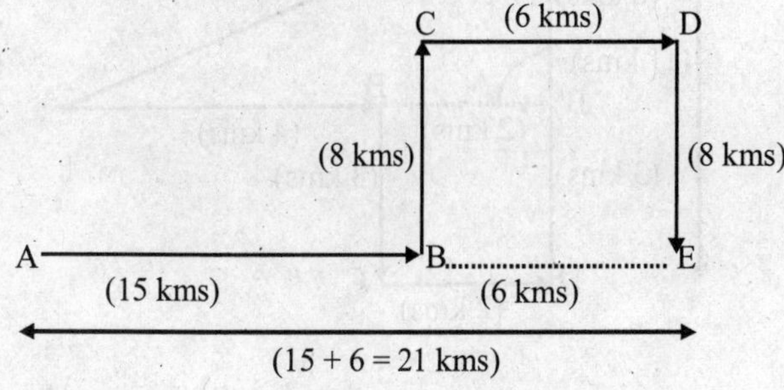

Total straight distance AE = AB + BE = 15 + 6 = 21 kms. As end point E is exactly in line with starting point (A) towards its right, Direction w.r.t. A is East. So Ans.: 21 kms East

b) **Calculating straight vertical distance:**

Format: Ravinder starts his journey and goes towards North. He covers 12 kms. And turns to his left. He further turns to left after covering 4 kms. He covers 16 kms. And then he turns left and covers 4 kms and reaches his destination.

Possible Questions:

1) How far is he from the starting point and in which direction?
2) Which direction is he facing at the end of the journey?

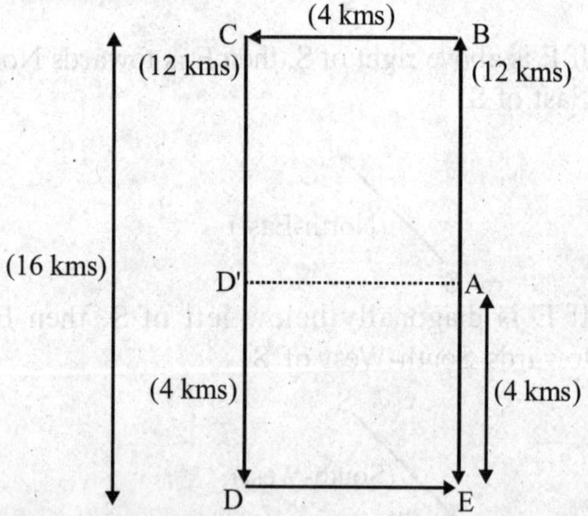

Distance to be calculated is AE = 4 kms. As End point E is just below in line with starting point A, direction w.r.t. starting point is South. As in distance DE, arrow is pointing towards East, Ravinder is facing East at the end of the journey.

Ans: 1) 4 kms. South 2) East.

c) **Calculating straight diagonal distance:**

Format: A man starts going towards West. He covers 4 kms and turns to his left. He covers 3 kms and turns right. After covering 2 kms, he finally turns right and covers 11 kms. How far is he from the starting point and in which direction?

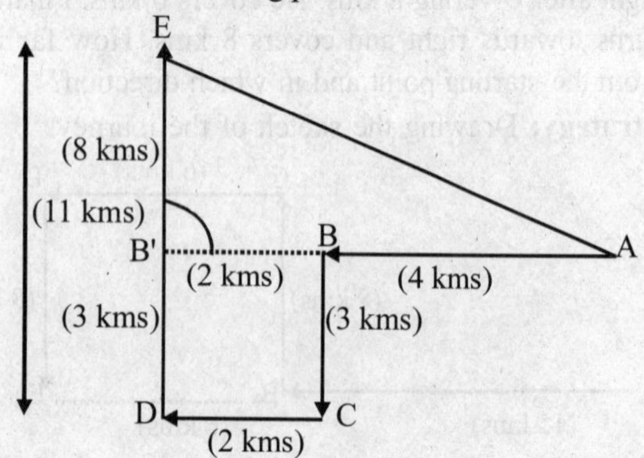

Here, the straight distance from the starting point A to the end point E is AE which is a diagonal distance. For calculating this a right angle triangle AB'E is carved in the sketch and formula of Pythagoras Theorem is applied to find out distance AE as follows:

$$AE = \sqrt{(AB')^2} + \sqrt{(B'E)^2} = AE$$

While putting the values:

$$AE = \sqrt{(6)^2} + \sqrt{(8)^2} = \sqrt{100} = 10 \text{ kms.}$$

As point E is towards diagonally left towards A, E is towards North-West of A

So Ans: 10 kms, North-West

In a nutshell, it is observed that in terms of straight distance and direction, either horizontal, vertical, or diagonal distance is to be calculated.

Positioning

In this type an account describes the positions of different subjects in different directions with respect to one another and some questions are asked after the account.

Format (I): There are five houses X, Y, Z, A, and B situated in different directions. B is in the south of Z. X is towards West of B. A is towards North of X. Y is towards West of A.

Possible Questions:

1) In which direction B is situated w.r.t Y?
2) In which direction Y is situated w.r.t. X?

Strategy:

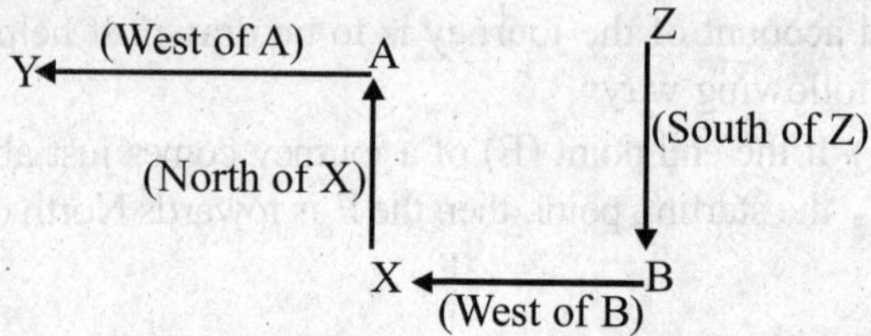

Ans: Q1: South-East

Q2: North-West

Format (II): P, Q, R, S, T, U, and V are seven branches of an office which are located in different parts of a region. T is situated 20 kms towards East of branch Q. S is 30 kms away in North of T. Branch R is 10 kms towards East of S. U is 15 kms in South of R. V is at a distance of 30 kms in West of U, and P is 20 kms away from V towards its North.

Possible Questions: 1) In which direction V is situated with respect to Q?

2) In which direction U is situated with respect to T?
3) In which direction P is situated w.r.t. S?
4) In which direction R is situated w.r.t. V?

5) In which direction S is situated w.r.t. U and V respectively?
6) How far is V situated from Q?
7) In which direction Q is situated with respect to S?
8) In which direction T is situated with respect to V?

Answers can be found by drawing the following sketch:

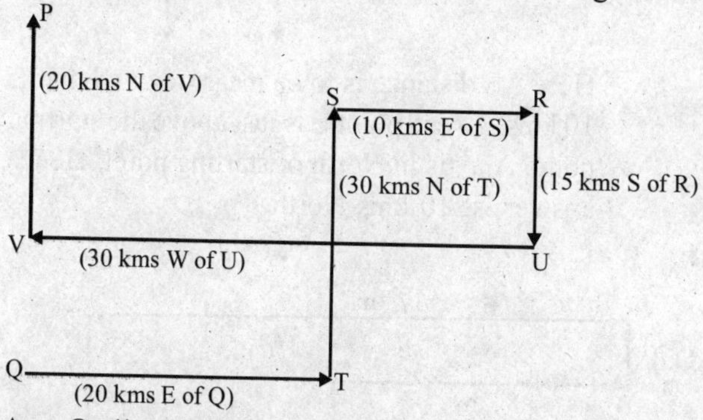

Ans:Q. 1) North
Q. 2) North-East
Q. 3) North-WestQ. 4) North-East
Q. 5) North-West, North-East
Q. 6) 15 kms
Q. 7) South-West
Q. 8) South-East

Turning Sequences

Questions on turning sequences are solved while following formulae studied in the chapter of prerequisites.

Format:

Q.1) A person starts journey while facing South. Which of the following turning sequences should he follow so that he/she should be facing South again at the end of the journey?
A) L-L-R-L-R-R-L-L B) R-L-R-R-L-R-L-L
C) R-R-L-R-L-R-L-R D) R-R-R-L-R-R-L-L

Q.2) A person starts journey while facing East. Which of the following turning sequences should he follow that he/she should be facing West at the end of the journey?
A) L-L-R-L-R-R-L-L
B) R-L-R-R-L-R-L-L
C) R-R-L-R-L-R-L-L
D) R-R-R-L-R-L-L-L

Q. 3) A person starts journey while facing East. Which of the following turning sequences should he follow that he/she should be facing North at the end of the journey?
A) L-L-R-L-L-R-L B) L-R-R-R-L-R-R
C) R-R-L-R-L-R-R D) R-R-L-L-R-R-L

Ans: Q. 1) B Q. 2) A Q. 3) D

Practice Exercise

General Questions Format

1. A person is going to North, he covers 10 kms and then he turns to his left and he covers 5 kms. He then turns right and covers 8 kms. Again he turns right and covers 15 kms. Finally he turns right and covers 18 kms. How far he is from the starting point and in which direction?
(A) 10 kms W (B) 15 kms N
(C) 10 kms E (D) 20 kms E

2. Ajay is going towards East, he covers 10 kms and turns right and covers 6 kms. Then he starts moving back and covers 16 kms, and then turns left and moves 10 kms. How far is he from the starting point and in which direction?
(A) 10 kms N (B) 16 kms S
(C) 10 kms S (D) 15 kms W

3. I am going towards West, after covering 8 kms, I turn to right and cover 3 kms, again I turn to right and cover 17 kms, again to right and cover 11 kms and finally to right and cover 9 kms. How far am I from the starting point and in which direction?
(A) 9 kms N (B) 8 kms S
(C) 9 kms S (D) 8 kms N

4. Starting from a point Raju walked 12 kms towards North. He turned right and walked 10 kms. He again turned right and walked 12 kms, and then he turned left and walked 5 kms. How far is he from the starting point?
(A) 27 kms E (B) 5 kms E
(C) 10 kms W (D) None of these

5. Arun starts driving towards West. After driving 100 kms, he turns towards North, and then turns towards East after driving 200 kms. He drives 100 kms more. How far is he from the starting point and in which direction?
(A) 200 kms N (B) 100 kms N
(C) 100 kms S (D) 200 kms S

6. Going towards North a cyclist covers 8 kms, then takes a right turn and goes 5 kms straight. He then turns right again and goes 8 kms; finally he takes a left turn to reach his office. In which direction is his office from the starting point?
(A) North (B) South
(C) East (D) West

7. A person is going to North-West. He covers 30 kms and turns left, covers 30 kms more and again turns left and further covers 30 kms. From that point he starts going towards the starting point. Which direction is he following?
(A) South-East (B) North-East
(C) East (D) North

8. A man performs Shirshasan and his face is towards East. His left hand is pointing towards
(A) East (B) West
(C) South (D) North

9. I am going towards West, If I follow the turning sequence: 'Left, Right, Right, Left, Left, Right', then which direction I would be facing at the end of my journey?
(A) North (B) East
(C) West (D) South

10. Geeta went 2 miles Northward from her house, then went 2 miles Eastward and reached her office. Reeta went 2 miles westward from her house and after walking 2 miles Northward reached the same office. In which direction is Reeta's house to Geeta's house?
(A) East (B) West
(C) South (D) North

KEY

1. C

15 kms
D E
8 kms
5 kms B
C
18 kms
10 kms
A F

Here AF distance is 10 kms and end point (F) is in the East of starting point (A).

2. A Distance to be calculated

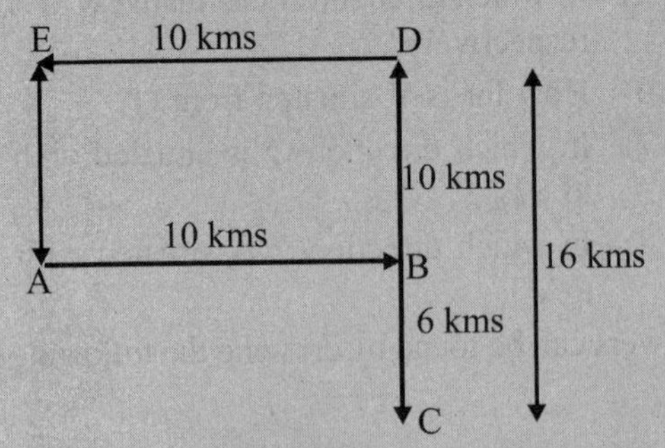

Here AE distance is to be measured and that is 10 kms. As end point E is just above the starting point, Ajay is in North of starting point. Hence answer is: 10 kms North.

3. B

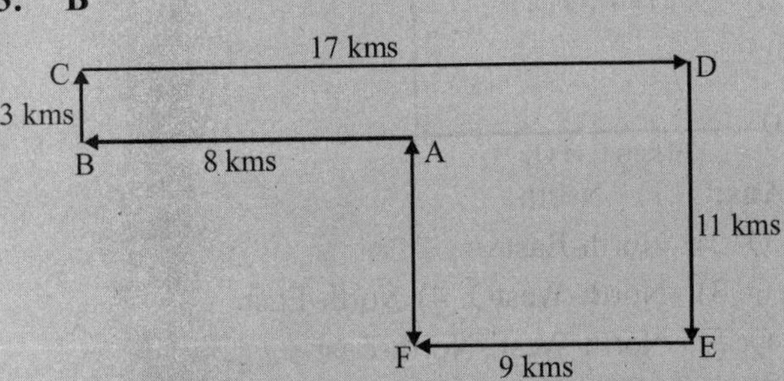

Here FA distance is to be measured and that is 8 kms and F is just below A so direction is South. Answer is 8 kms South and that is option B.

4. D

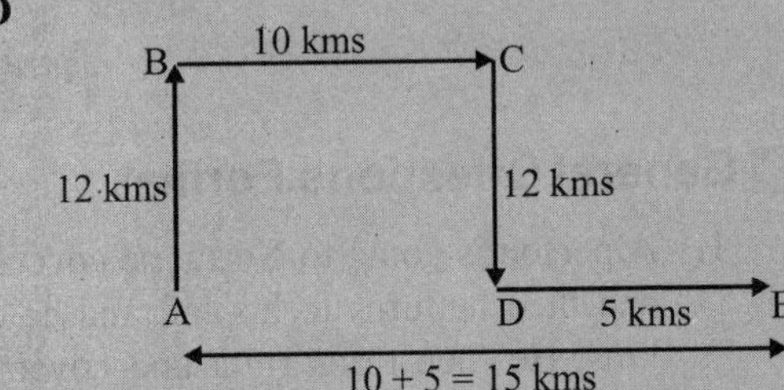

Here, distance AE is to be measured and that is 15 kms. As end point E is towards right of starting point A. Hence, E is in the east of A. Answer is 15 kms East

5. A

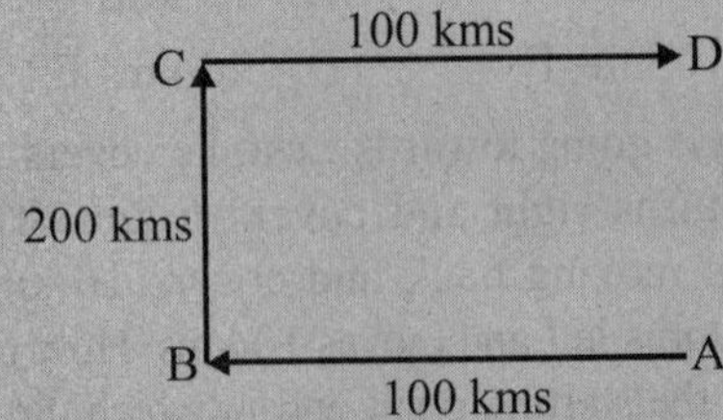

Distance to be measured is AD and that is 200 kms as it is parallel to distance BC which is also 200 kms, hence AD is 200 kms. As end point D is lying just above starting point A, D is in north of A. So answer is 200 kms N

6. C

B 5 kms
8 kms
8 kms
A
East

7. B

B
30 kms
30 kms
A
C
30 kms
D

In above sketch he starts moving towards starting point A after reaching D. So he is following North-East direction.

8. C In a normal posture if a person is facing East, his left side is towards north. As in Shirshasan there is 180?degree rotation, hence change in their directions, that is, now the hands will be pointing towards opposite directions. In normal posture if left hand points towards North, now it will be pointing towards South.

9. C From the knowledge of prerequisites we know that if there are equal number of left turns and right turns, then the direction towards which one is facing at start and end of journey is same. Similarly, in this question, the person performing journey is facing west at start of journey and there are three left turns and three right turns so the person at the end of journey will be facing West as he was facing at the start of the journey.

10. A

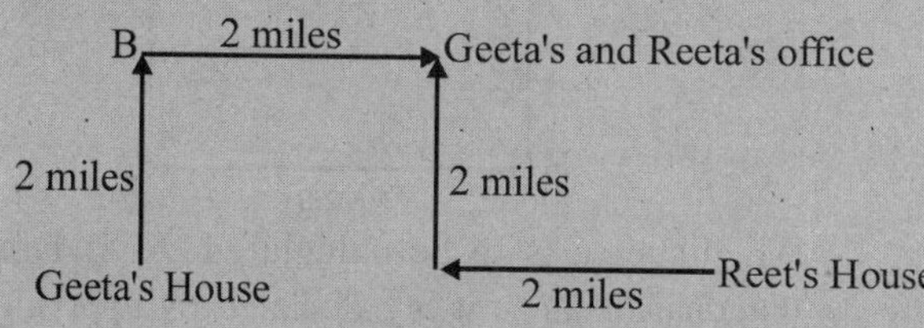

As Reeta's house towards right of Geeta's house and both the houses are in line, Reeta's house is in east of Geeta's house.

Questions Asked in Previous NET Exams

1. Gopal walks 20 m North. Then he turns right and walks 30 m. Then he turns right and walks 35 m. Again he turns left and walks 15 m. Then he again turns left and walks 15 m. The shortest distance between his original position and final one is **(UGC NET JULY 2018)**

   (A) 65 m (B) 55 m
   (C) 40 m (D) 45 m

2. A postman walked 20 m straight from his office, turned right and walked 10 m. After turning left he walked 10 m and after turning right walked 20 m. He again turned right and walked 70m. How far he is from his office? **(UGC NET NOVEMBER 2017)**

   (A) 40 m (B) 60 m
   (C) 20 m (D) 50 m

3. A person walks 10 m in front and 10 m to the right. Then every time turning to his left, he walks 5, 15 and 15 m respectively. How far is he from his starting point? **(UGC NET JULY 2016)**

   (A) 20 m (B) 15 m
   (C) 10 m (D) 5 m

4. Anil after travelling 6 km towards East from his house realised that he has travelled in a wrong direction, he turned and travelled 12 km towards West, turned right and travelled 8 km to reach his office. The straight distance of the office from his house is: **(UGC NET DECEMBER 2015)**

   (A) 20 km (B) 14 km
   (C) 12 km (D) 10 km

5. One day Prakash left home and walked 10 km towards south, turned right and walked 5 km, turned right and walked 10 km and turned left and walked 10 km. How many km will he have to walk to reach his home straight? **(UGC NET JUNE 2015)**

   (A) 30
   (B) 10
   (C) 20
   (D) 15

6. A man started walking frorn his house towards south. After walking 6 km, he turned to his left walked 5 km. Then he walked further 3 km after turning left. He then turned to his left and continued his walk for 9 km. How far is he away from his house?

(UGC NET JUNE 2014)

(A) 3 km (B) 4 km

(C) 5 km (D) 6 km

KEY

1. D

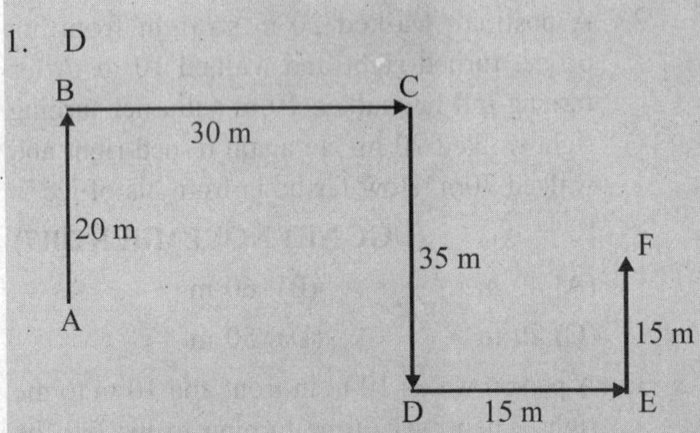

Distance AF is required to be measured. A and F are at same level so the straight distance between A and F is 45 (30 parallel to BC and 15 parallel to DE). So answer is choice D.

2. D In above question diagonal distance AE is to be measured. Here a right angle triangle is created. It is seen in the triangle side AH is 30 m.

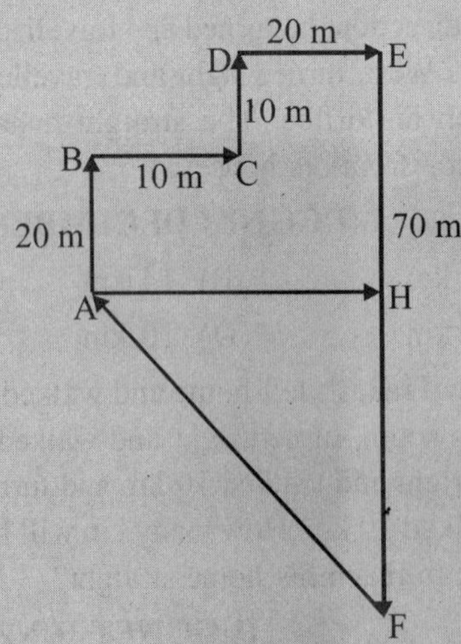

Side HF of triangle is 40 m. AF side will be equal to =

$$\sqrt{(AH^2)} + \sqrt{(HF^2)} \Rightarrow \sqrt{(30)^2} + \sqrt{(40)^2} = 50\text{m}$$

3. D

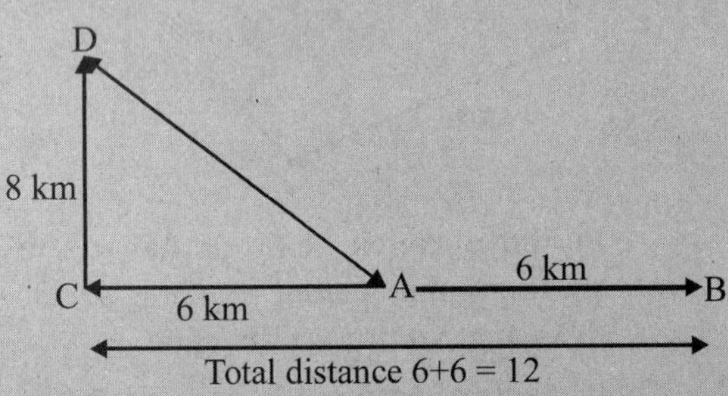

As it is clear from the figure distance AF is to be measured and that is 5 m and so is the answer,

4. D

D

8 km

C

A

6 km

B

6 km

Total distance 6+6 = 12

The required distance to be measured is DA. As this is diagonal distance, a right angled triangle is created. Side CD of the triangle measures 8 km, side AC of triangle measures 6 km. By applying Pythagoras Theorem formula answer will be 10 km.

5. D

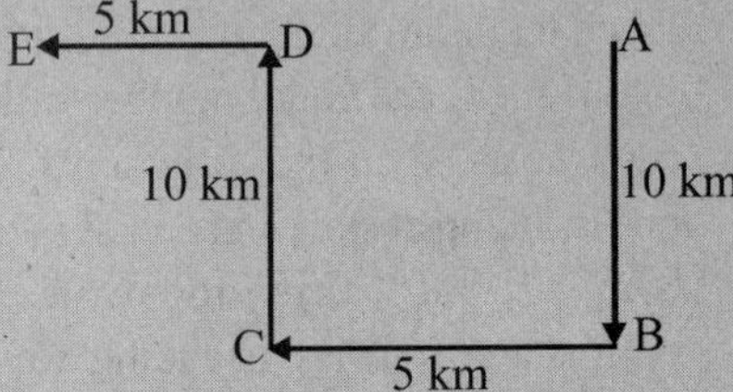

In above case distance AE is to be measured and that is 15 kms and so is the answer.

6. C

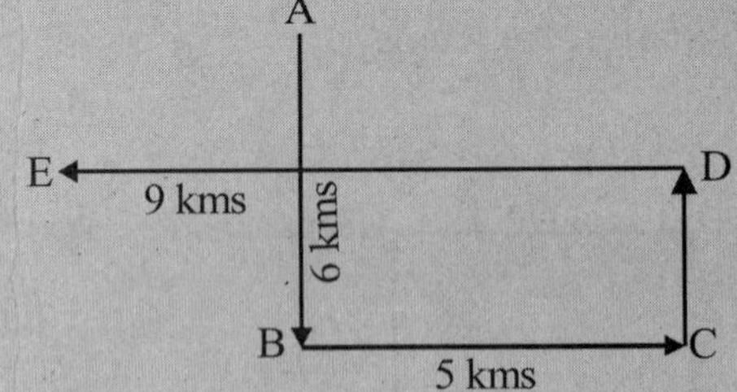

AE distance is to be calculated. As it is a diagonal distance it is calculated by applying Pythagoras theorem formula and answer will be 5 kms.

Coding-Decoding

CONCEPT

Coding is an activity to convert an original word or text message into already devised codes in the form of letters, words, numbers, signs, pictures, etc. to maintain secrecy for espionage. On the other hand, decoding is an activity to convert an encoded word or text message back into its original form. As coding and decoding is very meticulously done and requires intelligence, it has become an indispensable part of reasoning/mental ability tests of various competitive exams.

Format

Questions on coding and decoding are given in the format of giving a word with its code as a sample. Then the code of another word is asked and the candidate is to study the sample coding and while following the same pattern, one is to find out the code of the asked word. This is a universal pattern of questions in multiple choice answers format in every type of coding pattern.

Strategy

Various types of questions on this topic can be solved while using prerequisites of Letters and Numbers, and skill of Ordering, De-Ordering, and Substitution.

TYPES OF CODING-DECODING QUESTIONS IN COMPETITIVE EXAMS

Aspirants appearing in various competitive exams are asked the following types of questions on coding and decoding.

Replacement Coding

The major coding patterns of this type are Letter Coding, Number Coding, Word Coding, and Language Coding.

Letter Coding is the art replacing the original letters of a meaningful word with some other letters of the English Alphabet either in succeeding, preceding, or corresponding order to original letters to make a coded word. The pattern of replacement of letters further gives us two types of coding combinations, viz. Parallel Coding and Cross Coding.

a) Parallel Coding: In parallel coding the original word and the coded word proceed in the same direction. It is clear from the following example:

If a word DICTIONARY is encoded as EJDUJPOBSZ, then the word SECONDARY is encoded as?

Sol. Here, the given coding pattern is written as under:

	1	2	3	4	5	6	7	8	9	10
Main Word:	D	I	C	T	I	O	N	A	R	Y

Coded Word:	E	J	D	U	J	P	O	B	S	Z
	1	2	3	4	5	6	7	8	9	10

In above example the replacement pattern of the letters is in parallel mode, as first letter of the coded word is immediate succeeding to the first letter of the main word and so second with second, third with third, and so on. Similarly, parallel replacement may be in the preceding order or the corresponding order to the main word. So while following the same pattern, the code of the word SECONDARY is

	1	2	3	4	5	6	7	8	9
Main Word:	S	E	C	O	N	D	A	R	Y

Coded Word:	T	F	D	P	O	E	B	S	Z
	1	2	3	4	5	6	7	8	9

So the code of word SECONDARY is TFDPOEBSZ.

In above case we move from left to right in the main word as well as in the coded word in replacement patterns.

b) Cross Coding: In cross coding the replacement pattern of the coded word is diagonal to the proceeding of original word as is clear from the following example:

If a word AMBIGUOUS is encoded as TVPVHJCNB, then what is the code of word POLYCLINIC?

Here, the coding pattern of the sample word is:

	1	2	3	4	5	6	7	8	9
Main Word:	A	M	B	I	G	U	O	U	S

Coded Word:	T	V	P	V	H	J	C	N	B
	9	8	7	6	5	4	3	2	1

In above case the replacement pattern in the coded word is again succeeding order of letters in the main word but in a diagonal or cross fashion, i.e., the last letter of the coded word is immediate succeeding to first letter of the main word and so on. In cross coding we proceed from left to right in the main word and right to left in the coded word in all the replacement patterns. While following the same pattern the code of word POLYCLINIC is determined as follows:

	1	2	3	4	5	6	7	8	9	10
Main Word:	P	O	L	Y	C	L	I	N	I	C

Coded Word:	D	J	O	J	M	D	Z	M	P	Q
	10	9	8	7	6	5	4	3	2	1

So the code of POLYCLINIC is DJOJMDZMPQ.

Imp. While choosing whether a coding pattern in a given question belongs to parallel coding or cross coding, it is to be checked if the first letter of the main word is closer to first letter of the coded word in the replacement combination of succeeding, preceding, or corresponding order. In that case it is a case of parallel coding but if it is closer to the last letter of the coded word in the same manner, then it is a case of cross coding.

Replacement Ordering

As it has already been stated that it may be parallel coding or cross coding, the letters of the main word are replaced in succeeding, preceding, or corresponding order to create the coded word. Replacement ordering may be consecutive, with gap, or with alternative repetition. It is clear from the following examples:

1) If the code of a word GERMANY is FDQLZMX, then code of word PORTUGAL is ONQSTFZK.

   Explanation: It is a case of consecutive preceding order parallel coding.

2) If a word HALOGEN is encoded as KDORJHQ, then the code of word EXAMPLE is HADPSOH.

   Explanation: It is a case of replacement in succeeding order with the gap of two letters in parallel coding.

3) If a word SALUTE is encoded as HZOFGV, then the code of word BOARD is YLZIW.

   Explanation: Here the replacement is in corresponding order in parallel coding.

4) If a word PENCIL is encoded as JGALCN, then word COURSE will be encoded as CQPSMA.

   Explanation: In above case the replacement is in preceding order with the gap of one letter in cross coding.

5) If a word WONDERFUL is encoded as XNOCFQGTM, then code of word GENTLEMAN is HDOSMDNZO.

   Explanation: Here, the replacement is alternative repetition of succeeding order and preceding order respectively in parallel coding.

Number Coding

In this type letters in the original word are replaced by numbers in a certain pattern to create the coded word. It is clear from the following examples:

1) If word PAINT is coded as 74128, EXCEL is encoded as 93596. Then code of word ACCEPT is 455978.

   Explanation: The letters of word ACCEPT are one way or other common to the given words PAINT and EXCEL and accordingly the numbers replacing letters of these words also become of the common letters of the word ACCEPT.

2) If C = 3, N = 14, X = 24 then code of word FRANCE is 47, then code of word ENGLAND is 57.

   Explanation: Original position of the letters in succeeding order of alphabet is given. Taking this as a base, position of letters in the word FRANCE is sum up to get the given code in this way:

   Word: F R A N C E

   Position: 6 + 18 + 1 + 14 + 3 + 5 = 47

   In the same way the code of word ENGLAND is obtained.

3) If a word SUNSET is encoded like 343 then what is the code of word PUNCTUAL?

   1) 60 2) 64

   3) 69 4) 49

   Answer is choice no. 2, i.e., 64

   Explanation: Here, the letters of the original words are replaced simply by cube of 7. Similarly, on the same pattern the code of word PUNCTUAL comes out to be 64 as it is cube of 4 and no other choice is cube of any number. Here, the code may be square, prime number, or any other form of number.

Word Coding

There are two types of word coding:

• Substitution Coding • Elimination Coding

Substitution Coding

It gives a chain of words while substituting every preceding word with the new one and ultimately it is asked to find out the code of a particular word in the chain. It is clear from following examples:

1) If fan is called watch, watch is called table, table is called tumbler, tumbler is called cup, cup is called heater, heater is called book, book is called bangle, bangle is called toothpaste, and toothpaste is called car, then from which source will we get knowledge? Answer is **bangle**.

   Explanation: Above chain of words is just deceptive and thus has no chronological or sequential relation. The main target is to find out the name given to 'Book', which is a source of knowledge. Hence, bangle is the answer.

2) If driver becomes officer, officer becomes carpenter, carpenter becomes doctor, doctor becomes mason, mason becomes teacher, teacher becomes vender, vender becomes judge, judge becomes waiter, waiter becomes merchant, and merchant becomes beggar, then who will examine the patients? Answer is **carpenter**.

   Explanation: The main target is to detect the professional who has become doctor and so the answer is carpenter.

Elimination Coding **:** Here three or four statements of strange sounding words or numbers (codes) are given. Opposite to these strange words or numbers (codes) their meaning is given. The candidate is to ultimately find the code of a particular word in the question. It is clear from the following examples:

1) In a certain code language

   (A) pit, dar, na means **you are good**.

   (B) dar, tok, pa means **good and bad**.

   (C) tim, natok means **they are bad**.

   Then which code word stands for word **good**?

   Answer is 'dar'.

   Explanation: In such questions elimination method is used to find out encoded or decoded word. In this case code of word 'good' is to be determined. By concentrating on these set of statements it is found that word 'good' exists in statement A and statement B. It is also known that code of a word and its meaning exist in the same statement. It is thus ascertained that code of word 'good' exists in statement A and B. As 'good' is a common word in both the statements, a common code in statement A and B should be detected and that is 'dar'. 'dar' does not exist in statement C as word 'good' also does not exist in statement C.

2) In a certain code 786 means study very hard, 958 means hard work pays, and 645 means study and work. Then what is the code number of word **very**?

   Explanation: In the above example the code of the asked word is found by concentrating on the fact that in which particular statement asked word exists and then correlating it with its corresponding code and eliminating others the answer is determined. As the given codes do not convey the meaning of the words in the given order, eliminating uncommon codes and correlating common codes with the words strategy is used. In above example number 7 is determined as code of word 'very'.

Jumbled Coding

In this type of coding the letters of the original word are jumbled in different orders. The candidate is to study the sample coding as given and following the same pattern, the code of the asked word is to be found out. It is clear from the following examples:

1) If a word PICTURE is written like ERUTCIP, then the code of word GROUND is DNUORG.

   Explanation: The original word is written in reverse order and so is the asked word.

2) If Code of word UNTOWARD is NUTOAWRD then code of word PACKAGES is APCKGAES.

   Explanation: In the eight lettered sample word, first and third pair of letters is reversed and so the asked word becomes:

Main Sample word:	UN	TO	WA	RD
Coded Word:	NU	TO	AW	RD
		Similarly		
Main Asked Word:	PA	CK	AG	ES
Coded Word:	AP	CK	GA	ES

3) If a word SOLITUDE is encoded like OSILUTED, then code of word CANDIDATES will be ACDNDITASE.

   Explanation: Contrary to above case, here all the pairs of sample and asked word are reversed consecutively like:

Main Sample word:	SO	LI	TU	DE
Coded Word:	OS	IL	UT	ED
		Similarly		
Main Asked Word:	CA	ND	ID	AT ES
Coded Word;	AC	DN	DI	TA SE

4) If a word EUROPE is encoded as EPORUE then code of word SNACKS is SKCANS.

   Explanation: Sometimes a word has the same letter at the start and at the end just like word EUROPE. There both extreme letters are kept intact and letters in between them are jumbled. Coding-decoding in such cases is clear from following:

	1	2	3	4	5	6
Main Sample Word:	E	U	R	O	P	E
Coded Word:	E	P	O	R	U	E
	1	5	4	3	2	1

   Similarly, following the same order of jumbling, the code of asked word is created as:

	1	2	3	4	5	6
Main Asked Word:	S	N	A	C	K	S
Coded Word:	S	K	C	A	N	S
	1	5	4	3	2	6

   Similarly, other similar patterns of jumbling can be detected in questions.

Practice Exercise

General Questions Format

1. In a certain code, SWITCH is encoded as TVJSDG, then which word is written as CQFZE?
(A) BARED (B) BREAD
(C) BRAED (D) BRADE

2. In a certain code, a word REMOTE is written as EROMET, then which word will have code IPNCCI?
(A) NPIICC (B) PICCIN
(C) PINCIC (D) PICNIC

3. In certain code a wordCARROM is written as BZQQNL, what will be the code of word HOUSE?
(A) IPVTF (B) GNTRD
(C) INVRF (D) GPTID

4. In certain language PRABA is written as 27595, THILAK is 368451, then the code of BHARATHI is........
(A) 37536689 (B) 57686535
(C) 96575368 (D) 96573586

5. If PALE is 2134, EARTH is 41590, then PEARL is
(A) 29530 (B) 24153
(C) 25413 (D) 25430

6. If cook is called butler, butler is called manager, manager is called teacher, teacher is called clerk, and clerk is called principal, then who will teach in the class?
(A) cook (B) teacher
(C) manager (D) clerk

7. If rain is water, water is road, road is cloud, cloud is sky, sky is sea, and sea is path, then where do aeroplanes fly?
(A) Road (B) Sea
(C) Cloud (D) Water

8. If pen is table, table is fan, fan is chair, and chair is roof, then on which will we sit?
(A) Fan (B) Chair
(C) Roof (D) Table

9. If 'tee, pee, see' means 'Drink fruit juice', 'see, kee, lee' means 'Juice is sweet', and 'Lee, ree, mee' means 'He is intelligent', then what is the code of word 'sweet'?
(A) see (B) kee
(C) lee (D) pee

10. In a certain language, 134 means good and tasty, 478 means see good pictures, and 729 means pictures are faint. Then which number stands for see?
(A) 9 (B) 2
(C) 1 (D) 8

11. In a certain code a word HOUSE is written as INVRF, then how is word CROWD is written?
(A) DQPUE (B) DQPVK
(C) DQPVE (D) DQEPV

12. If a word TEN is encoded as 256, SIXTY as 19827, then how word SIXTEEN is encoded?
(A) 1965255 (B) 1963255
(C) 1982556 (D) 1963556

13. If a word MACHINE is encoded as 19-7-9-14-15-20-11, then what is the code of word DANCER?
(A) 13-7-20-10-11-25
(B) 11-7-20-16-11-24
(C) 10-7-20-13-11-24
(D) 10-7-20-9-11-24

14. In a certain code word NIMBUS is written as PWDJKP, then how is word RELICT written?
(A) QEKJGT (B) PFJLGT
(C) QEKMTG (D) None of these

15. In a certain code "lik dye pin" means "eat and drink", "pin bit sem" means "drink hot milk", "lik sem ani" means "milk and curd", then what is the meaning of word "eat"?
(A) lik (B) dye
(C) pin (D) can't be determined

16. If a word FRESCO is written as HUGVER, then what is code of word MURALS?
(A) OXTDNU (B) OYSDMV
(C) OXTCMV (D) OXTDNV

17. In a certain code a word PROSENCEPHALON is written as QSPTFODVKSZOLM. How is word NESTORIANISM written in that code?
(A) OFTVPSRZMRNH
(B) OFTVPSRZMRHN
(C) OETUPSRZMRHN
(D) OFTUPSRZMRHN

KEY

1. B It is a case of parallel coding. Given word SWITCH is written in the following way:

S W I T C H

T V J S D G

By observing the replacement pattern it is found that the first letter of the given word (S) is replaced by its immediate succeeding letter T but second word W is replaced by its immediate preceding letter V. This trend of replacing letters of original word by succeeding and preceding letter alternatively gives rise to the coded word. After understanding this, the word in question is considered. It is found out that an encoded word is given and its word is to be found. By adopting the same approach, but in reverse order, as adopted for word SWITCH, asked word is found and that is BREAD.

2. D This is a case of jumbled coding as it is shown in first jumbling:

Original Word: R E M O T E

Coded Word: E R O M E T

It is observed that the word REMOTE is a six lettered word and it is divided into pairs. Then these pairs are jumbled. On the other hand, question is about finding the original word by decoding the coded word. As given encoded word is also a six lettered word, its jumbled pairs are decoded to get word PICNIC.

Coded Word: I P N C C I

Original Word: P I C N I C

3. B Original Word: C A R R O M

Encoded Word: B Z Q Q N L

This a parallel coding in which original letters are replaced by their immediate preceding letters to form an encoded word. Similar approach is used to get code of word HOUSE and that is GNTRD.

4. C Letters of the word BHARATHI have been picked up from the given words PRABA and THILAK. Whatever digit is encoding the letters in word PRABA and THILAK would become code of letters constituting word BHARATHI. For example, letter B in the word PRABA has been encoded as digit 9, this code will become part of the word BHARA, as this word is starting with B. Digit 9 will become starting digit in this word. Similarly, code of other letters can be found to get full encoded word.

5. B Same as for question number 4 above.

6. D This is a case of substitution coding. Chain of substitutions given in the question has been given just to confuse the candidate. Here, different professionals have been renamed. Ultimate target is to find out new name (code) of teacher. As teacher has been given a name clerk, so answer is clerk. It is to be noted here that though professionals have been given new names, yet there is no effect on the original field of professionals. That is why 'clerk' is the answer.

7. C This question is a bit different from the previous question. There, different names were given to different subjects but there was no effect on the field they belonged. In the present question it is not mentioned 'called'; rather 'is' has been mentioned. This changes the original field of the affected subject. Here, question is "Where do aeroplanes fly". Aeroplanes fly in sky but now sky is cloud. So 'cloud' is the answer.

8. A Same as explained in question 7.

9. B This a case of elimination method. Code of word 'sweet' is to be found. After concentrating on the statements it is found that word 'sweet' is present in second statement only. Other words in the statement like 'juice' and 'is' are present in other statements also. Corresponding to word 'sweet' code 'kee' is present only in the second statement. Therefore, word 'kee' is code of word 'sweet'.

10. D Same as in question 9.

11. C Original Word: H O U S E

Encoded word: I N V R F

Above is a case of parallel coding. In this word the first replacement of H with I is succeeding order replacement but second replacement of O with N is a preceding order arrangement and this pattern of alternative succeeding and preceding order replacement goes on throughout the word.

Similar approach is applied to find out the code of word CROWD and that is DQPVE.

12. C Same as explained for question number 4 above.

13. D Original Word: M A C H I N E

Encoded Word: 19 7 9 14 15 20 11

This is a case of parallel coding in which code of a particular letter is formed by adding 6 in the original position of the letter. For example M = 19 (13 + 6), A = 7 (1 + 6), and so on. Same strategy is used to find out code of word DANCER and that is 10-7-20-9-11-24.

14. D Original Word: N I M B U S

Encoded Word: P W D J K P

Though first and the last letter of encoded word is same, yet it is found with the help of second letter I that it is a case of cross coding with alternative patterns of replacement. Further coding pattern goes like this: last two letters of encoded word P and K are succeeding with the gap of one letter to first two letters N and I of original word. But succeeding order pattern between M and J is different. J is preceding letter to M with the gap of two letters. So there are two patterns of replacement repeating alternatively. It is shown here:

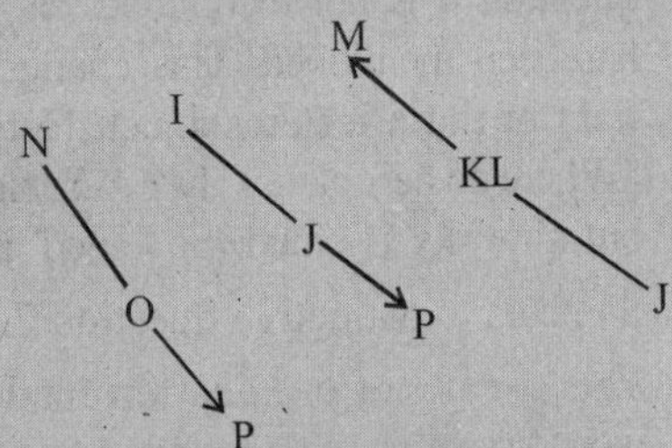

Again, coding pattern of coding B and U is same as for N and I. Coding of last letter S is same as coding of letter M in the original word. Same strategy is applied to construct code of word RELICT which is QEKIGT which is not among the answer choices, and hence answer is D.

15. B Same way as explained in question number 9 above.

16. D Original Word: F R E S C O

Encoded Word: H U G V E R

Above coding is parallel coding. Pattern of replacement is in succeeding order succession. First letter of encoded word H is succeeding with gap of one letter to first letter of original word. Second letter U of encoded word is succeeding to R with the gap of two letters and both the patterns repeat themselves alternatively. Similar approach is applied to the word MURALS and its code is OXTDNV.

17. D Original Word: P R O S E N C E P H A L O N

Encoded Word: Q S P T F O D V K S Z O L M

Above case is of parallel coding and the given word contains 14 letters and these have been divided into two equal parts. First 7 letters in the coded word are immediate succeeding letters to first seven letters of original word. Last seven letters of original and encoded word are corresponding to each other. Similer pattern is for word NESTORIANISM has 12 letters so answer is D.

Questions Asked in Previous NET Exams

1. If REASON is coded as 5 and GOVERNMENT as 9, than what is the code for ACCIDENT? **(UGC NET JUNE 2019)**

   (A) 6 (B) 7

   (C) 8 (D) 9

2. If RED is coded as 6720, then how would GREEN be coded **(UGC NET JUNE 2019)**

   (A) 16717209 (B) 1677209

   (C) 9207716 (D) 1677199

3. If HPU = 9, JNU = 9. Then DU = ? **(UGC NET DECEMBER 2019)**

   (A) 5 (B) 6

   (C) 4 (D) 7

4. If ABODE is coded as ADRHJ, then the code for AGRO will be: **(UGC NET DECEMBER 2018)**

   (A) AIVX (B) AIUS

   (C) AIST (D) AVCD

5. If the code of ALLAHABAD is DPQGOIKKO, then the code of BENGULURU will be **(UGC NET JULY 2018)**

   (A) ESBTBDIMF (B) MBDBFEIST

   (C) EISMBTDBF (D) ESBDFBTMI

6. If VARANASI is coded as WCUESGZQ, then the code of KOLKATA will be: **(UGC NET JULY 2018)**

   (A) LOQOZEH (B) HLZEOOQ

   (C) ZELHOQO (D) LQOOFZH

7. In a certain code, "COVALENT" is coded as BWPDUOFM. The code of "ELEPHANT" will be: **(UGC NET NOVEMBER 2017)**

   (A) QMUBIADH (B) QFMFUOBI

   (C) EPHNTEAS (D) MFUIQRTW

8. In a particular code, HOSPITALS is coded as HSOLSAPTI. The code of BIOLOGICALS will be **(UGC NET AUGUST 2016)**

   (A) BLICOALIOSG (B) BOLGICAILOS

   (C) SBLAOILOBCG (D) BSILOALCOIG

9. In certain code, SELECTION is coded as QCJCARGML. The code of AMERICANS will be **(UGC NET JULY 2016)**

   (A) YKCPGAYLQ (B) BNFSJDBMR

   (C) QLYAGPCKY (D) YQKLCYPAG

10. In certain code MATHURA is coded as JXQEROX. The code of HOTELS will be

(UGC NET JUNE 2015)

(A) ELIPQB (B) LEQIBP
(C) ELQBIP (D) LEBIQP

11. If STREAMERS is coded as UVTGALDQR, then KNOWLEDGE will be coded as

(UGC NET DECEMBER 2014)

(A) MQPYLCDFD (B) MPQYLDCFD
(C) PMYQLDFCD (D) YMQPLDDFC

12. Certain coding method, the word QUESTION is encoded as DOMESTIC. In this coding, what is the code word for the word RESPONSE? **(UGC NET JUNE 2014)**

(A) OMESUCEM (B) OMESICSM
(C) OMESICEM (D) OMESISCM

13. In certain code TEACHER is written as VGCEJGT. The code of CHILDREN will be

(UGC NET DECEMBER 2013)

(A) EKNJFTGP (B) EJKNFTGP
(C) KNJFGTP (D) None of these

14. In a certain code GALIB is represented by HBMJC. TIGER will be represented by

(UGC NET JUNE 2013)

(A) UJHFS (B) UHJSE
(C) JHUSF (D) HUJSE

15. If MOHAN is represented by the code KMFYL, then COUNT will be represented by

(UGC NET DECEMBER 2012)

(A) AMSLR (B) MSLAR
(C) MASRL (D) SAMLR

16. Given that in a code language, '645' means 'day is warm'; '42' means 'warm spring'; and '634' means 'spring is sunny'; which digit represents 'sunny' ? **(UGC NET JUNE 2012)**

(A) 3 (B) 2
(C) 4 (D) 5

17. If '367' means 'I am happy'; '748' means 'you are sad', and '469' means 'happy and sad' in a given code, then which of the following represents 'and' in that code?

UGC NET DECEMBER 2011)

(A) 3 (B) 6
(C) 9 (D) 4

18. If HOBBY is coded as IOBY and LOBBY is coded as MOBY; then BOBBY is coded as

(UGC NET JUNE 2011)

(A) BOBY (B) COBY
(C) DOBY (D) OOBY

19. If INSURANCE is coded as ECNARUSNI, how HINDRANCE will be coded?

(UGC NET DECEMBER 2010)

(A) CADNIHWCE (B) HANODEINR
(C) AENIRHDCN (D) ECNARDNIH

20. In a certain code, CLOCK is written as KCOLC. How would STEPS be written in that code? **(UGC NET JUNE 2009)**

(A) SPEST (B) SPSET
(C) SPETS (D) SEPTS

21. In a certain code, GAMESMAN is written as AGMEMSAN. How would DISCLOSE be written in that code?

(UGC NET DECEMBER 2008)

(A) IDSCOLSE (B) IDCSOLES
(C) IDSCOLES (D) IDSCLOSE

22. AGARTALA is written in code as 14168171, the code for AGRA is: **(UGC NET JUNE 2008)**

(A) 1641 (B) 1416
(C) 1441 (D) 1461

23. If in a certain language TRIVANDRUM is coded as 2 5 9 5 3 5 4 7 5 8, how would MADRAS be coded? **(UGC NET JUNE 2007)**

(A) 834536 (B) 834538
(C) 834530 (D) 834539

24. In a certain code, PAN is written as 31 and PAR as 35. In this code PAT is written as:

(UGC NET DECEMBER 2006)

(A) 30 (B) 37
(C) 38 (D) 39

25. In a certain code, FHQK means GIRL. How will WOMEN be written in the same code?

(UGC NET JUNE 2006)

(A) VNLDM
(B) FHQKN
(C) XPNFO
(D) VLNDM

KEY

1. B A code of a word is one less than number of letters in given word. For example word REASON has six letters and its code is 5. Similar logic is applicable to the other word in the question.

2. B Original Word: R E D

Encoded Version: 6 7 20

Here, original positions of the given three letters R, E, and D has been given and adding 2 in that, i.e., R = 20 (18 + 2), E = 7 (5 + 2), D = 6 (4 + 2). So code of RED can be written like:

R E D

20 7 6

Now this order has been inverted to frame the actual code as given in the question

So finally the code becomes: 6720

Similarly code of the given word GREEN is determined as follows;

G R E E N

Original position of letters with the addition of two: G = 9 (7+ 2), R = 20 (18+ 2), E = 7 (5 + 2), N = 16 (14 + 2). In the original order the positions become like this:

G R E E N

9 20 7 7 16

Inverted Version: 16 7 7 20 9

So the code is: 1677209

3. A HPU = 9, here original positions of H, P and U are taken in A to Z order i.e. H = 8, P = 16 and U = 21, then their sum is taken; 8 + 16 + 21 = 45. Then this sum is divided with 5

$$\frac{45}{5} = 9$$

Similarly JNU i.e 10 + 14 + 21 = 45, again divided with 5 to get 9

Now in the same way, DU $\Rightarrow 4 + 21 = 25$ and after dividing with 5, we get 5. So code of DU is 5 as in answer choice number 1.

4. B Coding mode is parallel coding in which original letters are replaced with their succeeding order letters with increasing gap. It is shown as follows:

Original Word: A B O D E

Encoded Word: A D R H J

While observing above, it is found that while proceeding in the parallel mode with succeeding letters replacement, gap among the letters is increasing in the following way:

There is 0 gap between A and A, there is gap of one letter C between B and D, there is gap of two letters (P and Q) between O and R and so on. Same logic is applied on the word AGRO to obtain the right code AIUS.

5. C

Original Word : A L L A H A B A D

Coded Word : D P Q G O I K K O

Above is a case of parallel coding. Just like above question, this question also follows a succeeding order pattern of replacement with increasing difference in gap. For example, first letter of encoded word D is succeeding to first letter of main word A with the gap of two letters B and C. Similarly, next letter P is succeeding to L with the gap of three letters M, N, and O and so on. Same logic is applied to word BENGULURU which is EISMBTDBF.

6. D Above is a case of parallel coding. Coding pattern is same as in previous questions 3 and 4. Here also there is replacement of letters of original word in succeeding order with increasing number of letters in the gap.

7. B

Original Word : C O V A L E N T

Coded Word : B W P D U O F M

Observing above it is detected that there is partial cross coding. This word contains 8 letters. It is divided into two equal halves of 4 letters each. Then cross coding with the replacement of succeeding letters is done for the first half and second half separately as shown below:

Original Word:

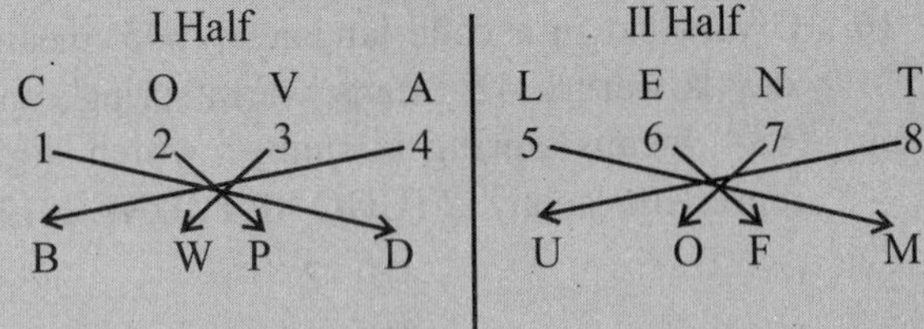

Encoded Word: B W P D O F M

Considering first half it is found that first letter of encoded word B is immediate succeeding to last letter of first half of original word, i.e., A. Further encoding goes like this and same pattern is adopted in the second half. Same logic is applied to get code of the word ELEPHANT and the correct code is QFMFUOBI.

8. D

Original Word : H O S P I T A L S

Encoded Word : H S O L S A P T I

This is a case of jumbled coding. A keen observation reveals that original word has been encoded by starting with the same letter and then alternatively picking up letters from left extreme and right extreme respectively as shown below:

Original Word :	1	2	3	4	5	6	7	8	9
	H	O	S	P	I	T	A	L	S
Encoded Word :	H	S	O	L	S	A	P	T	I
	1	9	2	8	3	7	4	6	5

Same logic is applied on the second given word BIOLOGICALS and the right code so found is BSILOALCOIG.

9. A

Original Word : S E L E C T I O N

Encoded Word : Q C J C A R G M L

It is a case of parallel coding. Here all letters of encoded word are preceding to all letters of original word with the gap of one letter in their respective relationship format. Same logic is applicable on the second given word AMERICANS.

10. C Coding pattern exactly same as in question number 8. The only difference is that the gap of replacement is of two letters instead of one letter.

11. B

Original Word : S T R E A M E R S

Encoded Word : U V T G A L D Q R

Above is a case of parallel coding. Above word contains 9 letters and letter A is the middle letter. Coding from letter S to A follows a pattern of succeeding letter with the gap of two letters for each letter. A is rewritten as A. After A, coding pattern changes. Each letter in the original word is replaced by its respective immediate preceding letter. Same logic is applied to given second word KNOWLEDGE to obtain the right code.

12. C Original Word : Q U **E** **S** T I **O** **N**

Coded Word : D O **M** **E** S T **I** **C**

Given Word : R **E** **S** P O N **S** **E**

This is a strange type of coding pattern. Here, there is no succeeding or preceding pattern of replacement. Here, the word has been encoded by taking common letters into consideration involving all the three words. Let us consider the bold letters in all the three words.

Letters E S are common in word QUESTION and RESPONSE as letters of DOMESTIC and QUESTION are same in number, letters M E are taken to have replaced ES. So in encoded version of RESPONSE, letters E and S are replaced with M and E as shown below:

Given Word : R E S P O N S E

Interim Coded Word : – M E – – – – –

Further, letters E and S of original word are written in reverse order in the given word, these letters will also be replaced with codes of E and S in reverse order as shown below:

Given Word : R E S P O N S E

Interim Coded Word : – M E – – – E M –

Now letters O and N in the original word has been encoded with letters I and C in the coded word. As letters O and N are present in the given word also, these are replaced with I and C in interim code word as shown below:

Given Word : R E S P O N S E

Interim Coded Word : – M E – I C E M –

Final Code Word : O M E S I C E M

As there is choice C where coded word is ending with ICEM, that is the answer.

13. B Original Word : T E A C H E R

Encoded Word : V G C E J G T

Above is a case of parallel coding. Here, every letter of coded word is succeeding to its respective letter in original word with the gap of one letter. Similar logic is applied to the given word CHILDREN to get the right code.

14. A Original Word : G A L I B

Encoded Word : H B M J C

Explanation: It is the simplest case of succeeding order coding in parallel coding mode. Each letter of coded word is immediate succeeding letter of its respective letter in original word. Similar logic is applied to find correct code of the given word TIGER.

15. A Original Word : M O H A N

Encoded Word : K M F Y L

This is a case of parallel coding. Each letter of the coded word is preceding to its respective letter of original word with the gap of one letter. Same logic is applied to the given word COUNT to detect the right code.

16. A Here target is to find code of word 'sunny'. This word is present in third statement only. There are three numbers in third statement, i.e., 6, 3, and 4. It is also observed that like word 'sunny', number 3 is also present in third statement only. So number 3 is code of word 'sunny'.

17. C Word 'and' is present in third statement only. Numbers present in third statement are 4, 6, 9. It is observed that like word 'and', number 9 is also present in third statement, so number 9 is the code of word 'and'.

18. B Original Words : HOBBY LOBBY

Coded Words : IOBY MOBY

It is concluded from above that in parallel coding mode, starting letters of encoded words are immediate succeeding to starting letters of original words. Further, one letter B is dropped in the encoded word. Same logic is applied code of given word BOBBY.

19. D

Original Word : I N S U R A N C E

Encoded Word : E C N A R U S N I

Above is a case of jumbled coding. Encoded word is written in reverse order of original word. Same logic is applied on the given word HINDRANCE to obtain the right code.

20. C Original Word : C L O C K

Encoded Word : K C O L C

Explanation: Like previous question this is also a case of jumbled coding. Here, letters of encoded word are reverse of the letters of original word. Similar logic is applied to find the code of the given word STEPS.

21. A

Original Word : G A M E S M A N

Encoded Word : A G M E M S A N

Above is a case of jumbled coding. Original word carries 8 letters which means 4 pairs. It is observed that in the encoded word first and third pairs of letters are jumbled whereas second and fourth pairs of letters are kept intact. Similar logic is applied to given word DISCLOSE, also carrying eight letters, and the right code is formed.

22. D Original Word : A G A R T A L A

Code Numbers : 1 4 1 6 8 1 7 1

Above is a case of number coding. Here, letters of original word are given random number codes. Letters in the word AGRA have been picked up from word AGARTALA. What number code is allotted to a particular letter, will remain same if any or all letters of original word is/are found in encoded word. Hence, same number which is coded is allotted to that/those common letter(s). For example, in the original word, A is allotted number code 1. Same number code 1 is allotted to letter A in the given word AGRA and so on. Similar logic is applied to other common letters between original and encoded word. In this way the correct number code is found, i.e., 1461.

23. A

Original Word : T R I V A N D R U M

Code Number : 2 5 9 5 3 5 4 7 5 8

Explanation: Just like in question number 21 above, all letters of given word MADRAS are common with original word TRIVANDRUM. Only letter 'S' is not common. In word TRIVANDRUM letter R appears twice and both the 'R's have been allotted different number codes. Earlier R is allotted number 5 and later R is allotted number 7. As letter 'S' is immediately succeeding letter to 'R', number code can be either 6 or 8. In all the answer choices letter 'R' is allotted number code 5. If R is 5 then S must be 6. Hence, choice A is the answer.

24. B Observation straightway establishes that this also a case of number coding. In every word first two letters P A are same with same code numbers. Last letter of each succeeding word is succeeding to last letter of preceding word with gaps of letters. Number of letters succeeding to previous letter is added to the position of original words. For example R is fourth succeeding letter to N so position of word PAR becomes 35 (31 + 4) and so on. Same logic is applied to given word PAT to find out the right code.

25. A Original Word : G I R L

Encoded Word : F H Q K

It is a case of parallel coding. Here, all letters of coded word are immediate preceding to letters of original word in the same order. Same logic is applied to the given word WOMEN and right code is found.

5 Relationship

CONCEPT

The questions on relationship test our knowledge about various blood and non-blood relations among which we survive. The purpose of asking questions on relationships is to test the cognitive ability of a candidate. Questions on relationship are asked in different formats in various competitive exams. Like other competitions, questions on relationship are also asked in NET Paper 1. After consulting previous NET papers, it has been found that questions on reasoning are confined to popular types and thus, are easy to understand and solve with correct answers. It is also a fact that questions on relationship is asked in almost every attempt of NET. Questions on relationship are asked in NET mainly from the following types:

1) Introduced Type
2) Accounted Type
3) Tabulated Type
4) Encoded Type

Strategy

Questions on relationship require a common strategy to solve them. It may be from introduced type or accounted type. A question on relationship involves many relationships and seeks to find out relationship of any two characters among a battery of characters related to one another in one respect or the other as given in a question. The most effective strategy to solve any question on relationship is to read the question and draw a sketch of relationship of all the characters in the question according to their generation and nature of relationship with one another. Each line of the drawn sketch signifies paternal, maternal, or in-law's relationships. Further, these lines also differentiate among different generations. On the basis of this, following types of relationships exist in the questions on relationship:

1) **Horizontal Relationship:** It is the relationship which exists within the same generation. It includes blood as well as non-blood relationship. For example: Relationship of brother, sister, spouse (husband and wife), brother-in-law, sister-in-law, etc. This relationship is called horizontal as it is diagrammatically expressed with a horizontal line.
2) **Vertical Relationship:** This relationship exists among different generations like relationship of parents with their children and grandchildren (Blood relationship) and relationship of son-in-law, daughter-in-law, mother-in-law, and father-in-law (Non-blood relationship). This is represented by drawing vertical or diagonal lines in the sketch.

Sketches of Relationships

1) **Horizontal Relationship:** A-------------B (Here A and B may be brothers, sisters, spouses, brother-sister, cousins, brothers-in-law, or sisters-in-law to each other.
2) **Vertical Relationship:**

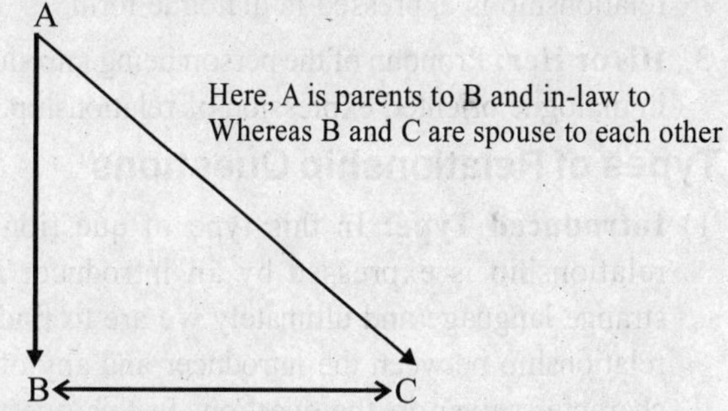

Caution

An aspirant is to be cautious while reading a question on relationship otherwise one is likely to commit mistakes. It is important to note that in order to detect correct relationship and gender; we are to totally depend upon the language and terms of relationship and gender as given in the question. ***There should not be any assumption about any person's relationship and gender, if it is not clear from the language of the question. Similarly, any missing link among relations given in the question should not be assumed to be there.*** For example, if it is given in the question that A is B's brother, it should not be assumed that B is also A's brother as B's gender is not clear in the question.

Relationship Terminology

Following relationship terms are used in questions on relationship. Understanding these terms will be conducive in solving questions on relationship confidently and correctly.

1. **Only:** A term 'Only' is used with following relationships in the question:

   Son (Only son means single male issue in the family, he may have sisters)

   Daughter (Only daughter means single female issue in the family, she may have brothers)

   Brother (Only brother means maximum two male issues in the family, they may have sisters)

   Sister (Only sister means maximum two female issues in the family, they may have brothers)

   Son-in-law (Only son-in-law means his wife is family's single married female issue, she may have unmarried sisters)

   Daughter-in-law (Only daughter-in-law means her husband is family's single married male issue, he may have unmarried brothers). Same logic is applicable to **Uncle, Aunt, Nephew, Niece, Cousin, Brother-in-law, and Sister-in-law.**

2. **My:** It is pronoun of the introducer, where the relationship is expressed in dialogue form.

3. **His or Her:** Pronoun of the person being introduced in dialogue oriented expression of relationship.

Types of Relationship Questions

1) **Introduced Type:** In this type of questions, a relationship is expressed by an introducer in a strange language and ultimately we are to find the relationship between the introducer and any of the characters given in the question. In this question, drawing of sketch can be started from either the introducer or from the person being introduced.

Format: Mohinder introduces a lady like this, "Her mother-in-law is the only daughter of my father's father-in-law."

Following possible questions can be asked on this relationship:

1) How is Mohinder related to the lady's mother-in-law?
2) How is the lady related to Mohinder?
3) How is Mohinder's father related to the lady?
4) How is the lady's mother-in-law related to Mohinder's father?

Strategy: First, following sketch of the relationship is drawn:

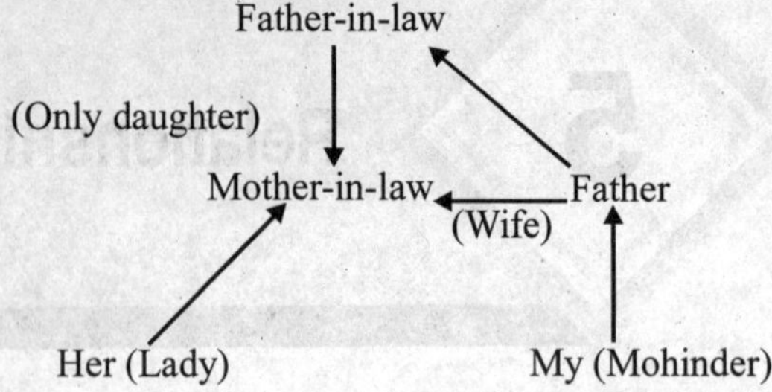

Ans:

1) Son
2) Can't be determined (Wife or sister-in-law)
3) Father-in-law
4) Wife

2) **Accounted type:** In this type also, a relationship among different members of a family is expressed in a strange language but without any introducer; rather some names are given to the characters and ultimately we are to detect the relation between any two characters. In this type one can start drawing the sketch of the very first two related characters and can proceed further by covering all the relationships in the given sequence and can complete the sketch.

Format: K's brother R is Q's grandson. S, sister of H is J's only daughter. M is the only son of K's grandfather. Q's son is married to J's daughter. Brother-in-law of H is father of two children. Q's daughter-in-law has a brother.

Possible questions:

1) How is J related to S?
2) How is M related to Q?
3) How is H related to M?
4) Who is Q's daughter-in-law?
5) How is K related to R?
6) How many brothers does R have?

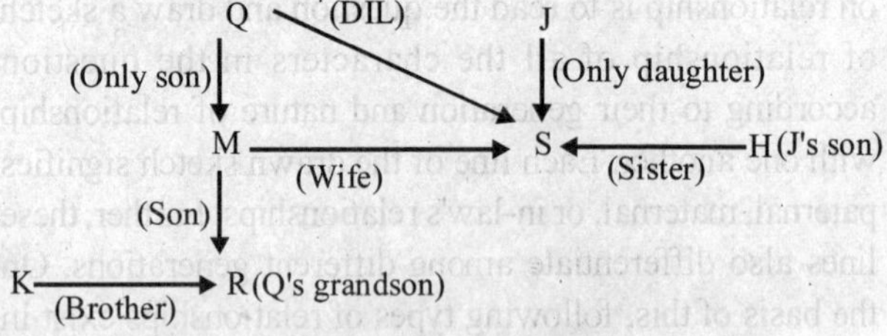

- DIL means Daughter-in-law

Ans:

1) Can't be determined (Father or mother, as gender is not clear)
2) Son
3) Brother-in-law

4) S
5) Can't be determined (Brother or sister, as gender is not clear)
6) Can't be determined (it is not clear whether R is Q's only son or not)

3) **Tabulated Type:** In this type a partial account of members of a family is given expressing their relationship and professions. This is followed by a set of questions to be answered. The clear information of the account is recorded in a table as it is and the remaining is derived from the given facts and then the questions are answered.

Format: There is a family of six persons A, B, C, D, E, and F. They are Salesman, Engineer, Lawyer, Accountant, Teacher, and Doctor but not in the same order. There are two married couples in the family. D, the Salesman is married to the Lady Teacher. The Doctor is married to the Lawyer. F, the Accountant is the son of B and brother of E. C, the Lawyer is the daughter-in-law of A. E is the unmarried Engineer. A is the grandmother of F.

Possible questions:

1) How is E related to F?
2) What is the profession of B?
3) What is the profession of A?
4) Which are the two couples?
5) How is D related to F?

Solution: Drawing a table from the given relationship account

A	B	C	D	E	F
F's and E's Grandmother, Teacher, D's wife, B's mother	Doctor, C's Husband, A's and D's son	Lawyer, A's and D's daughter-in-law, B's	Salesman, A' husband, E's and F's Grandfather, B's father	Unmarried Engineer, Grandchild of A and D	Accountant, B's son, E's brother, Grandson of A and D

Now the answers to the above questions can be given by using information recorded in the above table.

Ans:

1) Cannot be determined as E's gender is not clear
2) Doctor
3) Teacher
4) A & D and B & C
5) Grandfather

4) **Encoded type:** Here the relationship is expressed in codes using arithmetic signs (or other codes) and the questions are answered after understanding them.

Format: **Q + R means Q is father of R**

Q – R means Q is sister of R

Q × R means Q is brother of R

Q ÷ R means Q is mother of R

Possible questions: Consider the following equation:

M × N – J + S ÷ T

1) Who is aunt of S?
2) How is J related to M?
3) How is T related to N?
4) How is J related to T's mother?

Strategy: Understanding the given encoded relationship:

Q + R means first character Q is father of second character R, i.e., gender of R is unknown.

Q – R means first character Q is sister of second character R, i.e., gender of R is unknown.

Q × R means first character Q is brother of second character R i.e. gender of R is unknown.

Q ÷ R means first character Q is mother of second character R, i.e., gender of R is unknown.

Now following the above conditions, the relationship in the above equation can be decoded in the following relationships:

1) M × N means M is brother of N but N's gender is not clear
2) N – J means N is sister of J but J's gender is not clear
3) J + S means J is father of S but S's gender is not clear
4) S ÷ T means S is mother of T but T's gender is not clear

In all the above cases, it is established that ***gender of last character of any equation is always unknown.***

Drawing the sketch of the above relationship from above decoding:

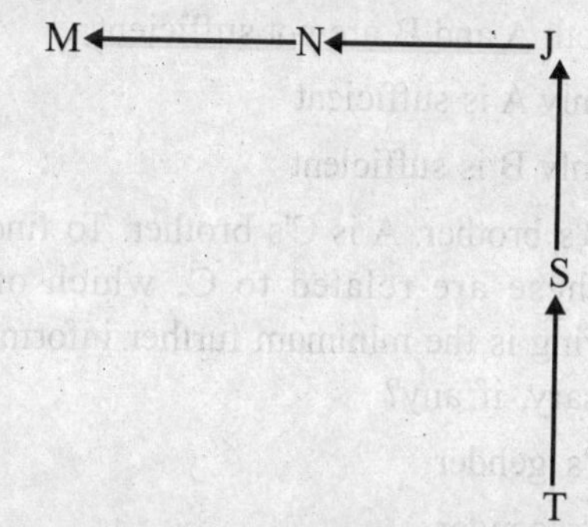

Ans:

1) N
2) Brother
3) Can't be determined as T's gender is not clear.
4) Father

Practice Exercise

General Questions Format

1. If F is brother of A, C is daughter of A, K is sister of F, and J is brother of C, then who is uncle of J?

   (A) F (B) C
   (C) K (D) A

2. Ravina tells Karishma, "Your sister is the daughter of my mother's brother". How is Krishma related to Ravina's mother's brother?

   (A) Daughter (B) Sister
   (C) Niece (D) Daughter-in-law

3. If A is brother of B, C is wife of D, who is father of A. Which of the following statements can be true?

   (A) D is father of B (B) A is son of C
   (C) C is mother of B (D) B is brother of A

4. Pointing towards a person in a photograph, Aruna said," He is the only son of the father of my sister's brother". How is that person related to Aruna?

   (A) Maternal uncle (B) Mother
   (C) Father (D) None of these

5. "Is C mother of D?". To find out the above answer which of the following information given in the statements A and B is/are sufficient?

   a. B has two children of which D is one.
   b. D's sister is daughter of C.

   (A) Both A and B together are needed
   (B) Both A and B are not sufficient
   (C) Only A is sufficient
   (D) Only B is sufficient

6. A is B's brother. A is C's brother. To find out how these are related to C, which of the following is the minimum further information necessary, if any?

   I. C's gender
   II. B's gender

   (A) Only I is necessary
   (B) Only II is necessary
   (C) Either I or II is necessary
   (D) Neither I and nor II is necessary

Direction (Q. 7-8): Read the given information and solve questions 7 and 8 below.

A is the father of C but C is not his son.
E is the daughter of C. F is the spouse of A.
B is the brother of C. D is the son of B.
G is the spouse of B. H is the father of G.

7. Who is the granddaughter of A?

   (A) D (B) B
   (C) H (D) E

8. Who is the son-in-law of H?

   (A) C (B) B
   (C) A (D) D

9. P is the father of Q. R is the mother of S. The sister of Q and T is S. Which of the following statements is **definitely not true**?

   (A) R is the wife of P
   (B) R has one daughter
   (C) S is the son of P
   (D) Q is the sister of T

10. Pointing to a woman, Abhijit said, "Her granddaughter is my brother's only daughter". How is the woman related to Abhijit?

    (A) Sister (B) Grandmother
    (C) Mother-in-law (D) Mother

11. A is B's brother, C is A's mother, D is C's father, F is A's son. How is B related to F's child?

    (A) Aunt (B) Cousin
    (C) Nephew (D) None of these

12. A is B's daughter. B is C's mother. D is C's brother. How is D related to A?

    (A) Father (B) Grandfather
    (C) Brother (D) None of these

KEY

1. **A** Drawing the sketch of the relationship:

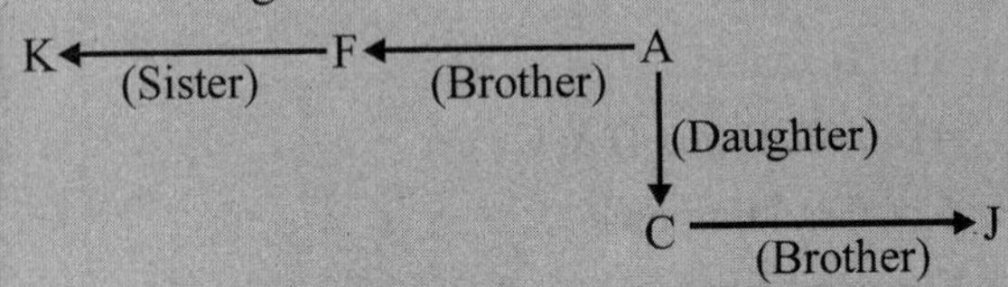

Sketch unveils that J is son of A and F is brother of A. So F is uncle of A.

Hence, choice A is the answer.

2. **A** Drawing the sketch:

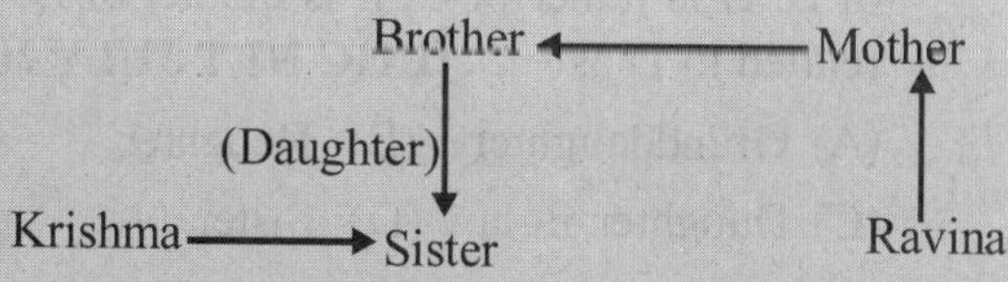

Ravina's mother's brother is Krishma's father. So Krishma is his daughter.
Hence, choice A is the answer.

3. **D** Drawing the sketch:

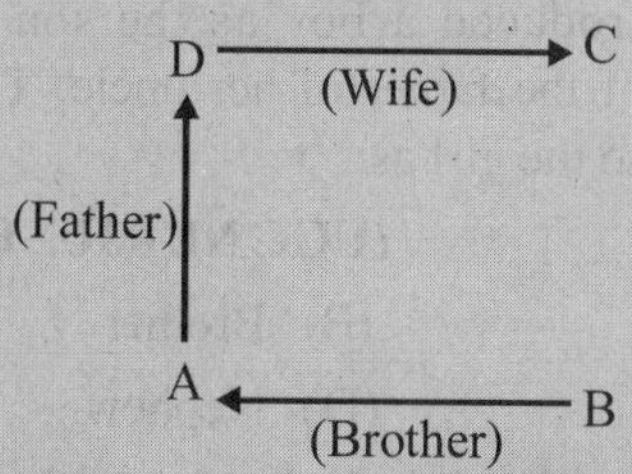

Concentrate on the word **'Can'** in the question and according to the sense conveyed by it in only statement D there is possibility of B being brother of A as B's gender is not given. Rest of the statements are definitely true. Hence, choice D is the answer.

4. **D** Drawing sketch of relationship:

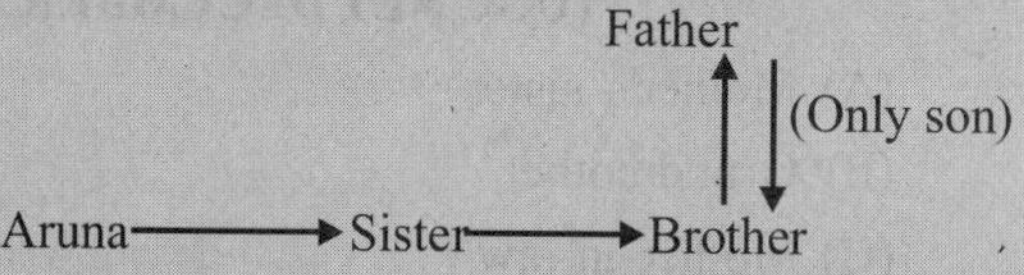

Sketch conveys clearly that the person who is father of the person in photograph is also father of Aruna and her sister. So all the children are brother/sisters to one another and the person in photograph is Aruna's brother and he is the only son also. Hence, choice D is the answer.

5. **B** In order to find whether C is mother of D, knowledge of D's gender is required, but D's gender is not given. Neither is it conveyed by statements 'a' and 'b'. So both 'a' and 'b' statements are not sufficient. Hence, choice B is the answer.

6. **B** It is not possible to state relationship of A and B to C, until B's gender is clear. So further information of B's gender is required. Hence, answer choice B is the answer.

Sketch of (7-8):

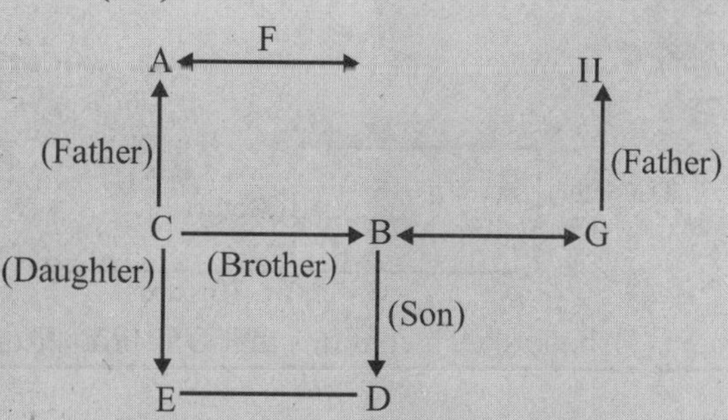

7. **D** Evident from the sketch

8. **B** Evident from the sketch

9. **C** **Sketch:**

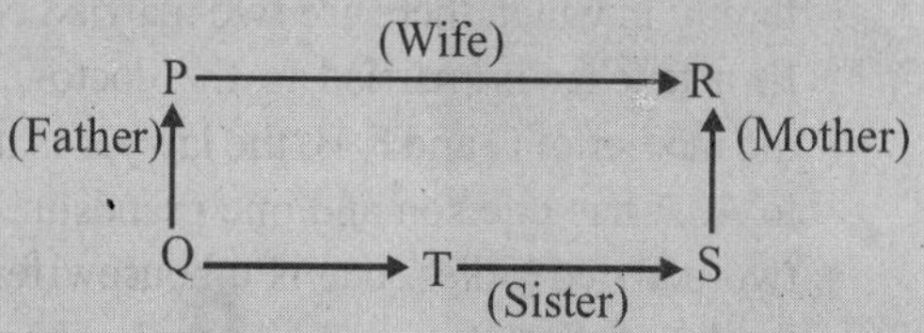

Only statement 3 is not definitely true as here S is shown as male whereas it is clear from above that S is female.

10. **D** **Sketch:**

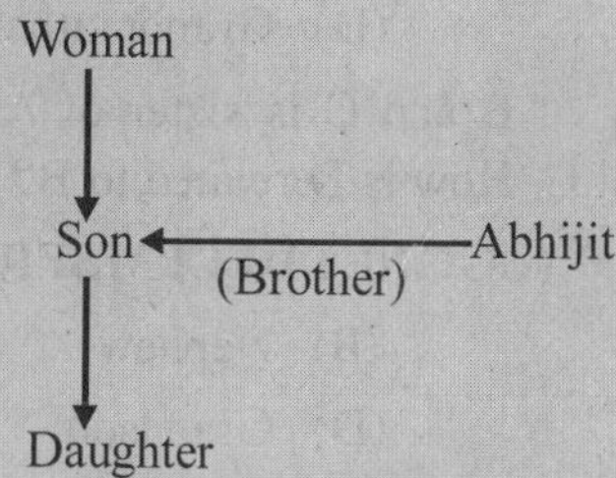

From above sketch it is clear that daughter of Abhijit's brother is grand-daughter of the woman under reference. As woman's son and Abhijit are brothers, the woman under reference is also mother of Abhijit. Hence, choice 4 is the answer.

11. **D** **Sketch:**

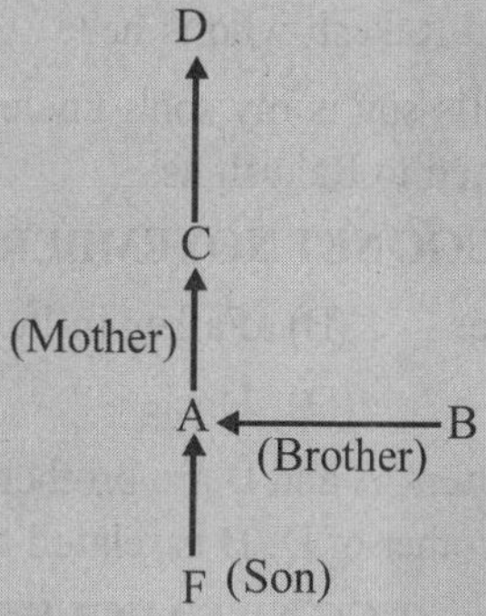

No such relation is evident from the sketch. Hence, choice 4 is the answer.

12. C Sketch:

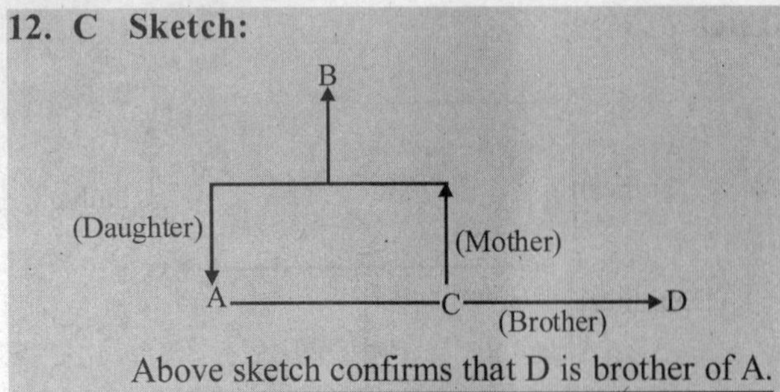

Above sketch confirms that D is brother of A.

Questions Asked in Previous NET Exams

1. A, B, C, D, E, and F are six members in a family in which there are two married couples. E, a teacher is married to the doctor, who is the mother of C and F. B, the lawyer is married to A. A has one son and one grandson. Of the two married ladies, one is a housewife. There is also one student and one male engineer in the family. How is A related to C?

   (UGC NET JUNE 2019)

   (A) Grandfather (B) Mother
   (C) Sister (D) Grandmother

2. A is father of B and C is sister of A. D is grandson of C. How is D related to B?

   (UGC NET DECEMBER 2019)

   (A) Uncle (B) Nephew
   (C) Cousin (D) Grandson

3. Introducing, Rakesh to her husband a woman said, "His brother's father is the only son of my grandfather". The woman is related to Rakesh as: **(UGC NET JULY 2018)**

   (A) Aunt (B) Mother
   (C) Sister (D) Daughter

4. Ajay is a friend of Rakesh. Pointing to an old man Ajay asked Rakesh who is he?

   Rakesh said "His son is my son's uncle". The old man is related to Rakesh as:

   (UGC NET NOVEMBER 2017)

   (A) Grandfather (B) Father-in-law
   (C) Father (D) Uncle

5. C and D are sisters. A and B are brothers. E is son of A and brother of D. B is related to C as

   (UGC NET AUGUST 2016)

   (A) Brother (B) Son
   (C) Uncle (D) Father-in-law

6. A is sister of B. F is daughter of G. C is mother of B. D is father of C. E is mother of D. A is related to D as **(UGC NET JULY 2016)**

   (A) Granddaughter (B) Daughter
   (C) Daughter-in-law (D) Sister

7. P and Q are brothers. R and S are sisters. The son of P is brother of S. Q is related to R as:

   (UGC NET DECEMBER 2015)

   (A) Son (B) Brother
   (C) Uncle (D) Father

8. A girl introduced a boy as the son of the daughter of the father of her uncle. The boy is related to the girl as:

   (UGC NET JUNE 2015)

   (A) Son (B) Brother
   (C) Uncle (D) Nephew

9. A is brother of B. B is the brother of C. C is the husband of D. E is the father of A. D is related to E as **(UGC NET DECEMBER 2014)**

   (A) Daughter (B) Daughter-in-law
   (C) Sister-in-law (D) Sister

10. A man pointing to a lady said, "The son of her only brother is the brother of my wife". The lady is related to the man as

    (UGC NET DECEMBER 2013)

    (A) Mother's sister
    (B) Grandmother
    (C) Mother-in-law
    (D) Sister of father-in-law

11. P is the father of R and S is the son of Q and T is the brother of P. If R is the sister of S, how is Q related to T ? **(UGC NET JUNE 2013)**

    (A) Wife (B) Sister-in-law
    (C) Brother-in-law (D) Daughter-in-law

12. E is the son of A, D is the son of B, E is married to C, C is the daughter of B. How is D related to E? **(UGC NET JUNE 2010)**

    (A) Brother (B) Uncle
    (C) Father-in-law (D) Brother-in-law

13. 'A' is father of 'C', and 'D' is the son of 'B'. 'E' is the brother of 'A'. If 'C' is the sister of 'D', how is 'B' related to 'E'?

    (UGC NET JUNE 2007)

    (A) Daughter (B) Husband
    (C) Sister-In-Law (D) Brother-In-Law

KEY

1. D A table of the given family account is drawn as follows:

A	B	C	D	E	F
Housewife, Married to lawyer, Has one son and one grandson	Lawyer, Married to A	Engineer or Student	Doctor, Mother of C and F	Teacher, Married to doctor	Engineer or Student

Relationship sketch:

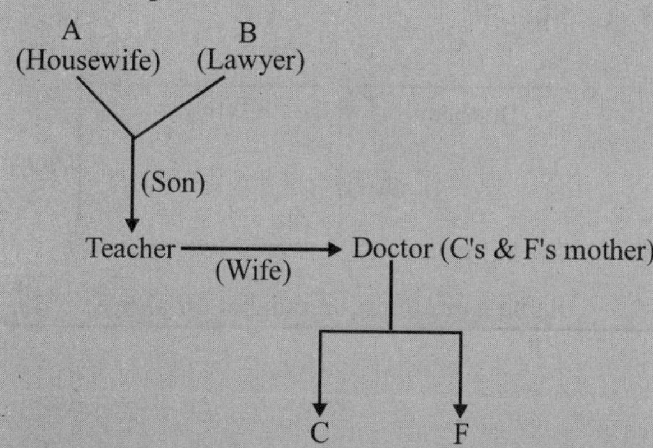

So A is grandmother of C.

2. B Above relationship is shown with the following sketch:

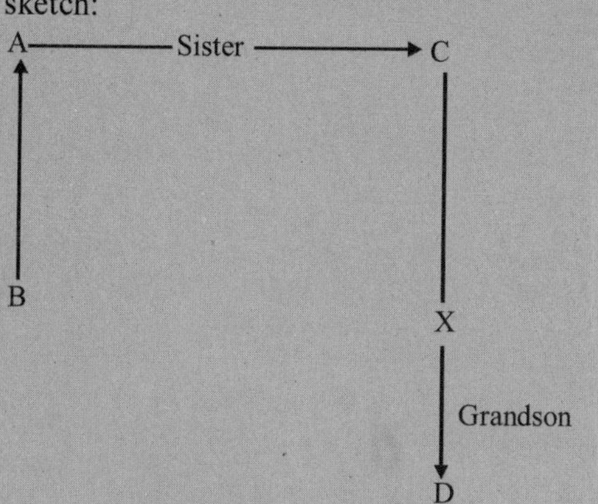

From above sketch it is clear that D is son of B's cousin X, so D is B's nephew. Hence choice number 2 is the answer.

3. C

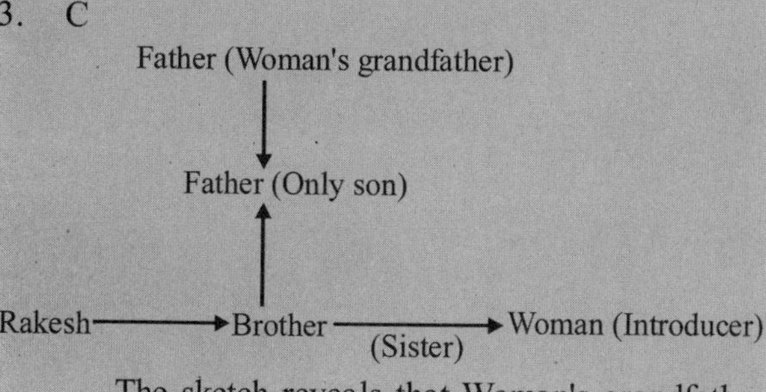

The sketch reveals that Woman's grandfather is Rakesh's grandfather also. So woman is Rakesh's sister. Hence, choice 3 is the answer.

4. C **Sketch:**

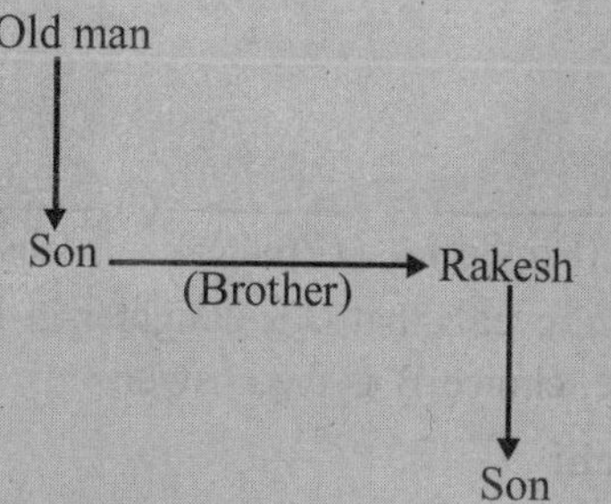

Rakesh is also old man's son that is why his son calls Rakesh's brother uncle. Hence, choice 3 is the answer.

5. C **Sketch:**

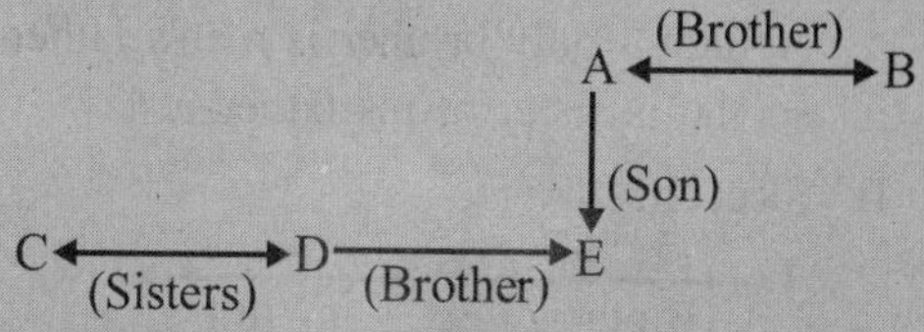

Being in upper generation, B is uncle of C. Hence, choice B is the answer.

6. A

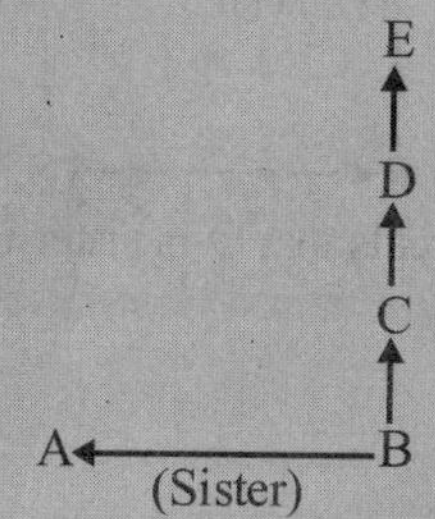

It is evident from the sketch that A is granddaughter to D as B, C, D, and E are in vertical blood relation to one another.

7. C **Sketch:**

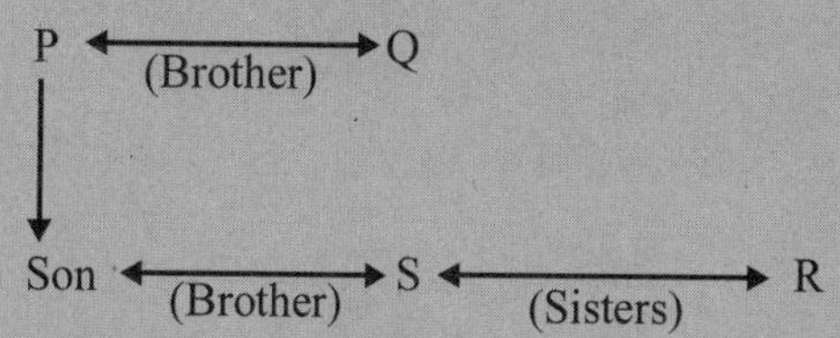

R is P's daughter and Q is P's brother, so Q is R's uncle.

8. B **Sketch:**

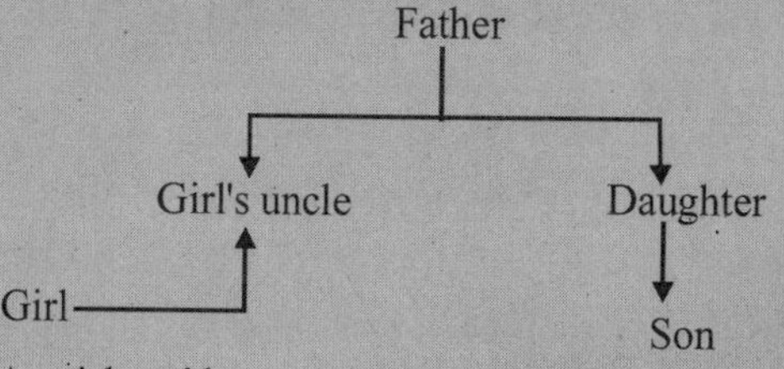

As girl and boy are in the same generation and are paternally related, boy is girl's brother.

9. B **Sketch:**

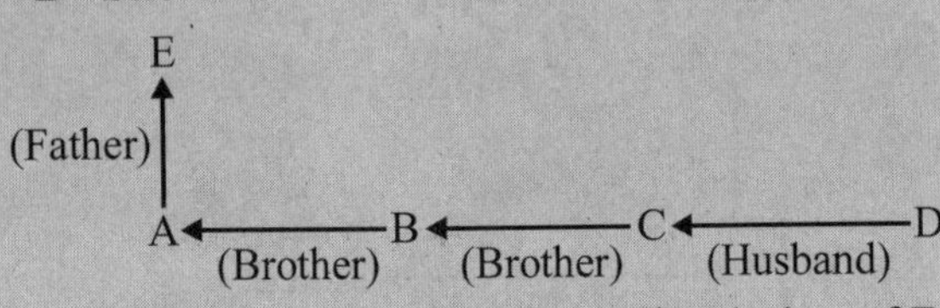

Sketch reveals that D is daughter-in-law of E. Hence, choice B is the answer.

10. D **Sketch:**

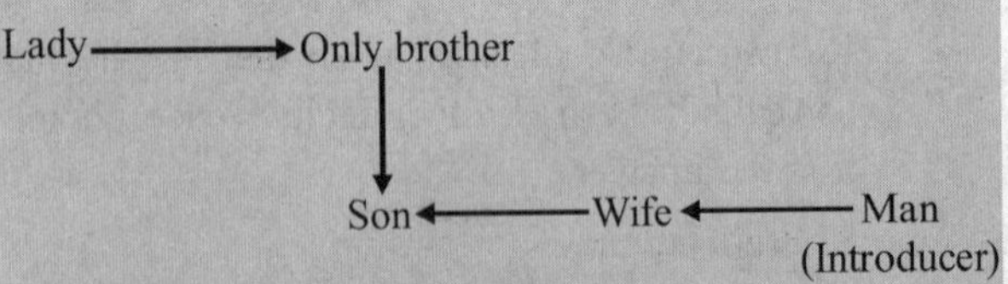

As lady's only brother is man's father-in-law, so she is sister of his father-in-law.

11. B **Sketch:**

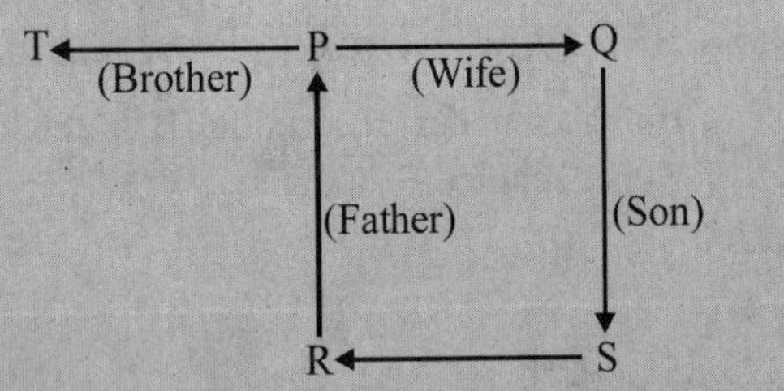

Sketch truly reveals that Q is sister-in-law of T.

12. D **Sketch:**

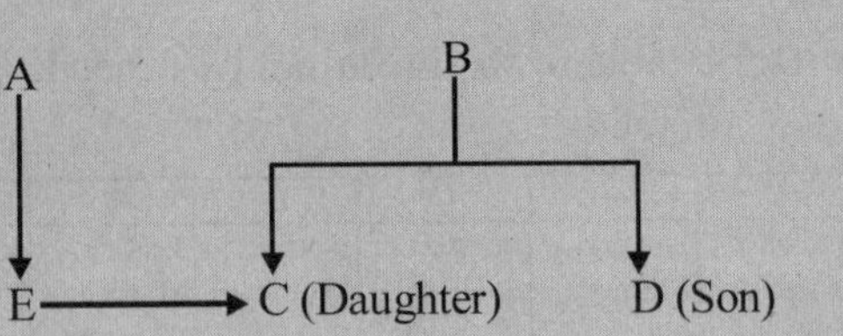

D is E's wife C's brother, so D is brother-in-law of E.

13. C **Sketch:**

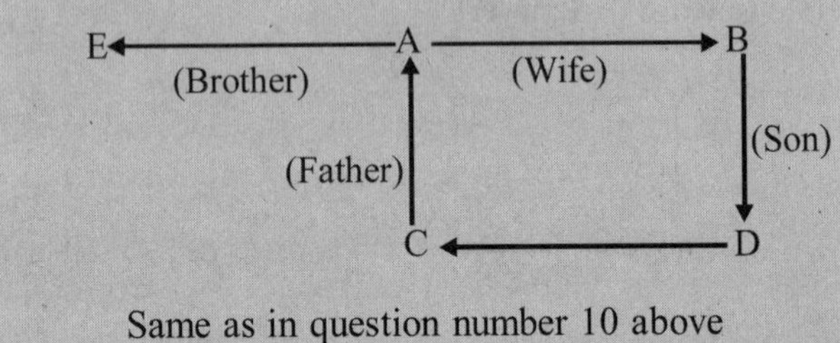

Same as in question number 10 above

6 Letter Series

CONCEPT

The question on letter series is based on the knowledge of prerequisites of letters. In this question a letter series is given in the succeeding or preceding order and then a question is asked to find out a letter either replacing a question mark or find out a particular letter towards left or right of any letter in the series.

TYPES OF LETTER SERIES

On the above basis, there are two types of letter series:

1) Alphabet Progression
2) Alpha numeric progression

1. Alphabet Progression

In this type a sequence of letters is given either in succeeding order or preceding order with a question mark either at the beginning, middle, or last of the series. One is to understand the trend of progression made by other letters in the series and then to replace the question mark with the letter which maintains the same trend in the series and that letter is the answer.

Strategy

While choosing a particular letter to replace the question mark, first of all one needs to identify whether the series is progressing in succeeding or preceding order and then to find out a particular letter while applying the knowledge of prerequisites of the alphabet. Trend of letters in progression series is given in the following ways:

1) **Continuous Progression:** In this series (given either in succeeding order or preceding order) every preceding letter is related to its immediate succeeding letter.

Example 1: Replace the question mark in the series:

F, H, J, L, ?, P, R, T

A) W B) M

C) O D) N

Solution: Here the answer will be N, as here series is progressing in succeeding order staring with F. The trend maintained in this series is that each succeeding letter is succeeding to its immediate preceding letter with gap of one letter. So after L the concerned letter is N while maintaining the trend in the series, which is in choice D.

Example 2: Replace the question mark in the series given below:

V, S, P, M, J, G, ?

A) D B) F

C) I D) None of these

Solution: While observing the above trend, it is found that the series starting with V is progressing in the preceding order with the gap of two letters between each preceding letter and succeeding letter. If the same trend is continued, the next letter to G is D which is falling in choice A so answer choice A is the answer.

Example 3: Complete the series given below:

D, E, G, J, N, S, ?

A) W

B) Y

C) U

D) Z

Solution: At the very first sight it is found that the letter series is progressing in succeeding order. Further, the trend set by progressing letters is that starting from D, each successive letter is succeeding to its immediate preceding letter with gap of letters increasing by 1 at each progress, i.e., there is no gap of letter between D and E. There is gap of one letter between E and G, of two letters between G and J and so on. In the same way, the desired letter replacing the question mark will be Y, hence choice B is the answer.

2) **Alternative Progression:** In this minimum two alternative series are given with the question mark. The required letter(s) will be belonging to that series which is in the range of the question mark.

Example 4: Replace the question mark

I, U, K, S, M, Q, ?, O, Q ?

A) N, P

B) M, Q

C) O, M

D) None of these

Solution: In above series there are two alternative series of letters

First: I, K, M, ?, Q

Second: U, S, Q, O, ?

In the first series letters are progressing in succeeding order with gap of one letter.

In second series letters are progressing in preceding order with the gap of one letter. So the required letter in the first series is O and in the second series is M. Hence, the answer is choice C.

Example 5: Find out the next item

P, F, N, Q, E, O, R, D, ?, ?

A) P, S B) C, R

C) T, U D) S, P

In the above question there are three series progressing alternatively

First: P, Q, R, ?

Second: F, E, D

Third: N, O, ?

It is clear from above trend that first and third series are in succeeding order at their respective position, whereas second series is in the preceding order. As the question marks are in the range of first and third series, the required letters are P and S. Hence, answer is choice A.

3) **Group Progression:** In this type, letters are given in groups in the succeeding or preceding order establishing intragroup or intergroup or both relationship among letters. Here ? is to be replaced by either whole group or particular letter(s) as directed in the question.

Example 6: R B G, S C H, T D I, U E ?

A) W B) J

C) F D) R

Solution: In the above relationship it is found that each successive group is establishing a succeeding intergroup relationship with its immediate preceding group as follows:

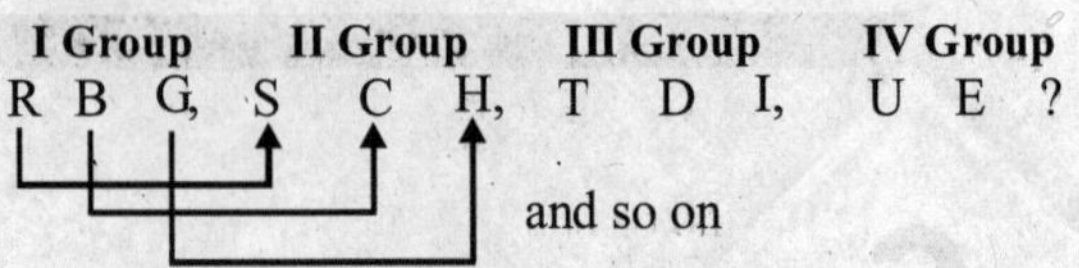

As II group is succeeding to I group, so is the III group with II group and so on. While maintaining the same trend the required letter to replace ? is J, hence choice B is the answer.

Example 7: Complete the series:

F G H, UTS, R B I, I Y R, K Q D, P J W, X D O, ?

A) WSJ

B) YOP

C) PVF

D) CWL

Solution: In above series, letters in II group are corresponding to letters in I group as shown below:

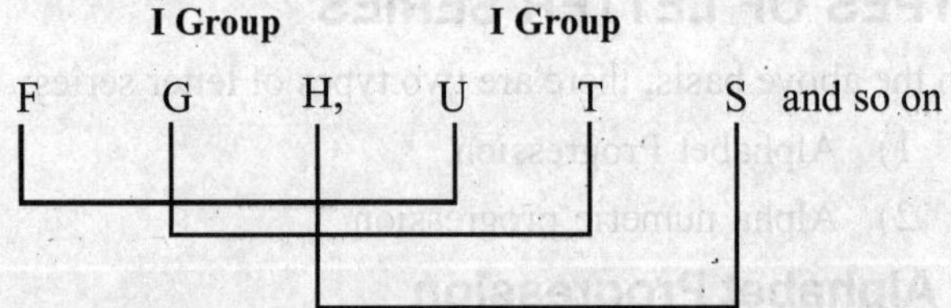

Same relationship is of IV group to III and so on. While maintaining the same trend the required group is CWL. Hence, answer choice D is the answer.

Example 8: What will come in place of ? in the following series?

K T D P, M R F N, O P H L, Q ? ? J

A) IJ B) RW

C) NJ D) PL

Solution: The pattern of relationship is that the first and third letter of each successive group is succeeding with the gap of one to the first and third letter of the each preceding group. Further, second and fourth letter of each successive group is preceding with the gap of one to second and fourth letter of each preceding group. This relationship of first two groups is shown as follows:

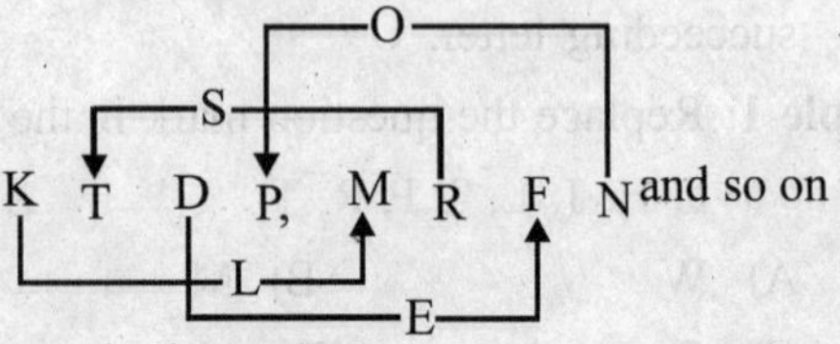

While maintaining the same trend, the letters replacing ?? are NJ. Hence, choice C is the answer.

2. Alpha-Numeric Progression

In this type of series, letters are given along with their respective succeeding or preceding order position and a trend is set up in the series. The required letter is obtained by maintaining the same trend.

Example 9: What will come next

F-6, U-21, J-10, Q-17, D-4, W-23, R-18, ?

A) I-9

B) T-13

C) B-6

D) None of these

Solution: The trend being followed in the above series is that each successive letter is corresponding to its previous letter. Also, number indicating position of each letter in A to Z order is given along with it. While maintaining the same trend, the required letter-number set to replace question mark is I-9 as I is corresponding to letter R and also has 9th position in alphabet in A to Z order. Hence, choice A is the answer.

Example 10: Replace the question mark in the following series:

D_4, G_7, J_{10}, M_{13}, P_{16}, S_{19}, ?

A) W_{23} B) V_{22}

C) Z_{26} D) X_{24}

Solution: In above series each successive letter is succeeding to its immediate previous letter with the gap of two letters. Further, A to Z order position of each letter in the alphabet is given. While maintaining the same trend the required letter-number set replacing ? is V_{22}, hence choice B is the answer.

Example 11: Complete the following series

Q-10, N-13, K-16, H-19, E-22, ?

a) A-26 B) Z-1

C) V-5 D) B-25

Solution: In above series each successive letter is preceding with gap of two letters to its immediate previous letter. Also, respective position of each letter in Z to A order is given along with it. Maintaining this trend, the letter-number set replacing the question mark is B-25 and hence, choice D is the answer.

Practice Exercise

General Questions Format

Complete the given series in the following questions:

1. Z, X, V, T, R, ?, ?

(A) O, K (B) N, M

(C) K, S (D) P, N

2. BDF, CFI, DHL, ?

(A) CJM (B) EIM

(C) EJO (D) EMI

3. YEB, WFD, UGF, SHH, ?

(A) QOL (B) QIJ

(C) TOL (D) QNL

4. U, O, I, ?, A

(A) E (B) C

(C) S (D) G

5. A, Z, X, B, V, T, C, R, ?, ?

(A) C,B (B) J,H

(C) B,H (D) P, D

6. CE, GI, KM, OQ, ?

(A) TW (B) TV

(C) SU (D) RT

7. Z Y X, U TS, PON, K, ?, ?

(A) H, G (B) H, I

(C) I, H (D) J, I

8. AZ, CX, FU,?

(A) IR (B) IV

(C) JQ (D) KP

9. JE, LH, OL, SQ, ?

(A) WV (B) WX

(C) VW (D) XW

10. BEH, KNQ, TWZ, ?

(A) IJL (B) CFI

(C) BDF (D) ADG

11. LXF, MTJ, NPN, OLR, ?

(A) PHV (B) PIU

(C) PJW (D) PKX

12. AB, BA, ABC, CBA, ABCD, ?
(A) ACBD (B) BACD
(C) CABD (D) DCBA

13. D-4, F-6, H-8, J-10 ,?
(A) K-12 (B) L-12
(C) L-14 (D) K-11

14. KM5, IP8, GS11, EVI4, ?
(A) BXI7 (B) BY17
(C) CY18 (D) CY17

15. W, U, S, Q, O, M, ?
(A) H (B) K
(C) P (D) None of these

16. CD, FG, IJ, LM, ? P
(A) O (B) N
(C) P (D) Q

17. E-5, H-8, K-11, N-14, Q-17, ?
(A) S-22 (B) T-20
(C) R-16 (D) P-18

18. ZAB, DEF, HIJ, LMN, ?
(A) S T U (B) P Q R
(C) N O P (D) U V W

19. WV, SR, ON, ?J
(A) M (B) H
(C) K (D) P

20. ADG, GJM, MPS, ?
(A) U Y S (B) S Y U
(C) V Y S (D) S V Y

KEY

1. D Letters are progressing in the preceding order with the gap of one letter between two consecutive letters.

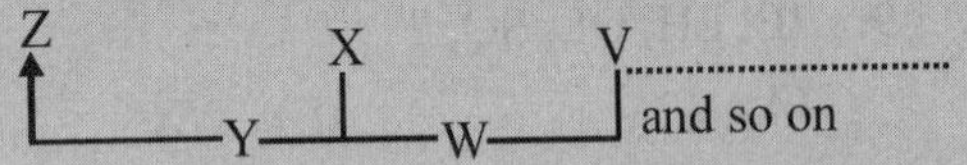

2. C This is a case of group progression in the succeeding order of letters. Each group of three letters is related to its succeeding group in the following pattern.

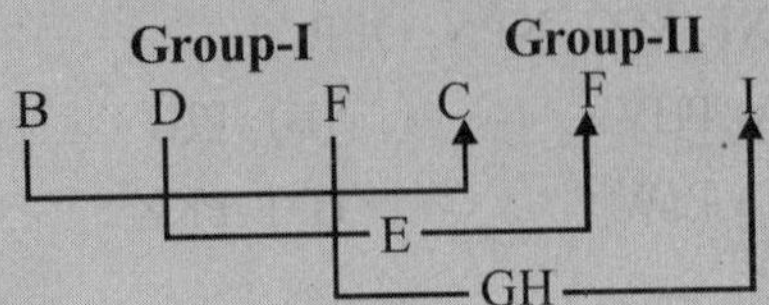

In the same way group II is related to group III and so on. Hence, option C is the answer.

3. B Here, the group progression has adopted the following pattern:

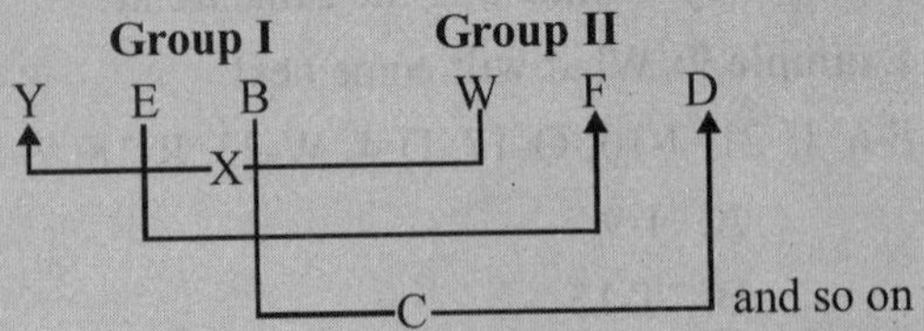

Group II has similar relation with group III, III with IV, and ultimately group QIJ is achieved. Hence, option A is the answer.

4. A These are vowel letters but one vowel letter is missing and that is the answer.

5. D There are three series progressing in succeeding order thus maintaining the following trend:

A Z X B V T C R ? ?

Series 1: A, B, C.....................I

Series 2: Z, V, R,....................II

Series 3: X, T,?..........................III

Letters of each series show a trend after the gap of two letters each time. By following trend of respective series question marks are replaced by P D. Hence, choice D is the answer.

6. C This twin letter group progression series grows in succeeding order where each latter of a preceding group maintains a difference of three letters with its corresponding letter in the succeeding group. This is shown as follows:

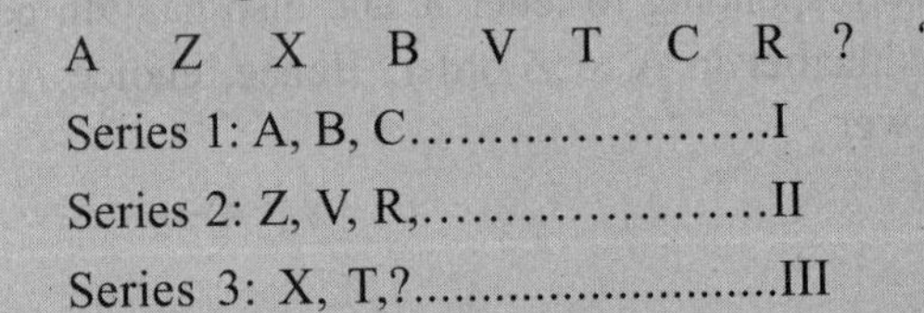

Group II and the following groups maintain the same trend with their respective succeeding group and desired pair SU. Hence, option C is the answer.

7. D In this group, progression series three letters in each group are related to three letters of next group in preceding order. Further, there is also a preceding order relation between the last letter of a group with the first letter of its immediate next group. It is shown below:

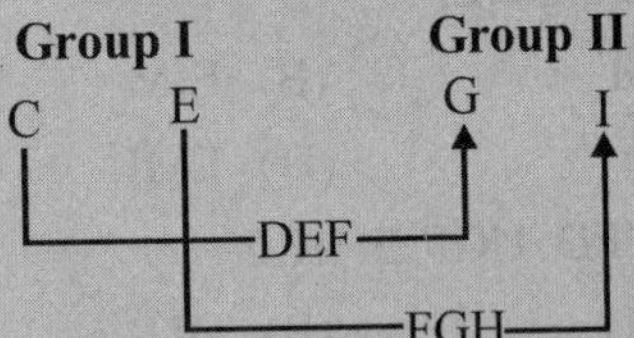

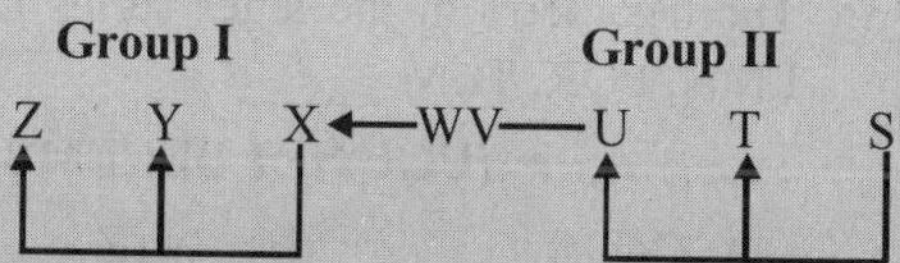

Similar pattern is followed in remaining groups and desired letters JI are achieved. Hence, option D is the answer.

8. C Each pair in the series is a pair of corresponding letters. First letter of each pair is progressing in succeeding order with gap of letters and the number of letters in the gap is increasing by one with each progression. For instance there is gap of one letter B between letters A and C, two letters D and E between C and F, and so on. Second letter in each group is corresponding to the first letter of the respective group. While maintaining this trend letters JQ are achieved. Hence, choice C is the answer.

9. D This is a twin group series in which letters are progressing in succeeding order with increasing gap at each progression. First and second letters of each succeeding group are progressing with increasing gaps of letters in their respective framework. For instance, to start with, there is gap of one letter K between J and L and so on whereas each second letter of each group maintain different pattern of progression. Difference of letters between each second letter of each group starts with the gap of two letters as is evident from the observing difference of letters F and G between E and H and increases by one at each progression. So while maintaining two parallel trends, desired letters XW are achieved. Hence, choice D is the answer.

10. B In this group progression series there is intra group and intergroup progression in succeeding order. The series follows following pattern:

Group I		Group II	Group III
B	E	H—IJ→K N Q	T W Z
└CD—	—FG—┘		

Above pattern is established in each group and hence answer is B.

11. A This is a three lettered group progression series. Letters are progressing in succeeding order in each group and have adopted the following pattern:

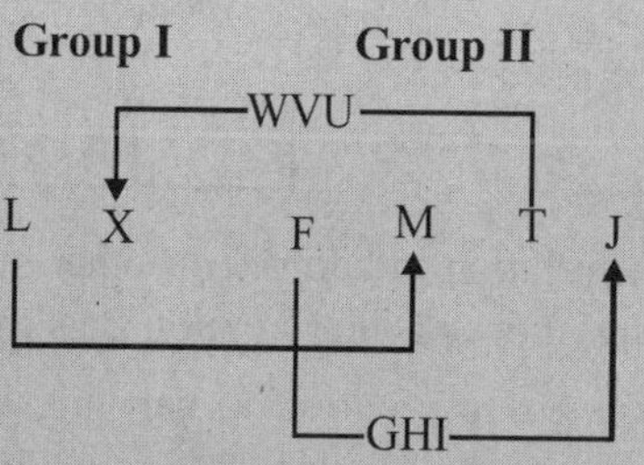

Similar trend is followed in other groups and answer PHV is achieved. Hence, option A is the answer.

12. D Each successive group is reverse of its immediate preceding group. So option D is the answer.

13. B Positions of letters proceeding from A to Z are given. Letters are proceeding in succeeding order with gap of one letter and position. Knowledge of prerequisites of reasoning helps in understanding and solving such questions. In this case series start with letter D and then it proceeds in the way discussed above. Hence, option B is the answer.

14. D This is group progression with letters in each group are alternatively related. That pattern is as follows:

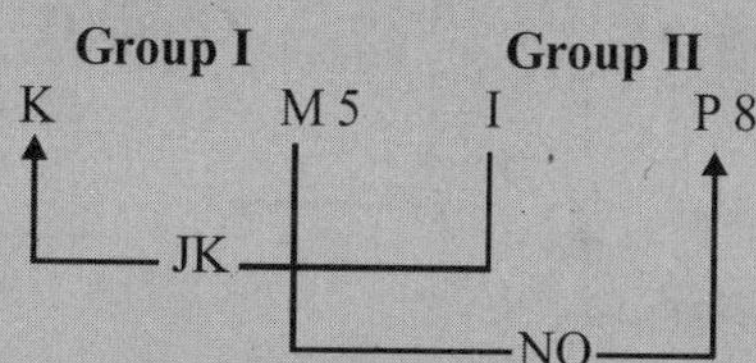

Above pattern is adopted in rest of the groups. Further, the number shown along with letters is increasing with 3. So choice D is the answer.

15. B If observed from right to left above series require K in place of ?. Hence, option B is the answer.

16. A

17. B

18. B This series is a three lettered group progression wherein each group is having succeeding order progression. Then last letter of each group is related to first letter of its immediate succeeding group with the pattern of succeeding order with the gap of one letter. Pattern of two such groups is shown here:

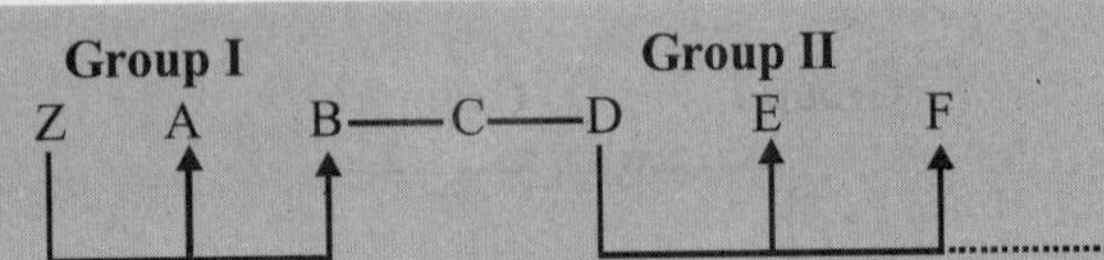

Same relation is adopted in other succeeding groups and we achieve option B as the answer.

19. C This a group progression carrying intragroup and intergroup relation as is found in question number 18 above. The only difference is that in question number 18 there are three letters in each group having succeeding order relationship whereas in this question there are two letters in each group having preceding order relationship.

20. D This is an intragroup and intergroup progression series having three complete groups of three letters each and fourth is to be determined by carrying forward the trend maintained in other groups. Besides having succeeding order relation among groups it has also been observed that last letter of each group becomes first letter of its immediate succeeding group which follows the succeeding order progression like preceding groups. Arrangement of two groups is shown below as illustration:

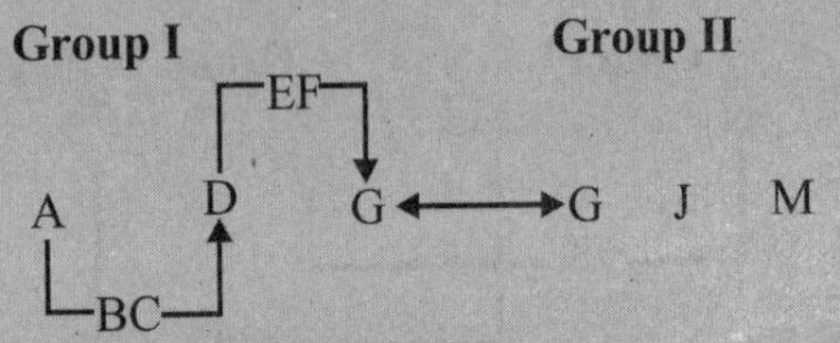

Similar pattern is followed in remaining succeeding groups and we get the desired group S V Y, hence option D is the answer.

Questions Asked in Previous NET Exams

1. Choose the missing term out of the given alternatives. **(UGC NET JUNE 2019)**

   TEF, UGH, __________, WKL

   (A) CMN (B) UJI
   (C) VIJ (D) IJT

2. Choose the missing term out of following JAK, KBL, LCM, MDN, __________

   (UGC NET JUNE 2019)

   (A) OEP (B) NEO
   (C) MEN (D) PFQ

3. The next term in the letter series DEF, HIJ, LMN, PQR, TUV, ______ is

   (UGC NET DECEMBER 2018)

   (A) XYZ (B) WYZ
   (C) WXY (D) YZA

4. The next term in the series XY, ABC, FGHI, ? is **(UGC NET JULY 2018)**

   (A) MNPQO (B) MNOPQ
   (C) PQOMN (D) NMPOQ

5. The next term in the series: ABD, DGK, HMS, MTB, SBL, ________ is:

   (UGC NET JULY 2018)

   (A) KZU (B) ZCA
   (C) ZKW (D) ZKU

6. The next term in the following series YEB, WFD, UHG, SKI, ? will be

   (UGC NET JANUARY 2017)

   (A) TLO (B) QOL
   (C) QLO (D) GQP

7. In the series AYD, BVF, DRH, GMJ, ? the next term is

   (UGC NET AUGUST 2016)

   (A) GLK (B) HLM
   (C) LHM (D) KGL

8. In the series AB, EDC, FGHI, ________? ________ OPQRST, the missing term is

   (UGC NET JULY 2016)

   (A) JKLMN (B) JMKNL
   (C) NMLKJ (D) NMKLJ

9. The next term in the series:

   (UGC NET DECEMBER 2015)

   B2E, D5H, F12K, H27N, ? is:

   (A) J561 (B) 162Q
   (C) Q62J (D) J58Q

10. The next term in the series: BA, ED, IH, NM, ___ is **(UGC NET DECEMBER 14)**

    (A) TS (B) ST
    (C) TU (D) SU

11. Complete the series BB, FE, II, ML, PP, ______ by choosing one of the following options given: **(UGC NET JUNE 2014)**

    (A) TS (B) ST
    (C) RS (D) SR

12. What will be the next term in the following?
DCXW, FEVU, HGTS, ?

(UGC NET DECEMBER 2009)

(A) AKPO (B) ABYZ
(C) JIRQ (D) LMRS

KEY

1. C This is a group progression series containing three letters each. Here, first letter of a group is related to the first letter of its immediate succeeding group in the succeeding order, then second with second and third with third. For instance, relation of first two groups is shown below:

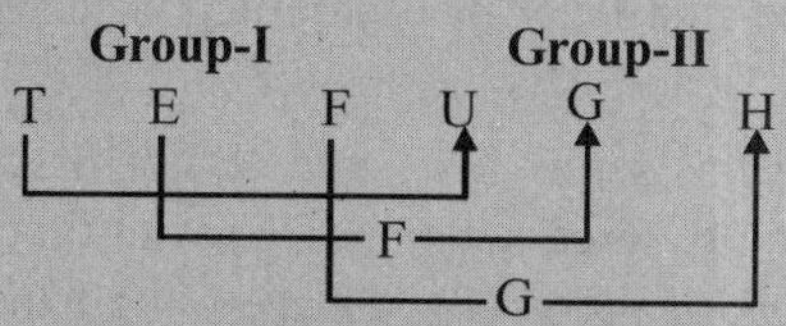

Same pattern is found in the succeeding groups. So option 3 is the answer.

2. B In this three group series, last letter of each group becomes first letter of its immediate succeeding group. Further, middle letter of a succeeding group is the immediate succeeding letter to the middle letter of the group immediate preceding to it. Further, last letter is immediate succeeding letter to the first letter in each group. Relationship of first two groups is shown below as instance:

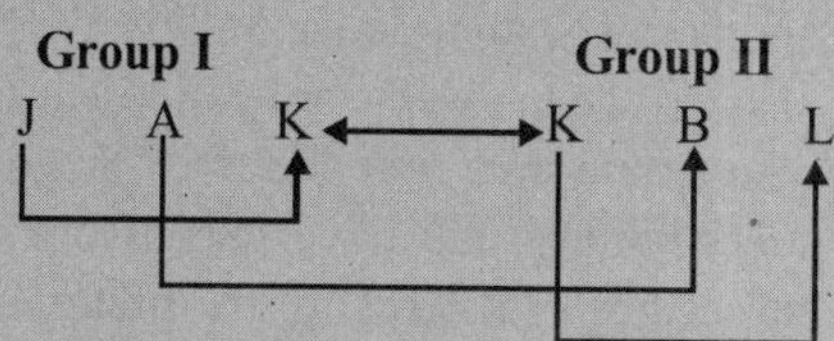

Similar pattern is adopted in remaining succeeding groups. Hence, option 2 is the answer.

3. A In this series there is group progression where each group is containing three letters. There is intergroup and intergroup relation. Second letter of a group is immediate succeeding to its immediate preceding letter of the group. Similar relation can be seen in the third letter of the same group with the second letter of the group. Further, first letter of a group is succeeding with a gap of one letter to the last letter of its immediate preceding group. Let us see the relation of first two groups in the following set-up.

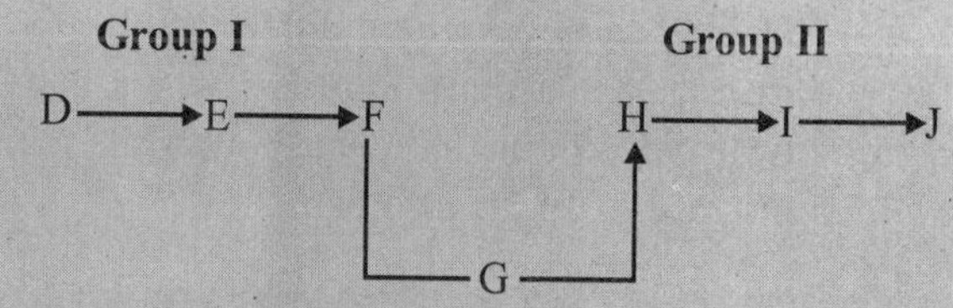

Similar relationship in other groups establishes that option 1 is the answer.

4. B Number of letters in each successive group is increasing by one. There also occurs intragroup and intergroup relation in the succeeding order. Gap of letters between the last letter of a group and first letter of immediately preceding group also increases by one at every progression. The relationship is shown as follows:

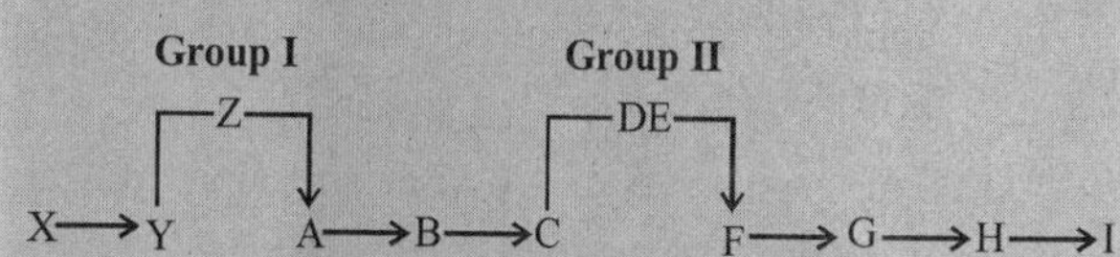

Similarly, group III and IV will progress and ultimately group MNOPQ is achieved. Hence, option 2 is the answer.

5. C There is intergroup relation in the succeeding order. Letters in each group increases by 1. It can be shown while picking up first three groups as follows.

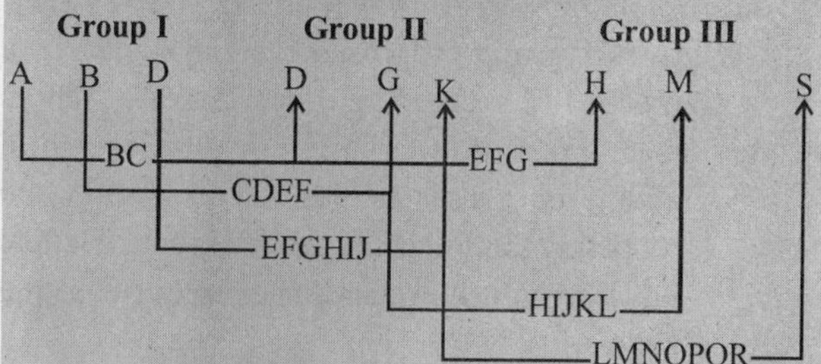

So the starting gap of letters between the first two letters of first two groups is of two letters, i.e., BC between A and D and this gap increases by 1 at the start of each group. Second two letters B and D of first and second group have four letter difference between them, i.e., CDEF. This difference also increases by 1 in succeeding groups. Further, two third letters D and K of group I and II have a difference of five letters EFGHIJ and in this case also difference increases by 1 in successive progressions. In this way group ZKW is achieved. Hence, option 3 is the answer.

6. B Each group containing three letters is showing succeeding and preceding order progression. Difference in the letters differs with different pairs of letters in the groups which can be understood in the following way while taking instance of first two groups:

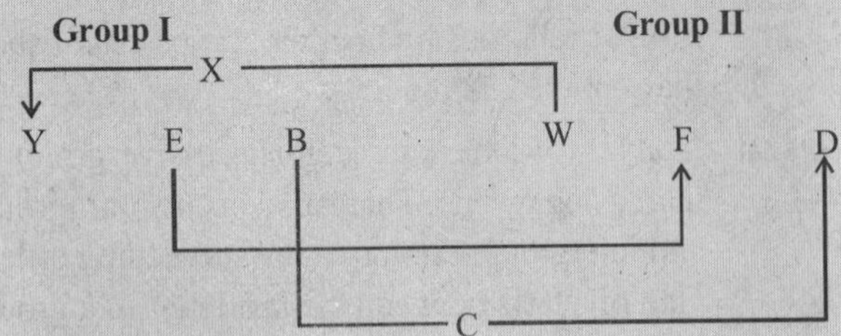

Similar trend with increasing number of letters is maintained in remaining groups and so we achieve the desired group QOL. Hence, option 2 is the answer.

7. D This is a series of group progression and each group has three letters each. Here, the first letter of each group is related in succeeding order with increasing by 1. Middle letter of each group is in preceding order with the gap of letters increasing by 1 at each progression and each third letter of the groups is progressing in succeeding group with a constant gap of one letter. Following this pattern the desired group KGL is achieved. Hence, option D is the answer.

8. C In this group progression series letters are proceed in succeeding order. Order of letters is reversed in alternative succession while adding one letter at each succession. While following this trend, the desired group of letters NMLKJ is achieved. Hence, option C is the answer.

9. D Here there is a letter series and another is number series. Both the series are separated and the trend is observed.

BE, DH, FK, HN, ?

This is an intergroup progression series and letters are progressing in succeeding order. First letters of each group are maintaining a gap of one letter. Second letters of each group are maintaining a gap of two letters. Number series goes like this:

2, 5, 12, 27, ?

Here the trend is: 2 x 2 + 1 = 5, 5 x 2 + 2 = 12, 12 x 2 + 3 = 27, 27 x 2 + 4 = 58

Putting the trends in given order of the series we achieve the desired group J58Q. Hence, option D is the answer.

10. A In this group progression, each group contains letters in reverse order. Gap of letters between the first letter of each group is increasing by 1. Hence, A is the answer.

11. A In this series first letter (B) of first pair has gap of three letters (CDE) with first letter of second group (F). On the other hand second letter B of first group has a gap of two letters (CD) with second letter E of second group. Same trend is followed in succeeding groups with change of number of letters in the alternative manner. Hence, option A is the answer.

12. C First two letters of each group are consecutive to each other and are written in reverse order as C and D are written DC. The last two letters are corresponding to the first two letters. In the first group corresponding letter of C is X and corresponding letter to D is W. These are also written in reverse order. Further, first letter of a group and first letter of its immediate succeeding group have gap of one letter in succeeding order as D of the first group and F of the second group have gap of one letter E between them. In the same way other groups are formed and we achieve the desired group of letters, i.e., JIRQ. Hence, option C is the answer.

7 Number Series

CONCEPT

Questions on number series requires to find a number to replace a question mark or blank space with an appropriate number in the given series, thus carrying forward the trend already maintained by the given series. Sometimes, it is asked to detect a wrong number in the series, which is not compatible to the prevailing trend of the series.

Questions on number series are being asked regularly in NET Paper 1. Due to this, understanding the concept and sufficiently practising this topic become an indispensable part of NET Paper 1 preparation. As different types of numbers are put in questions on number series, it is wise to be acquainted with different types of numbers and number system.

Types of Numbers

1) **Natural Numbers (N)**, (also called positive integers, counting numbers, or natural numbers); They are the numbers {1, 2, 3, 4, 5, …}
2) **Whole Numbers (W)**. This is the set of natural numbers, plus zero, i.e., {0, 1, 2, 3, 4, 5, …}.
3) **Integers (Z)**. This is the set of all whole numbers plus all the negatives (or opposites) of the natural numbers, i.e., {… , –2, –1, 0, 1, 2, …}
4) **Rational Numbers (Q)**. This is all the fractions where the top and bottom numbers are integers; e.g., $\frac{1}{2}, \frac{3}{4}, \frac{7}{2}, -\frac{4}{3}, \frac{4}{1}$

   [Note: The denominator cannot be 0, but the numerator can be].
5) **Real Numbers (R)**, (also called measuring numbers or measurement numbers). This includes all numbers that can be written as a decimal. This includes fractions written in decimal form e.g., 0.5, 0.75 2.35, { 0.073, 0.3333, or 2.142857.
6) **Prime Numbers** are numbers greater than 1 that can only be divided by themselves and 1 to give an integer answer. Example of these are **2, 3, 5, 7, 11, 13, 17, ….** Note that 2 is the first and only even prime number.
7) **Even Numbers:** A whole number exactly divisible by 2 is called even number.
8) **Odd Numbers:** A whole number which is not exactly divisible by 2 is called an odd number.
9) **Composite Numbers:** Numbers having more than two factors are called as composite numbers. **For example:** 4, 6, 8, 10, 15, 21, etc. are composite numbers.

Types of Number Series

1) *Continuous Series:* **In this type, each number in the series is related to its immediate succeeding number.**

Examples: What will come in place of question mark?

a) 6, 11, 21, 36, 56, ?

A) 78　　B) 65

C) 93　　D) 81

Solution:

6　11　21　36　56　?(81)

+5　+10　+15　+20　+25

Starting with 6, difference is increasing by 5 to get the next number. Every increasing number is added to the previous number to obtain next number of the series as is shown above. Hence, choice D is the answer.

b) 3, 9, 27, 81, ?

A) 144 B) 243

C) 155 D) None of these

Solution:

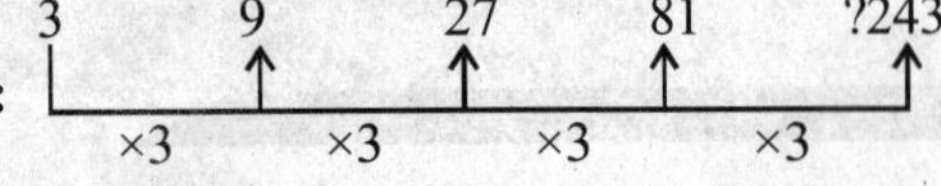

Starting with 3 every number is multiplied with 3 to get next number. Hence choice B is the answer

c) 3, 7, 15, 31, 63, ?

A) 125 B) 90

C) 127 D) 155

Solution:

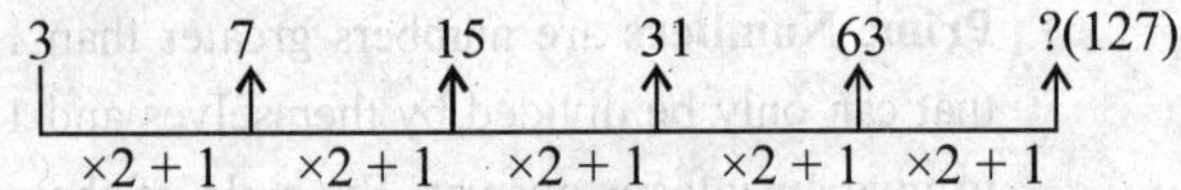

Starting with 3, every number is multiplied with 2 and 1 is added to the product to obtain immediate succeeding number and so on. Hence, choice C is the answer.

2) *Alternative Series:* **In this case more than one series is given to the candidate and the candidate is to follow the pattern of that series which comes in the range of the question mark.**

Example: 2, 20, 4, 18, 6, 16, 8, 14, 10, 12, 12, ?

A) 10 B) 15

C) 20 D) 17

Solution: There are two series in this question. Numbers of both the series are progressing in alternative succession.

Series 1: 2 4 6 8 10 12

Series 2: 20 18 16 14 12 ?(10)

From the above it is clear that ? is coming in the range of series 2. Hence, answer is choice A.

3) *Individual Operation Series:* **This series is found in continuous or alternative progression and basically tests the knowledge of squares or cubes. Squares or cubes are asked direct or with deviation.**

Example 1: 16, 25, 36, 49, 64, ?

A) 100 B) 144

C) 75 D) 81

Solution: Observing the trend it is found that number 16 is $(4)^2$ and after that a series of squares of 5, 6, 7, and 8. Next number which will maintain this trend is square of 9, i.e., 81. Hence, choice D is the answer.

Example 2: 0, 7, 8, 63, 24, 215, 49, ?

A) 513 B) 512

C) 511 D) 510

Solution: 0, 7, 8, 63, 24, 215, 48, ?

$(1)^2 - 1$ $(2)^3 - 1$ $(3)^2 - 1$ $(4)^3 - 1$ and so on

Here are two series operating alternatively. Starting with 0 there is square minus 1 for every even number and there is cube minus 1 for every even number. So the answer is choice C.

4) ***Parallel Series:*** In this type a series is divided into two equal halves, as the digit items including ? in the series are aggregated in even number, i.e., there are either 6 digits or 8 digits or so in the series so that it can be divided into two equal halves. Here, one half is complete and the other is incomplete as carrying?. Whatever trend is maintained in the complete half, same trend is to be maintained in the incomplete half and suitable number is to be found out, which will replace the question mark.

Example: 3, 6, 11, 80, ?, 165

A) 150 B) 160

C) 170 D) 180

Solution: As the given series is six digit series, it is divided into two equal halves:

3, 6, 11, 80, ?,(160) 165

×2 +5 ×2 +5

Here, the trend in complete side is that first number 3 is multiplied with 2 to get next number 6 and in that number 6, 5 are added to get the last number 11. This trend is applied to the incomplete side as shown above and answer 160 is obtained.

5) ***Prime Number Series:*** Knowledge of prime numbers as obtained from prerequisites helps one to understand and detect the trend maintained in such series. In such series one is to understand the trend in the progression and detect the number to replace?

A prime number series can be expressed while maintaining the following trends:

a) Ascending Order:

i) Without Gap: **29, 31, 37, 41, 43, ?**

A) 44

B) 45

C) 47

D) 51

Solution: Here C is the answer as it is ascending order series on prime numbers and according to this ordering 43 is immediately followed by 47.

ii) With Gap: **19, 29, 37, 43, 53, ?**

A) 57

B) 59

C) 61

D) 67

Solution: There is gap of one prime number between the two successive numbers in the above series.

This is shown below:

19 — 23 — 29 — 31 — 37 — 41 — 43 — 47 — 53 — 59 — ?(61)

Hence, choice C is the answer.

(Gap can be of more than one number also. In that case same strategy is to be applied to solve the question)

ii) With Gap: **19, 29, 37, 43, 53, ?**

A) 57

B) 59

C) 61

D) 67

b) Descending Order:

i) Without Gap: **61, 59, 53, 47, 43, ?**

A) 37 B) 31

C) 29 D) 41

Solution: Natural transition in descending order

ii) With Gap:**83, 73, 67, 59, 47, ?**

A) 41

B) 29

C) 31

D) 43

Solution: There is gap of one prime number between the two successive numbers in above series proceeding in descending order. This is shown below:

83 — 79 — 73 — 71 — 67 — 61 — 59 — 53 — 47 — 43 — ?(41)

As is clear from above, prime number 41 rightly replaces ? and hence, choice A is the answer.

In this series gap between two prime numbers may be more than one in ascending and descending order.

6) ***Fibonacci Series:*** This series is given in groups of numbers. Numbers in a particular group are put into mathematical operation on one another while maintaining a uniform pattern.

Example: 1, 3, 3, 2 , 3, 6, 3, 3, 9, 4, ?, 12

A) 2

B) 4

C) 3

D) 5

Solution: Here the groups are:

1,3,3 2,3,6 3,3,9 4,?,12

By observing these groups, it is found that in each group central number 3 is common in all groups and it is multiplied with first number to give third number in a group. In one group central multiplier is missing so choice C is the answer.

Practice Exercise

General Questions Format

1. 4, 16, 32, 128, 256, ?
(A) 1234 (B) 856
(C) 1024 (D) 1142

2. 2, 10, 30, 68, ?
(A) 128 (B) 130
(C) 136 (D) 140

3. 2, 18, 46, 98, ?
(A) 196 (B) 192
(C) 200 (D) None of these

4. 6, 9, 18, 45, ?
(A) 135 (B) 99
(C) 115 (D) 138

5. 18, 11, 24, 14, ?
(A) 32 (B) 26
(C) 30 (D) 34

6. 8, 9, 13, 22, ?
(A) 31 (B) 36
(C) 47 (D) 38

7. 2, 8, 16, 128, ?
(A) 2041 (B) 2045
(C) 2046 (D) 2048

8. 18, 54, 60, 30, 4, 12, ?, 9
(A) 23 (B) 18
(C) 11 (D) 16

9. 79, 71, 61, 53, ?, 37
(A) 51 (B) 49
(C) 47 (D) 43

10. 6, ?, 62, 123, 214, 341
(A) 11 (B) 25
(C) 36 (D) 47

11. 2, 9, 28, ?, 126, 217
(A) 36 (B) 42
(C) 56 (D) 65

12. 2, 8, 40, ?, 1680, 13440
(A) 80 (B) 120
(C) 160 (D) 240

13. 0.2, 0.04, 0.006, ?
(A) 0.007 (B) 0.008
(C) 0.0008 (D) 0.0012

14. 3, 4, 12, 45, ?, 1005
(A) 152 (B) 198
(C) 144 (D) 196

15. 4, 6, 12, 30, ?, 315, 1260
(A) 75 (B) 88
(C) 90 (D) 121

16. 27, 135, 45, 225, 75, ?
(A) 225 (B) 275
(C) 300 (D) 375

17. 10, 15, 24, ?, 54, 75, 100
(A) 37 (B) 39
(C) 31 (D) 33

18. 47, 119, 167, ?, 359, 527
(A) 279 (B) 281
(C) 283 (D) 287

19. 41, 31, ?, 17, 11, 5
(A) 19 (B) 21
(C) 23 (D) 27

20. 21, 16, 33, 41, 9, 4, 9, ?
(A) 19 (B) 17
(C) 11 (D) 23

21. 2, 6, 21, 88, 445, ?
(A) 2676 (B) 2570
(C) 2680 (D) 2476

22. 4, 6, 10, 18, 34,?
(A) 64 (B) 80
(C) 66 (D) 56

23. 286, 276, 262, 246, 226, ?
(A) 206 (B) 202
(C) 208 (D) 204

24. 5, 11, 35, 143, ?
(A) 710 (B) 719
(C) 715 (D) 716

25. 3, 4, 8, 17, 33, ?
(A) 60
(B) 63
(C) 64
(D) 58

KEY

1. **C** The first number is multiplied with 4 and second with 2 and this trend is alternatively repeated throughout the question. The trend is x 4 x 2 x 4 x 2.......

2. **B**

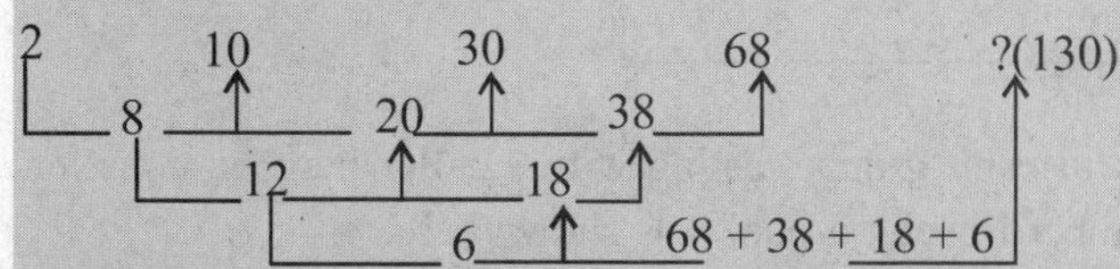

There is a stepping difference downwards until difference becomes constant or single digit. Trend ends at that step where difference becomes single digit. Sum of all differences (68 + 38 + 18 + 6) is 130 and this is the answer, i.e., choice B.

3. **C**

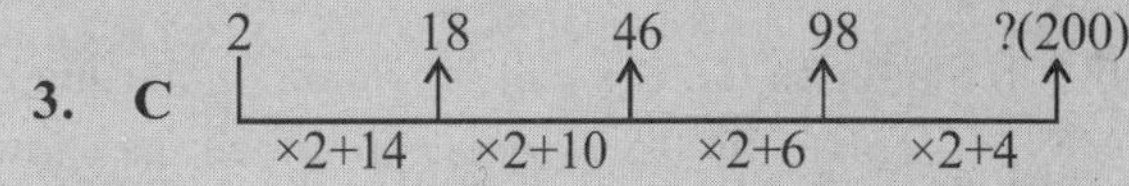

4. **A**

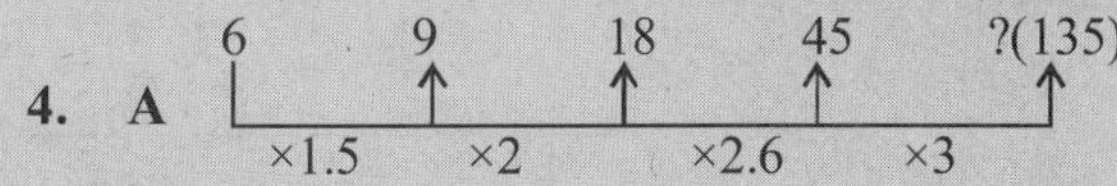

5. **C**

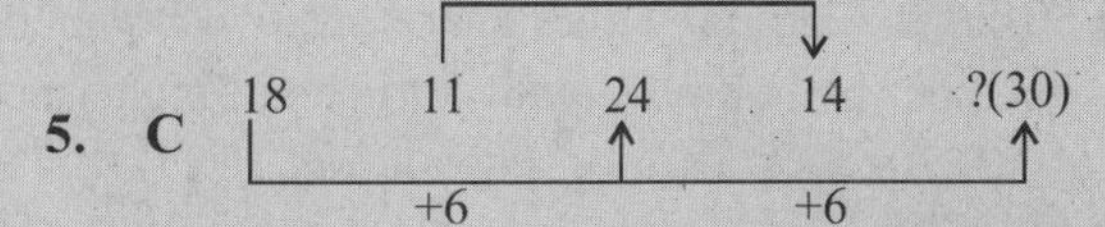

6. **D**

8 9 13 22 ?(38)

$+(1)^2$ $+(2)^2$ $+(3)^2$ $+(4)^2$

7. **D** $(2 \times 8 = 16,\ 8 \times 16 = 128,\ 16 \times 128 = 2048)$

8. **B** Parallel series progressing in following manner:

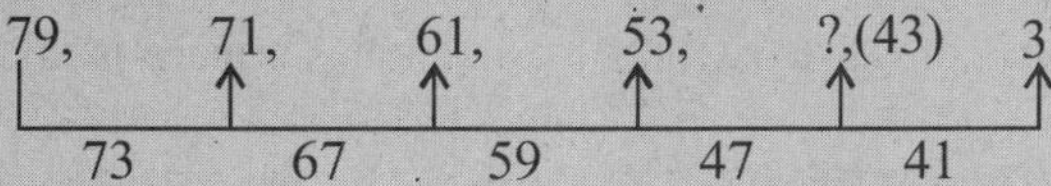

9. **D** Prime number sequence in descending order with the gap of one prime number.

79, 71, 61, 53, ?,(43) 37

73 67 59 47 41

10. **B** It is individual operation series in which figures nearing cubes of some figures are progressing as shown below:

6, ?,(25) 62,

$(2)^3 - 2$ $(3)^3 - 2$ $(4)^3 - 2$

123, 214, 341

$(5)^3 - 2$ $(6)^3 - 2$ $(7)^3 - 2$

11. **D** In this series one is added each time to cubes of given numbers in the series starting with 2, as shown below:

2, 9, 28,

$(1)^3 + 1$ $(2)^3 + 1$ $(3)^3 + 1$

?,(65) 126, 217

$(4)^3 + 1$ $(5)^3 + 1$ $(6)^3 + 1$

12. **D** Starting with 2 there is multiplication with 4, 5, 6, and so on at every progression as shown below:

2, 8, 40, ?,(240) 1680, 13440

×4 ×5 ×6 ×7 ×8

13. **C** At each step there is simultaneous addition of 0 and 2 after decimal as shown below:

0.2, 0.04, 0.006, ?(0.0008)

+.02 +.002 +.0002

14. **D** Starting with first number 3, series progresses by multiplying the number with minimum number of the series and adding its square to the product. Same trend is maintained during the series while increasing the number by 1 as shown below:

3, 4, 12, 45, ?,(196) 1005

×1 +(1)² ×2 +(2)² ×3 +(3)² ×4 +(4)² ×5 +(5)²

15. C In the series there is multiplication of starting number 4 with a fraction and then at each step multiplier is increased by 0.5 to get next number as shown here:

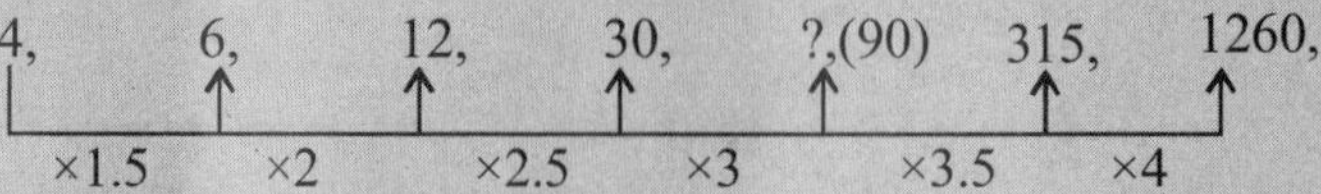

16. D This is a group series. There are two numbers in each group starting with smaller number. Smaller number is multiplied with 5 to obtain bigger number in each group. It is shown here:

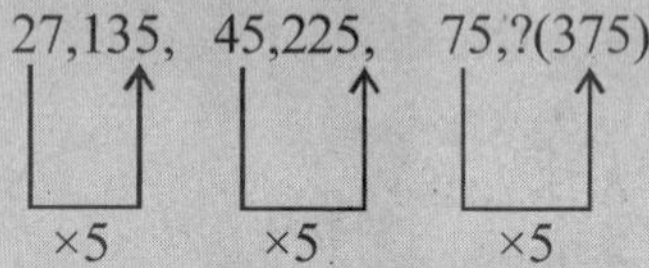

17. A This is a continuous series in ascending order wherein starting with addition of 5 in the first number 10. Further additions are maintaining addition while maintaining a difference of 4 taking first addition of 5 as base as shown below:

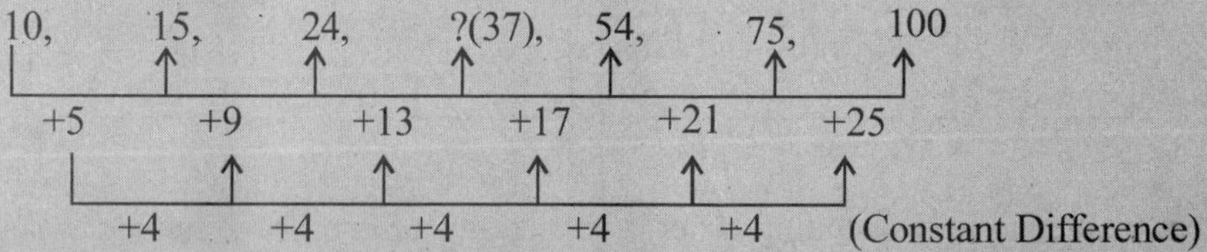

18. D In this series starting from 7 onwards each prime number's square is taken and 2 is deducted (minus 2).

47, 119, 167,

$(7)^2 - 2$ $(11)^2 - 2$ $(13)^2 - 2$

?, 359, 527

$(17)^2 - 2$ $(19)^2 - 2$ $(23)^2 - 2$

19. C Prime number series in descending order with the gap of one prime number.

20. B Parallel series with eight numbers. Trend in each half is same as shown below:

21 16 33 41 | 9 4 9 ?(17)

−5 ×2+1 +8 | −5 ×2+1 +8

21. A This continuous series in ascending order where in a number is multiplied with and added to first number of series simultaneously as shown below:

2, 6, 21, 88, 445, ?(2676)

×2 +2 ×3 +3 ×4 +4 ×5 +5 ×6 +6

22. C It is simple ascending order continuous series. Making an addition of 2 to the first number, each successive number is getting addition of number double to the previous one. It is shown below:

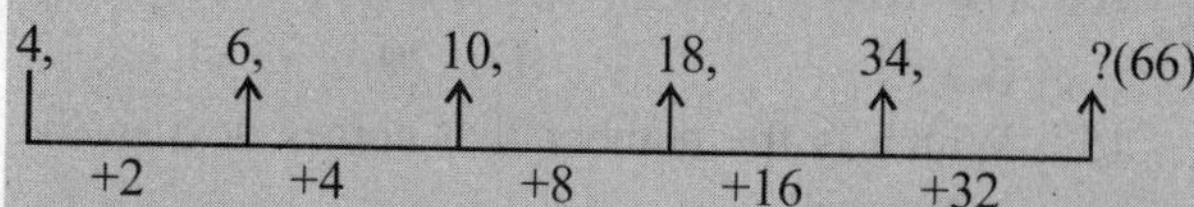

23. D It is descending order starting with subtraction of 10 and further deductions are made in a uniform pattern in alternative pattern of deductions. It is shown below:

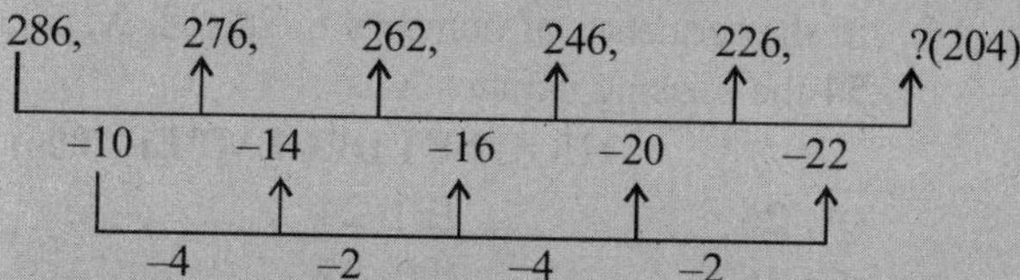

There is repetition of difference by – 4 and – 2 in alternative succession.

24. B It is a continuous series in ascending order. A universal trend is maintained in the series by simultaneous multiplication and addition to each number with two different numbers which set an increasing trend in whole of the series as shown below:

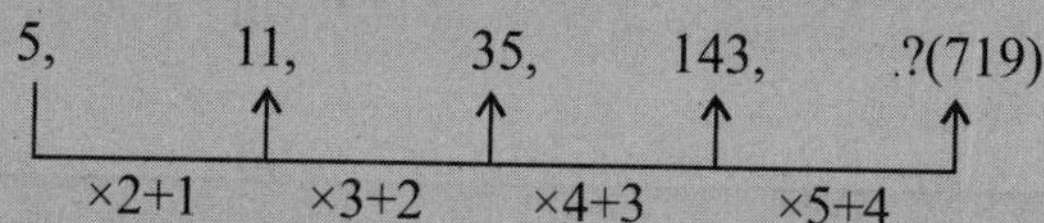

25. D It is a continuous series in ascending order. At each step square of a number is added to get next number. As series progresses, addition of squares of numbers are one number more than previous number as shown below:

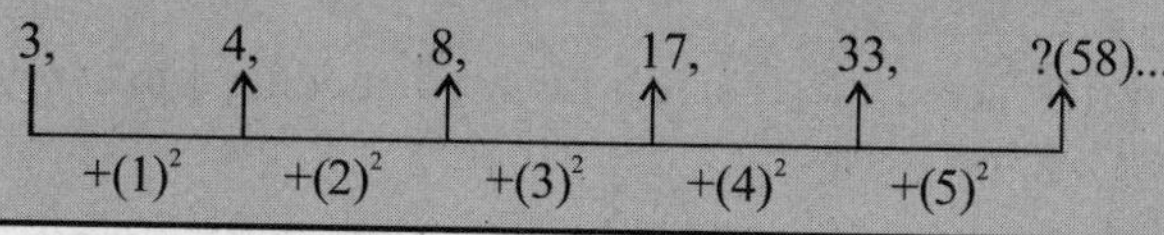

Questions Asked in Previous NET Exams

1. Which one is the wrong number in the given series?

   3, 13, 43, 53, 63, 83

   (UGC NET DECEMBER 2019)

   (A) 13 (B) 53
   (C) 63 (D) 83

2. In the series 1, 6, 15, 28, 45, ... the next term will be:

   (UGC NET NOVEMBER 2017)

   (A) 66 (B) 76
   (C) 56 (D) 84

3. The missing term in the series 1, 4, 27, 16, ?, 36, 343, … is

   (UGC NET JANUARY 2017)

   (A) 30 (B) 49
   (C) 125 (D) 81

4. The next term in the series : 2, 7, 28, 63, 126, _____ is

   (UGC NET DECEMBER 2014)

   (A) 215 (B) 245
   (C) 276 (D) 296

5. The missing term in the series 2, 7, 24, 77, ?, 723 is

   (UGC NET SEPTEMBER 2013)

   (A) 238 (B) 432
   (C) 542 (D) 320

6. The missing number in the series 40, 120, 60, 180, 90, ?, 135 is

   (UGC NET JUNE 2013)

   (A) 110 (B) 270
   (C) 105 (D) 210

7. The missing number in the series: 0, 6, 24, 60, 120, ?, 336, is

   (UGC NET DECEMBER 2012)

   (A) 240 (B) 220
   (C) 280 (D) 210

8. Which is the number that comes next in the following sequence?

   2, 6, 12, 20, 30, 42, 56, _____

   (UGC NET JUNE 2012)

   (A) 60 (B) 64
   (C) 72 (D) 70

9. What is the number that comes next in the sequence?

   2, 5, 9, 19, 37, ___

   (UGC NET DEC. 2011, DECEMBER 2009)

   (A) 76 (B) 74
   (C) 75 (D) 50

10. Find the wrong number in the sequence

(UGC NET DECEMBER 2008)

125, 127, 130, 135, 142, 153, 165

(A) 130 (B) 142

(C) 153 (D) 166

11. Find the next number in the following series:

2, 5, 10, 17, 26, 37, 50, ?

(UGC NET JUNE 2010, DECEMBER 2007)

(A) 63 (B) 65

(C) 67 (D) 69

12. Insert the missing number in the following:

3, 8, 18, 23, 33, ?, 48

(UGC NET JUNE 2009)

(A) 37 (B) 40

(C) 38 (D) 45

13. Insert the missing number in the following:

$\frac{2}{3}, \frac{4}{7}, ?, \frac{11}{21}, \frac{16}{31}$

(UGC NET DECEMBER 2008)

(A) $\frac{10}{8}$ (B) $\frac{6}{10}$

(C) $\frac{5}{10}$ (C) $\frac{7}{13}$

14. Insert the missing number in the following series:

4 16 8 64 ? 256

(UGC NET JUNE 2008)

(A) 16 (B) 24

(C) 32 (D) 20

15. Which is the number that comes next in the sequence?

9, 8, 8, 8, 7, 8, 6,

(UGC NET JUNE 2007)

(A) 5 (B) 6

(C) 8 (D) 4

16. In the sequence of numbers 8, 24, 12, X, 18, 54 the missing number X is:

(UGC NET DECEMBER 2006)

(A) 26 (B) 24

(C) 36 (D) 32

17. Insert the missing number:

$\frac{16}{32}, \frac{15}{33}, \frac{17}{31}, \frac{14}{34}$?

(UGC NET JUNE 2006)

(A) $\frac{19}{35}$ (B) $\frac{19}{30}$

(C) $\frac{18}{35}$ (D) $\frac{18}{30}$

KEY

1. C Only 63 is a composite number while others are prime numbers.

2. A

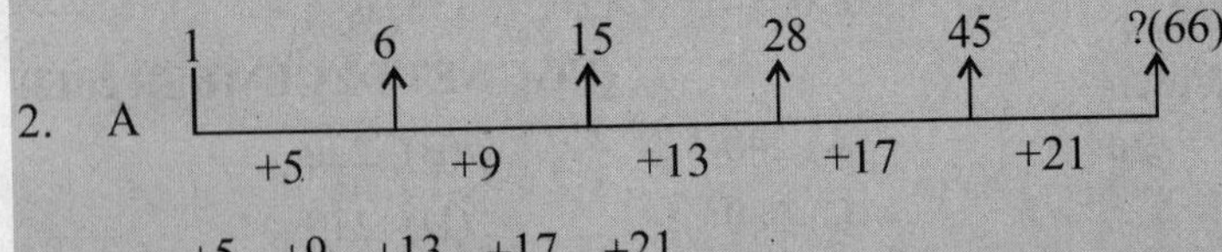

+5 +9 +13 +17 +21

Staring with difference of five from 1 to 6, further difference is increasing with 4, i.e., adding 4 to every preceding difference.

3. C

1 4 27 16 ? 36 343

$(1)^3$ $(2)^2$ $(3)^3$ $(4)^2$ $(5)^3$ $(6)^2$ $(7)^3$

So number 125 will replace? and that is answer choice number 3.

4. A

2 7 28

$(1)^3+1$ $(2)^3-1$ $(3)^3+1$

63 126 ____(215)

$(4)^3-1$ $(5)^3+1$ $(6)^3-1$

5. A

2 7 24 77 ?(238) 723

(2×3)+1 (7×3)+3 (24×3)+5 (77×3)+7 (238×3)+9

6. B It is a case of group number series. In each group there are two numbers. First number is multiplied with 3 to get second number. Same process is repeated in each group and required number is found out. It is shown as follows:

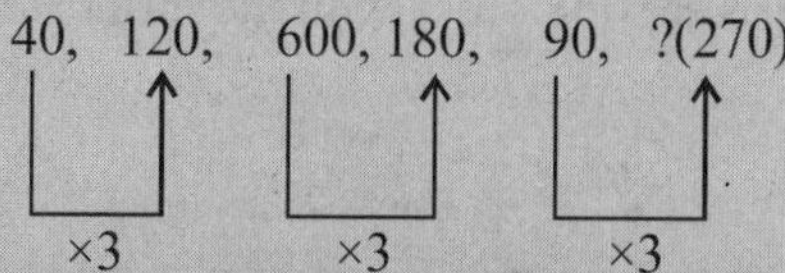

7. D This series is a case of stepping differences, i.e., constant difference between two numbers in series is obtained by stepping down the differences until difference in either becomes constant or becomes single digit difference. It is shown as follows:

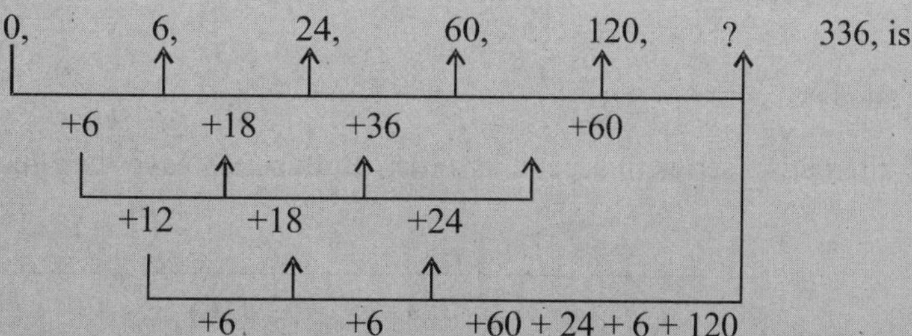

8. C This is a continuous series in ascending order wherein starting with first number 2 of the series we go on adding the numbers while maintain the difference of 2 throughout as shown below:

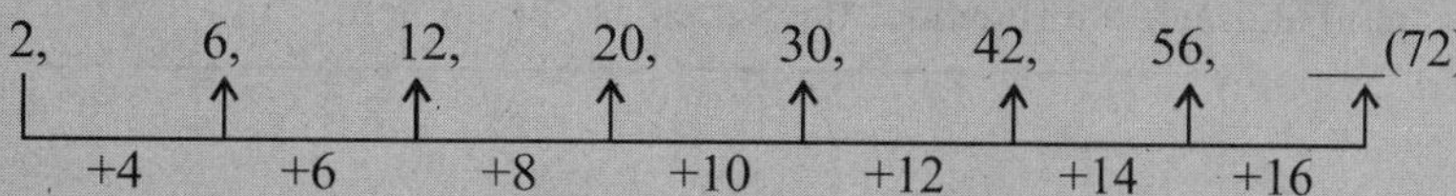

9. C This is continuous series in ascending order. Trend of the series goes like this each number is multiplied with 2 to get succeeding number but along with multiplication number 1 is alternatively added to and subtracted from the product. This is shown as follows:

2, 5, 9, 19, 37, __(75)

×2+1 ×2–1 ×2+1 ×2–1 ×2+1

10. D The series has uniform difference of prime numbers among the numbers in the series. And there is one number which is wrong and that is found as shown below:

125, 127, 130, 135, 142, 153, 165(166)

+2 +3 +5 +7 +11 +13

11. B This series is continuous ascending order series. It progresses when each number of the series is square of some number plus one and same trend is continued throughout the series as shown below:

2, 5, 10, 17,

$(1)^2+1$ $(2)^2+1$ $(3)^2+1$ $(4)^2+1$

26, 37, 50, ?(65)

$(5)^2+1$ $(6)^2+1$ $(7)^2+1$ $(8)^2+1$

12. C This is continuous ascending order series. Series progress with alternative addition of 5 and 10 as shown here:

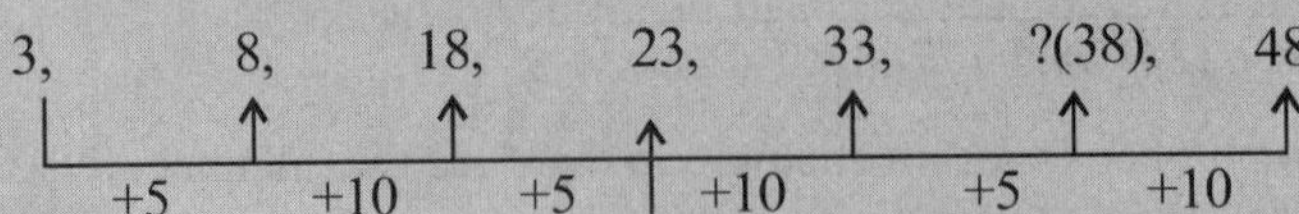

13. D This is series with fraction. Here numerators and denominators form their separate series and then are put in the form of fraction. Numerators progress in increasing order with the difference of 1 whereas denominators progress also in increasing order with the difference of 2. It is shown as follows:

Numerator Series:

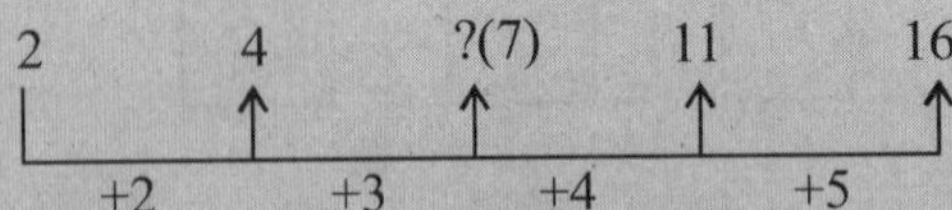

Denominator Series:

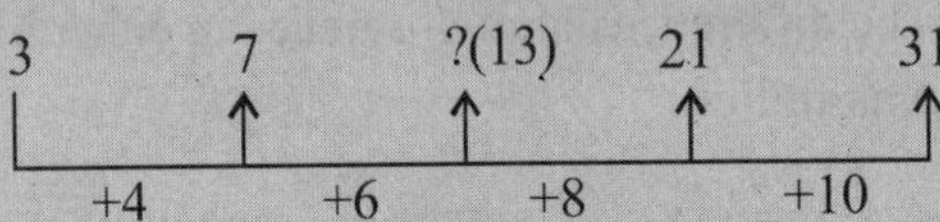

So the required number is $\frac{7}{13}$

14. A It is the case of alternative series in ascending order. Both series have their respective trends as shown below:

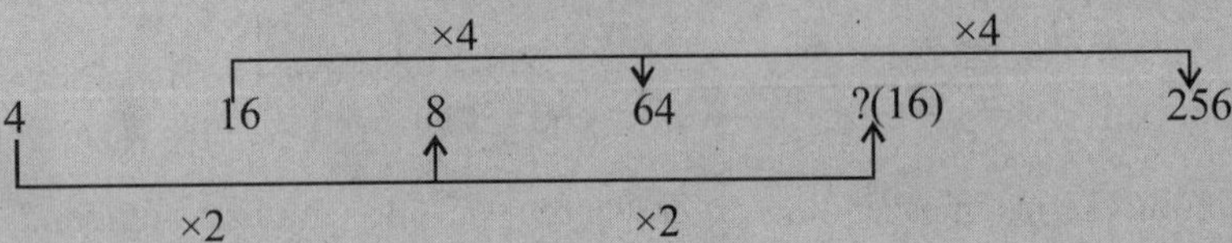

15. C It is a case of alternative series. One series is decreasing by one number whereas other series repeats the same number again and again throughout the series as shown here:

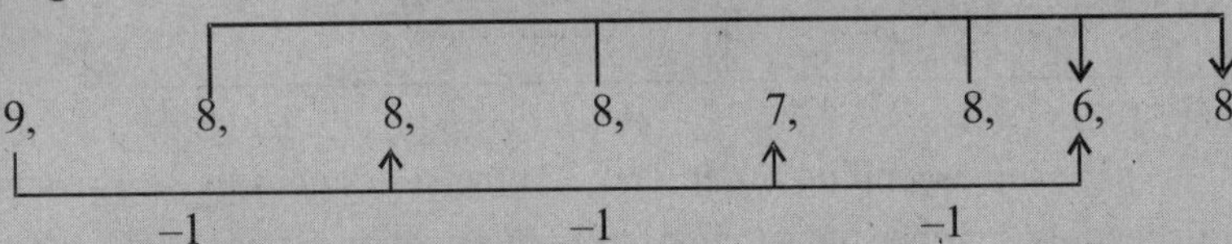

16. C It is a group series containing two numbers in each group. First number of each group is multiplied with 3 to get second number of each group as shown below:

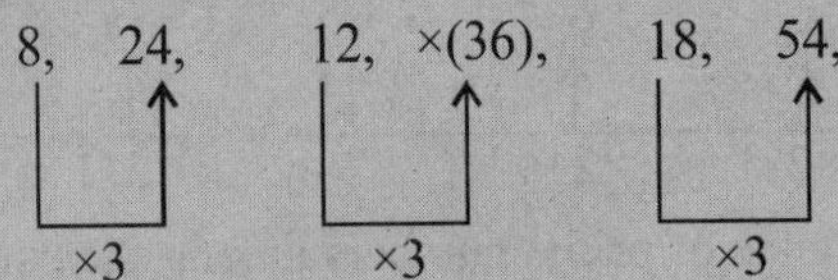

17. D This is a series having numerators and denominators. However, numerators and denominators have their respective series. There is no fractional result. Their respective series is shown as follows:

Numerator Series:

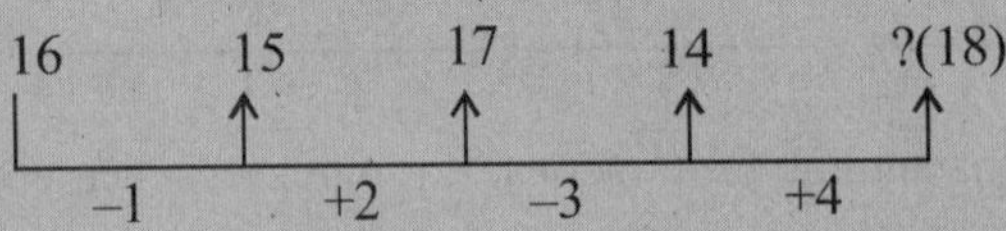

Denominator Series:

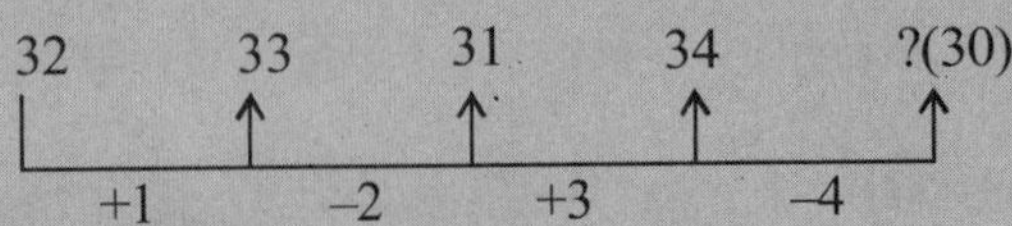

So the answer is: $\frac{18}{30}$

8 Assertion and Reason

CONCEPT

Questions on Assertion and Reason involves understanding of logical reasoning. In this question two statements are given. Out of these one statement is **Assertion (A)** and second one is **Reason (R)**. The statements are of general nature and describe some phenomena. Candidate is to read both A and R and decide whether:

(A) Both A and R are True and R is the correct explanation of A

(B) Both A and R are True but R is not the correct explanation of A

(C) A is True but R is False

(D) A is False But R is True

(E) Both A and R are False

Candidate is to choose one of the options as answer. Choosing correct answer requires candidate's intelligent observation, understanding of given phenomena in both statements, and correlating acumen to choose the right choice.

Significance

Generally, this question is asked in every reasoning paper, but it has been observed that this question has been regularly asked in NET Paper 1 and Paper 2 for the last many years. In Paper 1 this question is asked from Teaching Aptitude, Research Aptitude, Communication, Environment, and Higher Education. It may be asked from any topic, but thorough understanding and regular practice can enable a candidate to master this topic.

Strategy

A candidate is to clearly read both Assertion and Reason. While having thorough understanding of topic from which such question is asked, detecting a relation between the two can help one to find the correct answer. It can be easily ascertained that the phenomenon mentioned in assertion is the result or effect of phenomenon explained in R. A candidate is also supposed to detect independent truth of A and R without having any relation with each other. Further, it is also to be detected whether both A and R are true or false. Sometimes either only A or only R is false. Detecting any of all such forms of A and R will be possible only if the candidate is having complete knowledge of the topic which is stated in A and R.

In NET exam, questions on A and R are asked from theory section of the NET syllabus. There are questions from Teaching Aptitude, Research aptitude, Communication, ICT, People and Environment, and Higher education. In this chapter, questions on A and R from all these sections have been discussed individually with detailed solutions. As answer of this question is to be chosen from five given choices, let us take the answer choice wise examples and try to be convinced as to why a particular answer choice is the answer.

Case 1: Both A and R are true and R is the correct explanation of A

Assertion (A): A healthy teacher–learner interaction yields desired results.

Reason (R): A learner's success is the outcome of teaching–learning ethics adopted during teaching–learning process.

In above case it is evident from A and R that healthy interaction between the teacher and learner is possible if there is true adoption of teaching–learning ethics which ultimately yields the desired result, i.e., success. So here both A and R are true and R is the correct explanation of A.

Case 2: Both A and R are true but R is not correct explanation of A

Assertion (A): Greenhouse gases in the atmosphere trap harmful sunrays.

Reason (R): Carbon monoxide is one of the greenhouse gases.

In above case A is describing a phenomena of greenhouse gases with respect to harmful sunrays which is true. On the other hand, R is describing type of a gas belonging to the group of greenhouse gases. Here, it is quite clear that both A and R are true in their respective framework but R is not elaborating the phenomena described by A. Hence, it is concluded that both A and R are true but R is not correct explanation of A.

Case 3: A is true but R is false

Assertion (A): Dual mode universities impart formal and non-formal education.

Reason (R): Higher education being imparted in different institutes determines the literacy rate of a society.

It is true that dual mode universities offer formal and non-formal education; that's why these are known as dual mode universities. So A is true above. On the other hand R is not true because it is not higher education which determines the literacy rate, rather it is primary education index with which literacy rate is calculated while taking into consideration all literates with the age of seven and above. So R is not true.

Case 4: A is false but R is true

Assertion (A): Summative research is conducted at the beginning of a project.

Reason (R): Objective research is conducted while applying quantitative techniques.

In above case A is false as summative research is conducted after completion of a project to assess its success or failure. On the other hand, R is true because objective research is conducted on natural sciences whereas quantitative techniques are applied to obtain certain specific results.

Case 5: Both A and R are false

Assertion (A): Computer cannot be operated without installing modem.

Reason (R): Trojan is software used to install modem.

In above case both A and R is false. A is false as modem is a device of connectivity and is not used to install a computer. Similarly, R is also false as Trojan is a virus damaging computer software and not an installation software.

SUBJECT-WISE ILLUSTRATIONS OF ASSERTION AND REASON

Questions on assertion and reason have been being frequently asked in the NET paper. It has been observed that there are 4 to 5 questions asked in each attempt pertaining to Teaching Aptitude, Communication, ICT, People and Environment, Higher Education, and Research aptitude. Let us see some subject-wise illustrations as follows:

Assertion–Reason on Teaching Aptitude

Illustration 1

Assertion (A): Outcome-based Education (OBE) is a learner-centered teaching method.

Reason (R): Learners are motivated to learn with concentration and give their feedback.

(A) A is true but R is false

(B) Both A and R are true and R is the correct explanation of A

(C) A is false but R is true. Both A and R are true but R is not correct explanation of A.

Answer: B

Explanation: A is true as it introduces a learner-centered teaching method. R is also true as it explains how OBE is a learner-centered method, so choice B is the answer.

Illustration 2

Assertion (A): Understanding is a level of cognition wherein a learner starts giving feedback.

Reason (R): Different levels of cognitive development make the learner a rational thinker.

A) Both A and R are true and R is the correct explanation of A

B) A is true but R is false

C) Both A and R are true but R is not correct explanation of A.

D) A is false but R is true.

Answer: C

Explanation: Both A and R are true as per theories of cognitive development, but A and R are true in their respective framework. Hence, R does not explain the phenomenon mentioned in A.

Illustration 3

Assertion (A): Individual learning techniques of adolescent learners differ from those of adult learners.

Reason (R): Adult learners learn faster than adolescent learners.

(A) A is true but R is false
(B) Both A and R are true and R is the correct explanation of A
(C) Both A and R are true but R is not correct explanation of A
(D) Both A and R are false

Answer: D

Explanation: A is false as it is not necessary that learning techniques of learners change with growth in age. Difference in techniques of learning is commonly found even in the learners of the same age group. R is also false as it is reverse of what is written in A. Psychomotor skills determine the pace of learning and these are faster in adolescent learners as compared to adult learners.

Illustration 4

Assertion (A): SWAYAM PRABHA is a digital initiative from Government of India to provide universal accessibility to education at all levels.

Reason (R): Courses offered for learning under SWAYAM PRABHA are certified by the university of the concerned state.

(A) Both A and R are true and R is correct explanation of A
(B) A is true but R is false
(C) Both A and R are true but R is not correct explanation of A
(D) A is false but R is true

Answer: B

Explanation: A is conceptually true whereas R is not true as the SWAYAM PRABHA initiative does not cover the aspect of awarding certificates on the courses offered by it to be certified by any university.

Illustration 5

Assertion (A): Learners' characteristics cannot be detected without a sound teaching support system.

Reason (R): Teaching support system builds capacity in teachers to teach learners in an effective way.

(A) Both A and R are false
(B) Both A and R are true but R is not correct explanation of A
(C) A is false but R is true
(D) Both A and R are true and R is correct explanation of A

Answer: C

Explanation: A is false as teaching system does not detect the learners' characteristics; rather such characteristics help in education planning and its execution. R is true as it explains the meaning of the teaching support system.

Assertion–Reason on Research Aptitude

Illustration 1

Assertion (A): Simulative research is conducted on values prevailing in the society.

Reason (R): Various research works on values generally end in ambiguity.

(A) Both A and R are false
(B) Both A and R are true and R is correct explanation of A
(C) A is true but R is false
(D) A is false but R is true

Answer: A

Explanation: A is false as simulative research is conducted on simulators, a highly technical IT device involving computation models, whereas research on values involves qualitative techniques. R is also false as research on values is conducted with proper research methods which end in concrete findings.

Illustration 2

Assertion (A): Positivistic approach to research is objective in nature.

Reason (R): Knowledge of reality is obtained by applying scientific and quantitative research methods.

(A) Both A and R are true but R is not correct explanation of A
(B) A is true but R is false
(C) A is false but R is true
(D) Both A and R are true and R is correct explanation of A

Answer: D

Explanation: A is true as positivistic approach to research works on set principles and laws of nature. R correctly explains the objective nature of positivistic approach to research.

8.4 Assertion and Reason

Illustration 3

Assertion (A): Working hypothesis is a provisionally accepted hypothesis for further research.

Reason (R): Research design is prepared to distribute working hypothesis into subcategories.

(A) Both A and R are true but R is not correct explanation of A

(B) A is true but R is false

(C) Both A and R are false

(D) Both A and R are true but R is not correct explanation of A

Answer: B

Explanation: A is true as it defines working hypothesis and it helps in anticipating findings. R is false as Research design is an action plan for handing research efficiently, it does not distribute working hypothesis further.

Illustration 4

Assertion (A): Snowball sampling technique of data collection is used when size of the targeted population under study is very large.

Reason (R): Sampling technique of data collection depends upon the nature and size of the targeted population.

(A) Both A and R are true and R is correct explanation of A

(B) Both A and R are true and R is not correct explanation of A

(C) A is true but R is false

(D) A is false but R is true

Answer: D

Explanation: A is false as snowball sampling technique for data collection is used when size of targeted population is too small. On the other hand, sampling technique of data collection is chosen as explained in R.

Illustration 5

Assertion (A): Motivation of effective presentation of research work leads to thesis writing.

Reason (R): Thesis contains detailed account of research work from objectives to findings.

(A) Both A and R are true and R is the correct explanation of A

(B) A is true but R is false

(C) Both A and R are true but R is not correct explanation of A

(D) Both A and R are false

Answer: C

Explanation: A is true as explained in A and R is also true as explained in R but these are true in their respective framework only.

Assertion–Reason on Communication

Illustration 1

Assertion (A): Dyadic communication highlights the communicator's purpose.

Reason (R): Feedback is the measure of effective communication.

(A) Both A and R are true and R is the correct explanation of A

(B) Both A and R are true but R is not correct explanation of A

(C) A is true but R is false

(D) A is false but R is true

Answer: B

Explanation: Both A and R are true in their respective format.

Illustration 2

Assertion (A): A formal communication is never complete without phatic communication.

Reason (R): People greet one another before sharing actual message and wish after sharing it.

(A) Both A and R are true and R is correct explanation of A

(B) Both A and R are false

(C) Both A and R are true but R is not correct explanation of A

(D) A is true but R is false

Answer: A

Explanation: A mentions a form of communication and R explains its meaning.

Illustration 3

Assertion (A): Present day mass media of India works under the whip of autocracy.

Reason (R): Mission of 'Edutainment' can be fully achieved through mass media.

(A) A is true but R is false

(B) Both A and R are false

(C) Both A and R are true but R is not correct explanation of A

(D) A is false but R is true

Answer: D

Explanation: A is false as India is a democratic country and whip of autocracy does not exist for any sector. R is true as mass media agency like Prasar Bharati and print media are effective in providing education through entertainment to masses in India.

Illustration 4

Assertion (A): Hierarchy of an organisation observes all directions of communication.

Reason (R): Upward communication is more effective at executive level than subordinate level.

(A) Both A and R are false

(B) A is false but R is true

(C) A is true but R is false

(D) Both A and R are true but R is not correct explanation of A

Answer: C

Explanation: A is true as explained in A. R is false as upward communication is possible at all levels from subordinate to boss and every such communication is effective being statutory and formal in nature.

Illustration 5

Assertion (A): As communication is a flow, it is bound to get barriers.

Reason (R): Distance is the biggest barrier to present day communication.

(A) Both A and R are true but R is not correct explanation of A

(B) Both A and R are false

(C) Both A and R are true and R is the correct explanation of A

(D) A is false but R is true

Answer: B

Explanation: A is false as it is not mandatory for communication flow to get barriers. R is also false as with the advent of communication technology, distance is no more a barrier for present day communication.

Assertion–Reason on Information and Communications Technology

Illustration 1

Assertion (A): Computer is a machine used for solving various complex calculations.

Reason: (R): Computer system consists of hardware and software.

(A) Both A and R are false

(B) A is false but R is true

(C) Both A and R are true and R is correct explanation of AA is true but R is false

Answer: D

Explanation: A is true as mentioned in A. R is false as computer system consists of hardware, software, people, and data.

Illustration 2

Assertion (A): Various socio- economic factors are responsible for creating digital divide.

Reason (R): There is uneven distribution of access to Internet between various sections of the population.

(A) Both A and R are false

(B) A is true but R is false

(C) Both A and R are true and R is correct explanation of ABoth A and R are true but R is not correct explanation of A

Answer: C

Explanation: A is true as it mentions the concept of digital divide. R is true and explains meaning of digital divide.

Illustration 3

Assertion (A): Bhoomi is an ICT project started by Kerala Government.

Reason (R): Total land record has been computerised under the Bhoomi Project.

(A) A is true but R is false

(B) A is false but R is true

(C) Both A and R are true and R is correct explanation of A

(D) Both A and R are true but R is not correct explanation of A

Answer: B

Explanation: A is false as the Bhoomi Project has been started by Karnataka government. R is true as explained in R.

Illustration 4

Assertion (A): Information stored in the Internet is organised like memory in brain.

Reason (R): Internet allows people to perform any operation concerned with any field.

(A) Both A and R are false

(B) A is true but R is false

(C) A is false but R is true

(D) Both A and R are true and R is correct explanation of A

Answer: A

Explanation: A is false as information stored in internet is like pages of a book. R is false as for conducting operations on the computer, a particular software and not Internet is required.

Illustration 5

Assertion (A): E-Kalpa is a digital initiative started by Union Ministry of Human Resource Development (MHRD).

Reason (R): Higher education in India is being imparted through various digital initiatives by the government.

(A) Both A and R are true and R is the correct explanation of A

(B) Both A and R are true but R is not correct explanation of A

(C) Both A and R are false

(D) A is true but R is false

Answer: B

Explanation: Both A and R are true in their respective framework.

Assertion–Reason on People, Development and Environment

Illustration 1

Assertion (A): Ecological footprint determines the level of biodiversity of a region.

Reason (R): Continuous monitoring of ecological footprint prevents environmental pollution.

(A) Both A and R are true and R is correct explanation of A

(B) Both A and R are false

(C) A is true but R is false

(D) A is false but R is true

Answer: B

Explanation: A is false. Ecological footprint is man's demand for natural products. Ecological footprint does not determine level of biodiversity; rather excessive ecological footprint destroys ecosystem. R is also false as monitoring of ecological footprint does not prevent environmental pollution; rather reduction in it does it.

Illustration 2

Assertion (A): Climate experiences undesirable changes due to anthropogenic activities.

Reason (R): Human beings waste natural resources resulting in imbalance of ecosystem.

A) A is false but R is true

B) A is true but R is false

C) Both A and R are true and R is correct explanation of A

D) Both A and R are true but R is not correct explanation of A

Answer: C

Explanation: A is true as it is stating the impact on climate by a particular type of activity. R is true and explains the meaning and nature of anthropogenic activity.

Illustration 3

Assertion (A): E-waste is major contaminator of soil.

Reason (R): Soil pollution results in poor vegetation.

(A) Both A and R are true and R is correct explanation of A

(B) A is false but R is trueBoth A and R are true but R is not correct explanation of A

(C) Both A and R are false

Answer: C

Explanation: Both A and R are true in their respective format. A is true because of excessive littering and dumping of e-waste on ground which enters soil and damage its fertility. R states the effect of soil pollution on vegetation, hence does not explain A, yet it is true.

Illustration 4

Assertion (A): Groundwater floods occur due to excessive precipitation.

Reason (R): Flood mitigation measures reduce the loss occurred due to floods.

(A) Both A and R are true and R is the correct explanation of A

(B) Both A and R are true but R is not correct explanation of A

(C) A is true but R is false

(D) A is false but R is true

Answer: D

Explanation: A is false because groundwater floods occur when there is heavy and persistent rain whereas, precipitation is a process of fall of snow, water vapours, dew, etc. which does not carry an impact like heavy and persistent rainfall. R is true as explained in R.

Illustration 5

Assertion (A): International Solar Alliance is an effort of distributing solar energy among member countries.

Reason (R): International Solar Alliance was founded in Rome in 2015.

(A) A is false but R is true

(B) Both A and R are true but R is not correct explanation of A

(C) Both A and R are true and R is correct explanation of A

(D) A is true but R is false

Answer: D

Explanation: A is presenting fact of International Solar Alliance. R is false because alliance was founded in Paris in 2015.

Assertion–Reason on Higher Education

Illustration 1

Assertion (A): Higher education in India after independence has been taken as a measure of socio-economic development.

Reason (R): Specialised institutes of higher learning cropped up in India after independence.

(A) A is false but R is true

(B) Both A and R are true and R is correct explanation of A

(C) Both A and R are true but R is not correct explanation of A

(D) A is true but R is false

Answer: B

Explanation: A is true as explained in A. R explains A fully as growth of specialised institutes were open to prepare human resources in different socio-economic fields after getting specialised knowledge of a particular field.

Illustration 2

Assertion (A): Institutes of higher learning in India are provided low-cost funds under LEAP scheme.

Reason (R): Institutes of higher learning in India are collaborating with best foreign institutes for better research in higher education.

(A) Both A and R are false

(B) Both A and R are true and R is correct explanation of A

(C) A is false but R is true

(D) A is true but R is false

Answer: C

Explanation: A is false as scheme LEAP (Leadership for Academicians Programme) does not provide low-cost funds to institutes of higher learning. Rather, this scheme works for better leadership in the institutions. It is the scheme RISE (Revitalising Infrastructure and Systems in Education) under which low cost funds are provided. R is true as explained in R as such foreign collaborations are part of initiatives taken by the Government of India to improve research standards in Indian higher education.

Illustration 3

Assertion (A): Higher education in ancient India was not open to all.

Reason (R): Universities of ancient India imparted higher education in Pali language.

(A) A is true but R is false

(B) Both A and R are true but R is not correct explanation of A

(C) A is true but R is false

(D) Both A and R are false

Answer: A

Explanation: A is false as in Buddhist era higher education was not open to disabled and sick. R is false as Pali was a local language in ancient India. It was not considered language of scholars. It was Sanskrit, which became the medium of instruction in higher education system. Further, subjects like Mathematics, Science, and Polity were taught by various universities in India and these could not be taught in Pali due to their technical nature.

Illustration 4

Assertion (A): Deemed universities in India are allowed to award their own degrees.

Reason (R): As per UGC norms Administrative structure of a deemed university is same as of a full-fledged university.

(A) Both A and R are true and R is correct explanation of A

(B) Both A and R are true but R is not correct explanation of A

(C) A is true but R is false

(D) Both A and R are false

Answer: D

Explanation: A is false because a deemed university may or may not awarding degrees until these are allowed by UGC. R is also false as the administrative structure of a deemed university is not the same as many colleges and such institutions are declared deemed universities and these have different administrative structure. For example, deemed universities may not have vice-chancellors but a full-fledged university has a vice-chancellor.

Illustration 5

Assertion (A): Idea of Directive Principles of State Policy in Indian constitution is taken from Constitution of Ireland.

Reason (R): Directive Principles though not justiciable yet guarantee fundamental governance in promoting welfare of the people of India.

(A) Both A and R are true and R is correct explanation of A

(B) A is true but R is false

(C) A is false but R is true

(D) Both A and R are true but R is not correct explanation of A

Answer: D

Explanation: Both A and R are true within their respective framework. Both A and R are stating features of Directive Principles individually.

Practice Exercise

Assertion–Reason Format

1. **Assertion (A):** Quality of teaching in Indian universities is accredited by CABE.

   Reason (R): University education is no more confined to state or central universities.

   (A) Both A and R are true and R is correct explanation of A

   (B) Both A and R are true but R is not correct explanation of A

   (C) A is true but R is false

   (D) A is false but R is true

2. **Assertion (A):** Easy access to ICT has resulted in growth of heinous crimes during past few years.

   Reason (R): ICT has provided extra power to police enabling it to hit hard on crimes and criminals.

   (A) Both A and R are true and R is correct explanation of A

   (B) Both A and R are true but R is not correct explanation of A

   (C) Both A and R are false

   (D) A is true but R is false

3. **Assertion (A):** Communication between transgenders is termed as transpersonal communication.

   Reason (R): There are different types of communication as there are different types of communicators.

   (A) Both A and R are true and R is the correct explanation of A

   (B) Both A and R are true but R is not correct explanation of A

   (C) Both A and R are false

   (D) A is true but R is false

4. **Assertion (A):** Today e-waste is rapidly becoming a major pollutant.

   Reason (R): Widespread littering of e-waste is a big hindrance in the process of its safe and timely disposal.

   (A) Both A and R are true and R is correct explanation of A

   (B) Both A and R are true but R is not correct explanation of A

   (C) Both A and R are false

   (D) A is true but R is false

5. **Assertion (A):** A polished and refined classroom communication helps learners to learn faster.

   Reason (R): A teacher's communication in classroom is always polished and refined.

   (A) Both A and R are true and R is correct explanation of A

   (B) Both A and R are true but R is not correct explanation of A

   (C) A is true but R is false

   (D) A is false but R is true

6. **Assertion (A)**: Non-verbal communication is always part of verbal communication.

   Reason (R): Gestures showed in verbal communication provide strength to communication.

   (A) Both A and R are true and R is correct explanation of A

   (B) Both A and R are true but R is not correct explanation of A

   (C) A is true but R is false

   (D) Both A and R are false

7. **Assertion (A):** A research scholar writes a thesis to fulfill the research commitment he/she has made with his/her guide.

   Reason (R): Thesis is an evidence of research scholar's loyalty towards the guide.

   (A) Both A and R are true and R is correct explanation of A

   (B) Both A and R are true but R is not correct explanation of A

   (C) Both A and R are false

   (D) A is true but R is false

8. **Assertion (A):** Some of the courses being provided by the Central and State universities are the same.

   Reason (R): Central and State universities run those courses which cannot be run by an open university.

   (A) Both A and R are true and R is correct explanation of A

   (B) Both A and R are true but R is not correct explanation of A

   (C) A is true but R is false

   (D) A is false but R is true

9. **Assertion (A):** Some of the teaching traits are idealistic.

   Reason (R): Traits like teacher 'never loses temper' does not work in irritating situations.

   (A) Both A and R are true and R is correct explanation of A

   (B) Both A and R are true but R is not correct explanation of A

   (C) A is true but R is false

   (D) A is false but R is true

10. **Assertion (A):** UN has taken a soft stand towards developing countries as compared to developed countries in fixing targets to curb global warming.

    Reason(R): Industrial revolution is mainly responsible in making developed nations primary emitter of greenhouse gases.

    (A) Both A and R are true and R is correct explanation of A.

    (B) Both A and R are true but R is not correct explanation of A

    (C) Both A and R are false

    (D) A is true but R is false

11. **Assertion: (A):** Learning is not confined to closed classrooms.

    Reason (R): Constructivism believes in learning through interaction of peer groups.

    (A) Both A and R are true and R is correct explanation of A

    (B) Both A and R are true but R is not correct explanation of A

    (C) A is true but R is false

    (D) A is false but R is true

12. **Assertion (A):** Various socio-economic and cultural differences among members of today's society are influenced by the digital divide.

    Reason (R): Certain sections of the society can afford Internet facilities by virtue of their affluence.

    (A) Both A and R are true and R is correct explanation of A

    (B) Both A and R are true but R is not correct explanation of A

    (C) A is true but R is false

    (D) A is false but R is true

13. **Assertion (A):** Equity is one of the measures of good governance.

    Reason (R): All members including most vulnerable ones are empowered to improve and maintain their well-being.

    (A) Both A and R are true and R is correct explanation of A

    (B) Both A and R are true but R is not correct explanation of A

    (C) A is true but R is false

    (D) A is false but R is true

14. **Assertion (A):** Positivistic approach to research covers qualitative and quantitative techniques of research.

    Reason (R): Findings of research through positivistic approach are compatible to objectives of experimental and behavioral research works.

    (A) Both A and R are true and R is correct explanation of A

    (B) Both A and R are true but R is not correct explanation of A

    (C) Both A and R are false

    (D) A is true but R is false

15. **Assertion:** Downward flow of communication does not contribute much in the development of an organisation.

    Reason (R): Different flows of communication in an organisation are measures of its success.

    (A) Both A and R are true and R is correct explanation of A

    (B) Both A and R are true but R is not correct explanation of A

    (C) A is false but R is true

    (D) A is true but R is false

16. **Assertion (A):** All India Survey of Higher Education (AISHE) claims to achieve increasing Gross Enrolment Ratio (GER) in the sphere of higher education.

    Reasoning (R): Rashtriya Uchchatar Shiksha Abhiyaan (RUSA) has been implemented to establish more institutions of higher education in the wake of increasing GER.

    (A) Both A and R are true and R is correct explanation of A

    (B) Both A and R are true but R is not correct explanation of A

    (C) A is false but R is true

    (D) A is true but R is false

17. **Assertion (A):** Aerosols play an important role in climate change.

    Reason (R): Large-sized aerosols suspended in air block sunlight thus making earth's surface cool.

    (A) Both A and R are true and R is correct explanation of A

    (B) Both A and R are true but R is not correct explanation of A

    (C) A is false but R is true

    (D) A is true but R is false

18. **Assertion (A):** Structure of an argument varies with mood of syllogism.

    Reason (R): Categorical propositions constitute mood of syllogism.

    (A) Both A and R are true and R is correct explanation of A

    (B) Both A and R are true but R is not correct explanation of A

    (C) A is false but R is true

    (D) A is true but R is false

19. **Assertion (A):** Sending message through email is better than ordinary post.

    Reason (R): There is quick delivery of message without incurring any cost over it.

    (A) Both A and R are true and R is correct explanation of A

    (B) Both A and R are true but R is not correct explanation of A

    (C) A is false but R is true

    (D) A is true but R is false

20. **Assertion (A):** Beforehand knowledge of learners characteristics helps a teacher to decide whether he is to teach or not.

    Reasoning (R): Teaching stubborn learners is simply a wastage of time.

    (A) Both A and R are true and R is correct explanation of A

    (B) Both A and R are true but R is not correct explanation of A

    (C) Both A and R are false

    (D) A is true but R is false

KEY

1. D A is false as higher education bodies including university education standards are accredited by NAAC. R is true because due to liberalisation in education field, many private and deemed universities have been established to impart higher education.

2. B If ICT has equipped police with most advanced communication gadgets enabling it crack down various nexus and rackets, at the same time it has become one of the reasons of rise in crime rate and criminals are daring to commit heinous crimes.

3. C A is conceptually false. R is also false because there are different types of communication due to different types of communication purposes and channels. Same communicator is found to communicate from different platforms and channels.

4. A Both A and R are right as people do not take disposal of e-waste sincerely. They throw exhausted battery cells, batteries of mobile phone, computer parts, and other electronic devices around either on ground or in water bodies and this open disposal of e-waste is turning it a rapidly becoming major pollutant.

5. C A is true because classroom communication includes communication of both teacher as well as learners and a refined communication from both ends benefits learners to learn faster. R is false because here only teacher's communication is mentioned whereas classroom communication is a bilateral process. Moreover word 'always' also makes it doubtful to be true.

6. D Both A and R are false as both state about verbal communication which includes verbal as well as non-verbal communication. Gestures leave impact in oral communication only.

7. C Here both A and R are false because thesis is written not to fulfill personal commitment; rather it is written to obtain a research degree.

8. C A is true because some of the academic courses of central and state universities are common. R is not true as an open university is a full-fledged university and runs all courses in parallel to central and state universities.

9. A A is true and R rightly elaborates the fact mentioned in A.

10. A Assertion A is true as UNO is stricter with developed nations regarding allotment of time by the end of which emissions should be reduced to a certain percentage as UNO is of the view that due to Industrial Revolution, they started emitting greenhouse gases much earlier than developed countries. Now they have achieved development so they should immediately bring down emissions to the fixed percentage within time allotted. On the other hand, developing countries are still developing and to sustain them in the development process they need industry and manufacturing so the restrictions on emissions are quite soft as targets to reduce emissions and stipulated time. R provides correct explanation of A.

11. C A is true because learners do not learn from formal method only, rather they learn through social interaction. R is not true because constructivism does not propagate what is mentioned in R; rather propagates what is mentioned in A.

12. C A is false as it is not socio-economic differences which are influenced by digital divide; rather it is digital divide which is influenced by socio-economic and cultural differences among members of today's society. R is true as certain affluent sections of society naturally have access to internet and other ICT products and services as they can very well afford it.

13. A A mentions about equity as a measure of good governance and R correctly explains the concept of equity.

14. C Positivistic approach to research believes in using scientific and quantitative techniques and there is no room for qualitative or behavioral approaches. As both A and R in the question advocate that positivistic approach to research considers both quantitative and qualitative methods, that is why both A and R are false.

15. C A is totally false as every flow of communication is instrumental in determining the working health of an organisation. Communication flows in the hierarchy of an organisation determine its success or failure. Execution of directions from the superiors and prompt responses lead to success of an organisation. So A is not true. But R is true as it states the same thing which has been discussed for R.

16. B Both A and R are true in their respective framework. Both are separately showing evidence and policy based development in higher education.

17. A A defines aerosols being responsible for climate change. And R explains how aerosols change climate.

18. B Both A and R are two independent facts.

19. A A regards email better than ordinary post and R explains reason of it.

20. C Both A and R talk against the ethics of teaching and learning.

Questions Asked in Previous NET Exams

Questions on Assertion and Reason have been asked in different NET attempts from theory subjects like Teaching Aptitude, Research Aptitude, Logical Reasoning, Communication, ICT, People, Development, and Environment, and Higher Education. All such questions from NET Paper 1 attempts (2006 to 2019) have been covered in the practice section of all the concerned chapters. Aspirants can refer to those chapters.

9 Analytical Reasoning

CONCEPT

Analytical reasoning, also called Puzzle Test/ Miscellaneous Reasoning, is a part of a reasoning question paper. Such questions have also been part of NET Paper 1. It includes random questions on different aspects of reasoning, making an aspirant use quick decision-making skill while solving such questions. These questions aim at testing the cognitive ability of aspirants. Questions on comparisons of qualities, position of letters in the English alphabet, number puzzles, situation testing, logical reasoning, scheduling of an activity, relationship, fundamentals of mathematics, and any other question based on common sense and observation are asked in various competitive exams.

Strategy

An aspirant is to be fully equipped with overall knowledge of reasoning and basic mathematics. Wording and language of such questions matter a lot. As questions on analytical reasoning do not belong to any topic, aspirant should read every word of the question as some words help an aspirant in taking the right decision. Their use conveys the actual sense of a statement. For example, there is a difference in sense conveyed by words like All, Some, No, All not, Some Not, Most, Is, Am, Are, May, Can, Will, Shall, Generally, Often, and Usually. Any of these words present in any statement are decisive in giving correct answers.

EXAMPLES

Example 1: From the given words, select the word which cannot be formed using the letters of the given word.

ORDINALS

A) DINAR B) ADORN
C) SALON D) IDEAL

Solution: 'IDEAL', There is no 'E' in the given word.

Example 2: If "A" means "subtraction", "B" means "division", "C" means "addition", and "D" means "multiplication", then

330 B 6 A 32 C 45 D 12 = ?

A) 525 B) 547
C) 582 D) 563

Solution: 330 B 6 A 32 C 45 D 12

$\Rightarrow 330 \div 6 - 32 + 45 \times 12$

$\Rightarrow 55 - 32 + 540 \Rightarrow 563$

Example 3: I hire a taxi from my home to go to my workplace. The fare system in the city is such that for the first kilometre, I am charged Rs. 25, and after that, I am charged Rs. 6 per kilometre. If my workplace is 10 km far from my home, what amount do I have to pay if I go by taxi?

A) Rs. 64 B) Rs. 89
C) Rs. 90 D) Rs. 79

Solution: Total amount $= 25 + (10 - 1) \times 6 = 25 + 54 = 79$

Example 4: In a row of cars, red car is 14th from left and 23rd from right. How many cars are there in the row?

A) 36 B) 37
C) 35 D) 34

Solution: Total cars in the row $= 14 + 23 - 1 = 36$

B) Arrange the given words in the sequence in which they occur in the dictionary.

i. Fabric **ii. Face**
iii. Failure **iv. Faculty**

(A) iv, ii, i, iii (B) iii, iv, ii, i
(C) iv, iii, i, ii (D) i, ii, iv, iii

Solution: Fabric
Face
Faculty
Failure

Example 5: If 27 (15) 33
41 (13) 53

then what is the value of 'A' in 26 (A) 35?

(A) 16 (B) 13
(C) 14 (D) 11

Solution: $2 + 7 + 3 + 3 = 15$

$4 + 1 + 5 + 3 = 13$

$2 + 6 + 3 + 5 = 16$

Example 6: In the following number series how many 5s are there which are immediately preceded by a pair of numbers whose product is more than product of the pair of numbers immediately following 5?

3 4 5 3 5 7 8 5 1 9 5 2 4 5 5 1 2 3 5 4 2 5 7 5 6 3 2 5 4 7

A) 4 B) 5

C) 6 D) 2

Solution: (3 4 5 3 5 7 8 51 9 5 2 4 55 1 2 3 5 4 2 5 7 5 6 3 2 5 4 7)

The underlined 5s fulfil the condition.

Example 7: P, Q, R, and T answered an examination. In the results, Q was immediately followed by P but no one was there after P. R was ahead of Q but could not score as much as T. Who scored the second highest?

A) P B) R

C) Q D) T

Solution: (T > R > Q > P)

Direction: Read the following account and answer the question that follows:

M, V, K, D, T, J, and R are seven friends studying in different classes: III, IV, V, VI, VII, VIII, and IXth standards. Each of them likes different colours—Yellow, Blue, Red, White, Black, Green, and Violet. J likes Red and studies in class Vth. R likes Violet and studies in class IIIrd. M studies in class VIIIth and does not like either Green or Yellow. K likes White and does not study either in VIIth or in IVth. D studies in VIth and likes Black. T does not study in IVth. V does not like Green.

Example 8: What is M's favourite colour?

A) Red B) Yellow

C) Green D) Blue

Solution: It is clear by drawing a table as follows:

Friends	Class	Favourite Colour
M	VIIIth	Blue
V	IVth	Yellow
K	IXth	White
D	VIth	Black
T	VIIth	Green
J	Vth	Red
R	IIIrd	Violet

Example 9: Which one will replace the question mark?

5	4	7	8
6	9	5	10
3	7	2	?

A) 1 B) 4

C) 3 D) 6

Solution: $\frac{(5+4+7)}{2} = 8$

$\frac{(6+9+5)}{2} = 10$

$\frac{(3+7+2)}{2} = 6$

Practice Exercise

General Questions Format

1. Seven students P, Q, R, S, T, U, and V take a series of tests. No two students get similar marks. V always scores more than P. P always scores more than Q. Each time either R scores the highest and T gets the lowest or S scores the highest and U or Q scores the lowest. If S is ranked 6th and Q is ranked 5th, which of the following statements can be true?

(A) V is ranked first or fourth

(B) R is ranked second or third

(C) P is ranked second or fourth

(D) U is ranked second or fourth

Directions (Q. 2–3): There are six teachers A, B, C, D, E, and F in a school. Each of these teaches two subjects, one compulsory and the other optional. D's optional subject is History while three others have it as compulsory subject. E and F have Physics as one of their subjects. F's compulsory subject is Mathematics which is an optional subject of both C and E. History and English are A's subjects but in terms of compulsory and optional subjects they are just reverse of those of D. Chemistry is an optional subject of only one of them. The only female teacher in the school has English as her compulsory subject.

2. What is C's compulsory subject?

(A) History (B) Physics

(C) Chemistry (D) None of these

3. Who is lady teacher?

(A) D (B) B

(C) F (D) None of these

Directions (Q. 4–5) Arrange the following in a meaningful order.

4. 1. Birth 2. Death
3. Funeral 4. Marriage
5. Education
(A) 4 5 3 2 1 (B) 2 3 4 5 1
(C) 1 5 4 2 3 (D) None of these

5. 1. Site 2. Plan
3. Rent 4. Money
5. Building
(A) 4 1 2 5 3 (B) 3 4 2 5 1
(C) 2 3 5 1 4 (D) None of these

6. Jeewan is taller than Shyamal, who is taller than Akash. Radhika is shorter than Akash but taller than Raghu, who is taller than Srikant. Who is the tallest?
(A) Jeewan (B) Akash
(C) Radhika (D) Data inadequate

7. If the positions of the letters in the word TWINKLE are rearranged in the alphabetical order, then position of how many letters will remain unchanged?
(A) None (B) Three
(C) Two (D) one

8. 200 toffees are to be distributed among children of a class in equal number. If there were 15 children less, each child would have got 8 toffees. How many children are there in the class?
(A) 25 (B) 40
(C) 45 (D) Can't be determined

9. When X is added to Y, the result is 130% of X. What is the difference between the two numbers?
(A) 70 (B) 65
(C) 21 (D) Can't be determined

10. Day after tomorrow is my birthday. On the same day next week is a festival. Today is Sunday. What will be the day just after the festival?
(A) Tuesday (B) Sunday
(C) Wednesday (D) None of these

11. If 7 spiders make 7 webs in 7 days, then 1 spider will make 1 web in how many days?
(A) 1 day (B) 7 days
(C) 49 days (D) 3.5 days

12. If 47 × 56 = 7645, 78 × 32 = 8273 then 26 × 49 = ?
(A) 4629 (B) 6924
(C) 2964 (D) None of these

13. Ketan takes casual leave only on the first working day of every month. The office has weekly offs on Saturday and Sunday. In a month of 30 days, the first working day happens to be 3rd of the month and it is Tuesday. What will be the day for his next casual leave?
(A) Wednesday (B) Thursday
(C) Friday (D) None of these

14. From Shivaji Bus Terminus buses leave for Meerut every 25 minutes. The enquiry clerk told a passenger that a bus has left for Meerut 10 minutes past 2:00 PM. At what time will the next bus for Meerut leave from Shivaji Terminus?
(A) 2:25 PM (B) 2:40 PM
(C) 2:35 PM (D) None of these

Direction: Study the following information carefully and give answer to question that follows:

Six friends P, Q, R, S, T, and U have different numbers of shirts. The person who has the second highest number of shirts has 25 shirts. P has more shirts than Q but not the highest. S has more shirts than R and U but not more than Q. R has more shirts than only one person.

15. Who among the following has the third lowest number of shirts?
(A) S (B) R
(C) U (D) Q

Q. (16–20) Insert the missing number:

16. Which one will replace the question mark?
(A) 18
(B) 12
(C) 9
(D) 6

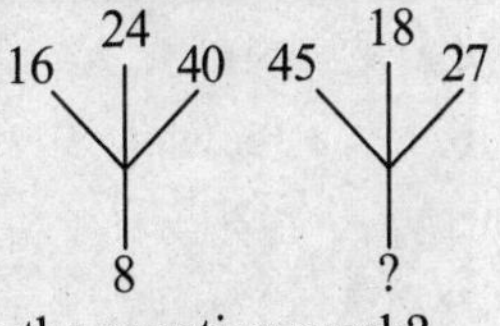

17. Which one will replace the question mark?
(A) 25
(B) 37
(C) 41
(D) 47

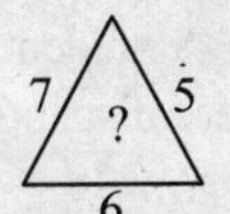

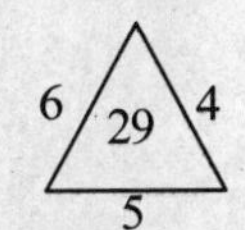

18. Which one will replace the question mark?
(A) 45
(B) 41
(C) 32
(D) 40

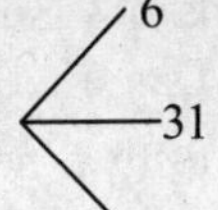

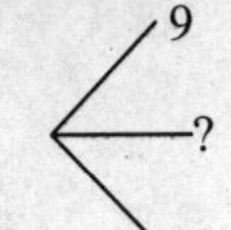

19. Which one will replace the question mark?

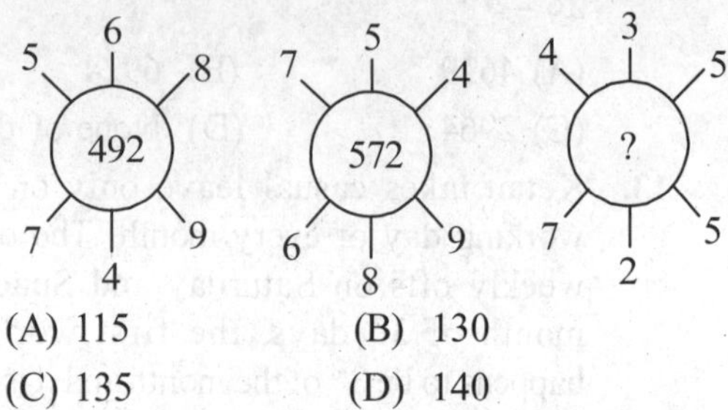

(A) 115 (B) 130

(C) 135 (D) 140

20. Which one will replace the question mark?

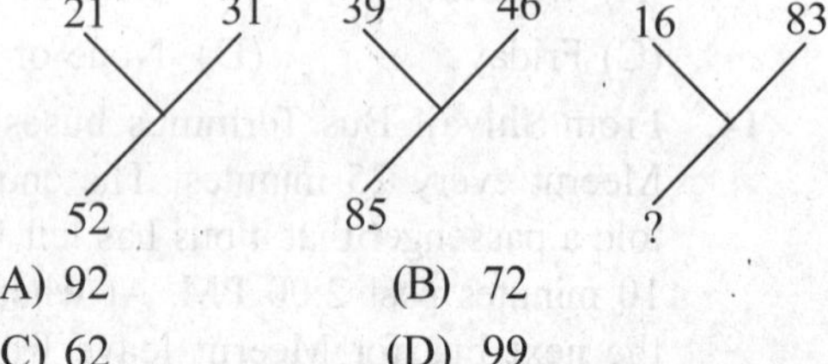

(A) 92 (B) 72

(C) 62 (D) 99

KEY

1. D Rank of Seven students: (In ascending order)

VII	VI	V	IV	III	II	I
T	S	Q	U/P	V/P	U/V	R
(Bottom)						(Top)

2. A

3. A Explanations to question numbers 2 and 3:

Answers are determined by drawing the following table:

TEACHER	COMPULSORY SUBJECT	OPTIONAL SUBJECT
A	HISTORY	ENGLISH
B	HISTORY	CHEMISTRY
C	HISTORY	MATHEMATICS
D	ENGLISH	HISTORY
E	PHYSICS	MATHEMATICS
F	MATHEMATICS	PHYSICS

4. C **5.** A

6. A Jeewan>Shyamal>Akash>Radhika> Raghu >Srikant

7. A

8. B Let total number of children x.

As 5 students are short, per student 8 toffees were distributed. So value of x:

$$\frac{200}{(x-15)} = 8 \Rightarrow 200 = 8(x-15) \Rightarrow x = 40$$

9. D

10. C Today is Sunday →Tomorrow is Monday → Day after tomorrow is Tuesday

So festival next week is also on Tuesday. Day just after the festival is Wednesday.

11. B Time taken to make a web is same irrespective of number of spiders

12. B In each case two extreme numbers across the multiplication sign are coming together. For example:

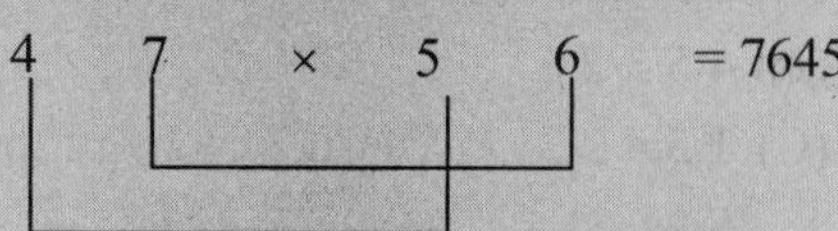

Similar approach is applied to other combinations to find out the right answer, i.e., choice 2.

13. D First working day of the month under question is Tuesday and date is 3rd. We know that after every seven days day of the week repeats itself. So in the present month after 3rd the next Tuesdays during the month will fall on 10th, 17th, and 24th. As month is of 30 days month will end with Monday. Tuesday is the first working day of next month so Ketan will take leave on Tuesday being first working day of the month. As none of the answer choices display Tuesday, answer is 'None of these'.

14. C Next bus for Meerut will be at 2:35 PM, earlier bus left at 10 minutes past 2:00 PM and the bus leaves for Meerut after every 25 minutes. So 25 minutes after 10 minutes past 2:00 PM is accomplished at 2:35 PM.

15. A T > P > Q > S > R > U

|
25

16. C $\frac{(12+18+30)}{10} = 6$; $\frac{(16+24+40)}{10} = 8$

Similarly, $\frac{(45+18+27)}{10} = 9$

17. C $(5 \times 3) + 4 = 19$

and $(6 \times 4) + 5 = 29$

Therefore, $(7 \times 5) + 6 = 41$

18. A $(15 \times 2 - 3) = 27$

$(31 \times 2 - 6) = 56$

and $(45 \times 2 - 9) = 81$

19. B $(5 \times 6 \times 8) + (7 \times 4 \times 9) = 492$

and $(7 \times 5 \times 4) + (6 \times 8 \times 9) = 572$

Therefore $(4 \times 3 \times 5) + (7 \times 2 \times 5) = 130$

20. D $21 + 31 = 52$ and $39 + 46 = 85$

Therefore, $16 + 83 = 99$

Questions Asked in Previous NET Exams

1. Among the five friends Vineet is taller than Monika but not as tall as Ram. Jacob is taller than Dilip but shorter than Monika. Who is the tallest in their group? **(UGC NET JUNE 2019)**
   (A) Ram (B) Monika
   (C) Vineet (D) Jacob

2. Ali buys a glass, a pencil box, and a cup and pays Rs. 21 to the shopkeeper. Rakesh buys a cup, two pencil boxes, and a glass and pays Rs. 28 to the shopkeeper. Preeti buys two glasses, a cup, and two pencil boxes and pays Rs. 35 to the shopkeeper. The cost of 10 cups will be **(UGC NET JANUARY 2017)**
   (A) Rs. 40 (B) Rs. 60
   (C) Rs. 80 (D) Rs. 70

3. Namita and Samita are brilliant and studious. Anita and Karabi are obedient and irregular. Babita and Namita are irregular but brilliant. Samita and Kabita are regular and obedient. Who among them is/are brilliant, obedient, regular, and studious? **(UGC NET DECEMBER 2014)**
   (A) Samita alone (B) Namita and Samita
   (C) Kabita alone (D) Anita alone

4. One writes all numbers from 50 to 99 without the digits 2 and 7. How many numbers have been written? **(UGC NET JUNE 2014)**
   (A) 32 (B) 36
   (C) 40 (D) 38

5. In this series 6, 4, 1, 2, 2, 8, 7, 4, 2, 1, 5, 3, 8, 6, 2, 2, 7, 1, 4, 1, 3, 5, 8, 6
   How many pairs of successive numbers have a difference of 2 each?
   (UGC NET DECEMBER 2013)
   (A) 4 (B) 5
   (C) 6 (D) 8

6. Ananaya and Krishna can speak and follow English. Bulbul can write and speak Hindi as Archana does. Archana talks with Ananya also in Bengali. Krishna cannot follow Bengali. Bulbul talks with Ananya in Hindi. Who can speak and follow English, Hindi, and Bengali?
   (UGC NET DECEMBER 2013)
   (A) Archana (B) Bulbul
   (C) Ananya (D) Krishna

7. Yadav, Arjun, Rajesh, and Kamal play cricket. Rajesh and Kamal play tennis but do not play football. Yadav does not play Badminton but plays golf. Arjun does not play tennis. Kamal sometimes plays badminton. Who does play only cricket? **(UGC NET SEPTEMBER 2013)**
   (A) Yadav (B) Arjun
   (C) Rajesh (D) Kamal

8. The odd numbers from 1 to 45 which are exactly divisible by 3 are arranged in an ascending order. The number at 6th position is **(UGC NET JUNE 2013)**
   (A) 18 (B) 24
   (C) 33 (D) 36

9. Suppose A means minus (–), B means multiplied by (x), C means divided by (/), and D means plus (+). The value of 90 D 9 a 29 C 10 B 2 is **(UGC NET DECEMBER 2012)**
   (A) 8 (B) 10
   (C) 12 (D) 14

10. If Ram knows that y is an integer greater than 2 and less than 7 and Hari knows that y is an integer greater than 5 and less than 10, then they may correctly conclude that **(UGC NET JUNE 2012)**
    (A) y can be exactly determined
    (B) y may be either of two values
    (C) y may be any of three values
    (D) there is no value of y satisfying these conditions

11. How many numbers between 100 and 300 begin or end with 2?
    (UGC NET DECEMBER 2011)
    (A) 100 (B) 110
    (C) 120 (D) 180

12. In a college having 300 students, every student reads 5 newspapers and every newspaper is read by 60 students. The number of newspapers required is **(UGC NET DECEMBER 2011)**
    (A) at least 30 (B) at most 20
    (C) exactly 25 (D) exactly 5

13. How many 8's are there in the following sequence which are preceded by 5 but not immediately followed by 3? **(UGC NET JUNE 2011)**
    5 8 3 7 5 8 6 3 8 5 4 5 8 4 7 6 5 5 8 3 5 8 7 5 8 2 8 5
    (A) 4 (B) 5
    (C) 7 (D) 3

14. If a rectangle were called a circle, a circle a point, a point a triangle, and a triangle a square, the shape of a wheel is **(UGC NET JUNE 2011)**

(A) Rectangle (B) Circle
(C) Point (D) Triangle

15. If 5472 = 9, 6342 = 6, 7584 = 6, what is 9236? **(UGC NET DECEMBER 2010)**

(A) 2 (B) 3
(C) 4 (D) 5

16. Three individuals X, Y, and Z hired a car on a sharing basis and paid Rs. 1,040. They used it for 7, 8, and 11 hours, respectively. What are the charges paid by Y? **(UGC NET DECEMBER 2009)**

(A) Rs. 290 (B) Rs. 320
(C) Rs. 360 (D) Rs. 440

17. There are five books A, B, C, D, and E. The book C lies above D, the book E is below A and B is below E. Which is at the bottom? **(UGC NET DECEMBER 2008)**

(A) E (B) B
(C) A (D) C

18. If an article is sold for Rs. 178 at a loss of 11%; what would be its selling price in order to earn a profit of 11%? **(UGC NET JUNE 2008)**

(A) Rs. 222.50 (B) Rs. 267
(C) Rs. 222 (D) Rs. 220

19. Which one of the following statements is completely nonsensical? **(UGC NET DECEMBER 2006)**

(A) He was a bachelor, but he married recently.
(B) He is a bachelor, but he married recently.
(C) When he married, he was not a bachelor.
(D) When he was a bachelor, he was not married.

20. Which of the following statements say the same thing? **(UGC NET DECEMBER 2006)**

(i) "I am a teacher" (said by Arvind)
(ii) "I am a teacher" (said by Binod)
(iii) "My son is a teacher" (said by Binod's father)
(iv) "My brother is a teacher" (said by Binod's sister)
(v) "My brother is a teacher" (said by Binod's only sister)
(vi) "My sole enemy is a teacher" (said by Binod's only enemy)

Choose the correct answer from the code given below:

Code:

(A) (i) and (ii) (B) (ii), (iii), (iv), and (v)
(C) (ii) and (vi) (D) (v) and (vi)

21. Which of the following are correct ways of arguing? **(UGC NET DECEMBER 2006)**

(i) There can be no second husband without a second wife.
(ii) Anil is a friend of Bob, Bob is a friend of Raj, hence Anil is a friend of Raj.
(iii) A is equal to B, B is equal to C, hence A is equal to C.
(iv) If everyone is a liar, then we cannot prove it.

Choose the correct answer from the code given here:

Code:

(A) (iii) and (iv) (B) (i), (iii), and (iv)
(C) (ii), (iii), and (iv) (D) (i), (ii), (iii), and (iv)

22. Which of the following statement/s are ALWAYS FALSE? **(UGC NET DECEMBER 2006)**

(i) The sun will not rise in the East some day.
(ii) A wooden table is not a table.
(iii) Delhi city will be drowned under water.
(iv) Cars run on water as fuel.

Choose the correct answer from the code given below:

Code:

(A) (i), (iii), and (iv) (B) Only (iii)
(C) (i), (ii), and (iii) (D) (ii) alone

23. Which of the following statements is/are absolutely impossible? **(UGC NET DECEMBER 2004)**

(a) A woman giving birth to her own grandchild
(b) A man attending his own funeral
(c) The sun not rising in the East someday
(d) Cars running without petrol

Chose the correct answer from the codes given below:

Codes:

(A) (a) and (b) (B) (c) and (d)
(C) (b) (D) (a)

24. Which of the following statements say the same thing? **(UGC NET DECEMBER 2004)**

a) "I am clever" (said by Rama)
b) "I am clever" (said by Raju)
c) "My son is clever" (said by Rama's father)
d) "My brother is clever" (said by Rama's sister)
e) "My brother is clever" (said by Rama's only sister)
f) "My sole enemy is clever" (said by Rama's only enemy)

Chose the correct answer from the codes given below:

Codes:

(A) (a), (c), (d), (e), and (f)
(B) (a) and (b)
(C) (d) and (e)
(D) (a) and (f)

KEY

1. A Comparison of heights of Vineet, Monika, Ram, Jacob, and Dilip as per conditions in the question:

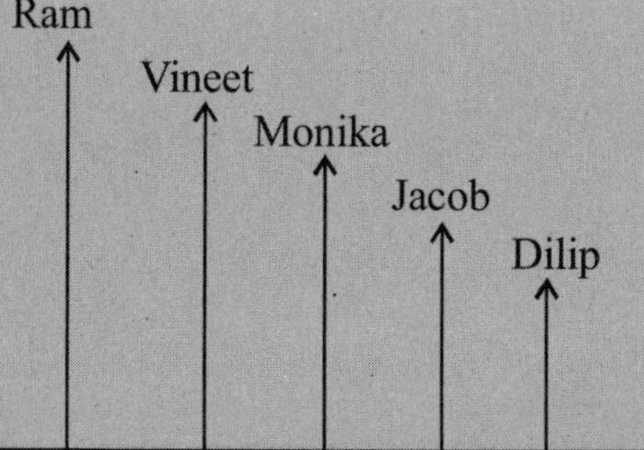

Heights of arrows indicate heights of five friends. As per condition in the question, above sketch of comparative heights has been drawn. According to this Ram is the tallest in the group.

2. D To solve this question pencil box is written as P, glass as G, and cup as C.

Ali's Purchase:

G + P + C = 21................I

Rakesh's Purchase:

G + 2P + C = 28..............II

From here price of a pencil box is:

28 – 21 = 7

So price of pencil box = Rs. 7

Preeti's Purchase:

2G + C + 2P = 35.....................III

Here, price of one glass: 35 – 28 = 7

Now when price of one P and one G is Rs. 7 each, then

Equation I reveals that price of one cup is Rs. 7

So price of 10 cups: 10 x 7 = Rs. 70

3. A This can be solved by drawing following table:

Name	Brilliant	Studious	Obedient	Regular
Namita	✓	✓		x
Samita	✓	✓	✓	✓
Anita			✓	x
Karabi			✓	x
Babita	✓			x
Kabita			✓	✓

4. A Number of digits from 50 – 59 except 52 and 57 = 8............(I)

Number of digits between 60 – 69 except 62 and 67 = 8 ....(II)

Number of digits between 80 – 89 except 82 and 87 = 8...........(III)

(Numbers between 70 and 79 are not considered as these are having 7 in them)

Number of digits between 90 – 99 except 92 and 97 = 8.............(IV)

Now the total number of digits from 50 to 99 = 32 (8 + 8 + 8 + 8)

5. C First pair: 6 and 4

Second pair: 4 and 2

Third pair: 5 and 3

Fourth pair: 8 and 6

Fifth pair: 1 and 3

Sixth pair: 8 and 6

6. C It can be solved by drawing following table:

Name	**Hindi**	**Bengali**	**English**
Ananya	✓	✓	✓
Krishna		×	✓
Bulbul	✓		
Archna	✓	✓	

7. B

Name	Cricket	Tennis	Football	Badminton	Golf
Yadav	✓			×	✓
Arjun	✓	×			
Rajesh	✓	✓	×		
Kamal	✓	✓	×	✓	

From above it is clear that Arjun plays cricket only.

8. C The first six odd numbers between 1 – 45 divisible by 3 in ascending order are:

3, 9, 15, 21, 27, 33

Hence 33 is at sixth position.

9. D The given equation is:90 D 9 A 29 C 10 B 2

After substituting the values equation is: $90 + 9 - 29 \div 10 \times 2$

$$\Rightarrow 99 - \frac{29}{10} \times 2 = 70$$

10. A Ram's Knowledge: $2 < y < 7$

Hari's Knowledge: $5 < y < 10$

Numbers between 2 and 7 = 3, 4, 5, 6

Numbers between 5 and 10 = 6, 7, 8, 9

Value of y must fulfil both the conditions above. According to that value of y cannot be 3, 4, or 5 as these values do not fulfil the second condition, i.e., 5 < **y**. It can also not be 7, 8, 9 as these values do not fulfil the condition that is **y** < 7. So value of **y** should be that number which should justify the knowledge of both Ram and Hari. That value is 6. So **y** = 6

11. B In this question numbers either beginning or ending with 2 are to be counted between 101 and 299. So the required numbers in the ascending order go like this:

102,112,122,132,142,152,162,172,182, 192 and after that 100 numbers from 200 t0 299

So the total numbers which are either starting or ending with 2 between 100 and 300 are 110.

12. C It is given that: Total number of students = 300

Every student reads 5 newspapers, total readability: $300 \times 5 = 1500$

Every newspaper covers 60 students.

So total number of required newspapers

$$= \frac{1500}{60} = 25$$

So exactly 25 newspapers are required.

13. A Underlining those 8's in the series which are preceded by 5 but not immediately followed by 3, then series look like this:

58375863854584765583587582 85

So there are 4 such 8s.

14. C Requires knowledge of coding-decoding

15. A Establishing equality between 5472 and 9:

$5 + 4 + 7 + 2 = 18$

Further segregating digits of number 18 like $1 + 8 = 9$

In this way 5472 = 9

Similarly: $6 + 3 + 4 + 2 = 15 \Rightarrow 1 + 5 = 6$

$7 + 5 + 8 + 4 = 24 \Rightarrow 2 + 4 = 6$

So $9 + 2 + 3 + 6 = 20 \Rightarrow 2 + 0 = 2$

16. B Total hours used by X, Y, and Z = 7 + 8 + 11 = 26

Total charges paid = 1040

Per hour charges: $\frac{1040}{26} = 40$

As Y used 8 hours, charges paid by Y: 40 x 8 = 320

17. B Position of books is like this:

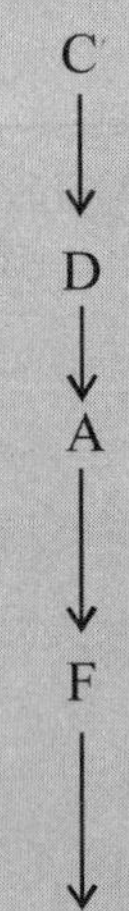

B Sol book B is at the bottom

18. C Let the cost price (CP) be x.

89% of x = 178

$$\Rightarrow \frac{89}{100} \times X = 178 \Rightarrow X = 178 \times \frac{100}{89} = 200$$

Now CP is 200 and profit 11%

So Selling price (SP) is: $\frac{111}{100} \times 200 = 222$

19. B Paradoxical statement yielding no sense.

20. B Statements are self-explanatory.

21. A Statements are self-explanatory.

22. A Statements are self-explanatory.

23. A Statements are self-explanatory.

24. A Statements are self-explanatory.

10 Profit and Loss

CONCEPT

Cost Price: The price at which an article is purchased, is called its **cost price**, abbreviated as **CP.**

Selling Price: The price at which an article is sold, is called its **selling price**, abbreviated as **SP.**

Profit or Gain: If SP is greater than CP, the seller is said to have a **profit** or **gain.**

Loss: If SP is less than CP, the seller is said to have incurred a **loss.**

IMPORTANT FORMULAE

1. Gain = (SP) – (CP)
2. Loss = (CP) – (SP)
3. Loss or gain is always reckoned on CP
4. Gain Percentage: (Gain %) = $\left[\frac{\text{Gain} \times 100}{\text{CP}}\right]$
5. Loss Percentage (Loss %) = $\left[\frac{\text{Loss} \times 100}{\text{CP}}\right]$
6. SP = $\left[\frac{(100 + \text{Gain\%})}{100} \times \text{CP}\right]$
7. SP = $\left[\frac{(100 - \text{Loss\%})}{100} \times \text{CP}\right]$
8. CP = $\left[\frac{100}{(100 + \text{Gain\%})} \times \text{SP}\right]$
9. CP = $\left[\frac{100}{100 - \text{Loss\%}} \times \text{SP}\right]$
10. If an article is sold at a gain of say 40%, then SP = 140% of CP
11. If an article is sold at a loss of say, 40% then SP = 60% of CP
12. When a person sells two similar items, one at a gain of say *x*%, and the other at a loss of x%, then the seller always incurs a loss given by:

$$\text{Loss\%} = \left(\frac{\text{Common Loss and Gain\%}}{10}\right)^2 = \left(\frac{x}{10}\right)^2$$

Practice Exercise

General Questions Format

1. By selling 45 lemons for Rs. 40, a man loses 20%. How many should he sell for Rs. 24 to gain 20% in the transaction?
   (A) 16 (B) 18
   (C) 20 (D) 22

2. If the cost price of 12 pens is equal to the selling price of 8 pens, the gain percent is?
   (A) 12% (B) 30%
   (C) 50% (D) 60%

3. The percentage profit earned by selling an article for Rs. 1920 is equal to the percentage loss incurred by selling the same article for Rs. 1280. At what price should the article be sold to make 25% profit?
   (A) Rs. 2000 (B) Rs. 2200
   (C) Rs. 2400 (D) Data inadequate

4. If 8 books bought at prices ranging from Rs. 200 to Rs. 350 per book are sold at prices ranging from Rs. 300 to Rs. 425 per book, what is the greatest possible profit that might be made in selling eight books?
   (A) 600 (B) 1200
   (C) 1800 (D) Data inadequate

5. Tarun got 30% concession on the labelled price of an article and sold it for Rs. 8750 with 25% profit on the price he bought. What was the labelled price?
   (A) 10000 (B) 12000
   (C) 13000 (D) 14000

6. If the cost price is 25% of selling price, then what is the profit percent?
   (A) 150% (B) 200%
   (C) 300% (D) 350%

7. The cost price of 20 articles is the same as the selling price of x articles. If the profit is 25%, then the value of x is:
   (A) 15
   (B) 16
   (C) 18
   (D) 25

8. A man buys oranges at Rs. 5 a dozen and an equal number at Rs. 4 a dozen. He sells them at Rs. 5.50 a dozen and makes a profit of Rs. 50. How many oranges does he buy?
   (A) 30 dozen (B) 40 dozen
   (C) 50 dozen (D) 60 dozen

9. A person incurs a loss of 5% by selling a watch for Rs. 1140. At what price should the watch be sold to earn 5% profit?
   (A) Rs. 1200 (B) Rs. 1230
   (C) Rs. 1260 (D) Rs. 1290

10. A trader sold an article at a loss of 5% but when he increased the selling price by Rs. 65 he gained 3.33% on the cost price. If he sells the same article at Rs. 936, what is the profit percentage?
    (A) 15% (B) 16.75%
    (C) 20% (D) Data insufficient

11. A retailer buys a radio for Rs. 225. His overhead expenses are Rs. 15. He sells the radio for Rs. 300. The profit percent of the retailer is
    (A) 10% (B) 50%
    (C) 25% (D) 52%

KEY

1. B Let SP of 45 lemons be Rs. x

Then, 80 : 40 = 120 : x

i.e., $\frac{80}{40}=\frac{120}{x} \Rightarrow 80x = 210 \times 40$

$\Rightarrow x = \frac{120 \times 40}{80} = 60$

For Rs. 60, lemons sold = 45

For Rs. 24, lemons sold = $\frac{45}{60} \times 24 = 18$

2. C We know we will need gain amount to get gain percent. So let us get gain first.

Let the cost price of 1 pen be Re 1

Cost of 8 pens = Rs. 8

Selling price of 8 pens = 12

Gain = 12 – 8 = 4

$\text{Gain\%} = \frac{\text{Gain}}{\text{cost}} \times 100 \Rightarrow \frac{4}{8} \times 100 = 50\%$

3. **A** Let CP be Rs. x

$$CP \Rightarrow \frac{1920-x}{x}\times 100 = \frac{x-1280}{x}\times 100$$

$1920 - x = x - 1280 \Rightarrow 2x = 3200$

$\Rightarrow x = 1600$

Required SP = 125% of Rs. 1600

$$= \frac{125}{100}\times 1600 = \text{Rs.} 2000$$

4. **C** Least cost price = Rs. (200 × 8) = Rs. 1600

Greatest Selling Price = Rs. (425 × 8)

= Rs. 3400

Required profit = Rs. (3400 – 1600) = Rs. 1800

5. **A** $\text{Cost Price} = \frac{100}{125}\times 8750 = 7000$

Let the labelled price be Rs. X

$$\text{Then } \frac{70}{100}\times X = 7000$$

$$\Rightarrow X = 7000\times\frac{100}{70} = 10000$$

6. **C** Let the SP = 100, then CP = 25, Profit = 75

$$\text{Profit\%} = \frac{75}{25}\times 100 = 300\%$$

7. **B** Let CP of each article be Re. 1, then CP of × articles = Rs. x

SP of × articles = Rs. 20.

Profit = Rs. $(20 - x)$

$$\frac{20-x}{x}\times 100 = 25 = 2000 - 100x = 25x$$

$\Rightarrow 25x + 100x = 2000 \Rightarrow x = 16$

8. **C** Cost price of 2 dozen oranges Rs. (5 + 4) = Rs. 9

Selling price of 2 dozen oranges = Rs. 11

Profit: 11 – 9 = 2

If profit is Rs. 2, oranges bought = 2 dozen

If profit is Rs. 50, oranges bought

$$= \frac{2}{2}\times 50 = 50 \text{ Dozen}$$

9. **C** Let CP be Rs. 100. First to calculate CP on 5% loss, by applying the formula:

$$CP = \left[\frac{100}{100 - \text{Loss\%}}\times SP\right]$$

$$\Rightarrow \left[\frac{100}{95}\times 1140\right] = 1200$$

Now new SP with 5% profit:

$$SP = \left[\frac{100 + \text{Gain\%}}{100} x CP\right]$$

$$\Rightarrow \left[\frac{105}{100}\times 1200\right] = 1260$$

Hence, desired SP is Rs. 1260

10. **C** 103.33 CP – 0.95 CP = 65

CP = Rs. 780

$$\text{Profit \%} = \left[\frac{936-780}{780}\times 100\right] = 20\%$$

11. **C** Cost price = (225 + 15) = 240

Selling price = 300

$$\text{Gain \%} = \frac{60}{240}\times 100 = 25\%$$

Questions Asked in Previous NET Exams

1. Sanjay sold an article at a loss of 25%. If the selling price had been increased by Rs. 175, there would have been a gain of 10%. What was the cost price of the article?

(UGC NET JUNE 2019)

(A) Rs. 350 (B) Rs. 400
(C) Rs. 500 (D) Rs. 750

2. A trader mixes three varieties of refined oil costing Rs. 100, Rs. 40, and Rs. 60 per litre in the ratio of 2 : 4 : 3 in terms of litre and sells the mixture at Rs. 66 per litre. What percentage of profit he makes?

(UGC NET JUNE 2019)

(A) 12% (B) 10%
(C) 9% (D) 8%

3. If an article is sold for Rs. 178 at a loss of 11%; what would be its selling price in order to earn a profit of 11%?

(UGC NET JUNE 2008)

(A) Rs. 222.50 (B) Rs. 267
(C) Rs. 222 (D) Rs. 220

KEY

1. 3 Let cost price = x

   Loss = 25%

   Profit = 10%

   Difference in sale price = 175

   So $\frac{110}{100}x - \frac{75}{100}x = 175 \Rightarrow 35x$

   $= 17500 \Rightarrow x = \frac{17500}{35} = 500$

   Therefore cost price is Rs. 500

2. B Ratio of oils in mixture= 2 : 4 : 3

   Selling price of mixture = Rs. 66 per litre

   Cost of oils per litre = Rs. 100, Rs. 40, and Rs. 60 respectively

   Total cost = 2 × 100 + 4 × 40 + 3 × 60

   = Rs. 540

   Total selling price = (66 × 9) = Rs. 594

   {here 9 = 2 + 4 + 3}

   Profit = Rs. (594 – 540) = Rs. 54

   Profit % = $\frac{54}{540} \times 100 = 10\%$

3. C Loss 11%

   SP = Rs. 178

   Loss: (100 – 11) = Rs. 89

   Finding out the cost price (CP)

   $= \frac{100}{89} \times 178 = 200$

   so the cost price is Rs. 200

   Now, if profit is 11%, then selling price

   $= \frac{111}{100} \times 200 = 222$

   Hence selling price for bringing 11% profit is Rs. 222, i.e., answer choice C

11 Ages

CONCEPT

Age of a subject whether living or non-living, is its total life span. As the time passes, number of years is added to the current age and life span starts getting shortened. In various competitive exams the questions on ages are related to present, past, and future age of human beings and are quite popular with the paper setters. Before going ahead, let us understand the relationship among the different phases of age:

(Imp: In all questions on ages, the age to be calculated is assumed to be x and value of x is solved while making an equation.)

Present Age: Current Age.

Let the present age of an individual be x. Present age in the question is indicated by using helping verb 'is' or 'are'.

Past Age: Age a few years ago. For example, 5 years ago, then an individual's age was x – 5. Past age in the question is indicated by use of words 'was' or 'were' or 'ago' or 'before'.

Future Age: Age after a few years. After 5 years, the individual's age will be x + 5. Future age is indicated in the question by using word 'after' or 'hence' or 'will' or 'shall'.

Practice Exercise

General Questions Format

1. The ratio of the ages of Mohan and Sohan is 3 : 4. Twelve years hence, their ages will be in the ratio of 5 : 6. What will be Sohan's age after 6 years?

(A) 30 (B) 55
(C) 32 (D) 45

2. Ramu was 4 times as old as his son 8 years ago. After 8 years, Ramu will be twice as old as his son. What are their present ages?

(A) 8, 16 (B) 16, 40
(C) 32, 16 (D) 16, 64

3. A man is four times as old as his son. Five years ago, the man was nine times as old as his son was at that time. What is the present age of the man?

(A) 40 (B) 49
(C) 52 (D) 32

4. The sum of the ages of Aruna and her mother is 49 years. Also, 7 years ago, the mother's age was 4 times Aruna's age. Find the present age of Aruna's mother.

(A) 25 (B) 35
(C) 40 (D) 45

5. The ages of A and B differ by 16 years. If 6 years ago, the elder one was 3 times as old as the younger one, find their present ages.

(A) 14, 30 (B) 16, 32
(C) 20, 40 (D) 55, 65

6. The ages of Ram and Mukta are in the ratio of 3 : 5. After 9 years, the ratio of their ages will becomes 3 : 4. The present age of Mukta (in years) is:

(A) 9 (B) 15
(C) 18 (D) 24

7. A father is twice as old as his son. 20 years ago, the age of the father was 12 times the age of the son. The present age of the father (in years) is:

(A) 44 (B) 32

(C) 22 (D) 45

8. One year ago, Mrs Promila was four times as old as her daughter Swati. Six years hence, Mrs Promila's age will exceed her daughter's age by 9 years. The ratio of the present ages of Promila and her daughter is:

(A) 9 : 2 (B) 11 : 3

(C) 12 : 5 (D) 13 : 4

9. Sachin was twice as old as Ajay 10 years back. How old is Ajay today if Sachin will be 40 years old 10 years hence?

(A) 20 years (B) 10 years

(C) 30 years (D) 40 years

10. If 6 years are subtracted from the present age of Gulzar and the remainder is divided by 18, then the present age of his grandson Anup is obtained. If Anup is 2 years younger to Mahesh whose age is 5 years, then what is the present age of Gulzar?

(A) 96 years (B) 84 years

(C) 48 years (D) 60 years

11. The total of the age of A, B, and C at present is 90 years. Ten years ago, the ratio of their ages was 1:2:3. What is the age of B at present?

(A) 40 years (B) 30 years

(C) 20 years (D) 18 years

KEY

1. **A** Let Mohan's age be 3x and Sohan's age be 4x

After 12 years Mohan's age is 3x+12 and Sohan's age is 4x + 12

Ages after 12 years = $\left(\frac{3x+12}{4x+12}\right) = \frac{5}{6}$

By cross multiplying value of x = 6So Mohan's present age is 6 × 3 = 18

Sohan's present age = 6 × 4 = 24

So Sohan's age after 6 years = 30

2. **B** 8 years ago, age of Ramu's son = x

Ramu's age = 4x

After 8 years age of Ramu's son = x + 16

Ramu's age = 4x + 16

- *16 years have been added as ages have been assumed to be x and 4x eight years ago. After 8 years means 8 years from now. So 8 years from past to present and 8 years from present to future. So 8 + 8 = 16*

After 8 years Ramu's and his son's age equation is:

2(x + 16) = 4x + 16

By solving for x value of x = 8

So 8 years ago age of Ram's son was 8 and Ramu's age was 4 × 8 = 32

Now their present ages are 8 + 8 = 16 and 32 + 8 = 40

Hence, choice number B is the answer.

3. **D** Let present age of son = x and present age of man = 4x

5 years ago son's age was x – 5 and man's age was 4x – 5

Equation of ages:

9(x – 5) = 4x – 5 by solving for x, value of x is 8. So man's present age = 8 × 4 = 32

Hence, choice number D is the answer.

4. **B** Given that Aruna's age + Mother's age = 49

Let Aruna's age = x

Age of Aruna's mother = 49 – x

7 years ago Aruna's age = x – 7 and mother's age = 49 – x – 7

Equation: 4(x – 7) = 49 – x – 7

While solving for x value of x = 14

So Aruna's present age = 14 and mother's present age = 49 – 14 = 35

So choice number B is the answer.

5. **A** Given that age of A and B differ by 16 years

Let elder's age = x

Younger's age = x – 16

6 years ago:

Elder's age = x – 6 and

Younger's age = x – 16 – 6

Equation:

3(x – 16 – 6) = x – 6

After solving for x, value of x comes out to be 30.

So elder's present age = 30 and younger's present age = 30 – 16 = 14.

Hence, choice number A is the answer.

6. B Given that ratio of Ram's and Mukta's age = 3 : 5

After 9 years their ratio will be 3 : 4

Let present ages of Ram and Mukta be 3x and 5x respectively.

After 9 years Ram's age = 3x + 9 and Mukta's age = 5x + 9

Equation: $\frac{(3x+9)}{(5x+9)} = \frac{3}{4}$

After solving for x value of x comes out to be 3.

So the present age of Ram is 3 × 3 = 9 and present age of Mukta is 5 × 3 = 15

Hence, choice number B is the answer.

7. A Given that father is twice the age of his son.

Let son's age = x and father's age = 2x

20 years ago son's age = x – 20.

Father's age = 2x – 20

As father was 12 times the age of his son, the equation is

12(x – 20) = 2x – 20

After solving for x, value of x is 22

Present age of son = 22

Present age of father = 2 × 22 = 44

Hence, choice number A is the answer.

8. D Given that 1 year ago Promila was 4 times the age of her daughter Swati.

Let Swati's age 1 year ago = x and Promila's age 1 year ago = 4x

After six years from present

Swati's age = x + 7 (1 + 6)

Similarly, Promila's age = 4x + 7 (1 + 6)

Equation: x + 7 + 9 = 4x + 7

After solving for x, value of x is 3

So 1 year ago Swati's age = 3 and Promila's age = 4 × 3 = 12

Present ages of Swati and Promila are 4 and 13 hence ratio is 13 : 4.

Hence, choice number D is the answer.

9. A Given that 10 years ago Sachin was twice the age of Ajay.

Let Ajay's age 10 years ago = x

Similarly, Sachin's age 10 years ago = 2x

After 10 years from now Sachin's age will be 40

Equation: 2x + 20 = 40

After solving for x, value of x comes out to be 10

So Ajay's present age = 10 + 10 = 20 years (as value of x pertains to the period 10 years back)

Hence, choice number A is the answer.

10. D While following instructions from the question, following equation is obtained:

$\frac{(\text{Gulzar's Age} - 6)}{18} = \text{Anup's Age}$

Let Gulzar's age = x

Filling the values in above equation we get:

$\frac{(x-6)}{18} = 3$

After solving for x, value of x = 60 and that is Gulzar's age.

Hence, choice number D is the answer.

11. B Given that total age of A, B, and C is 90 years.

10 years ago ratio of their ages was 1 : 2 : 3

Let their ages be 10 years ago: x, 2x and 3x

Total age of A, B, and C 10 years ago:

x + 2x + 3x = 90 – 30

While solving for x, value of x comes out to be 10

So B's age 10 years ago = 20

B's age at present = 30

So choice number B is the answer.

Questions Asked in Previous NET Exams

1. `A 50 year old man has a son whose age is 2/5 of his age. After how many years the ratio of the age of the man to his son will be 5/3?

(UGC NET DECEMBER 2019)

(A) 10 years (B) 15 years

(C) 20 years (D) 25 years

2. At present, a mother is 3 times older than her son. After 5 years, the sum of their ages will be 70 years. The age of the mother after 10 years will be **(UGC NET AUGUST 2016)**

(A) 40

(B) 55

(C) 45

(D) 60

3. At present a person is 4 times older than his son and is 3 years older than his wife. After 3 years the age of the son will be 15 years. The age of the person's wife after 5 years will be: **(UGC NET JUNE 2015)**

   (A) 50 (B) 42

   (C) 48 (D) 45

4. The mean of the ages of father and his son is 27 years. After 18 years, father will be twice as old as his son. Their present ages are **(UGC NET DECEMBER 2014)**

   (A) 42, 12 (B) 40, 14

   (C) 30, 24 (D) 36, 18

5. Anil is twice as old as Sunita. Three years ago, he was three times as old as Sunita. The present age of Anil is **(UGC NET DECEMBER 2013)**

   (A) 6 years (B) 8 years

   (C) 12 years (D) 16 years

KEY

1. D Age of the father 50. Age of the son

$= \frac{2}{5} \times 50 = 20$

So age of the son is 20 years.

Now let after X years ratio of age of father to his son will be 5/3. We get following equation

$= \frac{50+X}{20+X} = \frac{5}{3}$

By cross multiplying value of X is 25. So after 25 years the desired ratio will be achieved. Hence answer is choice number 4

2. B It is given that mother's age is thrice the age of the son.

Let Son's age = x

Mother's age = 3x

After 5 years sum of their ages will be 70

Equation: (x + 5) + (3x + 5) = 70.

After solving for x, value of x comes out to be 15.

Son's present age = 15

Mother's present age = 3 x 15 = 45

Mother's age after 10 years = 45 + 10 = 55

Hence, choice B is the answer.

3. A It is given that the person is 4 times the age of his son and 3 years older to his wife. Let the age of son = x. Age of father = 4x and age of wife = 4x – 3

After 3 years son becomes 15

Equation: x + 3 = 15.

Solving for x we get x = 12

Son's present age = 12

Father's present age = 4 × 12 = 48

Wife's present age = 48 – 3 = 45

Wife's age after 5 years = 45 + 5 = 50

Hence, choice A is the answer.

4. A It is given that averageage of father and son is 27.

Their total age = 2 × 27 = 54 years

Let son's age = x

Father's age = 54 – x

After 18 years father will be twice the age of the son

Equation: 2(x + 18) = (54 – x) + 18

After calculating for x, value of x comes out to be 12

So son's present age = 12

Father's present age = 54 – 12 = 42

Hence, choice A is the answer.

5. C It is given that Anil is twice as old as Sunita

Let Sunita's age = x and Anil's age = 2x

3 years ago Anil was three times as old as SunitaHere Sunita's age = x – 3 and Anil's age = 2x " 3

Equation: 3(x – 3) = 2x – 3

After solving value of x, x is = 6

So present age of Sunita = 6 and Anil's present age = 2 × 6 = 12

Hence, choice number C is the answer.

12 Ratio and Proportion

CONCEPT

The ratio is a comparison of two like terms in its simplest form. For example, we can compare the height of Ram and Shyam, we can compare the weight of Ram and Shyam, but we can't compare the height of Ram to the weight of Shyam.

A Ratio is denoted as a : b or $\frac{a}{b}$ where a is the antecedent and b is the consequent.

The two dots in the horizontal line are a colon which means **'is to'.**

Suppose a is 40 kg and b is 60 kg then the ratio of a and b will be written as 40 : 60

As the ratio is the comparison of two terms in its simplest form.

We can denote 40 : 60 = 2 : 3

Practice Exercise

General Questions Format

1. If Rs. 782 be divided into three parts, proportional to $\frac{1}{2}:\frac{2}{3}:\frac{3}{4}$, then the first part is:

(A) Rs. 182 (B) Rs. 190
(C) Rs. 196 (D) Rs. 204

2. The salaries A, B, and C are in the ratio 2 : 3 : 5. If the increments of 15%, 10%, and 20% are allowed respectively in their salaries, then what will be new ratio of their salaries?

(A) 3 : 3 : 10
(B) 10 : 11 : 20
(C) 23 : 33 : 60
(D) Cannot be determined

3. If 40% of a number is equal to two-third of another number, what is the ratio of first number to the second number?

(A) 2 : 5 (B) 3 : 7
(C) 5 : 3 (D) 7 : 3

4. The fourth proportional to 5, 8, 15 is:

(A) 18 (B) 24
(C) 19 (D) 20

5. Two numbers are in the ratio 3 : 5. If 9 is subtracted from each, the new numbers are in the ratio 12 : 23. The smaller number is:

(A) 27 (B) 33
(C) 49 (D) 55

6. The salaries of A, B, and C are in the ratio of 1 : 2 : 3. The salary of B and C together is Rs. 6000. By what percent is the salary of C more than that of A?

(A) 100% (B) 200%
(C) 300% (D) 400%

7. In a bag, there are coins of 25 p, 10 p, and 5 p in the ratio of 1 : 2 : 3. If there is Rs. 30 in all, how many 5 p coins are there?

(A) 50 (B) 100
(C) 150 (D) 200

8. Promod's collection contains US, Indian, and British stamps. If the ratio of US to Indian stamps is 5 to 2 and the ratio of Indian to British stamps is 5 to 1, what is the ratio of US to British stamps?

(A) 10 : 5 (B) 15 : 2
(C) 20 : 2 (D) 25 : 2

9. In a library, the ratio of number of story books to that of Non-storybooks was 4 : 3 and total number of Storybooks was 1248. When some more Storybooks were bought, the ratio became 5 : 3. Find the number of Storybooks bought.

(A) 312 (B) 321
(C) 936 (D) 1560

10. A dog takes 3 leaps for every 5 leaps of a hare. If one leap of the dog is equal to 3 leaps of the hare, the ratio of the speed of the dog to that of the hare is :

(A) 9 : 5 (B) 2 : 3
(C) 4 : 7 (D) 5 : 6

11. If 76 is divided into four parts proportional to 7, 5, 3, and 4, then the smallest part is:

(A) 12 (B) 15
(C) 16 (D) 19

12. What number has a 5 : 1 ratio to the number 10?

(A) 42 (B) 50
(C) 55 (D) 62

KEY

1. D Given ratio $= \frac{1}{2}:\frac{2}{3}:\frac{3}{4} = 6:8:9$

$\therefore$ 1st part = Rs. $\left(782 \times \frac{6}{23}\right)$ = Rs. 204

2. C Let A = 2k, B = 3k, and C = 5k

A's new salary $= \frac{115}{100}$ of 2k

$= \left(\frac{115}{100} \times 2k\right) \; \frac{23k}{10}$

B's new salary $= \frac{110}{100}$ of 3k

$= \left(\frac{110}{100} \times 3k\right) = \frac{33k}{10}$

C's new salary $= \frac{120}{100}$ of 5k

$= \left(\frac{120}{100} \times 5k\right) = 6k$

$\therefore$ New ratio $\left(\frac{23k}{10} : \frac{33k}{10} : 6k\right) = 23 : 33 : 60$

3. C Let 40% of $A = \frac{2}{3}B$

Then, $\frac{40A}{100} = \frac{2B}{3}$

$\Rightarrow \frac{2A}{5} = \frac{2B}{3} \Rightarrow \frac{A}{B} = \left(\frac{2}{3} \times \frac{5}{2}\right) = \frac{5}{3}$

$\therefore A : B = 5 : 3$

4. B Let the fourth proportional to 5, 8, 15 be x.

Then, 5 : 8 : 15 : x

$\Rightarrow 5x = (8 \times 15)$

$x = \frac{(8 \times 15)}{5} = 24$

5. B Let the numbers be 3x and 5x.

Then, $\frac{3x - 9}{5x - 9} = \frac{12}{23}$

$\Rightarrow 23(3x - 9) = 12(5x - 9)$

$\Rightarrow 9x = 99$

$\Rightarrow x = 11.$

$\therefore$ The smaller number = $(3 \times 11) = 33$

6. B Let the salaries of A, B and C be x, 2x and 3x respectively.

Then $2x + 3x = 6000 \Rightarrow x = 1200$

A's salary = Rs. 1200,

B's salary = Rs. 2400, and C's salary Rs. 3600

Excess of C's salary over A's

$= \left[\left(\frac{2400}{1200}\right) \times 100\right] = 200\%$

7. C Let the number of 25 p, 10 p, and 5 p coins be x, 2x, 3x respectively.

Then, sum of their values

$= \text{Rs.}\left(\frac{25x}{100} + \frac{10 \times 2x}{100} + \frac{5 \times 3x}{100}\right) = \text{Rs.}\frac{60x}{100}$

$\therefore \frac{60x}{100} = 30 \Leftrightarrow x = \frac{30 \times 100}{60} = 50$

Hence, the number of 5 p coins = (3×50)

$= 150$

8. D Indian stamps are common to both ratios. Multiply both ratios by factors such that the Indian stamps are represented by the same number. US : Indian = 5 : 2, and Indian : British = 5 : 1. Multiply the first by 5, and the second by 2. Now US : Indian = 25 : 10, and Indian : British = 10 : 2

Hence, the two ratios can be combined and US : British = 25 : 2

9. A Ratio of Storybooks to Non-storybooks is = 4 : 3

$$\frac{\text{Storybooks}}{\text{Non-Storybooks}} = \frac{4}{3} \Rightarrow \text{Non-Storybooks}$$

$$= \frac{3}{4} \text{x} 1248 = 936$$

Let M be the number of Storybooks to be added So the total Storybooks = 1248 + M After addition of Storybooks new ratio will be:

$$\frac{\text{Storybooks}}{\text{Non-Storybooks}} = \frac{5}{3} \Rightarrow \frac{1248+M}{936}$$

$$= \frac{5}{3} \Rightarrow \frac{3(1248+M)}{} = 5 \times 939.$$

So M = 312

10. A Dog : Hare = (3 × 3) leaps of hare : 5 leaps of hare = 9 : 5

11. A Given ratio = 7 : 5 : 3 : 4, Sum of ratio terms = 19

$$\text{Smallest part} = \frac{76}{19} \times 3 = 12$$

12. B $5:1 = x:10 \; \frac{5}{1} = \frac{x}{10}$ With cross multiplication $x = 50$

Questions Asked in Previous NET Exams

1. If x : y = 7 : 9 then 3x - 5y : 4x + y =?

(UGC NET DECEMBER 2019)

(A) $-\frac{24}{37}$ (B) $-\frac{22}{37}$

(C) $\frac{15}{22}$ (D) $\frac{42}{37}$

2. Two numbers are in the ratio of 3 : 5. If 9 is subtracted from the numbers, the ratio becomes 12 : 23. The numbers are

(UGC NET DECEMBER 2014)

(A) 30, 50 (B) 36, 60

(C) 33, 55 (D) 42, 70

KEY

1. C Ratios can be rewritten as; $\frac{x}{y} = \frac{7}{9}$ and $\frac{3x-5y}{4x+y}$

Putting values of x and y we get

$$\frac{(3\times7)-(5\times9)}{(4\times7)+9} = -\frac{24}{37}$$

2. C Let the numbers are 3x and 5 x. After subtracting 9 and with new ratio equation is:

$$\frac{(3x-9)}{5x-9} = \frac{12}{23} \Rightarrow 23(3x-9) = 12(5x-9)$$

Solving for x we get x = 11

After putting value of x in the original ratio, numbers are 33 and 55.

Hence, answer is C.

13 Time and Distance

CONCEPT

Concept of time, distance, and speed is a practical one. There are various living and non-living movable bodies like human beings, animals, various modes of road, rail, air, and sea transportation which are moving to finish a journey which is started by them. Movement of such bodies gives rise to three measurable concepts:

Distance: Distance is how far a moving body has moved from its starting point. Distance is measured in either kilometres or metres.

Time: How much time is taken by a moving body to cover a particular distance determines the concept of time. It is measured in hours (hrs), minutes (min), or seconds (sec).

Speed: It is a particular distance covered by a moving body in kilometres or metres per unit of a particular time period, i.e., hour, minute, or second. It is measured in kilometres per hour or kilometres or metres per minute or metres per second.

FORMAT AND FORMULAE

It is a fact that the present age is the age of race and speed. So the concepts of time, distance, and speed are regularly calculated. Calculation of these concepts is now part of question papers of quantitative aptitude of all competitive exams. Questions on this topic are formula based, i.e., out of these three variables of time, distance, and speed, two are given and one we are to calculate. Formulae on these variables can be studied as under:

1) Speed $= \frac{\text{Distance}}{\text{Time}}$ 2) Time $= \frac{\text{Distance}}{\text{Speed}}$

3) Distance = Speed × Time

Conversion of Variables

Distance: Distance is measured in either kilometres (kms) or in metres (m).

Conversion of A kms to A m = A × 1000 m

Conversion of A m to kms $= \frac{A}{1000}$ kms

Time: Conversion of A hrs to min = A × 60 min

Conversion of A min to sec = A × 60 sec

Conversion of A hrs to sec = A × 60 × 60

Conversion of A min to hrs $= \frac{A}{60}$ hrs

Conversion of A sec to min $= \frac{A}{60}$ min

Conversion of A sec into hrs. $= \frac{A}{60 \times 60}$ hrs

Conversion of speed of A kms/hr to m/sec

$$= \left[A \times \frac{1000}{3600}\right] = \left[A \times \frac{5}{18}\right] \text{m/sec}$$

Conversion of A m/sec to kms/hr

$$= \left[A \times \frac{3600}{1000}\right] = \left[A \times \frac{18}{5}\right] \text{kms/hr}$$

Some Concepts

Relative Speed: When two parallel moving bodies are simultaneously moving with different speeds, it is calculated in the following way:

1) **Relative speed of two parallel moving objects in the same direction:** When two bodies a and b, i.e., cars, buses, trains, etc. are moving parallel to each other in the same direction and speed of a is u kms/hr and that of b is v kms/hr. If u > v, then the relative speed of the two moving objects a and b is (u – v) kms/hr.

2) **Relative speed of two parallel moving objects in opposite direction:** When two objects a and b are moving parallel to each other with speed of u kms/hr. and v kms/hr respectively, then relative speed of a and b is (u + v) kms/hr.

3) **Time taken by two simultaneously moving objects:** It has been ascertained that for two simultaneously moving objects, relative speed is calculated. Sometimes it is asked to calculate time

taken by two simultaneously parallel moving objects to cross (meet at first time) each other. For calculating time, knowledge of distance is required. For that purpose length of either track, length of single object, or both the objects so given is considered as distance. In case of two different lengths, i.e., L_1 and L_2, total distance will be $L_1 + L_2$.

Average Speed

a) **When distance is same:** If a moving object moves from point a to b with a speed of x kms/hr and returns back from b to a with a speed of y kms/hr, then average speed of the object in the whole journey is

$$= \left[\frac{2xy}{x+y}\right] \text{kms/hr}$$

b) **When time is same:** If a moving object covers distance A with a speed of x kms/hr and distance B with speed of y kms/hr, then the average speed is calculated as:

$$\text{Average Speed} = \left[\frac{x+y}{2}\right] \text{kms/hr}$$

Ratio of Speeds of Two Moving Objects

When ratio of speeds of two moving objects A and B is a : b, then ratio of time taken by two objects to cover same distance is

$$\frac{1}{a} : \frac{1}{b} = b : a$$

Reaching Late or Early

When a person covers a certain distance having an average speed of x km/hr, he is late by x_1 hours but with a speed of y km/hr, he reaches his destination y_1 hours earlier, hence

Required distance = Product of two speeds x Difference between arrival times/Difference of two speeds

Finding Speed or Time Required After Crossing Each Other

If two persons or trains A and B start their journey at the same time from two points P and Q towards each other and after crossing each other they take a and b hours in reaching Q and P respectively, then

$$\frac{\text{A' Speed}}{\text{B' Speed}} = \frac{\sqrt{b}}{\sqrt{a}}$$

PROBLEMS ON TRAINS

Concept

This section on problems on trains is an extension to the concept of time and distance. In this section questions revolve around

1) Time taken by a running train, with a particular length and speed, to cross a vertical object like a tree, an electric pole, a man standing along track, or so.
2) Time taken by a running train, with a particular length and speed, to cross a horizontal object like a railway platform, tunnel, or bridge of a certain length.
3) Time taken by two running trains with their respective speeds and lengths, to cross each other when these are running in opposite direction to each other.
4) Time taken by a running train with a particular length and speed to cross a slower moving train with a respective speed and length.

Formulae

- Time taken by a train of length l metres to pass a pole or standing man or a signal post is equal to the time taken by the train to cover l metres.
- Time taken by a train of length l metres to pass a stationery object of length b metres is the time taken by the train to cover $(l + b)$ metres.
- Suppose two trains or two objects/bodies are moving in the same direction at u m/s and v m/s, where $u > v$, then their relative speed is $= (u - v)$ m/s.
- Suppose two trains or two objects bodies are moving in opposite directions at u m/s and v m/s, then their relative speed is $= (u + v)$ m/s.
- If two trains of length a metres and b metres are moving in opposite directions at u m/s and v m/s, then the time taken by the trains to cross each other $= \frac{(a+b)}{(u+v)}$
- If two trains of length a metres and b metres are moving in the same direction at u m/s and v m/s, then the time taken by the faster train to cross the slower train $= \frac{(a+b)}{(u-v)}$

***Important**: In case of each of the questions of trains, heterogeneous units are to be converted into homogeneous units. For instance, if speed of a train is given in kmph, whereas length of train (distance) is given in metres and time required is in seconds, then speed given in kmph is to be converted into metres per second by applying the formula discussed earlier.*

Practice Exercise

General Questions Format

1. A man reaches his office 20 min late, if he walks from his home at 3 km per hour and reaches 30 min early if he walks at 4 km per hour. How far is his office from his house?
   (A) 20 kms (B) 16 kms
   (C) 14 kms (D) 10 kms
2. Two boys starting from the same place walk at a rate of 5 kmph and 5.5 kmph respectively. What time will they take to be 8.5 km apart, if they walk in the same direction?
   (A) 15 hours (B) 16 hours
   (C) 17 hours (D) 18 hours
3. A man travelled from the village to the post office at the rate of 25 kmph and walked back at the rate of 4 kmph. If the whole journey took 5 hours 48 minutes, find the distance of the post office from the village in kms?
   (A) 40 (B) 30
   (C) 20 (D) 10
4. A man walks 6 km at a speed of $1\frac{1}{2}$ kmph, runs 8 km at a speed of 2 kmph, and goes by bus another 32 km. Speed of the bus is 8 kmph. Find the average speed of the man in kmph.
   (A) $5\frac{9}{12}$ (B) $4\frac{2}{13}$
   (C) $6\frac{4}{17}$ (D) None of these
5. A man in a train notices that he can count 41 telephone posts in one minute. If they are known to be 50 metres apart, then at what speed (km/hr) is the train travelling?
   (A) 60 (B) 100
   (C) 110 (D) 120
6. Two men A and B start from place X walking at $4\frac{1}{2}$ kmph and $5\frac{3}{4}$ kmph respectively. How many km apart they are at the end of $3\frac{1}{2}$ hours if they are walking in the same direction?
   (A) $2\frac{9}{7}$ (B) $3\frac{7}{5}$
   (C) $1\frac{3}{4}$ (D) $4\frac{3}{8}$
7. Two trains starting at the same time from two stations 200 km apart and going in opposite directions cross each other at a distance of 110 km from one of the stations. What is the ratio of their speeds?
   (A) 9 : 20 (B) 11 : 9
   (C) 11 : 20 (D) None of these
8. A man walks at a speed of 2 km/hr and runs at a speed of 6 km/hr. How much time will the man require to cover a distance of 20 $\frac{1}{2}$ km, if he completes half of the distance, i.e., $\left(10\frac{1}{4}\right)$ km on foot and the other half by running?
   (A) 12.4 hrs (B) 6.8 hrs
   (C) 10.7 hrs D 9.9 hrs
9. Jagan went to another town covering 240 km by car moving at 60 kmph. Then he covered 400 km by train moving at 100 kmph and then rest 200 km he covered by a bus moving at 50 kmph. The average speed during the whole journey was?
   (A) 36 kmph (B) 35 kmph
   (C) 72 kmph (D) 70 kmph
10. A bus covers its journey at the speed of 80 km/hr in 10 hours. If the same distance is to be covered in 4 hours, by how much the speed of the bus will have to increase?
    (A) 85 kmph (B) 95 kmph
    (C) 105 kmph (D) 120 kmph
11. In covering a distance of 30 km, Abhay takes 2 hours more than Sameer. If Abhay doubles his speed, then he would take 1 hour less than Sameer. Abhay's speed is:
    (A) 5 kmph (B) 6 kmph
    (C) 8 kmph (D) None of these

KEY

1. **D** Let two speeds be S_1 and S_2. Let two times be T_1 and T_2. Applying the formula:
   $$\frac{(S1 \times S2) \times (T1 - T2)}{S1 - S2} = \frac{10}{1} = 10\,\text{km}$$
2. **C** In this type of question we need to get the relative speed between them.
   The relative speed of the boys = 5.5 kmph – 5 kmph= 0.5 kmph

Distance between them is 8.5 km

$$\text{Time} = \frac{\text{Dis tan ce}}{\text{Speed}} = \frac{8.5 \text{ km}}{0.5 \text{kmph}} = 17 \text{ hrs}$$

3. C Average speed = $\frac{2xy}{x+y}$

Here x = 25 and y = 4

$$\Rightarrow \frac{2 \times 25 \times 4}{25+4} = \frac{200}{29} \text{km/hr}$$

Distance covered in 5 hours 48 minutes

$$= \text{Speed} \times \text{Time} = \left(\frac{200}{29}\right) \times \left(\frac{29}{5}\right)$$

Distance covered in 5 hours 48 minutes = 40 kms

Distance of the post office from the village

$$= \left(\frac{40}{2}\right) = 20 \text{ km}$$

4. B Man walked 6 km at 1.5 kmph, again he walked 8 km at speed of 2 kmph, and 40 km at a speed of 8 kmph.

Time taken individually:

$$\Rightarrow \frac{6}{1.5} = 4 \text{ m} \Rightarrow \frac{8}{2} = 4 \text{ m} \Rightarrow \frac{40}{8} = 5 \text{ m}$$

$$\text{Average speed of man} = \frac{\text{total dis tan ce}}{\text{total time}}$$

$$\Rightarrow \frac{54}{13} = 4\frac{2}{13} \text{ kmph}$$

5. D Number of gaps between 41 poles = 40So total distance between 41 poles = 40 × 50 = 2000 metre = 2 km

In 1 minute train is moving at 2 km/minute

Speed in hours = 2 × 60 = 120 km/hour

6. D Relative speed = $5\frac{3}{4} - 4\frac{1}{2} = 1\frac{1}{4}$

Time = $3\frac{1}{2}$ h

$$\text{Distance} = \frac{5}{4} \times \frac{7}{2} = \frac{35}{8} = 4\frac{3}{8} \text{ km}$$

7. B In the same time, they cover 110 km and 90 km respectively.

Therefore, ratio of their speeds = 110 : 90

= 11 : 9

8. B We know that

$$\text{Time} = \frac{\text{Dis tan ce}}{\text{Speed}}$$

$$\text{Required time} = \frac{\left(10\frac{1}{4}\right)}{2} + \frac{\left(10\frac{1}{4}\right)}{6}$$

$$= \frac{41}{8} + \frac{41}{24} = \frac{164}{24} = 6.8 \text{ hours}$$

9. D By car 240 km at 60 kmph

Time taken = $\frac{240}{60}$ = 4 hr

By train 400 km at 100 kmph

Time taken = $\frac{400}{100}$ = 4 hr

By bus 200 km at 50 kmph

Time taken = $\frac{200}{50}$ = 4 hr

So total time = 4 + 4 + 4 = 12 hr

and total speed = 240 + 400 + 200 = 840 km

Average speed of the whole journey = $\frac{840}{12}$

= 70 kmph

10. D Initial speed = 80 km/hr

Total distance = 80 × 10 = 800 km

New speed = $\frac{800}{4}$ = 200 km/hr

Increase in speed = 200 – 80 = 120 km/hr

11. A Let Abhay's speed be x km/hr

Then, $\frac{30}{x} - \frac{30}{2x} = 3$

$\Rightarrow 6x = 30 \Rightarrow x = 5$ km/hr

Questions Asked in Previous NET Exams

1. A man travelled from a village to the railway station at the rate of 20 kmph. He walked back at the rate of 5 kmph. If the whole journey took 5 hours, find out the distance of the railway station from the village.

(UGC NET JUNE 2019)

(A) 10 kms (B) 15 kms

(C) 20 kms (D) 40 kms

KEY

1. C Time = 5 hrs Let distance be x

Then $5 = \frac{x}{20} + \frac{x}{5} \Rightarrow x = 20\text{kms}$

PROBLEMS ON TRAINS

General Questions Format

1. A train 160 m long is running with a speed of 48 kmph. In what time will it pass a telegraph pole?
(A) 15 sec (B) 15min
(C) 12 sec (D) 30 sec

2. A train 180 m long is running with a speed of 54 kmph. In what time will it pass a tunnel 540 m long?
(A) 48 sec (B) 15 sec
(C) 12 sec (D) 5 sec

3. A train 100 m long is running with a speed of 70 kmph. In what time will it pass a man who is running at 10 kmph in the same direction in which the train is going?
(A) 5 sec (B) 10 sec
(C) 15 sec (D) 6 sec

4. A train 110m long is running with a speed of 60 kmph. In what time will it pass a man who is running at 6 kmph in the opposite direction in which the train is going?
(A) 23 sec (B) 20 sec
(C) 6 sec (D) 25 sec

5. A train 100 m long takes 7.2 sec to cross a man walking at a rate of 5 kmph in a direction opposite to that of the train. Find the speed of the train.
(A) 45 kmph (B) 50 kmph
(C) 75 kmph (D) 92 kmph

6. Two trains 132 m and 108 m in length are running towards each other on parallel lines, one at the rate of 32 kmph and another at 40 kmph. In what time will they be clear of each from the moment they meet?
(A) 45 sec (B) 55 sec
(C) 10 sec (D) 12 sec

7. A train 280 m long running with a speed of 63 kmph will pass an electric pole in:
(A) 160 sec (B) 16 sec
(C) 18 sec (D) 15 sec

8. A train 360 m long is running at a speed of 54 kmph. Time taken by the train to cross the tunnel 390 m long is
(A) 25 sec (B) 50 sec
(C) 30 sec (D) 35 sec

9. If a train 110 m long passes a telegraph pole in 3 sec, then the time taken (in sec) by it to cross a railway platform 165m long, is
(A) 3 (B) 4
(C) 5 (D) 7.5

10. If a train 700 m long is running at a speed of 72 kmph, and time taken by the train to cross the tunnel is 1 min, then the length of the tunnel is ……. metres.
(A) 700 (B) 600
(C) 550 (D) 500

11. A train takes 18 sec to pass completely through a station 162 m long and 15 sec through another station 120 m long. The length of the train is …….. metres.
(A) 70 (B) 80
(C) 90 (D) 100

12. A train 50 m long passes a platform 100 m long in 10 sec .The speed of the train (km/hr) is
(A) 10 (B) 15
(C) 54 (D) 100

13. A train 100 m long, running at 36 kmph takes 25 sec to pass the bridge. The length of the bridge (in metre) is:
(A) 90 (B) 144
(C) 150 (D) 540

14. A train 100 m long travels at 70 kmph. A man is running 10 kmph in the same direction is which the train is going. The train will pass the man in….
(A) 6 sec (B) 6.6 sec
(C) 7 sec (D) 8 sec

15. A train 270 m long is moving at a speed of 25 kmph. It will cross a man coming from the opposite direction at a speed of 2 kmph in…
(A) 28 sec (B) 24 sec
(C) 32 sec (D) 36 sec

16. Two trains of lengths 120 m and 80 m are running in the same direction with the velocities of 40 kmph and 50 kmph respectively. The time taken by them to cross each other is
(A) 60 sec (B) 72 sec
(C) 75 sec (D) 80 sec

17. A train covers a certain distance in 50 min, if it runs at a speed of 40 kmph on an average. The speed at which the train must run to reduce the time of journey to 40 min, will be:

(A) 50 kmph (B) 55 kmph

(C) 60 kmph (D) 70 kmph

18. If the speed of a train be 92.4 kmph, how many metres would it cover in 20 minutes?

(A) 61600 m (B) 30800 m

(C) 15400 m (D) none

19. A train 137 metres and 163 metres in length are running towards each other on parallel lines, one at rate of 42 kmph and another at 48 kmph. In what time will they be clear of each other from the moment they meet?

(A) 1 sec (B) 12 sec

(C) 13 sec (D) 2 sec

20. There are two towns A and B. Anil goes from town A to B at 40 kmph. He comes back to the starting point at 60 kmph. What is his average speed during the whole journey?

(A) 38 kmph (B) 48 kmph

(C) 58 kmph (D) 68 kmph

KEY

1. C **2. A** **3. D** **4. C** **5. A**

6. D Total length (Distance) = (132 + 108 = 240)
Relative speed = (32 + 40 = 72 kmph)
Therefore time taken to cross each other

$$= \frac{240 \times 18}{72 \times 5} = 12 \text{ sec}$$

7. B **8. B**

9. D First of all speed of the train is calculated on the basis of the first relationship:

$$\text{Speed} = \frac{110}{3}$$

Now time taken to cross the platform:

$$\frac{(110+165)}{\frac{110}{3}} \Rightarrow \frac{275 \times 3}{110} = 7.5 \text{sec}$$

10. D Time = 1 minute means 60 seconds

Let length of tunnel = x

Applying the formula: Distance = Speed × Time

$$(700 + x) = 72 \times \frac{5}{18} \times 60 = 500$$

11. C Here speed of the train is uniform. Let length of the train = x

$$\text{Equation: } \frac{162+x}{18} = \frac{120+x}{15} = 90$$

12. C **13. C** **14. A** **15. D** **16. B** **17. A**

Hint: Distance in kms is found from the first combination where time and speed is given. Here, minutes will be converted into hours. Then taking that distance so calculated, speed will be found from the second combination where time and distance are known to us.

18. B **19. B** **20. B**

Questions Asked in Previous NET Exams

1. A train leaves Agra at 5 am and reaches Delhi at 9 am. Another train leaves Delhi at 7 am and reaches Agra at 10:30 am. At what time do the two trains cross each other?

(UGC NET JUNE 2019)

(A) 6:36 am (B) 6:56 am

(C) 7 am (D) 7:56 am

KEY

1. D Let distance between Agra and Delhi = x kms

Speed of train from Agra to Delhi

$= \frac{x}{4}$ kmph (Difference of departure and arrival time is 4 hrs)

Speed of train from Delhi to Agra

$$= \frac{x}{\frac{7}{2}} = \frac{2x}{7} \text{kmph}$$

(Difference between departure and arrival time is 3.30 hrs, i.e., $\frac{7}{2}$ hrs)

Suppose trains meet at y hours after 5.00 am

$$\text{then } x = \left[\frac{x}{4} \times 2\right] + \left[\frac{2x}{7} \times (y-2)\right]$$

(There is difference of 2 hours in the departure time of both the trains).

$$\Rightarrow \frac{y}{4} + \frac{2(y-2)}{7} = 1 \Rightarrow 7y + 8(y-2) = 28$$

$$\Rightarrow 15y = 44 \Rightarrow y = \frac{44}{15} \text{hrs} \Rightarrow 2\text{hrs} - 56\text{min}$$

So both the trains meet at 7.56 am (Two hours after 5.00 am)

Simple Interest

CONCEPT

A borrower borrows certain amount from a lending agency (Bank, Finance Company, or Individual) to meet some financial requirements. Lending agency advances that amount for a certain period of time. Now the borrower is to repay the amount borrowed within agreed time period along with certain extra amount (EMI or full). That extra amount is known as interest. If the interest is imposed uniformly, it is called simple interest. Standard unit of expressing simple interest is percentage rate (R %).

TERMS USED IN OPERATION OF SIMPLE INTEREST

Principal (P): The original sum of money loaned/ deposited. This is also known as capital.

Interest (I): The amount of money that you pay to borrow money or the amount of money that you earn on a deposit.

Time (T): The duration for which the money is borrowed/deposited.

Rate of Interest (R): The percent of interest that you pay for money borrowed, or earn for money deposited.

FORMULAE

Rule 1) When P, T, and R are given and SI is to be calculated

$$\text{Simple Interest (SI)} = \frac{P \times R \times T}{100}\%$$

$$\text{Principal Amount (P)} = \left[\frac{100 \times SI}{R \times T}\right]$$

$$\text{Rate of Simple Interest (R)} = \left[\frac{100 \times SI}{P \times T}\right]$$

$$\text{Time Period (T)} = \left[\frac{100 \times SI}{P \times R}\right]$$

Rule 2) When total amount along with interest is to be paid at the end of an agreed period is to be calculated, we calculate the total amount (A) as follows:

Here P, R, and T are given.

$$A = P + SI$$

$$\text{Thus } A = P + \left[\frac{(P \times R \times T)}{100}\right]$$

Rule 3) If the interest on a sum of money is 1/x of the principal, and the number of years is equal to the rate of interest then rate can be calculated using the formula:

$$\sqrt{\left(\frac{100}{x}\right)}$$

Derivation for this result:

We know SI = {(P × R × T)/100}

Put SI = P/x ; and T = R

$$P/x = \left[\frac{(P \times R \times T)}{100}\right] \Rightarrow \left[\frac{(P \times R \times R)}{100}\right]$$

$$\Rightarrow \frac{P}{x} = \frac{P \times R \times R}{100}$$

$$R^2 = \frac{100}{x} \Rightarrow R = \sqrt{\frac{100}{x}}$$

Rule 4) The rate of interest for t_1 years is r_1%, t_2 years is r_2%, and t_3 years is r_3 %. If a man gets interest of Rs. x for ($t_1 + t_2 + t_3 = n$) years, then principal is calculated by the following formula:

$$\frac{x \times 100}{r_1t_1 + r_2t_2 + r_3t_3}$$

Derivation for this result:

$$x \times 100 = p[t_1\, r_1 + t_2\, r_2 + t_3\, r_3]$$

$$P = \frac{x \times 100}{[t_1r_1 + t_2r_2 + t_3r_3]}$$

Rule 5) Calculation of simple rate of interest, when a sum of money becomes X times in n years

$$\text{Rate of interest (R)} = \frac{100(x-1)}{n}$$

Rule 6) Calculation of time when a sum of money becomes x times at a given simple rate of interest in n years.

$$n = \frac{100(x-1))}{r}$$

Rule 7) Calculation of principal sum when the sum is put at certain rate of simple interest for certain period of time (n), had it be put at a higher/lower rate (r) it would have yielded x amount more/less.

$$P = \frac{X \times 100}{n \times r}$$

Rule 8) Calculation of time when a certain amount is invested for certain time but at different rates. When rate per annum is r_1 the amount becomes x_1 but at rate r_2 per annum, the amount becomes x_2.

Time, t, is given by the formula:

$$T = \left[\frac{(x_1 - x_2)}{(x_2 r_1 - x_1 r_2)}\right] \times 100$$

Rule 9) Calculation of interest when a person deposits A_1 amount at r_1% per annum and amount A_2 at r_2% per annum, then the rate of interest for the whole sum is

$$r = \left[\frac{(A_1 r_1 + A_2 r_2)}{(A_1 + A_2)}\right]$$

Practice Exercise

General Questions Format

Complete the given series in the following questions:

1. A man deposits Rs. 500 at 4% per annum and Rs. 600 at 5% per annum. Find the rate of interest for the whole sum.

(A) 40/11% (B) 30/11%

(C) 40/11% (D) 50/11%

2. A certain amount is invested for certain time. When invested at 9% it amounts to Rs. 200 but when it was invested at 2% it amounts to Rs. 50. Find the time.

(A) 300 years (B) 100 years

(C) 150 years (D) 250 years

3. If the simple interest on Rs. 500 increases by Rs. 10 when time increases by 4 years, find the rate per annum.

(A) 0.5% (B) 0.2%

(C) 0.3% (D) 0.7%

4. A man borrowed Rs. 24000 from two money lenders. For one loan, he paid 15% per annum and for the other 18% per annum. At the end of one year, he paid Rs. 4050. How much did he borrow at each rate?

(A) Rs. 16000 (B) Rs. 12000

(C) Rs. 15000 (D) Rs. 13000

5. A person takes a loan of Rs. 200 at 5% simple interest. He returns Rs.100 at the end of one year. In order clear his dues at the end of 2 years, he would pay:

(A) Rs. 100 (B) Rs. 105

(C) Rs. 115 (D) Rs. 110

6. How long will it take for a sum of money to grow from Rs.1250 to Rs.10000, if it is invested at 12.5% p.a. simple interest?

(A) 65 years (B) 56 years

(C) 45 years (D) 57 years

7. A certain sum of money amounts to Rs. 2500 in a span of 5 years and further to Rs. 3000 in a span of 7 years at simple interest. The sum is?

(A) Rs. 1800 (B) Rs. 2000

(C) Rs. 1400 (D) Rs. 1250

8. A sum of money invested for a certain number of years at 8% p.a. simple interest grows to Rs.180. The same sum of money invested for the same number of years at 4% p.a. simple interest grows to Rs.120 only. For how many years was the sum invested?

(A) 25 years

(B) 15 years

(C) 20 years

(D) 22 years

9. Reena took a loan of Rs. 1200 with simple interest for as many years as the rate of interest. If she paid Rs. 432 as interest at the end of the loan period, what was the rate of interest?

(A) 3.6 (B) 6

(C) 18 (D) None of these

10. How much time will it take for an amount of Rs. 450 to yield Rs. 81 as interest at 4.5% per annum of simple interest?

(A) 3.5 years (B) 4 years

(C) 4.5 years (D) 5 years

11. What will be the ratio of simple interest earned by certain amount at the same rate of interest for 6 years and that for 9 years?

(A) 1 : 3 (B) 1 : 4

(C) 2 : 3 (D) Data inadequate

KEY

1. D Here $A_1 = 500$ $A_2 = 600$ $r_1 = 4$ $r_2 = 5$

Applying the formula: $r = \left[\frac{(A_1r_1 + A_2r_2)}{(A_1 + A_2)}\right]$

$$\left[\frac{(500x4 + (600x5))}{500 + 600}\right]$$

$$\Rightarrow \left[\frac{(2000 + 3000)}{1100}\right] \Rightarrow \frac{5000}{1100} = \frac{50}{11}\%$$

2. A $X_1 = 200$ $r_1 = 9$ $X_2 = 50$ $r_2 = 2$

Applying the formula:

$$T = \left[\frac{(x_1 - x_2)}{(x_2r_1 - x_1r_2)}\right] \times 100$$

Putting the values:

$$T = \left[\frac{(200 - 50)}{(50x9 - 200x2)}\right] \times 100$$

$$\Rightarrow \left[\frac{150}{(450 - 400)}\right] \times 100$$

$$\Rightarrow \frac{150}{50} x100 = 300 years$$

3. A Here $T_1 - T_2 = 4$ $P = 500$ SI_1 - $SI_2 = 10$

Applying the formula:

$$SI_1 - SI_2 = \left[\frac{P \times R \times (T_1 - T_2)}{100}\right]$$ By putting values in it, we get:

$$10 = \left[\frac{500 \times R \times 4}{100}\right] \Rightarrow R = 0.5\%$$

4. C Let the sum at 15% be Rs. x and that at 18% be Rs. (24000 – x).

$$\left[\frac{(15 \times X \times 1)}{100}\right] + \left[\frac{(24000 - X) \times 18 \times 1}{100}\right]$$

$$= 4050 \Rightarrow 15X + 432000 - 18X = 405000$$

$$\Rightarrow X = 9000$$

Money borrowed at 15% = Rs. 9000

Money borrowed at 18% = (24000 – 9000) = Rs. 15000

5. C Here P = 200Rate (R) = 5 Time = 1+1

Amount to be paid:

$$Rs.\left[100 + \frac{200 \times 5 \times 1}{100} + \frac{100 \times 5 \times 1}{100}\right] = 115$$

6. B Simple interest is given by the formula SI $= \left(\frac{p \times n \times r}{100}\right)$, where p is the principal, n is the number of years for which it is invested, r is the rate of interest per annum

In this case, Rs. 1250 has become Rs.10,000

Therefore, the interest earned = 10,000 - 1250 = 8750

So applying SI formula:

$$8750 = \left[\frac{(1250 \times n \times 12.5)}{100}\right]$$

$$\Rightarrow n = \frac{700}{12.5} = 56 years$$

7. D 2500 in 5th year and 3000 in 7th year

So in between 2 years Rs. 500 is increased

$\Rightarrow$ for a year $\frac{500}{2} = 250$

So, per year it is increasing Rs. 250 then in 5 years $\Rightarrow 250 \times 5 = 1250$

Hence, the initial amount must be 2500 – 1250 = Rs. 1250

8. A $X_1 = 180$ $r_1 = 8$ $X_2 = 120$ $r_2 = 4$

Applying the formula:

$$T = \left[\frac{(x_1 - x_2)}{(x_2 r_1 - x_1 r_2)}\right] \times 100$$ Putting the values:

$$T = \left[\frac{(180-120)}{(120 \times 8 - 180 \times 4)}\right] \times 100$$

$$\Rightarrow \left[\frac{60}{(960-720)}\right] \times 100$$

$$\Rightarrow \left[\frac{60}{240}\right] \times 100 = 25\text{years}$$

9. B Let rate = R% and time = R years.

As R = T Then, $\left(\frac{1200 \times R \times R}{100}\right) = 432$

$$\Rightarrow 12R^2 = 432$$

$$\Rightarrow R^2 = 36$$

$$\Rightarrow R = 6$$

10. B Time = $\frac{(100 \times 81)}{(450 \times 4.5)}$

$$\Rightarrow \frac{8100}{2025} = 4\text{years}$$

11. C Let the principal be P and rate of interest be R%.

Required Ratio = $\left[\frac{P \times R \times 6/100}{P \times R \times 9/100}\right]$

$$= \frac{6PR}{9PR} = \frac{2}{3} = 2:3$$

15 Compound Interest

CONCEPT

Compound interest is the addition of interest to the principal sum of a loan or deposit, or in other words, interest on interest. It is the result of reinvesting interest, rather than paying it out, so that interest in the next period is then earned on the principal sum, plus previously accumulated interest.

FORMULAE TO CALCULATE COMPOUND INTEREST

Let Principal = P, Rate = R% per annum, Time = *n* years

1. **When interest is compound Annually:**

$$\text{Principal P}\left[1+\frac{R}{100}\right]^n$$

2. **When interest is compounded Half-yearly:**

$$\text{Amount} = P\left[1+\frac{R/2}{100}\right]^{2n}$$

3. **When interest is compounded Quarterly:**

$$P\left[1+\frac{R/4}{100}\right]^{4n}$$

4. **When interest is compounded Annually but time is in fraction, say $3\frac{2}{5}$ yrs.**

$$\text{Amount} = P\left[1+\frac{R}{100}\right]^3 \text{x} \left[1+\frac{2/5R}{100}\right]$$

5. **When Rates are different for different years, say R_1%, R_2%, and R_3% for 1st, 2nd, and 3rd year respectively.**

$$\text{Amount} = P\left[1+\frac{R_1}{100}\right]\text{x}\left[1+\frac{R_2}{100}\right]\text{x}\left[1+\frac{R_3}{100}\right]$$

6. **To find the sum when difference between the Compound Interest and Simple Interest is given with certain rate of interest compounded annually for a certain period of time.**

$$\text{Calculating CI} = P\left[1+\frac{R}{100}\right]^n - P$$

$$\text{Calculating SI}\left[\frac{\text{PxRxT}}{100}\right]$$

Thus putting equation, i.e., CI – SI = Difference and calculating the sum

Short Formula: To find the amount when difference between CI and SI is given for 2 years

$$\text{CI} - \text{SI} = P\left[\frac{R}{100}\right]^2$$

Formula for finding P when difference between CI and SI for 3 years is given

$$\text{CI} - \text{SI} = \frac{PR^2(300+R)}{(100)^3}$$

7. **Present worth of Rs. X due n years hence is given by:**

$$\text{Present Worth} = \frac{X}{\left[1+\frac{R}{100}\right]^n}.$$

Practice Exercise

General Questions Format

Complete the given series in the following questions:

1. Find the compound interest on Rs. 10,000 in 2 years at 4% per annum, the interest being compounded half-yearly.

   (A) 524.32 (B) 624.32
   (C) 724.32 (D) 824.32

2. Simple interest on a certain sum of money for 3 years at 8% per annum is half the compound interest on Rs. 4000 for 2 years at 10% per annum. The sum placed on simple interest is:

   (A) Rs. 1550 (B) Rs. 1650
   (C) Rs. 1750 (D) Rs. 2000

3. If the simple interest on a sum of money for 2 years at 5% per annum is Rs. 50, what is the compound interest on the same at the same rate and for the same time?

   (A) Rs. 51.25 (B) Rs. 52
   (C) Rs. 54.25 (D) Rs. 60

4. A sum of money invested at compound interest amounts to Rs. 650 at the end of the first year and Rs. 676 at the end of the second year. The sum of money is:

   (A) Rs. 600 (B) Rs. 540
   (C) Rs. 625 (D) Rs. 560

5. What will be the compound interest on a sum of Rs. 25,000 after 3 years at the rate of 12% p.a.?

   (A) Rs. 9000.30 (B) Rs. 9720
   (C) Rs. 10123.20 (D) Rs. 10483.20

6. If the simple interest on a sum of money at 5% per annum for 3 years is Rs. 1200, find the compound interest on the samė sum for the same period at the same rate.

   (A) 1261
   (B) 1271
   (C) 1281
   (D) 1291

7. Arun invested an amount of Rs. 8000 in a fixed deposit scheme for 2 years at compound interest rate 5% p.a. How much amount will Arun get on maturity of the fixed deposit?

   (A) 8600 (B) 8620
   (C) 8820 (D) None of these

8. Find the compound interest on Rs. 16,000 at 20% per annum for 9 months, compounded quarterly.

   (A) 2422 (B) 2522
   (C) 2622 (D) 2722

9. The difference between simple interest and compound interest on Rs. 1200 for one year at 10% per annum reckoned half-yearly is:

   (A) Rs. 2.50 (B) Rs. 3
   (C) Rs. 3.75 (D) Rs. 4

10. On a sum of money, the simple interest for 2 years is Rs. 660, while the compound interest is Rs.696.30, the rate of interest being the same in both the cases. The rate of interest is

    (A) 10% (B) 11%
    (C) 12% (D) 13%

11. Find compound interest on Rs. 7500 at 4% per annum for 2 years, compounded annually.

    (A) 612 (B) 712
    (C) 812 (D) 912

KEY

1. **D** Principal = Rs. 10000; Rate = 2% per half-year; Time = 2 years = 4 half-years

   Amount = 10000

   $$\left[1+\frac{2}{100}\right]^4$$

   $$\Rightarrow \left[10000\times\frac{51}{100}\times\frac{51}{100}\times\frac{51}{100}\times\frac{51}{100}\right]=10824.32$$

   CI = Rs. (10824.32 – 10000) = Rs. 824.32

2. C CI $= \text{Rs.}\left[4000 \times \left(1+\frac{10}{100}\right)^2 - 400\right]$

$= \text{Rs.}\left(4000 \times \frac{11}{10} \times \frac{11}{10} - 4000\right) = 840$

$\therefore$ Sum $= \text{Rs}\left(\frac{420 \times 100}{3 \times 8}\right) = \text{Rs.}1750$

3. A Sum $= \text{Rs.}\left(\frac{50 \times 100}{2 \times 5}\right) = \text{Rs.}500$

Amount $= \text{Rs.}\left[500 \times \left(1+\frac{5}{100}\right)^2\right]$

$= \text{Rs.}\left(500 \times \frac{21}{20} \times \frac{21}{20}\right)$

= Rs. 551.25

$\therefore$ CI = Rs. (551.25 – 500) = Rs. 51.25

4. C Simple Interest for one year = Compound Interest for one year

Interest on Rs. 650 for 1 year = 676 – 650 = Rs. 26

$SI = \frac{P \times R \times T}{100} \Rightarrow 26 = \frac{650 \times R \times 1}{100}$

$\Rightarrow R = \frac{26 \times 100}{650} = 4\%$

To find sum of money, following formula is applied:

$A = P\left[1+\frac{R}{100}\right]^n \Rightarrow P = \frac{A}{\left[1+\frac{R}{100}\right]^n}$

$\Rightarrow P = \frac{650}{\left[1+\frac{4}{100}\right]^1} = \frac{650}{\frac{26}{25}} = \frac{650}{26} \times 25 = \text{Rs.}625$

5. C Amount $\text{Rs.}\left[25000 \times \left(1+\frac{12}{100}\right)^3\right]$

$= \text{Rs.}\left[25000 \times \frac{28}{25} \times \frac{28}{25} \times \frac{28}{25}\right]$

= Rs. 35123.20

CI = Rs. (35123.20 – 25000) = Rs. 10123.20

6. A Here we are to find Principal from the given data applying SI formula:

$SI = \frac{P \times R \times T}{100} \Rightarrow 1200 = \frac{P \times 5 \times 3}{100}$

$\Rightarrow P = \frac{1200 \times 100}{15} = 8000$

Now P = 8000

Calculating compound interest at given rate and on given period.

$CI = 8000 \cdot \left[1+\frac{5}{100}\right]^3 = 9261$

$\Rightarrow 9261 - 8000 = 1261$

7. C Amount $= \text{Rs.}\left[8000 \times \left(1+\frac{5}{100}\right)^2\right]$

$= \text{Rs.}\left(8000 \times \frac{21}{20} \times \frac{21}{20}\right)$

= Rs. 8820

8. B Explanation: Principal = Rs. 16000; Time = 9 months = 3 quarters

Rate = 20% per annum = 5% per quarter

Amount $= 16000\left[1+\frac{5}{100}\right]^3 = 18522$

CI = Rs. (18522 – 16000) = Rs. 2522

9. B SI $= \text{Rs}\left(\frac{1200 \times 10 \times 1}{100}\right) = \text{Rs.}120$

CI $= \text{Rs.}\left[1200 \times \left(1+\frac{5}{100}\right)^2 - 1200\right]$

= 123

$\therefore$ Difference = Rs. (123 – 120)

= Rs. 3

10. B Explanation: Difference in CI and SI for 2 years

= Rs (696.30 – 660)

= Rs. 36.30. SI for one year = Rs 330

SI on Rs. 330 for 1 year = Rs. 36.30

Rate $= \left[\frac{100 \times 36.30}{330 \times 1}\right] = 11\%$

11. A Amount $= 7500\left[1+\frac{4}{100}\right]^2$

$\Rightarrow$ Amount $= 7500 \times \left[\frac{26}{25} \times \frac{26}{25}\right] = 8112$

therefore, CI = Rs. (8112 – 7500) = Rs. 612

Questions Asked in Previous NET Exams

1. A sum of money with compound interest becomes Rs. 2400 in one year and Rs. 3000 in two years. Find the principal amount.

   (UGC NET DECEMBER 2019)

   (A) 1900 (B) 1910
   (C) 1915 (D) 1920

KEY

1. D. Money with compound Interest of two years = 3000

Money with compound interest of one year = 2400

Difference = 600

Rs. 600 is simple interest as money with compound interest for first year becomes principal amount for second year and interest of one year is simple interest. By taking this value of R % is calculated by applying formula of simple interest:

$$\frac{P \times R \times T}{100} = SI$$

$$\Rightarrow \frac{2400 \times R \times 1}{100} = 600$$

$$\Rightarrow R = \frac{100 \times 6000}{2400} = 25\%$$

Now finding the principal amount P while applying compound interest formula for 1 year.

Here;

Money with CI = 2400, R = 25% Time (T) =1 year.

$$CI = P\left[1+\frac{R}{100}\right]$$

$$\Rightarrow 2400 \Rightarrow P\left[1+\frac{25}{100}\right]$$

By solving above P =1920

Unit VI

Logical Reasoning

1 Logic and Structure of Argument

LOGIC: INTRODUCTION

Whenever anyone makes a statement in a communication process, the recipient tries to find logic in it. Every recipient has his or her own way to find the logic in it. A statement appearing logical to someone may appear illogical to another recipient. It can be made clear by taking an example:

'Nitish is a hardworking person'.

The above statement is logical for that recipient who knows Nitish. As he is convinced that the statement maker is telling the truth, he would not argue over it. On the other hand, this statement is illogical to that recipient, who does not know Nitish. He is not convinced and argues with the statement maker as on which basis the statement maker is asserting this. Does he have some evidence to prove the truth of the statement? Now, the statement maker defends himself by making one or more statements further as evidence as follows:

1) **All employees of company A are hardworking.**
2) **Nitish is an employee of company A.**

Above two statements are evidences to prove the truth of the statement **'Nitish is a hardworking person'**. As statement number 1 and 2 fully support the original statements, that statement becomes logical. These evidences are sufficient enough to convince anyone and can satisfy any argument over it. Thus, it is observed from the above illustration that logic lies in that statement which convinces the recipient about the truth of the statement and there is no need to create any argument over it. That statement is taken to be illogical which cannot convince a recipient and reaction of the recipient comes in the form of an argument, which is to be satisfied by the statement maker while furnishing supportive evidences. Hence, logic is the ability to distinguish between true and false statements so made by a communicator.

Important Points to Remember

1) Argument is the basis of logic. When an argument is created over truth of a statement (assertion), the statement maker is to give evidence(s) to prove the truth of the statement he has made, which results into formation of a set of at least three statements.
2) In a set of statements, the statements given as evidences are called PREMISES. Premises generally support the assertion (given statement).
3) The very first statement made by a communicator is called ASSERTION, as it is given without evidence(s). If there is a need to prove its truth or logical validity, with supportive evidence(s), and when its validity is proved, it is called CONCLUSION, which is always the last statement in a set of statements.

TYPES OF LOGIC

There is a need to prove the truth of a statement only when there is an argument over its validity. Such an effort yields a set of statements comprising evidences and assertions. These sets of statements are seen through the following types of logic:

Deductive Logic

In this type of logic, an assertion or statement is made about a single subject. In case of an argument, its truth is proved by premises, which fully support the conclusion. Deductive logic works on the principle of **Certainty**. That means the given assertion certainly becomes true conclusion where premises given are fully supporting it. It is clear from the following example:

Assertion: Deepak is a rich man.

Now to satisfy an argument over it, the following premises are given:

1) All residents of colony X are rich.
2) Deepak is a resident of colony X.

Above premises are fully supporting the given assertion. And the set of statements so formed is as follows:

1) All residents of colony X are rich. (Premise 1)
2) Deepak is a resident of colony X. (Premise 2)
3) Therefore, Deepak is a rich man. (Conclusion)

Above set of statements belongs to deductive logic as the set starts with general subjects and ends with a specific or single subject.

Important Points to Remember

1) Premises always support the conclusion.
2) Truth of premises always yield true conclusion.
3) Premises are always true.
4) Conclusion is certainly true.

Inductive Logic

In inductive logic, an assertion, which turns out to be the conclusion, is **Probabaly True**. Here, premises do not fully support the conclusion. It is clear from the following illustration.

Assertion: All post graduates are appearing in the NET exam.

As an attempt to prove truth in it, following premises are given:

1) Navin, a post graduate, is appearing in the NET exam. (Premise1)
2) Surinder, a post graduate, is appearing in the NET exam. (Premise 2)
3) Therefore, all postgraduates are appearing in the NET exam. (Conclusion)

In the above case, on the basis of only two specific cases, a generalised conclusion has been drawn, which is not certainly true but is Probably True.

Important Points to Remember

1) Inductive logic works on the principle of PROBABILITY.
2) In a set of statements, one starts with specific subject(s) and ends with a generalised conclusion.

ARGUMENT AND ITS STRUCTURE

When one is trying to satisfy someone's argument in order to prove certainty in truth of the statement (assertion), he has made, then he is actually practicing **Deductive Logic**. So the structure of an argument displays the principle of deductive logic. Main motive behind creating an argument over an assertion is to ascertain whether the given statement is **TRUE or FALSE**. Such investigation yields a set of statements. An argument satisfying the process yields a set of either three statements or five statements.

Set of Three Statements

Let us consider the following set of statements:

1) NET qualified candidates become lecturers. (Premise1)
2) Sudhir wants to become a lecturer. (Premise 2)
3) Sudhir should qualify NET exam. (Conclusion)

Set of Five Statements

1) NET qualified candidates become lecturers. (Premise 1)
2) As a lecturer, one educates the society. (Premise 2)
3) NET qualified candidates educate the society. (Inference)
4) Sudhir wants to educate the society. (Premise 3)
5) Sudhir should qualify NET exam. (Conclusion)

Above statements show that structure of an argument in deductive logic consists of either three statements or five statements. The set of three statements depicts the traditional format where two premises are true and fully support the conclusion. On the other hand, set of five statements consists of premises, inference, and conclusion. Conclusion is the same in both the cases.

Important Points to Remember

1) Inference, in a set of five statements, is an interim conclusion derived from premises 1 and 2. It is a way to derive the final conclusion.
2) Third statement is always either inference (in case of five statements set) or conclusion (in case of three statements set). There cannot be a premise at either of these positions.
3) Statement number 4 in a set of five statements set is always a premise.
4) As the assertion maker is to prove its truth certainly, structure of the argument is found in deductive logic.

PROPOSITION: STRUCTURE

A proposition is any statement in a set of statements, i.e., premises, inference, and conclusions are all propositions. It is also called categorical proposition as the subject and the predicate in it designate some categories, due to which subject term and predicate term are called categorical terms. The structure of a categorical proposition can be studied in the following way:

A proposition: All students are intelligent.

Above proposition carries the following terms:

1) **Subject term:** As we find in general English structure, any living/non living noun or pronoun at the beginning of a sentence is the subject, here also it is the same. In the above proposition, **students** is the subject term (S).

2) **Predicate term:** A noun/pronoun/adjective at the end of a sentence is a predicate. Adjective **intelligent** is the predicate term in above proposition (P).

3) **Copula:** In general English, a sentence carries helping verbs like is, am, are, will, shall, and so on. In logic terminology, this helping verb of a proposition is called copula. In the above proposition, **are** is copula which connects subject term and predicate term.

Aristotelian Categories of Propositions

According to Aristotle, there are four categories of propositions in logic.

1) **Universal Affirmative Proposition:** If a proposition starts with **'All'** and is positive in nature and meaning, it is called Universal Affirmative and is denoted with **A**.

   Eg.: All students are intelligent. (All S is P)

2) **Universal Negative Proposition:** If a proposition starts with **'No'** and is negative in its nature and meaning, it is called Universal Negative and is denoted with **E**.

   Eg.: No student is intelligent. (No S is P)

3) **Particular Affirmative:** If a proposition starts with **'Some'**, it is called Particular Affirmative and is denoted with **I**.

   Eg.: Some students are Intelligent. (Some S is P)

4) **Particular Negative:** If a proposition starts with **'Some'** and carries negative meaning, it is called Particular Negative and is denoted with **O**.

   Eg.: Some students are not intelligent. (Some S is not P)

Square of Opposition

Above statements A, E, I, and O are having a logical relationship among them. That is shown with the following chart, called Square of Opposition.

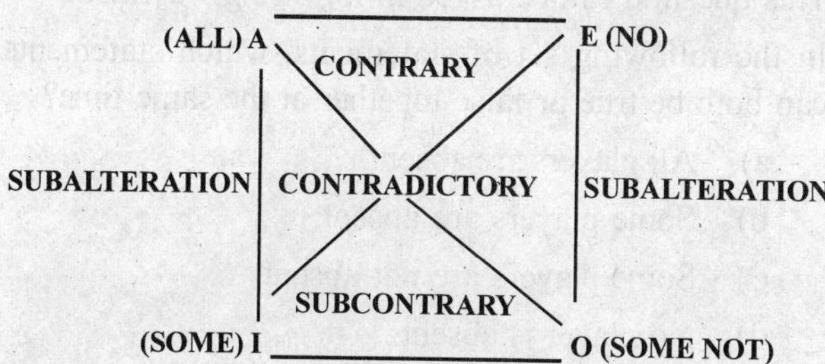

Relationship among different categories of proposition, as shown in the above Square of Opposition, is explained as follows:

1) **Contrary:**

Propositions A and E are **Contrary** to each other. This means that both **A** and E cannot be true at the same time but can be false together as **A** states universal positive statement, whereas **E** stands for universal negative statement. If **A** is true, **E** must be false and vice versa. For example, if a proposition **"All doctors are honest" (A)** is true, then proposition **"No doctor is honest" (E)** cannot be true and vice versa. This category establishes the relationship between **All** and **No.**

Example: Which of the following propositions are contrary to each other?

a) Some players are absent.
b) All players are absent.
c) Some players are not absent.
d) No player is absent.

A) a and d B) b and c
C) b and d D) a and c

Solution: As contrary relation is established between All and No, hence choice C is the answer.

This question can be asked in the following way also:

Example: Which of the two statements in the following set of statements cannot be true or false together at the same time?

a) Some players are absent.
b) All players are absent.
c) Some players are not absent.
d) No player is absent.

A) a and d B) b and c
C) b and d D) a and c

Solution: In the above case, the given condition of choosing statements indicates contrary relation, so choice **C** is the answer.

2) **Subcontrary:**

I and **O** are subcontrary to each other. It indicates that both propositions can be true together but both cannot be false together. In case **I** is true, **O** can also be true. If a proposition **"Some doctors are honest" (I)** is true, then **"Some doctors are not honest" (O)** is also true. Further, if a proposition **"Some animals are docile" (I)** is false, it does not mean that the proposition **"Some animals are not docile" (O)** is also false. This category indicates the relationship between Some are and Some not.

Example: Which of the following propositions are subcontrary to each other?

a) Some players are absent.
b) All players are absent.
c) Some players are not absent.
d) No player is absent.

A) a and d B) b and c
C) b and d D) a and c

Solution: As subcontrary relation is established between **Some are** and **Some not**, hence choice **D** is the answer.

This question can be asked in the following way also:

Example: Which of the two statements in the following set of statements can be true together but cannot be false together at the same time?

a) Some players are absent.
b) All players are absent.
c) Some players are not absent.
d) No player is absent.

A) a and d B) b and c
C) b and d D) a and c

Solution: In the above case, the given condition of choosing statements indicates subcontrary relation, so choice **D** is the answer.

3) Contradictory:

Propositions A and O are contradictory to each other and so are E and I. Propositions are contradictory to each other when both the proposition cannot be true or false together. If proposition **"All doctors are honest" (A)** is true, then **"Some doctors are not honest" (O)** is false (relation between A and O). Similarly, if proposition **"No doctor is honest" (E)** is true, then proposition **"Some doctors are honest." (I)** is false and vice versa (relation between E and I). This category establishes relation between **All** and **Some not** and secondly between **No** and **Some**.

Example: Which of the following propositions are contradictory to each other?

a) Some players are absent.
b) All players are absent.
c) Some players are not absent.
d) No player is absent.

Solution: Here, there will be two answers; one showing relationship between **All** and **Some not**, i.e., statement b and c. Another answer shows relation between **No** and **Some**. In that case, answer will be statements d and a. In the exam, there will be one case only, so that single answer choice may be selected.

This question can be asked in the following way also:

Example: Which of the two statements in the following set of statements cannot be true or false together at the same time?

a) Some players are absent.
b) All players are absent.
c) Some players are not absent.
d) No player is absent.

Solution: As above.

4) **Subalteration**:

There is subalteration relation between propositions **A** and **I** and between **E** and **O**. Two propositions are subaltern to each other when both can be true together or false together.

It means if **A** is true, then **I** is also true. Similarly, if **E** is true, **O** is also true. Again, if **A** is false, **I** is also false, and if **E** is false, then **O** is also false. But this relation does not hold good in reverse order, i.e., if proposition **I** or **O** is true or false, it does not mean that **A** or **E** would also be true or false accordingly. If proposition **"All doctors are honest" (A)** is true, then proposition **"Some doctors are honest" (I)** will also be true. In the same way, if proposition **"No doctor is honest" (E)** is true, then proposition **"Some doctors are not honest" (O)** will be true, but the same logic in reverse order, i.e., **I** to **A** or **O** to **E** is not possible.

Example showing Subalteration between A and I

Which of the following two statements in the following set of statements are subaltern to each other?

a) All players are absent.
b) Some players are absent.
c) Some players are not absent.
d) No player is absent.

A) b and d B) a and b
C) c and d D) a and d

Solution: As in this case, relationship is to be established between **All** and **Some**, answer choice **B** is the answer.

This question can be asked in following way also:

In the following set of statements, which statements can both be true or false together at the same time?

a) All players are absent.
b) Some players are absent.
c) Some players are not absent.
d) No player is absent.

A) b and d B) a and b
C) c and d D) a and d

Solution: As above.

Example showing Subalteration between E and O

Which of the following two statements in the following set of statements are subaltern to each other?

a) All players are absent.

b) No player is absent.

c) Some players are not absent.

d) Some players are absent.

A) b and c B) a and b

C) c and d D) a and d

Solution: As in this case, relationship is to be established between **No** and **Some not**, answer choice **A** is the answer.

This question can be asked in following way also:

In the following set of statements, which statements can both be true or false together at the same time?

a) All players are absent.

b) No player is absent.

c) Some players are not absent.

d) Some players are absent.

A) b and c B) a and b

C) c and d D) a and d

Solution: As above.

Above relationships of propositions can be shown with the following table also:

Proposition	TRUE	FALSE
Contrary	X X	√ √
Sub-contrary	√ √	X X
Contradictory	X X	X X
Subaltern	√ √	√ √

In the above table, √ indicates possibility of being true or false proposition and X represents non-possibility of being true or false proposition.

Important Points to Remember

1) In each of the relationships between two propositions, subject and predicate should be the same.
2) Category A proposition signifies 100% inclusion of the subject term in the predicate term.
3) Category E proposition signifies 100% exclusion of the subject term from the predicate term.
4) Category I and O signify partial inclusion and partial exclusion of the subject term in the predicate term.
5) Subaltern relation between two propositions is found in downward direction, that is, from A to I and from E to O. It does not hold good in upward direction.

Distribution of Terms

Subject and Predicate terms of a categorical proposition is either distributed or undistributed, depending upon the extent of the relationship between subject term with predicate term and vice versa.

A term is **distributed** when it informs about each and every member of the class mentioned in the subject or predicate term. On the other hand, a term is said to be undistributed when it does not inform about each and every member of the class mentioned in the subject or predicate term. This can be better understood with the following categorical prepositions:

1) **All computers are machines.**

   In this proposition, subject term computer is **distributed** because it is referring to all computers in the class or group. On the other hand, predicate term machines is **undistributed** because here, term machines is covering only computers and other machines are not being referred here.

2) **No computer is a machine.**

   Here, both subject and predicate term are distributed as subject term refers that all **computers** in the class are not **machines**, i.e., all members of the subject term are not at all part of the predicate term. Similarly, predicate **machines** is referring that all machines are not at all computers, i.e., all members of predicate term are not part of the subject term.

3) **Some Computers are machines.**

   In this proposition, both subject term computers and predicate term machines are undistributed as subject refers to some computers only and predicate refers to only those machines which are computers.

4) **Some computers are not machines.**

   In this proposition, subject term is undistributed as it refers to some computers only and not all computers. On the other hand, predicate term is distributed because it is referring to all machines which are not part of the subject term computers.

In universal propositions subject-term indistributed and in negative propositions predicate term indistributed

Quality and Quantity of a Categorical Proposition

Quantity of a proposition is indicated by the extent of coverage of subject and predicate in their relationship. It means that Universal Affirmative and Universal Negative propositions indicate their quantity. Universal affirmative and universal negative propositions answer the question-How many.

Universal affirmative includes 100% subject term in the predicate term.

Similarly, a Particular Affirmative and Particular Negative statement also indicate the extent of relationship of subject term with predicate term

Example: All animals are mortal.

It is clear from the proposition that 100% animals are part of mortals.

Example: Some animals are mortal.

Above proposition indicates that some members of subject term animals are part of predicate term mortal.

Example: No animal is mortal.

Above proposition excludes 100% subject term animals from predicate term mortal.

Example: Some animals are not mortal.

Above indicates that some members of subject term animals are not part of predicate term mortal.

Quality of a categorical proposition indicates how a subject term is related to the predicate term in that proposition. Nature of relationship of a subject term with predicate term is either Affirmative or Negative. So an affirmative proposition carries positive quality and a negative proposition carries negative quality.

Example: All graduates are officers.

Some graduates are officers.

Both of the above propositions are Affirmative in quality.

Example: No graduate is officer.

Some graduates are not officers.

Both of the above propositions are Negative in quality.

Important Points to Remember

1) Subject term is distributed in a universal proposition only if that proposition is either universal affirmative or universal negative.
2) A universal proposition is bigger in quantity than a particular proposition.
3) No is used both for quality and quantity.
4) Predicate term is distributed only in E and O type of proposition.

Distribution of terms and quantity and quality of categorical propositions is summarised as follows:

Proposition	Distribution		Quality	Quantity	Type of Proposition
	Subject	Predicate			
All S is P	Distributed	Undistributed	Affirmative	Universal	A
No S is P	Distributed	Distributed	Negative	Universal	E
Some S is P	Undistributed	Undistributed	Affirmative	Particular	I
Some S is not P	Undistributed	Distributed	Negative	Particular	O

TERMS IN THE STRUCTURE OF A DEDUCTIVE ARGUMENT

Structure of a deductive argument consists of at least three statements, out of which the first two statements are premises and last statement is conclusion. The premises and conclusion of this set of statements are known by different terms. It is clear from the following set of statements:

1) All persons are punctual.
2) Some persons are farsighted.
3) Therefore, some farsighted men are punctual.

Above set of statements consists of certain terms, viz. Major Term, Minor Term, and Middle Term.

1) **Major Term:** While considering the conclusion, it is found that 'punctual' is predicate and predicate of conclusion is called Major term.
2) **Minor Term:** Subject of the conclusion is 'men' and it is called Minor term.
3) **Middle Term:** Subject of both the premises are 'persons'. As it is common in both the premises, it is called Middle term. Middle term does not appear in the conclusion.
4) **Major Premise:** Premise which contains major term is the Major premise.
5) **Minor Premise:** Premise which contains minor term is the Minor premise.

Above set of statements are now viewed with terms in the following way:

1) All persons are punctual. (Major premise)
2) Some persons are farsighted. (Minor premise)
3) Therefore, some farsighted men are punctual.

In the above set of categorical propositions, **'punctual' is 'Major term', 'farsighted' is 'Minor term',** and **'persons' is 'Middle term'.**

MOOD OF SYLLOGISM

Mood of syllogism is determined by the categorical propositions. When a set of three statements is given in which first two are premises and third is a conclusion, category of each proposition is examined as categorised by Aristotle, i.e., whether proposition is of A, E, I, or O category. Then all the categories of propositions are collectively expressed in the order of the given set of propositions. It is clear from the following set of statements:

1) All students are hardworking. (Major premise)
2) Some students are intelligent. (Minor premise)
3) Some intelligent learners are hardworking. (Conclusion)

In the above set, proposition 1 is universal affirmative so has A category and also indicates type of major premise. Proposition 2 belongs to particular affirmative category so it is categorised as I. It also indicates the type of minor premise. Proposition 3 is conclusion and is of particular affirmative, i.e., I.

Now putting all the categories of propositions in the order from premise 1 to conclusion, i.e., first premise 1, second premise 2, and then conclusion, mood of syllogism is: AII. Mood of syllogism is expressed by three letters put together in the order as stated above. The correct order is: first proposition is major premise, second proposition is minor premise, and third proposition is conclusion.

FIGURE OF SYLLOGISM

Figure of syllogism or logic is determined by the different positions of the middle term in the structure of a deductive argument.

The different positions of the middle term determine the figure of the syllogism. There are four figures of syllogism as explained below:

First Figure: The middle term is the subject of the major premise and predicate of the minor premise.

Example: M – P (All human beings are teachers.)
S – M (All guides are human beings.)
Therefore S – P {All guides are teachers.}

Second Figure: Middle term is predicate of both the premises.

Example: P – M (All teachers are human beings.)
S – M (All guides are human beings.)
Therefore S – P {All guides are teachers.}

Third Figure: Middle term is subject of both the premises.

M – P (All human beings are teachers.)
M – S (All human beings are guides.)
Therefore S – P {All guides are teachers.}

Fourth Figure: Middle term is predicate of major premise and subject of minor premise.

P – M (All teachers are human beings.)
M – S (All human beings are guides.)
Therefore S – P {All guides are teachers.}

Figure-wise placement of middle term in all the four figures is summarised in the following table:

First Figure	Second Figure	Third Figure	Fourth Figure
M—P	P—M	M—P	P—M
S—M	S—M	M—S	M—S
S—P	S—P	S—P	S—P

In the above set, S is Subject, P is Predicate, and M is Middle Term.

Rule of Collar: This Rule of Collar is an easier way to remember position of Middle term (M), shown as follows:

First Figure	Second Figure	Third Figure	Fourth Figure
M–P S–M S–P	P–M S–M S–P	M–P M–S S–P	P–M M–S S–P

The lines so drawn above look like collar of a shirt.

Combination of Mood and Figure of Syllogism

Aristotle combined mood and figure of syllogism to find whether a particular form of syllogism is valid or invalid. There are 256 combinations of mood and figure which have led to two types of valid forms of syllogism-unconditional and conditional.

1) **Unconditionally Valid Form:** According to a mathematician Boolean's point of view, 15 forms in combination of mood and figure of syllogism are valid. These are also called 'Syllogistic Valid Forms'. These combinations are valid from Aristotelian view also. This combination is shown as follows:

First Figure	Moods: AAA, EAE, AII, EIO
Second Figure	Moods: EAE, AEE, EIO, AOO
Third Figure	Moods: IAI, AII, OAO, EIO
Fourth Figure	Moods: AEE, IAI, EIO

2) **Conditionally Valid Forms:** There are certain valid forms of syllogism in combination of mood with figure, which are valid only from Aristotelian point of view. There are 9 such combinations. It is shown as follows:

First Figure	Moods: AAI, EAO
Second Figure	Moods: AEO, EAO
Third Figure	Moods: AAI, EAO
Fourth Figure	Moods: AEO, EAO, AAI

So there are 24 (15+9) valid forms of combinations of mood and figure of syllogism.

Reconstruction of Syllogism from Given Mood and Figure

1) A I I - 2

Before reconstructing syllogism, it is to be checked whether given combination is valid or not?

In above combination AAI is mood and 2 is figure. This combination is valid only if AAI exists in 2nd figure in either conditionally or unconditionally valid table. On checking, it is found that A I I does not belong to second figure in either of the tables. Hence, it is an invalid form.

2) E I O - 4

Verification of above form reveals that above mood is found in fourth figure in unconditional validity table. So this form is valid. Now syllogism is reconsidered by adopting the following steps:

1) Construct the outline of syllogism from the given mood, where proposition E is major premise, proposition I is minor premise, and proposition O is conclusion.

E: No______ are______

I: Some______ are______

O: Some______ are not______

2) Follow the given figure to place middle term (M) in the set. The given figure is fourth figure, so according to that, M will be placed as follows:

E: No______ are_M______

I: Some_M___ are______

O: Some______ are not______

3) Finally, placing the major term (P) and minor term (S) as follows:

E: No__P___ are_M____(Major Premise)

I: Some_M___ are_S____(Minor Premise)

O: Some__S__ are not___P__(Conclusion)

TYPES OF ARGUMENT

1) **Analogous Argument:** If in a set of statements, premises mention an object, but conclusion does not mention that object exactly, but rather mentions some other object, which is similar to the object mentioned in the premises, then such an argument is called analogous argument. Such an argument is based on the principle of inductive logic where conclusion is probably true.

Example: Scooter is a convenient riding in narrow city lanes. (Premise)

Motorcycle is also a convenient riding in city narrow lanes. (Conclusion)

2) **Abductive Argument:** This argument is based on present circumstances. In this argument, conclusion is based on circumstantial premises. The conclusion so obtained is an assumption.

Example:

1) Munish is ignoring me these days.

2) I have never been bitter to him.

3) Munish must have some misunderstanding.

3) **Practical Argument:** In this set of argument, conclusion is based on speculative premises.

Example:

1) Property prices are rising these days.

2) These will start falling after achieving the apex.

3) One should sell one's property now.

4) **Cogent, Good, or Sound Argument:** Any valid deductive or inductive argument.

FALLACIES

A fallacy is a defect in the argument which makes the argument invalid. A fallacy may be occurring accidently or deliberately. A fallacy is called error if it occurs accidentally. On the other hand, if fallacy is created deliberately, it is called 'trick'. A trick is called 'Sophism'. Whether it is error or trick, a fallacy sabotages the validity of the argument and resultantly, argument becomes invalid. A fallacy whether occurring accidently or deliberately, makes an argument unsound and invalid. Further, maker of such an argument loses his/her credibility.

SOPHISM

A n argument which is apparently valid but is actually invalid. Such an argument is deliberately made invalid with an intension to deceive someone,

Types of Fallacies

1) Formal Fallacies
2) Informal Fallacies

Formal Fallacies

A formal fallacy is the fallacy of form and technical structure of an argument. In a way, it is the fallacy of reasoning. Premises do not support the conclusion or conclusion does not rightly follow from the premises in such an argument. Various defective structures of the argument containing formal fallacies can be seen as under:

Before viewing the invalid arguments, let us consider a valid argument:

Formally Valid Arguments:

A) True and Valid:

1) All fruits are perishable.
2) Mango is a fruit.
3) Therefore, mango is perishable.

Given above is true and valid argument because premises are practically true and fully support the conclusion.

B) False but Valid:

1) All fruits are vegetables.
2) Mango is a fruit.
3) Therefore, mango is a vegetable.

In the above argument, premise 1 is false but structure of argument is correct as here also, premises support the conclusion. If all fruits are vegetables and mango is one of these, then conclusion 'Mango is a vegetable' is valid.

Formally Invalid Arguments:

A) False and Invalid

1) Some fruits are vegetables.
2) Mango is a fruit.
3) Therefore, mango is a vegetable.

Above argument is formally invalid. Premise number 1 is practically false. Further, premise 1 states that 'Some fruits are vegetables'. It implies that some fruits are not vegetables. So conclusion 'Mango is a vegetable' cannot be valid as mango may not be part of 'Some fruits are vegetables'.

B) True but Invalid

1) Some fruits are perishable.
2) Mango is a fruit.
3) Therefore, mango is perishable.

In the above argument, premises 1 and 2 are true. Still, conclusion 'Mango is perishable' is not valid as premise 1 states that 'some fruits are perishable'. It implies that some fruits are not perishable and mango may not be part of 'Some fruits are perishable'.

Informal Fallacies

An informal fallacy is an unclear expression of an argument or misuse of language. It deals with the logic of usage of a word or language of a proposition. There are various ways of misuse of language, thus creating informal fallacies. There are the following types of informal fallacies:

a) **Fallacies of Presumption:** This is the fallacy which is created due to presumption of truth without evidence. Such fallacies can be expressed in the following ways:

1) **Interogative Assumption:** Let us consider the statement:

   'Does he confess that he has committed the crime?'

   There is no clarity about the ultimate answer of this question. Either of answer Yes or No is assumed. If answer is in Yes, it means that he accepts that he has committed the crime. If answer is in No, then it implies that he has committed the crime but does not accept it.

2) **Hasty Generalisation: Here are propositions:**

   'Being Punjabi he is non-vegetarian. All Punjabis are non-vegetarian.'

   These two propositions present an illustration of inductive logic and reflects a presumption about all on the basis of a single individual. So this becomes a case of hasty generalisation.

3) **Cause and Effect Assumption:** Consider the following propositions:

   'Due to rain we could not win the match. Rain is bad luck.'

   This expression is assumption of cause and effect.

4) **Slippery Slope Fallacy:** This fallacy occurs when consequences of an action are falsely assumed. Here falls the following type of propositions:

   'If examiner favours one student, he will have to help the whole class.'

5) **Sweeping Generalisation:** The propositions are:

   'Meditation relieves one from all tensions. So everyone should go for meditation'.

   Here, generalisation of a single premise makes the argument housed with fallacy of presumption.

6) **Tu Quoque Fallacy:** This fallacy arises when a person does not listen to one's advice but rather points out that person's faults who is giving advice.

This fallacy is also called 'you too' fallacy and 'look who's talking' fallacy. Let us consider the following propositions:

A to B, "Avoid tax evasion. It is an offence'.

B to A, 'Look who is advising me, who himself is facing charges of embezzlement of government funds'.

7) **Appeal to Ignorance:** Such fallacies are commonly found in routine communication on any subject. Such a fallacy is based on the logic that a particular theory or principle is true because it has not yet been proved false.

'Mr. A is declared innocent by the court as no evidence is found against him.'

In the above case 'Mr. A is innocent' is accepted as no evidence has proved it false.

8) **Circular Argument:** It is the argument which takes its truth from the argument itself.

'Cigarette smoking is injurious to health because this message is printed on the cigarette packet.'

9) **False Dilemma:** When someone presents the argument in such a way that one is left with only two options.

'If Raman does not retaliate to this attack by hooligans, he must be a coward.'

Now there are two options before Raman. He should either retaliate or earn the tag of coward.

b) **Fallacies of Ambiguity:** An argument carries a fallacy of ambiguity when the terms used are unclear in their meaning or convey more than one meaning. Such fallacies can be expressed in the following ways:

1) **Fallacies of Ascent:** In this case, meaning of the pivotal word in a proposition is not clear as it conveys more than one meaning.

'While roaming about in the forest he shot at the aimed animal'.

Here word shot is creating confusion as it is conveying more than one meaning. One meaning is that he shot at the animal with a gun. Second meaning is that he shot at the animal with a camera. He might have aimed at an animal as he was in the forest. It is not clear whether he killed the aimed animal or took photographs of the aimed animal.

2) **Equivocation Fallacies:** Such a fallacy arises in an argument when the same word or term is used at different places with different meanings.

I) 'People should be patient while relief work is in progress.'

II) 'Ambulance is taking the patient to a nearby hospital.'

In the first proposition, word patient means that people should keep patience during progress of the relief work. In the second proposition, word patient means that person who is not well and ambulance is taking him to hospital for treatment.

3) **Straw Man Fallacy:** This fallacy arises when the listener misunderstands the message of the communicator and misinterprets it, even referring to those subjects which were never intended by the communicator in his statement.

A says to B, 'I understand that you have a big friend circle but beware of selfish ones.'

B replies to A, 'I cannot believe that you will call my friends selfish.'

In the above case, B is overreacting by misunderstanding A's suggestion. A is not calling B's friends selfish and he was not even intending to do so. But B is misinterpreting A's suggestion.

c) **Fallacies of Relevance:** These fallacies are arising when irrelevant information is given to people by pursuing them to think emotionally rather than logically. Such fallacies are expressed in the following way:

1) **Appeal to Authority:** In this fallacy, statement maker, instead of giving attention to the importance of the argument, attaches content with a person known to have authority in a certain field in order to make the statement emphatic.

'Doctors believe that smoking is injurious for health. What does he think, he knows more than doctors?'

2) **Argumentum ad Populum:** In this, fallacy arises when the argument claims that some idea or belief is true because a majority of people believe that it is true.

'This school must be the best one as most of the people send their wards to this school.'

3) **Ad Hominem Fallacy:** This occurs when in a debate or argument, one participant attacks the other participant with accusations and abuses and the other participant retaliates while refuting all accusations with a feeling of insult. This fallacy is also known as Abusive fallacy or Attacking a person fallacy.

'Do not pay attention to this so-called doctor. He has not completed MBBS even.'

4) **Bandwagon Fallacy:** Such an argument advocates adopting current and modern trends.

'Present and modern education needs demand to send our wards to English medium schools. So we must send our wards to English medium schools for enabling them to survive in the modern world.'

5) **Gambler's Fallacy:** In such an argument, it is believed that if a particular event is occurring continuously in a series, then there is a probability of its occurring less frequently in the near future. This fallacy is also known as Monte Carlo fallacy.

'This dice has been coming up with number six at the top for the fifth time in a row. It has probability to come up with number one at the top if thrown for the sixth time.'

6) **Genetic Fallacy:** This fallacy accepts or rejects the truth of a concept on the basis of its history or origin rather than on the basis of its present meaning or merit.

'In spite of possessing appropriate qualification required for the post of Administrative Officer, he cannot be appointed as his ancestors survived as slaves to various kings who ruled India.'

7) **Red Herring Fallacy:** It is a deliberate attempt to introduce an irrelevant topic during the progress of an argument on some other topic with a motive to distract the attention of those participating in the discussion.

'A doctor to the audience," We should all go on fast for at least two days in a week to keep ourselves fit'.

Someone from the audience, "Sir, what has been the fate of the recent hunger strike by the doctors?"

8) **Weak Analogy:** Weak analogy arises when while participating in an argument, one in order to prove his or her point compares the similarities of two unlike subjects to prove his/her point. Such analogy is too weak to prove the point and makes the argument unsound and invalid.

'His parents beat him like the police beat a criminal.'

In the above case, there is no connection between beating by parents and beating by police. If parents beat their children, their motive is to reform their child as they are emotionally attached. On the other hand, police beats a criminal to make him confess to his crime. Moreover, the police does not have emotional attachment with the criminal. So such a comparison carries weak analogy and makes the argument totally invalid.

USES OF LANGUAGE

When an argument in logical reasoning is expressed, it is expressed in language. Language is the prime indicator of validity of an argument in logical reasoning. Further, it is the language which tells whether an argument so presented is deductive, inductive, analogous, cogent, circular, fallacious, logical, or illogical. Following are the ways in which language is used in logic:

1) **Descriptive Use:** In an argument, description of some subject or process is given. Describing an activity or subject is the basic requirement to assess whether an argument is valid or invalid. It is also known as informative use of language.

Example: Cars have steering wheel.

Parrots are green in colour.

In the above description, two subjects, car and parrot is given. Informative use of language is applicable to true and false statements. Rather, it helps in identifying truth of falseness of an argument. Let us see the following propositions:

1) A computer has an input device, output device, memory, and a central processing unit.
2) A goat has four horns.
3) Nepal is not a state of India.
4) A book has a cover, preface, table of contents, and chapters.

In the above case, propositions 1, 3, and 4 are true where language is giving right description of computer, Nepal, and book. On the other hand, proposition number 2 is wrong, as here language is giving wrong description of goat. So it is the descriptive or informative use of language which enables us to identify right and wrong proposition.

2) **Expressive Use:** Language is put to expressive use when one expresses one's emotions, feelings, and sentiments. Such feelings may convey a sense of achievement, loss, happiness, sadness, affection, hate, etc.

1) It's too bad !
2) It's awesome !
3) Take care.
4) Let's help the needy.
5) Proud of you !

Expressive use cannot be identified as true or false as these are qualitative features of concept. Further, expressive use of language is not informative as is concerned with emotions. This use of language is also known as emotive use of language.

3) **Directive use:** This use of language carries a sense of command, advice, request, and wish.
   1) Post this letter.
   2) May almighty help him.
   3) Kindly open the door.
   4) May I help you?

Such statements are carrying imperative mood and presupposes truth of proposition. For example, if someone says "Post this letter", then this truth is presupposed that the letter has not yet been posted.

CONNOTATION AND DENOTATION OF TERMS

Connotation: It is the sense of sentiments, emotions, customs, and rituals attached to a term or word, which is not the literary meaning of that term or word. For example: Consider word 'Bank'; its connotative sense is 'Faith'.

Denotation: It is the literary or dictionary meaning of a term or word. Example: Consider word 'Bank'. Its denotative sense is a person or an organisation which accepts deposits and advances loans. It also means a belt of land along the side of a river.

Relation between Connotation and Denotation

Emotional sense (Connotation) and literary meaning (Denotation) of a word go together. For example, let us consider a term 'Home'. Its literary meaning (denotation) is a dwelling, whereas its emotional sense (connotation) is family, as it is considered that there is no home without a family in which members are emotionally attached to one another. It is inferred from this that connotation of a term considers its qualitative or abstract aspect, whereas denotation depicts the physical or quantitative aspect.

Senses of Connotations

Positive sense: If a word signifies positive emotion, ritual, custom, or tradition, that is its positive connotation. For example, word 'Toast' signifies the gesture of honouring someone by people while eating and drinking together. On the other hand, its denotation is a slice of bread.

Negative sense: When a word signifies the feeling of hatred or any other negative emotion, it is said to be in negative connotation. For example, a word 'Mudslinging'. Connotative sense of this word is negative as it signifies defaming someone. Mudslinging is usually witnessed among the leaders of the opposite parties during electioneering. On the other hand, its literal meaning is smearing mud on someone's face.

Connotation and Denotation in Logic

Connotations and denotations are properties of a term in a proposition.

Connotation in Logic

It is a term signifying some properties or principles through which it is learnt how to apply that term correctly. Connotation of a term possesses some common properties which make that term applicable to objects concerned with that term and that term also possesses some essential properties without which that term cannot be applied to any subject concerned with the term. For example: Connotation of term 'Train' is a combination of its common qualities applied to every type of train (passenger, goods, etc.) and essential qualities like mechanics of train which enables the term Train applicable to this mode of transportation. Connotation is also known as 'Intension' as it refers to qualities intended by the term.

Connotation in a set of statements:

All watches convey time. (Common quality)

A watch must have a dial. (Essential quality)

Connotation of term watch: All objects having dial and conveying time are watches.

Denotation in Logic

Denotation of a term in logic is its application to various things. The general term is applicable to various things in such a way that such application conveys meaning of the term. The subjects or things to which a general term is applicable are called its denotations. For example: the term 'cutlery' is applicable to spoons, knives, forks, etc. All these items constitute meaning of cutlery so these items constitute the denotation of the term 'cutlery'. Similarly, denotation of 'cuisine' is all dishes to which the term is applicable. Denotation is also known as 'Extension' as it tells the extent of objects to which the term is applied.

Types of Connotation

(i) **Objective connotation:** Objective connotation covers all the known and unknown qualities of the term. But logic does not recognise the objective view as some qualities may not be essential. For example, consider a proposition that 'All human beings have two eyes'. Here, the objective connotation of all human beings is having two eyes, but if someone loses one eye in an accident, it does not mean that the person having lost one eye is no more a human being. So possessing two eyes for being a human being is not an essential quality or property for being a human being. Moreover, all animals are also having two eyes but these are not human beings.

(ii) **Subjective connotation:** Subjective connotation covers only those qualities of a term which are known to a particular user. This connotation is psychological in character. There are many users of an object and every individual associated with the term deciphers its attributes from an individual point of view. So connotation of a term varies from person to person. Subjective connotation cannot be accepted in logic, as there is no single connotation due to different views.

(iii) **Logical or conventional connotation:** Logical connotation is knowledge of essential and sufficient qualities of the term due to which the term is applicable to the object. Logical connotation is also known as Conventional connotation. Thinkers adopt conventional connotation in logic as the essential and sufficient qualities of a term are universally known, due to which the term is applicable to the object under consideration. For example, essential and sufficient qualities of a term 'Hospital' are availability of sufficient beds and proper treatment which are universally accepted. There is no inclusion of non-essential qualities like government hospital, private hospital, general hospital, specialised hospital, rural hospital, urban hospital, etc.

Relation between Connotation and Denotation

Connotation and denotation of a term are effectively related as explained by the following points:

1) **Connotation of a term determines its denotation:** Connotation of a term determines its denotation but reverse is not true. For example: Everyone knows the qualities intended by the term 'Ghosts' in the sense of its connotation. In this example, quality of ghosts is life after death in the form of a spirit. So the term is revealing qualities intended by the term Ghosts. The term also reveals the denotation of the term by revealing that all spirits are ghosts. But reverse is not possible as denotation 'All spirits are ghosts' does not reveal the qualities of the term Ghosts.

2) **Connotation and denotation are related in inverse proportion:** There is an inverse proportional relation between connotation and denotation. It means that an increase in connotation results into decrease in denotation and vice versa. It is seen in the following example given below.

Increase In Connotation Results In Decrease In Denotation:

Consider the term 'Students'. It refers to all students and is intending certain qualities. If connotation is increased by adding 'Hardworking' to the term, it becomes 'Hardworking students'. This leads to decrease in the extent (denotation) as now extension is confined to 'Hardworking students' only. By further increasing the connotation by adding another quality 'Intelligent', this further leads to narrow down the denotation to 'Intelligent and hardworking students'.

Decrease In Connotation Results Into Increase In Denotation:

While considering above example in reverse order, it will be observed that every decrease in connotation is leading to increase in denotation.

'Intelligent and hardworking students'

'Hardworking students'

'Students'

Exception: In some objects, any change (increase or decrease) in connotation of the term associated with these objects does not bring any change (decrease or increase) in its denotation. Sometimes, there is one-sided change in connotation or denotation. Both will inversely change only when they experience simultaneous change. For example, connotation of term 'two-wheeler' is all the essential and common qualities found in all the 'two-wheelers' like, cycle, scooter, motorcycles, mopeds, etc. Its denotation is all two-wheelers in the world. If some scooters are added in the stock, it will not to lead to decrease in the extent of denotation of the term 'Two-wheeler'.

Practice Exercise

General Questions Format

1. Inductive reasoning derives the conclusion with
   (A) Certainty (B) Authority
   (C) Validity (D) Probability
2. A logical defect in an argument is called
   (A) Syllogism (B) Fallacy
   (C) Premises (D) Inference
3. Consider the following statements:
   I) All teachers are graduates in school X.
   II) Mohan is a teacher in school X.
   What is the valid conclusion which can be drawn from the above statements?
   (A) School X employs only graduate teachers.
   (B) Mohan becomes a graduate to teach in school X.
   (C) Mohan is a graduate.
   (D) All graduate teachers are teaching in school X.
4. Which kind of logical reasoning is reflected from the situation in Q. 3 above?
   (A) Deductive
   (B) Inductive
   (C) Syllogistic
   (D) None of the above
5. An assertion does not necessarily need a/an
   (A) Inference (B) Evidence
   (C) Situation (D) Premise
6. Possibility of being TRUE or FALSE lies in a/an
   (A) Premise (B) Conclusion
   (C) Proposition (D) all Of the above
7. Which of the following is NOT TRUE?
   (A) A true premises can yield a false conclusion.
   (B) A general premise sometimes yields specific conclusion.
   (C) A general statement is the basis of an inductive argument.
   (D) Premises need an evidence in support of the claim they make.
8. In deductive reasoning, premises cannot start with adjective like
   (A) All (B) Only
   (C) No (D) Almost
9. Driving a conclusion from premises is generally termed as
   (A) Inference
   (B) Logic
   (C) Syllogism
   (D) None of the above
10. Syllogism is more significant in..............reasoning.
    (A) deductive (B) inductive
    (C) hypothetical (D) None of these
11. Which of the following statements can be taken as base for inductive reasoning?
    (A) Some students are intelligent
    (B) All leaders are rich
    (C) Majority of citizens is supporting us
    (D) X is a rich man
12. The statement, "X is a lecturer in college A" is likely to have a/an
    (A) inference (B) conclusion
    (C) evidence (D) All of the above
13. Which of the following is TRUE in the following proposition?
    All elephants are animals.
    (A) Subject term is undistributed whereas predicate term is distributed.
    (B) Both subject and predicate terms are undistributed.
    (C) Subject tern is distributed whereas predicate term is undistributed.
    (D) Both subject term and predicate terms are distributed.
14. Which of the following mood is valid in the third figure of unconditionally valid forms?
    (A) EAE
    (B) EAO
    (C) AEE
    (D) IAI

15. Consider the set of following arguments:

1) Mamta is not attending college these days.
2) She has never missed her college.
3) Mamta must have some emergency at home.

Above argument is

(A) Analogous (B) Fallacy
(C) Circular (D) Abductive

16. Mood "AEO" is valid in which of the following pair of figures of syllogism as per conditional valid norms?

(A) I - III (B) II - IV
(C) II - III (D) I - IV

17. Consider the statement:

All buildings provide shelter.

In terms of connotation and denotation, which quality does it possess?

(A) Connotation with essential quality
(B) Denotation with essential quality
(C) Connotation with common quality
(D) Denotation with common quality

18. Objective view of connotation is not accepted by scholars because the view is

(A) Paradoxical (B) Contradictory
(C) Ambiguous (D) Theoretical

19. Which of the following best explains the relation between connotation and denotation of terms in logic?

(A) An increase in connotation results in increase in denotation and vice versa.
(B) An increase in connotation does not change denotation.
(C) A decrease in denotation does not bring any change in connotation.
(D) An increase in connotation results in decrease in denotation and vice versa.

20. Which of the following is the result of a formal fallacy arising in a deductive argument?

a) Premise is false but conclusion is still valid
b) Premise is false and conclusion is invalid
c) Premise is true but conclusion is invalid

(A) Both a and b (B) a, b, and c
(C) Only b (D) Only c

21. Consider the following proposition:

Do not pluck flowers.

Which use of language is carried by the above proposition?

(A) Expressive
(B) Descriptive
(C) Directive
(D) Informative

22. Types of informal fallacies are given under Column I and their meaning are given under Column II. Study the fallacies under Column I and match with their correct meaning and choose the correct code:

	Column I (Fallacy)		Column II (Meaning)
a)	Bandwagon	I)	Attacking remarks
b)	Equivocation	II)	Irrelevant topic for discussion
c)	Ad Hominem	III)	Current trends
d)	Red Herring	IV)	Different uses of same word

Codes:	(a)	(b)	(c)	(d)
(A)	ii	iv	iii	i
(B)	i	ii	iii	iv
(C)	ii	iii	iv	i
(D)	iii	iv	i	ii

23. Uses of language in logical reasoning is vital because language

a) describes the composition of various arguments.
b) expresses emotional attachment with arguments and structures.
c) explains the difference between a true and false argument.
d) is the only means to convey the status of an argument.

(A) a and d only
(B) a, c, and d only
(C) b only
(D) c only

24. Which of the following best expresses the difference between formal and informal fallacies?
    (A) Formal fallacy arises accidently while informal fallacy arises deliberately.
    (B) Formal fallacy is related to faulty structure of argument while informal fallacy is misrepresentation of language of the argument.
    (C) Formal fallacy occurs in deductive reasoning while informal fallacy occurs in inductive reasoning.
    (D) Formal fallacy is temporary while informal fallacy is permanent.
25. In the structure of an argument, validity of conclusion is determined by
    (A) Language of assertion
    (B) Support from premises
    (C) Nature of argument
    (D) Presence of inference

KEY

1. D	2. B	3. C	4. A	5. B	6. D	7. C
8. B	9. C	10. A	11. D	12. A	13. C	14. D
15. D	16. B	17. C	18. A	19. D	20. B	21. C
22. D	23. A	24. B	25. B			

Assertion–Reason Format

1. **Assertion (A):** An analogous argument is deductive in nature.
   Reason (R): A deductive argument does not depend upon truth of premises.
   (A) Both A and R are true and R is correct explanation of A
   (B) A is false but R is true
   (C) A is true but R is false
   (D) Both A and R are true but R is not correct explanation of A
2. **Assertion (A):** Objective connotation is not acceptable in logic.
   Reason (R): All the essential qualities of a term are taken at their face value only.
   (A) Both A and R are true and R is correct explanation of A
   (B) Both A and R are false
   (C) Both A and R are true but R is not correct explanation of A
   (D) A is true but R is false
3. **Assertion (A):** A cogent argument does not necessarily contain valid conclusion.
   Reason (R): Validity of conclusion depends upon authenticity of premises.
   (A) Both A and R are false
   (B) A is true but R is false
   (C) A is false but R is true
   (D) Both A and R are true but R is not correct explanation of A
4. **Assertion (A):** An inductive argument is considered to be an assumption.
   Reason (R): Probability and assumption serve as evidences to prove validity of an inductive argument.
   (A) Both A and R are true and R is correct explanation of A
   (B) A is true but R is false
   (C) Both A and R are true but R is not correct explanation of A
   (D) Both A and R are false
5. **Assertion (A):** Middle term is the central point of consideration in the mood of syllogism.
   Reason (R): Categorical propositions are an integral part of mood of syllogism.
   (A) Both A and R are true and R is correct explanation of A
   (B) A is true but R is false
   (C) A is false but R is true
   (D) Both A and R are true but R is correct explanation of A
6. **Assertion (A):** An inference is not always a part of deductive argument.
   Reason (R): Inference acts as an interim conclusion only when an argument has five propositions.
   (A) Both A and R are false
   (B) A is true but R is false
   (C) Both A and R are true but R is not correct explanation of A
   (D) Both A and R are true and R is correct explanation of A

7. **Assertion (A):** Propositions A and I are subaltern to each other.

Reason (R): Subaltern propositions can be true together but cannot be false together.

(A) Both A and R are true and R is correct explanation of A

(B) A is true but R is false

(C) Both A and R are true but R is not correct explanation of A

(D) A is false but R is true

8. **Assertion (A):** Logical reasoning is theory of derived truth.

Reason (R): Truth is a derivative of experience.

(A) Both A and R are true but R is not correct explanation of A

(B) Both A and R are true and R is correct explanation of A

(C) Both A and R are false

(D) A is true and R is false

9. **Assertion (A):** Straw man fallacy is fallacy of presumption.

Reason (R): Misinterpreting someone's ideas generates a fallacy.

(A) A is true but R is false

(B) A is false but R is true

(C) Both A and R are true and R is correct explanation of A

(D) Both A and R are true but R is not correct explanation of A

10. **Assertion (A):** Circular argument is a conclusion-centred argument.

Reason (R): A conclusion-centred argument comes in support of truth of premises.

(A) A is true but R is false

(B) Both A and R are true but R is not correct explanation of A

(C) Both A and R are false

(D) A is false but R is true

11. **Assertion (A):** Square of Opposition illustrates the relation among categorical propositions.

Reason (R): Four categories of propositions involve affirmative and negative relationship among them.

(A) Both A and R are true and R is correct explanation of A

(B) Both A and R are true but R is not correct explanation of A

(C) Both A and R are false

(D) A is true but R is false

12. **Assertion (A):** Argument is the basis of deductive logic.

Reason (R): Premises in deductive logic depend upon the authenticity of assertion.

(A) A is true but R is false

(B) Both A and R are true and R is correct explanation of A

(C) A is false but R is true

(D) Both A and R are true but R is not correct explanation of A

13. **Assertion (A):** Language plays an important role in expressing nature of an argument.

Reason (R): Language differs with the nature of argument.

(A) Both A and R are true and R is correct explanation of A

(B) Both A and R are true but R is not correct explanation of A

(C) A is true but R is false

(D) Both A and R are false

14. **Assertion (A):** Comparison is the basis of analogous argument.

Reason (R): Similarity is the basis of analogous argument.

(A) Both A and R are true and R is correct explanation of A

(B) Both A and R are false

(C) A is true but R is false

(D) A is false but R is true

15. **Assertion (A):** Deductive argument contains an element of certainty.

Reason (R): Premises fully support the conclusion in deductive argument.

(A) Both A and R are true and R is the correct explanation of A

(B) Both A and R are true but R is not the correct explanation of A

(C) A is true but R is false

(D) A is false but R is true

KEY

1. C	**2.** A	**3.** C	**4.** D	**5.** C	**6.** D	**7.** B
8. C	**9.** B	**10.** C	**11.** A	**12.** A	**13.** C	**14.** D
15. A						

Questions Asked in Previous NET Exams

1. Inductive argument proceeds from **(UGC NET JUNE 2019)**
   (A) Universal to Particular
   (B) Particular to Universal
   (C) Universal to Universal
   (D) Particular to Particular

2. When subject and predicate of both the premises are the same but they differ in quality only, it is known as **(UGC NET JUNE 2019)**
   (A) Contradictories (B) Contraries
   (C) Subaltern (D) Superaltern

3. If proposition 'All republics are grateful' is taken to be true, then which of the following propositions can be false? **(UGC NET JUNE 2019)**
   (i) Republics are not grateful
   (ii) Some republics are not grateful
   (iii) No republics are grateful
   (iv) Some republics are grateful
   Select the correct answer from the options given below:
   (A) (i) only (B) (ii) only
   (C) (i), (ii), and (iii) (D) (ii) and (iii)

4. The proposition 'No red is black' is equivalent to which of the following propositions? **(UGC NET JUNE 2019)**
   (i) No black is red
   (ii) All red are black
   (iii) Some red are not black
   (iv) Red is not black
   Select the correct answer from the options given below:
   (A) (i), (ii), (iii), and (iv)
   (B) (iii) only
   (C) (i) and (iv)
   (D) (iv) only

5. The proposition 'All leaves are green.' is equivalent to which of the following propositions? **(UGC NET JUNE 2019)**
   a) No leaves are green
   b) No leaves are non-green
   c) No leaves are in other colour than green
   d) No green is leaf
   Select the correct answer from the options given below:
   (A) b, c, and d (B) a and b
   (C) b only (D) b and c

6. When subject and predicate of both the premises are same but they differ in quantity, it is known as **(UGC NET JUNE 2019)**
   (A) Subaltern (B) Contraries
   (C) Subcontraries (D) Contradictories

7. If proposition 'All pens are not pencils' is taken to be true, then which of the following prepositions can be false? **(UGC NET JUNE 2019)**
   (A) All pens are pencils
   (B) Some pencils are pens
   (C) No pen is pencil
   (D) Some pens are pencils

8. Identify the reasoning in the following argument: **(UGC NET JUNE 2019)**
   'Writing on paper is similar to writing on the board.'
   (A) Deductive
   (B) Hypothetical
   (C) Analogical
   (D) Inductive

9. No musicians are Japanese. **(UGC NET JUNE 2019)**
   All barbers are musicians.
   No barbers are Japanese.
   Identify the middle term in the above syllogism.
   (A) Subject in the first premise and predicate in the second premise
   (B) Predicate in the first premise and subject in the second premise
   (C) Predicate in both the premises
   (D) Subject in both the premises

10. The inference, "The Mouse is an animal .Therefore a large mouse is a large animal" commits which one of the following fallacies?

(UGC NET DECEMBER 2019)

(A) Straw Man
(B) Slippery slope
(C) Equivocation
(D) fallacy of Composition

11. In which of the following propositions, both can be true simultaneously but cannot be false simultaneously?

(UGC NET DECEMBER 2019)

(A) Contrary
(B) Contradiction
(C) Sub contrary
(D) Subaltern

12. "All tigers are animals". This is an example of which type of proposition?

(UGC NET DECEMBER 2019)

(A) Particular Negative
(B) Particular affirmative
(C) Universal Negative
(D) Universal affirmative

13. Under which of the conditions an argument may be valid? Select the correct answer from the code given below:

(UGC NET DECEMBER 2018)

Statements:

(a) When its conclusion and premises are true
(b) Even when its conclusion and one or more of its premises are false
(c) Only when its conclusion is true

(A) (c) alone (B) (a) and (b)
(C) (a) and (c) (D) (a) alone

14. Truth and falsity are attributes of:

(UGC NET DECEMBER 2018)

(A) Debates (B) Propositions
(C) Opinions (D) Arguments

15. Which one among the following is a presupposition in inductive reasoning?

(UGC NET JULY 2018)

(A) Law of identity
(B) Unchangeability in nature
(C) Harmony in nature
(D) Uniformity of nature

16. Which onc is not correct in the context of deductive and inductive reasoning?

(UGC NET JULY 2018)

(A) A deductive argument makes the claim that its conclusion is supported by its premises conclusively.
(B) A valid deductive argument may have all false premises and true conclusion.
(C) An inductive argument claims the probability of its conclusion.
(D) An inductive argument cannot provide us any new information about matters of fact.

17. If two propositions are connected in such a way that they cannot both be false although they may both be true, then their relationship is called **(UGC NET AUGUST 2016)**

(A) Contrary
(B) Subcontrary
(C) Contradictory
(D) Subalternation

18. Which one among the following is not a characteristic of a deductive type of argument?

(UGC NET AUGUST 2016)

(A) The conclusion follows from the premise/premises necessarily.
(B) The argument admits degree of complexity.
(C) The argument provides us knowledge about matters of fact.
(D) The argument must be either valid or invalid.

19. Select the code which states the condition of an invalid deductive argument:

(UGC NET AUGUST 2016)

(A) All the premises are true but the conclusion is false.
(B) Some of the premises are true but the conclusion is false.
(C) All the premises are false and the conclusion is also false.
(D) All the premises are true and the conclusion is also true.

20. Select the code which is not correct: **(UGC NET AUGUST 2016)**

An analogical argument is strengthened by

(A) increasing the number of entities.

(B) increasing the number of similar respects.

(C) reducing the claim made earlier stronger.

(D) making the conclusion stronger when premises remain unchanged.

21. Among the following propositions two are related in such a way that one is the denial of the other. Which are those propositions? Select the correct code: **(UGC NET JULY 2016)**

Propositions:

(a) All women are equal to men.

(b) Some women are equal to men.

(c) Some women are not equal to men.

(d) No women are equal to men.

Codes:

(A) (a) and (b) (B) (a) and (d)

(C) (c) and (d) (D) (a) and (c)

22. Select the code, which is not correct in the context of deductive argument with two premises: **(UGC NET JULY 2016)**

(A) An argument with one true premise, one false premise, and a false conclusion may be valid.

(B) An argument with two true premises and a false conclusion may be valid.

(C) An argument with one true premise, one false premise, and a true conclusion may be valid.

(D) An argument with two false premises and a false conclusion may be valid.

23. Given below are two premises, and four conclusions are drawn from them (taking singly or together). Select the code that states the conclusions validly drawn.

(UGC NET JULY 2016)

Premises:

(i) All religious persons are emotional.

(ii) Ram is a religious person.

Conclusions:

(a) Ram is emotional.

(b) All emotional persons are religious.

(c) Ram is not a non-religious person.

(d) Some religious persons are not emotional.

Codes:

(A) (a), (b), (c), and (d)

(B) (a) only

(C) (a) and (c) only

(D) (b) and (c) only

24. If the proposition 'All thieves are poor' is false, which of the following propositions can be claimed certainly to be true?

(UGC NET JULY 2016)

Propositions:

(A) Some thieves are poor.

(B) Some thieves are not poor.

(C) No thief is poor.

(D) No poor person is a thief.

25. Consider the following statement and select the correct code stating the nature of the argument involved in it:

(UGC NET JULY 2016)

To suppose that the earth is the only populated world in the infinite space is as absurd as to assert that in an entire field of millet, only one grain will grow.

(A) Astronomical (B) Anthropological

(C) Deductive (D) Analogical

26. Consider the argument given below:

'Pre-employment testing of teachers is quite fair because doctors, architects, and engineers who are now employed had to face such a testing.'

What type of argument is it?

(UGC NET DECEMBER 2015)

(A) Deductive (B) Analogical

(C) Psychological (D) Biological

27. Among the following propositions two are related in such a way that they can both be true, although they cannot both be false. Which are those propositions? Select the correct code.

(UGC NET DECEMBER 2015)

Propositions:

(a) Some priests are cunning.

(b) No priest is cunning.

(c) All priests are cunning.

(d) Some priests are not cunning.

Codes:

(A) (a) and (b) (B) (c) and (d)

(C) (a) and (c) (D) (a) and (d)

28. A cluster of propositions with a structure that exhibits some inference is called

(UGC NET DECEMBER 2015)

(A) An inference

(B) An argument

(C) An explanation

(D) A valid argument

29. "A man ought no more to value himself for being wiser than a woman if he owes his advantage to a better education, than he ought to boast of his courage for beating a man when his hands were tied." The above passage is an instance of **(UGC NET DECEMBER 2014)**

(A) Deductive argument

(B) Hypothetical argument

(C) Analogical argument

(D) Factual argument

30. By which of the following proposition, the proposition "Wise men are hardly afraid of death" is contradicted?

(UGC NET DECEMBER 2014)

(A) Some wise men are afraid of death.

(B) All wise men are afraid of death.

(C) No wise men is afraid of death.

(D) Some wise men are not afraid of death.

31. When in a group of propositions, one proposition is claimed to follow from the others, that group of propositions is called

(UGC NET DECEMBER 2014)

(A) An argument

(B) A valid argument

(C) An explanation

(D) An invalid argument

32. "If a large diamond is cut up into little bits, it will lose its value just as when an army is divided up into small units of soldiers, it loses its strength". The argument put above may be called as **(UGC NET JUNE 2014)**

(A) Analogical

(B) Deductive

(C) Statistical

(D) Causal

33. Given below are some characteristics of a logical argument. Select the code which expresses a characteristic which is not inductive in character.

(UGC NET JUNE 2014)

(A) The conclusion is claimed to follow from its premises.

(B) The conclusion is based on causal relation.

(C) The conclusion conclusively follows from its premises.

(D) The conclusion is based on observation and experiment.

34. If two propositions having the same subject and predicate terms can both be true but cannot both be false, the relation between those two propositions is called

(UGC NET JUNE 2014)

(A) Contradictory

(B) Contrary

(C) Subcontrary

(D) Subaltern

35. If two propositions having the same subject and predicate terms are such that one is the denial of the other, the relationship between them is called **(UGC NET DECEMBER 2013)**

(A) Contradictory (B) Contrary

(C) Subcontrary (D) Subalternation

36. When the conclusion of an argument follows from its premise/premises conclusively, the argument is called

(UGC NET DECEMBER 2013)

(A) Circular argument

(B) Inductive argument

(C) Deductive argument

(D) Analogical argument

37. Saturn and Mars are planets like the earth. They borrow light from the Sun and move around the Sun as the Earth does. So those planets are inhabited by various orders of creatures as the earth is.

What type of argument is contained in the above passage?

(UGC NET DECEMBER 2013)

(A) Deductive (B) Astrological

(C) Analogical (D) Mathematical

38. Given below are two premises. Four conclusions are drawn from those two premises in four codes. Select the code that states the conclusion validly drawn.

(UGC NET DECEMBER 2013)

Premises:

(i) All saints are religious. (Major)

(ii) Some honest persons are saints. (Minor)

Codes:

(A) All saints are honest.

(B) Some saints are honest.

(C) Some honest persons are religious.

(D) All religious persons are honest.

39. Choose the right code:

(UGC NET DECEMBER 2012)

A deductive argument claims that:

I. The conclusion does not claim something more than that which is contained in the premises.

II. The conclusion is supported by the premise/premises conclusively.

III. If the conclusion is false, then premise/premises may be either true or false.

IV. If premise/combination of premises is true, then conclusion must be true.

Codes:

(A) I and II

(B) I and III

(C) II and III

(D) All of the above

40. By which of the following proposition, the proposition 'Some men are not honest' is contradicted?

(UGC NET DECEMBER 2012)

(A) All men are honest.

(B) Some men are honest.

(C) No men are honest.

(D) All of the above.

41. Inductive logic studies the way in which a premise may

(UGC NET DECEMBER 2011)

(A) Support and entail a conclusion

(B) Not support but entail a conclusion

(C) Neither support nor entail a conclusion

(D) Support a conclusion without entailing it

42. Which of the following statements are true? Choose from the codes given below.

(UGC NET DECEMBER 2011)

1. Some arguments, while not completely valid, are almost valid.
2. A sound argument may be invalid.
3. A cogent argument may have a probably false conclusion.
4. A statement may be true or false.

Codes:

(A) 1 and 2 (B) 1, 3, and 4

(C) 4 alone (D) 3 and 4

43. A reasoning where we start with certain particular statements and conclude with a universal statement is called

(UGC NET DECEMBER 2010)

(A) Deductive reasoning

(B) Inductive reasoning

(C) Abnormal reasoning

(D) Transcendental reasoning

44. Which of the following is an example of circular argument? **(UGC NET JUNE 2010)**

(A) God created man in his image and man created God in his own image.

(B) God is the source of a scripture and the scripture is the source of our knowledge of God.

(C) Some of the Indians are great because India is great.

(D) Rama is great because he is Rama.

45. Lakshmana is a morally good person because____. **(UGC NET JUNE 2010)**

(A) he is religious (B) he is educated

(C) he is rich (D) he is rational

46. Two statements I and II given below are followed by two conclusions (a) and (b). Supposing the statements are true, which of the following conclusions can logically follow?

(UGC NET JUNE 2010)

I. Some religious people are morally good.

II. Some religious people are rational.

Conclusions:

(a) Rationally religious people are good morally.

(b) Non-rational religious persons are not morally good.

(A) Only (a) follows.

(B) Only (b) follows.

(C) Both (a) and (b) follow.

(D) Neither (a) nor (b) follows.

47. Certainty is ______.

(UGC NET JUNE 2010)

(A) an objective fact

(B) emotionally satisfying

(C) logical

(D) ontological

48. Deductive argument involves

(UGC NET DECEMBER 2009)

(A) Sufficient evidence

(B) Critical thinking

(C) Seeing logical relations

(D) Repeated observation

49. Inductive reasoning is based on or presupposes

(UGC NET DECEMBER 2009)

(A) Uniformity of nature

(B) God created the world

(C) Unity of nature

(D) Laws of nature

50. Logical reasoning is based on

(UGC NET DECEMBER 2008)

(A) Truth of involved propositions

(B) Valid relation among involved propositions

(C) Employment of symbolic language

(D) Employment of ordinary language

51. Two propositions with the same subject and predicate terms but different in quality are

(UGC NET DECEMBER 2008)

(A) Contradictory

(B) Contrary

(C) Subaltern

(D) Identical

52. The premises of a valid deductive argument ______. **(UGC NET DECEMBER 2008)**

(A) provide some evidence for its conclusion

(B) provide no evidence for its conclusion

(C) are irrelevant for its conclusion

(D) provide conclusive evidence for its conclusion

53. Syllogistic reasoning is

(UGC NET DECEMBER 2008)

(A) Deductive (B) Inductive

(C) Experimental (D) Hypothetical

54. Deductive reasoning proceeds from ______.

(UGC NET JUNE 2008)

(A) general to particular

(B) particular to general

(C) one general conclusion to another general conclusion

(D) one particular conclusion to another particular conclusion

55. Logical argument is based on

(UGC NET DECEMBER 2007)

(A) Scientific reasoning

(B) Customary reasoning

(C) Mathematical reasoning

(D) Syllogistic reasoning

56. A syllogism must have

(UGC NET JUNE 2007)

(A) Three terms (B) Four terms

(C) Six terms (D) Five terms

57. Copula is that part of proposition which denotes the relationship between

(UGC NET JUNE 2007)

(A) Subject and predicate

(B) Known and unknown

(C) Major premise and minor premise

(D) Subject and object

58. 'E' denotes

(UGC NET JUNE 2007)

(A) Universal negative proposition

(B) Particular affirmative proposition

(C) Universal affirmative proposition

(D) Particular negative proposition

59. Which of the following conclusions is logically valid based on statement given below?

(UGC NET JUNE 2006)

Statement: Most teachers are hardworking.

Conclusions:

(I) Some teachers are hardworking.

(II) Some teachers are not hard working.

(A) Only (I) is implied

(B) Only (II) is implied

(C) Both (I) and (II) are implied

(D) Neither (I) nor (II) is implied

60. Which of the following conclusions is logically valid based on statement given below?

(UGC NET JUNE 2006)

Statement: Most of the Indian states existed before independence.

Conclusions:

(I) Some Indian States existed before independence.

(II) All Indian States did not exist before independence.

(A) only (I) is implied

(B) only (II) is implied

(C) Both (I) and (II) are implied

(D) Neither (I) nor (II) is implied

61. Direction for this question:

Given below are two statements (a) and (b) followed by two conclusions (i) and (ii). Considering the statements to be true, indicate which of the following conclusions logically follow from the given statements by selecting one of the four response alternatives given below the conclusion.

(UGC NET JUNE 2006)

Statements:

(a) All businessmen are wealthy.

(b) All wealthy people are hardworking.

Conclusions:

(i) All businessmen are hardworking.

(ii) All hardly working people are not wealthy.

(A) Only (i) follows

(B) Only (ii) follows

(C) Both (i) and (ii) follow

(D) Neither (i) nor (ii) follows

KEY

1. B	**2.** B	**3.** C	**4.** C	**5.** D	**6.** A	**7.** A
8. C	**9.** A	**10.** C	**11.** C	**12.** D	**13.** D	**14.** B
15. D	**16.** D	**17.** B	**18.** C	**19.** A	**20.** D	**21.** D
22. B	**23.** C	**24.** B	**25.** D	**26.** B	**27.** D	**28.** B
29. C	**30.** B	**31.** A	**32.** A	**33.** C	**34.** C	**35.** A
36. C	**37.** C	**38.** C	**39.** A	**40.** A	**41.** A	**42.** D
43. B	**44.** D	**45.** B	**46.** D	**47.** A	**48.** A	**49.** B
50. A	**51.** B	**52.** A	**53.** A	**54.** A	**55.** D	**56.** A
57. A	**58.** A	**59.** C	**60.** B	**61.** A		

2 Venn Diagram

VENN DIAGRAM: CONCEPT

Venn diagram graphically represents the relationship among categorical propositions and is generally expressed with overlapping circles. There is overlapping of other figures also like squares, triangles, rectangles, etc. It was devised by English logician and philosopher John Venn. Each circle, triangle, or square in a Venn diagram represents an individual set of objects. If a smaller figure is embedded in a bigger figure, then the whole of the smaller figure is considered as subset of the bigger figure which is an independent set. Partial overlapping indicates the common characteristics of some objects of two independent sets. If two or more sets have nothing in common, then the sets are shown independent to one another. It can be shown as follows:

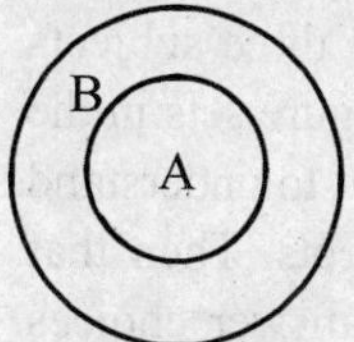

Here, A is subset of B, i.e., All A are B

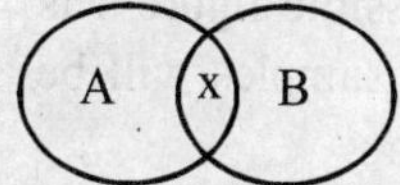

Here, A and B are independent sets.

However, x indicates that Some A are B and Some B are A

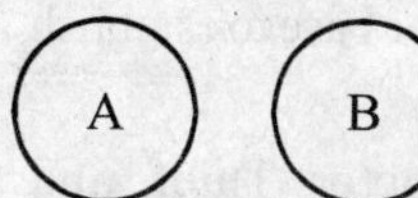

Here, A and B are independent sets and they share nothing between them

Significance of Venn Diagram

Venn diagram helps in understanding the relationship among categorical propositions introduced by Aristotle. Basic constituents of a categorical proposition are Subject term (S) and Predicate term (P). In a set of propositions, there is found another term, i.e., Middle term (M). Venn diagram expresses the relationship among these terms.

Expressing Relationships

Venn diagram expresses relationship among different terms of categorical propositions in terms of their quality and quantity in the following way:

1) Relationship between S and P and vice versa
2) Relationship between S and M and vice versa
3) Relationship between M and P and vice versa
4) Relationship between S and P through M and vice versa

Venn diagram expresses the above relationships as per quantity and quality of proposition in case of one, two, or three propositions as explained below:

Single Proposition Relationship

* **Universal Affirmative Proposition:**

Statement: All Cars are Automobiles.

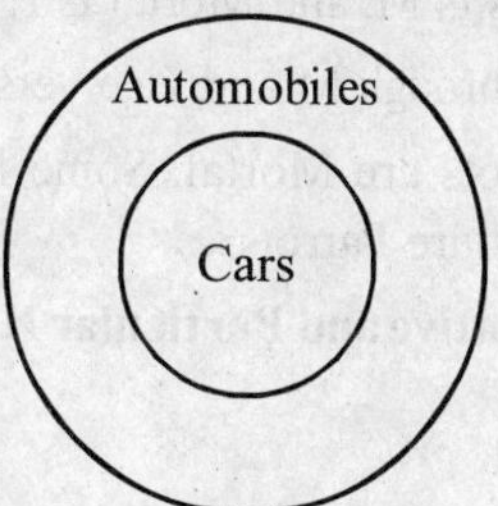

Here, Car is S and Automobile is P.

Here, All Cars are Automobiles and some Automobiles are Cars.

* **Particular Affirmative and Particular Negative Proposition:**

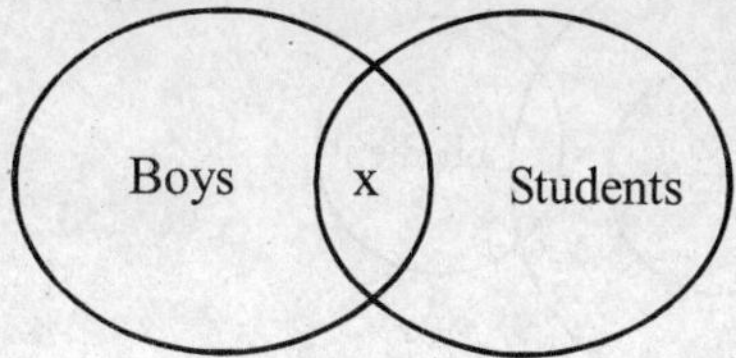

Statement: Some Boys are Students.

Here, Boys is S and Students is P.

Here, area x indicates that some boys are students and some students are boys. Similarly, remaining area of both the sets indicate that some boys are not students and some students are not boys.

* **Universal Negative Proposition:**

  Statement: No Rickshaw is Scooter.

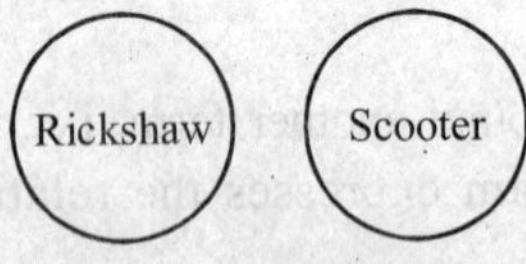

Here, Rickshaw is S and Scooter is P.

Here, no rickshaw is scooter and no scooter is rickshaw.

Two Proposition Relationship

* **Universal Affirmative Proposition:**

  Statements:

  All Parrots are Birds.

  All Birds are Mortal.

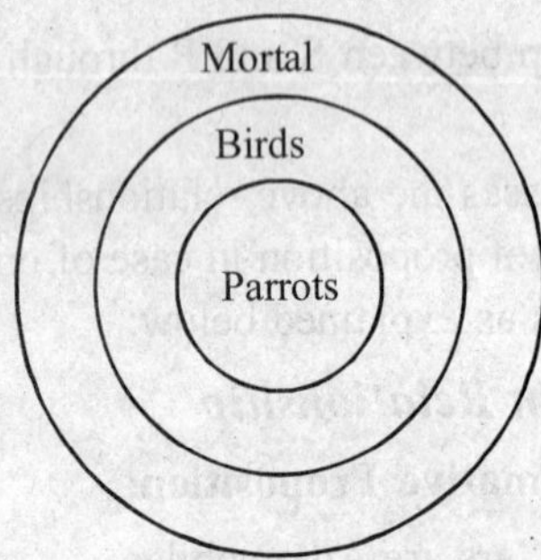

Here, Parrots is S, Birds is M, and Mortal is P.

Here, S is related to P through M and vice versa.

Relationship: All Parrots are Mortal. Some Mortals are Parrots. Some Birds are Parrots.

* **Particular Affirmative and Particular Negative Proposition:**

  Statements:

  Some Players are Students.

  Some Players are not Students.

  Some Obedient are Players.

  Some Obedient are not Players.

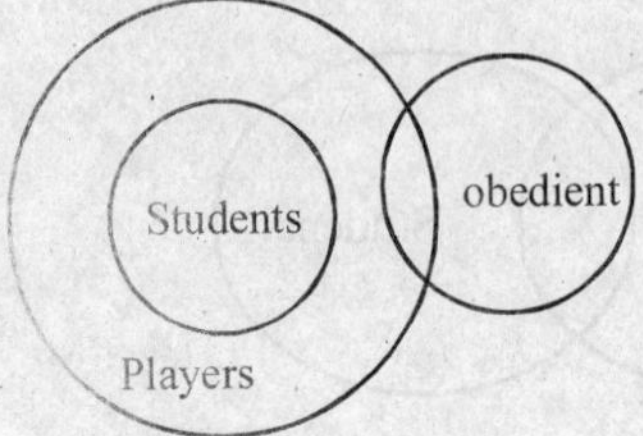

Relationship:

Some Players are Students. Some Players are not Students.

Some Obedient are Students. Some Obedient are not Students.

* **Universal Negative Proposition:**

  Statements:

  No Road is a Lane.

  No Lane is Street.

Relationship:

No Lane is Road.

No Street is Lane.

Part – I

SUITABLE MATCHING

INTRODUCTION

Questions on the 'Suitable matching' application of Venn diagram has been frequently asked in previous NET exams. The nature of questions is that three subjects are given, which are followed by four figure sets in the form of answer choices. An aspirant has to understand the relationship among the given subjects. Then that figure set will be picked up from the answer choices which are suitably matching with the relationship among those three subjects. There are 10 possible figure sets of such relationships. Each set with examples will be studied in this chapter.

CONCEPT

It is important to note that relationship among the given subjects is to be ascertained on the basis of their identity or recognition. There should be no other base to establish the relationship.

For example, if three subjects 'Doctor, Thief, and Grocer' are given, their relationship will be expressed with three separate circles as a set of Venn diagram because each of the three has their respective identity and recognition. They are different from one another as they have a different identity. Relationship should not be seen on the ground that as all of them are human beings, so they are related.

Set-I

Three subjects from any field are given. Along with them, three figure sets in the form of Venn diagrams are given. It is to be identified that which figure set best suitably expresses the relationship among the given subjects.

Let A, B, and C be the three subjects. Their possible relationship or non-relationship is elaborated with the help of the following figure sets.

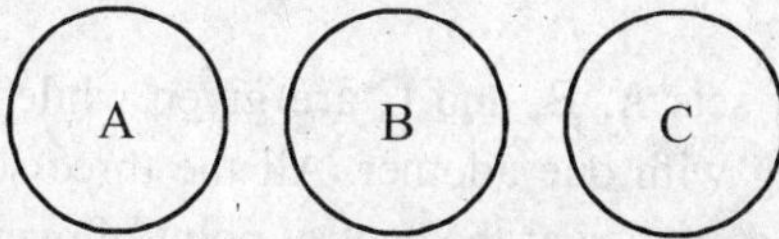

In the above set, A, B, and C have no relation with one another as indicated by three separate circles.

Example: Table, Beggar, River

Explanation: As all objects have a different identity, there is a separate circle for each subject.

Set- II

Here, three interlocking circles are expressing a relationship. Given below is a figure and example to help understand the relationship.

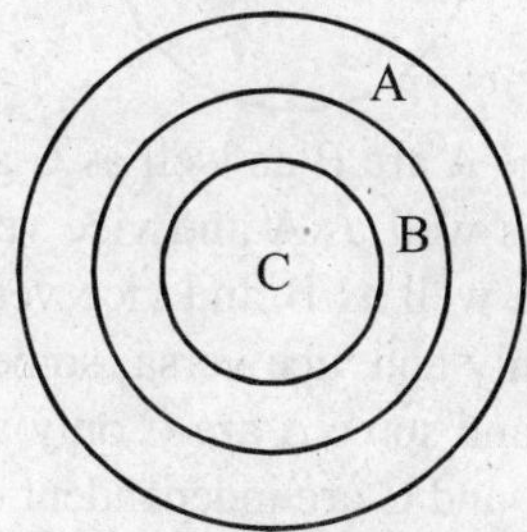

In the above set, all C are B and all B are A, but reverse is not true, i.e., all B are not C and all A are not B. Therefore, all A are also not C. However, some B are C and some A are B, threfore some A are C.

Example: Minute, Hour, Second

Explanation: Here, circle C stands for second, B for minute, and A for hour as all seconds are minutes and all minutes are hours.

Set- III

In the figure set below, three circles are given in such a way that circle B is sub-circle of circle A, and C is a separate circle partially overlapping with B.

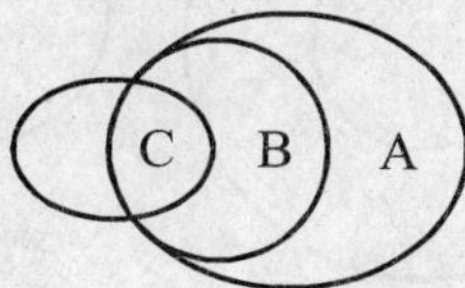

Here, All B are A but some A are B. Some C are B and some B are C, hence some A are C through B.

Example: Socialists, Earth, Country

Explanation: In this figure, set A is earth, B is country, and C is socialists. B is sub-circle of A which indicates that all countries are earth but whole earth is not countries as circle A is wider than B. C is partially overlapping B. It indicates that the part of C which is overlapping means some countries are socialists but some are not. The outer part of C indicates that some socialists are not countries, rather these can be socialist schools of thought, organisations, norms, etc.

Set- IV

In the figure set below, circles A and B are partially overlapped, whereas C is an independent circle.

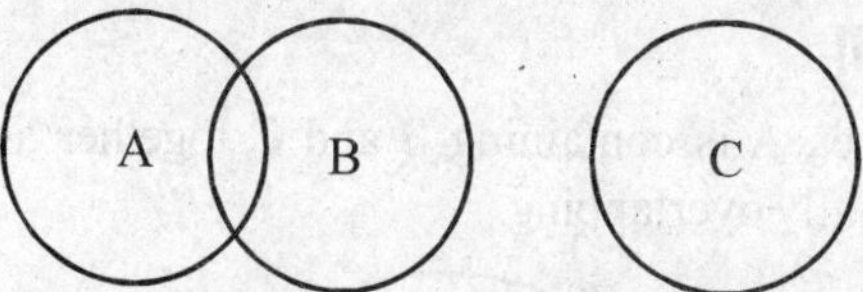

In the above case, some A are B and some B are A. Both have no relation with C and so has C with them.

Example: Male, Student, Bucket

Explanation: Circles A and B are partially overlapping, which indicates that some males are students and some students are males. C is separate as it has a separate identity of a non-living object, i.e., bucket.

Set-V

As given below, circles A and C are partially overlapping central circle B from its different sides.

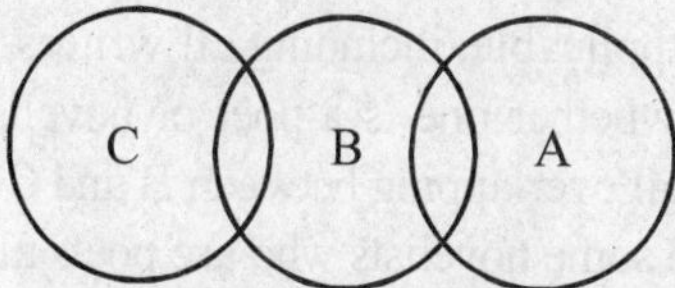

Here, some B are C and some B are A. Some B are independent of A and C. However, some C are B and some A are B, though A and C have no relation between them.

Example: Pet, Dog, Cat

Explanation: Circle B is pet and out of the other two, one is cat and other is dog. Central portion of B indicates those pets which are neither cats nor dogs. Partially overlapped portions of circle A and C with circle B indicate that these dogs and cats are pets, whereas others are stray.

Set- VI

Here, both circles C and B are contained (fully overlapped) in A.

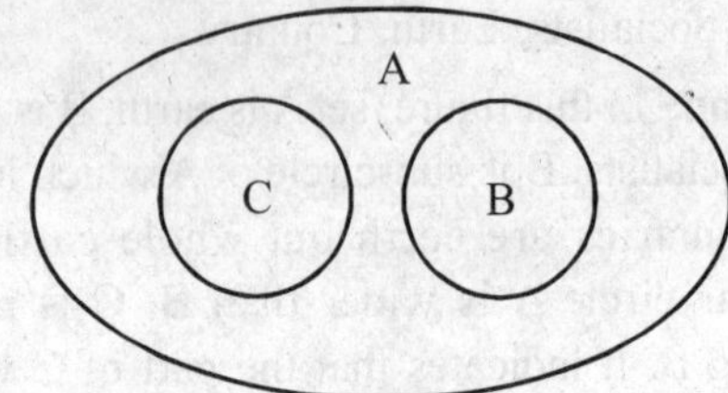

Here, all C and all B are A, but all A are neither B nor C. However, some A are C and some A are B. C and B are independent of each other.

Example: Bus, Jeep, Automobile

Explanation: Whether it is bus or jeep, both are included in automobile. So A is automobile and out of B and C, one is bus and another is jeep.

Set- VII

In this set, A is containing B and C together and they are partially overlapping.

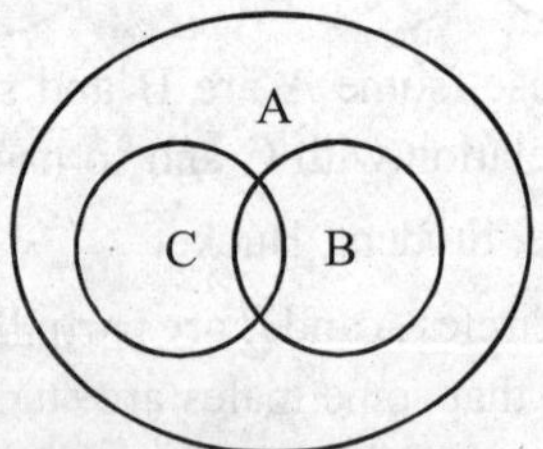

Here, all C are A and all B are A. All A are neither C nor B, but some A are C as well as B. Here also, some C are B and some B are C.

Example: Poet, Novelist, Writer

Explanation: A is writer which is a general term and universally applicable, including all writers. A contains B and C as whether one is a poet or novelist, both are writers. Partial overlapping between B and C establishes that there are some novelists who are poets also and vice versa and rest of them are independent of each of them.

Set - VIII

Set C is completely contained by set A. Set B is partially overlapping with C and A independently. Some part of set B is independent of overlapping.

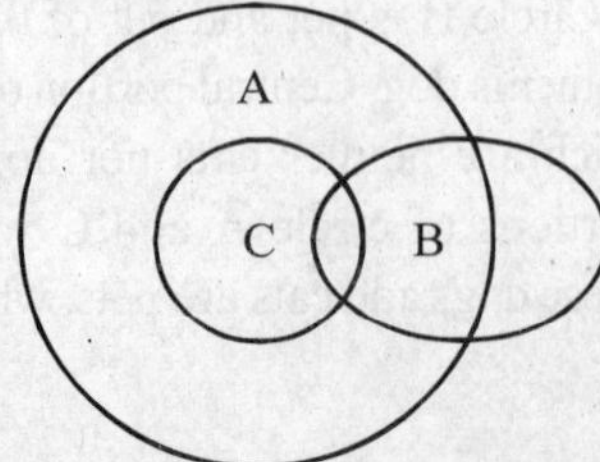

In the above case, all C are A but all A are not C. Some B are C as well as A and vice versa. Some B are only A and vice versa, whereas some B are independent of C and A.

Example: Brother, Student, Male.

Explanation: Here, set A is male, set C is brother, and set B is students. The figure establishes that all brothers (C) are males (A) and some students are brothers and also males (overlapping part of B and C inside A). Some students are males but not brothers (portion of B outside C) and some students are not males (non-overlapping part of B outside A).

Set-IX

In this set, sets A, B, and C are given while partially overlapping with one another. All the three sets share their characteristics at the central point of overlapping. Then two out of three are sharing their characteristics at each bilateral overlapping, leaving aside the third one. Some part of each set is independent of overlapping.

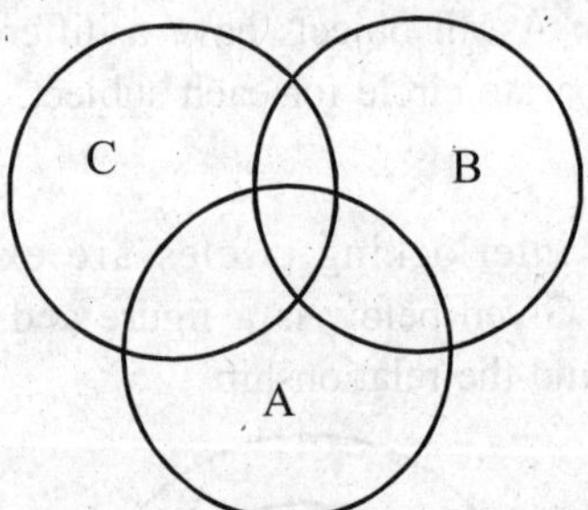

In this case, some A are B as well as C and vice versa. Some B are C as well as A and vice versa. Similarly, some C are A as well as B and vice versa. Here also, some A are B only and vice versa, some B are C only and vice versa, and some A are C only and vice versa. Still, some A, B, and C are independent of one another.

Example: Graduates, Officers, Govt. Employees

Explanation: As all the sets are open and neutrally overlapped, any set can be chosen as graduates, Govt. employees, and officers.

SET - X

Here, all B are A but all A are not B, rather some A are B. On the other hand, A and B both have

no relation with C as shown below.

Example: Cow, River, Animal

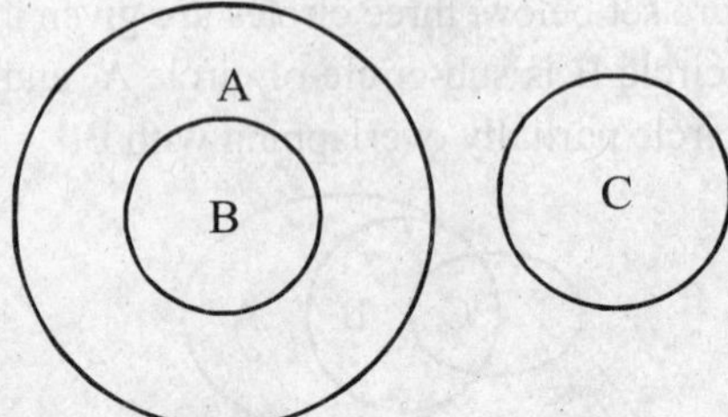

Explanation: In this set, A is animal, B is cow, and C is river. A and B are related, whereas C is an independent set.

Part – II

CLASS REPRESENTATION

CONCEPT

Class representation is another popular topic from Venn diagram, which is asked in the NET exam. In this, various geometrical figures (usually circles) are shown spatially overlapping with one another. Each figure in the given set represents a class.

Format

A figure set of three or four figures is given. Each figure represents a class of people. These classes generally belong to different professions and characteristics of people. The given figures partially overlap with one another. A number or a letter of English alphabet appears randomly in different parts of the figure. Numbers or letters cover the overlapped and independent area of each figure in the set. A number or letter covering a single or more than one figure represents class of single or more than one figure it covers. Then questions are asked about which letter or number covering a single or more than one figure represents a given class or classes. Two types of questions are asked on this topic:

1) Identifying one or more given classes represented by a number or letter
2) Statement on the basis of given figure set is given, and it is to be ascertained whether the statement is true or false.

STRATEGY OF CLASS REPRESENTATION

As and when a figure set is given, first of all it is reviewed that how many figures are there in the given set of the Venn diagram. Number of overlapped figures represents the same number of the given classes. For example, if in a Venn diagram set, four figures are partially overlapping with one another, there are four classes which figures are representing. As there is partial overlapping of each figure, some part of each figure is independent of overlapping. Overlapped part of each figure represents some part of the respective given class(es) and the part that is independent of overlapping represents some part of opposite class(es) covered in overlapping. Candidate should mark opposite class of each given class. This can be shown with the following example:

In the given figure set, △ represents Actors, ▭ represents Soldiers and ○ represents Bankers. Here, along with given classes, their opposite classes are also to be considered as:

Given Classes: Actors, Soldiers, and Bankers

Opposite Classes: Non-actors, Non-soldiers (civilians), and Non-bankers

In the given Venn diagram, triangle, rectangle, and circle are partially overlapping. This indicates that some proportion of given classes are sharing common characteristics with one another. Area of figures independent of overlapping indicate that this proportion of given classes does not have any common characteristics among them.

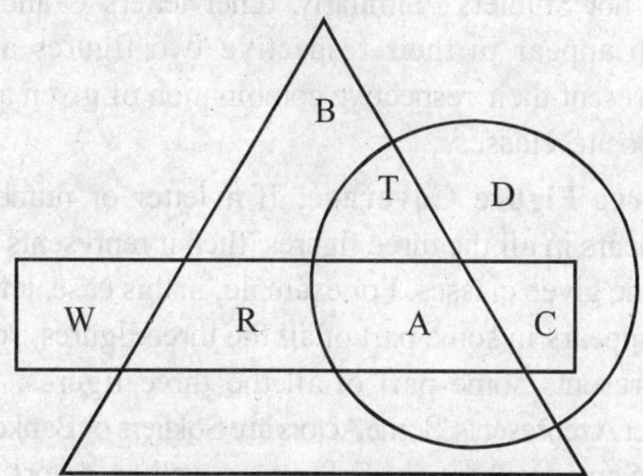

A further look at the figure set reveals that different overlapped and non-overlapped areas of figure sets are denoted by various letters of the English alphabet. These letters are representing single or more than one given classes depending on the number of figures they cover. Further, each letter does not only represent the given classes, but also represents the opposite classes depending on how many figures a letter is covering. So a letter or number represents a given class or classes in combination with opposite classes.

Class Representation Through Coverage of Figures in Three Figure Set

1) **One Figure Coverage:** If a letter or number appears in one figure only, then it represents the given class of that figure and opposite classes of other figures in which that letter or number is not appearing. For example, in the above case, letter B is appearing in triangle only. So it represents the given class of triangle, i.e., Actors, but along with this, it also represents the opposite classes of circle and rectangle, i.e., Non-bankers and Non-soldiers respectively. So classes represented by B are 'Some Actors who are neither Soldiers nor Bankers.' Similarly, the other letters D and W are also appearing in a single figure and they also represent their respective given and opposite classes in the way B is representing.

2) **Two Figure Coverage:** If a letter or number is appearing in two figures, then it represents the given classes of those two figures and opposite class of the figure in which it is not appearing. For example, letter T is appearing in circle and triangle and does not appear in rectangle. So T is representing given classes of circle and triangle, i.e., Actors and Bankers and also represents opposite class of rectangle, that is, Non-soldiers. So the classes represented by T are: 'Those Bankers who are Actors but not Soldiers'. Similarly, other letters C and R also appear in their respective two figures and represent their respective combination of given and opposite classes.

3) **Three Figure Coverage:** If a letter or number appears in all the three figures, then it represents all of the given classes. For example, in this case, letter A appears in some part of all the three figures, so it represents some part of all the three figures. So letter A represents 'Some Actors are Soldiers or Bankers' or 'Some Bankers are Soldiers as well as Actors' or 'Some Soldiers are Actors as well as Bankers'.

In a nutshell, each number in the above figure set represents possible cross combinations of Given Class (GC) and Opposite Class (OC) in the overlapped and independent areas of the figure set as follows:

I) GC-GC-GC (covers all the three GC figures)

II) GC-GC-OC (covers two GC figures only)

III) GC-OC-OC (covers one GC figure only)

Part – III

STATEMENTS & CONCLUSIONS (FALLACIES)

CONCEPT

A fallacy is created in a structure of deductive argument when in spite of premises being true, conclusion is false. Similarly, if the premises are false, even then the conclusion will be false as false premise can support a false conclusion only.

There have been questions on fallacies in various reasoning exams including NET Paper 1. Knowledge of logical reasoning helps one to solve questions on fallacies.

Format

Format of questions on fallacies is given in the form of a structure of deductive arguments. In the usual structure, there is a set of four statements, out of which first two are premises and the last two are conclusions, which are numbered I and II. A candidate is to read the statements and conclusions and decide whether conclusion(s) logically follow(s) from the premises. As the question is in MCQ form, the candidate is to choose the correct choice from the following answer choices:

A) If only conclusion I follows

B) If only conclusion II follows

C) If either conclusion I or II follows

D) If both conclusions I and II follow

E) If neither conclusion I nor II follows

STRATEGY

Though given statements in this type of question are practically not true, yet a logical relation exists between statements and conclusions. There also exists a relationship between the given statements also. In the chapter of logical reasoning, structure of a proposition, i.e., statement has already been studied. You might recall that a set of propositions contains subject term, middle term, and predicate term. Knowledge of logical reasoning and Venn diagram further helps in solving such questions. Candidate is to read the statements carefully, consider them true even if these are not, and understand the structure of each statement. It is also to be ascertained whether given premises or statements belong to A, E, I, or O category. Category of each statement influences the decision about validity of the given conclusions. It is also important to note fallacies in the given set of statements. Now let us discuss a set of propositions category-wise to understand how to judge validity of conclusion(s) in a given set of propositions.

1) **When both the Statements are of Universal Affirmative Category (A):**

Statement 1: All Cups are Plates.

Statement 2: All Plates are Glasses.

Conclusions:

I. Some Plates are Cups.

II. All Cups are Glasses.

A) If only conclusion I follows

B) If only conclusion II follows

C) If both conclusions I and II follow

D) If neither conclusion I nor II follows

Answer: C

Explanation: Let us draw Venn diagram of the two statements one by one.

Venn diagram of the first statement:

All Cups are Plates.

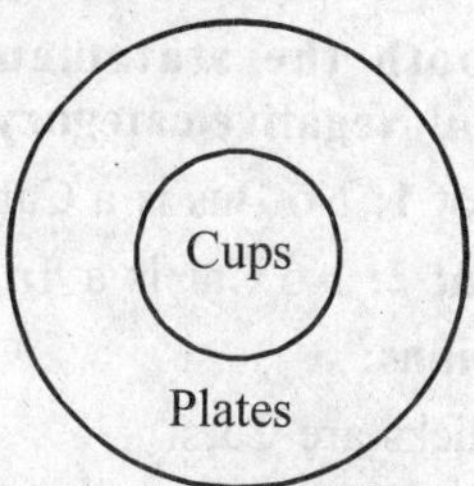

Venn Diagram of second statement:

All Plates are Glasses.

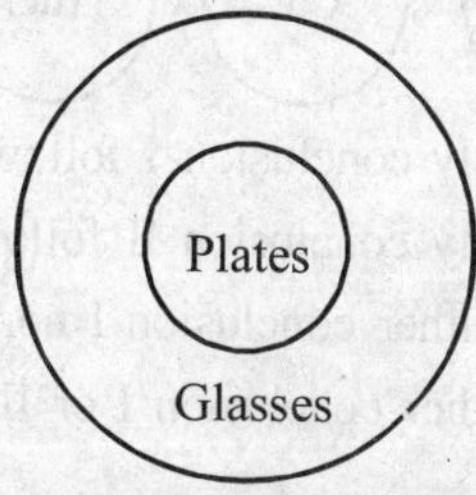

From the above statements it is found that middle term 'Plates' is the means of relationship between Glasses and Plates as it is equally distributed between the two. The combined Venn diagram of both the statements is as follows:

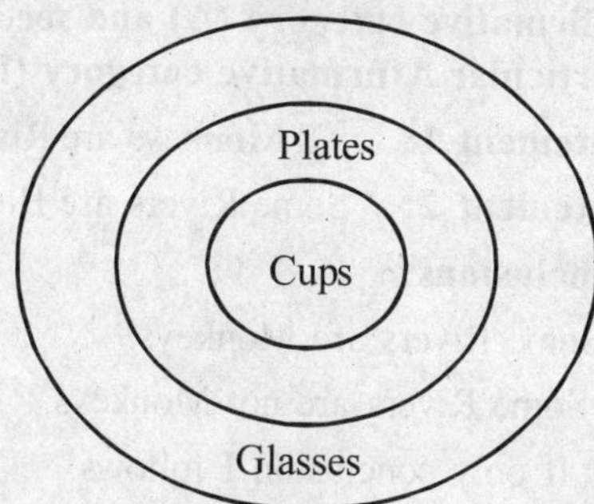

From the above diagram, the relationship among propositions is clear. Now given conclusions can be reviewed for deciding which conclusion(s) is/are valid.

Given conclusions are:

I. Some Plates are Cups.

II. All Cups are Glasses.

Decision about conclusions:

1) Venn diagram indicates that all Cups are Plates and all Plates are Glasses. Thus, it is established that middle term 'Plates' is equally distributed between subject of first statement, i.e., 'Cups' and predicate of the second statement, i.e., 'Glasses'.
2) In the above case, as one moves from the smaller circle to the bigger one, Universal Affirmative conclusion will be valid.
3) If one moves from the bigger circle to the smaller circle, the conclusion will be of category 'I' which states that 'Some Subjects (S) are Predicates (P)'. It also implies that this conclusion also conveys category 'O', i.e., Some S are not P.

Valid Conclusions: From the above, the following conclusions are valid and thus follow:

1) All Cups are Glasses.
2) Some Plates are Cups.
3) Some Glasses are Plates.

There is no other conclusion beyond these conclusions which will follow. Now we find that both the given conclusions are out of the three valid conclusions mentioned above. So in this case, answer to this question is C.

2) **When both the Statements belong to Particular Affirmative category (I):**

Statement 1: Some Boys are Tables.

Statement 2: Some Tables are Coaches.

Conclusions:

I. No Table is a Boy.

II. All Coaches are Boys.

A) If both conclusions I and II follow
B) Only conclusion I follows
C) If only either conclusions I or II follows
D) If neither conclusions I nor II follows

Answer: D

Explanation:

Venn diagram of first statement:

Some Boys are Tables.

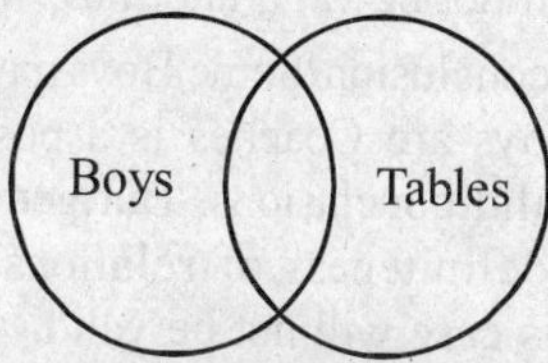

Venn diagram of second statement:

Some Tables are Coaches.

There is a possibility of two diagrams while considering the place of middle term 'Tables'.

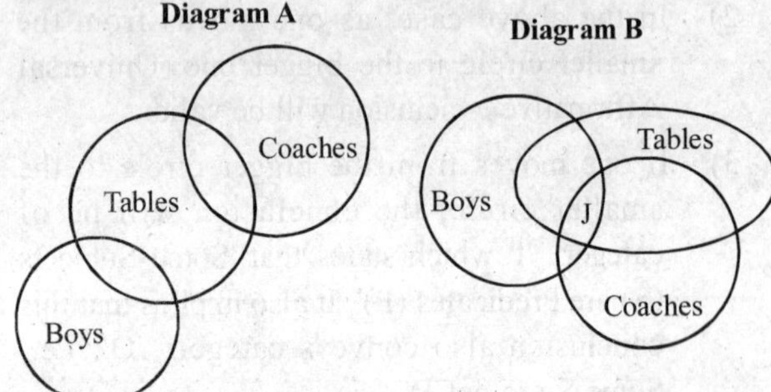

Decision about conclusions:

1) As and when predicate term 'Coaches' is shown in Venn diagram, relationship between Boys and Coaches becomes uncertain as here, common term is not equally distributed between Boys and Coaches.
2) In the cases where both statements start with 'Some', there is partial overlapping of sets due to which middle term 'Table' is not equally distributed between subject term 'Boys' and predicate term 'Coaches', thus creating uncertainty regarding any definite relationship between them.
3) Above two diagrams show that either of the two situations will happen as the second statement in the set does not clarify which Tables are Coaches; whether those who are not Boys (Diagram A) or those which are Boys also (Diagram B).
4) In case relationship of Diagram A prevails, then there is no relationship between Boys and Coaches, but on the other hand, if relationship of Diagram B prevails, then there is definitely a relationship existing between Boys and Coaches. It is shown at point 'J' in Diagram B, where there is partial overlapping of Coaches and those Boys which are Tables.
5) If this situation exists, then some Boys who are Tables are Coaches. But this is only a possibility and the other possibility of Diagram A where there is negative relation between Boys and Coaches cannot be denied.
6) So any conclusion which establishes a definite positive or negative relation between Boys and Coaches will not be valid and thus, will not follow.
7) If there is a conclusion 'Some Boys may be Coaches' or 'Some Boys are Coaches is a possibility', then these are valid conclusions. But generally in such questions, definiteness of relationship is shown which in this case will not be valid.

Valid Conclusions: From the above, following conclusions are valid and thus follow:

1) Some Coaches are Tables.
2) Some Tables are Boys.

It is because 'Some' is reversible. If it is true that 'Some Coaches are Tables', then its valid conclusion can be 'Some Tables are Coaches'.

Any other conclusion besides these will not follow. While finding given conclusions in the question, it is ascertained that neither conclusion I nor II follows. So answer is D.

3) **When both the statements belong to Universal Negative category (E)**

Statement 1: No Bus is a Car.

Statement 2: No Car is a Truck.

Conclusions:

I) All Trucks are Cars.

II) No Car is a Bus.

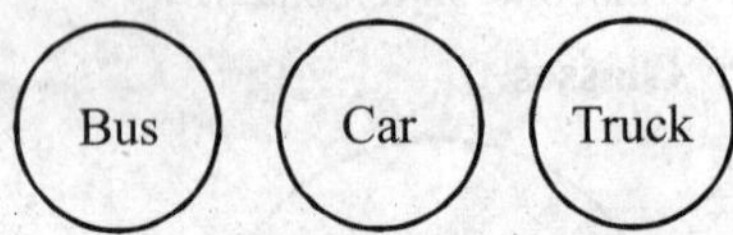

A) If only conclusion I follows
B) If only conclusion II follows
C) If neither conclusion I nor II follows
D) If either conclusion I or II follows

Answer: C

Explanation: As all the propositions are not related to one another, answer is C.

MIXED CASES

1) **When first statement is of Universal Affirmative category (A) and second is of Particular Affirmative category (I):**

Statement 1: All Monkeys are Rivers.

Statement 2: Some Rivers are Books.

Conclusions:

I) Some Rivers are Monkeys.

II) Some Rivers are not Monkeys.

A) If only conclusion I follows
B) If only conclusion II follows
B) If both conclusions I and II follow
D) If either conclusion I or II follows

Answer: D

Explanation: Drawing Venn diagram of first statement:

All Monkeys are Rivers.

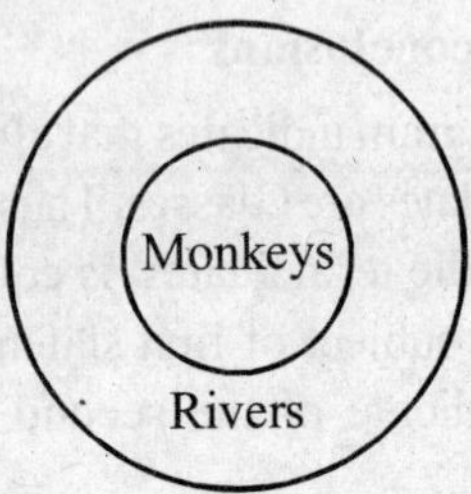

Drawing Venn diagram of second statement:

Some Rivers are Books.

On this statement there wisll be two diagrams:

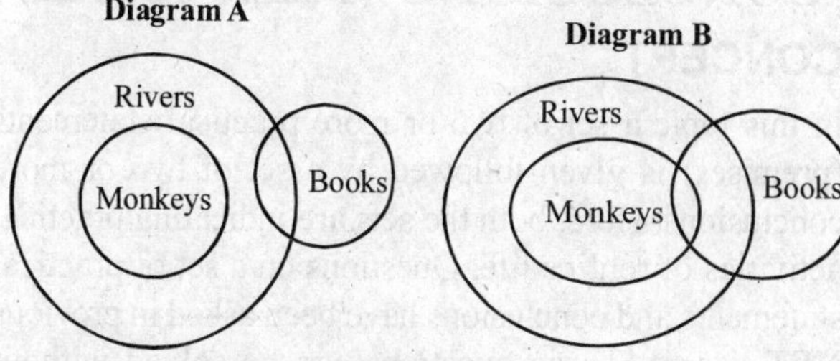

Decision about conclusions:

1) In this case, either of the above cases is possible.
2) If it is as in Diagram A above, there is no relation between Monkeys and Books.
3) If it is as in Diagram B above, then there is definite relation between some Monkeys and some Books.
4) However, in both diagrams A and B above, there is definite relation between Monkeys and Rivers.

Valid Conclusions: Following conclusions are valid in this case:

I) Some Rivers are Monkeys.

II) Some Books are Rivers.

No other conclusion is valid in the above case.

In this question given conclusions are:

I) Some Rivers are Monkeys.

II) Some Rivers are not Monkeys.

Here, as conclusion I is evident from both diagrams A and B, it definitely follows. Conclusion II is implication of conclusion I, i.e., if conclusion I is valid, it naturally conveys the sense of conclusion II, and on the other hand if conclusion II is accepted, it naturally conveys the sense of conclusion I. We cannot accept both the conclusions at the same time as it creates redundancy. In such cases where both the conclusions are valid and they convey the same sense, either of the two follows. So answer in this case is: 'Either conclusion I or II follows', i.e., Answer choice is D.

2. When first statement is of Particular Affirmative category (I) and second is of Universal Affirmative category (A):

Statement 1: Some Lanes are Streets.

Statement 2: All Streets are Bridges.

Conclusions:

I) Some Bridges are Lanes.

II) No Street is Lane.

A) If only conclusion I follows

B) If only conclusion II follows

C) If both conclusions I and II follow

D) If neither conclusion I nor II follows

Answer: A

Explanation: Drawing Venn diagram of first statement:

Some Streets are Lanes.

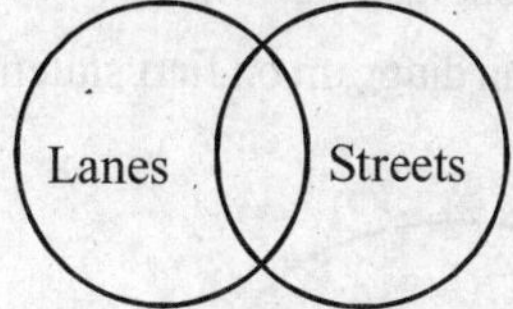

Drawing Venn diagram of second statement:

All Streets are Bridges.

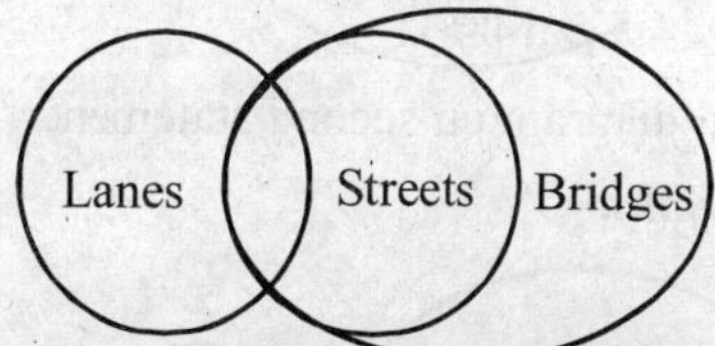

Decision about conclusions:

1) Both the diagrams reveal that some Lanes and some Streets are positively related, i.e., some Streets are definitely Lanes and also, some Lanes are definitely Streets.
2) As those Lanes which are Streets are also definitely Bridges, as is clear from Venn diagram of second statement, some Bridges are also definitely Lanes.

Valid Conclusions:

1) Some Streets are Lanes.
2) Some Lanes are Bridges.
3) Some Bridges are Lanes.
4) Some Bridges are Streets.

Now the given conclusions are:

I) Some Bridges are Lanes.

II) No Street is Lane.

It is found from the above statements that conclusion II is not among the valid conclusions, so only conclusion I is valid. Hence, answer choice A is the answer.

3) When first statement is of Universal Affirmative category (A) and second statement is of Universal Negative category (E).

Statement 1 : All Birds are Kites.

Statement 2: No Kite is a Ship.

Conclusions:

I) No Bird is Ship. II) Some Kites are Birds.

A) Only I conclusion follows

B) Only II conclusion follows

C) Both I & II conclusions follow

D) Neither I nor II conclusions follow

Explanation: Drawing Venn diagram on first statement:

All Birds are Kites.

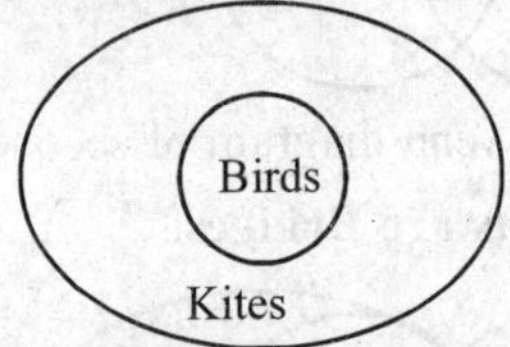

Drawing Venn diagram on second statement:

No Kite is a Ship.

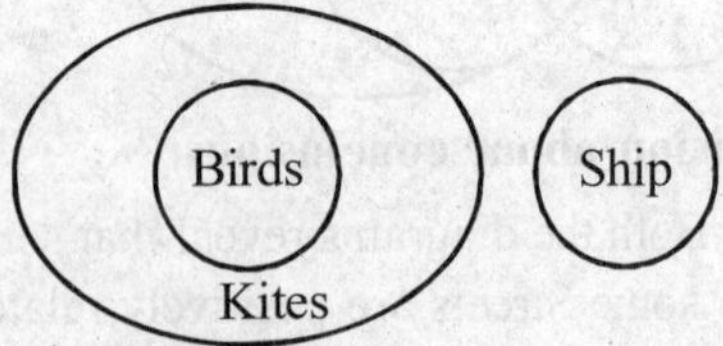

Decision about Conclusions:

1) Both of above diagrams reveal that there is a definitely positive relation between Kites and Birds.
2) Second diagram reveals that there is negative relationship of Kites with Ship.
3) As all Birds are Kites in the given statement 1, all Birds also have negative relationship with Ship.

Valid conclusions: Following are valid conclusions of this type:

1) No Bird is a Ship.
2) No Ship is a Kite.
3) No Ship is a Bird.
4) Some Kites are Birds.

We know that given conclusions are:

I) No Bird is Ship.

II) Some Kites are Birds.

As both the conclusions are among valid conclusions, the correct answer is 'Both conclusions I and II follow'. Hence, answer choice C is the answer.

Part – IV

STATEMENTS & CONCLUSIONS (PRACTICAL)

CONCEPT

In this topic a set of two or more practical statements (premises) is given followed by a set of two or more conclusions. Here, both the sets are indicating practical activities of routine life. Questions on a set of practical statements and conclusions have been asked in previous NET exams. These questions can be solved without using Venn diagram. The answer is to be chosen out of the following answer choices:

1. If only conclusion I follows
2. If only conclusion II follows
3. If either conclusion I or II follows
4. If neither conclusion I nor II follows
5. If both conclusions I and II follow

Strategy

While choosing answer choices, a candidate is to understand the practical aspect of the statements and accordingly, validity of the conclusion is to be decided. While deciding about the validity of the conclusions, one is to consider the practical aspect, experience related to the contents of the statements, understand the relationship of various elements, i.e., subject term, middle term (if any), and predicate term, and accordingly select the relevant answer choice. It should be also understood that whether conclusion is indicating certainty or probability of truth and a relevant conclusion must be supported by the premises. It is also to be considered whether the premises are belonging to A, E, I, or O category. Let us see how a relevant choice is to be understood.

1) Answer choice no. 1 is selected when it is found that only conclusion I naturally follows from the statements and conclusion II is neither naturally nor practically following from the statements.

Statements:

1) Some schools belong to the private sector.
2) All public sector schools are run either by state or central governments.

Conclusions:

I) Both public sector and private sector schools contribute in developing human resources.

II) Private sector schools are more efficient than public sector schools.

Here, only conclusion I follows because in both the premises, term 'schools' is middle term and it is evident that to whichever sector these may belong, schools are catering to education and thus, contributing in developing human resources. As conclusion II is not supported by the premises, it does not follow.

2) Answer choice no. 2 is selected when it is found that only conclusion II naturally follows from the statements and conclusion I is neither naturally nor practically following from the statements.

Statements:

1) No country can develop if there is misutilisation of resources.

2) Every country is blessed with some natural resources.

Conclusions:

I) Deteriorating law and order situation in every country leads to misutilisation of resources.

II) Proper utilization of resources will ensure development in any country.

In the above case, conclusion I is not supported by the premises because premise 1 is establishing proper utilization of resources as a measure for the development of an economy which comes as a natural transition in conclusion II only, whereas conclusion I is depicting the reason of misutilisation of resources which is not of the concern of any premise. Thus, conclusion II is fully supported by the premises. So conclusion II follows.

3) Choice number 3 is chosen when it is found that premises in the set are supporting both the conclusions but still cannot go with them at the same time as there is mutual exclusiveness or clash of opinion in the contents of conclusions and at one time, either of the conclusion can be drawn.

Statements:

1) Some welfare policies made by the government never reach the real beneficiaries.

2) Government has come up with Ujjwala scheme for the welfare of women.

Conclusions:

I. Women will get benefits of Ujjwala scheme.

II. Women will not get benefits of Ujjwala scheme.

In this case, both the premises are highlighting the welfare schemes being brought up by the government. But word 'Some' in the first premises creates the doubt about full coverage of beneficiaries under this scheme like 'Some' earlier schemes. So there is possibility that either conclusion I or II will follow.

4) Answer choice number 4 is chosen when no premise in the set supports the conclusions directly or indirectly. Conclusions are following neither practically nor logically from the premises.

Statements:

1) Tourist spots of India attract thousands of tourists from all over the world.

2) Some tourists visit only popular tourists spots of India.

Conclusions:

I. Unpopular tourist spots in India are unhygienic and poorly maintained.

II. Tourists visiting India feel insecure at some tourist spots.

Here, neither conclusion I nor II follow, because both the premises do not support the conclusions at all. Premise 1 highlights the international importance of tourist spots of India, whereas premise 2 reveals about selected choice of tourist spots by some tourists for any unknown reason. On the contrary, both the conclusions do not indicate any transformation from the given statements, so neither conclusion I nor II follows.

5) Answer choice no. 5 is chosen when both the conclusions follow the statements in their respective framework and there is no mutual exclusiveness or clash of opinion between them.

Statements:

1) All political leaders are supposed to be committed to their voters.

2) Voters are wooed by the leaders contesting elections.

Conclusions:

I) An election is one of the means to give committed leaders to voters.

II) Voters are decisive in deciding the fate of a contestant.

In above set of statements, both the premises are Universal Affirmative, i.e., A. These are fully supporting both the conclusions. Both the premises are highlighting the relation between an election and commitment and power of the voters, which is reflected in the conclusions. So both conclusions follow.

Practice Exercise

1. Which of the following is TRUE about Venn diagram?
   a) It helps in understanding relationship between various variables in categorical propositions.
   b) Subject term and Predicate terms of a proposition are the basis of the Venn diagram.
   c) In a single proposition, Venn diagram justifies the relation between Copula and Subject term.
   d) It establishes a relationship between Universal Affirmative Proposition with Particular Negative Proposition.

   (A) b and c only (B) a only
   (C) a, b, and c only (D) b and d only

2. Two partially overlapping sets of a single categorical proposition in a Venn diagram signify that Subject and Predicate are
   (A) Casually related
   (B) Independent of each other
   (C) Related in theory
   (D) None of the above

3. Which of the following is an integral part of Venn diagram showing relationship of categorical propositions?
   a) Copula b) Subject term
   c) Predicate term d) Middle term
   (A) b and c only (B) c only
   (C) a, b, c, and d (D) a, c, and d only

4. Venn diagram is a way to ____________ categorical propositions.
   (A) relate (B) show
   (C) define (D) understand

5. Which of the following aspects of categorical propositions are shown to be related in a Venn diagram?
   (A) Quantity (B) Quality
   (C) Both of them (D) Neither of them

Assertion–Reason Format

6. **Assertion (A):** Subject and Predicate terms of a categorical proposition are related.

   Reason (R): Venn diagram shows relationship between Subject and Predicate terms of a categorical proposition.

   (A) Both A and R are false
   (B) A is true but R is false
   (C) Both A and R are true and R is correct explanation of A
   (D) Both A and R are true but R is not correct explanation of A

7. **Assertion (A):** Copula is the basis behind drawing a Venn diagram to establish relationship between the Subject and Predicate terms.

   Reason (R): Subject and Predicate terms are related to determine the categorical proposition.

   (A) Both A and R are true and R is correct explanation of A
   (B) Both A and R are false
   (C) A is true but R is false
   (D) Both A and R are true but R is not correct explanation of A

8. **Assertion (A):** Embedded figure in a Venn diagram conveys a key relationship.

   Reason (R): A Universal Affirmative Proposition is part of any other proposition in a Venn diagram.

   (A) Both A and R are true and R is correct explanation of A
   (B) Both A and R are true but R is not correct explanation of A
   (C) A is true but R is false
   (D) A is false but R is true

9. **Assertion (A):** Aristotle's categorical propositions are understood with the help of a Venn diagram.

   Reason (R): Understanding a Venn diagram is the only way to understand categorical propositions.

   (A) Both A and R are false
   (B) Both A and R are true and R is correct explanation of A
   (C) A is true but R is false
   (D) A is false but R is true

10. **Assertion (A):** A Venn diagram significantly shows a negative relation between Subject and Predicate terms of a categorical proposition.

Reason (R): Subject and Predicate term of a categorical proposition are shown related to each other in a Venn diagram.

(A) Both A and R are true and R is correct explanation of A

(B) A is true but R is false

(C) Both A and R are true but R is not correct explanation of A

(D) A is false but R is true

KEY

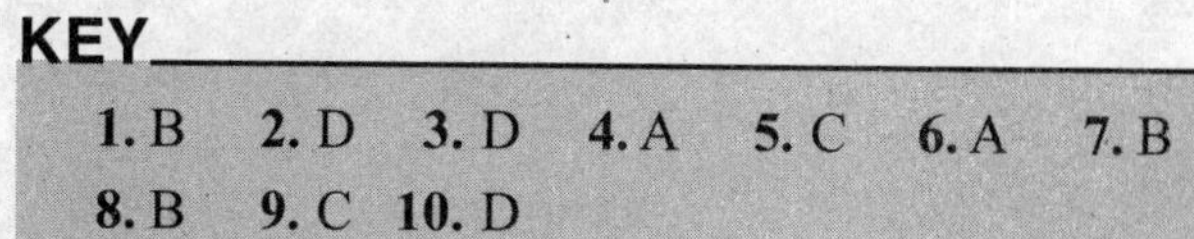

1. B 2. D 3. D 4. A 5. C 6. A 7. B 8. B 9. C 10. D

Part – I

DIRECTION: Read the subjects in the each of the following question and match with any one of the figure set given which best explains the relationship among the subjects in each question. (In case no figure expresses the suitable matching, then give the answer as option D (None of these)).

1. Education, Science, Literature

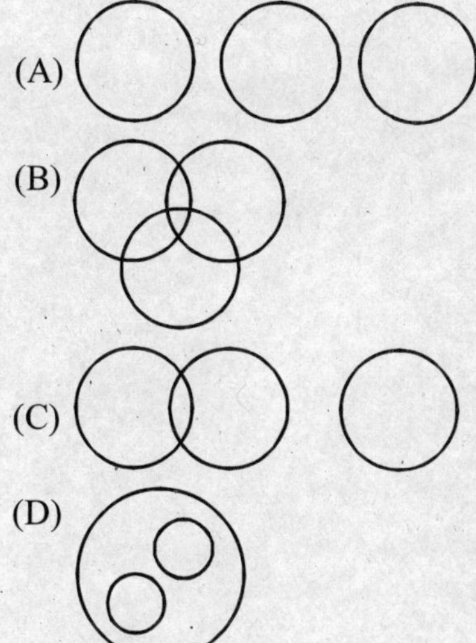

(A)

(B)

(C)

(D)

2. Officer, Player, Writer

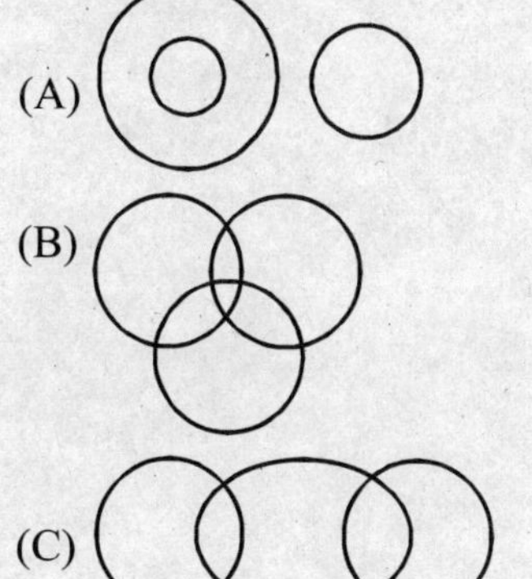

(A)

(B)

(C)

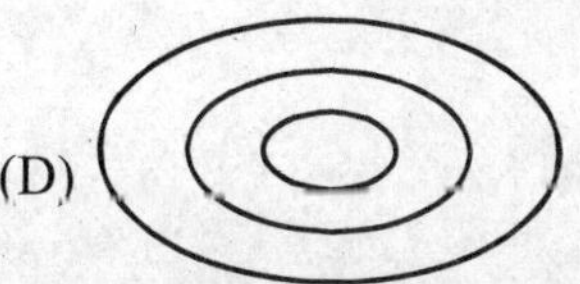

(D)

3. Male, Thief, Bridegroom

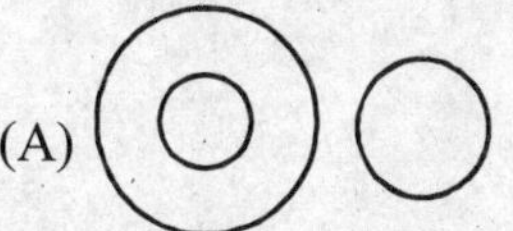

(A)

(B)

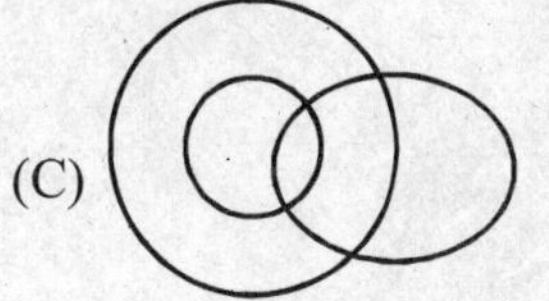

(C)

(D)

4. Sholay, Shillong, Shatabdi

(A)

(B)

(C)

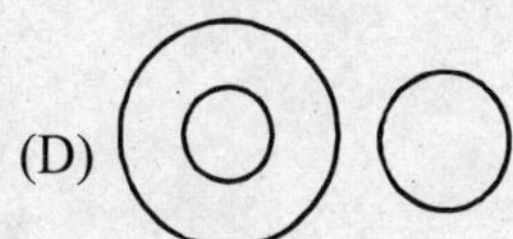

(D)

5. Doctor, Brother, Sister

(A)

(B)

(C)

(D) None of these

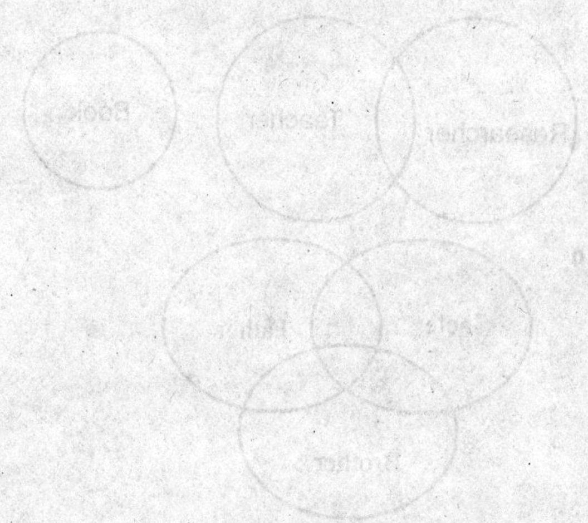

8. Here, out of two partially overlapped circles, one is teacher and the other is researcher. It establishes that some teachers are researchers and vice versa. Book is an object so it is represented by a separate circle.

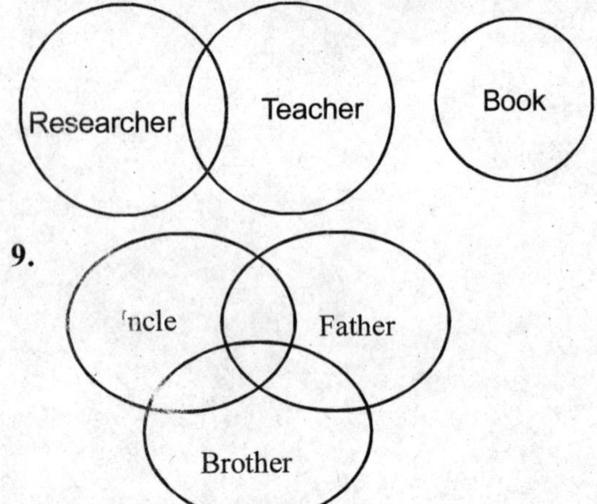

9.

10. In this case, big circle is force and out of two smaller circles inside the bigger circle, one is army and other is police.

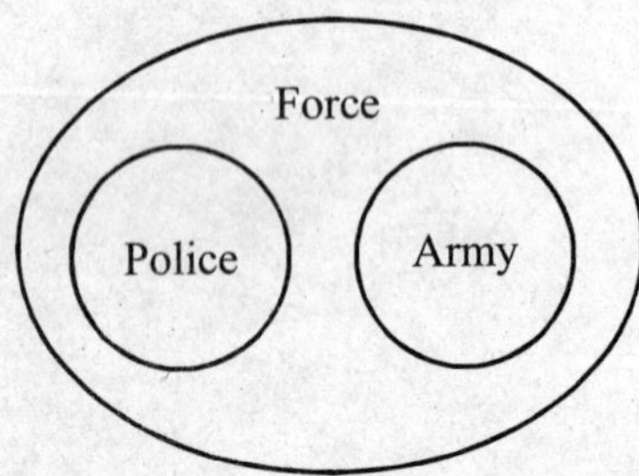

Above relationship establishes that whole police and army is force but whole force is not police and army only.

11. In this case, inner circle is shopkeeper and outer circle is trader. As a monk has no relation with worldly life, he is represented by a separate circle.

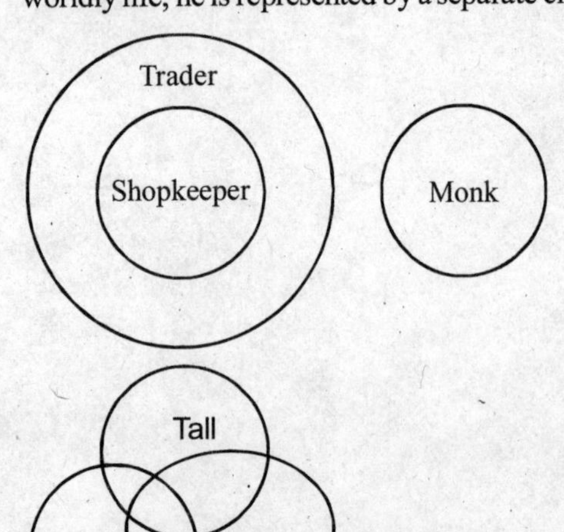

12.

Part – II

General Questions Format

DIRECTIONS (Q. 1-10): In the following figure set, Circle represents Teachers, Triangle represents Writers, and Square represents Actors. Observe the figure set carefully and give answers to the questions which follow the figure set.

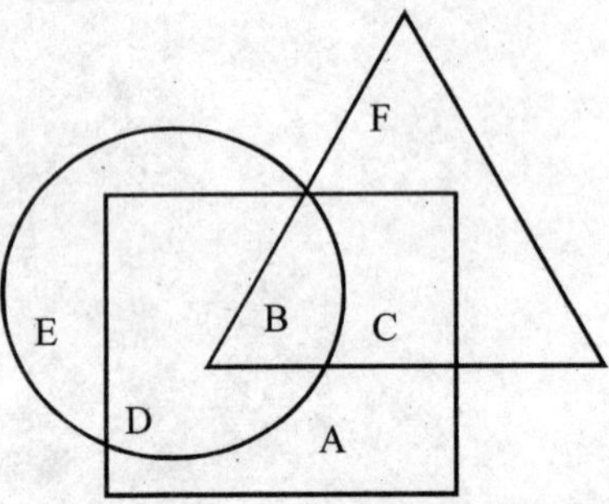

1. Which letter represents those Actors who are Writers but not Teachers?
(A) C (B) F
(C) E (D) A

2. Which letter represents those Teachers who are writers as well as Actors?
(A) D (B) C
(C) A (D) B

3. Which letter represents Non-writer, Non-actor Teachers?
(A) E (B) D
(C) F (D) Can't say

4. Which letter represents those Actors who are neither Writers nor Teachers?
(A) C (B) A
(C) D (D) B

5. Which letter represents those Teachers who are Actors but not Writers?
(A) F (B) D
(C) A (D) C

6. Which letter represents those Writers who are neither Teachers nor Actors?
(A) A (B) C
(C) B (D) F

7. Which of the statements is TRUE?
(A) Some Non-writers are not Actors.
(B) All Teachers are either Actors or Writers.
(C) No Actor is Non-teacher writer.
(D) All of the above

8. If letters representing the Teachers, who are Writers as well as Actors, Non-writer, Non-teacher Actors, and those Teachers who are Actors but not Writers are picked up and arranged in the same order, then which meaningful word comes out?

   (A) CABE (B) BADE
   (C) FADE (D) None of these

9. Which of the following statements is FALSE?
   (A) Some Non-teachers are Actors as well as Writers.
   (B) No Teacher is Actor alone.
   (C) All Actors are Non-teacher Writers.
   (D) All of the above

10. Which statement is TRUE?
    (A) Some Teachers are Non-actor Non-writers.
    (B) No Actor is Writer only.
    (C) Some Non-actors are Teachers, whereas some Actors are neither Teachers nor Writers.
    (D) All of the above

Directions Q. (11-16): In the following arrangement of figures, three circles A, B, and C are partially overlapping with each other and these are representing three different classes; A represents Vegetarians, B represents Officers, and C represents Postgraduates. Observe the following set carefully and give answers to questions, which follow the set.

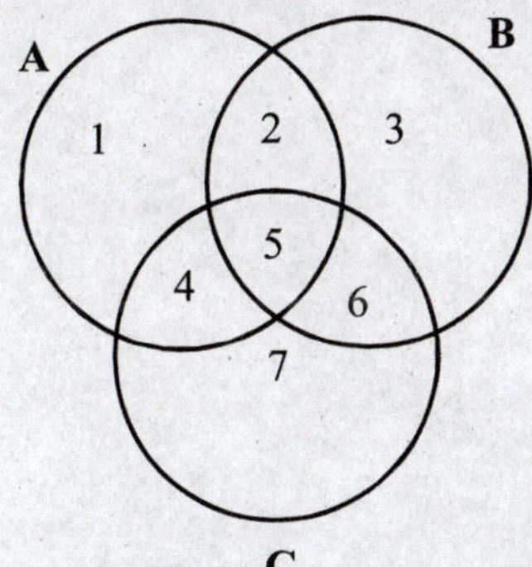

11. 'Some Vegetarian Officers in the set are Graduates'. This statement is
    (A) True (B) False
    (C) Probably true (D) Probably false

12. Which number represents Non-vegetarian Postgraduate Officers?
    (A) 6 (B) 3
    (C) 1 (D) 5

13. No 7 represents those Postgraduates who are
    (A) Vegetarian Officers
    (B) Non-vegetarian Non-officers
    (C) Vegetarian Non-officers
    (D) Non-vegetarian Officers

14. Which of the following statements in FALSE?
    (A) Some Vegetarian Officers are Postgraduates.
    (B) A Non-officer, who is Non-vegetarian, is a Postgraduate.
    (C) All Officers are either Postgraduates or Vegetarians, or both.
    (D) All of the above

15. Sum total of the numbers representing Vegetarian Non-officers is
    (A) 10 (B) 22
    (C) 8 (D) None of these

16. Which of the statement can be TRUE?
    (A) Some Vegetarian Postgraduates are Clerks.
    (B) No Postgraduate is Vegetarian alone.
    (C) Some Vegetarian Non-officers are Postgraduates whereas some Non-vegetarians are not Postgraduates.
    (D) All of the above

KEY

1. A	2. D	3. A	4. B	5. B	6. D	7. A
8. D	9. C	10. D	11. C	12. A	13. B	14. C
15. D	16. A					

Part – III

General Questions Format

1. Given below are two premises with four conclusions derived from them. Which of the following conclusions could be validly drawn from them?

   Premises:
   1. All Mountains are Cars.
   2. Some Cars are Scooters.

   Conclusions:
   a) All Scooters are Mountains.
   b) Some Mountains are Scooters is a possibility.
   c) Some Mountains are Cars.
   d) No Car is a Mountain.

   (A) b only (B) a and c only
   (C) b, c, and d only (D) a and d only

8. If letters representing the Teachers, who are Writers as well as Actors, Non-writer Non-teacher Actors and those Teachers who are Actors but not Writers are picked up and arranged in the same order, then which meaningful word comes out?

(A) CABE (B) BADE

(C) EADE (D) None of these

9. Which of the following statements is FALSE?

(A) Some Non-teachers are Actors as well as Writers

(B) No Teacher is Actor alone

(C) All Actors are Non-teacher Writers

(D) All of the above

10. Which statement is TRUE?

(A) Some Teachers are Non-actor Non-writers

(B) No Actor is Writer only

(C) Some Non-actors are Teachers, whereas some Actors are neither Teachers nor Writers

(D) All of the above

Directions Q. (11-16): In the following arrangement of figures, three circles A, B, and C are partially overlapping with each other and these are representing three different classes. A represents Vegetarians, B represents Officers, and C represents Postgraduates. Observe the following set carefully and give answers to questions, which follow the set.

11. 'Some Vegetarian Officers are the Postgraduates'. This statement is

(A) True (B) False

(C) Probably true (D) Probably false

12. Which number represents Non-vegetarian Postgraduate Officers?

(A) [illegible] (B) [illegible]

(C) 1 (D) 5

13. No. 7 represents those Postgraduates who are

(A) Vegetarian Officers

(B) Non-vegetarian Non-officers

(C) Vegetarian Non-officers

(D) Non-vegetarian Officers

14. Which of the following statements is FALSE?

(A) Some Vegetarian Officers are Postgraduates

(B) A Non-officer, who is Non-vegetarian, is a Postgraduate

(C) All Officers are either Postgraduates or Vegetarians, or both

(D) All of the above

15. Sum total of the numbers representing Vegetarian Non-officers is

(A) 10 (B) 22

(C) [illegible] (D) None of these

16. Which of the statements can be TRUE?

(A) Some Vegetarian Postgraduates are Officers

(B) No Postgraduate is Vegetarian alone

(C) Some Vegetarian Non-officers are Postgraduates, whereas some Non-vegetarians are not Postgraduates

(D) All of the above

KEY

[illegible]

Part–III

General Questions Format

1. Given below are two premises with four conclusions derived from them. Which of the following conclusions could be validly drawn from them?

Premises:

1. All Mountains are Cars.
2. Some Cars are Scooters.

Conclusions:

a) All Scooters are Mountains.
b) Some Mountains are Scooters is a possibility.
c) Some Mountains are Cars.
d) No Car is a Mountain.

(A) b only (B) a and c only

(C) b, c, and d only (D) a and d only

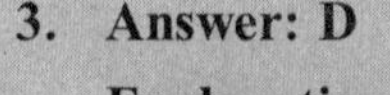

3. Answer: D

Explanation:

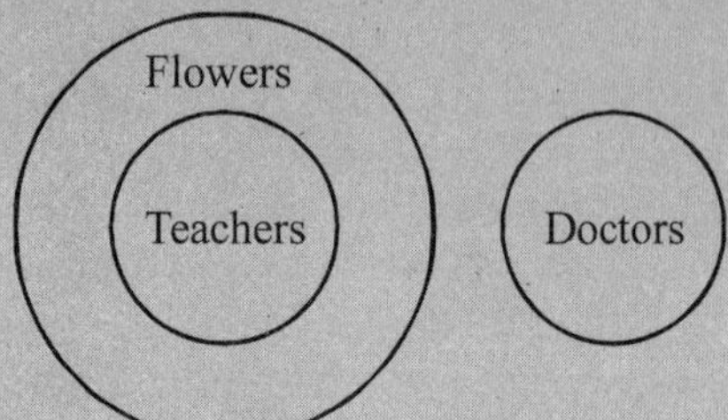

4. Answer: C

Explanation:

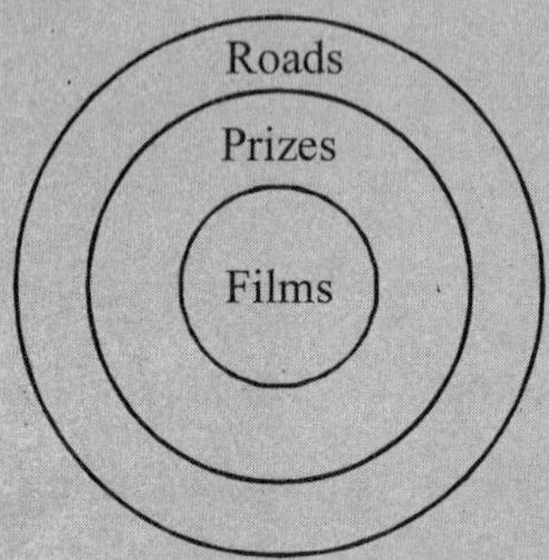

5. Answer: C

Explanation:

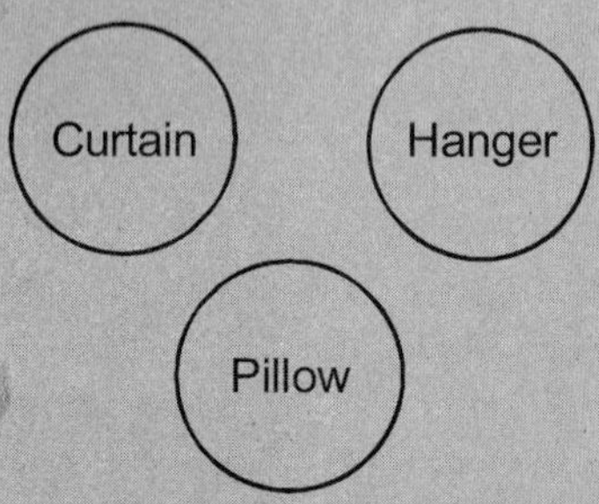

6. Answer: C

Explanation:

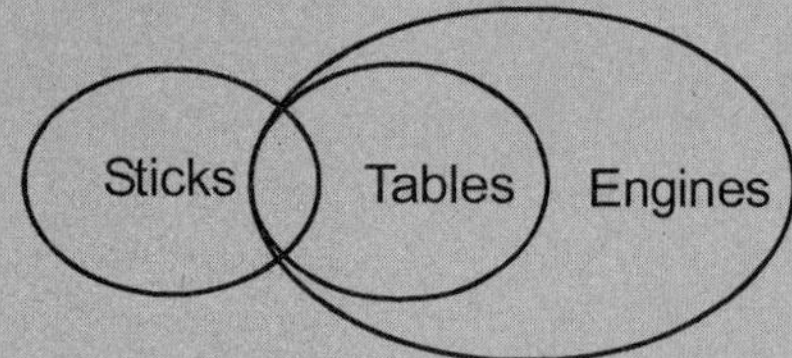

7. Answer: A

Explanation:

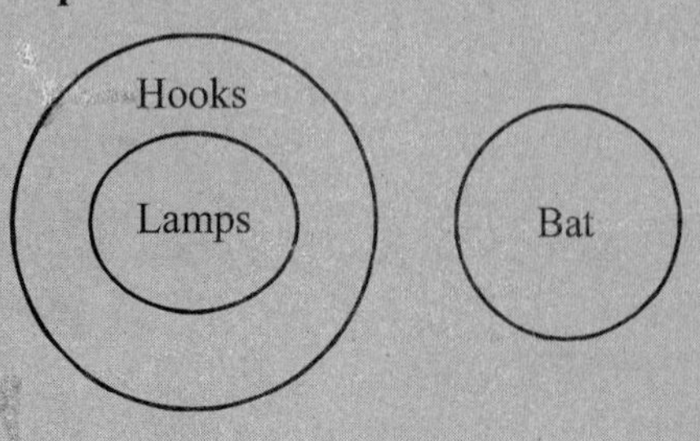

8. Answer: C

Explanation:

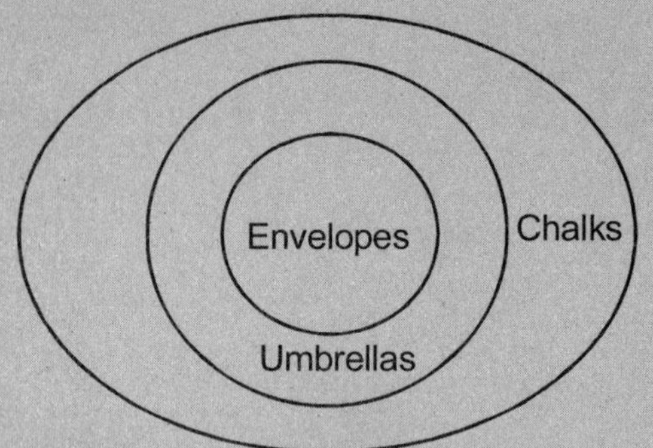

9. Answer: A

Explanation:

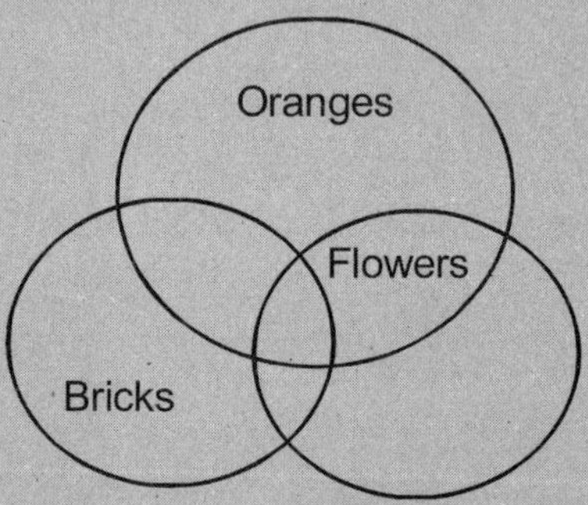

10. Answer: D

Explanation:

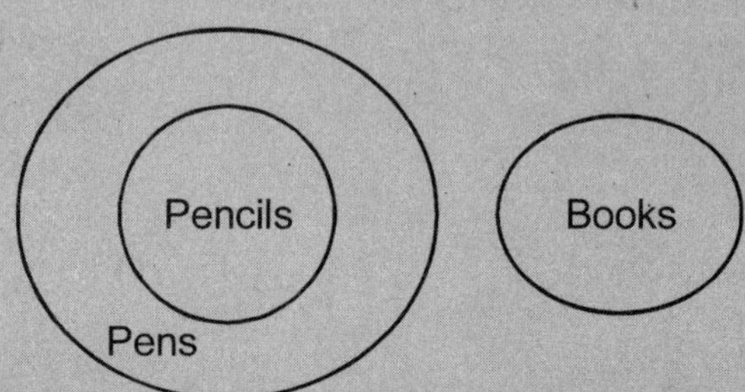

11. Answer D

Explanation:

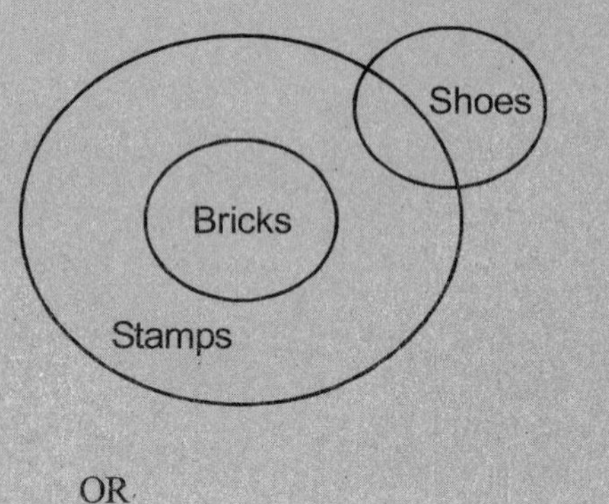

OR

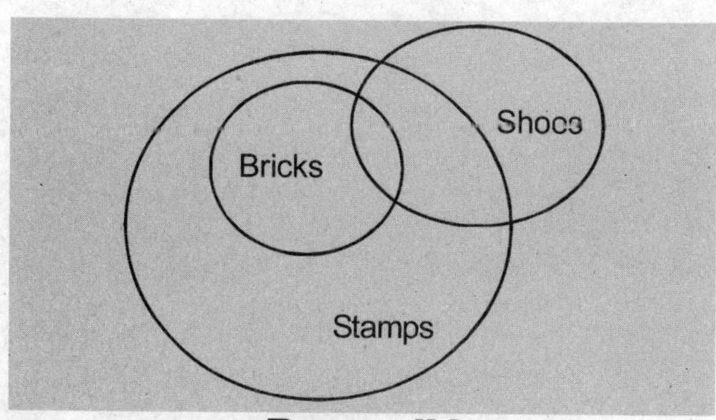

Part – IV

Directions: Find out which conclusion(s) can be logically drawn from the given statements in the following questions:

1. **Statements:**

Mr. A casually goes for morning walk.

He always meets Mr. B in the way.

Conclusions:

I. Mr. B casually goes for morning walk.

II. Mr. B regularly goes for morning walk.

(A) Both conclusions I and II follow

(B) Only conclusion II follows

(C) Only conclusion I follows

(D) Neither conclusion I nor II follows

2. **Statements:**

Only those hosts are hungry, who attend guests.

Only those guests are hungry, who are late.

Conclusions:

I. Some hosts are indifferent.

II. Some guests are punctual.

(A) Only conclusion I follows

(B) Only conclusion II follows

(C) Either conclusion I or II follows

(D) Both conclusions I and II follow

3. **Statements:**

Mr X is to attend a marriage ceremony.

At the same time he wants to enjoy a match on T.V.

Conclusions:

I. Mr. X will miss the marriage.

II. Mr. X will miss the match.

(A) Only conclusion I follows

(B) Only conclusion II follows

(C) Either conclusion I or II follows

(D) Both conclusions I and II follow

4. **Statements:**

Government has recently announced a welfare policy for the poor.

The poor are also beneficiaries of Public Distribution Scheme (PDS) launched by the government.

Conclusions:

I. The recently announced policy is different from PDS.

II. Government is concerned about the welfare of the poor only.

(A) Only conclusion I follows

(B) Only conclusion II follows

(C) Either conclusion I or II follows

(D) Both conclusions I and II follow

5. **Statements:**

Some of the teachers with long hair are males.

Rekha is a teacher with long hair.

Conclusions:

I. Rekha is male.

II. Rekha is female.

(A) Only conclusion I follows

(B) Only conclusion II follows

(C) Either conclusion I or II follows

(D) Both conclusions I and II follow

6. **Statements:**

Mohinder has applied for the job of a teacher in school X.

A teacher of school X must be a graduate.

Conclusions:

I. Mohinder is a graduate.

II. Mohinder is a postgraduate.

(A) Only conclusion I follows

(B) Only conclusion II follows

(C) Either conclusion I or II follows

(D) Both conclusions I and II follow

7. **Statements:**

There was a devastating hurricane in village X.

Most of the property in village X is damaged.

Conclusions:

I. There are frequent hurricanes in village X.

II. Wherever such hurricane occurs, it causes destruction.

10. If you want to select Hindi and English knowing Teachers, which of the following is to be selected?

(A) g (B) b
(C) c (D) e

11. If you want to select persons, who do not know English and are not Teachers, which of the region is to be selected?

(A) e (B) g
(C) b (D) a

Study the following Venn diagram and answer questions numbered 12 to 14.

Three circles representing Graduates, Clerks, and Government Employees are intersecting each other. The intersections are marked A, B, C, e, f, g, and h. Which part best represents the statements in questions 12 to 14? **(UGC NET DECEMBER 2008)**

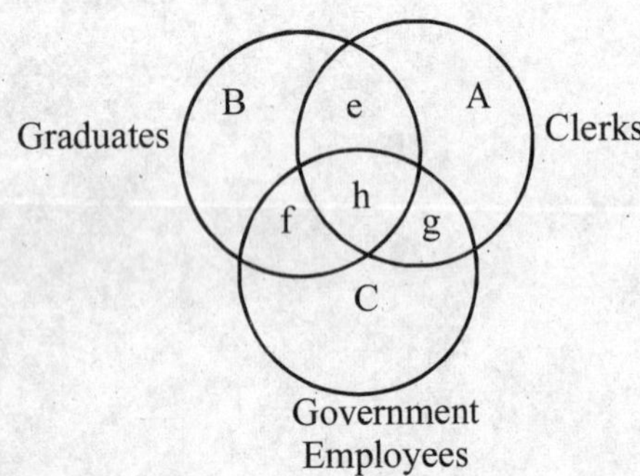

12. Some Graduates are Government Employees but not Clerks.

(A) h (B) g
(C) f (D) e

13. Some Clerks are Graduates as well as Government Employees.

(A) e (B) f
(C) g (D) h

14. Some Graduates are Clerks but not Government Employees.

(A) f
(B) g
(C) h
(D) e

KEY

1. D	2. B	3. B	4. A	5. C	6. A	7. C
8. C	9. A	10. C	11. B	12. C	13. D	14. D

Part – III

1. Given below are two premises with four conclusions derived from them. Which of the following conclusions could be validly drawn from them? **(UGC NET JUNE 2019)**

Premises:

I) All Fans are Tubes.

II) Bulbs are not Tubes.

Conclusions:

a) Fans are not Bulbs.

b) All Bulbs are Fans.

c) Fans are Bulbs.

d) No Tube is Bulb.

(A) a, b, c (B) a and d
(C) a only (D) b, c, and d

2. Given below are two premises (a) and (b). Four conclusions are drawn from them. Select the code that states validly drawn conclusion(s) taking the premises individually or jointly. **(UGC NET DECEMBER 2018)**

Premises:

(a) All Judges are Lawyers.

(b) No Doctors are Lawyers.

Conclusions:

(1) No Lawyers are Doctors.

(2) No Doctor are Judges.

(3) All Lawyers are Judges.

(4) Some Doctors are Judges.

(A) (1) and (3) (B) (1) and (2)
(C) (1) and (4) (D) (2) and (3)

3. Given below are two premises (a) and (b). From those two premises four conclusions (i), (ii), (iii), and (iv) are drawn. Select the code that states the conclusions validly drawn from the premises (taking singly or jointly). **(UGC NET JANUARY 2017)**

Premises:

(a) Untouchability is a Curse.

(b) All Hot pans are untouchable.

Conclusions:

(i) All Hot pans are a Curse.

(ii) Some untouchable things are Hot pans.

(iii) All Curses are Untouchability.

(iv) Some Curses are Untouchability.

Codes:

(A) (i) and (ii) (B) (ii) and (iii)
(C) (iii) and (iv) (D) (ii) and (iv)

4. Given below are two premises, with four conclusions drawn from them (taking singly or together). Which conclusions are validly drawn? Select the correct answer from the codes given below: **(UGC NET AUGUST 2016)**

Premises:

(i) All Bats are Mammals.
(ii) Birds are not Bats.

Conclusions:

(a) Birds are not Mammals.
(b) Bats are not Birds.
(c) All Mammals are Bats.
(d) Some Mammals are Bats.

Codes:

(A) (a), (b), and (d) (B) (b) and (d)
(C) (a) and (c) (D) (b), (c), and (d)

5. Given below are two premises and four conclusions drawn from those premises. Select the code that expresses conclusion drawn validly from the premises (separately or jointly). **(UGC NET JUNE 2014)**

Premises:

(a) All Dogs are Mammals.
(b) No Cats are Dogs.

Conclusions:

(i) No Cats are Mammals.
(ii) Some Cats are Mammals.
(iii) No Dogs are Cats.
(iv) No dogs are Non-mammals.

Codes:

(A) (i) only (B) (i) and (ii)
(C) (iii) and (iv) (D) (ii) and (iii)

6. Given below are two premises. Four conclusions are drawn from those two premises in four codes. Select the code that states the conclusion validly drawn.

(UGC NET DECEMBER 2013)

Premises:

(i) All Saints are Religious. (Major)
(ii) Some Honest persons are Saints. (Minor)

Conclusions:

(i) All Saints are Honest.
(ii) Somc Saints are Honest.
(iii) Some Honest persons are Religious.
(iv) All Religious persons are Honest.

Codes:

(A) (i) only (B) (i) and (ii)
(C) (ii) and (iii) (D) (iii) and (iv)

KEY

1. B **Explanation:**

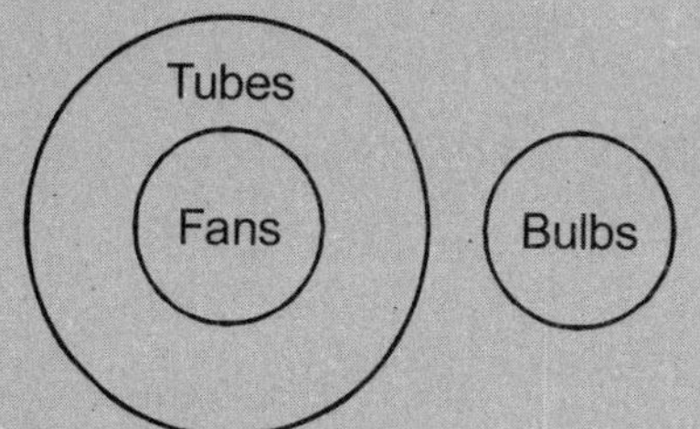

2. B **Explanation:**

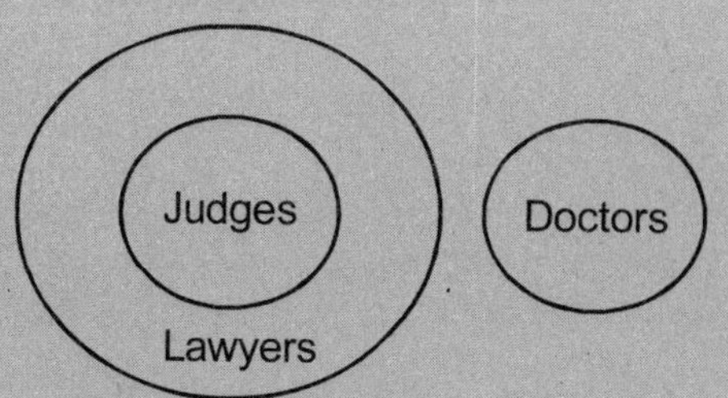

3. D **Explanation:**

Conclusion i is not valid as premises do not establish relationship between 'Hot pan' and a qualitative concept 'Curse'. Conclusion iii is also invalid as valid conclusion should be 'Some curses are untouchability'.

4. B Explanation:

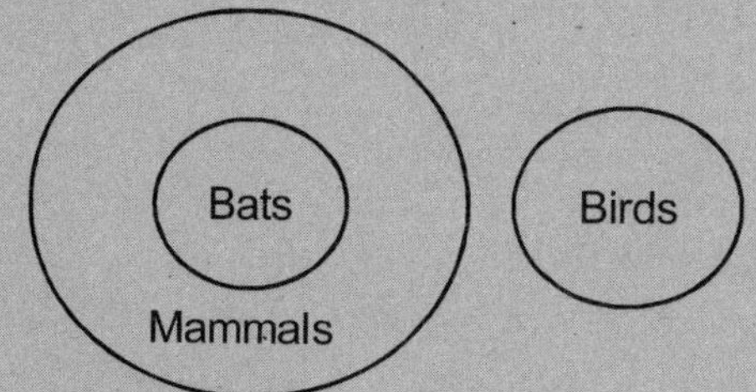

5. C **Explanation:**

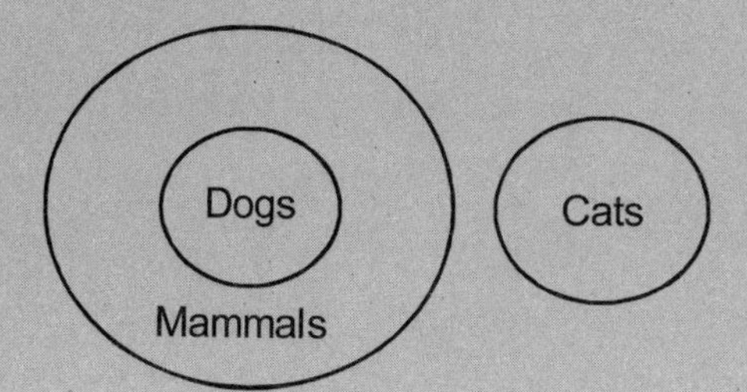

ANUMANA (INFERENCE)

According to Indian philosophy, Anumana is made of two words, i.e., Anu and Mana. Anu means 'after' and Mana means 'learning' (cognition). It means, whatever is learnt (cognized) after Praman is Anumana. In Indian philosophy, Anumana is the means of valid knowledge which is derived as a conclusion from given premises or evidences. Anumana derives the right knowledge by using reasoning. It illustrates the reasons to arrive at a new truth or knowledge through observation and previous truths. So Anumana is that knowledge which is attained after some other knowledge, i.e., perception. Anumana has a pivotal position in the Hindu School of Indian Logic (Nyaya).

Structure of Anumana

It has been established that Anumana is the means to obtain knowledge of reality through the previous knowledge of relation (concomitance) among the major term (Sadhya), minor term (Paksha), and middle term (Hetu). So the structure of Anumana is a set of premises containing major term (Sadhya) and minor term (Paksha) and the last statement is the conclusion. There are the following types of statements in the structure of Anumana:

1) Proposition or Hypothesis (Pratijna)
2) Reason or ground (Hetu)
3) Example or Illustration (Udaharana)
4) Application (Upanaya)
5) Conclusion (Nigamana)

Traditional Example

A traditional example, associated with this philosophy, illustrates the above structure:

1. Fire is there on the hill (the Pratijna?, hypothesis).
2. Because there is smoke on the hill (the Hetu, reason or probans).
3. Wherever there is smoke, there is fire; like a kitchen (the Udaharana, illustration of concomitance).
4. This hill is likewise smoky (the Upanaya, application of the rule).
5. Thus, fire is there on the hill (the Nigamana, conclusion).

In the above example, proposition number 1 is a hypothesis or theory (Pratijna) which is to be proved.

Now concentrating on statement number 5, which is a conclusion, it is found that fire is subject (minor term-Sadhna) and hill is predicate (major term-Sadhya). Now concentrating on premises, it is found that smoke is the middle term (Hetu).

Vyapti (Invariable Relation)

Vyapti establishes truth of the inference. Inference is not possible without Vyapti. Basis of Anumana is invariable relation between 'Hetu' and 'Sadhya' which is known as invariable concomitance (both occurring together) in Western Epistemology. This relation between Hetu and Sadhya is Vyapti. Vyapti establishes cause and effect relationship which leads to inference derived from previous knowledge (perception). For example: Where there is smoke there must be fire. Here, smoke is 'Hetu' (what is perceived) and fire is 'Sadhya' (which becomes basis of inference). Vyapti or relation between Hetu and Sadhya is established on the perceptual knowledge in the past as fire in the kitchen. This relation between Hetu and Sadhya is not reversible. Example: Where there is fire there must not be smoke, does not establish invariable concomitance between Hetu and Sadhya.

CONCOMITANCE

Concomitance is the term used in Western epistemology to construct structure of inference.In Indian logic there is concomitance between 'Hetu' and Sadhya'. It means hetu and sadhya are existing together to be conducive in drawing anumana (inference)

Hetvabhasa (Fallacies of Anumana)

A fallacy in the structure of Anumana (inference) is known as Hetvabhasa in the language of Indian logic. A fallacy exists when Hetu (reason) appears to be true but actually it is not. Nyaya sutra says that fallacies are resemblances of reason. Name 'Hetvabhasa' is given to fallacy in reason by Vatsyayana School. It is pointed out that Hetu so presented in the structure of inference does not possess the features of real Hetu, but it appears like Hetu. It is stated by different schools that a fallacy of the reason, i.e., middle term leads to fallacy in the inference. Vaisesika Sutra classifies three types of fallacies (Hetvabhasa):

1) Viruddha (Contradiction)
2) Asiddha (Unapproved)
3) Samdighda (Doubtful or inconclusive)

As Hetvabhasa is fallacy of reason or middle term, presence of Hetvabhasa in the structure of an argument make inference invalid. As in the example of fire on hill:

1) Fire is there on the hill (the Pratijna?, hypothesis).
2) Because there is lightning on the hill (the Hetu, reason or probans).
3) Wherever there is lightning, there is fire; like a kitchen (the Udaharana, illustration of concomitance).

4) This hill is likewise catching lightning (the Upanaya, application of the rule).

5) Thus, fire is there on the hill (the Nigamana, conclusion).

In the above set of statements, there is fallacy of Hetu or reason, i.e., middle term, because inference in a structure of Anumana is given on the basis of reason which has already been perceived. In the above example, lightning is Hetu and fire is Sadhya. Here, there is no concomitance between lightning and fire. It is true that lightning also becomes cause of fire but very rarely. Smoke is an indication of fire whereas lightning is not an indication of fire. In the above example, conclusion drawn on the basis of lightning as Hetu or middle term or reason, is invalid. Here, middle term lightning resembles smoke as cause of fire, but it is not reality.

Kinds of Anumana

1) Purvavat Anumana
2) Sheshavat Anumana
3) Samanyato Drushta Anumana

1) **Purvavat Anumana:** This is reasoning obtained from cause to effect. 'Purva' means first or preceding and 'Vat' means like. This means that effect is inferred from cause. In this philosophy, inference is future effect of present cause. So there is a cause and effect relationship between minor term (Sadhana) and major term (Sadhya). For example: If there are mosquitoes around, these become cause of malaria. Here, mosquitoes are the cause and malaria is the effect.

2) **Sheshavat Anumana:** In this philosophy, cause is inferred from its effect as word 'Shesha' means effect. Sometimes, the previous cause is inferred from present effect. For example, while finding a malaria patient, it is inferred that mosquitoes must have bitten him earlier.

3) **Samanyato Drushta Anumana:** This philosophy believes that an object changes its position due to movement when movement is not visible. For example, sun rises in the east in morning and changes its position to west in the evening due to movement of the earth where movement of the earth is not felt or visible.

SCHOOLS OF INDIAN LOGIC

There are six schools of Indian logic. These are also called Six schools of Hindu Philosophy.

1) ***Nyaya:*** *Nayaya is one of the six Hindu Schools of Indian philosophy or Logic. The school was propounded by Gautama. It portrays the means of acquiring right knowledge. It accepts there are four means of valid knowledge i. e. 1) Perception (Pratakshya). 2) Anumana (Inference) 3) Upmana (Comparison) 4) Shabda (Verbal testimony)*

2) ***Samkhya:*** *It is the oldest philosophypropounded by Kanada. The school has two entities 'Purush' (spirit) and 'Prakriti' (nature, energy). The school believes tha one can attain knowledge of self with meditation and concentration.*

3) ***Yoga:*** *Founder of this school is Patanjali. This works on the philosophy of disc ipline of body and mind through yoga.*

4) ***Vaisheshika:*** *Founder of this school is sage Kanada. This philosophy believes in atomic theory of Physics. It states that the whole universe will reduced to atoms and Brahmins will be instrumental in injecting consciousness in these atoms*

5) ***PurvaMimamsa:****This school establishes the authority of vedas. It states that every activity in the universe is governed by mantras and yajnas.*

6) ***UttaraMimamsa (Vedanta):*** *The school believes that world is unreal and the only reality is Brahmin*

UPAMANA (COMPARISON AND ANALOGY)

Upamana word is made of two words 'Upa' and 'Mana.' Upa means similarity and Mana means cognition or knowledge. In Indian logic, Upamana is accepted as another valid source of knowledge. It describes that analogy is another valid means of knowledge. Through this means, knowledge is attained by comparing two objects on the basis of similarity in their characteristics. A traditional illustration is given to clear the meaning of Upamana. A person comes to know about a word "Gavaya" (wild ox). He does not know the meaning of the word "Gavaya." He is told that Gavaya is an animal that looks like a cow. When that person happens to actually see a wild ox, he recollects that he has already been told that Gavaya (wild ox) is an animal resembling a cow; he fully understands the meaning of Gavaya. Various schools of Indian philosophy Nyaya, Vedanta, and Mimamsa admit Upamana as Pramana of valid knowledge. Gist of the concept of Upamana is obtaining knowledge by observing two similar subjects.

ARTHAPATTI (POSTULATION OR PRESUMPTION)

It is made of two words 'Artha' and 'Patti' where 'Artha' means fact and 'Patti' means assumption. Indian logic recognises Arthapatti as another Pramana of authentic knowledge of any subject in the world. It is postulation of an unknown fact in order to highlight the known fact which cannot be explained otherwise. Postulation and presumption is made according to prevailing circumstances. A traditional example of this is: We see a fat man who claims that he eats nothing in the day but he is getting fatter or sustains fat. As without eating he cannot maintain a certain level of fat, we postulate that the man eats at night. So we postulate his eating habit during night to highlight the known fact that the man under reference is fat or getting fatter. Arthapatti establishes that presuming about an unknown fact yields authenticity of the known fact. In the above example, postulating that the fat man is eating during night provides knowledge that 'The man is fat' and that must be true. Arthapatti is considered as an independent means of valid knowledge.

ANUPALABHDI (NON-PERCEPTION)

This Pramana provides valid knowledge through non-perception as an independent source of knowledge. This means of knowledge apprehends about absence (Abhava) of a subject. Advaita and Mimamsa schools of thought recognise Anupalabhdi as an independent source of knowledge (Pramana). Philosophy of Anupalabhdi states that non-perception of a subject is means to knowledge of apprehension of absence or non-existence (Abhava) of the subject. For example, sometimes it is said "There is no student in the class". It means that due to non-perception (Anupalabhdi), it was apprehension of non-existence (Abhava) of students from the class. Here, non-perception or non-apprehension is the means to provide apprehension of absence of students. Logic of the concept is that non-perception also gives authentic knowledge like perception. Sometimes, perception and non-perception both provide knowledge in their respective principles, as one is conscious of both. It is also mentioned that non-perception or non-apprehension (Anupalabhdi) means of knowledge is practised as a natural phenomenon experienced by one as non-perception is not an artificial or deliberate attempt.

SABDA (WORD TESTIMONY)

Sabda is an effective and independent means (Pramana) of providing authentic knowledge. It is verbal communication and is universally used. It is also called 'Apta-vakyas' (statement of a trustworthy person). Sabda is an independent means of providing valid knowledge by a trustworthy person who coveys the message correctly. Knowledge is provided either through oral or written mode. Philosophy of Sabda states that knowledge provided through words is valid if the person who is giving the message is trustworthy. Maximum information of the different fields in the world is conveyed and accepted through words, and this information is made valid with different evidences and statistics. There are various modes of providing knowledge through authentic words (Agama) like newspapers, journals, T.V., radio, educational institutions, persons, etc. Through these modes, words (Sabda) become means of effective communication, thus bringing awareness. Word testimony is valid only when source of information is authentic. If there is doubt on the validity of the message so conveyed, there are provisions to verify the same. When a genuine communicator conveys the message, the recipient should possess rich vocabulary and knowledge of grammar, sentence structure, and language of the communicator. Only then, the recipient can decide whether the message is valid or not.

TERMS OF INDIAN LOGIC

1) Apta-vakyas: Statement of a trustworthy person
2) Agama: Authentic word
3) Akanksha: Expectation
4) Pramata: Knower
5) Prameya: Object of knowledge
6) Pada: Word
7) Pratyaksha: Perception
8) Anumana: Inference
9) Hetvabhasa: Fallacy
10) Anupalabhdi: Non-perception
11) Abhava: Non-existent
12) Arthapatti: Postulation
13) Upamana: Comparison/Analogy
14) Gavaya: Wild ox
15) Yukti: Active process of gaining knowledge
16) Indriyarthasannikarsha: Gaining knowledge through sensory organs
17) Avyapadesya: Non-verbal
18) Hetu or Linga: Cause and middle term
19) Viruddha: Contradiction
20) Asiddha: Unproved
21) Samdighda: Doubtful or inconclusive
22) Anadhyavasaya: Indefinite judgement

Practice Exercise

General Questions Format

1. Which of the following is NOT TRUE about Anumana?
   a) Conclusion is based on evidences.
   b) Pratyaksha is the precondition for Anumana to attain right knowledge.
   c) Anumana propagates opposite to what is propagated by Nyaya school.
   d) Anumana paves a way to understand other means of valid knowledge.

   (A) only b (B) b and c only
   (C) a, d, and b (D) a, b, c, and d

2. Arrange the following in logical order
   (A) Hetu-Pratijna-Nigmana-Upanaya-Udaharana
   (B) Upanaya-Hetu-Udaharana-Pratijna-Nigamana
   (C) Pratijna-Hetu-Udaharana-Upanaya-Nigamana
   (D) Nigamana-Udaharana-Upanaya-Hetu-Pratijna

3. Name of some terms from Indian logic are given under Column I and their meaning are given under Column II. Match the term with its exact meaning and choose the correct answer from the codes given below.

Column I (Term)	Column II (Meaning)
a) Asiddha	i) Word
b) Pada	ii) Knower
c) Akanksha	iii) Unapproved
d) Pramata	iv) Expectation

Codes:	(a)	(b)	(c)	(d)
(A)	iii	ii	iv	i
(B)	i	iii	iv	ii
(C)	iv	ii	iii	i
(D)	iii	i	iv	ii

4. Knowledge through Sabda is considered valid if source of knowledge is ______.
   (A) accessible (B) an inference
   (C) authentic (D) a doctrine

5. Which of the following is NOT TRUE about Pratyaksha? It______.
   a) is ultimate proof of valid knowledge
   b) supplements the knowledge provided through Anumana
   c) works on the doctrine of Pratyksha and needs no Pramana
   d) is an experience rather than acquiring knowledge only

   (A) b and c only (B) All are true
   (C) b only (D) a, c, and d only

6. Consider the proposition:
   There is fire on the hill.
   What is the position of the above proposition in the structure of Anumana?
   (A) Upanaya (B) Hetu
   (C) Nigamana (D) Pratijna

7. Relation between Hetu and Sadhya is part of
   (A) Agma (B) Vyapti
   (C) Prameya (D) None of these

8. In the structure of Anumana, which is called the major term?
   (A) Sadhya (B) Hetu
   (C) Sadhana (D) Yukti

9. Which school of Indian logic believes in Atomic Theory of Physics regarding existence?
   (A) Nyaya (B) Samkhya
   (C) Vaisheshika (D) Uttara Mimamsa

10. Which of the following is TRUE about Arthapatti as a means of valid knowledge?
    a) Application of norms determining valid fact on assumptions about that fact
    b) Presuming about an unknown fact yields authenticity of the known fact
    c) An observed unknown fact later develops into a valid known fact
    d) Examining the validity of unknown fact paves the way for accepting validity of known fact

    (A) c and d only (B) d only
    (C) b only (D) b, c, and d only

11. Names of different schools of Indian logic are mentioned under Column I, and their meaning and illustrations are under Column II. Match each school of thought with its meaning and significance and choose the correct code given below:

Column I (School of thought)	Column II (Meaning/Illustration)
a) Samkhya	i) Atomic Theory
b) Nyaya	ii) Vedas
c) Vaisheshika	iii) Four means of valid knowledge
d) Purva Mimamsa	iv) Meditation

Codes:	(a)	(b)	(c)	(d)
(A)	iv	iii	i	ii
(B)	i	ii	iii	iv
(C)	ii	i	iv	iii
(D)	iii	ii	i	iv

12. Which of the following best explains the Indian Epistemology?

(A) Asking questions on the validity of source of knowledge

(B) Obtaining that means of knowledge which has been truly verified

(C) Attaining knowledge with reason

(D) Following path of sources of valid knowledge

13. In Indian logic 'Pramana' has base in evidence of

(A) Valid source of knowledge

(B) Right school of thought

(C) Rational approach to right knowledge

(D) None of these

14. According to Indian logic there is a single reliable source of knowledge and that is

(A) Anumana

(B) Sabda

(C) Pratyaksha

(D) Upamana

15. Which of the following is TRUE about 'Hetvabhasa'?

a) It is a fallacy of 'Hetu', i.e., fallacy of reason.

b) Hetu appears to be true but actually it is not.

c) This concept is given by Vatsyayana School of Thought.

d) Structure of 'Anumana' becomes invalid due to presence of 'Hetvabhasa'.

(A) c and d only (B) a, b, c, and d

(C) a, c, and d only (D) b and d only

16. Consider the statement- 'It describes that analogy is another valid means of knowledge'. This statement conveys information about which valid means of knowledge?

(A) Upamana (B) Arthapatti

(C) Anupalabhdi (D) Pratyaksha

17. Which of the following school(s) of India logic believe(s) that there are six means of valid knowledge?

(A) Mimamsa (B) Advaita

(C) Both (D) Neither

18. Names of different means of knowledge as given in Indian logic are given under Column I and their meanings are given under Column II.

Column I (Name)	Column II (Meaning)
a) Upamana	i) Non-perception
b) Hetvabhasa	ii) Postulation
c) Arthapatti	iii) Analogy
d) Anupalabhdi	iv) Fallacy

Codes:	(a)	(b)	(c)	(d)
(A)	ii	iv	iii	i
(B)	i	ii	iii	iv
(C)	iii	iv	ii	i
(D)	iv	iii	ii	i

19. In Indian logic, Arthapatti is taken as

(A) Hetu (B) Pramana

(C) Sadhya (D) Sadhana

20. In the structure of Anumana, there is existence of 'Major Term, Middle Term, and Minor Term'.

What are their names in the terms of Indian logic in that order?

(A) Sadhana, Hetu, Sadhya

(B) Sadhya, Hetu, Sadhana

(C) Hetu, Sadhya, Sadhana

(D) Sadhana, Sadhya, Hetu

KEY

1. A	2. C	3. D	4. C	5. C	6. D	7. B
8. A	9. C	10. C	11. A	12. C	13. D	14. C
15. B	16. A	17. C	18. C	19. B	20. B	

Assertion–Reason Format

1. **Assertion (A):** Epistemology is the basis of Indian logic.

   Reason (R): There are various questions in Indian logic with regard to attaining knowledge.

   (A) Both A and R are true and R is correct explanation of A

   (B) Both A and R are true but R is not correct explanation of A

   (C) A is true but R is false

   (D) A is false but R is true

2. **Assertion (A):** There is nothing in common between Indian logic and Western logic.

   Reason (R): What is perception in Indian logic is evidence in Western logic.

   (A) Both A and R are true and R is correct explanation of A

   (B) A is true but R is false

   (C) Both A and R are true but R is not correct explanation of A

   (D) Both A and R are false

3. **Assertion (A):** Pramana leaves no scope of further argument on obtaining right knowledge.

   Reason (R): Every school of Indian logic has accepted Pramana as a valid means of knowledge.

   (A) Both A and R are true and R is correct explanation of A

   (B) Both A and R are true but R is not correct explanation of A

   (C) Both A and R are false

   (D) A is true but R is false

4. **Assertion (A):** Hetvabhasa is fallacy of Hetu.

   Reason (R): In a fallacy there is no real Hetu but what is present appears like Hetu.

   (A) Both A and R are false

   (B) Both A and R are true but R is not correct explanation of A

   (C) A is true but R is false

   (D) A is false but R is true

5. **Assertion (A):** Purvavat Anumana is reasoning of cause and effect.

   Reason (R): Previous cause is inferred from present effect.

   (A) Both A and R are true and R is correct explanation of A

   (B) A is true but R is false

   (C) A is false but R is true

   (D) Both A and R are true but R is not correct explanation of A

6. **Assertion (A):** Pratyaksha is universally accepted as Pramana of valid knowledge.

   Reason (R): Sources of valid knowledge differ in different schools of Indian logic.

   (A) A is true but R is false

   (B) A is false but R is true

   (C) Both A and R are true and R is correct explanation of A

   (D) Both A and R are true but R is not correct explanation of A

7. **Assertion (A):** Upamana proves to be a source of valid knowledge through comparing two unlike subjects.

   Reason (R): Perception plays an important role in getting right knowledge through Upamana.

   (A) Both A and R are true and R is correct explanation of A

   (B) Both A and R are true but R is not correct explanation of A

   (C) A is true but R is false

   (D) A is false but R is true

8. **Assertion (A):** Sabda is an independent means of providing valid knowledge.

   Reason (R): Apta-vakyas make the valid knowledge universally accepted.

   (A) Both A and R are false

   (B) A is true but R is false

   (C) Both A and R are true and R is the correct explanation of A

   (D) Both A and R are true but R is not correct explanation of A

9. **Assertion (A):** Anupalabhdi sees non-perception as the valid knowledge about apprehension of absence of the subject.

   Reason (R): Non-perception always creates apprehension about missing the subject.

   (A) Both A and R are false

   (B) Both A and R are true but R is not correct explanation of A

   (C) A is true but R is false

   (D) A is false but R is true

10. **Assertion (A):** There is cause and effect relation between Hetu and Sadhya.

    Reason (R): Purvavat Anumana believes that present cause has its effect in future.

    (A) A is true but R is false

    (B) Both A and R are true and R is correct explanation of A

    (C) A is false but R is true

    (D) Both A and R are false

KEY

1. A **2.** D **3.** B **4.** D **5.** B **6.** D **7.** D **8.** C **9.** A **10.** B

Questions Asked in Previous NET Exams

1. Which of the following Parmanas is used by the classical Indian school of logic to prove the existence of God?

   (UGC NET DECEMBER 2019)

   (A) Arthapati (postulation)

   (B) Upamana (comparison)

   (C) Perception (pratyaksha)

   (D) Inference (anumana)

2. The term 'Yogaja' (Intuitive) pertains to which of the following 'Parmanas'?

   (UGC NETDECEMBER 2019)

   (A) Perception

   (B) Inference

   (C) Verbal Testimony

   (D) Comparison

3. Consider the following example given below:

   (UGC NET JUNE 2019)

   Dewadatta is growing fat.

   He does not eat food during the day.

   Therefore, he must be eating food during the night.

   Identify the logic involved in the example provided above by choosing the correct answer from options given below:

   (A) Arthapatti (B) Anupalabdi

   (C) Anumana (D) Sabda

4. Which of the following Parmanas is used by the classical Indian school of logic to prove the existence of God?

   (A) Arthapati (postulation)

   (B) Upamana (comparison)

   (C) Perception (pratyaksha)

   (D) Inference (anumana)

5. The term 'Yogaja' (Intuitive) pertains to which of the following 'Parmanas'?

   (A) Perception

   (B) Inference

   (C) Verbal Testimony

   (D) Comparison

KEY

1. D **2.** A **3.** A **4.** D **5.** A

Unit VII

Data Interpretation

1 Sources Acquisition and Classification of Data

CONCEPT

When a research scholar starts a research project, he primarily needs data on the subject under research. Nature of data to be acquired depends upon nature of the research project. Data are acquired from a source. Data collected from a source through different methods are then analysed as per requirement of the research project. A research work cannot be completed without acquisition of the compatible data. However, acquiring data is an extremely challenging work which needs exhaustive planning, rigorous work, understanding, determination, and more to have the capacity to complete the research project effectively. There are different types and classes of data, sources of data collection, and methods of data collection.

TYPES OF DATA

It is already known that nature of data required for research purpose is either quantitative or qualitative. Both qualitative and quantitative data are found in the following types:

1) Primary Data
2) Secondary Data

Primary Data

Primary Data is collected through direct interaction with the original source by the research scholar or investigator. This original source is the targeted population under study. It is that data which is collected for the first time by the research scholar for the inquiry in hand. This data is required for micro-level research work. It is also called 'Raw Data'.

Advantages of Primary Data

1) **Original Data:** The primary data are original and relevant to the topic of the research study, so the degree of accuracy is very high.
2) **Flexible:** Primary data is that data which can be collected from a number of ways like interviews, telephone surveys, focus groups, etc. It can be also collected across the national borders through emails and posts. It can include a large population and wide geographical coverage.
3) **Current and Updated Information:** Primary data is current and it can better give a realistic view to the researcher about the topic under consideration.
4) **Reliable:** Reliability of primary data is very high because these are collected by the concerned and reliable parties.

Disadvantages of Primary Data

1) **Limited Coverage:** For collection of primary data where interview is to be conducted, the coverage is limited and for a wider coverage, more number of researchers are required.
2) **Time-consuming:** A lot of time and effort is required for data collection. By the time the data is collected, analysed, and report is ready, the problem of the research becomes very serious or outdated. So the purpose of the research may be defeated.
3) **Design Problem:** It has design problems like how to design the surveys. The questions must be simple to understand and respond.
4) **Non-Cooperation from Respondents:** Some respondents do not give timely responses. Sometimes, the respondents may give fake, socially acceptable, and diplomatic answers and try to cover up the realities.
5) **Costly:** With more people, time, and effort involvement, the cost of the data collection goes high. The importance of the research may go down.
6) **No Control on Collection:** In some primary data collection methods, there is no control over the data collection. Incomplete questionnaires always give a negative impact on research.

Secondary Data

Secondary Data are of repetitive nature, i.e., investigator collects the data which are already collected by someone before him. In this type of collection, a research scholar is not to personally meet any one as he does in collection of primary data; rather he consults various books, journals, newspapers, research papers, thesis, etc. by visiting some library or any other such institution. Secondary data are collected for macro-level research projects. Collection of secondary data is also known as 'Data Mining.'

Advantages of Secondary Data

1) **Cheaper and Faster:** The primary advantage of secondary data is that it is cheaper and faster to access.
2) **Access to Quality Data:** It provides a way to access the work of the best scholars all over the world.
3) **Direction-Oriented:** Secondary data gives a frame of mind to the researcher that in which direction he/she should go for the specific research.
4) **Adds Value to Research:** Secondary data save time, effort, and money and adds to the value of the research study.

Disadvantages of Secondary Data

1) **Likely to be Unreliable and Inaccurate:** The data is collected by the third party (which may not be a reliable party), so the reliability and accuracy of data goes down.
2) **Not Universal:** Data collected in one location may not be suitable for the other one due to the variable environmental factor.
3) **Getting Obsolete:** With the passage of time, the data becomes obsolete and very old and not suitable to the current problem under study.
4) **Likely to Distort Results:** Secondary data collected can distort the results of the research. For using secondary data, a special care is required to amend or modify it for use.
5) **Issues of Authenticity and Copyright:** As the sources of collecting secondary data are globally spread and involve a large number of authors, reporters, and researchers, it can raise issues of authenticity and copyright.

TABULATED COMPARISON BETWEEN PRIMARY AND SECONDARY DATA

Basis of Comparison	Primary Data	Secondary Data
Meaning	Primary data refers to the first hand data gathered by the researcher himself/herself.	Secondary data means data collected by someone else earlier.
Data	Real-time/Current data	Past data
Process	Deeply involved	Quick and easy
Sources	Surveys, Observation, Experiments, Questionnaire, Interviews	Government Publications, Websites, Books, Journals, Articles, Unpublished records
Cost-effectiveness	Expensive	Economical
Collection Time	Long	Short
Specificity	Always specific to researcher's needs	May not be specific to researcher's needs
Available in	Crude/Raw form	Refined form
Accuracy and Reliability	More	Relatively less

LEVELS OF RESEARCH

There are broadly two levels of research projects undertaken by research scholars, i.e., micro-level and macro-level.

1) **Micro-level Research:** The subject of this research work is related to local level issues, the data of which can be obtained by interacting personally with the targeted population.
2) **Macro-level Research:** Research works dealing with the national or international level issues are macro-level research projects. Data for such projects cannot be acquired through direct interaction with the targeted population as the population is scattered over an inaccessibly wide extent.

Sources of Data

Whether qualitative or quantitative, data are collected from the following sources:

1) Primary Source
2) Secondary Source

Primary Source

Following sources provide primary data:

a) Individuals
b) Focus Groups
c) Audio-video Recordings
d) Speeches
e) Art Objects
f) Natural Evidences

Secondary Source

Data for macro-level research work is obtained from the following sources (including both published and unpublished information):

Published Statistics include:

a) Reports of inquiry committees and commissions
b) Official publications by the centre and local government
c) Publications of banks, trades associations, and stock exchanges
d) Publications of various journals and magazines
e) Reports of research scholars and research institutions
f) Official publications of foreign governments and international bodies
g) Publications of political parties

Unpublished Statistics include:

Information provided by records kept in public and private sector offices

Electronic Source includes:

a) e-journals, newspapers, and books
b) Websites

METHODS OF DATA COLLECTION

Primary Data Collection Methods

a) **Personal investigation (Interview):** The surveyor collects the data himself/herself. The data so collected is reliable but is suited for small projects. Researcher interviews the respondent in structured, semi-structured, or unstructured form
b) **Collection via Investigators:** Trained investigators are employed to contact the respondents to collect data.
c) **Questionnaires:** Questionnaires may be used to ask specific questions that suit the study and get responses from the respondents. These questionnaires may be mailed as well.
d) **Telephonic Investigation:** The collection of data is done through asking questions over the telephone to give quick and accurate information.
e) **Investigation by Post:** A research scholar sends the questionnaire to far-off sitting respondents by post and respondents send that back to the research scholar after filling the questionnaire.
f) **Observation:** In observation method, the information is sought by way of investigator's own direct observation without asking from the respondent. The main advantage of this method is that it is free from subjective biasness, as it is free from the respondent's willingness. It is, however, an expensive and time-consuming method. Moreover, the information provided by this method is very limited and some of the more busy people like executives may not be accessible for direct observation.
g) **Delphi Technique:** It is a forecasting technique wherein the researcher elicits the information from the panel of experts either personally or through a questionnaire sent through the mail. Here, each expert in his/her respective field is asked to give his/her opinions on the problem concerned and the consolidated view of all is used to reach for the most accurate answer.
h) **Focus Group Interview:** It is one of the widely used data collection methods wherein a small group of people, usually 6-12 members come together to discuss the common areas of the problem. Here, each individual is required to provide his idea and opinion on the issue concerned and reach a unanimous decision. In this interview, there is a moderator who regulates the discussion among the group members.
i) **Surveys:** Surveys are used to collect data from the target audience and gather insights into their preferences, opinions, choices, and feedback related to the subject under study. This method is used in market research where business houses get feedback from customers to assess future prospects of their products and services.

Secondary Data Collection Methods

Secondary data is collected by consulting various traditional and electronic sources. Data available in these sources are noted down by the research scholar for its use in the research project. The collected data may be qualitative or quantitative; the method of collecting secondary data is the same.

ACQUISITION OF DATA

Every research project has a targeted population from which data is to be obtained for further studies to complete the research. As size of targeted population is large, it is not possible for the researcher scholar to approach every member of the targeted population for fetching information due to cost and time constraints. So research scholar picks up a sample of data from the targeted population and uses that data for analysis throughout the research work by applying suitable methodology and whatever findings are resultantly obtained are generalised for the whole of the targeted population. Picking up data as a sample requires highly technical skills. Various sampling techniques are used to pick up the sample.

Types of Sampling

Sampling techniques are broadly divided into two techniques:

1) Probability Sampling
2) Non-Probability Sampling

Probability Sampling

In probability sampling, each member of the targeted population has a chance to be selected as a sample. This sampling technique is used where the targeted population is homogeneous. Probability sampling technique is not applicable in case targeted population is heterogeneous. For example, if a research scholar is studying the contribution of agricultural labour in the economy of Punjab, then it is taken as homogeneous population as targeted population includes only agricultural labour. It is easy to pick up the sample by using probability technique in which every member of agricultural labour has a chance to be selected as part of the sample. On the other hand, if a research scholar is studying the contribution of labour in Punjab's economy, then targeted population is not homogeneous as the term 'labour' includes every agricultural, industrial, household, construction, and every type of labour. Trying probability sampling technique will not yield desired result until research scholar divides this population into homogeneous groups. Following sampling techniques are used to pick up the sample:

1) **Simple Random Sampling:** Here, members of targeted population are selected randomly and every member of the said population has an equal chance of being selected in the sample. Let us suppose that there are total 100 members in a target population. Research scholar is to pick up a sample of 40 members. Then research scholar does not fix any criteria of selecting 40 members; rather he picks them up randomly. Each of the 100 members has a chance to be selected as one of the 40 members. Sometimes, a research scholar uses lottery method to pick up the sample randomly or randomly pick up required number of members from a sequential list.

2) **Stratified Random Sampling:** Sample data are picked up through stratified random sampling where target population is not highly homogeneous. Research scholar first divides the population into homogeneous subgroups on the basis of similarities among members, which are called strata and then randomly picks up a sample from each stratum. Let us consider the case where a research scholar is to access the contribution of labour in Punjab's economy. Here, the targeted population is heterogeneous as members of labour in Punjab differ in age, gender, nature of occupation, etc. Research scholar will first divide this population into homogenous subgroups on the basis of age, gender, nature of occupation, and then randomly collect data from each stratum.

3) **Systematic Sampling:** It is called systematic sampling as a systematic technique is followed to acquire sample data. If a researcher decides to select a member from after a fixed position or interval from the targeted population, he will use systematic sampling technique to pick up the sample. Member occurring after a fixed interval becomes nth member. If a researcher wants to select a member after an interval of 10 members in a targeted population of 100, the nth member becomes 10th element. Then he will select members at the following positions:

   Sample: 10th, 20th, 30th, 40th, 50th, 60th, 70th, 80th, 90th, and 100th

   Further, if a researcher is to select 20 members after a fixed interval at nth member from the target population of 100, he will divide the total population into a desired sample like this:

   100/20 = 5

   This means he will pick up every 5th member as nth member to complete the sample of 20 members.

4) **Cluster Sampling:** In this sampling technique a research scholar randomly collects data from targeted population (naturally or already divided into subgroups or clusters). Research scholar considers naturally divided subgroups as clusters. For example,

while studying the contribution of labourers in Punjab's economy, he will consider labour belonging to a particular region as one cluster irrespective of gender, occupation, and age. Similarly, labour belonging to a particular occupation or activity is considered another cluster irrespective of region, religion, caste, gender, etc. Similarly, he finds other such clusters and randomly collects data samples from each cluster. It is different from stratified random sampling technique on the grounds that in stratified sampling, research scholar himself/herself divides the targeted population into homogenous groups whereas in cluster sampling, naturally occurring subgroups of targeted population are considered clusters in spite of their heterogeneous characteristics. Further, stratified random sampling technique aims at achieving homogenous population groups whereas in cluster sampling, aim is to pick sample according to the convenience of the research scholar.

5) **Multistage Sampling:** Multistage sampling divides large populations into stages to make the sampling process more practical. It is a more complex form of cluster sampling which contains two or more stages in sample selection. In simple terms, in multistage sampling, large clusters of the population are divided into smaller clusters in several stages in order to make primary data collection more manageable. Even smaller clusters are divided further into the smallest cluster in the next stage depending upon the requirement and nature of research. It has to be acknowledged that multistage sampling is not as effective as true random sampling.

6) **Area Random Sampling:** Area random sampling technique is used when no complete information of targeted population is available. Then the total area housing targeted population is divided into subareas or clusters and then research scholar randomly picks up a sample from each subarea. For example, a research scholar is to study the contribution of labourers of Punjab to Punjab's economy. The number of labourers engaged in different occupations of Punjab may not be available, but a list of different occupations scattered over the whole area of Punjab is available. Then research scholar divides the total area of Punjab into subareas and randomly collects data regarding number of labourers engaged in different occupations of that subarea which can then be studied.

Non-Probability Sampling

In non-probability sampling, researcher does not randomly select the members from the targeted population. In this sampling technique no member of the targeted population gets an equal chance of being selected as a sample. A researcher selects the members as per his own choice and convenience. Following are some techniques of non-probability sampling:

1) **Purposive Sampling:** In this method of sampling the research investigator purposely selects certain units for study. In this type of method, it is the selection which is uppermost and nothing is left to chance. Here, the sample is picked up according to the purpose of research. This method is the most authenticated as the selection is based on a purpose under which the useful units are selected for study. This sampling method is useful where the population is small and finite. For example, if the purpose of study is engagement of teenage labourers in agriculture sector in Punjab, then only teenage labourers in the agriculture sector of Punjab will be covered for study.

2) **Convenience Sampling:** As the name suggests, this sampling technique covers those members/elements for study which are easily available to the research scholar. Here, samples are picked up as per convenience of the research scholar who aims to save time and cost involved in collecting data through random sampling technique. For example, a research scholar intends to study the contribution of labourers in Punjab to the economy of Punjab will study those labourers who are easily available for study.

3) **Snowball Sampling:** This is the sampling technique which is used to acquire data where size of target population is too small to fulfil the purpose of study and researcher does not know whereabouts of the members of the targeted population. In this case, research scholar approaches a member of the targeted population; he records data from him and then asks him to give reference of another such member so that he can approach him also to obtain the same data. After getting reference from that member, he approaches the second member, records data, and asks him also to give some reference, and so on. This sampling technique is also known as chain sampling. For example, if a researcher is to make a study of contribution of agricultural labour from Nepal in the economy of Punjab, he will hardly find any and if with his efforts he finds one, then he asks for some reference of another such member for approach and study.

4) **Quota Sampling:** In this sampling technique a quota of the members from the targeted population is fixed for study. A researcher does not carry forward his/her study beyond that quota. The quota may be fixed on the basis of age, gender, occupation, region, religion, income, etc. as per requirement of the study. For example, to study the contribution of labour in Punjab to the economy of Punjab, a researcher fixes a quota of 50 female labourers and 60 male labourers within the age group of 30-40 engaged in the agriculture sector. He will interview only those labourers who have been fixed in the quota fulfilling other conditions also.

CLASSIFICATION OF DATA

Data classification is the process of arranging data into homogenous groups or classes according to some common characteristics present in the data. For example, during the process of sorting letters in a post office, the letters are classified according to the cities and further arranged according to streets.

> *"Classification is the process of arranging data into sequences according to their common characteristics or separating them into different but related parts."*
>
> *Prof. Secrist*

Objectives of Data Classification

1) **Separating Similarities and Differences:** To consolidate the volume of data in such a way that similarities and differences can be quickly understood. Figures can consequently be ordered in a few sections holding common traits.
2) **Facilitating Comparison:** To facilitate comparison among different classes of data and draw inferences.
3) **Highlighting Important Characteristics:** To point out the important characteristics of the data at a flash.
4) **Priority to Prominent Data:** To give importance to the prominent data collected while separating the optional elements.
5) **Application of Statistical Technique:** To allow a statistical method on the material gathered.

Types of Data Classification

1) **Geographical Classification:** Under this type of classification, the data are classified on the basis of area or place, and as such, this type of classification is also known as areal or spatial classification. The areas may be in terms of countries, states, districts, or zones. This type of classification is suitable for those data which are distributed geographically relating to a phenomenon, viz. population, mineral resources, production, sales, students of universities, etc.
2) **Chronological Classification:** Under this type of classification, the data collected are classified on the basis of time of their occurrence. As such, the series obtained under this classification is purely known as a time series. This type of classification is suitable for those data which take place in course of time, viz. population, production, sales, results, etc. The different classes obtained under this classification are arranged in order of the time which may begin either with the earliest, or the latest period.
3) **Qualitative Classification:** Under this type of classification, the data obtained are classified on the basis of certain descriptive characters or qualitative aspects of a phenomenon, viz. gender, beauty, literacy, honesty, intelligence, religion, eyesight, etc. As such, this sort of classification is also otherwise known as 'descriptive classification'. Such type of classifications is usually two opposite classes (dichotomous) in nature in which the whole data are divided into two groups, viz. a group with the absence of the attitude such as blind and not blind, or deaf and not deaf, etc.
4) **Quantitative Classification:** Under this type of classification, the collected data are classified on the basis of certain variables, viz. marks, income, expenditure, profit, loss, height, weight, age, price, production, etc. which is capable of quantitative applications and measurements. It is also known as 'classification by variables'.

Some Vital Facts:

1) Purposive sampling is a non-probability sampling
2) In sampling, the lottery method is used for Randomisation.
3) When a research problem is related to heterogeneous population, the most suitable sampling method is Stratified Sampling.
4) Systematic sampling technique is generally followed when the population is finite.

Practice Exercise

General Questions Format

1. A research work without data is just like
   (A) Hospital without doctor
   (B) Lock without key
   (C) Body without blood
   (D) College without teacher

2. Which of the following is NOT TRUE about Primary Data?
   a) Primary data becomes basis of secondary data.
   b) It is also called 'Prime Data'.
   c) Methods of primary data collection emphasise on collecting original data.
   d) Qualitative data serves as a panacea for current problems.
   (A) Only a, c, and d (B) Only b
   (C) a, b, c, and d (D) Only d

3. Homogenous population is the precondition of which sampling technique?
   (A) Cluster Sampling
   (B) Stratified Sampling
   (C) Area Sampling
   (D) Systematic Sampling

4. Which of the following is NOT a source of Primary data?
   (A) Focus groups (B) Natural evidences
   (C) Art objects (D) Websites

5. Consider the following data obtained from an NGO:
   i) A blood donation camp was organised on 10-08-2019.
   ii) Free copies and pens were distributed to school children on 23-02-2019.
   iii) A seminar against drug menace was organised on 16-10-2019.
   Classification of this data will be called _____ Classification.
   (A) Chronological (B) Eventual
   (C) Systematic (D) Longitudinal

6. Natural subgrouping of a targeted population yield data through _____ sampling technique.
   (A) Stratified (B) Quota
   (C) Snowball (D) Cluster

7. Which of the following disadvantage of primary data establishes that researcher has no control over data collection?
   (A) Time-consuming
   (B) Design problem
   (C) Non-cooperation from respondents
   (D) Cost exceeding budget

8. Secondary data adds value to research as it
   (A) gives an opportunity to the research scholar to explore data from every corner of the world.
   (B) provides access to established works of world renowned scholars, authors, and scientists.
   (C) does not carry any apprehension of non-cooperation from the data source which creates deadlock in the progress of the research project.
   (D) aims at objective study which is relevant and unambiguous.

9. Which of the following justifies the logic of picking up samples from the targeted population for a research work?
   (A) Size of population is too large to be covered by the investigator
   (B) Taken sample represents the total population and its results are generalised to cover the whole population
   (C) Various statistical techniques are compatible to analyse small-sized data as is in a sample
   (D) All of the above

10. Which of the following is TRUE about Snowball Sampling?
    a) It makes research scholar to adopt a different approach to fetch data which is generally not adopted in case of other sampling techniques.
    b) Being applicable on too small-sized and scarce population, it increases the chances of manipulation of data in case a researcher fails to contact the original source.
    c) It is the least popular sampling technique among research scholars as it involves a lot of wastage of time, money, and energy in locating the actual source.

d) In spite of covering all the available members of the targeted population, the data so acquired does not yield adequate representation to be generalised after the analysis.

(A) Only c and d (B) Only a, c, and d
(C) Only a (D) a, b, c, and d

11. Which exclusive feature(s) of interview is/are conducive for a research scholar to meet the purpose of study?
a) It aims at fetching data which are instrumental in completing the research work of a researcher.
b) Interview is respondent-centred due to which respondent feels comfortable in furnishing true information.
c) Researcher gets genuine information as there is no scope of manipulation due to face-to- face interaction.
d) There is always room for fetching additional information through interview due to its broader scale to supplement the main data.

(A) Only b and d
(B) Only c
(C) a, b, c, and d
(D) Only a, b, and c

12. In which method of data collection researcher obtains information of experts?
(A) Focus group (B) Survey
(C) Observation (D) Delphi

13. Which of the following is NOT a non-probability method of sampling?
(A) Quota (B) Purposive
(C) Systematic (D) Snowball

14. A researcher is to study the impact of stress on performance of employees of different ages and occupations in private and public sector concerns in a metropolitan city. Which sampling method should he choose to acquire data?
(A) Cluster Sampling
(B) Stratified Random Sampling
(C) Systematic Sampling
(D) Multistage sampling

15. Consider the statements:
P: Classification of data helps in identifying the common characteristics of data.
Q: Similarities and differences in data can be studied after classification of data.
State whether:
(A) P is true but Q is false
(B) P is false but Q is true
(C) Both P and Q are true
(D) Both P and Q are false

KEY

1. C **2.** B **3.** B **4.** D **5.** A **6.** D **7.** A
8. B **9.** D **10.** C **11.** A **12.** D **13.** C **14.** B
15. C

Assertion–Reason Format

1. **Assertion (A):** Acquiring preliminary data involves interaction between research scholar and the respondent.
Reason (R): Research scholar interviews the respondent to acquire data on a questionnaire.
(A) Both A and R are true and R is correct explanation of A
(B) Both A and R are true but R is not correct explanation of A
(C) A is true but R is false
(D) A is false but R is true

2. **Assertion (A):** Concept of targeted population loses its relevance in snowball sampling.
Reason (R): Success of snowball sampling depends upon materialization of references.
(A) Both A and R are true but R is not correct explanation of A
(B) A is true but R is false
C) A is false but R is true
(D) Both A and R are true and R is correct explanation of A

3. **Assertion (A):** Data mining is one of the methods to acquire primary data.
Reason (R): A research work requiring primary data is effective in highlighting the lacunae of a system.

(A) Both A and R are false

(B) A is true but R is false

(C) A is false but R is true

(D) Both A and R are true but R is not correct explanation of A

4. **Assertion (A):** Classification of data facilitates comparison.

Reason (R): Geographical classification of data helps in demographic studies.

(A) Both A and R are true and R is correct explanation of A

(B) Both A and R are true but R is not correct explanation of A

(C) Both A and R are false

(D) A is true but R is false

5. **Assertion (A):** Sources of secondary data are transparent.

Reason (R): Secondary data obtained from any source is costlier and time-consuming.

(A) A is true but R is false

(B) A is false but R is true

(C) Both A and R are true and R is correct explanation of A

(D) Both A and R are true but R is not correct explanation of A

6. **Assertion (A):** Data acquisition is escapable in case of research on open source activities.

Reason (R): Open source activities yield that data which cannot be put to research.

(A) A is true but R is false

(B) A is false but R is true

(C) Both A and R are false

(D) Both A and R are true and R is correct explanation of A

7. **Assertion (A):** Targeted population becomes a norm-based population in systematic sampling.

Reason (R): Researcher selects members as samples after a fixed position or interval from the targeted population.

(A) A is true but R is false

(B) A is false but R is true

(C) Both A and R are true but R is not correct explanation of A

(D) Both A and R are true and R is correct explanation of A

8. **Assertion (A):** Multistage sampling is a complex form of stratified sampling.

Reason (R): Making subgroups of homogenous data is a standing condition of stratified sampling.

(A) Both A and R are true and R is correct explanation of A

(B) Both A and R are true but R is not correct explanation of A

(C) A is true but R is false

(D) A is false but R is true

9. **Assertion (A):** Dichotomy is the essential feature of qualitative data classification.

Reason (R): Various behavioral traits are classified in classification of qualitative data.

(A) Both A and R are true and R is correct explanation of A

(B) Both A and R are true but R is not correct explanation of A

(C) Both A and R are false

(D) A is false but R is true

10. **Assertion (A):** Data obtained from non-probability sampling technique is of a non-representative nature.

Reason (R): Non-probability sampling techniques do not recognize targeted population as a vital contributor of sampling.

(A) Both A and R are true but R is not correct explanation of A

(B) Both A and R are false

(C) A is true but R is false

(D) Both A and R are true and R is correct explanation of A

KEY

1. A **2.** C **3.** A **4.** B **5.** A **6.** C **7.** D **8.** D **9.** B **10.** A

Questions Asked in Previous NET Exams

1. Which one of the following is a non-probability sampling? **(UGC NET JUNE 2014)**

(A) Simple Random (B) Purposive

(C) Systematic (D) Stratified

2. In sampling, the lottery method is used for

(UGC NET DECEMBER 2013)

(A) Interpretation

(B) Theorisation

(C) Conceptualisation

(D) Randomisation

3. Which one of the following is a non-probability sampling method?

(UGC NET SEPTEMBER 2013)

(A) Simple Random Sampling

(B) Stratified Sampling

(C) Cluster Sampling

(D) Quota Sampling

4. Which of the following sampling methods is not based on probability?

(UGC NET JUNE 2013)

(A) Simple Random Sampling

(B) Stratified Sampling

(C) Quota Sampling

(D) Cluster Sampling

5. Which of the following sampling methods is based on probability?

(UGC NET DECEMBER 2012)

(A) Convenience Sampling

(B) Quota Sampling

(C) Judgement Sampling

(D) Stratified Sampling

6. Suppose you want to investigate the working efficiency of nationalised banks in India, which one of the following would you follow?

(UGC NET JUNE 2011)

(A) Area Sampling

(B) Multistage Sampling

(C) Sequential Sampling

(D) Quota Sampling

7. When a research problem is related to the heterogeneous population, the most suitable sampling method is:

(UGC NET DECEMBER 2008)

(A) Cluster Sampling

(B) Stratified Sampling

(C) Convenient Sampling

(D) Lottery Method

8. Which one is called non-probability sampling?

(UGC NET JUNE 2008)

(A) Cluster Sampling

(B) Quota Sampling

(C) Systematic Sampling

(D) Stratified Random Sampling

9. Which of the following sampling methods is appropriate to study the prevalence of AIDS amongst males and females in India in 1976, 1986, 1996, and 2006?

(UGC NET JUNE 2008)

(A) Cluster Sampling

(B) Systematic Sampling

(C) Quota Sampling

(D) Stratified Random Sampling

10. Which technique is generally followed when the population is finite?

(UGC NET DECEMBER 2007)

(A) Area Sampling Technique

(B) Purposive Sampling Technique

(C) Systematic Sampling Technique

(D) None of the above

KEY

1. B **2.** D **3.** D **4.** C **5.** D **6.** B **7.** B **8.** B **9.** B **10.** C

2 Quantitative and Qualitative Data

QUANTITATIVE DATA

Quantitative data is information of those variables which can be assigned numerical values and are put in mathematical calculations and statistical analysis. Various mathematical and statistical techniques are applied to analyse quantitative data. Data pertaining to natural sciences is quantitative in nature. Quantifiable data is always measurable in numerical units and such data is continuous data. Such data gives answer to questions like 'How Many?', 'How Much?', 'How Often', etc. Quantitative data is usually collected for statistical analysis using surveys, polls, or questionnaires sent across to a specific section of a population.

Characteristics of Quantitative Data

1) **Accurate:** As quantitative data is obtained and analysed through mathematical and statistical techniques, it comes up with an accurate level.
2) **Unambiguous:** There is no ambiguity in quantitative data due to its numerical measurements. Quantitative data on different quantifiable variables and indicators are expressed in specific numerical units which present a clear and relevant data.
3) **Authentic:** Quantitative data are collected and analysed with established and universally accepted and tested mathematical and statistical techniques, hence making data authentic.
4) **Based on Structured Instrument:** Structured instruments like questionnaire are used to obtain the quantitative data
5) **Representative in Nature:** Quantitative data are representative in nature. This means that data are collected from a sufficiently large-sized targeted population out of which data are picked up as sample. This sample represents the whole population and the results obtained after analysing this sample are generalised.
6) **Standard Format:** Data are in the form of numbers and statistics, often arranged in tables, charts, figures, or other non-textual forms.

Importance of Quantitative Data

1) **Facilitating Research:** Data are collected for research purpose. Quantitative data facilitates research and removes apprehension of any deadlock due to use of authentic mathematical and statistical techniques.
2) **Specific Results:** Most of the research works depend upon quantitative data as these yield specific results after data analysis.
3) **Accurate Hypothesis Testing:** Quantitative data with mathematical and statistical techniques yield accurate hypothesis testing establishing credibility of the research work. It is ascertained by the research scholar whether hypothesis is null or alternative.

Types of Quantitative Data

1) **Projection of Data:** While using mathematical and statistical tools, various predictions are made regarding progress in data. For example, when a product is launched in a market, predictions regarding its future sales and sustainability in the market are made by applying various mathematical tools.
2) **Calculation through Sensors:** Certain machines like computers are capable of converting any type of data into numerical units through its sensors.
3) **Counting Data:** It is a type of data in which counting is the basis of any conclusion, for example, how many people are online at a particular time.
4) **Measurable Data:** There are various data which are measured in different numerical units for analysis and research purpose. For example, data on height, temperature, size, etc. are measurable. A research scholar while following a particular methodology analyses data while measuring the variables.
5) **Qualitative Data with Quantitative Entity:** Data on certain qualitative subjects is also converted into quantitative entities. An example could be when a hotelier asks the guest to rate hospitality while giving marks from 1 to 10.

Methods of Quantitative Data Collection

While conducting research, a research scholar adopts different methods to collect data according to the nature of research. There are mainly two methods to collect quantitative data:

1) **Surveys:** A research scholar collects quantitative data by conducting survey on the population under study. Out of that the desired sample is picked up for further studies. Following are the types of surveys a research scholar conducts to acquire the desired data.

   a) **Longitudinal Survey:** In this survey, data on continuous variables under study are collected over a certain period of time. Here, data so collected pertains to two time periods depicting growth in that variable between the two time periods. For example, Census is conducted once in 10 years. Population is a continuous variable which is continuously changing and its growth is definitely studied by conducting a Census. If a census is conducted in 2011, the figures so collected are compared with the figures of previous Census in 2001. So growth of population is studied. This survey is called longitudinal survey.

   b) **Cross-sectional Survey:** In this method of data collection, data of a variable is collected for a particular time period. There is no comparison of the collected data with either past or future time period.

2) **Structured Interviews:** Quantitative data is also collected by conducting structured interview with the members of the targeted population. A questionnaire is prepared by the research scholar and he asks questions to the members of the targeted population and collects data. Interview can be face-to-face, online, or on telephone.

Analysis of Quantitative Data:

Quantitative data are analysed with different methods by a research scholar to reach the conclusion of his research work. There are the following methods with which quantitative data are analysed:

1) **Gap analysis:** Gap analysis uses a side-by-side matrix to depict quantitative data that helps in measuring the difference between expected performance and actual performance of any quantitative variable in terms of growth. This data analysis helps measure gaps in performance and the things that are required to be done to bridge this gap.

2) **Cross-tabulation:** Cross-tabulation is the most widely used quantitative data analysis method. It is a preferred method since it uses a basic tabular form to draw inferences between different data sets in a research study. It contains data that are mutually exclusive or has some connection with one another.

3) **Total Unduplicated Reach and Frequency (TURF) Analysis:** This method is used by business houses to assess the frequency and avenues by which their messages reach the customers and prospective customers to plan their business and advertisement strategies. Quantitative data collected through this method assesses the total market reach of a product.

4) **Trend analysis:** Trend analysis is a statistical analysis method that provides the ability to look at quantitative data that has been collected over a long period of time. This data analysis method helps collect feedback about data changes over time and it aims to understand the change in variables considering one variable remains unchanged. This method becomes the basis of experimental or ex-post facto method of research.

5) **Maximum Difference Scaling or MaxDiff Analysis:** The MaxDiff analysis is a quantitative data analysis method that is used by business houses to fathom customer preferences for a purchase in the best and worst preference scale due to which this method is also called the "best-worst" method. Company conducts survey and collects information regarding which is the best and which is the worst preference of the customer regarding purchase of a product. A questionnaire is prepared containing questions on preferences to be given by the customer. Message testing, customer satisfaction, brand preference, and product features are the common surveys where MaxDiff analysis is used to predict the outcome. This method is very similar to conjoint analysis but is much easier to implement and can be interchangeably used. The respondents are asked to pick the most and least important factors in the given answer options.

Advantages of Quantitative Data

1) **Conduct in-depth research:** Since quantitative data can be statistically analysed, it is highly likely that the research will be detailed and in-depth.

2) **Minimum bias:** There are instances in research, where personal bias is involved which leads to incorrect results. Due to the numerical nature of quantitative data, the personal bias is reduced to a great extent.

3) **Accurate results:** As the results obtained are objective in nature, they are extremely accurate.

QUALITATIVE DATA

Qualitative data are pieces of information regarding those variables which are neither expressed in numerical units nor any mathematical or statistical tool is applicable for their analysis. These data are collected in philosophical research on values, supernatural concepts, and behavioural traits. Qualitative data are not measurable but comparable.

Characteristics of Qualitative Data

1) **Ordinal in Nature:** Qualitative data are ordinal in nature, i.e., the data can be ordered and compared.
2) **Nominal Data:** Qualitative data are nominal in nature. They are used to label variables or denote certain variables. For example, sometimes gender, social status, marital status, economic position, ethnicity, etc. are denoted by qualitative data.
3) **Non-Numeral:** Qualitative data are collected through figures, charts, pictures, words or codes, audio-video recordings, text and documents, symbols, focus groups, interview transcripts, observation, and notes. These are non-numeral in nature.
4) **Categorical Nature:** Qualitative data are divided into groups. Examples of categorical data are race, sex, age group, and educational level.
5) **Observation-Oriented:** Qualitative data is observation-oriented. Data are collected through observation of various qualitative and behavioural traits of the sample subject.
6) **Exploratory in Nature:** Qualitative data being related to abstract phenomenon is exploratory in nature. Its exploration is deep-rooted and reaches those levels which cannot be reached with quantitative data.

Importance of Qualitative Data

1) **Base for Quantitative Data Analysis:** Qualitative data provides the means by which the researcher can quantify various concepts. Division of qualitative data into various categories enables the research scholar to choose a specific group for further quantifying the related concepts.
2) **Facilitates Study of Human Behaviour:** Importance of qualitative data is highlighted in the fact that these data facilitate study of human behavioural traits like emotions, values, ethics, etc. For overall development of society, research on changing human behaviour, trends in lifestyle, ethics, and values is equally essential. For this purpose, qualitative data are needed to bring reforms in the society which is not possible with quantitative data.
3) **Provides Broader Base for Study:** There is a need to study developments in cultural, religious, social, and ethnic disciplines of the society at a broader scale to assess the trends. This is possible with qualitative data.

Qualitative Data Collection Methods

Qualitative data collection methods are mainly focused on gaining insights, reasoning, and motivations, hence they go deeper in terms of research. Some of the leading methods of qualitative data collecting methods are explained below:

One-to-One Interviews: It is one of the most commonly used data collection instrument for qualitative research, mainly because of its personal approach. The interviewer or the researcher collects data directly from the interviewee on a one-to-one basis. The interview may be informal and unstructured (conversational). The questions asked are mostly spontaneous open-ended questions, with the interviewer letting the flow of the interview dictate the next question to be asked.

OPEN-ENDED QUESTIONS

Open-ended questions are defined as free-form survey questions that allows a respondent to answer in open text format such that they can answer based on their complete knowledge, feeling, and understanding. This means that response to this question is not confined to a set of structured options.

2. **Focus groups:** A researcher while undertaking research through qualitative data keeps focus on that group of persons to be interviewed who are currently part of the subject of study or are ex-associates. The group is limited to 6-10 people and a moderator is assigned to moderate the ongoing discussion. Depending on the data which is sorted, the members of a group may have something in common. For example, a researcher conducting a study on bureaucracy will choose members who are bureaucrats or were bureaucrats and have sufficient knowledge of the subject matter.
3. **Record-keeping:** This method of collecting qualitative data makes use of the already existing reliable documents and similar sources of information as the data source. This data can be used in a new research. This is similar to going to a library. There, one can go over books and other reference material to collect relevant data that is likely be used in the research.
4. **Process of observation:** In this qualitative data collection method, the researcher immerses himself/

herself in the setting where his respondents are, and keeps a keen eye on participants and takes down notes. This is known as the process of observation. Besides taking notes, other documentation methods, such as video and audio recording, photography, and similar methods can be used.

5. **Longitudinal studies:** This data collection method is performed on the same data source repeatedly over an extended period of time. It is an observational research method that goes on for a few years and in some cases, can go on for even decades. The goal of this data collection method is to find correlations through an empirical study of subjects with common traits.
6. **Case studies:** In this method, data is gathered by in-depth analysis of case studies. The versatility of this method is demonstrated in how this method can be used to analyse both simple and complex subjects. The strength of this method is how judiciously it uses a combination of one or more qualitative data collection methods to draw inferences.

Qualitative Data Analysis

There are two main approaches of qualitative data analysis:

1) **Deductive Approach:** The deductive approach involves analysing qualitative data based on a structural instrument (questionnaire) that is predetermined by the researcher. In this case, a researcher can use the questions as a guide for analysing the data. This approach is quick and easy and can be used when a researcher has a fair idea about the likely responses that he/she is going to receive from the sample population.
2) **Inductive Approach:** The inductive approach, on the contrary, is not based on a predetermined structure or set ground rules/framework. Here, researcher conducts an unstructured interview of the respondent. This is more time-consuming and a thorough approach to qualitative data analysis.

Advantages of Qualitative Data

1. **It helps in-depth analysis:** Qualitative data collected provide the researchers with in-depth analysis of subject matters. While collecting qualitative data, the researchers tend to probe the participants and can gather ample amount of information by asking the right kind of questions. From a series of question and answers, the data that is collected is used to draw conclusions.
2. **Understand what customers think:** Qualitative data helps the market researchers to understand the mindset of their customers. The use of qualitative data gives businesses an insight into why a customer purchased a product. Understanding customer language helps market research infer the data collected in a more systematic manner.
3. **Rich data:** Collected data can be used to conduct research in the future as well. Since the questions asked to collect qualitative data are open-ended questions, respondents are free to express their opinions which lead to collecting more information.

Disadvantages of Qualitative Data

1. **Time-consuming:** As collecting qualitative data is more time-consuming, fewer people are studied in comparison to collecting quantitative data and unless time and budget allow, a smaller sample size is included.
2. **Not easy to generalize:** Since fewer people are studied, it is difficult to generalize the results of that population.
3. **Is dependent on researcher's skills:** This type of data is collected through one-to-one interviews, observations, focus groups, etc. It relies on the researcher's skills and experience to collect information from the sample.

TABULATED DIFFERENCE BETWEEN QUALITATIVE AND QUANTITATIVE DATA

Basis of Comparison	Qualitative Data	Quantitative Data
Meaning	Qualitative data is the data in which the classification of objects is based on attributes and properties.	Quantitative data is the type of data which can be measured and expressed numerically.
Research Methodology	Exploratory	Conclusive
Approach	Subjective	Objective
Analysis	Non-Statistical	Statistical
Collection of Data	Unstructured	Structured
Determines	Depth of Understanding	Level of Occurrence
Asks	Why	How many/much
Sample	Small number of non-representative nature	Large number of representative nature
Outcome	Develops initial understanding	Recommends final course of action

Practice Exercise

General Questions Format

1. Which of the following is/are NOT TRUE about quantitative data?
   a) Quantitative data does not work where it is not possible to pick up a sample due to too small size of targeted population.
   b) Various mathematical and statistical tools become evidences of accuracy and authenticity of quantitative data analysis.
   c) Quantitative data obtained through structured instrument minimises the risk of incompatibility with objectives of a research work.
   d) Collection and analysis of quantitative data is easier, verifiable, and rectifiable.

   (A) Only c (B) Only a and d
   (C) None of these (D) Only a, c, and d

2. Consider the following statements and choose the appropriate answer choice:
   P: Structured instrument is an indispensable tool to obtain quantitative data.
   Q: Qualitative data is obtained as it provides basis for quantitative data analysis.

   (A) P is true but Q is false
   (B) A is false but Q is true
   (C) Both P and Q are false
   (D) Both P and Q are true

3. Which of the following is TRUE regarding difference between qualitative data and quantitative data?
   (A) Qualitative data is passive whereas quantitative data is active.
   (B) Qualitative data is an obligation whereas quantitative data is a prerogative.
   (C) Qualitative data is informatory whereas quantitative data is reformatory.
   (D) None of these

4. Various methods of qualitative data collection establish that qualitative data collected through
   (A) observation is more effective than collected through focus groups
   (B) any method yields the same results
   (C) recordkeeping method portrays compatibility of data with objectives of every new research
   (D) None of these

5. Answers to open-ended questions are based on respondents'
   a) feeling b) understanding c) knowledge

   (A) Only a and b (B) a, b, and c
   (C) Only b (D) Only c and b

6. Had there not been analysis of qualitative data there would not have been
   a) research on social evils leading to drafting and implementing of various reforms in the society
   b) study on various types of human behavioural traits helping in framing various statutes in social, economic, and judicial field
   c) market research on preferences of prospective customers regarding purchase of a product
   d) assessment of rituals of different communities preserving respective values and ethics as commitments to the community.

   (A) Only a and c (B) a, b, c and d
   (C) only b and d (D) Only d

7. Different methods of quantitative data analysis are given under Column I and their respective themes are given under Column II. Match the method of data analysis with its respective theme and choose the correct code among the given codes given below:

Column I (Method of analysis)	Column II (Theme)
a) TURF Analysis	i) Longitudinal Analysis
b) Gap Analysis	ii) Best-worst
c) MaxDiff Analysis	iii) Growth
d) Trend Analysis	iv) Popularity

Codes:	(a)	(b)	(c)	(d)
(A)	iii	ii	iv	i
(B)	iv	i	ii	iii
(C)	iv	iii	ii	i
(D)	i	iv	ii	iii

8. Which of the following is TRUE?
   a) Quantitative data determines in-depth study of a variable.
   b) Qualitative data classifies objects on the basis of attributes and properties.
   c) Quantitative data pertains to large-sized samples of non-representative character.
   d) Qualitative data recommends a final course of action as an outcome of analysis.

   (A) Only c (B) Only a and d
   (C) a, b, c, and d (D) only b

9. Statement: Can qualitative data be used as a base for quantitative data analysis?

Arguments I: Yes, there are some behavioural traits which can be put to quantitative analysis.

II. No, qualitative variables cannot be expressed in numerical terms due to their abstract nature.

(A) Only argument I is strong
(B) Only argument II is strong
(C) Both arguments I and II are strong
(D) Neither argument I nor II is strong

10. Which of the advantage makes qualitative data the most reliable data for research?

(A) Qualitative data paves way for study of human behaviour which is not possible with quantitative data.
(B) Unstructured format of qualitative data broadens the scope of study.
(C) Subjective nature of qualitative data enables a research scholar to successfully interact with focus groups for data collection.
(D) Qualitative data becomes the basis for creating awareness and bringing reforms in the society.

KEY

1. C **2.** A **3.** D **4.** D **5.** B **6.** A **7.** A **8.** D **9.** C **10.** A

Assertion–Reason Format

1. **Assertion (A):** Being objective in nature, quantitative data yield unambiguous results when put to analysis.

Reason (R): Quantitative data collected through surveys are the most reliable to get desired results.

(A) Both A and R are true and R is correct explanation of A
(B) Both A and R are true but R is not correct explanation of A
(C) A is true but R is false
(D) A is false but R is true

2. **Assertion (A):** Deductive approach to qualitative data analysis enables the research scholar to study the problem at a broader scale.

Reason (R): Studying a problem at a broader scale takes significance of quantitative data to the back seat.

(A) Both A and R are false
(B) A is false but R is true
(C) A is true but R is false
(D) Both A and R are true but R is not correct explanation of A

3. **Assertion (A):** Trend analysis of quantitative data is part of experimental method of research.

Reason (R): Researcher obtains feedback of changing trends in continuous variables while considering one variable unchanged.

(A) A is true but R is false
(B) A is false but R is true
(C) Both A and R are true but R is not correct explanation of A
(D) Both A and R are true and R is correct explanation of A

4. **Assertion (A):** Quantitative data showing growth in a variable is subject to analysis.

Reason (R): Trends showing growth in different variables also contain qualitative data.

(A) Both A and R are true and R is correct explanation of A
(B) Both A and R are true but R is not correct explanation of A
(C) Both A and R are false
(D) A is true but R is false

KEY

1. C **2.** A **3.** D **4.** B

Questions Asked in Previous NET Exams

1. Given below are two statements - one is labelled as Assertion (A) and other as Reason (R): **(UGC NET DEC 2019)**

Assertion (A): Sniffing may be used to steal data or information over a network.

Reason (R): Sniffing is the process of monitoring and capturing all data packets passing though given network.

In the light of above stated two statements, choose the correct option from the choices given below

(A) Both A and R are true and R is the correct explanation of A
(B) Both A and R are true and R is not the correct explanation of A
(C) A is true but R is false
(D) A is false but R is true

KEY

1. A

3 Data Interpretation & Graphic Representation
(Bar-Chart, Histograms, Pie-Chart, Table & Line-Chart)

DATA INTERRPRETATION

Data Interpretation is the process of making sense out of a collection of data that has been processed. This collection may be present in various forms like bar graphs, line charts and tabular forms, histograms, pie charts and other similar forms and hence needs an interpretation of some kind.

1. Bar Chart

A bar chart is used to represent data visually using bars of different heights or lengths. Data is graphed either horizontally or vertically, allowing viewers to compare different values and draw conclusions quickly and easily. A typical bar chart will have a label, axis, scales, and bars, which represent measurable values such as amounts or percentages. Bar graphs are used to display all kinds of data, from quarterly sales and job growth to seasonal rainfall and crop yields, exports, imports etc. Data on bar chart show growth in any variable over some period of time.

Nature of Questions Asked on Bar Charts:

In the above cases questions can be asked either by observing the data or by calculations. Following calculations are required to be made:

1) Percentage
2) Percentage Change (increase or decrease)
3) Average.
4) Ratio.

1) **Percentage:** Percent means per hundred. X percent can be expressed as; $\frac{X}{100}$

   Percentage is calculated with respect to a total number as:

   A is what % of B, Then: $\frac{A}{B} \times 100$

2) **Percentage Change:** Change in percentage is calculated as:

   i) Increase in percentage shows an increase i.e. a Smaller Figure (SF) grows into Bigger Figure (BG), then:

   $$\frac{BF - SF}{SF} \times 100$$

   ii) Decrease in percentage shows a decrease i.e. a Bigger Figure (BF) becoming Smaller Figure (SF), then:

   $$\frac{BF - SF}{BF} \times 100$$

3) **Average:** An average is per unit value of a subject. It is calculated as:

   Formula 1:Average= [Sum of observations / Number of observations]

   Formula 2:Total Sum= [Average x No. of observations]

4) **Ratio:** A ratio is calculated while keeping a common number as quotient between the two numbers as:

   Ratio between 15 and 9 is: 5 : 3

Practice Exercise

General Questions Format

1-5: Study the following graph of India's Trade carefully and answer the question given below it:

(UGC NET JUNE2009)

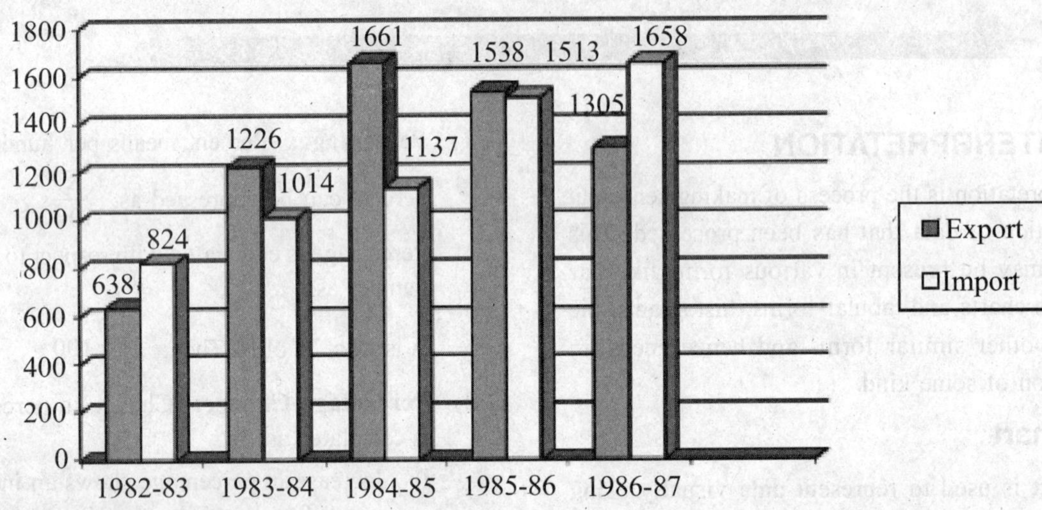

1. The export in 1985-86 was approximately how many times that of the year 1982-83?
   (A) 0.41 (B) 2.41
   (C) 0.55 (D) 1.84
2. In which of the following years was the gap in the imports and exports the least?
   (A) 1982-83 (B) 1983-84
   (C) 1984-85 (D) 1985-86
3. What is the ratio of years having above average exports to those having below average exports in the given period?
   (A) 3 : 2 (B) 4 : 1
   (C) 2 : 3 (D) 1 : 4
4. Which of the following statements is true about the graph?
   (A) There is a continuous rise in imports
   (B) from 1984-85 Exports are above average
   (C) till 1984-85 imports are below average
   (D) All of above
5. The imports in 1986-87 are approximately how many percent more than the imports of 1982-83?
   (A) 49 (B) 50
   (C) 201 (D) NOA

KEY

1. **B** $\frac{\text{Exports of } 1985-86}{\text{exports of } 1982-83} \Rightarrow \frac{1538}{638} = 2.41$
2. **D** It is a question on observation. It is found by observing bar chart that in 1985-86 there was minimum gap between exports and imports.
3. **A** Total of exports = 6368
   Number of years = 5
   Average = 1273.6
   It is observed from the table that years 1984-85, 1985-86 and 1986-87 have exports above average. Hence ratio of number of years having exports above average to number of years having exports below average is: 3 : 2
4. **D**
5. **D** applying the formula of %age increase:

$$\frac{\text{exports of } 1986-87 - \text{exports of } 1982-83}{\text{Exports of } 1982-83} \times 100$$

$$= \frac{1658-824}{824} \times 100 = 100\% \text{ (Approx.)}$$

There is no answer choice displaying this answer.

Questions Asked in Previous NET Exams

Study the following graph carefully and answer questions 1 to 3.

(UGC NET JUNE 2009)

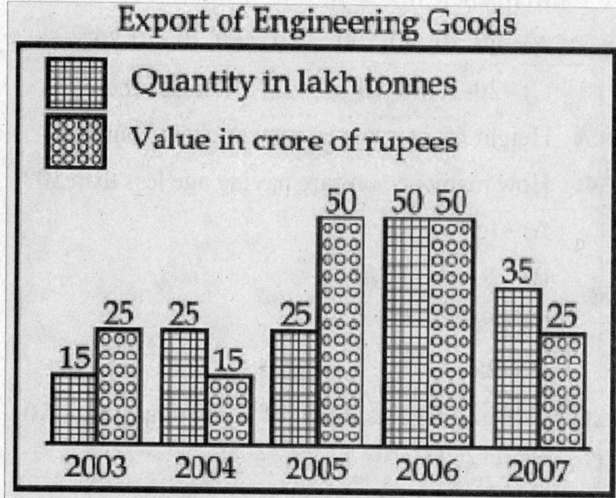

1. In which year the quantity of engineering goods' exports was maximum?
   (A) 2005
   (B) 2006
   (C) 2004
   (D) 2007
2. In which year the value of engineering goods decreased by 50 percent compared to the previous year?
   (A) 2004
   (B) 2007
   (C) 2005
   (D) 2006
3. In which year the quantity of exports was 100 percent higher than the quantity of previous year?
   (A) 2004
   (B) 2005
   (C) 2006
   (D) 2007

KEY

1. **B** This is an observation based question. Height of bar representing quantity exported of engineering goods is maximum in 2006.
2. **B** It is an observation question. It is found in the bar chart that value of exports engineering goods Fell to 25 cr. Rs. In 2007 from Rs.50 Cr. In 2006. So 50% fall in 2007.
3. **C** Observation based question. Heights of bars between 2005 and 2006, representing quantity of engineering products exported justify the answer i.e. increase from 25 lakh tonnes to 50 lakh tonnes.

2. Histograms

Histograms are graphs of a distribution of continuous data. Histograms can provide a visual display of large amounts of data that are difficult to understand in a tabular, or graph form. It was introduced by Karl Pearson in 1891. A **histogram** is a display of statistical information that uses rectangles (bins) to show the frequency of data items in successive numerical intervals of equal size. The width of the bin is determined by the range and may or may not be equal to the other bins. Hight of a bin indicates frequency of occurrence of a variable in that bin. In the most common form of **histogram**, the independent variable is plotted along the horizontal axis and the dependent variable is plotted along the vertical axis. As the frequency of the data occurrence is represented by a bar, hence it looks very much like a bar graph. This is clear from the following example: **Example:** The histogram given below shows the distribution of continuous variable age. A histogram is to be constructed from this data. Steps to construct histogram is shown below:

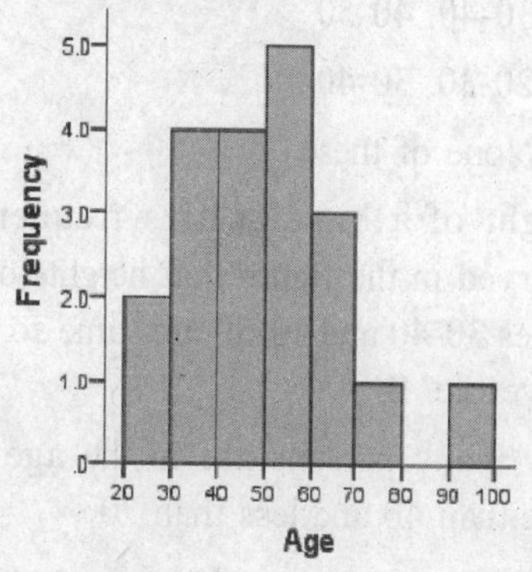

36 25 38 46 55 68 72 55 36 38
67 45 22 48 91 46 52 61 58 55

How to construct a histogram from a continuous variable?

To construct a histogram from a continuous variable one first needs to split the data into intervals, called **bins**.

In the example above, **age** has been split into bins, with each bin representing a 10-year period starting at 20 years.

Each bin contains the number of occurrences of scores in the data set that are contained within that bin.

For the above data set, the frequencies in each bin have been tabulated along with the scores that contributed to the frequency in each bin as stated below:

Bin	Frequency	Scores Included in Bin
20-30	2	25,22
30-40	4	36,38,36,38
40-50	4	46,45,48,46
50-60	5	55,55,52,58,55
60-70	3	68,67,61
70-80	1	72
80-90	0	-
90-100	1	91

Notice that, unlike a bar chart, there are no "gaps" between the bars (although some bars might be "absent" reflecting no frequencies). This is because a histogram represents a continuous data set, and as such, there are no gaps in the data.

Sample questions on above histogram:

1. Which ranges of age group experience same frequency?

   A) 70-80, 40-50

   B) 30-40, 40-50

   C) 20-30, 30-40

   D) None of these

Ans.B Height of a bin signifies frequency. It is observed in the figure that heights of bins of ranges 30-40 and 40-50 are same so that is the answer i.e. B

2. How many persons are in the age group of more than 40 and less than 70

   A) 10 B) 6

   C) 12 D) 20

Ans.C Above age group falls in the bins of 40-50, 50-60 and 60-70. Total of frequencies of these bins 4, 5 and 3.

Adding these frequencies 4+5+3 = 12. So answer is C

3. Which age groups experience minimum frequencies?

   A) 70-80, 90-100 B) 60-70, 70-80

   C) 20-30,40-50 D) None of these

Ans.A Height of intervals in answer choice number A.

4. How many persons are having age less than 50?

   A) 15

   B) 20

   C) 10

   D) 25

Ans.C Adding frequencies of ages less than 50 (4+4+2+) = 10

5. What is the total number of persons?

   A) 18

   B) 19

   C) 21

   D) 20

Ans.D Total of frequencies = 20

6. What is the percentage of persons with the age group of 40-50 of total persons?

   A) 40 B) 30

   C) 20 D) 35

Ans.C Total number of persons = 20

Total number of persons in the required age group = 4

Percentage: $\frac{4}{20} \times 100 = 20\%$

7. What is the ratio of frequencies with age group of less than 50 to the age groups of above fifty?

   A) 2 : 3 B) 4 : 7

   C) 1 : 1 D) 7 : 11

Ans.C Sum of frequencies in the age group less than 50 = 10

Sum of frequencies in the age group able 50 = 10

So ratio is 10 : 10 i.e. 1 : 1

Practice Exercise

A histogram is given below. Observe it carefully and give answers to the questions following histogram.

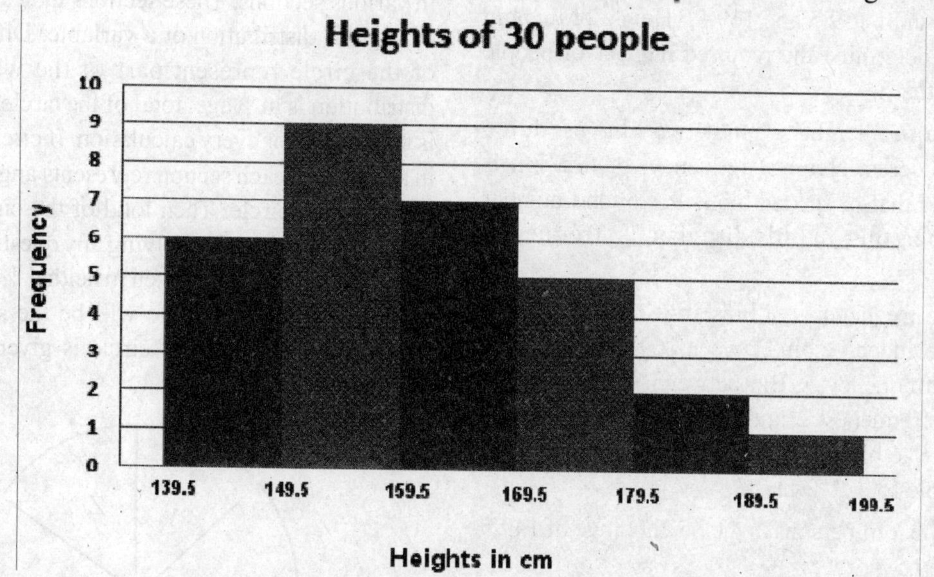

1. How many people have height between 159.5 and 169.5?
   (A) 4 (B) 7
   (C) 5 (D) None of these
2. How many people have heights less than 159.5 cm?
   (A) 15 (B) 20
   (C) 10 (D) 5
3. How many people have heights more than 169.5 cm?
   (A) 6 (B) 8
   (C) 12 (D) 3
4. What is the percentage of persons of height range of 149.5 -159.5 cm. of the persons with height range of 139.5-149.5 cm?
   (A) 125% (B) 110%
   (C) 165% (D) 150%
5. What percentage of people have heights between 149.5 and 179.5 cm?
   (A) 60% (B) 70%
   (C) 80% (D) None of these
6. What is the ratio of persons in height range of 179.5-189.5 cm to height range of 139.5-149.5 cm?
   (A) 2 : 5 (B) 1 : 4
   (C) 9 : 1 (D) 1 : 3
7. What is average of frequencies?
   (A) 3 (B) 5
   (C) 7 (D) 6
8. If two more persons are added in the height range of 169.5-179.5? What will be its effect on the present frequency of this range? It will
   (A) increase by 2
   (B) No change
   (C) decrease by 2
   (D) Data inadequate
9. How many times the number of persons in the height group of 139.5-149.5 are more than the number of persons in height group 139.5-149.5?
   (A) 4.63
   (B) 2.17
   (C) 5.00
   (D) 3.00
10. Which of the following is NOT TRUE about histogram? It
    (A) Differs from bar graph due to no gap in the rectangles
    (B) shows the distribution of continuous data
    (C) has independent variable along Y-axis and dependent variable along X-axis
    (D) was introduced by Karl Pearson.

KEY

1. **B** Here those people are considered who fall in the bin of 159.5 and 169.5. Height of this bin will determine the required number of people and that is 7.
2. **A** Here the heights of first two bins are to be considered. Height (frequency) of first bin is 6 and that of second bin is 9. So total number of persons in this bracket is frequency $6 + 9 = 15$
3. **B** Here frequencies of bins above 169.5 cm. are to be added i.e.bin between 169.5 to bin 179.5 has frequency 5. Bin between 179.5 to 189.5 has frequency 2 and frequency between bin 189.5 to bin 199.5 is 1. So required number of people $(5 + 2 + 1) = 8$
4. **D** Number of persons in the height range of 149.5 – 159.5 = 9

   Number of persons in the height range of 139.5 – 149.5 = 6

   Required %age $= \frac{9}{6} \times 100 = 150\%$
5. **B** Number of persons in the height range of 149. 5 – 179.5 = 9 + 7 + 5 = 21

   Required %age $= \frac{21}{30} \times 100 = 70\%$
6. **D** Number of persons in the height range of 179.5 – 139.5 = 2

   Number of persons in the height age group of 139.5 – 149.5 = 6

   The required Ratio: 2 : 6 i.e. 1 : 3
7. B Sum of frequencies = $(1 + 2 + 5 + 7 + 9 + 6) = 30$

   Number of frequencies = 6

   So average is $\frac{30}{6} = 5$
8. **A** Number of frequencies in a particular age group is the total number of persons in that range. So with addition of two more persons frequency will increase by 2
9. **D** Number of persons in height group of 139.5-149.5 = 6
10. **C** Consult text.

3. Pie-Chart

A pie chart is given in the form of a circle, distributed in various sections. These sections indicate a percentage or angular distribution of a variable. Different sections of the circle represent part of the whole circle. If distribution is in %age, total of the circle is 100 and this is taken base for every calculation. If circle is distributed in angles then each section represents angular proportion of the whole circle. Then total of the circle is 360 and this is taken as base for solving any question. Sometimes distribution of circle is given in neither %age nor angles, in that case total of circle will be the sum of units in which the distribution of circle is given.and that total will become:

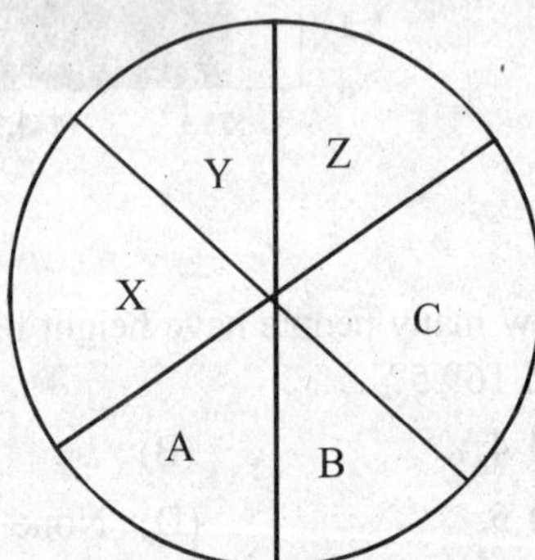

LET TOTAL OF CIRCLE = Z

Here A , B, C, X, Y, Z show the %age or angular or any other unit distribution of whole variable, which is represented by the whole circle. In this case also questions are asked the answer to which is given either through observation or calculation. Following type of calculation based questions are asked:

In %age Terms:

a) **Calculating Amount of a Percentage when total Amount and Percentage is given:**

   A % of Z is equal to?

   Formula: $\frac{A}{100} \times 2 = T$

b) **Calculating total variable when %age and its amount is given:**

   C% of a sum is R, what is sum

   Applying the formula:

   $$\frac{C}{100} x sum = R$$

   $$\Rightarrow Sum = Rx\frac{100}{C} = Z$$

In Angular Terms:

a) **Calculating Amount of an angle when total Amount and angle is given:**

A° of Z is equal to?

Formula: $\frac{A}{360} \times Z = T$

b) **Calculating total variable when angle and its amount is given:**

C° of a sum is R, what is sum

Applying the formula:

$\frac{C}{360}$xSum = R ⇒ Sum = Rx$\frac{360}{C}$ = Z

In Conversion Terms:

a) **Converting %age to Angle:** What is central angle of Y%?

Applying the Formula:

$\frac{Y}{100} \times 360 = M^o$

b) **Converting Angle to Percentage:** What is %age of M°

Applying the formula:

$\frac{M}{360} \times 100 = Y\%$

Practice Exercise

Q.1-5: The following questions are to be answers on the basis of the following diagrams. These graphs summarise the use of water by the average adult. Graph I indicates Water Intake and Graph II indicates Water output:

Graph-I

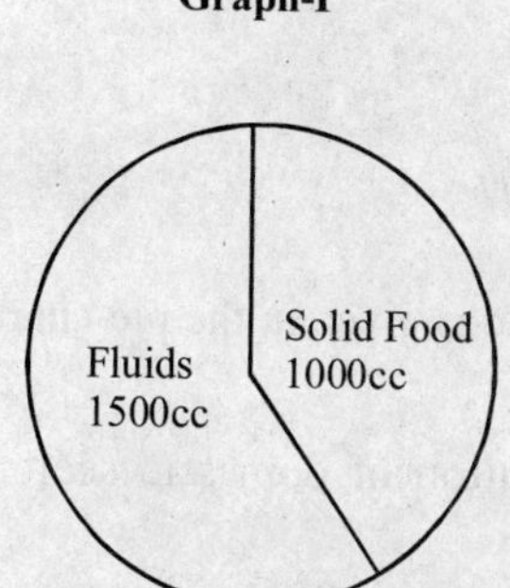

Graph-II

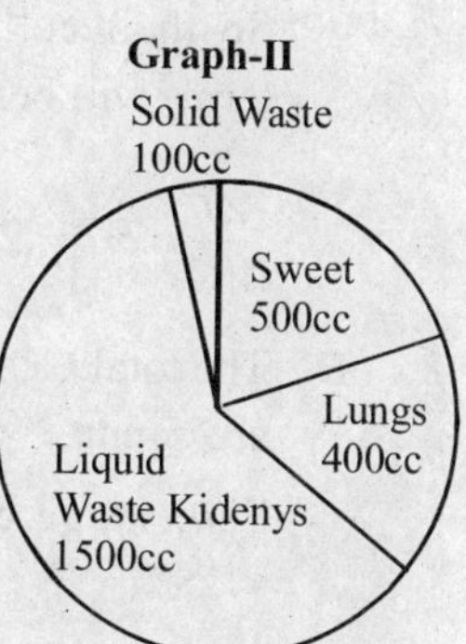

Total of I and II graph = 2500 cc each

1. What percent of the daily water output through the kidneys is the daily water intake in fluids?

   (A) 25% (B) 33%
   (C) 66% (D) 100%

2. What percent of the daily water output is water expired from the lungs?

   (A) 1.6% (B) 4%
   (C) 16% (D) 19%

3. What is the angle of the sector in Graph I representing daily water intake in solid food?

   (A) 72° (B) 103°
   (C) 120° (D) 144°

4. What is ratio of the angles of the sector in Graph II representing liquid wastes through kidneys to that of water output through sweat?

   (A) 1 : 3 (B) 3 : 1
   (C) 33 : 10 (D) 33 : 100

5. What percent of the daily water output through solid wastes is the daily water intake through solid food?

   (A) 100% (B) 10%
   (C) 1000% (D) 1%

KEY

1. **D** Daily Water output through kidneys: 1500 cc.
   Daily intake through fluids: 1500
   Calculating %age: $\frac{1500}{1500} \times 100 = 100\%$

2. **C** Daily water output: 2500cc
   Daily water expired from lungs: 400cc
   Required %age: $\frac{400}{2500} \times 100 = 16\%$

3. **D** Converting 1000cc into angle:
   $\frac{1000}{2500} \times 360 = 144^o$

4. **B** Liquid waste through liquid waste: 1500cc
   Water output through sweat: 500 cc
   Required Ratio: $1500 : 500 \Rightarrow 3 : 1$

5. **C** Required %age: $\frac{100}{100} \times 1000 = 1000\%$

Questions Asked in Previous NET Exams

The total electricity generation in a country is 97 GW. The contribution of various energy sources is indicated in percentage terms in the Pie Chart given below:

(UGC NET JUNE 2012)

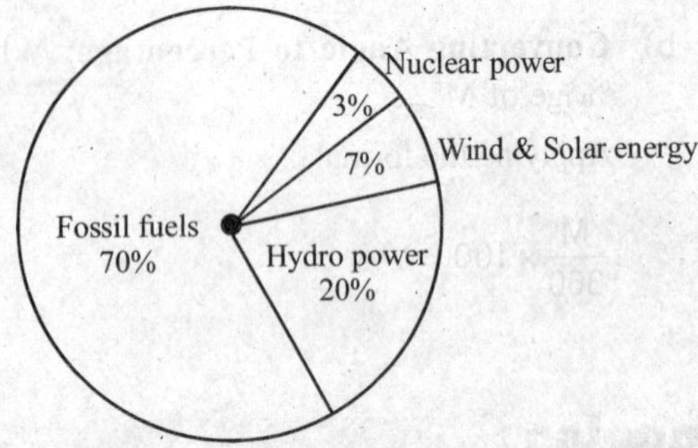

1. What is the contribution of wind and solar power in absolute terms in the electricity generation ?
   (A) 6.79 GW (B) 19.4 GW
   (C) 9.7 GW (D) 29.1 GW
2. What is the contribution of renewable energy sources in absolute terms in the electricity generation ?
   (A) 29.1 GW (B) 26.19 GW
   (C) 67.9 GW (D) 97 GW

The total CO_2 emissions from various sectors are 5 mmt. In the Pie Chart given below, the percentage contribution to CO_2 emissions from various sectors is indicated. **(UGC NET DECEMBER 2011)**

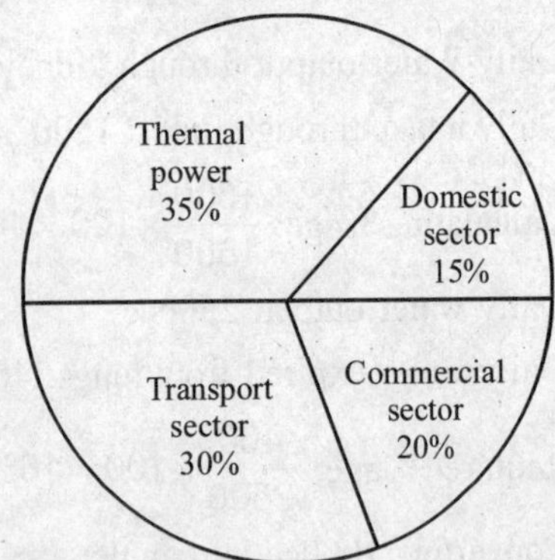

3. What is the absolute CO_2 emission from domestic sector?
   (A) 1.5 mmt (B) 2.5 mmt
   (C) 1.75 mmt (D) 0.75 mmt
4. What is the absolute CO_2 emission for combined thermal power and transport sectors?
   (A) 3.25 mmt
   (B) 1.5 mmt
   (C) 2.5 mmt
   (D) 4 mmt

KEY

1. A Share of wind and solar 7%.

Total electricity generation: 97GW

Amount of electricity generation by wind and solar resources:

$$\frac{7}{100} \times 97 = 6.79\text{GW}$$

2. B Renewable energy sources in the given pie-chart are wind and solar source and hydro source and their percentages are 7 and 20 respectively. Their collective contribution is 27%.

So their collective contribution in absolute terms will be:

$$\frac{27}{100} \times 97 = 26.19\text{GW}$$

3. D The total CO_2 emissions given in the pie-chart are 5mmt.

Percentage contribution of domestic sector = 15%

Contribution of domestic sector in absolute terms $= \frac{15}{100} \times 5 = 0.75\text{mmt}$

4. A In the given pie-chart %age contribution of CO_2 emissions of thermal power and transport sector is 35 and 30 respectively. Their combined contribution is (35+30) = 65%

Now combined contribution of thermal power and transport sector is $= \frac{65}{100} \times 5 = 3.25\text{mmt}$

4. Table Chart

In table chart growth of a variable in any field is shown over a period of time in a tabulated form. The table shows a positive or negative trend in a variable in social, economic, political, trade, cultural or any other field of life. Nature of questions asked on the table chart is same as on bar chart. There also have been observation and calculation based questions on percentage, change in percentage, average, ratio etc.

Practice Exercise

Q 6-10: Study the following table carefully and answer question 1-5

Year \ Discipline	Arts		Science		Commerce		Engineering		Agriculture	
	No.	%age Pass	No.	%age Pass	No.	%age Pass	No.	%age Pass	No.	%age Pass
2010	120	45	80	65	210	50	110	70	96	55
2011	145	50	140	60	180	55	148	68	120	53
2012	90	52	120	64	205	58	150	65	115	52
2013	105	40	95	54	170	45	120	80	85	46
2014	98	55	86	70	165	60	105	75	135	50
2015	84	58	105	55	196	52	135	72	102	65

1. What was the percentage decrease in the number of students passed under engineering discipline from 2011 to 2012?
   (A) 5 (B) 3
   (C) 6 (D) 2
2. In which of the following years was the number of students passed under commerce discipline exactly equal to the total number of students under Arts discipline in 2013?
   (A) 2015 (B) 2014
   (C) 2010 (D) 2011
3. In how many of the given years was the percentage of students passed under all the disciplines more than 50?
   (A) 2 (B) 3
   (C) 5 (D) 1
4. Approximately what was the difference in number of students passed under Agriculture discipline between 2011 and 2012?
   (A) 1 (B) 9
   (C) 8 (D) 4
5. What was the approximately percentage increase in the number of students under commerce discipline from 2014 to 2015?
   (A) 12 (B) 24
   (C) 20 (D) 15

KEY

1. **B** It is an observation based question. It is observed in the table chart that 68% students passed in engineering discipline where as 65% students passed in 2012. So percentage decrease is 3.
2. **C** Total number of students in arts discipline in 2013are 105. A close observation of the table chart reveal that in the year 2010 total number of students in the commerce discipline were 210 and out of them 50% passed and 50% of 210 is 105. So it is 2010 in which the number of candidates passed in commerce discipline is exactly equal to total number of students in arts in 2013.
3. **A** This is an observation based question. It is observed from the table that there are two such years i.e. 2012 and 2015 in which pass percentage is above 50 in all disciplines.
4. **D** Number of students passed in agriculture discipline in 2011 $= \frac{53}{100} \times 120 = 63.6$
   Number of students passed in agriculture discipline in 2012 $= \frac{52}{100} \times 115 = 59.8$
   Difference: 63.6 – 59.8 = 3.8
   Number of students in round figure = 4

5. C Applying formula of %age increase:

$$\frac{196-165}{165}\times 100 \Rightarrow \frac{31}{165}\times 100 = 18.78\%$$

Approximately 20%

Questions Asked in Previous NET Exams

Consider the following table that shows the total number of tickets sold of five movies P, Q, R, S and T across two cinema houses A and B on a particular day. In accordance with the table answer the questions that follow: **(UGC NET JUNE 2019)**

Sale of Cinema Tickets Cinema wise

Movies	Cinemas	
	A	B
P	200	300
Q	350	400
R	250	350
S	300	350
T	400	250

1. What is the difference between the total numbers of tickets sold of all movies together at cinema A and total number of tickets sold of all movies together at cinema B?
   (A) 170 (B) 180
   (C) 150 (D) 160
2. The number of tickets sold of movie T at cinema A is what percent of number of tickets of movie P sold at cinema A?
   (A) 220% (B) 200%
   (C) 210% (D) 190%
3. What is the ratio of number of tickets sold of movie P at cinema B to the number of tickets sold of movie Q at cinema B?
   (A) 2 : 3 (B) 3 : 4
   (C) 1 : 2 (D) 3 : 5
4. What is the average number of tickets sold at cinema B for movies T and S together?
   (A) 360 (B) 320
   (C) 300 (D) 340
5. What is the total number of tickets sold for movies Q and R together at both the cinemas A and B together?
   (A) 1050 (B) 1200
   (C) 1250 (D) 1350

KEY

1. C Total number of tickets sold at cinema A = 1500
   Total number of tickets sold at cinema B = 1650
   Difference of tickets sold = 150
2. B Number of tickets sold of movie T at cinema A = 400 ......(i)
   Number of tickets sold of movie P at cinema A=200 ....(ii)
   Percentage of (ii) to (i) $= \frac{400}{200}\times 100 = 200\%$
3. B Number of tickets sold of movie P at cinema B = 300
   Number of tickets sold of movie Q at cinema B = 400
   Required ratio: 300 : 400 i.e. 3 : 4
4. C Total number of tickets sold of movie S at cinema B = 350
   Total number of tickets sold of movie T at cinema B = 250
   Average:
   $$\frac{350+250}{2} \Rightarrow \frac{600}{2} = 300$$
5. D Total number of tickets sold of movie Q at both cinemas A and B together:
   (350 + 450) = 750
   Total number of tickets sold of movie R at both cinemas A and B together:
   (250 + 350) = 600
   Total number of tickets sold of movies Q and R from cinema A and B together:
   750 + 600 = 1350

Consider the following table that shows the production of fertilizer by a company (in 10000 tonnes) during the year 2011 to 2018. **(UGC NET JUNE 2019)**

Year:	2011	2012	2013	2014	2015	2016	2017	2018
Production of Fertilizer:	35	50	70	55	75	60	85	90

1. In which year percentage increase in production as compared to the previous year was maximum?
   1) 2012 2) 2013
   3) 2015 4) 2018

2. What was the approximate percentage increase in the production of fertilizer in 2018 compared to that in 2011?
   1) 157% 2) 165%
   3) 177% 4) 182%
3. In how many of the given years was the production of fertilizer more than the average production of the given years?
   1) 2 2) 3
   3) 4 4) 5
4. What was the percentage decline in the production of fertilizer from 2013 to 2014?
   1) 20.4% 2) 21.4%
   3) 22.6% 4) 24.2%
5. The average production of 2012 and 2013 was exactly equal to average production of which of the following pairs of years?
   1) 2011 and 2012 2) 2011 and 2017
   3) 2012 and 2014 4) 2015 and 2016

KEY

1. 1 %age increase from 2011 to 2012:

$$\frac{50-35}{35}\times 100 \Rightarrow \frac{15}{35}\times 100 = 42.8\%$$

%age increase from 2012 to 2013:

$$\frac{70-50}{50}\times 100 \Rightarrow \frac{20}{50}\times 100 = 40\%$$

%age increase from 2014 to 2015:

$$\frac{75-15}{55}\times 100 \Rightarrow \frac{20}{55}\times 100 = 36.3\%$$

%age increase from 2017 to 2018:

$$\frac{90-85}{85}\times 100 \Rightarrow \frac{5}{85}\times 100 = 5.8\%$$

From above it is clear that maximum %age increase was in 2012 over its previous year.

2. 1 %age increase in production from 2011 to 2018:

$$\frac{90-35}{35}\times 100 \Rightarrow \frac{55}{35}\times 100 = 157.4$$

Approx.157%

3. 3

$$\frac{35+50+70+55+75+60+85+90}{8} \Rightarrow \frac{520}{8} = 65$$

From the table chart it is evident there are 4 years viz. 2013, 2015, 2017 and 2018 in which production is more than average production i.e. 65.

4. 2 Percentage decline in production from 2013 to 2014:

$$\frac{70-55}{70} \Rightarrow \frac{15}{70}\times 100 = 21.4\%$$

5. 2 Average production of 2012 and 2013:

$$\frac{50+70}{2} = \frac{120}{2} = 60$$

Same average is found for years 2011 and 2017.

Directions : The following table gives the sale of computers of different types or brands over the years 2001-2007. Based on data answer the questions (1-5)

(UGC NET DECEMBER 2019)

Number of different types of computers sold (In Thousands)

Years	Types of Computers			
	Lenovo	Acer	IBM	HCL
2001	20	40	50	80
2002	30	25	60	70
2003	50	50	50	55
2004	60	70	40	35
2005	70	85	70	25
2006	80	45	80	20
2007	90	60	100	10

1. Name the type/brand of computer whose sale has decreased continuously over the years?
   1) Lenovo 2) Acer
   3) IBM 4) HCL
2. The percentage increase in the sale of Lenovo computers in 2007 compared to sales in 2001 is
   1) 200% 2) 250%
   3) 300% 4) 350%
3. The difference in the number of Acer computers sold in 2002 and 2005 is
   1) 15,000 2) 20,000
   3) 45,000 4) 60,000
4. In which year the percentage of Acer computers sold as to the total number of computers sold was maximum?
   1) 2003 2) 2004
   3) 2005 4) 2007
5. Name the type of computer for which the total sale in all the seven years is maximum?
   1) IBM 2) Lenovo
   3) Acer 4) HCL

KEY

1. D This question is to be answered by observing the sale trends of all computers from the year 2001 to 2007. Careful observation conveys that HCL computer has experienced continuous decrease in sale from 2001 to 2007, hence choice number 4 is the answer.

2. D Saleof Lenovo computers in 2001 = 20,000

   Sale of Lenovo computers in 2007 = 90,000

   Percentage increase of Lenovo computers from 2001 to 2007

   $$= \frac{90000-20000}{20000} \times 100 = 350\%$$

3. D This question is also to be answered through observation and observation reveals that sale of Acer computers in 2002 is 25,000 and sale in 2005 is 85,000 so the difference is 60,000

4. C Total number of acer computers sold over the years = 375000

   As in the year 2005, 85000 computers were sold and are maximum as compared to other years. So percentage sale of acer computers to the total sale is maximum in 2005 i.e 22.66%, whereas as percentage sale in 2003, 2004 and 2007 is 13.33%, 18.66% and 16% respectively.

5. A Total sale of Lenovo over the period = 400000

   Total sale of Acer over the period = 375000

   Total sale of IBM over the period = 450000

   Total sale of Lenovo over the period = 295000

   It is evident from above that total sale of IBM computers is maximum over the period of time, hence choice no. 1 is the answer.

Based on the below table, answer question No. 1, 2, and 3. (UGC NET DECEMBER 2018)

State	% of Villages not Electrified
A	25%
B	45%
C	20%
D	60%
E	55%
F	30%

1. How many States have at least 50% or more electrified villages?

   (A) 3

   (B) 2

   (C) 4

   (D) 1

2. Which State has twice the percentage of electrified villages in comparison to State D?

   (A) State A

   (B) State C

   (C) State B

   (D) State D

3. In the year 2000, the total number of villages in State D was 15,000. In the year 2010, the total number of villages had increased to 20,000 out of which 10,000 villages were yet to be electrified. The % of villages not electrified in 2010 in state D has thus________.

   (A) Not enough data

   (B) Gone up

   (C) Come down

   (D) Cannot be computed

KEY

1. C It is observation based question. It is observed that there are 4 states A, B, C and F in which at least 50% villages are electrified.

2. B In state D 60% villages are not electrified. This means 40% villages of state D are electrified. Table chart further reveals that in state C, 20% villages are not electrified. This means in state C, 80% villages are electrified, which is twice the %age of electrified villages in state D.

3. C It is given in the table that in state D, 60% villages are not electrified. In 2010,out of 20,000 villages in state D 10,000 were not electrified. This means 50% villages were not electrified in state D in 2010. So the %age of not electrified villages in state D has come down from 60% to 50%.

The table below embodies data on the production, exports and per capita consumption of rice in country P for the five years from 2012 to 2016. Answer questions 31 - 35 based on the data contained in the table. **(UGC NET JULY 2018)**

Year-wise Production, Exports and Per Capita Consumption of Rice

Year	Production (in million kg)	Exports (in million kg)	Per Capita Consumption (in kg)
2012	186.5	114	36.25
2013	202	114	35.2
2014	238	130	38.7
2015	221	116	40.5
2016	215	88	42

Where, Per Capita Consumption = (Consumption in million kg) / (Population in million) and consumption (in million kg) = Production - Exports.

1. The Percentage increase in the consumption of rice over the previous year was the highest in which year?
   (A) 2013 (B) 2014
   (C) 2015 (D) 2016
2. What is the population of the country in the year 2014 (in million)?
   (A) 2.64 (B) 2.72
   (C) 2.79 (D) 2.85
3. The ratio of exports to consumption in the given period was the highest in the year:
   (A) 2012
   (B) 2013
   (C) 2014
   (D) 2015
4. In which year, the population of country was the highest?
   (A) 2013
   (B) 2014
   (C) 2015
   (D) 2016
5. What is the average consumption of rice (in million kg) over the years 2012 - 2016?
   (A) 104
   (B) 102.1
   (C) 108
   (D) 100.1

KEY

1. B Explanation: Consumption of rice in
   2012 : 186.5 – 114 = 72.5
   2013 : 202 – 114 = 88
   2014 : 238 – 130 = 108
   2015 : 221 – 116 = 105
   2016 : 215 – 088 = 127
   Percentage Increase:
   2012-2013 = 21.37%
   2013-2014 = 22.72%
   2014-15 = 6.48%
   2015-2016 = 10.43%
   Hence year registering highest %age increase over previous year is 2014.
2. C Population in 2014:
   $$\frac{\text{Consumption in 2014}}{\text{Per capita income in 2014}}$$
   $$\Rightarrow \frac{108}{38.70} = 2.79$$
3. A Year wise Ratio of Exports to Consumption:
   2012 = 114 : 72.5 =1.5
   2013 = 114 : 88 = 1.2
   2014 = 130 : 108 = 1.2
   2015 = 116 : 105 = 0.9
   Thus the highest ratio is in 2012
4. D Population in:
   2013: $\frac{88}{35.20} = 2.5$ million
   2014: $\frac{108}{38.70} = 2.7$ million
   2015: $\frac{105}{40.50} = 2.5$ million
   2016: $\frac{127}{42} = 3.02$ million
   So the highest population is in year 2016
5. D Average consumption of rice from 2012 to 2016:
   $$\frac{72.5 + 88 + 108 + 105 + 127}{5}$$
   $$\Rightarrow \frac{500.5}{5} = 100.1 \text{ million tonnes}$$

5. LINE CHART

Line Graph or Chart is the innovative version of Bar Graph representation. For example in the following figure, If we connect the upper point of the first Bar to the upper point of the second Bar and then tie these dots, we will get a line. Repeating the procedure gives us the Line Graph representation. Line graph and bar graph are easy to comprehend.

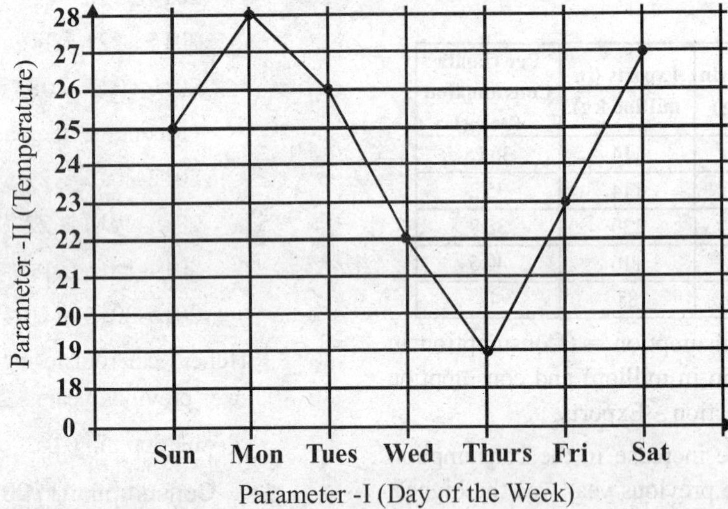

As stated above line chart is a version of bar graph, nature of concepts and questions on line chart is same as on bar graph. It is clear from the following example sets:

Practice Exercise

The following line graph gives the ratio of the amounts of imports by a company to the amount of exports from that company over the period from 1995 to 2001.

Ratio of Value of Imports to Exports by a Company Over the Years.

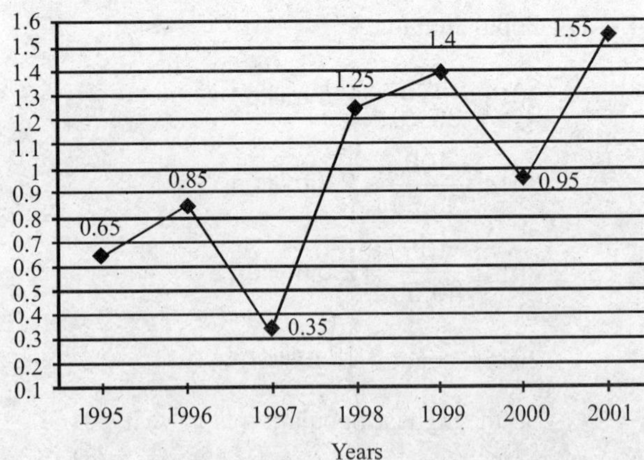

1. If the imports in 1998 was Rs. 250 crores and the total exports in the years 1998 and 1999 together was Rs. 500 crores, then the imports in 1999 was ?

   (A) Rs. 250 crores (B) Rs. 300 crores

   (C) Rs. 357 crores (D) Rs. 420 crores

2. The imports were minimum proportionate to the exports of the company in the year ?

   (A) 1995 (B) 1996

   (C) 1997 (D) 2000

3. What was the percentage increase in imports from 1997 to 1998 ?

   (A) 72 (B) 56

   (C) 28 (D) Data inadequate

4. If the imports of the company in 1996 was Rs. 272 crores, the exports from the company in 1996 was ?

   (A) Rs. 370 crores

   (B) Rs. 320 crores

   (C) Rs. 280 crores

   (D) Rs. 275 crores

5. In how many of the given years were the exports more than the imports ?

   (A) 1

   (B) 2

   (C) 3

   (D) 4

KEY

1. **D** The ratio of imports to exports for the years 1998 and 1999 are 1.25 and 1.40 respectively.

   Let the exports in the year 1998 = Rs. x crores.

   Then, the exports in the year 1999

   = Rs. (500 – x) crores.

   $\therefore 1.25 = \frac{250}{x}$

   $\Rightarrow x = \frac{250}{1.25} = 200$ [Using ratio for 1998]

   Thus, the exports in the year 1999

   = Rs. (500 – 200) crores = Rs. 300 crores.

   Let the imports in the year 1999 = Rs. y crores.

   Then, $1.40 = \frac{y}{300}$

   $\Rightarrow y = (300 \times 1.40) = 420.$

   $\therefore$ Imports in the year 1999 = Rs. 420 crores.

2. **C** The imports are minimum proportionate to the exports implies that the ratio of the value of imports to exports has the minimum value.

   Now, this ratio has a minimum value 0.35 in 1997, i.e., the imports are minimum proportionate to the exports in 1997.

3. **D** The graph gives only the ratio of imports to exports for different years. To find the percentage increase in imports from 1997 to 1998, we require more details such as the value of imports or exports during these years.

   Hence, the data is inadequate to answer this question.

4. **B** Ratio of imports to exports in the year 1996 = 0.85.

   Let the exports in 1996 = Rs. x crores.

   Then, $\frac{272}{x} = 0.85 \Rightarrow x = \frac{272}{0.85} = 320.$

   Exports in 1996 = Rs. 320 crores.

5. **D** The exports are more than the imports imply that the ratio of value of imports to exports is less than 1.

   Now, this ratio is less than 1 in years 1995, 1996, 1997 and 2000.

   Thus, there are four such years.

Questions Asked in Previous NET Exams

In the following chart, the price of logs is shown in per cubic metre and that of Plywood and Saw Timber in per tones. Study the chart and answer the following questions 1 and 2. **(UGC NET JUNE 2010)**

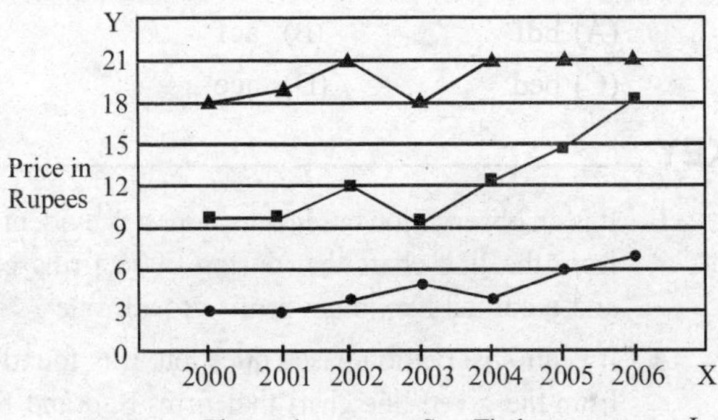

1. Which product shows the maximum percentage increase in price over the period?

   (A) Saw timber (B) Plywood

   (C) Log (D) None of the above

2. In which year the prices of two products increased and that of the third increased ?

   (A) 2000 (B) 2002

   (C) 2003 (D) 2006

KEY

1. **A** There is 100% increase in saw timber from 9 to 18 over the period
2. **C** It is an observation based question. It is observed that price of plywood and logs increased during the year 2003-04 and that of saw timber decreased during the same period

Study the following graph and answer questions numbered from 1 to 2: **(UGC NET DECEMBER 2008)**

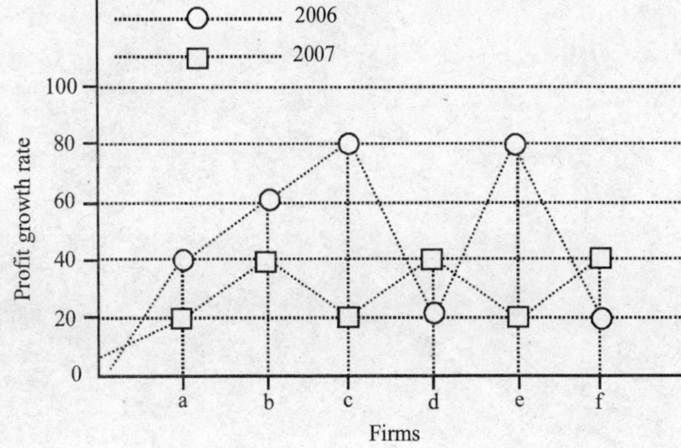

1. Which of the firms got maximum profit growth rate in the year 2006?

(A) ab (B) ce

(C) cd (D) ef

2. Which of the firms got maximum profit growth rate in the year 2007?

(A) bdf (B) acf

(C) bed (D) ace

KEY

1. B It is an observation based question. It is evident from the line chart that during 2006 firms c and e earned maximum profit growth rate

2. A It is an observation based question. It is found from the given line chart that firms b, d and f have maximum profit growth rate in 2007.

Study the following graph and answer question numbers 1 to 3: **(UGC NET DECEMBER 2006)**

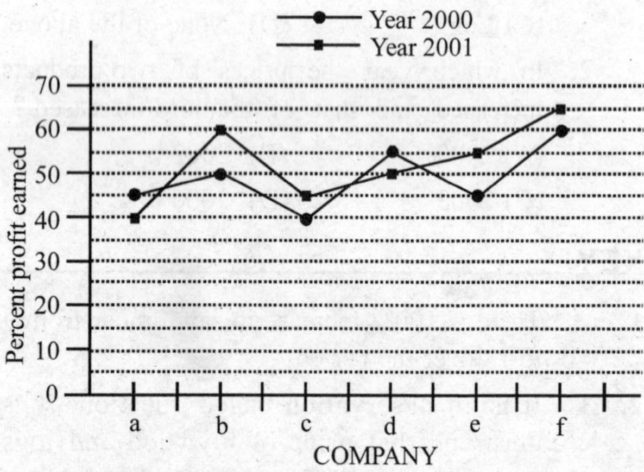

1. In the year 2000, which of the following Companies earned maximum percent profit?

(A) a (B) b

(C) d (D) f

2. In the year 2001, which of the following Companies earned minimum percent profit?

(A) a

(B) c

(C) d

(D) e

3. In the years 2000 and 2001, which of the following Companies earned maximum average percent profit?

(A) f

(B) e

(C) d

(D) b

KEY

1. D It is an observation based question. It is evident from the bar chart that in the year 2000, company f earned maximum profit percentage.

2. A It is clear from the chart that company a touched lowest level of profit %age of 40 in the year 2001.

3. A In the years 2001 and 2002, average of percent profit earned by

$$\text{Company f} = \frac{60+65}{2} = 62{,}50$$

$$\text{Company e} = \frac{45+55}{2} = 50$$

$$\text{Company d} = \frac{50+55}{2} = 52{,}50$$

$$\text{Company b} = \frac{50+60}{2} = 55$$

Maximum average earning of profit percent in the years 2000 and 2001 is by company f i.e. 62.50

4 Mapping of Data

CONCEPT

Data plays a pivotal role in making a research work accurately and successfully. When a research scientist undertakes the process of research, he/she identifies sources of data as per the requirement of the research. He/she is to collect data from different data collection systems. Then data collected from different fields is to be accumulated at one data model which is the targeted database. But due to different formats and computer languages, data may not be possible to be transformed into the targeted data model. Here, data mapping helps to create relationship between the data collected from one data field to that data field which is to receive it. Data mapping creates relationship between two data models and transforms data from source data model into targeted model in that format and computer language which is compatible to the targeted data model. Data mapping helps by relating data from one data collection system to the other one under target. For example, during a study on difference in cognitive abilities in boys and girls of 10th class students from different sections of a school, a sample from the target group is chosen. Data to be collected for the sample includes names of students, parents' names, family background, family income, number of boys and girls, attendance rate, punctuality, obedience level, understanding level, and level of reciprocity in class while attending lecture, habits, extent of inclination towards subjects currently studying, and motivation level. In data mapping each variable is called field. Data are collected from all these fields and will be transformed into a single field. Here, data mapping will help in data collection.

Significance of Data Mapping:

While conducting research, a research scholar collects data from various fields. After collection of data, the data are to be processed and analysed by applying different research and statistical tools. Data mapping is effective in making a research work accurate, authentic, and relevant to results obtained after processing accurate data. So, a research work can be made credible through data mapping. Further, significance of data mapping is listed as under:

1) Data mapping establishes the relationship between two variables from two different data fields. For example, two teachers having different addresses are working in the same hospital.
2) It drops any redundant irrelevant or false data and only accurate data is migrated for accurate and authentic results.
3) Data mapping ensures that a particular data format or pattern should not look like another data format or pattern. That means that data mapping gives a unique identity to a particular data. For example, in thesis writing 'ibid' should not have any other pattern than the one mentioned here.
4) Data mapping identifies and secures personal and private information like health issues, bank details, and pin numbers of debit and credit cards.

TERMS RELATED TO DATA MAPPING

Data Migration: Data migration is a process to migrate data from one data model to another data model. Data model from which data is to be migrated is called Source Data Model and the data model in which data are to be transferred is called Destination Data Model. Let us suppose that data is to be migrated from data model A to data model B. Then data model A is source data model and data model B is destination data model. Now let us continue with the above example of 10th class students. It is found that the whole information required for research is not available from a single data source. Data regarding academics is available in one data model and data regarding other features is available in the second model. These data can be related while migrating data to the destination model through data mapping software. So data mapping paves a way for data migration between the source data model and destination data model.

Data Warehousing: It is a technique of collecting data from different fields and storing at one data destination. Data warehousing is an electronic storage of a large amount of data including redundant and irrelevant information, collected from different fields by a research scholar.

Data Transformation: It is the process of transforming or converting data from the data format from source data model to destination data model in the format compatible to it. Under this process, not only format of data is transformed but computer language of source data model is also changed into the computer language of destination data model.

Data Integration: Data integration is the process of connecting data available in a new data model with the old data model. Data integration makes assessment easier and accurate.

DATA MAPPING SOFTWARE

Data mapping software is a converter of data. It converts the data into electronic interchangeable file format. The purpose is to facilitate matching of incoming data with the existing data in the data model. Conversion of data in the systems is done efficiently. Data mappings software converts any data from any field into data of any type, format, and size compatible to the receiving system, i.e., destination data model. The software drops the irrelevant and superfluous data fields and combines the data in new relevant fields. Due to data software there is no more need to transform data manually.

In a way, data mapping software consolidates data from different fields into a single field while separating redundant and irrelevant data fields. Some of the leading data mapping softwares available are Dell Boomi, Adeptia, HVR, Alooma, and IBM InfoSphere.

DATA MAPPING TECHNIQUES

1. **Manual Data Mapping:** In this technique, data mapping is done through hands. There is migration of data between the two data models by mapping manually.
2. **Semi-Automated Mapping:** In this technique, mapping is done between two semantically (language-wise) related data models.
3. **Automated Data Mapping:** It is a process in which data mapping is done between source of data and the targeted data model using a simple drag and drop model. In this process of data transformation, there is built-in data transformer in the model.

DRAG AND DROP DATA MODEL

Drag and drop is a built-in interface for data integration and mapping in a code-free environment. It provides advance level functions for development and testing. This device helps in data integration and data transformation automatically from source data model to destination data model.

Practice Exercise

General Questions Format

1. Which of the following is not TRUE about Data Warehousing? It........

a) is a data collection technique.

b) is an improvement over data integration.

c) is an electronic storage of data collected from various data fields.

d) helps a research scholar in data mapping.

(A) a and c only (B) b, c, and d only
(C) b and c only (D) b only

2. Data mapping helps a research work in the following ways. It

a) drops redundant and irrelevant information from data collected from different fields.

b) creates relation between two different data models for successful data transformation.

c) provides a unique format to the variables used in the research work to prevent copying.

d) identifies data and ensures its security to prevent these from leakage and being copied.

Arrange above points in the order of priority from the most important to the least one.

(A) d-b-a-c (B) a-d-c-b
(C) d-c-b-a (D) c-a-b-d

3. Which of the following will create deadlock in the way of data mapping?

a) Source data model and targeted data model

b) Format and computer language compatible to source data model

(A) Only a (B) Both a and b
(C) Only b (D) Neither a nor b

4. Which of the following is code-free data mapping?

(A) Automated (B) Manual

(C) Semi-automated (D) None of these

5. Find the odd choice among the following.

(A) HVR (B) Adeptia

(C) Zylix (D) Alooma

6. Which of the following statement(s) is/are TRUE?

a) Data integration is a substitute of data migration.

b) Data mapping is not possible when two data models under consideration understand different computer languages.

c) Drag and drop approach of data mapping facilitates hypothesis testing.

d) Unique formatting of data is another name of data mapping.

(A) Only b and d (B) Only c

(C) Only a and c (D) Only b, c, and d

7. Consider the statement "Data mapping has helped in consolidating data which used to be scattered before for want of data mapping technology leading to chaos and deadlocks."

The statement highlights the

a) Contribution of data mapping in bringing awareness for consolidating data for making a research work authentic and successful

b) Problems faced by the research scientists while managing scattered data for want of data mapping techniques

c) Role of data mapping in putting data in right order, thus removing all hindrances in the progress of data relating activities

d) Importance of data mapping in managing a scattered data to make it conducive for any activity demanding use of data

(A) c only (B) b and d only

(C) a and c only (D) a, b, c, and d

8. Suppose a research scientist wanted to collect data on names, age, and ailments of patients visiting clinic X. Data are to be collected from two incompatible data fields. Then which step of data mapping will be taken first?

(A) Data migration

(B) Data transformation

(C) Data integration

(D) Data warehousing

9. How does semantic relation between the source data model and destination data model affect data mapping?

(A) There is no need to change format and computer language for transferring data.

(B) Data mapping software will work faster to yield desired results as soon as possible.

(C) It makes data mapping possible even if two different data models contain too large and too small data.

(D) None of these

10. Tools of data mapping are given under Column I and their central meaning is given under Column II. Match the tool with its exact central meaning and choose your answer from the codes given below.

Column I	Column II
a) Data migration	i) Formatting
b) Data warehousing	ii) Transferring
c) Data transformation	iii) Linking
d) Data integration	iv) Storing

Codes:	(a)	(b)	(c)	(d)
(A)	ii	iv	i	iii
(B)	i	iii	iv	ii
(C)	ii	i	iv	iii
(D)	i	ii	iii	iv

11. Drag and drop model of data mapping is used in ________ data mapping.

(A) Designated

(B) Manual

(C) Semi-automated

(D) Automated

12. Major cause of recording redundant and irrelevant data for a research work is

(A) Carelessness of research scholar

(B) Non-cooperation from data source

(C) Communication gap between research scholar and data source

(D) Can't say

4.4 Mapping of Data

13. Which of the following data mapping tasks cover all the operations of data mapping?
(A) Data integration
(B) Data transformation
(C) Data warehousing
(D) None of these

14. Which of the following is TRUE about data mapping software?
a) It converts the data into electronic interchangeable file format.
b) It drops the irrelevant and superfluous data fields.
c) It consolidates data from different fields into a single field.
d) It separates redundant and irrelevant data fields
(A) c and d only (B) a and b only
(C) a, b, c, and d (D) a only

15. Which of the following data mapping tasks ensures an error-free transformation of the data?
(A) Data mapping software
(B) Data transformation
(C) Data warehousing
(D) Data migration

KEY

1. D	2. B	3. C	4. A	5. C	6. B	7. A
8. D	9. D	10. A	11. D	12. D	13. D	14. C
15. A						

Assertion–Reason Format

1. **Assertion (A):** Data mapping creates relation between two incompatible data models.
Reason (R): Data is transformed from one data model to another data model by making format and computer language compatible to targeted data model.
(A) Both A and R are true and R is the correct explanation of A
(B) Both A and R are true but R is not correct explanation of A
(C) A is true but R is false
(D) A is false but R is true

2. **Assertion (A):** Data mapping software filters the data collected from different data fields.
Reason (R): Old and new data models are connected in the data integration process.
(A) Both a and R are false
(B) A is true but R is false
(C) Both A and R are true but R is not correct explanation of A
(D) Both A and R are true and R is correct explanation of A

3. **Assertion (A):** Various tasks of data mapping are complementary to one another.
Reason (R): Data mapping follows a subjective approach in its various tasks.
(A) Both A and R are true but R is not correct explanation of A
(B) Both A and R are false
(C) A is true but R is false
(D) A is false but R is true

4. **Assertion (A):** Data are transformed into destination data model through data warehousing.
Reason (R): Data integration is the process of linking old data model with new data model.
(A) Both A and R are true and R is correct explanation of A
(B) A is true but R is false
(C) A is false but R is true
(D) Both A and R are false

5. **Assertion (A):** Transformation of data from source data model to destination data model is a highly technical operation.
Reason (R): For successful transformation, format and computer language compatible to destination data model is used.
(A) Both A and R are true and R is correct explanation of A
(B) Both A and R are true but R is not correct explanation of A
(C) Both A and R are false
(D) A is true but R is false

KEY

1. A	2. C	3. D	4. C	5. A

5 Data and Governance

CONCEPT

Governance in a social set-up aims at maintaining efficiency and transparency in the working of various public sector departments so that there should be regular and timely delivery of public utility services. Present age is digital age. So in the present age there is a need of smart governance. Government and other public sector agencies collect data from various sectors of the society like agriculture, industry, banking, health, education, households, etc. These data are used to draft and implement many welfare and development policies for the general public and sustainable socio-economic development of the country. So data has an indispensable relation with governance and is always instrumental in effecting smart governance. Introduction of computer and satellite technology in the social system has come up with efficient techniques of data acquisition, preservation, and utilisation which has facilitated the governing agencies to come up with perfect e-governance and smart governance.

DATA AND GOVERNANCE IN INDIA

Various general and digital initiatives of governance through data have been taken by India.

1) **National Data Sharing and Accessibility Policy (NDSAP):** It has been globally experienced that sharing of non-sensitive data of various central and state government departments with the public has resulted in desired socio-economic development of a country. Public sector agencies invest huge public investment in collecting data depicting growth in different sectors about which public must be acquainted with. Keeping in view the emphasis of the Government on engaging citizens in Governance Reforms, placing of non-strategic data in the public domain and the provisions of RTI Act 2005 for empowering the citizens to secure access to information under the control of public authority leading to the transparency and accountability in the working of every public authority, NDSAP was brought out by India.

   National Data Sharing and Accessibility Policy (NDSAP) was approved by the Union government in 2012. The sole objective of the policy to provide public easy access to the shareable government data and information collected by the central and state governments in human readable and machine readable forms. NDSAP, termed as the 'Open Data Policy' of Government of India, calls for proactive sharing of data by different government agencies, both at the national and sub-national levels. The scope of the policy extends to all data (except for information pertaining to the negative list) created by using public funds and owned by different government agencies, ministries, and departments of the Union and State Governments in India.

HUMAN READABLE AND MACHINE READABLE FORMAT

1) ***Human Readable Format:*** *This is presentation of data in that format which can be easily read by humans. Data in the human readable format is encoded in commonly readable text, i.e., ASCII (American Standard Code for Information Interchange) or Unicode.*

2) ***Machine Readable Format:*** *Machine readable data format data is presentation of data in that format which can be read by*

computers only and not by humans. It is governed by computer number system, i.e., binary number system. The OPEN Government Data Act 2019, passed in the USA defines machine-readable data as "data in a format that can be easily processed by a computer without human intervention while ensuring no semantic meaning is lost."

India has put all sorts of data in both the formats for enabling citizens to have easy access to this data to have stock of the e-governance situation.

2) **Open Government Data (OGD) Platform:** After NDSAP was notified in 2012, India launched OGD in 2012 in compliance to NDSAP provisions. OGD is an effective platform which supports and justifies 'Open Data' initiative of Government of India. The portal is required to be used by Government of India Ministries/Departments and their organizations to publish datasets, documents, services, tools, and applications collected by them for public use. It aims to increase transparency in the functioning of the Government and also open avenues for many more innovative uses of government data. The Open Government Data Platform India is a joint initiative of Government of India and US Government. Open Government Data Platform India is also packaged as a product and made available in open source for implementation by countries globally. The entire product is available for download at the Open Source Code Sharing Platform "GitHub". India has incorporated various appreciable elements on this platform like publishing data descriptions or metadata along with data, creating a citizens' engagement mechanism through feedback forms, bringing in Application Programming Interface, better known as APIs, for community involvement in refining the platform, etc. On the contrary, not much headway has been achieved in terms of publishing budget data in open formats on this platform. In the light of this fact, even states' performance is also dismal (except few states like Sikkim, Odisha, Telangana, Tamil Nadu, and Kerala which have made efforts to bring in their own open data policies keeping in line with the principles of NDSAP). But even for most of these States, (except Sikkim), budget data still remain confined in closed formats like PDF and are not published in formats prescribed by NDSAP like Excel (XLS), Comma Separated Values (CSV), and Open Document Formats for Spreadsheet (ODS).

OGD Modules

Open Government Data Platform India has 4 (four) major modules to facilitate sharing of data with the general public, as detailed below:

- **Data Management System (DMS)** - Module for contributing data catalogues by various government agencies for making those available on the front-end website after a due approval process through a defined workflow.
- **Content Management System (CMS)** - Module for managing and updating various functionalities and content types of the Open Government Data Platform of India.
- **Visitor Relationship Management (VRM)** - Module for collating and disseminating viewer feedback on various data catalogues.
- **Communities** - Module for community users to interact and share their enthusiasm and views with others, who share common interests as that of theirs.

APPLICATION PROGRAMMING INTERFACE (API)

API is a communication protocol between the client (user) and the server. It is a contract in which a client (user) makes a request in a specific format to achieve access to data and he gets a response in a specific format for initiating further to become part of the country's development process through data sharing.

DATA PRIVACY REGIME IN INDIA

The concept of '***Data Privacy***' is not specifically stated under existing Indian laws. The Indian courts have, from time to time, interpreted the concept of privacy with the interpretation of the right to life and personal liberty under Article 21 of the Constitution.

However, in 2017, the Supreme Court of Indian came up with a historic judgement declaring "Right to Privacy" an integral part of right to life and personal liberty under Article 21 of the Indian Constitution.

Data Privacy as Fundamental Right

In a gesture of good governance, the Supreme Court of India declared Right to Privacy as a fundamental right. It has been ordered by the apex court that Right to Privacy must be protected against state and non-state actors. Non-state actors include corporations, media organizations, business magnates, people's liberation movements, lobby groups, religious groups, aid agencies, and violent non-state actors such as paramilitary forces.

STATE AND NON-STATE ACTORS

__State actors__ are governments or their agencies of foreign countries. __Non-state actors__ include organizations and individuals that are not affiliated with, directed by, or funded through the government. These include corporations, private financial institutions, and NGOs, as well as paramilitary and armed resistance and terrorist groups. These individuals/ organisations have social, political, and economic power to influence national/ international policies but they are not allied with any particular country. Difference between state and non-state actors are converging as state actors support non-state actors whose ideologies converge with that of the state actors.

While the apex court declared "right to privacy" as a fundamental right, Justice Sanjay Kishan Kaul, while writing the judgement, also expressed apprehension of creation and growth of 'Digital Footprint' due to excessive dependence on the Internet. Online majors like Facebook, Uber, and Alibaba have "extensive knowledge of one's movements, searches, and conversations. Social network providers, search engines, e-mail service providers, are all examples of non-state actors that have extensive knowledge of users movements, financial transactions, conversations-both personal and professional, health, mental state, interest, travel locations, fares, and shopping habits," the judge said. He observed that as we move towards becoming a digital economy and increase our reliance on Internet-based services, "a deeper and deeper digital footprint is being created." "The access to information, which an individual may not want to give, needs the protection of privacy," Justice Kaul said.

DIGITAL FOOTPRINT

Digital footprint is the information about a particular person that exists on the Internet as a result of their online activity. It is one's online identity and individuality and is what makes one unique. It builds the online reputation, or impression, depending on the things one does online. It is important to be aware of it because anything posted online is permanent and stays there forever, regardless of being deleted.

Sensitive Personal Data or information (SPDI)

Right to Privacy is put in peril when non-state actors are successful in fetching one's SPDI through illegal means with some ulterior motive. SPDI is any information that is clearly about a particular person. To prevent this risk Information Technology Act (IT Act), 2000 was amended and SPDI Rules 2011 were framed. SPDI Rules only apply to corporate bodies and persons located in India and in a few cases, the rules only apply to relations between an individual and a body corporate, and not between two body corporates. As per these rules, following data are termed as 'Sensitive Personal Data or Information', which must be protected as a fundamental right against non-state actors:

- Passwords
- Financial information, such as bank account or credit card or debit card or other payment instrument details
- Physical, physiological, and mental health condition
- Sexual orientation
- Medical records and history
- Biometric information
- Any detail relating to the above as provided to body corporate for providing service

- Any information received under the above by body corporate for processing, storing, or processing under lawful contract or otherwise

As per SPDI Rules, a body corporate is required to obtain prior consent from the information provider (user) regarding the purpose of usage of the SPDI. Such information should be collected only if it is essential and required for a lawful purpose connected with the functioning of the body corporate. The body corporate is also required to take reasonable steps to ensure that the information provider has knowledge about the collection of information, the purpose of collection of such information, the intended recipients, and the name and address of the agency collecting and retaining the information. The information should be used only for the purpose for which it is collected and should not be retained for a period longer than what is required.

The SPDI Rules further make it mandatory that a body corporate handling SPDI shall provide a comprehensive privacy policy containing details such as the type of information collected, the purpose for collection of information, the disclosure policy, the security practices, and procedures followed, etc. The privacy policy is required to be clearly published on the website of the body corporate and made readily available to the information providers.

INFORMATION TECHNOLOGY (IT) ACT 2000

The Information Technology Act, 2000 or ITA-2000, or IT Act, was notified on October 17, 2000. It is the law that deals with cybercrime and electronic commerce in India. The Act provides a legal framework for electronic governance by giving recognition to electronic records and digital signatures. It also defines cybercrimes and prescribes penalties for them. It also outlines the Justice Dispensation Systems for cyber crimes.

SPDI and IT ACT 2000

Government of India notified Information Technology Rules in 2011 under Information Technology Act 2000 to protect SPDI. The Security Practices Rules require entities holding sensitive personal information of users to maintain certain specified security standards. IT Act legally obligates all stakeholders (i.e., any individual or organisation that collects, processes, transmits, transfers, stores, or deals with sensitive personal data) to adhere to its requirements.

IT Amendment Act 2008

IT Act 2000 was amended to further protect SPDI as it brought in new provisions such as Section 43A and Section 72A. Section 43A of the IT Act primarily deals with the compensation for negligence in implementing and maintaining 'reasonable security practices and procedures' in relation to 'sensitive personal data or information' ("SPDI") while Section 72A of the IT Act mandates punishment for disclosure of 'personal information' in breach of lawful contract or without the information provider's consent.

Personal Data Protection Bill 2018

Government has brought up the Personal Data Protection Bill 2018. The draft bill restricts and imposes conditions on the cross-border transfer of personal data, and suggests setting up of Data Protection Authority of India to prevent any misuse of personal information.

COBIT 5

COBIT 5 is a framework from the Information Systems Audit and Control Association (ISACA) for the management and governance of information technology (IT).

COBIT 5 and SPDI: India is securing SPDI with COBIT 5 framework to comply with provisions of IT Act 2008. ISACA has released guidelines for Indian enterprises for securing sensitive personal data by using COBIT 5.

ICT : Introduction, Advantages and Disadvantages

CONCEPT

Information and communications technology (ICT) is the tool to send and receive messages through technology-rich channels. Computer, being the fundamental component of ICT, has facilitated various communication activities round the world within the shortest possible time. With the passage of time, ICT has been adding many gadgets and modes of communication like computers, hardware, software and applications, laptops, palmtops, pagers, cellphones, television, satellite, social networking, SMS, e-mail, etc. ICT has brought in a revolution in human society.

Advantages of ICT

1) ***Making communication accessible worldwide:*** We can not only share information quickly and efficiently, but we can also bring down barriers of linguistic and geographic boundaries. The world has developed into a global village due to the help of information technology.

2) ***Keeping individuals always in touch:*** ICT gadgets like cellphones, Internet, etc. keep people in touch with one another. This has made many tasks easier and saved money. Now a family member is not to worry if the other member gets late.

3) ***Making various research projects more accurate and authentic:*** Research scholars and scientists now have an easy and authenticated access to information required for their research from any corner of the world. Such access makes their research accurate.

4) ***Making easy access to education:*** ICTs are a potentially powerful tool for extending educational opportunities, both formal and non-formal, to previously underserved constituencies-scattered and rural populations, groups traditionally excluded from education due to cultural or social reasons such as ethnic minorities, girls and women, persons with disabilities, and the elderly, as well as all others who for reasons of cost or because of time constraints are unable to enroll on campus.

5) ***Indispensable:*** Today, ICT has become indispensable for the overall development of all sectors of every country. Its indispensability is clearly indicated by the fact that one of the Sustainable Development Goals (SDG) of the UNO reads, **"Significantly increase access to information and communications technology and strive to provide universal and affordable access to the Internet in least developed countries by 2020."**

6) ***Promotion in mass media:*** There has been a remarkable improvement in the services rendered by mass media like TV, Radio, newspapers, etc. Their coverage of events have become live and quick. It is due to ICT that sources of mass media can have instant feedback on their coverage, programmes, etc.

7) ***Strengthening law and order machinery and defence:*** ICT has helped a lot in strengthening the law and order position. Devices like CCTV cameras, mobile phones, and Internet communication have helped the police to nab the culprits without much delay which was not possible in the absence of ICT. Similarly, in defence also, ICT is helping the forces to detect the location of the enemy through hi-tech communication systems.

8) ***Cost-effectiveness:*** Message services like e-mail and SMS are free, whereas other modes like postal and courier services charge for the service. Further, ICT devices are multi-purpose and multi-functional, due to which these prove to be economic to run a business, charity, and any other service.

9) ***Greater availability:*** Online access to different services for the common man has made these services available 24x7. One can purchase or sell any product or services at anytime and anywhere through online stores and shops. According to a World Bank report, more than 75% of the population of the world has access to mobile phones.

10) ***Bridging the cultural gap:*** Greater access to technology has helped to bridge the cultural gap by helping people from different cultures to communicate with one another, and allow for the exchange of views and ideas, thus increasing awareness and reducing prejudice.

8. Which Indian state has excelled in sharing budget data in open data policy?
   (A) Karnataka (B) Maharashtra
   (C) Odisha (D) Sikkim
9. What is the full form of NDSAP?
   (A) National Document Sharing and Accessibility Policy
   (B) National Data Showing and Accessibility Policy
   (C) National Data Sharing and Accessibility Policy
   (D) National Data Sharing and Availability Policy
10. Which of the following has been kept out of the jurisdiction of NDSAP?
   (A) Air India
   (B) National Archives of India
   (C) Atomic Energy Commission
   (D) Khadi & Village Industries Commission

KEY

1. C 2. C 3. D 4. D 5. A 6. A 7. B 8. D 9. C 10. C

Assertion–Reason Format

1. **Assertion (A):** Government of India has put data sharing in the provision of RTI Act.
   Reason (R): Aim is to engage citizens in governance reforms.
   (A) Both A and R are false
   (B) A is true but R is false
   (C) Both A and R are true but R is not correct explanation of A
   (D) Both A and R are true and R is correct explanation of A
2. **Assertion (A):** COBIT 5 secures sensitive personal data as per provisions of IT Act 2000.
   Reason (R): There is a provision of identifying non-state players in IT Act 2000 posing threat to sensitive personal data.
   (A) Both A and R are true and R is correct explanation of A
   (B) Both A and R are false
   (C) Both A and R are true but R is not correct explanation of A
   (D) A is true but R is false
3. **Assertion (A):** Governance through sharing of data is instrumental in overall socio-economic development.
   Reason (R): Various government agencies share data to clear bottlenecks in the path of development process.
   (A) A is true but R is false
   (B) A is false but R is true
   (C) Both A and R are true and R is correct explanation of A
   (D) Both A and R are true but R is not correct explanation of A
4. **Assertion (A):** Declaring Right to Privacy as fundamental right has replaced SPDI Rules.
   Reason (R): Incorporating Right to Privacy in fundamental rights is an effective evidence of good governance.
   (A) Both A and R are true and R is correct explanation of A
   (B) A is true but R is false
   (C) A is false but R is true
   (D) Both A and R are true but R is not correct explanation of A
5. **Assertion (A):** A deeper digital footprint is under higher risk of leakage.
   Reason (R): Various online destinations, frequently visited by the users, know all the sensitive personal data of the users.
   (A) Both A and R are true but R is not correct explanation of A
   (B) Both A and R are false
   (C) Both A and R are true and R is correct explanation of A
   (D) A is true but R is false

KEY

1. D 2. B 3. A 4. C 5. C

Unit VIII

Information and Communication Technology (ICT)

1.4 ICT : Introduction, Advantages and Disadvantages

8. If a visitor is talking on a mobile phone in a hospital, he is
(A) committing a crime.
(B) exercising his right to communicate.
(C) attending an urgent and unavoidable call.
(D) none of the above.

9. ICT equipment is the least useful for
(A) heart patients (B) cynics
(C) beggars (D) thieves

10. ICT has led to universal computerisation. It means that computer has
(A) attracted all and sundry
(B) established its importance all over
(C) taken over every major and minor operation related to any field
(D) All of the above

11. ICT communication is always a/an _________ communication.
(A) advanced (B) effective
(C) fundamental (D) emergent

12. Which of the following crimes is the direct outcome of ICT?
(A) murder (B) robbery
(C) abduction (D) intrigue

13. It is not advisable to keep mobile phone in the upper left pocket because it may arrest ______.
(A) blood circulation (B) heart beat
(C) blood pressure (D) respiration

14. What is the biggest contribution of ICT to human beings?
(A) Connectivity (B) Comfort
(C) Technology (D) Vigilance

15. Which of the following is the pivot of ICT?
(A) Computer (B) Satellite
(C) Message (D) Medium

16. Which of the following is NOT a general sign of online communication?
(A) wwf (B) .com
(C) @ (D) //

17. Various TV channels are encouraging viewers to communicate with them mainly through
(A) E-mail (B) Surfing
(C) SMS (D) Can't say

18. A welfare agency wants to educate the masses about ICT. The most effective way will be to ___.
(A) pursue the government to make ICT study compulsory in schools and colleges
(B) contact film stars to present shows on ICT education all over
(C) propagate the significance of ICT through various channels of mass media
(D) arrange ICT facilities for them at a subsidised rate

19. Some of the tools of ICT are
a. Television b. Mobile phone
c. Computer d. Pager
Arrange them in chronological order.
(A) d-c-b-a (B) b-a-d-c
(C) c-a-d-b (D) a-c-d-b

20. What is fundamentally required by a person, who is to work on Internet?
(A) Cyber café
(B) Internet connection
(C) Computer
(D) Knowledge of operating Internet

21. Which of the following is/are NOT TRUE about Information and communications technology? It _______.
i) is a revolution which has plugged various gaps in communication
ii) approaches stakeholders of communication technology enabling them to use it in business, social work, or any other field of life
iii) has enabled the mankind to pounce upon various obstacles in the way of smooth and error-free flow of information, message, or feedback at national or international level
iv) is a boon for sections of the society which survive with an ambition to achieve hassle-free achievements in communication while using respective communication technology devices
(A) i, iii, and iv (B) ii only
(C) i and iv only (D) i, ii, iii, and iv

22. "Access to ICT by 2020" has been adopted as a Sustainable Development Goal by the UNO. It signifies that ________.
i) many countries still have a poor access to ICT and the UNO has made it mandatory for the member states to achieve 100% access to ICT by 2020
ii) the UNO has directed the member countries that by 2020, digital connectivity among member countries should be achieved and global and national level digital divide should be eradicated

Practice Exercise

General Questions Format

1. Which of the following is NOT TRUE about Open Government Data Platform?

a) The platform has been launched as a joint venture with the French Government.

b) It was launched in compliance to the provisions of IT amendment Act 2008.

c) The platform aims at community involvement in drafting various development and welfare policies through API data sharing technique.

d) It was launched in 2015.

(A) Only b and d (B) Only a and b

(C) a, b, c, and d (D) Only b

2. Which of the following initiatives of the government has provided maximum security to SPDI?

(A) Data Protection Bill 2018

(B) IT Act 2000

(C) IT Act 2008

(D) IT Rules 2011

3. Digital Footprint is established as a result of

(A) sending and receiving frequent e-mails

(B) chatting on Facebook

(C) availing online public utility services

(D) all of these

4. According to The OPEN Government Data Act 2019, data sharing in

(A) machine readable format is better than human readable format

(B) human readable format is better than machine readable format

(C) both machine readable and human readable formats are equally significant in their respective framework.

(D) None of these

5. OGD modules are given under Column I and their associated fields are given under Column II. Match the module with its correct associated field and choose the right code among the given codes.

Column I (OGD Module)	Column II (Associated Field)
a) Data Management System (DMS)	i) Functionalities
b) Content Management System (CMS)	ii) Interaction
c) Visitor Relationship Management (VRM)	iii) Catalogues
d) Communities	iv) Feedback

Codes:

	(a)	(b)	(c)	(d)
(A)	iii	i	iv	ii
(B)	ii	iii	iv	i
(C)	iv	ii	iii	i
(D)	iii	iv	i	ii

6. Which of the following justify(ies) the purpose of governance through data sharing?

a) Public has the right to know about growth of different sectors in which huge taxpayers' money is invested.

b) Providing access to government data involves public opinion through feedback helping in drafting various welfare and development policies.

c) Government wants to make data sharing transparent and accept accountability for any lacuna in sharing data.

d) Various verdicts of the Supreme Court have made it mandatory for the government to share data as a tool of e-governance.

(A) Only a (B) Only a, c, and d

(C) a, b, c, and d (D) Only a and d

7. Which of the following is not included in the list of SPDI?

(A) Biometric information

(B) Pan Card

(C) Debit Card

(D) Credit Card

11) ***Creation of new jobs:*** Probably, the best advantage of ICT has been the creation of new and interesting jobs. Computer programmers, Systems analysts, Hardware and Software developers, and Web designers are just some of the many new employment opportunities created with the help of ICT.

12) ***Motivating to learn:*** ICT gadgets such as videos, television, and multimedia computer software that combine text, sound, and colourful, moving images can be used to provide challenging and authentic content that will engage the student in the learning process. Interactive radio likewise makes use of sound effects, songs, dramatisations, comic skits, and other performance conventions to compel the students to listen and become involved in the lessons being delivered.

Disadvantages of ICT

1) Making life more and more mechanical: As today ICT devices are governing every sphere of life, we are fast forgetting moral, social, and ethical values. Our whole life is being governed by machines where there is no room for emotions and sentiments.

2) Promoting national and international terrorism and other crimes: If on one hand ICT has strengthened communication network and has been successful in maintaining the law and order situation, at the same time there is rise in cybercrimes which are of very dangerous magnitude. The incidents of abductions, murders, and robberies have increased manifold due to easy communication access among criminals with the help of ICT gadgets.

3) Unhealthy impact on young generation: Various social networking sites are sharing obscene content which is spoiling the young generation.

4) Rapidly becoming health and safety hazard: Users are taking ICT devices for granted and they use them while driving, which has resulted in many fatal accidents on highways. Further, users have developed addiction for ICT devices and they continuously use them which leave a bad impact on their health. It leaves a harmful impact on the nervous system, sense of vision, and hearing. Their persistent use creates hypertension and heart problems which sometimes prove to be fatal.

5) Computer viruses: Various harmful bugs like virus, worms, Trojans, malware, spam, phishing, etc. damage the costly computer system and make the system corrupt, thus resulting in loss of very valuable information and data. Rivals inject such virus into a user's computer system by plotting intrigue against the user out of jealousy, hate, or feeling of hostility. Such bugs can cause chaos and disrupt our daily lives.

DIGITAL DIVIDE AND ICT

The issue of Digital Divide cropped up in late 1990s. It is the uneven distribution of access to ICT tools, particularly Internet, broadly between the rich and the poor. It is also the divide among different geographical, political, and cultural groups. Some groups by virtue of their affluence, education, and awareness have an edge over others regarding easy access to Internet or broadband. It is a divide between haves and have-nots of ICT. Further, it is a gap between 'ICT-empowered and ICT-excluded communities.' Those who have poor or no access to ICT or digital resources, lag behind those who have an easy access in this technology-centred society. Whether it is an issue of education, health, skill development, innovations, or research, only access to digital resources help in achieving the desired results. Digital divide is also visible between developing and developed countries. High cost of installation of quality Internet connection also becomes a basis of digital divide. In spite of tall claims by different governments of universal distribution of benefits of ICT by framing and implementing policies for providing universal and equal access of ICT and digital resources to all sections of population, yet there is digital divide between the rich and the poor, literates and illiterates, skilled and unskilled, and urban and rural population.

Digital Divide in India: *Digital divide is remarkably visible in India which is a multi-cultured, multi-religion, and multi-language country. The divide is between the urban and rural areas. According to a survey, more than 75% of Internet and broadband connections are in top 30 cities. The survey also finds that about 6% of the total population has access to telephone and less than 1% has access to personal computer. According to a report by World Information Society, Internet users in India are 11 per thousand, whereas this figure is 580 per thousand in Japan and 640 per thousand in the USA. Difference in the level of knowledge, skill, awareness, and education also becomes the basic causes of the divide. Growing population and delay in implementing the policies become other major reasons for digital divide in India.*

Steps to Reduce Digital divide in India: *There are many e-governance and related projects set up in various states to reduce digital divide in India, like the UNDP supported Jan Mitra scheme in Rajasthan, Choice in Chattisgarh, Lokmitra in Himachal Pradesh, RajNIDHI in Rajasthan, Lokvani in UP, SETU in Maharashtra, and Jai Kisan in Uttranchal.*

WORLD TELECOMMUNICATION AND INFORMATION SOCIETY DAY

Having signing of first International Telegraph Convention on 17 May, 1865 at Paris by the UN members at its background, World Telecommunication and Information Society Day is celebrated every year on 17 May. In the Paris convention, International Telegraph Union was established under the UNO. Later, it became International Telecommunication Union (ITU) with its headquarters at Geneva (Switzerland). The purpose of ITU has been advancing communication technology from telegraph to modern technology of satellite and online communication.

Purpose behind celebrating World Telecommunication and Information Society Day is to create awareness worldwide about the advantages of using Internet and other ICT devices and motivating maximum societies to use technologies tagged under ICT which will ultimately help in bridging the digital divide.

Some Vital Facts

1) ICT helps in international development by bridging the digital divide and providing equitable access to technologies.
2) Converging technologies that exemplify ICT include the merging of audio-visual, telephone and computer networks through a common cabling system.
3) ICT are the main instruments for the creation of computer networks and the applications based on them.
4) ICT supports the spread of information and knowledge, separating the content from the place where it belongs physically.
5) Information technology refers to the use of hardware and software for storage, retrieval. Processing and distributing information of many kinds

Practice Exercise

General Questions Format

1. Information technology is the need of the day because it ________.

(A) facilitates communication irrespective of distance between the sender and the receiver

(B) has solved all the problems of mankind

(C) generates a variety of entertainment channels for the viewers

(D) None of the above

2. Which of the following is NOT a component of modern communication technology?

(A) Walkie-talkie (B) Computer

(C) Mobile Phone (D) Binoculars

3. Which of the following is TRUE about ICT? It is a/an __________.

(A) Campaign (B) Revolution

(C) Breakthrough (D) Technology

4. Satellite TV is an example of_____ technology.

(A) less communication and more information

(B) less information and more communication

(C) more or less information and communication

(D) None of the above

5. ICT has solved the academic problems of the students and the teachers by:

(A) enabling them to openly interact with each other and decide about joining a foreign university.

(B) helping them to locate the foreign university or institution of their choice for getting admission in them.

(C) teaching them about the norms of foreign universities.

(D) furnishing them the complete information about the desired academic destination anywhere in the world.

6. ICT has helped in facilitating distance education as

(A) students can obtain lectures/notes through Internet in the shortest possible time at their doorstep itself.

(B) authorities imparting distance education arrange seats in the cyber cafes for the student getting such education for surfing.

(C) knowledge about ICT is imparted by adding this chapter in the curriculum.

(D) None of the above

7. If a stranger is found communicating on a mobile phone near a bank, it definitely indicates that he is

(A) making contact with his associates for looting the bank.

(B) talking with some of his friends in the bank itself.

(C) communicating with his near or dear ones sitting around or far away.

(D) can't say

2 Abbreviations and Terminology

1. ***Integrated Services Digital Network (ISDN):*** It is a telecommunications standard for the transmission of digital information over ordinary telephone lines, and the name for the digital telephone network. It contains channels for digitised speech, data, image, or video signals.
2. ***local area network (LAN):*** It is a communications system linking computers within a restricted geographical area such as a building or campus. This also allows computers to share information from a central source.
3. ***Peripheral:*** Hardware device which can be plugged into the computer to perform some additional function such as a disk drive, a printer, or an overlay keyboard
4. ***PoP (Point of Presence):*** It is a location and telephone number provided by an Internet Service Provider (ISP) for local dial-up access to the Internet by users. The more PoPs in the country, the more likely one is to pay local call rates.
5. ***Portable Document Format (PDF):*** It is used to store and transmit text and images with a set appearance, sometimes in order that documents appear exactly as in print with the same line endings and pagination. PDF files can be created and read using software such as Adobe Acrobat.
6. ***Server:*** It is a computer system that provides a particular service to devices on a network.
7. ***WAN:*** A network which links computers over a large geographical area, including telecommunication links such as satellites.
8. ***Wizard:*** It is an on-screen step-by-step guide that helps a user perform a particular task.
9. ***WORM (Write Once Read Many):*** It is a computer storage medium, optical disks on which information cannot be erased or amended once it has been recorded.
10. ***Bandwidth:*** A measure of the capacity of a communications channel. It is the range of frequencies that a channel can handle.
11. ***A virtual community, e-community, or online community:*** It is a group of people that primarily interact via communication media such as newsletters, telephone, email, Internet social network service, or instant messages rather than face to face, for social, professional, educational, or other purposes.
12. ***The Internet Message Access Protocol (IMAP):*** It is one of the two most prevalent Internet standard protocols for email retrieval.
13. ***Post Office Protocol (POP):*** It is an application-layer Internet standard protocol used by local email clients to retrieve email from a remote server.
14. ***ASCII:*** Stands for American Standard Code for Information Interchange. Computers can only understand numbers, so an ASCII code is the numerical representation of a character such as 'a' or '@' or an action of some sort. ASCII codes represent text in computers, communications equipment, and other devices that use text. ASCII was developed by the American Standards Association (ASA).
15. ***ACTS (Automatic Coin Telephone System):*** It is a public coin-operated telephone service that completes a variety of phone calls, times the calls, and collects payment without the aid of an operator.
16. ***Pascal:*** It is a third-generation language (3GL).
17. ***Arithmetic-Logic Unit (ALU):*** It is the part of a computer processor (CPU) that carries out arithmetic and logic operations.
18. ***ARPANET:*** It was the network that became the basis for the Internet. Based on a concept first published in 1967, ARPANET was developed under the direction of the US Advanced Research Projects Agency (ARPA).

KEY

1. A	2. D	3. C	4. D	5. D	6. A	7. D
8. D	9. B	10. C	11. A	12. D	13. B	14. A
15. B	16. A	17. C	18. C	19. D	20. D	21. B
22. C	23. C	24. B	25. A	26. A	27. D	28. D
29. C	30. C					

Assertion–Reason Format

1. **Assertion (A):** People generally misuse ICT facility.
   Reason (R): Positive thinking and a typical skill is required to rationally use ICT facility.
   (A) Both A and R are true and R is correct explanation of A
   (B) Both A and R are true but R is not correct explanation of A
   (C) A is true but R is false
   (D) A is false but R is true
2. **Assertion (A):** ICT has brought in digital connectivity and digital connectivity has brought in the world in close proximity.
   Reason (R): ICT devices are used to create connectivity in diversity.
   (A) Both A and R are true and R is correct explanation of A
   (B) Both A and R are true but R is not correct explanation of A
   (C) A is true but R is false
   (D) A is false but R is true
3. **Assertion (A):** Digital divide is the natural outcome due to some people being blessed with affluence and some who are not.
   Reason (R): Internet-empowered community can come forward to help Internet-deprived community to have access over it.
   (A) Both A and R are true and R is correct explanation of A
   (B) Both A and R are true but R is not correct explanation of A
   (C) Both A and R are false
   (D) A is true but R is false
4. **Assertion (A):** Advantages and disadvantages of ICT are paradoxical to one another.
   Reason (R): If ICT has facilitated communication on one hand, then on the other hand it has also caused communicable bottlenecks.
   (A) Both A and R are true and R is correct explanation of A
   (B) A is true but R is false
   (C) A is false but R is true
   (D) Both A and R are false
5. **Assertion (A):** Mobile phones are sported these days for the sake of sporting them.
   Reason (R): Various service providers are coming up with attractive budget plans to make mobile phone affordable by everyone.
   (A) Both A and R are true and R is correct explanation of A
   (B) Both A and R are true but R is not correct explanation of A
   (C) A is true but R is false
   (D) A is false but R is true
6. **Assertion (A):** International Telecommunication Union (ITU) was established for transforming communication.
   Reason (R): Communication through telegraph advanced to modern technology of satellite and online communication.
   (A) Both A and R are true and R is correct explanation of A
   (B) Both A and R are true but R is not correct explanation of A
   (C) A is true but R is false
   (D) A is false but R is true
7. **Assertion (A):** Adverse impact of ICT is ignorable in the wake of its potential to digitally sustain the world today.
   Reason (R): Every development has its own advantages and disadvantages.
   (A) Both A and R are true and R is correct explanation of A
   (B) Both A and R are true but R is not correct explanation of A
   (C) A is true but R is false
   (D) Both A and R are false
8. **Assertion (A):** Eradicating international digital divide has been one of the UN Millennium Development Goals.
   Reason (R): ICT is considered to be effective in eradicating various environmental problems.
   (A) Both A and R are true and R is correct explanation of A
   (B) Both A and R are true but R is not correct explanation of A
   (C) Both A and R are false
   (D) A is false but R is true

9. **Assertion (A):** Use of ICT facility can be taken as a promising step towards overall development of a society.

Reason (R): There is no dearth of ICT gadgets worldwide in spite of global digital divide.

(A) Both A and R are true and R is correct explanation of A

(B) Both A and R are true but R is not correct explanation of A

(C) A is true but R is false

(D) A is false but R is true

10. **Assertion (A):** Advent of ICT has shown its potential of employment generation in every sphere.

Reason (R): ICT has provided skilled personal required in different fields like health, agriculture, education, industry, and trading.

(A) Both A and R are true and R is correct explanation of A

(B) Both A and R are true but R is not correct explanation of A

(C) A is true but R is false

(D) A is false but R is true

11. **Assertion (A):** People watch television not only for enjoyment but also for increasing their general knowledge.

Reason (R): Various devices of information and communication technology are used to fulfill various motives.

(A) Both A and R are true and R is the correct explanation of A

(B) Both A and R are true but R is not correct explanation of A

(C) A is true but R is false

(D) A is false but R is true

12. **Assertion (A):** Rational use of ICT devices protects the user from accidents and health hazards.

Reason (R): A major disadvantage of ICT devices is the assassination of culture and values conserved by the pioneers of a society.

(A) Both A and R are true and R is the correct explanation of A

(B) Both A and R are true but R is not the correct explanation of A

(C) A is false but R is true

(D) A is true but R is false

13. **Assertion (A):** Road accidents, particularly on highways, are increasing, and in majority of cases these prove to be fatal.

Reason (R): Investigations reveal that majority of road accidents happen due to driver being busy in using ICT devices like mobile phone or laptop while driving.

(A) Both A and R are true and R is the correct explanation of A

(B) Both A and R are true but R is not the correct explanation of A

(C) A is true but R is false

(D) A is false but R is true

14. **Assertion (A):** Optimum utilisation of ICT lies on the user's optimum involvement in it.

Reason (R): Penetrating into the ICT world fetches overall development of the users and their society.

(A) Both A and R are true and R is correct explanation of A

(B) Both A and R are false

(C) A is true but R is false

(D) Both A and R are true but R is not correct explanation of A

15. **Assertion (A):** Introduction of ICT has made satellite communication possible across the world.

Reason (R): Satellite communication has resulted in a steep rise in cybercrimes.

(A) A is false but R is true

(B) Both A and R are true and R is correct explanation of A

(C) Both A and R are true but R is not correct explanation of A

(D) A is true but R is false

KEY

1. A **2.** C **3.** B **4.** D **5.** B **6.** A **7.** D **8.** D **9.** B **10.** A **11.** A **12.** B **13.** A **14.** B **15.** A

Questions Asked in Previous NET Exams

1. Which of the following statement(s) is/are true in respect to ICT? **(UGC NET JUNE 2019)**

P: ICT is an acronym that stands for Information and Competitive technology.

Q: The effective use of ICT to support learning in the inclusive education exemplifies good teaching for all learners.

(A) P only (B) Q only

(C) Both P and Q (D) Neither P nor Q

-a company that would set new standards of excellence in business accounting and lead the market as India's number one accounting software developer.

50. ***Virus:*** A program which can be transmitted between computers via networks (especially the Internet) or removable storage such as CDs, USB drives, floppy disks, etc., generally without the knowledge or consent of the recipient. Results may range from nothing noticeable to deliberate damage to systems and data.

51. ***WYSIWYG:*** It is an acronym for What You See Is What You Get. The term is used in computing to describe a system in which content displayed during editing appears very similar to the final output, which might be a printed document, web page, slide presentation, or even the lighting for a theatrical event.

52. ***1GL:*** (First Generation Language) is a machine-level programming language.

53. ***CAT (Computer-Assisted Translation or Computer-Aided Translation):*** It is a form of translation wherein a human translator translates texts using computer software designed to support and facilitate the translation process.

54. ***DAC:*** In electronics, a digital-to-analog converter is a device that converts a digital (usually binary) code to an analog signal (current, voltage, or electric charge). An analog-to-digital converter (ADC) performs the reverse operation.

55. ***DFD:*** It stands for data flow diagram. It is a graphical representation of the "flow" of data through an information system. DFDs can also be used for the visualisation of data processing.

56. ***ADSL:*** It stands for Asymmetric Digital Subscriber Line. It is a high-speed digital telephone connection that operates over an existing copper telephone line, allowing the same line to be used for voice calls. ADSL lines offer transmission speed, and are used mainly for Internet access.

57. ***Adware:*** It is a software that may have been installed on your computer by a remote computer, i.e., via the Web. Many free utilities that one downloads from the Internet will install hidden software that sends details of the websites one visits and other information from one's computer (which can include one's email address) to advertisers so they can target the user.

58. ***Apache:*** The most popular Web Server software on the World Wide Web. Apache runs mainly on Unix systems, although there is also a Microsoft Windows version.

59. ***Backup or Back Up:*** It means to copy a file or folder from one computer to another storage device, e.g., a CD-ROM, as a precaution in case a computer's hard drive fails or is infected by a virus.

60. ***Blended Learning:*** This term normally refers to combining Internet-based distance learning with face-to-face tuition but it may also be used to describe combining offline ICT-based materials with more traditional materials, such as books, audio cassettes, and video cassettes.

61. ***Bus:*** This is basically a set of parallel wires for connecting the Central Processing Unit (CPU) of a computer to all other input-output devices. Data can be transmitted in two directions, from and to the CPU.

62. ***CALL:*** Computer-Assisted Language Learning.

63. ***Google:*** A popular search engine. Probably the most widely used search engine on the Web. You can also use Google to find definitions of words.

64. ***Hub:*** A common connection point for networked computers and other devices. Hubs are used to connect devices in a Local Area Network (LAN).

65. ***ICT:*** Information and Communications Technology.

66. ***Interface:*** In computer jargon, it is a connection between two systems. It can be hardware or software. It may take the form of a plug, cable or socket, or all three, for example, where a printer or scanner is connected to a computer, and then it's a hardware interface. There are also software interfaces that enable one program to link with another, passing across data and variables. The term interface, also known as user interface, also describes the software that is used to enable human beings to communicate with a computer, for example, Microsoft Windows, which is a Graphical User Interface (GUI) in common use on personal computers.

iii) lack of awareness and knowledge about ICT, illiteracy, and conservatism in certain sections of the population in developing and least developed countries became basis for this SDG

iv) by 2020, even the least developed countries will also enjoy easy, affordable, and universal accessibility to Internet

(A) ii and iv only (B) i, iii, and iv

(C) iii and iv only (D) i, ii, iii, and iv

23. Which of the following is the least significant cause of Digital Divide in India

(A) Illiteracy (B) Poverty

(C) Overpopulation (D) Ignorance

24. What is true about uses of Information and communications technology?

i) ICT has narrowed down the gaps in the verbal and non-verbal communication.

ii) While using ICT, users feel more privileged as compared to non-users.

iii) Use of ICT devices take the users close to efficiency, authenticity, and reliability.

iv) There is no substitute of an ICT service provider due to its easy and uniform accessibility.

(A) i, ii, iii, and iv (B) None of the above

(C) ii and iv only (D) i, iii, and iv

25. Consider the statement: "Generation of employment opportunities by ICT has put full stop to the apprehensions of unemployment by ICT". This statement is a/an

i) ICT fact ii) Statutory fact

iii) Overdrawn fact iv) Promising fact

v) Hypothetical fact

Choose the right code:

(A) Only i & iv (B) Only i, iii, & iv

(C) Only ii, iii, iv & v (D) Only i, ii, & iv

26. Digital divide between the rich and the poor of a country and between a least developed country and a developed country is

(A) same as digital divide which is the result of similar circumstances at every level that create differences with respect to accessibility to Internet and other digital resources.

(B) different as local and international circumstances leading to digital divide are incompatible.

(C) same on some points like access to Internet and digital resources, whereas it is different on some points like digital divide between the affluent and the least affluent countries due to various socio-economic, political, cultural, and economic reasons.

(D) None of these

27. It is said that "Introduction of ICT has paved an easy access to education." Which education is being referred here?

i) Formal education

ii) Non-formal education

iii) Informal education

(A) i, ii, and iii (B) Only i and iii

(C) Only iii (D) Only i and ii

28. Which of the following ICT devices is found to be in minimum use in the present life?

(A) Joysticks (B) Desktops

(C) External mouse (D) Can't say

29. World Telecommunication and Information Society Day is celebrated on 17 May with an objective to ______.

i) bridge the gap of digital divide

ii) review all ICT devices used in offering public utility services worldwide

iii) enhance the use of ICT in strengthening defence and law and order situation worldwide

iv) assess the progress of various ICT pacts signed by the UN member countries

(A) i, ii, iii, and iv (B) Only iii

(C) Only i (D) Only i, iii, and iv

30. ICT schemes initiated by the government of India are given under Column I and the states in which these schemes have been started are given under Column II. Match the scheme with its state and choose the correct code given thereafter.

Column I (ICT Scheme)	Column II (State)
a) Jan Mitra	i) Himachal Pradesh
b) Lokmitra	ii) Uttar Pradesh
c) SETU	iii) Rajasthan
d) Lokvani	iv) Maharashtra

Codes:

	(a)	(b)	(c)	(d)
(A)	ii	iii	iv	i
(B)	i	iv	ii	iii
(C)	iii	i	iv	ii
(D)	iv	i	ii	iii

19. ***ARCNET:*** It is a widely-installed local area network (LAN) technology.
20. ***Dots per Inch (dpi):*** It is a measure of the sharpness (that is, the density of illuminated points) on a display screen of a computer.
21. ***Dynamic Data Exchange (DDE):*** It allows information to be shared or communicated between programs. For example, when you change a form in your database program or a data item in a spreadsheet program, they can be set up to also change these forms or items anywhere they occur in other programs you may use. In a nutshell, it is the transfer of data from one application to another.
22. ***Password:*** It is an unspaced sequence of characters used to determine that a computer user requesting access to a computer system is really that particular user. A password is typically somewhere between four and 16 characters.
23. ***Macro Virus:*** It is a computer virus that "infects" a Microsoft Word or similar application and causes a sequence of actions to be performed automatically when the application is started or something else triggers it. Macro viruses tend to be surprising but relatively harmless. A typical effect is the undesired insertion of some comic text at certain points when writing a line. A macro virus is often spread as an email virus.
24. ***CAD (Computer-Aided Design):*** Software used by architects, engineers, drafters, artists, and others to create precision drawings or technical illustrations. CAD software can be used to create two-dimensional (2-D) drawings or three-dimensional (3-D) models.
25. ***Taskbar:*** It is a visual device on the desktop that typically shows the user which applications (tasks) are currently active and running. Some taskbars, such as those in Windows operating systems, also include icons for commonly-used utilities such as the system clock and antivirus software. In some systems, the user is allowed to modify the contents, location, or appearance of the taskbar. In Apple operating systems, the term dock is used instead of taskbar.
26. ***Hang-up:*** Also called a hang, is a condition that sometimes occurs when computer programs conflict or do not run properly. The computer seems paralyzed. Clicking the mouse has no effect, regardless of where the arrow or cursor is placed.
27. ***Ctrl-Alt-Delete:*** In a personal computer with the Windows operating system, Ctrl-Alt-Delete is the combination of keyboard keys that the computer user can press at the same time to terminate an application task or to reboot the operating system (have it shut down and restart itself). The Ctrl-Alt-Delete key combination allows the user to terminate the "hung" application and, if that doesn't work, to reboot the system. The idea to use this key combination as a way to reboot a system originated with an IBM engineer, David Bradley, in 1980.
28. ***Reboot:*** It is a method to restart a computer and reload the operating system. The most common reasons to reboot are because the installation of new software or hardware requires it, or because applications are not responding for some reason. On computers running Windows, you can usually reboot by selecting "Turn off computer" from the Start menu and then clicking "Restart" in the window that pops up. Rebooting a computer through the menu option or the keystroke combination is sometimes referred to as a warm boot, perhaps because it is more gentle than the alternative cold boot (simply pressing the computer's power button once to turn it off and then again to turn it back on). On larger computers (including mainframes), the equivalent term for "boot" is "initial program load" (IPL) and for "reboot" is "re-IPL."
29. ***Octal:*** It is a term that describes a base-8 number system. An octal number system consists of eight single-digit numbers: 0, 1, 2, 3, 4, 5, 6, and 7. The number after 7 is 10. The number after 17 is 20 and so forth. In computer programming, the octal equivalent of a binary number is sometimes used to represent it because it is shorter.
30. ***Safe Mode:*** It is an alternate boot method for Windows operating systems that makes it easier to diagnose problems. The only startup programs loaded are the operating system and drivers for the mouse, keyboard, and display modes display. It is often possible to get a system to start in safe mode when it won't start normally. To start in safe mode, press the F8 key while the system is booting and select "safe mode" (or the safe mode option you want) from the menu that appears.

31. ***QWERTY Keyboard:*** It is the standard typewriter and computer keyboard in countries that use a Latin-based alphabet. QWERTY refers to the first six letters on the upper row of the keyboard.

32. ***E-Cycling:*** It is the practice of reusing, or distributing for reuse, electronic equipment and components rather than discarding them at the end of their life cycle.

33. ***MULTOS:*** It stands for "Multiple Operating System" and is an operating system that allows multiple application programs to be installed and to reside separately and securely on a smart card. Each program is isolated by the operating system so that no application can interfere with another one.

34. ***BGAN (Broadband Global Area Network):*** It is a mobile communications system created to transmit broadband wireless voice and data communications almost anywhere on the earth's surface.

35. ***Spyware:*** It is any technology that aids in gathering information about a person or organisation without their knowledge. On the Internet (where it is sometimes called a spybot or tracking software), spyware is programming that is put in someone's computer to secretly gather information about the user and relay it to advertisers or other interested parties. Spyware can get in a computer as a software virus or as the result of installing a new program.

36. ***Universal Business Language (UBL):*** It is a royalty-free set of documents. The primary purpose of UBL is to promote and support the global use of e-commerce documents.

37. ***E-commerce (Electronic Commerce or EC):*** It is the buying and selling of goods and services on the Internet, especially the World Wide Web.

38. ***E-tailing:*** It is the selling of retail goods on the Internet. Short for "electronic retailing."

39. ***Hacker:*** It is a term used by some to mean "a clever programmer" and by others, especially those in popular media, to mean "someone who tries to break into computer systems."

40. ***Desktop Publishing:*** It is the process of using the computer and specific types of software to combine text and graphics to produce documents such as newsletters, brochures, books, etc.

41. ***CCTV (Closed-Circuit Television):*** It is a television system in which signals are not publicly distributed; cameras are connected to television monitors in a limited area such as a store, an office building, or on a college campus. CCTV is commonly used in surveillance systems.

42. ***Celeron:*** It is the low-end (and low cost) member of the family of microprocessors from Intel.

43. ***Benchmark:*** It is the act of running a computer program that is specially designed to provide measurements for a particular operating system or application.

44. ***Linux:*** It is a Unix-like operating system that was designed to provide personal computer users a free or very low-cost operating system comparable to traditional and usually more expensive Unix systems.

45. ***Darwin:*** It is computer operating system released by Apple Inc. in 2000.

46. ***Sun OS:*** It is a version of the Unix operating system developed by Sun Microsystems.

47. ***Windows NT:*** It is a family of operating systems produced by Microsoft. Windows 3.1x and Windows 9x were 16-bit/32-bit hybrids. Windows 2000, Windows XP, Windows Server 2003, Windows Vista, Windows Home Server, Windows Server 2008, and Windows 7 are based upon the Windows NT system, although they are not branded as Windows NT.

48. ***Unix (officially trademarked as UNIX, sometimes also written as UNIX with small caps):*** It is a computer operating system originally developed in 1969 by a group of AT&T employees at Bell Labs.

49. ***Tally:*** It is the name of an accounting software. The Late Shri S. S. Goenka, founder of the company Peutronics Pvt. Ltd. set up Tally's software business in 1986. His able mentoring of his son Bharat resulted in the creation of software that would simplify the process of financial accounting and inventory. Determined to create and develop a simple business accounting software, Bharat spent months in the research and development of path breaking technologies, which would assist him in achieving his goals. His dedication and focus led to the development of a commercial product. It was at this stage that Peutronics Pvt. Ltd. metamorphosed into Tally Solutions

2. Which of the following statement(s) regarding the term ICT is/are true?

P: A digital divide is an economic and social equality with regard to access to, use of, or impact of ICT.

Q: ICT helps in international development by bridging the digital divide and providing equitable access to technologies.

(UGC NET JULY 2018)

Choose the correct answer from the following:

(A) P only (B) Q only

(C) Both P and Q (D) Neither P nor Q

3. Which of the following statements, regarding the term ICT is/are TRUE?

P: ICT is an acronym that stands for Indian Classical Technology.

Q: Converging technologies that exemplify ICT include the merging of audio-visual, telephone, and computer networks through a common cabling system.

(UGC NET JULY 2018)

(A) P Only (B) Q Only

(C) Both P and Q (D) Neither P nor Q

4. Read the following two statements:

(UGC NET JANUARY 2017)

I: Information and communications technology (ICT) is considered a subset of Information Technology (IT).

II: The 'right to use' a piece of software is termed as copyright.

Which of the above statement(s) is/are CORRECT?

(A) Both I and II (B) Neither I nor II

(C) II only (D) I only

5. Which of the following statements regarding the features of Information and communications technology (ICT) is/are true?

(UGC NET AUGUST 2016)

I. ICT are the main instruments for the creation of computer networks and the applications based on them.

II. ICT supports the spread of information and knowledge, separating the content from the place where it belongs physically.

III. The digital and virtual nature of most of ICT products allows the expenditure for them to be maximised.

(A) I and II only (B) I and III only

(C) II and III only (D) I, II, and III

6. The statement "the study, development, implementation, support, or management of computer-based information systems, particularly software applications and computer hardware" refers to

(UGC NET JULY 2016)

(A) Information Technology (IT)

(B) Information and collaborative technology (ICT)

(C) Information and data technology (IDT)

(D) Artificial Intelligence (AI)

7. Information and communications technology includes **(UGC NET DECEMBER 2006)**

(A) Online learning

(B) Learning through EDUSAT

(C) Web-based learning

(D) All of the above

8. Which of the following is the appropriate definition of Information Technology?

(UGC NET DECEMBER 2004)

(A) Information technology refers to the use of hardware and software for processing information.

(B) Information technology refers to the use of hardware and software for distribution of useful information.

(C) Information technology refers to the use of hardware and software for storage, retrieval, processing, and distributing information of many kinds.

(D) Information technology refers to the use the principles of physical sciences and social sciences for processing of information of many kinds.

9. ICT stands for

(UGC NET DECEMBER 2004)

(A) International communication technology

(B) Intera common technology

(C) Information and communications technology

(D) Inter connected terminals

KEY

1. B	**2.** B	**3.** B	**4.** B	**5.** A	**6.** A	**7.** D
8. C	**9.** C					

67. ***Menu:*** A list of options from which a computer user makes a selection in order to determine the course of events in a program.

68. ***Narrowband:*** A term used to describe a slow-speed connection to the Internet, normally via a modem and less than or equal to 64 Kbps.

69. ***Pixel:*** A contraction of picture element. What you see on a computer display screen is made up of thousands of coloured pixels or small dots, which can be set according to the user's choice to produce either low-resolution output, medium-resolution output, or high-resolution output, the usual combinations of pixels across each line of the screen (horizontal pixels) and down each line of the screen (vertical pixels) being 640 x 480, 800 x 600, 1024 x 768, and 1280 x 1024. Thus, the more pixels on the screen, the higher the resolution (i.e., producing a finer, sharper image) and the greater the variety of colours that can be displayed.

70. ***Portal:*** A Web page, website, or service that acts as link or entrance to other websites on the Internet. Typically, a portal includes an annotated catalogue of the websites and may also include a search engine, email facilities, a forum, and other services. Also known as a Gateway.

71. ***Search Engine:*** A search facility provided at a number of sites on the World Wide Web. Search engines enable the user to search the whole of the Web for keywords and phrases and to locate related websites. This is a useful facility for locating information.

72. ***Server:*** A computer which provides services to other computers, which are known as clients.

73. ***Twitter:*** A Microblogging facility that allows users to post very short texts (maximum 280 characters) containing snippets of information about what they are doing at a given moment, news items, links to websites, or comments on events, e.g. conferences and courses: http://twitter.com

74. ***Array:*** In data storage, an array is a method for storing information on multiple devices. In general, an array is a number of items arranged in some specified way -for example, in a list or in a three-dimensional table. In random access memory (RAM), an array is the arrangement of memory cells.

75. ***Database:*** A collection of information that is organised so that it can easily be accessed, managed, and updated. In one view, databases can be classified according to types of content: bibliographic, full-text, numeric, and images.

76. ***Binary Tree:*** A method of placing and locating files (called records or keys) in a database, especially when all the data is known to be in random access memory (RAM).

77. ***Queue:*** In computer technology, a queue is a sequence of work objects that are waiting to be processed.

78. ***TCP/IP:*** Stands for Transmission Control Protocol/Internet Protocol, which is the basic communication language or protocol of the Internet.

79. ***Stack:*** TCP/IP is frequently referred to as a "stack." This refers to the layers (TCP, IP, and sometimes others) through which all data passes at both client and server ends of a data exchange.

80. ***Linear Data Structure:*** It is a sequential list of elements in data like in Array.

81. ***Data Encryption:*** It is an information security tool on the Internet.

82. ***Watermark:*** A recognizable image or pattern in paper that appears as various shades of lightness/darkness when viewed by transmitted light (or when viewed by reflected light, atop a dark background), caused by thickness or density variations in the paper.

83. ***Data Hiding:*** It is an information security tool on Internet.

84. ***S/MIME (Secure Multi-Purpose Internet Mail Extensions):*** It is a secure method of sending email that uses the Rivest-Shamir-Adleman encryption system. S/MIME is included in the latest versions of the web browsers from Microsoft and Netscape.

85. ***Crash:*** A system malfunction in which the computer stops working and has to be restarted.

86. ***Ethernet:*** A protocol for fast communication and file transfer across a network.

87. ***i18n:*** Short for internationalization. "18" is for the number of letters between the i and the n.

88. ***Domain Name System (DNS):*** It is a database system that translates a computer's fully qualified domain name into an IP address. Networked computers use IP addresses to locate and connect to each other, but IP addresses can be difficult for people to remember. For example, on the web, it's much easier to remember the domain name www.amazon.com than it is to remember its corresponding IP address (207.171.166.48). DNS allows you to connect to another networked computer or remote service by using its user-friendly domain name rather than its numerical IP address.

89. ***Ethernet:*** It is a physical and data link layer technology for local area networks (LANs). Ethernet was invented by engineer Robert Metcalfe.

90. ***Token Ring:*** It is a local area network (LAN) in which all computers are connected in a ring or star topology and a bit- or token-passing scheme is used in order to prevent the collision of data between two computers that want to send messages at the same time. The Token Ring protocol is the second most widely-used protocol on local area networks after Ethernet.

91. ***FDDI (Fiber Distributed Data Interface):*** It is a set for data transmission on fiber optic lines in a local area network (LAN) that can extend in range up to 200 km (124 miles). The FDDI protocol is based on the token ring protocol. In addition to being large geographically, an FDDI local area network can support thousands of users.

92. ***Smart card:*** It is a plastic card about the size of a credit card, with an embedded microchip that can be loaded with data, used for telephone calling, electronic cash payments, and other applications, and then periodically refreshed for additional use. A smart card contains more information than a magnetic stripe card and it can be programmed for different applications. Some cards can contain programming and data to support multiple applications and some can be updated to add new applications after they are issued. It works with COS, i.e., Card Operating System.

93. ***Internet Protocol version 4 (IPv4):*** It is the fourth revision in the development of the Internet Protocol (IP) and the first version of the protocol to be widely deployed. It is at the core of standards-based Internet working methods of the Internet. As of 2012, IPv4 is still the most widely deployed Internet Layer protocol.

94. ***IPv6 (Internet Protocol version 6):*** It is a revision of the Internet Protocol (IP) developed by the Internet Engineering Task Force (IETF). IPv6 is intended to succeed IPv4, which is the dominant communications protocol for most Internet traffic as of 2012. IPv6 was developed to deal with the long-anticipated problem of IPv4 running out of addresses. IPv6 implements a new addressing system that allows for far more addresses to be assigned than with IPv4. Each device on the Internet, such as a computer or mobile telephone, must be assigned an IP address in order to communicate with other devices. With the ever-increasing number of new devices being connected to the Internet, there is a need for more addresses than IPv4 can accommodate. IPv6 uses 128-bit addresses, allowing for 2128, or approximately 3.4×1038 addresses. IPv4 uses 32-bit addresses, allowing for only 4,294,967,296 unique addresses worldwide. IPv6 was intended to replace the widely used Internet Protocol Version 4 (IPv4) that is considered the backbone of the modern Internet. IPv6 is often referred to as the "next generation Internet" because of its expanded capabilities and its growth through recent large scale deployments.

95. ***POP3 (Post Office Protocol 3):*** It is the most recent version of a standard protocol for receiving email. POP3 is a client/server protocol in which email is received and held for you by your Internet server. Periodically, you (or your client email receiver) check your mailbox on the server and download any mail, probably using POP3. This standard protocol is built into most popular email products, such as Eudora and Outlook Express. It's also built into the Netscape and Microsoft Internet Explorer browsers.

96. ***Internet Message Access Protocol (IMAP):*** It provides the user more capabilities for retaining email on the server and for organising it in folders on the server. IMAP can be thought of as a remote file server. POP and IMAP deal with the receiving of email and are not to be confused with the Simple Mail Transfer Protocol (SMTP), a protocol for transferring email across the Internet. You send email with SMTP and a mail handler receives it on your recipient's behalf. Then the mail is read using POP or IMAP. Most webmail service providers such as Hotmail, Gmail, and Yahoo! Mail also provide IMAP and POP3 service.

97. ***Internet Explorer:*** Web browser that made its debut in 1995 as Microsoft's response to Netscape, one of the first graphical-based web browsers and, at the time, the dominant browser in use with control of over 90 percent of the market. Initially called Microsoft Internet Explorer (MSIE), the latest official release of IE is Internet Explorer 11.

98. ***Compiler:*** It is a program that translates a source program written in some high-level programming language (such as Java) into machine code (machine language) for some computer architecture (such as the Intel Pentium architecture). The generated machine code can be later executed many times against different data each time.

99. ***Virtual Memory:*** It is a feature of an operating system that enables a process to use a memory (RAM) address space that is independent of other processes running in the same system, and use a space that is larger than the actual amount of RAM present, temporarily relegating some contents from RAM to a disk, with little or no overhead.

100. ***Graphics Interchange Format (better known by its acronym GIF):*** It is a bitmap image format that was introduced by CompuServe in 1987 and has since come into widespread usage on the World Wide Web due to its wide support and portability.

101. ***Electronic Bulletin Board (EBB):*** It is a communication system that allows parties to view pipeline information through personal computers and phone lines. An online connection allows information to be viewed on a screen to the user, and allows the user to react by entering data, requesting new data, and/or requesting files to be transferred.

102. ***Multimedia Messaging Service (MMS):*** It is a standard in mobile messaging. Like SMS (Short Message Service), MMS is a way to send a message from one mobile to another. The difference is that MMS can include not just text, but also sound images and video. It is also possible to send MMS messages from a mobile phone to an email address.

103. ***Virtual Reality (VR):*** Sometimes referred to as immersive multimedia, is a computer-simulated environment that can simulate physical presence in places in the real world or imagined worlds. Most current virtual reality environments are primarily visual experiences, displayed either on a computer screen or through special stereoscopic displays, but some simulations include additional sensory information, such as sound through speakers or headphones. Some advanced, haptic systems now include tactile information, generally known as force feedback in medical, gaming, and military applications. Furthermore, virtual reality covers remote communication environments which provide virtual presence of users with the concepts of telepresence and telexistence or a virtual artifact.

104. ***Virtual University:*** It provides higher education programs through electronic media, typically the Internet. The first virtual university in India was set up in Tamil Nadu.

105. ***DOCX:*** The .docx extension is assigned to Microsoft Word documents created in the 2007 edition of Microsoft Word (and all later editions).

106. ***Extensible Markup Language (XML):*** It is a markup language that defines a set of rules for encoding documents in a format that is both human-readable and machine-readable. It is defined in the XML 1.0 Specification.

107. ***World Wide Web Consortium (W3C):*** It is the main international standards organisation for the World Wide Web (abbreviated WWW or W3).

108. ***FTP:*** It is an acronym for File Transfer Protocol. As the name suggests, FTP is used to transfer files between computers on a network. One can use FTP to exchange files between computer accounts, transfer files between an account and a desktop computer, or access online software archives.

109. ***PNG (pronounced ping as in ping-pong; for Portable Network Graphics):*** It is a file format for image compression that, in time, is expected to replace the Graphics Interchange Format (GIF) that is widely used on today's Internet.

110. ***BMP File Format:*** Also known as bitmap image file or device independent bitmap file format or simply a bitmap, is a raster graphics image file format used to store bitmap digital images.

111. ***Graphical User interface (GUI):*** It is a type of interface that allows users to interact with electronic devices through graphical icons and visual indicators.

112. ***JPEG:*** Short for Joint Photographic Experts Group, and pronounced jay-peg. JPEG is a lossy compression technique for colour images. Although it can reduce files sizes to about 5% of their normal size, some detail is lost in the compression.

113. ***TIFF (Tagged Image File Format):*** It is a computer file format for storing raster graphics images, popular among graphic artists, the publishing industry, and both amateur and professional photographers in general.

114. ***Raster Graphics Image:*** It is a dot matrix data structure representing a generally rectangular grid of pixels, or points of colour, viewable via a monitor, paper, or other display medium. Raster images are stored in image files with varying formats.

115. ***Read-Only Memory (ROM):*** It is a class of storage medium used in computers and other electronic devices. Data stored in ROM can only be modified slowly, with difficulty, or not at all, so it is mainly used to distribute firmware (software that is very closely tied to specific hardware, and unlikely to need frequent updates).

116. ***BIOS (Basic Input/Output System):*** It is a set of computer instructions in firmware which control input and output operations. BIOS software is stored on a ROM chip on the motherboard. It is specifically designed to work with each particular model of computer, interfacing with various devices that make up the complementary chipset of the system. In modern computer systems, the BIOS contents are stored on flash memory so that the contents can be rewritten without removing the chip from the motherboard.

117. ***Flash memory:*** It is an electronic non-volatile computer storage medium that can be electrically erased and reprogrammed.

118. ***EEPROM (also written E2PROM and pronounced "e-e-prom", "double-e prom", "e-squared", or simply "e-prom"):*** Stands for Electrically Erasable Programmable Read-Only Memory and is a type of non-volatile memory used in computers and other electronic devices to store small amounts of data that must be saved when power is removed.

119. ***Media Access Control Address (MAC Address):*** It is a unique identifier assigned to network interfaces for communications on the physical network segment. It may also be known as an Ethernet hardware address (EHA), hardware address, or physical address.

120. ***Interface:*** It is a device or program enabling a user to communicate with a computer.

121. ***Network interface controller (NIC, also known as a Network Interface Card, Network Adapter, LAN Adapter, and by similar terms):*** It is a computer hardware component that connects a computer to a computer network.

122. ***Institute of Electrical and Electronics Engineers (IEEE):*** It is a professional association with its corporate office in New York City. Today it is the world's largest association of technical professionals with more than 400,000 members in chapters around the world. Its objectives are the educational and technical advancement of electrical and electronic engineering, telecommunications, computer engineering, and allied disciplines.

123. ***IEEE 802:*** Refers to a family of IEEE standards dealing with local area networks and metropolitan area networks.

124. ***Lossy Compression or Irreversible Compression:*** It is the class of data encoding methods that uses inexact approximations and partial data discarding to represent the content. These techniques are used to reduce data size for storage, handling, and transmitting content.

125. ***CSS:*** It stands for Cascading Style Sheets. CSS describes how HTML elements are to be displayed on the screen, paper, or in other media. CSS saves a lot of work. It can control the layout of multiple web pages all at once.

126. ***Massive Open Online Course (MOOC):*** It is an online course aimed at unlimited participation and open access via the web. In addition to traditional course materials such as filmed lectures, readings, and problem sets, many MOOCs provide interactive courses with user forums to support community interactions among students, professors, and teaching assistants (TAs) as well as immediate feedback to quick quizzes and assignments. MOOCs are a recent and widely researched development in distance education which were first introduced in 2006 and emerged as a popular mode of learning.

127. ***Digital Empowerment:*** It is an innovative digital empowering project that uses a creative approach to teaching basic ICT skills and provides an effective entry route for learners, who are disengaged with the learning process, or who are unconfident with new technologies.

128. ***Cloud:*** It often refers to the Internet, and more precisely to some data center full of servers that is connected to the Internet.

129. ***AltaVista:*** It is a popular search engine on the Web. In addition to full-text searches, AltaVista can also search graphic images and tell you who is linked to your own Web pages. AltaVista's search robot, known as Scooter, can look at and collect data from three million Web pages per day. It was established in 1995. It became one of the most-used early search engines, but lost ground to Google and was purchased first by Overture and then by Yahoo! in 2003.

130. ***Mac OS:*** It is the computer operating system for Apple Computer's Macintosh line of personal computers and workstations.

131. ***Listserve:*** Computer program that automatically distribute an email message to individuals who are part of a list; messages can usually only be sent or received by members of the list.

132. ***Logic bomb:*** It is a piece of code inserted into an operating system or software application that implements a malicious function after a certain amount of time, or specific conditions are met. Logic bombs are often used with viruses, worms, and trojan horses to time them to do maximum damage before being noticed.

133. ***Boot Sector Virus:*** It is a type of virus that infects the boot sector of floppy disks or the Master Boot Record (MBR) of hard disks (some infect the boot sector of the hard disk instead of the MBR).

134. ***Network Media:*** It is any audio, video, images or text, used on a computer network, like the Internet. It almost always requires a computer to send and receive, as well as a community of people to create and consume the content.

135. ***Convergence:*** It is the integration of two or more different technologies in a single device or system, i.e., combination of computing, telecommunications, and media in a digital atmosphere.

136. ***Online Communication:*** It is instant messaging. This mode of communication is an enhanced method of the chat. Messages can be conveyed through a special software to any user who is part of the same instant messaging network. Both users have to be connected to the relevant network to be able to communicate online.

137. ***Cyber Venting:*** A process by which disgruntled employees set up websites to provide a forum for complaints. The term invented for this is cyber venting (venting their anger by electronic means).

138. ***Cyber Ranting:*** Relieving pressure by ranting and raving in a blog, tweet, text message, or other posting through the Internet.

139. ***Recall:*** In memory, this refers to the mental process of retrieval of information from the past. Along with encoding and storage, it is one of the three core processes of memory. There are three main types of recall: free recall, cued recall, and serial recall.

140. ***Poor Recall:*** In web search, finding a large number of documents with very little relevant information.

141. ***Web Crawler (also known as a Web Spider or Web Robot):*** It is a program or automated script which browses the World Wide Web in a methodical, automated manner. This process is called Web crawling or spidering.

142. ***Boolean Logic:*** It is a form of algebra in which all values are reduced to either TRUE or FALSE. Boolean logic is especially important for computer science because it fits nicely with the binary numbering system, in which each bit has a value of either 1 or 0.

143. ***Fuzzy logic:*** It is a form of many-valued logic in which the truth values of variables may be any real number between 0 and 1. It is employed to handle the concept of partial truth, where the truth value may range between completely true and completely false. By contrast, in Boolean logic, the truth values of variables may only be the integer values 0 or 1. The term fuzzy logic was introduced with the 1965 proposal of fuzzy set theory by Lotfi Zadeh.

144. ***Bluetooth Technology:*** A Bluetooth® device works by using radio waves instead of wires or cables to connect with one's cell phone, smartphone, or computer. Bluetooth is a wireless short-range communications

technology standard found in millions of products people use every day -including headsets, smartphones, laptops, and portable speakers.

145. ***Value-Added Network (VAN):*** It is a private network provider (sometimes called a turnkey communications line) that is hired by a company to facilitate electronic data interchange (EDI) or provide other network services. Before the arrival of the World Wide Web, some companies hired value-added networks to move data from their company to other companies.

146. ***VoIP:*** It stands for "Voice Over Internet Protocol," and is an advanced technology that allows businesses and staff to communicate more effectively than is possible with traditional phone lines. This technology is also referred to as IP Telephony as it uses Internet protocols to transmit packets of data.

147. ***Voice Portal (sometimes called a Vortal):*** It is a Web portal that can be accessed entirely by voice.

148. ***SITE:*** It stands for Satellite Instructional Television Experiment and was an experimental satellite communication project lunched in India in 1975, designed jointly by NASA and the Indian Space Research Organisation (ISRO). The project made available informational television programmes to rural India.

149. ***Wiki:*** A system that allows collaborative modification of its content and structure directly from the web browser. It is a website or database developed collaboratively by a community of users, allowing any user to add and edit content. The term comes from the word "wikiwiki," which means "fast" in the Hawaiian language. A wiki website operates on a principle of collaborative trust. The simplest wiki programs allow users to create and edit content. More advanced wikis have a management component that allows a designated person to accept or reject changes. The best known example of a wiki website is Wikipedia.

150. ***VLE (Virtual Learning Environment):*** It is a set of teaching and learning tools designed to enhance a student's learning experience by including computers and the Internet in the learning process.

151. ***Generations of Computers:*** With respect to evolution of computers through different time spans, there are five definable generations of computers:

A. **1940-1956: First Generation -Vacuum Tubes:** These early computers used vacuum tubes as circuitry and magnetic drums for memory. As a result they were very big in size and used to occupy a space of about a room. These were very costly to maintain.

B. **1956- 1963: Second Generation -Transistors:** During 1950s, vacuum tubes in computers were replaced by compact transistors. This period was termed as second generation of computers. Although first invented in 1947, transistors weren't used significantly in computers until the end of the 1950s. They were a big improvement over the vacuum tube.

C. **1964-1971: Third Generation-Integrated Circuits:** By this phase, transistors were now being miniaturised and put on silicon chips (called semiconductors). This led to a massive increase in speed and efficiency of these machines. These were the first computers where users interacted using keyboards and monitors which interfaced with an operating system, a significant leap up from the punch cards and printouts. This enabled these machines to run several applications at once using a central program which functioned to monitor memory.

D. **1972-2010: Fourth Generation-VLSI Microprocessors:** The fourth generation of computers is marked by the use of Very Large Scale Integrated (VLSI) circuits. VLSI circuits having about 5000 transistors and other circuit elements and their associated circuits on a single chip made it possible to have microcomputers of the fourth generation. Fourth Generation computers became more powerful, compact, reliable, and affordable. As a result, it gave rise to personal computer (PC) revolution. This revolution can be summed in one word: Intel. The chip-maker developed the Intel 4004 chip in 1971, which positioned all computer components (CPU, memory, and input/output controls) onto a single chip. What filled a room in the 1940s now fit in the palm of the hand. The Intel chip housed thousands of integrated circuits. The year 1981 saw the first ever computer (IBM) specifically designed for home use and 1984 saw the Macintosh introduced by Apple. Microprocessors even moved beyond the realm of computers and into an increasing number of everyday products. In this generation Time sharing, Real time, Networks, and Distributed Operating System were used. All the Higher level languages like C and C++, DBASE, etc. were used in this generation.

E. **2010- : Fifth Generation - Artificial Intelligence (AI):** AI is a reality made possible by using parallel processing and superconductors. Leaning to the future, computers will be radically transformed again by quantum computation, molecular, and nano technology. In the fifth generation, the VLSI technology became ULSI (Ultra Large Scale Integration) technology, resulting in the production of microprocessor chips having ten million electronic components. This generation is based on parallel processing hardware and AI (Artificial Intelligence) software. AI is an emerging branch in computer science, which interprets means and methods of making computers think like human beings. All the higher level languages like C and C++, Java, .Net, etc. are used in this generation.

152. *AW Files:* Answer Wizard files are data files saved in the .aw format using an application developed by Microsoft. The Microsoft Answer Wizard Builder software is used to create these AW files, and this application can also be installed and used to open these .aw files.

153. *A MOV File:* It is a common multimedia container file format developed by Apple and compatible with both Macintosh and Windows platforms.

154. *MP4 File Format:* MP4 file extension is an MPEG-4 video file format. MP4s are one of the more common video file formats used for downloading and streaming videos from the Internet.

155. *Audio Formats:* There are a number of different types of Audio files as given below:

I) **wav** - standard audio file format used mainly in Windows PCs. Commonly used for storing uncompressed (PCM), CD-quality sound files

II) **mp3** - the MPEG Layer-3 format is the most popular format for downloading and storing music

III) **ogg** - a free, open source container format supporting a variety of codecs

IV) **gsm** - designed for telephony use in Europe, gsm is a very practical format for telephone quality voice

V) **au** - the standard audio file format used by Sun, Unix, and Java

VI) **aiff** - the standard audio file format used by Apple

VII) **wma** - the popular Windows Media Audio format owned by Microsoft

VIII) **aac** - the Advanced Audio Coding format is based on the MPEG-4 audio standard owned by Dolby

IX) **ra** - a Real Audio format designed for streaming audio over the Internet

X) **dss** - the Digital Speech Standard files which are an Olympus proprietary format

XI) **msv** - a Sony proprietary format for Memory Stick compressed voice files

156. *Blu-ray:* It is an optical disc format designed to display high definition video and store large amounts of data. **Blu-ray** is the successor to DVD.

157. *.org:* Top level domain for non-profit organisations.

158. *.net Framework:* It is a software development platform developed by Microsoft. The framework was meant to create applications, which would run on the Windows Platform. The first version of the .NET framework was released in the year 2002.

159. *.edu:* Top level domain for education.

160. *.com:* It is the most common and most recognised domain suffix. It stands for "commercial" and is used by mostly commercial websites. However, anyone who wants to register a domain name can register a name ending in .com, whether their site is going to be used for commercial purposes or not.

161. ***Web 2.0 Applications:*** Web 2.0 is the term used to describe a variety of websites and applications that allow anyone to create and share online information or material they have created. A key element of the technology is that it allows people to create, share, collaborate, and communicate. Web 2.0 differs from other types of websites as it does not require any web design or publishing skills to participate, making it easy for people to create and publish or communicate their work to the world. Web 2.0 examples include hosted services (Google Maps),Web applications (Google Docs, Flickr), Video sharing sites (YouTube), wikis (MediaWiki), blogs (WordPress), social networking (Facebook), folksonomies (Delicious), Microblogging (Twitter), podcasting (Podcast Alley), and content hosting services.

162. ***WhatsApp Messenger:*** It is a cross-platform instant messaging application that allows iPhone, BlackBerry, Android, Windows Phone, and Nokia smartphone users to exchange text, image, video, and audio messages for free.

163. ***Google Talk:*** It is Google's free chat and instant messaging application available on multiple platforms, including Android, Mac OS 10.5 or later, Linux, Windows (Server 2003, XP, and later) and Google Chrome OS. Google Talk also provides support for Voice over Internet Protocol (VoIP) or PC-to-PC calls. Mobile platforms, such as Android and BlackBerry, include Google Talk on most compatible devices. Google Talk is also known as Gtalk.

164. ***Viber:*** It is a free to download app that allows users to make free calls, send texts, pictures, and video messages to other Viber users. It works on both mobile and computer and can be used to connect with people around the world.

165. ***Decryption:*** Decryption is the process of taking encoded or encrypted text or other data and converting it back into text that the user or the computer can read and understand.

166. ***Encryption:*** It is the process of encoding a message or information in such a way that only authorised parties can access it and those who are not authorised cannot.

167. ***Google Chrome:*** It is a web browser which is based on the open source Chromium project. Google released Chrome in 2008 and issues several updates a year. It is available for Windows, Mac OS X, Linux, Android, and iOS operating systems. The Google Chrome browser takes a sandboxing-based approach to Web security. Each open website runs as its own process, which helps prevent malicious code on one page from affecting others (or the computer operating system at large). The browser also supports Web standards such as HTML5 and cascading style sheets (CSS).

168. ***Bing:*** It is a search engine from Microsoft that was launched on May 28, 2009. Microsoft calls it a "Decision Engine," because it's designed to return search results in a format that organises answers to address your needs. When you search on Bing, in addition to providing relevant search results, the search engine also shows a list of related searches on the left-hand side of the Search Engine Results Pages (SERP). You can also access a quick link to see recent search history. Bing uses technology from a company called Powerset, which Microsoft acquired.

169. ***Yahoo:*** It is an Internet portal that incorporates a search engine and a directory of World Wide Websites organised in a hierarchy of topic categories. As a directory, it provides both new and seasoned Web users the reassurance of a structured view of hundreds of thousands of websites and millions of Web pages. It also provides one of the best ways to search the Web for a given topic. Since Yahoo is associated with the most popular Web search sites, if a search argument doesn't lead to a Yahoo topic page, it will still lead to results from the six or seven popular search engine sites Yahoo links to.

170. ***Google:*** It is a multinational, publicly-traded organisation built around the company's hugely popular search engine. Google's other enterprises include Internet analytics, cloud computing, advertising technologies, and Web app, browser, and operating system development.

171. ***TCP (Transmission Control Protocol):*** It is a standard that defines how to establish and maintain a network conversation via which application programs can exchange data. TCP works with the Internet Protocol (IP), which defines how computers send packets of data to each other.

172. ***Netiquette:*** It is etiquette guidelines for posting messages to online services, and particularly Internet newsgroups. It is also called Internet Ethical protocol.

173. ***Webmercial:*** It is an online video commercial that promotes a service or product.

174. ***Network Society:*** It is the expression coined in 1991 related to the social, political, economic and cultural changes caused by the spread of networked, digital information and communications technologies. The term network society was coined by Jan van Dijk in his 1991 Dutch book De Netwerkmaatschappij (The Network Society) and by Manuel Castells in The Rise of the Network Society (1996), the first part of his trilogy The Information Age.

175. ***Solaris:*** It is the computer operating system that Sun Microsystems provides for its family of Scalable Processor Architecture-based processors as well as for Intel-based processors. Sun has historically dominated the large UNIX workstation market. As the Internet grew in the early 1990s, Sun's SPARC/Solaris systems became the most widely installed servers for websites.

176. ***.doc:*** It is shorthand for a word document. It is a file extension associated with WordPad and other word processing programs. Microsoft Word is a good example of a word processor that can view .doc files.

177. ***txt file:*** It is a standard text document that contains unformatted text. It is recognised by any text editing or word processing program and can also be processed by most other software programs. TXT files are often created and opened using Microsoft Notepad and Apple TextEdit.

178. ***Simple Mail Transfer Protocol (SMTP):*** It is a protocol for sending email messages between servers. Most email systems that send mail over the Internet use SMTP to send messages from one server to another; the messages can then be retrieved with an email client using either POP or IMAP.

179. ***Apache HTTP Server:*** It is an open-source and free web server software that powers around 46% of websites around the world. The official name is Apache HTTP Server, and it's maintained and developed by the Apache Software Foundation.

180. ***Fedora Linux:*** It is a popular open source Linux-based operating system. Fedora is designed as a secure, general purpose operating system. Fedora is said to be the second-most commonly used Linux distribution, after Ubuntu.

181. ***Ubuntu:*** It is an open source Linux operating system. Ubuntu is considered a good for beginners. The operating system was intended primarily for personal computers (PCs) but it can also be used on servers. The word "ubuntu" is from the African Zulu language and translates as "humanity to others."

182. ***Open Source Operating System:*** It is an operating system that uses code that is freely-distributed and available to anyone to use, even for commercial purposes. Examples: Apache HTTP, Android, Mozilla Firefox, Linux, OpenOffice, Mozilla Thunderbird, and WordPress.

183. ***Closed-Source:*** Operating systems that use code that is proprietary and kept secret to prevent its use by other entities. Traditionally, they are sold for a profit.

184. ***Router:*** It is a physical or virtual appliance that passes information between two or more packet-switched computer networks. A router inspects a given data packet's destination, Internet Protocol address (IP address), calculates the best way for it to reach its destination, and then forwards it accordingly. A router is a common type of gateway. It is positioned where two or more networks meet at each point of presence on the Internet.

185. ***Switch:*** In the context of networking, it is a high-speed device that receives incoming data packets and redirects them to their destination on a local area network (LAN).

Practice Exercise

General Questions Format

1. Which of the following is TRUE about Telecommunications? It ________.
   (A) needs an electronic medium for communication
   (B) is a communication over long distances
   (C) involves communication about Telebrands
   (D) All of the above

2. Nibble is a/an ________.
   (A) software
   (B) zooming device
   (C) unit of measurement
   (D) processor

3. TPS stands for ________ Process System.
   (A) Total (B) Transaction
   (C) Terminal (D) Technology

4. Computer virus is a/an ________.
   (A) disorder (B) file
   (C) program (D) command

5. Which signals are received and transmitted by a satellite?
   (A) Radio (B) Television
   (C) Remote sensing (D) All of the above

6. Yahoo helps in
   (A) assembling a computer.
   (B) playing multimedia.
   (C) international communication.
   (D) All of the above

7. Antivirus software is used to ________ a virus.
   (A) destroy (B) stop
   (C) reverse (D) ignore

8. Which of the following is a programming language?
   (A) WAN (B) PABX
   (C) CBT (D) ALGOL

9. ROM stands for
   (A) Read on Memory
   (B) Revise only Memory
   (C) Restore of Memory
   (D) None of these

10. A computer processing and storing a large amount of information of many users at the same time is called
    (A) Supercomputer (B) Mainframe
    (C) Macintosh (D) None of these

11. Another name of monitor is
    (A) VDU (B) VGA
    (C) RAM (D) LCD

12. A pixel contributes in making ________ in television or computer.
    (A) sound (B) picture
    (C) circuit (D) none of these

13. ISDN is a service of transmitting signals and that is used in ________.
    (A) telephones (B) computer
    (C) televisions (D) can't say

14. Plotter is a/an ________ device.
    (A) output (B) input
    (C) obsolete (D) none of the above

15. Solo santry is a/an
    (A) processor (B) computer
    (C) antivirus (D) multimedia device

16. Mosaic has been original creator of
    (A) pop-ups (B) WWW
    (C) Java (D) bug

17. When a computer appears to do nothing, it is in the state of ________.
    (A) churning (B) prodigy
    (C) portal (D) none of these

18. ICT devices compatible of wireless communication among them are ________ compatible devices.
    (A) nibble (B) payload
    (C) stylus (D) none of these

19. Which of the following is required for running a Blog?
    (A) Website (B) Write-up
    (C) Publishing (D) All of the above

20. DDR stands for
    (A) Data Double Rate (B) Direct Data Release
    (C) Double Data Rate (D) Detect Data Rate

21. BASIC is a computer ________.
    (A) bug (B) language
    (C) virus (D) none of these

22. Clipboard is a part of ________.
    (A) monitor (B) website
    (C) RAM (D) modem

23. Status of an Internet connection is tested by
(A) ALGOL (B) PING
(C) IP (D) TPS

24. Compressing a computer file is called
(A) Zip (B) Chip
(C) FAQ (D) Firewall

25. Norton is a/an ______.
(A) website (B) processor
(C) antivirus (D) none of these

KEY

1. B	**2.** C	**3.** B	**4.** C	**5.** D	**6.** C	**7.** B
8. D	**9.** D	**10.** B	**11.** A	**12.** B	**13.** A	**14.** A
15. C	**16.** B	**17.** A	**18.** D	**19.** D	**20.** C	**21.** B
22. C	**23.** B	**24.** A	**25.** C			

Assertion–Reason Format

1. **Assertion (A):** The cache contains information stored by a web browser on the hard disk.

Reason (R): One does not have to download the same material again and again.

(A) Both A and R are true and R is correct explanation of A
(B) Both A and R are true but R is not correct explanation of A
(C) A is true but R is false
(D) A is false but R is true

2. **Assertion (A):** Every website has a homepage.

Reason (R): Homepage is mandatory for every website.

(A) Both A and R are true and R is correct explanation of A
(B) Both A and R are true but R is not correct explanation of A
(C) Both A and R are false
(D) A is true but R is false

3. **Assertion (A):** Macintosh computer is popular in the field of accounting and finance.

Reason (R): Macintosh was introduced in 1984 to take over a typical computer field.

(A) Both A and R are true and R is correct explanation of A
(B) A is false but R is true
(C) Both A and R are true but R is not correct explanation of A
(D) A is true but R is false

4. **Assertion (A):** Media Lab Asia is an Internet initiative by India.

Reason (R): Indians want to avail the most advanced benefits of Internet.

(A) Both A and R are true and R is correct explanation of A
(B) Both A and R are true but R is not correct explanation of A
(C) A is true but R is false
(D) A is false but R is true

5. **Assertion (A):** Touchpad in a laptop acts as a computer mouse.

Reason (R): A laptop without a touchpad needs an external mouse.

(A) A is true but R is false
(B) A is false but R is true
(C) Both A and R are true and R is correct explanation of A
(D) Both A and R are true but R is not correct explanation of A

6. **Assertion (A):** Downloading is an integral feature of a computer.

Reason (R): Majority of Internet operations belong to downloading.

(A) Both A and R are true and R is correct explanation of A
(B) Both A and R are true but R is not correct explanation of A
(C) A is true but R is false
(D) Both A and R are false

7. **Assertion (A):** Macro virus is a relatively less harmful virus.

Reason (R): There is insertion of unwanted comic text while typing normal text.

(A) Both A and R are true and R is correct explanation of A
(B) Both A and R are true but R is not correct explanation of A
(C) A is true but R is false
(D) A is false but R is true

8. **Assertion (A):** Taskbar is a software used by architects.

Reason (R): A particular software is required to make a computer operation successful.

(A) Both A and R are true and R is correct explanation of A

(B) Both A and R are true but R is not correct explanation of A

(C) A is true but R is false

(D) A is false but R is true

9. **Assertion (A):** Rebooting of a computer saves it from strokes arising due to voltage fluctuation.

Reason (R): CPU of a computer controls the entire rebooting operation.

(A) Both A and R are true and R is correct explanation of A

(B) Both A and R are false

(C) Both A and R are true but R is not correct explanation of A

(D) A is true but R is false

10. **Assertion (A):** E-cycling is a rational step to prevent atmospheric pollution.

Reason (R): Electronic waste is reused rather than discarding it in the open at the end of its life cycle.

(A) Both A and R are true and R is correct explanation of A

(B) Both A and R are true but R is not correct explanation of A

(C) A is true but R is false

(D) A is false but R is true

11. **Assertion (A):** Spyware is an antivirus which protects a computer system from leakage of a user's personal information.

Reason (R): There are software which when installed in someone's computer extract one's personal information without one's knowledge.

(A) Both A and R are true and R is correct explanation of A

(B) Both A and R are true but R is not correct explanation of A

(C) A is false but R is true

(D) A is true but R is false

12. **Assertion (A):** Spam is the abuse of electronic messaging systems.

Reason (R): Spam has gained a commercial value over the past.

(A) Both A and R are true and R is correct explanation of A

(B) Both A and R are true but R is not correct explanation of A

(C) Both A and R are false

(D) A is true but R is false

13. **Assertion (A):** Windows XP is a software to make operations of a computer virus-free.

Reason (R): Microsoft Corporation has been launching various versions of Windows.

(A) Both A and R are false

(B) Both A and R are true and R is correct explanation of A

(C) A is true but R is false

(D) A is false but R is true

14. **Assertion (A):** Internet files are generally compressed or zipped.

Reason (R): Compressed files take up less hard drive space and takes less time to transfer to another computer.

(A) A is true but R is false

(B) A is false but R is true

(C) Both A and R are true but R is not correct explanation of A

(D) Both A and R are true and R is correct explanation of A

15. **Assertion (A):** A virtual university provides higher education programs through electronic media, typically the Internet .

Reason (R): The first virtual university in India was set up in Tamil Nadu.

(A) Both A and R are true and R is correct explanation of A

(B) Both A and R are true but R is not correct explanation of A

(C) A is true but R is false

(D) A is false but R is true

16. **Assertion (A):** MMS includes text, audio, and video messages.

Reason (R): Transfer of data from mobile phone to an email address has been made possible due to introduction of MMS service.

(A) Both A and R are true and R is correct explanation of A

(B) A is true but R is false

(C) Both A and R are true but R is not correct explanation of A

(D) A is false but R is true

17. **Assertion (A):** Virtual reality is the presence of reality on a computer screen through stimulators.

Reason (R): Users are acquainted with the concept of telepresence through virtual reality.

(A) Both A and R are true and R is correct explanation of A

(B) Both A and R are true but R is not correct explanation of A

(C) Both A and R are false

(D) A is false but R is true

18. **Assertion (A):** FTP is a computer software to clear virus-corrupted files and transfer them to a safer hard disk.

Reason (R): Files are transferred from a computer to a network under a protocol.

(A) Both A and R are true and R is correct explanation of A

(B) Both A and R are true but R is not correct explanation of A

(C) A is true but R is false

(D) A is false but R is true

19. **Assertion (A):** Opening of web browser is governed under HTTP.

Reason (R): Hypertext Transfer Protocol is the set of rules for transferring files on the World Wide Web.

(A) Both A and R are true and R is correct explanation of A

(B) Both A and R are true but R is not correct explanation of A

(C) A is true but R is false

(D) Both A and R are false

20. **Assertion (A):** Ethernet is a communication device in the computer to build a network other than LAN.

Reason (R): Ethernet was designed by Microsoft Corporation in 1997.

(A) Both A and R are true and R is correct explanation of A

(B) Both A and R are true but R is not correct explanation of A

(C) A is true but R is false

(D) Both A and R are false

KEY

1. A	2. C	3. B	4. A	5. A	6. D	7. A
8. D	9. B	10. A	11. C	12. B	13. A	14. D
15. B	16. B	17. C	18. D	19. A	20. D	

Questions Asked in Previous NET Exams

1. Which of the following best describes the wiki? **(UGC NET JUNE 2019)**

(A) A system that allows users to add information on to a website but does not change any pre-existing information.

(B) A system that allows collaborative modification of its content and structure directly from the web browser.

(C) A system that serves as a publically accessible personal journal for an individual.

(D) A system that monitors the modification of content within a blog.

2. Which is spyware with respect to computer software? **(UGC NET JUNE 2019)**

(A) Software that aims to gather information about a person without his/her knowledge and that may send such information to another entity.

(B) Legitimate software that allows companies to monitor and supervise the computers of their employees from a central location.

(C) Software used to disrupt computer operation or gain access to private computer systems.

(D) A computer program hidden within another seemingly harmless program that produces copies of itself and inserts them into another programs or files.

3. Anjali's teacher uses VLE, a software tool design to deliver courses online. The acronym VLE stands for **(UGC NET JUNE 2019)**

(A) Video Learning Environment

(B) Visual Learning Environment

(C) Virtual Learning Environment

(D) Visual Local Environment

4. A/An__________is a computer programme that spreads by inserting copies of itself into other executable codes or documents.

(A) operating system (B) computer virus

(C) firewall (D) antivirus

5. Match the following: **(UGC NET JUNE 2019)**

Set I	**Set II**
a) First Generation	i) Transistor
b) Second Generation	ii) VLSI microprocessor
c) Third Generation	iii) Vacuum tube
d) Fourth Generation	iv) Integrated circuit

Select the correct option from the following

	(a)	(b)	(c)	(d)
(A)	iii	iv	i	ii
(B)	iii	i	iv	ii
(C)	iii	i	ii	iv
(D)	i	iii	iv	ii

6. Which of the following is not a/an web browser? **(UGC NET JUNE 2019)**
(A) Internet Explorer
(B) Mozilla Firefox
(C) Google Chrome
(D) Yahoo

7. Which of the following file format is not a video file format? **(UGC NET JUNE 2019)**
(A) .AW (B) .MOV
(C) .MP4 (D) .JPEG

8. Which of the following is most suitable for being designated as Fourth Generation language?
(A) ALGOL (B) Java
(C) C (D) SQL

9. Which of the following are audio formats? **(UGC NET DECEMBER 2018)**
(a) .wav (b) .aac
(c) .wmv (d) .fiv
Codes:
(A) (b) and (c) (B) (a) and (b)
(C) (a) and (d) (D) (c) and (d)

10. A small text stored on a user's computer by some websites in order to recognise and keep track of user's preferences is called: **(UGC NET DECEMBER 2018)**
(A) Cookie (B) Report
(C) Log (D) History

11. Which of the following statement(s) is/are true with regard to websites? **(UGC NET JULY 2018)**
P: A blog is a website that consists of posts in reverse chronological order.
Q: A wiki is a website that is designed to allow people to collaborate easily.
Choose the correct answer from the following:
(A) P only (B) Q only
(C) Both P and Q (D) Neither P nor Q

12. With regard to computer memory, which of the following statement(s) is/are TRUE?
P: Read-Only Memory (ROM) is 'volatile' memory.
Q: Random Access Memory (RAM) is 'volatile' memory.
R: Secondary memory is 'volatile' memory. **(UGC NET JULY 2018)**
(A) P only (B) Q only
(C) P and Q only (D) P and R only

13. What is the full form of USB as used in computer related activities? **(UGC NET NOVEMBER 2017)**
(A) Universal Security Block
(B) Universal Serial Bus
(C) United Serial Bus
(D) Ultra Security Block

14. What is the name of a webpage address? **(UGC NET NOVEMBER 2017)**
(A) Directory (B) Protocol
(C) URL (D) Domain

15. Which of the following domains is used for profit businesses? **(UGC NET NOVEMBER 2017)**
(A) .net (B) .edu
(C) .com (D) .org

16. With regard to a word processing software, the process of combining static information in a publication together with variable information in a data source to create one merged publication is called **(UGC NET JANUARY 2017)**
(A) Electronic mail (B) Data sourcing
(C) Mail merge (D) Spam mail

17. DVD technology uses an optical media to store the digital data. DVD is an acronym for **(UGC NET JANUARY 2017)**
(A) Digital Vector Disc
(B) Digital Volume Disc
(C) Digital Versatile Disc
(D) Digital Visualization Disc

18. Which of the following is a characteristic of Web 2.0 applications?

(UGC NET JANUARY 2017)

(A) Multiple users schedule their time to use Web 2.0 applications one by one.

(B) Web 2.0 applications are focused on the ability for people to collaborate and share information online.

(C) Web 2.0 applications provide users with content rather than facilitating users to create it.

(D) Web 2.0 applications use only static pages.

19. Random Access Memory (RAM), a form of computer storage, is a ______ memory.

(UGC NET AUGUST 2016)

(A) non-volatile (B) volatile

(C) permanent (D) secondary

20. In computer networking, HTTP is referred to as a stateless protocol as servers do not maintain any information about past client requests. HTTP is an acronym for

(UGC NET AUGUST 2016)

(A) Hyper Text Translation Protocol

(B) Hypertext Transfer Protocol

(C) High Terabyte Transfer Protocol

(D) Hypervisor Test Translation Protocol

21. The software used to navigate through the web is known as **(UGC NET AUGUST 2016)**

(A) Website (B) Web browser

(C) Internet (D) World Wide Web

22. ______ is a type of memory circuitry that holds the computer's start-up routine.

(UGC NET JULY 2016)

(A) RIM (Read Initial Memory)

(B) RAM (Random Access Memory)

(C) ROM (Read-Only Memory)

(D) Cache Memory

23. An ASCII is a character-encoding scheme that is employed by personal computers in order to represent various characters, numbers, and control keys that the computer user selects on the keyboard. ASCII is an acronym for

(UGC NET JULY 2016)

(A) American Standard Code for Information Interchange

(B) American Standard Code for Intelligent Information

(C) American Standard Code for Information Integrity

(D) American Standard Code for Isolated Information

24. The process of copying files to a CD-ROM is known as ______. **(UGC NET JULY 2016)**

(A) Burning (B) Zipping

(C) Digitising (D) Ripping

25. An unsolicited email message sent to many recipients at once is a ______

(UGC NET JULY 2016)

(A) Worm (B) Virus

(C) Threat (D) Spam

26. Which of the following is an open source software? **(UGC NET DECEMBER 2015)**

(A) MS Word (B) Windows

(C) Mozilla Firefox (D) Acrobat Reader

27. Which of the following enables us to send the same letter to different persons in MS Word?

(UGC NET DECEMBER 2015)

(A) Mail join (B) Mail copy

(C) Mail insert (D) Mail merge

28. Which of the following is an instant messaging application? **(UGC NET DECEMBER 2015)**

(a) WhatsApp (b) Google Talk

(c) Viber

Select the correct answer from the codes given below:

(A) (a) and (b) only (B) (b) and (c) only

(C) (a) only (D) (a), (b), and (c)

29. Which of the following is not open source software? **(UGC NET JUNE 2015)**

(A) Apache HTTP server

(B) Internet Explorer

(C) Fedora Linux

(D) OpenOffice

30. Encoding or scrambling data for transmission across a network is known as:

(UGC NET JUNE 2015)

(A) Decryption (B) Protection

(C) Detection (D) Encryption

31. Which is an instant messenger that is used for chatting? **(UGC NET JUNE 2015)**

(A) Google Talk (B) AltaVista

(C) MAC (D) Microsoft Office

32. CSS stands for (UGC NET DECEMBER 2014)
(A) Cascading Style Sheets
(B) Collecting Style Sheets
(C) Comparative Style Sheets
(D) Comprehensive Style Sheets

33. MOOC stands for (UGC NET DECEMBER 2014)
(A) Media Online Open Course
(B) Massachusetts Open Online Course
(C) Massive Open Online Course
(D) Myriad Open Online Course

34. gif, jpg, bmp, and png are used as extensions for files which store (UGC NET DECEMBER 2014)
(A) Audio data (B) Image data
(C) Video data (D) Text data

35. Digital empowerment means (UGC NET DECEMBER 2014)
(i) Universal digit literacy
(ii) Universal access to all digital resources
(iii) Collaborative digital platform for participative governance
(iv) Probability of all entitlements for individuals through cloud

Choose the correct answer from the codes given below:
(A) (i) and (ii) only
(B) (ii) and (iii) only
(C) (i), (ii), and (iii) only
(D) (i), (ii), (iii), and (iv)

36. Which one of the following is not a search engine? (UGC NET DECEMBER 2014)
(A) Google (B) Chrome
(C) Yahoo (D) Bing

37. The acronym FTP stands for (UGC NET JUNE 2014)
(A) File Transfer Protocol
(B) Fast Transfer Protocol
(C) File Tracking Protocol
(D) File Transfer Procedure

38. Which one of the following is not a/an image/graphic file format? (UGC NET JUNE 2014)
(A) PNG (B) GIF
(C) BMP (D) GUI

39. The first web browser is (UGC NET JUNE 2014)
(A) Internet Explorer (B) Netscape
(C) World Wide Web (D) Firefox

40. When a computer is booting, BIOS is loaded to the memory by
(A) RAM (B) ROM
(C) CD-ROM (D) TCP

41. Which one of the following is not the same as the other three? (UGC NET JUNE 2014)
(A) MAC address (B) Hardware address
(C) Physical address (D) IP address

42. Identify the IP address from the following:
(A) 300 215 317 3 (B) 302.215@ 417 5
(C) 202.50.20.148 (D) 202 - 50 - 20 - 148 Q

43. Internal communication within institutions is done through (UGC NET DECEMBER 2013)
(A) LAN (B) WAN
(C) EBB (D) MMS

44. Virtual reality provides (UGC NET DECEMBER 2013)
(A) Sharp pictures
(B) Individual audio
(C) Participatory experience
(D) Preview of new films

45. The first virtual university of India came up in (UGC NET DECEMBER 2013)
(A) Andhra Pradesh (B) Maharashtra
(C) Uttar Pradesh (D) Tamil Nadu

46. GIF stands for (UGC NET SEPTEMBER 2013)
(A) Global Information Format
(B) Graphics Information Format
(C) Graphics Interchange File
(D) Graphics Interchange Format

47. The Internet ethical protocol is called ___. (UGC NET SEPTEMBER 2013)
(A) net protocol (B) netiquette
(C) net ethics (D) net morality

48. Commercial messages on the net are identified as (UGC NET SEPTEMBER 2013)
(A) Net ads
(B) Internet commercials
(C) Webmercials
(D) Viral advertisements

49. Manuel Castells was the first to use the term **(UGC NET SEPTEMBER 2013)**
(A) Internet society (B) Electronic society
(C) Network society (D) Telematic society

50. Which one of the following is not an operating system? **(UGC NET SEPT. 2013)**
(A) IBM AIX (B) Linux
(C) Sun Solaris (D) Firefox

51. A computer program that translates a program statement by statement into machine language is called a/an **(UGC NET JUNE 2013)**
(A) Compiler (B) Simulator
(C) Translator (D) Interpreter

52. Compiler is a software which converts ______. **(UGC NET JUNE 2013)**
(A) characters to bits
(B) high level language to machine language
(C) machine language to high level language
(D) words to bits

53. Virtual memory is **(UGC NET JUNE 2013)**
(A) an extremely large main memory.
(B) an extremely large secondary memory.
(C) an illusion of extremely large main memory.
(D) a type of memory used in supercomputers.

54. 'WWW' stands for **(UGC NET JUNE 2013)**
(A) work with web (B) word wide web
(C) world wide web (D) worth while web

55. A hard disk is divided into tracks which is further subdivided into **(UGC NET JUNE 2013)**
(A) Clusters (B) Sectors
(C) Vectors (D) Heads

56. ALU stands for **(UGC NET DECEMBER 2012)**
(A) American Logic Unit
(B) Alternate Local Unit
(C) Alternating Logic Unit
(D) Arithmetic-Logic Unit

57. Computer virus is a **(UGC NET DECEMBER 2012)**
(A) Hardware (B) Bacteria
(C) Software (D) None of these

58. The file extension of MS-Word document in Office 2007 is ______. **(UGC NET DECEMBER 2012)**
(A) .pdf (B) .doc
(C) .docx (D) .txt

59. ______ is a protocol used by email clients to download emails to your computer. **(UGC NET DECEMBER 2012)**
(A) TCP (B) FTP
(C) SMTP (D) POP

60. TCP/IP is necessary if one is to connect to the **(UGC NET JUNE 2012)**
(A) Phone lines (B) LAN
(C) Internet (D) Server

61. Each character on the keyboard of computer has an ASCII value which stands for **(UGC NET JUNE 2012)**
(A) American Stock Code for Information Interchange
(B) American Standard Code for Information Interchange
(C) African Standard Code for Information Interchange
(D) Adaptable Standard Code for Information Change

62. Which of the following is not a programming language? **(UGC NET JUNE 2012)**
(A) Pascal (B) Microsoft Office
(C) Java (D) C++

63. Internet Explorer is a type of **(UGC NET JUNE 2012)**
(A) Operating system (B) Compiler
(C) Browser (D) IP address

64. POP3 and IMAP are email accounts in which **(UGC NET JUNE 2012)**
(A) One automatically gets one's mail everyday
(B) One has to be connected to the server to read or write one's mail
(C) One only has to be connected to the server to send and receive email
(D) One does not need any telephone lines

65. HTML is used to create ____. **(UGC NET DECEMBER 2011)**
(A) machine language program
(B) high level program
(C) web page
(D) web server

66. The term DNS stands for **(UGC NET DECEMBER 2011)**
(A) Domain Name System
(B) Defense Nuclear System
(C) Downloadable New Software
(D) Dependent Name Server

67. IPv4 and IPv6 are addresses used to identify computers on the Internet. Find the correct statement out of the following:
(UGC NET DECEMBER 2011)
(A) Number of bits required for IPv4 address is more than number of bits required for IPv6 address.
(B) Number of bits required for IPv4 address is same as number of bits required for IPv6 address.
(C) Number of bits required for IPv4 address is less than number of bits required for IPv6 address.
(D) Number of bits required for IPv4 address is 64.

68. High level programming language can be converted to machine language using which of the following?
(UGC NET DECEMBER 2011)
(A) Oracle (B) Compiler
(C) Mat lab (D) Assembler

69. DNS in Internet technology stands for
(UGC NET JUNE 2011)
(A) Dynamic Name System
(B) Domain Name System
(C) Distributed Name System
(D) None of these

70. HTML stands for **(UGC NET JUNE 2011)**
(A) Hypertext Markup Language
(B) Hyper Text Manipulation Language
(C) Hyper Text Managing Links
(D) Hyper Text Manipulating Links

71. Which of the following is type of LAN?
(UGC NET JUNE 2011)
(A) Ethernet (B) Token Ring
(C) FDDI (D) All of the above

72. Which of the following statements is true?
(UGC NET JUNE 2011)
(A) Smart cards do not require an operating system.
(B) Smart cards and PCs use some operating system.
(C) COS is a smart card operating system.
(D) The communication between the reader and the card is in full duplex mode.

73. S/MIME in Internet technology stands for
(UGC NET DECEMBER 2010)
(A) Secure Multipurpose Internet Mail Extensions
(B) Secure Multimedia Internet Mail Extension
(C) Simple Multipurpose Internet Mail Extension
(D) Simple Multimedia Internet Mail Extension

74. Which one of the following is not an Internet Service Provider (ISP)?
(UGC NET DECEMBER 2010)
(A) MTNL (B) BSNL
(C) ERNET India (D) Infotech India Ltd

75. The set of computer programs that manage the hardware/software of a computer is called
(UGC NET DECEMBER 2010)
(A) Compiler system
(B) Operation system
(C) Operating system
(D) None of these

76. Which one of the following is an example of operating system? **(UGC NET JUNE 2010)**
(A) Microsoft Word (B) Microsoft Excel
(C) Microsoft Access (D) Microsoft Windows

77. Which one of the following is different from other members? **(UGC NET JUNE 2010)**
(A) Google (B) Windows
(C) Linux (D) Mac

78. Bit stands for **(UGC NET DECEMBER 2009)**
(A) Binary information term
(B) Binary digit
(C) Binary tree
(D) Bivariate theory

79. Which one of the following is not a linear data structure? **(UGC NET DECEMBER 2009)**
(A) Array (B) Binary tree
(C) Queue (D) Stack

80. Which one of the following is not a network device? **(UGC NET DECEMBER 2009)**
(A) Router (B) Switch
(C) Hub (D) CPU

81. Which of the following is not related to information security on the Internet?
(UGC NET DECEMBER 2009)
(A) Data encryption
(B) Water marking
(C) Data hiding
(D) Information retrieval

82. What do you need to put your web pages on the WWW? **(UGC NET JUNE 2009)**
(A) A connection to Internet
(B) A web browser
(C) A web server
(D) All of the above

83. What is blog? **(UGC NET JUNE 2009)**
(A) Online music
(B) Intranet
(C) A personal or corporate website in the form of an online journal
(D) A personal or corporate Google search

84. Firewalls are used to protect a communication system against ______. **(UGC NET DEC. 2008)**
(A) unauthorised attacks
(B) virus attacks
(C) data-driven attacks
(D) fire attacks

85. The accounting software "Tally" was developed by **(UGC NET DECEMBER 2008)**
(A) HCL (B) TCS
(C) Infosys (D) Wipro

86. Errors in a computer programme are called **(UGC NET DECEMBER 2008)**
(A) Follies (B) Mistakes
(C) Bugs (D) Spam

87. HTML is basically used to design **(UGC NET DECEMBER 2008)**
(A) Web page (B) Websites
(C) Graphics (D) Tables and frames

88. Information, a combination of graphics, text, sound, and animation is called **(UGC NET DECEMBER 2008)**
(A) Multiprogramme (B) Multifacet
(C) Multimedia (D) Multiprocess

89. WYSIWYG - describes the display of a document on screen as it will actually print: **(UGC NET JUNE 2008)**
(A) What you state is what you get
(B) What you see is what you get
(C) What you save is what you get
(D) What you suggest is what you get

90. Which of the following is not a computer language? **(UGC NET JUNE 2008)**
(A) PASCAL (B) UNIX
(C) FORTRAN (D) COBOL

91. A keyboard has at least **(UGC NET JUNE 2008)**
(A) 91 keys (B) 101 keys
(C) 111 keys (D) 121 keys

92. CoralDRAW is a popular **(UGC NET JUNE 2008)**
(A) Illustration programme
(B) Programming language
(C) Text programme
(D) None of the above

93. CD-ROM stands for **(UGC NET DECEMBER 2007)**
(A) Computer Disk Read Only Memory
(B) Compact Disk Read Over Memory
(C) Compact-Disc Read-Only Memory
(D) Computer Disk Read Over Memory

94. WWW represents **(UGC NET DECEMBER 2007)**
(A) who what and where
(B) weird wide web
(C) word wide web
(D) world wide web

95. Data can be saved on backing storage medium known as: **(UGC NET DECEMBER 2007)**
(A) Compact Disk Recordable
(B) Computer Disk Rewritable
(C) Compact Disk Rewritable
(D) Computer Data Rewritable

96. RAM means: **(UGC NET DECEMBER 2007)**
(A) Random Access Memory
(B) Rigid Access Memory
(C) Rapid Access Memory
(D) Revolving Access Memory

97. Which part of the Central Processing Unit (CPU) performs calculations and makes decisions? **(UGC NET JUNE 2007)**
(A) Arithmetic-Logic Unit
(B) Alternating Logic Unit
(C) Alternate Local Unit
(D) American Local Unit

98. "Dpi" stands for **(UGC NET JUNE 2007)**
(A) Dots per inch
(B) Digits per unit
(C) Dots pixel inch
(D) Diagrams per inch

99. The process of laying out a document with text, graphics, headlines, and photographs is involved in **(UGC NET JUNE 2007)**
(A) Deck Top Publishing
(B) Desk Top Printing
(C) Desktop Publishing
(D) Deck Top Printing

100. Transfer of data from one application to another line is called **(UGC NET JUNE 2007)**
(A) Dynamic Disc Exchange
(B) Dodgy Data Change
(C) Dogmatic Data Exchange
(D) Dynamic Data Exchange

101. LAN stands for: **(UGC NET DECEMBER 2006)**
(A) Local And National
(B) Local Area Network
(C) Large Area Network
(D) Live Area Network

102. Which of the following statement is correct? **(UGC NET DECEMBER 2006)**
(A) Modem is a software.
(B) Modem helps in stabilising the voltage.
(C) Modem is an operating system.
(D) Modem converts the analog signal into digital signal and vice versa.

103. Networked media exist in interconnected _____. **(UGC NET JUNE 2006)**
(A) social environments
(B) economic environments
(C) political environments
(D) technological environments

104. The combination of computing, telecommunications, and media in a digital atmosphere is referred to as: **(UGC NET JUNE 2006)**
(A) online communication
(B) integrated media
(C) digital combine
(D) convergence

105. Using websites to pour out one's grievances is called: **(UGC NET JUNE 2006)**
(A) cyber venting (B) cyber ranting
(C) web point (D) web plea

106. In web search, finding a large number of documents with very little relevant information is termed: **(UGC NET JUNE 2006)**
(A) poor recall
(B) web crawl
(C) poor precision rate
(D) poor web response

107. The concept of connect intelligence is derived from: **(UGC NET JUNE 2006)**
(A) virtual reality
(B) fuzzy logic
(C) Bluetooth technology
(D) value-added networks

108. Use of an ordinary telephone as an Internet appliance is called: **(UGC NET JUNE 2006)**
(A) voice net (B) voice telephone
(C) voice line (D) voice portal

109. Video transmission over the Internet that looks like delayed live casting is called: **(UGC NET JUNE 2006)**
(A) Virtual video (B) Direct broadcast
(C) Video shift (D) Real-time video

110. 'SITE' stands for: **(UGC NET JUNE 2006)**
(A) System for International Technology and Engineering
(B) Satellite Instructional Television Experiment
(C) South Indian Trade Estate
(D) State Institute of Technology and Engineering

KEY

1. B	**2.** A	**3.** C	**4.** B	**5.** B	**6.** D	**7.** D
8. D	**9.** B	**10.** A	**11.** C	**12.** B	**13.** B	**14.** C
15. C	**16.** C	**17.** C	**18.** B	**19.** B	**20.** B	**21.** B
22. C	**23.** A	**24.** A	**25.** D	**26.** C	**27.** D	**28.** D
29. B	**30.** D	**31.** A	**32.** A	**33.** C	**34.** B	**35.** D
36. B	**37.** B	**38.** D	**39.** B	**40.** B	**41.** D	**42.** C
43. A	**44.** C	**45.** D	**46.** D	**47.** B	**48.** C	**49.** C
50. D	**51.** A	**52.** B	**53.** C	**54.** C	**55.** B	**56.** D
57. C	**58.** C	**59.** D	**60.** C	**61.** B	**62.** B	**63.** C
64. C	**65.** C	**66.** A	**67.** C	**68.** B	**69.** B	**70.** A
71. D	**72.** B	**73.** A	**74.** D	**75.** C	**76.** D	**77.** A
78. B	**79.** B	**80.** D	**81.** B	**82.** D	**83.** C	**84.** A
85. B	**86.** C	**87.** A	**88.** C	**89.** B	**90.** B	**91.** B
92. D	**93.** C	**94.** D	**95.** C	**96.** A	**97.** A	**98.** A
99. C	**100.** D	**101.** B	**102.** D	**103.** D	**104.** D	**105.** A
106. A	**107.** D	**108.** C	**109.** D	**110.** B		

3 Fundamentals of Computer

INTRODUCTION

A computer is an electronic device used to process data and convert the data into information that is useful to the people. It is a programmable machine that can store, retrieve, and process data. It is controlled by programmed instructions. Computers come in various varieties, including personal computers, tiny computers, laptops, supercomputers, etc. A complete computer system consists of hardware, software, people, and data. A computer is based on the binary numbering system, which consists of just two unique numbers, 0 and 1. All operations that are possible in the decimal system (addition, subtraction, multiplication, and division) are equally possible in the binary system.

PARTS OF A COMPUTER

A complete computer system has four parts:

I) ***Hardware:*** The mechanical devices that make the computer are called hardware. In other words, hardware is any part of the computer that one can touch. For example, keyboard, printer, monitor, speakers, mouse devices, etc. Hardware consists of interconnected electronic devices that one can use to control the computer operations input and output.

II) ***Software:*** It is a set of electronic instructions consisting of complex codes (also known as programs) that makes the computer perform tasks. It means software tells the computer what to do.

III) ***Users:*** Computer operators are its users. No computer is totally autonomous.

IV) **Data:** Data consists of raw facts, which the computer stores and reads in the form of numbers. The computer manipulates data according to the instructions stored in the software and forwards it for use by people or another computer. Data can consist of numbers, letters, sounds, or images. Whatever type of data is entered into a computer, computer converts it into numbers, i.e., the entered data become digital.

Note:

> *A computer File is a set of data or program instructions that has been given a name*
>
> *A file that the user can open and use is called Document.*

Hardware Components

A computer contains four types of hardware components described as follows:

Processing Devices

1) ***Processor:*** Processor of a computer is like its "Brain" as it organises and carries out instructions that come from either the user or the software. In personal computers, the processor usually consists of one or more microprocessors (sometimes called 'chip'). Microprocessor is plugged into the motherboard of the computer.
2) ***Motherboard:*** It is a rigid rectangular board containing a number of tiny electronic and other components.
3) ***Central Processing Unit (CPU):*** It is the processor. It interprets and carries out the basic instructions that operates a computer. The CPU performs millions of calculations every second. The CPU contains the Control Unit and the Arithmetic-Logic Unit (ALU). Practically, Intel Pentium is the most important CPU. Other types include Intel Celeron, VIA Cyrix, and AMD Athlon. Today, all CPUs are microprocessors. (A microprocessor is a complete computer on a silicon chip.)

Memory

Memory is a temporary storage place for data, instructions, and information. When a program is launched, it is loaded into and run from memory. The most common type of memory is called Random Access Memory (RAM). It is also sometimes called read/write memory. Data are both written to and read from memory. RAM needs constant power supply.

Amount of RAM contained in a computer affects the speed and power of the computer. The more RAM a computer has, the faster it can perform certain tasks. The most common measurement unit for describing a computer's memory is Byte. Processor interprets data while these are in RAM. However, RAM is volatile, i.e., it loses its contents when the power is switched off from the computer. Data should be copied from RAM to the hard disk in order to save it. Though most of personal computers have 64 to 128 megabyte (MB) of RAM, yet amount of RAM required is according to the nature of job taken from a computer, i.e., for business users at least 64 MB and for multimedia and graphic applications at least 256 MB of RAM is required. RAM has two forms-Dynamic RAM (DRAM) and Static RAM (SRAM). SRAM is faster than DRAM.

Memory and Disc:

Both computer memory and disk space are measured in units of bytes or its multiples. But there is a difference between the two. For example "12800 KB RAM" refers to the amount of main memory the computer provides to its CPU whereas "128 MB disk" symbolises the amount of space that is available for the storage of files, data, and other types of permanent information.

Input and Output Devices

Input devices accept data and instructions from the user or from another computer system (such as a computer from the Internet).

Output devices return processed data back to the user or to another computer. Input devices include keyboard, mouse, trackballs, touchpads, joysticks, scanners, digital cameras, and microphones. A computer generates several types of outputs depending on the hardware and software being used in the computer. Output devices include monitor, printer, and speakers. Some types of hardware can act as both input and output devices. A major example of this type of device is touch screen, a type of monitor that displays text or icons one can touch. Touch screens are popular in museums and libraries.

Communication Devices:

Communication devices are devices that can act as both input and output devices, which connect one computer to the other. Process of such connection is called Networking. The most common of such devices include modem, a device which enables computers to communicate through telephone lines or cable television systems and Network Interface Cards (NICs).

Storage Devices

A computer, along with performing the functions of processing and presenting the data, also needs a place to store the program files containing vital information. The most common storage mediums are hard disk, magnetic disk, disk drive, floppy disk, Compact Disc Read-Only Memory (CD-ROM) drive-the most common type of storage device after hard disk, Compact Disc Recordable (CD-R) drive, Compact Disc-ReWritable (CD-RW), and Digital Video Disk (DVD).

Software Components

Software are the instructions for the computer. A series of instructions that perform a particular task is called a program. The two major categories of software are system software and application software.

1) ***System Software:*** It consists of programs that control the operation of the computer. It means that system software is the operating system of the computer. Examples of operating system include Windows XP, Windows 7, the Macintosh Operating System, UNIX, LINUX OS/2, DOS (Disk Operating System), Android, Windows 8,Windows 10 (NT), iphone, etc.
2) ***Application Software:*** It tells the computer how to accomplish specific tasks, such as word processing or drawing, for the user. Examples of popular application program include Microsoft Office (Word, Excel, PowerPoint), CorelDraw, AutoCAD, 7-Zip, Adobe Acrobat Pro, Adobe Reader, and Google Chrome.

CLASSIFICATION OF COMPUTERS

Computers can be classified based on the technology being used and the way they are designed to perform the various tasks. Computers can be categorised into digital, analog, and hybrid based on their design and working:

- **Digital Computers:** These are the modern computers which are capable of processing information in discrete form. In digital technology, data which can be in the form of letters, symbols, or numbers is represented in binary form, i.e., 0s and 1s. The digital computers are used in industrial, business, and scientific applications. They are quite suitable for large volume data processing.
- **Analog Computers:** These computers are used to process data generated by ongoing physical processes, i.e., these computers can be used to

process continuously varying data like temperature and pressure. Thermometer can be taken as an example of analog computer which measures continuous rise and fall in mercury level indicating change in temperature. Analog computers are well suited for simulating systems. A simulator helps to conduct experiments repeatedly in a real-time environment. Some of the common examples are simulations in aircrafts, nuclear power plants, and hydraulic and electronic networks.

- **Hybrid Computers:** These use both analog and digital technology. It has the speed of an analog computer and the accuracy of a digital computer. It may accept digital or analog signals but an extensive conversion of data from digital to analog and analog to digital has to be done. Hybrid computers are used as a cost-effective means for complex simulations.

Classification of Digital Computers

- **Microcomputers:** These are also known as personal computers. These types of digital computers use a microprocessor (a CPU on a single chip) and include both desktops and laptops. These computers can work on small volume of data, are very versatile, and can handle a variety of applications. These computers are being used as work stations, CAD, multimedia, and advertising applications.

  Example: portable computers such as PDAs (Personal Digital Assistants) and tablets
- **Minicomputers:** These computers can support multiple users working simultaneously on the same machine. These are mainly used in an organisation where computers installed in various departments are interconnected. These computers are useful for small business organisations.
- **Mainframes:** These computers are large and very powerful computers with very high memory capacity. These can process huge databases such as census at an extremely fast rate. They are suitable for big organisations, banks, industries, etc. and can support hundreds of users simultaneously on the network.
- **Supercomputers:** These are the fastest and very expensive computers. They can execute billions of instructions per second. These are multiprocessor, parallel systems suitable for specialised complex scientific applications involving huge amounts of mathematical applications such as weather forecasting.

MEASUREMENT OF COMPUTER MEMORY UNITS

Units of Memory

There are the following types of units of memory:

Bit

Byte

Kilobyte

Megabyte

Gigabyte

Terabyte

Petabyte

Exabyte

Zettabyte

Yottabyte

Bit: The computer memory units start from bit. A bit is the smallest memory unit to measure data stored in main memory and storage devices. A bit can have only one binary value out of 0 and 1.

Nibble: A nibble is four binary digits or half of an eight-bit byte. A nibble can be conveniently represented by one hexadecimal digit.

Byte: Byte is not a part of hardware but it is a unit of measuring the amount of RAM, i.e., amount of information a device can store. One byte is one character. A character can be a number, letter, or symbol. One byte consists of eight bits (binary digits). A bit is the smallest unit of information a computer can process. In computer systems, a unit of data that is eight binary digits long is known as a byte. A byte is abbreviated with a big "B" whereas a bit is abbreviated with a small "b". Computer storage is generally measured in multiples of byte. For example, a 640 MB hard drive holds a nominal 640 million bytes (or megabytes) of data. Byte multiples are made up of exponents of 2 and generally expressed as a "rounded off" decimal number. For example, two megabytes or 2 million bytes are actually 2, 097, 152 (decimal) bytes.

Word: A computer word, like a byte, is a group of fixed number of bits processed as a unit, which varies from computer to computer but is fixed for each computer. The length of a computer word is called word-size or word length. It may be as small as 8 bits or may be as long as 96 bits. A computer stores the information in the form of computer words.

Kilobyte: The kilobyte is the smallest unit of memory measurement but greater than a byte. A kilobyte is 10^3 or 1, 000 bytes abbreviated as 'K' or 'KB'. It antecedes the megabyte, which contains 1, 000, 000 bytes. One kilobyte is technically 1, 000 bytes, therefore, kilobytes are often used synonymously with kibibytes, which contain exactly 1, 024 bytes. This is approximately equal to one page of a textbook.

Kilobytes are mostly used to measure the size of small files. For example, a simple text document may contain 10 KB of data and therefore it would have a file size of 10 kilobytes. Graphics of small websites are often between 5 KB and 100 KB in size. Individual files typically take up a minimum of four kilobytes of disk space.

Megabyte: One megabyte is equal to 1, 000 KBs and antecedes the gigabyte (GB) unit of memory measurement. A megabyte is 10^6 or 1, 000, 000 bytes and is abbreviated as "MB". 1 MB is technically 1, 000, 000 bytes, therefore, megabytes are often used synonymously with mebibytes, which contain exactly 1, 048, 576 bytes (One million + characters). This is approximately equal to one book. Megabytes are mostly used to measure the size of large files. For example, a high resolution JPEG image might range in size from 1-5 megabytes. A 3-minute song saved in a compressed version may be roughly 3 MB in size, and the uncompressed version may take up to 30 MB of disk space. A compact disc's capacity is measured in megabytes (approx. 700 to 800 MB), whereas the capacity of most other forms of media drives, such as hard drives and flash drives, is generally measured in gigabytes or terabytes.

Gigabyte: One gigabyte is equal to 1, 000 MBs and precedes the terabyte (TB) unit of memory measurement. A gigabyte is 10^9 or 1, 000, 000, 000 bytes and is abbreviated as "GB". 1 GB is technically 1, 000, 000, 000 bytes, therefore, gigabytes are used synonymously with gibibytes, which contain exactly 1, 073, 741, 824 bytes (characters). This is approximately equal to a bunch of books in a bookstand. Gigabytes, are sometimes also abbreviated as "gigs" and are often used to measure a storage device's capacity, e.g., a standard DVD drive can hold 4.7 GBs of data. Storage devices that hold 1, 000 GB of data or more are measured in terabytes.

Terabyte: One terabyte is equal to 1, 000 GBs and precedes the petabyte (PB) unit of memory measurement. A terabyte is 10^{12} or 1, 000, 000, 000, 000 bytes and is abbreviated as "TB". 1 TB is technically 1 trillion bytes, therefore, terabytes and tebibytes are used synonymously, which contains exactly 1, 099, 511, 627, 776 bytes. This is approximately equal to an entire bookstand.

Mostly, the storage capacity of large storage devices is measured in terabytes. Around 2007, consumer hard drives reached a capacity of 1 terabytes. Now, HDDs are measured in terabytes, for e.g., a typical internal HDD may hold 2 terabytes of data whereas some servers and high-end workstations that contain multiple hard drives may even have a total storage capacity of over 10 terabytes.

Petabyte: One petabyte is equal to 1, 000 TBs and precedes the exabyte unit of memory measurement. A petabyte is 10^{15} or 1, 000, 000, 000, 000, 000 bytes and is abbreviated as "PB". A petabyte is lesser in size than a pebibyte, which contains exactly 1, 125, 899, 906, 842, 624 or (2^{50}) bytes.

Most of the storage devices can hold a maximum of a few TBs, therefore, petabytes are rarely used to measure memory capacity of a single device. Instead, PBs are used to measure the total data stored in large networks or server farms. For example, Internet giants like Google and Facebook store more than over 100 PBs of data on their data servers.

Exabyte: One exabyte is equal to 1, 000 PBs and precedes the zettabyte unit of memory measurement. An exabyte is 10^{18} or 1, 000, 000, 000, 000, 000, 000 bytes and is abbreviated as "EB". Exabytes are lesser than exbibytes, which contain exactly 1, 152, 921, 504, 606, 846, 976 or (2^{60}) bytes.

The exabyte unit of memory measurement is so large, that it is not used to measure the capacity of storage devices. Even the data storage capacity of the biggest cloud storage centres is measured in PBs, which is a fraction of 1 EB. Instead, exabytes measure the amount of data over multiple data storage networks or the amount of data that is being transferred over the Internet for a certain amount of time. For e.g., several hundred exabytes of data is transferred over the Internet every year.

Zettabyte: One zettabyte is equal to 1, 000 exabytes or 10^{21} or 1, 000, 000, 000, 000, 000, 000, 000 bytes. Zettabyte is little bit smaller than zebibyte that contain 1, 180, 591, 620, 717, 411, 303, 424 or (2^{70}) bytes and is abbreviated as "ZB". One zettabyte contains one billion TBs or one sextillion bytes. That means it will take one billion one terabyte hard drives to store one zettabyte of data. Generally, zettabyte is used to measure the large amounts of data and all the data in the world is just a few zettabytes.

Yottabyte: One yottabyte is equal to 1, 000 zettabytes. It is the largest SI unit of memory measurement. A yottabyte is 10^{24} zettabytes or 1, 000, 000, 000, 000, 000, 000, 000, 000 bytes and is abbreviated as "YB". It is little bit smaller than yobibyte, which contains exactly 1, 208, 925, 819, 614, 629, 174, 706, 176 bytes or (2^{80}) bytes.1 yottabyte contains one septillion bytes which is exactly same as one trillion TBs. It is a very large number that humans can evaluate. There is no practical use of such a large measurement unit because all the data in the world is made of just a few zettabytes.

Brontobyte: A brontobyte is a unit of data that represent a very large number of bytes. It is often compared to approximately 1000 yottabytes; the specific number being 1,000,000,000,000,000,000,000,000,000 10^{27} bytes.

Geopbyte: This is currently the largest possible measurement for data storage.

One geopbyte is 1024^{10} or 1267650600228229401496703205376 bytes. Or simply, 10^{30} bytes. One geopbyte is equal to 1024 brontobytes.

Summary

Unit	Equivalent
1 Kilobyte (KB)	1,024 bytes
1 Megabyte (MB)	1,048,576 bytes
1 Gigabyte (GB)	1,073,741,824 bytes
1 Terabyte (TB)	1,099,511,627,776 bytes
1 Petabyte (PB)	1,125,899,906,842,624 bytes

Comparison of Memory Units

Kilobyte (KB)

1 KB = 1024 Bytes

Megabyte (MB)

1 MB = 1024 KB

Gigabyte (GB)

1 GB = 1024 MB

`Terabyte (TB)

1 TB = 1024 GB

Petabyte (PB)

1 PB = 1024 TB

Exabyte (EX)

1 EB = 1024 PB

Zettabyte (ZB)

1 ZB = 1024 EB

Yottabyte (YB)

1 YB = 1024 ZB

Brontobyte (BB)

1 BB = 1024 YB

Geopbyte (GB)

1 GB = 1024 BB

Data Hierarchy

Data stored in computer systems form a hierarchy extending from a single bit to a database, the major record-keeping entity of a firm. Each higher rung of this hierarchy is organised from the components below it. Data hierarchy from top to bottom is shown as follows:

1) A **database** is a collection of files
2) A **file** is made up of records
3) A **record** is made up of fields
4) A **field** is made up of characters
5) A **character** is made up of bytes
6) A **byte** is made up of bits

Some Vital Facts

1) 960x1024 is the exact number of bytes contained in a computer with memory of 960 Kbytes.
2) Computer is an electronic device that can store, retrieve and process both qualitative and quantitative data quickly and accurately.
3) Computers on an internet are identified by IP address
4) A computer add and compare its data in hard disk
5) 8 number system is usually followed in a typical 32-bit computer
6) In a Computer a byte generally consists of 8 bits
7) A confidential file is deleted from a workstation by dragging the file into the recycle bin and empty the recycle bin
8) Worm is a virus type that is capable of shifting from one computer to another without user interaction.

Practice Exercise

General Questions Format

1. Computers are basically used as a source of

(A) research (B) computation
(C) entertainment (D) demonstration

2. Which of the following is NOT part of hardware?

(A) Program (B) Keyboard
(C) Mouse (D) Monitor

3. Which of the following is NOT true about computer?

(A) Its main components are hardware and software.
(B) Processor is just like the heart of a computer.
(C) Every sphere of life is dependent on the computer.
(D) The skill of communication has obtained the maximum benefit from the computer.

4. Which of the following is NOT type of a computer?

(A) Laptop (B) Supercomputer
(C) Tiny computer (D) Athlon computer

5. A complete computer system includes

(A) Hardware, Software, and Data
(B) Hardware, Software, and People
(C) Processor, Monitor, and People
(D) None of the above

6. CYRIX is a type of

(A) Processor (B) Monitor
(C) Motherboard (D) Printer

7. If the data in a computer is to be permanently stored, then it must be shifted from

(A) Hard disk to RAM
(B) RAM to Hard disk
(C) Processor to RAM
(D) RAM to Processor

8. Monitor is a/an __________ device of the computer system.

(A) latest (B) integral
(C) output (D) input

9. Byte is a unit of computer's __________.

(A) programming (B) storage
(C) memory (D) all of the above

10. Computer manipulates the data according to the instructions stored in:
(A) Processor (B) Motherboard
(C) CPU (D) None of these

11. Which of the following is TRUE about RAM?
(A) It is volatile.
(B) It stands for Random Apex Memory.
(C) Improvement in RAM reduces the age of the computer.
(D) It is measured in megabyte.

12. Touch screen is an example of ______ device.
(A) input (B) output
(C) both (D) none of the above

13. Characters in one megabyte are equal to
(A) one book (B) bookshelf
(C) one page (D) none of these

14. Types of output generated by a computer depends upon ________.
(A) hardware (B) software
(C) both (D) none of these

15. Networking is connecting ________.
(A) input to output
(B) mouse to CPU
(C) one computer to another
(D) one computer to a satellite

16. Data in a computer becomes digital when it is converted into ________.
(A) binary digits (B) letters
(C) words (D) none of these

17. Modem is a device of ______.
(A) computation (B) confirmation
(C) communication (D) calculation

18. CD-ROM is a device for storing:
(A) Document (B) File
(C) Data (D) All of the above

19. CPU stands for __________ Processing Unit.
(A) Calculation (B) Communication
(C) Common (D) None of these

20. Software used in the computer is also known as ________.
(A) soft disk (B) program
(C) mouse (D) UPS

21. Memory units are given under Column I and bytes represented by these units are given under Column II. Match the memory units with bytes it represents and choose the correct code from the codes given below.

Column I (Memory unit)	Column II (Represented bytes)
a) Exabyte	i) 1024 Megabyte
b) Brontobytes	ii) 1024 Exabyte
c) Zettabyte	iii) 1024 Yottabyte
d) Gigabyte	iv) 1024 Petabyte

Codes:	(a)	(b)	(c)	(d)
(A)	ii	iv	iii	i
(B)	iv	iii	ii	i
(C)	i	ii	iv	iii
(D)	iii	i	ii	iv

22. Which of the following is NOT TRUE?
a) Analog computers are suitable for simulating systems.
b) Kilobyte is approximately equal to one textbook.
c) Mac computers are totally autonomous.
d) A bit is the remotest unit of information a computer can process.
(A) c and d only (B) a only
(C) a and c only (D) b, c, and d only

23. Consider the following statements:
a) The computer manipulates data according to the instructions stored in the software.
b) A click of the mouse by the user on a software of choice yields desired results.
c) Input devices accept data and instructions from the user or from other computer systems.
d) A rational user of a computer copies data from the RAM to the hard disk for saving data.
Which of the above statement explains the complete computer system?
(A) d (B) a
(C) b (D) c

24. DOS stands for
(A) Disk Operating System
(B) Double Operating System
(C) Data Operating System
(D) None of these

25. Which of the following is NOT a feature/features of minicomputer?
a) It supports a small number of users working alternatively on the same machine.
b) it is used in organisations.
c) It is capable of providing connectivity to all departments of an organisation.

d) It is useful for small business organisations.

(A) b and c (B) a only

(C) a, c, and d only (D) a, b, c, and d

26. Find the odd choice.

(A) Windows XP (B) Android

(C) Adobe Acrobat (D) UNIX

KEY

1. B	2. A	3. B	4. D	5. D	6. A	7. B
8. C	9. C	10. D	11. A	12. C	13. A	14. C
15. C	16. A	17. C	18. D	19. D	20. B	21. B
22. D	23. C	24. A	25. B	26. C		

Assertion–Reason Format

1. **Assertion (A):** All computer operations are based on binary numbers.

Reason (R): Binary numbers are two unique numbers, 0 and 1.

(A) Both A and R are true and R is correct explanation of A

(B) Both A and R are true but R is not correct explanation of A

(C) A is true but R is false

(D) A is false but R is true

2. **Assertion (A):** Input and output devices of a computer complete the communication process.

Reason (R): Touch screen is an input and output device.

(A) Both A and R are true and R is correct explanation of A

(B) Both A and R are true but R is not correct explanation of A

(C) A is true but R is false

(D) A is false but R is true

3. **Assertion (A):** Bytes in a computer indicate its storage capacity.

Reason (R): Mac computers have the maximum storage capacity.

(A) Both A and R are true and R is correct explanation of A

(B) Both A and R are false

(C) A is true but R is false

(D) A is false but R is true

4. **Assertion (A):** Mainframes are large and very powerful computers installed by banks.

Reason (R): Huge databases are to be processed by banks by supporting hundreds of users simultaneously on a network.

(A) Both A and R are false

(B) Both A and R are true but R is not correct explanation of A

(C) Both A and R are true and R is correct explanation of A

(D) A is true but R is false

5. **Assertion (A):** System software works faster than application software.

Reason (R): Operating system of a computer determines the speed of the system and application software.

(A) A is true but R is false

(B) Both A and R are false

(C) Both A and R are true and R is correct explanation of A

(D) Both A and R are true but R is not correct explanation of A

6. **Assertion (A):** RAM is a volatile memory slot in a computer.

Reason (R): RAM transfers memory to a permanent memory slot hard disk.

(A) Both A and R are true and R is correct explanation of A

(B) Both A and R are true but R is not correct explanation of A

(C) Both A and R are false

(D) A is true but R is false

7. **Assertion (A):** Analog computer is not successful in processing static data.

Reason (R): Simulation in aircrafts is compatible to analog computers.

(A) Both A and R are true and R is correct explanation of A

(B) Both A and R are true but R is not correct explanation of A

(C) A is true but R is false

(D) A is false but R is true

8. **Assertion (A):** Arithmetic-Logic Unit (ALU) is part of CPU.

Reason (R): Users still prefer to install traditional CPUs due to their high speed and efficiency.

(A) A is true but R is false

(B) A is false but R is true

(C) Both A and R are true but R is not correct explanation of A

(D) Both A and R are false

9. **Assertion (A):** For graphic applications, a computer must be equipped with a higher RAM than usual.

   Reason (R): A personal computer cannot handle graphic applications.

   (A) Both A and R are true and R is correct explanation of A

   (B) Both A and R are true but R is not correct explanation of A

   (C) A is true but R is false

   (D) A is false but R is true

10. **Assertion (A):** Modem is a communication device.

    Reason (R): Computers are enabled to communicate through different line and cable systems.

    (A) Both A and R are correct and R is correct explanation of A

    (B) Both A and R are true but R is not correct explanation of A

    (C) A is true but R is false

    (D) A is false but R is true

KEY

1. A **2.** D **3.** D **4.** C **5.** B **6.** D **7.** B **8.** A **9.** C **10.** A

Questions Asked in Previous NET Exams

1. A computer has main memory of 960 KB. What is the exact number of bytes contained in this memory? **(UGC NET JUNE 2019)**

   (A) 960 x 8 (B) 960 x 1000

   (C) 960 x 1024 (D) 960 x 1024 x 1024

2. In computer related activities, which of the following is inappropriate for describing a language translator? **(UGC NET DECEMBER 2019)**

   (A) Assembler (B) Compiler

   (C) Interpreter (D) Codec

3. In a computer, if 8 bits are used to specify address in memory, the total number of addresses will be: **(UGC NET DECEMBER 2018)**

   (A) 8 (B) 256

   (C) 216 (D) 512

4. A confidential file needs to be deleted from a workstation. Which is the most effective way to ensure this? **(UGC NET JULY 2018)**

   (A) Rename the file

   (B) Compress the file and back-up to tape

   (C) Copy and paste the file into the recycle bin and empty the recycle bin

   (D) Drag the file into the recycle bin and empty the recycle bin

5. A virus type that is capable of shifting from one computer to another without user interaction is known as a **(UGC NET JULY 2018)**

   (A) Worm (B) Trojan

   (C) Logic bomb (D) Boot sector

6. Put the following units of storage into the correct order, starting with the smallest unit first and going up to the largest unit: **(UGC NET JULY 2018)**

   (a) Kilobyte (b) Byte

   (c) Megabyte (d) Terabyte

   (e) Gigabyte (f) Bit

   Give your answer from the following code:

   (A) (f), (b), (a), (c), (d), (e)

   (B) (f), (b), (a), (d), (e), (c)

   (C) (f), (b), (a), (c), (e), (d)

   (D) (f), (b), (a), (d), (c), (e)

7. With regard to computer memory, which of the following statement(s) is/are TRUE? **(UGC NET JULY 2018)**

   P: Read-only Memory (ROM) is 'volatile' memory.

   Q: Random Access Memory (RAM) is 'volatile' memory.

   R: Secondary memory is 'volatile' memory.

   (A) P only (B) Q only

   (C) P and Q only (D) P and R only

8. The data storage hierarchy consists of: **(UGC NET NOVEMBER 2017)**

   (A) Bits, bytes, fields, records, files, and databases

   (B) Bits, bytes, records, fields, files, and databases

   (C) Bits, bytes, fields, files, records, and databases

   (D) Bytes, bits, fields, records, files, and databases

9. Which of the following correctly lists computer memory types from highest to lowest speed? **(UGC NET JANUARY 2017)**
   (A) Secondary Storage; Main Memory (RAM); Cache Memory; CPU Registers
   (B) CPU Registers; Cache Memory; Secondary Storage; Main Memory (RAM)
   (C) CPU Registers; Cache Memory; Main Memory (RAM); Secondary Storage
   (D) Cache Memory; CPU Registers; Main Memory (RAM); Secondary Storage

10. If one gigabyte is equal to 2^{30} bytes of data storage, then 1024 terabytes is equal to ___ bits of data storage. **(UGC NET AUGUST 2016)**
   (A) 2^{50} (B) 2^{53}
   (C) 2^{40} (D) 2^{56}

11. In a computer, a byte generally consists of: **(UGC NET DECEMBER 2015)**
   (A) 4 bits (B) 8 bits
   (C) 16 bits (D) 10 bits

12. Which of the following represents one billion characters? **(UGC NET JUNE 2015)**
   (A) Terabyte (B) Kilobyte
   (C) Megabyte (D) Gigabyte

13. A gigabyte is equal to **(UGC NET JUNE 2013)**
   (A) 1024 megabytes (B) 1024 kilobytes
   (C) 1024 terabytes (D) 1024 bytes

14. Minimum number of bits required to store any 3 digit decimal number is equal to ___. **(UGC NET JUNE 2012)**
   (A) 3 (B) 5
   (C) 8 (D) 10

15. 1 GB is equal to **(UGC NET DECEMBER 2010)**
   (A) 2^{30} bits (B) 2^{30} bytes
   (C) 2^{20} bits (D) 2^{20} bytes

16. Which number system is usually followed in a typical 32-bit computer? **(UGC NET JUNE 2010)**
   (A) 2 (B) 8
   (C) 10 (D) 16

17. Where does a computer add and compare its data? **(UGC NET JUNE 2010)**
   (A) CPU (B) Memory
   (C) Hard disk (D) Floppy disk

18. Computers on an Internet are identified by ________. **(UGC NET JUNE 2010)**
   (A) e-mail address (B) street address
   (C) IP address (D) None of the above

19. Which is the largest unit of storage among the following? **(UGC NET DECEMBER 2009)**
   (A) Terabyte (B) Megabyte
   (C) Kilobyte (D) Gigabyte

20. The 'brain' of a computer which keeps peripherals under its control is called: **(UGC NET DECEMBER 2007)**
   (A) Common Power Unit
   (B) Common Processing Unit
   (C) Central Power Unit
   (D) Central Processing Unit

21. Which of the following is the appropriate definition of a computer? **(UGC NET DECEMBER 2006)**
   (A) Computer is a machine that can process information.
   (B) Computer is an electronic device that can store, retrieve, and process both qualitative and quantitative data quickly and accurately.
   (C) Computer is an electronic device that can store, retrieve, and quickly process only quantitative data.
   (D) Computer is a machine that can store, retrieve, and process quickly and accurately only qualitative information.

KEY

1. C	2. D	3. B	4. D	5. A	6. C	7. B
8. A	9. C	10. B	11. B	12. D	13. A	14. D
15. B	16. A	17. A	18. C	19. A	20. D	21. B

ICT : Communication and Conferencing
(Basics of Internet, Intranet, Email, Audio and Video Conferencing)

CONCEPT

Advent of information and communications technology has refined the concept and style of communication. Today, digital means of communication have eradicated various lacunae and barriers found in the traditional communication. In fact, communications technology is acting as a fathometer of effective communication today. Various means like intranet, Internet, email, audio and video conferencing, etc. have been strong contributors in making communication effective. Every sector of present day society, viz. agriculture, manufacturing, trading, banking, insurance, household, education, health, etc. are making strides due to effective communication through various means of satellite technology. Intra-sector and inter-sector connectivity is the major contribution of digital communication. All these means are discussed here one by one.

INTERNET

Internet is a facility to share information through computer networking, covering local, regional, national, and global jurisdiction. It means that Internet is a worldwide telecommunications system that provides connectivity for millions of other, smaller networks; therefore, the Internet is often referred to as a 'network of networks'. It allows computer users to communicate with one another across distance and computer platforms. Millions of computers are connected globally which form a network in which any computer can communicate with any other computer as long as both are connected to the Internet. Connecting a computer to the Internet is called going online.

Background:

The Internet began in 1969 as the U.S. Department of Defense's Advanced Research Projects Agency (ARPA) to provide immediate communication within the Department in case of war. Computers were then installed at U.S. universities with defence related projects. As scholars began to go online, this network changed from military use to scientific use. As ARPANET grew, administration of the system became distributed to a number of organisations, including the National Science Foundation (NSF). This shift of responsibility began the transformation of the science oriented ARPANET into the commercially minded and funded Internet used by millions today.

Tools of Internet

1. **Electronic Mail (Email):** It was one of the original uses of the Internet. By assigning individual addresses to users, the routing system of the Internet is able to direct messages from user to user.
2. **File Transfer Protocol (FTP):** It is one of the standard languages of the Internet which determines how files are transferred from one location to another.
3. **Hyper Text Markup Language (HTML):** It is a set of codes which World Wide Web browsers use to display documents in a rich format.
4. **Hypertext Transfer Protocol (HTTP):** This is the language used by the World Wide Web to transfer files during a client-server session.
5. **Listserv:** This is an automated mailing list to which Internet users can subscribe and will receive mail from regularly. Listservs are often designed for the purpose of participating in discussions about specific topics.
6. **Transmission Control Protocol/Internet Protocol (TCP/IP):** This is the language which is the heart of the Internet, and allows computers to exchange information by using the different Internet tools.
7. **TELecommunication NETwork (TELNET):** This protocol allows users to log in to host computers remotely over the Internet. Telnet applications are available for most operating systems and are typically provided with Internet access accounts.
8. **Gopher:** This is an application-layer protocol that provides the ability to extract and view Web documents stored on remote Web servers. Gopher was conceived in 1991 as one of the Internet's first data/file access protocols to run on top of a TCP/IP network.

9. **Newsgroup:** This is an Internet-based discussion around an individual, entity, organisation, or topic. Newsgroups enable remotely connected users to share, discuss, and learn about their topic of interest by exchanging text messages, images, videos and other forms of digital content. Newsgroups are also referred to as USENET (User Network) newsgroups. Usenet is a collection of user-submitted notes or messages on various subjects that are posted to servers on a worldwide network.
10. **World Wide Web (WWW):** The World Wide Web is a client-server application system which transfers text, graphics, and sound files through the Hypertext Transfer Protocol. The WWW clients are called web browsers. There are many available, such as Mosaic and Netscape, both of which are compatible with Macintosh and Unix PCs. Probably, the most popular of all Internet tools is the World Wide Web.

Requirements for Connection to the Internet

a) A computer
b) An account with an Internet service provider
c) A modem
d) A telephone line
e) Suitable software

Internet Service Provider

A connection to the Internet is provided by an Internet Service Provider (ISP). The connection is provided to users for a fee. ISPs use a server, which is a computer with high storage capacity and memory. It is connected with other servers installed at different places in the world through satellites. ISPs also allow users to store mail on their servers.

Advantages of Internet

Communication: The main advantage of Internet is the faster communication than any other devices. It's an instant process. Communication in the form of video calls, emails, etc. is possible using Internet. Thus, there is no specific region that can be accessed. It is accessible all over the world. Hence, because of this global issues are reduced, since video conferencing is possible where everyone across the world can be in a single place and can solve out a problem.

Information: The Internet is the source of knowledge. All kinds of information is present in it. It is easily accessed and can be searched more to get additional knowledge. Information like educational related information, government laws, market sales, stocks and shares, new creations, etc. is gathered from a single place.

Learning: The Internet has now become a part of education. Education like home schooling is easily carried out using Internet. Teachers can upload their teaching videos in the Internet and is accessed by people across the world which is helpful for all students. The marks are also released in the Internet since releasing marks for the whole institution in notice boards will create chaos.

Entertainment: The Internet is now the most popular form of entertainment. Movies, songs, videos, games, etc. is available in Internet for free. Social networking is also possible using Internet. Hence, there is tons of entertainment that is available online on the Internet.

Social network: The social networking is the sharing of information to people across the world. Apart from being an entertainment website, it has many uses. Any job vacancy, emergency news, ideas, etc. can be shared in the website and the information gets passed on quickly to a wide area. Also, the social networking websites are used for easy communications. Example: Facebook and Twitter.

E-commerce: All business deals can be carried in the Internet like transaction of money, etc. This is called E-commerce. Online reservations, online ticket booking for movie, etc. can be done easily. It saves us lots of time. Online shopping is now the latest trend in Internet world where products from dresses to household furniture is available at the doorstep.

E-governance: Government has taken many digital initiatives to provide public utility services online. This has increased efficiency and transparency in the working of various government departments. E-governance has benefitted many people through digital initiatives.

Disadvantages of Internet

Information loss: The information crucial to us or any important files can be easily taken by the hackers. There is no exact proof for the security for the details we store like account number, passwords, etc. hence, sensitive information must be carefully stored by the people.

Spam: The unnecessary emails, advertisements, etc. sometimes are said to be spam because they have the ability to slow down the system and make the users to face lots of problems. Spam makes the people get more confused since important emails are also stored along with spam.

Virus attacks: The malware or virus threats are so deadly that it affects the system to a great extent. It immediately deletes all important files and finally the system ends up being crashed. The virus attack is possible in three ways. One, it attacks selected files. Two, it harms the executable boot files, and most dangerous of all is the macro virus which has the ability to replicate and expand to all parts of the files.

Virtual world: The people using Internet often will forget the difference between the virtual and real world. This causes the people to get depressed quickly and it leads to social isolation and obesity problems. The obesity is due to the lack of any physical exercises. So it's better to play outdoors rather than on the Internet.

Internet in india

Origin of Internet in India dates back to 1986 when it was launched in the form of Educational Research Network (ERNET) meant only for the use of educational and research communities. It was a joint undertaking of the Department of Electronics (DoE) of the Government of India, and the United Nations Development Program (UNDP), which provides technical assistance to developing nations. On 15th August 1995, Videsh Sanchar Nigam Ltd. (VSNL) formally launched Internet service for the Indian public.

Present status of Internet in India is as follows:

- 2/3rd of Internet users in India are in the age group of 12-29 years.

  Amazingly, a higher proportion of this age group is seen in rural India. This is indicative of the fact that there is potential for growth in this segment.
- Internet consumption at home is still prevalent across urban and rural population
- 1/3rd of the urban population is accessing Internet while travelling
- At a state level, Delhi NCR has registered the highest Internet penetration followed by Kerala, Haryana, Himachal Pradesh, and Punjab
- States in the East, except Assam and North East, have low Internet penetration.
- Among the cities, Mumbai and Delhi top the list with 11.7 million and 11.2 million Internet users' respectively. Bengaluru and Kolkata with 6.1 million users are third, followed by Chennai with 5.4 million Internet users.

Security Threats to Internet

Though technology has facilitated communication by making it online through the Internet, yet there are technical and man-made threats to the security of Internet which not only damages the computer system of the user but also puts personal information of the subscriber of the Internet at risk of leakage, making ground for misusing the technology leading towards crimes. There are the following major threats to the Internet:

1. **Computer virus:** Computer viruses are pieces of software that are designed to be spread from one computer to another. They're often sent as email attachments or downloaded from specific websites with the intent to infect the subscriber's computer- and other computers on his/her contact list-by using systems on the user's network. Viruses are known to send spam, disable one's security settings, and corrupt and steal data from one's computer, including personal information such as passwords, even going as far as to delete everything on his/her hard drive.
2. **Rogue security software:** This threat is posed from scammers committing frauds through the Internet. Rogue security software is malicious software that mislead users to believe there is a computer virus installed on their computer or that their security measures are not up-to-date. Then they offer to install or update users' security settings. They'll either ask him/her to download their program to remove the alleged viruses, or to pay for a tool. Both cases lead to actual malware being installed on one's computer.
3. **Computer worms:** Computer worms are pieces of malware programs that replicate quickly and spread from one computer to another. A worm spreads from an infected computer by sending itself to all of the computer's contacts, then immediately to the contacts of the other computers. Paradoxically, they are not always designed to cause harm; there are worms that are made just to spread. Transmission of worms is also often done by exploiting software vulnerabilities.
4. **Phishing:** Phishing is a method of social engineering with the goal of obtaining sensitive data such as passwords, usernames, and credit card numbers. The attacks often come in the form of instant messages or phishing emails designed to appear legitimate. The recipient of the email is then tricked into opening a malicious link, which leads to the installation of malware on the recipient's computer. It can also obtain personal information by sending an email that appears to be sent from a bank, asking to verify your identity by giving away your private information.

5. **Trojan horse or "Trojan":** It is a malicious bit of attacking code or software that tricks users into running it willingly, by hiding behind a legitimate program. It spreads often by email; it may appear as an email from someone one knows, and when one clicks on the email and its included attachment, one immediately downloads malware to one's computer. Trojans also spread when one clicks on a false advertisement. Once inside in one's computer, a Trojan horse can record one's passwords by logging keystrokes, hijacking one's computer gadgets, and stealing any sensitive data one may have on his computer.
6. **Rootkit:** It is a collection of software tools that enables remote control and administration-level access over a computer or computer networks. Once remote access is obtained, the rootkit can perform a number of malicious actions; they come equipped with keyloggers, password stealers, and antivirus disablers. Rootkits are installed by hiding in legitimate software: when one gives permission to that software to make changes to one's operating system, the rootkit installs itself in his computer and waits for the hacker to activate it. Other ways of rootkit distribution include phishing emails, malicious links, files, and downloading software from suspicious websites.
7. **Adware and spyware:** Adware is any software that is designed to track data of one's browsing habits through advertisements and pop-ups. Adware collects data with one's consent-and is even a legitimate source of income for companies that allow users to try their software for free, but with advertisements showing while using the software. The presence of adware on one's computer is noticeable only in the pop-ups, and sometimes it can slow down the computer's processor and Internet connection speed. When adware is downloaded without consent, it is considered malicious. Spyware works similarly to adware, but is installed on a computer without the user's knowledge. It can contain keyloggers that record personal information including email addresses, passwords, and even credit card numbers, making it dangerous because of the high risk of identity theft.

Leading Internet Service Providers

World

1. **AT & T:** It is US-based and the world's largest Internet service provider and media entertainer. **Taglines: "Your World Delivered", "Mobilising Your World", "Rethink Possible."**
2. **Verizon:** The Verizon network delivers access to blazing-fast Internet speeds, along with superior reliability and performance. It is the 100% fiber-optic network that brings one the Internet as it should be. It allows consumers to use their telephone and Internet service simultaneously over the same telephone line while benefitting from Internet connection speeds significantly faster than dial-up. This service was launched in 1998 in the USA.

   Tagline: "Can you hear me now?"
3. **Hughes:** It is the global leader in broadband satellite technology and services for home, office, enterprise, and service providers around the world.
4. **Frontier Communication:** Frontier offers broadband Internet, digital television service, and computer technical support to residential and business customers.
5. **Spectrum:** It is a USA-based broadband service provider.
6. **CenturyLink, Inc.:** It is a technology company based in the USA. It was founded in 1930. It offers communications, network services, security, cloud solutions, and voice and managed services.
7. **Xfinity:** It is a trade name of Comcast Cable Communications, a subsidiary of the Comcast Corporation, used to market consumer cable television, Internet, telephone, and wireless services which are provided by the company.

   Rankings of 2019: Above ISPs have been adjudged best in different fields of providing Internet services as follows:

   a) AT & T Internet: Best Customer services

   b) Verizon: Best for Fiber Internet

   c) HughesNet: Best for Satellite Internet

   d) Frontier: Best for Cheap Internet Service

   e) Centurylink: Best for Business

   f) Comcast Xfinity: Fastest Top Speed Cable

India

1) **Bharat Sanchar Nigam Limited (BSNL):** BSNL is the only service provider, making focussed efforts and planned initiatives to bridge the rural-urban digital divide in the ICT sector. In fact, there is no telecom operator in the country to beat its reach with its wide network giving services in every nook and corner of the country and operates across India except New Delhi and Mumbai. BSNL serves its customers with a wide bouquet of telecom services

namely Wireline, CDMA mobile, GSM mobile, Internet, and Broadband. Wi-Fi is yet another type of high speed Broadband access technology from BSNL, which enables citizens to access very Affordable, Anywhere and Anytime, high speed broadband services. BSNL Broadband launched its services on 14 January 2005 as DataOne.

Tagline: "Connecting India Faster", 'Behtar Sewa Ki Nai Lagan."

2. **Mahanagar Telephone Nigam Limited (MTNL):** MTNL was set up on 1st April, 1986 by the Government of India to upgrade the quality of telecom services, expand the telecom network, introduce new services, and to raise revenue for telecom development needs of India's key metro cities of Delhi and Mumbai. MTNL is the principal provider of fixed-line telecommunication service in the two metropolitan cities of Delhi and Mumbai. It offers mobile services in the city of Delhi including four peripheral towns Noida, Gurgaon, Faridabad, and Ghaziabad, and the Mumbai city along with the areas falling under the Mumbai Municipal Corporation, New Mumbai Corporation, and Thane Municipal Corporation. During the year 1999, MTNL brought in the most widely using service called Internet (Network of Networks), the extreme level of information exchange.

   Tagline: "Transparency makes us different."

3. **Tata Communications:** It was formerly called VSNL (Videsh Sanchar Nigam Limited), and is an Indian telecommunications company. It is part of the Tata Group. Tata's communications network spans more than 500,000 km of subsea fiber and more than 210,000 km of terrestrial fiber. It provides network services and software-defined network platforms, such as Ethernet, SD-WAN, Content Delivery Network (CDN), Internet, Multiprotocol Label Switching (MPLS), and Private Line.

4. **Bharti Airtel Limited:** Bharti Airtel Ltd. is a leading global telecommunications company with operations in 18 countries across Asia and Africa. Headquartered in New Delhi, India, the company ranks amongst the top 3 mobile service providers globally in terms of subscribers. In India, the company's product offerings include 2G, 3G, and 4G wireless services, mobile commerce, fixed line services, high speed home broadband, DTH, and enterprise services including national and international long distance services to carriers. In the rest of the geographies, it offers 2G, 3G, 4G wireless services, and mobile commerce.

   Tagline: "Express Yourself"

5. **Reliance Communications:** Reliance Communications owns and operates a nationwide telecommunications network to offer services to retail and enterprise customers, including fixed-line services, national and international long-distance connectivity, broadband services, and enterprise solutions.

   Taglines: 'Total Network", "Karlo Duniya Muthi Mein"

6. **Reliance Jio Infocomm Limited:** Reliance Jio Infocomm Limited, is an Indian telecommunications services company wholly owned by Reliance Industries and headquartered in Mumbai, Maharashtra, India. It operates a national LTE network with coverage across all 22 telecom circles. It does not offer 2G or 3G service, and instead provides service on its 4G network. In September 2019, Jio launched a fiber to the home service, offering home broadband, television, and telephone services.

   Tagline: "4G liyo to Jio", 'Digital Life"

7. **Asianet Communications:** Initiated in1993, Asianet Communications has 43,000 clients under its coverage area. It is one of the ISPs in India that offers an extensive range of broadband services to both corporates and homes.

8. **You Telecom:** YOU Broadband, owned by You Telecom, is one of the initial ISO 9001:2000 licensed Internet firms. It guarantees quality services to its customers with greater downloading and uploading speed. It is among one of the firms to have end-to-end network setting and a power to keep its clients connected even while they are travelling.

9. **Tata Teleservices:** The company was established in 1996 with headquarters at Mumbai to provide broadband services. However, due to heavy losses, Tata Teleservices Maharashtra Limited was merged into Bharti Airtel in July, 2019.

10. **Videocon Telecom:** the company was launched in 2010 at Mumbai. Videocon Telecom is rendering broadband services under brand name "Connect".

    Original Tagline: "Pakdo Life Ka Har Signal"

11. **Idea Cellular:** This broadband service provider belongs to Aditya Birla group.

    Taglines: "An idea can change your life", "What an idea sirji"

SEARCH ENGINE

A search engine is a web-based tool that enables users to locate information on the World Wide Web. A user enters keywords or key phrases into a search engine and receives a list of Web content results in the form of websites, images, videos, or other online data.

Leading Search Engines

1. **Google:** Google is the biggest search engine in the world. It is currently holding a whopping 88.47 per cent of the worldwide search engine market share. The search engine was created in 1996. The name "Google" is derived from the word "googol". A googol is a mathematical term meaning "10 raised to the power of 100" or 1 with 100 zeros after it. The company has developed many other software solutions such as Google Drive. It owns YouTube, has developed a line of smartphones and laptops, and has even created self-driving cars. Google also powers other search engines-including Ask, which is the sixth largest search engine in the world.
2. **Yandex:** It's the most popular search engine in Russia with 55% of total Russian search traffic, closely followed by Google. The search engine is also popular in Ukraine, Belarus, Kazakhstan, Uzbekistan, and Turkey. Yandex provides more than 70 different services, including tools such as Yandex Disk, a cloud-based storage service similar to Google Drive. The name "Yandex" was adopted in 1993 and stands for "Yet Another iNDEXer."
3. **Bing:** Bing is the second largest search engine in the world with an 8.04 per cent market share. While Bing is small in comparison to Google, it maintains a respectable market share in many countries. The search engine is owned and operated by Microsoft and has its origins in the previous search engines MSN Search and Windows Live Search.

   Tagline: "Bing is for Doing", "Bing and Decide"
4. **Ask:** It is the sixth largest search engine in the world with a 0.72 per cent market share-100 times smaller than Google and 10 times smaller than Bing. Based at USA, it was founded in 1996. The search engine was created as a question/answer service.
5. **Yahoo:** It is the fourth largest in the world with about 4% share in the global market. It was floated in 1994. Original name of the search engine was "Jerry and David's Guide to the World Wide Web". It was renamed Yahoo which stands for stands for "Yet Another Hierarchical Organized Oracle."

   Tagline: "Do you Yahoo?"
6. **Baidu:** It is the third largest search engine and China's largest one. The search engine has a sobriquet "The Famous Firewall of China".
7. **Naver:** Naver began in 1999 as the first web portal in Korea to develop and use its own search engine. Today, the Naver Corporation provides a multitude of services, such as an email client, encyclopaedia, children's search engine, and news web portal.
8. **AOL:** It is short for "America Online" and came into existence in 1985.

   Tagline: "AOL on" and "It's on..."
9. **Seznam:** This search engine and web portal is hugely popular in the Czech Republic. In fact, it was the leading search engine there until Google came along.
10. **DuckDuckGo:** This search engine is all about privacy. DuckDuckGo distinguishes itself from other search engines by not profiling its users.
11. **Lycos:** Lycos is known for emailing, web hosting, social networking, and entertainment websites.

WEB BROWSER

A web browser is a software program that allows a user to locate, access, and display web pages. Browsers are used primarily for displaying and accessing websites on the Internet. Browsers translate web pages and websites delivered using Hypertext Transfer Protocol (HTTP) into human-readable content. They also have the ability to display other protocols and prefixes, such as Secure HTTP (S-HTTP) and File Transfer Protocol (FTP).

Leading Web Browsers

1. **Google Chrome:** It is a cross-platform web browser developed by Google. It was first released in 2008 for Microsoft Windows, and was later ported to Linux, macOS, iOS, and Android.
2. **Mozilla Firefox:** It is a free and open source web browser which is made by the Mozilla Foundation It works on common operating systems, such as Windows, macOS, Linux, and Android.
3. **Opera:** It is an Internet browser developed by Opera Software and was first released on April 1, 1995. It is designed for desktops and mobile platforms, and is a popular choice for mobile phones. Opera claims to be the fastest browser on earth. It is compatible to Microsoft, Android, and Linux operating systems.

4. **Safari:** It is a graphical web browser developed by Apple.
5. **Internet Explorer:** It is an Internet browser that allows users to view web pages on the Internet. Users can also utilise Internet Explorer to listen to and watch streaming content, access online banking, make purchases over the Internet, and much more. It was first introduced on August 16, 1995, by Microsoft.
6. **Slimjet:** It is a powerful and one of the best browsers around. It has inbuilt extensions to ease Internet browsing. Powered by Blink Engine, Slimjet supports all Chrome Apps, plus a bundle of more extensive built-in apps.
7. **Maxthon:** It is a fast browser with a lot of features and reliable user interface. Powered by Maxthon Cloud Engine, it offers seamless browsing and downloads and works on all platforms.
8. **SlimBrowser:** It is a popular choice for users who like speed and security. It is based on Internet Explorer's Trident Engine and is a robust and powerful browser. It flaunts better usability features and speed compared to the Internet Explorer browser.
9. **Netscape:** It is originally published by AOL and has released its latest version based on Mozilla Firefox. It is fast, secure, and is a choice of many users online.
10. **UC:** It is a popular browser for both desktop and mobile devices. Tabbed browsing and fast startup make it a popular choice for thousands of users. Full download manager and full screen browsing adds on nicely.

INTRANET

Intranet is defined as a private network of computers within an organisation with its own server and firewall. It is a computer network for sharing corporate information, collaboration tools, operational systems, and other computing services only within an organisation. The outside world has no access to the intranet. Every company or organisation has its own intranet network. Only members or employees of the company or organisation or selected customers or clients have access to computers in the company's intranet network. Use of technology in intranet is the same as that used in Internet. In a way, an intranet of a particular organisation is its compact Internet which is confined to the world of that organisation while having no connection with the outside world.

FIREWALLS

A firewall is a network security system designed to prevent unauthorised attack to or from a private network. Firewalls can be implemented as both hardware and software, or a combination of both. Network firewalls are frequently used to prevent unauthorised Internet users from attacking private networks connected to the Internet, especially intranets. All messages entering or leaving the intranet pass through the firewall, which examines each message and blocks those that do not meet the specified security criteria.

Features of Intranet

1. **Document and Content Management**

   This is the main feature/function of any Intranet system. An Intranet system should store and manage company documents in the form of files, pdfs, spreadsheets, etc. It acts as a gateway of knowledge allowing employees to store, access, and share the content and documents securely and easily with just a few clicks.

2. **Search Capability**

   A good Intranet system should have an enterprise search feature. The search feature helps employees pull the information related to content or people by searching through specific keywords or phrases, categories, filtering the tagged content, etc. A good Search feature also enables employees to find items stored on the intranet even when they don't know what exactly they are looking for using 'suggested search results'.

3. **Information Generator**

   An Intranet system should allow members to generate and view information as and when required. Timely request processing and form processing are important tasks to be performed every now and then. An Intranet with good information generation capabilities allows employees to access business information such as forms, workflows, employee details, reports, etc. and respond to business tasks more rapidly and efficiently.

4. **Security**

   Every company has some sort of confidential data such as company plans and policies, personnel information, and financial data, which is shared only on a need-to-know-basis. A good Intranet should have tight password protected security layers that blocks unauthorised access and relieves you from the worries of data misuse and theft.

5. **Integration**

An intranet system must integrate business critical information and KRAs such as total sales, revenue generated, expenses incurred, traffic generated, etc. This will help employees get up-to-date information about their company in order to make wise decisions. It will also help in responding to many business needs at a time and in generating real-time reports by refreshing and integrating company information whenever any essential data changes.

6. **Sharing and Collaboration**

Where there are great employees, there are great ideas and opinions which should be shared with other members. A good Intranet should not miss the great feature of sharing and collaboration since Intranet is the only platform where communication flows in different ways, i.e., top to bottom, bottom to top, peer to peer, etc. Moreover, to make sharing a non-stop process, organisations should incorporate a blogging feature in their Intranet since it will help employees to share, view, and comment on the posts of internal as well as external participants.

7. **Social Networking**

Companies are recognising the value of social networking and social sharing over the Internet. Moreover, with the increasing demand of bringing the social networking inside the corporate walls in order to create awareness about the company online as well as to include it in the marketing strategy, companies should look for an Intranet system that supports social networking. With appropriate access of each social site in the Intranet, employees can connect with people, create a sense of community, and build a brand image at no cost.

8. **Available on Cloud 24x7**

A good Intranet should not limit its access within the corporate boundaries. Rather, it should be deployed on Cloud to make it available to employees 24x7 so that they do not lose the connectivity with their organisation when they are away from the office. This will help them in responding and acting on information and reports on time through their laptop, mobile phone, home PC, or any other network.

Advantages of Intranet

1. **Easy, Fast , and Economic:** Intranet is an easy, economical, and fast system of communication within the enterprise. It offers opportunities to keep every concerned individual informed, irrespective of the location. It also helps in reducing travel time as the communication between employees in the business enterprise can be more frequent and less expensive, particularly when the persons desiring to communicate are located far away from each other.
2. **Automatic service of information:** It serves information automatically and thus, an employee or member of the organisation cannot come with the excuse that he/she does not know or has missed some important information. Thus, demand for information is more frequent and detailed.
3. **No room for grapevine communication:** Intranet replaces grapevine as it permits inter-employee communication with more transparency and free expression of views. It enables employees at various levels to pose problems/questions, participate in discussions, and contribute answers to thorny problems of the company. The concept of collective expertise can be given a concrete shape with the help of the Intranet.
4. **Improvement in productivity:** It improves productivity of the employees, particularly management staff. With Intranet, the managers can spend more time in analysing information and not in seeking information and waiting for its delivery.
5. **Eradicates latency:** Intranet helps in eliminating the delay (latency) in communication of information in the enterprise and makes the flow of information need-driven rather than availability-driven.

Disadvantages of Intranet

1. **Risk of security:** One of the major disadvantages is the risk of security to the corporate information resource. The intranet exposes the corporate information resource to the risk of loss of privacy and even unauthorised alteration. The Intranet technology is still quite fragile and the risk of security and privacy of information on Intranet is higher.
2. **Ineffective work culture:** Intranet poses another challenge before the enterprise and that relates to the need to change the work culture for effectiveness of the Intranet. The executives, particularly at the top level of the managerial hierarchy are in the habit of delegating the handling of information, including mail to their secretaries, who are neither competent nor accountable.
3. **Dereliction of duty by subordinates:** Quite often, the emails are printed out by the secretaries and dumped on the table of the executive by the secretary. The practice of sharing passwords with secretaries could be fatal for the executive and the enterprise, in case of an overambitious or dissatisfied secretary. Another cultural change that is necessary is in the speed of response.

4. **Delay in response and disposal of references:** As the Intranet communications are convenient and less expensive, the number of mails/queries is likely to increase and if these are not responded to quickly, they will pile up and the order will give way to chaos in the enterprise.

EMAIL

Email is a short name for electronic mail. Email is the sending and/or receiving a message in the form of a text, files, pictures, and other attachments which is sent through a telecommunication network to a particular individual or a group on an email address.

History of Email

Email was developed by an American computer programmer Raymond Tomlinson in 1971. He created email as part of ARPANET. Tomlinson is considered to be the 'Father of email.'

Email in India

In India, email was first used in 1986, when a dial-up link for email exchange was set up between National Center for Software Technology (NCST) and IIT Bombay. Credit of bringing email to India goes to Rajiv Gavai, the then professor of Physics in the USA. Once launched in 1986, all Education and Research Network (ERNET) participating agencies, Indian institute of science (IISc), Bangalore, five IITs (Indian Institutes of Technology) at Delhi, Bombay, Kanpur, Kharagpur, and Madras, and the Department of Electronics (DoE) stared using email. EMAIL TERMS + ABBREVIATIONS

1) ***Simple Mail Transfer Protocol SMTP:*** *It is an Internet standard for the sending of email messages*
2) ***Majordomo:*** *It is software designed to manage and maintain Internet mail groups and discussion and mailing lists on the Internet.*
3) ***POP3:*** *It is the latest standard and can send and receive email only using POP.*
4) ***Server:*** *It is an instance of a computer program or device that accepts and responds to requests made by another program, known as a client.*
5) ***Phishing:*** *It is a term used to describe a malicious individual or group of individuals who scam users. They do so by sending emails or creating web pages that are designed to collect an individual's online bank, credit card, or other login information.*
6) ***ESP:*** *Email Service Provider.*
7) ***POP:*** *Post Office Protocol is one of the most commonly used protocols used to receive email on many email clients.*
8) ***IMAP:*** *Internet Message Access Protocol.*
9) ***Snail mail:*** *It is slang for the traditional paper mail sent by a postal service.*
10) ***Joe job:*** *It is a term used to describe a spam message.*
11) ***POP2:*** *It was an early standard of POP that was only capable of receiving email and required SMTP to send email*
12) ***FNEA:*** *Full Name and Email Address.*
13) ***MIME:*** *Multipurpose Internet Mail Extensions.*
14) ***Push email:*** *It is a term for any email system that actively transfers new email to the client.*
15) ***Graymail:*** *It is bulk email.*
16) ***Pine:*** *It is a program for accessing email and newsgroups.*
17) ***Postmaster:*** *It is a person who is the administrator of an Internet mail server and deals with errors in the processing of email messages.*
18) ***Snooze of an email:*** *It is a process that will temporarily remove them from one's inbox -it will come back to the top of your inbox at the time you set it.*

Sending and Receiving Email Messages

Email messages are sent and received under SMTP, POP3, and IMAP protocols. SMTP protocol is meant for sending mails, and POP3 and IMAP for receiving mails stored in a mailbox. For sending messages, an email is opened and there appears a + sign on the upper left corner of the screen. When the user reaches that + sign, word 'compose' appears. When that word is clicked, the whole box containing space with 'To', 'Cc', 'Bcc', 'From', 'Subject', and space for composing message is given which is sufficient even for sizeable messages. Email is sent or received by adopting the following steps:

1. **Use of email client:** For sending and receiving email messages, an email client (also known as email program like Mozilla Thunderbird or Microsoft Outlook) is to be used.
2. **Need of server:** A server belonging to a particular Internet service provider (ISP) is needed to store and deliver messages.

EMAIL CLIENT (EMAIL PROGRAM)

An email program enables one to send, receive, and manage one's messages. This program has a capability to send and receive email via World Wide Web. Members are not charged for this service. When the user gets himself registered with this service, he gets a password and an account. The user is responsible for keeping his password confidential. The user can change the password at any time and also set up a new account and close the old one.

Popular email Clients (Programs):

1) ***Mozilla Thunderbird:*** *Thunderbird is a free email application that's easy to set up and customise. It is developed by Mozilla Firefox.*
2) ***DreamMail:*** *It is a complete email client with all the templates, i.e., templates of business, meetings, romantic events, and friendly and smiley messages. It also contains search engines and RSS (Really Simple Syndication) reader enabling the user to get news and updated content on a subject. This client was created by Dream Software Studio.*
3) ***Microsoft Outlook:*** *This is also a mail program to send and receive messages. It is also used to manage personal data. Microsoft Outlook was introduced to the public in 1997.*
4) ***Mail app for Windows 10:*** *This mail client includes all features required from a client to manage the flow of email messages.*
5) ***Mailbird:*** *It is an email client compatible for windows 7, 8, and 10.*
6) ***eM Client :*** *It is a fully-featured email client with a modern and easy-to-use interface. eM Client also offers calendar, tasks, contacts, and chat.*
7) ***Webmail (or web-based email):*** *It is an email client implemented as a web application running on a web server. Examples of webmail software are RoundCube and SquirrelMail.*

3. **Connecting Email Client to Server:** One needs to connect the email client with a server to download new email and storing old email online.
4. **Writing Email Message:** Message is written in the following manner:

   a) **Typing of Address:** Sender types his/her address in the space mentioning 'From' and address of the prospective recipient is typed in the space mentioning 'To' along with some sign and name of the service provider. Format of both the addresses is same. Here are examples of some formats of email address:

      i) kumarsahu123@yahoo.com

      ii) recruit_ gov.19@state.in

      iii) autosales.dreamcars@gmail.com

      iv) help@ins.com

FORMAT and BREAK DOWN OF EMAIL ADDRESS

Email: floodrelief.cm@pbgov.in

Above address can be broken down into the following parts:

1) ***Part before sign @:*** *Part before @ sign is the alias, user, group, or department of a company or government. In the given example, the part before @ indicates flood relief account or department.*
2) ***@:*** *This sign is used as a divider in the email address. It is used in all SMTP email addresses.*
3) ***Part after sign @:*** *It is the domain name to which user belongs. Sometimes, the domain is the actual name of the user (as in this case domain is pbgov), which indicates Punjab government. Sometimes, domain of an Internet service provider (ISP) is given which has been subscribed by the user and here, ISP represents user. For example: @gmail.com, @yahoo.com.*

   b) **Cc:** Cc stands for 'Carbon Copy'. This means copy of the message is also being sent to someone who is not the main addressee. For example, if a sender wants to send an email to the chairman of an organisation, but at the same time he also wants to bring that message to the notice of the Managing director of the same concern. He will address the chairman in the space mentioning 'To' and at the same time he will click 'Cc' mentioned at the right corner of the column of 'To'. A separate space with the letter 'Cc' appears and here the sender types the name of the Managing Director. In this way the message reaches both the chairman and the Managing Director.

   c) **Bcc:** This stands for "Blind carbon copy". It is sent to that recipient whom the user wants should not know who else has received the copy. This option is very rarely used.

d) **Subject:** Email is not sent without subject. Subject depicting the gist of the main message is typed in the space provided for subject.

e) **Message Body:** It is the location where the sender types his/her main message.

f) **Reply and Forward:** There is a space below the area meant for composing the message. In the said area, two columns are given for reply to all and forward.

5) **Attachments:** There is a bar below the area where the message is composed. This bar has an attachment sign. Any attachment like a folder, zip file, pictures, audios, videos, etc. compatible to the composed message are sent by clicking on the attachment signs.

Domain Name System

Domain name system is the process of converting the domain name in the web address format. Domain names are converted into web domain format by using domain suffixes, which are approved by The Internet Assigned Numbers Authority (IANA). IANA has approved the following domain suffixes and these have been put as Top Level Domains (TLD):

1) ***.com:*** *Stands for "Commercial". This is the most common domain suffix. This used by commercial websites.*
2) ***.org:*** *Stands for "Organisation." This domain is meant for non-profit organisations.*
3) ***.net:*** *This stands for "Networking". This domain is obtained by organisations involved in networking technologies.*
4) ***.edu:*** *Stands for "Education". This is meant for educational institutions.*
5) ***.gov:*** *Stands for "Government"*
6) ***.mil:*** *Stands for "Military."*

Other Domain Suffixes:

1) ***.in:*** *Stands for "India."*
2) ***.ac:*** *Stands for 'Academic"*
3) ***.int:*** *Stands for "International organisation"*

Receiving of an Email Message

As a prospective recipient receives signal of a message, the recipient opens his/her email domain and goes to the Inbox. He clicks there, opens inbox, and reads the message and replies accordingly. The message so received indicates time and date of sending the message by the sender.

Norms of a Valid Email Message

Following norms make an email address valid:

1) An email must have a username followed by @ (the at sign) which is followed by the domain name with a domain suffix.
2) The username cannot be longer than 64 characters long, and the domain name cannot be longer than 254 characters.
3) There should be only one @ sign in an email address.
4) The space and special characters: ( ) , : ; <> \ [ ] are allowed. Occasionally, a space, backslash, and quotation mark work, but must be preceded with a forward slash. Although valid, some email providers do not allow these characters.
5) The username and email addresses as a whole cannot begin or end with a period.
6) The email must not have two or more consecutive periods.

Advantages of Email

There are many advantages of email regarding the usage of email versus postal mail. Some of the main advantages are listed below.

1) **Free delivery:** Sending an email is virtually free, outside the cost of Internet service. There is no need to buy a postage stamp to send a letter.
2) **Global delivery:** Email can be sent to nearly anywhere around the world, to any country.
3) **Instant delivery:** An email can be instantly sent and received by the recipient over the Internet.
4) **File attachment:** An email can include one or more file attachments, allowing a person to send documents, pictures, or other files with an email.
5) **Long-term storage:** Emails are stored electronically, which allows for storage and archival over long periods of time.
6) **Environmentally friendly:** Sending an email does not require paper (paperless), cardboard, or packing tape, thus conserving paper resources and protecting environment.

Leading Email Service Providers

1) **Gmail:** Gmail is the best email service provider at present. Gmail is a simple, secure, user-friendly, and very reliable email service by Google. The email content is provided under POP and IMAP protocols. It offers 15 GB of storage space with the free email account, with services like Calendar and Drive

(where one can save attachments from the emails), and offers feature-rich apps for mobile devices. It supports built-in chat functionality that allows for voice and video chat as well. Gmail was released on 1stApril, 2004. It was created by Paul T. Buchheit, an American computer engineer.

2) **Zoho Mail:** Zoho Mail offers an excellent, free email account with 5 GB storage. Zoho Mail is a completely ad-free email service and if the storage space is insufficient, one has the option to pay for additional storage space at affordable rates. It has been created by Zoho Corporation, USA.

3) **Outlook.com (Formerly Hotmail):** Outlook.com is an email service from Microsoft that offers free email accounts for personal use. It is the redesigned Hotmail and Windows Live Hotmail email service which offers an advertisement-supported web client and feature-rich apps for Windows, iOS, and Android platforms.

4) **Mail.com:** This was created by the German Internet Company United Internet in 1995. Mail.com offers a free, advertising-supported email service with unlimited storage for emails, choice of over 200 domains, online file storage, and collection of emails from other accounts.

5) **Yahoo Mail:** Yahoo email service was launched in 1997 by its parent American company Yahoo! Yahoo Mail provides four different email plans: three for personal use and another for businesses. The outstanding feature for Yahoo Mail is the ability to create 500 disposable email addresses. By covering over 280 million users worldwide, Yahoo mail has become the third largest email service provider in the world.

6) **GMX (Global Mail eXchange):** This free email service was established in 1997. It is owned by United Internet AG, Germany. The mail is accessible through POP3 and IMAP4 protocols. In addition to an email address, each GMX account includes a Mail Collector, Address Book, Organiser, and File Storage.

7) **ProtonMail:** ProtonMail was established in 2014 in Switzerland. It is an End-to-End Encrypted Email (E2EE). It is a communication system in which only the communicating users can read the message. The server is accessible through email client Webmail. The objective of ProtonMail is secured, encrypted, and private email. It offers a free mail account with 500 MB storage.

8) **AOL Mail:** America Online email service provider was established in 1993. It offers a free email account with unlimited storage along with other regular features of other service providers. AOL is one of the first public email service providers. It provides knowledge of latest events under the head "Today on AOL."

9) **Yandex Mail:** Yandex mail is a free email service provider from Russia. It was launched in 2000. The free email account of Yandex Mail comes with 10 GB storage, an integrated calendar, and a linked account with Yandex Disk for storing your documents.

10) **Tutanota:** Launched in 2011, it is a free encrypted email service from Germany. It is an ad-free email service and relies on premium subscriptions which offer many more features than free accounts including Inbox rules, aliases, custom domains, and even an unlimited search. Main focus of this service provider is security.

11) **iCloud Mail:** This mail service is provided to users of Apple device. iCloud is built in every apple device. Once the user is connected with the service through an Apple device, it offers all features and services of other email service providers. iCloud ID is also built-in, hence user need not create any separate ID. This guarantees security of the content in any form stored in the mail. If any user's Apple ID does not end with @icloud.com, @me.com, or @mac.com, he/she must set up an @icloud.com email address before he/she can use Mail on iCloud.com.

2019 RANKINGS OF LEADING EMAIL SERVICE PROVIDERS

1.	*Gmail*
2.	*Outlook*
3.	*Yahoo*
4.	*Zoho*
5.	*AOL*
6.	*Mail.com*
7.	*ProtonMail*
8.	*GMX*
9.	*iCloud*
10.	*Yandex*

Email Versus Webmail

Though Email and Webmail are the services on Internet, which are used for sending and receiving of emails, yet there is some difference in the nature of their providing service:

Email Client	Webmail
A computer program that allows users access to their emails on a desktop computer	Allows users access to their emails via device's web browser
Emails are accessible without Internet access	Access to emails requires an Internet connection
Emails can be backed up to the computer	Emails can be backed up in the Email Server (Gmail, AOL, and Yahoo are webmail servers)
Needs an up-to-date antivirus program to scan emails	Emails are automatically scanned for viruses by the service provider

WEB CONFERENCING

Web conferencing or Internet conferencing is one of the online services by which one can start a live meeting or conference virtually. All one needs in this case is a stable Internet connection, a device, and a software or tool by which one will be able to connect to other clients, partners, or employees for the meeting. This conferencing has an edge over traditional conferences.

Types of Web Conferencing:

1) Audio Conferencing
2) Video Conferencing

Audio Conferencing

Audio conferencing is a teleconference between two or among more than two people, groups, parties, etc. through ICT devices. Audio conferencing can be conducted either through the telephone line or the Internet by using devices such as phones or computers. In audio conferencing, even one person can be talking to many persons at the same time. Participants of conference may be vertical or horizontal hierarchy of an organisation, friend, associates, etc. Audio conference may be formal and non-formal. If one only wants to listen, he/she just needs speakers. If he/she decides to speak as well, he/she may need a microphone as well. In this age of advancing communication technology, audio conferences play a decisive role in success of business, services, government schemes, and other works. Such conferences have become indispensable and convenient for government officials, business persons, and all sections of the population as it is now costly and non-feasible to physically go to attend a conference.

Features of Audio Conferencing

Following features of audio conference makes it successful:

1) **Starting/Stopping Conference by the Leader:** It is the leader or chairman of the conference who starts the conference dialling in a communication device. It is the leader who also stops the conference by signing off.
2) **Multi-Dialling Out:** After the start of conference, leader can resort to single or multiple-dialling from the phone book.
3) **Locking/Unlocking:** There is provision of locking of conference to avoid additional participants. Conference can also be unlocked for resuming the proceedings any time during the conference.
4) **Question and Answer Session:** Question and answer session is started by responding to the question of one participant. Other participants are put on mute for ensuring noise-free and smoothly-flowing communication.
5) **Mute/Unmute:** There is a provision to put one or more than one participant on mute in the interest of barrier-free communication. Further, mute mode can be unmuted at any time during the conference.
6) **Auto Recording:** Minutes of the meeting are automatically recorded by opening application of recording of phone or any other device of teleconferencing.
7) **Blast Dialling:** There is a provision of dialling a large number of people in a single attempt in case of a large-scale conference.
8) **Automated Post Conference:** All post conference reports like attendance record and call duration record are provided to the participants of the conference.
9) **Entry/Exit Tones:** There is a provision of tones in the form of signal, ring tone, or music signifying entry to and exit from the conference.
10) **Lecture Mode:** In case a conference covers a large number of participants, all the participants except leader or speaker are placed into "Listen Only" mode so that the content being delivered by the leader/ speaker can be heard and understood properly.
11) **Music:** A melodious music is played until the start of the conference. This signifies that those participants who have already been connected may not feel monotonous while waiting for the rest of

the participants or leader of the conference. Stopping of the music signifies that all the participants and leader have arrived and the conference is going to be started.

12) **Pre-Conference Host Room:** Participants who get connected are provided with Pre-Conference Host Room, where they are to wait for the start of the conference. In this room participants can talk to one another or conference operator. They can discuss on issues likely to be on the agenda of the conference before the start of the conference

13) **Only Listed Participants Allowed:** A list of participants is provided to the conference operator at least 24 hours before the conference through call or in a Microsoft® Excel or Comma-Separated Values (CSV) format.

14) **Attendance Reports:** A report regarding each conference call including caller ID, entry and exit times, and a link to listen to the MP3 recording of the conference is mailed to the conference leader after each call.

Leading Audio Conferencing Service Providers

1) **eZ Talks:** It is popular for arranging cloud meetings and is situated in Hong Kong.
2) **Infinite Conferencing:** It is one of the largest audio conference providers in the world. It is known for designing audio conferences for small business houses. Developed by Infinite, it is situated in the USA.
3) **Arkadin Anytime:** It s a multinational audio conferencing service provider having offices in many countries including USA, Singapore, Malaysia, India, etc. It is the biggest service provider in India. Arkadin Anytime is a great proof that the audio conferencing providers in India can develop an accessible and reliable communication software.
4) **OpenVoice:** It is a UK-based quality service provider. OpenVoice is highly permissive, allowing conferences with up to 500 participants.
5) **WebEx:** It offers very well-optimised audio conferencing.
6) **Budget Conferencing:** This arranges teleconferencing for those who cannot spend much on such conferencing. It arranges meetings up to 300 participants.

Leading Audio Conferencing Service Providers in India

1) **Door Sabha Nigam Limited (DSNL):** Leading audio conferencing service provider, situated in India with head office at Chennai.
2) **Tata Tele:** High quality audio conferencing service provider from Tata group. Due to service of instant meeting access, the provider ensures seamless conferences.
3) **Vodafone Audio Conferencing Service:** It provides a reliable, cost-effective audio conference solution that connects a concern's workforce across geographies and time zones.
4) **Eagle Conferencing:** Eagle conferencing was established in 2005 with its main offices at Mumbai and Bengaluru. Its main target is to provide audio conference to small-to-medium size companies that carry out businesses in India and individual clients.

Audio Conferencing Tools

1) Workplace by Facebook
2) GlobalMeet
3) West
4) OpenVoice
5) Spike
6) MobileDay
7) CallHippo
8) LoopUp
9) Brring Conferencing
10) Cloud Phone

Advantages of Audio Conferencing

1) **Cost-Effective:** It is cost-effective. Even enterprises with limited budgets can also avail the benefit of audio conferencing. As conferencing is online, it does not incur any commuting cost to the participants.
2) **Instant Connection:** Participants sitting at any corner in the world come in contact with one another instantly.
3) **Easy Utilisation:** Use of ICT devices meant for audio conferencing is easy to use. There is no need of any heavy installation. Handy communication devices can be taken anywhere and audio conference can be held even while travelling or roaming outside.
4) **Conference Recording:** As proceedings of the conference are recorded, no participant can miss any content and conference proves to be successful.
5) **Time Saver:** Such conferences save much of the time of the participants due to instant connection and the same message is conveyed to all the participants instantly at the same time.

6) **Economic way of communication:** Audio conferencing is an economic way of communication as it saves heavy expenses a company has to incur on trips of its officials to attend the conference.

7) **More Effective than Traditional Conference:** Due to all its digital features discussed above, an audio conference is more effective than a traditional conference.

Disadvantages of Audio Conferencing

1) **No display of non-verbal gestures of communication:** There is a physical interaction of participants in the traditional conference. In such conferences there is blending of verbal and non-verbal communication which helps in putting one's point with conviction and thus is effective. Such gesture is lacking in audio conferencing and sometimes the communication remains no more effective and the conference may end in a fiasco.

2) **No guarantee of active participation:** As participants cannot see one another, there is no surety that they are actively participating in the conference, due to which the whole purpose of the conference is lost.

3) **Risk of entropy:** As all the participants are connected through electronic devices, there is a risk in break of communication due any snag developed even in a single device. Any break in the communication can occur due to defect in any device. Power breakdown in regular or backup supply can also break communication which leads to confusion, tension, chaos, and thus, whole conference experiences futility. There is no such risk in traditional conferences.

4) **Distortion of sound quality:** Due to any fault in telephone lines or any background noise, there is distortion in the sound quality and it becomes difficult to convey and receive the message.

Video Conferencing

Video conferencing is that teleconferencing in which two or more persons or groups sitting at different places talk, hear, and view one another on a monitor or screen with the help of compatible audio and video devices. Video conference can be organised on mobile phone, laptop, desktop, or any such electronic device. Video conference is held by individuals, government departments, corporate houses, welfare organisations, and all others in the organised or unorganised sectors.

Background: The first ever video conferencing was used in 1961 by NASA during the first manned space flight. However, video conference was introduced as a commercial package for the first time at a World Fair in 1968.

Equipment Required for a Video Conference:

1) Computer or Video Conferencing Machine
2) Webcam or Camera
3) Monitor
4) External Microphone
5) Broadband Connection

Types of Video Conferencing Systems

Different video types of video conferences are held to fulfil the objectives of the conference. As video conferencing is the need of today, every individual or every group involved in different activities hold these conferences. There are the following types of video conference, which are held to achieve different objectives:

1) **Telepresence Video Conferencing:** This type of conference is held when a meeting is to be hosted as closely as possible, even if the participants are not present in the same room. Large screens are used and cameras are positioned at eye level. The result is a videoconference set-up that appears as if all the participants are sitting in the same room and around the same table.

2) **Integrated Video Conferencing System:** Integrated video conferencing systems are designed generally for group video conferencing where there's a centralised location for the equipment. The entire main camera, displays, and other peripheral videos are mounted in the main conference location. Integrated video conferencing systems are typically ideal for boardroom and classroom conferences.

3) **Desktop Video Conferencing System:** As an important one of the types of video conferencing systems, desktop video conferencing system is very popular with people on-the-go and typical office workers. Within this option there are two choices available: a software client on one's desktop or a hardware codec that doubles as one's computer monitor. By using this type of set-up, the video conferencing system is brought right into one's personal computer while still pulling off a full-motion conference.

4) **Service-based Video Conferencing System:** For serviced-based systems, the provider, which often is a telecom carrier, handles majority of the control when it comes to the network set-up. This means less work on the leader's end. He just pays for the solution and his provider manages it for him making it more convenient, especially if he does not want to bother with the technicalities.

Leading Video Conferencing Service Providers

As the success of every field, especially business, depends upon perfect, noise-free and seamless video conferencing, various service providers have started organising desired video conferencing for the clients. Some of the leading service providers are stated below:

1) **ezTalks** is the world's leading online video conferencing provider that is powerful yet very easy to use. It offers full portfolio products including Meetings, Rooms, and Webinars to facilitate the unified communication in every sphere. While the Meetings enables the leader to host unlimited HD video conferencing with anyone, anytime, and anywhere, ezTalks offer high-quality video and audio with live broadcasting supported from any device. Not only this, video conferencing provider is full of features and user-friendly.

WEBINAR

> *The word 'webinar' is a blend of 'web' and 'seminar'. A webinar is an event held on the Internet which is attended exclusively by an online audience. This distinguishes it from a webcast, which also includes the presence of a physical audience. Other terms used as alternatives for webinar are web event, online seminar, webcast, web lecture, and virtual event.*

2) **Zoom** is a big player in the industry of web/video conferencing. Zoom provides a free plan for web conferencing that offers the significant advantage to new startups and small and medium enterprises.

3) **VideoCentric** is a web conferencing service provider of UK. This web conferencing service can be controlled by voice commands where users can use their voice to start or end the meetings. For businesses, voice commands over video conferencing help create real work environment during meetings and make video conferencing more authentic.

4) **TrueConf** is used by 5000 companies around the world. TrueConf server is specially designed to work for corporate networks as it offers UltraHD video conferencing as well as cross-platform client applications, and offers convenient collaboration tools. Another feature it offers is, Address Book with status and photos. It has a very flexible administration, and the best part is that all of these features are for free.

5) **VCNow** is a product of unified collaboration services, and it provides unified communication and collaboration services. It supports features like virtual meeting rooms, video, audio and web conferencing. VCNow is a leading web conferencing service provider in India, and it is recommended by industry-leading professionals of video conferencing in India. Their services include video conferencing centres, managed video conferencing services, webcast and streaming services, virtual classrooms, etc. VCNow offers loud and clear audio in the video conferencing, making it real easy and professional.

Video Conferencing Tools

1. Google Hangouts
2. ezTalks
3. Skype
4. Anymeeting
5. WebEx Meetings
6. Tokbox
7. ooVoo
8. MeetingBurner

Advantages of Video Conferencing

1. **No time constraint:** Video conferencing can be conducted at any time of the day. Time differences between countries do not matter when people use this method of communication because they do not actually need to travel to attend meetings.
2. **Dramatic travel saving:** Not only is video conferencing a direct replacement for many in-person business trips, but there is also virtually no cost for people to be involved in a virtual meeting, as you can easily bring them together.
3. **Easy communication:** People can use video conferencing to communicate with anyone with HD video and other collaboration tools such as whiteboard, text exchange, file sharing, media sharing, screen sharing, remote control, electronic voting, conference recording, etc.
4. **Increased productivity:** By eliminating time and district barriers, meetings can be held anytime, anywhere, and with anyone. In this way, meetings are shorter and more effective. And also, with the rich collaboration tools, decisions can be made faster.

Disadvantages of Videoconferencing

1. **Lack of personal interaction:** Some meetings require a personal touch to be successful. Video conferencing can be less personal than meeting face-to-face, and it can be possible to miss out on vital body language when you're struggling with a pixelated image or stuttering video.

2. **Technical problems:** The major disadvantages are the technical difficulties associated with smooth transmissions that could result from software, hardware, or network failure. Remote connections are sometimes known to be hampered by environmental changes. On some occasions, the absence of technical support personnel creates difficulty for participants who are unfamiliar with the videoconferencing technological concepts.

3. **International time zones:** One of the very real disadvantages of using video conferencing is that if one communicates regularly with people in other countries, one will be available at different times to them. Unfortunately, without the skills of a time lord, there's not really a practical way to overcome this.

4. **High cost of setup:** Setting up video conferencing in an office can be a bit expensive for small-sized companies. Simple features can fit into the budget, but if advanced features are required, then a substantial amount of expenditure must be done.

Some Vital Facts

1) Unsolicited advertising sent to a large number of recipients is called 'Spam'
2) Blind Carbon Copy means the users specified in the Bcc: field will get the e-mail but will not see the addresses in the to: and cc: fields.
3) comdomains is used for - profit businesses.
4) Firewalls are used to protect a communication network system against unauthorized attacks

Practice Exercise

General Questions Format

1. Which of the following is NOT true about search engine Bing?

a) It is the fourth largest channel in the world.
b) It is smaller than Google.
c) Microsoft operates this search engine.
d) It has its origin in MSN research.

(A) c and d only (B) a, c, and d only
(C) a only (D) b and d only

2. According to 2019 rankings, which is the third largest search engine?

(A) Gmail (B) IOL
(C) Yahoo (D) Zoho

3. Which of the following is TRUE about web conferencing?

a) There is demand from technology today that web conferencing is the key to success of any sphere.
b) Web conferencing has eradicated various myths regarding online communication.
c) Various tools of web conferencing create virtual reality in the web conferences.
d) Hardships of traditional conferences were improved upon in web conferences.

(A) b, c, and d only
(B) c and d only
(C) a, b, c, and d
(D) c only

4. Which of the following is a webmail server?

(A) AOL (B) Google
(C) Yahoo (D) All of these

5. Which of the following is NOT a feature of audio conferencing?

(A) Blocking (B) Muting
(C) Recording (D) Waiting

6. Consider the statement "Credit of putting custom of traditional communication to the backseat goes to ICT". State whether the statement is

(A) True, because ethics of ICT demand a transformation from traditional to hi-tech communication customs
(B) False, because no technology can eradicate customs of a society in the name of modernisation
(C) True, because hi-tech communication today is the backbone of success of every field
(D) False, because ICT cannot overpower traditions unless there is mass awareness about it.

7. Internet was used for the first time to manage __________ operations.

(A) defence (B) space
(C) banking (D) research

8. Internet is also referred as

(A) superpower of network
(B) network in network
(C) power of network
(D) none of these

9. Which of the following is TRUE about status of Internet in India?

(A) Delhi NCR has registered the highest Internet penetration followed by Kerala.

(B) 2/3rd of Internet users in India are in the age group of 12-29 years.

(C) States in the East, except Assam and North East, have low Internet penetration.

(D) All of the above are true.

10. Which of the following is NOT TRUE about intranet?

a) Outside world has no access to intranet.

b) Use of technology in intranet is the same as that used in Internet

c) Every company dealing in like products and services are interconnected.

d) It is a private network of computers within an organisation.

(A) a and d only (B) c only
(C) a, c, and d only (D) b, c, and d only

11. Virtual world created by Internet affects human______.

(A) vision (B) aptitude
(C) business (D) health

12. Email terms are given under Column I and their meaning is given under Column II. Match the email term with its meaning and choose the correct code from the codes given below:

Column I (Email Terms)	Column II (Meaning)
a) Graymail	i) Postal mail
b) Snail mail	ii) Removal of a mail from inbox
c) Snooze	iii) Bulk mail
d) Majordomo	iv) Internet mail groups

Codes:	(a)	(b)	(c)	(d)
(A)	ii	i	iii	iv
(B)	iii	i	ii	iv
(C)	i	iv	iii	ii
(D)	iv	iii	ii	i

13. **Statement:** Has web conferencing been successful in overcoming limitations of traditional conferencing?

Arguments:

I. Yes, web conferencing never ends in fiasco.

II. No, risk of break in connectivity still exists as it existed in traditional conferencing.

(A) Only argument I is strong

(B) Only argument II is strong

(C) Both argument I and II are strong

(D) Neither argument I nor II is strong

14. What was the former name of Tata Communications?

(A) Bharat Sanchar Anusthan

(B) Tata telecommunications

(C) Videsh Sanchar Nigam

(D) Tata DoCoMo

15. Name of Internet service providers are given under Column I and their taglines are given under Column II. Match the service provider with taglines and choose the correct code among the codes given below.

Column I (Name of Service Provider)	Column II (Tagline)
a) Reliance Communication	i) Transparency Makes Us Different
b) BSNL	ii) Express Yourself
c) MTNL	iii) Karlo Duniya Muthi Mein
d) Bharti Airtel	iv) Behtar Sewa Ki Nai Lagan

Codes:	(a)	(b)	(c)	(d)
(A)	iii	i	iv	ii
(B)	ii	iv	iii	ii
(C)	i	iiii	ii	iv
(D)	iii	iv	i	ii

16. Which of the following ensures a barrier-free, seamless, and successful video conferencing?

(A) A reputed service provider

(B) An IT graduate conference leader

(C) Maximum attendance

(D) Ethics of web communication

17. Which of the following is NOT a correct email address?

(A) serviceauto.rupam 23@thapar,grp

(B) foodpb_4dine@yahoo.com

(C) plot123.udpchd@gov.in

(D) nigam.serv71@expo2019

18. Which of the following is a web browser?
(A) Slimjet (B) Lycos
(C) Safari (D) Opera

19. Which of the following is TRUE?
(A) Gopher protocol was raised to compete with the popular Transmission Control Protocol.
(B) FTP stands for File Termination Protocol.
(C) The most popular Internet tool is World Wide Web.
(D) World Wide Web uses HTML language to transfer files.

20. Which of the following is a webmail server?
(A) AOL (B) Gmail
(C) Yahoo (D) All of these

21. Which of the following is NOT TRUE regarding Intranet?
a) Intranet is used just like Internet but without any foreign contribution in its operation.
b) A company installing and using intranet targets efficiency, transparency, and sincerity in work culture of the company.
c) Jurisdiction of intranet operation is governed by the expansion plan of the concerned company.
d) There is no comparison between the intranet operations in terms of jurisdiction and feasibility being practised in two different intranet equipped companies.
(A) c and d only (B) a, b, c, and d
(C) a and b only (D) b, c, and d only

22. Consider the following statements:
i) Internet and other means of web networking establish faster connection campaigns among the users as compared to traditional means of establishing connection.
ii) Search engines and web browsers have enabled users in attempting to locate any address on the earth which was not possible in traditional ways of sending messages.
iii) Internet service providers are ensuring prompt and perennial connectivity which was a distant dream during the days of traditional means of establishing connectivity.
iv) Web domains have brought up the concept of address in the coded format for security reasons which was not possible in sending messages though traditional means.

Which of the above statements fully justifies the transformation of traditional practices of sending messages into an age of digital connectivity?
(A) iii (B) iv
(C) i (D) ii

23. Consider the following statements:
P: An Intranet with good information generation capabilities allows employees to access business information.
Q: A security-equipped Intranet should not encourage sharing and collaboration.
(A) Both P and Q are true
(B) P is true but Q is false
(C) Neither P nor Q is true
(D) P is false but Q is true

24. Which of the following domain suffix is Top Level Domain (TLD)?
(A) .ac (B) .org
(C) .int (D) .in

25. In an email address, part of address before @ signifies
(A) Domain (B) Divider
(C) User (D) Suffix

26. Names of the Internet service providers (ISP) are given under Column I and their ranking remarks 2019 are given under Column II. Match the ISP with its ranking remark and choose the correct code from the codes given below:

Column I (ISP)	Column II (Remarks)
a) AT & T	i) Best customer service
b) Verizon	ii) Best for fiber Internet
c) Frontier	iii) Best for cheap Internet services
d) Centurylink	iv) Best for business

Codes:

	(a)	(b)	(c)	(d)
(A)	ii	iii	i	iv
(B)	iii	i	iv	ii
(C)	i	iii	ii	iv
(D)	i	ii	iii	iv

27. In India, email was introduced in the year
(A) 2002 (B) 1986
(C) 1968 (D) None of these

28. Consider the statement: "A webinar is an event held on the Internet which is attended exclusively by an online audience".
Which of the following evidences fully support the ethics of Webinar?
(A) An application of Internet is being routed through an Internet Service Provider (ISP)
(B) An Internet protocol which binds the audience to attend the event online
(C) Internet has made it possible to establish bilateral communication even without direct interaction
(D) Events like webinar have defined a distinction between online and offline audience

KEY

1. C	2. C	3. D	4. D	5. A	6. C	7. A
8. D	9. D	10. D	11. D	12. B	13. D	14. C
15. D	16. D	17. A	18. B	19. C	20. D	21. B
22. A	23. B	24. B	25. C	26. D	27. B	28. C

Assertion–Reason Format

1. **Assertion (A):** Internet has made the whole world a global village.
Reason (R): Service providers, browsers, and search engines have facilitated global connectivity.
(A) Both A and R are true and R is correct explanation of A
(B) Both A and R are true but R is not correct explanation of A
(C) A is true but R is false
(D) A is false but R is true

2. **Assertion (A):** Electronic means of sending messages are not always desirable.
Reason (R): Sender of a message also sends his/her affections with it.
(A) Both A and R are true and R is correct explanation of A
(B) Both A and R are true but R is not correct explanation of A
(C) Both A and R are false
(D) A is true but R is false

3. **Assertion (A):** Participants may not be actively participating in an audio conferencing.
Reason (R): Audio conferencing service providers provide waiting slot to waiting participants.
(A) Both A and R are true but R is not correct explanation of A
(B) Both A and R are true and R is correct explanation of A
(C) A is true but R is false
(D) A is false but R is true

4. **Assertion (A):** Computer means of sending messages are environment-friendly.
Reason (R): There is no use of paper in sending messages through computer means.
(A) Both A and R are true and R is correct explanation of A
(B) Both A and R are true but R is not correct explanation of A
(C) Both A and R are false
(D) A is false but R is true

5. **Assertion (A):** Some parts of an email address are superfluous.
Reason (R): Junk mail increases the superfluous content in the inbox.
(A) Both A and R are true and R is correct explanation of A
(B) Both A and R are true but R is not correct explanation of A
(C) A is true but R is false
(D) A is false but R is true

6. **Assertion (A):** A web browser displays a website on a computer screen.
Reason (R): Internet service providers enable a web browser to locate a website.
(A) Both A and R are true and R is correct explanation of A
(B) Both A and R are true but R is not correct explanation of A
(C) Both A and R are false
(D) A is false but R is true

7. **Assertion (A):** In video conferencing, audio visual means are used to make the conference a success.
Reason (R): Video conference overcomes the limitations of audio conferencing.

(A) Both A and R are true and R is correct explanation of A

(B) Both A and R are true but R is not correct explanation of A

(C) A is true but R is false

(D) A is false but R is true

8. **Assertion (A):** A company installs intranet for security reasons.

Reason (R): Intranet becomes basis for evaluating the performance of employees of an organisation.

(A) Both A and R are true but R is not correct explanation of A

(B) Both A and R are true and R is correct explanation of A

(C) Both A and R are false

(D) A is true but R is false

9. **Assertion (A):** Where there is Internet there is networking.

Reason (R): Facility of Internet has made users networking addicts.

(A) Both A and R are true and R is correct explanation of A

(B) Both A and R are true but R is not correct explanation of A

(C) Both A and R are false

(D) A is false but R is true

10. **Assertion (A):** An email client enables one to send and receive messages.

Reason (R): Domain suffixes complete the email address on which the message is to be sent or received.

(A) Both A and R are correct and R is correct explanation of A

(B) Both A and R are correct but R is not correct explanation of A

(C) A is true but R is false

(D) A is false but R is true

11. **Assertion (A):** There is a risk of grapevine communication in an intranet-equipped organisation.

Reason (R): Employee unions in loggerheads with the management misuse intranet technology.

(A) Both A and R are true and R is correct explanation of A

(B) Both A and R are true but R is not correct explanation of A

(C) A is true but R is false

(D) Both A and R are false

12. **Assertion (A):** No participant of an audio conference misses any content of the conference proceedings.

Reason (R): Recording of the conference proceedings is accessible to participants.

(A) Both A and R are true and R is correct explanation of A

(B) Both A and R are true but R is not correct explanation of A

(C) A is true but R is false

(D) A is false but R is true

13. **Assertion (A):** File attachment facility in email makes decoding of the message easier for the recipient of message.

Reason (R): Attached picture is a stronger decoder than attached text.

(A) Both A and R are true and R is correct explanation of A

(B) Both A and R are true but R is not correct explanation of A

(C) A is true but R is false

(D) A is false but R is true

14. **Assertion (A):** Web conferencing materialises conferences in virtual reality.

Reason (R): Virtual reality is the ultimate solution to communication barriers in traditional conferencing.

(A) Both A and R are true and R is correct explanation of A

(B) Both A and R are true but R is not correct explanation of A

(C) A is true but R is false

(D) A is false but R is true

15. **Assertion (A):** Spam is the most ridiculous creation of Internet services.

Reason (R): Inbox bears the burden of spam to keep Internet connectivity intact.

(A) Both A and R are true and R is correct explanation of A

(B) Both A and R are correct but R is not correct explanation of A

(C) A is true but R is false

(D) A is false but R is true

KEY

1. A	2. C	3. A	4. A	5. D	6. A	7. A
8. C	9. D	10. B	11. D	12. A	13. C	14. B
15. C						

Questions Asked in Previous NET Exams

1. In the context of email, what is 'spam'?

(UGC NET JULY 2018)

(A) The act of overloading an email server by using denial-of-service attacks

(B) Email messages that are infected with viruses

(C) A large quantity of messages that do not reach the recipient

(D) Unsolicited advertising sent to a large number of recipients

2. Given the following email fields, which of the email addresses will 'swami' be able to see when he receives the message?

(UGC NET JULY 2018)

To... ram@test.com

Cc... raj@test. com; ravi@test.com

Bcc... swami@test. com; rama@test. com

Codes:

(A) ram@test. com

(B) ram@test. com; raj@test. com; ravi@test. com

(C) ram@test. com; rama@test. com

(D) ram@test. com; rama@test. com; raj@test. com; ravi@test. com

3. Which of the following domains is used for profit businesses?

(UGC NET NOVEMBER 2017)

(A) net

(B) edu

(C) com

(D) org

4. With regard to email, what does Bcc: mean?

(UGC NET AUGUST 2016)

(A) Blind Computer Communication: The users specified in the Bcc: field will get the email and see the addresses in the To: and Cc: fields.

(B) Blind Carbon Copy: The users specified in the Bcc: field will get the email and see the addresses in the To: and Cc: fields.

(C) Blind Computer Communication: The users specified in the Bcc: field will get the email but it will be an audio file because this is how blind people get email.

(D) Blind Carbon Copy: The users specified in the Bcc: field will get the email but will not see the addresses in the To: and Cc: fields.

5. Which one of the following is not a search engine?

(UGC NET DECEMBER 2014)

(A) Google (B) Chrome

(C) Yahoo (D) Bing

6. Firewalls are used to protect a communication network system against:

(UGC NET DECEMBER 2008)

(A) Unauthorised attacks

(B) Virus attacks

(C) Data-driven attacks

(D) Fire attacks

7. An Email address is composed of:

(UGC NET JUNE 2008)

(A) two parts (B) three parts

(C) four parts (D) five parts

8. Which of the following is the appropriate format of URL of email?

(UGC NET DECEMBER 2006)

(A) www_mail.com

(B) www@mail.com

(C) WWW@mail.com

(D) www.mail.com

KEY

1. D	2. A	3. C	4. D	5. B	6. A	7. A
8. B						

5 ICT Number Systems

NUMBER SYSTEMS

Decimal Number System

Decimal number system works on the theory of base ten numbers starting with 0. The numbers proceed like 0, 1, 2, 3, 4, 5, 6, 7, 8, 9. All these numbers are single digit numbers. Any higher number to 9 is expressed with 10 and so on. When the number series attains 19, number higher to 19 is expressed with 20 and so on. This means that decimal number remains between 0 and 9 in any row.

Any decimal number indicating base 10 is shown like this: $\mathbf{(D)_{10}}$

Here, D is any decimal number.

A decimal number is used in computer operation after converting it into binary number.

Binary Number System

Binary is a base two number as it has only two digits, i.e., 0 and 1. Computer operation is based on binary number system. Binary number proceeds from 0 to 1.

Binary number is expressed as $\mathbf{(B)_2}$

Here, B is any binary number

Octal Number System

Octal number system is an base eight system. Here, there are eight digits from 0 to 7

0, 1, 2, 3, 4, 5, 6, 7

Octal number system is used in computer operations after being converted into binary numbers. In octal numbers, immediate higher number to 7 is 10 then 11, 12, 13, 14, 15, 16, 17, 20, 21, and so on. After attaining 7 in any row the higher number is obtained by prefixing the next digit with 0 and so on. In any case an octal number runs from 0 to 7.

An octal number is expressed as: $\mathbf{(O)_8}$

Here, O is any octal number.

Hexadecimal Number System

Another computer related number is hexadecimal number system as a hexadecimal number can be converted into binary numbers and so on. This number system uses digits of decimal number system from 0 to 9, after that letters like A, B, are used to achieve 16th position and again 0 is used as next number in the series by prefixing a 1 or 2 and so on. The digits are shown below:

0, 1, 2, 3, 4, 5, 6 7, 8, 9 A, B, C, D, E, F, 10,11,12,13,14,15,16,17,18,19,1A,1B, and so on

It is represented with 16 base: $\mathbf{(H)_{16}}$

CONVERSION

There are frequent questions in exams regarding conversion of one of the above numbers to any other number. Such conversions are also made for various computer operations. It is, therefore important to understand the methods of such conversions

Conversion in Binary Number System

Binary number is expressed with base two as in binary number there are only two numbers, i.e., 0 and 1. Actually these are two symbols of the binary number system. Though there are two numbers in binary number system, yet digit 2 is not expressed in binary number system. The numbers so expressed are 0 and 1. So in binary system 10 is equal to 2 in decimal number system. Binary numbers viz-a-viz decimal numbers are expressed as follows:

Binary	0	1	10	11	100	101	110	111	1000	1001	1010
Decimal	0	1	2	3	4	5	6	7	8	9	10

Conversion of Decimal Number to Binary Number

There are two methods of conversion: Division Method and Table Method. Let us take an example to convert decimal number 38 to binary number.

Division Method

As the base number of a decimal number is 2, go on dividing the given decimal by 2 until there is zero remainder. Binary number is obtained by picking up the quotient and reminder of the last division and remainders of the other divisions from bottom to top as shown by arrow below.

```
2 | 38
2 | 19---0 ◄
2 | 9----1
2 | 4----1
2 | 2----0
2 | 1----0
```

Binary number of decimal number 38 is 100110

Table Method

In this method decimal number is converted into binary number through the following steps:

1) Draw the table and put 2^0 in the last column and proceed to left as shown below.
2) Chose the number close to but less than given decimal number.
3) Mark 1 in the column of chosen number and subtract that number from the given decimal number.
4) Consider the remainder from above and choose the number close to but less than the remainder and repeat the process until the difference is zero.
5) Finally put zero in all the vacant columns towards right of the column where 1 was first marked and obtain the desired binary number in left to right order.

Binary number of 38 is calculated with table method as follows:

2^8	2^7	2^6	2^5	2^4	2^3	2^2	2^1	2^0
256	128	64	32	16	8	4	2	1

Number close to but less than given decimal number 38 is 32. So 38 – 32 = 6 and 1 is marked below 32.

2^8	2^7	2^6	2^5	2^4	2^3	2^2	2^1	2^0
256	128	64	32	16	8	4	2	1
			1					

As in the above case remainder is 6, now a number close to but less than 6 is chosen which is 4. Now 4 is subtracted from 6 and 1 is marked below 4

2^8	2^7	2^6	2^5	2^4	2^3	2^2	2^1	2^0
256	128	64	32	16	8	4	2	1
			1			1		

Same procedure is repeated by choosing number close to but less than 4 and that number is 2. Again1 is marked below 2 in the table and 2 – 2 = 0

2^8	2^7	2^6	2^5	2^4	2^3	2^2	2^1	2^0
256	128	64	32	16	8	4	2	1
			1			1	1	

After achieving difference zero, process is stopped and 0 is marked in all the vacant columns towards right of column having 32.

2^8	2^7	2^6	2^5	2^4	2^3	2^2	2^1	2^0
256	128	64	32	16	8	4	2	1
			1	0	0	1	1	0

So binary number of decimal number 38 is 100110

Solved Examples

Example 1: Convert decimal number 80 to binary number.

As binary number has base 2, number 80 will be subsequently divided by two in the following manner:

Division Method:

```
2 | 80
2 | 40--0 ◄
2 | 20----0
2 | 10----0
2 | 5---0
2 | 2----1
2 | 1----0
```

So Binary Number of decimal number 80 is 1010000

Table Method:

2^8	2^7	2^6	2^5	2^4	2^3	2^2	2^1	2^0
256	128	64	32	16	8	4	2	1
		1	0	1	0	0	0	0

80 – 64 = 16 – 16 = 0

So binary number of decimal number 80 is 1010000

Example 2: Convert decimal number 46 to binary number.

2^8	2^7	2^6	2^5	2^4	2^3	2^2	2^1	2^0
256	128	64	32	16	8	4	2	1
			1	0	1	1	1	0

Here the number close to 46 is 32, so 46 – 32 = 14 Now closest number to 14 is 8, so 14 – 8 = 6 Closest number to 6 is 4 so 6 – 4 = 2, further 2 – 2 = 0, so the binary number is 101110

Division Method:

```
2 | 46
2 | 23--0 ◄
2 | 11--1
2 | 5--1
2 | 2--1
2 | 1--0
```

So the binary number is 101110

Example 3: Convert decimal number 118 into binary number.

Division Method:

2	118
2	59----0
2	29----1
2	14----1
2	7------0
2	3------1
2	1------1

Binary Number is 1110110

Table Method:

2^8	2^7	2^6	2^5	2^4	2^3	2^2	2^1	2^0
256	128	64	32	16	8	4	2	1
		1	1	1	0	1	1	0

Given decimal number is: 118. Following all the steps, which go like this:

118 – 64 = 54, 54 – 32 = 22, 22 – 16 = 6, 6 – 4 = 2, 2 – 2 = 0

Hence binary number is: 1110110

Conversion of Number with Fraction

Example 1: Convert decimal number 120.63 into binary number.

Division Method:

First converting the number before fraction point, i.e., 120

2	120
2	60--0
2	30--0
2	15--0
2	7--1
2	3--1
2	1--1

Binary number is 1111000

Table Method:

2^8	2^7	2^6	2^5	2^4	2^3	2^2	2^1	2^0
256	128	64	32	16	8	4	2	1
		1	1	1	1	0	0	0

Following the steps:

120 – 64 = 56, 56 – 32 = 24, 24 – 16 = 8, 8 – 8 = 0

So binary number of 120 is 1111000

Now the fraction number 0.63 is converted into binary number through following steps:

1) Multiply the decimal number with 2.
2) If the value is more than 1, then 1 is to be separated from rest of the product.
3) If the value is less than 1, then 0 is to be put before fraction figure
4) Again multiplying the fractional figure with 2 and put either zero or 1 as binary number.
5) Count binary number from top to bottom.

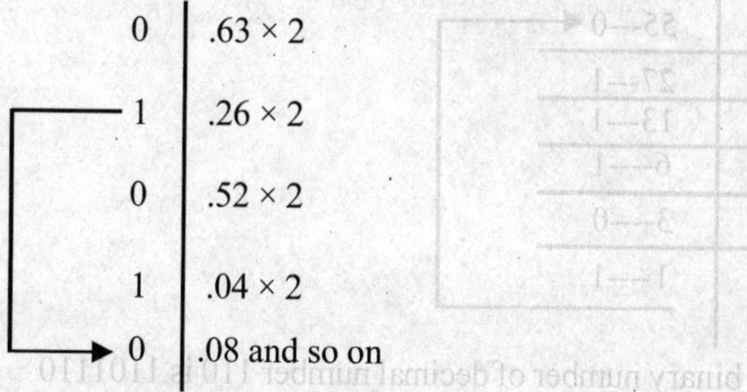

So binary number is 1010

So binary number of decimal number 120.63 is 1111000.1010

Example 2: Convert decimal number 96.81 into binary number.

Division Method:

First converting the first figure 96 into binary number:

2	96
2	48--0
2	24--0
2	12--0
2	6--0
2	3--0
	1--1

Binary number of 96 is 1100000

Table Method:

2^8	2^7	2^6	2^5	2^4	2^3	2^2	2^1	2^0
256	128	64	32	16	8	4	2	1
		1	1	0	0	0	0	0

96 – 64 = 32, 32 – 32 = 0

So binary number of decimal number 96 is 1100000

Now calculating binary number of decimal number 0.81

Multiplication Method: 0.81 × 2

1 .62 × 2
1 .24 × 2
0 .48 × 2
0 .96 × 2
1 .92 × 2 and so on

Binary number is 0.11001

So the binary number of decimal number 96.81 is 1100000.11001

Example 3: Convert decimal number 110.62 into binary number.

First, calculate binary number of 110

Division Method:

2	110
2	55---0
2	27---1
2	13---1
2	6----1
2	3----0
2	1----1

So the binary number of decimal number 110 is 1101110

Table Method:

2^8	2^7	2^6	2^5	2^4	2^3	2^2	2^1	2^0
256	128	64	32	16	8	4	2	1
		1	1	0	1	1	1	0

Number closest but less than 110 is 64, so 110 – 64 = 46, 46 – 32 = 14, 14 – 8 = 6, 6 – 4 = 2, 2 – 2 = 0

Hence the binary number of decimal number 110 is 1101110

Now Calculation of fractional part 0.62 as follows:

Multiplication Method:

0	.62 × 2
1	.24 × 2
0	.48 × 2
0	.96 × 2
1	.92 × 2
1	.84 and so on

So binary equivalent of decimal number 0.62 is 10011

Binary equivalent of 110.62 is 1101110.10011

IMPORTANT POINTS TO REMEMBER

1) If a decimal number without fraction is converted into binary number with Division Method, 0s and 1s so obtained as reminders after the last step of division are counted from bottom to top.
2) When a fraction part of a decimal number is converted into binary number, then 0s and 1s so obtained as reminders after last step of division, counting is made from top to bottom.

Conversion of a Binary Number to Decimal Number

Sometimes there is a question in the exam to convert a binary number to a decimal number. This can be done in the following way:

Example 1: Convert a binary number 1001110 into a decimal number.

Step1. Draw the decimal number table:

2^8	2^7	2^6	2^5	2^4	2^3	2^2	2^1	2^0
256	128	64	32	16	8	4	2	1

Step 2: Put the value of given binary number putting one digit in one column proceeding from right to left.

Table Method:

2^8	2^7	2^6	2^5	2^4	2^3	2^2	2^1	2^0
256	128	64	32	16	8	4	2	1
		1	0	0	1	1	1	0

Step 3: Adding decimal number where binary value number 1 is underneath and ignoring the number which has value 0 underneath it.

64 + 8 + 4 + 2 = 78.

So 78 is the decimal number of binary number 1001110

Example 2: Convert a binary number 1001101 into a decimal number.

Solution: While following the above steps:

2^8	2^7	2^6	2^5	2^4	2^3	2^2	2^1	2^0
256	128	64	32	16	8	4	2	1
		1	0	0	1	1	0	1

64 + 8 + 4 + 1 = 77

So 77 is the decimal number of binary number 1001101

Example 3: Convert binary number 1110110 into decimal number.

Solution: Following the same steps:

2^8	2^7	2^6	2^5	2^4	2^3	2^2	2^1	2^0
256	128	64	32	16	8	4	2	1
		1	1	1	0	1	1	0

64 + 32 + 16 + 4 + 2 = 118

So 118 is the decimal number of binary number 1110110

Example 4: Convert binary number 1110011 into decimal number.

Solution:

2^8	2^7	2^6	2^5	2^4	2^3	2^2	2^1	2^0
256	128	64	32	16	8	4	2	1
		1	1	1	0	0	1	1

64 + 32 + 16 + 2 + 1 = 115

So 115 is decimal number of binary number 1110011

Example 5: What is the decimal number of binary number 11001100?

Solution:

2^8	2^7	2^6	2^5	2^4	2^3	2^2	2^1	2^0
256	128	64	32	16	8	4	2	1
	1	1	0	0	1	1	0	0

Obtaining the decimal number:

128 + 64 + 8 + 4 = 204

So 204 is the decimal number of binary number 11001100

Conversion Of Binary Number With Fraction Into Decimal Number

If a binary number with fractions is to be converted into decimal number, then following steps are followed:

Decimal table of fractions is drawn as follows:

2^{-1}	2^{-2}	2^{-3}	2^{-4}	2^{-5}	2^{-6}	2^{-7}	2^{-8}

1) Consider fractional part of given binary number. Digits in the fraction are considered to proceed from left to right.
2) Each digit of fraction is picked up one by one and is put in each column of above table starting from extreme left and proceeding to right by putting one digit in one column.
3) Those fractions are picked up which have 1 underneath and those are neglected which have 0 beneath them. Then picked up fractions are added to get the desired decimal number of fractional part of the given binary number

DECIMAL VALUES OF FRACTIONS FOR CONVERSION FROM BINARY TO DECIMAL NUMBER

$2^{-1} = \frac{1}{2} = 0.50 \quad 2^{-2} = \frac{1}{4} = 0.25 \quad 2^{-3} = \frac{1}{8} = 0.125$

$2^{-4} = \frac{1}{16} = 0.0625 \quad 2^{-5} = \frac{1}{32} = 0.03125$

$2^{-6} = \frac{1}{64} = 0.01562 \quad 2^{-7} = \frac{1}{128} = 0.0078$

$2^{-8} = \frac{1}{256} = 0.0039$

Above values are calculated to make calculations easier and these values can be put in each column of the decimal table in the following way:

2^{-1}	2^{-2}	2^{-3}	2^{-4}	2^{-5}	2^{-6}	2^{-7}	2^{-8}
0.50	0.25	0.125	0.0625	0.03125	0.01562	0.00781	0.00390

Example 1: Convert binary number 0.1101 into decimal number.

Solution: While following above steps, each digit of fractional part is picked up and is inserted in the following table:

2^{-1}	2^{-2}	2^{-3}	2^{-4}	2^{-5}	2^{-6}	2^{-7}	2^{-8}
0.50	0.25	0.125	0.0625	0.03125	0.01562	0.00781	0.00390
1	1	0	1				

Now fraction values of those columns are picked up and added which have 1. Fractional values of columns with 0 are not considered because their result is always 0.

So 0.50 + 0.25 + 0.0625 = 0.8125. As only fractional part is to be considered as there is no integer in the given binary number, hence answer is 0.8125

Decimal fraction of binary fraction 0.1101 is 0.8125

Example 2: What is decimal number of binary number 0.110?

Solution:

2^{-1}	2^{-2}	2^{-3}	2^{-4}	2^{-5}	2^{-6}	2^{-7}	2^{-8}
0.50	0.25	0.125	0.0625	0.03125	0.01562	0.00781	0.00390
1	1	0					

0.50 + 0.25 = 0.75

So decimal number of binary number 0.110 is 0.75

Example 3: Convert binary number 0.1001 into decimal number.

Solution:

2^{-1}	2^{-2}	2^{-3}	2^{-4}	2^{-5}	2^{-6}	2^{-7}	2^{-8}
0.50	0.25	0.125	0.0625	0.03125	0.01562	0.00781	0.00390
1	0	0	1				

0.50 + 0.0625 = 0.5625

So decimal number of binary number 0.1001 is 0.5625

Example 4: Convert binary number 0.1111 into decimal number.

Solution:

2^{-1}	2^{-2}	2^{-3}	2^{-4}	2^{-5}	2^{-6}	2^{-7}	2^{-8}
0.50	0.25	0.125	0.0625	0.03125	0.01562	0.00781	0.00390
1	1	1	1				

0.50 + 0.25 + 0.125 + 0.0625 = 0.9375

So 0.9375 is the decimal number of binary number 0.1111

Example 5: Convert binary number 0.00101 into decimal number.

2^{-1}	2^{-2}	2^{-3}	2^{-4}	2^{-5}	2^{-6}	2^{-7}	2^{-8}
0.50	0.25	0.125	0.0625	0.03125	0.01562	0.00781	0.00390
0	0	1	0	1			

0.125 + 0.03125 = 0.15625

So decimal number of binary number 0.00101 is 0.15625

Conversion of Binary Fractions with Integer Value into Decimal Number

Example 1: Convert binary number 1100111.0101

Solution: Above number has integer as well as fractional value. Integer and fraction valued binary number is separately converted into decimal number.

First, integer value is converted as it has been converted earlier. **1100111**

2^8	2^7	2^6	2^5	2^4	2^3	2^2	2^1	2^0
256	128	64	32	16	8	4	2	1
		1	1	0	0	1	1	1

64 + 32 + 4 + 2 + 1 = 103

So integer part of the given binary number 1100111 is converted into decimal number 103

Now converting the fraction part 0.0101

2^{-1}	2^{-2}	2^{-3}	2^{-4}	2^{-5}	2^{-6}	2^{-7}	2^{-8}
0.50	0.25	0.125	0.0625	0.03125	0.01562	0.00781	0.00390
0	1	0	0				

0.25 + 0.0625 = 0.3125

Decimal number of fraction part of binary number 0.0101 is 0.3125

By joining the integer and fraction part of binary number 1100111.0101, its complete conversion into decimal number comes out to be 103.3125

Example 2: Convert binary number 0111001.11010

Solution: First converting the integer part, i.e., 0111001

2^8	2^7	2^6	2^5	2^4	2^3	2^2	2^1	2^0
256	128	64	32	16	8	4	2	1
		0	1	1	1	0	0	1

32 + 16 + 8 + 1 = 57

Now converting the fraction part 0.11010

2^{-1}	2^{-2}	2^{-3}	2^{-4}	2^{-5}	2^{-6}	2^{-7}	2^{-8}
0.50	0.25	0.125	0.0625	0.03125	0.01562	0.00781	0.00390
1	1	0	1	0			

0.50 + 0.25 + 0.0625 = 0.8125

Combining bothinteger and fraction values, the complete conversion comes out to be 57.8125

So decimal number of binary number 0111001.11010 is 57.8125

Example 3: What is decimal number of binary number 1101001.01011?

Solution: Converting the integer part 1101001

2^8	2^7	2^6	2^5	2^4	2^3	2^2	2^1	2^0
256	128	64	32	16	8	4	2	1
		0	1	1	1	0	0	1

64 + 32 + 8 + 1 = 105

Converting the fraction part 0.01011

2^{-1}	2^{-2}	2^{-3}	2^{-4}	2^{-5}	2^{-6}	2^{-7}	2^{-8}
0.50	0.25	0.125	0.0625	0.03125	0.01562	0.00781	0.00390
0	1	0	1	1			

0.25 + 0.0625 + 0.03125 = 0.34375

Complete conversion of binary number 1101001.01011 into decimal number is 105.34375

IMPORTANT POINTS TO REMEMBER

1) While converting fraction part of a binary number into decimal number, table starts with 2^{-1} instead of 2^{-0} because 2^{-0} gives value 1 and 1 does not express fraction.
2) When an integer part of a binary number is to be converted into decimal number, then each digit is entered in the columns of the decimal table in right to left order.
3) When fraction part of a binary number is to be converted into decimal number, then each digit of the fractional part is entered in the columns of the decimal table in left to right order.

Conversion of Decimal Number into Octal Number

As octal number has base 8, a decimal number is converted into octal number through the following steps:

1) Divide the given decimal number with 8 and get quotient with remainder. Remainder may be any natural number or zero
2) Go on dividing the quotients so obtained until quotient is less than 8.
3) Put zero in place of quotient and take the last quotient (which is less than 8) as remainder.
4) Count all the remainders so obtained from bottom to top. That will be the octal number of the given decimal number.

Solved Examples

Example 1: Convert a decimal number 48 into octal number.

Dividing 48 with 8 as shown below:

```
8 | 48
--+------
8 | 6------0
--+------
8 | 0------6
```

In above case after every division, first figure on left side is quotient, i.e., 6 and figure on the right side is remainder, i.e., 0. As 6 is smaller than 8, further division is not possible. So in the last step quotient 6 is taken as reminder after putting 0 in place of quotient. Now proceeding from bottom we get 60. Hence, 60 is the octal number of decimal number 48

Example 2: Convert decimal number 123 into octal number.

Solution: Dividing 123 with 8 as follows:

```
8 | 123
8 | 15-------3
8 | 1--------7
8 | 0------1
```

While proceeding from bottom to top, the octal number so obtained is 173

So octal number of decimal number 123 is 173

Example 3: What is the octal number of decimal number 325?

Solution:

```
8 | 325
8 | 40----------5
8 | 5------------0
  | 0---------5
```

The octal number of decimal number 325 is 505

Example 4: Convert decimal number 1137 to octal number.

Solution:

```
8 | 1137
8 | 142-----------1
8 | 17-------------6
8 | 2-------------1
  | 0-----------2
```

So 2161 is the octal number of decimal number 1137

Conversion of Decimal Number with Fraction to Octal number

Steps:

1) Consider the given fraction and multiply with 8, which is the base of octal number system.
2) Separate the carry and fraction so obtained with above multiplication.
3) Go on multiplying the quotient so obtained with 8 and go on separating carry and fraction at each step.
4) This process can be repeated up to fourth or fifth fraction place depending upon the demand of the question.
5) Pick up all carries in top to bottom order and that will be octal version of a fractional decimal number.

Example 1: Convert 0.27 decimal number into octal number.

```
0 | .27 x 8 = 2.16 (Here 2 is carry and is
  |  separated in next step)
2 | .16 x 8 = 1.28 (Here 1 is carry)
1 | .28 x 8 = 2.24 (2 is carry)
2 | .24 x 8 = 1.92
1 | .92 x 8 = 7.36
7 | .36
```

Further calculation can be stopped here as it has already reached five places of fraction. While picking up carries from top to bottom it comes out to be 21217

So 0.21217 is the octal number of decimal number 0.27

$(0.27)_{10} = (0.21217)_8$

Example 2: Convert decimal number 46.34 into octal number.

Solution: In above case first of all octal number of integer is solved. This can be solved in the following way:

```
8 | 46
8 | 5------6
  | 0------5
```

So octal number of integer part of decimal number 46 is 56

Now finding out octal number of the fraction part of given decimal number, i.e., 0.34

```
0 | .34 x 8 = 2.72
2 | .72 x 8 = 5.76
5 | .76 x 8 = 6.08
6 | .08 x 8 = 0.64
```

Calculation is stopped here as in the last step there is no carry. Taking carries from top to bottom the octal number so obtained is 0.256

So 56.256 is the octal number of decimal number 46.34

$(46.34)_{10} = (56.256)_8$

Conversion of Octal Number to Decimal Number

This conversion can be made with the following expansion table:

8^4	8^3	8^2	8^1	8^0
4096	512	64	8	1

Values beyond 8^4 is not shown in the table as a very big conversion is not generally asked in the exam.

Steps:

1) Consider the given octal number and enter each digit one by one in the above expansion table in left to right order.
2) Multiply number in a particular column with its power of eight.
3) Add all the products so obtained to get the desired number.

Solved Examples

Example 1: Convert the octal number 60 into decimal number.

8^4	8^3	8^2	8^1	8^0
4096	512	64	8	1
			6	0

Obtaining the desired decimal number:

0 x 1 + 8 x 6 = 48

So 48 is the decimal number of octal number 60

$$(60)_8 = (48)_{10}$$

Example 2: Convert octal number 173 to decimal number.

Solution:

8^4	8^3	8^2	8^1	8^0
4096	512	64	8	1
		1	7	3

1x 3 + 8 x 7 + 64 x 1 = 123

So octal number 173 is converted into decimal number 123

$$(173)_8 = (123)_{10}$$

Example 3: Convert octal number 505 into decimal number.

Solution:

8^4	8^3	8^2	8^1	8^0
4096	512	64	8	1
		5	0	5

1x 5 + 8 x 0 + 64 x 5 = 325

So octal number 505 is converted into decimal number 325

$$(505)_8 = (325)_{10}$$

Example 4: Convert octal number 2161 into decimal number.

Solution:

8^4	8^3	8^2	8^1	8^0
4096	512	64	8	1
	2	1	6	1

Further: 1 x 1 + 8 x 6 + 64 x 1 + 512 x 2 = 1137

So 1137 is the decimal number of octal number 2161

$(2161)_8 = (1137)_{10}$

Conversion of Octal Number with Fractions to Decimal Number

An octal number with fraction can be converted into decimal while knowing about result of the values of fractions in the expansion table shown as follows:

8^{-1}	8^{-2}	8^{-3}	
0.125	0.0156	0.0019	

In above table 8^{-1} means $\frac{1}{8}$, 8^{-2} means $\frac{1}{64}$, and 8^{-3} means $\frac{1}{512}$ and so on

Here, values up to 8^{-3} have been taken because denominator beyond this value becomes too big to be asked in the exam.

Steps:

1) Consider the given number and draw the expansion table of fractions.
2) Pick up the fractional part and put one digit in one column in left to right order.
3) Multiply the digit so picked up with value of the respective column.
4) Add up all the products so obtained to get the desired decimal number.

Solved Examples

Example 1: Convert an octal number 0.38 into decimal number.

Solution:

8^{-1}	8^{-2}	8^{-3}	
0.125	0.0156	0.0019	
3	8		

3 x 0.125 + 8 x 0.0156 = 0.4998

So 0.499 is the decimal number of octal number 0.38

$(0.38)_8 = (0.499)_{10}$

Example 2: Convert octal number 672.51 into decimal number.

Solution: First of all integer 672 is converted to decimal number with expansion table:

8^4	8^3	8^2	8^1	8^0
4096	512	64	8	1
		6	7	2

1 x 2 + 8 x 7 + 64 x 6 = 442

Now solving the fraction part 0.51 with the help of expansion table

8^{-1}	8^{-2}	8^{-3}	
0.125	0.0156	0.0019	
5	1		

5 x 0.125 + 1 x 0.0156 = 0.6406

Taking both the values, integer and fractions together, the number becomes 442.6406

So 442.6406 is the decimal number of octal number 672.51

$(672.51)_8 = (442.6406)_{10}$

Conversion of Decimal Number into Hexadecimal Number

A decimal number with base 10 is converted into Hexadecimal number with base 16 by taking the following steps:

Steps:

1) Consider the given decimal number and divide it by 16.
2) Consider the quotient and reminder so obtained.
3) Divide the quotient with 16 again to get fresh quotient and remainder.
4) Go on repeating division with 16 until quotient is either zero or a number less than 16.
5) The desired hexadecimal number is obtained by picking up reminders from bottom to top.

Solved Examples

Example 1: Convert decimal number 54 into hexadecimal number.

```
16 | 54
16 | 3------6
     0--------3
```

Solution: In the above operation, 3 is quotient and 6 is remainder and so is 3. Taking these remainders in bottom to top order, the number so obtained is 36.

Hence 36 is the hexadecimal number of decimal number 54

$(54)_{10} = (36)_{16}$

Example 2: What is hexadecimal number of decimal number 82?

Solution:

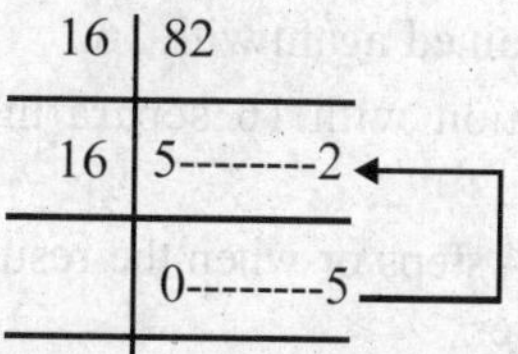

So 52 is the hexadecimal number of decimal number 82

$(82)_{10} = (52)_{16}$

Example 3: What is hexadecimal number of decimal number 169?

Solution:

```
16 | 169
16 | 10---------9
     0----------10
```

Remainders so obtained in bottom to top are 109

As 10 is written as A in hexadecimal number system, number becomes A9

So hexadecimal number of decimal number 169 is A9

$(169)_{10} = (A9)_{16}$

Example 4: Convert decimal number 1210 to hexadecimal number.

Solution:

```
16 | 1210
16 | 75--------10
16 | 4------------11
16 | 0-------------4
```

While picking up remainders from bottom to top the number so obtained is 41110

As 10 is A and 11 is B in hexadecimal number system, the number becomes 4BA

So 4BA is hexadecimal number of decimal number 1210

$(1210)_{10} = (4BA)_{16}$

Conversion of Decimal Number with Fractions to Hexadecimal Number

This conversion is completed by the following steps:

Steps:

1) Consider the given decimal number with fraction.
2) If fraction has integer with it then separate the integer part from fraction part.
3) Multiply the fraction part with 16.

4) If product comes with an integer then treat that integer as carry and separate it from fractional part.
5) Divide the fraction so obtained again with 16.
6) Go on dividing the fraction with 16 separating carry.
7) Repeat the process up to 4 steps or when the result is zero, whichever is earlier.
8) Stop multiplication and count carries so obtained from top to bottom and get the desired number.

Solved Examples

Example 1: Convert decimal number 0.38 to hexadecimal number.

Solution:

0	.38 x 16 = 6.08 (Here 6 is carry)
6	.08 x 16 = 1.28 (Here 1 is carry)
1	.28 x 16 = 4.48 (Here 4 is carry)
4	.48 x 16 = 7.68
7	.68

Here, multiplication is stopped as 0 has not been obtained.

Counting carries in top to bottom order, the number so obtained is 0.6147

So hexadecimal number of decimal number 0.38 is 0.6147

$$(0.38)_{10} = (0.6147)_{16}$$

Example 2: Convert decimal number 846.61 to hexadecimal number.

Solution: First, the integer part 846 is converted to hexadecimal number.

16	846	
16	52	14
16	3	4
	0	3

Hexadecimal number so obtained by picking up reminders in bottom to top order is 3414

As 14 is written as E in hexadecimal system, number becomes 34E

So 34E is hexadecimal number of integer part of decimal number 846

Now solving the fraction part:

0	.61 x 16 = 9.76 (Here 9 is carry)
9	.76 x 16 = 12.16 (12 is carry)
12	12 .16 x 16 = 2.56 (2 is carry)
2	.56 x 16 = 8.96 (8 is carry)
8	.96

Calculation here is stopped as it has achieved four carry points. Picking up carries from top to bottom is 9 12 2 8. As 12 is written with C here, the desired number is 0. 9C28

So 0.9C28 is the hexadecimal number of fraction part of decimal number 0.61

Now after combining fraction with integer part the whole number becomes 34E.9C28

So 34E.9C28 is the hexadecimal number of decimal number 846.61

$$(846.61)_{10} = (34E.9C28)_{16}$$

Conversion of Hexadecimal Number to Decimal Number

Steps:

Draw the expansion table of hexadecimal number system as shown below:

16^3	16^2	16^1	16^0

1) Fill the value of 16 with respective power starting from extreme right

16^3	16^2	16^1	16^0
4096	256	16	1

2) Pick up the given hexadecimal number, then starting from right, fill one digit in each column of above table starting from right of the table.
3) Multiply each digit with respective power of 16 and add all the results to get the desired decimal number.

Solved Examples

Example 1: What is the decimal number of hexadecimal number 7B3?

Solution: Drawing the expansion table and entering the given hexadecimal number:

16^3	16^2	16^1	16^0
4096	256	16	1
	7	B	3

As B = 11 in the hexadecimal system, putting that value in above box:

16^3	16^2	16^1	16^0
4096	256	16	1
	7	11	3

Now 1 x 3 + 16 x 11 + 256 x 7 = 1971

So 1971 is the decimal number of hexadecimal number 7B3

$$(7B3)_{16} = (1971)_{10}$$

Example 3: Convert hexadecimal number CEB to decimal number.

Solution:

16^3	16^2	16^1	16^0
4096	256	16	1
	C	E	B

Further:

16^3	16^2	16^1	16^0
4096	256	16	1
	12	14	11

1 x 11 + 16 x 14 + 256 x 12 = 3307

So 3307 is decimal number of hexadecimal number CEB

$$(CEB)_{16} = (3307)_{10}$$

Conversion of Hexadecimal Number with Fraction to Decimal Number with Fraction

First consider some fractional values of hexadecimal system:

$16^{-1} = \frac{1}{16} = 0.0625 \quad 16^{-2} = \frac{1}{256} = 0.0039$

$16^{-3} = \frac{1}{4096} = 0.00024$

Generally, conversion will not be asked beyond this value, further operation is stopped here.

Steps:

1) Consider the given hexadecimal number and then draw expansion table as follows:

16^{-1}	16^{-2}	16^{-3}
0.0625	0.0039	0.00024

2) Put each digit of fraction value in above table in left to right order.

3) Multiply each digit with respective value of 16 from left to right.

4) Add up all the values so obtained and get the desired number.

Solved Examples

Example 1: Convert hexadecimal number 0.9C2 to decimal number.

Solution:

16^{-1}	16^{-2}	16^{-3}
0.0625	0.0039	0.00024
9	C	2

Further:

16^{-1}	16^{-2}	16^{-3}	
0.0625	0.0039	0.00024	
9	12	2	

0.0625 x 9 + 0.0039 x 12 + 0.00024 x 2 = 0.612

So 0.612 is the decimal number of hexadecimal number 0.9C2

Example 2: What is the decimal number of hexadecimal number 8F2.3A?

Solution: Solving the integer part first:

16^3	16^2	16^1	16^0
4096	256	16	1
	8	F	2

Further:

16^3	16^2	16^1	16^0
4096	256	16	1
	8	15	2

1 x 2 + 16 x 15 + 256 x 8 = 2290

Hence 2290 is the decimal number of integer part of hexadecimal number of 8F2

Further:

16^{-1}	16^{-2}	16^{-3}	
0.0625	0.0039	0.00024	
3	A		

Further:

16^{-1}	16^{-2}	16^{-3}
0.0625	0.0039	0.00024
3	10	

$0.0625 \times 3 + 0.0039 \times 10 = 0.2265$

Now combining the integer and fraction part so obtained, number becomes: 2290.2265

So 2290.2265 is the decimal number of hexadecimal number 8F2.3A

$$(8F2.3A)_{16} = (2290.2265)_{10}$$

Conversion of Octal Number to Binary

An octal number has base 8. Before converting any octal number, a binary equivalent table is drawn by adopting the following steps:

1) Corresponding to that a binary equivalent table is to be drawn starting from 2^0 to 2^2 as shown below.

Octal Number	Binary Equivalent		
	2^2	2^1	2^0

2) Binary equivalents should be written in right to left order starting with 2^0.
3) As octal number has base 8 which is 2^3, binary equivalent so drawn for conversion should be less than 2^3.
4) Now primary octal numbers are written in the table as shown below:

Octal Number	Binary Equivalent		
	2^2	2^1	2^0
0	4	2	1
1			
2			
3			
4			
5			
6			
7			

5) Binary equivalent of each number is written under binary equivalent table as follows:

Octal Number	Binary Equivalent		
	$2^2(4)$	$2^1(2)$	$2^0(1)$
0	0	0	0
1	0	0	1
2	0	1	0
3	0	1	1
4	1	0	0
5	1	0	1
6	1	1	0
7	1	1	1

6) Binary equivalent is obtained for each octal number by considering the power of binary equivalent. For example, octal number 0 has 0 in binary equivalent as there is no zero result in the binary equivalent. Hence, none of the binary equivalent is required.
7) Binary equivalent 2^0 has result 1, it is required for octal number 1. So number 1 is written under 2^0 and 0 under other equivalents as these are not required. So binary number of octal number 1 is 001. Similarly, octal number 2 requires binary equivalent 2^1 as it produces result 2. Hence number 1 will be put under 2^1 and put zero under other equivalents as these are not required. So binary numbed of octal number 2 is 010
8) Octal number 3 is converted to binary as per its requirement of binary equivalent. As 3 is 2 +1, 1 is put under binary equivalents 2^0 and 2^1 as their total is 3 and 0 is put under binary equivalent 2^2 as it is not required. So binary equivalent of octal number 3 is 011. Binary equivalents of other octal numbers are obtained in the same way. Resultantly, above table is drawn.

Example: Convert octal number 57 to binary number.

Solution: Considering the given number 57.

Digits of this number 57 are separated as 5 and 7. Now the values of 5 and 7 are obtained from binary equivalent table. Here binary value of 5 is 101 and that of 7 is 111. By combining these, binary number so obtained is 101111.

So binary number of octal number 57 is 101111

$$(57)_8 = (101111)_2$$

Number Conversion Table

Decimal Base-10	Binary Base-2	Octal Base-8	Hexadecimal Base-16
0	0	0	0
1	1	1	1
2	10	2	2
3	11	3	3
4	100	4	4
5	101	5	5
6	110	6	6
7	111	7	7
8	1000	10	8
9	1001	11	9
10	1010	12	A
11	1011	13	B
12	1100	14	C
13	1101	15	D
14	1110	16	E
15	1111	17	F
16	10000	20	10
17	10001	21	11
18	10010	22	12
19	10011	23	13
20	10100	24	14
21	10101	25	15
22	10110	26	16
23	10111	27	17
24	11000	30	18
25	11001	31	19
26	11010	32	1A
27	11011	33	1B
28	11100	34	1C
29	11101	35	1D
30	11110	36	1E
31	11111	37	1F
32	100000	40	20

SIGNED MAGNITUDE FORM

In general, we represent the positive (unsigned) numbers without any sign indication and negative numbers with 'minus' (negative sign) sign before them. For example, 7 is a positive number and –7 is a negative number. But these are not applicable for computing in the digital systems like, computers, as the data is represented in binary number system. So to represent the sign a special notation is required. Such expression is called Signed Magnitude form. Signed magnitude form of number is expressed in two forms:

Signed Magnitude Expression

In signed magnitude form, a binary number has a sign bit at its Most significant Bit (MSB). Signed binary numbers are expressed with positive and negative signs. Positive number is represented with '0' at its most significant bit (MSB).

Negative number is represented with '1' at its most significant bit (MSB).

Example 1: What is signed magnitude binary form of decimal number +8?

Solution: As the given number is having + sign, it is expressed with 0 in sign bit. The binary number of +8 in signed magnitude form is expressed as follows:

Sign Bit	Actual binary
0	1000 (4-bit)

Signed Magnitude Form of +8 is 01000

Example 2: What is signed magnitude binary form of decimal number –8?

Solution: As the given number has negative sign before it, it is represented with sign 1.

Sign Bit	Actual Binary
1	1000 (4 bits)

Signed Magnitude Form of –8 is 11000

1's and 2's Complement of Signed Magnitude Form

A) 1's complement of signed form binary number is expressed by reversing the binary number, i.e., 1s are made 0s and 0s are made 1s.

Example: Binary number of 9 is 1001. Its 1's complement is expressed as follows:

Binary number:		1	0	0	1
1's Complement Form:		0	1	1	0
Signed Form Expression:	0	0	1	1	0

Examples of 1's Complement

Example 1: –33 = ?

33 is represented as $(100001)_2$

In 8-bit notation, it is represented as $(0010\ 0001)_2$

Now, –33 is represented in one's complement as $(1101\ 1110)_2$

Example 2: –127 = ?

In 8-bit notation, 127 is represented as $(0111\ 1111)_2$

Now, –127 is represented in one's complement as $(1000\ 0000)_2$

Example 3: –1 = ?

1 is represented as $(001)_2$

In 8-bit notation, it is represented as $(0000\ 0001)_2$

Now, –1 is represented in one's complement as $(1111\ 1110)_2$

B) 2's complement is expressed by adding 1 to 1's complement so found in binary number.

Example 2:

1's complement of 9 is 0110

2's complement expression: 0110 + 0001 = 0111

Signed magnitude form: 00111

Examples of 2's Complement

Example 1: –33 = ?

33 is represented as $(100001)_2$

In 8-bit notation, it is represented as $(0010\ 0001)_2$

Now, –33 is represented in one's complement as $(1101\ 1110)_2$

Adding 1 (0000 0001) to it,

The result is $(1101\ 1111)_2$

Therefore, the two's complement of the number –33 is $(1101\ 1111)_2$.

Example 2: –127 = ?

In 8-bit notation, 127 is represented as $(0111\ 1111)_2$

Now, –127 is represented in one's complement as $(1000\ 0000)_2$

Adding 1 (0000 0001) to it,

The result is $(1000\ 0001)_2$

Therefore, the two's complement of the number –127 is $(1000\ 0001)_2$

Example 3: –1 = ?

1 is represented as $(001)_2$

In 8-bit notation, it is represented as $(0000\ 0001)_2$

Now, –1 is represented in one's complement as $(1111\ 1110)_2$

Adding 1 (0000 0001) to it,

The result is $(1111\ 1111)_2$

Therefore, the two's complement of the number –1 is $(1111\ 1111)_2$

Generally, signed magnitude form is expressed in 8-bit binary number. If a number is of lower bit, then sufficient 0s are prefixed to make it 8-bit.

Practice Exercise

General Questions Format

1. Convert the binary number 0000.1010 to decimal.
   (A) 0.10 (B) 0.55
   (C) 0.50 (D) 0.625
2. The decimal equivalent of binary 1010000 is ________.
   (A) 96 (B) 80
   (C) 78 (D) 84
3. Convert the binary number 1011.1110 to decimal.
   (A) 11.875 (B) 11.675
   (C) 13.875 (D) 13.75
4. What is the decimal value of 2^{-2}?
   (A) 0.5 (B) 0.125
   (C) 0.2 (D) 0.25
5. Convert the decimal number 12.125 to binary.
   (A) 1100.0110 (B) 1110.0010
   (C) 1100.0010 (D) 1010.1100
6. Which binary value equals 2^{-2}?
   (A) 0000.0010 (B) 0010.0000
   (C) 0000.1000 (D) 0000.0100
7. Convert the decimal number 6.75 to binary.
   (A) 0110.1100 (B) 0111.1100
   (C) 0110.0110 (D) 0110.1010
8. How many symbols are used in the hexadecimal number system?
   (A) sixteen (B) six
   (C) ten (D) twelve
9. The hexadecimal equivalent of a decimal 13 is ________.
   (A) "C" (B) "D"
   (C) "E" (D) "F"
10. Convert decimal 213 to binary.
    (A) 1100101
    (B) 0111001
    (C) 11010101
    (D) 11100011

11. Convert decimal 19 to binary.
(A) 00010011 (B) 00010100
(C) 00100011 (D) 00011001

12. The hexadecimal equivalent of a decimal 11 is ________.
(A) "A" (B) "B"
(C) "C" (D) "D"

13. What is the decimal value of 2^3 ?
(A) 4 (B) 8
(C) 2 (D) 6

14. Which binary value equals 24?
(A) 00010000 (B) 00010100
(C) 00010001 (D) 00001000

15. Convert decimal 31 to octal.
(A) $(37)_8$ (B) $(43)_8$
(C) $(33)_8$ (D) (30)8

16. The decimal equivalent of binary 110101 is ________.
(A) $(47)_{10}$ (B) $(53)_{10}$
(C) $(49)_{10}$ (D) $(59)_{10}$

17. What is the decimal value of 2^{-1}?
(A) 0.1 (B) 0.25
(C) 0.5 (D) 0.05

18. What is the decimal value of 2^1?
(A) 1 (B) 4
(C) 2 (D) 0

19. Convert the binary number 1010.1100 to decimal.
(A) 12.65 (B) 10.875
(C) 10.55 (D) 10.75

20. What is the decimal value of 2^5?
(A) 10 (B) 20
(C) 16 (D) 32

21. The hexadecimal equivalent of decimal 128 is ________.
(A) $(82)_{16}$ (B) $(80)_{16}$
(C) $(85)_{16}$ (D) $(90)_{16}$

22. Convert decimal 36 to binary.
(A) 00110100 (B) 01000010
(C) 00100100 (D) 01100010

23. Convert decimal 20 to octal.
(A) 16 (B) 10
(C) 18 (D) 24

24. How many unique numeric symbols are used in the decimal number system?
(A) unlimited (B) nine
(C) one (D) ten

25. The decimal equivalent of binary 1000110 is ________.
(A) 126 (B) 110
(C) 134 (D) 144

26. The decimal equivalent of binary 0010111 is ________.
(A) $(48)_{10}$ (B) $(22)_{10}$
(C) $(19)_{10}$ (D) $(23)_{10}$

27. Convert decimal 101 to binary.
(A) 00111011 (B) 01100101
(C) 01101111 (D) 01110011

28. Which binary value equals 2^6?
(A) 00001100 (B) 0000110
(C) 01000000 (D) 00100000

29. What is the decimal value of 2^6?
(A) 128 (B) 36
(C) 32 (D) 64

30. What numeric symbols are used in the binary number system?
(A) 0 through 8 (B) 0, 1, 2
(C) 1, 2 (D) 0, 1

31. Which binary value equals 2^{-1}?
(A) 1.0000 (B) 0.0010
(C) 0.0001 (D) 0.1000

32. Convert decimal 58 to binary.
(A) 00011110 (B) 00111010
(C) 00111100 (D) 00101110

33. What is binary form of decimal number +28 in signed magnitude form?
(A) 010101 (B) 111010
(C) 011100 (D) 0011101

34. What is binary form of decimal number +53 in signed magnitude form (1's complement)
(A) 0 110111 (B) 0010100
(C) 0111101 (D) 0000010

35. What is binary form of decimal number –78 in signed magnitude form (2's complement)
(A) 00100011 (B) 01000111
(C) 11110111 (D) 00000001

KEY

1. D	2. B	3. A	4. D	5. C	6. D	7. A
8. A	9. B	10. C	11. A	12. B	13. B	14. A
15. A	16. B	17. C	18. C	19. D	20. D	21. B
22. C	23. D	24. D	25. C	26. D	27. B	28. C
29. D	30. D	31. D	32. B	33. C	34. D	35. A

Questions Asked in Previous NET Exams

1. What is the decimal equivalent of binary number 1100110?

(UGC NET JUNE 2019)

(A) 102 (B) 204
(C) 153 (D) 5

2. Which of the following statement(s) is/are TRUE? **(UGC NET JANUARY 2017)**

S1: The decimal number 11 is larger than the hexadecimal number 11.

S2: In the binary number 1110.101, the fractional part has the decimal value as 0.625.

(A) SI only (B) S2 only
(C) Both S1 and S2 (D) Neither S1 nor S2

3. If the binary equivalent of the decimal number 48 is 110000, then the binary equivalent of the decimal number 51 is given by

(UGC NET EXAM JULY 2016)

(A) 110011 (B) 110010
(C) 110001 (D) 110100

4. Which one of the following represents the binary equivalent of the decimal number 25?

(UGC NET EXAM JUNE 2015)

(A) 11011 (B) 10101
(C) 01101 (D) 11001

5. Binary equivalent of decimal number 35 is

(UGC NET EXAM DECEMBER 2014)

(A) 100011 (B) 110001
(C) 110101 (D) 101011

6. Which one of the following is correct?

(UGC NET DECEMBER 2012)

(A) $(17)_{10} = (17)_{16}$ (B) $(17)_{10} = (17)_8$
(C) $(17)_{10} = (10111)_2$ (D) $(17)_{10} = (10001)_2$

7. If $(y)_x$ represents a number y in base x, then which of the following numbers is smallest of all? **(UGC NET DECEMBER 2011)**

(A) $(1111)_2$ (B) $(1111)_8$
(C) $(1111)_{10}$ (D) $(1111)_{16}$

8. The binary equivalent of $(-19)_{10}$ in signed magnitude system is

(UGC NET JUNE 2011)

(A) 11101100 (B) 11101101
(C) 10010011 (D) None of these

9. The octal number system consists of the following symbols:

(UGC NET JUNE 2011)

(A) 0 – 7 (B) 0 – 9
(C) 0 – 9, A – F (D) None of the above

10. The hexadecimal number system consists of the symbols

(UGC NET DECEMBER 2010)

(A) 0 – 7 (B) 0 – 9, A – F
(C) 0 – 7, A – F (D) None of these

11. The binary equivalent of $(-15)_{10}$ is (2's complement system is used)

(UGC NET DECEMBER 2010)

(A) 11110001 (B) 11110000
(C) 10001111 (D) None of these

12. Which one of the following represents the binary equivalent of the decimal number 23?

(UGC NET JUNE 2010)

(A) 01011
(B) 10111
(C) 10011
(D) None of the above

KEY

1. A	2. B	3. A	4. D	5. A	6. D	7. A
8. D	9. A	10. B	11. A	12. B		

6 Digital Initiatives in Higher Education

CONCEPT

Higher education in India is rapidly heading towards leading a digital life. Keeping pace with current requirements, Indian government is making a huge investment in bringing latest communications technology in this field. Today, higher education is no more confined to books and traditional classrooms. Various digital initiatives have been taken by the Indian government which has incorporated the concept of digital content and smart classrooms. Indian government is pursuing the target of cent per cent digitisation of higher education by roping in information and communications technology in the sphere of higher education. As every sphere of life is enjoying digital age today, teaching and learning field is no more an exception. Due to various digital initiatives being taken by India to make information and communications technology lifeline of higher education, students and teachers are being given the facilities of e-learning, online education, e-teaching, digital libraries, etc. In spite of this, still a lot is to be achieved in digitisation of higher education due to infrastructural, administrative, academic, and faculty bottlenecks. Continuous efforts of India can remove these bottlenecks also. Following digital initiatives have been taken by India:

1) **e-ShodhSindhu:**

   The Union Ministry of Human Resource Development (MHRD) formed e-ShodhSindhu on the recommendation of an Expert Committee. This initiative was created by merging three initiatives, namely UGC-INFONET Digital Library Consortium, NLIST (National Library and Information Services Infrastructure for Scholarly Content), and INDEST (Indian National Digital Library in Engineering Sciences and Technology)-AICTE (All India Council for Technical Education) Consortium. The e-ShodhSindhu will continue to provide current as well as archival access to more than 15,000 core and peer-reviewed journals and a number of bibliographic, citation, and factual databases in different disciplines from a large number of publishers and aggregators to its member institutions, including centrally-funded technical institutions, universities, and colleges that are covered under 12(B) and 2(f) Sections of the UGC Act.

2) **Virtual Labs:**

   Another digital initiative of MHRD is Virtual Labs project under the aegis of National Mission on Education through Information and Communications Technology (NMEICT). This project is a consortium activity of twelve participating institutes and IIT Delhi is the coordinating institute. It is a paradigm shift in ICT-based education. For the first time, such an initiative has been taken up in remote experimentation. Under Virtual Labs project, over 100 Virtual Labs consisting of approximately 700+ web-enabled experiments were designed for remote operation and viewing. The intended beneficiaries of the projects are:

   - All students and faculty members of Science and Engineering Colleges who do not have access to good lab facilities and/or instruments.
   - High-school students, whose inquisitiveness will be triggered, possibly motivating them to take up higher?studies.
   - Researchers in different institutes who can collaborate and share resources.
   - Different engineering colleges who can benefit from the content and related teaching resources.

There is no requirement of creating any additional infrastructure to set up Virtual Labs for conducting experiments. One computer terminal with broadband Internet connectivity is all that is needed to perform the experiments remotely. The simulations-based experiments can be accessed remotely via the

Internet. The Virtual Labs has been designed to give students a feel of the real laboratory. Unlike traditional lab set-up, students can perform the same experiment as many as times as they wish individually. Students are even able to perform experiments involving sophisticated and costly equipment generally not readily available in every college. Web-based and video-based courses address the issue of teaching to some extent. Conducting joint experiments by two participating institutions and also sharing costly resources has always been a challenge. With the present day Internet and computer technologies, the above limitations can no more hamper students and researchers in enhancing their skills and knowledge. This would help in learning basic and advanced concepts through remote experimentation. Internet-based experimentation further permits use of resources-knowledge, software, and data available on the Web, apart from encouraging skilful experiments being simultaneously performed at points separated in space (and possibly, time). Over 205 Virtual Labs in 9 Engineering and Science disciplines, comprising about 1515 experiments are operational and currently being accessed by more than 6 lakh students.

3) **Baadal:**

It is a digital initiative developed and maintained by IIT Delhi. It is a cloud orchestration and virtualisation management software initiated by MHRD under NMEICT scheme. It ensures optimum utilisation of the infrastructure and speeds up the development and deployment of eGov applications for academic needs. It is hosted in NIC data-centre. Main features of Baadal are:

- Monitoring of dynamic resource utilisation
- An integrated workflow system for request and commissioning of virtual machines
- Facilities for suspend, resume, shutdown, power off, power on, and specifying resource requirement of virtual machines

4) **Global Initiative of Academic Networks (GIAN):**

Govt. of India approved a new program titled Global Initiative of Academic Networks (GIAN) in higher education aimed at tapping the talent pool of scientists and entrepreneurs internationally to encourage their engagement with the institutes of higher education in India so as to augment the country's existing academic resources, accelerate the pace of quality reform, and elevate India's scientific and technological capacity to global excellence. GIAN has been launched to invite world famous foreign academics to premier Indian institutes by providing global exposure and knowledge sharing by renowned professors with students and faculty. Many courses are taught by foreign faculty from different countries under this program.

5) **The National Programme on Technology Enhanced Learning (NPTEL):**

It was initiated by seven Indian Institutes of Technology (Bombay, Delhi, Kanpur, Kharagpur, Madras, Guwahati, and Roorkee) along with the Indian Institute of Science, Bangalore in 2003. Five core disciplines were identified, namely, civil engineering, computer science and engineering, electrical engineering, electronics and communication engineering, and mechanical engineering and 235 courses in web/video format were developed in this phase.

The main goal of NPTEL Phase II (2009-14) was to build on the engineering and core science courses launched previously in NPTEL Phase I. An additional 600 web and video courses were created in all major branches of engineering and physical sciences at the undergraduate and postgraduate levels, and management courses at the postgraduate level. Several improvements such as indexing of all video and web courses and keyword search were implemented. NPTEL was first conceived in 1999 to offer web and video based online courses. Anyone can access these courses without any fee or eligibility requirement. The lectures are delivered by renowned professors from IITs and leading institutes. NPTEL was the first of its kind successful MOOC-type platform to stream online lectures.

Highlights:

- Largest online repository in the world of courses in engineering, basic sciences, and selected humanities and social sciences subjects
- Online web portal http://nptel.ac.in-more than 471 million+ views
- Youtube channel for NPTEL -most subscribed educational channel, 1.5 million+ channel subscribers, 404 million+ views

- More than 56000 hours of video content
- Most accessed library of peer-reviewed educational content in the world
- 52000+ hours of transcribed content; 51000+ hours of subtitled videos

6) **e-PG Pathshala:**

Another landmark digital initiative of the MHRD is e-PG Pathshala under its National Mission on Education through ICT (NMEICT). The project is being executed by the UGC. The content and its quality being the key component of education system, high quality, curriculum-based, interactive e-content in 70 subjects across all disciplines of social sciences, arts, fine arts and humanities, natural and mathematical sciences, linguistics, and languages have been developed by the subject experts working in Indian universities and other R&D institutes across the country. Every subject has a team of principal investigator, paper coordinators, content writers, content reviewers, language editors, and multimedia team.

7) **Atal Ranking of Institutions on Innovation Achievements (ARIIA):**

ARIIA is an initiative of Ministry of Human Resource Development (MHRD), Govt. of India to systematically rank all major higher educational institutions and universities in India on indicators related to "Innovation and Entrepreneurship Development" amongst students and faculties. ARIIA ranking will certainly inspire Indian institutions to reorient their mindset and build ecosystems to encourage high quality research, innovation, and entrepreneurship. More than quantity, ARIIA will focus on quality of innovations and will try to measure the real impact created by these innovations nationally and internationally. Moreover, ARIIA will set the tone and direction for institutions for future development for making them globally competitive and in the forefront of innovation.

8) **The National Institutional Ranking Framework (NIRF):**

NIRF was approved by the MHRD and launched by Honourable Minister of Human Resource Development on 29th September 2015.This framework outlines a methodology to rank institutions across the country. The methodology draws from the overall recommendations and broad understanding arrived at by a Core Committee set up by MHRD, to identify the broad parameters for ranking various universities and institutions. The parameters broadly cover "Teaching, Learning, and Resources", "Research and Professional Practices", "Graduation Outcomes", "Outreach and Inclusivity", and "Perception".

9) **IMPRINT:**

Adopting engineering and technology as the vehicle to addressing the societal needs and achieving national prosperity, MHRD has drafted a new and catalytic scheme called IMPacting Research INnovation and Technology or IMPRINT. IMPRINT is a first-of-its-kind Pan-IIT and IISc joint initiative to develop a

(a) New Education Policy, and

(b) Roadmap for Research

to solve major engineering and technology challenges in selected domains needed by the country.

IMPRINT scheme has ten domains which represent the most important areas relevant to our country in order to enable, empower, and embolden the nation for ***inclusive growth and self-reliance***. The first phase of IMPRINT is dedicated to creating a policy document defining the scope, strategy, and mandate for pursuing engineering challenges in the country and not developing a specific technological product or process. The real engineering pursuit will ensue in the second phase. Each technology domain of IMPRINT along with the underlying themes, targets, and topics embedded in them represent the immediate goals before the nation for engineering innovation and intervention. However, the principal motto remains the same for each domain: (a) to create an education policy for inculcating scientific temperament and innovation skill, and (b) to develop the research roadmap for technology preparedness.The Domains and Coordinators of IMPRINT, steered by IIT Kanpur (as the national coordinator), are: (i) Health care: IIT Kharagpur (ii) Information and Communication Technology: IIT Kharagpur (iii) Energy: IIT Bombay (iv) Sustainable Habitat: IIT Roorkee (v) Nano-technology Hardware: IIT Bombay (vi) Water Resources and River systems: IIT Kanpur (vii) Advanced Materials: IIT Kanpur

(viii) Manufacturing: IIT Madras (ix) Security and Defense: IIT Madras (x) Environmental Science and Climate Change: IISc, Bangalore.

10) **VIDWAN:**

VIDWAN has been launched to strengthen teaching and research in India. It is the premier database of profiles of scientists/researchers and other faculty members working at leading academic institutions and other R&D organisation involved in teaching and research in India. It provides important information about expert's background, contact address, experience, scholarly publications, skills and accomplishments, researcher identity, etc. The database is developed and maintained by Information and Library Network Centre (INFLIBNET) with financial support from the National Mission on Education through ICT (NMEICT). The database would be instrumental in selection of panels of experts for various committees and taskforce established by the Ministries/Govt. establishments for monitoring and evaluation purposes. The 'Information and Library Network' (INFLIBNET) Centre took the initiative. The objectives of VIDWAN is to i) collect academic and research profiles of scientists, faculty, and research scientists working in leading academic and R&D organisations in India and abroad; ii) quickly and conveniently provide information about experts to peers, prospective collaborators, funding agencies, policy makers, and research scholars in the country; iii) establish communication directly with the experts who possess the expertise needed by research scholars; iv) identify peer reviewers for review of articles and research proposals; and v) create information exchanges and networking opportunities among scientists. Further, the availability of a single point expert database will help the policy makers and funding agencies in decision-making and policy intervention. R&D organisations include IITs, CSIR, DRDO, etc.

11) **Spoken Tutorial:**

It is a multi-award winning educational content portal. Here, one can learn various Free and Open Source Software all by oneself. Self-paced, multi-lingual courses ensure that anybody with a computer and a desire for learning, can learn from any place, at any time, and in a language of one's choice. Spoken Tutorial project aims to teach various free and open source software through small length audio and video tutorials. The idea is that what one sees and hears can be better comprehended by the human mind. Each tutorial is approximately of ten minutes screencast explaining the use/working of software along with recorded narration for self-learning. The target audience is anyone who wants to learn IT concepts. The various tutorials in spoken tutorials are on LibreOffice (open word processor), Scilab, Linux, LaTeX, PHP, MySQL, Python, etc. These tutorials are provided free of cost on the project website. Spoken tutorial project has also collaborated with many institutes all over India by dubbing the content in various regional languages. The spoken tutorials are available in English, Hindi, and many state languages of India.

12) **FOSSEE (Free/Libre and Open Source Software for Education):**

FOSSEE project promotes the use of Free/Libre Open Source Software (FLOSS) tools to improve the quality of education in our country. The aim is to reduce dependency on proprietary software in educational institutions. The use of FLOSS tools is encouraged through various activities to ensure replacement of commercial software by equivalent FLOSS tools. The FOSSEE project is part of the National Mission on Education through Information and Communications Technology (ICT) and Ministry of Human Resource Development (MHRD), Government of India. FOSSEE project sanctioned to IIT Bombay has been promoting use of open source software in educational institutions and the domain is (http://fossee.in). It does this through instructional material, such as spoken tutorials, documentation, such as textbook companions, awareness programmes, such as conferences, training workshops, and internships. Textbook Companion (TBC) is a collection of code for solved examples of standard textbooks. About 2,000 college students and teachers have participated in this activity and close to 1,000 TBCs have been created in Scilab and Python alone. FOSSEE has made all the TBCs open source and has made them available for free download. Scilab and Python TBCs are also on the cloud, so that one needs only a browser to access/execute the codes of TBC. FOSSEE is promoting the well established open source software, i.e., OpenFOAM, an alternative to the proprietary software Fluent for computational fluid dynamics; and DWSIM, an alternative to the proprietary software Aspen Plus, for chemical process simulation. FOSSEE has also undertaken several new open source software activities as well: raising Scilab toolboxes to that of Matlab; development of eSim, an electronic design automation software, an alternative to ORCAD; and development of Sandhi, a software for data acquisition and control, an alternative to LabVIEW. The FOSSEE team works on open source hardware projects, such as Open PLC and Arduino as well. Through all of these projects, a large number of students across the country have been trained.

13) **e-Acharya:**

The INFLIBNET Centre has developed a web-based interface called "e-Acharya: Integrated e-Content Portal" for all e-content projects, developed/funded under the National Mission of Education through ICT. There are more than 50 projects on e-content under NMEICT which are developed/being developed in various subject disciplines (science, arts, engineering, social science, etc.) through various Indian institutes/ universities/colleges. e-Acharya, also called 'Integrated e-Content Portal' of NMEICT, is the official repository of NMEICT e-content and all content produced under NMEICT. It is being put at this Repository platform at INFILIBNET Centre Gandhinagar, so to apply basic tenets of preservation for digital content, implement standard Metadata scheme of different types for the digital content, and ensure their long-term availability. All the Project Investigators awarded development of e-content under. NCERT shall provide e-content Links to e-Acharya and it will be ensured that all the content including e-Books are made available on e-Acharya. The e-Acharya besides being a repository of content shall also have the Metadata of all these contents and it shall form a vertical of 'National Digital Library' (NDL), being implemented by IIT Kharagpur. The e-Acharya shall be backed by a robust 24X7 Data Centre, which shall be integrated with NMEICT, Cloud network, set up at NIC/NKN Data Centre by the IIT Delhi and called 'Baadal'. The MOOCs being produced under NMEICT shall also be uploaded on e-Acharya.

14) **Educational TV and Radio Broadcasting:**

Education satellite (EDUSAT) was the first exclusive satellite launched for broadcasting classroom educational content for distance learning in year 2004. **Gyan Darshan** is a satellite channel of DD India to telecast programmes in association with IGNOU. It airs programs related to open and distance education courses offered by IGNOU. **Gyan Dhara** is an Internet-based live discussion service for students where they can participate by asking questions through email or telephone. **Gyan Vani** is an FM-based radio service airing programs related to higher and technical education. **Swayam Prabha** is a bouquet of Direct-to-Home channels launched recently for transmitting high quality educational content without any charges. **Consortium for Education Communication (CEC)** is also running 24-hours **Vyas channel** for transmitting educational content for undergraduate classes. CEC has also established media centres in various universities across the country to produce high quality educational video content.

15) **Talk to a Teacher:**

This project running at IIT, Bombay has three major components: Researchoscope (RS), Courses on View (COV), and Ask a Question (AAQ). RS is a series of lectures under which Ph.D. scholars of IIT Bombay exhibit their work by giving talks about their research work. The video archives of talks on various subjects of science and engineering are available. The graduates speak for about 40 minutes to discuss details of their research work and also invite questions in the last 10 minutes. COV project provides free access to Engineering and Science courses recorded live in the classrooms of IIT Bombay. AAQ is a one of its kind initiative in which learners can ask questions in various fields of science and engineering from faculty members of IIT Bombay. The questions can be asked during live sessions as well as offline in forum discussions. The project gives an opportunity to students from various engineering colleges to interact face-to-face with the faculty of IIT Bombay. Talk to a

Teacher developed by IIT Bombay, is an initiative of the National Mission on Education through ICT, funded by MHRD to provide free access to a few selected graduate and postgraduate courses, taught at IIT Bombay by distinguished faculty members and scholars. It uses A-VIEW collaboration tool developed by Amrita University for providing virtual classrooms to the faculty across the country. These courses can be viewed absolutely free of charge at lower bandwidths on a personal computer/laptop having a headphone and Internet connection. Registration is not required as it does not have any evaluation/certification process. The courses are recorded live in the classrooms of IIT Bombay and may not reflect the entire content of the course. Apart from the core courses in Engineering and Computer Science disciplines, the program also covers Humanities and Social Sciences discipline. More than 80,000 teachers have been trained, so far, under this project, involving synchronous delivery of courses from IIT Mumbai and IIT Kharagpur.

16) **e-Yantra:**

It is yet another digital initiative sponsored by MHRD under the National Mission on Education through ICT program. It is an initiative by IIT Bombay that aims to create the next generation of embedded systems engineers with a practical outlook to help provide practical solutions to some of the real world problems. The project is implemented to incorporate robotics into engineering education with the objective of engaging students through exciting hands-on application of mathematics, computer science, and engineering principles. Creation of robotic platforms has been very successfully demonstrated during Phase I of the project. Presently, e-Yantra has been implemented in 100 colleges. e-Yantra is creating skills by setting up lab infrastructure for project-based learning and training teachers in these 100 engineering colleges. Going ahead, MHRD sees the core skills developed by IIT Bombay as generating, distributing, and analysing content to further create manpower with practical skills. All the projects and code are available on the e-Yantra web-site www.e-yantra.org as open source content.

17) **National Digital Library (NDL):**

NDL of India is a free and open collection of e-books, research papers from IISc, Bangalore, various state education board books, and previous year question papers of UPSC/GATE/JEE exams. The books are available in English as well as in many Indian languages. Full e-books in pdf format can be downloaded and read in offline mode. A Project titled "Development of National Digital Library of India, Towards Building a National Asset" has been sanctioned to IIT, Kharagpur under NMEICT by MHRD. National Digital Library in India aims to collect, preserve, and disseminate the entire intellectual output of our country and provide online access from school level to post graduate level, including technical education. The project aims to develop (i) overall framework to collate a large number of e-contents for school, college, and higher education, e-content, virtual library, covering needs of learners with differing abilities (ii) Design and development of "OAI-PMH" Server for Metadata Harvesting, Indexed, etc. (iii) serve as a pan-India virtual teaching-learning-evaluation-knowledge platform and for key national assets, and (iv) collect resources from other Ministries such as Ministry of Culture, Health, Rural Development and Department of Science and Technology on this portal. There are more than 72 lakh digital books available through the NDL. The contents cover almost all major domains of education and all major levels of learners from school level to the highest level of education including lifelong learners. More than 15 lakh students have registered themselves in the NDL. The NDL is available through a mobile app too.

18) **Shodhganga:**

Shodhganga is an online and open repository of research theses uploaded by all Indian universities. It has been made mandatory by UGC to upload full thesis work of all scholars before awarding any research degree. Even synopsis of the research project proposals can be uploaded on ShodhGangotri, which is also part of this initiative. The research work of Ph.D. scholars all over India is available in open repository and can be accessed freely by anyone.

19) **National Knowledge Network (NKN):**

NKN is multi-gigabit Internet backbone for higher education and research network to aid resource sharing and multidisciplinary research. Various CSIR research laboratories, atomic energy institutions, IITs/, universities, and higher learning institutes are digitally interconnected via NKN, so that researchers, professors, scientists, and students can work closely with each other via streaming of lectures, information sharing, and collaborative research. With such seamless digital connectivity, classroom sessions, video conferences, digital library, and guest lectures can be delivered to all connected institutions. NKN has the capacity to connect as many as 30,000 to 40,000 universities and laboratories all over India. Virtual classrooms are set up in all connected institutions for knowledge dissemination.

20) **Quality Enhancement in Engineering Education (QEEE):**

QEEE program is run through IIT Madras, where live lectures are delivered through dedicated bandwidth to students of top 10% engineering colleges by the faculty of IIT. The coursepack also include tutorials, virtual labs, e-books, quizzes and assignments, and Bridge courses. Students are evaluated at the end of the course through proctored examination by local faculty members and a certificate is also awarded to all successful candidates.

21) **ShodhGangotri:**

Under the initiative called **"ShodhGangotri"**, research scholars/research supervisors in universities are requested to deposit electronic version of approved synopsis submitted by research scholars to the universities for registering themselves for the Ph.D. programme. The repository on one hand, would reveal the trends and directions of research being conducted in Indian universities, and on the other hand, it would avoid duplication of research. Synopsis in "ShodhGangotri" would later be mapped to full-text theses in **"Shodhganga"**. As such, once the full-text thesis is submitted for a synopsis, a link to the full-text theses would be provided from ShodhGangotri to "Shodhganga".

22) **National Academic Depository (NAD):**

National Academic Depository (NAD) is an initiative of Ministry of Human Resources Development, Govt. of India (MHRD) to facilitate digital issuance, storage, access, and verification of Academic Awards issued by Academic Institutions. NAD is a Unique, Innovative, and Progressive initiative under "Digital India" theme towards achieving Digital enablement of the Education Records. NAD aspires to make the vision of Digital Academic Certificates for every Indian a reality. This touches the lives of Indian youth and empowers them with Digital, Online, Trusted, and Verifiable Certificates which are accessible in a secure manner at all times. NAD promises to do away with difficulties/inefficiencies of collecting, maintaining, and presenting physical papers.

23) **e-Kalpa:**

Another MHRD/NMEICT initiative named "e-Kalpa" creating Digital-Learning Environment for Design in India has successfully demonstrated the achievement of the following project objectives, on completion of its Phase I:

1. Digital online content for learning Design with e-Learning programs on Design
2. Digital Design Resource Database including the craft sector
3. Social networking for Higher Learning with collaborative Learning Space for Design
4. Design inputs for products of National Mission in Education through ICT.

The content of e-Kalpa website named "D'source" includes 160 Courses on Design Learning in different domains, more than 400 Resources in the form of fine examples of Design and Crafts, 110 Case studies of Design Projects undertaken by professionals and design students, 50 Video Lectures and Presentations by subject experts, and 600 examples of a Visual Gallery that has documented works of the rich tradition of art and design seen across different regions of India.

Practice Exercise

General Questions Format

1. The aim of National Digital Library in India is to provide online access to:
   (A) post graduate level students the best subject and general content collected from the best sources of India.
   (B) students as well as adults gaining education from any source by collecting best possible content from the most intellectual sources of India.
   (C) school and college level students attaining technical education the subject-wise relevant content, just like in a library, collected from various IITs in the country.
   (D) None of these.

2. Which of the following are three major components of the digital initiative 'Talk to the Teacher'?
   (A) Researchoscope, Courses on View, Ask a Question
   (B) Academicia, Curriculum Proposal, Ask a Question
   (C) Researchoscope, Teacher Intro, Authenticity Profile
   (D) Courses on View, Teacher Intro, Content Feasibility

3. Which of the following digital initiative has been taken by the government of India for creating next generation engineers?
   (A) e-Acharya (B) e-Kalpa
   (C) e-Yantra (D) e-ShodhSindhu

4. Which of the following is TRUE about Virtual Labs?
   a) Labs are working under aegis of MHRD.
   b) There is no requirement of creating separate infrastructure for these labs.
   c) IIT Kharagpur is the coordinating institute.
   d) These labs are covered under a consortium of 15 participating units.

   (A) b and d only
   (B) a and b only
   (C) a, c, and d only
   (D) a, b, c, and d

5. Which of the following is NOT feature of digital initiative 'Baadal'?
   (A) Dynamic resource utilisation
   (B) Integrated workflow system for attending requests
   (C) Digitisation of providing online content
   (D) Commissioning of virtual machines

6. e-Kalpa initiative has been started to facilitate learning in ____.
   (A) architecture
   (B) medical science
   (C) finance and banking
   (D) design and craft

7. National Academic Repository will facilitate provision of various academic services except
   (A) issuing academic awards
   (B) digital enablement of education records
   (C) providing trusted and verifiable academic certificates
   (D) pursuing universities and colleges to encourage providing online academic services

8. Which of the following is NOT TRUE about 'Spoken Tutorial'?
   a) It is a portal to Free and Open Source Software.
   b) One can learn from anywhere, at any time, and in the language of one's choice.
   c) Coaching is given in the form of online text which can be downloaded without any cost.
   d) Idea behind this initiative is to develop online perception in learners' minds.

   (A) c and d only (B) a, b, c, and d
   (C) b only (D) a and d only

9. What is the full form of digital initiative FOSSEE?
   (A) Free/Libral and Open Source Software for Education
   (B) Free/Libre and Open System Software for Education
   (C) Formal/Libre and Open Source Software for Education
   (D) Free/Libre and Open Source Software for Education

10. Which academic online centre is associated with e-Acharya?

(A) NMEICT (B) INFLIBNET
(C) NDL (D) NIRF

11. Which of the following is TRUE?

(A) Synopsis of a thesis are deposited to ShodhGangotri.

(B) QEEE is a portal started for promoting elementary engineering education to qualify IIT entrance exams.

(C) Shodhganga is a repository of research theses mandated by UGC.

(D) Gyan Darshan is an educational channel telecasted jointly by DD and UGC.

12. Under Column I below, various digital initiatives in higher education by India are given and under Column II concept of initiative is given. Match the digital initiative with its concept and choose the correct code among the codes given below:

Column I (Digital Initiative)	Column II (Concept)
a) VIDWAN	i) Pooling of scientists and entrepreneurs
b) IMPRINT	ii) Ranking of institutions of higher education
c) ARIIA	iii) Engineering and technology as a panacea
d) GIAN	iv) Profile of researchers and teachers

Codes:	(a)	(b)	(c)	(d)
(A)	iv	iii	ii	i
(B)	iii	ii	iv	i
(C)	iv	i	ii	iii
(D)	i	iv	iii	ii

13. Why does India need digital initiatives in the field of higher education?

a) There is a need to prevent rapidly increasing brain drain.

b) Higher education needs dynamic approach which is possible due to digital initiatives.

c) Digital initiatives will narrow down the digital divide among students.

d) Diversification of higher education is the need of the day and this is possible through digital initiatives

Arrange above initiative evidences in descending order of priority.

(A) d-a-b-c (B) c-d-a-b
(C) a-b-d-c (D) d-b-c-a

14. Consortium Education communication (CEC) is running which 24-hours educational channel?

(A) Gyan Darshan (B) Gyan Dhara
(C) Vyas (D) Swayam Prabha

15. What is the other name of 'Integrated e-Content Portal'?

(A) e-Kalpa (B) e-ShodhSindhu
(C) e-Acharya (D) e-Yantra

16. Find the wrong pair.

(A) Baadal - IIT Delhi
(B) FOSSEE - IIT Guwahati
(C) e-Acharya - IIT Kharagpur
(D) IMPRINT- IIT Kanpur

17. Following are two objectives of digital initiative IMPRINT. Which of these two is FALSE?

a) Create an education policy for inculcating scientific temperament and innovation skill.

b) Develop the research roadmap for technology preparedness.

(A) Only a (B) Only b
(C) Both a and b (D) Neither a nor b

18. Which of the following is NOT an objective of VIDWAN?

(A) Collecting academic and research profiles of scientists, faculty, and research scientists working in or retired from leading academic and R&D organisations in India and abroad

(B) Creating information exchanges and networking opportunities among scientists

(C) Quickly and conveniently providing information about experts to various agencies and bodies

(D) Establishing communication directly with the experts who possess the expertise needed by research scholars

19. A journey from ShodhGangotri to Shodhganga is a journey of

(A) Research to Findings

(B) Synopsis to Thesis

(C) Experiment to Award

(D) Design to Craft

20. National Knowledge Network (NKN) works on the principle of

(A) Setting virtual classrooms

(B) Connecting CSIR laboratories with its key projects

(C) Resource sharing and multidisciplinary research

(D) All of the above

21. What is the status of the following statements with reference to ShodhGangotri?

a) Accepts original version of synopsis of research from the research scientists

b) Reveals the trends and directions of research being conducted in Indian universities

c) Avoids duplication of research

(A) Only a and c are true but b is false

(B) Only b and c are true but a is false

(C) All a, b, and c are true

(D) All a, b, and c are false

22. A-VIEW collaboration tool has been developed for which of the following digital initiatives?

(A) E-Yantra

(B) Shodhganga

(C) National Digital Library

(D) Talk to a Teacher

23. "Setting up lab infrastructure for project based learning" is the objective of which digital initiative?

(A) e-Yantra (B) NKN

(C) QEEE (D) Virtual Laboratory

KEY

1. D	**2.** A	**3.** C	**4.** B	**5.** C	**6.** D	**7.** D
8. A	**9.** D	**10.** B	**11.** C	**12.** A	**13.** D	**14.** C
15. C	**16.** B	**17.** D	**18.** A	**19.** B	**20.** C	**21.** B
22. D	**23.** A					

Assertion–Reason Format

1. Assertion (A): India has made huge investment in introducing digital initiatives in higher education

Reason (R): Higher education in India is in transformation from a traditional phase to a phase with hundred per cent digitisation.

(A) Both A and R are true and R is correct explanation of A

(B) Both A and R are true but R is not correct explanation of A

(C) A is true but R is false

(D) A is false but R is true

2. Assertion (A): Information and Communications Technology has provided global connectivity to digital initiatives for higher education

Reason (R): Digital content and smart classroomshave motivated learners of higher education to create an atmosphere of e-learning and research.

(A) Both A and R are true and R is correct explanation of A

(B) Both A and R are false

(C) Both A and R are true but R is not correct explanation of A

(D) A is true but R is false

3. Assertion (A): Gyan Darshan has made distance education accessible to all.

Reason (R): Countrywide classrooms are telecasted on different subjects with the help of Education Satellite (EDUSAT).

(A) Both A and R are true and R is correct explanation of A

(B) Both A and R are true but R is not correct explanation of A

(C) A is false but R is true

(D) A is true but R is false

4. Assertion (A): FOSSEE advocates achieving and maintaining quality in higher education.

Reason (R): Use of Open Source Software in higher education is a boon for seekers of computer knowledge at undergraduate and postgraduate level.

(A) Both A and R are true and R is correct explanation of A
(B) Both A and R are true but R is not correct explanation of A
(C) A is true but R is false
(D) A is false but R is true

5. **Assertion (A):** Top 10 engineering colleges of India are covered under QEEE.

   Reason (R): Enhancement of quality in engineering education will help in bringing economic development in India.

   (A) Both A and R are true and R is correct explanation of A
   (B) Both A and R are true but R is not correct explanation of A
   (C) A is true but R is false
   (D) A is false but R is true

6. **Assertion (A):** Initiative of Virtual Labs is a paradigm shift in ICT-based education.

   Reason (R): For the first time, such an initiative has been taken up in remote experimentation.

   (A) Both A and R are true but R is not correct explanation of A
   (B) Both A and R are true and R is correct explanation of A
   (C) A is true but R is false
   (D) Both A and R are false

7. **Assertion (A):** e-PG Pathshala works under NMEICT.

   Reason (R): Students and teachers develop an easy access to quality content collected from national and international sources.

   (A) Both A and R are true and R is correct explanation of A
   (B) Both A and R are true but R is not correct explanation of A
   (C) A is true but R is false
   (D) A is false but R is true

8. **Assertion (A):** NPTEL is the largest online repository in the world of courses in engineering.

   Reason (R): Video courses have been created in all branches of Computer Engineering.

   (A) Both A and R are true and R is correct explanation of A
   (B) Both A and R are true but R is not correct explanation of A
   (C) A is true but R is false
   (D) A is false but R is true

9. **Assertion (A):** Digital initiative GIAN has been launched to invite world famous foreign academics to premier Indian institutes.

   Reason (R): Institutions of higher learning in India need foreign faculty for want of Indian faculty.

   (A) Both A and R are true and R is correct explanation of A
   (B) Both A and R are true but R is not correct explanation of A
   (C) A is true but R is false
   (D) A is false but R is true

10. **Assertion (A):** 'Talk to a teacher' is a digital initiative developed by IIT Madras.

    Reason (R): Virtual classrooms project has been developed by Amrita University in 'Talk to a Teacher' initiative.

    (A) Both A and R are true and R is correct explanation of A
    (B) Both A and R are true but R is not correct explanation of A
    (C) A is true but R is false
    (D) A is false but R is true

KEY

1. B **2.** B **3.** A **4.** C **5.** D **6.** A **7.** A
8. C **9.** C **10.** D

Questions Asked in Previous NET Exams

1. GIAN (Global Initiative of Academic Networks) has been launched by government of India in order to____.

   (UGC NET JUNE 2019)

   (A) encourage Indian scholars to learn abroad
   (B) discourage Indian scholars from researching in India
   (C) encourage global scholars to engage with their counterparts in India
   (D) encourage global scholars to engage with Indian scholars abroad

2. Which of the following is an online storehouse of all academic awards like certificates, diplomas, degrees, marksheets, etc.?

(UGC NET JUNE 2019)

(A) SWAYAM
(B) National Digital Library
(C) National Academic Library
(D) National Academic Depository

3. The purpose of ICT use in education is to

(UGC NET DECEMBER 2019)

(1) attract students
(2) make teaching interesting
(3) optimistic learning outcomes
(4) promote technology culture in teaching

4. Which of the following tools is a collaboration tool for providing virtual classroom?

(UGC NET DECEMBER 2019)

(1) A – Lab (2) A – View
(3) A – Tutor 4) A – Learner

5. Which of the following terms is related to the digital learning environment for design?

(UGC NET DECEMBER 2019)

(1) e-Vidwan (2) e-Acharya
(3) e-Kalpa (4) e-yantra

KEY

1. C **2.** D **3.** C **4.** B **5.** C

7 ICT and Governance

CONCEPT AND SIGNIFICANCE

Today, ICT has become an inseparable means of providing public services by various government, semi-government, and other organisations. Efficient, convenient, and timely services provided through ICT have become a symbol of good governance. Governance through sound ICT set-up has become a guarantee of overall socio-economic development. Like other countries, India is also exploring the potential of ICT for achieving a desired socio-economic development. The best use of ICT in governance is to bring transparency, efficiency, and accountability in public services.

ICT AND INDIA

Background

India entered digital governance era in 1975 when it started using computers in government services. Computer support system was introduced in government departments to facilitate planning and National Informatics Centre (NIC) was established in 1976 for this purpose. Launching of National Informatics Centre Network (NICNET) in 1987 provided the main thrust for e-Governance. This was followed by the launch of the District Information System of National Informatics Centre (DISNIC) programme to computerise all district offices in the country for which free hardware and software was offered to the State Governments. NICNET was extended via the State capitals to all district headquarters by 1990. In the ensuing years, with ongoing computerisation, tele-connectivity and Internet connectivity established a large number of e-Governance initiatives, both at the Union and State levels. NICNET has linked all the departments of the State Governments, Central Government, and around 625 District Administrations of India. Andhra Pradesh was the first state in the country to take up e-Governance in a systematic manner.

Current Status of e-Governance

According to Economic Survey 2018-19, India is spending about 6% of its GDP to develop ICT and more than 3 million people are employed in IT sector resulting into 8% growth in this sector. In spite of this, as per ICT Development Index (IDI), published by UN agency International Telecommunication Union, India ranked 134 in 2018 out of 176 countries. Major reason of this dismal position is digital divide. However, while pursuing the target of Digital India (Slogan-"Power to Empower") and ensuring good governance through ICT, central and state governments have come up with various schemes and action plans. Some of the steps have been taken by India in the following categories:

1) G2G: Government to Government Initiatives
2) G2C: Government to Citizen Initiatives
3) G2B : Government to Business Initiatives

G2G: GOVERNMENT TO GOVERNMENT INITIATIVES

G2G initiatives have been adopted to make government's internal procedures more efficient. Under these initiatives, government departments and undertakings share data electronically. The objective is to facilitate data access and data sharing. Following digital programmes have been started under G2G initiatives:

a) **SmartGov (Andhra Pradesh):** It has been developed to streamline operations and enhance efficiency through workflow automation and knowledge management for implementation in the Andhra Pradesh Secretariat.
b) **Khajane Project in Karnataka:** It is a comprehensive online treasury computerisation project of the Government of Karnataka. The project has resulted in the computerisation of the entire treasury related activities of the State Government and the system has the ability to track every activity right from the approval of the State Budget to the point of rendering accounts to the government.
c) **e-Procurement:** Ministry of Commerce and Industry (Department of Commerce) has been nominated as the Nodal Ministry for implementation of e-Government Procurement (e-GP) Mission Mode Project (MMP). The vision of the e-Procurement MMP is "To create a national initiative

to implement procurement reforms, through the use of electronic Government procurement, so as to make public procurement in all sectors more transparent and efficient".

d) **e-Municipalities:** It is a unique initiative of the Government of India conceptualised under the umbrella of the overall National e-Governance Plan (NeGP) and the Jawaharlal Nehru National Urban Renewal Mission (JNURM) aimed at improving operational efficiencies within Urban Local Bodies (ULBs).

e) **e-Panchayat:** This is an e-Governance initiative for the rural sector providing a comprehensive software solution attempting automation of Gram Panchayat functions. It is a platform for Panchayat representatives to connect with the rest of the world, which aims to bring out the local voices by empowering the local communities to showcase and share local social, cultural, and economic practices, stories, and challenges.

National e-Governance Plan

> *Government of India formulated National e-Governance Plan in 2006. This is an initiative of the government to provide all government services available to the citizens of India through electronic media. Although the early years of the plan did not receive much traction, it laid down the foundation for building a technology-enabled knowledge economy.*
> *Motto of the Plan:* ***"Public Services Closer Home"***

G2C: GOVERNMENT TO CITIZEN INITIATIVES

a) **National Land Records Modernisation Programme (NLRMP):** A project for Computerisation of Land Records (CLR) was launched in 1988-89 with the intention to remove the inherent flaws in the manual system of maintenance and updation of Land Records. In 1997-98, the scheme was extended to tehsils to start distribution of Records of Rights to landowners on demand. The focus of the entire operation has always been to employ state-of-the-art information technology (IT) to galvanise and transform the existing land records system of the country.

b) **Bhoomi Project:** This project has been started by Karnataka government to computerise the total land records of Karnataka so that farmers can get any information regarding land online. The project has been of great success as Karnataka's more than 6.7 million farmers have been covered. The project has been sponsored by the Ministry of Rural Development, Government of India along with Karnataka government. The project is one of the examples of e-Governance.

c) **Gyandoot:** It is a government-to-citizen, intranet-based service portal, implemented in the Dhar district of the state of Madhya Pradesh, India, in January 2000. The project was designed to extend the benefits of information technology to people in rural areas by directly linking the government and villagers through information kiosks. The kiosks provide access to a variety of government services, such as registration of complaints and submission of applications for the issuance of certificates and loans. Data on prices of agricultural crops in different markets are also available. Gyandoot pioneered the idea of rural telecentres in India. The project concept has been replicated by other information and communications technologies (ICT) development initiatives in India. Gyandoot was very successful in the early years of its implementation, and the project was awarded the Stockholm Challenge Information Technology (IT) award in 2000 for public service and democracy.

d) **Lokvani Project in Uttar Pradesh:** It is a public-private partnership project at Sitapur District in Uttar Pradesh which was initiated in November, 2004. Its objective is to provide a single-window, self-sustainable e-Governance solution with regard to handling of grievances, land record maintenance, and providing a mixture of essential services.

e) **Project FRIENDS (Fast, Reliable, Instant, Efficient Network for Disbursement of Services) in Kerala:** It is a single-window facility providing citizens the means to pay taxes and other financial dues to the State Government. The services are provided through FRIENDS Jan Sevana Kendrams located in the district headquarters.

f) **e-Mitra Project in Rajasthan:** It is an integrated project to facilitate the urban and the rural masses with maximum possible services related to different state government departments through Lokmitra-Janmitra centers/kiosks.

g) **eSeva in Andhra Pradesh:** This project is designed to provide 'Government to Citizen' and 'e-Business to Citizen' services. The highlight of the eSeva project is that all the services are delivered online to consumers/citizens by connecting them to the respective government departments and providing online information at the point of service delivery. The project has facilitated the payment of civic utility bills including electricity, sewerage, and water bills, and various taxes including property tax and octroi, etc.

h) **Admission to Professional Colleges -Common Entrance Test (CET):** With the rapid growth in the demand as well as supply of professional education, the process of admission to these institutions became a major challenge in the early 1990s. Recourse was then taken to ICT to make the process of admission transparent and objective. One of the pioneering efforts was made by Karnataka. The State Government decided to conduct a common entrance test based on which admission to different colleges and disciplines was made.

i) **e-Health and e-Medicine:** As WHO has recognised e-health or e-medicine as an indispensable ICT tool for accelerating efficient and timely health services, India has implemented it under the Ministry of Health and Family Welfare. Under this service of e-Governance, besides providing hi-tech health services, health education is also rendered. The ultimate target of e-health is to reach the remotest possible patients through telecentres and kiosks.

j) **Akshaya Project:** It was the first e-literacy project of India, which was launched in Malappuram district of Kerala in 2002. This was a district-wise project with the aim to have at least one member of each family to be computer literate in the district. Today, Malappuram is the first e-literate district of India. This was India's first ICT project to reach masses, particularly rural masses. Akshaya centres are offering public utility services also.

k) **E-Public Distribution System:** Computerisation of the PDS is envisaged as an end-to-end project covering key functional areas such as supply chain management including allocation and utilisation reporting, storage and movement of food grains, grievance redressal and transparency portal, digitisation of beneficiary database, Fair Price Shop automation, etc.

l) **e-District:** This is one of the 31 Mission Mode Projects under National e-Governance Plan (NeGP) with the DeitY, GoI being the nodal ministry. This project aims at providing support to the basic administrative unit, i.e., District Administration by undertaking back end computerisation to enable electronic delivery of high volume citizen centric government services which would utilise the three infrastructure pillars of State Wide Area Networks (SWAN), State Data Centers (SDCs), and Common Service Centers (CSCs) to deliver services to the citizen at their doorsteps.

m) **M-Governance:** This is the use of mobile or wireless to improve Governance service and information "anytime, anywhere". M-governance mobile app is used and mobile is taken as an input supplying device in the form of feedback and suggestions on the state of public services offered by various departments of the government. This helps the departments in making decisions and plans to provide public services as required by the public.

n) **Crime and Criminal Tracking Network & Systems (CCTNS):** It is an MMP project aiming at creating a comprehensive and integrated system for enhancing the efficiency and effective policing at all levels and especially at the Police Station level through adoption of principles of e-Governance, and creation of a nationwide networked infrastructure for evolution of IT-enabled state-of-the-art tracking system.

o) **Pradhan Mantri Jan Dhan Yojana (PMJDY):** This scheme has been launched with the aim of providing basic banking amenities to everyone, by providing accounts, debit cards, and accidental insurance coverage worth ? 1 lakh. This is envisioned as a move to empower Indian citizens and head towards inclusive growth.

p) **Direct Benefit Transfer (DBT):** Under this scheme, consumers will receive subsidies directly into their bank accounts, while the subsidised goods will be sold at market prices. This will reduce pilferage, adulteration, and other malpractices, while ensuring that subsidies reach the people who need them.

q) **DigiLocker:** This service was launched as an important facility to store crucial documents like Voter ID card, Pan card, BPL card, driving license, education certificates, etc. in the cloud. The 10 MB personal storage space is linked to the Aadhar number of the user.

r) **The Digital Saksharta Abhiyan or National Digital Literacy Mission (NDLM) Scheme:** This has been formulated to impart IT training to 52.5 lakh persons, including Anganwadi, ASHA workers, and authorised ration dealers in all the States/UTs across the country. The initiative aims at training non-IT literate citizens to become IT literate to enable their active and effective participation in the democratic, developmental process, and enhance their livelihood too.

s) **e-Granthalaya:** This is an Integrated Library Management Software developed by National Informatics Centre (NIC), Ministry of Electronics and Information Technology, Government of India. The application is useful for automation of in-house activities of libraries and to provide various online member services. The software provides built-in Web OPAC interface to publish the library catalogue over the Internet. The software is UNICODE Compliant and thus, supports data entry in local languages.

t) **Direct Cash Transfer (DCT):** To facilitate disbursements of Government entitlements like MGNREGA, Social Security pension, Handicapped Old Age Pension, etc. of any Central or State Government bodies, using Aadhaar and authentication thereof as supported by UIDAI.

u) **Aadhaar Enabled Payment System (AEPS):** It is a payment service empowering a bank customer to use Aadhaar as his/her identity to access his/her respective Aadhaar enabled bank account and perform basic banking transactions like balance enquiry, cash deposit, cash withdrawal, and remittances through a business correspondent.

v) **e-Sampark:** This is a mechanism to connect the government directly with citizens across India by running mailer, outbound dialing, and SMS campaigns. The platform is used for sharing informational and public service messages. The concept of e-Sampark has been introduced to establish proactive communication by digitisation of campaigns. The multi-faceted platform facilitates not only a seamless communication between the government and citizens, but also maintains a database of contacts of the nodal officers, representatives, and citizens. In addition, users can also view the previous campaigns conducted.

w) **Himmat App:** It is an initiative by Delhi police, especially for women. This is an emergency service, comprised of an android emergency application, which can send a distress call or emergency message to Delhi Police officials and specified contact or group in an emergency situation faced by a woman. The Police personnel will get these SOS alerts and locations on a portal and as a SMS on their mobile phones as well.

x) **Telecentres:** Various telecentres have been opened across the country in order to facilitate the access to Internet and other digital resources by the poor. State of Tamil Nadu has implemented Sustainable Access in Rural India (SARI) project. Under SARI project, rural people are offered various, free ICT services like computer education, e-mail, web browsing, and other related services.

y) **IRCTC Connect:** In order to cater to the growing demand of railway passengers to make the ticketing application more user-friendly and faster, Indian Railway Catering and Tourism Corporation (IRCTC) Connect was created by Union ministry of Railways. The new app with several add-on features is based on the next generation e-ticketing system. Synchronised with the ticketing website, the app facilitates options for searching and booking train tickets, checking existing reservations or cancelling them, and getting upcoming journey alerts.

z) **MeghRaj:** Government of India has started an ambitious initiative-"GI Cloud" which has been named as 'MeghRaj'. The focus of this initiative is to accelerate delivery of e-services in the country while optimising ICT spending of the Government. This will ensure optimum utilisation of the infrastructure and speed up the development and deployment of eGov applications.

G2B: GOVERNMENT TO BUSINESS (G2B) INITIATIVES

a) **e-Procurement Project in Andhra Pradesh and Gujarat:** This is a project to reduce the time and cost of doing business for both vendors and the government.

b) **MCA21:** This is an initiative which has been taken by the Ministry of Corporate Affairs. The project aims at providing an easy and secure online access to all registry related services provided by the Union Ministry of Corporate Affairs to corporates and other stakeholders at any time and in a manner that best suits them.

c) **eBiz:** This initiative is being implemented by Infosys Technologies Limited (Infosys) under the guidance and aegis of Department of Industrial Policy and Promotion (DIPP), Ministry of Commerce & Industry, Government of India. The focus of eBiz is to improve the business environment in the country by enabling fast and efficient access to Government-to-Business (G2B) services through an online portal. This will help in reducing unnecessary delays in various regulatory processes required to start and run businesses.

NINE PILLARS OF DIGITAL INDIA

1) ***Broadband Highways***

In the rural areas, the broadband highways would be implemented through Department of Telecommunications (DoT); with a capital expenditure of Rs. 32,000/- crores. The rural broadband highways intend to cover 250,000 Gram Panchayats.

2) ***Universal Access to Mobile Connectivity***

The ongoing programmes in the area of access to phones would be focused towards increasing network penetration and coverage. Universal access to mobile connectivity would be implemented through Department of Telecommunications (DoT); with a capital expenditure of Rs. 16,000/- crores and coverage of about 42,300 villages.

3) ***Public Internet Access Programme-National Rural Internet Mission***

CSCs would be made viable through multi-functional end-points for service delivery through Gram Panchayats. Implemented through DeitY (data.gov.in), it would cost Rs. 4,750 crores to increase the present reach of 130,000 to 250,000 villages..

4) ***e-Governance: Reforming Government through Technology***

Government would take up Business Process Re-engineering (BPR) using IT to improve transactions, including form simplification and reduction, online applications and tracking, developing interface between departments, use of online repositories like school certificates and voter identity cards, and integration of services and platforms like Unique Identification Authority of India (UIDAI).

5) ***e-Kranti: Electronic Delivery of Services***

The present ongoing programme (NeGP) would be revamped to cover various elements to bring e-Kranti. This would include fostering technology in the areas of planning, agriculture, education, health, financial inclusion, justice, and security. The technology for planning would include GIS-based decision-making and National GIS Mission Mode Project.

6) ***Information for All***

The pillar of 'Information to all' would encompass making information online and hosting websites and documents. This would result into an easy and open access to information by the public in general along with development of open data platforms.

7) ***Electronics Manufacturing: Target NET ZERO IMPORTS by 2020***

In India, the existing structure needs strengthening in order to boost electronic manufacturing; the target being 'NET ZERO Imports' in this domain in the days to come. This would be an ambitious goal which would require coordinated action on many fronts like taxation, incentives, economies of scale, and elimination of cost disadvantages.

8) ***IT for Jobs***

The objectives of this pillar is to train people in smaller towns and villages for IT sector jobs, setting up of BPO in each of the North-East states in order to foster ICT-enabled growth, train service delivery agents to run viable businesses delivering IT services, and to train rural workforce to cater to their own needs and hence create a telecom-ready workforce. These initiatives would be implemented mainly through DoT and DeitY.

9) ***Early Harvest Programmes***

Some of the immediate measures which can be realised soon are covered in this pillar of 'Early harvest programmes'. These would be the measures such as creating an IT platform targeted to elected representatives along with all the Government employees covering 1.36 crore mobiles and 22 lakh emails through development of a mass messaging application. Other measures would primarily include technological improvements such as modification of Government greetings to e-Greetings, implementation of biometric attendance in all government offices, Wi-Fi in all universities, secured emails within government, standardised government email design, public Wi-Fi hotspots, transformation of school books to eBooks, SMS-based weather information, SMS-based disaster alerts, and a national portal for lost & found children.

Practice Exercise

General Questions Format

1. G2G initiative SmartGov has been adopted and implemented in

(A) Maharashtra (B) Punjab

(C) Uttrakhand (D) Andhra Pradesh

2. What is the motto of the National e-Governance Plan?

(A) Public Services Closer Home

(B) Public Services at Your Doorstep

(C) Digital India Smiling India

(D) Early Disposal Easy Life

3. MMP stands for

(A) Major Mode Project

(B) Mission Mode Project

(C) Mode Mission Project

(D) Main Mission Project

4. Which union ministry is a nodal agency for e-procurement? Union Ministry of......

(A) Agriculture

(B) Food processing

(C) Commerce & Industry

(D) Micro and Small Enterprises

5. Which of the following is NOT an objective of e-Panchayat initiative?
   a) Automation of Gram Panchayat functions
   b) Conducting an e-census of the village after every two years
   c) Connecting panchayat representatives to the rest of the world
   d) Providing Internet connection to poor families of the village to narrow down digital divide

   (A) c and d only (B) a, c, and d only
   (C) b and d only (D) b only

6. Which of the following is NOT covered under Khajane Project of Karnataka?
   a) Computerisation of all sorts of State treasury grants issued to freedom fighters
   b) Computerisation of all treasury records and activities
   c) Online disposal of every type of bill pending in treasury
   d) Online display of treasury proposals for the State budget

   (A) a, c, and d only (B) c only
   (C) b and c only (D) a only

7. Which of the following best explains the relationship between ICT and governance?
   (A) ICT brings reforms not only in the working of various departments, rather people also start showing faith in governance
   (B) ICT governance aims at bringing transparency, efficiency, and accountability in performing public services.
   (C) ICT is effective in creating awareness among people regarding concept of governance through various apps and websites.
   (D) Governance becomes good governance with the help of a sound ICT set-up.

8. Which of the following initiative is NOT covered under G2C?
   (A) e-Sampark (B) DigiLocker
   (C) Himmat App (D) MCA21

9. Which of the following is TRUE?
   a) Under Digital Saksharta Abhiyan IT training is imparted to marginalised communities.
   b) CCTNS project aims at imparting online IT training to those police personnel who are not IT-literate.
   c) DigiLocker is the only service where the allotted storage space is to be linked with the user's Pan card.
   d) e-Granthalaya is an Integrated Library Management Software developed by National Informatics Centre(NIC).

   (A) d only (B) b and c only
   (C) a, b, and d only (D) c only

10. Various digital initiatives operational under e-Governance are given under Column I and nature of service provided by them is given under Column II. Match the digital initiative with its respective nature of service and choose the correct code from the given codes.

Column I (Digital Initiative)	**Column II (Nature of Service)**
a) Akshaya Project	i) Knowledge Management
b) SmartGov	ii) e-literacy
c) MCA21	iii) Social security
d) DCT	iv) Registry related service

Codes:

	(a)	(b)	(c)	(d)
(A)	i	iv	ii	iii
(B)	iii	i	ii	iv
(C)	iv	iii	ii	i
(D)	ii	i	iv	iii

11. Which of the following is NOT provided under Pradhan Mantri Jan Dhan Yojana?
    (A) Credit card (B) Debit card
    (C) Health insurance (D) e-Banking

12. e-Sampark is
    (A) a mobile app through which any foreign tourist in danger in any part of India can contact police by sending an emergency alarm to the nearest police station.
    (B) a health department initiated online domain of a panel of doctors who can be contacted through DeitY in case of a serious road accident.
    (C) an e-mechanism to connect the government directly with citizens across India by running mailer, outbound dialling, and SMS campaigns for sharing public services messages.
    (D) a khoya-paya app through which concerned authorities are contacted regarding lost and found children.

13. With regard to which product a target of Net Zero Imports by 2020 has been set under Digital India initiative?

(A) Pharmaceuticals (B) Electronics
(C) Garments (D) None of these

14. Which of the following is NOT TRUE about Bhoomi Project?

a) The project has been started by Karnataka government.
b) The project envisages computerisation of land records of natives of Karnataka.
c) The project has been sponsored by the Union Ministry of Rural development.
d) The project aims to provide online information to farmers regarding their land.

(A) b only (B) c and d only
(C) a and b only (D) All are true

15. What is the full form of NLRMP?

(A) National Land Records Maintain Programme
(B) National Land Resources Modernisation Programme
(C) National Land Records Modernisation Programme
(D) Nodal Land Records Modernisation Process

16. Which G2C e-Governance initiative earned the honour of winning Stockholm challenge information technology (IT) award in 2000?

(A) Bhoomi Project (B) Lokvani
(C) e-Mitra (D) Gyandoot

17. Types of e-Governance initiatives are given under Column I and the digital initiatives belonging to the type are given under Column II. Match the type with the initiative belonging to it and choose the correct code among the given codes.

Column I (Type of e-Governance)	Column II (Digital Initiative)
a) G2C	i) e-Panchayat
b) G2G	ii) MCA21
c) G2B	iii) Lokvani

Codes:

	(a)	(b)	(c)
(A)	ii	i	iii
(B)	iii	i	ii
(C)	i	ii	iii
(D)	ii	iii	i

18. Which state first conducted Common Entrance Test (CET) for admission to professional colleges?

(A) Maharashtra (B) Karnataka
(C) Bihar (D) Kerala

19. What is TRUE about beginning of e-Governance era in India?

a) India entered the digital governance era in 1975.
b) National Informatics Centre was established in 1976.
c) Andhra Pradesh was the first state in the country to take up e-Governance in a systematic manner.
d) National Informatics Centre Network (NICNET) was the pivotal force behind launching e-Governance in India.

(A) a, b, c, and d (B) a, c, and d only
(C) c only (D) b and d only

20. According to Economic Survey 2018-19 India is spending about _______% of its GDP to develop ICT.

(A) 4 (B) 10
(C) 6 (D) 1

KEY

1. D	2. A	3. B	4. C	5. C	6. A	7. B
8. D	9. A	10. D	11. C	12. C	13. B	14. A
15. C	16. D	17. B	18. B	19. A	20. C	

Assertion–Reason Format

1. **Assertion (A):** e-Governance in India has not made much headway.

Reason (R): Indians are not technology conscious.

(A) Both A and R are true and R is correct explanation of A
(B) Both A and R are true but R is not correct explanation of a
(C) Both A and R are false
(D) A is true but R is false

2. **Assertion (A):** Today all the public utility services in India are covered under e-Governance initiatives.

Reason (R): Digitisation of public services ensures the efficient, transparent, and timely delivery of amenities to general public.

(A) Both A and R are true and R is correct explanation of A

(B) Both A and R are true but R is not correct explanation of A

(C) A is true but R is false

(D) A is false but R is true

3. **Assertion (A):** e-Governance in India has provided more teeth to statutes governing the public utility services.

Reason (R): Indian people are very well aware about benefits of e-Governance.

(A) Both A and R are true but R is not correct explanation of A

(B) A is true but R is false

(C) A is false but R is true

(D) Both A and R are false

4. **Assertion (A):** Efficient execution of digital initiatives is an indicator of good governance.

Reason (R): Good governance makes efficient execution of digital initiatives possible.

(A) Both A and R are true and R is correct explanation of A

(B) Both A and R are true but R is not correct explanation of A

(C) A is true but R is false

(D) A is false but R is true.

5. **Assertion (A):** Computerisation of land records has proved to be a boon for land owners.

Reason (R): Land owners can check any detail of their land online.

(A) Both A and R are true and R is correct explanation of A

(B) Both A and R are true but R is not correct explanation of A

(C) A is true but R is false

(D) Both A and R are false

6. **Assertion (A):** Increasing population of India is affecting the successful execution of various e-Governance initiatives.

Reason (R): Rapidly increasing demand over supply of public utility services is causing unnecessary delays and inefficient execution of initiatives.

(A) Both A and R are true and R is correct explanation of A

(B) Both A and R are true but R is not correct explanation of A

(C) A is false but R is true

(D) A is true but R is false

7. **Assertion (A):** G2G initiatives provide basis for executing G2C initiatives efficiently in e-Governance.

Reason (R): Actual beneficiaries of e-Governance initiatives avail advantages of both G2G and G2C initiatives.

(A) Both A and R are true and R is correct explanation of A

(B) Both A and R are true but R is not correct explanation of A

(C) A is false but R is true

(D) A is true but R is false

8. **Assertion (A):** MGNREGA wages are disbursed under DBT initiative.

Reason (R): All disbursements in e-Governance are made through Aadhaar linkage.

(A) Both A and R are true but R is not correct explanation of A

(B) Both A and R are true and R is correct explanation of A

(C) A is false but R is true

(D) Both A and R are false

9. **Assertion (A):** The main thrust behind launching of e-Governance in India had been NICNET.

Reason (R): NICNET connected all government departments paving way for launching various e-Governance initiatives.

(A) Both A and R are true and R is correct explanation of A

(B) Both A and R are true but R is not correct explanation of A

(C) Both A and R are false

(D) A is true but R is false

10. **Assertion (A):** India needs to spend more on e-Governance initiatives.

Reason (R): There is a need to launch initiatives to educate people regarding e-Governance.

(A) Both A and R are true and R is correct explanation of A

(B) Both A and R are true but R is not correct explanation of A

(C) Both A and R are false

(D) A is false but R is true

KEY

1. C **2.** A **3.** C **4.** B **5.** A **6.** A **7.** D
8. C **9.** A **10.** B

Unit IX

People, Development and Environment

Development, Environment and Human Interaction

INTRODUCTION

Environment: In the simplest concept environment is surroundings provided to all organisms including human beings by nature. Environment is the given conditions in which one survives and grows. Whatsoever is affecting an organism is environment.

Development: Development is directly related to the state of an economy. If the per capita income is rising, leading to rise in Gross Domestic Product (GDP) and in the Gross National Product (GNP), then it is ascertained that the economy is developing.

Relation between Environment and Development: There is a natural relationship between development and environment. Nature has provided resources which help in the development and environment protection. Earth through its lithosphere, hydrosphere, atmosphere, and biosphere is providing fresh air, clean water, land, fertile soil oil, petroleum, coal, wood, livestock, minerals, ores, and metals to man for their rational use to fetch growth by maintaining a clean environment. An economy mainly has an agriculture sector, industrial sector, and services sector. Production of various products in these sectors needs use of various natural resources mentioned above. There is a vicious circle between the environment and economic development. Neat and clean environment (in all its forms) protects natural resources for production and rational use of resources provides a neat and clean environment.

Practically, relation of environment with development is not healthy. Man, due to his lust for rapid economic gains, has misutilised and overutilised nature's resources which has resulted in pollution in all the spheres of the earth. Due to pollution, development process is hampered as polluted environment attacks plants, animals, and human health in the form of various fatal diseases. For the past few years the whole world has been concerned about this catastrophic situation. Major national and international agencies, particularly United Nations, has set certain development goals to be achieved by both developed and developing nations.

DEVELOPMENT GOALS

As the development process in an economy sets in, there is growth of population which yields rise in demand for consumer goods and services. Such rise in demand disturbs the equilibrium between demand and supply. Due to rapidly increasing population, demand also rises with the same pace, but on the other hand, due to scarcity of resources, supply does not increase so rapidly. This results in various social and economic evils like poverty, illiteracy, diseases, crimes, and other evils. Economies in order to increase supply to fulfil rising demand resort to overutilization of resources resulting in deforestation, excess use of fertilizers and pesticides, contamination of water by various factories, and using chemicals in production of various goods. All this hampers development on one hand, and on the other hand pollutes the natural resources. Resultantly, there is grave presence of the above evils. A customary discrimination against the fair sex is also visible in many societies. While eyeing on all these factors, United Nations chalked out development goals to eradicate all these social, economic, and ecological evils from the societies.

Millennium Development Goals (MDGs)

United Nations called a Global Summit of the member countries in September 2000 at its headquarters in New York. In the summit, eight millennium goals were set up, which were to be achieved by 2015. The declaration is popularly known as Millennium Declaration. The then 189 member countries endorsed these goals and agreed to achieve them by 2015. The goals were:

1) To eliminate extreme poverty and hunger
2) To achieve universal primary education
3) To empower women and promote gender equality
4) To reduce child morality
5) To promote maternal health
6) To fight malaria, HIV/AIDS, and other diseases
7) To promote environmental sustainability
8) To develop a global partnership for development

UNDP & MDGs

UNO designated its development agency United Nations Development Programme (UNDP) the job of a scorekeeper of MDGs. UNDP was to monitor the progress in achievement of MDGs in different countries within the stipulated time. UNDP not only monitored the progress in this direction, it also extended help to the countries in achieving the goals. It further established a liaison between the UN policy teams and the member countries party to the millennium declaration. Achievement of MDGs was further initiated through United Nations Development Assistance Frameworks (UNDAFs)

MDGs and India

India being signatory to the Millennium declaration worked sincerely towards achieving MDGs with United Nations Development Programme (UNDP) assistance. India was successful in achieving some MDGs. India could reduce poverty by half, however target of reducing hunger was not successfully met. Other areas of MDG, in which India could make effective progress were gender parity in primary school enrolment, providing clean drinking water, reduction in child mortality by two-third, combatting HIV/AIDS, malaria, and other diseases, chalking out policies and programmes for sustainable development, and inviting private partnership in various fields, particularly in information and technology sector. In other areas, though progress was not remarkable, yet there had been consistent efforts to achieve desired progress in that direction.

SUSTAINABLE DEVELOPMENT GOALS (SDGs)

Success of Millennium Development Goals motivated United Nations to give a call to the member nations to sign another declaration comprising 17 Sustainable Development Goals. These goals give a universal call to bring peace and prosperity, end of poverty, and protection of the earth. These goals touch some new areas like achieving economic inequality, peace and justice, environment and climate change, innovations, ensuring parities in income, consumption, and other related areas.

SDGs were adopted by member countries in United Nations conference on Sustainable Development in Rio de Janerio (Brazil) in 2012. As per the declaration, SDGs were to be adopted from the year 2016 and these were to be achieved by 2030. These are also known as 'Agenda 2030'. It means that from 2016, SDGs were going to replace MDGs. There was a clear-cut call to work on these SDGs to combat economic, environmental, political, and technology challenges, which was the need of the hour.

Following are the SDGs:

1) No poverty
2) Zero hunger
3) Good health and well-being
4) Quality education
5) Gender equality
6) Clean water and sanitation
7) Affordable and clean energy
8) Decent work and economic growth
9) Industry, innovation, and infrastructure
10) Reduced inequalities
11) Sustainable cities and communities
12) Responsible consumption and production
13) Climate action
14) Life below water
15) Life on land
16) Peace justice and strong institutions
17) Partnerships for goals

1) **No poverty:** The goal aims at eradicating poverty by 2030. According to UN estimate, more than 600 million people in the world are living on or below poverty line. This goal can be achieved worldwide by providing basic amenities to these people, reducing caste and regional disparities restraining people to work and earn in a particular region, etc.

2) **Zero hunger:** There is a huge number of belts in the world where people, particularly children, are undernourished. Aim of the goal is to eradicate all forms of hunger by 2030. Under this goal, efforts can be made in producing sufficient food through efficient agriculture planning and through application of appropriate technology.

3) **Good health and well-being:** In the wake of outbreak of various fatal diseases worldwide like AIDS/HIV, malaria, measles in children, tuberculosis, the goal aims to eradicate these diseases and make the world healthy by 2030, This is being achieved to cover all diseases under effective medical treatment, efficient medical skill, and creating awareness through health and sex education. The mission is to achieve this goal through care, cure, and prevention.

4) **Quality education:** Realizing that education is an effective force in bringing development in all sectors, the goal aims to provide access to primary, secondary, and higher education to all by 2030. The aim is also to provide vocational education. As far as the education sphere is concerned, there should be no disparity on ground of wealth, gender, region, and religion. The goal is targetting to provide free primary and secondary education to all.

5) **Gender equality:** The goal aims to end all types of discriminations against women in all fields. Crimes against women are to be tackled through stringent legislations and their implementation. Discrimination against women is proving a big hurdle in the path of sustainable economic development.

6) **Clean water and sanitation:** Water scarcity and bad sanitation is depriving millions of people worldwide of good health and hence becoming a strong contributing factor in efforts for sustainable development. The goal aims to provide affordable drinking water and neat and clean hygiene and sanitation to all by 2030 by developing proper technology and infrastructure.

7) **Affordable and clean energy:** Affordable and clean energy will be ensured to all by investing in solar, thermal, wind, hydroelectric, and other renewable sources of energy.

8) **Decent work and economic growth:** In order to bring workforce out of forced labour, slavery, and human trafficking, the goal aims to encourage entrepreneurship and hence creating humane work conditions and economic growth with suitable planning and its implementation.

9) **Industry, innovation, and Infrastructure:** Due to rapidly increasing urbanisation, investment in industry, technology, infrastructure, and services is becoming indispensable. The goal aims to effect balanced investment in consumer goods, core, infrastructure, and technology fields. Investment in transport, energy sector, and scientific innovations will be other areas of priority. Such efforts will lead to efficiency in use of energy and generate maximum employment opportunities. Goal aims to increase the employment in renewable energy sector from about 2 million to about 20 million by 2030. There will be increase in the processing industry of agricultural products particularly in developing countries. The goal also aims to provide easy and affordable access to information and communication technology, particularly Internet, in the least developed countries by 2020.

10) **Reduced Inequalities:** Today, income inequality is rapidly rising around the world in general and in developing countries in particular. The goal aims to reduce this inequality by pursuing sound policies and action plans-Making sound and universal regulations for free flowing of money in the economies and making investments in the fields in which employment opportunities are created for low income groups. Such laws should be enacted which discourage monopolist practices in the economic field. And the goal vows to achieve it by 2030.

11) **Sustainable cities and communities:** This goal aims at managing the burden on cities of large-scale exodus of rural population to urban areas. Due to large-scale migration, many cities, rather big cities, are coming up. Therefore, there is a need to bring reforms in the economic, civic, transport, hygiene fields, creation of greenbelts, and mitigating environmental hazards to accommodate migrants, particularly in developing countries. Developing sustainable cities and settling down communities in humane conditions is the aim of this goal. There is UN prediction that in the coming decade, there would undergo over 80% urban expansion.

12) **Responsible consumption and production:** Another requirement of sustainable development is efficiency in managing natural resources. Such resources are limited and demand their rational use but a lot of resources are wasted during production and consumption process. Lot of food is wasted. As per a UN study, about 1.5 billion tonnes of food is wasted per year in the world and over 2 billion people are undernourished and remain hungry. Situation is found to be grave in developing and underdeveloped countries. Further, lot of non-biodegradable waste like plastic in all its forms is thrown openly after use and a large-scale littering is visible all over. Such disposals result in air and water pollution. Excessive deforestation and wastage of water for enhancing production also yields catastrophic results. This goal aims to motivate producers to invest in industry which recycles the waste and produce suitable goods.

13) **Climate action:** Abrupt climate change is fast becoming a big hurdle in attaining sustainable development. As the whole world is on a production spree, emissions of greenhouse gases is also rising, resulting in global warming, floods, tsunamis, cyclones, landslides, and other hazards. Target of this goal is to put efforts to reduce ecological footprint. Here also, the present way of production and consumption are against ecological norms. Target is to change the ways of production and consumption to bring a favourable ecosystem.

ECOLOGICAL FOOTPRINT

Ecological Footprint is man's demand for everything which nature produces i.e. productive land, vegetables, fruits, water, protein products like chicken, egg, fish, livestock, land for creating infrastructure in urban areas and jungle to absorb emission of carbon dioxide from fossil fuels. Excessive ecological footprint i.e. excess demand for resources for economic gain, leads to overutilization and wastages of natural resources yielding disturbance of ecosystem. Reduction in ecological footprint will balance demand and supply mechanism.

14) **Life below water:** The goal aims to reduce marine pollution.

15) **Life on land:** Life on the earth is largely depending on vegetation, milk, and meat products. Availability of all these in sufficient quantity depends upon proper growth of plants, their retention, afforestation, and availability of productive and fertile land. But due to overutilization and wastage of resources, there is acute shortage resources and products required to sustain life on the earth. The goal's aim is to maintain natural habitat and earth's ecosystem to attain sustainable life on the earth.

16) **Peace, justice, and strong institutions:** Sustainable development can be achieved only amid sound law and order situation. If there is anarchy, violence, terrorist activities, trans- border killings, illegitimate use of arms, sexual violence, and other crimes against women, development process will be completely sabotaged as unlawful activities hamper the spirit of entrepreneurship in every sector resulting in an economy in rubbles. As such unlawful activities are prevalent in various belts of the world, particularly in developing countries, the goal aims to work for bringing strict laws against such activities. Further, awareness about human rights will also work in a useful way to nab such actions. There will be a focus on creating a liaison between the governments and communities to jointly find a productive solution in the interest of sustainable development.

17) **Partnerships for goals:** Due to advancement in communication technology, nations of the world today are well connected and in a way, the world today has become a global village. While keeping this state of affairs in sight, the goal aims at increase in the international trade, not only among developed countries but between developed and developing countries also. There should be exchange of technology, manpower, and services among developing countries also. That is, there must be acceleration in North-South and South-South investment. Policy-making should aim at liberal foreign direct investment, and joint ventures in every sector of the economy. There must be bilateral and multilateral trade agreements. Coveted level of development can be achieved by partnerships at the international level and this is the pivotal aim of this goal.

UNDP AND SDGs

UNDP is playing the same role in getting SDGs implemented as it played in case of MDGs. UNDP is helping the member countries in achieving the goals within stipulated period of time. UNDP is providing necessary support to the countries in planning crusade against poverty, economic inequalities, wastage of natural resources, harmful climate change, crimes and violence UNDP is also assisting member countries to build up an atmosphere of gender equality, education, rational use of energy resources, provision of neat and clean water, sound financial health, inviting foreign collaborations, maintaining peace and sound law and order. It assists in sound policy framework under which there is a provision for private and public sector work together in the interest of overall development.

SDGs AND INDIA

During various national and international meetings, India has been strongly stating that it is fully committed to achieve SDGs by 2030. The target is to achieve overall development. Targets have been fixed to ensure participation of every sector and section of the population in the development process. Primary agency supervising the progress in SDGs is NITI Aayog. NITI Aayog has come up with the schemes of developing those areas which are covered by SDGs, i.e., economy, social sector, and environment. Government-sponsored schemes have been framed to achieve these goals. State governments have also been advised to work in this direction and their progress is reviewed in various meetings. India, equipped with effective policies and programmes, is sure to achieve these goals within the stipulated time. India's initiatives to achieve SDGs by the stipulated time are explained as follows:

Goal 1. No Poverty: India has been initiating efforts to reduce poverty for many years. Eradicating poverty had been the major target of the Indian planning system. Several anti-poverty programmes have been implemented. As poverty is directly related to unemployment in India and both are significantly found in rural areas, India through Mahatma Gandhi National Rural Employment Guarantee Act generated over 2 billion person days of employment during 2018-19. Further, there have been initiatives to enhance agricultural infrastructure and implementing livelihood-based opportunities. It resulted into employment and income to the poor, thereby attacking poverty by empowering the poor. Similarly, other action plans helping in reducing poverty include housing for all by 2022, direct financial assistance to poor householders, easy access to education, health and nutrition, particularly women and children who are the most vulnerable section among the poor, provision of pension and insurance, provision of safe drinking water, and sanitation.

Goal 2. Zero hunger: There have been various programmes to enhance nutrition, particularly among school going children and other vulnerable sections of undernourished population, for e.g., initiatives like Food Security Act, Midday meal, and Public Distribution System. 100 million school children are covered under Midday meal scheme and 800 million people are covered by Public Distribution System under which food grains are provided at an affordable price. Further, National Mission for Sustainable Agriculture (NMSA) is coming up with climate change sustainable strategies, thus increasing agricultural productivity and food production leading to achieve zero hunger.

Goal 3. Good health and well-being: Efforts to achieve this goal are housed in the the National Health Policy 2017. The policy targets the universalization of primary health and reduction in infant mortality, particularly infants under 5. A health insurance policy covering up to Rs. 10,000 for the people living below poverty line is also being implemented. The government has also set a target of immunising all unimmunised and partially immunised children against vaccine-preventable diseases by 2020.

Goal 4. Quality education: While pursuing SDG 4, India is making progress in universalization of primary education. The current National Education Policy is sharing this target of universalization of education with SDG 4. There has been improvement in enrolment of girls at primary and elementary level of education. India has already achieved 100% enrolment of boys and girls at primary level education. Youth literacy rate is touching 94% for males and 92% for females. India's most successful and leading education scheme Sarv Shiksha Abhiyaan is making strides and aims at achieving universal quality education for all. In addition to this another scheme under the name Rashtriya Uchttar Shiksha Abhiyaan (RUSA) has been yielding satisfactory results in the field of higher education. Gross enrolment Ratio (GER) is increasing at every level of education. Further, quality teacher training programmes have been implemented to raise the standard of teaching. Students from different countries are taking admission in various quality education institutes like IGNOU, IITs, AIIMS, IIMs, etc.

Goal 5. Gender equality: In the wake of discrimination against women and heinous crimes against women, Indian government has launched various schemes for welfare of women and creating gender parity. Various schemes like Beti Bachao Beti Padhao (Save the Girl Child Educate the Girl Child) vows to ensure safety and education of the girl child so that women may stand in equation with males. Other initiative has been taken to generate more employment in schemes like Standup India and MGNREGA. The biggest hindrance to achieve gender equality was illiteracy of Indian women. A number of initiatives were taken by the government with the help of NGOs and private sector in the direction of creating awareness in women regarding literacy and education. Resultantly, at present, more than 60% Indian women are literate and aware about their potential. While proceeding towards achieving SDG 5, other important schemes initiated by India for the prosperity and protection of women are Sukanya Samriddhi Yojana and Janani Suraksha Yojana. These schemes will be really proving a milestone in the journey to achieve gender equality and target of SDG 5 will be met within the stipulated time.

Goal 6. Drinking water and sanitation: According to World Bank report, 520 million people in India had been defecating in the open, the number which is the highest in the world. India has already taken initiative in the direction with various schemes. India has launched Swachh Bharat Abhiyaan to make India 100% Open Defecation-Free (ODF) before the end of the stipulated time. With 100% ODF India, there will be remarkable improvement in sanitation. There has been a programme to provide safe drinking water with name National Rural Drinking Water Programme (NRDWP) and for conservation of waters of river Ganga, Namami Gange programme has been launched.

Goal 7. Clean and affordable energy: India has launched National Solar Mission to achieve SDG 7.

Goal 8. Decent work and economic growth: India is an agrarian economy and majority of its population depends upon agriculture. Despite that, agricultural productivity is not enjoying a satisfactory level. India has initiated various programmes in this direction. There is enhancement in public investment and introduction of technology in the agriculture sector. Programmes have also been initiated to enhance employment in the non-farm sector. Due to implementing various women welfare programmes, women labour force is on the increase which is very effective in the development process. According to a report by the McKinsey Global Institute (2015), if India increases its female labour force participation rate by 10 percentage points by 2025, its GDP could rise by as much as 16 per cent as compared to the business-as-usual scenario. Similarly in industry, services, technology, and household sectors, India is achieving economic development. Various schemes supporting this are National Skill Development Mission, Deen Dayal Upadhyaya Antodaya Yojana, Atal Innovation Mission, and MGNREGA.

Goal 9. Industry, innovation, and infrastructure: India has launched programmes under which every mode of transport, i.e., roadways, railways, airways, and waterways are being expanded. Action plans have been launched to bring road connectivity and electricity to rural areas. Digitisation of India, particularly rural India, is being effected through mobile connectivity and Internet. Target is to make India a digital powered society. Through 'Make in India' programme, India is soon going to become an information and communication technology and manufacturing hub in the line to achieve SDG 9. Manufacturing sector is another promising sector. The current Manufacturing Policy has the target to raise the output from 18% of GDP to 25% of GDP by 2025. Further, there has been increase in foreign direct investment (FDI) through 'Make in India' programme, which has helped India sustaining an average growth rate of 7.5% in the last three years. Under Pradhan Mantri Mudra Yojana, easy credit has been granted to aspiring entrepreneurs, thus creating self employment opportunities in small-scale industrial sector. Other programmes to strengthen industry, innovation and infrastructure are Startup India and Atal Innovation Mission.

Goal 10. Reduced inequalities: India has taken initiative to reduce economic inequalities by launching 'Jan Dhan Yojana.' Under this scheme easy credit is provided to small entrepreneurs, thereby increasing their income and reducing economic inequalities.

Goal 11. Sustainable cities and communities: There has been rapid increase in urban population mainly due to mass exodus of rural people to cities. According to a projected estimate India will add 416 million urban dwellers between 2018 and 2050. It has been further projected that by 2030, there will be seven mega cities in India with a population above 10 million each. Along with urbanisation, slum areas are also rapidly developing. To achieve sustainable development in this direction India is implementing Smart City Mission, the Jawaharlal Nehru national Urban Mission, and the Atal Mission for Rejuvenation and Urban Transformation (AMRUT).

Goal 12. Sustainable production and consumption: There has been imbalance in production in India as India accounts for 18% of world's population and 4% of world's water resources. Additionally, India is responsible for maximum emissions of carbon dioxide and other greenhouse gases in the world. India has taken steps with a target of reducing emission intensity of its GDP by 33-35% by 2030. To achieve this, India ratified the Paris Agreement. India has launched schemes like National Policy on Bio-fuels and National Clean Energy Fund (NCEF) through which natural resources can be efficiently used.

Goal 13. Climate action: Being one of the highest emitter of carbon dioxide globally, India has been taking initiatives to reduce emissions and bring it down to the permissible level. Signing of Paris Agreement is one example. Besides this, India has launched National Action Plan on Climate Change (NAPCC) and National Mission for Green India in order to achieve SDG 13.

Goal 14. Life Below water: India towards achievement of SDG 14, has initiated various programmes to flourish Blue Revolution. According to a National Report to the Convention of Biological Diversity, India is the second largest producer of fish in the world. To sustain and improve upon this position, India has launched programmes like Sagarmala Project (Blue Revolution) under which India's ports and coastlines are getting improved and connected. Further, India has adopted a National Plan for the Conservation of Aquatic Ecosystems to conserve marine ecosystem. India is committed to protect its 7,517 kms. of its coastline and protect biodiversity below water while assessing the level of marine pollution through Coastal Ocean Monitoring and Prediction System. Through National Oil Spill- Disaster Contingency Plan, oil spills are managed so that oil spill may not harm aquatic life. National Fisheries Action Plan (NFAP) provides livelihood to the fishing community and promotes ecological integrity of the marine ecosystem.

Goal 15. Life on land: Due to increasing population and large scale deforestation, India is losing land biodiversity. India has initiated various programmes to protect biodiversity on land. These programmes include National Afforestation Programme and a national programme on the Integrated Development of Wildlife Habitats which are core projects aimed at the conservation of land ecosystems. Two specific schemes-Project Tiger and Project Elephant are being implemented. India is also implementing Nagoya Protocol and Aichi Targets of the Convention on Biological Diversity (CBD).

Goal 16. Peace, justice, and strong institutions: This SDG demands lessening of burden of pending cases on Indian High Courts and the Supreme Court. In this direction India has taken initiative in the form of Pragati Platform, and development of infrastructure facilities for the Judiciary including Gram Nyayalays for villages.

Goal 17. Partnerships for the goals: With the motive of achieving this SDG, India is actively going for international partnership. India is member of various UN agencies and is actively participating in UN programmes and global summits. Further, India is member of Shanghai Cooperation Organization and BRICS and its New Development Bank. India has also implemented incentive-based policies to pave way for foreign companies to invest in India. India's expertise is open to neighbouring countries for their development. Launching of South Asia Satellite in 2017 will help in sharing of vital data among neighbouring countries like Nepal, Bangladesh, Bhutan, Sri Lanka, Maldives, and Afghanistan. India is also coming up with international technology trade pacts with the countries like France, UK, Israel, China, and others. India is aware that SDG 17 and other SDGs can be achieved with international cooperation.

Thus, India is working for achieving SDGs and the prime role is being played by NITI Aayog, which is making plans to develop those sectors which are covered by SDGs.

HUMAN-ENVIRONMENT INTERACTION

Man is interacting with the environment every second and this interaction is natural. Man survives while using various natural resources like air, water, timber, energy, and livestock. Nature has provided these resources to man for their rational use, thereby maintaining a healthy lifecycle and keeping the environment clean. Unfortunately, human interaction with environment is not healthy.

People are overutilising limited resources leading to large-scale wastage of resources. Man is more conscious about economic gains, which he is ready to achieve even at the cost of precious resources and clean environment. As population is rapidly increasing, there is more and more demand for consumer goods and production of these goods require more land for opening more industries, which results in excessive deforestation. Pure water is being contaminated by various chemical factories and tanneries which deposit the waste in various water bodies. People are using plastic and dispose it openly. Disposing plastic openly is dangerous for the environment. There is overutilization of non-renewable resources like metals, oil, petroleum, natural gas, etc. People do not realise that once these resources are exhausted, nothing will be left for the future generation. Further, there is large-scale wastage of water also. As the man is now living in a contaminated environment, it results in various diseases like cancer, liver infections, and respiratory disorders. Man is also using plastic which is non-biodegradable. When it is used and thrown in the open, it releases greenhouse gases while reacting with heat of the sun. It is equally harmful if disposed in water.

Present nature of human interaction with the environment needs reformation. People should themselves realise that they are polluting the environment for their vested interest and this polluted environment is in turn becoming fatal for them. There is need to change peoples' ideology and mass media like radio, television, and newspapers can be very much effective. Resultantly, people can take voluntary initiative to clean the environment by realising its importance. Such action will help the government also to implement various environment protection schemes as government alone cannot do effective work in this direction unless people voluntarily go with it.

Some Vital Facts

1) Developing a global partnership for development was one of the Millennium Development Goals.
2) Sustainable development is use of natural resources judiciously so that they are available for future generations.
3) SDGs are formally known as "Transforming Our World: 2030 Agenda."

Practice Exercise

General Questions Format

1. While working to achieve Millennium Development Goals, India could make remarkable progress in
   (A) Gender parity
   (B) Provision of clean drinking water
   (C) Reduction in child morality
   (D) All of the above
2. Man's life support system depends upon..... resources
   (A) natural (B) biodegradable
   (C) renewable (D) environmental
3. Which of the following is TRUE about the environment?
   (A) There are some natural forces, which protect the environment.
   (B) Excessive dependence of man on natural resources is depleting it.
   (C) Environment is the mother of natural resources.
   (D) Environment examines the life cycles of organisms including man.
4. Which of the following human actions is proving fatal for the environment?
   (A) Wastage of natural resources
   (B) Using non-renewable resources
   (C) Regularly interacting with the environment
   (D) All of the above
5. People can be effective in protecting the environmental depletion by
   (A) launching protests against the government for not tackling the problem seriously.
   (B) advising others to avoid the willful wastage of natural resources.
   (C) keeping vigil over those who deliberately pollute the environment.
   (D) none of the above.
6. Overutilisation of some of the natural resources carries an apprehension of
   (A) exhaustion (B) over-interaction
   (C) wastage (D) diseases
7. How can we relate (A) environment, (B) pollution, and (C) natural resources?
   (A) C is part of A and B affects both of them
   (B) A creates C but B destroys C
   (C) B destroys A in case C is not in the way
   (D) A protects C from B
8. People-Environment interaction is desirable only when it
   (A) ensures the man's dependence on the environment.
   (B) is likely that biodegradable resources are going to be exhausted.
   (C) paves way for minimum wastage of natural resources.
   (D) is propagated by the media.

9. Excessive ecological footprint leads to
(A) destruction of natural resources.
(B) more emission of carbon dioxide from fossil fuels.
(C) imbalance in nature's demand and supply mechanism.
(D) outbreak of various respiratory diseases.

10. SDG number 14 basically aims to achieve
(A) shelter for migratory population from rural to urban areas.
(B) development of big cities to absorb excess population migrating to urban areas.
(C) development of sustainable marine and coastal ecosystems.
(D) creation of new and expanded civic bodies in order to widely chalk out settlement plans for migratory population.

11. A polluted environment always causes
(A) inconvenience (B) diseases
(C) shortage (D) wastage

12. Pollution is the result of man's.........action.
(A) natural
(B) routine
(C) unavoidable
(D) none of the above

13. If the plastic is not discarded after one use, it can
(A) become more harmful.
(B) check environmental pollution.
(C) lose the property of non-biodegradability.
(D) attract attention of authorities banning its use.

14. Which of the following best explains the relationship between environment and development?
(A) Development is possible amid neat and clean environment.
(B) Dynamic nature of environment gives rise to dynamic development process.
(C) Environment and development are two sides of the same coin.
(D) Natural resources creating the environment restrict their overutilization for development.

15. Providing suitable environment to mankind is a/an..........contribution of the earth.
(A) original (B) fundamental
(C) ultimate (D) intimate

16. An environment-friendly society is always
(A) possible (B) desirable
(C) affordable (D) appreciable

17. Which of the following is TRUE?
(A) Environmental and water pollution are substitutes of each other.
(B) Natural resources act as stimulants for man to enhance his economic interests resulting in pollution.
(C) Voluntary efforts to curb pollution will lead to saving precious natural resources.
(D) Renewable natural resources do not have risk of misutilisation.

18. Which of the following is NOT TRUE about SDG: Responsible Consumption and Production?
(A) Setting of industries for recycling waste
(B) Fixing quota of resources helping in production and consumption process to ensure minimum wastage
(C) Ensuring proper feeding of hungry and undernourished population
(D) Disposing of large-scale littering all around including plastic

19. Which of the following pair is wrong?
(A) SDG 5 - Gender Equality
(B) SDG 2 - Zero Hunger
(C) SDG 16 - Life on Land
(D) SDG 11 - Sustainable Cities and Communities

20. How does NITI Aayog work on achievement of SDGs?
(A) Framing plans for the development of those sectors and sections which are covered by SDGs
(B) Having proper liaison with UNDP to seek guidance in achieving these goals
(C) Arranging training for SDG concerned personnel to motivate them to efficiently achieve SDGs
(D) All of the above

21. What is sustainable development?
   (A) The development that meets the needs of the present without compromising the ability of future generations to meet their own needs
   (B) To conserve natural resources and to develop alternate sources of power while reducing pollution and harm to the environment
   (C) The practice of developing land and construction projects in a manner that reduces their impact on the environment by allowing them to create energy-efficient models of self-sufficiency
   (D) All of the above

22. Which of the following is correct, if we only achieve two out of three pillars of Sustainable Development?
   (A) Social + Economic Sustainability = Equitable
   (B) Social + Environmental Sustainability = Bearable
   (C) Economic + Environmental Sustainability = Viable
   (D) All of the above

23. Human interaction with the environment is unhealthy on account of
   (A) overutilization of natural resources
   (B) indifference towards environment protection policies
   (C) misutilising non-biodegradable stuff like plastic
   (D) None of the above

24. Which of the following statement best explains the relationship between environment and development?
   (A) Environment sustained by natural resources provide a conducive ground for rational use of resources in production of goods and services resulting in rise of per capita income and GDP.
   (B) Environment and development sustain each other with the help of natural resources.
   (C) Per capita income and GDP grow in an environment full of resources conducive in maximum investment.
   (D) Availability of renewable and non-renewable resources in the environment pave way for investment in consumer goods industries which is ultimately taken as a development indicator.

26. Sustainable Development Goals are also known as
   (A) Millennium Declaration
   (B) Agenda Rio 2012
   (C) Agenda 2020
   (D) Agenda 2030

27. Which of the following is TRUE about India's action plan for achieving SDG 5-'Gender Equality'?
   i) Indian women have been motivated to adopt legal course for crimes against them by men.
   ii) India has launched Janani Suraksha Yojana to provide pre-natal and post-natal care to working women during maternity leave.
   iii) Schemes like 'Standup India' and MNGREGA are helping millions of women to seek employment even in male dominated fields.
   iv) Government is granting school and college going girls study scholarships at par with male students under 'Beti Bachao, Beti Padhao' scheme.
   (A) ii and iii only
   (B) None of the above
   (C) i. ii, iii, and iv
   (D) ii only

28. India being signatory to Nagoya Protocol, is working to protect
   (A) Air
   (B) Water
   (C) Biodiversity
   (D) Threatened species

29. Which of the following best justifies India's initiative to achieve SDG 17?
   (A) Launching of South Asia Satellite
   (B) International trade and technology pacts
   (C) Membership of BRICS
   (D) None of the above

30. Match the schemes launched by India given under Set I with the concerned SDG given under Set II and select the right code:

Set I (Schemes)	Set II (SDG)
a) Sagarmala Project	i) Peace, Justice, and Strong Institutions
b) Pragati Platform	ii) Industry, Innovation, and Infrastructure
c) National Policy on Bio-fuels	iii) Life below Water
d) Make in India	iv) Sustainable Production and Consumption

Codes:	(a)	(b)	(c)	(d)
(A)	ii	i	iv	iii
(B)	iii	iv	i	ii
(C)	iii	i	iv	ii
(D)	ii	iv	iii	i

KEY

1. D **2.** A **3.** B **4.** A **5.** D **6.** A **7.** C
8. C **9.** C **10.** C **11.** B **12.** D **13.** B **14.** A
15. C **16.** B **17.** C **18.** B **19.** C **20.** A **21.** D
22. D **23.** A **24.** A **25.** D **26.** D **27.** B **28.** C
29. A **30.** C

Assertion–Reason Format

1. **Assertion (A):** Rapidly increasing population pollutes the environment.

   Reason (R): Opening of more and more industries is leading to large-scale deforestation.

   (A) Both A and R are true and R is the correct explanation of A
   (B) Both A and R are true but R is not correct explanation of A
   (C) A is true but R is false
   (D) A is false but R is true

2. **Assertion (A):** Ecological footprint is not necessarily posing threat to the environment.

   Reason (R): Various natural resources act as determinants of ecological footprint.

   (A) Both A and R are true and R is the correct explanation of A
   (B) Both A and R are true but R is not correct explanation of A
   (C) A is true but R is false
   (D) A is false but R is true

3. **Assertion (A):** Human rights Awareness is the prime agenda in developing countries since recent past.

   Reason (R): Achieving sustainable development is a mission for people of developing countries.

   (A) Both A and R are true and R is the correct explanation of A
   (B) Both A and R are true but R is not the correct explanation of A
   (C) A is true but R is false
   (D) Both A and R are false

4. **Assertion (A):** Present interaction of people with the environment is not healthy.

   Reason (R): Mass media can be effective in changing people's outlook towards the environment.

   (A) Both A and R are true and R is the correct explanation of A
   (B) Both A and R are true but R is not the correct explanation of A
   (C) A is true but R is false
   (D) A is false but R is true

5. **Assertion (A):** UNDP is helping the member countries in defining SDGs.

   Reason (R) : Performance of member countries in achieving SDGs is evaluated by UNDP.

   (A) Both A and R are true and R is the correct explanation of A
   (B) Both A and R are true but R is not the correct explanation of A
   (C) A is true but R is false
   (D) A is false but R is true

KEY

1. A **2.** A **3.** D **4.** B **5.** C

Questions Asked in Previous NET Exams

1. **Statement I:** The Millennium Development Goals were adopted by the United Nations in the year 2010.

   Statement II: Developing a global partnership for development was one of the Millennium Development Goals

   (UGC NET JUNE 2019)

   Which of the above statement (s) is/are correct?

   (A) Only I (B) Only II

   (C) Both I and II (D) Neither I nor II

2. Which of the following statements best explains the concept of sustainable development?

   (A) Use of natural resources minimally

   (B) Use of natural resources for our benefit

   (C) Use of natural resources judiciously so that they are available for future generations

   (D) Preserve natural resources for our future generations

3. Sustainable Development Goals (SDGs) are formally known as **(UGC NET JULY 2018)**

   (A) Transforming Our World: 2030 Agenda

   (B) Sustainable Living For All: 2022 Agenda

   (C) Life Of Dignity For All: 2022 Agenda

   (D) One Planet, One People: 2030 Agenda

4. **Assertion (A):** Sustainable development is critical to well-being of human society.

   Reason (R): Environmentally sound policies do not harm the environment or deplete the natural resources.

   (UGC NET JANUARY 2017)

   Choose the correct code:

   (A) Both (A) and (R) are correct and (R) is the correct explanation of (A).

   (B) Both (A) and (R) are correct, but (R) is not the correct explanation of (A).

   (C) (A) is true and (R) is false.

   (D) (A) is false and (R) is true.

5. **Assertion (A):** The problems of environmental sustainability are difficult to resolve.

   Reason (R): Our understanding of how environment works and how different human choices affect the environment is inadequate.

   (UGC NET AUGUST 2016)

   Choose the correct code:

   (A) Both (A) and (R) are correct and (R) is the correct explanation of (A).

   (B) Both (A) and (R) are correct, but (R) is not the correct explanation of (A).

   (C) (A) is true and (R) is false.

   (D) (A) is false and (R) is true.

6. Sustainable development goals have specific targets to be achieved by

   (UGC NET JULY 2016)

   (A) 2022

   (B) 2030

   (C) 2040

   (D) 2050

KEY

1. B **2.** C **3.** A **4.** B **5.** A **6.** B

2 Anthropogenic Activities

INTRODUCTION

While surviving among natural resources, man indulges in various activities to earn his livelihood. In the race of fetching maximum economic gain, man misutilises and overutilises the natural resources which leave a bad impact on the environment. Resultantly, there are many changes in climate. The impact on environment and climate caused by human activities is called 'anthropogenic activities'. Such activities like deforestation, release of greenhouse gases by burning fossil fuels, excessive use of fertilizers and pesticides in agricultural operations, emission of carbon monoxide, lead, asbestos, and other pollutants through the smoke of vehicles and chimneys of various factories result in pollution and environment degradation.

IMPACT OF ANTHROPOGENIC ACTIVITIES ON THE ENVIRONMENT

As population on the earth is increasing, human interference in the nature's phenomena is also increasing, thereby leaving unhealthy, rather catastrophic impact on the environment. Impact of anthropogenic activities on the environment can be seen as follows:

1) **Climate change:** Anthropogenic activities have resulted in change in climate. There is increase in various industries to produce various goods in response to increasing demand. Installation of factories basically need more land which is already limited. To house such production units, large-scale deforestation is practiced. Deforestation disturbs the natural climate balance. Further, emissions of greenhouse gases lead to rise in the global temperature. This has brought severe irregularities in the duration of a particular season in a particular belt of the world. Such activities are responsible for various natural disasters like hurricanes, cyclones, and tsunamis leading to large-scale destruction of life and property.
2) **Water pollution:** Chemical wastes and garbage, sewage, and discarded plastic are thrown into various water bodies and ultimately drained into seas and oceans, posing a huge threat to aquatic life. Another reason of pollution in water bodies is excessive use of fertilizers which reaches water bodies through rain, soil erosion, and dust storms. Ultimate destination of any pollutant in any water body is oceans and seas.
3) **Air pollution:** Another dangerous impact of anthropogenic activities is air pollution. Human activities involving burning of fossil fuels and automotive and factory exhausts are creating respiratory diseases. Smog created due to stubble burning is also leaving a devastating impact on the atmosphere.

SMOG

Smog is a type of air pollution arising when smoke gets mixed with fog. Smoke arising due to emission of various gases due to burning of stubble, fossil fuels, and automotive exhausts. A hazy layer in the air is spread out when sunrays react with nitrogen oxides and sulphur dioxide in the atmosphere.

4) **Overpopulation:** Burden of population on the planet is continuously increasing. Decrease in the death rates due to better and accessible medical facilities is resulting in overpopulation. More the population, more is the land needed, leading to more deforestation. Absence of trees imbalances the ecosystem. In a situation of

few trees, less will be the absorption of carbon dioxide released by human activities. Further, overpopulation will necessitate more and more use of fossil fuels, hence more release of greenhouse gases. Increase in carbon dioxide will pose a threat to terrestrial life and in some species, there will be an apprehension of their extinction due to loss of their habitat.

5) **Global warming:** As man is depending on fossil fuels to have energy, greenhouse gases are emitted to raise the global temperature. Due to rise in earth's temperature almost by 2 degree celsius, polar ice melts and excess water fills up oceans, resulting into tsunamis.
6) **Acid rain:** When gases like carbon dioxide, sulphur dioxide, and nitrogen oxide are released into the atmosphere due to anthropogenic activities, they react with water vapours in the atmosphere to give acids like carbonic acid and sulphuric acid. After becoming acidic, water vapours become heavy and fall down on the earth in the form of acid rain. When acid rain falls on any body part, it causes skin diseases. It damages plant foliage, it spoils the paints of cars and other materials, and it fades the lustre of marble statues.
7) **Changes in the genetic structure of species:** At present, anthropogenic activities are concentrating on modification of genes of plant species through genetic engineering techniques. In order to get rapid growth, man uses more and more fertilizers which lead to soil pollution and water pollution.

Editor: The text inside the following textbox is invisible, please look into it.

GMO

Every plant or animal species have a genetic structure with which it grows naturally. Human being for its vested interest modifies the DNA of the species to give artificial growth. Such organisms are Genetically Modified Organisms (GMO). Purpose behind modification in genetic structure particular of plant species is to speed up their growth artificially and their growth even in the off season, resisting change in season and making that species an all season species so that maximum economic gain be fetched.

8) **Depletion of ozone layer:** Ozone layer in the atmosphere protects the earth and mankind from various hazardous rays of the sun. Activities of mankind resulting in global warming result in depletion of the ozone layer which is becoming helpless in filtering hazardous sun rays and these are directly coming to the earth. This leads to various fatal diseases for man.
9) **Acidification of oceans:** Carbon dioxide released by human activities acidifies oceans when it mixes up with ocean water to make carbonic acid. This acidification becomes fatal for aquatic life.
10) **Deforestation:** As the population is increasing, more and more land is required to accommodate new population. This results in large-scale deforestation. Forests give us oxygen and absorb carbon dioxide. Human beings, animals, and plants cannot survive in the absence of oxygen. Forests serve as home to many animals also. Absence of forests creates apprehension of their extinction.

Some Vital Facts

1) Agriculture is that anthropogenic activity accounts for more than 2/3rd of global water consumption.
2) Watershed Development Approach is the most comprehensive approach to address the problems of man-environment interaction
3) Ecological footprint is the area of productive land and water to meet the resources requirement.
4) In urban areas, smog episodes occur frequently in winters.
5) In winters, a lot of biomass is burnt by people for heating purposes or to keep themselves warm.

Practice Exercise

General Questions Format

1. Which of the following is TRUE about biodiversity?
   (A) Diverse population of various species interact to bring reason of survival for one another.
   (B) Increasing human population and migration to urban areas leads to mismatch in different species.
   (C) Diverse range of various animal and plant species need their respective habitat and genetic strength for survival.
   (D) All of the above

2. Which anthropogenic activity is least harmful for the environment?
   (A) Using fertilizers and pesticides to fetch maximum crop yield
   (B) Burning of fossil fuels to obtain energy
   (C) Migration of rural population to urban areas
   (D) None of these

3. Which of the following phenomenon, set in due to anthropogenic activities, is correct?
   (A) Burning of fossil fuels result in global warming which depletes the ozone layer.
   (B) Increasing urbanisation leads to large-scale deforestation leading to loss of biodiversity.
   (C) Greenhouse gases mixed with the ocean water bring acid rain.
   (D) Global warming results in various skin and other fatal diseases caused by the terrestrial heat.

4. Plantation of genetically modified plant species results in
   (A) deforestation (B) soil pollution
   (C) growth of weeds (D) none of these

5. Release of which gas into the atmosphere does not form acid rain?
   (A) Nitrogen Oxide
   (B) Hydrogen Oxide
   (C) Sulphur Dioxide
   (D) Carbon Dioxide

6. Anthropogenic activities are given under Column I and their outcome is given under Column II. Match the activity with its result.

Column I (Anthropogenic Activity)	Column II (Outcome)
a) Deforestation	i) Water pollution
b) Burning of fossil fuels	ii) Extinction
c) Sewage	iii) Loss of biodiversity
d) Wastage of resources	Iv) Global warming

Codes:	(a)	(b)	(c)	(d)
(A)	ii	iv	iii	i
(B)	iii	ii	iv	
(C)	iv	iii	i	ii
(D)	iii	iv	i	ii

7. Consider the following statements:
   i) Ozone layer in the atmosphere protects the earth and mankind from various hazardous rays of the sun.
   ii) Overpopulation necessitates more and more use of resources to preserve and protect biodiversity.
   iii) Anthropogenic activities create an impact on the environment which result in reduction in the proportionate emissions responsible for global warming.
   iv) Acidification of oceans is the result of acid rain falling down on sea surface, after greenhouse gases react with water vapours in the atmosphere to form acids.

   Which of the above statement(s) is TRUE?
   (A) ii and iv only
   (B) i only
   (C) ii, iii, and iv
   (D) i and iii only

KEY

1. C **2.** D **3.** B **4.** B **5.** B **6.** D **7.** B

Assertion–Reason Format

1. **Assertion (A):** Deforestation leads to extinction of animals.

   Reason (R): Loss of biodiversity in a region is actually migration of animals towards a suitable habitat.

   (A) Both A and R are true and R is correct explanation of A

   (B) A is true but R is false

   (C) Both A and R are true but R is not correct explanation of A

   (D) A is false but R is true

2. **Assertion (A):** Anthropogenic activities become less intensive with the development of a region.

   Reason (R): Economic development and environment degradation are substitutes.

   (A) Both A and R are true and R is the correct explanation of A

   (B) Both A and R are false

   (C) A is true but R is false

   (D) A is false but R is true

3. **Assertion (A):** Burning of fossil fuels is a deliberate attempt by man for economic gains.

   Reason (R): Various respiratory diseases are a result of burning of fossil fuels.

   (A) Both A and R are true and R is correct explanation of A

   (B) Both A and R are true but R is not correct explanation of A

   (C) Both A and R are false

   (D) A is false but R is true

KEY

1. A **2.** B **3.** B

Questions Asked in Previous NET Exams

1. **Assertion (A):** In urban areas, smog episodes occur frequently in winters.

   Reason (R): In winters, a lot of biomass is burnt by people for heating purposes or to keep themselves warm.

   (UGC NET NOVEMBER 2017)

   Choose the correct answer from the code given below:

   (A) Both (A) and (R) are true but (R) is not the correct explanation of (A)

   (B) (A) is true and (R) is false

   (C) Both (A) and (R) are false

   (D) Both (A) and (R) are true and (R) is the correct explanation of (A)

2. Which of the anthropogenic activity accounts for more than 2/3rd of global water consumption?

   (UGC NET DECEMBER 2014)

   (A) Agriculture

   (B) Hydropower generation

   (C) Industry

   (D) Domestic and municipal usage

3. The most comprehensive approach to address the problems of man-environment interaction is one of the following:

   (UGC NET DECEMBER 2013)

   (A) Natural Resource Conservation Approach

   (B) Urban-industrial Growth Oriented Approach

   (C) Rural-agricultural Growth Oriented Approach

   (D) Watershed Development Approach

4. Ecological footprint represents

   (UGC NET DECEMBER 2011)

   (A) Area of productive land and water to meet the resources requirement

   (B) Energy consumption

   (C) CO2 emissions per person

   (D) Forest cover

KEY

1. A **2.** A **3.** D **4.** A

3 Environmental Issues

INTRODUCTION

Environment and the various issues associated with it are the subject of concern at present. Issues may be the same but their magnitude differs with the area these belong to.

LOCAL ISSUES

Local environment issues include all the environment-threatening issues within the municipal jurisdiction. It is duty of the local government body to address local environment issues, which are listed as follows:

1) Disposal of sewage and other waste
2) Menace of stray animals
3) Overflowing sewers
4) Creating greenbelts and parks
5) Stringent action against littering
6) Drainage of stranded water yielding many communicative ailments from mosquitoes
7) Proper arrangement of parking to avoid overcrowding of vehicles resulting in various environmental problems
8) Disposal of stray garbage heaps here and there within the municipal jurisdiction
9) Water pollution
10) Air pollution

All the above local level issues should be addressed with proper planning and installation of waste treatment plants by the municipal authorities.

REGIONAL ISSUES

There are different regions in the world in the form of continents. Regional environmental issues touch the broader part of environmental concerns. Following are some regional issues:

1) Overutilisation of natural resources
2) Achievement of sustainable development
3) Overpopulation in urban areas leading to shortage of land
4) Air pollution
5) Water pollution
6) Greenhouse effect
7) Increasing poverty
8) Lack of healthcare facilities and education
9) Deforestation leading to loss of biodiversity and soil infertility
10) Extinction of species due to loss of their habitat

BIODIVERSITY

As the name suggests Biodiversity (Biological + Diversity) is the diverse range of life including plants, animals, small organisms surviving on all spheres of the earth i.e. on land, in air and in water. Biodiversity is growth of different species in their respective habitat (natural suitable surroundings). Biodiversity also covers genetic strength of various plants and animal species. Preserving and protecting biodiversity is important as various plant and animal species provide food to human being. Additionally many herbs provide drugs. It must be protected in any case. Deforestation is the biggest threat to biodiversity.

GLOBAL ENVIRONMENTAL ISSUES

Though many of the global environment issues are coinciding with regional and local environmental issues, yet some have global coverage.

1) Climate change
2) Global warming
3) Air pollution
4) Marine pollution
5) Depletion of ozone layer
6) Nuclear pollution
7) Aftermath of natural hazards
8) Water pollution

It may be a local or regional or global environmental challenge, but there is a need to nail it at its source through effective planning and implementation.

Practice Exercise

General Questions Format

1. Which of the following is NOT a global environmental issue?
   (A) Climate change
   (B) Disposal of sewage
   (C) Nuclear pollution
   (D) Loss of biodiversity
2. Which of the following is NOT TRUE about environmental issues?
   (A) Environmental issues hamper economic development.
   (B) Regional issues take the shape of global issues if they remain unattended for a long time.
   (C) Local environmental issues do not interfere with regional and global issues.
   (D) Environmental issue of any level poses a threat to biodiversity.
3. The human activity, among the following, which causes maximum environmental pollution having regional and global impacts, is:
   (A) Urbanisation (B) Industrialisation
   (C) Agriculture (D) Mining

KEY

1. B **2.** C **3.** B

Assertion–Reason Format

1. **Assertion (A):** Local environment issues do not need long-term planning.
   Reason (R): Different level environmental issues may be the same but these differ in magnitude.
   (A) Both A and R are false
   (B) Both A and R are true and R is correct explanation of A
   (C) A is true but R is false
   (D) Both A and R are true but R is not correct explanation of A
2. **Assertion (A):** Global environmental issues can be managed through global talks.
   Reason (R): An untackled local environmental issue becomes a global issue one day.
   (A) Both A and R are true and R is correct explanation of A
   (B) Both A and R are true but R is not correct explanation of A
   (C) A is true but R is false
   (D) Both A and R are false

KEY

1. D **2.** D

4 Pollution and Waste: Types, Impact and Control

INTRODUCTION: CONCEPT

Any harmful effect on various species like human beings, animals, or plants due to undesirable change in our surroundings is **Pollution**. Pollution is the result of anthropogenic activities practiced for economic gains.

Background

Pollution is, by and large, not a natural phenomenon. Nature has blessed us with the neatest possible environment that helps in the healthy growth of mankind, animals, and plants. We are fortunate enough to be inhabitants of the earth, the only planet that has made possible the birth and survival of man, animals, and plants due to its unique features like possessing a conducive atmosphere and natural and useful resources in all its spheres viz. lithosphere, hydrosphere, atmosphere, and biosphere. But as we are heading towards modernisation and developing lust for short-term economic gains, we have started contaminating the clear and neat natural environment. In the name of exploitation of natural resources for human welfare, the resources are rather being destroyed. During the last few decades we have polluted our air, water, and land with a variety of waste products. The planet which had been once the protector of our lifeline is now fast becoming a hub of pollutants, which are fatally hazardous. And for bringing such a catastrophic situation, only man is responsible.

Types Of Pollution

1) Air pollution
2) Water pollution
3) Noise pollution
4) Soil pollution
5) Marine pollution
6) Thermal pollution
7) Groundwater pollution

DIFFERENT KINDS OF POLLUTION

Air Pollution

Air pollution is caused by the presence of undesirable solid or gaseous particles in the air up to the extent which is sufficient to affect health of various species surviving on the earth. Air pollution is caused due to natural and man-made reasons. Natural reasons like volcanic eruptions and forest fires do fill the air with dust and other pollutants, but the stay of these pollutants is very short in the atmosphere as these are washed away with rain. Pollutants deposited in the air by human activities persistently stay in the atmosphere and pose various dangers for the species and become effective in bringing undesirable changes in climate. As air pollution is directly concerned with the atmosphere, it becomes mandatory to study the structure of the atmosphere.

Structure of the Atmosphere

Atmosphere has four layers if seen from bottom to top, i.e., Troposphere, Stratosphere, Mesosphere, and Thermosphere.

Troposphere is the lowest or innermost layer of the atmosphere. Earth's weather is contained in this layer. Life is surviving in this layer. This layer contains 75% of air along with clouds and water vapours. Boundary of this layer is called Tropopause. Pollutants of the air remain in this layer. This layer extends up to about 20 kms.

Stratosphere is the next layer extending up to about 50 km above the earth's surface. This layer contains ozone which absorbs harmful ultraviolet sun rays, thus protecting us from skin cancer and many other fatal diseases. This layer of atmosphere is suitable for aeroplanes as it does not carry turbulence. Boundary of this layer is called Stratopause.

Mesosphere is a thin layer of atmosphere. This layer contains little nitrogen and oxygen. Boundary of this layer is called Mesopause. This layer extends up to about 80 kms.

Thermosphere is the uppermost layer of the atmosphere. It is hot because it is getting direct sunlight. This layer extends upward up to about 600 kms.

COMPOSITION OF EARTH'S ATMOSPHERE

Atmosphere of the earth comprises of various gases in this proportion: 78% Nitrogen, 21% Oxygen, and 1% Argon along with traces of Nitrous oxide, Krypton, Ozone, Carbon dioxide, Hydrogen, Methane, Helium, Neon, Carbon Monoxide, Iodine, and Water vapours.

Sources of Air Pollution

Point source pollution: Point source pollution is caused when pollutants are released into air by a single identifiable source. Example: emissions from a factory. As in this case source can be identified being a single one, it is easier to find ways to eradicate this pollution.

Nonpoint source pollution: Nonpoint source air pollution occurs when pollutants are introduced into the air from different sources, some of which cannot be identified. Example: If a region is experiencing smog which may be coming from different sources like emissions from automobiles, factories, burning of stubble, etc. and such sources are unidentifiable. As in this pollution source cannot be identified, it becomes more difficult to eradicate this pollution. Here, authorities try all the measures required for all possible sources to address such air pollution.

Control Measures

As air pollution is caused mainly due to emissions and burning of fossil fuels, various measures to control this menace can be taken:

1) **Adopting renewable energy resources:** As air pollution is caused mainly due to emissions and burning of fossil fuels, energy can be obtained by switching over to renewable sources which are environment-friendly.
2) **Recycling of waste:** Discarded waste products like garbage, plastics, etc. react with sunlight and air to produce air pollutants. There should be installation of treatment and recycling plants to produce various products from them.
3) **Avoid wastage of electricity:** Electricity is produced by burning fossil fuels. Sensible usage of electricity without wastage will reduce burning of fossil fuels and hence cause less air pollution.
4) **Sharing vehicles:** People going for jobs or any other work on their vehicles should be educated and motivated to share vehicles in rotation which will reduce automotive emissions which are hazardous for the environment.
5) **Using public transport mode:** Vehicle owners and others should be appealed to use public transport instead of their own vehicles separately, leading to reduction of vehicular emissions.
6) **Treatment devices in vehicles:** Vehicular exhausts contain pollutants like carbon monoxide, lead, asbestos, etc. which after creating air pollution generates many fatal diseases, so fuel filter treatment devices should be installed in the vehicles.
7) **Stringent laws against public smoking:** Smoking in the public should be prohibited by enacting strict regulations.

LONDON SMOG

London faced a severe environmental disaster in December 1952 called Great Smog of London or Killer Fog of 1952. Due to high pressure wind system, a thick fog covered London at ground level. This fog got mixed with smoke coming out of chimneys, furnaces, and burning of coal for domestic purposes. Smog stayed for five days. It caused severe hardships for the residents. Due to thickness of the smog, visibility level was reduced to zero. There were about 12,000 deaths due to suffocation, bronchial asthma, and pneumonia and more than 150,000 fell ill. Most of the casualties were among infants and elderly population. Zero visibility paralysed the total transport system, schooling, and business and people had to confine themselves in their houses.

Pea-Souper

Pea-souper is thick smog of yellow, green, or black colour caused due to air pollution. It contains various solid particles and gases like sulphur dioxide due to burning of fossil fuels like coal during industrial processes. Pea-souper is a poisonous fog which leads to death and respiratory diseases. Pea-souper, though less intensive, is the same as London smog.

Air Pollution in India

Air pollution in India is caused by burning coal, wood, automotive exhausts, traffic congestion, and stubble burning. The smoke arising out of these sources pollutes Indian air. Overpopulation of India is also becoming a strong contributor to air pollution. Overburdened by population, India is facing a steep increase in demand for various goods and services. To fulfil this demand, more and more industries are being set up leading to large-scale deforestation. Production and plying of more vehicles are resulting in more and more carbon monoxide emissions leading to air pollution and loss of natural habitat of many species. As far as emission of greenhouse gases is concerned, India is one of the leading countries.

WHAT STATISTICS AND STUDIES SAY

World Health Organisation (WHO) furnished a list of 15 cities of the world having maximum particulate pollution. Out of these 15 cities, 14 belonged to India.

As per Environmental Performance Index 2016, out of 180 top countries plagued with air pollution, Indian ranked 141.

According to State of India's Environment (SoE) 2018, India is ranking 177th among top 180 countries with air pollution.

As per Washington Post study, on average, life expectancy of Indian people has cut short by 5.3 years due to air pollution. Those in two districts east of Delhi-Hapur and Bulandshahr-have their life expectancy cut short by 12 years, which is the greatest reduction in the world due to air pollution.

As per report of a social work organisation Greenpeace, NCR Delhi, Sonbhadra (U.P.), Singrauli (Madhya Pradesh), and Talcher-Angul (Odisha) are among the world's largest nitrogen oxide air pollution hotspots.

As reported by Central Pollution Control Board (CPCB) in 2018, Air Quality index (AQI) was poorer in Kolkata as compared to AQI in Delhi. Average AQI in Kolkata was 295 parts per million (ppm) against 287 ppm in Delhi.

$PM_{2.5}$ AND PM_{10}

Particulate Matter (PM) is mixture of fine solid and liquid particles suspended in air from different man-made and natural actions like burning of fuels, reaction of gases with water vapours in atmosphere, dust storms, forest fires, and vehicular and factory emissions. These fine particles enter lungs through breathing and cause various respiratory diseases. PM is measured in micrometres. There are two types of PM.

$PM_{2.5}$ is that atmospheric particulate matter which has a diameter of less than 2.5 micrometres which is more than 100 times thinner than human hair. $PM_{2.5}$ consists of super fine particles that enter the whole body through lungs. These particles are so fine that these are visible only through the microscope.

PM_{10} is that particulate matter which is less than 10 micrometres in diameter. It is 30 times thinner than human hair. These particles are coarse particles and enter the lungs. PM_{10} is safer than $PM_{2.5}$.

Major Polluted Cities of India

According to air pollution data released by WHO about top 15 cities of world, 14 cities are from India. $PM_{2.5}$ level of Kanpur is found to be 173 (micrograms per cubic metre) and thus tops the list. $PM_{2.5}$ level of Delhi is 143 (micrograms per cubic metre) fixes it at 6th position.

Control Measures taken by India

With the start of 2019, India launched 'Clean Air India Initiative'. Under this initiative a campaign will be launched to curb air pollution in Indian cities. This initiative will be a joint venture of India and Netherlands under which Indian entrepreneurs in partnership with Dutch companies will be working to clean Indian air. This initiative is a collaborative project of Get in the Ring, a platform for startups, Government of Netherlands, Startup India, and INDUS forum, an online matchmaking platform of Indian and Dutch companies. Under this initiative there is a target of achieving reduction in $PM_{2.5}$ and PM_{10} by 20 to 30% by 2024. There is also a target of curbing air pollution of NCR-Delhi, the air of which is getting severe pollution from the smoke of stubble burning in neighbouring Punjab and Haryana states. There is a plan to install recycling plants in these states so that instead of burning it, stubble is recycled to get useful products like paper and packaging material.

Water Pollution

When human activities result in undesirable changes in the quality and composition of water, which make it unfit for drinking and any other purpose and make it a health hazard for organisms, it is said to be polluted.

Water is a precious natural resource which is indispensable for survival of man, animals, plants, and all organisms. Proportion of pure surface water available for survival is just 0.3%. Man is persistently polluting and wasting water as water is being taken for granted.

Man is contaminating pure water by introducing various chemicals and sewage into water bodies like rivers, canals, lakes, ponds, etc. and making it unfit for drinking and washing purposes. These chemicals are waste effluents coming out of various chemical factories and tanneries and after getting mixed with clean water it creates various waterborne diseases for man, animals, and plants.

Sources Of Water Pollution

1) **Water-soluble inorganic chemicals:** Various chemicals, acids, and toxic metals such as mercury and lead and salts introduced in the water make water unsafe to drink and pose threat of various fatal ailments and pose danger to aquatic life.
2) **Sediment of suspended matter:** Soil particles due to soil erosion are deposited on surface water in different water bodies and remain suspended in the water. These obstruct the sunlight reaching the aquatic plants and hamper the photosynthesis activity due to which growth of these plants is put in peril.
3) **Pathogens:** Different wastes discharged in water generate various harmful bacteria, virus, protozoa, and parasitic worms which pose threat to aquatic life.
4) **Inorganic plant nutrients:** There are phosphates and nitrates soluble in water and they result in growth of weed and algae. These unwanted plants' growth depletes the quality, taste, and odour of water. Such growth wipes out oxygen from water. This weed also affects the quality and taste of drinking water supplied to households by clogging water pipes.
5) **Hot water:** Many chemical industries and distilleries run the cold water in chambers to cool the hot liquids. When due to transfer of heat cold water becomes hot, then that hot water is inducted into water bodies. Temperature of water in the water bodies then rises, and pose threat to aquatic life by wiping out oxygen of that water.
6) **Oxygen-depleting wastes:** There are oxygen-bearing bacteria in water. When wastes are deposited in water, these oxygen-bearing bacteria fight with this waste to maintain immunity of water. In this process lot of oxygen is depleted resulting in threat to aquatic life.
7) **Oil:** Oil spillage on roads also pollutes surface water as this oil falls into water bodies.
8) **Organic chemicals:** Organic chemicals like detergents, pesticides, gasoline, plastic, gas, etc. when deposited in clean water due to various human activities (like mishandling of chemicals and illegitimately), badly pollute clean water.
9) **Human source:** A large amount of water is used by man for various domestic purposes. This water when becomes waste is discharged through drains into various water bodies. Here, when this waste water gets mixed with litter like plastic, paper, etc. it becomes municipal waste or sewage. This sewage pollutes clean water. Though sewage is a big source of water pollution, yet the biggest source of water pollution is agricultural activity.

Control Measures

Whether it is water pollution or any other, voluntary efforts to control it is much more effective than enforced measures. Water pollution can be controlled rather than prevented by taking a few voluntary and enforced steps as follows:

1) Plastic littering in various water bodies like lakes, canals, ponds, etc. should be avoided.
2) Excessive use of fertilizers and pesticides should be avoided.
3) Toilets should not be used as bins by throwing domestic waste into these as this disposal waste through drains of toilets ends up landing in water bodies, thus resulting in pollution.
4) Stringent regulations should be made for curbing illegal disposal of chemical effluents into water bodies.
5) Maximum trees should be planted to prevent soil erosion due to which eroded soil descends on surface water. Additionally, more plantations of trees will contain the flow of waste water to clean water bodies.
6) Disposal of cooking oil and fat into kitchen sinks should be avoided.
7) Wastage and overutilisation of water should be avoided.
8) There should be proper treatment of sewage and other wastes to avoid deposits of toxic elements in water bodies.
9) Potassium permanganate should be dissolved in water to disinfect it.
10) Maximum energy saving gadgets like washing machines should be used which save water and reduce the quantity of waste water.
11) Disposal of dead bodies into rivers should be prohibited.

EUTROPHICATION

When water of lakes, rivers, or any other water body is enriched with nutrient salts like nitrate and phosphorus and these results in growth of algae and weeds, this development is called 'Eutrophication'. Algae and weeds pose great threat to the aquatic life and the ecosystem. Eutrophication changes the composition, taste, and odour of surface water to a harmful extent. On one hand, eutrophication is a natural and slow process, on the other hand, nitrate and phosphorus induction into water bodies by man-made activities accelerate eutrophication. Excessive use of fertilizers is responsible for rapid eutrophication. Remains of nitrate and phosphorus on land are swept away with rain water and discharged into water bodies. Another reason of rapid eutrophication is that when minerals and other nutrient-rich sewage is discharged directly to water bodies, this paves way for eutrophication. This can be treated with the methods of treating contaminated water.

Water Pollution in India

It has been estimated that the biggest source of water pollution in India is untreated sewage. About 75% of India's water is polluted due to sewage. Whenever there is mention of water pollution in India, rivers of India emerge as frontrunners.

SEWAGE

Sewage is waste water as a residual of different human activities like washing, bathing, cleansing, sanitation, etc. This waste water travels to sewers through drainage pipes of houses and work places and ultimately mingles with clean water of water bodies to pollute it. Sewage is also called municipal waste.

Among rivers of India it is the Ganges which is housing maximum pollution. Various chemical industries and tanneries situated on banks of river Ganga throw their effluents into it. Further, disposal of dead bodies in the river becomes another major source of its contamination. Other gravely polluted rivers of India include Yamuna, Mahi, and Tapi.

WATERAID SURVEY

WaterAid, an international organisation working on water sanitation and hygiene, made a survey of water pollution in India. It has reported that about 80% of India's surface water is polluted. Report has further revealed that such a high intensity of surface water pollution is giving birth to diseases like cholera, dysentery, jaundice, and diarrhoea. Undernutrition among most of the children is also due to water pollution.

India's Initiative

Under National Water Quality Monitoring Programme (NWQMP), Central Pollution Control Board along with State Pollution Control Boards is monitoring the quality of water bodies in India. Following steps have been taken in this direction:

1) A network to monitor and assess water quality in different water bodies has been set up.
2) An online system to monitor discharge of effluents in rivers has been installed.
3) Financial assistance for setting up sewage and effluent treatment plants has been granted.
4) Various aquatic conservation plans have been executed.

MAJOR ACTION PLANS

1) ***Ganga Action Plan (GAP):*** *GAP was launched in 1986. The objective was to clean the river of various toxic effluents and untreated sewage by taking all possible measures needed to enforce cleanliness drive.*

2) ***Yamuna Action Plan (YAP):*** *This plan was launched in 1993. This is a joint venture of government of India and Japan. In this plan the river is to be cleaned up in multi-phase succession.*

3) ***National River Conservation Plan (NRCP):*** *This plan was launched in 1995 to prevent pollution of rivers. This centrally sponsored plan covers 40 rivers along 20 states.*

4) ***National Lake Conservation Plan (NLCP):*** *The plan was launched in 2001. The objective of the plan was to conserve the lakes and clean the polluted and degraded lakes in India.*

5) ***National Wetlands Conservation Programme (NWCP):*** *The scheme was launched in 1987 with the objective of conservation and management of wetlands.*

6) ***National Plan for Conservation of Aquatic Ecosystem (NPCA):*** *This plan was launched in 2013 by merging NLCP and NWCP.*

Soil Pollution

Soil is such a gift of nature which has no substitute. Soil comprises various precious components like minerals, micro- and macroorganisms, and organic and inorganic material, which sustains life of plants. Soil pollution is contamination of soil due to human and natural activities.

Causes of Soil Pollution

1) **Excessive use of fertilizers and pesticides:** In order to attain speedy growth of agricultural produce, man is using excess fertilizers and pesticides. Strong chemicals in these contaminate the soil and pierce themselves deep in the soil resulting in degradation of soil quality and thus loss of fertility.
2) **Industrial waste:** industries generally dump waste in the soil which leads to degrading quality of soil by contaminating it.
3) **Deforestation:** Trees are soil fixtures. Soil is not carried away by winds if there is sufficient number of trees. Deforestation results in soil erosion during dust storms. Due to soil erosion, land no more remains suitable for growth of plants and vegetation.
4) **Acid rain:** When acid rain showers containing sulphuric acid and carbonic acid fall on soil, it contaminates the soil by dissolving its nutrients.
5) **Littering and domestic waste:** Frequent and large-scale littering here and there contaminates soil and domestic waste is another big cause of soil pollution.
6) **Radioactive waste and dust:** Explosions resulting from nuclear tests release radioactive waste and dust which is deposited, hence polluting soil.
7) **e-waste:** Discarded electronic gadgets like mobile phones, computers, tablets, and others comprise electronic waste and these result in contamination of soils. Heavy metals like cadmium, copper, and lead particles get mixed with soil making it highly toxic.

Effects of Soil Pollution

1) **Deterioration in plant life:** When soil is persistently contaminated, it loses components like nutrients which support plant life. Due to contamination of soil, it becomes impossible to cultivate any vegetation. Soil pollutants shorten the life span of plants and as plantation vanishes due to soil pollution, animals living on plants also die.
2) **Severe hazard for human health:** Crop produced on contaminated soil becomes toxic. When human beings obtain food from such crops or meat of animals, which have already consumed affected plants, it causes skin cancer, liver ailments, and digestive disorders and hence threatens human life. Consumption of lead and mercury contained in the produce of a crop from contaminated soil impair kidney and liver functions.
3) **Loss of soil fertility:** Due to various human activities like mining, lot of toxic chemical and metallic components mix with the soil resulting in total loss of soil fertility.
4) **Loss of business and livelihood:** Crops grown on contaminated soil are not fit for human consumption. Such crops have to be discarded, which results in loss of business and badly affects livelihood of many depending on agricultural produce.
5) **Causing air and water pollution:** Soil contaminated with various hazardous components discharge volatile compounds to contributing further to air pollution. Similarly, contaminated soil when mixed with water in lakes, rivers, canals, etc. creates water pollution.
6) **Increase in salinity of soil:** Excessive use of fertilizers and pesticides in agricultural operations results in increase in the quantity of salts in soil. Soil is already containing salt. Irrigation and agricultural activities deposit nitrates and phosphates in soil further and increase the salt content in soil. Due to this plants grown on such soil become unable to absorb soil moisture. Plants and vegetation grown with salt pollutants in soil become poisonous and pose greater threat to human health if such stuff is consumed.

Measures to Control Soil Pollution

1) **Forestation:** Forestation drives should be initiated to prevent soil erosion and flooding. Trees and grass should be grown on slopes meeting water bodies.
2) **Use of organic fertilizers and pesticides:** Use of biofertilizers and pesticides should be used instead of poisonous and chemical ones.
3) **Avoid littering:** Littering of various wastes should be avoided. Rather, wastes should be properly dumped to avoid its contact with soil.
4) **Awareness about hygiene:** General public should be motivated to be hygienic and use toilets, which will reduce open defecation, a major cause of soil pollution.

5) **Recycling of wastes:** Waste recycling plants should be installed to avoid waste and hence soil pollution.

6) **Legal measures:** Stringent regulations should be enforced to check illegitimate handling of chemicals, illegal mining, and industrial and construction activities.

7) **Prohibitions on use of toxic chemicals and pesticides:** There should be ban on toxic chemicals and pesticides. Ban should also be there on nuclear explosions releasing radioactive waste and dust.

Polychlorinated Biphenyls (PCBs)

PCBs are chlorinated synthetic chemicals which are used as coolant in electric equipment, paints and adhesives, etc. PCBs have emerged as very toxic soil pollutants which remain in soil for a long time. PCB are deposited in soil surrounding those buildings where adhesives are used to plug in leakages (caulking) and fall on soil due to mishandling. PCBs are also concentrated in the soil of e-waste shredding sites. Retention of PCBs in soil results in loss of soil protein. Prolonged exposure to soil containing PCBs has very harmful effects on human, animal, and plant health. PCBs can enter bodies through inhalation and consuming PCBs-affected water (as PCBs are present in air and water also). Their stay in bodies results in fatal skin diseases and blood cancer.

Soil Pollution in India

Indian soil is found to be plagued with all pollutants due to various man-made activities causing soil pollution. According to a study by SRM University Tamil Nadu, the concentration of PCBs in Indian soil is twice the global concentration. It has been further found in the study that Chennai alone generates about 47000 tonnes of e-waste contaminating soil. Similarly, big cities like Mumbai, Delhi, and Kolkata have alarming level of PCBs concentration.

Thermal Pollution

Thermal pollution is a form of water pollution. Various chemical factories and distilleries circulate cold water in a chamber coinciding chamber of hot liquid or chemical so produced. Due to convection, heat of liquid or chemical is transferred resulting in cooling down of liquid or chemical and heating of water. Then hot water is discharged into water bodies. Contamination suffered by cold water of any water bodies from hot water is called thermal pollution. Hot water eats up oxygen of normal water in any river, canal, or stream and puts aquatic plant and animal life in danger.

Causes of Thermal Pollution

1) **Water as cooling agent:** In justifying definition of thermal pollution, different plants and industries use water as cooling agent and when extremely hot water is discharged into water bodies, it raises temperature of cold water, hence creating thermal pollution.

2) **Deforestation:** Shades of trees protect water in various water bodies from direct exposure to the sun. Deforestation results in exposure of water bodies to the sun and hence temperature of water rises and results in thermal pollution.

3) **Natural causes:** Natural actions like volcanic eruptions discharge hot lava into seas and oceans, thereby raising their temperature.

4) **Soil erosion:** When soil is continuously getting deposited in water bodies due to soil erosion, water level rises and gets more exposure of the sun, hence there is rise in its temperature.

5) **Discharge of waste water into water bodies:** During summer, roads, pavements, and sloped surfaces leading to water bodies become hot. When waste water is discharged to water bodies after flowing over a hot surface, temperature of water rises causing thermal pollution.

Effects of Thermal Pollution

1) **Loss of oxygen dissolved in water:** Most strong and direct effect of thermal pollution is fall in proportion of oxygen dissolved in water, thus creating suffocation for aquatic life and creating anaerobic environment due to which plants and animals in water die.

AEROBIC AND ANAEROBIC ENVIRONMENT

Aerobic environment exists when free oxygen is around and organisms grow in oxygen, and cold or normal water of water bodies create an aerobic environment for aquatic life.

Anaerobic environment is environment when there is no oxygen around. Hot water when discharged into water bodies creates anaerobic environment for aquatic life leading to suffocation and their death.

2) **Mass killing of aquatic species:** Extreme hot water results in mass killing of fishes and other species.

3) **Loss of biodiversity:** Due to rise in temperature of water in a particular water body, the species migrate to other water bodies, thereby loss of biodiversity results.

4) **Imbalance in food chain:** As a consequence of thermal pollution, there is rise in metabolic rate of organisms under which organisms consume more food, thus disturbing the food chain leading to ecological imbalance.

Control Measures

1) **Developing ponds for storing hot water:** Industries and plants using water as a cooling agent can develop ponds for storing hot water instead of discharging it into water bodies. That water can be reused after it loses temperature.

2) **Tree plantation along banks of water bodies:** Maximum tree plantation along banks of water bodies keep water under shade and protect it from the heat of the sun and there is no rise in its temperature.

3) **Preference in using oil as coolant:** Oil as a coolant can be used instead of water. Oil can be reused also.

Groundwater Pollution

A lot of water flows underground and is found in soil and surface under rocks. When there is rainfall, some water which is falling on ground fills the pores of soil and seeps down. Groundwater, being considered as fresh water for drinking and washing purpose is used by pumping it out through bore wells, tube wells, and submersible pumps. When different pollutants (like chemicals of fertilizers, pesticides, oil, and gasoline) reach groundwater, while seeping through soil and aquifers, and pollute groundwater, groundwater pollution occurs.

AQUIFER

An aquifer is a sand and bedrock layer underground through which groundwater flows. This layer of water has permeable rocks, i.e., such bedrock has openings through which liquids and gases can pass through. Pollutants reach groundwater through aquifers and pollute ground water.

Causes of Groundwater Pollution

1) Excessive use of fertilizers and pesticides
2) Leakage of underground storage tanks containing oil and gasoline
3) Littering and e-waste dumped in the soil approaching aquifers
4) Untreated municipal wastewater and sewage flowing through roads and reaching aquifer sites
5) Absence of sewer system at some localities (referring to septic system under which human waste is drained away underground), may reach groundwater leading to groundwater pollution.
6) Garbage and other waste material from landfills reach groundwater to contaminate groundwater.

Effects of Groundwater Pollution

1) **Human health hazard:** Polluted groundwater if consumed, comes as a major health hazard. Polluted groundwater results in arsenic poisoning which causes serious liver ailments like cirrhosis, skin cancer, spleen enlargement, and other fatal diseases. Entry of chromium and lead in body through groundwater leads to serious mental disorders. Joints are damaged due to excessive consumption of fluoride. Blue baby syndrome is developed due to consumption of groundwater containing nitrate. Consumption of groundwater mixed with sewage results in various viral and bacterial diseases.

BLUE BABY SYNDROME

Blue baby syndrome is developed in infants. Consumption of groundwater or surface water containing nitrates develops this syndrome. In this, skin of infants turn blue due to decrease in haemoglobin in infant's blood. This is also known as infant methemoglobinemia. Baby turns blue because blood is unable to carry oxygen around the body. As there is increase in concentration of nitrates due to excessive use of fertilizers and pesticides, this syndrome is commonly found in rural areas. Use of water from wells is also responsible for this disease which proves fatal for infants.

2) **Threat to economy:** Due to contamination of groundwater, water remains no more suitable for consuming and irrigation. As it affects plant and animal life, human beings and animals either die or migrate and subsequently, economic value of that land depreciates. Similarly, many industries depend upon groundwater for their smooth running. Due to contamination of groundwater, quality of the product is affected, hence depreciating its value and fall in demand for such products.

3) **Increasing toxic content in surface water:** Contamination of groundwater increases toxic content in surface water in rivers, lakes, and streams posing threat to aquatic life.

4) **Fall in agricultural productivity:** High salinity in water leads to decrease in soil and agricultural productivity resulting in fall in yield.

Control of Groundwater Pollution

1) Underground tanks containing oil should be regularly checked and any leakage should be immediately repaired.
2) Waste material should not be dumped on the ground.
3) Preference should be given to use biofertilizers and pesticides instead of chemical ones.
4) Treatment plants to recycle municipal and urban waste should be installed.
5) Regulations against indiscriminate littering should be enacted.

Groundwater Pollution in India

According to a study made by Central Groundwater Board of India along with Duke University USA, there has been huge presence of uranium in groundwater in India. According to an estimate, in India, about 50% of domestic needs in urban area and more than 80% of rural areas are fulfilled by groundwater. Average level of groundwater development in India is 30%. However, some states have exploited it in much higher percentage like Punjab 90%, Rajasthan 50%, Tamil Nadu 66%, Lakshadweep 60%, and Haryana 85%. But groundwater pollution is increasing in India. A study by Central Groundwater Board has found alarming concentration of the following pollutants in groundwater in different states of India.

Groundwater Contamination in India

Sr. No.	Name of Pollutant	Affected States
1	Iron	Karnataka, Chhattisgarh, West Bengal, Assam Orissa, Jharkhand, North Eastern States
2	Nitrate	Andhra Pradesh, Himachal Pradesh, Delhi, Kerala, Tamil Nadu, Rajasthan, Punjab, West Bengal, Uttar Pradesh
3	Arsenic	West Bengal Assam, Chhattisgarh, Uttar Pradesh
4	Salinity	Gujarat, Haryana, Rajasthan, Punjab
5	Fluoride	Madhya Pradesh, Odisha, Rajasthan, Kerala, Punjab, West Bengal
6	Uranium	Rajasthan Andhra Pradesh, Odisha, Gujarat, Kerala, Tamil Nadu, Pondicherry, Goa, Haryana, West Bengal

- Maximum cases of arsenic poisoning due to groundwater pollution are reported from West Bengal.

India's Initiative

1) **Water (Prevention and Control of Pollution) Act, 1974:** The Act was enforced with the objective to protect water resources from pollution. This Act prohibits discharge of any pollutant directly or indirectly into any water body and sewer.
2) **Environment Protection Act, 1986:** This Act also forbids emission and depositing of water pollutants into water bodies.
3) **National Project on Aquifer Management:** Under this project, there is regular mapping of aquifers to assess the quality and quantity of groundwater. Objective is that through proper resource management plans and governance, purity of aquifers is to be ensured to preserve pollution-free groundwater resources.
4) **Setting up Arsenic Task Force:** To eradicate arsenic poisoning from groundwater of West Bengal, Arsenic Removal Units (ARU) were set up to meet the objective through Arsenic Task Force.
5) **Scheme to remove salinity:** Under this scheme, effective initiatives were taken to eradicate salinity in groundwater of Gujarat by changing cropping pattern, regular uplifting of underground water, etc.
6) **Groundwater (Sustainable Management) Bill, 2017:** The Bill aims at giving regulatory control of groundwater management to local bodies for its sustainable management. The Bill also recognises that to have access to pure water is a fundamental right of citizens and it is a matter of trust for them as water sustains their lives. The Bill also recommends decentralising the control of groundwater resources and protection of water at aquifer level.
7) **Establishment of Central Groundwater Authority:** Under Section 3 (3) of Environment Protection Act, 1986, Central Groundwater Authority has been established to control and manage development of groundwater resources in the country.

Noise Pollution

Noise pollution is any unwanted noise dumped into the atmosphere resulting in health hazards. Noise pollution is measured in Decibel (dB). There are various sounds around us. Every sound is not an unwanted noise. There is no noise pollution from a sound until it is unbearable and leaves a bad impact on health. According to WHO standards, a sound level up to 70 dB do not leave any harmful effect on ears and health. It is said that continuous exposure to sound level with more than 85 dB for 8 hours at a stretch is damaging.

Sources of Noise Pollution

1) Traffic and transportation (road, railways, and airways)
2) T.V., radio, and telephone
3) Firecrackers
4) Loudly played music systems
5) Horns and sirens
6) Social, political, and religious functions and gatherings
7) Factories and industries

Effects of Noise Pollution on Human Health

1) Overexposure to sound and noise causes damage to ears resulting in temporary or permanent hearing loss.
2) Continuous noise of traffic and music at night disturbs sleep which results in harmful effects on human body due to insufficient and frequently disturbed sleep.
3) Persistent noise pollution from any source at any time puts pressure on nervous system and bloodstream resulting in hypertension, stress, and depression.
4) Children become soft targets of noise pollution. Due to noise pollution children suffer from impaired hearing.
5) Workers at various work places experience fall in their efficiency due to noise pollution as they develop mental fatigue from unwanted noise.

Effect on Wildlife and Marine Life

Noise of steamers, ships, oil drills, and devices to detect seismic and volcanic belts is high enough to create a bad impact on marine life. Wildlife (particularly animals staying near cities and villages) are disturbed by noise of traffic, industries, machines, and fire crackers.

Measures to Control Noise Pollution

1) Prolonged use of earphones should be avoided.
2) Noise should be reduced at source.
3) Sound-proof devices should be used in the areas filled with persistent high-level noise.
4) Recipient should be protected.

Decibel Levels of Common Sounds

dB	Environmental Condition
0	Threshold of hearing
10	Rustle of leaves
20	Broadcasting studio
30	Bedroom at night
40	Library
50	Quiet office
60	Conversational speech
70	Average radio
74	Light traffic noise
90	Subway train
100	Symphony orchestra
110	Rock band
120	Aircraft takeoff
146	Threshold of pain

Permitted Noise Levels - Ambient Noise Levels dB

Zone	Daytime	Nighttime
Silent Zone	50	40
Residential Zone	55	45
Commercial Zone	65	55
Industrial Zone	75	70

A standard safe time limit has been set for exposure to various noise levels. Beyond this 'safe' time, continuing exposure over a period of a year will lead to hearing loss.

Duration	dBA
8 hours	90
4 hours	93
2 hours	96
1 hour	99
30 minutes	102
15 minutes	105
7 minutes	108
4 minutes	111
2 minutes	114
1 minute	117
30 seconds	120

Noise Pollution in India

With the rapid increase in population, Indian people are experiencing high concentration of noise pollutants along with other pollutants. In response to increase in demand, due to increase in population, more industries are being established, more social and religious functions are being organised, and there is incoming of more sound-featured electronic devices like television, mobile phones, etc. This is leading to increase noise levels coming from loud music, sirens, traffic horns, noise of machineries, etc. Indian cities are being regularly filled with unbearable sound levels. According to a Central Pollution Control Board (CPCB) study, Mumbai is among the noisiest cities in the world. It is followed by Lucknow, Hyderabad, Delhi, and Chennai. The study states that these cities have exceeded the limit of permitted noise level by 100%. Medical reports by experts say that average age of deafness in India has reduced to 50 from earlier 60-65. Noise pollution is becoming a fast potential killer in India.

Permissible Noise levels in India

Nature of Area	Permitted Level (dB) During Day and Night Respectively
Residential Area	50 and 45
Commercial Area	65 and 55
Industrial Area	75 and 70
Silent Zones	50 and 40

Initiative by India

1. **Enactment of The Noise Pollution (Regulation and Control) Rules, 2000**

   Indian government enacted The Noise Pollution (Regulation and Control) Rules, 2000, under which following conditions were laid down to curb noise pollution:

   1) There will be notification of Ambient Air Quality with respect to noise pollution by the state governments.
   2) There will be no use of loud speaker or public address system during night between 10 PM to 6 AM without taking permission from the concerned authority.
   3) Categorisation of residential, commercial, and industrial areas will be done by the concerned state government.
   4) An area up to 100 meters around hospitals and educational institutes was declared silent zone.
   5) Anyone caught violating these provisions will be liable for punishment.
   6) It would be the responsibility of the concerned states to initiate efforts to ensure maintaining of permitted noise levels in different areas.

2. **Setting up National Ambient Noise Monitoring Network (NANMN)**

   Government of India set up NANMN in 2011 to monitor noise pollution, particularly in big and metro cities round the clock. This was to be materialised with the help of CPCB and State Pollution Control Boards.

3. **Plan to Reduce Permissible Sound Limit of Horns**

   Ministry of Road Transport and Highways has planned to reduce maximum permissible sound level of horns below 100 dB against a limit of 93 dB and 112 dB under Central Motor Vehicle Rules, 1989. It has been estimated by experts that horns are the major source of noise pollution in India.

Nuclear (Radioactive) Pollution

When various atomic tests are undertaken, there is nuclear explosion which results into radioactive waste and nuclear dust mixing with air, hence causing nuclear pollution. It has been estimated due to nuclear pollution about 15 to 20% radioactive particles enter into atmosphere and continue to fall on the earth for years together.

Effects of Nuclear Pollution

1) Dangerous and fatal impact on human lives causing genetic disorders and its traces are found in many coming generations.
2) Harmful impact on plants
3) As nuclear waste and dust is discharged in water bodies, it results in poisoning of water.
4) It adds strongly to global warming.
5) Death of animals, when they graze plantation affected by nuclear waste

Prevention of Nuclear Pollution

Nuclear pollution can be prevented by enacting strict laws regarding nuclear tests. Nuclear tests should be allowed in utmost need in the interest of peaceful and healthy use of nuclear energy.

One of the most important and dangerous type of pollution is nuclear pollution. Nuclear pollution is produced by nuclear explosions which are carried out for performing nuclear tests and which are used for making nuclear weapons. Due to this explosion, about 15 to 20% of the radioactive particles enter into the atmosphere. Once they enter into the air they continue to fall on the earth after about every 6 months up to several years.

WASTES AND TYPES OF WASTE

Waste is any material which is discarded after basic use. This waste if not treated, badly effects environment resulting in air pollution and water pollution. There are different types of wastes.

Solid Waste

During various human activities, different solid products are used and their residual is discarded as it becomes unwanted. Such unwanted sold material is solid waste. It includes garbage, waste kitchen material like disposable utensils, bottles, wrappers, plastic and other bags, empty containers, cans of various products, rags, torn footwear, newspapers, etc. Solid waste turns out to be harmful for the environment if not treated timely and properly. Solid waste can be put to three categories:

1) **Content:** Whether the waste is wood, glass, metal, paper, plastic, organic material, etc.
2) **Origin:** If it belongs to household, industry, institution, construction, or commercial emergence
3) **Nature:** Whether it is hazardous or non-hazardous in terms of being toxic or non-toxic, flammable, or inflammable, radioactive, infectious, etc.

Municipal Solid Waste

Any solid waste which is not hazardous is called municipal solid waste. MSW is coming from kitchens, business establishments, industries, and institutes. MSW is collected and disposed of in routine. Every domestic waste is MSW. MSW does not include industrial waste and debris. It includes empty cans, discarded vegetables, eggshells, bones, wooden pieces, paper, and aluminium foil. Different items of MSW take respective time in degeneration, which is shown in the table below:

Degeneration Time Of MSW

Sr. No.	Name of waste	Degeneration Time (Approx.)
1	Woollen Clothes	One Year
2	Paper	10 Days to One Month
3	Plastic	One Million Years
4	Cotton Clothes	2 to 5 Months
5	Wood	10 to 15 Years
6	Kitchen Waste (Vegetables, Fruits)	1 to 2 Weeks
7	Metal Cans (Tin, Aluminium)	100 to 500 Years

According to a study by The Energy and Resources Institute (TERI) New Delhi, at present Indian cities generate 62 million tonnes of MSW per year and by 2047 this will touch 260 million tonnes per year. Further according to a report by The Union Ministry of Environment and Forests submitted to the Parliament that about 80% of MSW is collected and 20-28% of it is processed and treated.

Disposal of MSW is becoming challenging with increase in population. Improper and inadequate disposal harms the environment. Due to modern lifestyle, products in present day market are packed in tins, plastic bags, and aluminium foils. As these are non-biodegradable, they take hundreds of years for degeneration. Majority of Indian cities do not possess sufficient facilities to transport MSW. Further, landfills are not properly managed and neither are these empty to accommodate waste.

LANDFILL

Landfill is an area created with engineering skill to bury solid waste without harming human health and environment. Here, solid waste is buried for long time to generate energy from it. Landfill is not just a dump.'

Mangement of MSW

Littering and municipal waste is prohibited to be thrown openly. So it is to be collected through organised methods and reduced, recycled, and disposed in landfills. These are the stages of MSW management:

1) **Collection:** MSW is collected at the source. It is collected either through community bin method, house-to-house collection, or periodic collection with prior information of day and timings. It is collected by municipal bodies either directly or by a private or public sector agency authorised by the government.
2) **Storage:** MSW is stored in storage facilities created by municipal authorities. It is stored in this way that it should not become an environment and health and environment hazard. Municipal authorities install different coloured bins for storing, transporting, reducing, recycling, and disposal of a particular type of MSW. As such waste is carrying components of different nature, different coloured bins are installed. Biodegradable waste is stored in green coloured bin, recyclable waste is stored in white coloured bin, and other wastes are stored in black coloured bin. There is no option for manual handling.
3) **Processing:** Biodegradable waste is processed through different methods:
   i) **Composting:** it is a process under which biodegradable and organic component of MSW is degraded as per microbiological norms by

creating an aerobic environment. In this process of degradation, bacteria are used to separates the organic component into water and carbon dioxide. Due to this, large amount of heat and water vapours are produced. While supplying sufficient oxygen and maintaining optimum temperature, process ends by giving a product called compost which is used as manure to increase soil fertility. This process also results in reduction in waste by a huge volume.

ii) **Pulverisation:** In this method, solid waste so collected is grinded by grinding machines which ultimately converts solid waste into powder. This changes volume and physical characteristics of MSW. Then this powder is disposed of in landfills.

iii) **Incineration:** Solid waste is burnt in a furnace called incinerator after separating combustible material from non-combustible ones. Due to high temperature, all harmful bacteria, pathogens, and pests in the waste are destroyed. However, there is a risk of air pollution due to high rising fumes.

iv) **Vermicomposting:** In this waste management method, organic matter, vegetables, and bedding material (newspapers, soil, or sawdust) are kept in a covered bin and earthworms are released into the bin. Earthworms digest these vegetables and bedding material and in excretion, produce rich compost called 'worm castings'. This process is repeated after getting compost.

v) **Anaerobic digestion:** It is a natural process under which organic matter in the waste is broken to release biogas. Biogas is a renewable energy source from which energy produced is used for cooking and generating electricity. Residue of biogas, digestate is used as a fertilizer.

4) **Disposal:** Non-biodegradable and non-recyclable waste is disposed in landfills with utmost care as due to poor handling, any leakage in the open will contaminate the environment and human health.

5) **Management at Source:** Various MSW generators like households, business establishments, industrial houses, and other sources should be educated through awareness campaigns to manage waste in an intelligent way at their respective ends. Mass media and NGOs can play an important role in making such campaigns successful.

6) **Salvaging:** Under this process the waste is recycled to produce new products.

Municipal Solid Waste in India

According to an estimate by World Bank, India generates 150000 tonnes of MSW per day. Mumbai becomes the world's fifth most wasteful city. Out of the total waste generated, about 80% is collected and about 30% is treated and the rest is dumped in landfills. The report further states that at this rate of waste generation, India's daily waste generation will touch 377000 tonnes by 2025. Sole responsibility of such a large quantity waste generation lies with rapid urbanisation and industrialisation.

Further, states of India are not taking MSW management seriously. According to a study by Urban Affairs Ministry, only eight states in the country process more than 50% of the garbage generated by their cities. States like West Bengal, Tamil Nadu, Haryana, Bihar, Andhra Pradesh, Odisha, and Jharkhand do not process even 10% of their total MSW. However, Chhattisgarh processes more than 70% of MSW followed by Telangana, Sikkim, and Goa.

According to study by Center for Science and Environment (CSE) Delhi, Indian landfills are overfilled with garbage and waste and cannot accommodate any more. Disposing MSW on already overfilled landfills create environment, water, and groundwater pollution.

India's Initiative in MSW Management

1) **Municipal Solid Wastes (Management and Handling) Rules, 2000:** Under these rules Municipalities are responsible to collect, segregate, store, transport, process, and dispose municipal solid waste.

2) **Solid Waste Management Rules (SWM) Rules, 2016:** Previous rules covered solid waste of municipal area. These rules widen the area coverage beyond municipal area. These rules also include ports and harbours, state and central government organisations, defence establishments, religious places, pilgrimages, areas belonging to railways, airports, and every notified area and industry. Under these rules, following regulations have been earmarked for waste generators, which are to be complied with:

   a) In case an event is organised for more than 100 persons, the organiser will have to ensure segregation of waste at source and that segregated waste is to be handed over to waste collector.

b) Burning, burying, or throwing waste openly here and there, public spaces, and water bodies by waste generator is prohibited.

c) It will be mandatory for hawkers and vendors and other petty businessmen to keep containers for putting the waste generated out of their business activity and hand it over to waste collector daily.

d) All restaurants, hotels, and other such establishments will segregate the waste at source and handover the recyclable material to the unit authorised for recycling and other waste should be treated with proper methods.

3) **Steps under Swachh Bharat Abhiyan:** Various initiatives have been taken under Swachh Bharat Abhiyan to make India open defecation free. Building up toilets and 100% door-to- door collection of waste has been enforced and that has yielded results.

4) **Waste-to-Energy Project (WtE):** Waste-to-Energy project has been installed and about 90 MW is being generated from waste. This production will rise as according to an estimate by Union Ministry of New and Renewable Energy, estimated potential from sewage is about 200 MW and it is about 1500 MW from MSW.

Hazardous Waste

Hazardous wastes are those wastes which pose a threat to human life and environment. Such wastes include wastes from refineries, paper mills, chemical manufacturing companies, plastic manufacturing factories, etc. When mishandled, they pose a great threat to human lives and the environment.

Types of Hazardous Waste

1) **Waste prone to reaction:** There are certain wastes like gunpowder and nitroglycerine which are prone to react with air and may cause explosion. These wastes release toxic gases and can cause explosion during routine operations.

2) **Household wastes:** These wastes include old batteries, paint tins, old medicines, medicine bottles, shoe polish containers, and old fire crackers.

3) **Toxic waste:** Toxic wastes causes harm to human health, particularly children who experience biological changes. Such wastes are equally harmful to animals. Such wastes include remains of pesticides and heavy metals.

4) **Wastes prone to ignition:** Certain wastes of gasoline, alcohol, paints, and thinners are prone to ignition during handling and disposal.

5) **Corrosive wastes:** Wastes of acids, bases, and alkalis are corrosive in nature. Due to leakage or mishandling or disposal, if such wastes fall on human being, animals, plants, or any other marble and metallic objects, their corrosive action creates corrosion of skin, paints, lustre of marble structures, and statues.

Hazardous Waste Management

1) **Physical treatment:** In physical treatment non-hazardous components are separated from hazardous components in the waste. This is the change in physical form of the waste and chemical composition is not altered. Here, materials are separated to be treated through chemical and biological treatment.

2) **Chemical treatment:** In this treatment, chemical composition of the waste is changed to make it less hazardous. Chemical treatment is eco-friendly as it can be carried out at source and it produces minimum emissions. Various techniques like neutralisation, de-chlorination, oxidation, and precipitation are used.

3) **Biological treatment:** In this process microorganisms are used to decompose the waste into elements like carbon dioxide, water, and simple organic and inorganic elements.

Hazardous Waste in India

According to an estimation of Union Ministry of Environment and Forests, there are about 71000 industries and these are generating about 8 million metric tonnes hazardous waste per annum. Leading states in generating hazardous wastes are Andhra Pradesh, Tamil Nadu, Uttar Pradesh, and Bihar.

India's initiative: Hazardous Waste (Management, Handling and Transboundary Movement) Rules, 2008

Government of India notified Hazardous Waste (Management, Handling and Transboundary Movement) Rules 2008 as an action plan of National Environment Policy, 2006. Under these rules the following provisions were notified:

1) Industries can store hazardous wastes maximum up to 90 days unless permission is obtained by concerned State Pollution Control Board.

2) Industries should explore strategies to reuse, recover, and recycle hazardous waste.

3) Management, treatment, and recycling facilities will be launched under public-private partnership.

4) Setting up of common Treatment, Storage, and Disposable Facilities (TSDFs):State governments will promote TSDFs with central subsidy. TSDFs have already been established in 16 states.
5) Interstate movement of hazardous waste will be permitted on mutual agreement basis.
6) Establishment of regulatory and institutional framework for better waste management.
7) Preparation of technical guidelines for better management of hazardous waste.
8) Development of GIS based National Hazardous Waste Inventorisation System (NHWIS)
9) **Capacity Building Project:** Union Ministry of Environment and Forests has developed a World Bank aided project "Capacity Building for Industrial Pollution Management" under which hazardous waste management is also being applied.
10) **Implementation of Provisions of Basel Convention:** India being signatory to Basel Convention to manage and minimise hazardous waste is implementing regulations to control transboundary movement of hazardous wastes among states.

BASEL CONVENTION

On 22 March 1989, an international treaty on the control of transboundary movement of hazardous waste and its disposal was signed in a convention at Basel (Switzerland) by 187 countries and India is one of them. This convention is popularly known as Basel Convention. Agenda of this convention was preventing the transborder transfer of hazardous waste among nations. Another item of the agenda was to minimise the toxic content of this waste before its disposal. The objective was to protect human health and environment from adverse effects of hazardous waste.

Biomedical Waste

Biomedical wastes are wastes of hospitals which are generated during diagnosis, surgery, and immunisation of human beings and animals. Biomedical wastes are also generated during medical research and experiments. The wastes include discarded bandages, syringes, human excreta, discarded gloves, mercury from broken thermometers, blood and tissue removed from operating rooms, contaminated and expired medicines and vaccines, discarded lencets and needles, human and animal tissues discarded during medical treatment process, amputated human and animals body parts, swabs, and leakage of radiotherapy or research liquid from labs during research process. These wastes are highly infectious in nature and can prove fatal if infected by these. It has been estimated that on an average, if a hospital generates 4 kg of waste, I kg out of it is infectious.

Sources of Biomedical Wastes

1) Hospitals
2) Doctors and dentist office
3) Mortuaries
4) Nursing homes
5) Clinics and Polyclinics
6) Diagnostic laboratories
7) Veterinary hospitals
8) Cattle breeding centers

Effects of Biomedical Wastes

1. **Effects on human health:** Due to being highly infectious in nature, biomedical wastes leave a dangerous impact on human health by resulting in fatal diseases like gastro infections (Salmonella), Streptococcus pneumonia, measles, skin infections, AIDS, genital infections, and meningitis. These diseases are fatal in nature and these are transmitted in human bodies through breath, saliva, inhaled secretions, skin secretions, blood transmission, and hepatitis.
2. **Effects on animals and biodiversity:** Various biomedical wastes reach various habitats, lakes, and rivers due to mishandling of such wastes. These result in destruction of wildlife and loss of biodiversity.
3. **Contamination of groundwater:** These biomedical wastes reach groundwater through aquifers due to poor maintenance of landfills. When these wastes are buried, ill-managed landfills pave way for such wastes to reach the groundwater. Rainfall is also a contributor in such groundwater pollution.
4. **Causing air pollution:** Sometimes biomedical wastes are burnt to destroy them. But if these wastes are burnt without incineration management, this burning generates pollutants which pollute air and this becomes a major biohazard.
5. **Radioactive pollution:** Various diseases require radiotherapy. Similarly, radioactive material is used during various medical researches. Leakage of radioactive material due to mishandling causes radioactive pollution.

Disposal of Biomedical Waste

There are three stages of disposing biomedical waste:

Stage 1

Collection and segregation: It always safest to collect biomedical waste at the point of generation. Then it is to be segregated to put in different containers earmarked for disposal of such wastes. Putting such waste in the wrong container will pose a threat to pollute the environment and harm human health. According to provisions in 'The Biomedical Waste (Management and Handling) Rules, 1998', Indian government has issued guidelines to choose a particular coloured container for a particular type of biomedical waste as given below:

Cardboard box with blue marking: Discarded glass vials and other glass waste should be disposed in this container.

Yellow bag: Blood bags, bandages, dressings, human anatomical waste, cotton swabs with body fluids are to be discarded in this bag.

White puncture proof container: Sharp objects, needles, surgical knives, blades or any other sharp-ended waste should be put in this container.

Red bag: Tubes, syringes without needles, surgery gloves, and intravenous tubes and sets are to be discarded in this bag.

Black Bags: Non-biomedical wastes like discarded office stationary, disposable glasses, plates, hospital kitchen waste, etc. are to be disposed off in this bag.

Stage 2

Storage and Transportation: After segregation, the containers of biomedical wastes are picked up and transported to the storage site. While picking up the segregated waste, it is ascertained which waste is disposable and which is reusable. Accordingly it is treated. Storing site should be far away from the human and animal settlements. Wastage should be carefully handled even at the transportation stage. Any leakage or spilling will cause havoc.

Stage 3

Treatment and Disposal: Certain biomedical wastes can be decontaminated and can be treated for reuse. These can be decontaminated with incineration (burning), thermal processing (autoclaving), or through chemical treatment.

Biomedical Waste Management in India

According a report submitted by the Ministry of Health and Family Welfare to the Lok Sabha, maximum biomedical waste is generated in Maharashtra followed by Karnataka, Tamil Nadu, and Kerala. On an average India generates about 6 lakh kg biomedical waste daily.

Union Ministry of Environment and Forests enacted **Biomedical Waste Management Rules, 2016** under Environment Protection Act, 1986. The rule makes it mandatory for all waste generators to pre-treat the waste at source. The rules further mandates barcode system for proper control. Jurisdiction of these rules is over all persons who generate, collect, receive, store, transport, treat, dispose, or handle biomedical waste in hospitals, nursing homes, clinics, dispensaries, veterinary institutions, animal houses, pathological laboratories, blood banks, Ayush hospitals, research or educational institutions, health camps, blood donation camps, first aid rooms, forensic laboratories, and research labs. The rules further make it obligatory for occupier to ensure the following:

i) Waste should be handled in such manner that it should not be harmful to human and animal health and also should not contaminate environment.
ii) Waste should be directly transported to the place of storage without any secondary handling.
iii) Waste like laboratory waste, blood samples, and blood bags should be given pre-treatment and disinfected or sterilised before disposal.
iv) Biomedical waste should not be disposed along with municipal solid waste.
v) Hospital staff should be properly trained in handling the waste.
vi) Bags and containers containing biomedical waste should be covered under barcode system to ensure to be disposed off within one year from the date of notification of these rules.
vii) Chlorinated plastic bags, gloves, and blood bags should be phased out within two years from the date of notification of these rules.

Biomedical Waste Management Rules, 2016 were amended to improve the management of waste in the interest of environment protection and resulted in **Biomedical Waste Management Rules (Amendment), 2018.** The rules state that generators of biomedical waste will not use chlorinated plastic bags and gloves after March 27, 2019. Further, blood bags were exempted from being phased out as prescribed in earlier rules.

INCINERATION AND AUTOCLAVING

INCINERATION: *Incineration is a technology through which waste is hurnt to obtain energy. Burning or combusting of waste is done in the presence of oxygen. Waste is burnt in an incinerator in a controlled temperature. Due to burning, waste material is converted into flue gas, particles, and ash. The recovered products are further used to produce electricity. India's largest incineration plant is situated in New Delhi.*

AUTOCLAVING: *It is a process in which biomedical or other waste is given high-pressure steam to sterilise it. Temperature is made too high to kill harmful organisms and bacteria. After autoclaving, waste becomes free from harmful organisms and bacteria and it can be used for producing energy or electricity.*

Liquid Waste

Liquid waste is defined as any discarded waste in liquid form. Liquid waste comprises kitchen, municipal, and industrial wastewater, sewage, sludges, discarded oil, grease, liquid detergents, and liquid hospital waste. Wastewater comprises of organic and inorganic material. This waste is mixture of various liquid wastes, some of which are infectious, some are radioactive, and some are toxic. There should be safe disposal of liquid waste, i.e., it should not create harmful effect on human, animal and environmental health.

Sources of Liquid Waste

1) **Storm water:** Storm water is contaminated as it comprises of various pollutants like soil, remains of wear and tear of rubber tyres of vehicles, litter, faecal matter, and oil from vehicles.
2) **Residential areas:** It is domestic wastewater generated due to cooking, washing, bathing, and discarded water of any such activity by the residents. Grey water (water from kitchen and bathrooms) and black water (water from toilet) coming from pipes and sewers is also a form of liquid waste.
3) **Commercial areas:** Wastewater is generated from different human activities in business establishments, market places, theatres, cinemas, multiplexes, shops, companies, and institutions. This wastewater contains fats, oils, and grease.
4) **Industrial areas:** Liquid waste is generated during the manufacturing process. This liquid waste contains various toxic chemicals which are harmful to the human health and the environment.

ORGANIC AND INORGANIC MATTER IN WASTE

Both solid and liquid waste contains mixture of organic and inorganic matter which are separated during treatment stages.

Organic matter: *That matter is organic which contains carbon, nitrogen, and oxygen. The components of organic matter comprise the matter which lived a life and now it is dead. Example: wood, fish, meat, dead plants, and vegetables. Still, there is certain matter which is made from organic material like paper and card, which is made from wood and dead plants. Further, plastic (obtained from fossils of plants and animals) is also organic. Organic material is naturally decomposed by bacteria.*

Inorganic matter: *Inorganic material in the waste does not contain carbon and has mineral origin. Example: Glass, metals, ceramics, bricks, clay, chalk, minerals, salts, iron, calcium, sand, and other chemical and mineral material.*

Effects of Liquid Waste

1) **Health risk:** Liquid waste contaminate surface water, groundwater, soil, and air which result in various respiratory, neuro, skin, and heart diseases.
2) **Groundwater pollution:** Untreated and unmanaged liquid waste when deposited in landfills, reaches groundwater through aquifers.
3) **Air pollution:** Foul smell emitted by liquid waste contaminate and thus cause air pollution. Further, gases emitted by liquid waste also cause air pollution resulting in storms, heat waves, etc.
4) **Surface water pollution:** Leakage or spilling of oil gets deposited in water bodies, thus making water toxic and changing the composition of water.
5) **Greenhouse gases:** Untreated and unmanaged liquid waste emits greenhouse gases resulting in global warming leaving an adverse impact on climate which lead to unnatural changes in climate.
6) **Economic loss:** Mismanagement of liquid waste amounts to violation of environmental statutes and regulations. Any such waste generator is imposed fine of lakhs of rupees by the concerned authority, thus leading to huge economic loss because of poor handling of liquid waste.
7) **Soil contamination:** Liquid wastes reaching the ground penetrate deep into the soil, thus contaminating soil and resulting in loss of fertility. Further, soil is exposed to various toxic chemicals of liquid waste. This restricts plants' growth and vegetation grown on such soil becomes unsuitable for consumption.

Liquid Waste Management

1) **Incineration:** Hazardous liquid waste is treated through incineration. Production of heat in the furnace results in separation of hazardous waste such as scrap material, acids, oils, and other chemicals and leaves behind clean water.
2) **Transportation:** Industries and other units transport the liquid waste to the liquid disposal company where it can be treated by any method.
3) **Sedimentation:** The liquid waste generated by any source is put into a sediment sink which leads to separation of water from solid waste. Then water is treated and solid waste is deposited into landfills.
4) **Solidification:** Liquid waste is solidified by adding fly ash, sawdust, lime dust, etc. Then it becomes easier to treat it and dispose it.
5) **Disposal:** Liquid waste disposal companies are hired by factories generating liquid waste for treatment and disposal. Factories maintain a fleet of trucks for transporting liquid waste.
6) **Dewatering:** Non-hazardous liquid waste is treated by dewatering. Liquid waste is put in a huge bag and water is separated and solid waste is sent to landfills.
7) **Composting:** When water is separated from solids in liquid waste, residual organic matter is converted into organic fertilizer which is rich in nitrogen, potassium, and sodium.
8) **Root zone:** Liquid waste of kitchen and bathroom is treated with root zone method. In this method liquid is put in a sedimentation tank and it is filtered for reuse.

Three Stages of Sewage Treatment

I) ***Primary treatment:*** *In primary treatment wastewater is treated. Certain heavy particles in wastewater settle down and certain lighter components like oil. ghee, grease, etc. float on the water. At this stage, settled and floating particles are separated from wastewater.*

II) ***Secondary treatment:*** *At this stage microorganisms are separated from wastewater through* ***biofiltration*** *process. Then residual wastewater is discharged for tertiary treatment. This treatment is also known as* ***biological treatment****. Duration of this treatment is longer than primary treatment.*

III) ***Tertiary treatment:*** *In this stage wastewater is further filtered through* ***microfiltration*** *to remove microorganisms, which could not be separated in primary and secondary treatment, to make wastewater 100% suitable for discharging into streams, lakes, and canals. In this stage certain chemicals are also used to purify wastewater. This treatment is done to ensure that now water is totally pollutants-free.*

Liquid Waste in India

As India is a rapidly fast developing economy, there is fast growth in various industries. With increase in more industries, business establishments, companies, multiplexes, and housing complexes, liquid waste generation is also increasing along with other wastes. In the race to fetch maximum economic gain, people are ignoring WASH (Water, Sanitation, and Hygiene) norms.

Liquid Waste Management in India

India is propagating Swachh Bharat Abhiyan norms in urban and rural areas to manage liquid waste along with solid waste. Indian government's efforts to create awareness about WASH indicators and comparing of building toilets have yielded results in managing liquid and solid waste. According to a report by Union Ministry of Drinking Water and Sanitation, 25 states have declared themselves open defecation free (ODF) and over five lakh villages have become ODF.

Electronic Waste (e-waste)

Due to fast change in communication technology, various electronic gadgets are coming up making previous ones obsolete. This is resulting in e-waste plethora. Electronic waste or e-waste comprises abandoned electronic products which have crossed their expiry date or have become out of fashion like discarded televisions, computers, laptops, VCRs, mobile phones, fax machines, copiers, monitors, computer key boards, CPUs, electronic batteries, and cameras. Some articles of e-waste can be reused, resold, recycled, and refurbished.

Effects of e-waste

1) **Harmful effects on human health:** Discarded electronic products contain many toxic elements which damage human health. The toxic elements include lead, mercury, cadmium, arsenic, chlorine, bromine, lithium, and PCBs. Such elements enter human body

through contaminated air (inhalation of toxic fumes), soil, water, and groundwater. These elements cause various fatal diseases and disorders in the human body. Mercury attacks kidneys and reproductive system, lead damages blood and nervous system, bromine imbalances thyroid hormone system and causes cancer, arsenic attacks skin and respiratory system, cadmium reduces cognition power in children, and chlorine damages tissues. Such elements also reduce immunity and human body catches various infections caused by bacteria and virus. Burning of electronic waste emits cancer-generating fumes. Workers working on e-waste dumps or landfills become the soft targets.

2) **Effect on air:** Generally, e-waste is thrown openly or dumped in a landfill. When e-waste heats up due to solar heat, it emits toxic fumes which enter the atmosphere and pollute air due to which harmful effects of polluted air crop up which damage various systems of human beings and animals.
3) **Harmful effect on surface water and groundwater:** Due to improper disposal of vicarious e-waste items, toxic and carcinogenic elements seep into the soil and reach groundwater. On the other hand, surface water in various water bodies is polluted as contaminated groundwater while flowing, mixes with stream, canal, pond, or river water. This contaminated water becomes a major health hazard for human beings and flora and fauna.
4) **Soil pollution:** Heavy metals and toxic chemicals of e-waste enter soil and pollute soil. These non-biodegradable elements settle in the soil for a long period, hence posing danger for fertility of soil, human, animal, and plant life.

E-waste Management

1) **Recycling:** Discarded electronic devices can be reused after recycling. E-waste is recycled after picking up and separating usable and unusable components by dismantling various electronic devices. Dismantled parts of various devices can be assembled again to produce a device which can be brought into use. Some devices need minor repair and these can be reused after proper repair and can also be put for sale. In this process, all steel components are picked up through a magnet. Glass is separated from plastic. Dismantled components can be resold as raw material for various electronic devices. Recycling is done with utmost care so that separated components may not pose any danger to the environment and health of flora and fauna and human beings. Separated plastic, glass, and metals are sent to respective recyclers for further usage.
2) **Refurbishing:** Discarded electronic devices are picked up and renovated (refurbished) by using engineering skill and then these can be resold at nominal prices. Discarded televisions, cameras, laptops, printers, etc. can be refurbished.
3) **Selling out old devices rather than throwing them:** One may sell one's old television, computer, camera, etc. through various online websites or directly to the people who need such devices at a reasonable price. This will help in reducing quantum of e-waste.
4) **Disposal in exchange offers:** Old or out-dated electronic devices can be given back to the company offering exchange offers. This will reduce e-wastage.
5) **Principle of three R's:** Waste can be well managed by adopting the principle of three R's, i.e., Reduce, Reuse, and Recycle. This principal can be adopted for managing other kinds of wastes also.

MAJOR E-WASTE GENERATING COUNTRIES

According to a study by ASSOCHAM-NEC in 2018, India is among the first five countries generating e-waste. China is at the top and India's position is fourth. China is followed by the USA, Japan, India, and Germany.

E-Waste in India

According to The Global E-Waste Monitor (2017) report published by the United Nations University, India generates approximately 2 million tons e-waste per annum. 80% of it is personal devices. Among the top e-waste producing countries, India stands 5th after USA, China, Japan, and Germany. According to a study by ASSOCHAM, 70% of total e-waste in India comprises of computer equipment, followed by telecommunication equipment and phones (12%), electrical equipment (8%), medical equipment (7%), and remaining is household e-waste. It has been further estimated that people are discarding their electric and electronic devices much faster. Resultantly, volume of waste is growing at about 21% per annum. As per this report by 2020 volume of e-waste from old computers will increase by 500%, from discarded mobile phones will be 18% higher, from abandoned televisions about 2 times higher, and from discarded refrigerators will double of their present level.

India's Initiative

1. **E-Waste (Management and Handling) Rules, 2011:** Union Ministry of Environment and Forests notified E-Waste (Management and Handling) Rules, 2011. The rules hold producer of electric and electronic devices, responsible for recycling and reducing e-waste in the country. Further, producer is to make consumer aware about hazardous components of the product. In the case of consumers like hotels, enterprises, big companies, and government who purchase e-products in bulk, they are made responsible for recycling and reducing e-waste. Producers are also to give brochures to consumers for handling the electronic products, dos and don'ts, and guidelines to prevent e-waste. Bulk users and producers will be ensuring that generated e-waste will be sent to authorised collection centres or producers will buy them back. Producers and bulk consumers will have to maintain the record of generated e-waste and the same will have to be furnished to State Pollution Control Boards or Pollution Control Committees.
2. **E-Waste (Management) Rules, 2016:** In these rules, the concept of Extended Producer Responsibility (EPR) was incorporated under which the producers of Electrical and Electronic Equipment (EEE) were made responsible to fulfil the targets specified in the rules to collect back e-waste and to ensure that the collected e-waste will be channelised to authorised recyclers. Collection target either in weight or number, under EPR plan will be 30% of total quantity of waste generated during the first two years of implementation of rules 40% during third and fourth years, 50% during fifth and sixth years, and 70% during seventh years and onwards. Further, state governments were also made responsible to ensure safety, health, and skill development of the workers engaged in dismantling and recycling operations. Urban local bodies (Municipal corporations/committees/councils) were made responsible to collect the orphan e-waste and channelise to authorised recycler or dismantler.
3. **E-waste (Management) Amendment Rules, 2018:** Government of India notified this amendment on 22nd March, 2018. Under this amendment, targets under EPR plan were revised. The revised targets were made applicable on 1st October 2017. The phase-wise collection of e-waste in weight will be 10% of the quantity of waste generated as specified in EPR during 2017-18 with a 10% increase every year until 2023. From 2023 onwards target will be 70% as specified in EPR plan.

Some Vital Facts

1) Unregulated small scale industry is the major source of pollution in rivers of India.
2) Household waste, Sanitation residue, Waste from streets and Construction and demolition debris comprises Municipal Solid waste (MSW)
3) The dominant source of pollution due to oxides of Nitrogen (NOX) in urban areas is road transport.
4) Agriculture activity contributes to water pollution more than any other throughout world.
5) In mega cities of India, the dominant source of air pollution is municipal waste.

Practice Exercise

General Questions Format

1. Which of the following statements is/are TRUE?
   i) Nonpoint source pollution is more hazardous than point source pollution.
   ii) Different layers of atmosphere are significant in determining the extent of global warming due to presence of greenhouse gases in the atmosphere.
   iii) Harmful ultraviolet rays from sun are absorbed in the stratosphere.
   iv) Atmosphere comprises less than 1% nitrous oxide.
   (A) i and iii only (B) iii and iv only
   (C) ii and iv only (D) All of the above
2. Which of the following justifies the status of Municipal Solid Waste (MSW) in India?
   (A) There is a big gap in collection and treatment of MSW.
   (B) MSW is fast becoming an indicator of modern lifestyle.
   (C) Majority of cities have developed facilities to transfer MSW under Swachh Bharat Abhiyan.
   (D) North-eastern states generate less MSW than north-western states.
3. Which provision(s) of Solid Waste (Management) Rules, 2016 establish(es) that poor handling of Municipal Solid Waste is responsible for loss of biodiversity?
   i) In case an event is organised for more than 100 persons, the organiser will have to ensure segregation of waste at source and see that segregated waste is to be handed over to waste collector.
   ii) Burning, burying, or throwing waste openly here and there, public spaces, and water bodies by waste generator is prohibited.
   iii) It will be mandatory for hawkers and vendors and other petty businessmen to keep containers for putting the waste generated out of their business activity and hand it over to waste collector daily.
   iv) All restaurants, hotels, and other such establishments will segregate the waste at source and handover the recyclable material to the unit authorised for recycling and other waste should be treated with proper methods.
   (A) ii and iv (B) i, ii, iii, and iv
   (C) only ii (D) only iv
4. Secondary treatment of wastewater is also known as
   (A) Biological treatment
   (B) Preliminary treatment
   (C) Secondary treatment
   (D) Tertiary treatment
5. Which bacteria consumes organic matter as their food, and thus oxidise it to produce a stable end product?
   (A) Viruses
   (B) Aerobic bacteria
   (C) Anaerobic bacteria
   (D) Rotifers
6. To curb air pollution in urban India, India has launched 'Clean Air India Initiative' as a joint venture with which country?
   (A) China (B) Netherlands
   (C) Fiji (D) Indonesia
7. What is the full form of NWQMP initiative taken by India to curb water pollution?
   (A) National Water Quality Management Programme
   (B) National Water Quality Monitoring Policy
   (C) National Water Quality Monitoring Programme
   (D) National Wastewater Quality Monitoring Parity
8. What was the central agenda of Basel Convention?
   (A) Recycling e-waste and producing eco-friendly goods and their exchange among member countries
   (B) Curbing transborder exchange of synthetic raw material for various industries resulting in air, water, and groundwater pollution

(C) Control of transboundary movement of hazardous waste and its disposal

(D) Making it obligatory to member countries to obtain licences for exchanging recycled waste in reuse and resale policy

9. Which of the following is NOT a step to check air pollution?

(A) Installation of fuel filter devices in vehicles

(B) Initiating legal action against individuals or organisations responsible for generating pollutants in the air

(C) Cycling discarded material like plastic in order to avoid its reacting with sunlight and producing air pollutants

(D) Judicious use of resources produced after burning fossil fuels

10. According to an estimate by Ministry of Road and Transport, horns of................are the biggest source of noise pollution in India.

(A) Cars (B) Trucks

(C) Buses (D) All of the above

11. In disposal of biomedical waste, yellow bag is kept for disposing

(A) bandages

(B) glass vials

(C) syringes without needles

(D) surgical knives

12. Air quality depicting PM2.5 is hazardous to

(A) Railway drivers (B) Old people

(C) Miners (D) All of the above

13. According to Union Ministry of Environment and Forests, which Indian state tops in generating hazardous waste?

(A) Tamil Nadu (B) Uttar Pradesh

(C) Maharashtra (D) Andhra Pradesh

14. India has launched 'Capacity Building for Industrial Pollution Management' with the help of

(A) WHO (B) World Bank

(C) UNESCO (D) ADB

15. Which of the following is NOT TRUE about air pollution?

i) Air pollution decreases the proportion of oxygen in the atmosphere.

ii) Point source air pollution is easier to address as compared to nonpoint source pollution.

iii) Though there are common sources of air pollution, yet a major source of air pollution varies from country to country.

iv) The most effective method of eradicating air pollution is pulverisation.

(A) ii and iii (B) i, ii, iii, and iv

(C) i and iv (D) i, iii, and iv

16. Thinner particles responsible for deteriorating the air quality resulting in the damage of vital body organs are referred as ....PM

(A) 20.5 (B) 2.5

(C) 10.5 (D) 15.5

17. The easiest method of disposal of garbage is

(A) Landfilling (B) Vermiculture

(C) Burning (D) Incineration

18. India enacted Extended Producer Responsibility (EPR) for the management of

(A) Liquid waste (B) Solid waste

(C) Hazardous waste (D) E-waste

19. Ambient Air Quality Index monitors which other pollution besides monitoring air pollution?

(A) Water pollution (B) Noise pollution

(C) Soil pollution (D) Thermal pollution

20. Types of wastes are given under Column I and their respective treatment technique is given under Column II. Match the type of waste with the respective method of its treatment.

Column I (Type of Waste)	Column II (Treatment Technique)
a) Liquid waste	i) Refurbishing
b) E-waste	ii) Vermicomposting
c) Biomedical waste	iii) Sedimentation
d) Municipal solid waste	iv) Segregation

Codes:

	(a)	(b)	(c)	(d)
(A)	i	ii	iv	iii
(B)	i	iv	ii	iii
(C)	iii	i	iv	ii
(D)	ii	iii	iv	i

21. Which of the following three R's are conducive to make pollution-free environment?

(A) Recreate, Restore, Recycle

(B) Resource, Resale, Reduce

(C) Reduce, Reuse, Recycle

(D) Recall, Random, Reconstruct

22. The best method of treating non-biodegradable waste is

(A) Dumping (B) Recycling

(C) Burying (D) Burning

23. Types of MSW is given under Column I and its degeneration time is given under Column II. Match MSW under Column I with its degeneration time under Column II.

Column I (Name of MSW)	**Column II (Degeneration Time)**
a) Wood	i) one year
b) Kitchen waste	ii) 200 years
c) Metal cans	iii) 15 years
d) Woollen clothes	iv) 2 weeks

Codes:	(a)	(b)	(c)	(d)
(A)	ii	iv	iii	i
(B)	i	ii	iv	iii
(C)	iv	ii	i	iii
(D)	iii	iv	ii	i

24. India's largest incineration plant is situated in

(A) Bangalore

(B) New Delhi

(C) Mumbai

(D) Kanpur

25. Eutrophication is the result of

(A) natural activities

(B) human activities

(C) both natural and human activities

(D) None of these

26. Yamuna Action Plan is a joint venture of India and

(A) Japan

(B) Russia

(C) Israel

(D) Norway

27. While taking CPCB report as an evidence on noise pollution in India, which of the following orders of cities is TRUE starting with the noisiest city?

(A) Mumbai > Lucknow > Hyderabad > Delhi > Chennai

(B) Delhi > Hyderabad > Mumbai > Chennai > Lucknow

(C) Chennai > Mumbai > Hyderabad > Delhi > Lucknow

(D) Hyderabad > Chennai > Lucknow > Mumbai > Delhi

28. Blue baby syndrome is developed in children due to presence of

(A) excess chlorine in drinking water

(B) deficient sulphate in drinking water

(C) excess nitrate in drinking water

(D) excess heavy metals in drinking water

29. In which method of MSW disposal, earthworms are used?

(A) Vermicomposting

(B) Pulverisation

(C) Incineration

(D) Composting

30. Which country tops the world in generating e-waste?

(A) Japan (B) India

(C) China (D) USA

31. India launched National Ambient Noise Monitoring Network (NANMN) to curb noise pollution in

(A) Urban and rural belts neighbouring railway stations and bus stands

(B) Rural belts neighbouring highways and railway tracks.

(C) Urban and rural belts neighbouring hospitals and educational institutions

(D) None of the above

32. What is the source of grey water in liquid waste?

(A) Kitchen and bathroom

(B) Toilet

(C) Sewer

(D) Laundries

33. Which of the following is TRUE about pollution?

i) Once it is resulted in any sphere, it victimises some innocent organisms on the behest of some unnatural activities by vested interests.

ii) It is result of unwanted lust and race for short-term gain ending in destruction of ecosystem and loss of biodiversity.

iii) It is such a force which forces man to realise what damages he has been doing to the environment and himself with his hypocritical approach to use of rare and precious natural resources.

iv) Triggered by anti-eco forces, it is interference in the natural existence and working of natural resources, which lose their vitality to serve nature naturally.

(A) i and iv (B) ii, iii, and iv
(C) i, ii, and iii (D) i, ii, iii, and iv

34. Enrichment of water bodies with nutrient salts leading to growth of algae is called

(A) Pulverisation
(B) Eutrophication
(C) Anaerobic digestion
(D) Autoclaving

35. In composting, volume of solid waste is

(A) Reduced (B) Enhanced
(C) Burnt (D) Removed

KEY

1. B	**2.** A	**3.** C	**4.** A	**5.** B	**6.** B	**7.** C
8. C	**9.** B	**10.** D	**11.** A	**12.** D	**13.** C	**14.** B
15. B	**16.** B	**17.** D	**18.** B	**19.** C	**20.** C	**21.** C
22. B	**23.** D	**24.** B	**25.** C	**26.** A	**27.** C	**28.** C
29. A	**30.** C	**31.** D	**32.** A	**33.** D	**34.** B	**35.** A

Assertion–Reason Format

1. Assertion (A): Sediments of suspended matter contaminate water of streams and rivers.

Reason (R): Deforestation is the major cause of soil erosion.

(A) Both A and R are true and R is the correct explanation A
(B) Both a and R are true and R is not correct explanation of A
(C) A is true but R is false
(D) Both A and R are false

2. Assertion (A): All sources of air pollution are identified and treated to curb air pollution.

Reason (R): Emissions from factories and vehicles are major sources of air pollution.

(A) Both A and R are true and R is the correct explanation of A
(B) Both A and R are true but R is not correct explanation of A
(C) A is false but R is true
(D) A is true but R is false

3. Assertion (A): Organic material of solid and liquid waste has biological origin.

Reason (R): Solid or liquid wastes are treated through incineration.

(A) Both A and R are true and R is the correct explanation of A
(B) Both A and R are true but R is not the correct explanation of A
(C) A is true but R is false
(D) Both A and R are false

4. Assertion (A): Landfills and aquifers are natural ground openings for disposal of solid and liquid waste.

Reason (R): Treating solid and liquid waste through incineration is precondition to its disposal in landfills and aquifers.

(A) Both A and R are true and R is the correct explanation of A
(B) Both A and R are true but R is not correct explanation of A
(C) A is true but R is false
(D) Both A and R are false

5. Assertion (A): People generally exchange their old televisions, cameras, computers, and mobile phones with new ones in various exchange offers.

Reason (R): Exchange offers on old electric and electronic devices are responsible for rapid increase in e-waste.

(A) Both A and R are true and R is the correct explanation of A
(B) Both A and R are true but R is not correct explanation of A
(C) A is true but R is false
(D) A is false but R is true

6. **Assertion (A):** Oxygen depletion in water bodies put aquatic life in danger.

   Reason (R): Distilleries and chemical factories discharge hot water into water bodies.

   (A) Both A and R are true and R is correct explanation of A

   (B) Both A and R are true but R is not correct explanation of A

   (C) A is true but R is false

   (D) A is false but R is true

7. **Assertion (A):** Every noise in a public gathering creates noise pollution.

   Reason (R): Public gatherings should be organised in a soundproof hall.

   (A) Both A and R are true and R is correct explanation of A

   (B) Both A and R are false

   (C) A is false but R is true

   (D) Both A and R are true but R is not correct explanation of A

8. **Assertion (A):** Biomedical waste and e-waste are hazardous.

   Reason (R): Improper management of wastes carry a number of apprehensions.

   (A) A is true but R is false

   (B) A is false but R is true

   (C) Both A and R are false

   (D) Both A and R are true and R is correct explanation of A

9. **Assertion (A):** Pollution in Indian rivers is an outcome of the social set-up of our society.

   Reason (R): Various action plans to clean Indian rivers have yielded results.

   (A) Both A and R are false

   (B) A is true but R is false

   (C) Both A and R are true but R is not correct explanation of A

   (D) Both A and R are true and R is correct explanation of A

10. **Assertion (A):** Air pollution in Delhi is nonpoint source pollution.

    Reason (R): Residents of Delhi are visiting doctors with complaints of breathlessness.

    (A) Both A and R are true and R is correct explanation of A

    (B) A is false but R is true

    (C) Both A and R are true but R is not correct explanation of A

    (D) Both A and R are false

KEY

1. B **2.** C **3.** B **4.** D **5.** C **6.** A **7.** B **8.** D **9.** C **10.** B

Questions Asked in Previous NET Exams

1. Which of the following is considered as major source of pollution in rivers of India?

   (UGC NET JULY 2018)

   (A) Unregulated small-scale industry

   (B) Untreated sewage

   (C) Agricultural run-off

   (D) Thermal power plants

2. Municipal Solid Waste (MSW) comprises of

   (UGC NET JULY 2018)

   (i) Household waste

   (ii) Sanitation residue

   (iii) Waste from streets

   (iv) Construction and demolition debris

   Choose the correct answer from the code given below:

   Code:

   (A) (i), (ii), and (iii)

   (B) (i) and (iii)

   (C) (i), (iii), and (iv)

   (D) (i), (ii), (iii), and (iv)

3. The dominant source of pollution due to oxides of Nitrogen (NOx) in urban areas is

   (UGC NET JANUARY 2017)

   (A) Road transport

   (B) Commercial sector

   (C) Energy use in industry

   (D) Power plants

4. Which of the following is the largest source of water pollution in major rivers of India?

   (UGC NET JULY 2016)

   (A) Untreated sewage

   (B) Agriculture run-off

   (C) Unregulated small-scale industries

   (D) Religious practices

5. **Assertion (A):** People population control measures do not necessarily help in checking environmental degradation.

   Reason (R): The relationship between population growth and environmental degradation is rather complex.

   (UGC NET DECEMBER 2015)

   Choose the correct answer from the following:

   (A) Both (A) and (R) are true and (R) is the correct explanation of (A)

   (B) Both (A) and (R) are true but (R) is not the correct explanation of (A)

   (C) (A) is true but (R) is false

   (D) (A) is false but (R) is true

6. Which activity contributes to water pollution more than any other throughout the world ?

   (UGC NET SEPTEMBER 2013)

   (A) Agriculture

   (B) Hydroelectric power generation

   (C) Industry

   (D) Urbanisation

7. Which of the following parameters is not used as a pollution indicator in water?

   (UGC NET JUNE 2012)

   (A) Total dissolved solids

   (B) Coliform count

   (C) Dissolved oxygen

   (D) Density

8. In mega cities of India, the dominant source of air pollution is **(UGC NET JUNE 2011)**

   (A) Transport sector

   (B) Thermal power

   (C) Municipal waste

   (D) Commercial sector

9. The Ganga Action Plan was initiated during the year **(UGC NET JUNE 2011)**

   (A) 1986

   (B) 1988

   (C) 1990

   (D) 1992

10. Which of the following pairs regarding typical composition of hospital wastes is incorrect?

    (UGC NET DECEMBER 2008)

    (A) Plastic: 9–12%

    (B) Metals: 1-2%

    (C) Ceramic: 8-10%

    (D) Biodegradable: 35-40%

KEY

1. B	**2.** D	**3.** A	**4.** A	**5.** A	**6.** A	**7.** D
8. A	**9.** A	**10.** A				

5 Climate Change and Its Dimensions

INTRODUCTION

The United Nations Framework Convention on Climate Change (UNFCCC), which provides an outline to the parties to address the causes of climate change, defines climate change as "a change of climate which is attributed directly or indirectly to human activity that alters the composition of the global atmosphere and which is in addition to natural climate variability observed over comparable time periods". When there is rise in earth's average temperature, it is referred to as change in climate. Such a climate change results in 'Global Warming'. This climate change is visible in rise in sea levels, droughts, and various effects on the environment. Climate change is basically a change in statistical properties of the climate system. Statistical properties include average temperature, average rainfall, variability in precipitation (water vapours falling on the earth like rain, snow, hailstorm, etc.), and extremities of winter and summer. If a change in these statistical properties of climate persists for a long period, say about 30 years, it is known as 'Climate Change'.

Editor: The text inside the following textbox is invisible, please look into it.

PARTS OF CLIMATE SYSTEM

Climate system of any region on this earth or of the earth as a whole generates climate. Climate system has five parts:

1) ***Cyrosphere:*** *Cyrosphere comprises of total snow and ice on the earth. This includes glaciers, snow cover, ice sheet and sea ice. The sphere plays a major role in determining climate. It reflects solar radiations back to space. Due to accumulation and melting of sea, there is variation in sea level.*
2) ***Biosphere:*** *it is the sphere which comprises the whole animal and plant kingdom on land, water and air. Biosphere also helps in determining climate. Plant kingdom stores carbon dioxide and thus contributes in determining and setting carbon cycle. Transfer of water to atmosphere is possible due to sufficient growth of plants.*
3) ***Atmosphere:*** *Atmosphere containing various gases like nitrogen, oxygen, carbon dioxide ,argon and water vapours play the strongest part in determining climate due to extremities in temperature, rainfall etc. Wind currents move heat from one region to the other due to heating and cooling of air currents*
4) ***Hydrosphere:*** *All small and enormous water bodies like oceans also determine climate being part of the climate system. Water bodies particularly oceans help in storing and transporting energy. As oceans engulf huge amount of heat, there is prevention from abrupt change in temperature.*
5) ***Lithosphere:*** *This sphere comprises land surface which is constituting plains, mountains, soil. Land and soil mixture are effective in absorbing some sun rays and reflecting back others. Winds traveling over earth's surface leave a great impact on lithosphere due to composition of lithosphere. Though not sizable yet lithosphere's contribution in determining climate is not deniable. Movement of winds over surface of the earth results in carrying air over plains and mountains for effecting rainfall and precipitation*

Causes of Climate Change

There are natural and man-made causes of climate change.

1) **Volcanic eruptions:** Nature and cycle of climate is affected by volcanic eruptions. On one side molten hot lava is released during eruptions and on the other hand, gases and dust particles enter the atmosphere. Sulphur dioxide released during volcanic eruptions

enters the stratosphere and has a cooling effect on the earth and particles like ash and other particles divert the sunlight away from the sun by shading it. Along with that, greenhouse gases like carbon dioxide released during eruptions lead to rise temperature of the earth, and hence result in global warming.

2) **Human activities:** There is release of carbon dioxide and other greenhouse gases to the atmosphere due to burning of fossil fuels during various human activities. This results in global warming. Due to global warming, there is abrupt change in climate.

3) **Variation in solar radiations:** Out of total solar radiations received by the earth, some are absorbed by it while some are reflected back as thermal radiations. There exists a balance between incoming and outgoing radiations to sustain a climate. Any imbalance between such radiations cause change in climate. Research works say that 70% of radiations are absorbed by the lithosphere, hydrosphere, and atmosphere. 30% of these are reflected back by ice, snow, roof terraces, ocean surface, sand, clouds, and atmospheric aerosols. But greenhouse gases trap these reflected radiations and do not let them return back to space. Due to this climate change occurs, visible in global warming and melting of polar ice leading to rise in sea levels, which further affect marked changes in climate

Editor: The text inside the following textbox is invisible, please look into it.

AEROSOLS

Aerosols or atmospheric aerosols are tiny particles solid or droplets suspended in the earth's atmosphere. These are released into atmosphere by natural or anthropogenic activities. Aerosols like dust, volcanic ash, carbon particulates released due to forest fires and fog are natural. Anthropogenic aerosols are emissions from factories and vehicles, carrying air pollutants and soot. Aerosols play an important role in climate change as these are transported by air currents. The extent of change in climate depends on size, location and composition. Large sized aerosols obstruct the sun light hence making surface cool. Some aerosols, which are light coloured like sulphate aerosols, reflect back the sun rays to space again making earth cool. On the other hand dark coloured aerosols like black carbon or soot absorb the sunrays and hence warm the atmosphere. Dark coloured or black aerosols remain suspended in air and travel through air but heavy ones fall on the surface of earth due to gravity and settled down on snow, ice or desert. Due to this deposition of black aerosols on cyrosphere and desert, neither cyrosphere nor desert is able to reflect back solar radiations (albedo). This will lead to increase in terrestrial heat and hence global warming.

4) **Movement in tectonic plates:** Lithosphere is composed of large-sized, irregular-shaped rock plates called tectonic plates. These keep on moving at a uniform speed of 2–5 centimetres per year. Radioactive decay in the core of earth produces heat which becomes the force behind shifting of the tectonic plates. These plates also move due to convection currents below them. Movement or shifting of tectonic plates bring change in ocean currents which results in generation of more and more heat. Further, shifting of tectonic plates result in more volcanic eruptions due to which a greater amount of carbon dioxide and sulphur dioxide is released into the atmosphere resulting in rise in temperature. On the contrary, any lazy movement of tectonic plates lead to fall in temperature.

ALBEDO

Albedo is the extent of reflection of a light ray by a surface. Shining and light coloured surfaced has high albedo and black and dark coloured surface has lower albedo as such surface absorbs the light rather than reflecting it. Albedo contributes in climate change also. White and light coloured surface of earth like snow, sea & polar ice and desert have high albedo as they reflect more solar radiations back into the space and does not let the surface temperature rise. On the other hand black surface such as rocks or dark aerosols settled on snow, mountains or any other surface absorb sun radiations thereby rising the temperature of the earth resulting in global warming.

Effects of Climate Change

1) **Release of more carbon dioxide by lithosphere and hydrosphere:** Oceans absorb a huge amount of carbon dioxide and put a constraint on global warming. Similarly, forests on land absorb carbon dioxide. Due to climate change, oceans heat up and there is

abnormal concentration of carbon dioxide. Excess that is not absorbed by oceans and oceans become acidic, posing threat to aquatic life. Trees and forests absorb carbon dioxide, minimising the risk of global warming. Due to large-scale deforestation, trees are not left to absorb carbon dioxide. Further, dead plants emit carbon dioxide leading to huge deposits of carbon dioxide in the atmosphere. Being the major greenhouse gas, carbon dioxide deposits in the atmosphere result in global warming.

2) **Melting of polar ice:** Climate change is more marked at North Pole and South Pole. Ice caps on these poles melt to deposit more and more water in oceans, leading to disasters like tsunamis.
3) **Threat to aquatic life:** Due to rise in earth's temperature, ocean is warmed and temperature rises above the normal limit of 1° celsius. Oceans are already in the risk zone as far as aquatic life is concerned, with temperature already above 1° celsius and likely to touch 1.5° celsius. This climate change ultimately victimises aquatic life.
4) **Threat of species extinction and loss of biodiversity:** Climate changes resulted due to deforestation leave a harmful impact on plant and animal life. Deforestation poses a great threat to survival of animal and plant species. Various plant and animal species depend on trees and forests for their survival. These forests are the natural habitat of many animals. When due to persistent and large-scale deforestation, nothing is left to feed the species; they either become extinct or migrate to a better habitat, marking loss of diversity. According to an estimate by Intergovernmental Panel on Climate Change, with a 1.5° celsius average rise in global temperature, about 30% of animal and plant species will be at risk of extinction.
5) **Bad Impact on cyrosphere:** The whole cyrosphere of the earth experiences the harmful effect of climate change. Rise in temperature melts glaciers, ice sheets, and snow. This leads to abnormal rise in sea levels. Ice in the sea melts and generates black water which absorbs more and more sunlight, due to which ocean water temperature rises rapidly, developing various unnatural climatic processes like cycle of rapid melting and heating.
6) **Threat to threatened species:** Many threatened species are surviving in different habitats on this earth. There is apprehension of losing these rare species as these species do not get enough time to adapt to a particular climate due to quick and abrupt changes in climate.
7) **Disturbing water channel:** Change in climate disturbs the normal water channel due to frequent floods and droughts. Moreover, sea ice on melting releases black water which absorbs more heat.
8) **Ill effects on human health:** With the warming of atmosphere due to climatic changes, heat waves set in. Heat waves bring extremely hot summers which results in many deaths and ailments. Due to heat, certain bacteria enter freshwater which survive and grow in warm fresh water and cause various infections. Urban areas plagued by smog also become the source of various respiratory diseases.
9) **Damage of infrastructure:** Extremities of temperature and seasons due to climatic changes damage infrastructure. Such extremities put excess load on electric supply devices and cables, resulting in disruption in smooth electric supply.
10) **Threat to agriculture:** Changing weather conditions present a great challenge to farmers. What crop is to be cultivated depends by and large on climate suitable to that crop. Rapidly changing climate badly affects growth of crops and other agricultural products. Due to change in climate, rains become unpredictable and untimely rains ruin the crops. Such climatic changes are also responsible for growth of weeds, which interfere in the growth of crops and destroy them.

CLIMATE CHANGE AND ITS DIMENSIONS

A change in climate has many dimensions apart from ecological and health dimensions. Any normal or abnormal change in climate has the following two types of dimensions:

1) Socio-economic dimensions
2) Political dimensions

Socio-economic Dimensions

"Parties should protect the climate system for the benefit of present and future generations of humankind, on the basis of equity and in accordance with their common but differentiated responsibilities and respective capabilities". This has been stated by the United Nations Framework Convention on Climate Change (UNFCCC). In this quotation it has been made mandatory for countries and societies to protect climate as a precaution against abrupt changes in climate which may sabotage progress of various socio-economic issues and projects. Socio-economic dimensions of climate change are discussed as follows:

i) Health
ii) Human rights
iii) Gender equality
iv) Housing
v) Water, food security, and nutrition
vi) Employment and livelihood.
vii) Migration of workforce
viii) Education
ix) Infrastructure

i) **Health:** Unnatural and abnormal climate change affects human health. There are different sections surviving in the society. These sections of the society have a huge social and economic gap. The privileged and affluent sections of the society make prior arrangements against climate changes and they do not become victims of unhealthy impact of climate changes. The most vulnerable lot is the marginalised and poor sections of the society. Marginalised sections includes women, children, refugees, nomadic people, people living in water-scarce areas, migrants, people with physical and mental handicaps, minorities, and the poor. Major determinants of health are safe drinking water, secure food, and shelter security. These determinants are badly damaged due to change in climate. Resultantly, marginalised section of the society becomes victim of various infectious and fatal diseases because they cannot afford means to protect them. Everyone should be protected while maintaining equity as emphasised in the UNFCCC mandate.

ii) **Human rights:** UNFCCC mandate to member countries emphasises protection of climate in the interest of protection of mankind, so everyone should enjoy right to live, food, and shelter. In case of adverse effect of climate change, human beings and their rights must be protected. This provision should be included in mitigation policies of climate change. Here again, the vulnerable section of the society should be given proper attention to make it secured in normal and abnormal change in climate and bring resilience.

iii) **Gender equality:** Climate changes affect women more than men. Women are assigned subordinate status as compared to men, particularly in developing countries. Livelihood of the poorest population is dependent upon local natural resources. As women constitute the majority in the poorest population, they are always exposed to jobs requiring use of natural resources. Adverse effects of climate change create more sufferings and hardships for women as compared to men. Women belonging to the poorest population have less access to medicine and treatment in case they fall ill due to any adversity in climate. Such women have restrictions on studying also. In spite of this, women tolerate and continue to work in the fields as well as in the house with patience. Women are the front line sufferers of climate adversities, but they face these and become capable of finding out ways of mitigating natural disasters with their experience and also adapt to the changes. Women also possess leadership qualities and can take constructive decisions. But male-dominated societies do not feel any need to consult them. While keeping in consideration elevation of women's status in such societies, UN has asked member countries to work for gender equality and this is also one of the Sustainable Development Goals for 2030 or Agenda 2030.

iv) **Housing:** Marginalised section of a society's population has either poor dwellings or no dwellings as majority of the marginalised section is very poor. Due to this reason, this section becomes the primary party to face any change in climate. Most of the damage done to this section is due to absence of houses or shelter. Members of this section develop many ailments only due to the fact that they do not possess any shelter to protect themselves from prolonged and persistent exposure to climate change. Provision of housing for the marginalised section should be kept in various policies made to manage climate changes as sustainable development is basically attached with the lot of this section of population. Further, along with provision of housing, such architecture should be planned which may resist the impact of natural calamities effected due to abnormal change in climate.

v) **Water, food security, and nutrition:** Climate changes bring droughts and hurricanes and extremities in temperature, which prey on food and water security and nutrition of vulnerable sections of the society. Drastic changes in climate directly affect agriculture production and productivity. Due to this, there is apprehension of hunger epidemic and undernutrition. Destruction of crops and allied products and degradation in crop quality due to unpredicted rains create scarcity of food and droughts. Also, floods create scarcity of drinking water. Due to scarcity, food and water go beyond the access of the vulnerable sections. Such calamities deprive the agrarian population from its livelihood also. Children are deprived of required nourishment. Scarcity also raises prices of available foodstuff and cereals, which the poor cannot afford. In the World Food Summit, 1996, it has already been defined that food security is intact when every section of the population can afford nutritious and sufficient food and it has access to such food any time it wants. For sustainable development, this definition should be materialised in the disaster management and climate change policies to ensure this food and water security for everyone.

vi) **Employment and livelihood:** It has been categorically mentioned in Sustainable Development Goals (Agenda 2030) that poverty eradication is a must for achieving sustainable development. Poverty arises due to unemployment or absence of means of livelihood. Change in climate threatens employment and livelihood. Majority of the population, particularly in developing countries, depend upon agriculture for their livelihood and earnings. Due to droughts, floods, hurricanes, and other calamities, people have to migrate to safer and prospective .places where they can earn livelihood.

vii) **Migration of workforce:** As observed earlier, climate changes enforce affected people to migrate to near or far places to earn their livelihood which is lost at the primitive place of settlement. There is migration of coastal workforce also due to hurricanes, rising sea levels, and cyclones. Migratory workforce from rural areas or low-lying coastal areas prefers to settle down in cities where they hope for an alternative livelihood. Migration of this labour puts load on the already settled or native labour. Migratory labour enters into temporary contracts even at lower wages. As this workforce is poor, it compromises on substandard material for its housing. Sometimes, such people put their life into grave risk while residing in under-construction buildings or under bridges and flyovers and some start residing on footpaths and sidelanes. Such sites are prone to accidents and crimes, particularly against women. They also do not halve any access to legal rights, due to which they cannot get any legal remedy in case of any mishappening. Due to residing in unsanitary surroundings, they develop risk of serious ailments and pose threat of proliferation of infectious diseases all around. A sound policy framework is required to provide for safety and protection of the workforce which is enforced to migrate due to abnormal changes in climate.

viii) **Education:** Member of every society has right to education in today's legislature. Climate changes strongly hinder the education stream. Adverse impact of changes in climate like droughts, floods, rise in sea levels, hurricanes, and extremities of temperature deprives the school and college going students of their right to education. Due to calamities, schools and colleges are closed for an indefinite period. Affluent sections of the society send its wards to high profile schools and colleges in case of such emergency as it can afford their exorbitant fees. On the contrary, the poor who cannot afford such a high fee have to either wait patiently for normalcy to again send their children to the same school or college or to migrate to slums in the urban areas to find some community school or colleges. In both the cases, education of students is interrupted and they cannot cope up on resuming their education.

ix) **Infrastructure:** Development of infrastructure in any society is an indicator of its progress in socio-economic sectors. A sound infrastructure in transportation, health, communication, commerce and banking, education, law and order, and defence guarantees security and reasonably affordable lifestyle to every section of the society. Abnormal changes in climate damage this infrastructure. Flyovers, bridges, dams, railway tracks, hospitals, schools, colleges, banks, communication towers, railway stations, airports, and defence establishments are either demolished or destroyed by various erroneous changes in climates like droughts, floods, hurricanes, tsunamis, extremities of temperature, and cyclones. All such catastrophes disrupt national and international trade, hamper regular study and education, create various infectious diseases, halts road, rail, and air transport, and deteriorate law and order situation. It also results in people not getting proper health treatment, contamination of surface and groundwater, embargo to communication flow, starvation, mass deaths, and steep rise in crime rate. Here again, a sound mitigating policy is required to protect means of socio-economic development including all sections of the population. Only then sustainable socio-economic development can be achieved.

UNFCCC

UN framework Convention on Climate Change (UNFCCC) is an international treaty, which aims at finding solution to problems created by climate change. It has been first international treaty on climate change. Main target was to reduce emission of greenhouse gases by industrialised countries all over the world and prevent human interference in the natural climate. The convention for signature in 1992 and the treaty was signed in 1994 at the Earth summit at Rio. Mandate of UN FCCC says, "Stabilise greenhouse gas concentrations in the atmosphere at a level that would prevent dangerous anthropogenic (human-induced) interference with the climate system"

Political Dimensions

As per Intergovernmental Panel on Climate Change (IPCC), political dimension of climate change is concerned with formation of sound adaptation and mitigation policies and good governance. Climate changes create havoc which put the total social, political, economic, health, defence, and all other systems out of gear. All systems of the country are interdependent. Political system is the parent system of all other systems. If there is a sound political system with good governance and result-oriented policies, any natural or man-made abnormality in climate can be faced and its consequences may be addressed. Following policy frameworks are included in political dimensions.

Adaptation Policies

Adaptation is reducing vulnerability towards harmful effects of climate change. Due to abrupt climate changes, natural disasters have been occurring without warning. With passage of time there has been development in technology and communication means. With the help of this technology, now it is possible to anticipate catastrophic consequences of abrupt changes in climate. The United Nations Framework Convention on Climate Change (UNFCCC) defines adaptation as "adjustment in natural or human systems in response to actual or expected climatic stimuli or their effects, which moderates harm or exploits beneficial opportunities. Various types of adaptation can be distinguished, including anticipatory and reactive adaptation, private and public adaptation, and autonomous and planned adaptation". An adaptation policy ensures drafting of approaches and means aiming at minimising or preventing the anticipated damages of climate changes. Adaptation policy contains:

i) Cultivation of crops which can tolerate droughts
ii) Planting those species of trees which are less vulnerable to storms and hurricanes and fire
iii) Efficient use of scarce resources
iv) Preparing roads, rail tracks, dams, and other infrastructure with such an engineering skill that these erections are able to resist floods, drainage, and global warming
v) Improvement in vigil on climate-sensitive diseases and controlling measures
vi) Developing wetlands as buffer against sea level rise and floods
vii) Reducing dependence on a single source of energy
viii) Rational use of water through proper storage of drinking water, expanding rainwater harvesting, and improvement in irrigation efficiency
ix) Crop diversification resulting in reduction of vulnerability to climate changes, as certain crops date-wise and type-wise escape harmful effects of climate change

According to Intergovernmental Panel on Climate Change (IPCC) Assessment Report, government of UNFCCC signatory countries are coming up with sound adaptation policies on climate change.

Mitigation Policies

Mitigation policies on climate change target to restrict the rate of global warming and its effects. Global warming is the result of various anthropogenic activities emitting greenhouse gases, particularly carbon dioxide, responsible for global warming. As per IPCC estimate, energy supply is the major source of carbon emissions, i.e., 25%, followed by industry -19%, forestry -17%, agriculture-13%, transport-13%, residential and commercial buildings-8%, and waste and waste water-3%. UNFCCC mandate also points towards preventing interference of anthropogenic activities in the ecosystem generating dangerous results. While highlighting the importance of mitigation measures against abnormal climate change, the IPCC's 2014 Assessment Report states, "Mitigation is a public good; climate change is a case of the 'tragedy of the commons'". This means that selfish and vested interest of human beings waste scarce natural resources, and emit greenhouse gases in the atmosphere resulting in harmful climate changes, which could have been used in a better way, if these could be used for the common interests. Mitigation policy framework involves the following traits:

i) **Carbon pricing:** Major cause of global warming is human emission of greenhouse gases, particularly carbon dioxide. Government is to make a policy to charge price of carbon emitted by human beings through industries and automobiles. This price is charged as a compensation of health loss, crop damage, and loss of property which are resulted by global warming, floods, rise in sea level, and droughts. Various governments are experiencing that carbon pricing is becoming instrumental in reducing emissions and transition of carbonised societies to decarbonised ones has already started in. It is also known as carbon taxing. This step will help in reducing source of greenhouse gases like burning of fossil fuels for producing electricity which is used in heating, transportation, and other anthropogenic activities.

ii) **Increase in carbon sinks:** Carbon sinks are natural absorbents of carbon dioxide or separate carbon dioxide from atmosphere. Carbon sinks include forests, plants, soil, and oceans. Mitigation policy should aim at maximum forestation and reforestation.

iii) **Eradicating fossil fuels in a phased manner:** Switching over to renewable energy sources will help restrictions on emissions of greenhouse gases.

IPCC

Intergovernmental Penal on Climate Change (IPCC) came into existence in 1988. The penal was created by the United Nations Environment Programme (UNEP) and the World Meteorological Organisation (WMO). IPCC provides knowledge of science of climate change to the governments of all member countries of the UNO or WMO. Knowledge provided by the IPCC helps the member countries to plan appropriate adaptation and mitigation measures against climate change. Knowledge provided by IPCC also helps various countries to undergo climate change related pacts and agreements.

CLIMATE CHANGE AND INDIA

Climate changes affect India the maximum as India is among those countries which are most vulnerable to change in climate. One of the major reasons is India's emergence as a leading economy of the world. Major reasons include increasing density of economic activity and majority of population earning its livelihood from natural resources. According to an estimate by World Bank, pressure on India's water, soil, forests, and air is likely to be the highest in the world by 2020.

Effects of Climate Change on India

1) **Effect on farmers' income:** Adverse effects of climate changes in the agricultural field are jeopardising government of India's plan to double the farmers' income by 2022. According to Economic Survey 2017-18, climate change will reduce farmers' income by 15 to 18% in the near future due to fall in quality and quantity of crops. This fall would be sharper in unirrigated areas. There it would be 20 to 25%. The survey further observes that with 1 degree celsius rise in terrestrial temperature, there will be fall in farmers' income by 6.2% in kharif season and 6% in rabi in unirrigated areas.

2) **Fall in agricultural productivity:** Abrupt changes in climate and rise in temperature are making monsoons unpredictable. This is creating imbalance in rainfall distribution. Some states are getting frequent and untimely rainfalls creating floods, whereas some states

are experiencing frequent droughts. Floods and landslides of Uttrakhand in 2013, floods in Chennai in 2015, droughts of Maharashtra, Gujarat, Jharkhand, and Chhattisgarh, and floods of Kerala in 2018 are some devastating mishappenings of climate change. This has reduced agricultural productivity resulting in steep fall in crop yield. States like Chhattisgarh, Odisha, Jharkhand, and some belts of north-western India have experienced significant fall in crop yield. Various belts in coastal states like Maharashtra, Tamil Nadu, Andhra Pradesh, West Bengal, and Goa are meeting the same fate due to rise in oceanic level.

3) **Fall in living standards:** Climate changes are becoming a reason for the falling living standards of the poor population of India which is mostly depending on agriculture and other natural resources.

   According to a report, published in The Hindustan Times, by Muthukumara Mani, a leading economist in the World Bank, Indian states like Chhattisgarh and Madhya Pradesh have experienced the greatest decline in living standards of the poor and tribal population. Decline in these states has been more than 9%. This is followed by Rajasthan, Uttar Pradesh, and Maharashtra.

4) **Fall in GDP:** While reviewing a special report of Intergovernmental Panel on Climate Change (IPCC), Dr Roxy Mathew Koll, a scientist at the Indian Institute of Tropical Meteorology, Pune says that India is fast becoming a hotspot of global warming along with China and Pakistan. At the present rate of rise in temperature, there is apprehension of droughts, floods, and heat waves which will result in fall in crop yield which will further reduce India's GDP from 2–10%.

5) **Stress on water resources:** Climate change is fast putting stress on the already scarce water resources of India which are only 4% of the world's water resources. Himalayan rivers of India like Brahmaputra, Ganga, Ravi, Beas, Satluj, and other Indus rivers depend upon water obtained due to melting of snow. Rise in temperature results in early and fast melting of snow and fresh water is wasted in the form of floods which puts stress on water resources and create scarcity of water. Urbanisation, industrialisation, expansion in agriculture, economic development, and rapidly increasing population has resulted in a steep rise in demand for water in India. Agriculture is the largest consumer of water. About 83% of total water available in India is used for agriculture. Equally important is the groundwater. Over 85% of rural needs and about 50% of urban needs are met by groundwater in India. Stress on water due to global warming is drying aquifers and the water table is going down.

6) **Damage to tourist spots and other infrastructure in coastal states:** India's tourist intensive states like Goa, Maharashtra, Gujarat, Odisha, Kerala, and Andhra Pradesh are badly affected due to climate changes. There is risk of damage to tourist spots and other infrastructure due to cyclones, tsunamis, and other natural calamities. Such damages will not only result in loss of human, animal, and plant lives but also a huge loss to revenue generated from tourism. It has been estimated that a one metre rise in sea level in Goa will result in loss of revenue to the tune of 8000/- crores and Maharashtra will lose revenue of about 200000/- crores.

CLIMATE RESILIENCE

Climate resilience is to reduce and address vulnerability of different sections of population, states, nations to climatic changes. Intergovernmental Penal on Climate Change (IPCC) defines climate resilience as "capacity of social, economic , and environmental systems to cope with a hazardous event or trend or disturbance, responding or reorganizing in ways that maintain their essential function, identity, and structure, while also maintaining the capacity for adaptation, learning, and transformation." So climate resilience is the capacity of different systems of a society to face, resist and respond to any adversity in climate. Climate resilience is found in various adaptation and mitigation measures initiated by the societies. Resilience requires addressing vulnerability to climate change without hampering socio-economic and political growth of a society.

Policy Measures By India

Adaptation Measures

While adopting adaptation measures, India adopted issues close to the IPCC agenda of science of climate changes and anticipation of climate change risks and their management. Union ministry of Environment and Forests, while drafting adaptation measures, targetted fathoming nature and intensity of vulnerability in India. Adaptation measures are required to combat and conquer rise in sea level, health risks, floods, extremity of temperature, storms, hurricanes, cyclones, and terrestrial and oceanic warming. India has come up with the following adaptation plans and measures against climate change:

i) **National Action Plan on Climate Change (NAPCC):** Government of India launched NAPCC in June 2008, focussing on adaptation and mitigation measures against abrupt climate changes while protecting poor and vulnerable sections of the population, maintaining high growth rate, and achieving an objective for sustainable development. NAPCC earmarked eight missions as an initiative to address climate changes through adaptation and mitigation:

a) National Solar Mission
b) National Mission for Enhanced Energy Efficiency
c) National Mission on Sustainable Habitat
d) National Water Mission
e) National Mission for Sustaining the Himalayan Ecosystem
f) National Mission for Green India
g) National Mission for Sustainable Agriculture
h) National Mission on Strategic Knowledge for Climate Change

Out of these eight missions defined by NAPCC, five of these are focussing on adaptation measures:

a) **National Water Mission:** Under this mission, initiatives will be taken to increase water usage efficiency by 20%, thus achieving optimum use of water. Further there is target of recycling waste water and implementation of Integrated Water Resource Management (IWRM).

b) **National Mission on Strategic Knowledge for Climate Change:** This mission aims at adopting an institutional approach for generating data and knowledge of science of climate change along with knowledge of adaptation and mitigation measures. Such knowledge will also help to better understand adaptation measures against harmful effects of climate change. The mission proposes creation of Climate Science Research Fund with which research works can be undertaken with international collaboration. The mission aims to encourage private sector also in funding research works. The mission aims to create hi-tech knowledge networks for sharing, communicating, and exchanging knowledge on changes in climate.

c) **National Mission for Sustainable Agriculture:** India is an agrarian country and more than 60% of its population depends on agriculture. As the agriculture sector is worst affected by harmful effects of climate change, there is a need to take adaptation measures like improvement in agricultural productivity in rain-fed belts, developing climate-resilient crops, water use efficiency, livelihood diversification, nutrient management, and expansion of weather insurance mechanisms to protect it. Indian Council of Agricultural Research (ICAR) has been undertaking adaptation and mitigation measures for sustainable development of agriculture in India. ICAR launched a network project 'National Innovations on Climate Resilient Agriculture (NICRA)' in 2011. NICRA has been concentrating on four prospective areas: improving crop production, livestock and fisheries, institutional innovations to make farmers self-reliant for adaptation against climate change, and natural resource management. The project has four components viz. technology demonstration, capacity building, sponsored competitive grants, and strategic research.

d) **National Mission for Sustaining Himalayan Ecosystem:** Glaciers are a major source of water in the Himalayan rivers and thus, major source of water supply. These become perennial due to regular deposits of water generated due to melting of snow and glaciers. But due to global warming, the cryosphere experiences fast melting and thus deposit of a huge amount of water into rivers and water bodies. This raises their level and excess water is overflown in the form of floods, cyclones, and tsunamis. Thus, cryosphere comes under recession. To create a check on warming, this mission aims at increasing forest cover, biodiversity conservation, and all other ecological measures in the Himalayan region.

e) **National Mission for "Green India":** Under this mission there has been a target of afforestation of about 5 million hectares of degraded forests and expansion in forest cover from 23% at present to 33%.

f) **MNREGA Initiative:** The Mahatma Gandhi National Rural Employment Guarantee Act (MNREGA) is a scheme which guarantees 100 days of employment with standard wages to the poorest in rural areas in a financial year. By guaranteeing employment to the poorest section of the population in rural areas, MNREGA is acting as an adaptation measure for the most vulnerable section of the population against harmful effects of climate change.

g) **Adaptation Measures in UNDAF States:** United Nations Development Assistance Framework (UNDAF) from 2008 to 2012 has adopted seven Indian states namely Odisha, Chhattisgarh, Rajasthan, Uttar Pradesh, Jharkhand, Madhya Pradesh, and Bihar. United Nations Development Programme (UNDP) is undertaking adaptation measures in these Indian states against abnormal climate changes. This programme was followed by United Nations Development Action Framework (UNDAF), 2013-17. This programme adopted two more states viz. Maharashtra and Assam, and added them to the previous seven states. Now the total states covered had been nine. In all these states, UNDP in collaboration with Niti Aayog, has initiated adaptation measures like food and nutrition security, gender equality, governance, and sustainable development against unpredictable changes in climate.

NAF

> *India created National Adaptation Fund (NAF) in 2014 with an allocation of Rs. 100 crores.It was created to finance the expenditure incurred in national and state level implementation of adaptation measures particularly in those areas which are the most vulnerable to climate change.*

Mitigation Measures

Following mitigation measures have been adopted by India:

a) **Integrated Energy Policy, 2006:** India is fast developing economy and as far as size of the economy is concerned, India stands as the fourth largest economy in the world and third largest emitter of greenhouse gases. Rising population is increasing demand and acceleration in production of various goods and services is resulting in increasing growth rate. A huge amount of energy is needed for sustainable development. This energy is obtained through burning fossil fuels. This results in GHG emissions. In spite of this, India is not the leading GHG emitter globally. India's GHG emissions vary between 65% to 70%, and it is estimated that by 2020 this percentage will be 70%. As per the present emission quantum; India emits about 4% of global GHG emissions. Source-wise percentage of total emissions goes like this: 58% from energy, industry 22%, agriculture 17%, and waste 3%. On per capita basis, Indian emissions are below the G20 world average. Still, India has been taking various mitigating steps to reduce GHG emissions. India adopted Integrated Energy Policy, 2006 under which the following provisions are applicable:

i) Speedy development of nuclear and hydro power to generate clean energy

ii) Promoting energy efficiency in all sectors

iii) Plantation of biofuels and attention towards generating energy from renewable resources

iv) Adopting mass transportation approach

v) Acquiring various technologies on clean energy

vi) Emphasis on Research and Development to strengthen combating against climate changes India has committed on international platform to reduce emission intensity of its GDP by 20 to 25% by 2020.

b) **National Clean Energy Fund (NCEF):** For encouraging and financing initiatives for clean energy and funding research in the field of clean energy, Indian government created this fund. In this a cess of Rs. 400/- is imposed on per tonne coal domestically produced or imported.

c) **State Action Plan on Climate Change (SAPCC):** In 2009, Indian government decentralised plans on climate change. States have drafted their plans according to their topography and extent of vulnerability. All possible adaptation and mitigation measures are being taken by states. 30 states have formulated their SAPCCs. Union Ministry of Environment and Forests has accessed a budget of Rs. 11 lakh crores to fund SAPCCs.

d) **Securing resilience in agriculture:** India has launched a project worth Rs. 65000/- crore to reduce greenhouse gases from agriculture during 2018-25.

e) **Curbing emissions from shipment:** In April 2018, India along with 196 other countries signed an agreement in London to reduce carbon dioxide emissions by 50% from shipping by 2050.

The Prime Minister's Council on Climate Change (PMCCC) has asserted to create awareness of stakeholders affected by changes in climate. Stakeholders include sections of population, government agencies, private sector players, scientists, industry, agriculture sector, and various communities. Draft of the council aims at the following:

i) A sustainable development strategy should be prepared to protect the most poor and vulnerable sections of society

ii) Economic growth should be achieved through ecological stability

iii) Inviting international cooperation in research and exchange of technology on climate change

iv) Developing suitable technology for effectively implementing adaptation and mitigation strategy

IWRM

Integrated Water Resources Management (IWRM) is a policy framework conceived for efficient use of scarce water resources and improve water usage efficiency. Global Water Partnership (GWP) has defined IWRM as, "a process which promotes the coordinated development and management of water, land and related resources, in order to maximise the resultant economic and social welfare in an equitable manner without compromising the sustainability of vital ecosystems." Basic concept of IWRM doctrine is that different uses of scarce water are interrelated and it must be used rationally in order to give sustainable development. IWRM principles were adopted and recommended in the International Conference on Water and the Environment at Dublin (Ireland) in 1992 [also called Dublin Principles] and under Agenda 21 in the World Summit on Sustainable Development at Rio de Janeiro (Brazil), in 1992. Fundamental principles aim at the following:

1) Social equity: Different sections of the population are surviving in the society and each individual from every section of the population should be provided equal access to scarce water resources. Marginalised section of the society comprises of poor people, women, children, and elderly who are most vulnerable to the changes in climate. IWRM aims to provide equal share of water resources to every user of water for sustainable human beings. This can be achieved by ensuring participation of users, planners, researchers, and scientists in making sound policies on allocation of water resources rationally and equally.

2) Economic efficiency: Financial and water resources are scarce, particularly in developing economies. IWRM aims to provide financial and water resources to all the users of resources in the society. As water resources help in developing major economic sectors like agriculture, industry, household, and services sector, water resources should be considered as an economic good and be allocated to all sectors, maintaining sustainability of the economy and planning growth leading to rise in GDP.

3) Ecological sustainability: Abrupt changes in climate are resulting into loss of habitat and biodiversity. IWRM aims to maintain ecological sustainability through adaptation measures to prevent any loss of habitat and biodiversity.

Some Vital Facts

1) Climate change has its implication for forest fires.
2) The most significant impact of volcanic eruption has been felt in the form of change in weather.

Practice Exercise

General Questions Format

1. Which of the following statement(s) is TRUE?
   a) Oceans absorb a huge amount of greenhouse gases and put constraint on global warming.
   b) Black water generated after melting of sea ice absorbs more sunlight resulting in rise in sea level.
   c) Smog, deforestation, and burning of fossil fuels are results of abnormal climate changes.
   d) Tolerable rise in oceanic temperature due to climate changes is below 1° celsius.

   (A) a and d (B) a, b, c, and d
   (C) b and d (D) b, c, and d

2. Which of the following is TRUE about climate change?
   a) Climate changes are the means of formulating adaptation and mitigation policies.
   b) Adverse effects of climate change lead to loss of resilience in socio-economic sectors.
   c) Emission of greenhouse gases are the primary indicator of climate changes.
   d) Loss of biodiversity due to climate change does not mean killing of biodiversity.

   (A) a, b, c, and d (B) a and c
   (C) a, c, and d (D) b and d

3. Aim of UNFCCC is to
   (A) make member countries share the idea of curtailing GHG emissions in various UN meetings
   (B) reduce GHG emissions resulting in abrupt climatic changes with catastrophic results
   (C) dictate the signatory countries to the agreement to adopt IPCC doctrine
   (D) None of these

4. How will switching over to renewable sources of energy from conventional sources of energy affect changes in climate?
   (A) Changes in climate will become predictable.
   (B) Climate changes will be less harmful.
   (C) Vulnerability to climate changes will be addressed in a more effective way.
   (D) There will be no change in climate.

5. The basic objectives of The United Nations Framework Convention on Climate Change (UNFCCC or FCCC) is:
   (A) To stabilise the melting ice of Antarctic Ocean
   (B) To stabilise greenhouse gas concentrations in the atmosphere at a level that would prevent dangerous anthropogenic interference with the climate system
   (C) Reduce the carbon emission up to the level of 1992
   (D) Stabilise the ozone layer depletion

6. Which of the following statements is/are correct about National Mission for a Green India or Green India Mission (GIM)?
   1. National Mission for a Green India is under the Prime Minister's Council on Climate Change.
   2. It is one of the eight Missions outlined under the National Action Plan on Climate Change (NAPCC).

   (A) Only 1 (B) Only 2
   (C) Both 1 and 2 (D) Neither 1 nor 2

7. Dublin Principles are related to
   (A) Integrated water management
   (B) Reduction of vulnerability to climate change
   (C) Reduction in GHG emissions
   (D) Research in the field of environment

8. Coping up with adverse effects of climate change is called
   (A) Resilience (B) Albedo
   (C) Sequestering (D) Exacerbating

9. What is TRUE about climate change?
   (A) Climate change can be reversed if proper adaptation measures have been taken.
   (B) Anthropogenic activities are making the poorest and marginalised sections of the population most vulnerable to climate changes.
   (C) Socio-economic and political dimensions are putting science of climatic change into the back seat.
   (D) None of these

10. Which of the following statements about the 'National Adaptation Fund for Climate Change' is NOT correct?

(A) The fund is meant to assist national and state level activities to meet the cost of adaptation measures.

(B) This scheme has been taken as a Central Sector Scheme.

(C) The Indian Council of Agricultural Research is the national level entity for the fund.

(D) The fund was created in 2014.

11. Which of the following is TRUE about carbon tax?

a) It is levied on producers of those products which are produced by using conventional sources of energy.

b) Agricultural, industrial, and household sectors fall under the jurisdiction of carbon tax.

c) Carbon tax is charged as compensation to health loss, crop damages, loss of biodiversity, and destruction of property.

d) Carbon tax has proved to be an effective tool in restricting unpredictability in climate change.

(A) a, c, and d (B) a, b, c, and d

(C) b and d (D) b, c, and d

12. Name of entity is given under Column I and nature of climatic change activity is given under Column II. Match the entity with its nature of activity.

Column I (Name of Entity)	Column II (Nature of Activity)
a) UNFCCC	i) Scientific knowledge of climate change
b) IPCC	ii) Awareness about impacts of climate change
c) NCEF	iii) Solution to problems of climate change
d) PMCCC	iv) Financing initiatives to address adversities

Codes:

	(a)	(b)	(c)	(d)
(A)	ii	iii	iv	i
(B)	iii	iv	i	ii
(C)	i	ii	iii	iv
(D)	iii	i	iv	ii

13. Which of the following is NOT TRUE about climate change? It

a) is alteration in global atmosphere.

b) results into global warming.

c) is attributed to human activities.

d) is measured in terms of atmospheric pressure.

(A) Only c (B) Only d

(C) a, c, and d (D) a, b, c, and d

14. Climate resilience is a part of the

(A) relief work carried on to manage destruction due to climate change

(B) prohibitions imposed on certain activities of people residing in vulnerable belts

(C) adaptation and mitigation measures adopted to combat destructive climate change

(D) subject to be discussed in various national and international summits on climate change

15. Which of the following is TRUE?

(A) What crop is to be cultivated depends by and large on climate suitable to that crop.

(B) IPCC plans adaptation and mitigation measures against climate change for member countries of UNO.

(C) Change in climate disturbs the normal water channel due to heavy precipitation and release of black water.

(D) Indian government decentralised plan on climate change in 2009.

16. Which climate change control agency has appealed the countries to protect climate?

(A) Prime Minister's Council on Climate Change (PMCCC)

(B) United Nations Development Action Framework (UNDAF)

(C) National Action Plan on Climate Change (NAPCC)

(D) The United Nations Framework Convention on Climate Change (UNFCCC)

17. Intergovernmental Panel on Climate Change (IPCC) states that, "Climate change is a case of the tragedy of commons". This implies that

(A) Common people are the most vulnerable to climate change, thus meeting tragic consequences.

(B) Vested interests are responsible for unnatural climate change, thus wasting scarce resources which could have been used for common interest and welfare.

(C) Climate change is the result of certain common phenomena set up by global warming leading to disasters like floods, tsunamis, hurricanes, and sea cyclones resulting in tragedies.

(D) Various common occupations like labour, porting, vending, and carpentry become the front line casualty of climate change and their occupations meet a tragic end.

18. Which of the following is NOT a provision(s) of draft on awareness of climate change prepared by the Prime Minister's Council on Climate Change (PMCCC)?

a) Allocating funds for mitigating effects of climate change, to the tune of 5% of the total outlay of disaster management, in each annual budget

b) Preparing a sustainable development strategy to protect most vulnerable sections of the society

c) Achieving economic growth through ecological stability

d) Inviting international cooperation in research and exchange of technology on climate change

e) Developing suitable technology for effectively implementing adaptation and mitigation strategies

(A) c and d only (B) a, c, d, and e

(C) a only (D) b, c, and e only.

19. Which of the following is NOT a socio-economic dimension of climate change?

(A) Housing

(B) Heritage

(C) Employment

(D) Education

20. National Mission on Strategic Knowledge for Climate Change has proposed for the creation of

(A) Climate Change Sensor System

(B) Climate Resilience Monitoring System

(C) Climate Science Research Fund

(D) Climate Science University

KEY

1. C	**2.** C	**3.** B	**4.** B	**5.** B	**6.** B	**7.** A
8. A	**9.** D	**10.** C	**11.** B	**12.** D	**13.** B	**14.** C
15. C	**16.** D	**17.** B	**18.** C	**19.** B	**20.** C	

Assertion–Reason Format

1. Assertion (A): Migration of rural workforce to urban areas is an indicator of climate change.

Reason (R): Climatic changes test the vulnerability of the poorest and marginalised population depending on natural resources for its livelihood.

(A) Both A and R are true and R is the correct explanation of A

(B) Both A and R are true but R is not correct explanation of A

(C) A is true but R is false

(D) A is false but R is true

2. Assertion (A): Scientific knowledge of climatic changes helps in drafting and implementing effective adaptation and mitigation policies by various governments.

Reason (R): IPCC provides scientific knowledge of climate and climatic changes to governments of UN member countries.

(A) Both A and R are true and R is the correct explanation of A

(B) Both A and R are true but R is not the correct explanation of A

(C) A is true but R is false

(D) Both A and R are false

3. Assertion (A): Different sections of the population should have equal access to scarce water resources.

Reason (R): IWRM is an initiative to work for ensuring rational and uniform distribution of scarce water resources.

(A) Both A and R are true and R is correct explanation of A

(B) Both A and R are true but R is not correct explanation of A

(C) A is true but R is false

(D) Both A and R are false

4. **Assertion (A):** Current climate changes are not natural, thus cause harm.

Reason (R): Climate changes used to be soothing a few years ago.

(A) Both A and R are true and R is the correct explanation of A

(B) Both A and R are correct but R is not correct explanation of A

(C) A is true but R is false

(D) A is false but R is true

5. **Assertion (A):** An effective action plan on climate change is needed to mitigate the adversaries of climate change.

Reason (R): The Central Government has decentralised the National Action Plan on Climate Change for better results through respective State Action Plans.

(A) Both A and R are true and R is correct explanation of A

(B) A is true but R is false

(C) Both A and R are true but R is not correct explanation of A

(D) A is false but R is true

6. **Assertion (A):** Oceans can absorb any amount of carbon dioxide released in the atmosphere.

Reason (R): Ocean water becomes acidic due to absorption of carbon dioxide.

(A) Both A and R are true and R is the correct explanation of A

(B) A is false but R is true

(C) Both A and R are true but R is not correct explanation of A

(D) Both A and R are false

7. **Assertion (A):** Climate change and education are related in the same way as builder and destroyer are related.

Reason (R): Climate change of any magnitude does not hamper imparting of education.

(A) Both A and R are true and R is the correct explanation of A

(B) Both A and R are true but R is not correct explanation of A

(C) Both A and R are false

(D) A is true but R is false

8. **Assertion (A):** Curbing emissions is a fundamental initiative to prevent undesirable changes in climate.

Reason (R): Disastrous climate changes in developing countries are due to higher rate of emissions in comparison to developed countries.

(A) A is true but R is false

(B) A is false but R is true

(C) Both A and R are true and R is correct explanation of A

(D) Both A and R are true but R is not correct explanation of A

9. **Assertion (A):** Every anthropogenic activity is not necessarily a cause of climate change.

Reason (R): A short-lived climate change is not harmful.

(A) Both A and R are true and R is correct explanation of A

(B) Both A and R are true but R is not correct explanation of A

(C) A is true but R is false

(D) Both A and R are false

10. **Assertion (A):**Persistent and prolonged exposure to climate changes results in ill-health.

Reason (R): Marginalised population needs dwellings as a shelter to protect it from environmental diseases.

(A) A is true but R is false

(B) A is false but R is true

(C) Both A and R are correct but R is not correct explanation of A

(D) Both A and R are correct and R is correct explanation of A

KEY

1. D **2.** A **3.** A **4.** C **5.** A **6.** B **7.** C
8. A **9.** D **10.** D

Questions Asked in Previous NET Exams

1. As part of National Climate Change Policy, Indian government is planning to raise the installed capacity of renewable energy by the year 2030 to **(UGC NET DECEMBER 2015)**
   (A) 175 GW
   (B) 200 GW
   (C) 250 GW
   (D) 350 GW
2. In order to avoid catastrophic consequences of climate change, there is general agreement among the countries of the world to limit the rise in average surface temperature of earth compared to that of pre-industrial times by **(UGC NET JUNE 2014)**
   (A) 1.5°C to 2°C
   (B) 2.0°C to 3.5°C
   (C) 0.5°C to 1.0°C
   (D) 0.25°C to 0.5°C
3. By the year 2022, the Climate Change Action Plan of Government of India aims at installing **(UGC NET SEPTEMBER 2013)**
   (A) 20,000 MW of wind power
   (B) 25,000 MW of wind power
   (C) 20,000 MW of solar power
   (D) 10,000 MW of solar power
4. The phrase "tragedy of commons" is in the context of **(UGC NET JUNE 2013)**
   (A) tragic event related to damage caused by release of poisonous gases
   (B) tragic conditions of poor people
   (C) degradation of renewable free access resources
   (D) climate change
5. Climate change has implications for **(UGC NET JUNE 2010)**
   1. soil moisture 2. forest fires
   3. biodiversity 4. ground water

   Identify the correct combination according to the code:

   Codes:
   (A) 1 and 3 (B) 1, 2, and 3
   (C) 1, 3, and 4 (D) 1, 2, 3, and 4
6. The most significant impact of volcanic eruption has been felt in the form of: **(UGC NET DECEMBER 2006)**
   (A) change in weather
   (B) sinking of islands
   (C) loss of vegetation
   (D) extinction of animals

KEY

1. A **2.** A **3.** C **4.** C **5.** B **6.** A

6 Pollutants and Their Impact

WHAT ARE POLLUTANTS?

Pollutants are solid, liquid, or gaseous particles which are present in air or water in a quantity greater than natural abundance. Excessive presence of pollutants leaves a harmful impact on the environment. Pollutants present in air (outdoors and indoors) are inhaled by people while breathing. Even a minute particulate inhaled with air, can leave a fatal impact on human beings and animals. Pollutants present in water spread out all over and these are carried away with the flow of water and reach seas and oceans. Pollutants, whether present in air or water, harmfully affect human, animal, and plant health. In addition, pollutants are effective in attacking luster of historical marble statues and other structures. Pollutants are also responsible for damaging the paints of buildings and vehicles. Different types of pollutants in the air (outdoors and indoors) and water with their harmful impacts are mentioned below:

Air Pollutants Of Outdoor Pollution and Their Impact

As per environmental standards, following are the various types of pollutants:

1) **Degradable or non-persistent pollutants:** These can be rapidly broken down by natural processes. Eg: domestic sewage, discarded vegetables, etc.
2) **Slowly degradable or persistent pollutants:** Pollutants that remain in the environment for many years in an unchanged condition and take decades or longer to degrade. E.g., DDT and most plastics.
3) **Non-degradable pollutants:** These cannot be degraded by natural processes. Once they are released into the environment, they are difficult to eradicate and continue to accumulate. E.g., toxic elements like lead or mercury.

TYPES OF POLLUTANTS

Air pollutants are found in two types:

1) Primary Pollutants
2) Secondary Pollutants

Primary Pollutants

Primary pollutants are emitted directly from identifiable sources either naturally (dust storms, volcanic eruptions, etc.) or man-made sources (emissions from vehicles and industries). These pollutants account for 90% of global air pollution. The following types of primary pollutants are present:

a) **Carbon monoxide:** Carbon monoxide (CO) is an odourless, colourless gas which forms when the carbon in fuels doesn't completely burn. It is usually generated by motor vehicles and industry but can also be formed during bushfires. Indoors, carbon monoxide is formed by unflued (without chimney) gas heaters, wood-burning heaters, and are contained in cigarette smoke. The largest anthropogenic source of carbon monoxide is emissions from automobiles, boats, ships, and aeroplanes. Carbon monoxide levels are typically highest during cold weather, because cold temperatures make combustion less complete and traps pollutants close to the ground.

   Impact on human health: Continuous exposure to CO leads to chest pain, impaired vision, and dizziness. Cigarette smoking is responsible for the greatest exposure to carbon monoxide. Exposure to air containing even 0.001 percent of carbon monoxide for several hours can cause collapse, coma, and even death. As carbon monoxide remains attached to hemoglobin in blood for a long time, it accumulates and reduces the oxygen-carrying capacity of blood. This impairs perception and thinking, slows reflexes, and causes headaches, drowsiness, dizziness, and nausea. Carbon monoxide in heavy traffic causes headaches, drowsiness, and blurred vision.

b) **Carbon dioxide:** Carbon dioxide (CO_2) is an odorless and colorless gas. Atmospheric carbon dioxide derives from multiple natural sources including volcanic outgassing, the combustion of organic matter, and the respiration processes of living aerobic organisms; man-made sources of carbon dioxide come mainly from the burning of various fossil fuels for power generation and transport use.

Impact on human health: Carbon dioxide emissions impact human health by displacing oxygen in the atmosphere. Breathing becomes more difficult as carbon dioxide levels rise. In closed areas, high levels of carbon dioxide can lead to health complaints such as headaches. Continuous exposure to carbon dioxide leads to weakening of the defence mechanism of body and depression of central nervous system which can be fatal.

c) **Nitrogen dioxide:** Nitrogen dioxide is a highly reactive gas formed by emissions from motor vehicles, industry, unflued gas heaters, and gas stove tops. High concentrations can be found especially near busy roads and indoors where unflued gas heaters are in use. Other indoor sources can be from cigarette smoke or from cooking with gas. Outdoors, nitrogen dioxide contributes to the formation of ground-level ozone (O_3) as well as particulate matter pollution.

Impact on human health: Nitrogen dioxide is a highly respiratory irritant gas. Nitrogen oxides can irritate the lungs, aggravate asthma or chronic bronchitis, and also increase susceptibility to respiratory infections such as asthma, influenza, or common colds. Its exposure also increases frequency of asthma attacks.

d) **Sulphur dioxide:** It is a highly reactive gas with a pungent and irritating smell. It is produced by burning of fossil fuels in power plants and in other industrial activities, petroleum extraction and refining; paper manufacturing; municipal incinerating; and ore smelting for metal extraction. Natural process like decomposition and combustion of organic matter and volcanic eruptions also produce sulphur dioxide. It is one of the pollutants depleting the environment and leaving harmful impacts on the human body.

Impact on human health: Sulphur dioxide irritates nose, throat, and lungs. It worsens any existing respiratory disease like asthma. It can cause bronchitis and cardiovascular diseases.

e) **Hydrogen fluoride:** Hydrogen fluoride is a colourless gas, which has a sharp, pungent smell. It is highly toxic and irritating, but non-flammable. It is released from both anthropogenic activities and natural phenomenons. It is released naturally from volcanic eruptions but its quantity is too small to have any adverse impact. On the other hand, major quantity is releases from various anthropogenic activities like emissions from high temperature industrial process, thermal power plants, combustion of products containing fluorine compounds like plastics and rubber, fire extinguishing agents, aerosol propellants, and other chemicals.

AEROSOL PROPELLANTS

Aerosol propellants are gases (usually carbon dioxide or nitrous oxide) which are compressed with other substances in a steel or aluminum can. These gases and substances release through a valve of the can when pressure is released by pushing the nozzle. These propellants and substance contained in the container are released in the form of spray. Examples: room sprays, body sprays, detergent sprays, foam sprays, etc.

Impact on human health: Hydrogen fluoride enters the human body either by inhalation of air containing hydrogen fluoride or by dermal contact with hydrofluoric acid (dissolved form of hydrogen fluoride). Dermal contact with hydrofluoric acid occurs mainly in the occupational setting. Inhalation of air containing hydrogen fluoride can cause irritation of the eyes, nose, and throat. Exposure to high levels may cause muscle spasms and can damage the lungs and heart and in extreme cases, can result in death.

f) **Volatile Organic Compounds (VOCs):** These compounds contain carbon-containing gases and vapours but excluding carbon dioxide, carbon monoxide, and chlorofluorocarbons. VOCs are released from burning fuel such as gasoline, wood, coal, or natural gas. They are also released from many consumer products like paints and thinners, cigarettes, cleaners and disinfectants, air fresheners, building material and furnishings, printers, photostat machines, pesticides, moth repellents, dry cleaning fluids, adhesives, glues, etc.

Impact on human health: Whether used or kept unused, released VOCs leave harmful impacts on human health. Exposure to VOCs through air or dermal contact, results in irritation of eyes and respiratory attack, headache, dizziness (feeling faint or weak), visual disorders, memory problems, damage to kidney and liver system, cancer, skin allergy, dyspnoea (difficulty in breathing), fatigue, emesis (vomiting), nausea, etc.

g) **Methane:** Methane is a colourless gas. At low concentrations it is odourless, but it has a sweet smell at high concentrations. At mixtures more than about 5-15% in air, it becomes explosive. It has a lifetime of around ten years because it is only very gradually destroyed by other chemicals in air. Methane is one of the components of volatile organic compounds (VOCs). It is produced both naturally and from man's activities.

Source: One of the main sources of methane into the environment is from the natural decomposition of plant and animal matter in airless conditions. This occurs in marshes, rice paddies, pounds, open grounds, and filthy water channels. The biggest man-made source of methane is from waste dumped in landfills. Methane is also released during the mining and distribution of fossil fuels (coal, oil, and gas).

Impact on human health: At normal environmental concentrations, methane has no impacts on human health. At extremely high (artificial) concentrations in an enclosed space, the reduction in oxygen levels could lead to suffocation as it displaces oxygen in air. It can also result in rapid heartbeat, clumsiness, emotional imbalance, and fatigue.

h) **Ammonia:** Ammonia is a common naturally occurring substance. It is also manufactured by man. At normal environmental conditions, pure ammonia is a colourless, pungent-smelling, caustic (corrosive) gas. It is stored under high pressure as a liquid. It is highly soluble in water and reacts with acids to form ammonium salts.

Source: The major source of ammonia is natural, i.e., from decaying organic matter and from the excreta of humans and animals. Man-made sources such as from the use of fertilisers and waste disposal sites or industrial processes, are smaller.

Impact on human health: Exposure to ammonia either through air or dermal contact at environmental concentrations does not have adverse effects on health. However, exposure to high concentrations following an accidental release or in occupational settings could cause irritation of the eyes, nose, and throat as well as burning of the skin where there is direct contact.

i) **Particulate Matter (PM):** Particulate matter consists of extremely small solid particles and liquid droplets suspended in air. These vary in size and shape and are usually classified according to size categories: typically less than or equal to 10 micron, PM_{10}; and less than or equal to 2.5 micron, $PM_{2.5}$ (1 micron = 1 millionth of a meter).

$PM_{2.5}$ AND PM_{10}

Above concepts have been widely explained in Chapter 4 of this Unit.

Composition: A variety of components including soot, nitrates, sulphates, organic chemicals, inorganic salts, metals, soil or dust particles, and allergens (such as fragments of pollen or mould spores), silica, asbestos, liquid sprays, mist, etc.

Source: Particulate matter comes from combustion processes, including vehicle exhaust, from waste incineration, building constructions, mining, thermal power stations, stone crushing, quarrying processes, and from other industrial processes. Some particulates are released naturally from forest fires, volcanoes, and from dust storms.

Impact on human health: Particulate matter affect human health differently due to its being different in size. PM_{10} particles are minute enough to enter nose and throat and reach lungs and create respiratory diseases. On the other hand, $PM_{2.5}$ are so minute that they reach the blood stream once these enter the human body. Once PM enters the human body, it can cause irritation of eyes, nose, and throat, aggravating existing diseases like asthma and other lung diseases, heart attacks, and arrhythmias (irregular heart beat) in people with heart disease.

j) **Lead:** Pure lead is a bluish-white metal. It is very dense, soft, highly malleable (bendable), ductile (can be drawn into wires), but does not conduct electricity or heat very well. Although lead is resistant to corrosion, it dissolves slowly in water.

Source: Anthropogenic activities like metal production and processing and emissions from thermal power plants can release lead. Lead used to be released in a large amount from vehicular exhausts when vehicles were fuelled with leaded fuel. Now this source is no more effective as vehicles are now getting unleaded fuel. Now domestic sector is also no more a source of lead as lead pipes have been replaced by PVC pipes and various chemicals like paints, etc. used in homes are also lead-free. Small amounts are released naturally from the earth's crust, from volcanoes, and from forest fires.

Impact on human health: Lead is a cumulative poison which affects the central nervous system. Routine exposure to lead from old lead pipes, dust from industries using lead, and working in factories using lead proves to be a strong health hazard. It increases the risk of premature birth, reduces birth weight, induces learning difficulties, inhibits growth, damages the kidneys, causes weakness in the joints, affects the memory, damages the male reproductive system, causes abortions, and is a potentially carcinogenic (cancer-bearing matter).

k) **Mercury:** Mercury is a silvery-white metal which is a liquid at room temperatures. Mercury vapours are readily released from the liquid. It is odourless and non-flammable.

Source: The main sources of mercury in air and water are from waste incineration, chlorine manufacture, in mercury cells, metal production, coal combustion, from dental surgeries and crematoria, from hospitals and clinics, and from industrial processes using mercury. Small amounts are released naturally from the earth's crust.

Impact on human health: Mercury is toxic to humans. It damages the nervous system, lungs, and kidneys. Exposure usually occurs through consumption of contaminated fish or grain, but can also occur through inhalation of mercury vapours, particularly at workplaces where mercury is used. Extreme exposure due to an accidental release or at workplaces can cause death. Some types of mercury compounds are more toxic than others: for example, methyl mercury rapidly accumulates in the brain. Exposure to both organic and inorganic forms may also be carcinogenic.

MINAMATA DISASTER

It is what happened more than 64 years ago when the most horrific mercury poisoning disaster the world has ever seen took place in Minamata, Japan.

In May 1956, four patients from the city of Minamata on the west coast of the southern Japanese island of Kyushu were admitted to hospital with the same severe and baffling symptoms. They suffered from very high fever, convulsions, psychosis, loss of consciousness, coma, and finally death. As time went on, more and more people became sick and many died. Doctors were puzzled by the strange symptoms and terribly alarmed. It was finally determined that the cause was mercury poisoning.

Mercury was in the waste product dumped into Minamata Bay on a massive scale by a chemical plant. The mercury contaminated the fish living in Minamata Bay. People ate the fish, were themselves contaminated, and became ill. Local bird life as well as domestic animals also perished. In all, 900 people died and 2,265 people were certified as having directly suffered from mercury poisoning-now known as Minamata disease.

l) **Chlorofluorocarbons (CFCs):** Chlorofluorocarbons (CFCs) are a group of compounds which contain the elements chlorine, fluorine, and carbon. At room temperatures, they are usually colourless gases or liquids which evaporate easily. They are generally unreactive and stable, non-toxic, and non-flammable. CFCs are also a part of the group of chemicals known as the volatile organic compounds (VOCs).

Source: Most CFCs have been released to the atmosphere through the use of aerosols containing them and as leakages from refrigeration equipment. Other releases may occur from industries producing and using them and other products containing them. There are not thought to be any natural sources of CFCs to the environment.

Impact on human health: Chlorofluorocarbons enter the body primarily by inhalation of air containing chlorofluorocabons, but can also enter by ingestion of contaminated water, or by dermal contact with chlorofluorocarbons. Inhalation of high levels of chlorofluorocarbons can affect the lungs, central nervous system, heart, liver, and kidneys. Symptoms of exposure to chlorofluorocarbons can include drowsiness, slurred speech, disorientation, tingling sensations, and weakness in the limbs. Exposure to extremely high levels of chlorofluorocarbons can result in death. Ingestion of chlorofluorocarbons can lead to nausea, irritation of the digestive tract, and diarrhoea. Dermal contact with chlorofluorocarbons can cause skin irritation and dermatitis. Chlorofluorocarbons are involved in the destruction of the stratospheric ozone layer resulting in increased exposure to UV radiation which is known to cause skin cancer.

Secondary Pollutants

Secondary pollutants are not emitted directly to atmosphere, as these are produced in the atmosphere when chemical reactions take place among primary pollutants. Different secondary pollutants are given as under:

a) **Ground level ozone:** Naturally occurring ozone exists in the upper atmosphere of the earth and protects mankind and other organisms from harmful UV sunrays by filtering them. On the other hand, ground level ozone or surface ozone acting as a secondary pollutant leaves harmful impact on human beings and other organisms. It is also a component of smog.

Source: Ground level ozone is formed by chemical reactions between oxides of nitrogen (NOx) and volatile organic compounds (VOC). This happens when primary pollutants emitted by cars, power plants, industrial boilers, refineries, chemical plants, and other sources chemically react in atmosphere in the presence of sunlight.

Impact on human health: Ground level ozone is a toxic and irritating gas. It causes irritation in eyes, nose, and throat. It also causes chronic bronchitis. It impairs functioning of the liver and causes an uneasy feeling in chest and airway inflammation.

b) **Acid rain:** Primary pollutants such as oxides of sulphur, nitrogen, and carbon react with water vapours in the atmosphere and produce nitric acid, sulphuric acid, and carbonic acid. Then water vapours become acidic and become heavier, and fall down in the form of precipitation-snow, dew, or rain.

Impact on human health: Acids in the precipitation are corrosive in nature. They cause irritation of eyes and skin through dermal contact. It can also cause irritation in the lungs and can damage them.

c) **Peroxyacyl nitrates or PANs:** PANs are created in the atmosphere when VOCs react with nitrogen oxide.

Impact on human health: PANs have many adverse effects in the human body such as reduced respiratory function and eye irritation, and may also causing impaired breathing and other lung problems. Human exposure to PANs occurs in urban areas where automobile and industrial emissions are high.

Cumulative Impact of Air Pollutants on Animals, Plants, Objects, and Environment

1) **Animals:** Pollutants like hydrogen fluoride is ingested by wild animals or cattle. They develop a disease 'Fluorosis' in which teeth and bones are affected. Exposure to certain pollutants like methane and carbon monoxide causes irritation in eyes, nose, throat, and lungs leading to suffocation and death.

2) **Plants:** Air pollutants like oxides of nitrogen become dangerous for plants. High levels of nitrogen oxides damage plant life. Acid rain damages vegetation. Leaves of crop plants are damaged when gaseous pollutants enter pores of plants. Chronic exposure of the leaves to air pollutants can break down the waxy coating that helps prevent excessive water loss and leads to damage from diseases, pests, drought, and frost. Such exposure interferes with photosynthesis and plant growth, reduces nutrient uptake, and causes leaves to turn yellow, brown, or drop off altogether. At a higher concentration of sulphur dioxide, majority of the flower buds become stiff and hard. They eventually fall from the plants, as they are unable to flower. Acid deposition can damage tree foliage directly.

3) **Objects:** Acid rain created by air pollutants like oxides of nitrogen, sulphur, and carbon has corrosive nature, and thus destroys colour of buildings. It also destroys the luster of marble statues and buildings. Further, acid rain spoils the paint of vehicles.

4) **Environment:** Pollutants like nitrogen dioxide is involved in the formation of ground level ozone. Atmospheric changes induced by pollution contribute to global warming, a phenomenon which is caused due to the increase in concentration of certain gases like carbon dioxide, nitrogen oxides, and methane. Observations of the earth have shown beyond doubt that atmospheric constituents such as water vapor, carbon dioxide, methane, nitrogen oxides and chloroflurocarbons (CFCs) trap heat in the form of infrared radiation near the earth's surface. This is known as the **'Greenhouse Effect'**. Pollutants like CFCs have serious environmental consequences. Their long lifetimes in the atmosphere mean that some end up in the higher atmosphere (stratosphere) where they can destroy the ozone layer, thus reducing the protection it offers the earth from the sun's harmful UV rays. CFCs also contribute to Global Warming (through "the Greenhouse Effect").

Greenhouse Gases: *Water vapor, carbon dioxide, ground level ozone, methane, nitrogen oxides, and chloroflurocarbons (CFCs).*

Greenhouse Effect: *Greenhouse gases trap heat in the form of infrared radiation near the earth's surface. This is known as the 'Greenhouse Effect'. The phenomenon is similar to what happens in a greenhouse. The glass in the greenhouse allows solar radiation to enter which the objects inside absorb. These objects radiate heat in the form of terrestrial radiation, which does not pass out through the glass. The heat is therefore trapped in the greenhouse increasing the temperature inside and ensuring the luxuriant growth of plants.*

Global Warming: *It is a gradual increase in the overall temperature of the earth's atmosphere generally attributed to the greenhouse effect caused by increased levels of carbon dioxide, CFCs, and other greenhouse gases by trapping the sun's heat in the atmosphere. Due to excess rise in temperature of the earth, global warming is becoming global warning.*

POLLUTANTS OF INDOOR AIR POLLUTION

Indoor air pollution is the degradation of indoor air quality by harmful chemicals and other materials; it can be up to 10 times worse than outdoor air pollution. This is because contained areas enable potential pollutants to build up more than open spaces. Some common air pollutants and their impact on health are given as under:

1) **Excess moisture:** Excess moisture creates dampness in the house or building. It damages wall paint and furniture and encourages growth of termite and fungi. It destroys woodwork and accelerates rusting of metallic installations It is a health hazard also. It results in depression, respiratory diseases, and allergies.
2) **Radon:** It is highly radioactive gas. It is generated in soil and enters houses through the ground. It results in cancer.
3) **Combustion products:** Gas-fired appliances, including furnaces, water heaters, cooking ranges, and some dryers, produce carbon dioxide, carbon monoxide, nitrous oxides, and water vapor. If the appliance is not vented properly to the outside, they leave a harmful impact on the human health. (Impacts have already been explained earlier in this chapter)
4) **Volatile Organic Compounds (VOCs):** Furniture, carpets, curtains which yield smell, smell of cooking oil, hair oil, plastic objects in the form of kitchenware and bathroom ware, medicines, smell of cooking processes, and all types of sprays in the house yield VOCs which also leave harmful impacts on the human health.

CONTROLLING AIR POLLUTANTS IN INDIA

Government of India has been taking steps to contain air pollutants as explained below:

1) The Air (Prevention and Control of Pollution) Act, 1981 act was passed to control air pollution.
2) In 2015, Government of India, together with IIT Kanpur la unched the National Air Quality Index.
3) In 2019, India launched 'The National Clean Air Programme' (NCAP) with tentative national target of 20%-30% reduction in $PM_{2.5}$ and PM_{10} concentrations by 2024, considering 2017 as the base year for comparison.
4) The Central Pollution Control Board (CPCB) monitors four air pollutants, namely sulphur dioxide (SO2), oxides of nitrogen (NOx), suspended particulate matter (SPM), and respirable particulate matter (PM_{10}). These are target air pollutants for regular monitoring at 308 operating stations in 115 cities/towns in 25 states and 4 Union Territories of India. The monitoring of these pollutants is carried out for 24 hours.
5) Decreasing trends have been found in sulphur dioxide and nitrogen dioxide in Delhi, Bhopal, and Prayagraj.

National Air Quality Index

National Air Quality Index (AQI) was launched on 17 October 2014 to disseminate information on air quality in an easily understandable form for the general public. The measurement of air quality is based on eight pollutants, namely, Particulate Matter (PM10), Particulate Matter (PM2.5), Nitrogen Dioxide (NO2), Sulphur Dioxide (SO2), Carbon Monoxide (CO), Ozone (O3), Ammonia (NH3), and Lead (Pb). National Air Quality Index (AQI) transforms complex air quality data of eight pollutants into a single number (index value), nomenclature, and colour in the following manner:

Index Value	***Status***	***Colour***
(0-50)	*Good*	*Sea Green*
(51-100)	*Satisfactory*	*Dark Green*
(101-200)	*Moderately Polluted*	*Dark Pink (Mauve)*
(201-300)	*Poor*	*Yellow*
(301-400)	*Very Poor*	*Bright Red*
(401-500)	*Severe*	*Maroon*

WATER POLLUTANTS

Impact of Water Pollutants

Impact on human health:

Various water pollutants have different harmful impact on human health. Different chemicals have different effects depending on their locations and kinds.

1) Bacterial, viral, and parasitic diseases like typhoid, cholera, encephalitis, poliomyelitis, hepatitis, skin infection, and gastrointestinal diseases spread through polluted water.
2) Nitrogenous chemicals are responsible for cancer and blue baby syndrome.
3) Lead-contaminated water damages central nervous system when such contaminated water is used.
4) Acid rain when it falls on humans can cause irritation in eyes, nose, and throat. It also results in skin allergies.

Impact on animals:

1) Water pollutants become harmful to the fish and animals that need the water to survive.
2) Organic pollutants deplete oxygen of water which results in death of fish and other aquatic animals.

3) Acid rain causes irritation in eyes, nose, and throat of animals on which drops of acid rain falls.
4) Wild and stray animals have to drink water from water bodies as they are surviving on water. While drinking contaminated water from these water bodies, they fall ill and even die.

Impact on plants:

1) Particulates suspended in water obstruct the sunlight entering water. This hampers the photosynthesis process and aquatic plants cannot grow and meet premature death.
2) Acid rain falling on plants damages the plant structure. Acid rain being corrosive destroys the leaves and flowers.
3) Excess use of fertilizers and pesticides in water for irrigation reduces the soil productivity which results in reduction in crop yield.

Impact on objects:

Acid rain destroys paints of vehicles, luster of marble statues, and structures.

TYPES OF WATER POLLUTANTS

There are two types of water which are attacked by respective pollutants as given below:

1) Pollutants of Surface Water
2) Pollutants of Ground Water

Pollutants of Surface Water and Their Impact

Following types of water pollutants are discussed below:

a) **Disease causing agents:** These are pathogens which include bacteria, viruses, protozoa, and parasitic worms that enter water from domestic sewage and untreated human and animal wastes.
b) **Organic pollutants or oxygen-depleting wastes:** These are pollutants which originate from domestic sewage (raw or treated), urban run-off, industrial (trade) effluents, and farm wastes. Sewage effluents are the primary and greatest source of organic materials discharged to freshwaters. Large populations of bacteria use up the oxygen present in water to degrade these wastes. In the process this degrades water quality. If too much organic matter is added to the water, all the available oxygen is used up. This causes fish and other forms of oxygen-dependent aquatic life to die.
c) **Inorganic plant nutrients:** These are water-soluble nitrates and phosphates that cause excessive growth of algae and other aquatic plants. They may interfere with the use of the water by clogging water intake pipes, changing the taste and odour of water, and cause a build-up of organic matter. As the organic matter decays, oxygen levels decrease and fish and other aquatic species die.
d) **Water-soluble inorganic chemicals:** These are acids, salts, and compounds of toxic metals such as mercury and lead. High levels of these chemicals can make the water unfit to drink, harm fish and other aquatic life, reduce crop yields, and accelerate corrosion of equipment where this water is used.
e) **Sediment of suspended matter** is another class of water pollutants. These are insoluble particles of soil and other solids that become suspended in water. This occurs when soil is eroded from the land. High levels of soil particles suspended in water interferes with the penetration of sunlight. This reduces the photosynthetic activity of aquatic plants and algae disrupting the ecological balance of the aquatic bodies.
f) **Acid Rain:** It is another pollutant of rain water. It contains various acids which are toxic and corrosive in nature. When acid rain falls on any organism, it leaves harmful impacts.

Pollutants of Groundwater

Groundwater pollutants reach the groundwater through aquifers and contaminate the water. Presently, maximum consumers in rural and urban areas are depending on groundwater. It is a matter of concern if pollutants have access to groundwater. Following pollutants pollute the groundwater:

1) **Sewage and Industrial waste storage above or near aquifer:** Toxic elements of urban run-off, sewage, and industrial waste-carrying chemical and metallic pollutants reach the groundwater through the aquifer nearby and reach groundwater and pollute it.
2) **Lack of sanitary landfills:** Landfills are places on land where domestic and commercial waste is buried to be disposed of later. Ordinary landfills pose a great threat of groundwater pollution as waste particles go down through bottom of landfills and pollute groundwater. Only sanitary landfills can save groundwater from getting polluted.
3) **Excessive fertilizers and pesticides:** Excessive fertilizer and pesticides used in agricultural operations go down through soil and contaminate groundwater.
4) **Oil and gasoline:** Due to leakage of underground oil and gasoline storage tanks, these pollutants go down and pollute the groundwater. Oil spilled on ground due to accidents of tankers also reaches groundwater through aquifers.

5) **Mining wastes:** Mining wastes containing dust, metallic particles, and other wastes also reach groundwater through aquifers and pollutes groundwater.

SANITARY LANDFILL

A sanitary landfill is a pit with a protected bottom where trash is buried in layers and compressed to make it more solid. The main purpose of a sanitary landfill is to ensure waste is safe by reducing the harm from accumulated waste and allowing safe decomposition. A sanitary landfill has a protected bottom which prevents groundwater pollution by not letting the pollutants go down to pollute groundwater.

Impact of Groundwater Pollutants on Human Health, Animals, and Plants

Groundwater pollutants contaminate it. Any disease caused by the consumption of polluted groundwater is called arsenic poisoning. Arsenic poisoning causes fatal diseases like skin erosion, liver and spleen enlargement, cirrhosis of the liver, diabetes, goiter, and skin cancers. Maximum cases of arsenic poisoning are reported from West Bengal. Groundwater pollutants have the same effect on animals and plants as surface water pollutants, which has been discussed earlier in this chapter.

CONTROL ON WATER POLLUTANTS IN INDIA

Central Pollution Control Board of India is responsible to take measures to monitor and contain pollutants. Following measures have been taken in this direction:

1) **De**

1) **Pollutant Monitoring Stations:** CPCB in collaboration with concerned SPCBs/PCCs established a nationwide network of water quality monitoring comprising 1245 stations in 27 States and 6 Union Territories on rivers all over the country. The monitoring is done on a monthly or quarterly basis for surface water and half-yearly basis for groundwater. The monitoring network covers 250 Rivers, 78 Lakes, 6 Tanks, 26 Ponds, 8 Creeks, 19 Canals, 19 Drains, and 382 Wells. It has been found that organic pollutants dominate in creating pollution in water bodies. The grossly polluted rivers on specific stretches are Sabarmati, Godavari, Satluj, Yamuna, Cauvery, Ganga, Krishna, Tapi, Mahanadi, and Brahmani whereas relatively clean rivers are Mahi, Narmada, Brahmaputra, and Beas with respect to organic and bacterial pollution.

2) **Global Environment Monitoring System (GEMS):** GEMS was started in 1978 under which Water Programme was launched to clean rivers from pollutants.

3) **National Programme of Monitoring of Indian National Aquatic Resources System (MINARS):** The programme was started in 1984 to monitor water quality of water of water bodies. Network of 870 monitoring stations have been accomplished under this programme.

4) **Three-tier Monitoring Programme:** To obtain satisfactory results in getting rid of water pollutants, presently, the inland water quality monitoring network is operated under a three-tier programme, i.e., GEMS, Monitoring of Indian National Aquatic Resources System (MINARS), and Yamuna Action Plan.

WATER POLLUTANTS UNDER CPCB SCANNER

Surface Water: *Pathogens, Eutrophication, Oxygen-depleting wastes*

Groundwater: *Fluoride, Nitrate, Arsenic, Nitrate*

Some Vital Facts

1) Untreated sewage is considered to be the biggest source of river pollution in India.
2) Chlorofluorocarbons are neither produced naturally nor by industrial activity.
3) Suspended fine particles are the major cause of respiratory diseases.
4) Road transport is the dominant source of pollution due to oxides of nitrogen in urban areas.
5) Surface ozone (being part of smog in urban areas) irritates eyes and respiratory tract of human beings.
6) Unvented gas stoves, wood stoves, and kerosene heaters are the sources of nitrogen oxide indoor pollution.
7) Transport is the main source of carbon monoxide in urban areas.
8) Agricultural activity contributes maximum to water pollution than any other activity.
9) Emissions from road transport contribute maximum in the formation of surface ozone.
10) The smog in cities in India mainly consists of oxides of nitrogen and unburnt hydrocarbons.
11) Sulphur dioxide affects the respiratory tract in human beings.
12) Maximum soot (black carbon) is released from thermal power plants.

Practice Exercise

General Questions Format

1. Which of the following is CORRECT?
   a) Non-persistent air pollutants are not harmful.
   b) Plastic is a pollutant which mixes with greenhouse gases in the atmosphere and is responsible for climate change.
   c) Air pollutants like lead and mercury cause major damage on human health as these remain persistent in the atmosphere for ever.
   d) Sewage is a non-degradable pollutant which releases a toxic gas radon which cause heart related ailments which are usually fatal.

   (A) c only (B) b and c only
   (C) a, b, c, and d (D) all are incorrect
2. A matter does not become pollutant until it
   (A) remains suspended in atmosphere
   (B) is not degraded by natural process
   (C) is misused in anthropogenic activities
   (D) all of the above
3. Which of the following is NOT an impact of air pollutants?
   (A) Changes in climate
   (B) Respiratory diseases
   (C) Formation of stratospheric ozone
   (D) Destroying luster of objects
4. Which of the following is TRUE about chlorofluorocarbons (CFCs)?
   a) There is no known natural source of producing CFCs.
   b) CFCs are produced during burning of fossil fuels.
   c) CFCs are effective in destroying surface level ozone.
   d) CFCs serve as antidote to skin infections due to exposure of skin to harmful UV sun rays.

   (A) c and d only
   (B) a only
   (C) a, b, and d only
   (D) c only
5. Consider following statements:
   Statement P: Exposure to carbon monoxide causes incurable diseases like anemia.
   Statement Q: Carbon monoxide pollution accounts for 90% of global air pollution.
   (A) Both P and Q are correct
   (B) P is correct but Q is wrong
   (C) Q is correct but P is wrong
   (D) Both P and Q are wrong
6. Which of the following is/are TRUE ?
   a) Primary pollutants are more harmful than secondary pollutants.
   b) Secondary pollutants are more harmful than primary pollutants.
   c) Primary pollutants cease to exist at high temperature.
   d) Concentration of secondary pollutants is high in tropics.

   (A) a and c only (B) a, c, and d only
   (C) d only (D) a only
7. As per National Air Quality Index norms, 2014, quality index of a pollutant having sea green colour is assessed as
   (A) Poor (B) Good
   (C) Satisfactory (D) Severe
8. Which of the following pollutant is not assessed under National Air Quality Index norms?
   (A) Lead (B) Methane
   (C) Ammonia (D) Carbon monoxide
9. India has pledged to reduce $PM_{2.5}$ and PM_{10} by_______% by 2024.
   (A) 10–15 (B) 30–35
   (C) 20–30 (D) None of these
10. Radon is a primary pollutant causing________ pollution.
    (A) indoor air (B) outdoor air
    (C) surface water (D) groundwater
11. In which of the following cities concentration of sulphur dioxide and nitrogen dioxide has decreased as per CPCB report?
    (A) Indore (B) Jalandhar
    (C) Bhopal (D) None of these

12. Which of the following serve (s) as aerosol propellant?

(A) Carbon dioxide (B) Nitrous oxide

(C) Both of these (D) None of these

13. Which of the following pollutants does not have harmful impact on human health at normal environmental concentrations?

(A) Methane (B) Lead

(C) Carbon monoxide (D) Sulphuric acid

14. What is the most destructive harm caused by greenhouse gases?

(A) These react with water vapours to form acid rain which leave corrosive impact on human skin.

(B) There is depletion of ozone layer due to greenhouse gases, thus unable to protect mankind from dangerous UV sunrays.

(C) Anthropogenic activities release them in atmosphere and contribute in abrupt climate changes.

(D) Greenhouse gases trap heat of the sun at the surface leading to global warming which is instrumental in causing various natural hazards.

15. Names of air pollutants are given under Column I and their impacts on human health are given under Column II. Match the pollutant with its impact correctly and choose the correct answer choice among the codes given below:

Column I (Pollutant)	**Column II (Impact)**
a) Lead	i) Dyspnoea
b) Carbon monoxide	ii) Minamata disease
c) VOCs	iii) Attacking central nervous system
d) Mercury	iv) Sluggish reflexes

Codes:	(a)	(b)	(c)	(d)
(A)	ii	iv	i	iii
(B)	iii	iv	i	ii
(C)	iv	iii	ii	i
(D)	i	iv	iii	ii

16. Which of the following is TRUE about a pollutant? A pollutant

a) is a short-lived bacteria or virus which dies while depleting oxygen of water.

b) is hidden in all disposable objects like plastics and attacks when these objects are disposed of in the open.

c) is the result of those anthropogenic activities which have commercial interest.

d) is a major destroyer of renewable energy resources, thus hampering various natural processes in lithosphere, hydrosphere, atmosphere, and biosphere.

(A) c and d only (B) b only

(C) a, b, c, and d (D) None of the above

17. Concentration of pollutants in air and water is increasing day by day. It implies that

a) Race for economic gains is getting accelerated leading to more anthropogenic activities, thus adding to the stock of pollutants.

b) Various laws and regulations of controlling pollutants are not being implemented in letter and spirit.

c) There is hardly any voluntary initiative for containing concentration of pollutants from individuals either due to lack of awareness or motivation.

d) There is a slow process of switching over from non-renewable energy resources to renewable energy resources for producing electricity

(A) a, c, and d only (B) b and d only

(C) a, b, c, and d (D) c only

18. Which of the following is a secondary pollutant?

(A) Carbon dioxide (B) Surface ozone

(C) VOCs (D) Methane

19. A pollutant whether in air or water, when comes in contact with human beings, it

(A) attacks different systems in body

(B) changes their lifestyle

(C) makes them aware about the damage

(D) all of these

20. Maximum cases of arsenic poisoning from groundwater pollution are reported from

(A) West Bengal (B) Odisha

(C) Uttrakhand (D) Madhya Pradesh

KEY

1. A	2. D	3. C	4. A	5. D	6. D	7. B
8. B	9. C	10. A	11. C	12. C	13. A	14. D
15. B	16. D	17. D	18. B	19. D	20. A	

Assertion–Reason Format

1. **Assertion (A):** Air and water pollutants are harmful.

   Reason (R): Anthropogenic activities are a matter of concern today.

   (A) Both A and R are true and R is correct explanation of A

   (B) Both A and R are true but R is not correct explanation of A

   (C) A is true but R is false

   (D) A is false but R is true

2. **Assertion (A):** Indoor air pollutants are not easy to eradicate.

   Reason (R): Outdoor and indoor air pollutants are the same.

   (A) A is true but R is false

   (B) A is false but R is true

   (C) Both A and R are true and R is correct explanation of A

   (D) Both A and R are true but R is not correct explanation of A

3. **Assertion (A):** Government initiatives like GEMS and MINARS will help in reducing $PM_{2.5}$ and PM_{10}.

   Reason (R): Pollutants present in air or water in India are different from pollutants present in air and water of advanced countries.

   (A) Both A and R are true and R is correct explanation of A

   (B) Both A and R are true but R is not correct explanation of A

   (C) Both A and R are false

   (D) A is true but R is false

4. **Assertion (A):** Indian rivers are still polluted.

   Reason (R): Indian air is still polluted.

   (A) Both A and R are true and R is correct explanation of A

   (B) Both A and R are true but R is not correct explanation of A

   (C) A is true but R is false

   (D) A is false but R is true

5. **Assertion (A):** Pollutants of air and water affect human health differently.

   Reason (R): Airborne and waterborne diseases are on the increase.

   (A) Both A and R are false

   (B) Both A and R are true and R is correct explanation of A

   (C) A is true but R is false

   (D) Both a and R are true but R is not correct explanation of A

6. **Assertion (A):** Reduction in $PM_{2.5}$ and PM_{10} will resolve breathing problems of people.

   Reason (R): India has launched National Clean Air Programme targeting reduction in $PM_{2.5}$ and PM_{10} by 10–20% by 2030.

   (A) A is true but R is false

   (B) Both A and R are true and R is correct explanation of A

   (C) Both A and R are false

   (D) Both A and R are true but R is not correct explanation of A

7. **Assertion (A):** Urban area smog is the result of anthropogenic activities in villages surrounding a city.

   Reason (R): After getting affected by smog, people in urban areas have been raising voice against anthropogenic activities in surrounding villages.

   (A) Both A and R are true and R is correct explanation of A

   (B) A is true but R is false

   (C) Both A and R are false

   (D) A is false but R is true

8. **Assertion (A):** Pollutants polluting indoor air are fatally dangerous.

   Reason (R): Radon is a radioactive gas that forms in soil and enters the houses through the ground.

   (A) A is true but R is false

   (B) Both A and R are false

   (C) Both A and R are true but R is not correct explanation of A

   (D) Both A and R are true and R is correct explanation of A

9. **Assertion (A):** Aerosol propellants have become part of modern living style.

Reason (R): Compressed aerosols when released leave a refreshing impact.

(A) Both A and R are true and R is correct explanation of A

(B) A is true but R is wrong

(C) Both A and R are true but R is not correct explanation of A

(D) Both A and R are false

10. **Assertions (A):** Aquifers near sanitary landfills do not pose threat of groundwater pollution.

Reason (R): Arsenic poisoning is the result of groundwater pollution.

(A) A is false but R is true

(B) Both A and R are true but R is not correct explanation of A

(C) A is true but R is false

(D) Both A and R are true and R is correct explanation of A

KEY

1. A **2.** A **3.** C **4.** B **5.** B **6.** A **7.** C
8. D **9.** A **10.** A

Questions Asked in Previous NET Exams

1. Methane, greenhouse gas is emitted from

(a) landfills (b) construction debris

(c) wet lands (d) e-waste

Choose the correct statements from the options given below **(UGC NET JUNE 2019)**

(A) (a), (b) and (d) (B) (a), (c) and (d)

(C) (a) and (c) only (D) (a) and (d) only

2. Which is the major source of marine pollution? **(UGC NET JUNE 2019)**

(A) Agricultural run-off

(B) Oil spill

(C) Industrial waste water

(D) Sewage

3. Methane, greenhouse gas is emitted from

(a) landfills (b) constructiondebris

(c) wet lands (d) e-waste

Choose the correct statements from the options given below **(UGC NET DECEMBER 2019)**

(A) (a), (b) and (d) (B) (a), (c) and (d)

(C) (a) and (c) only (D) (a) and (d) only

4. **Assertion (A):** Indoor air pollution is serious hazard.

Reason (R): The dispersal of air pollutants is rather limited in indoor environment.

Choose the correct answer from the code given below: **(UGC NET JULY 2018)**

(A) Both A and R are true and R is the correct explanation of A

(B) Both A and R are true and R is not the correct explanation of A

(C) A is true and R is false

(D) Both A and R are false

5. Which of the following is considered as major source of pollution in rivers of India? **(UGC NET JULY 2018)**

(A) Unregulated small-scale industry

(B) Untreated sewage

(C) Agricultural run-off

(D) Thermal power plants

6. Which of the following pollutant gases is not produced both naturally and as a result of industrial activity? **(UGC NET NOVEMBER 2017)**

(A) Nitrous oxide

(B) Methane

(C) Carbon dioxide

(D) Chlorofluorocarbons

7. **Assertion (A):** In urban areas, smog episodes occur frequently in winters.

Reason (R): In winters, a lot of biomass is burnt by people for heating purposes or to keep themselves warm.

Choose the correct answer from the code given below: **(UGC NET NOVEMBER 2017)**

(A) Both A and R are true but R is not the correct explanation of A

(B) A is true and R is false

(C) Both A and R are false

(D) Both A and R)are true and R is the correct explanation of A

8. Which of the following pollutants is the major cause of respiratory disease? **(UGC NET NOVEMBER 2017)**

(A) Nitrogen oxides

(B) Carbon monoxide

(C) Volatile organic compounds

(D) Suspended fine particles

9. The dominant source of pollution due to oxides of nitrogen (NOx) in urban areas is

(UGC NET JANUARY 2017)

(A) Road transport
(B) Commercial sector
(C) Energy use in industry
(D) Power plants

10. The arsenic pollution in groundwater in Bangladesh and parts of India is due to

(UGC NET AUGUST 2016)

(A) Industrial waste
(B) Thermal power plants
(C) Natural sources
(D) Agricultural practices

11. Among the following air pollutants, which directly impacts human health as well as climate? **(UGC NET AUGUST 2016)**

(A) Soot
(B) Sulphur dioxide
(C) Oxides of nitrogen
(D) Chlorofluorocarbons

12. Which of the following is the largest source of water pollution in major rivers of India?

(UGC NET JULY2016)

(A) Untreated sewage
(B) Agriculture run-off
(C) Unregulated small-scale industries
(D) Religious practices

13. Identify the air pollutant in urban areas which irritates eyes and also respiratory tract of human beings. **(UGC NET JULY 2016)**

(A) Particulate matter
(B) Oxides of nitrogen
(C) Surface ozone
(D) Carbon monoxide

14. Inside rural homes, the source/sources of nitrogen oxide pollution may be:

(UGC NET DECEMBER 2015)

(a) Unvented gas stoves
(b) Wood stoves
(c) Kerosene heaters

Choose the correct code:

(A) (a) and (b) only (B) (b) and (c) only
(C) (b) only (D) (a), (b), and (c)

15. Which of the following pollutants can cause cancer in humans?

(UGC NET DECEMBER 2015)

(A) Pesticides (B) Mercury
(C) Lead (D) Ozone

16. In the recently launched Air Quality Index in India, which of the following pollutants is not included? **(UGC NET JUNE 2015)**

(A) Chlorofluorocarbons
(B) Carbon monoxide
(C) Fine particulate matter
(D) Ozone

17. Which of the following cities has been worst affected by urban smog in recent times ?

(UGC NET JUNE 2014)

(A) Paris (B) London
(C) Los Angeles (D) Beijing

18. The primary source of organic pollution in fresh water bodies is

(UGC NET EXAM JUNE 2014)

(A) run-off from urban areas
(B) run-off from agricultural farms
(C) sewage effluents
(D) industrial effluents

19. One of the anthropogenic sources of gaseous pollutants chlorofluorocarbons (CFCs) in air is **(UGC NET DECEMBER 2014)**

(A) Cement Industry
(B) Fertilizer industry
(C) Foam industry
(D) Pesticide industry

20. The major source of the pollutant gas, carbon monoxide (CO), in urban areas is

(UGC NET DECEMBER 2013)

(A) Thermal power sector
(B) Transport sector
(C) Industrial sector
(D) Domestic sector

21. Which activity contributes to water pollution more than any other throughout the world?

(UGC NET SEPTEMBER 2013)

(A) Agriculture
(B) Hydroelectric power generation
(C) Industry
(D) Urbanisation

22. Which of the following is a source of emissions leading to the eventual formation of surface ozone as a pollutant?

(UGC NET JUNE 2013)

(A) Transport sector

(B) Refrigeration and air-conditioning

(C) Wetlands

(D) Fertilizers

23. The smog in cities of India mainly consists of

(UGC NET JUNE 2013)

(A) Oxides of sulphur

(B) Oxides of nitrogen and unburnt hydrocarbons

(C) Carbon monoxide and SPM

(D) Oxides of sulphur and ozone

24. 'Minamata disaster' in Japan was caused by pollution due to

(UGC NET DECEMBER 2012)

(A) Lead (B) Mercury

(C) Cadmium (D) Zinc

25. Chromium as a contaminant in drinking water in excess of permissible levels, causes

(UGC NET JUNE 2012)

(A) Skeletal damage

(B) Gastrointestinal problem

(C) Dermal and nervous problems

(D) Liver/Kidney problems

26. Irritation in eyes is caused by the pollutant

(UGC NET JUNE 2012)

(A) Sulphur dioxide (B) Ozone

(C) PAN (D) Nitrous oxide

27. Which is the source of chlorofluorocarbons?

(UGC NET JUNE 2012)

(A) Thermal power plants

(B) Automobiles

(C) Refrigeration and air-conditioning

(D) Fertilizers

28. Which of the following pollutants affects the respiratory tract in humans?

(UGC NET DECEMBER 2011)

(A) Carbon monoxide (B) Nitric oxide

(C) Sulphur dioxide (D) Aerosols

29. In mega cities of India, the dominant source of air pollution is **(UGC NET JUNE 2011)**

(A) transport sector

(B) thermal power

(C) municipal waste

(D) commercial sector

30. The constituents of photochemical smog responsible for eye irritation are

(UGC NET DECEMBER 2010)

(A) SO_2 and O_3 (B) SO_2 and NO_2

(C) HCHO and PAN (D) SO_2 and SPM

31. Maximum soot is released from

(UGC NET DECEMBER 2009)

(A) Petrol vehicles

(B) CNG vehicles

(C) Diesel vehicles

(D) Thermal power plants

32. Surface ozone is produced from

(UGC NET DECEMBER 2009)

(A) Transport sector

(B) Cement plants

(C) Textile industry

(D) Chemical industry

33. The maximum emission of pollutants from fuel sources in India is caused by:

(UGC NET DECEMBER 2006)

(A) Coal

(B) Firewood

(C) Refuse burning

(D) Vegetable waste products

KEY

1. C	2. D	3. C	4. A	5. B	6. D	7. A
8. D	9. A	10. C	11. A	12. A	13. C	14. D
15. B	16. A	17. D	18. C	19. A	20. B	21. A
22. A	23. B	24. B	25. D	26. A	27. C	28. C
29. C	30. C	31. D	32. A	33. C		

7 Natural Energy Resources

SOURCES OF ENERGY: CONCEPT

Various sources of energy play a pivotal role in the development of a society. Whether it is an individual or the whole society, all need energy provided by different sources.

Importance of Energy

Energy is important for individuals and society for attaining a better quality of life and to achieve various social and economic goals. A progressive production of various consumer and producers' goods and services in the field of agriculture, industry, power supply, infrastructure, health, education, information and communication technology, nuclear discoveries, and space exploration, sustains on the continuous supply of energy from different sources.

SOURCES OF ENERGY

Mainly there are two major sources of energy:

1) Renewable
2) Non-renewable

Both sources can be studied in detail as follows:

Renewable Sources of Energy

Renewable sources of energy cover all natural sources which provide energy. Such resources are not harmful as they do not pollute the environment and these are not costly either. Renewable energy is harnessed mainly for electricity generation, providing energy to rural areas, heating of water, and transportation. Different renewable energy sources are discussed as follows:

1. **Solar Energy:** Solar energy is captured by using photoelectric panels or Solar Photovoltaic (SPV) cells to produce electricity for household sector and working sector or business sector. Sun is the biggest source among the renewable sources of energy. Solar energy helps to meet the day-to-day power needs. Direct solar energy is effective in human and plants' growth.

International Solar Alliance: *The Alliance was founded in November 2015 at Paris in consequence to India's proposal. Known as 'Paris Declaration', the alliance covers more than 122 countries which are situated on or near Tropic of Cancer and Tropic of Capricorn. By virtue of this, these countries receive maximum solar energy. Under this alliance, the member countries including India resolved to share power generation and technology used by harnessing solar energy, thus reducing cost of power generation, and increasing quality and quantity of energy for all.*

Indian Scenario:

India is harvesting solar energy for various power needs. In June 2018, India's solar energy capacity was 23 GW. India has already attained fifth position in solar energy capacity in the world. India has fixed an ambitious and optimistic target of achieving 100 GW by 2022. Initiating operations in this direction, India is expecting achievement of an additional 19 GW solar capacity and 38 GW installed capacity in 2019 through new installations of various solar projects. Installation of world class solar power plants is an effective step towards achieving this target.

Solar Power Parks in India

1) ***Bhadla Solar Park:*** *The park has been situated in Jodhpur, Rajasthan. With a capacity of 2255 MW, the park is one of the largest in the world.*
2) ***Charanka Solar Park:*** *With a capacity of 1100 MW, the park is situated in Gujarat. It is the fourth largest in the world.*
3) ***Kurnool Solar Park:*** *The park with a capacity of 1000 MW is situated in Panyam Mandal, Andhra Pradesh.*
4) ***Rewa Solar Plant:*** *Commissioned in Rewa district of Madhya Pradesh in 2018, the park has a capacity of 750 MW*

5) ***Kamuthi Solar Park:*** *The park is situated in Madurai, Tamil Nadu. It has capacity of 648 MW*

6) ***Pavagada Solar Park:*** *The park has been installed in Karnataka with a capacity of 600 MW*

7) ***Welspun Solar Park:*** *It is situated in Madhya Pradesh with a capacity of 151 MW*

8) ***Sakri Solar Park:*** *The park is situated in Maharashtra. It has capacity of 125 MW*

9) ***Banasura Floating Solar Park:*** *The largest floating solar plant in India, is situated in Wayanad, Kerala.*

10) ***Mirzapur Solar Park:*** *Situated in U.P. with a capacity of 75 MW, it is the largest plant in U.P.*

Upcoming : *NP Kunta Ultra Mega Solar Park, Ananthapur, Andhra Pradesh (1500 MW), Kadapa Ultra Mega Solar Park, Andhra Pradesh (650 MW), Sambhar Ultra Mega Solar Park, Rajasthan (4000 MW)*

Wind Energy: Wind energy is harnessed through turbines installed in wind farms. Turbines are connected to generators to produce electricity for various purposes. Wind as a renewable source of energy is cheap and freely available. Wind energy is clean and non-polluting as mechanical energy of wind is converted to electric energy without burning fossil fuels. Further, wind as a renewable source is cost-effective, requires a small piece of land, and requires less water as compared to solar plants. Due to this, wind is treated as the best source of energy.

Indian Scenario: India has established wind farms in different states to convert wind energy to electricity. Major states contributing to a sizeable share of wind energy are Madhya Pradesh, Rajasthan, Maharashtra, Karnataka, Andhra Pradesh, Gujarat, Telangana, and Tamil Nadu. Tamil Nadu has the maximum installed capacity of about 7633 MW. Indian government has fixed target of generating 60 GW power by 2022.

2. Geothermal Energy:

It is another clean and environment friendly energy coming from beneath the earth. High temperature under the earth heats up the groundwater which converts it into steam. This is natural heat of the earth arising from the deposits of dust and gas billions of years ago. Heat is also produced with decay of radioactive matter present in the rocks under the earth. Geothermal energy is found in shallow depth in hot water and miles deeper where rocks under the surface of the earth are in the hot molten form called magma. Energy is harnessed from hot water, hot fluids, and steam under the earth. Turbines are used to capture energy, which is converted to electricity through generators.

Indian Scenario: According to an estimate by Geological Survey of India (GSI), Puga valley in Ladakh (J&K) is the most promising location of geothermal energy. As per the survey, the other promising locations fall in Tapti, Son, Mahanadi, and Godavari river basins, Himalayas, and Cambay (Gujarat). As per an estimate, India has a potential of 10,000 MW of geothermal energy.

3. Hydrogen Energy:

As a renewable energy source, hydrogen is available in plenty. Hydrogen energy is used to supply power to household, agriculture, industry, services, transportation, and aviation.

Indian Scenario: Ministry of New and Renewable Energy (MNRE) has initiated steps to harness and use hydrogen energy. Research projects have been initiated on various aspects of hydrogen. Work is also being done to produce and store hydrogen energy to use it as fuel for generating electricity. Under National Hydrogen Energy Road Map (NHERM) programme, India has set a target of generating 1000 MW electricity from hydrogen by 2020. Further, there has also been a target of running 1 million hydrogen-driven vehicles.

4. Tidal Energy:

Tidal energy is obtained from energy hidden in tides while these are rising or falling. As capturing tidal energy is possible only in the coastal regions, electricity generated from tides have limited jurisdiction.

Indian Scenario: Potential areas of tidal energy in India are Gulf of Cambay in Gujarat, Gulf of Kutch, and Sunderbans stretch of Gangetic delta in West Bengal. As per an estimate, India has a potential of 8000 MW of tidal energy.

5. Wave Energy:

Another renewable source energy is wave energy. Like tidal energy, it also has limited jurisdiction, i.e., only coastal areas. Energy is obtained at ocean sites by placing energy-capturing instruments at the surface and then the mechanical energy so obtained is converted to electric energy.

Indian Scenario: There is a rich scope of generating wave energy in India due to its over 7000 km coastline. With the present technology, India can aspire to produce

40 to 60 MW of energy. Under an ambitious plan of Department of Ocean Development, a plant at Vizhinjam inTrivandrum (Kerala) has been set up.

6. Hydroelectric Energy:

Hydroelectric energy is produced by fetching electricity from the potential energy of falling or flowing water by constructing dams over various water bodies like rivers, streams, etc. This energy is also renewable and environment-friendly.

Indian Scenario: India is successfully obtaining energy from water for various purposes like supply of electricity to households, government, and business sectors, and irrigation, washing, etc. for which various hydroelectric multipurpose dams have been erected. While possessing a potential of 148,700 MW , India has attained 7th position in the world in hydroelectric power.

Major Hydroelectric Dams in India:

Sr.No.	Name of the Dam	River	State	Remarks
1	Hirakud	Mahanadi	Odisha	One of the world's longest man- made dams
2	Bhakra	Satluj	Himachal Pradesh	Serves Punjab, Haryana, Rajasthan
3	Rihand	Rihand	U.P.	Multipurpose
4	Tungabhadra	Tungabhadra	Karnataka	Serves Andhra Pradesh and Karnataka
5	Rana Pratap	Chambal	Rajasthan	Serves M.P. and Rajasthan Sagar
6	Gandhi Sagar	Chambal	M.P.	-------
7	Nagarjunasagar	Krishna	Andhra Pradesh	--------
8	Kosi	Kosi	Bihar	Serves Bihar and Nepal
9	Farakka Barrage	Ganges	West Bengal	Water sharing with Bangladesh
10	Tehri	Bhagirathi	Uttarakhand	Highest dam in India
11	Sardar Sarovar	Narmada	Gujarat	Serves M.P., Rajasthan, Maharashtra, Gujarat World's second highest gravity dam
12	Srisailam	Krishna	Andhra Pradesh	Third largest capacity dam in India
13	Pandoh	Beas	Himachal Pradesh	---------
14	Maharana	Beas	Himachal Pradesh	Also known as Pong Dam Pratap Sagar
15	Nizam Sagar	Manjira	Telangana	------------------
16	Salal	Chenab	J&K	
17	Chamera	Ravi	Himachal Pradesh	----------------------------
18	Nathpa Jhakri	Satluj	Himachal Pradesh	India's largest hydropower plant
19	Idukki	Periyar	Kerala	India's first arch dam
20	Nangal	Satluj	Punjab	------------------
21	Massanjore	Mayurakshi	Jharkhand	-------------------
22	Ranjit Sagar	Ravi	Punjab	Also known as Thein dam Serves Punjab and J&K
23	Panchet	Damodar	Jharkhand	-------------------

8. Biomass Energy:

Organic material of plants and animals composes biomass. Energy from biomass is obtained by burning biomass. Biomass energy can be developed with minimum cost. Carbon dioxide is released from burning biomass.

Indian Scenario: In India, currently about 500 million tonnes of biomass is produced. Out of the total energy produced in India, 32% is derived from biomass. In the current scenario, potential of producing biomass energy in India is about 18000 MW.

Biogas: *Organic matters like sewage, animal waste, agriculture waste, food waste, etc. experience decomposition by bacteria in the absence of oxygen (anaerobic digestion), thus yielding a mixture of gases like Methane and Carbon dioxide. This mixture is called Biogas.*

Biogas is a renewable source of energy and is used as a fuel for cooking, gas engines, electric generation, and transportation, and as an agent in refrigeration. Biogas is eco-friendly as it does not pollute air, soil, and water.

Non-Renewable Sources of Energy

Non-renewable sources are the sources which are found under the earth. Due to their nature and limited availability, such resources never reproduce once they are exhausted. Fossils under the earth yield coal, petroleum, and gas and these are called **fossil fuels**. Another non-renewable source is uranium which yields nuclear or atomic energy. Once these are exhausted, they never grow again. Major sources of non-renewable energy are given as follows:

1) Coal:

Coal is that fossil fuel, which is available in abundance and is used as a fuel for cooking and a source to produce electricity through thermal plants. Capacity of thermal plants to produce electricity depends on coal availability.

Indian Scenario: India fetches coal by extracting it from various coal mines in India. India can boast on possessing fifth largest coal reserves in the world. At present, India stands fourth in the world in coal production in the world.

MAJOR COAL MINES IN INDIA

MINE LOCATION	*STATE*
1) Jharia	*Jharkhand*
2) Dhanbad	*Jharkhand*
3) Daltonganj	*Jharkhand*
4) Talcher	*Odisha*
5) Singrauli	*Madhya Pradesh*
6) Korba	*Chhattisgarh*
7) Ranigunj	*West Bengal*
8) Yellandu	*Andhra Pradesh*
9) Kakri	*Uttar Pradesh*
10) Wardha	*Maharashtra*

2) Oil, Petroleum, and Natural Gas:

Oil, petroleum, and natural gas are used as fuel for various purposes and are always high in demand.

Indian Scenario: India is the third largest consumer of crude oil and petroleum products in the world. According to an estimate, 80% of total electricity generation is from fossil fuels.

3) Nuclear Energy:

Nuclear energy is produced in plants through nuclear fusion and nuclear fission from uranium. Nuclear fission is more commonly used. Nuclear energy is used for various preliminary and advanced purposes, varying from household needs to advance science and technology needs. Nuclear energy does not emit greenhouse gases as emitted by burning of fossil fuels.

Indian Scenario: Presently, India has 7 nuclear plants and 22 nuclear reactors. In the field of nuclear energy, India has installed capacity of about 7000 MW.

Nuclear Power Plants in India

1)	*Kalapakkam*	-	*Tamil Nadu*
2)	*Kakrapar*	-	*Gujarat*
3)	*Tarapur*	-	*Maharashtra*
4)	*Kudankulam*	-	*Tamil Nadu*
5)	*Rawatbhata*	-	*Rajasthan*
6)	*Kaiga*	-	*Karnataka*
7)	*Narora*	-	*Uttar Pradesh*

COMPARATIVE CONSUMPTION OF ENERGY IN INDIA

In India, source wise consumption of energy is as follows:

Coal (Thermal) ----57%, Natural Gas-------45%, Crude Oil (Petroleum)----28%,

Hydroelectricity----4%, Renewable----3%, Nuclear-----1%

FLORAL KINGDOM IN INDIA

Forests

India is affluent in the floral kingdom. Botanical Survey of India (BSI) has established that there are about 50,000 species of plants in India. These include all types of plants along with herbs having medicinal value. Angiosperms (having about 18,000 species) is the largest group of plants in India's floral kingdom. Forest area covers about 24% of India's total geographical area. With respect to forest coverage, India stands 10th in the world. Different types of forests are found in India.

Distribution of Forests in India

1) **Humid Deciduous Forests:** These are found in Western Ghats, Assam, West Bengal Plateau, and Ganga region of Bihar. Example: Shirish, Sal, Neem, Teak, Mango
2) **Mangrove Forests:** The densest growth is in the Delta of Sundarbans. The other areas are deltas of Krishna, Cauvery, Godavari, Mahanadi, and Brahmaputra. Example: Hogla, Keora

3) **Scrub and Thorny Forests:** These are found in the areas where there is no regular rain. Desert areas of Rajasthan and Gujarat experience the growth of the forest. Example: Cactus, Babul, Palm

4) **Dry Deciduous Forests:** Their main belt of concentration is Tamil Nadu, Rajasthan, Maharashtra, Madhya Pradesh, and Karnataka. Example: Amaltas, Tendu, Rosewood, Satinwood

5) **Evergreen Forests:** These forests are found in Western Ghats, Andaman & Nicobar, and Terai belt of Eastern Ghats. Example; Bamboo, Rubber

6) **Himalayan Vegetation:** These vegetation are found in the Himalayas

7) **Desert Vegetation:** These are found in the Thar desert of Rajasthan. Example: Cacti

National Forest Policy, 2018

Union Ministry of Environment, forest and Climate Change has come up with Draft National Forest Policy, 2018. This aims at bringing minimum one-third of the total geographical area of the country under forest cover. There is provision of strict rules regarding protection of dense forest cover. Strategy of the policy will be to deal with international challenges to climate change. Conservation and protection of forest wealth is the main agenda of the policy. Another point of emphasis in the policy is to provide ecological security to present and future generations through rational management of forests. Environmental stability and conservation of biodiversity is the pivotal objective of the policy.

HERBS WITH MEDICINAL VALUES

PLANT SPECIES	*MEDICINAL VALUE*
1) Autumn crocus	*Anti-cancer agent*
2) Penicillium fungi	*Analgesic, general antibiotic*
3) Papaya	*Regulating digestion*
4) Opium poppy	*Analgesic*
5) Cocoa	*Analgesic*
6) Pineapple	*Reducing tissue inflammation*
7) Yellow Cinchona	*Antimalarial*
8) Indian snakeroot	*Reduces high blood pressure*
9) Belladonna	*Reduces intestinal pain*
10) Mint rubefacient	*Reduces pain, regulate blood supply*

FAUNAL KINGDOM OF INDIA

Zoological Survey of India illustrates the presence of various animal species in India. According to an estimate, India has about 90,000 animal species including mammals, reptiles, aves, pisces, arthropods, and others.

Faunal Distribution In India

1) **Bengal Tiger** is found in Madhya Pradesh, Uttranchal, West Bengal, Rajasthan, and Kerala.
2) **Sambar Deer** is found in almost all regions of India and mainly in Haryana.
3) **Kala Hiran** is found all over India.
4) **Indian Rhino** is found in Assam and other North Eastern states.
5) **Asiatic Lion** is found in Gir Forests, Gujarat.
6) **Indian Elephant** is found in Kerala, Tamil Nadu, Uttar Pradesh, and Assam.
7) **Nilgai** is found in Central and Northern India.
8) **Great Indian Bustard** is found in Rajasthan and Madhya Pradesh.
9) **Great Hornbill** is found in Kerala.
10) **Asiatic Wild Ass** is found in Great Rann of Kutch in Gujarat.
11) **Indian Red Panda** is found in the Himalayas.

National Wildlife Parks in India

1) *Sundarbans National Park----West Bengal (Tiger Reserve)*
2) *Manas National Park----Assam*
3) *Pench National Park----Madhya Pradesh*
4) *Rajaji National Park----Uttarakhand.*
5) *Sariska Wildlife Sanctury-----Rajasthan (Tiger Reserve)*
6) *Nagarhole National Park-------Karnataka*
7) *Gir National Park ----------------Gujarat (Asiatic Lion)*
8) *Kaziranga National Park--------Assam (One-horned Rhino)*
9) *Tadoba Tiger Reserve-----------Maharashtra*
10) *Wayanad Wildlife Sanctuary---Kerala*

11) *Silent Valley National Park------Tamil Nadu*
12) *Ranthambore Tiger Reserve---Rajasthan.*
13) *Corbett National Park-------------Uttarakhand (Tiger Reserve)*
14) *Bhandavgarh National Park-----Madhya Pradesh (Tiger Reserve)*
15) *Keoladeo National Park ------------Rajasthan (Siberian Crane)*
16) *Kanha National Park---------------Madhya Pradesh*
17) *Periyar National Park---------------Kerala*
18) *Dudhwa National Park-------------Uttarakhand*
19) *Madumalai National Park----------Tamil Nadu*
20) *Jaldapara Wildlife Sanctury--------West Bengal*
21) *Singalila National Park--------------Darjeeling (West Bengal)*
22) *Bandipur National Park--------------Karnataka*
23) *Wild Ass Sanctuary---------------------Gujarat*

***Endangered Species:** Endangered species are those species which are likely to become extinct. Following are the endangered species in India:*

1) *Blackbuck*
2) *Asiatic Lion*
3) *Snow Leopard*
4) *Nilgiri Tahr*
5) *Lion-tailed Macaque*
6) *One-horned Rhinoceros*
7) *Bengal Tigers*

National Wildlife Action Plan 2017-2031

Union Ministry of Environment, Forest and Climate Change launched National Wildlife Plan 2017-2031. This is the third action plan in the series. Main emphasis of the plan is to monitor the impact of climate changes on wildlife and how the unhealthy impact can be mitigated. Special emphasis of the plan would be recovery of threatened species by conserving their habitats. The plan will also address the issue of human-wild animal conflict which is rising for want of proper monitoring and care of wildlife habitats. On an ambitious note, participation of private sector in wildlife conservation will be encouraged during the action plan.

Wildlife Protection Act, 1972

In order to protect wildlife and control illegitimate activities like poaching, Government of India enacted an Act of Parliament, i.e., Wildlife Protection Act, 1972. This Act has jurisdiction over both flora and fauna.

BIOSPHERE

Biosphere is one of the spheres of the earth among lithosphere, hydrosphere, and atmosphere. Biosphere covers the total plant and animal life existing in all other spheres of the earth.

Biosphere conservation is the process of protecting the diverse flora and fauna, including endangered species. There are two types of conservation: In-situ Conservation and Ex-situ Conservation.

- **In- situ Conservation:** In-situ conservation is the practice of protecting the species in their natural habitat. This process encourages species to develop in their natural habitat. There is no outside interference. In-situ conservation is done by creating national parks, wildlife sanctuaries, and biosphere reserves.
- **Ex-situ Conservation:** Under this, the species are kept outside their natural habitat. In ex-situ conservation, humans' involvement is there to conduct research, particularly on protection of endangered species. In this programme, botanical gardens, zoological gardens, and zoos are created.

Biosphere Reserves

Biosphere reserves are structures erected on land and in coastal belts to protect various floral and faunal species, including the endangered species. These are established under legislation, so they are protected reserves.

UNESCO'S INITIATIVE

UNESCO launched a Man and Biosphere (MAB) programme in 1970, where the term Biosphere was used. This is the scientific and intergovernmental programme to improve human-environment relations. MAB programme aims at conducting research and experiments to conserve biosphere by creating Biosphere Reserves. Target is to protect different species of flora and fauna.

Biosphere Reserves in India

Sr No.	Name of Biosphere	Location	Prominent Species
1	Nokrek National Park	Garo Hills Meghalaya	Red Panda
2	Achanakmar-Amarkantak	Chhatisgarh Madhya Pradesh	Cricket Frog
3	Gulf of Mannar	Between India and Srilanka Laccadive Sea	Sea Turtle
4	Nilgiri	Western Ghats, Nilgiri Hills	Lion-tailed Macaque, Nilgiri Tahr
5	Sundarbans	Between river Ganges and Brahmaputra	One of the largest Mangrove forest in the world. UNESCO Heritage site
6	Similipal	Northeast Odisha	Gaur, Barking deer
7	Great Nicobar	Nicobar Island	Nicobar Megapode Giant Robber Crab
8	Pachmari	Satpura Range. M.P.	Leopard, Tiger, Indian Giant Squirrel
9	Nanda Devi	Northeast of Uttrakhand	UNESCO World heritage site. Snow Leopard.
10	Cold Desert	Himachal Pradesh (Western Himalaya)	Snow Leopard
11	Dihang-Dibang	Arunachal Pradesh (Eastern Himalaya)	NA
12	Seshachalam Hills	Andhra Pradesh (Eastern Ghats)	NA
13	Manas	Assam (Eastern Himalayas)	Red Panda, Golden Langur
14	Khangchendzonga	Sikkim (Eastern Himalayas)	Snow Leopard
15	Agasthyamalai	Kerala (Western Ghats)	Elephant, Nilgiri Tahr
16	Dibru-Saikhowa	Assam (East Himalaya)	Tiger, Capped Langur, Jungle Cat
17	Panna	Madhya Pradesh	Sloth Bear, Sambhar
18	Little Rann of Kutch	Gujarat	Indian Wild Ass

Some Vital Facts

1) Tidal power is the source of renewable power which can be developed with minimum cost.
2) Rajasthan receives the highest solar radiation in the country.
3) India has the fifth largest installed wind power in the world.
4) The maximum amount of wind power is contributed by Tamil Nadu.

Practice Exercise

General Questions Format

1. Kosi hydroelectric project has been started by Bihar with cooperation from
(A) Nepal (B) Bhutan
(C) China (D) Maldives

2. Kanha National Park is situated in
(A) Rajasthan (B) Madhya Pradesh
(C) Maharashtra (D) Karnataka

3. In which state Hirakud dam has been built?
(A) Punjab (B) Bihar
(C) Orissa (D) None of these

4. Dry deciduous forests are mainly found in
(A) Tamil Nadu (B) Odisha
(C) Himachal (D) Jharkhand

5. Rewa Solar Park has been installed in
(A) Karnataka (B) Maharashtra
(C) Odisha (D) Madhya Pradesh

6. Tehri dam is built over the river
(A) Gomti (B) Kosi
(C) Bhagirathi (D) Narmada

7. Which of the following is NOT a fossil fuel?
(A) Petroleum (B) Coal
(C) Wood (D) Gas

8. Gir Forest is known for
(A) Elephants (B) Lions
(C) Deer (D) Rhinoceros

9. Participating states in the Chambal river project are
(A) Haryana & Rajasthan
(B) M.P. & Gujarat
(C) Odisha & West Bengal
(D) Rajasthan & M.P.

10. Which of the following herbs helps in relieving pain?
(A) Papaya (B) Belladonna
(C) Fungi (D) Cinchona

11. Talcher coal mine is situated in
(A) Gujarat (B) Odisha
(C) Jharkhand (D) West Bengal

12. Bandipur National Park is situated in
(A) Gujarat (B) Rajasthan
(C) Assam (D) Karnataka

13. Bamboo is an example of _______ forests.
(A) deciduous (B) scrub and thorny
(C) mangrove (D) evergreen

14. India has fixed a target of achieving 100 GW of solar energy by
(A) 2022 (B) 2025
(C) 2019 (D) None of these

15. Which of the following is NOT TRUE about faunal distribution in India?
(A) Indian Red Panda is found in Assam
(B) Asiatic Lion is found in Gujarat
(C) Nilgai is found in Central India
(D) Great Indian Bustard is found in Rajasthan

16. According to an estimate by Geological Survey of India (GSI), ________ valley in Ladakh (J&K) is the most promising location of geothermal energy.
(A) Nathu la (B) Puga
(C) Dha Hanu (D) Markha

17. Evergreen forests are found in
(A) Himachal Pradesh (B) Kerala
(C) Sundarbans (D) Western Ghats

18. Bhakra Nangal Project is a joint venture of
(A) Rajasthan, Himachal, Punjab
(B) Punjab and Haryana
(C) Punjab, Haryana, Rajasthan
(D) None of the above

19. Ranjit Sagar Dam serves the states of
(A) Haryana and J & K
(B) Punjab and J&K
(C) U.P. and Rajasthan
(D) None of these

20. Great Hornbill is the state bird of
(A) Kerala (B) Punjab
(C) J & K (D) U.P.

21. Bhandavgarh National Park is situated in
(A) Odisha (B) Rajasthan
(C) Madhya Pradesh (D) U.P.

22. UNESCO'S MAB Programme emphasises
    (A) conserving biosphere
    (B) minimising human animal conflict
    (C) impact of climate change on biosphere
    (D) All of the above

23. Which of the following is NOT covered in National Wildlife Action Plan 2017-2031 launched by government of India?
    (A) Mitigation of bad impact of climate change on animals
    (B) Creating proper habitat for migratory birds
    (C) Addressing human-animal conflicts
    (D) Recovering threatened species

24. International Solar Alliance has been formed to
    (A) supply the harnessed solar energy to the member countries at a cheaper rate
    (B) fulfill the solar energy needs of those countries which do not get sufficient solar energy by virtue of their geographical location
    (C) reduce the cost of technology for member countries in producing electricity from solar energy
    (D) All of the above

25. What is India's ranking in the world in terms of possessing solar energy capacity?
    (A) 7th (B) 10th
    (C) 4th (D) 2nd

26. Which of the following gases is released by biogas?
    (A) Sulphur dioxide (B) Nitrogen
    (C) Methane (D) Ozone

27. SPV technique is used to harness ____ energy.
    (A) tidal (B) geothermal
    (C) solar (D) hydro

28. Which of the following provision(s) is/are NOT TRUE about National Forest Policy, 2018?
    a) Strict regulations regarding protection of dense forest cover
    b) Provision of ecological security to present and future generations
    c) Enhancement of tree plantation at least by 20% as compared to previous forest policy
    d) Providing suitable habitat to herbs with medicinal values
    (A) a and d only (B) b only
    (C) a, c, and d only (D) c and d only

29. Under NHERM programme, India has set a target to generate 1000 MW energy from hydrogen by
    (A) 2030 (B) 2025
    (C) 2022 (D) 2020

30. Anaerobic digestion in biomass results into production of
    (A) Sulphur dioxide and Methane
    (B) Carbon dioxide and Methane
    (C) Ozone and Methane
    (D) Nitric oxide and Methane

KEY

1. A	2. B	3. C	4. A	5. D	6. C	7. C
8. B	9. D	10. B	11. B	12. D	13. A	14. A
15. A	16. B	17. D	18. C	19. B	20. A	21. C
22. A	23. B	24. A	25. C	26. C	27. C	28. D
29. D	30. B					

Assertion–Reason Format

1. **Assertion (A):** Biogas is a mixture of Methane and Carbon dioxide.

   Reason (R): Biogas is a renewable source of energy.
   (A) Both A and R are true and R is the correct explanation of A
   (B) Both A and R are true but R is not correct explanation of A
   (C) A is true but R is false
   (D) A is false but R is true

2. **Assertion (A):** Maximum hydroelectric dams are built over perennial rivers.

   Reason (R): Himalayan rivers never go dry as these are snow-fed.
   (A) Both A and R are true and R is correct explanation of A
   (B) Both A and R are true but R is not correct explanation of A
   (C) Both A and R are false
   (D) A is true but R is false

3. **Assertion (A):** In-situ biosphere conservation takes species away from their natural habitat.

   Reason (R): Narrowing down of biosphere conservation has resulted into extinction of rare species worldwide.

   (A) Both A and R are true but R is not correct explanation of A
   (B) Both A and R are true and R is correct explanation of A
   (C) Both A and R are false
   (D) A is true but R is false

4. **Assertion (A):** Delta of Sundarbans is known for deciduous forests.

   Reason (R): Rivers flowing through Sundarbans delta nourish Amaltas trees.

   (A) Both A and R are true and R is correct explanation of A
   (B) Both A and R are true but R is not correct explanation of A
   (C) Both A and R are false
   (D) A is true but R is false

5. **Assertion (A):** Some non-renewable sources of energy are available in abundance.

   Reason (R): Coal as a source of energy is used maximum among all non-renewable sources of energy.

   (A) Both A and R are false
   (B) Both A and R are true and R is correct explanation of A
   (C) Both A and R are true but R is not correct explanation of A
   (D) A is true but R is false

6. **Assertion (A):** India has maximum potential of producing energy from wind.

   Reason (R): Wind is the cheapest source of energy.

   (A) Both A and R are true and R is correct explanation of A
   (B) Both A and R are true but R is not correct explanation of A
   (C) A is true but R is false
   (D) Both A and R are false

7. **Assertion (A):** Harnessing energy from renewable sources is cheaper than from non-renewable sources.

   Reason (R): Non-renewable sources of energy sources should be used rationally and saved for future generations.

   (A) Both A and R are true and R is correct explanation of A
   (B) Both A and R are true but R is not correct explanation of A
   (C) A is true but R is false
   (D) A is false but R is true

8. **Assertion (A):** Energy harnessed from any source is ultimately used for generating electricity.

   Reason (R): Electricity generated from thermal plants is cheaper than generated through hydroelectric dams.

   (A) Both A and R are true and R is correct explanation of A
   (B) Both A and R are true but R is not correct explanation of A
   (C) A is true but R is false
   (D) Both A and R are false

9. **Assertion (A):** Faunal population of a region needs a suitable biosphere reserve for survival.

   Reason (R): Endangered species kept in biosphere reserves no longer remain endangered.

   (A) Both A and R are true and R is correct explanation of A
   (B) Both A and R are true but R is not correct explanation of A
   (C) A is true but R is false
   (D) A is false but R is true

10. **Assertion (A):** National parks in India should be provided with sufficient funds.

    Reason (R): Species kept in national parks need proper care in terms of diet and health.

    (A) Both A and R are true and R is correct explanation of A
    (B) Both A and R are true but R is not correct explanation of A
    (C) Both A and R are false
    (D) A is true but R is false

KEY

1. B **2.** A **3.** C **4.** C **5.** B **6.** D **7.** B
8. D **9.** C **10.** A

Questions Asked in Previous NET Exams

1. The target set by Indian government for generating power from wind energy by the year 2022 is **(UGC NET JUNE 2019)**
   (A) 60 GW (B) 50 GW
   (C) 40 GW (D) 15 GW
2. Efficiency of electrical power generation is least amongst the following sources of energy in case of **(UGC NET JUNE 2019)**
   (A) Solar (B) Wind
   (C) Geothermal (D) Nuclear
3. The share of which of the following sources of energy in electricity generation at present is the least? **(UGC NET DECEMBER 2019)**
   (A) Thermal (B) Solar and Wind
   (C) Hydro (D) Nuclear
4. Biosphere reserves are:
   (i) area comprising terrestrial marine and coastal ecosystems
   (ii) monitored by national governments
   (iii) areas where threatened animals and plants are kept in their habitat
   (iv) wildlife sanctuaries
   Choose the correct statements from the options given below: **(UGC NET DECEMBER 2019)**
   (A) (i) and (ii) (B) (ii) and (iii)
   (C) (iii) and (iv) (D) (i) and (iv)
5. A source of renewable power which can be developed with minimum cost is **(UGC NET DECEMBER 2018)**
   (A) Wind mills (B) Tidal power
   (C) Biomass power (D) Geothermal energy
6. In terms of their contribution to the total power generation in India, Identify the correct sequence of energy sources : Thermal Power Plants (TPP), Large Hydropower Projects (LHP), Nuclear Energy (NE), and Renewable Energy (RE) which includes solar energy, wind energy, biomass, and small hydropower projects. **(UGC NET JULY 2018)**
   (A) TPP > RE > LHP > NE
   (B) TPP > LHP > RE > NE
   (C) LHP > TPP > RE > NE
   (D) LHP > TPP > NE > RE
7. Consider the following statements and select the correct answer from the code given below: **(UGC NET JUNE 2014)**
   (i) Rajasthan receives the highest solar radiation in the country.
   (ii) India has the fifth largest installed wind power in the world.
   (iii) The maximum amount of wind power is contributed by Tamil Nadu.
   (iv) The primary source of uranium in India is Jaduguda.
   (A) (i) and (ii) (B) (i), (ii), and (iii)
   (C) (ii) and (iii) (D) (i) and (iv)
8. By the year 2022, the Climate Change Action Plan of Government of India aims at installing **(UGC NET DECEMBER 2013)**
   (A) 20,000 MW of wind power
   (B) 25,000 MW of wind power
   (C) 20,000 MW of solar power
   (D) 10,000 MW of solar power
9. Match List - I with List - II and find the correct answer from the codes given below: **(UGC NET SEPTEMBER 2013)**

List - I (Biosphere Reserve)	**List - II (Area of Location)**
a. Nilgiri	i. Deccan Peninsula
b. Manas	ii. Chhattisgarh
c. Similipal	iii. Eastern Himalayas
d. Achanakmar-Amarkantak	iv. Western Ghats

Codes:

	(a)	(b)	(c)	(d)
(A)	i	ii	iii	iv
(B)	ii	iii	iv	i
(C)	iii	iv	ii	i
(D)	iv	iii	i	ii

10. The second most important source after fossil fuels contributing to India's energy needs is **(UGC NET DECEMBER 2012)**
    (A) Solar energy
    (B) Nuclear energy
    (C) Hydropower
    (D) Wind energy

11. Which of the following sources of energy has the maximum potential in India?

(UGC NET DECEMBER 2011)

(A) Solar energy
(B) Wind energy
(C) Ocean thermal energy
(D) Tidal energy

12. The Great Indian Bustard bird is found in

(UGC NET DECEMBER 2009)

(A) Thar Desert of Rajasthan
(B) Coastal regions of India
(C) Malabar coast
(D) Delta regions

13. Which one of the following non-conventional energy sources can be exploited most economically?

(UGC NET DECEMBER 2009)

(A) Solar
(B) Wind
(C) Geothermal
(D) Ocean Thermal Energy Conversion (OTEC)

14. Match List-I with List-II and select the correct answers from the codes given below:

(UGC NET DECEMBER 2008)

List-I (National Parks)	**List-II (States)**
(a) Periyar	(i) Odisha
(b) Nandan Kanan	(ii) Kerala
(c) Corbett National Park	(iii) Rajasthan
(d) Sariska Tiger Reserve	(iv) Uttarakhand

Codes:	(a)	(b)	(c)	(d)
(A)	ii	i	iv	iii
(B)	i	ii	iv	iii
(C)	iii	ii	i	iv
(D)	i	ii	iii	iv

15. The Great Indian Bustard Bird is found in

(UGC NET DECEMBER 2007)

(A) Thar desert of India
(B) Coastal regions of India
(C) Temperate forests in the Himalayas
(D) Tarai zones of the Himalayan foothills

16. Match the List-I (Dams) with List-II (Rivers) in the following:

(UGC NET DECEMBER 2005)

List-I (Dams)	**List-II (Rivers)**
a) Bhakra	i) Krishna
b) Nagarjunasagar	ii) Damodar
c) Panchet	iii) Satluj
d) Hirakud	iv) Bhagirathi
e) Tehri	v) Mahanadi

Codes:	(a)	(b)	(c)	(d)	(e)
(A)	v	iii	iv	ii	i
(B)	iii	i	ii	v	iv
(C)	i	ii	iv	iii	v
(D)	ii	iii	iv	i	v

KEY

1. A **2.** C **3.** B **4.** A **5.** C **6.** A **7.** B **8.** C **9.** D **10.** C **11.** A **12.** A **13.** A **14.** A **15.** A **16.** B

8 Natural Hazards and Disasters and Their Mitigation

INTRODUCTION

Natural hazards and natural disasters are transitionally related. In a way, natural hazards give rise to natural disasters. Any unwanted and unhealthy development in the natural ecosystem is the mother of natural hazards and natural disasters. These can be understood separately.

Natural Hazards

Natural hazards are unwanted and unhealthy developments in the natural ecosystem due to abrupt changes in climate. Any abnormality found and felt in routine and smooth development of lithosphere, atmosphere, or hydrosphere is termed as a natural hazard. Natural hazards include earthquakes, floods, volcanic eruptions, tsunamis, hurricanes, cyclones, droughts, and famines and epidemics. Natural hazards may be occurring at local, regional, national, or international level.

Natural disasters

Natural disasters are harmful and fatal impacts of natural hazards can be felt on the socio-economic and political systems, humans, livelihood, flora and fauna, infrastructure, health systems and services, education system finance and banking, indigenous and foreign trade, communication set-ups, law and order, and defence of a region where natural hazard in any form occurs. There is total breakdown and serious disruptions in policy framework being implemented to achieve sustainable development.

TYPES OF NATURAL HAZARDS AND DISASTERS

As natural hazards give birth to natural disasters, types of natural hazards also include types of natural disasters. Following are the types of natural hazards and disasters:

1) **Hydro-Meteorological:** Hazards occur due to abnormal movements in atmosphere and hydrosphere resulting in floods, cyclones, hurricanes, landslides, droughts, and tidal waves yielding disasters like loss of human, animal, and plant kingdom, loss of diversity, damage to property, degradation of ecosystem, and damage to socio-economic fabric.
2) **Biological:** Biological disasters are spread through infections, which occur through infestation of insects carrying pathogenic organisms and microorganisms, bacteria, and virus and such infections become epidemics. Disasters under this category include mass loss of human lives due to development of communicative diseases, skin ailments, injuries, and other infectious diseases. These further results in hampering progress of development efforts in different sectors of the society.
3) **Geo-Physical:** This type includes hazards occurring due to various movements inside the earth covering lithosphere and hydrosphere resulting in earthquakes, tsunamis, and volcanic eruptions. These hazards generate disasters like destruction of life, property, large-scale fires, demolition of buildings getting reduced to rubble, fatal accidents, loss of animal and plant life, and washing away of movable and immovable belongings.

Mitigation

Mitigation policies are measures to reduce the vulnerability towards natural hazards and disasters along with measures acting as a buffer to harmful effects of natural hazards and disasters. Nature of mitigation depends upon the nature of natural hazards. Though there are some common effects of various natural hazards, yet type of mitigation measures taken are according to the nature of natural hazard and disaster.

MAJOR NATURAL HAZARDS AND DISASTERS FLOODS

Flood is forceful overflowing of huge volume of water on a dry land (overflowing over coastal and river banks) putting the total terrestrial life out of gear.

Types of Floods

a) **Coastal Floods:** Coastal floods occur in areas close to the sea, ocean, or any large-sized water body. Water from the sea or ocean is pushed towards the coast by hurricane or severely flowing winds. Pushing of tidal waves to the shore by hurricanes and storms is called storm surge and it is the major cause of coastal floods. Huge volume of water pushed to the shore enters low-lying areas in full force. Global warming is another cause of coastal floods as sea level rises and overflows in the form of flood. Such floods result in loss of life and property at a large scale. Coastal floods can be mild, moderate, and major. Intensity of disaster emerging out of floods depends upon the degree of floods.

b) **River Floods:** River floods occur due to longer period of heavy rainfall at a stretch and huge volume of water is discharged into rivers and streams and these water bodies are filled with water beyond their capacity and excess water overflows in the form of flood. Such floods are also known as fluvial floods or riverine floods. Such floods also occur due to early and excess melting of ice due to rise in terrestrial temperature resulting in deposit of excess water into rivers and streams. Riverine floods are also caused due to landslides falling into rivers resulting in overflowing of water. Intensity of river floods depends upon intensity and duration of precipitation. River floods are categorised into:

Catastrophic floods: These are caused due to collapse of dams, infrastructure, or damages incurred due to earthquakes and volcanic eruptions.

Flash floods: On the other hand, these occur without or little warning. Such floods are the most common and dangerous. Such floods occur due to prolonged rainfall raising water level and water flows with full force. Intensity of these floods depends upon intensity of rainfall and topography of the affected region. Urban areas housing huge and dense cement erections obstruct free drainage of flood water which creates havoc due to intensive force of water flow. Stones and debris carried by this full force of water makes flash floods even more dangerous.

Surface floods: Groundwater floods occur due to prolonged and continuous rainfall. Such rainfall transforms into flood when excess rainwater overpowers the water absorption capacity of the ground. When the ground is no more in capacity to absorb rainwater, excess water is transformed into flood. Such floods are also called pluvial or surface water floods.

Overbank floods: These occur when water of different water bodies overflows over their banks resulting in flood. These floods are also commonly occurring floods.

PRECIPITATION

Precipitation is the falling down of water vapours present in the atmosphere. These water vapours fall down on the ground in different forms viz. rain, drizzling, freezing rain (ice crystals falling on the earth and melting into liquid after coming into contact with warmer air), snow, sleet (pallets of ice), and hail. When atmosphere is filled with water vapours beyond its capacity, precipitation occurs as water vapours in any form and fall down due to gravitation pull of the earth. Precipitation is produced when air rises and gets cooled due to fall in temperature and low pressure. Moisture in the air is condensed into clouds.

c) **Groundwater floods:** Groundwater floods occur due to prolonged and continuous rainfall. Such rainfall transforms into flood when excess rainwater overpowers the water absorption capacity of the ground. When the ground is no more in capacity to absorb rainwater, excess water is transformed into flood.

Effects of Floods

As flooding is a natural hazard, it leaves an unhealthy impact on the affected region as a whole. The effects of flooding are:

1) Loss of human, animal, and plant life
2) Disruptions in transport and communication system
3) Damage to roads, bridges, sewer system, flyovers, and other infrastructural erections
4) Shortage of safe drinking water
5) Halting economic, business, and banking activities and loss of livelihoods
6) Degradation of environment and ecosystem
7) Outbreaking of epidemics, particularly malaria and other infectious diseases
8) Disruptions in supply of electricity and basic amenities leading to acute food shortage
9) Waterlogging and blockage of sewerage system giving rise to various diseases
10) Chronic wetness to houses situated in urban areas

11) Loss of habitats and biodiversity
12) Disruption in health services and shortage of medicines
13) Decay of waste matter due to improper drainage, further paving way for various infectious diseases
14) Damage to crops, thus aggravating crisis on different sections of the affected region

Mitigation

Flood is that hazard which incurs structural and non-structural damages. Mitigation measures are taken for minimising the harmful impacts on structural and non-structural spheres. Structural and non-structural mitigation measures are taken according to the nature of flood and location and geography of the affected region.

Structural Flood Mitigation

Structural flood mitigation covers construction of roads, bridges, dams, levees, and other infrastructural erections with such an architectural skill so that these structures may resist the harmful impacts of floods and dilute the impacts. Structural measures include:

Maintaining existing infrastructure: Existing infrastructure receiving flood water like culverts, levees, creeks, and fills must be properly maintained for ensuring free drainage of excess water in case flood occurs. Floodwalls can be constructed to control flood water. Regular checking and maintenance of sewer system help in mitigating floods. Various openings in levees, floodwalls, and culverts can be plugged in with closures to prevent flood water flowing towards residential complexes.

Voluntary efforts: Residents of low-lying or flood-prone areas can construct and maintain their houses and other establishments as a mitigation measure. There can be installation of solid fencing to keep flood water away from homes. Level of windows should be high enough to prevent flood water from entering homes through windows. Domestic waste or sewage can be treated and disposed properly, so as to block the flow of water. Use of check valves also prevent blockage in the sewer and water can flow freely. Electricity installations should be fitted at an elevation to avoid short-circuiting.

Arrangements of easy access to essential services: Regular checking and maintenance of roads and paths facilitating uninterrupted movement of ambulances, fire tenders, and other such essential services vehicles in case of emergency arising out of flooding.

Levee: *A levee is a wall of bricks and stones erected to prevent flood water from entering residential areas and houses. Levees are erected to prevent flow of water overflown from water bodies. Prevented water can be used in irrigation and other agricultural activities.*

Culvert: *A culvert is a pipe-type structure made of soil or concrete built under a road or railway track to allow free drainage of water from one side of the road or railway track to the other side. Proper maintenance of culverts helps drainage of flood water also to protect roads or railway tracks from damaging due to flood water flowing over roads or railway tracks.*

Creek: *A creek is a narrow water channel which is sheltered. Water in a creek remains within its banks. Tributary of a river is also called creek. Creek is also found in marshy areas.*

Fill: *Fill is a land dug behind the levee to accommodate prevented flood water and divert it for irrigation and agricultural activities.*

Floodwall: *A floodwall is constructed with concrete and steel to withstand pressure of flood water. Objective is to prevent water from entering inhabited areas.*

Non-Structural Flood Mitigation

These consist of certain mitigation measures without involving flood defence systems developed for structural erections. Following measures are included in non-structural mitigation measurements:

1) **Flood Modelling:** This is a mitigation measure taken in advance to assess the intensity, area, and type of possible floods. Here, data on rainfall is collected. It is also assessed whether the area that is likely to be affected by floods has roads, bridges, agricultural fields, and residential or commercial buildings. It is also assessed whether ground under study is a hilly area and how many drainage joints are there through which flood water will flow. Data is collected through remote sensing. Flood modelling is concentrated on the following enforcements:
   a) Assessment of sewer network
   b) Assessment of breaches in dams
   c) Assessment of capacity of culverts, fills, and floodwalls

d) Drawing hazard maps for those urban areas which are the most likely to be affected by floods.

e) Assessment of the type of soil of the possible affected area

f) Assessing flood route

g) Adopting dual drainage model to manage risks of floods in urban areas

DUAL DRAINAGE MODEL

Dual drainage model is an application in flood modelling for urban areas prone to floods. In dual drainage model, assessment of minor drainage and major drainage is made through which flood water will flow in case of flood. Minor drainage is the sewer network and major drainage network consists of various drainage channels on the surface like streets, lanes, roads, and other such channels over which that flood water flows which is in excess to flood water flowing through pipes of sewers. Assessment of water flowing through both draining channels in the event of floods is made, which helps in planning risk management measures. Flood water simultaneously flows on the surface and in pipes of sewers and both minor and major drainage channels interact at an inlet made to take flowing water to a common drainage channel. Dual drainage model helps in managing risks of flood, as an advance assessment of water runoff is made and it lessens the damages during flood as dual drainage channels divide the volume and smothers force of the flood water.

2) **Flood insurance:** Disastrous impact of floods comprise of ailments, loss of human life, damage to moveable and immovable properties, crops, industrial goods, and loss of business. An insurance policy against all these odds can help in compensating any such loss and damage.

3) **Mass awareness:** Mass media can educate people about harmful impacts of floods and precautions to be taken to mitigate damages. Sufficient websites may be created by the authorities to proliferate full knowledge of floods.

4) **Survey of properties in flood-prone areas:** A survey of housing and business properties established in the flood-prone areas will help in making people understand harmful impacts of floods. Accordingly, residents, business persons, and insurers can plan risk management steps and compensation of losses.

5) **Statutes against construction in flood-prone areas:** Flood-prone areas can be identified and restrictions on construction in such areas can be imposed through suitable land use statutes and legislations.

6) **Installation of advance warning system:** Advance warning systems can be installed to alert general public about apprehensions of flood and people may shift their families and belongings to safer places in time.

FLOODS IN INDIA

Irregular monsoons in India have made floods the most commonly occurring natural hazard. As monsoon rainfall is concentrated in three to four months, i.e., June to September (comprising 80% of total rainfall), it leads to floods. According to an estimate by the Rashtriya Barh Ayog, total flood-prone area on the eve of 12th Five year Plan has increased to 49.8 million hectares from about 38 million hectare in 1958, thus registering an increase by 25%. Major flood-prone areas fall in:

1) **Peninsular river basin:** This belt comprises Cauvery, Krishna, Mahanadi, Godavari, Tapti, Narmada, and Penna rivers along with coastal regions of Kerala, Andhra Pradesh, Odisha, Karnataka, and Tamil Nadu. Odisha is affected by overflowing waters of rivers Baitarani and Brahamani. Water from these rivers attack the thickly populated region surrounded by these rivers and cause large-scale damage. Coastal states are also under the influence of floods created by tropical cyclones.

2) **North-west river basin:** Beas, Jhelum, Ravi, and Satluj rivers falling in this belt receive sufficient quantum of rainwater, ultimately transforming into flood.

3) **Ganga basin:** Northern belt of India falls in this basin. It comprises rivers originating in the north and flowing towards east. Besides Ganga, other rivers and tributaries becoming source of floods are Yamuna, Kosi, Ghagra, Gandak, Sharda, Burhi Gandhak, Damodar, and Mahananda. These rivers cause floods in Haryana, Delhi, Uttar Pradesh, Bihar, and West Bengal.

4) **Brahmaputra and Barak basin:** West Bengal and north-eastern states like Assam, Manipur, Sikkim, and Arunachal Pradesh come under the influence of floods due to excess water overflowing banks of Brahmaputra and Barak, Jaldakha, and Teesta rivers.

Causes of Floods in India

Though there are common causes behind floods in India also, yet its location and diverse topography specifies some causes as follows:

1) **Heavy and prolonged rainfall:** Heavy and prolonged rainfalls during monsoons flood northern plains of India. Himalayan rivers are snow-fed rivers. They are already overfilled with snow melted water and heavy and prolonged rains further increases load of water in these rivers and thus, it floods. Peninsular rivers Narmada, Tapti, Krishna, Cauvery, and Mahanadi on the other hand have shallow beds due to their flowing over harsh topographic belts. Due to this, these are not able to accommodate much water and thus, water overflows during heavy rains in flood-prone areas of Madhya Pradesh, Gujarat, Odisha, and other peninsular river states. Rainy months even make water to overflow banks of otherwise dry rivers Ghaggar and Markanda, generating floods. Low-lying areas of the Punjab and Haryana are flooded with excess water due to heavy downpours.
2) **Silting of rivers:** Another cause of rainfalls in India is silting of rivers. Himalayan rivers, particularly Teesta, Kosi, and Torsa carry silt and sand with them resulting in raising the river bed, which is unable to absorb more water which overflows in the form of flood. Deposition of sand and silt lessens the speed of the flood water which is stranded and spread over even the fertile land, thus making it barren.
3) **Drain congestion:** Poorly maintained and obsolete drainage system also becomes one of the major causes of floods in urban areas. Water is blocked in the already congested and narrow drains and excess water flows over the surface in form of floods. Chennai floods of 2015 were caused due to blockage in drains which created havoc resulting in death toll of more than 400 people. Lack of clearing of drainage in Punjab and Haryana in the intensively cultivated areas also paves way to floods.
4) **Deforestation:** Forests help in limiting the speed of flood water. Deforestation in the river catchment areas in hilly areas in Himachal Pradesh, Uttarakhand, Western Ghats, and Chhota Nagpur Hills causes floods.
5) **Landslides:** Landslides in Himalayan and other mountainous regions cause floods. Devastating floods of Uttarakhand in 2013 were the result of landslides falling into rivers of the region.
6) **Cloudbursts:** A huge volume of water falls into rivers due to cloudbursts, thus overflowing their banks. Frequently occurring flash floods in Kullu region of Himachal Pradesh set in due to cloudbursts.
7) **Cyclones:** Coastal regions of West Bengal, Tamil Nadu, Andhra Pradesh, and Odisha are experiencing floods due to cyclones. Cyclones accompanied by strong winds raise tidal level and there is inundation in these regions.

INDIA'S FLOOD HISTORY

India and Indians suffered a lot due to some devastating floods in the past years.

1) ***Gujarat Floods 1979:** Floods were caused due to failure of Machhu Dam.*
2) ***Bihar Flood 1987, 2017:** Source of flood had been river Kosi. Due to large-scale destruction, river Kosi got sobriquet "Sorrow of Bihar". Water overflow from river Gandak had also been responsible for floods. Heavy rains in Bihar during monsoons have made Bihar the most flood-prone state in India.*
3) ***Assam Floods 1998***
4) ***Maharashtra Floods 2005:** Overall loss worth Rs. 550/- crores.*
5) ***Himalayan Flash Floods 2012:** Caused by cloudburst. It affected all Himalayan states.*
6) ***Jammu & Kashmir Floods 2014***
7) ***Assam Floods 2012 and 2015:** These floods ware caused by overflowing of the Brahamaputra and its tributaries due to heavy rainfall. It affected habitat of Kaziranga National Park also.*
8) ***Uttarakhand Floods 2013:** Devastating floods took the whole state under its influence. Caused due to landslides, it damaged the famous Kedarnath Temple besides damaging crops, property, infrastructure and large-scale loss of human, animal, and plant life.*
9) ***Chennai floods 2015***
10) ***Gujarat Floods 2015:** Gir Forest National Park was severely affected.*
11) ***West Bengal Floods 2017:** Cyclone Komen was responsible for floods.*
12) ***Mumbai floods 2017:** Heavy rainfall due to climate change became cause of floods.*
13) ***Gujarat Floods 2017:** Heavy influx of water into Dharoi and Dantiwada dam became the reason of flood.*
14) ***Kerala Floods 2018:** The most devastating flood affecting all the 14 districts of the state.*

Flood Mitigation in India

Management of floods in India were adopted with the launching of National Programme of Flood Management in 1954 and it became part of Five Year Plans. Besides taking general structural and non-structural measures to mitigate floods, Indian government has been coming up with certain policy frameworks to manage floods in India according to its vulnerability to floods on the basis of its topography, wide variation in flood distribution, and intensity of damages suffered by urban and rural areas.

Policy framework: A two-tier policy framework is adopted to manage floods in India. State governments and the central government both play a major role in planning and executing flood mitigation policies. State government, being better versed with their respective local conditions, are entrusted with the primary responsibility to manage floods. For this, states come up with flood management plans and implement these as per their requirement. States use their resources to make and execute such plans. Central government provides technical and non-technical advice. In addition to the above, the central government has drafted the following policies:

1) **Policy Statement-1954:** After devastating floods of 1954, government of India constituted an expert committee on flood management. The committee submitted policy statement in the Parliament, in which the parliament was appraised with the prevailing flood situation in the country with a strategy to manage floods and relieve the country of this hazard.
2) **Policy Statement-1958:** Expert Committee on Flood Management submitted its report in 1957 and its recommendations were considered as policy in 1958. The policy provided :
   a) Installation of flood forecasting and early warning systems
   b) Amalgamating flood management schemes with general water plans to ensure effective implementation of flood control schemes
   c) Drafting and implementing policy exclusively to manage floods in urban areas
   d) Prioritising soil conservation in Himalayas along with their foothills, Deccan Plateau, and Indo-Gangetic plain and catchment areas of multipurpose dams
   e) Proper designing, protection, and execution of embankments. These are an effective means of flood management.

Catchment Area and Embankment

Catchment Area: *It is an area of land which is filled with water during rains. The area is surrounded by hills. Rainwater flows over this catchment area and ultimately falls into rivers or streams. Catchment area also houses water from melting of snow. It is a low-lying area from where water coming due to any atmospheric phenomenon converges to the catchment area for ultimately joining a water body.*

Embankment: *An artificial mound or wall of stone adjacent to a road or any land area or dam to block flood water and preventing it from going to the road or adjoining area. This also referred as a levee or dyke.*

3) **National Water Policy (NWP):**
   a. **NWP-1987:** The National Water Resources Council adopted this policy. The policy recommended implementation of non-structural measures like installation of early warning system, providing flood cushion in the water storage projects, and protecting embankments.
   b. **NWP-2002:** While upholding the recommendations of NWP (1987), the National Water Resources Council adopted an updated National Water Policy in 2002. The policy provisions and recommendation included preparing a master plan of flood control for the flood-prone areas, making and enforcing strict regulations for housing and business establishments in the flood-prone areas, applying suitable technology by the states and the central governments to minimise soil and land erosion by various water bodies, i.e., rivers and seas, and modernising and expansion of flood forecasting activities.
   c. **NWP-2012:** NWP-2012 was adopted by the National Water Resources Council. The council again carried forward the provisions of NWP-1987 and NWP-2002 along with additional provisions like diverting part of flow of flood water to other rivers where there is no apprehension of havoc, creating reservoirs behind dams over rivers prone to floods, creating a channel parallel to town or river to dilute the strength of damage and destruction by flood water, monitoring the drainage system, and repairing and clearing congestions wherever necessary.

Flood plain zoning: The Central Water Commission has asked for flood plain zoning. It is earmarking zones of flood-prone areas and proposing permissible economic and development activities to achieve minimum damage in case of floods.

Flood proofing: It is raising the level of houses and other establishments above the flood level. Flood proofing has been implemented in various villages of West Bengal, Uttar Pradesh, Assam, and Bihar.

Flood Mitigation Bodies

1) **National Flood Commission (Rashtriya Barh Ayog):** Indian government created the commission in 1976 to manage floods while applying, administrative, and technical tools. The main task of the commission was to adopt a scientific and administrative approach to flood control. The commission was to draw a national plan of flood control specifying priorities. The commission submitted its report regarding flood control measures. The commission emphasise coordinated role of the state and the central governments in controlling floods. The major recommendations included preparing separate flood damage reports for the protected and unprotected areas, suitable legislation on flood management, and proper fund maintenance.
2) **Central Water Commission (CWC):** This commission was created in 1945. It works under the union Ministry of Water Resources, River Development, and Ganga Rejuvenation. The commission works for conservation, control, and utilisation of water resources for the purpose of flood control besides other purposes of irrigation, navigation, and supply of drinking water.
3) **Ganga Flood Control Commission (GFCC):** India created the commission in 1972 under the Ministry of Ministry of Water Resources, River Development, and Ganga Rejuvenation. Its main task is to prepare and implementing plans to control flooding in the Ganga basin.
4) **Brahmaputra Board:** The board was created as a statutory body in 1980 to control flooding in the Brahmaputra and the Barak basins covering all North-eastern states. The Board works under the Ministry of Water Resources, River Management, and Ganga Rejuvenation.
5) **Farakka Barrage Project Authority:** The authority was created in 1961 to divert the excess water of the Ganga to the Bhagirathi-Hoogly river system in order to prevent soil erosion and flooding in the basin. The authority works under the Ministry of Water Resources, River Development, and Ganga Rejuvenation.
6) **National Disaster Management Authority (NDMA):** It was created in 2005 with the Prime Minister as its chairman. The authority is to draft and implement plans regarding addressing of various disasters including floods.

CYCLONES

Cyclones or tropical cyclones are development of low atmospheric pressure systems over oceans and seas in the tropical and subtropical regions. Cyclones are characterised with strong winds moving at an average speed of 63 km/hr. Cyclones are also taken to be winds spiralling inward around a center of low atmospheric pressure zone. The center of the low pressure zone is called 'Eye of a storm'. These winds rotate clockwise in Southern Hemisphere and anti-clockwise in Northern Hemisphere. Tropical cyclones travel about 300-500 km a day. The diameter of a cyclone is between 100 to 2000 kms. Tropical cyclone is characterised by strong and high speed winds, heavy rain, rising tide level, and storm surge. Strong blowing of winds sometimes touch a speed of 200 to 300 km/hr, thus proving a devastating natural hazard. Cyclones also raise sea level by 20-25 feet above normal level. A cyclone occurs in tropical and subtropical regions which are hot being near to the equator. As water of tropical and subtropical seas and ocean is hot at the surface, cyclones occur after obtaining heat and energy from warm waters of seas and oceans. As cyclone is circular whirl of the spiralling air, the word cyclone has been derived from Greek word 'kuklos', which means coiling of a snake. Henry Piddington, a British meteorologist coined the word 'Cyclone.'

***Tropical regions** are the regions on the earth near the equator. These regions fall between Tropic of Cancer (In northern hemisphere) and Tropic of Capricorn (In southern hemisphere).*

***Subtropical regions** are the regions falling between 25° to 40° both in northern hemisphere and southern hemisphere.*

***Equator:** It is an imaginary horizontal line drawn in the middle of the earth. Equator is also called 0° latitude. Equator divides the earth horizontally into northern hemisphere and southern hemisphere. Equator is the hottest region of the earth as the sun's rays vertically fall on it.*

Tropic of Cancer: *It is a line parallel to the equator, drawn at about 23° in the northern hemisphere.*

Tropic of Capricorn: *It is another line drawn parallel to the equator at about 23° in the southern hemisphere. Countries falling between Tropic of Cancer and Tropic of Capricorn are hot due to being close to the Equator.*

Types of Cyclones

1) **Tropical Cyclone:** Cyclone occurring in tropical and subtropical regions is tropical cyclone.
2) **Polar Cyclones:** Such cyclones occur in the polar regions like Greenland, Antarctica, and Siberia. These cyclones are less harmful as these occur in sparsely populated areas. These are stronger in winter months.
3) **Mesocyclones:** As meso means middle, mesocyclone occurs when a part of the thunderstorm cloud is spinning and eventually generates a tornado. Mesocyclone is a way or means to generate a tornado. It is in the middle of two types of storms.

CYCLONES, HURRICANES, TYPHOONS, TORNADOES, WILLY-WILLIES

Hurricanes, Typhoons, Tornadoes, and Willy-Willies are also cyclones. There is no difference in a cyclone and any of these storms. A cyclone gets different names in different regions in which it is occurring.

Cyclone: *A cyclone is called cyclone in Indian Ocean and South Pacific Ocean.*

Hurricane: *A cyclone is called hurricane in Atlantic Ocean and West Indian islands in Caribbean Sea.*

Typhoon: *A cyclone is called typhoon in Pacific Ocean and China Sea.*

Tornado: *A cyclone is called tornado in Southern USA and Guinea lands of West Africa.*

Willy-Willy: *A cyclone is called Willy-Willy in waters in Australia.*

Causes of Cyclones

Main cause of the cyclone is rise in sea temperature. When the temperature rises above 27° C, cyclone sets in. The air over the surface of the sea rises up after getting warm. Rising air also carry sizeable moisture. Lifting of warm air creates low pressure zone with a center. Strong winds start spiralling around the low pressure zone and hence tropical cyclone occurs.

Effects of Cyclones

As cyclone is a natural hazard, it yields the following disasters:

1) Drowning of human beings, animals, vegetation, houses, and other masonry structures
2) Soil erosion and reduction in soil fertility
3) Contamination of drinking water
4) Disruption in various services like transport, communication, banking, trade, health, and power supply
5) Damage to public and private property
6) Outbreak of epidemics resulting in serious illness and deaths
7) Storm surge (abnormal rise of sea level) resulting in flash floods (flood water inundates into low-lying areas near coast and causes havoc)
8) Damage to embankments, flood walls, and other flood management structures
9) Large-scale rains and landslides
10) Degradation of ecosystem
11) Paralysis of civic system and services

CATEGORY OF CYCLONES AND DAMAGES

Category 1: *Wind speed between 80 to 120 km/hr. This cyclone damages some houses and trees.*

Category 2: *Wind speed between 120 to 165 km/hr. Significant damages to houses, crops, and trees*

Category 3: *Wind speeds between 165 to 220 km/hr. Heavy structural damages to buildings, houses, and infrastructure*

Category 4: *Wind speed between 220 to 280 km/hr. Damage to various services like communication, power supply, health, and banking*

Category 5: *Wind speed above 280 km/hr. Widespread damage to all sectors in rural and urban areas*

Mitigation Measures

Cyclones are characterised by storm surge. Storm surge creates floods in the low-lying areas near the coasts. All structural and non-structural measures taken for flood management are taken for tropical cyclone management.

WORLD HISTORY OF CYCLONES

Sr. No.	*Name of Cyclone*	*Affected Country/Region*	*Year*
1.	*Bhola*	*East Pakistan*	*1970*
2.	*Nina*	*China*	*1975*
3.	*Urir Char*	*Bangladesh*	*1985*
4.	*Katrina*	*USA*	*2005*
5.	*Mala*	*Myanmar, Thailand*	*2006*
6.	*Nargis*	*Myanmar*	*2008*
7.	*Hayian*	*Philipines*	*2013*
8.	*Patricia*	*USA, Mexico*	*2015*
9.	*Harvey*	*Belize, Suriname,*	*2017*
		Honduras, Guyana, USA	*2017*
10.	*Maria*	*Dominica, Puerto Rico, UK, France, USA*	*2017*
11.	*Kong-Rey*	*Philippines, South Korea*	*2018*
12.	*Yutu*	*Philippines, South China Sea*	*2018*
13.	*Mona*	*Fiji, Tonga*	*2019*
14.	*Pabuk*	*Vietnam, Malaysia, Thailand, Myanmar*	*2019*

CYCLONES IN INDIA

Coastal belt of India experiences tropical cyclones. India has a coastline of 7516 kms. Out of this, about 5400 km of the coastline is prone to cyclones. About 8% of total land are of India is prone to cyclones. Tropical cyclones in India account for 10% of total tropical cyclones in the world. Cyclones in India occur at the east coast and west coast. East coast is more vulnerable to cyclones than west coast. On the east coast, West Bengal, Odisha, Tamil Nadu, and Pondicherry are prone to cyclones. On the west coast, Gujarat, Goa, Karnataka, and Kerala are vulnerable. Cyclones occur between April and May and between October and December in India.

About two-third of the cyclones that occur in the Indian coastline occur in the Bay of Bengal. The Indian Ocean is one of the six major cyclone-prone regions of the world.

Cyclone Management in India

1) **Warning System:** India possesses the best warning system in the world. Indian Meteorological Department (IMD) not only forecasts the cyclones, but also estimates and categorises the cyclones and warnings are issued accordingly. Cyclones in the Bay of Bengal and Arabian Sea are predicted by Area Cyclone Warning Centres (ACWC) and Cyclone Warning Centres working under IMD. The National Cyclone Warning Centre (NCWC), New Delhi acts as a coordinator between the two. Cyclone warning is disseminated by several means such as satellite-based disaster warning systems, radio, television, telephone, fax, high priority telegram, public announcements, and bulletins in press. These warnings are disseminated to the general public, the fishing community (especially those in the sea), port authorities, commercial aviation, and the government machinery.
2) **Detection of low pressure in advance:** Low pressure is detected in advance through satellite tracking system and accordingly mitigation measures are taken along with evacuating population of target area and shifting it to safer places.
3) **Coastal belt plantation:** Green belt plantation along the coastal line in a scientific interweaving pattern can reduce the effect of the hazard. Providing a cover through green belt sustains less damage. Forests act as a wide buffer zone against strong winds and flash floods. Without the forest, the cyclone travel freely inland. The lack of protective forest cover allows water to inundate large areas and cause destruction. With the loss of the forest cover each consecutive cyclone can penetrate further inland.

4) **National Cyclone Risk Mitigation Project (NCRMP):** NCRMP has been launched by the government as a mitigation measure against the cyclones. Under this project all suitable structural and non-structural measures to mitigate the effects of cyclones in all coastal states and UTs are carried out. National Disaster Management Authority (NDMA) under the Ministry of Home Affairs is executing this project. 13 states and UTs have been identified according to vulnerability and frequency of occurrence of cyclones.

CYCLONE HISTORY OF INDIA

Sr. No.	*Name of Cyclone*	*Affected State/Region*	*Year*
1.	*Nisha*	*Tamil Nadu*	*2008*
2.	*Phyan*	*Tamil Nadu, Maharashtra, Gujarat*	*2009*
3.	*Bijli*	*West Bengal, Odisha*	*2009*
4.	*Laila*	*Andhra Pradesh, Tamil Nadu*	*2010*
5.	*Thane*	*Tamil Nadu*	*2011*
6.	*Nilam*	*Tamil Nadu, Andhra Pradesh*	*2012*
7.	*Helen*	*Andhra Pradesh*	*2013*
8.	*Phailin*	*Andhra Pradesh, Odisha*	*2013*
9.	*Lehar*	*Andaman Nicobar, Tamil Nadu*	*2013*
10.	*Hudhud*	*Andhra, Odisha, Madhya Pradesh, Chhattisgarh*	*2014*
11.	*Nada*	*Tamil Nadu*	*2016*
12.	*Kyant*	*Odisha*	*2016*
13.	*Vardah*	*Andaman & Nicobar, Tamil Nadu, Andhra Pradesh*	*2016*
14.	*Ockhi*	*Tamil Nadu, Kerala, Gujarat*	*2017*
15.	*Maarutha*	*Andaman Nicobar*	*2017*
16.	*Phethai*	*Andhra Pradesh, Odisha*	*2018*
17.	*Gaja*	*Tamil Nadu, Andhra Pradesh*	*2018*
18.	*Titli*	*Odisha, Andhra Pradesh*	*2018*
19.	*Fani*	*Odisha*	*2019*
20.	*Vayu*	*Gujarat Coast*	*2019*

DROUGHT

Drought is either absence or deficiency of rainfall from its normal pattern in a region for an extended period of time leading to general suffering in the society. It is imbalance between demand that people place on natural supply of water and natural event that provides the water in a given geographical region. Though drought is a natural disaster, its effects are made worse in developing countries by overpopulation, overgrazing, deforestation, soil erosion, excessive use of ground and surface water for growing crops, and loss of biodiversity. Effects of drought exist for months or years together. As droughts badly affect food production, it reduces life expectancy.

Types of Droughts

1) **Meteorological drought:** It is simply deficit of rainfall. Drought occurs when dry weather pattern overpowers the other climatic conditions. It is the least severe type of natural hazard as it does not demolish buildings and infrastructure like other disasters. Considerable absence of moisture in the atmosphere is the measure of drought. Lack of precipitation, dry winds, and rise in temperature are effective in occurrence of drought. This drought is an alarm of water shortage. If conditions of drought persist for some time, an acute water shortage is the apprehension. This drought occurs for a short period but becomes the base for other types of droughts.

2) **Hydrological drought:** Low level of water in various water bodies like streams, rivers, reservoirs, and groundwater results in hydrological drought. Though hydrological drought is a natural phenomenon, yet anthropological activities are also effective in occurrence of hydrological drought. Prolonged meteorological drought becomes the base of hydrological drought as meteorological drought leads to shortage of surface water. Changes in land use and land degradation are measures of the magnitude and frequency of this drought.

3) **Agricultural drought:** This drought occurs when moisture level in soil becomes insufficient to maintain average crop yield. Agricultural drought is the first signal of drought during span of meteorological drought. This drought is also outcome of soil-water deficit and reduced water level of reservoirs and groundwater. This drought hampers germination and reduces crop yield. First impact of agricultural drought is on rainfed areas, then on irrigated areas. Further, its impacts slowly spread into social fabric as the availability of drinking water diminishes. This results in reduction in energy production, ground water depletion, food shortage, health reduction and loss of life, increased poverty, reduced quality of life, and social unrest leading to migration.

4) **Socio-economic drought:** This type of drought occurs due to imbalance between demand and supply of consumer goods. Supply of various economic goods like water, foodgrains, fish, energy, and power depend upon the climatic conditions. Any abnormality in climate due to any reason creates imbalance. As drought is the outcome of scanty rainfall, poor precipitation, low level of water in water bodies due to abrupt climatic changes, demand exceeds supply in such an hour of emergency. Reduction in production of hydroelectric energy results in reduction in the production of essential and consumer goods. Further, growth in population also affects balance between demand and supply.

Causes of Drought

1) **Insufficient rainfall:** The foremost cause of a drought is insufficient and unevenly distributed rainfall.

2) **Climate changes:** There have been unpredictable and abrupt changes due to various human eco-hostile activities leading to global warming, thus resulting in droughts. Weather gets dry due to rise in temperature of the earth and prolonged droughts set in.

3) **Human activities:** Major human activity is deforestation for grabbing more and more land to erect concrete jungles. Forests act as an effective partner of water cycle. They help in storing water and make vital contribution in maintaining moisture in the atmosphere. But deforestation leads to wiping out the whole moisture by evaporation from the atmosphere and there are droughts as a result. Excessive farming is also responsible for droughts as overfarming leads to soil erosion due to which soil loses its power to hold water.

4) **Overexploitation of surface water resources:** Overutilisation of water from rivers and other water bodies for various purposes reduce the water level leading to droughts. Hydroelectric dams using water for various purposes lead to fall in water level.

Impacts of Droughts

1) Environmenal Impact
2) Economic Impact
3) Social Impact

1) **Environmental impact:** Droughts result in loss of biodiversity, damages to various animal and plant species, wildlife habitat, and degradation of landscape quality. Some of the impacts are short-lived as things become normal as drought ends. Soil erosion and degradation of landscape quality are permanent impacts, whereas loss of biodiversity and wildlife habitat leading to migration is short-lived as when circumstances return to normalcy, migrated animals come back.

2) **Economic impact:** Due to dependence on surface and groundwater, agriculture and allied sectors experience various damages due to shortage of water created by drought. Due to poor agricultural yield, there is reduction in farmers' income and farmers resort to debt from private money lenders, banks, and other financial institutions. Similarly, traders supplying agricultural products to farmers also experience reduction in their business. Further, there is reduction in overall business also leading to decrease in supply of goods. Prices of goods rise due to their shortage. Fallout of this situation is found in the form of unemployment. Fall in the level of water in rivers reduces navigation and hampers transportation of goods. Fall in income of people, particularly farmers, increase credit risk for credit institutions.

3) **Social impact:** Droughts compel the population of drought-ridden areas to migrate to urban areas. Further, conflict among people rises over water. There is reduction in public health and safety. There is outbreak of many diseases due to insect infestation. Migration to urban areas increases pressure on urban areas which arises poverty, unemployment, and social conflicts and unrest. Generally migrants do not return, thus depriving rural areas of human resources.

Mitigation Measures

1) **Public awareness and education:** If the community is aware of the do's and don'ts, then half of the problem is solved. This includes awareness on the availability of safe drinking water, water conservation techniques, agricultural drought management strategies like crop contingency plans, and construction of rainwater harvesting structure. Awareness can be generated by the print, electronic, and folk media.
2) **Drought monitoring:** It is continuous observation of the rainfall situation, availability of water in the reservoirs, lakes, rivers, etc. and comparing with the existing water needs in various sectors of society.
3) **Expansion of irrigation facilities:** This reduces the drought vulnerability. Land use based on its capability helps in optimum use of land and water and can avoid the undue demand created due to their misuse.
4) **Prediction:** Prediction about droughts through various warning systems enables people and government to take necessary precautionary steps to minimise the impact of drought. Predictions results in conducting water and moisture surveys in atmosphere and soil and availability of water for domestic, irrigation, and other purposes.
5) **Impact assessment:** Impact assessment includes reviewing public health, risk factors, extent of damage to flora and fauna, and water quality and quantity. Impact assessment helps in taking adequate steps by the government to provide relief to the affected population in terms of finance, food, and medical aid.
6) **Responsive measures:** Such measures include better drought monitoring, better water and crop management, augmentation of water supplies with groundwater, increased public awareness and education, intensified watershed and local planning, reduction in water demand, and water conservation.
7) **Conservation of water and soil:** Conservation practices minimise the disruption of the soil's structure, composition, and natural biodiversity, thereby reducing erosion and soil degradation, surface runoff, and water pollution.
8) **Herd management:** Herd management is an important strategy for drought mitigation. Factors to be considered include the expected drought duration, the current water and food supplies, the composition and body condition of the herd, and the financial resources available. Accordingly, steps are taken to protect the herd from catastrophes of drought.

DROUGHTS IN INDIA

In India, the droughts have been proven to be the deadliest natural disaster. Since 18th, 19th, and 20th centuries droughts in India have claimed millions of precious lives. India has been an agrarian country, so agriculture is the major occupation. Agricultural operations totally depend upon rainfall and water supply. Shortage of water either due to continuously falling water level or uneven distribution of rainfall result in droughts and then famine, causing mass deaths. According to Union Ministry of Agriculture and Farmers' Welfare, drought is a state of water shortage for human, cattle, and agriculture consumption resulting in economic losses, particularly in agriculture. According to the ministry, if rainfall is 19% below the normal level, there is failure to sustain moisture level in soil, thus leading to drought. It has been observed that in the recent years, frequency of drought has increased in Uttar Pradesh, Bihar, Karnataka, Maharashtra, and Kerala.

Drought-Prone Areas

About one-sixth of total geographical area of India representing 12% of total population is drought-prone. These areas receive an annual rainfall up to 60 cm. Maximum drought-prone area falls into arid, semi-arid, and sub-humid regions of the country.

DROUGHT-PRONE REGIONS OF INDIA

1) ***Arid region:** It is hot sandy region of the country comprising Great Indian Desert (Thar desert) of Rajasthan, Gujarat, Punjab, and Haryana.*
2) ***Semi-arid region:** This region possesses drought-prone area which is larger than the arid region. This region comprises Andhra Pradesh, Tamil Nadu, Karnataka, and Rajasthan.*

> 3) ***Sub-humid region:*** *In this region, rainfall is in summer and varies from 65 cm to 250 cm from west to east. In summer, temperature rises above 45° centigrade. This region comprises foothills of Himalayas, plains of the Punjab and Haryana touching the Himalayas, Rajasthan east of the Aravalli region, Uttar Pradesh, Bihar, and northern part of West Bengal and Assam.*

Causes of Droughts

Droughts occur in India due to the following reasons:

1) **Location:** Certain regions of India are located in the drought-prone belt. Such areas receive an annual rainfall up to 60 cms. Irrigation Commission has identified more than 70% districts of the country which are drought-prone. States to which these districts belong are Rajasthan, Odisha, Andhra Pradesh, Karnataka, and Maharashtra.
2) **Insufficient rainfall:** Various regions of India experience scanty rainfall which becomes a major cause of drought.
3) **Variation in monsoon rainfall:** This becomes another major reason of drought in India. Regions like interior Odisha, western Jharkhand, Chhattisgarh, Madhya Pradesh, Haryana, Punjab, Kutch in Gujarat, eastern Karnataka, and western Andhra Pradesh experience variability of rainfall leading to droughts.
4) **Delay in the onset of monsoon:** Traditional farming and lifestyle patterns place heavy reliance on the timely arrival of monsoon. So even if the monsoon is delayed by a week, it causes a major upset in the farming communities and causes drought and famine. These delays however are a fairly common occurrence in areas that get marginal rainfall. The areas most affected are Punjab, Haryana, the Indo-Gangetic plains, Bundelkhand, eastern Rajasthan, eastern Gujarat, Madhya Pradesh, south Bihar, Jharkhand, interior West Bengal, Odisha, Andhra Pradesh, interior Karnataka, and eastern Tamil Nadu.
5) **Breaks in monsoon:** Even within the monsoon, if there are long dry periods, that too can cause drought in affected areas. This may happen due to a reduction in the speed of the rain-laden winds, or a diversion in the route. The damage to crops is usually extensive.
6) **Areal difference in monsoon:** A deviation in the route of monsoon winds, or an early withdrawal of the monsoon too can have similar repercussions on an area. If the monsoon hangs over east Uttar Pradesh for a longer period of time, then west U.P. or Haryana are adversely affected.

Impact of Droughts

1) **Environmental Impact:** Drought puts flora and faunal life into peril. In central India, life of national bird of India, the peacock, is at continuous risk. During 2013 and 2016 more than 60 peacocks died in Morena district of Madhya Pradesh during summer drought. Further, droughts compel the farmers to extract aquifers to get groundwater, but this increases the stress level on aquifers and groundwater is depleted. This further leads to land subsidence and loss of springs and wetlands. This impact is visible in Aravalli region of Rajasthan. It has also been experienced that change in environment of one region or country leads to change in environment of other region or country. It is on record that air pollution from Europe contributes to droughts in India.
2) **Social impacts:** Droughts strongly affect the social structure of the affected region. There have been evidences of migration of population from drought-affected regions in Madhya Pradesh and Maharashtra to urban areas, thus increasing pressure on urban population which leads to depression, social unrest, and chaos in the society.
3) **Economic impacts:** Agricultural share in India's GDP has fallen considerably due to reduced crop yield resulting from droughts. Droughts not only affect agricultural production but also destroy the prospects of allied activities like dairy farming and cattle farming. Drought shrinks the volume of fodder and other components of cattle and other farming animals' diet, due to which there is large-scale death of cattle as happened in many drought-affected villages in Bundelkhand in 2016.

ENSO Impact and Droughts

> *El Nino-Southern Oscillation (ENSO) is a natural event which occurs in equatorial Pacific Ocean in every two or five years. El Nino is a natural event which raises the sea water temperature of the tropical Pacific Ocean. Due to rise in the temperature of oceanic water, atmosphere near equator dries up which leads to drought. Another natural event La Nina is opposite to El Nino as it reduces the sea water temperature. Droughts are associated with El Nino event. El Nino contributes to droughts in India as well as other countries falling in the range of the equatorial Pacific Ocean.*

SOME STATISTICS ON DROUGHTS IN INDIA

1) *11 states have been declared as drought-affected. The states are Uttar Pradesh, Madhya Pradesh, Rajasthan, Odisha, Chhattisgarh, Andhra Pradesh, Telangana, Maharashtra, Karnataka, Gujarat, and Jharkhand.*
2) *93% of total districts each of Chhattisgarh and Karnataka are drought-affected. These are followed by Jharkhand (92%) and Odisha and Madhya Pradesh (90%).*
3) *In terms of absolute numbers, Uttar Pradesh has highest number of drought-affected districts (50) followed by Madhya Pradesh (45).*

Drought Management in India

The Union Ministry of Agriculture is the nodal Ministry in respect of monitoring and managing drought conditions. Following are leading drought management strategies adopted by the government of India:

1) The National Disaster Response Fund (NDRF) and State Disaster Response Fund (SDRF) constituted under Disaster Management Act, 2005 provide immediate drought relief to the affected people.
2) For combating the adverse financial impacts of drought, the National Agricultural Insurance Scheme (NAIS) was introduced in 1999 and Weather Based Crop Insurance Scheme in 2007.
3) The Drought Management Group was constituted to coordinate the efforts to deal with drought in various states.
4) The National Disaster Management Cell monitors the drought situation in different states.
5) National Calamity Contingency Fund from the Government deals with calamities of a severe nature.
6) Drought-Prone Areas Programme and Desert Development Programme use the plans prepared on the basis of the integrated estimation.
7) Research institutions like the International Crops Research Institute for the Semi-arid Tropics (ICRISAT); Central Arid Zone Research Institute; Indian Grassland and Fodder Research Institute; Indian Council of Forestry Research and Education, etc. are some of institutes that are involved in drought management.
8) The National Mission for A Green India, aims at improving the quality of forest cover.
9) The Mahatma Gandhi National Rural Employment Guarantee Scheme (MGNREGS) has a strong focus on land, water, and afforestation activities.
10) Integrated Watershed Management Programme (IWMP) has targeted development of 75 million hectares of rainfed/degraded area in a phased manner during 2007- 2027.
11) Every block in drought-affected areas has been taken up as an intensive Block under Deendayal Antyodaya Yojana.
12) The Pradhan Mantri Fasal Bima Yojana was approved in order to better protect farmers in times of unforeseen crises, including drought.
13) National Hydrology Project (NHP) has been launched to build the capacity of the government agencies in water resources management through the use of information systems and adoption of state-of-the-art technologies including remote sensing.
14) Pradhan Mantri Krishi Sinchayee Yojana has been launched for the period between 2015 and 2020. It aims at expanding cultivable area under assured irrigation (Har khet ko pani) and improve on-farm water use efficiency to reduce wastage of water.
15) Neeranchal National Watershed Project has been initiated with the assistance of World Bank. The project seeks to support Integrated Watershed Management Program (IWMP) through technical assistance to improve incremental conservation outcomes and agricultural yields.

EARTHQUAKE

Due to sudden release of energy stored in the earth's crust, seismic waves are produced, resulting in shaking of lithosphere and that is known as earthquake. An earthquake is considered to be a destructive natural hazard.

Magnitudes of Earthquakes and their Impact

Magnitude of an earthquake is measured with Richter's Scale. Following are different magnitudes of earthquakes with their respective impact:

Magnitude	Earthquake Effects
2.5 or less	Usually not felt, but can be recorded by seismograph
2.5 to 5.4	Often felt, but only causes minor damage
5.5 to 6.0	Slight damage to buildings and other structures
6.1 to 6.9	May cause a lot of damage in very populated areas
7.0 to 7.9	Major earthquake. Serious damage

8.0 or greater	Great earthquake. Can totally destroy communities near the epicenter

Magnitude Classes of Earthquakes

Earthquakes are also classified in categories ranging from minor to great, depending on their magnitude.

Class	**Magnitude**
Great	8 or more
Major	7–7.9
Strong	6–6.9
Moderate	5–5.9
Light	4–4.9
Minor	3–3.9

BASI C EARTHQUAKE TERMS

1) ***Seismology:*** *It is the study of earthquakes and seismic waves moving around the earth.*
2) ***Seismograph:*** *It is an instrument used to detect and record earthquakes. It is also called Seismometer.*
3) ***Richter Scale:*** *An American scientist Charles F. Richter developed Richter Scale in 1935 to compare magnitude of earthquakes.*
4) ***Hypocenter:*** *It is the point within the earth's crust where earthquake rupture starts.*
5) ***Epicenter:*** *It is a point on the earth's surface just above the hypocenter.*
6) ***Harmonic Tremor:*** *It is the continuous occurring of earthquakes simultaneously with volcanic eruptions. These can be measured with a seismograph.*
7) ***Aftershocks:*** *These are earthquakes occurring in a sequence after the largest earthquake.*
8) ***Foreshocks:*** *These are small earthquakes occurring in a sequence before the largest earthquake.*
9) ***Mainshock:*** *It is the largest earthquake occurring before or after sequences of foreshocks and aftershocks.*
10) ***Crust:*** *It is the outermost major layer of the earth, ranging from about 10 to 65 km in thickness worldwide. The uppermost 15-35 km of crust is brittle enough to produce earthquakes.*
11) ***Plate Tectonics:*** *These are the thin large rocky plates under the earth which move relative to one another. Any abnormality in their movements results in earthquake.*
12) ***Rayleigh Wave:*** *It is a seismic surface where ground is shaken in an elliptical motion.*
13) ***Teleseismic monitoring:*** *This is a technique pertaining to seismically image earthquakes at distances greater than 1,000 km from the measurement site.*
14) ***Seismicity:*** *This refers to the geographic and historical distribution of earthquakes.*
15) ***Intensity:*** *This is a number (written as a Roman numeral) describing the severity of an earthquake in terms of its effects on the earth's surface and on humans and their structures.*
16) ***Liquefaction:*** *This refers to soil attaining characteristics of liquid due to increasing pore pressure during earthquake. Soil loses its solidity in this process.*

Intensity of Earthquake

Intensity of an earthquake signifies its severity. It is measured with Modified Mercalli scale or Rossi-Forel scale. Different intensities are shown below:

Magnitude	**Modified Mercalli Intensity**	**Description**
0-1.9	–	micro-not felt
2.0-2.9	I	minor-rarely felt
3.0-3.9	II-III	minor-noticed by a few people
4.0-4.9	IV-V	light-felt by many people, minor damage possible
5.0-5.9	VI-VII	moderate-felt by most people, possible broken plaster and chimneys
6.0-6.9	VII-IX	strong-damage variable depending on building construction and substrate
7.0-7.9	IX-X	major -extensive damage, some buildings destroyed
8.0-8.9	X-XII	great -extensive damage over broad areas, many buildings destroyed
9.0 and above	XI-XII	great-extensive damage over broad areas, most buildings destroyed

Causes and Types of Earthquakes

1) **Tectonic earthquakes:** These earthquakes occur due to abnormality in movement of plate tectonics. These are the most commonly occurring earthquakes worldwide.
2) **Induced earthquakes:** These earthquakes are the result of human activity like tunnel construction and implementing geothermal projects.
3) **Volcanic earthquakes:** These earthquakes occur due to volcanic eruptions. These are not dangerous and destructive like tectonic volcanoes. They are felt only within the hypocenter as they occur near the surface of the volcano.
4) **Collapse earthquakes:** These earthquakes are the result of caving in of buildings or roads. Subsidence becomes the primary cause of these earthquakes.
5) **Explosion earthquakes:** These earthquakes occur due to explosion of nuclear and chemical devices.

Effects of Earthquakes

1) **Ground rupture:** This effect of the earthquake actually breaks the earth's surface. This leads to damage to roads, railway tracks, airport runways, and supply pipelines of various amenities like water, cooking gas, etc. It also damage electricity and telephone wiring.
2) **Ground shaking:** It is the foremost effect of earthquakes. Shaking of ground results in collapse of buildings, landslides, and falling of trees leading to large-scale loss of lives, livestock, property, and infrastructure.
3) **Subsidence, liquefaction, and allied effects:** As a strong effect of earthquakes, subsidence of ground and liquefaction of soil, there exists a danger to railway lines, airports, buildings, sinking of buildings, etc.
4) **Landslides:** Landslides are also a fallout of earthquakes. Landslides destroy buildings built on hills and other buildings which come in the way. Landslides also block roads and railway lines.
5) **Tsunamis:** Though there is ground shaking and rupture due to earthquakes, yet major impact of earthquakes is in the oceans. Tsunamis are sea waves coming towards the beach. Starting waves are gentle but these are followed by abrupt and aggressive ones. Sea surface water moves vertically with a massive force in an earthquake. Sea water reaches up to a height of 100 feet and higher. Sea waves of tsunamis carry people, vehicles, buildings, animals, and other living/non-living objects along with them. Tsunamis pose a threat of grave natural hazard around the world in general and around Pacific Ocean in particular.
6) **Damage to social and economic order:** As earthquakes result in a huge and universal damages, health and socio-economic order is badly damaged. It results in diseases, deaths, starvation, unemployment, chaos, and deterioration of law and order.

Mitigation Measures

Earthquake mitigation measures are typically intended to reduce both casualties and damage in future earthquakes. Some broad earthquake mitigation measures include:

1) **Structural:** Though no building can be constructed 100% earthquake-safe, yet buildings can be made maximum earthquake-resistant up to a certain extent. This can be accomplished by selecting a proper structural configuration. Various experimental techniques can be used to test the response of buildings to verify their resistance to earthquakes. One such technique is earthquake shaking table.
2) **Non-structural:** A construction plan of each building should be made while adhering to the policy guidelines and its approval should be taken from concerned authorities. Building codes should be adopted. There should be formulation of guidelines for earthquake resistant construction and for retrofitting while specifying the selection of site, foundation, construction material, trained engineers, architects, and masons. Further, there should be guidelines for concerned authorities about land use planning, monitoring of construction work, and controlling of settlements in hazard-prone areas to avoid fatalities and loss of property.
3) **Seismic retrofitting:** Seismic retrofitting is the modification of existing structures to make them more resistant to seismic activity, ground motion, or soil failure due to earthquakes.

Besides the above broad measures, certain particular measures are also taken as follows:

Pre-Disaster Preventive Measures

1) **Long-term measures:**
   a) Re-framing buildings codes, guidelines, manuals, and byelaws and their strict implementation-Tougher legislation for highly seismic areas
   b) Incorporating earthquake-resistant features in all buildings at high-risk areas
   c) Making all public utilities like water supply systems, communication networks, electricity lines, etc. earthquake-proof-Creating alternative arrangements to reduce damages to infrastructure facilities

d) Constructing earthquake-resistant community buildings and buildings (used to gather large groups during or after an earthquake) like schools, dharamshalas, hospitals, prayer halls, etc., especially in seismic zones of moderate to higher intensities

e) Supporting R&D in various aspects of disaster mitigation, preparedness, and prevention and post-disaster management

f) Evolving educational curricula in architecture and engineering institutions and technical training in polytechnics and schools to include disaster related topics

2) Medium-term measures:

a) Retrofitting of weak structures in highly seismic zones

b) Preparation of disaster-related literature in local languages with dos and don'ts for construction

c) Getting communities involved in the process of disaster mitigation through education and awareness

d) Networking of local NGOs working in the area of disaster management

Post-Disaster Preventive Measures

1) Maintenance of law and order, prevention of trespassing, looting, etc.
2) Evacuation of people
3) Recovery of dead bodies and their disposal
4) Medical care for the injured
5) Supply of food and drinking water
6) Temporary shelters like tents, metal sheds etc.
7) Repairing lines of communication and information
8) Restoring transport routes
9) Quick assessment of destruction and demarcation of destroyed areas, according to the grade of damage
10) Cordoning off severely damaged structures that are liable to collapse during aftershock

RETROFITTING

Retrofitting means 'providing something with a component or feature to a building, not fitted during manufacture or adding something that it did not have when first constructed'. It is often used in relation to the installation of new building systems, such as heating systems, but it might also refer to the fabric of a building, for example, retrofitting insulation or double glazing.

Retrofitting has come to prominence in recent years as part of the drive to make buildings more thermal efficient and sustainable. This can help cut carbon emissions, make it cheaper and easier to run buildings, and can contribute to overcoming poor ventilation and moisture problems, therefore improving the health of occupants. It can also increase building adaptability, durability, and resiliency.

Major Earthquake-Prone Countries

(In descending order of frequency)

1) Japan
2) Nepal
3) India
4) Ecuador
5) Philippines
6) Pakistan
7) El Salvador
8) Mexico
9) Turkey
10) Indonesia

EARTHQUAKES IN INDIA

India, due to its geophysical setting, is highly prone to earthquakes of varying intensities. The country has faced several devastating earthquakes in the past resulting in a large number of deaths and severe property damage. As per the current seismic hazard map of the country, about 60% of India's land area is prone to moderate to severe earthquakes. Some of the devastating earthquakes are mentioned below:

1) **2015 India/Nepal Earthquake:** Indian states which were affected included Bihar, Uttar Pradesh, and Delhi. Operation 'Maitri' was launched as a rescue operation.

2) **2011 Sikkim Earthquake:** This occurred near the border of Nepal and Sikkim. The earthquake was also felt across north-eastern India with a moment magnitude of 6.9.

3) **2005 Kashmir Earthquake:** This was considered as the deadliest earthquake to hit South Asia since 1935 with a registered moment magnitude of 7.6.

4) **2004 Indian Ocean Earthquake:** This earthquake and tsunami was one of the most devastating natural disasters in India and also the deadliest tsunami in recorded history affecting people in 14 countries around the Indian Ocean.

5) **2001 Bhuj Earthquake:** This is also known as Gujarat earthquake which occurred on 26 January 2001 on the Republic Day of India at 08:46 AM IST. The earthquake with a registered moment magnitude of 7.7 destroyed nearly 400,000 homes and damaged millions of structures.

6) **1999 Chamoli Earthquake:** This was the strongest earthquake to hit the foothills of the Himalayas in more than 90 years and the state of Uttarakhand.
7) **1997 Jabalpur Earthquake:** This occurred near Kosamghat village and Jabalpur and Mandla were the worst affected districts.
8) **1993 Latur Earthquake:** This primarily affected the districts of Latur in Maharashtra state of western India.
9) **1991 Uttarkashi Earthquake:** This affected the Gharwal regions of Uttarakhand flanked by the Tons river, damaging and destroying thousands of homes.
10) **1941 Andaman Islands Earthquake:** This primarily struck the Andaman Islands and also nearby Bangladesh, Myanmar, and Thailand. Andaman Islands are part of the earthquakes, cyclones, tsunamis, floods, and home to the only active volcano in India.
11) **1975 Kinnaur Earthquake:** This had a magnitude of 6.8 causing extensive damage in Himachal Pradesh with epicentre in Kinnaur district.
12) **1967 Koynanagar Earthquake:** 1967 Koynanagar earthquake in Maharashtra occurred near the site of Koyna dam and damaged the Koynanagar township.
13) **1956 Anjar Earthquake:** This affected the town of Anjar in Kutch and caused maximum damage in Anjar along with largely destroyed houses in Bhuj, Kera, and Bhachau.
14) **1934 Bihar-Nepal Earthquake:** This was one of the worst earthquakes in India and also in Nepal, damaging major towns of Kathmandu and Darbhanga.
15) **1905 Kangra Earthquake:** This earthquake killed more than 20,000 people and occurred in the Kangra Valley and the Kangra region of Himachal Pradesh.

Earthquake Zones in India

Earthquake-prone areas of the country have been identified on the basis of scientific inputs relating to seismicity, earthquakes occurred in the past, and tectonic set-up of the region. Based on these inputs, Bureau of Indian Standards has grouped the country into four seismic zones, viz. Zone II, III, IV, and V. Of these, Zone V is seismically the most active region, while Zone II is the least. Broadly, no area of India has been classified as Zone I.

Zone - V comprises entire north eastern India, parts of Jammu and Kashmir, Himachal Pradesh, Uttaranchal, Rann of Kutch in Gujarat, part of North Bihar, and Andaman & Nicobar Islands.

Zone - IV covers remaining parts of Jammu and Kashmir and Himachal Pradesh, National Capital Territory (NCT) of Delhi, Sikkim, northern parts of Uttar Pradesh, Bihar, and West Bengal, parts of Gujarat, and small portions of Maharashtra near the west coast and Rajasthan.

Zone - III comprises Kerala, Goa, Lakshadweep islands, remaining parts of Uttar Pradesh, Gujarat , West Bengal, parts of Punjab, Rajasthan, Madhya Pradesh, Bihar, Jharkhand, Chhattisgarh, Maharashtra, Odisha, Andhra Pradesh, Tamil Nadu, and Karnataka.

Zone - II covers the remaining parts of the country.

Earthquake Mitigation in India

1) **National Building Code (NBC) of India 2016:** This code provides guidelines for regulating the building construction activities across the country. It serves as a Model Code for adoption by all agencies involved in building construction works. The Code mainly contains administrative regulations, development control rules, general building requirements, and fire safety requirements. The NBC 2016 contains chapters on development control rules and general building requirements, fire and life safety, building materials, structural design, construction management practices, and safety and building services.
2) **Rapid Visual Screening (RVS):** In the wake of earthquakes risk in India, there was a need to identify buildings posing risk of earthquakes. Technique of RVS is applied to assess the vulnerability of rapidly increasing buildings in leading cities of India. It covers ill-conceived erected structures. It also examines whether all the safety measures have been taken by the builder. If in RVS, any vulnerability in the building(s) is found, then timely corrective measures are taken to make it hazard-resistant.
3) **Seismic Monitoring Network:** A seismic monitoring network has been established by Indian Meteorological Department, National Geophysical Research Institute, Department of Science and Technology, Bhabha Atomic Research Centre, and Regional Research Laboratory. These stations are recording useful seismic data, which enables to determine the location of epicentre and depth of hypocentre.

VOLCANIC ERUPTIONS

What is a Volcano?

A volcano is an opening in the earth's crust through which lava, volcanic ash, and gases escape. More than 80% of total surface of the earth is of volcanic origin.

What is a Volcanic Eruption ?

Below a volcano, hot liquid magma containing gases rises to the earth's surface and comes out through the vent in the form of lava. As magma rises, pressure falls and gases escape along with magma. Escaping of this matter from inside the earth is called volcanic eruption. Volcanic eruption occurs through a weak point of the earth's crust. Volcanic eruption is a dangerous natural hazard. During volcanic eruption, ash clouds are sent out along with lava and volcanic bombs. All these are capable of causing huge damage to human life and property.

Categories of Volcanoes

On the basis of eruption frequency, volcanoes are observed in three categories:

1) **Active volcano:** An active volcano is a volcano that has had at least one eruption during the past 10,000 years. An active volcano might be erupting or dormant. An erupting volcano is an active volcano.
2) **Dormant volcano:** A dormant volcano is an active volcano that is not erupting, but supposed to erupt again.
3) **Extinct volcano:** An extinct volcano has not had an eruption for at least 10,000 years and is not expected to erupt again in a comparable time scale of the future.

Hazards of Volcano

1) **Lava:** Lava or molten rock, though moving slowly, can destroy buildings and infrastructure. However, it does not pose a direct threat to people.
2) **Pyroclastic flows:** Pyroclastic flows are hot avalanches of rock, ash, and gas that travel down volcano slopes at high speeds. They may be very dangerous close to a volcano.
3) **Phreatic explosions:** These are explosions caused by interaction of water with magma.
4) **Lahars:** Lahars are hot or cold mixtures of water and volcanic debris that form when volcanic materials interact with water, ice, snow, or loose wet sediments. Lahars are most dangerous close to a volcano, but large lahars may rapidly travel many tens of metres per second along river valleys, so they can pose a threat to people and infrastructure far beyond the volcano's slopes.
5) **Jokulhlaups:** These are large abrupt floods of water from glacial lakes or from beneath glaciers. They may be triggered when a volcano erupts under a glacier.
6) **Landslides:** Landslides and other collapses of large parts of a volcano may occur with or without accompanying eruptions, and may transform into lahars if significant water is available. Because many volcanoes are steep and unstable, landslides frequently pose a hazard even when a volcano is dormant (not erupting).
7) **Volcanic earthquakes:** These are the result of the movement of magma or fluids underground, and are often too small to detect without instruments. As these seismic activities occur before eruption of a dormant volcano, these are effective means to predict eruptions and monitor volcanoes.
8) **Tsunamis:** Tsunamis are water waves that can result from submarine eruptions or from volcanic landslides into large bodies of water resulting in water coming out with a force while maintaining a noticeable height and flowing towards settlements, thus destroying them.
9) **Volcanic gases:** These gases bubble out of lava or escape through soil or vents in the ground. The most common volcanic gases are water vapour, carbon dioxide, sulphur dioxide, hydrogen, hydrogen sulphide, and carbon monoxide. Some of these gases are irritating or poisonous, or cause breathing problems, and the release of sulphur dioxide causes acid rain to form. Over long time periods, volcanic gases affect climate, bringing undesirable and unhealthy changes in it.
10) **Tephra:** It consists of rock fragments ejected from a volcano. Volcanic ash is tephra, which is smaller than 2 mm (and may be as small as thousandths of a millimetre), while larger fragments are called lapilli or bombs and blocks. Blocks and bombs fall to the earth within a few kilometres of a volcano, but ash is ejected high into the atmosphere.

Volcanic Zones on the Earth`

1) **Ring of Fire:** Ring of fire or Pacific Ring of Fire is a horseshoe-shaped path along Pacific Ocean housing maximum volcanoes and seismic activities, setting most frequent earthquakes. Ring of Fire is also called Circum-Pacific Belt. 75% of earth's total volcanoes, i.e., above 450, fall in this zone.

RING OF FIRE

Ring of Fire is a path along the Pacific Ocean. It is so called as maximum volcanic and seismic activity takes place along the edge of this ring. This ring is 40,000 kms.(24,900 miles) long. It passes through New Zealand, Philippines, Japan, Alaska, and along western part of North and South America. Ring of Fire is situated in the 'Subduction Zone' of tectonic plates. Here, plates have converging border and one plate is compressed underneath another plate. The compressed plate (oceanic plate) melts rocks under it and rocks become magma, and due to being very near to the earth's crust comes out as lava and this is volcanic eruption.

2) **Mediterranean Zone:** This zone passes across Asia, entering India. Other countries falling in this zone of volcanoes are Italy, Greece, and Turkey.
3) **Mid-Atlantic Ridge Zone:** Iceland falls in this zone.

Effects of Volcanic Eruptions

Unlike other natural disasters, volcanic eruptions have both harmful and beneficial effects.

Harmful Effects:

1) **Loss of lives and property:** Volcanic eruptions near human settlements destroy lives and property. Residents of the affected region are evacuated to safer places during volcanic activity.
2) **Negative impact on ozone layer:** Ash discharged into stratosphere leaves a negative impact on the ozone layer which in turn becomes responsible for global warming.
3) **Destruction of landscapes:** Dense smoky clouds carry ash as a result of volcanic eruption, and natural scenery and landscaping is totally destroyed.
4) **Formation of lahars:** Ash and mud get mixed with rain and melting snow to form lahars. Lahars are fast-flowing matter posing threat to buildings and infrastructure.
5) **Creating other disasters:** Volcanic eruptions become the cause of earthquakes, floods, and landslides.
6) **Cause of respiratory diseases:** Large amount of dust and ash develops respiratory disease for the persons coming under the influence of eruptions.
7) **Unhealthy changes in climate:** Prolonged, big, and frequent eruptions bring unhealthy change in climate and make it unpredictable.

Beneficial Effects

1) **Boosts tourism:** Volcano sites present a beautiful landscape and scenery. Tourists are attracted to visit sites of volcanic eruptions after a volcano goes extinct.
2) **Rich potential of geothermal energy:** Places close to eruption sites have rich potential of geothermal energy which is a renewable source of energy and can be exploited to generate electricity.
3) **Enrich soil fertility:** Some ash is mixed with soil or lava and soil becomes rich in nutrients. This increases soil fertility and result in rich yield of agricultural crops.
4) **Source of life:** As volcanic gases have created water and atmosphere, these serve as source of life on earth.

Mitigation Measures

1) **Preparation of hazard maps:** This map helps to assess whether a volcano is potentially hazardous.
2) **Monitoring of volcanoes:** Monitoring of volcanoes through satellites should be done. If any change in temperature or sulphur dioxide emissions is detected, warnings can be issued. Concerned residents can be evacuated to safer places.
3) **Educating people:** General public can be educated about volcanoes and create awareness about dangerous consequences of eruptions. This can be achieved through mass media.
4) **Drafting emergency plans:** For potentially dangerous volcanoes, emergency plans can be made and notified through wide publicity.
5) **Early warning systems:** Early warning systems as a prevention measure can be installed.

Volcanoes in India

In India there are 7 volcanoes, given as follows:

Sr. No.	Name of Volcano	State	Status
1.	Barren Island	Andaman Islands	Active (2017)
2.	Narcondam	Andaman Islands	Dormant
3.	Baratang	Andaman Islands	Active (2003)
4.	Deccan Traps	Maharashtra	Dormant
5.	Dhinodhar Hills	Gujarat	Extinct
6.	Dhosi Hill	Haryana	Extinct
7.	Tosham Hills	Haryana	Extinct

LANDSLIDE

A landslide is defined as the mass movement of a part of rock, debris, soil, or earth down a slope. Landslides are a type of 'mass wasting', which denotes any down-slope movement of soil and rock under the direct influence of gravity.

Causes of Landslide

Though landslides are caused due to various natural phenomena, yet human activity also causes landslides. However, there are the following causes of landslides:

Natural Causes

1) **Earthquakes:** Seismic activities have always been a main cause of landslides throughout the world. Any time plate tectonics move, the soil that covers them moves with it. When earthquakes occur on areas with steep slopes, many times the soil slips causing landslides. Furthermore, ash and debris flows caused by earthquakes can also trigger mass movement of soil.
2) **Heavy rainfall:** When sloped areas become completely saturated by heavy rainfall, many times landslides can occur. Without the aid of mechanical root support, the soil simply runs off when it contains too much water.
3) **Weathering:** It is a natural procedure of wearing out of rocks due to which rocks become weak. Climatic hazards like acid rain also weaken rocks. Thus, weak rocks start descending from the top of a hill and are termed as landslide.
4) **Erosion:** It is caused by the continuous flow of water through hills and mountains due to rain or melting of snow. The slope support weakens and can't hold a rock or debris and such matter start coming down the slope.
5) **Volcano:** In volcanic eruption, soil on hills start moving downward, thus causing landslide.
6) **Forest fires:** Forest fires result in soil erosion and bring floods which also become cause of landslide.

Human Causes

1) **Clear cutting:** Clear cutting is a technique of timber harvesting that eliminates all old trees from the area. This technique is dangerous since it decimates the existing mechanical root structure of the area.
2) **Mining:** Mining activities that utilise blasting techniques contribute mightily to landslides. Vibrations emanating from the blasts can weaken soils in other areas and they become susceptible to landslides. The weakening of soil means a landslide can occur anytime.

Effects of Landslide

Like other natural hazards, landslide also creates harmful effects, which are explained as follows:

1) **Loss of life:** Communities living at the foot of hills and mountains are at a greater risk of death by landslides. A substantial landslide carries along huge rocks, heavy debris, and heavy soil with it. This kind of landslide has the capacity to kills lots of people on impact.
2) **Impact on river ecosystem:** Rock particles and debris fall into rivers and interrupt their natural flow. Due to blockage of flow of river water, river habitats like fishes die. People depending on river water for drinking and washing face shortage of water and water contamination.
3) **Traffic jams:** Rocks and debris fall down and block highways and create long traffic jams and it takes hours to clear the highway and roads. Commuters, patients, students, and other people going for various jobs face difficulty in reaching their destination in time. Further, shortage of essential goods and services is created as vehicles carrying these get struck in jams for hours together.
4) **Destroying landscape:** Landslides leave behind distorted landscapes.
5) **Destruction of infrastructure:** Landslides crush buildings and other infrastructure coming in the way of falling rocks and stones and create loss of lakhs of rupees. In addition to this, there is huge damage to roads, railway tracks, and vital offices.

Types of Landslides

1) **Slides:** This is a kind of mass movement whereby the sliding material breaks away from underlying stable material. It means that material on hills loses depth and starts falling down the slope.
2) **Topples:** These landslides occur when topple of rocks occur (that is, balance of rocks fails and rocks topple down).
3) **Lateral spreads:** These are gently falling rocks and soil.
4) **Flows:** Flows occur when the entire soil mass is deformed and start flowing downwards. Deformation of entire mass of soils on hills is due to seismic activity leading to liquefaction or heavy and persistent rains.

Mitigation Measures

Mitigation measures against landslide hazards must aim at careful analysis of landslides. Stabilisation of landslides is required to be achieved through proper layout plans. Rehabilitation should be planned and executed on the basis of these studies. Following are certain rehabilitation measures:

1) **Stabilising slopes with vegetation:** Afforestation on slopes helps a lot to prevent hazards of landslides. Trees through their roots absorb water even during precipitation. This helps in strengthening the hold of rocks as there is no danger of development of any crack or shrinkage. Planting deciduous trees helps to prevent hazards of landslide.
2) **Increasing stability of slopes:** Stability of slopes can be increased by reducing extra soil on the slope helping in landslide. This mitigation measure is taken when there is a dangerous situation and there is total failure of the slope and slide area is small. Man-made cuts and constructing terraces help to stabilise the slope.
3) **Drainage of landslides:** Developing proper drainage will regulate the flow of water and this prevents landslide.
4) **Drainage system at surface:** Proper drainage at surface prevents the extra water on surface from entering landslide area and this minimises chances of landslides.
5) **Dewatering earth material:** Landslides can be prevented by dewatering the earth material on slopes to prevent the rapid flow downwards. Horizontal drains with tiles can be constructed.
6) **Erecting walls:** Walls can be erected to smother the speed of the landslide flow at the landslide spot. These walls are also called dikes, cribs, or bulkheads. These walls are erected at those landslide spots which are near highways and railway tracks. The purpose is to prevent the landslide earth material from falling on highways or railway tracks.

LANDSLIDES IN INDIA

According to Geological Survey of India (GSI), 12% of total land area of India is susceptible to landslides. Major landslide-prone areas of India include:

1) Western Ghats and Konkan Hills (Tamil Nadu, Kerala, Karnataka, Goa, and Maharashtra)
2) Eastern Ghats (Araku region in Andhra Pradesh)
3) Eastern and North-east Himalayas (Darjeeling (West Bengal) and Sikkim and Arunachal Pradesh)
4) North-west Himalayas (Uttarakhand, Himachal Pradesh, and Jammu and Kashmir)
5) Naga-Arakkan mountain belt in the states of (Nagaland, Manipur, Mizoram, and Tripura)
6) Plateau margins of Peninsular India and Meghalaya plateau in North-east India

Causes of Landslides

In India, maximum landslides occur in Himalayas. Main reason besides rains is collusion of Indian and Eurasian tectonic plates. Being situated at the border of two plates, there are frequent earthquakes in the Himalayan belt leading to landslides.

Effects of Landslides

Landslides in India have same effects as has already been mentioned above. In addition to those certain effects, according to India's typical social and economic set-up and environmental system, there is damage to sewage disposal system, supply line of water, electricity, and communication. As in India the most vulnerable section of the population to any natural disaster comprises labourers, women, and children, they are affected in the form of deaths, diseases, outbreak of epidemics, loss of work, destruction of crops, starvation, and demolishing of dwellings. This devastating effect of landslides turns the economy also. Government has to spend millions of rupees in providing compensation to the affected population, and in repairs or reconstruction of buildings, and other infrastructure affected due to landslides.

Mitigation Measures in India

India has initiated the following steps to mitigate and manage landslides:

1) **Introduction of early warning systems:** Government has installed the second early warning system in Sikkim. The first was installed in Munnar (Kerala) in 2009. As per experts, the country needs about 500 such systems to manage landslides.
2) **Instrumentation network:** An instrumentation network for monitoring landslides has been installed by the Central Scientific Instruments Organisation (CSIO) at Mansa Devi, Haridwar.
3) **Landslide hazard mapping:** Department of Science and Technology (DST) has carried out landslide hazard mapping in Sutlej Valley (Himachal Pradesh), Kumaon and Gharhwal (Uttarakhand), Konkan Railway Region (Maharashtra), and North-eastern states of Manipur, Nagaland, Mizoram, Sikkim, and Arunachal Pradesh. Data maps are used for disaster management activities.
4) **Landslide safe route brochures:** Landslide safe route brochures have been prepared for guiding officials installing communication lines in hilly areas so that landslide may not snap them.

5) **National Landslide Risk Mitigation Project (NLRPM):** Government approved NLRMP is being run by National Disaster Management Authority (NDMA).

6) **Awareness programmes:** Government is periodically organising landslide mitigation awareness workshops, seminars, and other programmes for various government departments and NGOs and common people.

7) **Implementation of Landslip Prevention and Mitigation (LPmit) Programme:** Indian scientists studied Honkong's Landslip Prevention and Mitigation Plan and have implemented it in landslide-prone areas. The results are promising. There has been drastic reduction in magnitude of landslides and losses.

8) **National Geotechnical Facility (NGF):** NGF has been initiated at Dehradun by the Department of Science and Technology (DST) in collaboration with Norwegian Geotechnical Institute. It is a hi-tech facility to provide plans to save people from natural hazards like landslides.

TSUNAMI

The term 'Tsunami ' has been derived from a Japanese term 'Tsu' meaning 'harbour' and 'nami' meaning 'waves'. Tsunamis are popularly called tidal waves but they actually have nothing to do with the tides. These waves which often affect distant shores, are originated by rapid displacement of water from the lake or the sea either by seismic activity, landslides, volcanic eruptions, or large meteoroid impacts. Whatever the cause may be, sea water is displaced with a violent motion and swells up, ultimately surging over land with great destructive power. When approaching the sea coast, tsunami can reach up to a height of 100 feet. In the deep sea, tsunami has been recorded to travel with a speed of 700 kms/hr. Settlements within the vicinity of 30 metres from the source of tsunamis experience maximum damage. The force of the water can raze everything in its path. It is normally the flooding effect of the tsunami that causes major destruction to the human settlements, roads, and infrastructure, thereby disrupting the normal functioning of the society.

Causes of Tsunami

1) **Earthquakes:** Direct cause of tsunamis are earthquakes (This has been discussed under effects of earthquakes earlier in this chapter).

2) **Landslides:** Another major reason of tsunamis are landslides. These landslides occur either under water or originate above the sea and then plunge into sea water, displacing a huge volume of water. In the history of tsunami produced due to landslide, the most mammoth tsunami ever produced had been tsunami of Lituya Bay, Alaska in 1958.That tsunami had height of 1720 feet.

3) **Volcanic eruption:** As maximum volcanic activity is observed in Pacific Ocean (Ring of Fire), volcanic eruptions in the sea or near the seashore cause forceful vertical displacement of huge volume of water in the form of tsunamis.

Effects of Tsunami

1) **Double damage:** While coming from the sea to the seashore settlements, tsunami results in huge damage to the settlements. It again results in similar damage while withdrawing towards the sea. Withdrawing tsunami waves towards the ocean sweep establishments, foundations of buildings, and destroy beaches.

2) **Putting transportation out of gear:** As airports, railway tracks, highways, roads, and bridges are destroyed as an effect of tsunami, there is shortage of essential goods, services, and medical aid due to lack of importation.

3) **Impact on public health system:** Tsunami results in mass deaths of people either being washed away with waves or drowning as water inundates into houses or being crushed under giant waves or debris.

4) **Impact on sewerage system:** Sewerage system is badly affected as there is large-scale destruction of sewerage pipes.

5) **Loss of livelihood:** As population settled near seashores depend on the sea for its livelihood, various tools like boats, nets, etc. are destroyed, so there is huge loss of livelihood. Similarly, people indulging in agricultural activities also experience crop loss and loss of livelihood.

6) **Impact on economy:** Banks, insurance companies, markets, industries, stock markets, and other such organisations are also badly affected under the influence of tsunami. Total production and trading activity comes to a halt, thus shattering the economy of the affected region or country.

Mitigation Measures

Although a tsunami cannot be prevented, the effect of a tsunami can be reduced through community preparedness, timely warnings, and effective response.

TSUNAMIS IN INDIA

India does not have a noticeable history of tsunamis, except report of some high rising waves along with earthquakes. The earliest tsunami was reported in Bay of Bengal in 1881. In 1945, Gulf of Kutch of Gujarat experienced water waves of 11 meters height and Mumbai experienced waves of 2 meters height. In 2004, an earthquake in north Indian Ocean created a giant tsunami which made excessive damage to many coastal areas of Indonesia, India, Malaysia, Maldives, Sri Lanka, and Thailand. A trans-oceanic tsunami was observed over areas beyond the Ocean limit of origin. More than 2,30,000 people lost their lives in the above countries which is a record.

Mitigation Measures in India

National Disaster Management Authority (NDMA) has earmarked tsunami hazard zones covering coastal states. Further, tsunami risk assessment is made while assessing vulnerability to tsunamis where natural and man-made structures falling in tsunami hazard zones are at stake. The main factors to reduce potential losses due to tsunami are AWARENESS and PREPAREDNESS. The practical applications of this tsunami risk assessment, in both quantitative and qualitative terms, for implementation into mitigation strategies for the terrestrial and marine environments include:

1. Building Codes (potential damage due to wave action and flooding)
2. GIS Mapping
3. Land-use Planning (taking note of wave action and flooding)
4. Disaster Planning (in identified hazard zones)
5. Emergency Management
6. Emergency Personnel Training (necessary aspects relevant to marine situations)
7. Rescue and Response (marine situations related to shipping, cargo, tourists, inter-islands fishing community, and recreational boating)
8. Insurance Needs
9. Community Education
10. Simulated Tsunami Exercises

AVALANCHES

An avalanche is a mass of snow that slides rapidly down an inclined slope, such as a mountainside or the roof of a building. Avalanches are triggered by either natural forces (e.g., precipitation, wind drifting snow, or rapid temperature changes) or human activity. In mountainous terrain, they are among the most serious hazards to human life and property. Avalanches are sometimes called snowslides.

Types of Avalanches

1) **Large-scale avalanches:** These are caused by very heavy rains, which threaten localities, buildings, and communication links in all or parts of a valley. These occur spontaneously on the uphill mountain slopes and according to the meteorological conditions.
2) **Small-scale avalanches:** These are avalanches restricted to smaller local areas, which are mostly triggered by man in the course of his professional or sporting activities.

Effects of Avalanches

Extent of damage may be widespread or restricted depending upon the intensity of snowslides or causes those set in avalanches. Still, the damages from avalanches are observed as under:

1) Interruption in communication links
2) Damage to roads and railway tracks
3) Destruction of infrastructure
4) Interruption in telecommunication links
5) Interruption in supply of essential services
6) Loss of human lives
7) Closure of roads and highways and creation of traffic jams
8) Bad impact on economy of the region

Mitigation Measures

There are certain regions in the world, particularly snow-fed regions and cold countries which are always under the threat of avalanches. Such countries should establish institutions where different level courses in avalanche engineering should be started to study these in depth and come out with possible mitigation measures. Further, awareness about pros and cons of avalanches can help in taking remedial measures after avalanches.

Avalanche Zones

- ***Red Zone** - The most dangerous zone where snow avalanches are most frequent and have an impact pressure of more than 3 tonnes per square metre*
- ***Blue Zone** - Where the avalanche force is less than 3 tonnes per square metre and where living and other activities may be permitted with connection of safe design but such areas may have to be vacated on warning*
- ***Yellow Zone** - Where snow avalanche occur only occasionally*

Avalanche-Prone Areas in India

The Himalayas are well known for the occurrence of snow avalanches, particularly Western Himalayas, i.e., the snowy regions of Jammu and Kashmir, Himachal Pradesh, and western Uttar Pradesh.

- **Jammu and Kashmir:** Higher reaches of Kashmir and Gurez valleys, Kargil, Ladakh, and some of the major roads

- **Himachal Pradesh:** Chamba, Kullu-Spiti, and Kinnaur are vulnerable areas
- **Uttrakhand:** Parts of Tehri Garhwal and Chamoli districts are vulnerable areas

Disaster Management Bodies in India

- **National Disaster Management Authority (NDMA)**

  Working as an agency of Union Ministry of Home Affairs, NDMA works for planning and execution of mitigation measures against various natural disasters. It further works for strengthening India's power to resist natural disasters. The agency is responsible for framing policies, laying down guidelines and best practices, and coordinating with the State Disaster Management Authorities (SDMAs) to ensure an effective and distributed approach to disaster management.

- **National Institute of Disaster Management (NIDM)**

  NIDM is a premier institute for training and capacity development programs for managing natural disasters in India, on a national as well as regional basis. NIDM also serves as international SAARC Disaster Management Centre (SDMC) and works as focus for its operation and planning. UGC has worked out with NIDM and developed a model curriculum for strengthening disaster management in higher education and research. Most Central Universities have established Centre for Disaster Management under their School of Environmental Studies.

- **National Disaster Response Force (NDRF)**

  For the purpose of specialised response to a threatening disaster situation or disasters/emergencies (both natural and man-made) such as those of chemical, biological, radiological, and nuclear origin, National Disaster Response Force (NDRF) has been constituted.

Some Vital Facts

1) Avalanches belong to the category of geophysical hazards
2) Tsunami is geo-physical natural hazard.
3) Chemical contamination is not a natural hazard
4) Volcanic eruptions have the highest potential to cause damage to humans.
5) In case of earthquakes, an increase of magnitude 1 on Richter Scale implies a ten-fold increase in the amplitude of seismic waves.
6) Flash floods are caused when the atmosphere is convectively unstable and there is considerable vertical wind shear
7) Hydro-meteorological natural hazards cause maximum damage to property and lives
8) The most recurring natural hazard in India is floods.
9) Himalayan region is in the very high risk zone of earthquakes.
10) Change in weather is the most significant impact of volcanic eruption.

Practice Exercise

General Questions Format

1. Semi-arid areas of our country are prone to

(A) Earthquakes (B) Floods
(C) Forest fires (D) None of these

2. The most frequently occurring natural hazards in India are

(A) Floods (B) Earthquakes
(C) Cyclones (D) Droughts

3. Mitigation measures against natural hazards must be initiated by

(A) Government
(B) People
(C) Voluntary agencies
(D) All of the above

4. Eastern part of India is the most prone to

(A) Cyclones (B) Floods
(C) Drought s (D) Earthquakes

5. Which of the following is NOT TRUE about structural mitigation against floods?

a) Structural measures taken to protect infrastructure
b) Plugging in of openings in levees and culverts
c) Construction of separate sewers for flood water ensuring its uninterrupted flow
d) Constructing floodwells to accommodate flood water to be put into different uses separately

(A) b and d only (B) c and d only
(C) a, c, and d only (D) b only

6. Consider the following statements:

   Statement R: Among various causes of landslides, only weathering is manageable.

   Statement S: Landslides of hydrosphere are less intensive than landslides of lithosphere.

   (A) Both R and S are true

   (B) Both R and S are false

   (C) R is true but S is false

   (D) R is false but R is true

7. Name of cyclone is given under Column I and name of state which a cyclone hit is given under Column II. Match the cyclone with its state which it hit in the past and select the correct code among given codes.

Column I (Name of Cyclone)	**Column II (Name of affected State)**
a) Kyant	i) Andaman & Nicobar
b) Helen	ii) Tamil Nadu
c) Lehar	iii) Odisha
d) Nisha	iv) Andhra Pradesh

Codes:	(a)	(b)	(c)	(d)
(A)	ii	iv	iii	i
(B)	iii	ii	iv	i
(C)	iii	iv	i	ii
(D)	iv	i	iii	ii

8. An earthquake with a magnitude of 4.0-4.9 is

   (A) minor and rarely felt

   (B) moderate and felt by many people

   (C) major with extensive damage and felt by all

   (D) light with minor damage and felt by many people

9. Consider the following activities:

   a) prolonged and continuous rainfall

   b) early and excess melting of snow

   c) landslides

   d) occurring with prior warning

   Above activities are characteristics of which type of floods?

   (A) Coastal floods (B) Flash floods

   (C) Surface floods (D) River floods

10. Tephra is one of the hazards of

    (A) Drought (B) Volcanic eruption

    (C) Earthquake (D) Tsunami

11. Following are some schemes started by the government of India as mitigation measures against natural hazards.

    a) Integrated Watershed Management Programme (IWMP)

    b) National Calamity Contingency Fund

    c) Weather Based Crop Insurance Scheme

    d) Pradhan Mantri Fasal Bima Yojana

    Which of the above scheme(s) is meant for drought mitigation?

    (A) a and c only (B) a, b, and d only

    (C) c only (D) a, b, c, and d

12. Which of the following zones of earthquakes in India is the most active?

    (A) Zone II (B) Zone V

    (C) Zone III (D) Zone IV

13. Biggest tsunami in the history ever occurred was in

    (A) Hawaii (B) Luxemburg

    (C) Alaska (D) None of these

14. Which of the following is TRUE about cyclones striking India?

    (A) Indian cyclones account for about 25% of total cyclones in the world.

    (B) West coast is more vulnerable to cyclones than east coast.

    (C) About 8% of total area of India is cyclone-prone.

    (D) Cyclones in India affect the whole coast length.

15. Which Indian state has maximum number of drought-prone districts?

    (A) Gujarat (B) Bihar

    (C) Odisha (D) Uttar Pradesh

16. Consider the following statements:

    Statement X: A dormant volcano becomes active after 1000 years of dormancy.

    Statement Y: An active volcano is one that has erupted at least once in the last 10000 years.

    (A) X is true but Y is false

    (B) Both X and Y are true

    (C) Both X and Y are false

    (D) X is false but Y is true

17. Which of the following statement(s) is/are true?
   a) Geophysical natural hazards give rise to hydro-meteorological hazards.
   b) Biological hazards are man-made hazards.
   c) No natural hazard occurs independently.
   d) Geophysical hazards have their roots not only in lithosphere but also in hydrosphere.

   (A) d only (B) b and d only
   (C) a, b, c, and d (D) a and c only

18. Rapid Visual Screening (RVS) is a hazard mitigation technique used against
   (A) Floods (B) Volcanic eruptions
   (C) Avalanches (D) Earthquakes

19. While taking frequency and intensity into consideration, which natural hazard causes minimum human deaths?
   (A) Tsunami (B) Droughts
   (C) Floods (D) Earthquakes

20. India falls in which volcanic zones of the earth?
   (A) Mediterranean zone
   (B) Ring of Fire
   (C) Mid-Atlantic zone
   (D) None of these

21. Which is the common mitigation measure for all types of natural hazards?
   (A) National Building Code
   (B) Zoning
   (C) Mapping
   (D) Rehabilitating

22. Which anthropogenic activity (ies) become(s) cause of a natural hazard?
   a) Deforestation
   b) Emission of greenhouse gases
   c) Excessive use of fertilizers and pesticides
   d) Overutilisation of non-renewable resources

   (A) b and c only (B) a, c, and d only
   (C) a and b only (D) b only

23. Neeranchal National Watershed Project has been funded by
   (A) International Monetary Fund
   (B) World Bank
   (C) Asian Development Bank
   (D) None of these

24. Which of the following regions of India is/are maximum drought-prone?
   (A) Arid (B) Semi-arid
   (C) Sub-humid (D) All of these

25. Which of the following natural hazard is assessed in Red Zone?
   (A) Avalanches (B) Floods
   (C) Tsunamis (D) Droughts

KEY

1. D	**2.** A	**3.** D	**4.** A	**5.** B	**6.** B	**7.** C
8. D	**9.** D	**10.** B	**11.** D	**12.** B	**13.** C	**14.** C
15. D	**16.** D	**17.** A	**18.** D	**19.** B	**20.** A	**21.** D
22. C	**23.** B	**24.** D	**25.** A			

Assertion–Reason Format

1. **Assertion (A):** There should not be population settlements in the areas prone to natural hazards.

   Reason (R): Different natural hazards claim thousands of lives in different parts of the world every year.

   (A) Both A and R are correct and R is correct explanation of A
   (B) Both A and R are true but R is not correct explanation of A
   (C) A is true but R is false
   (D) A is false but R is true

2. **Assertion (A):** Volcanic eruptions are effective in climate change.

   Reason (R): Maximum seismic activity is observed along the Pacific Ocean.

   (A) Both A and R are true and R is correct explanation of A
   (B) Both A and R are true but R is not correct explanation of A
   (C) A is true but R is false
   (D) A is false but R is wrong

3. **Assertion (A):** Every natural hazard ends at its mitigation.

   Reason (R): Vulnerability of a region to a natural hazard determines its mitigation.

   (A) Both A and R are true and R is correct explanation of A
   (B) A is true but R is false
   (C) Both A and R are true but R is not correct explanation of A
   (D) A is false but R is true

4. **Assertion (A):** Hydro-Meteorological natural hazards are enduring.

   Reason (R): Enduring hydro-meteorological natural hazards are more destructive than other natural hazards.

   (A) Both A and R are true and R is correct explanation of A

   (B) A is true but R is false

   (C) Both A and R are false

   (D) A is false but R is true

5. **Assertion (A):** National Geotechnical Facility (NGF) has been installed at Dehradun.

   Reason (R): NGF has been installed in collaboration with Swiss Geotechnical Institute.

   (A) Both A and R are true and R is correct explanation of A

   (B) A is true but R is false

   (C) Both A and R are false

   (D) A is false but R is true

6. **Assertion (A):** Droughts occur due to El-Nino impact.

   Reason (R): El-Nino is a natural event raising temperature of ocean water in Pacific Ocean.

   (A) Both A and R are true and R is correct explanation of A

   (B) Both A and R are true but R is not correct explanation of A

   (C) Both A and R are false

   (D) A is true but R is false

7. **Assertion (A):** Sewerage system in urban areas acts as mitigation channel against floods.

   Reason (R): Flooding has played havocs in cities with poor and obsolete sewer system.

   (A) Both A and R are true and R is correct explanation of A

   (B) Both A and R are true but R is not correct explanation of A

   (C) Both A and R are false

   (D) A is true but R is false

8. **Assertion (A):** Natural hazards give rise to natural disasters.

   Reason (R): Natural disasters can be managed but natural hazards cannot be.

   (A) Both A and R are false

   (B) Both A and R are true and R is correct explanation of A

   (C) A is true but R is false

   (D) A is false but R is true

9. **Assertion (A):** Various government sponsored schemes implementing natural hazard mitigation measures cover all types of natural hazards.

   Reason (R): There has been remarkable reduction in natural hazards due to such schemes.

   (A) Both A and R are true and R is correct explanation of A

   (B) Both A and R are true but R is not correct explanation of A

   (C) A is true but R is false

   (D) A is false but R is true

10. **Assertion (A):** Effects of volcanic eruption are both beneficial and harmful.

    Reason (R): Eruption of a dormant volcano leaves same effects as left by an active volcano.

    (A) Both A and R are true and R is correct explanation of A

    (B) Both A and R are true but R is not correct explanation of A

    (C) Both A and R are false

    (D) A is true but R is false

KEY

1. A **2.** B **3.** D **4.** C **5.** B **6.** A **7.** A **8.** C **9.** C **10.** B

Questions Asked in Previous NET Exams

1. Which of the following belongs to the category of geophysical hazards?

   (UGC NET JUNE 2019)

   (A) Infestation (B) Avalanches

   (C) Invasive species (D) Diseases

2. National Disaster Management Authority is an agency of the Ministry of

   (UGC NET DECEMBER 2019)

   (A) Jal Shakti

   (B) Home Affairs

   (C) Earth Science

   (D) Housing and Urban Affairs

3. An earthquake of a magnitude in the range of 6·0-6·9 on the Richter Scale is considered **(UGC NET JULY 2018)**
(A) Moderate (B) Strong
(C) Major (D) Great

4. Which of the following types of natural disasters has no definite beginning and end? **(UGC NET JULY 2018)**
(A) Earthquakes (B) Landsides
(C) Hurricanes (D) Droughts

5. Which of the following natural hazards is not hydro-meteorological? **(UGC NET JANUARY 2017)**
(A) Snow avalanche (B) Sea erosion
(C) Tropical cyclone (D) Tsunami

6. Which of the following phenomena is not a natural hazard? **(UGC NET DECEMBER 2015)**
(A) Wildfire
(B) Lightning
(C) Landslide
(D) Chemical contamination

7. 'Lahar' is a natural disaster involving **(UGC NET JUNE 2014)**
(A) eruption of large amount of material
(B) strong winds
(C) strong water waves
(D) strong winds and water waves

8. The National Disaster Management Authority functions under the Union Ministry of **(UGC NET JUNE 2014)**
(A) Environment (B) Water Resources
(C) Home Affairs (D) Defence

9. Match List - I and List - II and select the correct answer from the codes given below: **(UGC NET JUNE 2014)**

List - I	List - II
a. Flood	1. Lack of rainfall of sufficient duration
b. Drought	2. Tremors produced by the passage of vibratory waves through the rocks of the earth
c. Earthquake	3. A vent through which molten substances come out
d. Volcano	4. Excess rain and uneven distribution of water

Codes:

	(a)	(b)	(c)	(d)
(A)	4	1	2	3
(B)	2	3	4	1
(C)	3	4	2	1
(D)	4	3	1	2

10. Which of the following types of natural hazards have the highest potential to cause damage to humans ? **(UGC NET JUNE 2013)**
(A) Earthquakes
(B) Forest fires
(C) Volcanic eruptions
(D) Droughts and floods

11. In the case of earthquakes, an increase of magnitude 1 on Richter Scale implies **(UGC NET DECEMBER 2012)**
(A) a ten-fold increase in the amplitude of seismic waves.
(B) a ten-fold increase in the energy of the seismic waves.
(C) two-fold increase in the amplitude of seismic waves.
(D) two-fold increase in the energy of seismic waves.

12. Which of the following is not a natural hazard? **(UGC NET DECEMBER 2011)**
(A) Earthquake
(B) Tsunami
(C) Flash floods
(D) Nuclear accident

13. Flash floods are caused when **(UGC NET JUNE 2011)**
(A) the atmosphere is convectively unstable and there is considerable vertical wind shear
(B) the atmosphere is stable
(C) the atmosphere is convectively unstable with no vertical windshear
(D) winds are katabatic

14. Volcanic eruptions affect

(UGC NETDECEMBER 2010)

(A) atmosphere and hydrosphere

(B) hydrosphere and biosphere

(C) lithosphere, biosphere, and atmosphere

(D) lithosphere, hydrosphere, and atmosphere

15. Which type of natural hazards cause maximum damage to property and lives ?

(UGC NET JUNE 2010)

(A) Hydrological

(B) Hydro-meteorological

(C) Geological

(D) Geo-chemical

16. The most recurring natural hazard in India is

(UGC NET DECEMBER 2009)

(A) Earthquakes

(B) Floods

(C) Landslides

(D) Volcanoes

17. Which of the following region is in the very high risk zone of earthquakes?

(UGC NET JUNE 2009)

(A) Central Indian Highland

(B) Coastal region

(C) Himalayan region

(D) Indian desert

18. Which one of the following is not associated with earthquakes?

(UGC NET DECEMBER 2008)

(A) Focus (B) Epicenter

(C) Seismograph (D) Swells

19. Which one of the following natural hazards is responsible for causing highest human disaster?

(UGC NET DECEMBER 2007)

(A) Earthquakes (B) Volcanic eruptions

(C) Snow storms (D) Tsunami

20. Which one of the following is appropriate for natural hazard mitigation?

(UGC NET JUNE 2007)

(A) International aid

(B) Timely warning system

(C) Rehabilitation

(D) Community participation

21. The most significant impact of volcanic eruption has been felt in the form of:

(UGC NET DECEMBER 2006)

(A) change in weather

(B) sinking of islands

(C) loss of vegetation

(D) extinction of animals

KEY

1. B	**2.** B	**3.** B	**4.** A	**5.** D	**6.** D	**7.** A
8. C	**9.** A	**10.** C	**11.** A	**12.** D	**13.** A	**14.** D
15. B	**16.** B	**17.** C	**18.** D	**19.** A	**20.** B	**21.** A

9 National and Global Initiatives for Environment Protection

ENVIRONMENT PROTECTION: A MISSION

In the Indian Constitution, Directive Principles of State Policy under Article 48 state that "State shall endeavour to protect and improve the environment and to safeguard the forests and wildlife of the country". Similarly, one of the Fundamental Duties in the Constitution under Article 51-A states that "It shall be the duty of every citizen of India to protect and improve the natural environment including forests, lakes, rivers and wildlife and to have compassion for living creatures."

India has truly followed the above Directive Principles and has been coming out with various Acts and Rules for protecting the environment. Adopting it as a mission and various initiatives in the direction of environment protection have been taken in the form of various pacts and agreements signed at national and international level. Besides, India has not only been participating in various national and international summits organised by various UNO and other agencies, but has also been presenting concrete suggestions and viewpoints to protect the environment. Various NGOs and individuals have also been active in working for environment protection while following the above Article 51-A of the Indian Constitution. Further, both private and public sectors individually and jointly are also effectively participating in this mission. Media, of course is playing a very vital role in creating awareness in masses about environment protection. Various initiatives taken by India and other countries in different forms as mentioned above can be viewed as follows:

NATIONAL LEVEL INITIATIVES: ACTS AND RULES

Environment Protection Act (1986)

This Act was passed by the Parliament in wake of the 1984 Bhopal gas leakage tragedy, in which lakhs of people died within one night due to the fatal effect of gas leaked from the plant of Union Carbide India Ltd. It was realised that environment protection norms were not being fully followed by owners of factories and other establishments. Need was felt to enact an Act with more teeth to prevent such tragedies and to work for environment protection. Resultantly, the Parliament passed the Environment Protection Act, which was enforced on November 19, 1986 under Article 253 of the Indian Constitution. It was extended to the whole of India. The Act was passed to provide for the protection and improvement of the environment and all matters concerned with that.

The Act gives certain powers to the central government to take measures for the purpose of protecting and improving the quality of the environment and to prevent environmental pollution.

Editor: The text inside the following textbox is invisible, please look into it.

UMBRELLA LEGISLATION

Environment Protection Act 1986 is called 'Umbrella Legislation'. It is so called because because it provides the framework to the central government in order to make the coordination between different states as well as the central authorities established under different acts like water act and air act etc. It also plugs in loopholes of other acts The purpose is to control the pollution from the all sources so that the quality of environment can be improved.

This Act empowers the central government for

1) Setting standards for emissions and discharges of pollution in the atmosphere by any person carrying on an industry or activity
2) Regulating the location of industries
3) Management of hazardous wastes
4) Protection of public health and welfare

5) Issuing time to time notifications under the Environment Protection Act for the protection of ecologically-sensitive areas
6) Examination of such manufacturing process and raw material which are likely to cause environmental threats
7) Carrying out research and investigation related to environmental pollution problems
8) Collection and dissemination of information on environmental pollution
9) Defining ecological-sensitive areas as restricted region as it has defined Aravalli regions in Alwar (Rajasthan), coastal sensitive zones, and Doon valley in Uttarakhand
10) Initiating coercive action against violators of the Act as the Act has a provision of 5 year imprisonment or a fine of Rs. I lakh or both
11) Laying down standards for discharge of environmental pollutants
12) Establishing environmental laboratories
13) Laying down procedures and safeguards for handling hazardous substances .

Environmental (Protection) Rules, 1986

Under these rules, the central government prohibits or restricts establishment of any industry and raw material used in the manufacturing process which is a threat to the biological diversity of that area.

Water (Prevention and Control of Pollution) Act, 1974

The Act was enacted as a Central Act passed by the Parliament in 1974. The Act was enacted to:

a) Prevent and control water pollution
b) Maintain whole amount level of water
c) Constitute the Central Pollution Control Board and State Pollution Control Boards

Air (Prevention and Control of Pollution) Act, 1981

This is a central Act of Parliament, which provides for the prevention and control of air pollution and maintaining the good quality of air. This Act is also called 'Air Act'.

National Action Plan on Climate Change (NAPCC)

(Kindly refer to Chapter 5 of Unit-IX for full length discussion on the above.)

INTERNATIONAL PLANS/EFFORTS

The Montreal Protocol on Substances That Deplete the Ozone Layer

This Protocol is a multi-lateral agreement. It is a historic protocol which controls the production and consumption of about 100 man-made chemicals declared as ozone depleting substances (ODS). Such substances attack the stratosphere when released into the atmosphere, and thus depletes the ozone layer as ozone layer is contained in the stratosphere. The Protocol was signed on 15 September, 1987. It is the only UN treaty which has been ratified by every member state. Further, it is a UNO directive to every member state that consumption and production of ODS will be regulated in a phased manner with different time schedules for developing and developed member countries. It is also the responsibility of each member country to comply with the directive in letter and spirit. Main provisions regarding control of ODS include:

a) Specific responsibilities related to the phase out of the different groups of ODS
b) Control of ODS trade
c) Annual reporting of data
d) National licensing systems to control ODS imports and exports
e) Binding, time-targeted, and measurable commitments for both groups of countries

Current Status of the Protocol

Member countries have been successful in phasing out ODS. But on the other hand, ODS has been replaced by emissions of hydrofluorocarbons (HFCs). HFCs, which are part of greenhouse gases, are more than twenty times more harmful than ODS and hundreds to thousands time more harmful than carbon dioxide in affecting unfavourable and unhealthy climate changes. Then a need was felt to amend the directives of Montreal Protocol of 1987.

Amendment to Address Hydrofluorocarbons (HFCs) Under Montreal Protocol

A summit of 197 member countries was held at Kigali (Rwanda) on October 15, 2016. In the summit, the member countries adopted the amendment. Under the amendment, countries committed to cut the production and consumption of HFCs by more than 80 per cent over the next 30 years. Under the amendment, developed countries will reduce HFC consumption beginning in 2019. Most developing countries will freeze consumption in 2024, with a small number of developing countries with unique circumstances freezing consumption in 2028. The plan also provides financing to certain countries, to help them transition to climate-friendly alternatives. Major elements of the Kigali Amendment include:

- Innovative and flexible structure
- Ambitious phasedown schedule
- Incentive for early action
- Broad participation
- Enforcement and accountability
- Multiple opportunities to increase ambition

The United Nations Conference on Sustainable Development (Rio Summit)

During the last few years, the world witnessed evaporation of resources sustaining development due to harmful anthropogenic activities. There was a need to save resources for sustainable development. Resultantly, the United Nations Conference on Sustainable Development-or Rio+20-took place in Rio de Janeiro, Brazil on 20-22 June, 2012. It resulted in a resolution focussing on ways to achieve sustainable development by implementing suitable measures in this direction. Following are the leading decisions of the resolution:

1) Launching a process to develop a set of Sustainable Development Goals (SDGs), which will be an improvement and supplement to the Millennium Development Goals and converge with the Post-2015 Development Agenda
2) Adopting fundamental and prioritised guidelines on Green Economy Policies
3) Establishing an intergovernmental process under the General Assembly to prepare options on a strategy for sustainable development financing
4) Strengthening the United Nations Environment Programme (UNEP) on several fronts with action to be taken during the 67th session of the General Assembly on 18th September, 2012
5) Establish a high-level political forum for sustainable development.
6) Submission to the United Nations to launch such a work programme in which progress in the area of Sustainable Development Goals is to be assessed by linking it with the growth of Gross Domestic Product (GDP) of the concerned country
7) Adoption of the 10-year framework of programmes on sustainable consumption and production patterns
8) Progressive decisions in main and allied areas of SDGs like energy, food security, oceans, and cities

The Rio+20 conference was successful to attract attention of thousands of members and representatives of the UN system. Result was obtained in the form of various voluntary commitments from all over the world to help in effectively achieving sustainable development goals within the stipulated time period which opened the doors of global partnerships for advanced sustainable development.

Convention on Biological Diversity (CBD)

With a sole motive of initiating actions to achieve a sustainable future, convention of Biological Diversity (Convention of Biodiversity in short) is a multi-national agreement. It was opened for signature at the Earth Summit in Rio de Janeiro on 5 June, 1992 and entered into force on 29 December, 1993. CBD is an international legally binding treaty on member countries. There are 168 signatories and 196 Parties to CBD. Ultimate authority of CBD is Conference of the Parties (COP). Three-fold objectives of CBD include:

1) Conservation of biodiversity
2) Sustainable use of biodiversity
3) Fair and equitable sharing of benefits arising from the use of genetic resources

Being a concern of humanity in general, CBD seeks to ensure biodiversity at all levels by covering:

- Ecosystems, species, and genetic resources
- Biotechnology including what is covered through Cartagena Protocol on Biosafety
- All possible domains like science, politics, education, agriculture, trading, manufacturing, social and cultural set-up, and any other sphere and activity directly or indirectly related to biodiversity

Editor: The text inside the following textbox is invisible, please look into it.

CURRENT ON CBD

Fourth session of the United Nations Environment Assembly was held at Nairobi (Kenya) from March11-15, 2019. In the session Ms. Cristiana Pa?ca Palmer, Executive Secretary, Convention on Biological Diversity urged the dignitaries to work jointly for checking rapidly falling biodiversity and prepare post-2020 biodiversity framework.

Supplementary Agreements to CBD Cartagena Protocol on Biosafety

***The Cartagena Protocol on Biosafety** to the Convention on Biological Diversity is an international treaty governing the movements of living modified organisms (LMOs) resulting from modern biotechnology from one country to another. It was adopted on 29 January 2000 at Cartagena (Columbia), as a supplementary agreement to the Convention on Biological Diversity and entered into force on 11 September 2003.*

***Living Modified Organism (LMO):** LMO is a living organism which is genetically modified to develique genetic structure with engineering of biotechnology. LMO causes great harm to human beings as any genetically modified plant grows as weed. LMO is same as GMO (already discussed in chapter 2 of this unit)*

Nagoya Protocol

The Nagoya Protocol on Access to Genetic Resources and the Fair and Equitable Sharing of Benefits Arising from their Utilisation to the Convention on Biological Diversity is a supplementary agreement to the Convention on Biological Diversity. It provides a transparent legal framework for the effective implementation of one of the three objectives of the CBD: the fair and equitable sharing of benefits arising out of the utilisation of genetic resources. It is also known as Nagoya Protocol on Access and Benefit Sharing (ABS), and was adopted on 29 October, 2010 in Nagoya, Japan and entered into force on 12 October, 2014.

National Biodiversity Authority

The National Biodiversity Authority (NBA) was established in 2003 by the Central Government to implement India's Biological Diversity Act (2002). The NBA is a statutory body and it performs facilitative, regulatory, and advisory function for the Government of India on the issue of conservation, sustainable use of biological resources, and fair and equitable sharing of benefits of use. Headquarters are at Chennai (Tamil Nadu). The International Day for Biological Diversity (or World Biodiversity Day) is a United Nations-sanctioned international day for the promotion of biodiversity issues. It is currently held on May 22.

Kyoto Protocol

Kyoto Protocol is an international agreement as an extension to United Nations Framework Convention on Climate Change (UNFCCC) of 1992. The protocol made reduction in greenhouse gases (GHG) emissions binding on the Parties. Parties were to ensure reduction in GHG emissions within a stipulated period of time. Primary aim was to reduce global warming by reducing the concentration of greenhouse gases in the atmosphere to that level which would prevent dangerous anthropogenic interference with the climate system. The Kyoto Protocol applies to the six greenhouse gases listed in Annex A: Carbon dioxide (CO_2), Methane (CH_4), Nitrous oxide (N_2O), Hydrofluorocarbons (HFCs), Perfluorocarbons (PFCs), and Sulphur hexafluoride (SF_6).

While recognising that developed and industrialised countries had been primarily responsible for emissions as having a long history of running factories emitting GHG for over 150 years, the Protocol imposes heavier burden on developed nations under the slogan of **"common but differentiated responsibilities"**.

The Kyoto Protocol was adopted in Kyoto, Japan, on 11 December, 1997 and entered into force on 16 February, 2005. The detailed rules for the implementation of the Protocol were adopted at Conference of the Parties (COP) 7 in Marrakesh, Morocco, in 2001, and are referred to as the "Marrakesh Accords". Its first commitment period started in 2008 and ended in 2012.

Doha Amendment

Second amendment to Kyoto Protocol was adopted at Doha (Qatar) on 8th December, 2012. Doha amendment was the start of the second commitment period by the Parties from 1 January, 2013 to 31 December, 2020.

Under the Protocol, countries must meet their targets primarily through national measures. However, the

Protocol also offers them additional means to meet their targets by way of three market-based mechanisms. These mechanisms are:

- International Emissions Trading
- Clean Development Mechanism (CDM)
- Joint Implementation (JI)

International Emissions Trading: As per the Protocol, the commitment is to reduce or limit GHG emissions. Each country is allowed an emission quota. Here, the countries with spare emissions sell their unused quota to the countries which have overachieved their targets. As the leading greenhouse gas affecting change in climate is carbon dioxide, countries prefer to trade in carbon. Thus, carbon is traded like a commodity and this is called 'Carbon Market'.

The Clean Development Mechanism (CDM): Under this mechanism, a country is allowed to implement its emission reduction project in developing countries. With this, that country earns saleable Certified Emission Reductions (CER) credits, each equal to one tonne of carbon dioxide which is considered towards meeting Protocol targets. For example, a rural electrification project by installing solar panels rather than burning fossil fuels will earn CER for the country which has implemented this emission reduction project.

Joint Implementation: Two countries on an emission reduction mission can earn emission reduction units by jointly implementing their emission reduction projects.

Paris Agreement

Parties to the UNFCCC reached a historic agreement in Paris on 12 December, 2015 at COP 21. The resolution was to combat climate change with determined action and investment to set a sustainable low carbon future. It was also resolved to assist developing countries in attaining the mission of reducing emissions affecting changes in climate, particularly carbon dioxide. It was for the first time that Paris Agreement brought all the countries together, initiating determined efforts to combat unhealthy climate change.

Aims of the Agreement

1) Pivotal aim of the Paris Agreement has been to strengthen the global response to challenges imposed by climate change and reduce the global temperature below 2 degrees Celsius and further below 1.5 degree Celsius
2) To increase the ability of countries to deal with the impacts of climate change
3) To finance flows consistent with low GHG emissions and climate-resilient pathway

What is Needed to Achieve the Above Goals

1) Appropriate mobilisation and provision of financial resources
2) A new technology framework
3) Enhanced capacity-building
4) Supportive action by developing countries and the most vulnerable countries

The Paris Agreement requires all Parties to put forward their best efforts through **"nationally determined contributions" (NDCs)** and to strengthen these efforts in the years ahead. This includes requirements that all Parties report regularly on their emissions and on their implementation efforts. There will also be a global stocktake every 5 years to assess the collective progress towards achieving the purpose of the Agreement and to inform further individual actions by the Parties.

Opening of the Agreement

The Paris Agreement was opened for signature on 22 April 2016-Earth Day-at UN Headquarters in New York. It entered into force on 4 November, 2016.

Crucial Areas

Paris Agreement earmarked certain thrust areas of combating climate change as follows:

- **Long-term temperature goal:** The Paris Agreement, in seeking to strengthen the global response to climate change, reaffirms the goal of limiting global temperature increase to well below 2 degrees Celsius, while pursuing efforts to limit the increase to 1.5 degrees.
- **Global peaking and 'climate neutrality':** To achieve this temperature goal, Parties aim to reach global peaking of greenhouse gas emissions (GHGs) as soon as possible. This is done in recognition of the fact that peaking will take longer for developing country. Parties will strive to achieve a balance between anthropogenic emissions by sources and removals by sinks of GHGs in the second half of the century.

GLOBAL PEAKING

As per Paris Agreement parties to agreement must achieve peak emissions by 2020 after that emission will start declining. Late achieving of global peaking will delay decline in emissions and it will become difficult to combat global warming. As emissions start declining rapidly after achieving peak level, only then it will be possible to maintain average rise in temperature between 1,5 degree Celsius and 2 degree Celsius.

"CLIMATE NEUTRL NOW" - INITIATIVE

Climate neutral now initiative was launched by UNFCCC in 2015.The initiative aims at encouraging and supporting every action being taken towards reducing emissions to target level and maintain rise in temperature less than 2 degree Cesius.and achieve climate resilience by mid-century. This is also the basic target of Paris Agreement. The initiative invites citizens, companies and organisations to work for achieving climate neutrality by reducing their carbon footprint.

- **Mitigation:** The Paris Agreement establishes binding commitments by all Parties to prepare, communicate, and maintain a nationally determined contribution (NDC), and to pursue domestic measures to achieve them. It also prescribes that Parties shall communicate their NDCs every 5 years and provide information necessary for clarity and transparency. Developed countries should continue to take the lead by undertaking absolute economy-wide reduction targets, while developing countries should continue enhancing their mitigation efforts, and are encouraged to move toward economy-wide targets over time in the light of different national circumstances.
- **Sinks and reservoirs:** The Paris Agreement also encourages Parties to conserve and enhance, as appropriate, sinks and reservoirs of GHGs, including forests.
- **Voluntary cooperation/Market- and non-market-based approaches:** The Paris Agreement recognises the possibility of voluntary cooperation among Parties to allow for higher ambitions and sets out principles-including environmental integrity, transparency, and rigorous accounting-for any cooperation that involves internationally the transfer of mitigation outcomes. It establishes a mechanism to contribute to the mitigation of GHG emissions and support sustainable development, and defines a framework for non-market approaches to sustainable development.
- **Adaptation:** The Paris Agreement establishes a global goal on adaptation-of enhancing adaptive capacity, strengthening resilience, and reducing vulnerability to climate change in the context of the temperature goal of the Agreement. It aims to significantly strengthen national adaptation efforts. It recognises that adaptation is a global challenge faced by all. All Parties should engage in adaptation, including by formulating and implementing National Adaptation Plans, and should submit and periodically update an adaptation communication describing their priorities, needs, plans, and actions. The adaptation efforts of developing countries should be recognised.
- **Loss and damage:** The Paris Agreement recognises the importance of averting, minimising, and addressing loss and damage associated with the adverse effects of climate change, including extreme weather events and slow onset events, and the role of sustainable development in reducing the risk of loss and damage.

Finance, technology, and capacity-building support: The Paris Agreement reaffirms the obligations of developed countries to support the efforts of developing countries Parties need to build clean, climate-resilient futures, while for the first time encouraging voluntary contributions by other Parties. Provision of resources should also aim to achieve a balance between adaptation and mitigation. In addition to reporting on finance already provided, developed country Parties commit to submit indicative information on future support every two years, including projected levels of public finance. The Agreement also provides that the Financial Mechanism of the Convention, including the Green Climate Fund (GCF), shall serve the Agreement. International cooperation is needed on climate-safe technology.

Developing countries will also be encouraged to implement such technology enhancing climate resilience. Climate change education, training, as well as public awareness, participation, and access to information about any provision of the Agreement is also to be enhanced under the Agreement.

- **Transparency, implementation, and compliance:** The Paris Agreement relies on a rigorous transparency and accounting system to provide clarity on action and support by Parties, with flexibility for their differing capabilities of Parties. In addition to reporting information on mitigation, adaptation, and support, the Agreement requires that the information submitted by each Party undergoes international technical expert review. The Agreement also includes a mechanism that will facilitate implementation and promote compliance in a non-adversarial and non-punitive manner, and will report annually to the CMA.
- **Global stocktake:** A 'global stocktake', to take place in 2023 and every 5 years thereafter, will assess collective progress toward achieving the purpose of the Agreement in a comprehensive and facilitative manner. It will be based on the best available science and its long-term global goal. Its outcome will inform Parties to update and enhance their actions and support and enhance international cooperation on climate action.

International Solar Alliance

(The above topic has been discussed in Chapter 7: "Natural and Energy Resources" of Unit-IX)

SOME OTHER NATIONAL/INTERNATIONAL ACTS, PROTOCOLS, SUMMITS/CONFERENCES

1) **National Green Tribunal Act, 2010** is an Act of the Parliament of India which enables creation of a special tribunal to handle the expeditious disposal of the cases pertaining to environmental issues.
2) **The Water (Prevention and Control of Pollution) Act** was enacted in 1974 to provide for the prevention and control of water pollution, and for maintaining or restoring the wholesomeness of water in the country.
3) **The Ozone Depleting Substances (Regulation and Control) Rules, 2000,** have been laid down for the regulation of production and consumption of ozone depleting substances.
4) **The Wildlife Protection Act, Rules 1973 and Amendment 1991** provides for the protection of birds and animals and for all matters that are connected to it, whether it be their habitat or the waterhole or the forests that sustain them.
5) **The Batteries (Management and Handling) Rules, 2001** relate to rules which shall apply to every manufacturer, importer, re-conditioner, assembler, dealer, auctioneer, consumer, and bulk consumer involved in the manufacture, processing, sale, purchase, and use of batteries or components so as to regulate and ensure the environmentally safe disposal of used batteries.
6) **The Environment (Siting for Industrial Projects) Rules, 1999** lay down detailed provisions relating to areas to be avoided for siting of industries, precautionary measures to be taken for site selection, as also the aspects of environmental protection which should have been incorporated during the implementation of the industrial development projects.
7) **The National Environment Tribunal Act, 1995** has been created to award compensation for damages to persons, property, and the environment arising from any activity involving hazardous substances.
8) **The Water (Prevention and Control of Pollution) Cess Act, 1977** provides for the levy and collection of cess or fees on water intensive industries and local authorities.
9) **The Atomic Energy Act, 1962** deals with development, control, and use of atomic energy for the welfare of people of India and radioactive waste.
10) **Geneva Protocol, 1925** is a treaty prohibiting the use of chemical and biological weapons in international armed conflicts. It was signed at Geneva on 17 June, 1925 and entered into force on 8 February, 1928.
11) **The Comprehensive Nuclear-Test-Ban Treaty (CTBT) 1996** is a multilateral treaty that bans all nuclear explosions, for both civilian and military purposes, in all environments. It was adopted by the United Nations General Assembly on 10 September, 1996, but has not entered into force, as eight specific states have not ratified the treaty.
12) **The Convention on Assistance in the Case of a Nuclear Accident or Radiological Emergency** is a 1986 treaty of the International Atomic Energy Agency (IAEA), whereby states have agreed to provide notification to the IAEA of any assistance that they can provide in the case of a nuclear accident that occurs in another state that has ratified the treaty.

13) **Protocol to the 1979 Convention on Long-Range Transboundary Air Pollution Concerning the Control of Emissions of Nitrogen Oxides or Their Transboundary Fluxes**, opened for signature on 31 October, 1988 and entered into force on 14 February, 1991. It was to provide for the control or reduction of nitrogen oxides and their transboundary fluxes. It was concluded in Sofia, Bulgaria.

14) **The Vienna Convention for the Protection of the Ozone Layer, 1985** is a multilateral environmental agreement signed in 1985 that provided frameworks for international reductions in the production of chlorofluorocarbons due to their contribution to the destruction of the ozone layer and resulting increase in the threat of skin cancer.

15) **Espoo Convention, 1991** is a United Nations Economic Commission for Europe (UNECE) convention signed in Espoo, Finland, in 1991 that entered into force in 1997. The Convention sets out the obligations of Parties- that is, States that have agreed to be bound by the Convention-to carry out an environmental impact assessment of certain activities at an early stage of planning. It also lays down the general obligation of States to notify and consult each other on all major projects under consideration that are likely to have a significant adverse environmental impact across boundaries.

16) **United Nations Conference on Environment and Development (UNCED)**, 1992 byname Earth Summit, was a conference held at Rio de Janeiro, Brazil (June 3-14, 1992), to reconcile worldwide economic development with protection of the environment. The Earth Summit was the largest gathering of world leaders as of 1992, with 117 heads of state and representatives of 178 nations in all attending. By means of treaties and other documents signed at the conference, most of the world's nations nominally committed themselves to the pursuit of economic development in ways that would protect the Earth's environment and non-renewable resources.

AGENDA-21

Agenda 21 is a non-binding action plan of the United Nations with regard to sustainable development. It is a product of the Earth Summit (UN Conference on Environment and Development) held in Rio de Janeiro, Brazil, in 1992. It is an action agenda for the UN, other multilateral organization, and individual governments around the world that can be executed at local, national, and global levels.

The "21" in Agenda 21 refers to the 21st century. It has been affirmed and had a few modifications at subsequent UN conferences. Its aim is achieving global sustainable development. One major objective of the Agenda 21 initiative is that every local government should draw its own local Agenda 21. Since 2015, Sustainable Development Goals are included in the Agenda 2030

17) **United Nations Conference on the Human Environment,1972** byname **Stockholm Conference**, was the first United Nations (UN) conference that focused on international environmental issues. The conference, held in Stockholm, Sweden, from June 5 to 16, 1972, reflected a growing interest in conservation issues worldwide and laid the foundation for global environmental governance. The final declaration of the Stockholm Conference was an environmental manifesto that was a forceful statement of the finite nature of Earth's resources and the necessity for humanity to safeguard them. The Stockholm Conference also led to the creation of the United Nations Environment Programme (UNEP) in December 1972 to coordinate global efforts to promote sustainability and safeguard the natural environment.

18) **The World Summit on Sustainable Development (WSSD)**, held in Johannesburg during 26 August and 4 September, 2002, was the biggest event of its kind organised by the United Nations to date. A major objective of the WSSD was to set out strategies for greater and more effective implementation of Agenda 21, negotiated in Rio ten years ago.

Practice Exercise

General Questions Format

1. Which of the following is NOT TRUE about Montreal Protocol?

a) The Protocol works for controlling production and consumption of man-made oxygen depleting substances (ODS).

b) It was signed in October 1989.

c) Parties to the agreement have replaced ODS with environment-friendly substances HFCs.

d) Only half of the UN member countries ratified the agreement due to technical hitches.

(A) c only (B) a, b, c, and d

(C) b and c only (D) a, b, and c only

2. Which of the following treaty prohibits use of chemical and biological weapons in international conflicts?

(A) CTBT

(B) Vienna Convention

(C) Stockholm Conference

(D) Geneva Protocol

3. Environment Protection Act was enacted in the wake of

(A) Bhopal gas leak tragedy

(B) Latur earthquake

(C) Ladakh avalanche

(D) Jaisalmer drought

4. Which of the following Protocols regulates the movement of LMOs?

(A) Geneva Protocol (B) Cartagena Protocol

(C) Nagoya Protocol (D) None of these

5. "Agenda 21" focusses on

(A) Marine pollution

(B) GHG emissions

(C) Sustainable development

(D) Deforestation

6. International Biodiversity Day is observed on

(A) 16 October (B) 10 January

(C) 23 September (D) 22 March

7. Names of conventions are given below under Column I and their objectives are given under Column II. Match the name of the convention with its objective and chose the correct code from the codes given below:

Column I	Column II
a) Stockholm Conference	i) Environment and Development
b) Earth Summit	ii) Reducing CFCs
c) Espoo Convention	iii) Environmental Governance
d) Vienna Convention	iv) Environmental Impact Assessment

Codes:

	(a)	(b)	(c)	(d)
(A)	i	iii	iv	ii
(B)	ii	iii	iv	i
(C)	iii	i	iv	ii
(D)	iv	ii	i	iii

8. Which of the following environmental Acts is called 'Umbrella Legislation'?

(A) The National Environmental Tribunal Act

(B) The Water (Prevention and Control of Pollution) Act

(C) The Atomic Energy Act

(D) None of these

9. Which Protocol asked to work with the slogan "common but differentiated responsibilities"?

(A) Nagoya (B) Kyoto

(C) Geneva (D) Paris

10. Which summit has its roots in Earth Summit, 1992?

(A) Johannesburg (B) Paris

(C) Rio (D) Stockholm

11. Which of the following greenhouse gas is not covered under Kyoto Protocol?

(A) Nitrous oxide

(B) Methane

(C) Carbon dioxide

(D) None of these

12. Which of the following regions has been declared as restricted region in Environment Protection Act,1986?

(A) Arid (B) Aravalli

(C) Marshy (D) Tropic

13. Agenda 21 states that

a) Every party to various UN conventions should submit a monthly report on progress in achieving millennium development goals to UNFCCC.

b) Developed Countries should launch campaigns to help developing countries in reducing emissions to the level set by the Earth Summit.

c) Parties to the Earth Summit should execute efforts at global, national, and local level to achieve sustainable development.

d) Local governments should draw their local 'Agenda 21' to move effectively and faster to achieve Agenda 2030.

(A) c only (B) a and d only

(C) c and d only (D) All of the above

14. 'Climate Neutral Now' initiative has been launched by

(A) Intergovernmental Panel on Climate Change

(B) National Action Plan on Climate Change

(C) Prime Minister's Conference on Climate Change

(D) United Nations Framework Convention on Climate Change

15. Doha Amendment is related to

(A) Kyoto Protocol (B) Cartagena Protocol

(C) Geneva Protocol (D) Nagoya Protocol

16. United Nations Environment Programme (UNEP) was created after UN meeting at....

(A) Doha (B) Stockholm

(C) Johannesburg (D) Paris

17. Which environmental concern has been a common agenda in different conventions and summits convened by either UNO or its agencies?

(A) Climate change (B) Loss of biodiversity

(C) Ozone depletion (D) None of these

18. Among different goals set in Paris Agreement, what does the goal of 'Adaptation' signify?

a) Though adaptation is a big challenge, it can be pursued to achieve climate resilience.

b) Though adaptation is a time-consuming process, is has to be pursued before taking mitigation measures.

c) Adaptation aims to strengthen national adaptation efforts.

d) Adaptation yields desirable results if followed as per priority with respect to the degree of vulnerability of subjects to climate change.

(A) a, c, and d only

(B) a, b, c, and d

(C) c and d only

(D) None of these

19. Consider the following statements:

Statement P: Kyoto Protocol allows discretion to Parties as far as its ratification is concerned.

Statement Q: Kyoto Protocol states that developing countries are responsible for increase in GHG emissions.

(A) Both P and Q are true

(B) Both P and Q are false

(C) P is true but Q is false

(D) P is false but Q is true

20. Consider a question: "Are 'National Green Tribunal Act, 2010' and 'The National Environment Tribunal Act, 1995' the same?"

Chose the most logical answer from the following answers:

(A) Yes, as both examine the legalities in taking mitigation measures against adverse changes in climate.

(B) No, as their dates of enactment are different.

(C) Yes, as both have been created to follow legal course of action in case ecological norms are violated by an individual, industry, and trading houses.

(D) No, as NGT Act deals with general environmental issues, whereas NET Act deals with compensation for accidents from using hazardous substances.

KEY

1. B	2. D	3. A	4. B	5. C	6. D	7. A
8. D	9. B	10. A	11. D	12. B	13. C	14. D
15. A	16. B	17. D	18. A	19. B	20. D	

Assertion–Reason Format

1. **Assertion (A):** Indian Constitution fixes responsibility on the government and citizens of India to safeguard the environment and resources.

   Reason (R): Violations of environmental norms either by the government or by the citizens are justiciable.

   (A) Both a and R are true and R is correct explanation of A

   (B) Both A and R are true but R is not correct explanation of A

   (C) A is true but R is false

   (D) A is false but R is true

2. **Assertion (A):** Environment depletion is one of the leading issues of concern for the world today.

   Reason (R): Compliance of various multinational Protocols, Agreements, and Acts for protecting The environment have not yielded any positive results due to subjective approach in tackling environmental threats.

   (A) Both A and R are true but R is not correct explanation of A

   (B) Both A and R are true and R is correct explanation of A

   (C) A is true but R is false

   (D) A is false but R is true

3. **Assertion (A):** Montreal Protocol is a pledge against Ozone Depleting Substances (ODS).

   Reason (R): ODS directly attacks the stratosphere containing ozone, resulting in ozone depletion.

   (A) Both A and R are false

   (B) Both A and R are true and R is correct explanation of A

   (C) A is false but R is true

   (D) Both A and R are true but R is not correct explanation of A

4. **Assertion (A):** Early peaking of emissions ensures stability in climate.

   Reason (R): Paris Agreement advocates global peaking of emissions.

   (A) Both A and R are true and R is correct explanation of A

   (B) A is true but R is false

   (C) A is false but R is true

   (D) Both A and R are true but R is not correct explanation of A

5. **Assertion (A):** Doon valley in Uttarakhand has been declared an eco-sensitive region in Environment Protection Act, 1986.

   Reason (R): Any type of illegal installation in an eco-sensitive region is a punishable offence.

   (A) Both A and R are false

   (B) Both A and R are true but R is not correct explanation of A

   (C) A is true but R is false

   (D) Both A and R are true and R is correct explanation of A

6. **Assertion (A):** Nagoya Protocol is a supplementary agreement of Kyoto Protocol.

   Reason (R): Conservation of biological diversity has been advocated in various international environment protocols.

   (A) A is false but R is true

   (B) A is true but R is false

   (C) Both A and R are true and R is correct explanation of A

   (D) Both A and R are true but R is not correct explanation of A

7. **Assertion (A):** Had there been no protocols on environment protection, there would not have been survival of humans on the earth today.

   Reason (R): Protocols have covered every threat of environment depletion to humans.

   (A) Both A and R are false

   (B) Both A and R are true and R is correct explanation of A

   (C) Both A and R are true but R is not correct explanation of A

   (D) A is true but R is false

8. **Assertion (A):** Anthropogenic activities are kept out of jurisdiction of some protocols on environment depletion.

   Reason (R): Kyoto Protocol and Paris Agreement consider role of anthropogenic activities in increasing emissions to an alarming level.

   (A) Both A and R are true and R is correct explanation of A
   (B) Both A and R are true but R is not correct explanation of A
   (C) A is true but R is false
   (D) A is false but R is true

9. **Assertion (A):** Rio+20 Summit focusses on achieving Sustainable Development Goals (SDGs).

   Reasoning (R): Millennium Development Goals (MDGs) were focussed in all the summits prior to Rio+20 Summit.

   (A) Both A and R are true and R is correct explanation of A
   (B) Both A and R are true but R is not correct explanation of A
   (C) A is false but R is true
   (D) A is true but R is false

10. **Assertion (A):** Environment protection era started with Environment Protection Act, 1986.

    Reason (R): Similarly, conservation of biodiversity was started with Convention of Biodiversity.

    (A) Both A and R are true and R is correct explanation of A
    (B) Both A and R are true but R is not correct explanation of A
    (C) A is true but R is false
    (D) Both A and R are false

KEY

1. C **2.** C **3.** B **4.** D **5.** B **6.** B **7.** B **8.** D **9.** D **10.** D

Questions Asked in Previous NET Exams

1. Which one of the following conferences/ summit is also known as UN Conference on Sustainable Development (UNCSD)?

   (UGC NET JUNE 2019)

   (A) The Stockholm Conference 1972
   (B) Rio de Janerio Conference 1972
   (C) Johannesburg Summit 2002
   (D) Rio+20 Conference 2012

2. In which country, the recent international agreement on phasing out Hydrofluorocarbons (HFCs) was signed?

   (UGC NET JANUARY 2017)

   (A) Rwanda
   (B) Morocco
   (C) South Africa
   (D) Algeria

3. Kyoto Protocol is related to

   (UGC NET JUNE 2013)

   (A) Ozone depletion
   (B) Hazardous waste
   (C) Climate change
   (D) Nuclear energy

4. Nagoya Protocol is related to

   (UGC NETDECEMBER 2012)

   (A) Climate change
   (B) Ozone depletion
   (C) Hazardous waste
   (D) Biodiversity

KEY

1. D **2.** A **3.** C **4.** D

10 Environment : Miscellaneous Facts

Leading Environment Terms

Landfill : A site that is specially designed to dispose of waste and operates with a licence granted by the Environmental Protection Agency (EPA)

Ecosystem : A community of organisms that depend on each other and the environment they inhabit

Carbon offset : A unit, equal to one tonne of carbon dioxide, that individuals, companies, or governments buy to reduce short-term and long-term emissions of greenhouse gases. The payment usually funds projects that generate energy from renewable sources such as wind or flowing water.

Abatement : Reducing the degree or intensity of, or eliminating, pollution

Radon : A common radioactive gas emitted from ordinary soils and rock. Radon has no smell, taste, or colour and can seep into homes, building up to dangerous levels if there is not enough ventilation. Being exposed to high levels of radon gas over a long period of time increases the risk of developing lung cancer.

Effluent : Liquid wastes such as sewage and liquid waste from industries

WEEE : Short for Waste Electrical and Electronic Equipment (WEEE), which are any unwanted devices

Backyard burning : An illegal method of getting rid of household waste, possibly in an attempt to save on bin charges that releases levels of pollutants into the air (thus harming air quality and risking the health of those burning the waste and of their neighbours)

Fossil fuels : Fuels –such as coal, gas, peat, and oil - that are formed in the ground over a long time from dead plants and animals and are used up once they are burned for energy

Sustainable development : Development using land or energy sources in a way that meets the needs of people today without reducing the ability of future generations to meet their own needs

Green design : A design, usually of a building, that includes environmentally-friendly features such as solar panels, skylights, or recycled building materials

Biodiversity : A short form of the phrase 'biological diversity', which means the variety of life on this planet and how it interacts within habitats and ecosystems. Biodiversity covers all plants, animals, and microorganisms on land and in water.

Particulate matter : A name given to fine solid or liquid particles that pollute the air and are added to the atmosphere by natural and man-made processes at the earth's surface. Examples of particulate matter include dust, smoke, soot, pollen, and soil particles.

Habitat : The area occupied by a community or species (group of animals or plants), such as a forest floor, desert, or seashore

Biodegradable waste : Organic waste, typically coming from plant or animal sources (for example food scraps and paper), which other living organisms can break down

Hazardous waste : Waste that poses a risk to human health or the environment and needs to be handled and disposed of carefully. Examples include oil-based paints, car batteries, weed killers, bleach, and waste electrical and electronic devices

Dioxins : Highly toxic chemicals that can be formed in small amounts from forest fires or volcanoes but more often are produced unintentionally from industrial activities and from incinerating waste and burning fossil fuels

Noxious gases : Poisonous gases that can harm people and the environment. Some gases have a strong smell, for example, sulphur dioxide and methane, while others, such as carbon monoxide, do not have any smell at all.

Fuel poverty : Being unable to heat a home to a safe and comfortable level because of low household income or having to spend more than 10% of household income to heat a home to a comfortable level because the home is not energy- efficient

Carbon footprint

A measure of the impact our activities have on the environment, especially climate change, often reported as the units of tonnes (or kg) of carbon dioxide each of us produces over a given period of time

Organic food

Plants and animals that are grown or reared without the use of synthetic fertilisers, pesticides, or hormones

Bring bank

A place where one can bring materials for recycling, for example glass, newspapers, heavy cardboard, and textiles

Conservation

Preserving or protecting animals and resources such as minerals, water, and plants through planned action (such as breeding endangered species) or non-action (such as not letting taps run unnecessarily)

Mulch

Leaves, straw, or compost used to cover growing plants to retain moisture and improve fertility of soil

Draught-proofing

A way to stop heat from escaping a home, for example, by sealing window frames and using draught excluders under doors

Reforestation

The process of planting trees in forest lands to replace those that have been cut down

Carbon count

A measure of the amount of carbon dioxide you produce through your lifestyle every day, for example through driving or using electrical appliances and lighting

Litter

Waste that is thrown away carelessly, mainly made up of plastic, metal, glass, paper, or food. Common examples are chewing gum and cigarette butts.

MBT

Short for 'Mechanical biological treatment', which is a way of sorting and treating waste. The waste is first sorted mechanically into materials that can and cannot be recycled. Any waste that can be recycled is then broken down biologically, often through composting, while the rest is usually sent to the landfill.

Carbon neutral

A situation that arises when the amount of carbon dioxide released into the air equals the amount of carbon dioxide removed from the air, for example, by planting trees, or the amount saved by using renewable energy sources to produce the same amount of energy.

Black bin (Grey bin)

A bin used by certain local authorities to collect waste that cannot be recycled or composted

Brown bin

A bin used by some local authorities to collect organic waste such as food and light garden waste

Compost

A rich soil-like material produced from decayed plants and other organic matter, such as food and animal waste, that decomposes (breaks down) naturally. Most food waste can be put into compost, but one should not include meat, bones, cheese, cooking oils, and fish. These may take a long time to break down and attract unwanted pests.

Cryptosporidium

A tiny parasite that can infect people if it is present in drinking water

Green bin

A bin used by certain local authorities to collect dry cardboard, paper, tins, and other recyclable waste, including certain plastics

Stubble burning

A deliberate burning of straw stubble that is left after harvesting paddy or wheat to dispose it off. Stubble burning is a serious health hazard as it releases toxic pollutants into the atmosphere generating respiratory diseases and becomes a major cause of air pollution.

Fly ash

A by-product from burning coal in thermal power generating plants. During combustion, mineral impurities in the coal (clay, feldspar, quartz, and shale) fuse in suspension and float out of the combustion chamber with the exhaust gases. As the fused material rises, it cools and solidifies into spherical glassy particles called fly ash. Fly ash is considered to be stronger, more environmental-friendly, and durable cement as compared to Portland cement. It is the most widely used construction material in the world. Fly ash is being very effectively and economically used in building components such as bricks, cement, doors, door-frames, etc. Fly ash is also being used in construction of roads and embankments with some design changes. It is also used as raw material in agricultural and wasteland development.

ENVIRONMENTAL DAYS

Day	Date
World Wetlands Day	February 2
World Water Day	March 22
Earth Day	April 22
International Migratory Bird Day	May 3
Greenery Day	May 4
International Day for Biological Diversity (World Biodiversity Day)	May 22
World Environment Day	June 5
World Oceans Day	June 8
Global Wind Day	June 15
World Population Day	July 11
International Day for the Preservation of the Ozone Layer	September 16
World Rivers Day	September - last Sunday
World Habitat Day	October - first Monday (Oct. 7, 2019)
International Day for Natural Disaster Reduction	October-second Wednesday (Oct.13, 2019)
International Day of Climate Action	October 24
International Day for Preventing the Exploitation of the Environment in War and Armed Conflict	November 6
World Soil Day	December 5
International Mountain Day	December 11
Hiroshima Day	August 6
World Forestry Day	March 21
World Health day	April 7
World Aids Day	December 1
World Resources Day	March 23
World Atmosphere Day	April 10
World Migratory Bird Day	Two-day event in second weekend of May
Van-Mahotasav Saptah	01-07 July
World Nature Day	October 3
International Tiger Day	July 29
World Lion Day	August 10

THE UNO THEMES FOR WORLD ENVIRONMENT DAY IN DIFFERENT YEARS

Sr. No	Year	Theme	Host Country
1	2019	Air Pollution	China
2	2018	Beat Plastic Pollution	India
3	2017	Connecting People with Nature	Canada
4	2016	Go Wild for Life	Angola
5	2015	Seven billion Dreams- One Planet-Consume with Care	Italy
6	2014	Raise Your Voice, not the Sea Level	Barbados
7	2013	Think, Eat, Save. Reduce Your Foodprint.	Mongolia
8	2012	Green Economy	Brazil
9	2011	Forest: Nature at your Service	India
10	2010	Many Species. One Planet. One Future	Rwanda

UNITED NATIONS INTERNATIONAL YEARS WITH ENVIRONMENTAL DESIGNATIONS

Sr. No	Year	Designated as
1	2017	International Year of Sustainable Tourism for Development
2	2016	International Year of Pulses
3	2015	International Year of Soils
4	2014	International Year of Family Farming
5	2013	International Year of Water Cooperation
6	2012	International Year of Sustainable Energy for All
7	2011	International Year of Forests
8	2010	International Year of Biodiversity
9	2008	International Year of Planet Earth

LEADING ENVIRONMENT RELATED MOVEMENTS IN INDIA

Chipko Movement

- **Place:** In Chamoli district and later at Tehri-Garhwal district of Uttarakhand
- **Aim:** A movement to protect the trees on the Himalayan slopes from the axes of contractors of the forest

  Gist: Mr. Sunderlal Bahuguna enlightened the villagers by conveying the importance of trees in the environment which checks the erosion of soil, cause rains, and provides pure air. The women of Advani village of Tehri-Garhwal tied the sacred thread around trunks of trees and they hugged the trees, hence it was called 'Chipko Movement' or 'Hug the tree movement'.

Narmada Bachao Andolan (NBA)

- **Year:** 1985
- **Place:** Narmada river, which flows through the states of Gujarat, Madhya Pradesh, and Maharashtra
- **Aim:** A social movement against a number of large dams being built across the Narmada river
- **Gist:** Protest was against the building of Sardar Sarovar Dam over river Narmada as there was no rehabilitation plan for the population which was to be displaced from the dam site. Afterwards, there were also protests against the project for its being hazardous to the environment.

Appiko Movement

- **Year:** 1983
- **Place:** Uttara Kannada and Shimoga districts of Karnataka state
- **Aim:** A movement against the felling and commercialisation of natural forest and the ruin of ancient livelihood
- **Gist:** Known as southern version of Chipko Movement, this movement was also against cutting of trees. To save trees people hugged the trees. The movement is termed as the southern version of Chipko Movement.

Save Silent Valley Movement

- **Year:** 1973
- **Place:** Silent Valley, an evergreen tropical forest in the Palakkad district of Kerala, India
- **Aim:** A movement in order to protect the Silent Valley, the moist evergreen forest from being destroyed by a hydroelectric project

  Gist: Movement against the Kerala State Electricity Board's proposal to erect a hydroelectric dam over Kunthipuzha river which ran through the Silent Valley, thus creating apprehensions of destroying the Silent Valley forest

Jungle Bachao Andolan

- **Year:** 1982
- **Place:** Singhbhum district of Bihar
- **Aim:** A movement against governments decision to replace the natural Sal forest with Teak
- **Gist:** The tribals of Singhbhum district of Bihar started the protest when the government decided to replace the natural Sal forests with the highly-priced Teak. This move was called by many as "Greed Game Political Populism". Later this movement spread to Jharkhand and Odisha.

Tehri Dam Conflict

- **Year:** 1978
- **Place:** Bhagirathi river near Tehri in Uttarakhand
- **Aim:** A movement against the displacement of town inhabitants and environmental consequence of the weak ecosystem

  Gist: Tehri dam attracted national attention in the 1980s and the 1990s. The major objections include seismic sensitivity of the region, submergence of forest areas along with Tehri town, etc. Despite the support from other prominent leaders like Sunderlal Bahuguna, the movement has failed to gather enough popular support at national as well as international levels.

Swachh Bharat Abhiyan (Clean India Mission)

It is the mission to clean up India's cities by launching effective cleaning campaigns while cleaning roads, streets, and infrastructure of each Indian city. The mission was launched on October 2, 2014 at Rajghat, New Delhi by the Prime Minister Sh. Narendra Modi. It is the largest mission to clean India involving 3 million government employees, students, individuals, public and private sector organisations, NGOs, and other philanthropic bodies and actvists to clean up 4041 cities, towns, and associated rural areas. Objectives of the mission include:

a) Elimination of open defection through construction of house-owned and community-owned toilets
b) Establishing an accountable mechanism of monitoring toilet use
c) Eradicating manual scavenging
d) Encouraging private sector participation
e) Generating awareness leading to behavioural change
f) Augmenting capacity utilisation for urban local bodies (ULBs)

Being run by the government of India, the mission aims to achieve an Open Defecation-Free (ODF) India by 2 October 2019, the 150th anniversary of the birth of Mahatma Gandhi, by constructing 90 million toilets in rural India at a projected cost of Rs. 1.96 lakh crore (US$30 billion). The mission will also contribute to India reaching Sustainable Development Goal Number 6 (SDG 6), i.e., "Clean Water and Sanitation". The mission contains two sub-missions: Swachh Bharat Abhiyan

"Gramin" or rural), which operates under the newly formed Ministry of Jal Shakti; and Swachh Bharat Abhiyan (Urban), which operates under the Ministry of Housing and Urban Affairs.

Swachh Bharat Abhiyan (SBA)

Swachh Sarvekshan 2019

According to Swachh Sarvekshan 2019, Indore (Madhya Pradesh) has been declared the cleanest city of India for the third time. Indore is followed by Ambikapur (Chhattisgarh).

LEADING ENVIRONMENTAL ACTIVISTS OF INDIA

Various environment activists have been associated with different movements and activities. Names of certain activists along with their association with mission/ movements/activities are given as under:

- **Chipko Movement:** Sundarlal Bahuguna, Gaura Devi, Sudesha Devi, Bachni Devi, Chandi Prasad Bhatt, Govind Singh Rawat, Dhoom Singh Negi, Shamsher Singh Bisht, and Ghanasyam Raturi
- **Narmada Bachao Andolan:** Medha Patkar, Baba Amte
- **Conservation of Birds:** Dr. Salim Ali, a well-known ornithologist. He earned a title "Birdman of India". He was awarded Padma Bhushan and Padma Vibhushan. He was instrumental in creating the Bharatpur Bird Sanctury.
- **Wildlife Conservation:** S.P. Godrej worked for wildlife conservation. He has been awarded with Padma Bhushan in 1999.
- **Cultivar Conservation:** Dr. M.S. Swaminathan worked for conservation of cultivar plants. Though he was a well-known agriculture scientist, he also worked for wildlife conservation.
- **Conservation of Community Biodiversity Registers:** Madhav Gadgil was an exponent of this. He was awarded with Volvo Environment Prize from Sweden.
- **Environmental Legalities:** M.C. Mehta is an ecology lawyer. He has been fighting various cases in the court in defence of environmental issues. He is well known for filing public interest litigations for the cause of environment conservation. He won the battles regarding protection of Taj Mahal and cleaning up Ganga.
- **Tehri Dam Conflict:** Sunderlal Bahuguna worked for rehabilitation of displaced population from the dam site.
- **Save Silent Valley Movement:** The Kerala Sastra Sahitya Parishad (KSSP), an NGO, and the poet-activist Sughathakumari played an important role in the Silent Valley protests.
- **Appiko Movement:** Pandurang Hegde

ENVIRONMENTAL INSTITUTIONS IN INDIA

1) Agency for Non-conventional Energy and Rural Technology (ANERT), Thiravanthapuram (Kerala)
2) Wildlife Trust of India, Noida (U.P.)
3) Wildlife Institute of India, Dehradun (Uttarakhand)
4) The Energy and Resources Institute (TERI), New Delhi
5) Central Pollution Control Board, New Delhi
6) National Biodiversity Authority, Chennai (Tamil Nadu)
7) National Tiger Conservation Authority, New Delhi
8) Forest Survey of India, Dehradun (Uttarakhand)
9) Central Zoo Authority of India, New Delhi
10) National Green Tribunal, New Delhi
11) Botanical Survey of India, Kolkata
12) Zoological Survey of India, Kolkata
13) Bombay Natural History Society (BNHS), Mumbai
14) World Wide Fund for Nature (WWF-India), New Delhi
15) Center for Science and Environment (CSE), New Delhi.
16) Bharati Vidyapeeth Institute of Environment Education and Research (BVIEER), Pune
17) Salim Ali Center for Ornithology and Natural History (SACON), Coimbatore (Tamil Nadu)
18) Kalpavriksh (NGO), Pune

ENVIRONMENTAL POLICIES IN INDIA

1. **The National Environment Policy (NEP), 2006:** This policy by the Ministry of Environment and Forests (MoEF) aims at mainstreaming all environmental concerns into developmental activities. It emphasises conservation of resources, and points that the best way to aid conservation is to ensure that people dependent on resources obtain better livelihoods from conservation, than from degradation of the resources. It argues that environmental degradation often leads to poverty and poor health outcomes among populations.

2. **National Conservation Strategy and Policy Statement on Environment and Development, 1992:** This policy reviews the dimension of environmental problems and illustrates the action taken by the government to address those problems. Action includes strategies and approaches. This policy also reviews development with respect to environment, i.e., development process may not leave an unhealthy impact on the environment.
3. **Policy Statement for Abatement of Pollution, 1992:** This policy statement was adopted in 1992 and urges to take pollution prevention measures while using hi-tech and latest methods. Some of the prevention measures include minimisation of waste, promotion of clean and low-waste technologies, resorting to reusing, recycling, environment audit, keeping natural resources account, and developing human resources. The policy statement states that total pollution prevention is possible with a combination of command and control methods, promotion of awareness, voluntary regulations, and fiscal measures.
4. **Draft National Forest Policy (NFP), 2018:** This policy released by the Union Ministry of Environment, Forests and Climate Change has the following objectives:
   i) Bringing one-third of India's total geographic area under forest with scientific interventions
   ii) Enforcing strict regulations for protecting the forest cover
   iii) Focussing on international challenges to climate change
   iv) Ensuring public-private partnership in undertaking afforestation and reforestation in degraded forest areas
5. **National Water Policy, 2012:** This was drafted by the Union Ministry of Water Resources and has the following features:
   i) Framing of water framework law strengthening optimum development of inter-state rivers
   ii) Treating water as an economic good so as to promote its conservation and efficient use because water fulfils the basic needs-consumption and irrigation
   iii) Designing water management plan as an adaptation strategy in the wake of climate change
   iv) Developing water footprint and water auditing to ensure its efficient use
   v) Setting up of Water Regularity Authority and making reuse and recycling of waste water incentive-oriented
   vi) Removing disparity of water supply in rural and urban areas
   vii) Community participation in conserving and managing water resources
   viii) Providing adequate grant to states for updating technology for planning and managing water resources

INDIA'S ENVIRONMENTAL PLEDGES

1) Achieving target of installing 175 GW renewable energy by 2022
2) While declaring her Intended Nationally Determined Contribution (INDC), India has pledged to reduce emission intensity of greenhouse gases per unit GDP by 33 to 35% from 2005 level by 2030, whereas it was 20-25% by 2020
3) Pledging to generate at least 40% from non-fossil fuels like solar, wind, and bio-fuels by 2030
4) Increasing forest cover rapidly to create an additional carbon sink by 2030, to absorb 2.5 to 3 billion tonnes of carbon dioxide
5) Under the "National Clean Air" programme, particulates suspended in air causing air pollution, will be reduced by 20-30% by 2024
6) Eliminating all single-use plastic by 2022

UNION MINISTRIES OF INDIA ASSOCIATED WITH ENVIRONMENTAL ISSUES

1) **Ministry of Environment, Forest and Climate Change:** The primary concerns of the Ministry are implementation of policies and programmes relating to conservation of the country's natural resources, including its lakes and rivers, its biodiversity, forests and wildlife, ensuring the welfare of animals, and the prevention and abatement of pollution. While implementing these policies and programmes, the Ministry is guided by the principle of sustainable development and enhancement of human well-being.
   Union Minister: Prakash Javadekar
   Minister of State: Babul Supriyo
2) **Ministry of Jal Shakti** is a Ministry under Government of India which was formed in May 2019 under the second Modi ministry. This was formed by merging of two ministries; Ministry of Water Resources, River Development and Ganga Rejuvenation and Ministry of Drinking Water and Sanitation. The new Ministry will encompass issues

ranging from providing clean drinking water, international and inter-states water disputes, to the Namami Gange project aimed at cleaning Ganga and its tributaries, and sub-tributaries.

Union Minister: Gajendra Singh Shekhawat

3) **Ministry of New and Renewable Energy (MNRE):** This is the nodal Ministry of the Government of India for all matters relating to new and renewable energy. The broad aim of the Ministry is to develop and deploy new and renewable energy for supplementing the energy requirements of the country.

Union Minister: Raj Kumar Singh

4) **Ministry of Home Affairs (MHA):** Along with other functions to ensure security to the country, states, and individuals from any internal and external threat, the Ministry also works for natural and man-made disasters management through National Disaster Management Authority (NDMA).

Union Minister: Amit Shah

Some Vital Facts

INTERNATIONAL CONFERENCES AND CONVENTIONS ON ENVIRONMENTAL ISSUES DURING 2019 AND 2020

	Name of conference	Date/ Month & Year	Venue	Agency
1)	SDG Summit	24-25, September, 2019	New York (USA)	UNO
2)	Conference on Empowering People as agents of more effective Climate action.	9, December, 2019	Madrid (Spain)	UNO
3)	UN Climate Change conference	2-13, December, 2019	Madrid (Spain)	UNO
4)	Barcelona Convention COP 21 on Marine Pollution	2-5, December, 2019	Naples, Italy	UNO
5)	Conference on Addressing Environmental Harms: The Business and Human rights Connection	26, November, 2019	Geneva, Switzerland	UNO
6)	SEA(South East Asia) Solutions	11-14 November, 2019	Bangkok, Thailand	UNO
7)	GEO-6	6-9 November, 2019	Oaxaca, Mexico	UNO
8)	Parties to Montreal Protocol	4-8 November, 2019	Rome, Italy	UNO
9)	Climate Action Summit	23 September, 2019	New York, USA	UNO
10)	UN Trade Forum: SDGs and Climate Change	9-13 September, 2019	Geneva, Switzerland	UNO
11)	Convention to Combat Desertification-COP 14	2-13 September, 2019	New Delhi, India	UNO
12)	World Water Week Theme: "Water for society - including all."	25-30 August, 2019	Stockholm, Sweden	UNO
13)	Global landscape Forum	22-23 June, 2019	Bonn, Gemany	UNO
14)	Conference of Parties to the United Nations Framework Convention on Climate Change	2-14 December, 2019	Kotawice, Poland	UNO
15)	The *GRIHA Summit,	17-18 December, 2019	New Delhi	The energy and resource Institute (TERI)

*GRIHA- Green rating for integrated Habitat Assessment

UNO designated October, 31 as WOLD CITIES DAY. 2019 Theme: Changing the world: innovations and better life for future generations

International Day of Forests 21, MayTheme 2019 'Forest and Education"

Vital Statistics:

1) 80% of agricultural land is used for livestock feed
2) Cities produce 60-80% of global greenhouse gas emissions.
3) Only 12 % cities across the globe have air quality measures that meet WHO standards.
4) Plastic packaging accounts for 50% of plastic waste.
5) Illegal wildlife trade is the fourth largest transnational crime after drugs, weapons and human trafficking.

Practice Exercise

General Questions Format

1. Preserving or protecting animals and resources such as minerals, water, and plants through planned action is termed as

(A) Habitat (B) Conservation
(C) Biodiversity (D) Ecosystem

2. 'Swachh Bharat Abhiyan (Urban)' works under which union Ministry?

(A) Ministry of Environment, Forests and Climate Change
(B) Ministry of Jal Shakti
(C) Ministry of Housing and Urban Affairs
(D) Ministry of New and Renewable energy

3. Names of environmental terms are given under Column I and their meaning/significance is given under Column II. Match the term with its exact meaning/significance and choose the correct code from the given codes.

Colum I (Environmental Term)	Column II (Meaning/ Significance)
a) Effluent	i) Toxic radioactive gas
b) Radon	ii) Reducing pollution
c) Landfill	iii) Liquid waste
d) Abatement	iv) A place to dump waste

Codes:

	(a)	(b)	(c)	(d)
(A)	ii	iv	i	iii
(B)	i	ii	iii	iv
(C)	ii	iii	i	iv
(D)	iii	i	iv	ii

4. Consider these two statements:

Statement P: M.C. Mehta is well-known for cultivar conservation.

Statement Q: Pandurang Hegde is known for his legal battle as an attorney against environmental violations.

(A) Both P and Q are true
(B) Both P and Q are false
(C) P is true but Q is false
(D) P is false but Q is true

5. TERI stands for

(A) The Energy and Resources Institute
(B) The Energy and Research Institute
(C) Tehri Energy and Research Institute
(D) The Electricity and Resource Institute

6. "Go Wild for Life" was theme of which year's World Environment day celebrations?

(A) 2018 (B) 2014
(C) 2016 (D) 2011

7. Which of the following is NOT TRUE about Draft National Forest Policy, 2018?

a) Bringing one-third area of India under forests
b) Focussing on international challenge of plastic pollution
c) Enforcing strict regulations against development of genetically modified plantation in forests
d) Encouraging private-public partnership in forestation and reforestation

(A) a, c, and d only (B) b and c only
(C) a, b, c, and d (D) d only

8. Fossil fuel includes

a) peat b) coal

c) gas d) oil

(A) c and d only (B) b and c only

(C) b only (D) a, b, c, and d

9. Find the wrong pair in the following pairs

(A) World Nature Day - August 6

(B) World Forestry Day - March 21

(C) World Atmosphere Day - April 10

(D) World Lion Day - August 10

10. Gajendra Singh Shekhawat is Union Minister of

(A) Environment, Forest and Climate Change

(B) New and Non-renewable Energy

(C) Jal Shakti

(D) Home Affairs

11. Which of the following is NOT a task of Union Ministry of Environment, Forests and Climate Change?

a) Conservation of country's natural resources

b) Harnessing energy from renewable resources to protect habitat of plants and wild animals, thus preventing loss of biodiversity

c) Ensuring welfare of animals

d) Prevention and abatement of pollution

(A) b only (B) b, c, and d only

(C) a, b, c, and d (D) a, c, and d only

12. Consider the statement "National Water Policy 2012 will be successfully providing safe drinking water to the common man". This statement is

(A) Definitely false (B) Probably false

(C) Probably true (D) Definitely true

13. Black bin contains that waste which

(A) can be recycled but cannot be composted

(B) cannot be recycled but can be composted

(C) can be neither recycled nor composted

(D) can be either recycled or composted

14. Which city has topped in cleanliness in Swachh Sarvekshan 2019?

(A) Bangaluru (B) Indore

(C) Ambikapur (D) Ahmedabad

15. New ministry of Jal Shakti has been created by merging ministries of

(A) Water Resources and Sanitation

(B) Water conservation and Energy Resources

(C) Environment and Sanitation

(D) Environment and Water resources

KEY

1. B	2. C	3. D	4. B	5. A	6. C	7. B
8. D	9. A	10. C	11. A	12. C	13. C	14. B
15. A						

Assertion–Reason Format

1. **Assertion (A):** A theme based World Environment Day is celebrated every year.

Reason (R): One of the major causes of environment depletion is ignorance and lack of motivation.

(A) Both A and R are true and R is correct explanation of A

(B) Both A and R are true but R is not correct explanation of A

(C) A is true but R is false

(D) A is false but R is true

2. **Assertion (A):** Carbon offset helps in achieving sustainable development.

Reason (R): Use of energy from non-renewable sources does not guarantee sustainable development.

(A) Both A and R are false

(B) Both A and R are true and R is correct explanation of A

(C) A is true but R is false

(D) Both A and R are true but R is not correct explanation of A

3. **Assertion (A):** Most of the environmental activists have been working for promoting India's environmental status in the world.

Reason (R): India has lost its global environmental status due to anthropogenic activities.

(A) Both A and R are true and R is correct explanation of A

(B) Both A and R are false

(C) A is true but R is false

(D) A is false but R is true

4. **Assertion (A):** Backyard burning has the same effects on the atmosphere as stubble burning.

   Reason (R): Burning of fossil fuels strongly contribute in air pollution.

   (A) Both A and R are true and R is correct explanation of A

   (B) Both A and R are true but R is not correct explanation of A

   (C) A is true but R is false

   (D) A is false but R is true

5. **Assertion (A):** Apikko movement was initiated in 1987.

   Reason (R): The movement has been termed as southern version of Chipko Movement.

   (A) Both a and R are false

   (B) A is true but R is false

   (C) A is false but R is true

   (D) Both A and R are true but R is not correct explanation of A

KEY

1. A **2.** D **3.** B **4.** B **5.** C

Questions Asked in Previous NET Exams

1. A green building

   i) uses minimum amount of energy

   ii) generates waste

   iii) consumes a lot of water

   iv) conserves natural resources

   (v) creates space for healthy living

   Choose the correct statements from the options given below: **(UGC NET DECEMBER 2019)**

   (A) (i), (ii) and (iii) (B) (i), (iv) and (v)

   (C) (ii), (iii) and (v) (D) (ii), (iv) and (v)

2. 'Fly ash' produced in thermal power plants is an eco-friendly resource for use in:

   (UGC NET JULY 2018)

   (a) Agriculture as micronutrient

   (b) Wasteland development

   (c) Dam and water-holding structures

   (d) Brick industry

   Choose the correct answer from the code given below:

   (A) (a), (b), and (d) only

   (B) (b), (c), and (d) only

   (C) (a), (c), and (d) only

   (D) (a), (b), (c), and (d)

3. As part of Intended Nationally Determined Contributions, Indian government through additional forest and tree cover has resolved to create an additional carbon sink (in terms of carbon dioxide equivalent) by year 2030 to the extent of **(UGC NET AUGUST 2016)**

   (A) 3.5 to 4 billion tonnes

   (B) 2.5 to 3 billion tonnes

   (C) 1.5 to 2 billion tonnes

   (D) 1 to 1.5 billion tonnes

4. Match List - I and List - II and identify the correct code:

   (UGC NET DECEMBER 2014)

a.	World Health Day	i.	16th September
b.	World Population Day	ii.	1st December
c.	World Ozone Day	iii.	11th July
d.	World AIDS Day	iv.	7th April

Codes:

	(a)	(b)	(c)	(d)
(A)	i	ii	iii	iv
(B)	iv	iii	i	ii
(C)	ii	iii	iv	i
(D)	iii	iv	ii	i

5. 'Chipko' movement was first started by

   (UGC NET DECEMBER 2010)

   (A) Arundhati Roy

   (B) Medha Patkar

   (C) Ila Bhatt

   (D) Sunderlal Bahuguna

KEY

1. B **2.** D **3.** B **4.** B **5.** D

Unit X

Higher Education System

Institutions of Higher Learning & Education in Ancient India

HIGHER EDUCATION IN ANCIENT INDIA

Religion was the base of higher education in ancient India. There had been prominently three religions, i.e., Hinduism, Buddhism, and Jainism. Religion-oriented higher education in ancient India had been instrumental in transmitting knowledge to the people, thus transforming ancient Indian society. Mainly there were two doctrines of education in ancient India, i.e., Brahminical Education and Buddhist Education. The education was imparted in oral mode. The other mode was 'chintan' or thinking.

METHODS OF TEACHING

1) ***Maukhik (Oral):*** *Teachers used to explain the concept orally. Students were to memorize the content. The main emphasis was on pronunciation.*
2) ***Chintan (Thinking):*** *This method was used in higher studies. Teachers used to motivate the students to retain the content, so taught, in the mind through thinking.*
3) ***Manan (Reflection):*** *This method of teaching was practised to impart higher education and was meant for highly intelligent students. Through this method students were motivated to discuss, debate, solve given problems, and indulge in storytelling and research.*

Doctrines of Education

Brahminical Education

This education flourished in Vedic period. Knowledge of Vedic text was transmitted orally. Pupils or learners used to get admissions in Ashramas, Gurukuls, Pathshalas, and temples for primary education and for higher education students used to go to 'Viharas' and 'Universities'. Their teachers were 'Rishis', or 'Gurus' and they hailed from Brahmin families. Pupils used to leave their houses to take admissions in educational institutions for the first time after 'Upanayana' ceremony or 'Initiation' ceremony as learners were going to settle down in ashramas to acquire initial knowledge. At this stage they acquired primary studies followed by higher education. Women were at parity with men in all spheres of education. Sanskrit was the medium of instruction. As the caste system was prevalent, Sanskrit was considered to be the language of scholars and Brahmins were considered scholars.

In the later Vedic period, as priesthood developed, higher education was concentrated on learning about rituals and other rites of religion performed by priests. The main subjects of higher education were technical aspects of worship and sacrifice. In this period, Brahmins were the teachers and the subjects of study were all rituals in religion.

Teaching elaborate rituals became subject of study in higher education in the beginning of classical period (600–300 BC). During this period, education of all levels was monopolised by Brahmins. There was imparting of medical education also as explained in Sushruta Samhita (a Sanskrit text on medicine and surgery in ancient India, written by Sushruta).

Buddhist Education

Religion and secularism were the central themes of Buddhist education. Education was imparted in monasteries and viharas. Though education was open to all, yet it was not imparted to the disabled and the sick. Monks used to control the entire education system besides imparting education as teachers. Education emphasised on development of personality traits and morality and the content of education was inspired from teachings of Buddha. Buddhist education gained popularity as it was open to all. Further, education laid emphasis on a good, moral life. Curriculum of Buddhist education includes Vinaya (codes of self-training in controlling mind, words, and action), Sutta (group discourse), and Abhidhamma (working on Buddhist doctrine). In a nutshell, Buddhist education aimed at achieving morality, deep thought, and wisdom.

PALI CANON OF BUDDHISM

Pali canon is the collection of religious texts (scriptures) preserved in Pali language. The texts completely belong to the Theravada Buddhist tradition.

Theravada Buddhist Tradition: *This word belongs to Pali language. It consists of two words; 'Thera' means doctrine and 'vada' means elders. So it is a 'Doctrine of Elders'. There is a school of thinkers who conservatively follow this doctrine preserved as Pali canon. It signifies that this school of thinkers follow Buddha's early teachings. Theravadas believe in individual salvation as Buddha was an ordinary man and not God, who attained Nirvana. This is also called Hinayana Buddhism. Theravada Buddhism had been popular in Sri Lanka, Thailand, and Myanmar. Presently it is becoming popular in the West.*

Buddhist texts include various subjects like Astronomy, Arithmetic, Lokayata, Astrology, Vedas, Magic, Medicine, Samkhya,, Army skills, Arts & Crafts skills, Nyaya, and Vaisheshika.

Lokayata: *It means 'Philosophy of People.' This school of thinkers believe in materialism, i.e., matter is sustaining the world. Any change in the mental or physical build-up is based on phenomena of matter.*

Samkhya: *It is the philosophy of gaining knowledge. It believes that pratyaksha (perception), anumana (inference), and sabda (words) are the valid sources of gaining knowledge.*

Vaisheshika: *it is the school of thought which believes that perception and inference are the valid means of gaining knowledge.*

INSTITUTIONS OF HIGHER LEARNING & EDUCATION

1) **Vikramshila University:** Vikramshila university or vihara was established by king Dharampala of Pala dynasty around 8th century BC in Magadh. This university was known for rendering 'Tantra Shastra.' The university later took form of six colleges. Besides Tantra Shastra, the university was imparting education in Grammar, Logic, and Philosophy. On the occasion of Samavartana (Convocation), degrees were awarded to graduates and post- graduates.
2) **Nadia University:** It is also known as Nabadwip University. This university was built at the confluence of the Ganga and the Jalangi river in Bengal. It was built up after the destruction of Nalanda and Vikramshila Universities. Main subjects of study were Logic, Vyakran, Political Science, and Law. At the university site there had been three centres of learning, viz. Gopalpur, Nabadwip, and Shantipur. There have been evidences of students studying for 20 years in the university.
3) **Mithila University:** This had been a prominent centre of learning and culture in ancient India. Prominently, Brahamanical System of education was adopted here. It is believed to be existing during days of Raja Janak (father of Sita). Subjects of Literature, Science, Nyaya Shastra (Jurisprudence), and Tarka Shastra (Logic) were taught. The university was known for Nyaya Shastra and Tarka Shastra. Noted Indian mathematician and philosopher Gangesha Upadhyaya eastablished New School of Logic in the university. It was difficult to qualify exams as syllabus and studies were tough. Students could get degrees only after passing Salaka Pariksha (Test). The university gained popularity all over for teaching Nyaya Shastra (Jurisprudence) and Tarka Shastra (Logic).
4) **Nalanda University:** This university was an outstanding centre of learning in Bihar (near Rajgriha). Having its roots in Buddhism, Nalanda university was a prominent centre of learning. In addition to teaching Buddhist studies, other subjects being taught were Martial Art, Mathematics, Astronomy, Fine Arts, and Politics. The university was at its apex during the Gupta Dynasty. Gupta king Kumaragupta is considered to be the founder of the university. It was built in 5 century CE. Students from Tibet, China, Greece, and Persia used to come to study in this 2000 year-old university. Admission to the university was not within everyone's reach. Students seeking admission to the university had to sit in an entrance exam. Chinese traveller Hieun-Tsang studied in the university for 5 years. He wrote in his account that only 20% of the candidates were used to be selected for admission. Minimum age required for admission was 20. University was residential. There were monasteries, classrooms, meditation halls, dormitories, and 10 temples in the campus. Subjects offered for studies were Samkhya, Sanskrit, Logic, Buddhism, Martial Art, Lokayata, Vaisheshika, Medicine, and many more. University was having capacity to accommodate 10,000 students and 2,000 teachers. Lakes and gardens were spread over all the compounds which were eight in number. Library of the university covered three multi-storey buildings and one of the buildings had nine storeys. This great centre of learning was destroyed by a Turkish plunderer Bakhtiyar Khilji in 12th century AD.
5) **Takshshila or Taxila university:** Foundation of Takshshila or Taxila University is believed to be laid down by Daryodhana. Taxila is now in Pakistan. This university proudly housed various scholars,

politicians, statespersons, and other personalities. Grammarian Panini, economics and political advisor Chanakya, author Vishnu Sharma, physician Charak, surgeon Jivaka, and Mauryan emperor Chandragupta Maurya had been students of Taxila University. Various subjects like Vedas, Agriculture, Army Skills, Commerce, Archery, Vedanta, Vyakran, and Ayurveda were taught. About 10,000 students from China, Arabia, and Greece studied in the university. Hun invader Toramana destroyed the university in late 5th century BC. This is the oldest university of the world.

6) **Odantapuri University:** This centre of learning was established by Gopala of Pala dynasty in 7th century in Maghada. Vedic scriptures and Buddhism were taught in this university.

7) **Somapura University:** This university was established by Dharampala of Pala dynasty in later 7th century. This university had been bigger than Nalanda university. Subjects taught were related to Hinduism, Jainism, and Buddhism. The university flourished up to 12th century until it was destroyed by Muslim plunderers.

8) **Vallabhi University:** Kings of Maitraka dynasty built up Vallabhi University. Various subjects like Economics, Book-keeping, Commerce, Politics, Law, Science and Medical science, and Vyakaran, were taught in the university. Graduates from this university were considered to be intelligent and hardworking. They were offered high ranking posts in the King's court. The university was destroyed by Arab invaders.

9) **Bikrampur University:** This university was established by Dharampala at Munshiganj in Bengal, now in Bangladesh. This university attracted students from China, Tibet, Nepal, and Thailand. Subjects on Buddhism were taught in the university.

10) **Pushpagiri University:** This university is considered to be established by king Ashoka. It was established in Kalinga (Odisha). The campus was built over three hills namely Ratnagiri, Lalitgiri, and Udayagiri. Buddhist monk Prajna spent some time in this university. Chinese traveller Xuanzang, who travelled to India mentioned this university in his account.

11) **Jagaddala University:** This university was established by the Pala king Rampala in 11th century in Northern Bengal (now situated in Bangladesh). Various subjects including Sanskrit were taught in the university.

12) **Morena Golden Triangle University:** This university was established in 8th century in Morena district of Chambal division of Madhya Pradesh. The university was established within three temples; Mitavali, Padavali, and Bateshwar. The temples were known as Golden Triangle. The temples appear to be golden when sunrays fell on them. Astrology and Mathematics were taught in the university.

13) **Telhara University:** This university was established at Telhara in Bihar. This university was an excellent centre of research. According to Tibetan accounts, this university is 3000 years old. It was destroyed in 12th century BC by Bakhityar Khilji.

Practice Exercise

General Questions Format

1. Which university of ancient India was known for teaching Nyaya Shastra (Jurisprudence) and Tarka Shastra (Logic)?

(A) Vallabhi University
(B) Nalanda University
(C) Mithila University
(D) Pushpagiri University

2. Which of the following modes of teaching in ancient India was the most effective at higher education level?

(A) Manan mode aiming to improve understanding level of students enabling them to acquire cognitive abilities for discussions or debates
(B) Oral mode aiming at strengthening their fundamental traits of learning, making them capable of learning through manan mode
(C) Chintan mode motivating students to enhance their concentration and retention power through meditation for better learning of higher education concepts
(D) All of these

3. Which of the following traditions helped in flourishing of higher education in ancient India?

a) Upanayana b) Vinayana
c) Theravada d) Abhidhamma

(A) a and c only (B) a, b, c, and d
(C) None of these (D) a, c, and d only

4. Kings of which dynasty established maximum universities in ancient India?

(A) Maitraka (B) Gupta
(C) Kushan (D) Pala

5. Which of the following statement(s) is/are NOT TRUE about higher education in ancient India?

i) Higher education was religion-based.
ii) Mode of education was oral.
iii) A learner was introduced to education after Nayana ceremony.
iv) Higher education institutions flourished under the aegis of Theravada Buddhism.

(A) i and iii only (B) iii and iv only
(C) All of these (D) i, iii, and iv

6. Inclusion of Lokayata, Samkhya, and Vaisheshika as subjects of study in Buddhist education signifies that

(A) Buddhist education aimed to develop cognitive power in learners
(B) There was a need to introduce pedagogical subjects in Buddhist education system
(C) Without these subjects it was difficult to learn Theravada Buddhism
(D) Buddhist education aimed to impart secular education along with religious one

7. Names of universities of ancient India are given under Column I. Match them with their respective location given under Column II and choose the right code given below:

Column I (Name of university)	Column II (Location)
a) Nadia University	i) Kalinga
b) Odantapuri University	ii) Bengal
c) Pushpagiri University	iii) Bihar
d) Telhara University	iv) Magadha

Codes:	(a)	(b)	(c)	(d)
(A)	iii	iv	i	ii
(B)	ii	iii	iv	i
(C)	i	ii	iv	iii
(D)	ii	iv	i	iii

8. Imparting of training for group discussion in Buddhist Education system is known as

(A) Vinaya (B) Abhidhamma
(C) Sutta (D) None of these

9. Which university of ancient India was known for teaching Tantra Shastra?

(A) Golden Triangle (B) Vikramshila
(C) Nalanda (D) Bikrampur

10. Which University of India was following Brahminical system of education?

(A) Mithila (B) Vikramshila
(C) Jagaddala (D) Pushpagiri

11. There are two statements P and Q.

P: King of the founder dynasty used to deliver degrees to passouts of a particular University in ancient India.

Q: Prevailing caste system deprived many of higher education in ancient India.

(A) Both P and Q are correct
(B) Both P and Q are wrong
(C) P is correct but Q is wrong
(D) P is wrong but Q is correct

12. According to Tibetan accounts, which university of ancient India had been an excellent centre of research?

(A) Bikrampur (B) Jagaddala
(C) Telhara (D) Pushpagiri

13. Which of the following statement(s) is/are true with respect to Taxila University?

i) The university was established after the destruction of Nalanda University.
ii) The university was in its later years converted into six colleges.
iii) Noted mathematician and philosopher Gangesha Upadhyaya established New School of Logic in the university.
iv) Noted statesman of ancient India, Chanakya had been a student of the university.

(A) iv only (B) ii only
(C) i, ii, and iv only (D) i, ii, iii, iv

14. Convocation organised by the universities of ancient India was literally known as

(A) Resayana (B) Samavartana
(C) Drishtyana (D) None of these

15. Graduates of which ancient Indian university were offered administrative posts in the king's court?

(A) Nalanda (B) Odantpuri
(C) Vallabhi (D) Sompura

16. Which of the following universities of ancient India acclaimed international recognition?

(A) Odantapuri
(B) Somapura
(C) Vikramshila
(D) Bikrampur

17. Which of the following is TRUE about higher education and primary education in ancient India?
    a) Higher education was imparted in 'Viharas' whereas primary education was imparted in 'Ashramas'.
    b) Higher education was imparted by 'Rishis' whereas primary education was imparted by 'Gurus'.
    c) Ceremony of 'Upanayana' was performed at the beginning of higher education whereas ceremony of 'Yajranayana' was performed at the beginning of primary education.
    d) Higher education was imparted in Sanskrit language whereas primary education was imparted in Pali language.

    (A) a and c only (B) b and d only
    (C) a only (D) a, b, c, and d

18. Which of the following statement(s) is/are TRUE?
    (A) Telhara university was established as an excellent centre of research in ancient India.
    (B) Somapura University was established by King Ashoka.
    (C) Brahmanical scriptures were taught in Odantapuri University.
    (D) Graduates from Pushpagiri University were used to be offered high ranking posts.

19. Which university of ancient India had admission to students through entrance exam?
    (A) Nalanda (B) Taxila
    (C) Vikramsila (D) Pushpagiri

20. Panini, the grammarian, was associated with which ancient Indian university?
    (A) Vallabhi (B) Somapura
    (C) Telhara (D) Taxila

21. Identify the wrong pair
    (A) Gangesha Upadhaya-Mithila University
    (B) Hieun Tsang-Nalanda University
    (C) Chanakya-Taxila University
    (D) Xuanzang-Vallabhi University

22. Which method of teaching was practised for highly intelligent students to impart higher education in ancient India?
    (A) Chintan (B) Maukhik
    (C) Manan (D) All of these

23. Buddhist monk Prajna studied in which ancient Indian university?
    (A) Mithila (B) Pushpagiri
    (C) Taxila (D) Bikrampur

24. What can be appropriately asserted about establishment and working of universities as institutions of higher learning and education in ancient India?
    i) There was a blend of perfect administration, discipline, teaching, and research in the universities.
    ii) University set-up of ancient India is reflected in present day university set-up in India.
    iii) Higher education and learning in various fields got a fillip during university era of ancient India.
    iv) Universities proved to be a channel of recognition for scientists, research scholars, mathematicians, foreign travellers, philosophers, and students.

    (A) i, ii, and iv only (B) ii and iv only
    (C) i, iii, and iv only (D) i, ii, iii, and iv

25. Which university of ancient India had the capacity to accommodate 10000 students and 2000 teachers at the same time?
    (A) Vikramshila (B) Nalanda
    (C) Vallabhi (D) Odantapuri

KEY

1. C	2. A	3. C	4. D	5. B	6. A	7. D
8. C	9. B	10. A	11. D	12. C	13. A	14. B
15. C	16. D	17. C	18. A	19. A	20. D	21. D
22. C	23. B	24. D	25. B			

Assertion–Reason Format

1. **Assertion (A):** Higher education in ancient India was channelized through different subjects.

   Reason (R): Curriculum of universities of ancient India had been learner-friendly.

   (A) Both A and R are true and R is the correct explanation of A
   (B) Both A and R are true but R is not correct explanation of A
   (C) A is true but R is false
   (D) A is false but R is true

2. **Assertion (A):** Present system of higher education has its roots in higher education system of ancient India.

   Reason (R): Research-based education was rendered by universities of ancient India.

(A) Both A and R are true and R is the correct explanation of A
(B) Both A and R are true but R is not correct explanation of A
(C) A is false but R is true
(D) A is true but R is false

3. **Assertion (A):** Epistemology had been the base of Buddhist Education in ancient India.
Reason (R): Higher education in ancient India covered study of valid sources of gaining knowledge.
(A) Both A and R are true and R is the correct explanation of A
(B) Both A and R are true but R is not correct explanation of A
(C) A is false but R is true
(D) Both A and R are false

4. **Assertion (A):** Universities of ancient India were divided on drawing curriculum of subjects to be taught.
Reason (R): Imparting of higher education was influenced by Brahminical and Buddhist system of education.
(A) Both A and R are true and R is the correct explanation of A
(B) Both A and R are true but R is not correct explanation of A
(C) A is true but R is false.
(D) A is false but R is true

5. **Assertion (A):** Higher education brought various reforms in the ancient society of India.
Reason (R): Graduates passouts from different universities in ancient India created awareness against various social evils in the society.
(A) Both A and R are true and R is the correct explanation of A
(B) Both A and R are true but R is not the correct explanation of A
(C) A is true but R is false
(D) A is false but R is true

6. **Assertion (A):** Religion was the base of higher education in ancient India.
Reason (R): In spite of different religions, higher education flourished in ancient India.
(A) Both A and R are false
(B) A is true but R is false
(C) A is false but R is true
(D) Both A and R are true but R is not correct explanation of A

7. **Assertion (A):** Higher education in ancient India was imparted through Chintan method of teaching.
Reason (R): The aim of higher education was to enhance the power of retention and concentration in students.
(A) A is false but R is true
(B) Both A and R are true and R is correct explanation of A
(C) A is false but R is true
(D) Both A and R are false

8. **Assertion (A):** Gurukuls were budding universities of ancient India.
Reason (R): Students studying in gurukuls were awarded degrees by the affiliating universities.
(A) Both A and R are true and R is correct explanation of A
(B) Both A and R are true but R is not correct explanation of A
(C) Both A and R are false
(D) A is true but R is false

9. **Assertion (A):** Beginning of classical period witnessed the universalisation of higher education in ancient India.
Reason (R): Teaching elaborated rituals became subject of study in higher education in this period.
(A) Both A and R are true and R is correct explanation of A
(B) Both A and R are true but R is not correct explanation of A
(C) A is true but R is false
(D) A is false but R is true

10. **Assertion (A):** University education in ancient India laid the foundation of research and innovations.
Reason (R): Culture of university education in ancient India was developed by Mauryan kings.
(A) A is true but R is false
(B) A is false but R is true
(C) Both A and R are true but R is not correct explanation of A
(D) Both A and R are true and R is correct explanation of A

KEY

1. B **2.** C **3.** C **4.** A **5.** A **6.** D **7.** B
8. C **9.** D **10.** A

2 Evolution of Higher Learning and Research in Post-Independence India

INTRODUCTION

India has been considered a coveted seat of higher learning for Indians as well as foreign learners since ancient times. While reviewing the socio-economic development of ancient, medieval, and modern India, it is found that establishment of various universities and colleges are the sufficient evidences to establish that higher education has been playing an effective role in achieving socio-economic development of India. Though roots of establishing institutions of higher learning in India were in the ancient period, yet higher education system in post-independence India was influenced by the British higher education system. However, evolution of higher learning since 1947 can be viewed through the following channels:

1) Higher Education and Five Year Plans
2) Commissions and Committees in higher education

HIGHER EDUCATION AND FIVE YEAR PLANS

Era of planning in independent India was started with the establishment of Planning Commission in 1950. While adopting development models for various sectors, education in general and higher education in particular was also considered a major developmental issue which could be effective in setting up a sound socio-economic sector.

First Five Year Plan (1951-56)

The plan emphasised to develop higher education according to the national needs. 9% of total outlay of the plan was allotted for growth of higher learning and education. Number of universities at the start of the plan was 27, which increased to 32 by the end of the plan. Number of colleges in 1956 was 772. Trend of acquiring higher education increased. Enrolment for higher education increased to 7,20,000 in the final year of plan from 4,20000 during 1950-51.

Second Five Year Plan (1956-61)

During second Five Year Plan there was tremendous increase in the number of students in universities and colleges. The plan emphasised to raise the standard of university and college education. 18% of the total outlay of second plan was allocated for higher education. By the end of the plan, number of colleges was increased to 1050. Number of measures was taken by the University Grants Commission (UGC) to improve quality of college and university education. Some of the measures had been improvement in infrastructure, establishing three year degree course, organising tutorials and seminars, provision of hostel facilities, scholarships for research, and salary for university teachers. Along with general higher education, technical higher education was also given due emphasis. Adequate resources were provided for research in science. Special emphasis was given to encourage women participation in graduate and postgraduate streams. Various university level courses in

Home Science, Music and Painting were introduced. The percentage of women enrolment in universities thus increased from 13% in 1955–56 to 17% in 1960–61.

IIT KHARAGPUR

Indian Institute of Technology (IIT) Kharagpur (W. Bengal) was established during First Five Year Plan, i.e., in the year 1951. It was the first IIT to be established in India.

Third Five Year Plan (1961-66)

During third Five Year Plan, 18% of total plan outlay was allotted for higher education. It was emphasised during the plan that education in general and technical education was the tool to achieve socio-economic development. University Grants Commission (UGC) helped universities to start new postgraduate courses in science and technology. Resultantly, there was 70% increase in the enrolment in science stream at postgraduate level.

Indian Institute of Advanced Study (IIAS)

IIAS was established by the Union Education Ministry in 1965 at Shimla, i.e., during Third Five Year Plan.

Fourth Five Year Plan (1969-74)

Main emphasis of fourth plan in the field of higher education was consolidation and improvement in higher education. This was to be achieved through increasing strength of staff of libraries and laboratories. Further, it was also the aim to increase facilities in libraries and laboratories. The plan proposed to start centres of advanced studies with the help of universities.

Fifth Five Year Plan (1974-79)

The plan emphasised to provide higher education to weaker sections of the society. This was to be achieved by establishing evening colleges and correspondence courses. There was also plan to strengthen postgraduate education and research through science service centres, common computer facilities, and workshops. The plan also emphasised to step up programmes of university level faculty development through orientation courses, summer institutes, and seminars.

Sixth Five Year Plan (1980-85)

The plan put special emphasis on higher education. Redesigning undergraduate courses and launching employment oriented programmes in higher education was the main target of the plan. There were programmes to enhance research in various subjects and fields to achieve sustainable development. Research and study programmes covered new areas of knowledge. There was improvement in infrastructure of universities, particularly their laboratories and libraries. Education was linked with work and productivity so that first degree holders may not face difficulty in getting jobs. Higher education was taken as a measure of social and economic development as it is effective in generating human resources in the form of administrators, doctors, engineers, management experts, and teachers and other nation builders. Due to implementation of various programmes, enrolment in higher education increased from 2.5 million in 1977–80 to 3.5 million in 1984-85. In order to provide easy access to higher education by all, State Institutes of Educational Technology (SIET) were set up in Gujarat, Maharashtra, Orissa (Odisha), Andhra Pradesh, Uttar Pradesh, and Bihar. SIETs used to produce educational programmes for television and telecast was made through INSAT. One hour daily programme on higher education was telecast for the benefit of all associated with higher education. A scheme was launched in 1984-85 to strengthen the infrastructural facilities for postgraduate education in science and technology within the university system.

INDIAN INSTITUTE OF MANAGEMNENT (IIM) LUCKNOW

Indian institute of Management (IIM) Lucknow was established in 1984, i.e., During Sixth Five Year plan. In 2005, IIM Lucknow became the first IIM to set up a satellite campus exclusively for executive education in Noida and Delhi NCR region.

Seventh Five Year Plan (1985-90)

The plan emphasised to impart higher education to weaker sections and first time degree seekers from backward areas. The plan aimed at raising the standard of higher education. The plan also had a target of taking higher education to maximum learners through open universities, correspondence courses, and part-time teaching. The area of concentration was to impart higher education through non-formal means of international standards like Indira Gandhi National Open University (IGNOU). Further, emphasis was on promoting postgraduate education in science and technology. The plan also felt the need of imparting training to teachers rendering higher education. There was emphasis on faculty development while designing training curriculum to impart knowledge of latest techniques of teaching. Another area of concentration during the plan was reforming the examination system and establishing autonomous colleges. Need was also felt to bring maximum students from scheduled caste and scheduled tribe communities under the fold of higher education.

Indira Gandhi National Open University (IGNOU)

IGNOU was established in the year 1985, i.e., initial year of Seventh Five Year Plan with headquarters at New Delhi.

As a result of the above efforts, enrolment of students in affiliated colleges was 36.93 lakhs and 7.3 lakhs in universities by the end of the plan. Enrolment of SCs/STs was 10%. About 5 lakh students were enrolled in correspondence courses and open universities, out of which 1 lakh students were enrolled in IGNOU. By the end of this plan, 106 colleges had been granted autonomous status. Grant to central universities, 95 state universities, and 3000 colleges was released by the

UGC. In compliance to National Policy on Education (NPE), 1986 and Programme of Action (POA) 1992, State Council of Higher Education (SCHE) was created in Andhra Pradesh. 48 academic staff colleges were created throughout the country to provide orientation and training to in-service teachers. Sufficient assistance was given under various programmes like Centres for Advance Studies (CAS), Department of Special Assistance (DSAs), and Committee on Strengthening of Infrastructure in Science and Technology (COSIST). Broadcasting of an educational programme under the name 'Countrywide Classroom' was started by the UGC through its 7 audio-visual centres. Several degree courses in computer science were started with the help of Department of Electronics. IGNOU was successful in fetching students from the disadvantaged groups like women, people living in hilly and backward regions, and handicapped ones with an enrolment of 1.64 lakhs in 1992 (Annual Plan). Government spent about Rs. 1200 crore on higher education during the plan.

Eighth Five Year Plan (1992-97)

This plan vowed to adopt an integrated approach to higher education. The emphasis was

a) to make higher education system financially self-supporting
b) promotion of value education
c) making higher education responsive to current socio-economic needs
d) to work to constitute National Council of Higher Education (NCHE) as recommended in National Policy on Education (NPE)
e) streamlining management in universities
f) arranging orientation courses for college and university teachers
g) Initiating efforts to establish National Assessment and Accreditation Council (NAAC) as proposed in NPE and POA
h) carrying forward CAS, DSA, and COSIST programmes
i) implementing Model Curricula for all streams
j) implementing recommendations of Working Group (constituted by the Planning Commission) to improve undergraduate courses in science and technology and teaching of mathematics in universities and colleges
k) initiating programmes of starting vocational courses in open universities according to rural needs
l) carrying forward all programmes started during previous plan(s)
m) implementing the suggestions of the Core Group (constituted by the Planning Commission) to promote value education in colleges and universities while consulting Ministry of Human Resource Development (MHRD), UGC, NCERT, and Association of Indian Universities (AIU)
n) enhancing research and other facilities in colleges and universities
o) Initiating plan to promote research in humanities in IIAS
p) Pursuing establishment of National Testing Service (NTS) for conducting competitive exams for various service thus delinking degrees as requirement for services
q) mobilising information and library network INFLIBNET

INFLIBNET

University Grants Commission (UGC) established Information and Library Network (INFLIBNET) Centre in 1991 (Annual Plan) at Gandhinagar (Gujarat), on the recommendation of Yash Pal Committee. INFLIBNET is indulging in modernising university libraries in India. INFLIBNET connects libraries with information centres of universities through a high speed data network across the nation. It is an ultramodern and hi-tech channel of communication among academicians and research scientists. Initially, it worked as a project of Inter-university Centre of Astronomy and Astrophysics (IUCCA). In 1996, it was given the status of an autonomous centre of UGC.

As a result of above efforts 8th Five Year Plan succeeded in:

i) restructuring syllabi to meet the current requirements of education
ii) enhancing coverage of INFLIBNET
iii) implementing Model Curricula in different subjects
iv) expanding schemes of women education at degree level
v) setting up of National Assessment and Accreditation Council (NAAC)
vi) implementing programmes to improve and modernise management in universities
vii) increasing in number of universities and colleges, i.e., in 1996-97 there were 228 universities and 6759 affiliated colleges.

viii) increasing the enrolment through distant mode of learning to 15 lakh

ix) achieving total enrolment of 6 million in colleges and universities

x) introducing career oriented courses at first degree level in 31 universities and 1000 colleges covering 40,000 students

xi) implementing programmes of fixing minimum qualification of teachers, increasing their competencies through Academic Staff Colleges

xii) establishing Distance Education Council under IGNOU to support open universities

xiii) introducing degree courses in agriculture, computer application, education, management, engineering, nutrition, and nursing in open universities

xiv) establishing Staff Training and Research Institute of Distance Education (STRIDE)

xv) establishing Indian Institute of Technology (IIT) Assam in 1994

xvi) improving infra structural facilities in Regional Engineering colleges to make them centres of excellence for research

NAAC

National Assessment and Accreditation Council (NAAC) was established in 1994 (during 8th Five Year Plan) by UGC on recommendation of NPE & POA. Headquarter of NAAC is at Bengaluru (Karnataka).

Ninth Five Year Plan (1997-2002)

The plan emphasised improving the quality of higher education, improving governance in universities, expansion of higher education in unserved areas and covering disadvantaged groups in such areas, improving syllabi to establish its relevance with practical requirements, implementing model code of governance to reduce political influence in colleges and universities, establishing autonomous colleges, and training of teachers. In relation to above mentioned targets, Ninth plan achieved the following:

i) Separate university for science and technology

ii) Converting various leading departments in open universities into independent open universities

iii) Increasing number of technical and management education institutions to meet the increasing demand for engineering courses, particularly IT courses

iv) Launching National Human resource Development Programme in IT in the year 2000

Tenth Five Year Plan (2002-07)

Following objectives were drawn to develop higher education further:

i) Increasing number of study centres to motivate maximum women to pursue higher learning

ii) Providing access to education for students of north-eastern region through open education system

iii) Initiating skill-oriented courses at higher studies level

iv) Starting professional degree courses in information technology, genetic engineering, biotechnology, biomedicine, applied psychology, tours & travel, physical education, and sports

v) Widening scope of Academic Staff Colleges to train college and university teachers

vi) Supporting NET Exam conducted by UGC and increasing number of research fellowships

vii) Developing IT orientation in higher education by providing Internet connectivity to colleges

viii) Setting up of open universities by the IGNOU in those regions/states where there is no such university

ix) Expanding Gyan Darshan and Gyan Vani services

GYAN DARSHAN & GYAN VANI

Gyan Darshan: *It is an educational telecast of Doordarshan, which imparts education of all levels through video lectures. The telecast is made throughout the country. It is the joint venture of Doordarshan and IGNOU.*

Gyan Vani: *It is an educational FM service broadcasting lectures in all subjects for the students seeking education of any level. The lectures and related content is prepared by IGNOU, other educational institutions, NGOs, government, and semi government and are broadcast by All India Radio.*

x) Raising enrolment in higher education of 18-23 year age group of students from 6% at the start of the plan to 10% by the end of the plan

xi) Drawing relevant curriculum, vocationalisation, and networking on the use of information technology

xii) Inviting private participation in Universities and deemed universities

xiii) Working for internationalisation of Indian education

Due to above efforts Tenth Five Year Plan achieved following:

i) In persuasion to increase number of institutions of higher learning, the plan witnessed growth in this direction. Resultantly, there had been 378 universities, 18064 colleges, faculty strength of 4 lakh and thus, this achievement made Indian higher education system one of the largest in the world.

ii) In spite of establishment of various institutional learning, Gross Enrolment Ratio (GER) with 11% did not stand at satisfactory level as compared to world average of 23%.

iii) Increase in the share of private unaided institutions of higher learning increased from 42% in 2001 to 63% in 2006.

iv) Central Institute of English and Foreign Languages (CIEFL) and state universities of Arunachal Pradesh, Tripura, Manipur, and Allahabad were converted into central universities.

v) National Institute of Educational Planning and Administration (NIEPA) was converted into deemed university.

vi) Due to private participation, there was tremendous increase in the technical and management institutions.

vii) University of Roorkee was converted to IIT Roorkee, thereby making it seventh IIT in the country.

viii) Indian Institute of Information Technology, Design and Manufacturing was established at Jabalpur.

ix) Private universities imparting technical education were made operational.

Eleventh Five Year Plan (2007-12)

In spite of achieving many feats in higher education during previous plans, India had been experiencing various shortcomings in higher education system, like lack of efficient management in institutions of higher learning, inappropriate quality, poor GER, and inadequate access to higher education by disadvantaged groups. In the light of these shortcomings, 11th plan laid emphasis on

i) Achieving desired quality in higher and technical education

ii) Inviting private participation and enhancing public spending in higher education

iii) Initiating major institutional and policy reforms which had been wanting attention since long

iv) Making higher education pocket friendly for all aspirants of higher education

v) Achieving 15% GER by the year 2011-12

vi) Universalisation of semester system

vii) Restructuring NET/SET to admit good quality teachers in sufficient number

viii) Autonomy and accountability in higher education institutions

ix) Setting up 8 new IITs and 7 new IIMs

x) Launching of National Mission on Education through ICT to increase ICT coverage to all universities and colleges.

xi) Working for making universities fully electronic with digital campuses

PRIVATE SECTOR PARTICIPATION IN HIGHER EDUCATION

1) *Birla Institute of Technology and Science (BITS), Pilani was set up by noted industrialist G.D. Birla in early 1900s.*

2) *The Tata Institute of Social Sciences (TISS) was established in 1936.*

3) *Indian Institute of Science (IISc), Bengaluru was established and Tata Institute of Fundamental Research (TIFR), Mumbai were established by J.R.D. Tata.*

4) *Santiniketan, presently Viswa-Bharati University, was founded by Nobel Laureate Rabindranath Tagore in early 1900s.*

5) *Xavier Labour Relations Institute (XLRI), one of the finest management schools in India, was founded in 1949 by Fr Quinn Enright in Jamshedpur.*

Eleventh plan achieved following feats:

i) Increase in enrolment in formal and non-formal institutions of higher learning

ii) GER in higher education increased from 12% in the year 2006-07 to 18% in the year 2011-12

iii) Increase in higher education capacity due to increase in higher education institutions by the central and state governments and private sector. Such institutes grew by 58% during the plan

iv) Significant growth of private institutions-95 private state universities, 17 private deemed universities, and 7818 private colleges were established during the plan period.

v) The plan established a unique feat of historic increase in the number of central institutions in a single plan. The government established 65 new institutions.

vi) Centre supported states to establish universities and colleges but states established 89 universities and 4024 colleges on their own during the plan period.

vii) Increase in enrolment in higher education (in both formal and non-formal means) by 9.3 million.

Twelfth Five Year Plan (2012-17)

The plan drew the following targets:

i) Focussing on three Es-expansion, equity, and excellence as a paradigm change. The three Es approach will be applied to central state and private institutes as central institutes account for 2.6% of total enrolment, state institutes account for 38.5%, and remaining by private institutes.

ii) Enhancing quality of higher education

iii) Imparting occupation-based education to make youth self-sufficient

iv) Granting autonomy to the institutions with accountability in case of poor quality higher education.

v) Ensuring a minimum standard of academic quality with expansion of higher education

vi) Ensuring access to higher education for all sections of population including the disadvantaged

vii) Creating additional capacity to absorb maximum aspirants

viii) Working for bringing excellence in teaching-learning process

ix) Bringing changes in organisations through access and equity

x) Continuing with the objectives and programmes of 11th Five Year Plan

xi) Implementing centrally sponsored schemes like Rashtriya Uchchatar Shiksha Abhiyan (RUSA), Technical Education Quality Improvement Programme (TEQIP), National Mission Education through ICT (NMEICT), Talk to Teacher (TTT) project, and Pandit Madan Mohan Malaviya National Mission on Teachers and Teaching (PMMMNMTT)

xii) Expansion of Skill Based Programmes including Community Colleges

xiii) Developing strategy of internationalisation of higher education covering faculty-student exchange programme and institutional collaboration

Due to above efforts the plan achieved following:

i) According to All India Survey on Higher Education (AISHE) 2017-18 there are 903 universities, 39050 colleges, and 1001 stand-alone institutions at the end of the plan.

ii) Appreciable progress with the approach of 'Three Rs' was witnesses as GER increased from 11.5% in 2005-06 to 25.8% during 2017-18.

iii) 600 universities were covered under NMEICT.

iv) More than one lakh teachers were trained under Talk to Teacher (TTT) project.

v) The issue of shortage of quality faculty was taken up under Pandit Madan Mohan Malaviya National Mission on Teachers and Teaching (PMMMNMTT).

vi) National Institutional Ranking framework was established in 2015 to improve quality of higher education.

vii) Second phase of TEQIP was launched under which institutes of technical higher education were strengthened by ensuring better governance, better teacher-student ratio, and increasing employability.

viii) National Digital Library was launched in 2017 and with the help of IIT Kanpur and all universities were connected with the library to provide digital learning material. This would be beneficial for institutions from backward areas.

ix) Distance enrolment at the end of the plan was 11% of the total enrolment in higher education.

HIGHEST ENROLMENT

According to All India Survey of Higher Education (AISHE) 2017-18, Uttar Pradesh topped in students enrolment percentage in higher education followed by Maharashtra and Tamil Nadu.

xiv) During the plan period, six Indian institutes of management , i.e., one each at Amritsar (Punjab), Sirmour (H.P.), Vishakhapatnam (AP), Bodh Gaya (Bihar), Bhubaneswar (Odisha), and Nagpur (Maharashtra).

xv) 20 Indian Institutes of Information Technology (IIITs) were approved during the plan period.

COMMISSIONS, COMMITTEES, AND POLICY FRAMEWORKS IN HIGHER EDUCATION IN INDIA

1) **Wardha Education Scheme (First Committee's Report):** An All-India National Education Conference was convened at Wardha in October 1937 under the presidentship of Gandhiji to consider his proposed scheme of self-supporting education. It passed the following resolutions: (a) that free and compulsory education be provided for seven years on a nation-wide scale; (b) that the medium of instruction be the mother tongue; (c) that the Conference endorsed the proposal made by Gandhiji that the process of education throughout this period should centre round some form of manual and productive work and that all the other abilities to be developed or training to be given should, as far as possible, be integrally related to the central handicraft chosen with due regard to the environment of the child; (d) that the Conference expects that this system of education will be gradually able to cover the remuneration of the teachers. The age of entry to school should be 7 years and the standard attained at the end of 7 years schooling should approximate to the Matriculation (less English). Main stress was on basic education, i.e., Nai Talim.
2) **Dr. Radhakrishnan Commission (The University Education Commission) 1948-49:** This commission recommended a strong programme of physical education and sports in universities and colleges. It also recommended the setting up of UGC and rural universities.
3) **The National Committee on Women's Education, 1958:** The problems of education of girls and women in the country, acquired a new significance since the attainment of Independence. The Educational Panel of the Planning Commission, in July 1957, recommended that "a suitable Committee should be appointed to go into the various aspects of the question relating to the nature of education for girls at the elementary, secondary, and adult stages and to examine whether the present system was helping them to lead a happier and more useful life". This was the first commission on women education after independence. The Conference of the State Education Ministers in 1957 also agreed that a special committee should be appointed to examine the whole question of women's education. The National Committee on Women's Education was accordingly set up by the Government in May 1958, with Shrimati Durgabai Deshmukh as Chairman. The Committee, in its report published in 1959, recommended that the highest priority should be given to establishing a parity between the education of boys and girls and a bold and determined effort should be made by the Centre and the States to face the difficulties and magnitude of the problem.
4) **Education Commission 1964-66:** In view of the important rote of education in the national development and in building up a truly democratic society, the Government considered it necessary to survey and examine the entire field of education in order to realise a well-balanced, integrated, and adequate system of national education capable of making a powerful contribution to all aspects of national life. To achieve these objectives speedily, the Government of India in October 1964, set up an Education Commission. The Commission in particular was to advise the Government on the national pattern of education and on the general policies for the development of education at all stages-ranging from the primary to postgraduate stage and in all its aspects besides examining a host of educational problems in their social and economic context. The Commission was, however, not to examine legal and medical education. The Commission, under the chairmanship of Dr. D. S. Kothari, Chairman. University Grants Commission, consisted of 17 members. The major recommendations of the commission include education and productivity, education and research, and education for national reconstruction.
5) **National Education Policy Review Committee:** The Central Govt. appointed this committee in 1990 under the Chairmanship of Acharya Ramamurthi. The committee recommended decentralization of education management, equity and social justice, and participative social order in the education system.
6) **Prof Yash Pal Committee:** It was set up in 1992 to suggest measures for restructuring higher education in the country. The committee has made several suggestions, including scrapping of regulatory bodies like the UGC and AICTE, granting full autonomy to universities, and instituting a national commission to supervise them. The commission would be a constitutional body like the

Election Commission. The thrust was to give full autonomy to universities which would function as self regulatory bodies and would be vested with all academic responsibilities. They would design the function and structure of programmes, including medical and engineering courses. The Commission would oversee the functioning of the universities and act as a facilitator for proper growth of higher education and research.

7) **National Knowledge Commission (NKC)** was constituted under the chairmanship of Sam Pitroda on 13th June 2005 with a time frame of three years, from 2nd October 2005 to 2nd October 2008. However, the commission submitted its report in 2006. As a high-level advisory body to the Prime Minister of India, the National Knowledge Commission has been given a verdict to guide policy and direct reforms, with a focus to major areas such as education, science and technology, agriculture, industry, e-governance, etc. Easy access to knowledge, creation and preservation of knowledge systems, dissemination of knowledge, and better knowledge services are the main concerns of the commission. The aim of the National Knowledge Commission is to enable the development of a vibrant knowledge-based society. This requires both a tangible improvement in existing systems of knowledge and creating avenues for generating new forms of knowledge. The report concentrated on the need for excellence in the system, expansion of the higher education sector in the country, and providing access to higher education for larger numbers of students. For achieving this, NKC recommended that higher education system needs an enormous expansion of opportunities, to around 1500 universities nationwide, that would enable India to attain a gross enrolment ratio of at least 15 per cent by 2015. It also recommended establishing an Independent Regulatory Authority for Higher Education (IRAHE). The IRAHE must be at an appreciable distance from the government and independent of all stakeholders including the concerned Ministries of the Government. The IRAHE would have to be established by an Act of Parliament, and would be responsible for setting the criteria and deciding on entry to higher education which is otherwise plagued by barriers. It would be the only agency that would be authorized to accord degree granting power to higher education institutions. It further observed that the expansion of our system of higher education is not possible without enhanced levels of financing. This must necessarily come from both public and private sources. It also recommended the creation of 50 National Universities that can provide education of the highest standard with at least 10 universities in first 3 years. As motivators for the rest of the nation, these universities shall train students in a variety of disciplines, including humanities, social sciences, basic sciences, commerce, and professional subjects, at both the undergraduate and postgraduate levels. National Universities can be established in two ways, by the government, or by a private sponsoring body that sets up a Society, Charitable Trust, etc. Another recommendation is that universities should be required to revise or restructure curricula at least once in three years. Annual examinations, which test memory rather than understanding, should be supplemented with continuous internal assessment which could begin with a weight of 25 per cent in the total to be raised to 50 per cent over a stipulated period. Universities must become the hub of research to create cooperation between teaching and research that enrich each other. This requires not only policy measures but also changes in resource allocation, reward systems, and mindsets. The elements of infrastructure that support the teaching-learning process, such as libraries, laboratories, and connectivity, need to be monitored and upgraded on a regular basis. A further observation was that a major aim of the higher education system must be to ensure that access to education for economically and historically socially underprivileged students is enhanced in a substantially more effective manner. Education is the fundamental mechanism for social inclusion through the creation of more opportunities. It is, therefore, essential to ensure that no student is denied the opportunity to participate in higher education due to financial constraints. Institutions of higher education should be encouraged to adopt a need-blind admissions policy. This would make it unlawful for educational institutions to take into account any financial factor while deciding whether or not to admit a student. There must be a well-funded and extensive National Scholarship Scheme targeting economically underprivileged students and students from historically socially disadvantaged groups.

NEED-BLIND ADMISSION POLICY

This policy is adopted in the USA. It has also been recommended by the Knowledge Commission. Under this policy a university or college does not consider the financial status of the candidate while considering about admission to an applicant.

8) **The National Commission for Higher Education and Research (NCHER) Bill, 2010:** This is an Act to provide for the determination, co-ordination, maintenance of standards in, and promotion of higher education and research, including university education, technical, and professional education other than agricultural [and medical] education, and for that purpose, to establish the National Commission for Higher Education and Research. It is to further promote the autonomy of higher educational institutions for the free pursuit of knowledge and innovation, and for facilitating access, inclusion, and opportunities to all, and providing for comprehensive and holistic growth of higher education and research in a competitive global environment through reforms and renovation; and to provide for an advisory to aspirants in the academic atmosphere. The head office of the Commission shall be at New Delhi. The Commission shall consist of a Chairperson and six other Members. NCHER is being set up on the recommendation of the Yash Pal committee. The committee, which was set up to suggest reforms in the higher education sector, had also recommended that the commission be a constitutional entity to ensure the absolute autonomy along the lines of the Election Commission of India.

9) **National Mission on Education through ICT (NMEICT):** The National Mission on Education through Information and Communication Technology (NMEICT) has been envisaged as a Centrally Sponsored Scheme to make full use of the potential of ICT, in teaching and learning process for the benefit of all the learners in Higher Education Institutions at any time in any mode. This was expected to be a major intervention in enhancing the Gross Enrolment Ratio (GER) in Higher Education by 5 percentage points during the XI Five Year Plan period. The three cardinal principles of Education Policy viz., access, equity, and quality could be served well by providing connectivity to all colleges and universities, providing low cost and affordable access-cum-computing devices to students and teachers, and providing high quality e-content free of cost to all learners in the country. NMEICT encompasses all the three elements. The Mission has two major components: providing connectivity, along with provision for access devices, to institutions and learners; and content generation. It seeks to bridge the digital divide, i.e., the gap in the skills to use computing devices for the purpose of teaching and learning among urban and rural teachers/learners in the Higher Education domain.

Some Vital Facts

1) Fourth five year plan of India has given special emphasis on "Education and Manpower."
2) Education Commission under the Chairmanship of Dr. D.S. Kothari was set up in 1964.
3) The National Knowledge Commission (NKC) was established in 2005.
4) NMEICT stands for National Mission on Education through ICT.
5) The recommendation of National Knowledge Commission for the establishment of 1500 universities is to ensure increase in student enrolment in higher education.
6) According to Radhakrishnan Commission, the aim of higher education is to develop the democratic values, peace and harmony.
7) National Council for Women's Education was established in 1958.
8) Networking of libraries through electronic media is known as INFLIBNET.
9) Another name of Basic Education or NaiTalim isWardha Education Plan

Practice Exercise

General Questions Format

1. NAAC was established on the recommendation of
   (A) University Grants Commission
   (B) Kothari Education Commission
   (C) National Commission for Higher Education
   (D) None of these

2. Which of the following was/were an achievement in the field of higher education during 11th Five Year Plan?
   a) Increase in enrolment in formal and non-formal institutions of higher learning
   b) Establishment of National Institutional Ranking Framework
   c) Fixing minimum qualifications of teachers for higher education institutions
   d) Launching of National Digital Library
   (A) a and c only (B) c, b, and d only
   (C) a only (D) c and d only

3. Periods of Five Year Plans are given under Column I and their main objectives are given under Column II. Match the Five Year Plans with their respective objectives and choose the correct answer choice given in the codes given below:

Column I	Column II
a) Eighth Five Year Plan	i) Establishing autonomous colleges
b) Ninth Five Year Plan	ii) Promotion of value education
c) Twelfth Five Year Plan	iii) Maximising women participation in higher education
d) Tenth Five Year Plan	iv) Expansion, Equity, and Excellence

Codes:	(a)	(b)	(c)	(d)
(A)	iii	ii	i	iv
(B)	i	ii	iii	iv
(C)	ii	iii	i	iv
(D)	ii	i	iv	iii

4. Which Indian Institute of management became the first institute to install satellite campus?
   (A) IIM Mumbai (B) IIM Lucknow
   (C) IIM Indore (D) IIM Amritsar

5. Which of the following fully justifies the evolution of higher education in post-independence India?
   (A) Higher education was developed as a pivotal means to develop overall development of the country.
   (B) There was a need to develop skills in administration, engineering, medical, and science fields for development of industry, agriculture, and other sectors of the country.
   (C) Higher education was considered a sector which required regular but step-wise development with each Five Year Plan.
   (D) Development of education was taken as a challenge as it could exalt status of India at the international level.

6. Indian Institute of Advanced Study (IIAS) was established during ______ Five Year Plan.
   (A) Fourth (B) Second
   (C) Sixth (D) Third

7. Which of the following is NOT one of the missions of NMEICT?
   (A) Providing connectivity to all universities and colleges
   (B) E-training to university and college teachers
   (C) Providing low cost and affordable access-cum-computing devices to students and teachers
   (D) Providing high quality e-content free of cost to all learners in the country

8. Which of the following is TRUE about status of higher education during Sixth Five Year Plan?
   a) There was focus on redesigning undergraduate courses and launching employment generation programmes were the main targets.
   b) There was target of improving universities, particularly laboratories.
   c) There was target to establish evening colleges to impart education to weaker sections.
   d) There was emphasis on increasing staff strength in libraries of colleges and universities.
   (A) a and b only (B) a, c, and d only
   (C) c only (D) None of these

9. Establishment of National Commission for Higher Education and Research was recommended by ________ Committee.

(A) Gokhale (B) Kothari
(C) Yash Pal (D) Narsimhan

10. Target of separate university of science and technology was achieved during ________.

(A) Sixth Five Year Plan
(B) Eleventh Five Year Plan
(C) Eighth Five year plan
(D) Ninth Five Year Plan

11. Which of the following streams is not covered by the proposed National Commission for higher Education and Research (NCHER) for promotion of higher education and research?

(A) Commerce (B) Medical
(C) Engineering (D) Liberal arts

12. According to All India Survey on Higher Education (2017-18), which Indian state tops in student enrolment percentage in higher education?

(A) Karnataka (B) Maharashtra
(C) Gujarat (D) Uttar Pradesh

13. INFLIBNET has been established by

(A) NCERT (B) UGC
(C) MHRD (D) CBSE

14. Which body on higher education for the first time recommended establishing a sports university in India?

(A) Yash Pal Committee
(B) Secondary Education Commission
(C) Kothari Commission
(D) Dr. Radhakrishnan Commission

15. Which Five Year Plan drafted the objective of setting National Testing Service (NTS)?

(A) 5th (B) 8th
(C) 10th (D) 12th

16. INFLIBNET was established on the recommendation of ________ Committee.

(A) Yash Pal (B) Mudaliar
(C) Kothari (D) Pitroda

17. IIT Kharagpur was established during________ Five Year Plan of India.

(A) second (B) sixth
(C) first (D) fifth

18. During which Five Year Plan University of Arunachal Pradesh was converted into central university?

(A) 8th (B) 10th
(C) 6th (D) 12th

19. Which of the following is TRUE regarding evolution of higher education in post-independence India?

a) Higher education development was allotted developmental opportunities in spite of post-independence challenges to India.
b) Efficient planning strategy and setting up of various committees and commissions resulted in desired and promising development of higher education after independence.
c) Specific target-oriented planning to develop higher education yielded promising results.
d) Emphasis on professional and vocational education was instrumental in developing the circumstances of higher education players.

(A) a and c only (B) b and c only
(C) a, b, c, and d (D) c only

20. Which of the following scheme(s) of higher education has/have been implemented during 12th Five Year Plan?

a) RUSA b) NPE
c) NMEICT d) NLM

(A) a and c only (B) a, c, and d only
(C) b and d only (D) a, b, c, and d

21. What had not been feature(s) of the National Commission for Higher Education and Research (NCHER) Bill 2010?

a) Autonomy to higher education institution to pursue knowledge and research freely
b) Growth in higher education through reforms and renovation
c) Promoting higher education including university, technical, agricultural, and medical education
d) Equal opportunities and easy access to all for learning higher education

(A) b and c only (B) a, c, and d only
(C) d only (D) c only

22. The first Committee to be constituted after independence by the Government of India on Women's Education was

(A) Dr. Radhakrishnan Commission

(B) The Mudaliar Commission

(C) The Sri Prakasa Committee

(D) Dr. Durgabai Deshmukh Committee

23. National Education Commission was set up under the chairmanship of

(A) Dr. D. S. Kothari

(B) Sam Pitroda

(C) Prof. Yash Pal

(D) Dr. A. Lakshmanswamy Mudaliar

24. What was the key recommendation of Prof. Yash Pal Committee?

(A) Reconstitution of UGC

(B) Starting matric classes in colleges

(C) Full autonomy to universities

(D) Promotion of Nai Talim

25. Which of the following programme(s) was/were promoted in the field of higher education during 7th Five Year Plan?

a) Centres of Advanced Studies (CAS)

b) Technical Education Quality Improvement Programme (TEQIP)

c) Department of Special Assistance (DSA)

d) Committee on Strengthening of Infrastructure for Science and Technology (COSIST)

(A) Only c and d (B) a, b, c, and d

(C) Only a, c, and d (D) Only b

26. Consider the following targets of higher education:

i) To enhance Gross Enrolment Ratio (GER) in higher education

ii) To provide connectivity to all universities and colleges

iii) To meet out the principles-Access, Equity, and Quality

To which organisation of higher education do these principles belong?

(A) NCTE (B) AISHE

(C) INFLIBNET (D) NMEICT

27. Constitution of National Council of Higher Education (NCHE) was recommended during which Five Year Plan?

(A) 8th (B) 3rd

(C) 12th (D) 10th

28. Which of the following is NOT TRUE about growth of higher education during Second Five Year Plan?

a) There was tremendous increase in number of students in colleges and universities.

b) Adequate resources were allocated for research in science.

c) There was renovations of those colleges and universities which were in a dilapidated condition.

d) Emphasis was given to ensure women participation in graduate and undergraduate streams.

(A) c only (B) b, c, and d only

(C) a only d) b and c only

29. AISHE stands for

(A) All India Society on Higher Education

(B) All India Survey on Higher Education

(C) All India Survey on Hi-tech Education

(B) All India Seminar on Higher Education

30. National Education Policy Review Committee was appointed under the Chairmanship of

(A) Dr. D.S. Kothari

(B) Acharya Ramamurthi

(C) Prof. Yash Pal

(D) Dr. A. Lakshmanswamy Mudaliar

KEY

1. D	2. A	3. D	4. B	5. B	6. D	7. B
8. A	9. C	10. D	11. B	12. D	13. B	14. D
15. B	16. A	17. C	18. B	19. B	20. A	21. D
22. D	23. A	24. C	25. C	26. D	27. A	28. A
29. B	30. B					

Assertion–Reason Format

1. Assertion (A): Various institutes of higher education were established during Five Year Plans in India.

Reason (R): India was to achieve self-sufficiency in various specialised fields in post-independence era.

(A) A is true but R is false

(B) Both A and R are false

(C) Both A and R are true and R is correct explanation of A

(D) Both A and R are true but R is not correct explanation of A

2. **Assertion (A):** Higher education was not allotted its due share in Five Year Plans.

   Reason (R): Increasing population hampered growth of higher education in post-independence India.

   (A) Both A and R are false

   (B) A is false but R is true

   (C) Both A and R are true and R is the correct explanation of A

   (D) Both A and R are true but R is not correct explanation of A

3. **Assertion (A):** Post-independence development in higher education has been more or less a carry forward of the British model of education.

   Reason (R): Various bodies on higher education set up after independence could leave a weak impact on higher education system of India.

   (A) Both A and R are false

   (B) Both A and R are true but R is not correct explanation of A

   (C) A is true but R is false

   (D) A is false but R is true

4. **Assertion (A):** India set up various commissions to suggest reforms in higher education after independence.

   Reason (R): Recommendations of all commissions have been inspired by the idea of Nai Talim.

   (A) Both A and R are true and R is the correct explanation of A

   (B) Both A and R are true but R is not correct explanation of A

   (C) A is true but R is false

   (D) A is false but R is true

5. **Assertion (A):** The purpose of higher education is to promote critical and creative thinking abilities among students.

   Reason (R): These abilities ensure job placements.

   (A) Both A and R are correct and R is the correct explanation of A

   (B) Both A and R are correct but R is not the correct explanation of A

   (C) A is true and R is false

   (D) A is false and R is true

6. **Assertion (A):** National Commission on Women Education did not suggest a concrete measure for ensuring women participation in higher education.

   Reason (R): Women voluntarily participated in higher education streams after independence.

   (A) Both A and R are true and R is correct explanation of A

   (B) Both A and R are false

   (C) A is true but R is false

   (D) A is false but R is true

7. **Assertion (A):** There has been a cyclic evolution of higher education in India after Independence.

   Reason (R): In spite of a well-defined education policy, there was not much headway in the growth of higher education in India.

   (A) Both A and R are true and R is correct explanation of A

   (B) Both A and R are true but R is not correct explanation of A

   (C) Both A and R are false

   (D) A is true but R is false

8. **Assertion (A):** Advent of ICT has affected universalisation of higher education in independent India.

   Reason (R): Digital divide among aspirants of higher education has been narrowed down.

   (A) Both A and R are true but R is not correct explanation of A

   (B) A is true but R is false

   (C) A is false but R is true

   (D) Both A and R are true and R is correct explanation of A

9. **Assertion (A):** Significance of imparting higher education through non-formal means was realised during the 7th Five Year Plan.

   Reason (R): Indira Gandhi National Open University was established during the 7th Five Year Plan.

   (A) Both A and R are true and R is correct explanation of A

   (B) Both A and R are true but R is not correct explanation of A

   (C) A is true but R is false

   (D) A is false but R is true

10. **Assertion (A):** Knowledge Commission has recommended need-blind admission policy in universities and colleges.

    Reason (R): There should be a universal admission policy suitable to every pocket.

    (A) Both A and R are true and R is correct explanation of A

    (B) Both A and R are true but R is not correct explanation of A

    (C) A is true but R is false

    (D) A is false but R is true

KEY

1. C **2.** B **3.** A **4.** C **5.** A **6.** B **7.** C **8.** D **9.** A **10.** B

Questions Asked in Previous NET Exams

1. Which of the following Five Year Plans of India has given special emphasis on "Education and Manpower"? **(UGC NET JUNE 2019)**

   (A) Third Five Year Plan

   (B) Fourth Five Year Plan

   (C) Second Five Year Plan

   (D) Fifth Five Year Plan

2. In which year Education Commission under the Chairmanship of Dr. D.S. Kothari was set up? **(UGC NET DECEMBER 2018)**

   (A) 1960 (B) 1955

   (C) 1952 (D) 1964

3. The National Knowledge Commission (NKC) was established in which year?

   (UGC NET DECEMBER 2018)

   (A) 1998 (B) 2007

   (C) 2000 (D) 2005

4. NMEICT stands for

   (UGC NET DECEMBER 2015)

   (A) National Mission on Education through ICT

   (B) National Mission on e-Governance through ICT

   (C) National Mission on e-commerce through ICT

   (D) National Mission on e-government through ICT

5. The recommendation of National Knowledge Commission for the establishment of 1500 universities is to

   (UGC NET DECEMBER 2009)

   (A) create more teaching jobs

   (B) ensure increase in student enrolment in higher education

   (C) replace or substitute the privately managed higher education institutions by public institutions

   (D) enable increased movement of students from rural areas to urban areas

6. According to Radhakrishnan Commission, the aim of higher education is

   (UGC NET DECEMBER 2008)

   (A) To develop the democratic values, peace, and harmony

   (B) To develop great personalities who can give their contributions in politics, administration, industry, and commerce

   (C) Both (A) and (B)

   (D) None of these

7. National Council for Women's Education was established in: **(UGC NET JUNE 2008)**

   (A) 1958 (B) 1976

   (C) 1989 (D) 2000

8. Networking of libraries through electronic media is known as: **(UGC NET JUNE 2007)**

   (A) INFLIBNET

   (B) LIBINFNET

   (C) Internet

   (D) HTML

9. Another name of Basic Education or Nai Talim is **(UGC NET DECEMBER 2004)**

   (A) Compulsory Education

   (B) New Education Policy

   (C) Wardha Education Plan

   (D) Sarva Shiksha Abhiyan

KEY

1. B **2.** D **3.** D **4.** A **5.** B **6.** A **7.** A **8.** A **9.** C

3 Learning Programmes in India

(Oriental, Conventional and Non-Conventional)

ORIENTAL LEARNING

Oriental learning is the study of culture, language, religion, people, history, and archaeology of Near Eastern and Far Eastern societies like Japan, China, Korea, etc. in general. These societies are considered to be rich in culture and heritage and scholars from other parts of the world used to study their heritage.

Oriental Learning in India

Like Near Eastern and Far Eastern countries, India also possesses a rich cultural heritage and scholars from all over the world, particularly Europe, come to study all traits of Indian Culture, i.e., Indology.

INDOLOGY

Indology is the study of rich cultural heritage of India. India has been renowned in the world since ancient times regarding its rich culture comprising religion, values, rituals, customs, preaching, discourses, epistemology, arts, and science. Indian culture, values, and rituals had been major subjects of study during ancient times. Scholars from many countries like China, Tibet, and Central Asia used to join ancient Indian universities like Nalanda, Takshila, and Vaisali to learn Indian culture and values. Though with the passage of time Indian society attained modernism and the days of ancient mode of teaching remained no more, yet aura of Indian cultural heritage did not diminish. Many scholars from Europe during the British rule got an opportunity to study Indology in the oriental language of Prakrit and Sanskrit. Scholars even obtained and learnt through manuscripts where there was no proper written account.

Actually it was the British, the colonial rulers, who formally created the subject Indology at the end of the 18th century, when the English scientist William Jones (1746-1794) founded the Asiatic Society of Bengal in Kolkata in 1784.

So scholars from Europe in 18th, 19th, and early 20th centuries revived the study of Indology which had gone to oblivion due to transformation of Gurukul society to Modern society. They used to obtain these manuscripts and then got them published. Where publishing was not possible, the manuscripts were used to be protected with some devices. As the precedent set in, study of Indology continued in India even after independence and even today, many oriental learning programmes are being conducted by various institutes. These institutes maintain well-stocked libraries housing indigenous literature and the literature obtained from various other Near Eastern and Far Eastern countries as these institutes not only involve research and study of Indology but also oriental learning in general.

Institutes of Oriental learning in India

1) Adyar Library and Research Center- Chennai
2) Asiatic Society-Kolkata
3) Bhandarkar Oriental Research Institute-Pune
4) Ganganath Jha Kendriya Sanskrit Vidyapeeth-Allahabad
5) Kuppuswami Sastri Research Institute-Chennai
6) Madras Sanskrit College
7) Mythic Society-Bengaluru
8) Oriental Institute-Vadodara
9) Oriental Research Institute and Manuscripts Library-Thiruvananthapuram
10) Oriental Research Institute-Mysuru
11) Sanskrit Academy-Chennai
12) Sanskrit Sahitya Parishad-Kolkata
13) The Sanskrit College University-Kolkata
14) Saraswati Mahal Library- Thanjavur
15) Vishveshvaranand Vishva Bandhu Institute of Sanskrit and Indological Studies-Hoshiarpur

CONVENTIONAL LEARNING

Classroom learning is called Conventional Learning. It is a traditional way of learning through teacher-centric methods of teaching.

Conventional Learning Programmes in India

Learning through books is a conventional way of learning as it has been a tradition. Also, various colleges and universities of India are rendering classroom teaching. Students are learning science, commerce, management, law, liberal arts, linguistics, etc. from books during classroom teaching and this is the conventional learning.

NON-CONVENTIONAL LEARNING

Non-conventional learning is considered so in two accounts:

1) When learning is acquired through modes other than classroom learning: Modes of self-learning, online learning, and all other modes of learning which are away from traditional mode of learning, i.e., teacher-centred classroom teaching is considered non-conventional. Even learning through videos, audios, and other technology devices are also part of non-conventional learning.
2) When learning is acquired in those subjects, fields, and activities which are not traditionally taught: It includes degree or diploma courses in those professions which on one hand open avenues of novel careers which are far more lucrative, secured, philanthropic, and status- oriented and on the other hand, provides an opportunity to serve mankind.

Non-Conventional Learning Programmes in India

Various non-conventional programmes are being run by various institutes offering courses other than the traditional ones as explained below:

1) **Gerontology:** Gerontology is the study that includes the social, emotional, and life aspects of ageing that aims to help the elderly. There are promising career opportunities in Gerontology. Ramnarain Ruia College (Mumbai), Tata Institute of Social Sciences, and Calcutta Metropolitan Institute of Gerontology are offering diploma and degree courses in Gerontology. Candidates after obtaining degrees or diploma in Gerontology are absorbed in leading national and international-level hospitals, old care homes, NGOs, and many other public sector and private sector organisations.
2) **Gandhian Thought:** Institute of Gandhian Studies (Wardha), Department of Gandhian Thought (Nagpur University), and other like institutes are offering diploma and degree courses in Gandhian studies that deal with the study of the life, philosophy, and methodology of Mahatma Gandhi, his days and strategy of freedom struggle, his belief in non-violence and cleanliness, etc. Candidates after obtaining diploma or degree in Gandhian thought are taken by various public sector and private sector institutes or organisations undertaking research in Gandhian thought or working on the principles of Gandhian thought.
3) **Ethical Hacking:** Many national and international level IT firms are looking for personnel skilled in ethical hacking. These hackers hack the system for security reasons. The companies are recruiting engineers who are good at cracking passwords (social media accounts), unlocking a closed system, or decoding multiple codes to detect a crime. Various institutes are offering courses in ethical hacking. Indian School of Ethical Hacking (Kolkata), NIIT, and Arizona Infotech (Pune) are some institutions imparting courses in ethical hacking.
4) **Spa Management:** Spa as a career is gaining popularity. People in present day life are full of tension. As spa relieves tension, many tension-ridden people visit spa centres. Many institutes like Ananda Spa Institute (Hyderabad) and Orient Spa Academy (Jaipur) are some leading institute offering courses in Spa Management.
5) **Carpet Technology:** Carpets have been a significant indicator of Indian culture and heritage and is giving prospective business in India and broad. In order to further improve technology of carpet manufacturing, Indian Ministry of Textiles has set up a course on carpet technology. The course supports the carpet industries by developing skilled labourers and technical support. The syllabus covers the technical understanding of fibres, the process of dyeing, washing, and more. After completing the course, candidates are well-placed in various public sector

and private sector houses manufacturing or trading in carpets. The Indian Institute of Carpet Technology, Allahabad and Indian Institute of Carpet Technology, Srinagar are some leading institutes offering courses in carpet technology.

6) **Museology:** Museums are a great source of attraction for the tourists, so they promise a decent career. A good number of aspirants complete courses in Museology. Museology is the study of museums. The course offers the knowledge of managing museums and museum collections. One needs to have a proper understanding of history and culture to opt for this profession. The Maharaja Sayajirao University (Vadodara), Jiwaji University (Gwalior), Aligarh Muslim University, UP University of Kolkata, and Banaras Hindu University are some leading institutes imparting education in Museology.

Practice Exercise

General Questions Format

1. Which of the following is TRUE about non-conventional learning?

a) Non-conventional means of teaching ensure better career opportunities than conventional means.

b) There is a provision of Public Contact Programme in non-conventional teaching-learning process.

c) Courses offered in non- conventional learning process carry scope of self-occupation.

d) Non-conventional learning is the secondary stage of conventional learning.

(A) Only c (B) Only b and d

(C) a, b, c, and d (D) Only b and c

2. Some institutes of oriental learning are given under Column I and the names of cities in which they are situated are given under Column II. Match an institute with its location and choose the correct code from the codes given below:

Column I (Institute)	**Column II (City)**
a) Saraswati Mahal Library	i) Kolkata
b) Mythic Society	ii) Vadodara
c) Government Sanskrit College	iii) Chennai
d) Oriental Institute	iv) Bengaluru
	v) Thanjavur

Codes:

	(a)	(b)	(c)	(d)
(A)	iii	iv	i	ii
(B)	ii	v	i	iii
(C)	iv	ii	iii	v
(D)	v	iv	i	ii

3. Learning Indology is part of

(A) Conventional Learning

(B) Oriental Learning

(C) Non-conventional Learning

(D) Contemporary Learning

4. Which of the following is/are NOT TRUE?

a) Conventional learning cannot be replaced with oriental learning.

b) Non-conventional learning programmes have been initiated in India to enhance employment opportunities in India.

c) Eastern countries invite scholars from Europe to promote oriental learning.

d) Had there not been British rule in India, there would not have been concept of Indology.

(A) a and d only (B) c only

(C) b and d only (D) a, c, and d only

5. Which of the following is NOT an institute of Oriental Learning?

(A) Ramnarain Ruia College

(B) Mythic Society

(C) Adyar Research Centre

(D) Asiatic Society

6. Which of the following non-conventional learning course is offered in Tata Institute of Social Sciences?
(A) Gerontology (B) Ethical Hacking
(C) Museology (D) Carpet Technology

7. Which of the following is/are TRUE?
a) Indology is the study of rich cultural heritage of the Indian subcontinent.
b) Oriental learning programmes in India are inspired from the British legacy in India.
c) Study of Gandhian thought is imparted by institutes of non-conventional learning.
d) Conventional learning programmes in India are customary and perennial.
(A) Only c (B) Only c and d
(C) Only a, c, and d (D) Only b

8. Indology was originally compiled in oriental languages of
(A) Prakrit and Sanskrit
(B) Brahmi and Sanskrit
(C) Pali and Sanskrit
(D) Gautami and Sanskrit

9. William Jones had been founder of
(A) Mythic Society
(B) Oriental Institute
(C) Adyar Library
(D) Asiatic Society

10. Consider the fact: Non-conventional learning system is surpassing the conventional learning system. What is the background behind the above fact?
(A) Stronger career appeal is making non-conventional learning more popular.
(B) Non-conventional learning system is gaining popularity as it involves learner-centric methods of teaching whereas conventional learning system involves teacher-centric method of teaching.
(C) Non-conventional learning system provides ample opportunities to learners to exploit their talent and skill which is not found in conventional learning system.
(D) All of the above

11. Which country's culture is studied under oriental learning?
(A) Japan
(B) Canada
(C) Australia
(D) Brazil

12. Which of the following non-conventional learning programmes aim at philanthropy?
(A) Gandhian Thought
(B) Ethical Hacking
(C) Gerontology
(D) All of these

13. Indology has its roots in
(A) Mythic Society
(B) Asiatic Society
(C) Adyar Research Centre
(D) Oriental Institute

14. Conventional learning programmes in India are justifying
(A) Universalisation of education
(B) Conglomeration of Gurukul mode of learning
(C) Consolidation of vocational learning with academic learning
(D) All of these

KEY

1. A	2. D	3. B	4. B	5. A	6. A	7. B
8. C	9. D	10. D	11. A	12. D	13. B	14. C

Assertion–Reason Format

1. **Assertion (A):** European scholars used to visit India to learn Indology during British era.
Reason (R): Indology is study of rich cultural heritage of India.
(A) Both A and R are true and R is correct explanation of A
(B) Both A and R are true but R is not correct explanation of A
(C) A is true but R is false
(D) A is false but R is true

2. **Assertion (A):** Non-conventional learning sometimes has a philanthropic aim.

   Reason (R): A non-conventional learning of Gerontology aims at helping the elderly and ageing members of the society.

   (A) Both A and R are true and R is correct explanation of A

   (B) Both A and R are true but R is not correct explanation of A

   (C) A is false but R is true

   (D) Both A and R are false

3. **Assertion (A):** European scholars laid the foundation of oriental learning in the world.

   Reason (R): Oriental learning in India was initiated by the Europeans in India too.

   (A) Both A and R are true and R is correct explanation of A

   (B) Both A and R are true but R is not correct explanation of A

   (C) A is true but R is false

   (D) A is false but R is true

4. **Assertion (A):** Oriental learning in post-independence India is enjoying the status it had in pre-independence India.

   Reason (R): Institutes of oriental learning in post-independence India are truly carrying forward the ethics of oriental learning of pre-independence India.

   (A) Both A and R are true and R is correct explanation of A

   (B) Both A and R are true but R is not correct explanation of A

   (C) Both A and R are false

   (D) A is true but R is false

5. **Assertion (A):** Conventional and non-conventional learning have same destination in spite of conceptual difference in them.

   Reason (R): Both conventional and non-conventional learning are acquired to fetch a secured and promising career.

   (A) Both A and R are true and R is correct explanation of A

   (B) Both A and R are true but R is not correct explanation of A

   (C) A is true but R is false

   (D) Both A and R are false

KEY

1. B **2.** A **3.** D **4.** C **5.** A

Questions Asked in Previous NET Exams

1. Identify the distinctive feature of traditional method of Indian education from the following list **(UGC NET DECEMBER 2019)**

   (A) 'Direct perception of truth" - both as means and end.

   (B) Making everything on 'Trust'

   (C) Evolving one way of earning

   (D) Following Nyaya Philosophy with deductive - Inductive Process

2. Which of the following forms a necessary component of Conventional Education System? **(UGC NET JUNE 2019)**

   (A) Learning from books

   (B) Learning from teacher

   (C) Learning from thinking

   (D) Learning through instructional material

KEY

1. A **2.** A

Education Concepts and Kinds
(Professional, Technical, Skill-Based, Value and Environmental Education)

MEANING OF EDUCATION

The word education has been derived from a Latin word 'Educare', which means to bring up. So education is an experience, which one undergoes throughout his life. It not only provides knowledge but also develops learner's personality like a guardian. As rightly stated by Swami Vivekanand, "*Education is the manifestation of the perfection already in man*"

Significance of Education

1) Developing learner's overall knowledge, experience, and personality
2) Measure of progress in the different fields of society
3) Helping in eradicating regressive and orthodox traditions, customs, and rituals
4) Only means of creating awareness about various innovations and reforms in every walk of life

Forms of Education

1) **Formal Education:** (Education provided in a classroom in schools, colleges, universities, etc.)
2) **Non-Formal Education:** (Education provided through post, TV, newspapers, radio, etc.)
3) **Informal Education:** (Education one attains from experiences of life, i.e., education one gets from one's parents, elders, friends, associates, strangers, daily life events, etc. at any place and any time)

Stages of Formal and Non-Formal Education

1) **Primary Education:** (School level Education, based on the principle of three 'R's, i.e., Reading, Writing, and Arithmetic and also emphasis on teaching general manners and physical and mental development)
2) **Secondary Education:** (Pre-University Education, i.e., +1, +2)
3) **Tertiary Education:** (Higher University Level Education after +2)

DIFFERENT CONCEPTS OF EDUCATION

Professional Education

As a society develops, a lot of socio-economic needs come up, which are to be fulfilled for growth of the society. Such needs are fulfilled through certain activities which are developed into different professions as needs vary in nature and approach to their fulfilment requires a particular skill. Resultantly, various professions come up like education, banking, health, commerce, law, industry, agriculture, engineering, pharmacy, nursing, computer science, etc. These professions are needed to be managed by the persons possessing a requisite qualification needed to manage that profession.

Professional qualification is acquiring a specialised knowledge of the skills required to handle a particular profession. Such knowledge is acquired by joining specialised education institutes and attending classroom, laboratory, and practical training. In the present age of satellite communication technology, professional education is acquired through ICT means also.

Technical Education

Technical education is different from academic education. This education is imparted under the formal and non-formal education systems. Imparting of this education is encouraged from rapid increase in industrialization and population leading to problem of unemployment, urbanisation, and modernization in different traditional and non-traditional occupations. There has been need of developing various technologies in different fields like agriculture, industry, communication, commerce, aviation, health, energy, education, banking, transportation, etc. For the development of technologies, there is a need to learn them first of all. With this objective, technical education is imparted at different levels of education. Up to primary and secondary level the motive of imparting technical education is a sort of providing introduction to various concepts of technical education. Technical education is acquiring the knowledge of a skill and engineering of a particular field through a specialized channel.

Technical Education in India

Indian government set up All India Council for Technical education (AICTE) in 1945 to maintain the standard of technical education. The development of technical education has been one of the major achievements of the post-independence period. Major achievement of this period is the creation of the All India Council for Technical Education in 1945. The Report of the Scientific Manpower Committee in 1947 had a far-reaching influence on this development. A further impetus was given by the Engineering Personnel Committee (1956) and the Committee for Postgraduate Engineering Education and Research (1961). The development of technical education as it relates to industry was promoted through the Apprentices Act (1961), the Industrial Training Institutes (ITIs), and junior technical schools at the skilled worker level and the spread of polytechnics at the technician level. Another significant factor that helped this development was the assistance received from friendly countries and international organizations.

At present, technical education in India is imparted by educational institutions enjoying international goodwill on the basis of highly competent, skilled, and professional faculty. Besides IITs, following are some institutions imparting technical education in India:

1) Indian Institute of Science (IISc), Bengaluru
2) Indian Institute of Information Technology and Management (IIITM), Gwalior
3) Indian Institute of Information Technology (IIIT), Allahabad
4) Indian School of Mines (ISM), Dhanbad
5) School of Planning and Architecture (SPA), New Delhi
6) National Institute of Foundry and Forge Technology (NIFFT), Ranchi
7) National Institute for Training and Industrial Engineering (NITIE), Mumbai
8) Technical Teachers' Training Institutes (TTTIs)
9) North Eastern Regional Institute of Science and Technology (NERIST)
10) Sant Longowal Institute of Engineering and Technology (SLIET), Punjab
11) SRM Institute of Science and Technology, Chennai

Startup India Plan

Department of Science and Technology (DST) and Ministry of Human Resource Development (MHRD) has jointly taken an initiative for promoting establishment of Research Parks/Technology Business Incubators /Startup Centres. In this regard, National Experts Advisory Committee (NEAC) has approved 13 Startup Centres, 16 Technology Business Incubators (TBIs), and 6 Research Parks under Startup India Scheme.

Skill-Based (Vocational) Education

Vocational education or skill-based education is a form of education in which people are provided with practical skills which will allow them to engage in careers which involve manual or practical abilities. Vocational education is very close to technical education. It is imparted at primary, secondary, and senior secondary level for introducing the concepts of various occupations to the students. However, it is imparted at graduate and postgraduate level to enable the students to become skilled in disciplines of different occupations. Main motive of imparting education in various occupations is to enable the candidates either to find a suitable job in a particular occupation or start their own viable unit. Different apex level institutes and universities are imparting such education at degree or postgraduate diploma level education in fashion technology, garments technology, pharmaceuticals, medical science, nursing, food technology, communication technology, creative arts, interior designing, business management, hotel management, etc.

Skill Based (Vocational) Education in India

In India, vocational training is imparted under the supervision of Directorate General of Training (DGT). The Directorate General of Training (DGT) in Ministry of Skill Development and Entrepreneurship is the apex organization for development and coordination at National level for the programmes relating to vocational training, including Women's Vocational Training. Industrial Training Institutes are under the administrative and financial control of State Governments or Union Territory Administrations. DGT also operates Vocational Training Schemes in some of the specialized areas through field institutes under its direct control. Development of these programmes at national level, particularly in the area concerning common policies, common standards and procedures, training of instructors, and trade testing are the responsibility of the DGT. Its portal is: https://dgt.gov.in/

Skill India

Skill India is a campaign launched by the Prime Minister on 15 July 2015 which aims to train over 40 crore people in India in different vocational skills by 2022. It includes various initiatives of the government like "National Skill Development Mission", "National Policy for Skill Development and Entrepreneurship, 2015", "Pradhan Mantri Kaushal Vikas Yojana (PMKVY)", and the "Skill Loan Scheme".

SKILL DEVELOPMENT INITIATIVES

1) ***National Skill Development Corporation (NSDC):*** *NSDC is a not-for-profit public limited company incorporated on July 31, 2008. NSDC aims to promote skill development by catalyzing creation of large, quality, and for-profit vocational institutions. Further, the organisation provides funding to build scalable and profitable vocational training initiatives. Its mandate is also to enable a support system which focuses on quality assurance, information systems, and train the trainer academies either directly or through partnerships. NSDC acts as a catalyst in skill development by providing funding to enterprises, companies, and organizations that provide skill training. It also develops appropriate models to enhance, support, and coordinate private sector initiatives.*

2) ***Pradhan Mantri Kaushal Vikas Yojana (PMKVY):*** *PMKVY is the flagship scheme of the Ministry of Skill Development & Entrepreneurship. The objective is to enable many Indian youth to take up industry-relevant skill training that will help them in securing a better livelihood. Individuals with prior learning experience or skills will also be assessed and certified under Recognition of Prior Learning (RPL). Under this Scheme, Training and Assessment fees are completely paid by the Government.*

Distance Education

Distance education is a modern system of non-formal education. It is imparted through correspondence or postal courses, contact programmes, electronic media, like radio, television, video, and audio cassettes, etc. and other audio visual aids. In the age of advanced communication technology, distance education is imparted online through various websites, apps, and portals. The terms which are used for distance education and distance education institutes are: Distance Learning, Distance Teaching, Open Education, Open Learning, Open School, Open University, University of the Air, University without Walls, Tele University, Out of school education, Correspondence Learning, Correspondence School, and Correspondence teaching.

Objectives

- To carry the school/college to the pupil or to take the fruits of useful learning to the very doorstep of the pupils
- To provide a suitable path for wider opportunities in education, especially in higher education
- To provide an efficient and less expensive process of education
- To provide facilities to pursue higher education to all qualified and willing persons who had failed to join regular college/university courses due to personal and economic reasons

Distance Education in India

Open and Distance Learning (ODL) system of the country consists of Indira Gandhi National Open University(IGNOU), State Open Universities (SOUs), Institutions, and Universities offering education and includes Correspondence Course Institutes (CCIs) in conventional dual mode universities. Various open universities in India are named below along with their year of establishment:

1) Dr. B.R. Ambedkar Open University Hyderabad, Andhra Pradesh (1982)
2) Indira Gandhi National Open University, New Delhi (1985)
3) Vardhman Mahaveer Open University Kota, Rajasthan (1987)
4) Nalanda Open University Patna, Bihar (1987)
5) Yashwantrao Chavan Maharashtra Open University, Nasik, Maharashtra (1989)
6) Madhya Pradesh Bhoj Open University, Bhopal, Madhya Pradesh (1991)
7) Dr. Babasaheb Ambedkar University, Ahmedabad, Gujarat (1994)
8) Karnataka State Open University, Mysuru, Karnataka (1996)
9) Netaji Subas Open University, Kolkata, West Bengal (1997)
10) U.P. Rajarshi Tandon Open University, Allahabad, UP (1999)
11) Tamil Nadu Open University, Chennai, Tamil Nadu (2002)
12) Uttarakhand Open University, Haldwani, Uttarakhand (2005)
13) Krishna Kanta Handiqui State Open University, Guwahati, Assam (2005)
14) Pandit Sunderlal Sharma (Open) University (PSSOU), Bilaspur, Chhattisgarh (2005)

Sakshat

Sakshat is a One Stop Education Portal in distance learning launched on October 30, 2006 by the then President of India to facilitate lifelong learning for students, teachers, and those in employment or in pursuit of knowledge free of cost to them.

The object of Sakshat is to cater to the learning needs of more than 50 crore people through a proposed scheme of 'National Mission on Education through Information and Communication Technology (NMEICT). The scheme is to provide connectivity to all institutions of higher learning to world of knowledge in the cyberspace, to leverage the potential of ICT in providing high quality knowledge modules with right e-content and to address to the personalized needs of learners, in order to take care of their aspirations. These modules are to be delivered through 'Sakshat'.

Value Education

This refers to the providing of education about moral and ethical values in the formal, non-formal, and informal ways. In the present day society modernization has put moral values like respect, appreciation, generosity, loyalty, sympathy, kindness, friendship, honesty, obedience, etc. to backseat and such education is fast becoming part of history. There is a need to revive this education also along with the education in other fields in order to really justify the meaning and significance of education.

VALUES

Values are virtues, ideals, and qualities on which actions and beliefs are based. Values are guiding principles that shape one's world outlook, attitudes, and conduct. The moral values present a true perspective of the development of any society or nation. They tell as to what extent a society or nation has developed itself.

Objectives of Value Education

1. Full development of child's personality in its physical, mental, emotional, and spiritual aspects
2. Inculcation of good manners and responsibility and cooperative citizenship
3. Developing respect for individual and society

4. Inculcating a spirit of patriotism and national integration
5. Developing a democratic way of thinking and living
6. Developing tolerance towards and understanding of different religious faith
7. Developing a sense of human brotherhood at social, national, and international levels
8. Helping children to have faith in themselves and in some supernatural power and order that is supposed to control this universe and human life
9. Enabling children to make moral decision on the basis of sound moral principles

Value Education in India

Various institutes of oriental learning are imparting value education.

Environmental Education

Environment today is a global issue of discussion as it is being polluted by anthropogenic activities posing grave threat to humans, flora, and fauna. To create awareness about maintaining a healthy environment, there is a need to educate people about the environment. Environmental education is imparted in an organised method. It is imparting knowledge about nature and natural resources comprising the ecosystem. Environment education also imparts knowledge about human interaction with natural resources, nature of interaction, and its effect on natural resources and the ecosystem. Ultimate aim of environmental education is to impart knowledge as to how sustainable development can be achieved.

Environmental Education (EE) in India

Environment education in India was made compulsory in formal education in schools through a Supreme Court judgement in 2003. Further, various measures have been taken by the government of India.

1) The **Centre for Environment Education** (CEE) in India was established in August 1984 as a Centre of Excellence supported by the Ministry of Environment and Forests. The organisation works towards developing programmes and materials to increase awareness about the environment and sustainable development. The head office is located in Ahmedabad.
2) **Environmental Orientation to School Education (EOSE):** Government of India launched EOSE. Through this programme it was expected to orient school children to their immediate environment using locale-specific examples and materials. To do so, a range of activities were initiated including production of locale-specific print materials, training modules, practical activities, and so on. The Ministry of Human Resource Development, Govt. of India had appointed three Nodal Agencies to implement the Scheme. Environmental education (EE) has been introduced as a regular course in formal school education system in India following the directive of the Honourable Supreme Court of India.
3) **Environment Education and Research:** There are various institutes in India imparting environmental education and undertaking research in environment. Some of the leading institutes are mentioned below:
   a) **G.B. Pant National Institute of Himalayan Environment & Sustainable Development:** The institute was established in 1988, as an autonomous Institute of the Ministry of Environment, Forest and Climate Change (MoEF&CC), Govt. of India at Almora (Uttarakhand).
   b) **The Indian Institute of Forest Management (IIFM):** It is a sectoral management institute, which constantly endeavours to evolve knowledge useful for the managers in the area of Forest, Environment and Natural Resources Management and allied sectors.
   HQ: Bhopal (MP)
   c) **Environment Protection Training and Research Institute (EPTRI):** It was set up in 1992 as an independent registered society by the Andhra Government with assistance from the Government of India.
   HQ: Hyderabad

d) **The Bombay Natural History Society (BNHS), Mumbai:** It was founded on 15 September, 1883. It is one of the largest non-governmental organizations in India engaged in conservation and biodiversity research.

e) **World Wide fund for Nature-India (WWF India), New Delhi:** The WWF India was initiated in 1969 in Mumbai, after which the headquarters were shifted to Delhi with several states' Divisional and Project offices spread across India. In the early years it focused attention on wildlife education and awareness. It runs several programmes, including the nature clubs of India program for school children and works as a think tank and lobby force for environmental and development issues.

f) **Centre for Science and Environment (CSE), New Delhi:** CSE is a public interest research and advocacy organization based in New Delhi. CSE researches into development that is both sustainable and equitable. It has published a major document on the State of India's Environment, the first of its kind to be produced as a citizen's report on the environment. It also publishes a popular magazine called 'Down to Earth' which is a science and environment fortnightly.

g) **C.P.R. Environmental Education Centre, Chennai:** The CPREEC was set up in 1988 (CPREEC) is a Centre of Excellence of the Ministry of Environment and Forests (MoEF), Government of India. It conducts a variety of programs to increase awareness and knowledge of public, i.e., school children, local communities, and women as main key target groups about the various aspects of environment. Its programs include components on wildlife and biodiversity issues.

h) **Bharati Vidyapeeth University, Institute of Environment Education and Research, Pune:** Bharati Vidyapeeth University, Institute of Environment Education and Research, Pune was established in 1994. This is part of the Bharati Vidyapeeth Deemed University. Its major focus is to spread the message of the need for pro-environmental action in society at large through a dual strategy of formal and non-formal integrated activities. BVIEER is a one of a kind institution that caters to the need of Environment Education at all levels (PhD, M.Sc., and Diploma).

i) **The Salim Ali Center for Ornithology and Natural History (SACON):** It is an autonomous organization with headquarters at Coimbatore. It is a national centre for information, education, and research in ornithology and natural history in India.

j) **Wild Life Institute of India (WII), Dehradun:**

Is an autonomous institution of (Ministry of Environment, Forest and Climate Change) MoEFCC, GOI, established in 1982. It is an internationally acclaimed institution, which offers training programmes, academic courses, and advisory in wildlife research and management. The Institute is actively engaged in research across the country on biodiversity related issues.

k) **Kalpavriksh:** This NGO was initially Delhi-based. Now it is working from Pune and is active in several other parts of India. Kalpavriksh worked on a variety of fronts: education and awareness, investigation and research, direct action and lobbying, and litigation with regard to environment and development issues.

Some Vital Facts

1) In 2003, Environment education in India was made compulsory in formal education system througha Supreme Court of India order
2) The purpose of value education is best served by focussing on concern over human values.
3) The aim of value education is to inculcate moral values in students.
4) The aim of vocationalization of education ismaking liberal education job-oriented
5) Value education makes a student good citizen.

Practice Exercise

General Questions Format

1. Which of the following is TRUE about Value Education? It is ....
   a) an effort not only to kindle spirit of morality and ethics in learner's mind; but rather motivate him to keep it alive throughout life.
   b) a message establishing that value education is playing second fiddle in the society with the advent of advanced communication technology.
   c) imparting knowledge about various moral, social, and ethical values through social and mass media to awaken the citizens.
   d) a narrative setting trends in adopting those values of society which have been a source of motivation for various civilizations to achieve pervasiveness in their existence.

   (A) Only b and d (B) a, b, c, and d
   (C) Only a (D) Only b

2. Sakshat is a government of India portal to impart
   (A) Value education
   (B) Environmental education
   (C) Technical education
   (D) Distance education

3. Which of the following truly explain(s) the significance of education? It.......
   a) is conducive in bringing reforms in the society.
   b) becomes a means and reason of various innovations leading to further development of the society.
   c) develops learner's knowledge, personality, and experience.
   d) gives opportunity to the learners to realise their respective goals to survive in the society with knowledge and skill.

   (A) a, b, c, and d
   (B) Only a and c
   (C) Only b
   (D) Only d

4. Under Skill India Programme, government of India has fixed a target of training 40 crore people in different vocational skills by the year
   (A) 2025 (B) 2022
   (C) 2020 (D) 2030

5. The ultimate aim of environmental education is to impart knowledge as to how
   (A) sustainable development can be achieved
   (B) biodiversity can be protected from the impact of unpredictable climate change
   (C) overutilization of non-renewable resources can be curbed
   (D) None of the above

6. Which of the following is/are NOT objective(s) of distance education?
   a) Providing an efficient, less expensive, and accessible process of gaining education
   b) Motivating dropouts of formal education stream to join distance education stream
   c) Providing research opportunities to those scholars who are physically challenged
   d) Providing a suitable path to wider opportunities in education, especially in higher education

   (A) Only a, c, and d
   (B) Only d
   (C) Only a, b, c, and d
   (D) Only b and c

7. Which of the following is/are TRUE?
   a) Tertiary education is imparted to make learners aware about various specialized streams to be joined after higher secondary education.
   b) The oldest open university of India is situated in Bihar.
   c) Vocational training is imparted in India under Directorate General of Training (DGT).
   d) Startup India plan is a joint initiative of MHRD and Department of Science and Technology.

   (A) Only c (B) Only c and d
   (C) Only a, c, and d (D) Only b

8. Name of institutions imparting technical education are given under column I and names of their headquarters are given under Column II. Match the institute with its headquarter and choose the correct code given below:

Column I (Institute)	Column II (Headquarter)
a) Indian Institute of Information Technology and Management (IITM)	i) Bengaluru
b) Indian Institute of Science (IISc)	ii) Gwalior
c) Indian School of Mines (ISM)	iii) Allahabad
d) Indian Institute of Information Technology (IIIT)	iv) Dhanbad
	v) Mumbai

Codes:	(a)	(b)	(c)	(d)
(A)	i	iv	ii	iii
(B)	ii	iii	v	i
(C)	ii	i	iv	iii
(D)	v	iii	ii	i

9. Consider these statements P & Q:

P: The word education has been derived from a German word 'Educare'.

Q: Informal education is imparted through correspondence or satellite.

(A) Both P and Q are true
(B) P is false but Q is true
(C) Both P and Q are false
(D) P is true but Q is false

10. Which of the following is NOT TRUE about 'Startup India' scheme? It is

(A) to promote Technology Business Incubators (TBI)
(B) to establish Startup Business Centers
(C) to be implemented through National Experts Advisory Committee (NEAC)
(D) a joint venture of Ministry of Human Resource Development and Ministry of Skill Development and Entrepreneurship

11. Which of the following is NOT one of the factors which encouraged imparting of technical education?

(A) Unemployment in rural areas resulting in migration of rural labour to urban areas
(B) Modernisation in traditional and non-traditional occupations
(C) Rapid industrialisation
(D) Rapid addition in job seekers due to rapid increase in population

12. Which of the following is the significance of Formal Education?

a) Developing learner's overall knowledge, experience, and personality
b) Promoting teacher-centric methods in the class for beginners for their better learning and grasping
c) Ensuring dyadic communication through healthy and effective interaction in the class
d) Only means of creating awareness about ethics of learning in the class

(A) a, b, c, and d (B) Only a and c
(C) Only d (D) Only a, b, and c

13. Which among the following is the oldest open university?

(A) Indira Gandhi national Open University
(B) Dr. B.R. Ambedkar Open University
(C) Nalanda Open University
(D) Kota Open University

14. Which institute of environmental education is the only institute which caters to the need of environmental education from the level of diploma to Ph. D?

(A) Environment Protection Training and Research Institute (EPTRI)
(B) C.P.R. Environmental Education Centre
(C) The Indian Institute of Forest Management (IIFM)
(D) Bharati Vidyapeeth University, Institute of Environment Education and Research

15. In 2003, Environment Education in India was made compulsory in formal education system through a/an

(A) Supreme court judgement
(B) Constitutional amendment
(C) UNO directive
(D) Initiative by Green Tribunal

KEY

1. C	2. D	3. B	4. B	5. A	6. D	7. B
8. C	9. C	10. D	11. A	12. B	13. B	14. D
15. A						

Assertion–Reason Format

1. **Assertion (A):** Informal education does not categorise a teacher and a student.

   Reason (R): Experience is the measure of one's qualification in informal education.

   (A) Both A and R are true and R is correct explanation of A

   (B) Both A and R are true but R is not correct explanation of A

   (C) A is true but R is false

   (D) A is false but R is true

2. **Assertion (A):** Need to impart technical education becomes more intensive as the society progresses.

   Reason (R): There is rapid increase in urbanisation and industrialisation with passage of time.

   (A) Both A and R are true and R is correct explanation of A

   (B) Both A and R are true but R is not correct explanation of A

   (C) Both A and R are false

   (D) A is true but R is false

3. **Assertion (A):** Value education helps in conserving moral and ethical values in the present day hi-tech society.

   Reason (R): Modernisation proves to be suicidal for education values in the society.

   (A) Both A and R are true and R is correct explanation of A

   (B) Both A and R are true but R is not correct explanation of A

   (C) Both A and R are false

   (D) A is true but R is false

4. **Assertion (A):** Skill-based education is rapidly replacing technical education in India.

   Reason (R): Various initiatives taken by India in skill-based education have muffled the initiatives of higher education.

   (A) Both A and R are true and R is correct explanation of A

   (B) Both A and R are true but R is not correct explanation of A

   (C) Both A and R are false

   (D) A is true but R is false

5. **Assertion (A):** Environmental education helps a society in keeping vigil over environmental pollution.

   Reason (R): Ignorance of environmental issues become a motive behind imparting environmental education.

   (A) Both A and R are false

   (B) Both A and R are true but R is not correct explanation of A

   (C) Both A and R are true and R is correct explanation of A

   (D) A is false but R is true

6. **Assertion (A):** Universalisation of skill-based education is an ambitious project of India.

   Reason (R): Skill India project aims to train 40 crore people in different vocational skills by 2022.

   (A) A is true but R is false

   (B) A is false but R is true

   (C) Both A and R are true but R is not correct explanation of A

   (D) Both A and R are true and R is correct explanation of A

7. **Assertion (A):** Tertiary education is imparted to produce specialised manpower.

   Reason (R): Various sectors of the society contributing in its development need specialised manpower due to which development becomes possible.

   (A) Both A and R are true and R is correct explanation of A

   (B) Both A and R are true but R is not correct explanation of A

   (C) A is true but R is false

   (D) Both A and R are false

8. **Assertion (A):** Technical education is an advanced form of skill-based education.

   Reason (R): Career avenues are more certain in skill-based education than technical education.

(A) Both A and R are false
(B) A is true but R is false
(C) Both A and R are true but R is not correct explanation of A
(D) Both A and R are true and R is correct explanation of A

9. **Assertion (A):** Distance education is more or less a non-conventional form of education.

Reason (R): Non-conventional education can be imparted through classroom teaching.

(A) Both A and R are true and R is correct explanation of A
(B) Both A and R are true but R is not correct explanation of A
(C) Both A and R are false
(D) A is false but R is true

10. **Assertion (A):** Institution of education is not perennial.

Reason (R): Paradigm shift in a society justifies the early abolition of institution of education.

(A) Both A and R are false and R is correct explanation of A
(B) Both A and R are true but R is not correct explanation of A
(C) A is true but R is false
(D) Both A and R are false

KEY

1. B **2.** A **3.** D **4.** C **5.** A **6.** D **7.** A **8.** C **9.** B **10.** D

Questions Asked in Previous NET Exams

1. The purpose of value education is best served by focussing on **(UGC NET JAN 2017)**
(A) Cultural practices prevailing in the society
(B) Norms of conduct laid down by a social group
(C) Concern for human values
(D) Religious and moral practices and instructions

2. The best way for providing value education is through **(UGC NET JULY 2016)**
(A) Discussions on scriptural texts
(B) Lecture/discourses on values
(C) Seminars/symposia on values
(D) Mentoring/reflective sessions on values

3. The aim of value education is to inculcate in students **(UGC NET DECEMBER 2011)**
(A) the moral values
(B) the social values
(C) the political values
(D) the economic values

4. The aim of vocationalisation of education is: **(UGC NET DECEMBER 2007)**
(A) preparing students for a vocation along with knowledge
(B) converting liberal education into vocational education
(C) giving more importance to vocational than general education
(D) making liberal education job-oriented

5. Value education makes a student: **(UGC NET JUNE 2007)**
(A) Good citizen
(B) Successful businessman
(C) Popular teacher
(D) Efficient manager

KEY

1. C **2.** D **3.** A **4.** D **5.** A

5 Policies, Governance and Administration

PART – I

BODIES FOR HIGHER EDUCATION IN INDIA

CONCEPT

Desirable progress in higher education depends upon quality of teaching rendered by highly efficient, professional, and specialised faculty as higher education involves learning and achievement of expertise in various specialised streams. At the same time, growth of higher education is equally dependent on good governance of various higher education bodies. It is the structure and skill of governance of such institutions which takes higher education to the apex and helps these institutions in earning international goodwill. Following account illustrates structure of governance in leading bodies of higher education.

SOME STATUTORY BODIES IN THE FIELD OF HIGHER EDUCATION

University Grants Commission (UGC)

UGC was formed in 1945 to supervise the work of three central universities of Aligarh, Banaras, and Delhi. The UGC was established on the recommendation of University Education Commission (1948-49), which was set up under the chairmanship of Dr. S. Radhakrishnan. The commission was to report on Indian university education and suggest improvements and extensions. UGC was thus first established in 1953 to cover all central and other universities in terms of allocating grants-in-aid. It was inaugurated by Maulana Abul Kalam Azad, the then Union Minister of Education, Natural Resources and Scientific Research and then ultimately it was established in 1956 as a statutory body under an Act of Parliament. UGC was entrusted with the job of maintaining a particular standard of university education while determining that standard. Organisational structure of UGC consists of a Chairman, a Vice-Chairman, and other official staff.

UGC operates through its regional centres at Bengaluru, Pune, Bhopal, Kolkata, Guwahati, and Hyderabad. UGC is carrying the twin responsibilities of granting aids to universities and maintaining standards of university education through coordination, planning, and application. UGC is regulating distance higher education through Distance Education Bureau (formerly Distance Education Councils). In order to make justice with its responsibilities, UGC performs the following functions:

1) Maintaining standard of university education by promoting and coordinating university education
2) Determining and ensuring standard teaching, evaluation, and research in universities
3) Monitoring the standard of education in universities and colleges
4) Advising government in formulating and implementing policies of higher education
5) Establishing equation between central and state governments on one hand and institutions of higher education on the other hand HQ: New Delhi

***Faculty Recharge Programme:** It has been noticed by the Government of India that there has been steep decline in research environment in Indian Universities and stagnation of faculty and infrastructure. The Government of India, through the University Grants Commission, has decided to launch a new Programme called "UGC Faculty Recharge Programme" to redress this situation. This is a pressing requirement since majority of our Universities, especially State Universities, have not recruited faculty on a significant scale for a long time and are in danger of losing more than a generation of researchers. Under this scheme, new recruitments of faculty will be made.*

National Assessment and Accreditation Council (NAAC)

It was recommended in the National Policy on Education (1986) and Programme of Action (POA) 1992 that there should be an autonomous body to grade standard of higher education in universities and colleges. NAAC was established in 1994 as an autonomous body. It is governed though a General Council (GC) and an

Executive council (EC). Eminent and seasoned academicians, policy makers, and administrators in the education field are members of these councils. UGC grants fund and other facilities to a university or college on the basis of accreditation marked by NAAC. NAAC evaluates the institutions for its conformance to the standards of quality in terms of its performance related to the educational processes and outcomes, curriculum coverage, teaching-learning processes, faculty, research, infrastructure, learning resources, organisation, governance, financial well-being, and student services. NAAC's accreditation helps different higher education institutes to improve upon shortcomings in imparting higher education. Headquarters of NAAC is in Bengaluru.

NAAC Mission

- To arrange for periodic assessment and accreditation of institutions of higher education or units thereof, or specific academic programmes or projects
- To stimulate the academic environment for promotion of quality of teaching-learning and research in higher education institutions
- To encourage self-evaluation, accountability, autonomy, and innovations in higher education
- To undertake quality-related research studies, consultancy, and training programmes
- To collaborate with other stakeholders of higher education for quality evaluation, promotion, and sustenance

Promotion of Core Values

NAAC undertakes to promote the following core values among the institutes of higher education of the country:

- Contributing to National Development
- Fostering Global Competencies among Students
- Inculcating a Value System among Students
- Promoting the Use of Technology
- Quest for Excellence

The Indian Council of Agricultural Research (ICAR)

Established in 1929, ICAR is an autonomous body under Department of Agricultural Research and Education (DARE). Responsible for proliferation of agricultural education, it grants opportunities to scientists to undertake research in Agricultural Engineering, Crop Science, Fisheries, Animal Sciences, Natural Resource Management, and Horticulture. Union Minister of Agriculture is its President. Its headquarters is at New Delhi.

Indian Council of Philosophical Research (ICPR)

The council was started as in 1981 to regulate research in Philosophy. It also provides funds for various research projects in Philosophy.

HQ: New Delhi

Indian Council of Social Science Research (ICSSR)

In order to promote and regulate research in social sciences, ICSSR was established in 1969.

HQ: New Delhi

The All India Council for Technical Education (AICTE)

Though set up in 1945, AICTE was granted status of a statutory body and established in 1987 through an Act of Parliament. Its main functions included planning, managing, and promoting technical education in India conducive in national development. As an apex level advisory body, it conducts surveys on facilities available in technical and education field. The body also implements government policy for development of technical education. Architecture, town planning, management, applied art and craft, engineering and technology, pharmacy, information technology, hotel management, and catering technology are covered under technical education. AICTE is governed by a Chairman, Vice-Chairman, and Member-Secretary. Its headquarters is in New Delhi.

National Board of Accreditation (NBA)

NBA was established by the AICTE in the year 1994, in order to assess the qualitative competence of the programmes offered by educational institutions from diploma level to post-graduate level in engineering and technology, management, pharmacy, architecture, and related disciplines, which are approved by AICTE.

Indian Council of Historical Research (ICHR)

ICHR offers fellowships to young scientists to undertake research in different areas of history. It was established in 1972 under Societies Registration Act. The council is governed by a chairman and 18 members. Chairman and members are selected among eminent historians. Its regional centres are working at Bengaluru and Guwahati.

HQ: New Delhi

The National Council For Teacher Education (NCTE)

This is another statutory body created by Government of India by an act of Parliament in 1995 in compliance to the proposals given in National Policy on Education, 1986 and Programme of Action (POA) 1992. The body is to improve and maintain the standards of teacher education. Its headquarters is in Delhi and it is governed by Chairperson, Vice-Chairperson, and Member Secretary.

HQ: New Delhi

The Distance Education Council (DEC)

Established in 1985, DEC is an apex body for the Open and Distance Learning (ODL) system in the country. The Council was constituted under the Indira Gandhi National Open University Act (1985), to act as an apex body for the ODL system. It is responsible for promotion, coordination, and maintenance of standards of the ODL system. The Vice Chancellor of IGNOU is the exofficio Chairperson of DEC. In June 2013, University Grants Commission has taken over DEC, by establishing Distance Education Bureau which will govern the distance education programmes in India. HQ: New Delhi

National Council of Rural Institutes (NCRI)

In order to regulate and promote rural higher education on the vision of Mahatma Gandhi, the Central Government established NCRI in 1995. While complying with the provisions and recommendation in National Policy of Education (NPE) 1986, the council is preparing curriculum for various courses in rural theoretical and practical higher education to be rendered by different universities and institutions.

HQ: Hyderabad

LEADING INSTITUTES IN THE FIELD OF HIGHER EDUCATION

Indian Institute of Advanced Study (IIAS)

IIAS is a residential centre for undertaking advance research in Humanities, Indian Culture, Religion, and Social and Natural Sciences. It was established in 1964 at Shimla (HP) by Ministry of Education, Government of India. A Governing Body administers the institute.

HQ: Shimla

The Indira Gandhi National Open University (IGNOU)

IGNOU was established in 1985 through an Act of Parliament. IGNOU is imparting higher education through distant means. Its mandate includes:

1) Promoting standard of open education
2) Proliferating education not only throughout the country but abroad also under the mission of Universalisation of Education
3) Ensuring education access to every section of the society
4) Approaching those education seekers who are economically poor and impart education at affordable cost
5) Maintaining high quality and latest technology in rendering education

HQ: New Delhi

Indian Institutes of Technology (IIT)

IITs are rendering higher education in different fields of engineering. For example, IITs are situated in Jodhpur (Rajasthan), Patna (Bihar), Bhubaneswar (Odisha), Mandi (HP), Indore (MP), Palakkad (Kerala), Tirupati (Andhra Pradesh), Bhilai (Chhattisgarh), Kharagpur (West Bengal), Ropar (Punjab), Banaras Hindu University (U.P), Roorkee (Uttarakhand), Guwahai (Assam), Kanpur (UP), Chennai (Tamil Nadu), Delhi, Mumbai (Maharashtra), Hyderabad (Telengana), and Goa. An IIT council governs all IITs with Union HRD Minister as its Chairman. However, at a particular, IIT level a Board of Governors administers the routine work of an IIT.

The National University of Educational Planning and Administration (NUEPA)

NUEPA is a deemed to be university established by the Ministry of Human Resource Development. Its earlier name was National Institute of Educational Planning and Administration. Its establishment is associated with the UNESCO's regional centre for Educational Planners and Administration started in 1960-61 for taking care of educational needs of South Asia. The organisation was renamed as Asian Institute of Educational Planning and Administration in 1965. Government of India took over this institute from UNESCO in 1970. The institute was named as National Staff College for Educational Planners and Administration. The institute was restructured with its present name in 1979.

The NUEPA as an autonomous organisation emphasises on planning, management, and capacity-building in educational policy, through research, training, consultancy, and dissemination. It offers part-time and full-time Ph. D. The NUEPA structure is based on nine academic and one administrative unit. Union MHRD Minister is Chairman (Chancellor) of the university. University has a Vice-Chancellor, a Board, and a Registrar as far as its organisational structure is concerned.

HQ: New Delhi

All India Institute of Medical Sciences (AIIMS)

AIIMS was established as an autonomous body through an Act of Parliament in 1956. It was established on the recommendations of Bhore Committee with the help of financial assistance from New Zealand. It imparts undergraduate and postgraduate level medical education. The Act, under which AIIMS has been established, authorises it to award its own degrees. AIIMS imparts training to teachers to teach in various medical colleges. At higher level, research in medical and paramedical field is also undertaken at AIIMS. Main thrust of AIIMS is to achieve self-sufficiency in medical education in the best interest of the nation. AIIMS has New Delhi as its headquarter.

Indian Institute of Information Technology Design and Manufacturing Kurnool (IIITDM Kurnool, Andhra Pradesh)

It was established in 2015 to regulate, promote education in information technology, engineering and design, and manufacturing relating engineering.

Indian Institute of Science (IISc)

Established in 1909, IISc is imparting higher education and research in science, management, designing, and engineering. It is located at Bengaluru (Karnataka). Besides being a deemed to be university, it enjoys the status of Small University and has been included among the top 10 small universities in the world by England based Times Higher Education Supplement (THES).

Indira Gandhi National Tribal University (IGNTU)

The university was established at Amarkantak (Madhya Pradesh) to impart standard higher education to tribal population of the country.

Indian Institutes of Management (IIMs)

An IIM is registered under Societies Registration Act. It is an autonomous body. IIMs are governed by IIM council which is headed by Union HRD Minister. IIMs offer postgraduate and doctoral courses in management. IIMs are situated in Amritsar (Punjab), Jammu (J & K), Rohtak (Haryana), Sirmaur (HP), Kashipur (Uttarakhand), Lucknow (U.P.), Udaipur (Rajasthan), Ahmedabad (Gujarat), Gaya (Bihar), Indore (M.P.), Raipur (Chhattisgarh), Nagpur (Maharashtra), Shillong (Meghalaya), Ranchi (Jharkhand), Kolkata (W. Bengal), Sambalpur (Odisha), Visakhapatnam (Andhra Pradesh), Bengaluru (Karnataka), Kozhikode (Kerala), and Tiruchirapalli (Tamil Nadu).

UNIVERSITIES IN INDIA

Universities in India are playing a vital role in providing and spreading higher education across the nation. There are different categories of universities in India, viz. Central Universities, State Universities, Deemed Universities, Private Universities, Agriculture Universities, Technical Universities, and Medical Universities.

Central Universities in India

A Central University is established by the Central Government through an Act of Parliament. While establishing a Central University, Government of India justifies the task of making way for providing and spreading higher education to meet the state of universalisation of higher education. Organisational structure of a Central University consists of the President of India, who acts as a Visitor. He is empowered to send members in the Executive Committee, Senate, Selection Committee, and other bodies organised to perform the smooth functioning of a university.

Central Universities in India

1. Aligarh Muslim University, Aligarh
2. Assam University, Silchar
3. Babasaheb Bhimrao Ambedkar University, Lucknow
4. Banaras Hindu University, Varanasi
5. Central Agricultural University, Imphal
6. Central University of Gujarat, Gandhinagar
7. Central University of Haryana, Mahendragarh
8. Central University of Himachal Pradesh, Kangra
9. Central University of Jammu, Samba, Jammu
10. Central University of Jharkhand, Ranchi
11. Central University of Karnataka, Gulbarga
12. Central University of Kashmir, Srinagar
13. Central University of Kerala, Kasaragod
14. Central University of Orissa, Koraput
15. Central University of Punjab, Bathinda
16. Central University of Rajasthan, Ajmer
17. Central University of South Bihar, Patna
18. Central university of Tamil Nadu, Tiruvarur
19. Dr. Harisingh Gour Vishwavidyalaya, Sagar, MP
20. English & Foreign Languages University, Hyderabad
21. Guru Ghasidas Vishwavidyalaya, Bilaspur
22. Hemwati Nandan Bahuguna Garhwal University, Uttarakhand
23. Indian Maritime University, Chennai
24. Indira Gandhi National Open University, New Delhi

25. Jamia Millia Islamia, New Delhi
26. Jawaharlal Nehru University, New Delhi
27. Mahatma Gandhi Antarrashtriya Hindi Vishwavidyalaya, Wardha
28. Mahatma Gandhi Central University, North of Ganga, Bihar
29. Manipur University, Imphal
30. Maulana Azad National Urdu University, Hyderabad
31. Mizoram University, Aizwal
32. Nagaland University, Zunheboto
33. Nalanda University, Rajgir, Bihar
34. North Eastern Hill University, Shillong
35. Pondicherry University, Puducherry
36. Rajiv Gandhi National Aviation University, Amethi, UP
37. Rajiv Gandhi University, Itanagar
38. Sikkim University, Gangtok
39. South Asian University, New Delhi
40. Tezpur University, Tezpur
41. The Indira Gandhi National Tribal University, Anuppur
42. Tripura University, Tripura
43. University of Allahabad, Allahabad
44. University of Delhi, Delhi
45. University of Hyderabad, Hyderabad
46. Visva Bharati, Shantiniketan, West Bengal
47. Delhi University, New Delhi

State Universities in India

A State University is formed by the state government under the State Legislature Act. Its organisational structure is the same as in other universities.

Deemed Universities in India

Central government declares certain educational institutes as deemed universities on the recommendation of the UGC. Only that institute is recommended for being deemed university which fulfils the standard norms fixed by UGC. Such a university is established under Section(3) of the University Grants Commission Act, 1956. Deemed universities are allowed to design syllabus, their own course plans, and take their own decision regarding admission and fees. Some deemed universities are also allowed to award degrees under their own name. UGC provide financial assistance to some of them. If a deemed university continues to perform well and fulfils the UGC norms and statutes, it attains the status of a full-fledged university.

Private University

Private universities are also UGC-approved institutes. However, such universities do not run on central or state funds. They can grant degrees but cannot have off-campus colleges or affiliate an institution/college. "They can establish off-campus centre(s) within the concerned State after their existence of five years and with the prior approval of the University Grants Commission," states the UGC website. Unlike state and central universities which have a 'Chancellor' as the head, a private university is always headed by 'President' or 'Chairperson'. A private university is formed by the UGC. It is not allowed to have affiliated colleges.

Unitary Universities in India

A unitary university is a single campus university. Such a university can open its own college or colleges which are known as university colleges. Single campus universities are mainly providing postgraduate courses and research.

Affiliating Universities in India

An affiliating university has departments of different subjects in its campus. Such a university may have a college or colleges in its campus. An affiliating university has various colleges affiliated to it falling in its jurisdiction. Such universities offer undergraduate as well as postgraduate courses and research.

Subject Universities in India

A lot of subject universities have been established in India in order to pave way for high esteem research opportunities in a particular subject. Agricultural universities, medical universities, technical universities, and veterinary universities are a few examples of this type. These universities indulge in research to meet the specialisation parameters of national and international level.

Open Universities in India

Such universities have been established in India to facilitate access to education for those students who cannot join formal education stream in a university campus or colleges, due to various limitations. An open university is the channel to impart online education.

AIU (Association of Indian Universities)

Association of Indian Universities was formed in 1925 with an idea of bringing together all the universities on a common platform emerged from the deliberations of a Conference of the Vice Chancellors of Universities convened by Lord Reading, the then Viceroy of India at Shimla. It is an organisation and association of major universities that is based in Delhi that evaluates the courses, syllabi, standards, and credits of foreign Universities pursued abroad and equates them in relation to various courses offered by Indian Universities. The AIU is mainly concerned with the recognition of Degrees/Diplomas awarded by the Universities in India, which are recognised by the University Grants Commission, New Delhi, and abroad for the purpose of admission to higher degree courses in Indian Universities. It is also a registered society under the Societies Registration Act, 1860 with the membership of Indian Universities. It acts as a bureau of information exchange in higher education and brings out a number of useful publications, including the Universities Handbook, research papers, and a weekly journal titled University News. It is also empowered to grant Associate Membership to universities of the neighbouring countries of India.

1) ***Single Mode University:*** *Single mode university is that university which imparts education to distant students only through distance education means. All open universities are single mode universities.*

   Single Mode Universities in India: *All open universities in India are Single Mode Universities.*

2) ***Dual mode University:*** *A Dual mode university imparts classroom education as well as distance education.*

   Dual Mode Universities in India: *All universities using both modes in imparting education are dual mode universities in India.*

3) ***Mixed Mode University:*** *A mixed mode university imparts education through regular campus programmes, distance education through traditional methods like printed material and contact classes, and then education through the increasingly popular technology-based online degree.*

4) ***Meta University:*** *The main purpose of the Meta University is to share learning E-sources with different Universities by using the latest technologies available in order to enable the students to benefit from the learning resources available in different institutions. The University Grants Commission (UGC) is the apex regulatory body. So Meta University concept marks paradigm shift in Higher Education in India. It is based on premise that 'Whole is Greater than Sum of Parts'. This concept allows students to move between various universities.*

Specialised Universities in India

1) National Sports University, Imphal (Manipur)
2) Indian National Defence University, Gurugram (Haryana)
3) National Rail and Transportation Institute (Deemed University), Vadodara (Gujarat)
4) S.N.D.T Women's University, Mumbai (Maharashtra)
5) National Law University, Delhi
6) M.C. National University of Journalism & Communication, Bhopal (MP)

Foreign Language Universities in India

1) Jawaharlal Nehru University (New Delhi) - Spanish, French, Russian, and Chinese.
2) Delhi University (Delhi) - French, German, and Spanish
3) English and Foreign Language University (Hyderabad) - Japanese, Russian, Persian, Turkish, and Korean.
4) Banaras Hindu University - Chinese, Japanese, and Russian
5) Jamia Milia Islamia University (Delhi) - Russian, Spanish, and Portuguese
6) University of Calcutta - Chinese, Japanese, German, Persian, etc. Only Russian is the subject which is taught from the start.
7) IGNOU (New Delhi) - Arabic and French
8) Pune University - French, German, Russian
9) University of Mumbai - French and German
10) Visva Bharati University, Shantiniketan (WB) - French, Arabic, Roman, German

GOVERNANCE OF UNIVERSITIES IN INDIA

A university generally has following pattern of governance:

The Visitor: In case of central university, the President of India is the visitor. Governor of a particular state represents visitor of a state university.

The Chancellor: Chancellor of a university is the governor of the state in which a university falls. The Governor of a state is the chancellor of a central university also which falls in that particular state. Vice-President of India is the Chancellor of Delhi universities. In some universities distinguished academicians or scientists are appointed as Chancellors by the Visitor (The President of India). Visva Bharti (Shantiniketan, West Bengal) is the only central university, where Prime Minister is the Chancellor. A chancellor is the head of administrative and academic affairs of a university.

The Vice-Chancellor: Vice-Chancellor of a university is in-campus head of the academic and administrative affairs of the university including affiliated colleges. Vice Chancellor is the CEO of academic and administrative affairs of a university. Vice-Chancellor is appointed by the President of India (Governor of the state). A name of the incumbent is chosen from among the panel of three, sent by the concerned state government to the chancellor of the concerned university. Vice-Chancellor is the head of various bodies functioning in the university, viz. Academic Council, senate, Syndicate, or any other body functioning in the University.

Pro Vice-Chancellor: Pro-Vice Chancellor enjoys the powers of Vice-Chancellor in his absence due to any reason. He is appointed by the Chancellor after consulting Vice-Chancellor of the concerned university. He functions on behalf of the Vice-Chancellor.

Dean: A full-time teacher of the university is appointed as dean by the Vice-Chancellor. A dean is to work at micro-level of different academic and administrative affairs. There can be Dean Academic Affairs, Dean Sports, Dean Faculty, Dean Colleges, etc.

Registrar: Registrar of a university is a full-time officer to deal with the day to day affairs of a university. He is appointed by the state government from acclaimed civil servants, Assistant or Deputy Registrars, teachers, or academicians. He is the custodian of records of the university. He is ex-officio member-secretary of various bodies in the university. He also convenes the meetings of various bodies. He is also responsible to make various correspondences with various departments, bodies, and personnel regarding issues of the concerned university. He is to exercise all powers vested to him as per the university statute.

The Court or the Senate: With about 100 members among registered graduates, heads of departments, college Principals, representatives of industries, Senate is a routine policy-making body. It regulates teaching and research in a university. It also approves awarding of degrees and it also maintains standards of university awards. Chancellor and Vice-Chancellor are its ex-officio members.

The Executive Council or the Syndicate: Syndicate is the body which has control on finance and administration. it can sign or break contracts on behalf of university. It also recommends affiliation of a college with the university. It is also responsible for maintaining law and order in university. It has about 20 members among representatives of colleges, deans, Vice-Chancellor as its Chairman and Pro Vice-Chancellor as members.

The Academic Council: As the name indicates, this is the body which forms norms regarding declaration of results and making proposals to enact statutes on various academic issues. It acts as an advisor to university on academic issues like course design, introduction of new courses, etc. The body consists of Vice-Chairman as its Chairman. Other members include Principal of the colleges and Heads of Departments.

Central Advisory Board of Education (CABE)

CABE is the oldest advisory body to government on education planning and implementation. It was established in 1920. The board passed through different reconstitution phases in 1935, 1990, and 2004. Union Human Resource Development Minister is the Chairman, Union Human Resources Development Minister of State is the Vice-Chairman, and Ministers of Education from different states are its members. In its report in June 2005, the board advocated autonomy for institutions of higher education.

Commonwealth of Learning (COL)

Commonwealth countries created this body to develop and share open learning at international level. Established in 1988, its headquarter is in Canada. The body is funded by Commonwealth countries with India ranking third in terms of providing funds, after UK and Canada.

Some Vital Facts

1) The premier organisation established in India to deal with capacity building and research in planning and management of education in India and South Asia is NUEPA.
2) The modern Indian university was established in 1857
3) The main aim of the faculty recharge scheme of UGC was to Address the shortage of faculty in higher education institution.
4) The University Grants Commission (UGC) was formally inaugurated on 28 December 1953 by Sh. MaulanaAbulKalam Azad.
5) India's first National Rail and Transportation University is situated in Gujarat.
6) NUEPA deals with "capacity building programme" on Educational Planning.
7) The President has the power to nominate some members to the Executive Committee or the Board of Management of a central university. University.
8) Distance Education Council (DEC) was established in 2013.

9) National Assessment and Accreditation Council is an autonomous institution and It is tasked with the responsibility of assessing and accrediting institutions of higher.
10) Union Public Service Communication (UPSC) is a Constitutional body.
11) There are 4 regional Offices of National Council of Teacher Education.
12) There are 7 regional Offices of University Grants Commission of India.
13) Universities in India are funded by the UGC.
14) IGNOU telecasts interaction educational programmes through its own channel.
15) University Grants Commission (UGC) and National Council of Teachers' Education (NCTE) have signed an MOU for Accreditation of Teacher Education Institutions in India
16) The Kothari Commission's report was entitled as 'Education and National Development.'
17) An open university is a single mode university.
18) According to Radhakrishnan Commission, the aim of Higher Education is to develop the democratic values, peace and harmony and great personalities who can give their contributions in politics, administration, industry and commerce
19) NAAC is an autonomous institution under the aegis of UGC
20) The University Grants Commission was constituted on the recommendation of Dr. Sarvpalli Radhakrishnan Commission

PART – II

HIGHER EDUCATION: MISCELLANEOUS FACTS

HIGHER EDUCATION

Higher education is that education which is imparted after Secondary education though formal and non-formal means. Such an education is imparted either by a university or an education body enjoying the status of a university. The National Policy on Education (1986) characterises higher education as a 'crucial factor for survival' providing the Indian people with "an opportunity to reflect on the critical, social, economical, cultural, moral, and spiritual issues". It also states that goals of higher education in India are Access, Equity, Quality and Excellence, Relevance, Value Based Education, and Compulsory and Free Education.

Structure of Higher Education

In the Indian system, higher education includes the education imparted after 10+2 stage-ten years of primary and secondary education followed by two years of higher secondary education. The first degree, the Bachelor's degree, is obtained after three years study in case of liberal arts, and four years in the case of most professional degrees (four and half in case of medicine and five/six in case of law). The Master's programme is usually of two years duration. The research degrees (M. Phil and Ph. D.) take variable time depending upon the individual student.

General Status of Higher Education in India

The Department of Higher Education, MHRD, is responsible for the overall development of the basic infrastructure of Higher Education sector, both in terms of policy and planning. Under a planned development process, the Department looks after expansion of access and qualitative improvement in the Higher Education, through world class Universities, Colleges, and other Institutions. India's higher education system today is the ***third largest in the world***, after the United States and China. The main governing body at the tertiary level is the University Grants Commission, which enforces its standards, advises the government, and helps coordinate between the centre and the state. Accreditation for higher learning is overseen by 15 autonomous institutions established by the University Grants Commission.

CURRENT STATUS OF HIGHER EDUCATION IN INDIA

Current status of higher education in India is evident from the latest All India Survey on Higher Education (AISHE) 2018-19 released by the HRD Ministry.

All India Survey on Higher Education (AISHE) 2018-19

To portray the status of higher education in the country, Ministry of Human Resource Development has been conducting an annual web-based All India Survey on Higher Education (AISHE) since 2010-11. The survey covers all the Institutions in the country engaged in imparting of higher education. Following are the key findings of AISHE 2018-19:

1) There are 993 Universities, 39931 Colleges and 10725 Standalone Institutions.
2) 298 Universities are affiliating, i.e., having Colleges.
3) 385 Universities are privately managed. 394 Universities are located in rural areas.
4) 16 Universities are exclusively for women, 3 in Rajasthan, 2 in Tamil Nadu, and 1 each in Andhra Pradesh, Assam, Bihar, Delhi, Haryana, Himachal Pradesh, Karnataka, Maharashtra, Odisha, Uttarakhand, and West Bengal.

5) There are 548 General, 142 Technical, 63 Agriculture and Allied, 58 Medical, 23 Law, 13 Sanskrit, and 9 Language Universities
6) The top 8 States in terms of highest number of colleges in India are Uttar Pradesh, Maharashtra, Karnataka, Rajasthan, Haryana, Tamil Nadu, Gujarat, and Madhya Pradesh.
7) Total enrolment in higher education has been estimated to be 37.4 million with 19.2 million males and 18.2 million females. Female constitute 48.6% of the total enrolment.
8) Gross Enrolment Ratio (GER) in Higher education in India is 26.3%, which is calculated for 18-23 years of age group. GER for male population is 26.3% and for females, it is 26.4%.
9) Uttar Pradesh comes at number one with the highest student enrolment followed by Maharashtra and Tamil Nadu.
10) The total number of foreign students enrolled in higher education is 47,427. Highest share of foreign students come from the neighbouring countries of which Nepal is at the top.
11) At Ph.D. level, maximum numbers of students out-turn is in Science stream followed by Engineering and Technology. On the other hand, at PG level, maximum students out-turn is observed in Social Science and Management stream comes at number two.
12) Share of female students is lowest in Institutions of National Importance followed by State Private Open Universities, Deemed Universities-Government.

HIGHER EDUCATION

NATIONAL EDUCATION POLICY – 2020

Introduction:

Education is a progressive and dynamic phase in human life and a society. A society cannot develop without making suitable policies for imparting and reforming education. Development of all sectors of a country is sustained on development in education and its system. Further diversification of education eradicates various socio-economic evils. A nation always needs continuous and comprehensive review of education system and sound periodic education policies to make education a synonym of overall development. Post-independent India also realised reforming impact of implementing education policy and thus came up with three education policies in primary, secondary and higher education level. Prior to National Education Policy (NEP) 2020, earlier national education policies had been NEP 1968 and NEP 1986 and Programme of Action (POA) 1992

National Education Policy (NEP) 1968:

NEP 1968 was drafted on the recommendation of Education Commission (1964-66) under the chairmanship of Dr. D. S. Kothari, the then chairman of the UGC. It was approved by the Parliament in July 1968. It introduced 10+2+3 pattern.

National Education Policy (NEP) 1986:

NEP 1986 was adopted by the Parliament in May 1986. The policy called for "special emphasis on the removal of disparities and to equalise educational opportunity," especially for Indian women, Scheduled Tribes (ST) and the Scheduled Caste (SC) communities i.e. access and equity.

Programme of Action 1992:

POA 1992 covered under NEP 1986 aimed at conducting a common entrance exam on all India basis for admission to professional and technical programmes in the country.

National Education Policy (NEP) 2020 :

Draft: Union HRD Ministry constituted a committee in June 2017, under the chairmanship of Dr. Kasturirangan to prepare a draft of new education policy. The Committee submitted its report on May 31, 2019. The report proposes an education policy, which seeks to address the challenges of: (i) access, (ii) equity, (iii) quality, (iv) affordability, and (v) accountability faced by the current education system.

Approval: NEP 2020 was approved by the Parliament on 29th July, 2020. It is the first education policy of 21st century.

Aims:

1) To increase state expenditure on education from around 4% to 6% of the GDP
2) Transforming Indian education system by 2040.
3) Revising and revamping of all aspects of the education structure, including its regulation and governance
4) Creating a new system that is aligned with the aspirational goals of 21st century education, including Sustainable Development Goal (SDG) – 4
5) Building upon India's traditions and value systems.
6) Development of the creative potential of each individual, the 'foundational capacities 'of literacy and numeracy and 'higher-order' cognitive capacities along with social, ethical, and emotional capacities and dispositions.
7) Providing all students, irrespective of their place of residence, a quality education system, with particular focus on historically marginalized, disadvantaged, and underrepresented groups

8) Empowering teachers and help them to do their job as effectively as possible and ensuring livelihood, respect, dignity, and autonomy.

Doctrine of the Policy:

1) Promoting each student's holistic development in both academic and non-academic spheres.
2) Giving the highest priority to achieving Foundational Literacy and Numeracy by all students by Grade 3.
3) No customary separations between arts and sciences, between curricular and extra-curricular activities, between vocational and academic streams so that students may choose any combination of subjects according to their talent and choice.
4) Ensuring multidisciplinary and a holistic education across the sciences, social sciences, arts, humanities, and sports.
5) Emphasis on conceptual understanding rather than rote learning.
6) Developing ethics, values and scientific temper in the mind of students.
7) Focus on regular formative assessment for learning rather than the summative assessment that encourages today's 'coaching culture.
8) Promoting multilingualism and the power of language in teaching and learning.
9) Taking teachers and faculty as the heart of the learning process – their recruitment, continuous professional development, positive working environments and service conditions.
10) Extensive use of technology in teaching and learning, removing language barriers, increasing access for special students and educational planning and management.
11) Full equity and inclusion as the cornerstone of all educational decisions to ensure that all students are able to survive and progress in the education system.
12) Implementing a 'light but tight' regulatory framework to ensure integrity, transparency, and resource efficiency of the educational system through audit and public disclosure.
13) Changing the name of Ministry of Human Resources Development (MHRD) to Ministry of Education.
14) Lok Vidya', i.e., important vocational knowledge developed in India, will be made accessible to students. The education ministry, would constitute a National Committee for the Integration of Vocational Education (NCIVE)

HOLISTIC EDUCATION

Holistic education is based on the premise that each person finds identity, meaning, and purpose in life through connections to the community, to the natural world, and to spiritual values such as compassion and peace. Holistic education aims to call forth from people who have love for life and a passionate love of learning.

Provisions of this Policy

School Education:

This policy provides to dismantling the present 10+2 structure in school education and replace it with a new pedagogical and curricular restructuring of 5+3+3+4 covering ages 3-18 as shown by following table:

Sr. No.	Level	Age	Class	Type
1	4	14 - 18	9 - 12	Secondary
2	3	11-14	6 - 8	Middle
3	3	8 - 11	3 – 5	Preparatory
4	5	3 - 8	Pre-school to 2	Foundational

Currently, children in the age group of 3-6 are not covered in the 10+2 structure as Class 1 begins at age 6. In the new 5+3+3+4 structure, a strong base of Early Childhood Care and Education (ECCE) from age 3 is also included, which is aimed at promoting better overall learning, development, and well-being.

Other Provisions:

1) A National Curricular and Pedagogical Framework for Early Childhood Care and Education (NCPFECCE) for children up to the age of 8 will be developed by NCERT.
2) Ensuring universal access to high-quality Early Childhood Care and Education (ECCE) across the country.
3) Attaining foundational literacy and numeracy for all children and to achieve universal foundational literacy and numeracy in primary schools by 2025.
4) Achieving 3 R's (Reading, Writing and Arithmetic) at foundation level.
5) National Mission on Foundational Literacy and Numeracy will be set up by the Union Ministry of Education.
6) Digital Infrastructure for Knowledge Sharing (DIKSHA) will provide high quality resources for fundamental literacy and numeracy.
7) Digital libraries will also be established and school libraries will be set up in villages

8) Through initiatives such as the Sarva Shiksha Abhiyan (now the Samagra Shiksha) and the Right to Education Act, gross enrolment ratio (GER) will be increased in schools.

9) Experiential learning will be implemented like hands-on learning, arts-integrated and sports-integrated education and story-telling-based pedagogy.

10) In secondary schools students will be given increased flexibility and choice of subjects to study - including subjects in physical education, the arts and crafts, and vocational skills.

11) A National Assessment Centre, PARAKH (Performance Assessment, Review, and Analysis of Knowledge for Holistic Development) will be set up, as a standard-setting body under Ministry of Education that fulfils the basic objectives of setting norms, standards, and guidelines for student assessment and evaluation for all recognized school boards of India.

12) A new and comprehensive National Curriculum Framework for Teacher Education(NCFTE) 2021, will be formulated for streamlining learner-centred curriculum

13) By 2030, the minimum degree qualification for teaching in schools will be a 4-year integrated B.Ed. degree.

14) An autonomous body, the National Educational Technology Forum (NETF), will be created to provide a platform for the free exchange of ideas on the use of technology to enhance learning, assessment, planning, administration.

HIGHER EDUCATION

NEP 2020 looks for revising the whole higher education system to rejuvenate it in order to impart quality higher education.

Motto: "Equity and inclusion."

Provisions:

1) **Establishing Multidisciplinary Higher Education Institutions (HEIs):** The pivotal emphasis of the policy is to discard the present set up of HEIs and create multidisciplinary universities and college, each of which will have more than 3000 or more students. There will a multidisciplinary university or college in each district or near it by 2030. There will be no more nomenclature of unitary, deemed, single mode or dual mode universities. All the universities will be converted into multidisciplinary universities and this is the highest priority of this policy. Such HEIs will have subjects of all the streams, even of specialist universities and will be research oriented. These will offer undergraduate and graduate programmes, with high quality teaching, research, and community engagement. Stand-alone agricultural universities, legal universities, health science universities, technical universities, and stand-alone institutions in other fields, shall aim to become multidisciplinary institutions offering holistic and multidisciplinary education. All institutions offering either professional or general education will aim to organically evolve into such institutions in an integrated manner by 2030. Technical education will, thus, also aim to be offered within multidisciplinary education institutions and programmes and have a renewed focus on opportunities to engage deeply with other disciplines.

2) **Graded Autonomy to Colleges:** Colleges will be graded according to accreditation and will be granted financial and administrative autonomy accordingly, which will be called graded autonomy and will be ultimately converted into multidisciplinary institution.

3) **Phasing out College Affiliation System:** College affiliation system will be phased out in 15 years. It will be phased out through a system of graded autonomy. Each affiliating university will be monitoring the working of its affiliated colleges so that they can develop their capabilities and achieve minimum yardsticks in academic and curricular matters.

4) **Colleges to Grant Degrees:** The policy proposes that in a due course of time, every college will be developed into either an autonomous degree-granting College, or constituent college of a university - in the latter case, it would be fully a part of the university. With appropriate accreditations, autonomous degree-granting Colleges could convert into Research-intensive or Teaching-intensive Universities, if they so aspire.

5) **Raising Gross Enrolment Ratio:** Poor Gross Enrolment Ratio (GER) in higher education stream is a serious matter of concern. The policy envisages raising GER in higher education from the present 26.3% to 50% by 2035.

6) **Holistic Undergraduate Education:** Holistic undergraduate education will be imparted with flexible curriculum of 3 or 4 years with multiple exit options. There will be a provision of awarding certificate/diploma/degree on abandoning the

studies by a student after 1st year, 2nd year and third year respectively.

7) **Discontinuing M.Phil.** M. Phil. Programme will be discontinued and all undergraduate, postgraduate and Ph.D. level programmes will be interdisciplinary.

8) **Academic Bank of Credits**: An Academic Bank of Credits will be established to facilitate storing of Credits under Choice Based Credit system (CBCS) thus bringing more flexibility in CBCS. The bank will digitally store the academic credits earned from various recognized HEIs enabling an HEI to award degrees taking into account credits earned.

9) **Multidisciplinary Education and Research Universities (MERUs):** MERUs will be established as models of the best education of international standard. MERUs will be set up at par with IITs and IIMs. They will also help set the highest standards for multidisciplinary education across India.

10) **The National Research Foundation:** To develop a strong research culture and building perennial research capacity The National Research Foundation (NRF) will be created as an apex body. It will fund outstanding research works and develop research culture in universities and colleges. The NRF will be governed, independently of the government, by a rotating Board of Governors consisting of the very best researchers and innovators across fields. The NRF will competitively fund research in all disciplines.

11) **Higher Education Commission of India (HECI):** The policy envisages to set up Higher Education Commission of India (HECI) as a single overarching umbrella body for entire higher education, excluding medical and legal education. Public and private (HEIs) will be governed by same norms. HECI will have following four independent verticals (bodies) under it:

   i) **National Higher Education Regulatory Council (NHERC):** It will function as the common, single point regulator for the higher education sector including teacher education and excluding medical and legal education.

   ii) **National Accreditation Council (NAC)**: It will function as a 'meta-accrediting body' Accreditation of institutions will be based primarily on basic norms, public self-disclosure, good governance, and outcomes.

   iii) **Higher Education Grants Council (HEGC):** It will carry out funding and financing of higher education based on transparent criteria. HEGC will be entrusted with the disbursement of scholarships and developmental funds.

   iv) **General Education Council (GEC):** It will frame expected learning outcomes for higher education programmes, also referred to as 'graduate attributes'. A National Higher Education Qualification Framework (NHEQF) will be formulated by the GEC and it shall be in synchronization with the National Skills Qualifications Framework (NSQF) to ease the integration of vocational education into higher education.

Some Definitions

NEP 2020 defines certain HEIs as follows:

1) **University:** A university will mean a multidisciplinary institution of higher learning that offers undergraduate and graduate programmes, with high quality teaching, research, and community engagement.

2) **Research Intensive University:** That university will be research intensive which will place equal emphasis on teaching and research

3) **Teaching Intensive University:** That university will be teaching intensive which will place greater emphasis on teaching but still conduct significant research.

4) **Autonomous Degree Granting College:** An Autonomous degree-granting College (AC) will be that large multidisciplinary institution of higher learning that will grant undergraduate degrees and will be primarily focused on undergraduate teaching.

12) **University Entrance Exams by NTA:** National Testing Agency (NTA) will conduct common entrance tests for university entrance in science, arts, humanities, specialised and vocational subjects twice a year.

13) **Indian Institute of Translation and Interpretation (IITI):** There is a proposal for etablishing Indian institute of Translation and Interpretation (IITI) while laying emphasis on Sanskrit and other Indian languages.

14) **Campuses of Best Universities in other Countries:** India's best universities will be allowed to set their campuses in other countries. Universities will be chosen according to their accreditation given to them according to their performance.

15) Three Types of HEIs: The policy proposes to three types of multidisciplinary HEIs i.e. Research-intensive universities, Teaching-intensive universities and autonomous degree granting colleges.

16) "Light but Tight" Regulation: At present various higher education regulatory bodies like UGC, NAAC, AICTE, NBA etc come up with various regulations which in one way or other affect autonomy of HEIs and used to clash with one another also.. This policy proposes to frame "Light but Tight" regulations through a single regulator to enforce less regulations and grant more autonomy to HEIs. These regulations will be based on transparent public disclosure, extensive use of technology, etc. The policy envisages gradual autonomy through suitable accreditations for all higher education institutions (HEIs).

17) International Students Office: In the interest of promoting India as a global study destination providing premium education at affordable costs, the policy provides to set up an International Students Office at each institution hosting foreign students.

18) Foreign Universities in India: As per the provision of the policy, universities of other countries falling among top 100 universities of the world will be allowed to set up their campuses in India.

19) Multidisciplinary IITs: In order to impart more holistic and multidisciplinary education the policy envisages that IITs will admit students of arts and humanity. Students of arts and humanities will aim to learn more science.

20) All HEIs to be Multidisciplinary by 2040: The policy proposes that all HEIs will become multidisciplinary by 2040.Such HEIs will aim at admitting thousands of students with minimum 3000 students.

Multidisciplinary Institution

A Multidisciplinary institution mean a multidisciplinary institution that offers undergraduate and postgraduate programmes, with high quality teaching, research, and community engagement.

21) Discretion of Open Distance Learning (ODL): Running ODL will be at discretion of institutions, if they are accredited to do so.They will have to improve access, increase GER, and provide opportunities for lifelong learning (SDG 4)

22) Holistic and Multidisciplinary Education: The policy proposes to impart such education which would develop all capacities of human beings - intellectual, aesthetic, social, physical, emotional, and moral in an integrated manner. Such an education will help developing all round individuals that possess critical capacities in fields across the arts, humanities, languages, sciences, social sciences, and professional, technical, and vocational fields with skill of communication.

23) Flexible Curriculum: HEIs will come up with flexible curriculum along with course options for the students, in addition to rigorous specialization in a subject or subjects. In curricula of all HEIs there will be credit-based courses and projects in the areas of community engagement and service, environmental education, and value-based education. This will help in achieving holistic and multidisciplinary education.

24) Global Citizenship Education (GCED): In order to create awareness and understanding of global issues in students, GCED will be imparted in HEIs. So that students may work for creating peaceful, tolerant, inclusive, secure, and sustainable societies.

25) Flexible Master's Programme: HEI's will offer flexible Master's programme. Those students who will complete 3 year Bachelor's programme, for them there will be 2 year Master's programme with second year completely devoted to research. Those students who will complete 4 year Bachelor's programme, they will be eligible for 1 year Master's programme. Finally there will be a provision for 5 year integrated Bachelor's/Master's programme.

26) Focus on Research and Innovations: HEIs will focus on research and innovation by setting up start-up incubation centres; technology development centres; centres in frontier areas of research; greater industry-academic linkages; and interdisciplinary research including humanities and social sciences research. Given the scenario of epidemics and pandemics, it is critical that HEIs take the lead to undertake research in areas of infectious diseases, epidemiology, virology, diagnostics, instrumentation, vaccinology and other relevant areas.

27) Revision in the Choice Based Credit System (CBCS): CBCS will be revised in the interest of innovation and flexibility.HEIs will adopt a criterion based grading system which will assess student achievement based on the learning goals for each programme, making the system fairer and outcomes more comparable. HEIs shall also move away from high-stakes examinations towards more continuous and comprehensive evaluation.

28) **Internationalisation at Home:** The policy proposes to achieve the goal of "Internationalisation at Home" by attracting maximum students from other countries by HEIs and provide them global quality education. International students studying in India will be provided greater mobility to students in India who may wish to visit, study at, transfer credits to, or carry out research at institutions abroad, and vice versa. Courses and programmes in subjects, such as Indology, Indian languages, AYUSH systems of medicine, yoga, arts, music, history, culture, and modern India, internationally relevant curricula in the sciences, social sciences, and beyond, meaningful opportunities for social engagement, quality residential facilities and on-campus support, etc. will be expedited.

29) **Liberty to Faculty:** Faculty will be given full freedom to frame curriculum and devise teaching methods while complying with the approved framework, including textbook and reading material selections, assignments, and assessments.

30) **Compatible Teacher Student Ratio:** Teaching duties also will not be excessive, and student-teacher ratios not too high, so that the activity of teaching remains pleasant and there is adequate time for interaction with students yielding an excellent and productive teaching-learning process.

31) **Reward of Service:** Teachers coming up with excellent performance will be rewarded with various incentives like promotions, increments, recognitions, and movement into institutional leadership. Meanwhile, faculty not delivering on basic norms will be held accountable.

32) **Transparency in Faculty Recruitment:** HEIs will recruit faculty while maintaining transparency. However a 'tenure-track' i.e., suitable probation period shall be put in place to further ensure excellence. There shall be a fast-track promotion system.

33) **Emphasis on Socially and Economically Disadvantaged Groups (SEDGs):** In order to fulfil the commitment of equity and inclusion in higher education, special attention will be given to SEDGs in imparting quality education. For this following initiatives will be taken:

i) Setting clear targets for higher GER for SEDGs
ii) Establishing high quality HEIs in those districts/ areas which contain large number of SEDGs
iii) Providing more financial assistance and scholarships to SEDGs in both public and private HEIs
iv) Make admissions processes and curriculum more comprehensive.
v) Develop bridge courses for students that come from disadvantaged educational backgrounds.

34) **More Exposure to Vocational Education:** HEIs will offer vocational courses either on their own or in partnership with industry and NGOs.The policy provides that at least 50% of learners through the school and higher education system shall have exposure to vocational education by 2025.

35) **B.Voc. Degree Programme to Continue:** The B.Voc. degrees introduced in 2013 will continue to exist, but vocational courses will also be available to students enrolled in all other Bachelor's degree programmes, including the 4-year multidisciplinary Bachelor 's programmes. HEIs will also be allowed to conduct short-term certificate courses in various skills including soft skills.

36) **Teacher Education:** The policy proposes that all multidisciplinary HEIs will offer B.Ed. programmes in collaboration with other departments. The HEI offering the 4-year integrated B.Ed. may also run a 2-year B.Ed., for students who have already received a Bachelor's degree in a specialized subject. A 1-year B.Ed. may also be offered for candidates who have received a 4-year undergraduate degree in a specialized subject. Teachers will be trained through technology programmes like SAWAYAM and DIKSHA

37) **HEIs to be Non-Profit Entity:** In order to curb commercialisation of education, the policy provides that all HEIs, public or private, will be complying with same regulation of audit and inspection. They will be declared non-profit entity and surplus funds if any will be reinvested in education sector. Process of charging fee particularly by private HEIs, will be transparent and fully disclosed.

38) **HEIs to Work with Effective Governance and Leadership:** The policy provides that measures will be taken at all HEIs to ensure leadership of the highest quality and promote an institutional culture of excellence. a Board of Governors (BoG) shall be established consisting of a group of highly qualified, competent, and dedicated individuals having proven capabilities and a strong sense of commitment to the an accredited institution. The

BoG of an institution will be empowered to govern the institution free of any external interference, make all appointments including that of head of the institution, and take all decisions regarding governance.

CURRENT SCHEMES AND PORTALS IN HIGHER EDUCATION

Rashtriya Uchchatar Shiksha Abhiyan (RUSA)

Rashtriya Uchchatar Shiksha Abhiyan (RUSA) is a Centrally Sponsored Scheme (CSS), launched in 2013 aimed at providing strategic funding to eligible state higher educational institutions. The central to states funding (in the ratio of 60:40 for general category States, 90:10 for special category states and 100% for union territories) is norm-based and outcome dependent. The funding flows from the central ministry through the state governments/union territories to the State Higher Education Councils before reaching the identified institutions. The funding to states is made on the basis of critical appraisal of State Higher Education Plans, which would describe each state's strategy to address issues of equity, access, and excellence in higher education.

Objectives

The salient objectives of RUSA are to:

- Improve the overall quality of state institutions by ensuring conformity to prescribed norms and standards and adopt accreditation as a mandatory quality assurance framework
- Usher transformative reforms in the state higher education system by creating a facilitating institutional structure for planning and monitoring at the state level, promoting autonomy in State Universities, and improving governance in institutions
- Ensure reforms in the affiliation, academic, and examination systems
- Ensure adequate availability of quality faculty in all higher educational institutions and ensure capacity-building at all levels of employment
- Create an enabling atmosphere in the higher educational institutions to devote themselves to research and innovations
- Expand the institutional base by creating additional capacity in existing institutions and establishing new institutions, in order to achieve enrolment targets
- Correct regional imbalances in access to higher education by setting up institutions in unserved and underserved areas
- Improve equity in higher education by providing adequate opportunities of higher education to SC/STs and socially and educationally backward classes, promote inclusion of women, minorities, and differently abled persons

RUSA would create new universities through upgradation of existing autonomous colleges and conversion of colleges in a cluster. It would create new model degree colleges, new professional colleges, and provide infrastructural support to universities and colleges. Faculty recruitment support, faculty improvements programmes, and leadership development of educational administrators are also an important part of the scheme. In order to enhance skill development, the central scheme of Polytechnics has been subsumed within RUSA. A separate component to synergise vocational education with higher education has also been included in RUSA. Besides these, RUSA also supports reforming, restructuring, and building-capacity of institutions in participating states.

National Research Professorship (NRP)

Government of India had instituted the scheme of National Research Professorship in 1949 to honour distinguished academics and scholars in recognition of their contribution to knowledge. Persons of real eminence, who have attained the age of 65 years and have made outstanding contributions in their respective fields and are still capable of productive research, are considered for appointment as National Research Professors.

Scheme for Incentivising State Governments for Expansion of Higher Education Institutions

A scheme is being introduced for incentivising States for establishing new higher educational institutions/ expanding existing higher educational institutions. This new Scheme will provide central assistance to the State Governments in the ratio of 1:2 (1:1 for Special Category States) for establishing new higher educational institutions/expanding existing higher educational institutions. The physical targets for XI Plan and XII Plan included new universities, colleges, and engineering colleges as well as expansion of existing colleges.

Scheme for Strengthening Science Based Higher Education and Research in Universities

Looking at the declining quality and quantum of scientific research in India, an Empowered Committee under the Chairmanship of Prof. M.M. Sharma was constituted for rejuvenation of Basic Scientific Research in Universities. Based on the recommendations of the Task Force, action for strengthening science-based education and research in Universities has been initiated. The main objective of the scheme is to promote excellence in research in higher education by supporting research programmes of the University and College teachers in various disciplines.

Community College Scheme

Central Government initiated to set up Community Colleges based on the recommendation of Committee of State Education Ministers, set up in 2012. Government of India decided to establish 200 community colleges on pilot basis from the academic session 2013-14. The Government of India (MHRD) and the Government of UK also signed a MoU on a framework for development of Community Colleges under UK India Education Research Initiative (UKIERI). These colleges provide education above the secondary level and below the degree level with appropriate skills, keeping in view the needs of the local industry and community, thereby leading to gainful employment and options for horizontal and vertical mobility. The model scheme on community colleges as conceptualised by MHRD has been shared with UGC and AICTE for funding them to make them functional from the academic session 2013-14. UGC would fund the community colleges hosted in a college while AICTE would fund the polytechnics hosting the community college.

Scheme for Promotion of Academic and Research Collaboration (SPARC)

It aims at improving the research ecosystem of India's higher educational systems by facilitating academic and research collaboration between Indian institutions and the best institutions of the world from 28 selected countries to jointly solve problems at national and/or international relevance. SPARC proposes to enable productive academic cooperation among participating nations.

Global Initiative of Academic Networks (GIAN)

In order to facilitate fundamental and socially relevant research in India, a lot of emphasis is being laid to strengthen collaboration between Indian Research groups with Top research groups in the world, so that India scientists and students can interact with the finest minds in the world. With this objective in mind, MHRD (Ministry of Human Resource Development, Government of India) in 2015 launched GIAN, under which an International academician can visit an Indian Institute for one to two weeks to offer a course. The response was overwhelming, as apart from the course, the Indian students and academicians got a chance to interact with the International Faculty.

Visiting Advanced Joint Research (VAJRA)

The Science and Engineering Research Board (SERB), a Statutory body of the Department of Science and Technology (DST) launched a 'Visiting Advanced Joint Research (VAJRA) Faculty Scheme' in 2017 to connect the Indian academic and research and development (R&D) systems to the best of global science and scientists for a sustained international collaborative research. The scheme offers adjunct/visiting faculty assignments to overseas scientists, faculty members, and R&D professionals including Non-resident Indians (NRI) and Overseas Citizen of India (OCI) to undertake high quality collaborative research in cutting-edge areas of science and technology, including interdisciplinary areas of priority such as energy, water, health, security, nutrition, materials and manufacturing, etc. with one or more Indian collaborators of public funded academic and research institutions of India.

Leadership for Academicians Programme (LEAP)

Union Ministry of Human Resource Development launched Leadership for Academicians Programme (LEAP). It is three weeks (2 weeks domestic and 1 week foreign training) leadership development training programme for second level academic functionaries in different higher education institutes. It will make Higher Education Institutions (HEIs) perform their roles of developing better students who will be future nation builders. It would provide senior faculty the required leadership and managerial skills including skills of problem-solving, handling stress, team-building work, conflict management, communication, understanding the complexity and challenges of governance in HEIs, and general administration. It will be implemented through 15 National Institute Ranking Framework (NIRF) top-ranked Indian Institutions namely, IIT Bombay, IIT Kanpur, IIT Kharagpur, IIT Roorkee, IISER Kolkata, NIT Trichy, JNU; IIT (BHU), Delhi University, TISS Mumbai, University of Hyderabad, NIEPA, Jamia Milia Islamia, BHU, and AMU.

Annual Refresher Programme in Teaching (ARPIT)

Annual Refresher Programme in Teaching (ARPIT) is a major and unique initiative of online professional development of 15 lakh higher education faculty using the MOOCs platform SWAYAM in a phased manner. For implementing ARPIT, 75 discipline-specific institutions have been identified and notified as National Resource Centres (NRCs) in the first phase.

Revitalising Infrastructure and Systems in Higher Education (RISE)

RISE scheme was announced in Union Budget 2017-18. It aims to lend low-cost funds to government higher educational institutions. Under it, all centrally-funded institutes (CFIs), including central universities, IITs, IIMs, NITs, and IISERs can borrow from a Rs 1,00,000 crore corpus over the next 4 years to expand and build new infrastructure. It will be financed via restructured Higher Education Financing Agency (HEFA), a non-banking financial company.

Pandit Madan Mohan Malviya National Mission on Teachers and Teaching (PMMMNMTT)

The Mission envisages to address comprehensively all issues related to Teachers, Teaching, Teacher Preparation, Professional Development, Curriculum Design, Designing and Developing Assessment & Evaluation methodology, Research in Pedagogy, and developing effective Pedagogy. This will be one of the major thrust areas of action of the Government. The Mission would address, on the one hand, current and urgent issues such as supply of qualified teachers, attracting talent into teaching profession, and raising the quality of teaching in schools and colleges. On the other hand, it is also envisaged that the Mission would pursue long-term goals of building a strong professional cadre of teachers by setting performance standards and creating top class institutional facilities for innovative teaching and professional development of teachers. The mission was launched during XII Five Year Plan.

Impacting Research Innovation and Technology (IMPRINT)

Adopting engineering and technology as the vehicle to addressing the societal needs and achieving national prosperity, MHRD drafted a new and catalytic scheme called **IMPRINT**. It is a first-of-its-kind Pan-IIT and IISc joint initiative to develop a (a) New Education Policy, and (b) Roadmap for Research to solve major engineering and technology challenges in selected domains needed by the country.

Skills Acquisition and Knowledge Awareness for Livelihood Promotion (SANKALP)

SANKALP is a centrally sponsored scheme of Ministry of Skill Development & Entrepreneurship (MSDE). It is an outcome focused scheme marking shift in government's implementation strategy in vocational education and training from inputs to results. SANKALP aims to implement the mandate of the National Skill Development Mission (NSDM).

Impactful Policy Research in Social Science (IMPRESS)

The Ministry of Human Resource Development (MHRD) launched a new scheme called IMPRESS (Impactful Policy Research in Social Science) to promote policy research in social science. The Indian Council of Social Science Research had been entrusted with the task of implementing and monitoring the scheme IMPRESS.

Startup India Plan

Department of Science and Technology (DST) and Ministry of Human Resource Development (MHRD) has jointly taken an initiative for promoting establishment of Research Parks/Technology Business Incubators/ Startup Centres. In this regard, National Expert Advisory Committee (NEAC) has approved 13 Startup Centres, 16 Technology Business Incubators (TBIs), and 6 Research Parks under Startup India scheme.

PORTAL-india.gov.in

This portal is very helpful in getting information related to the elementary, secondary, higher secondary, higher and adult education, etc. One can also find details of educational institutions, courses, admission procedure, scholarships, student loans, technical and medical education, and vocational studies, etc. Detailed information related to foreign scholarships, exchange programmes and universities, etc. is provided. Related documents and forms are also available.

Celebrating International and National Days of Education

International Day of Education - 24th January

National Education Day - 11th November

(11 November is birth anniversary of Maulana Abul Kalam Azad)

Civil Services Day - 21st April

National Youth Day - 12th January (Birthday of Swami Vivekanand)

Teachers Day - 5th September (Birthday of Dr. Radhakrishnan)
World Teachers Day - 5th October
International Students Day - 17thNovember

LEADING INSTITUTES AND STATUTORY BODIES OF HIGHER LEARNING AND RESEARCH IN INDIA

1) Avinashlingam Institution for Home Science and Higher Education for Women (Deemed university)---**Coimbatore (Tamil Nadu)**
2) English and Foreign Languages University---**Hyderabad (Telengana)**
3) Central Institute of Fisheries Education---**Mumbai (Maharashtra)**
4) Central Institute of Higher Tibetan Studies---**Varanasi (UP)**
5) Dayalbagh Educational Institute--- **Agra (UP)**
6) Gandhi Gram Rural Institute---**Dindigul (Tamil Nadu)**
7) Indian Agricultural Research Institute--- **Pusa (New Delhi)**
8) Indian Veterinary Research Institute---**Izatnagar (UP)**
9) Indian Institute of Science--- **Bangalore (Karnataka)**
10) Indian School of Mines--- **Dhanbad (Jharkhand) (This is now IIT)**
11) International Institute for Population Sciences---**Mumbai (Maharashtra)**
12) National Dairy Research Institute--- **Karnal (Haryana)**
13) National Museum Institute of History of Art Conservation and Museology---**New Delhi**
14) Rashtrya Sanskrit Vidyapeetha---**Tirupati (Andhra Pradesh)**
15) School of Planning and Architecture--- **New Delhi**
16) Sh. SatyaSai Institute of Higher learning---**Anantpur (Andhra Pradesh)**
17) Sh. Lal BahadarShastriRashtrya Sanskrit Vidyapeeth--- **New Delhi**
18) Tata Institute of Social Sciences--- **Mumbai (Maharashtra)**
19) Thapar Institute of Engineering and Technology (Deemed University)---**Patiala (Punjab)**
20) All India Institute of Medical Sciences---**New Delhi**
21) Indian Statistical Institute---**Kolkata (West Bengal)**
22) Indian Institute of Technology--- **New Delhi, Kanpur (UP), Kharagpur (West Bengal), Chennai (Tamil Nadu) and Mumbai (Maharashtra)**
23) Post Graduate Institute of Medical Education and Research--- **Chandigarh**
24) Sanjay Gandhi Postgraduate Institute of Medical Sciences--- **Lucknow (UP)**
25) Institute of Armament Technology--- **Pune (Maharashtra)**
26) National Institute of Educational Planning and Administrators--- **New Delhi**
27) Indian Council of Historical Research (ICHR)---**New Delhi**
28) Indian Council of Philosophical Research (ICPR)---**New Delhi**
29) Indian Institute of Advanced Study--- **Shimla (Himachal Pradesh)**
30) Indian Council of Social Science Research (ICSSR)---**New Delhi**
31) National Institute of Fashion Technology--- **New Delhi, Bangalore, Calcutta, Chennai, Gandhinagar (Gujarat)**
32) Indian Academy of Sciences--- **Bangalore (Karnataka)**
33) Indian National Science Academy---**New Delhi**
34) Indian National Academy of Engineering---**New Delhi**
35) National Academy of Sciences--- **Allahabad (UP)**
36) Indian Science Congress Association---**Kolkata (West Bengal)**
37) Advanced Centre for Treatment, Research and Education in Cancer--- **Mumbai (Maharashtra)**
38) Harish-Chandra Research Institute---**Allahabad (UP)**
39) Institute of Mathematical Sciences---**Chennai (Tamil Nadu)**
40) National Institute of Ocean Technology---**Chennai (Tamil Nadu)**
41) National Centre for Polar and Ocean Research---**Goa**

42) National Institute of Immunology---**New Delhi**
43) National Brain Research Centre---**Gurgaon (Haryana)**
44) Institute of Life Sciences---**Bhubneshwar (Orissa)**
45) Armed Forces Medical College---**Pune (Maharashtra)**
46) College of Military Engineering--- **Pune**
47) College of Defence Management---**Secunderabad (Andhra Pradesh)**
48) Rashtriya Indian Military College--- **Dehradun (Uttarakhand)**
49) National Institute of Agricultural Marketing---**Jaipur (Rajasthan)**
50) Central Institute of Fisheries, Nautical and Engineering Training---**Kochi (Kerala)**
51) Central Institute of Coastal Engineering for Fishery---**Bengaluru**
52) Central Island Agricultural Research Institute---**Port Blair (Andaman & Nicobar)**
53) All India Institute of Hygiene and Public Health---**Kolkata**
54) National Judicial Academy---New Delhi & **Bhopal (MP)**
55) National Fire Service College---**Nagpur (Maharashtra)**
56) National Institute of Criminology and Forensic Science---**New Delhi**
57) V.V. Giri National Labour Institute---**Noida (UP)**
58) Central Institute of Plastics Engineering & Technology---**Amritsar (Punjab)**
59) National Vocational Training Institute---**Noida**
60) Indian Institute of Mass Communication---**New Delhi**
61) Film and Television Institute of India---**Pune**
63) Satyajit Ray Film and Television Institute---**Kolkata**
64) Indian Institute of Maritime Studies--- **Navi Mumbai**
65) Marine Engineering and Research Institute---**Kolkata, Mumbai**
66) Lal Bahadur Shastri College of Advanced Maritime Studies and Research---**Mumbai**
67) National Institute of Aviation Management and Research---**New Delhi**
68) Indira Gandhi Rashtrya Uran Academy---**Fursatganj (UP)**
69) Indian Institute of Tourism and Travel Management---**New Delhi**
70) National Institute of Water Sports---**Goa**
71) Netaji Subhas National Institute of Sports---**Patiala (Punjab)**
72) Lakshmibai National College of Physical Education---**Thiruvanthapuram (Kerala)**
73) National Environmental Engineering Research Institute---**Nagpur**
74) Banasthali University---**Vanasthali (Rajasthan)**
75) SNDT (Shrimati Nathibai Damodar Thackersey) Women's University---**Mumbai, Pune (First Women's University in India)**
76) Lovely Professional University---**Jalandhar (Punjab)**
77) Mahatma Gandhi Antarrashtrya Hindi Vishvidyalya---**Vardha (Maharashtra)**
78) English and Foreign Languages University---**Hyderabad (Andhra Pradesh)**
79) National Law Institute---**Hyderabad (Andhra Pradesh)**
80) National Judicial Academy---**Bhopal (MP)**
81) National Savings Institute---**Nagpur**
82) Dr. Harisingh Gaur University---**Sagar (Madhya Pradesh)**
83) M.S. (Maharaj Sayajirao) University---**Vadodara (Gujarat)**
84) J.N. (Jai Narayan) Vyas University---**Jodhpur (Rajasthan)**
85) National Institute of Technical Teachers Training and Research (NITTTR)---**Chandigarh**
86) National Law University---**Delhi**
87) M.C. National University of Journalism and Communication---**Bhopal (MP)**

NIRF

The National Institutional Ranking Framework (NIRF) was approved by the MHRD and launched on 29th September 2015. This framework outlines a methodology to rank institutions across the country. The methodology draws from the overall recommendations and broad understanding arrived at by a Core Committee set up by MHRD.

NIRF RANKING - 2020 (Top Rank)

1) ***Overall:*** *Indian Institute of Technology Madras (Chennai)*
2) ***University:*** *Indian Institute of Science, Bengaluru*

3) ***College:*** *Miranda House, Delhi*
4) ***Engineering:*** *Indian Institute of Technology Madras (Chennai)*
5) ***Management:*** *Indian Institute of Management Ahmedabad*
6) ***Law:*** *National Law School of India University, Bengaluru*
7) ***Pharmacy:*** *Jamia Hamdard, New Delhi*
8) ***Architecture:*** *Indian Institute of Technology Kharagpur (W. Bengal)*
9) ***Medical:*** *All India Institute of Medical Sciences, New Delhi*

Some Vital Facts

1) Full form of SANKALP is Skills Acquisition and Knowledge Awareness for Livelihood Promotion
2) GIAN has been launched by the government of India to encourage global scholars engage with their counterparts in India.
3) RUSA was launched in 2013 with the purpose to provide strategic funding to eligible state higher educational institutions.
4) Access, equity, quality and excellence, relevance and value based education are goals of higher education in India.
5) Civil Service Day is celebrated in India on 21st April.

CONSTITUTIONAL BODIES IN INDIA

Constitutional bodies are those bodies which are mentioned in the constitution and their these are established under an article mentioned in the constitution. These bodies derive power from the constitution. Constitution will have to be amended in order to bring any change in their structure or composition.

1. Attorney General

Articles	76
Composition	–
Tenure and Removal	Not mentioned in the constitution. Holds office during the pleasure of President.
Further Appointment	YES
Powers	Has privileges of a MP, Right of audience in all courts in the territory of India, both houses of parliament, joint sitting of parliament (NOT entitled right to vote)
Additional Information	He can do Private practice but defend criminal cases only with GoI permission

2. Comptroller and Auditor General (CAG)

Articles	148
Composition	–
Tenure and	6yrs or 65 age
Removal	Same as that of SC Judge
Further Appointment	NO
Powers	Audits the accounts related to Consolidated fund of India and states (UTs with legislative assemblies), Contingency fund as well as Public accounts fund of centre and states. Advisor role regarding accounts to president
Additional Information	His certification regarding net proceeds of any tax or duty is final.

3. Election Commission

Articles	324
Composition	Chief Election Commissioner + Other commissioners (appointed by president)
Tenure and Removal	Determined by president (Presently 65 yrs age or 6yrs)
Further Appointment.	YES
Powers	Advisory role in case of disqualification of MP's and MLA's; EC certifies the general elections to the assembly can't be held on account of difficulties. Mere advisory not binding
Additional Information	CEC and EC's all enjoy same remuneration and previleges.

4. Finance Commission

Articles	280
Composition	Chairman (Experience in public affairs) + 4 members (Judges of HC, specialized knowledge of economics, accounts and finances of govt)
Tenure and Removal	–
Further Appointment	YES
Powers	Advisory regarding distribution of taxes between centre and states
Additional Information	It takes into consideration both capital and revenue requirements of state in formulating devolution

5. National Commission for SC's

Articles	338
Composition	Chairman , Vice Chairman, Three others
Tenure and Removal	For a term of three years. Pleasure of president
Further Appointment	YES
Powers	Quasi-judicial body ; Monitors and reports working of constitutional safeguards for SC's (including OBC's and ST's)
Additional Information	While investigation and inquiry, has all the powers of a civil court

6. National Commission for ST's

Articles	338-A
Rest of the Information	Same as above (that of Commission for SC's)

7. Special officer for Linguistic Minorities

Articles	350B
Composition	Commissioner assisted by deputy commissioner and assistant commissioner
Tenure and Removal	Not mentioned by Constitution. Pleasure of president.
Further Appointment	YES
Powers	Monitors and reports working of constitutional safeguards for linguistic minorities

8. Union Public Service Commission

Articles	315 – 323
Composition	9 – 11 members including Chairman.
Tenure and Removal	65 yrs of age / 6 yrs of service. President shall refer the reason for removal to the SC which conducts enquiry and advises president on removal. (The advice of the president)
Further Appointment	They are eligible only for appointment within SPSC and UPSC (Chairman of UPSC is not eligible for another term)
Powers	Advisory powers, recruitment of All India Services, Central services, public services of centrally administered territories.
Additional Information	Advice tendered by UPSC is not binding on the govt. But reasons for rejected recommendations has to be tabled in parliament.

9. State Public Service Commission

Articles	315-323
Tenure and Removal	62yrs of age/6 yrs of service; Appointed by govt but Removal by president.
REST	Same

NON-CONSTITUTIONAL BODIES

Non-constitutional bodies are created by an act of parliament or state legislative assembly. These bodies are also called **Statutory Bodies** as they derive power from the statute (Act or Law) under which these have been created. Some of the statutory bodies are explained below:

Statutory Posts/Bodies in India

1) The **Solicitor General of India** is the Indian government's chief legal advisor, and its primary lawyer in the Supreme Court of India. The Solicitor General of India is the secondary law officer of the country, assists the Attorney General, and is himself assisted by several Additional Solicitors General of India. Like the Attorney General for India, the Solicitor General and the Additional Solicitors General advise the Government and appear on behalf of the Union of India in terms of the Law Officers (Terms and Conditions) Rules, 1972. However, unlike the post of Attorney General for India, which is a Constitutional post under Article 76 of the Constitution of India, the posts of the Solicitor General and the Additional Solicitors General are merely statutory. Appointments Committee of the Cabinet appoints the Solicitor General.
2) **National Human Rights Commission:** The National Human Rights Commission (NHRC) of India was established on 12 October, 1993. The statute under which it is established is the Protection of Human Rights Act (PHRA), 1993 as amended by the Protection of Human Rights (Amendment) Act, 2006.
3) **National Commission for Women:** The National Commission for Women was set up as statutory body in January 1992 under the National Commission for Women Act, 1990
4) **National Commission for Minorities:** NCM was set up under National Commission for Minorities Act 1992. Five religious communities viz. muslims, Christians, Sikhs, Bhuddists and Zoroastrians(Parsis) are covered by the commission
5) **National Commission for Backward Classes:** National Commission for Backward Classes (NCBC) was initially constituted by the Central Govt by The National Commission for Backward

Classes Act, 1993 (27 of 1993). The present Commission (8th) has been accorded Constitutional Status and constituted through "The Constitution (One Hundred and Second Amendment) Act, 2018", whereby Article 338B has been inserted, forming a Commission for the socially and educationally backward classes to be known as NCBC.

6) **National Green Tribunal:** The National Green Tribunal has been established on 18.10.2010 under the National Green Tribunal Act 2010 for effective and expeditious disposal of cases relating to environmental protection and conservation of forests and other natural resources including enforcement of any legal right relating to environment and giving relief and compensation for damages to persons and property

7) **University Grants Commission (UGC):** The University Grants Commission of India is a statutory body set up by the Indian Union government in accordance to the UGC Act 1956 under Ministry of Human Resource Development, and is charged with coordination, determination and maintenance of standards of higher education.

8) **Central Information Commission (CIC)** is not a constitutional body but an independent body, which look into complaints and appeals pertaining to offices, public sector undertakings, financial institutions etc., under the government and the Union territories. *The Central Information commission was established in 2005 by the Government of India under the provisions of the Right to Information Act (2005).* The Central Information Commission is plays an important role in maintaining transparency in the system of the governance which is essential in the democracy. Such kind of transparency is necessary to check corruption, nepotism, oppression and misuse or abuse of the authority. **The President of India appoints the Chief Information commissioner and the information commissioners on the recommendation of the committee consisting of the Prime Minister as chairperson, the leader of the opposition in the Lok Sabha and union cabinet ministers nominated by the Prime Minister.**

9) **The NITI Aayog** (National Institution for Transforming India), is a think tank of the Government of India established on 1 January 2015 as a replacement for the Planning Commission to give suggestions to the Governments at the central and state levels with relevant strategic, directional and technical advice across the spectrum of key elements of policy / development process. The Prime Minister of India heads the Aayog as the Ex-officio Chairperson.

GOOD GOVERNANCE

Good Governance is an approach to government that is committed to creating a system founded in justice and peace that protects individual's human rights and civil liberties. According to the United Nations, Good Governance is measured by the eight factors of Participation, Rule of Law, Transparency, Responsiveness, Consensus Oriented, Equity and Inclusiveness, Effectiveness and Efficiency, and Accountability.

Tools or Characteristics of Good Governance

Participation requires that all groups, particularly those most vulnerable, have direct or representative access to the systems of government. This manifests as a strong civil society and citizens with the freedom of association and expression.

Rule of Law is exemplified by impartial legal systems that protect the human rights and civil liberties of all citizens, particularly minorities. This is indicated by an independent judicial branch and a police force free from corruption.

Transparency means that citizens understand and have access to the means and manner in which decisions are made, especially if they are directly affected by such decisions. This information must be provided in an understandable and accessible format, typically translated through the media.

Responsiveness simply involves that institutions respond to their stakeholders within a reasonable time frame.

Consensus Oriented is demonstrated by an agenda that seeks to mediate between the many different needs, perspectives, and expectations of a diverse citizenry. Decisions needs to be made in a manner that reflects a deep understanding of the historical, cultural, and social context of the community.

Equity and Inclusiveness depends on ensuring that all the members of a community feel included and empowered to improve or maintain their well-being, especially those individuals and groups that are the most vulnerable.

Effectiveness and Efficiency is developed through the sustainable use of resources to meet the needs of a society. Sustainability refers to both ensuring social investments carry through and natural resources are maintained for future generations.

Accountability refers to institutions being ultimately accountable to the people and one another. This includes government agencies, civil society, and the private sector all being accountable to one another as well.

Practice Exercise

PART-I

BODIES FOR HIGHER EDUCATION

General Questions Format

1. CABE is a/an
   (A) university
   (B) policy-making body
   (C) education programme
   (D) none of these
2. UGC was founded in
   (A) 1956 (B) 1963
   (C) 1953 (D) 1950
3. Which of the following is NOT the activity of NAAC?
   (A) Research in education planning
   (B) Arranging seminars and workshops in education
   (C) Training to academicians
   (D) None of the above
4. NCTE stands for National Council for .... Education
   (A) Technical (B) Theoretical
   (C) Teacher (D) Topical
5. Indian Institute for Advanced Study is governed by
   (A) Ministry of Human Resources
   (B) State Education Department
   (C) Himachal University
   (D) None of these
6. Which of the following fields is covered by AICTE?
   (A) Architecture (B) Town planning
   (C) Management (D) All of the above
7. ICAR undertakes research in
   (A) Industry (B) Agriculture
   (C) Astronomy (D) Infrastructure
8. AIIMS was established under an Act of
   (A) Medical Council of India
   (B) Union Health Ministry
   (C) Parliament
   (D) None of these
9. NAAC has been established by
   (A) AIU (B) UGC
   (C) IIAS (D) IIT
10. Which of the following state does not have IIM?
    (A) Orissa (B) UP
    (C) West Bengal (D) Karnataka
11. Number of IITs working in India is
    (A) 16 (B) 20
    (C) 18 (D) 5
12. CABE frames policy matters in the field of..........education.
    (A) elementary (B) secondary
    (C) technical (D) all of the above
13. Which of the following is a central university?
    (A) Jawaharlal Nehru (B) Aligarh Muslim
    (C) Visva Bharati (D) All of the above
14. Which of the following is one of the regional centres established by ICHR?
    (A) Chennai (B) Lucknow
    (C) Chhatisgarh (D) Guwahati
15. National Education Commission (1964-65) recommended that there should be at least one .... university in each Indian state.
    (A) womens' (B) agriculture
    (C) open (D) deemed
16. An institution which is conferred the status of a university is called .... University.
    (A) Assumed (B) Esteemed
    (C) Deemed (D) None of these
17. CSIR promotes.......research in the country.
    (A) Industrial (B) Informatory
    (C) Intellectual (D) None of these
18. NUEPA is a..............university.
    (A) central (B) deemed
    (C) state (D) open
19. The President of India act as .... of the central universities.
    (A) Chancellor (B) Consultant
    (C) Visitor (D) None of these

20. CABE was created to establish parity between
   (A) UGC and universities
   (B) Central and State universities
   (C) deemed and regular universities
   (D) None of these

21. The .... of a university presides over the convocation.
   (A) Vice-Chancellor (B) Registrar
   (C) Dean (D) Chancellor

22. Which of the following administrative body of a university enjoys the status of a court?
   (A) Senate
   (B) Syndicate
   (C) Academic Council
   (D) None of the above

23. Which administrative post is NOT mandatory for a university?
   (A) Vice-Chancellor (B) Pro Vice-Chancellor
   (C) Registrar (D) Dean

24. Registered graduates of a university become part of which administrative body?
   (A) Senate
   (B) Syndicate
   (C) Academic Council
   (D) All of the above

25. Which of the following functions is performed by the Academic Council of a university?
   (A) Determining the admission qualifications
   (B) Classifying the study courses
   (C) Determining the pattern of evaluation and awarding of degrees
   (D) All of the above

KEY

1. B	2. C	3. B	4. C	5. D	6. D	7. B
8. C	9. B	10. A	11. B	12. D	13. D	14. D
15. B	16. C	17. A	18. B	19. C	20. B	21. D
22. A	23. B	24. A	25. D			

Assertion–Reason Format

1. **Assertion (A):** Governance of higher education bodies aims at research and development.

   Reason (R): Human resources are shaped as prospective research scientists by various higher education bodies.
   (A) Both A and R are true and R is correct explanation of A
   (B) Both A and R are true but R is not correct explanation of A
   (C) A is true but R is false
   (D) A is false but R is true

2. **Assertion (A):** UGC declares certain education institutions as deemed universities.

   Reason (R): An institution declared as a deemed university is taken as a regular university in transit.
   (A) Both A and R are true and R is correct explanation of A
   (B) Both A and R are true but R is not correct explanation of A
   (C) Both A and R are false
   (D) A is true but R is false

3. **Assertion (A):** NAAC is an accreditation agency of MHRD.

   Reason (R): NAAC's accreditation helps different higher education institutes to improve upon shortcomings in imparting higher education.
   (A) A is false but R is true
   (B) A is true but R is false
   (C) Both a and R are true and R is correct explanation of A
   (D) Both A and R are true but R is not correct explanation of A

4. **Assertion (A):** Granting autonomy to institutions of higher education is one of the recommendations of CABE.

   Reason (R): CABE, a think tank of UGC, is allotted the task of assessing scope of granting autonomy to bodies for higher education.
   (A) Both A and R are true and R is correct explanation of A
   (B) Both A and R are true but R is not correct explanation of A
   (C) A is false but R is true
   (D) A is true but R is false

5. **Assertion (A):** NUEPA is a central deemed university.

   Reason (R): Union MHRD minister is Chancellor of NUEPA.

(A) Both A and R are true and R is correct explanation of A

(B) Both A and R are true but R is not correct explanation of A

(C) Both A and R are false

(D) A is false but R is true

6. **Assertion (A):** COL is an international learning organisation created by Commonwealth.

Reason (R): India being a member of Commonwealth tops the list among funding agencies.

(A) A is true but R is false

(B) A is false but R is true

(C) Both A and R are true and R is correct explanation of A

(D) Both A and R are true but R is not correct explanation of A

7. **Assertion (A):** Central and State universities have the same structure of governance.

Reason (R): There is a common Chancellor of a state and central universities if they are falling in the same state.

(A) Both A and R are false

(B) Both A and R are true but R is not correct explanation of A

(C) Both A and R are true and R is correct explanation of A

(D) A is true but R is false

8. **Assertion (A):** DARE is a supervising agency of Indian Council of Philosophical Research (ICPR)

Reason (R): Union I & B Minister is the President of ICPR.

(A) Both A and R are false

(B) Both A and R are true and R is correct explanation of A

(C) A is true but R is false

(D) A is false but R is true

9. **Assertion (A):** Senate of a university is designated as court of the university.

Reason (R): Senate maintains the standards of university awards.

(A) Both A and R are true but R is not correct explanation of A

(B) Both A and R are true and R is correct explanation of A

(C) A is true but R is false

(D) A is false but R is true

10. **Assertion (A):** One of India's objective has been to regulate and promote rural higher education on the vision of Mahatma Gandhi.

Reason (R): National Council of Rural Institutes (NCRI) was established by the Central Government in 1995.

(A) A is true but R is false

(B) A is false but R is true

(C) Both A and R are true but R is not correct explanation of A

(D) Both A and R are true and R is correct explanation of A

KEY

1. B **2.** C **3.** A **4.** D **5.** B **6.** A **7.** C **8.** A **9.** A **10.** D

Questions Asked in Previous NET Exams

1. The premier organisation established in India to deal with capacity-building and research in planning and management of education in India and South Asia is **(UGC NET JUNE 2019)**

(A) AIU (B) SAARC University

(C) NUEPA (D) Nalanda University

2. In which year the modern Indian university got established? **(UGC NET JUNE 2019)**

(A) 1957 (B) 1857

(C) 1947 (D) 1964

3. The main aim of the faculty recharge scheme of UGC was to: **(UGC NET JUNE 2019)**

(A) Address the shortage of faculty in higher education institution

(B) Upgrade the teaching skills of the faculty

(C) Upgrade the research infrastructure for the faculty in colleges and universities

(D) Strengthen the academia-industry linkage

4. The University Grants Commission (UGC) was formally inaugurated on 28 December 1953 by whom among the following?

(UGC NET DECEMBER 2018)

(A) Sh. Maulana Abul Kalam Azad

(B) Dr. Rajendra Prasad

(C) Mrs. Indira Gandhi

(D) Dr. S. Radhakrishan

5. The mandate of the University Grants Commission (UGC) includes **(UGC NET JULY 2018)**

(i) Disbursing grants to Universities and colleges

(ii) Recognising and monitoring technical institutions

(iii) Funding research centres in Universities

(iv) Managing various scholarship programmes

Choose the correct answer from the code given below:

Code:

(A) (i), (ii), and (iv) (B) (i), (iii), and (iv)

(C) (i), (ii), and (iii) (D) (i), (ii), (iii) and (iv)

6. Which one of the following States is going to have India's first National Rail and Transportation University?

(UGC NET JULY 2018)

(A) Uttar Pradesh (B) Maharashtra

(C) Bihar (D) Gujarat

7. Which of the following statements are correct about deemed universities?

(UGC NET JANUARY 2017)

(a) The Governor of the State is the Chancellor of deemed universities.

(b) They can design their own syllabus and course work.

(c) They can frame their own guidelines regarding admission and fees.

(d) They can grant degrees.

Select the correct answer from the codes given here:

Codes:

(A) (a), (b), and (c) (B) (b), (c), and (d)

(C) (a), (c), and (d) (D) (a), (b), (c), and (d)

8. Which of the following core values among the institutions of higher education are promoted by the NAAC (National Assessment and Accreditation Council) ?

(UGC NET JULY 2016)

(a) Contributing to national development

(b) Fostering global competencies among students and teachers

(c) Inculcating a value system among students and teachers

(d) Promoting the optimum utilisation of the infrastructure

Select the correct answer from the codes given below:

(A) (b), (c), and (d) (B) (a), (b), and (c)

(C) (a), (c), and (d) (D) (a), (b), (c) and (d)

9. The University Grants Commission was established with which of the following aims?

(UGC NET JUNE 2015)

a) Promotion of research and development in higher education

b) Identifying and sustaining institutions of potential learning

c) Capacity-building of teachers

d) Providing autonomy to each and every higher educational institution in India

Select the correct answer from the codes given below:

(A) (b), (c), and (d)

(B) (a), (b), and (d)

(C) (a), (b), (c) and (d)

(D) (a), (b), and (c)

10. Which of the following institutions are empowered to confer or grant degrees under the UGC Act, 1956?

(UGC NET DECEMBER 2014)

1. A university established by an Act of Parliament

2. A university established by an Act of Legislature

3. A university/institution established by a linguistic minority

4. An institution which is a deemed to be university

Select the correct answers from the codes given below:

(A) 1 and 2 (B) 1, 2, and 3

(C) 1, 2, and 4 (D) 1, 2, 3, and 4

11. Which of the following organisations deals with "Capacity-building programme" on Educational Planning?

(UGC NET DECEMBER 2014)

(A) NCERT (B) UGC

(C) NAAC (D) NUEPA

12. Which of the following statements are correct about a Central University?

(UGC NET JUNE 2014)

1. Central University is established under an Act of Parliament.
2. The President of India acts as the visitor of the University.
3. The President has the power to nominate some members to the Executive Committee or the Board of Management of the University.
4. The President occasionally presides over the meetings of the Executive Committee or Court.

Select the correct answer from the code given below:

Codes:

(A) 1, 2, and 4

(B) 1, 3, and 4

(C) 1, 2, and 3

(D) 1, 2, 3, and 4

13. Which one of the following Councils has been disbanded in 2013?

(UGC NET DECEMBER 2013)

(A) Distance Education Council (DEC)

(B) National Council for Teacher Education (NCTE)

(C) National Council of Educational Research and Training (NCERT)

(D) National Assessment and Accreditation Council (NAAC)

14. Which of the following statements are correct about the National Assessment and Accreditation Council? **(UGC NET DECEMBER 2013)**

1. It is an autonomous institution.
2. It is tasked with the responsibility of assessing and accrediting institutions of higher education.
3. It is located in Delhi.
4. It has regional offices.

Select the correct answer from the codes given below:

Codes:

(A) 1 and 3 (B) 1 and 2

(C) 1, 2, and 4 (D) 2, 3, and 4

15. Which of the following statements about the Union Public Service Commission are correct?

(UGC NET SEPTEMBER 2013)

1. UPSC is a Constitutional body.
2. It serves as an advisory body.
3. It is called upon to advise the Government in regard to representation of the Scheduled Castes and Scheduled Tribes in the Civil Service.
4. It is consulted on appointments of Chairman and members of Tribunals and Commissions.

Select the correct answer from the codes given below:

Codes:

(A) 1, 2, and 3 (B) 1, 2, and 4

(C) 1, 3, and 4 (D) 1 and 2

16. Which one of the following statements is not correct about the University Grants Commission (UGC)? **(UGC NET JUNE 2013)**

(A) It was established in 1956 by an Act of Parliament.

(B) It is tasked with promoting and coordinating higher education.

(C) It receives Plan and Non-Plan funds from the Central Government.

(D) It receives funds from State Governments in respect of State Universities.

17. Indian Institute of Advanced Study is located at **(UGC NET JUNE 2012)**

(A) Dharmshala (B) Shimla

(C) Solan (D) Chandigarh

18. Indicate the number of Regional Offices of National Council of Teacher Education.

(UGC NET JUNE 2012, SEPTEMBER 2013)

(A) 4 (B) 5

(C) 6 (D) 8

19. Indicate the number of Regional Offices of University Grants Commission of India. **(UGC NET DECEMBER 2011)**
   (A) 10 (B) 7
   (C) 8 (D) 9
20. Most of the Universities in India are funded by **(UGC NET JUNE 2011)**
   (A) Central Government
   (B) State Governments
   (C) University Grants Commission
   (D) Private bodies and Individuals
21. Which of the following organisations looks after the quality of Technical and Management education In India? **(UGC NET JUNE 2011)**
   (A) NCTE (B) MCI
   (C) AICTE (D) CSIR
22. Most of the Universities in India **(UGC NET DECEMBER 2010)**
   (A) conduct teaching and research only
   (B) affiliate colleges and conduct examinations
   (C) conduct teaching/research and examinations
   (D) promote research only
23. The accreditation process by National Assessment and Accreditation Council (NAAC) differs from that of National Board of Accreditation (NBA) in terms of **(UGC NET JUNE 2010)**
   (A) Disciplines covered by both being the same, there is duplication of efforts.
   (B) One has institutional grading approach and the other has programme grading approach.
   (C) Once get accredited by NBA or NAAC, the institution is free from renewal of grading, which is not a progressive decision.
   (D) This accreditation amounts to approval of minimum standards in the quality of education in the institution concerned.
24. The University which telecasts interaction educational programmes through its own channel is **(UGC NET DECEMBER 2009)**
   (A) Osmania University
   (B) University of Pune
   (C) Annamalai University
   (D) Indira Gandhi National Open University (IGNOU)
25. Who has signed an MOU for Accreditation of Teacher Education Institutions in India? **(UGC NET DECEMBER 2009)**
   (A) NAAC and UGC (B) NCTE and NAAC
   (C) UGC and NCTE (D) NCTE and IGNOU
26. The Kothari Commission's report was entitled on: **(UGC NET JUNE 2009)**
   (A) Education and National Development
   (B) Learning to be adventure
   (C) Diversification of Education
   (D) Education and socialisation in democracy
27. Which of the following is not a Dual mode University? **(UGC NET JUNE 2009)**
   (A) Delhi University
   (B) Bengaluru University
   (C) Madras University
   (D) Indira Gandhi National Open University
28. According to Radhakrishnan Commission, the aim of Higher Education is: **(UGC NET DECEMBER 2008)**
   (A) To develop the democratic values, peace, and harmony
   (B) To develop great personalities who can give their contributions in politics, administration, industry, and commerce
   (C) Both (A) and (B)
   (D) None of these
29. NAAC is an autonomous institution under the aegis of: **(UGC NET JUNE 2008)**
   (A) ICSSR
   (B) CSIR
   (C) AICTE
   (D) UGC
30. National Council for Women's Education was established in: **(UGC NET JUNE 2008)**
   (A) 1958 (B) 1976
   (C) 1989 (D) 2000
31. The government established University Grants Commission by an Act of Parliament in the year **(UGC NET JUNE 2007)**
   (A) 1980 (B) 1948
   (C) 1950 (D) 1956

32. The University Grants Commission was constituted on the recommendation of:

(UGC NET DECEMBER 2006)

(A) Dr. Sarvapalli Radhakrishnan Commission
(B) Mudaliar Commission
(C) Sargeant Commission
(D) Kothari Commission

KEY

1. C	**2.** B	**3.** A	**4.** A	**5.** B	**6.** D	**7.** B
8. B	**9.** C	**10.** C	**11.** D	**12.** C	**13.** A	**14.** B
15. C	**16.** D	**17.** B	**18.** A	**19.** B	**20.** C	**21.** C
22. C	**23.** C	**24.** D	**25.** B	**26.** A	**27.** D	**28.** C
29. D	**30.** A	**31.** D	**32.** A			

PART-II

MISCELLANEOUS FACTS

1. National Education Policy 2020 has changed the name of HRD Ministry to

(A) Ministry of Education and Research
(B) Human resources Ministry
(C) Ministry of Education
(D) Ministry of Education for Human Resources

2. Which of the following is TRUE about higher education?

a) Higher education is imparted through formal and informal means
b) There is ample scope of research in every stream of higher education
c) Higher education is imparted to shape future bureaucrats, planners, and leaders
d) There is no mode of education other than higher education when acquiring specialisation is considered.

(A) Only c (B) a, c, and d
(C) b and d (D) a, b, c and d

3. India's higher education system is the third largest in world after USA and

(A) China (B) Canada
(C) Japan (D) Australia

4. National Policy of Education 1986 characterises higher education as

(A) basic force behind specialisation
(B) motivating stimulant for research
(C) crucial factor for survival
(D) indispensable trait for existence

5. Which portal of government of India furnishes information regarding education of any level and of any stream

(A) ind.edu.in
(B) india.gov.in
(C) eduindia.ac.in
(D) edcanindia.gov.in

6. National Education Policy 2020 has provided for establishing HECI. What is the full form of HECI?

(A) Higher Education Commission of India
(B) Holistic Education commission of India
(C) Higher Education Council of India
(D) Holistic Education Council of India

7. Given below are two statements on provisions of National Policy of Education 2020:

Statement I. Launching of 'Lok Vidya' programme under which cultural and value education will be made accessible to students.

Statement II. Implementing a 'light but tight' regulatory framework to ensure integrity, transparency, and resource efficiency of the educational system through audit and public disclosure.

In the light of above statements choose the most appropriate answer from the options given below

(A) Both Statement I and Statement II are correct
(B) Both Statement I and Statement II are incorrect
(C) Statement I is correct and Statement II is incorrect
(D) Statement I is incorrect and Statement II is correct

8. According to AISHE 2018-19, which state has maximum number of women universities?

(A) Andhra Pradesh
(B) Rajasthan
(C) Kerala
(D) Punjab

9. Names of current schemes of higher education are given under Column I and their associated area is given under Column II. Match the name of scheme with its respective area of association and choose the correct code among the given codes.

Column - I (Scheme)	Column - II (Associated Area)
a) GIAN	i) Aiming to lend low-cost funds to government higher educational institutions
b) SANKALP	ii) Academic and research collaboration between Indian institutions and the best institutions of the world
c) RISE	iii) Collaboration between Indian Research groups with top research groups in the world
d) SPARC	iv) Government's implementation strategy in vocational education and training from inputs to results
	v) Connect the Indian academic and research and development (R&D) systems to the best of global science and scientists for a sustained international collaborative research

Codes:	(a)	(b)	(c)	(d)
(A)	iii	v	i	ii
(B)	ii	iv	v	iii
(C)	i	iii	iv	ii
(D)	iii	iv	i	ii

10. Which of the following is/are NOT provision(s) of National Policy of Education 2020 regarding higher education ?

(I) Multi-phased autonomy to colleges

(II) Establishing a National Assessment Centre PARAKH to give assessment guidelines to universities all over India.

(III) Raising GER to 50% by 2035.

(IV) Establishing Academic Bank of Credits.

(V) Revising time span of M.Phil. Programme

(VI) Conducting of university entrance exams by NTA

(VII) Strengthening college affiliation system

(A) I-II-V-VII (B) III-II-V-VI
(C) I-II-IV-III (D) III-II-VI-VII

11. Which of the scheme has been launched by the government of India for promoting research in social sciences?

(A) LEAP (B) IMPRESS
(C) IMPRINT (D) VAJRA

12. National Education Day is celebrated on 11 November to commemorate

(A) launching of National Policy of Education 1986

(B) launching of POA 1992

(C) birthday of Maulana Abul Kalam Azad

(D) establishment of Union Ministry of Education

13. According to AISHE 2018-19, which stream yields maximum number of Ph. D holders?

(A) Science

(B) Commerce

(C) Engineering & Technology

(D) Liberal Arts

14. Which of the following is/are TRUE about PMMMNMTT?

a) It is a mission to address teacher issues related to teachers

b) It was launched during XII Five Year Plan

c) It works for research in Pedagogy

d) It will pursue goals of building a strong professional cadre of teachers by setting performance standards

(A) a, b, c, and d (B) Only a
(C) Only a and d (D) Only d

15. Which of the following is NOT one of the objectives of RUSA?

(A) Ensuring reforms in the affiliation, academic, and examination systems

(B) Improving equity in higher education through participation by every section of aspirants

(C) Upgrading old state universities having obsolete infrastructure with funding from State Higher Education councils

(D) Organising faculty improvements programmes and leadership development of educational administrators

KEY

1. C	2. D	3. A	4. C	5. B	6. A	7. D
8. B	9. D	10. A	11. B	12. C	13. A	14. A
15. C						

Assertion–Reason Format

1. **Assertion (A):** Recently introduced schemes of higher education in India have earned a global status for it.

   Reason (R): Majority of schemes has enhanced avenues of research in higher education.

   (A) Both A and R are true and R is correct explanation of A

   (B) Both A and R are true but R is not correct explanation of A

   (C) A is true but R is false

   (D) A is false but R is true

2. **Assertion (A):** AISHE (2018-19) has presented a gloomy picture on current GER in Indian universities and colleges.

   Reason (R): GER for girls has been found to be higher than GER for boys.

   (A) Both A and R are true and R is correct explanation of A

   (B) Both A and R are true but R is not correct explanation of A

   (C) A is false but R is true

   (D) A is true but R is false

3. **Assertion (A):** Implementation of RUSA has given a fillip to state higher education system.

   Reason (R): State higher education system has been waiting for such a scheme since long.

   (A) Both A and R are true and R is correct explanation of A

   (B) Both A and R are true but R is not correct explanation of A

   (C) Both A and R are false

   (D) A is true but R is false

4. **Assertion (A):** National Policy of Education 2020 provides for no customary separation between social science and natural science streams for students.

   Reason (R): The policy goes for ensuring multidisciplinary and a holistic education for students across streams of vivid nature in the interest of increasing employment opportunities

   (A) Both A and R are true and R is correct explanation of A

   (B) Both A and R are true but R is not correct explanation of A

   (C) A is false but R is true

   (D) A is true but R is false

5. **Assertion (A):** Union HRD Ministry has launched Leadership for Academicians Programme (LEAP)

   Reason (R): Leadership and managerial skills are provided to senior faculty members in colleges or universities.

   (A) Both A and R are true and R is correct explanation of A

   (B) Both A and R are true but R is not correct explanation of A

   (C) A is true but R is false

   (D) A is false but R is true

KEY

1. B **2.** C **3.** D **4.** A **5.** A

Questions Asked in Previous NET Exams

1. In which of the following 'One nation one standard 'is mentioned as 'mantra' to ensure national standards and quality?

   (UGC NET DECEMBER 2019)

   (A) National Policy on education - 1968

   (B) National Policy on education - 1986

   (C) National Policy for Skill Development and entrepreneurship - 2015

   (D) NITI Aayog - 20017 to 18 to 2019 - 2020

2. Which of the following provides the overreaching vision that provides vision that guides research into socially relevant areas?

   (UGC NET DECEMBER 2019)

   (A) ARIIA (B) IMPRINT

   (C) NIRF (D) SWAYAMPRABHA

3. Expansion of SANKALP is

   (UGC NET JUNE 2019)

   (A) Sanskrit Awareness and Knowledge Acquisition of Language Programme

   (B) Skills Acquisition and Karate Awareness for Livelihood Promotion

(C) Skills Acquisition and Knowledge Awareness for Livelihood Promotion

(D) Sanskrit awareness and Knowledge Acquisition for Livelihood Promotion

4. GIAN (Global initiative of Academic Networks) has been launched by government of India in order to **(UGC NET DECEMBER 2018)**

(A) encourage Indian scholars to learn abroad

(B) discourage Indian scholars from researching in India

(C) encourage global scholars engage with their counterparts in India

(D) encourage global scholars engage with Indian scholars abroad

5. Which of the following was launched in 2013 with the purpose to provide strategic funding to eligible state higher educational institutions?

(UGC NET DECEMBER 2018)

(A) Rashtriya Madhyamik Shiksha Abhiyan

(B) All India Council for Technical Education

(C) Rashtriya Uchchatar Shiksha Abhiyan

(D) Sarva Shiksha Abhiyan

6. Which of the following are the goals of higher education in India?

(UGC NET NOVEMBER 2017)

(a) Access

(b) Equity

(c) Quality and Excellence

(d) Relevance

(e) Value-based Education

(f) Compulsory and Free Education

Select the correct answer from the code given below:

(A) (a), (b), (e), and (f)

(B) (a), (b), (c), (d), and (e)

(C) (a), (b), (c), (d), (e), and (f)

(D) (a), (b), and (e) only

7. Which of the following are the objectives of Rashtriya Uchchatar Shiksha Abhiyan (RUSA)?

(UGC NET DECEMBER 2015)

(a) To improve the overall quality of state institutions

(b) To ensure adequate availability of quality faculty

(c) To create new institutions through upgradation of existing autonomous colleges

(d) To downgrade universities with poor infrastructure into autonomous colleges

Select the correct answer from the codes given below:

(A) (a), (b), (c), and (d)

(B) (a), (b), and (c)

(C) (a), (c), and (d)

(D) (a), (b), and (d)

8. Civil Service Day is celebrated in India on:

(UGC NET JUNE 2015)

(A) 7th July (B) 21st April

(C) 24th April (D) 21st June

KEY

1. C **2.** B **3.** C **4.** C **5.** C **6.** C **7.** B **8.** B

Some Updated Vital Facts

1) The Swayam Prabha is a group of 34 DTH channels now.
2) Ministry of Education has launched an e-governance platform SAMARTH to provide quality education to students across all Universities & Higher Education Institutions (HEIs).
3) COP 25 Summit on Climate change has been held in Madrid (Spain).
4) "PARAM Shivay" is the name of the first Supercomputer designed and built under National Supercomputing Mission (NSM) by C-DAC at Indian Institute of Technology (BHU), Varanasi. It was dedicated to the scientific and research community of the nation
5) The Mission of Unnat Bharat Abhiyan is to enable higher educational institutions to work with the people of rural India in identifying development challenges and evolving appropriate solutions for accelerating sustainable growth.
6) Green Muffler is a technique of reducing noise pollution by planting 4-6 dense rows of trees around the populated areas or noisy places.
7) The highest percentage of Carbon Dioxide is emitted by China, followed by USA, India, Russia and Japan.
8) MOODLE stands for Modular Object-Oriented Dynamic Learning Environment. It was founded and developed by Martin Dougiamas in 2002. It was designed to provide educators, administrators, and learners with an open, robust, secure and free platform to create and deliver personalized learning environments.
9) SQL stands for Structured Query Language. SQL lets one access and manipulate databases.
10) China is the world leader in producing wind energy, with over a third of the world's capacity. India ranks fourth. Tamil Nadu tops in India
11) The top five countries of the world producing solar power chronologically are China, the United States, India, Japan, and Germany. Karnataka tops in India.
12) The US is the leading producer of geothermal energy across the world.
13) China is the leading producer of hydropower in the world. India ranks 5th. Himachal tops in India.
14) The USA is the world leader in producing nuclear energy. India stands at the 13th place
15) Iceland tops the world in producing renewable energy. India ranks third.
16) CPS stands for Characters per second. It is used in data entry to evaluate human computer typing speeds.
17) Photochemical smog is a mixture of pollutants that are formed when nitrogen oxides and volatile organic compounds (VOCs) react to sunlight, creating a brown haze above cities. It tends to occur more often in summer.
18) NEAT stands for National Educational Alliance for Technology. It is a public-private partnership (PPP) scheme launched by Ministry of Education for using technology for better learning outcomes in Higher Education.
19) A predatory Journal takes advantage of authors by asking them to publish for a fee without providing peer-review or editing services.
20) The File Transfer Protocol (FTP) is a standard network protocol used for the transfer of computer files between a client and server on a computer network.
21) The 2021 United Nations Climate Change Conference, also known as COP26, is the 26th United Nations Climate Change conference. It is scheduled to be held in Glasgow, Scotland from 1 to 12 November 2021 under the presidency of the United Kingdom.
22) COP24 conference took place from 2-16 December 2018 in Katowice, Poland. The main goal of the COP24 summit was to adopt a package of implementing rules for the Paris Agreement
23) As per Swachh Survekshan 2020 Chhattisgarh won the title of India's cleanest state for second time in a row and Indore is India's cleanest city for the fourth time in a row.

24) Swachh Survekshan is conducted by Ministry of Urban Development.

25) The Learning Management System (LMS) has been launched in December 2020 by the Karnataka government in digital mode. It will be implemented in government colleges within the state. It is said to be the first of its kind initiative in the country aimed at encouraging digital learning and improving the Gross Enrolment Ratio (GER) in higher education.

26) The Internet of things (IOT) explains the network of sensor fitted physical objects, software, and other technologies for the purpose of connecting and exchanging data with other devices and systems over the Internet.

27) Maximum performance Test is designed to test the limits of the knowledge and abilities of an examinee.

28) Typical Response Test is designed to measure things like personality, behaviour, attitudes or interests of the examinee.

29) New media is any media - from newspaper articles and blogs to music and podcasts - that are delivered digitally. From a website or email to mobile phones and streaming apps, any internet-related form of communication can be considered new media. It has made online learning independent

30) Black carbon aerosols are primary air pollutants.

NTA UGC NET PAPER - 1

(Date : 08-10-2022)

Directions (Q. 1 to 5) : The following table shows the percentage (%) distribution of total population, literate males and literate females in six cities A-F. In all cities together total population, number of literate males and number of literate females are 1.5 crore, 40 lakh and 25 lakh respectively. Ratio of males to females among the total population is 8 : 7. Based on the data in the table, answer the questions 1-5.

City	(%) Population (Out of 1.5 crore)	(%) Literate Males (Out of 40 lakh)	(%) Literate Females (Out of 25 lakh)
A	16%	18%	24%
B	18%	12%	18%
C	21%	20%	12%
D	15%	16%	16%
E	20%	19%	20%
F	10%	15%	10%

1. Number of literate males of city E as a percentage of number of literate females of city F is

(a) 240% (b) 118%

(c) 304% (d) 32.89%

2. The difference between literate population and illiterate population of city C is

(a) 8.5 lakh (b) 9.5 lakh

(c) 10.5 lakh (d) 20.5 lakh

3. Number of literate males of city D is........% more than number of literate females of city D.

(a) 160 (b) 60

(c) 61.538 (d) 120

4. Literate population of city E is..................% of the population of E

(a) 40 (b) 64

(c) 26 (d) 42

5. The illiterate population of city A is

(a) 10 lakh (b) 14.2 lakh

(c) 16.8 lakh (d) 18 lakh

6. Kinesics, when used, will communicate a person's

A. Social status

B. Level of involvement

C. Emotional Quotient

D. Political mobility

E. Language ambiguity

Choose the correct answer from the options given below:

(a) A, B, C only (b) B, C, D only

(c) D, C, E only (d) A, D, E only

7. In a certain code scheme "UNIVERSITY" is coded as "EIINRSTUVY". How INSTITUTION will be coded in the same coding scheme?

(a) IIINNOSTTTU (b) IININOSUTTT

(c) INIINOSTUTT (d) IINNIOSTTTU

8. A destructive computer program that masquerades as a useful application is called

(a) Virus (b) Worm

(c) Trojan (d) Firmware

9. Previous National Education Policy 1986 was modified in the year

(a) 1990 (b) 1992

(c) 1987 (d) 1996

10. Given below are two statements:

Statement I : language and other symbolic means of communication are surely social products.

Statement II : Communication media always provide the feel-good factor to their users.

In the light of the above statements, choose the correct answer from the options given below:

(a) Both statement I and statement II are true

(b) Both statement I and statement II are false

(c) Statement I is true but statement II is false

(d) Statement I is false but statement II is true

11. Which of the following forms of categorical propositions is valid?
A. Some S is not P B. Some S is P
C. No S is P D. All S is P
Choose the correct answer from the options given below:
(a) A, B and C only (b) B, C and D only
(c) A, C and D only (d) A, B, C D

12. A True Zero Point is a feature of
(a) Nominal Scale (b) Ratio Scale
(c) Interval Scale (d) Ordinal Scale

13. In communication, channel richness is the highest in case of
(a) Television
(b) Newspaper
(c) face-to-face conversation
(d) Formal reports

14. The proposition 'All things are non-eternal, because they are knowable' is fallacious because
(a) The middle term is non-exclusive
(b) The middle term is too narrow
(c) The middle term is too wide
(d) It involves a contradictory middle term

15. When a research study is conducted to know about an unknown area and collect information, it is known as
(a) Pilot study (b) Feasibility study
(c) Explanatory study (d) Exploratory study

16. Which of the following is a semantic barrier?
(a) Blurred image on television
(b) Unclear printing in newspaper
(c) Static broadcasting
(d) Redundancy in writing

17. What does the symbol (cc) signify?
(a) copyright material
(b) copyable material
(c) creative commons
(d) copying commons

18. Which of the following is a teacher-centered method?
(a) Problem solving
(b) Discussion method
(c) Inquiry approach
(d) Demonstration method

19. Which of the following are similarity elements in both qualitative and quantitative research?
A. Answering research questions
B. Preference to macro data.
C. Do not suffer from issues of error
D. Importance to transparency
E. Exploration of variation
Choose the correct answer from the options given below:
(a) A, B, C only (b) B, C, D only
(c) A, D, E only (d) A, B, E only

20. A sum of Rs. 16800 is divided in two parts. One part is lent at a simple rate of interest of 6% per annum and other part at 8% per annum. After 2 years the total sum received is Rs, 19,000. Find the sum lent at rate of 6% and 8% respectively.
(a) 12200, 4600 (b) 11000, 5800
(c) 12000, 4800 (d) 4800, 12000

21. Which of the following are common criteria of tests?
A. Administrative condition
B. All questions of higher order thinking skills.
C. Time limit
D. Nature of questions
E. Marks allocation
Choose the correct answer from the options given below:
(a) A, C, D only (b) B, C, D only
(c) B, C, D, E only (d) A, C, D, E only

22. Find the next term in the series given below:
5, 9, 14, 20, 27, 35, ?
(a) 62 (b) 70
(c) 44 (d) 42

23. The Acts of incorporation passed in 1857 provided for the establishment of universities of Calcutta, Bombay and Madras on the model of
(a) Cambridge University
(b) University of Harvard
(c) Oxford University
(d) University of London

24. Given below are two statements:

Statement I : Triangulation is described as that of researchers taking different perspectives in answering research questions.

Statement II : Triangulation is expected to produce knowledge from different insights to promote quality research.

(a) Both statement I and statement II are true
(b) Both statement I and statement II are false
(c) Statement I is true but statement II is false
(d) Statement I is false but statement II is true

25. Which of the following are Sustainable Development Goals (SDGs)?

A. No poverty
B. Zero hunger
C. Employment to everyone
D. Quality education
E. Gender equality

(a) A, B, C only (b) A, B, C, D only
(c) A, B, D, E only (d) C, D, E only

26. The average weight of 30 persons is increased by 2 kg when one of them whose weight is 40 kg is replaced by a new person. What is the weight of new person?

(a) 98 kg (b) 100kg
(c) 102 kg (d) 95 kg

27. Which logical informal fallacy is committed in the following argument-"No one has shown that aliens did not create the crop circles. So the crop circles must have been made by the aliens?"

(a) Begging the question
(b) Appeal to ignorance.
(c) Fallacy of accident
(d) Appeal to authority

28. The most important fallout of university reforms under whose leadership was the first official announcement of the future education policy of the Government of India to reduce the tension created among the educated Indians by the process of his university reforms?

(a) Charles Wood
(b) Hunter
(c) Curzon
(d) Dalhousie

29. Identify the correct sequence of the following elements in the mass communication process?

A. Selective exposure
B. Selective attention
C. Cognitive dissonance
D. Congruent information
E. Conformation of bias

(a) B A D C E (b) A E C B D
(c) C D E B A (d) E C A B D

30. Indian national Ambient Air Quality standards stimulate the maximum permissible limit of annual mean concentration of PM 2.5 to be

(a) 60 $\mu g/m^3$ (b) 45 $\mu g/m^3$
(c) 40 $\mu g/m^3$ (d) 25 $\mu g/m^3$

31. Which of the following are unethical in the context of research?

A. seeking informed consent of respondents
B. Offering incentives to respondents.
C. Coercing respondents for sensitive personal information.
D. Hiding the research purpose from respondents
E. Maintaining confidentiality.

Choose the correct answer from the options given below:

(a) A, B, C only (b) B, C, D only
(c) C, D, E only (d) A, B, D only

32) Which of the following recognized for the first time that the government should give 'frank and cordial support' to female education and take effective measures for its expansion?

(a) Women's Indian Association
(b) All India Women's Conference
(c) The Woods dispatch
(d) National Council of Women

33. Given below are two statements:

Statement I : Aristotelian syllogism has three terms.

Statement II : Nyaya syllogism has five terms.

In the light of above statements, choose the most appropriate answer from the options given below:

(a) Both statement I and statement II are true
(b) Both statement I and statement II are false
(c) Statement I is true but statement II is false
(d) Statement I is false but statement II is true

34. Given below are two statements, One is labelled as Assertion (A) and the other is labelled as Reason (R)

Assertion (A) : One of the objective of higher education is to promote critical and creative thinking abilities in the students

Reason (R) : Critical and creative thinking abilities are developed by rote learning

In the light of above statements, choose the most appropriate answer from the options given below:

(a) Both A and R are correct and R is the correct explanation of A
(b) Both A and R are correct but R is not correct explanation of A
(c) A is correct but R is not correct
(d) A is not correct but R is correct

35. Wind energy

A. is an intermittent energy
B. is extremely useful at remote and isolated places
C. does not depend on weather
D. is a clean energy
E. does not have any environmental impact at all.

Choose the most appropriate answer from the options given below:

(a) A, B, C only (b) A, B, D only
(c) B, C, D only (d) C, D, E only

36. Consider the worksheet below:

	A	B	C	D	E	F
1	Data	Result				
2	-4					
3						
4						

If a user wants to do following

i. Print "Within Budget" in cell B3 if the value in cell A2 is less than or equal to zero.
ii. Print "Over Budget" in cell B3 if value in cell A2 is greater than 100; then what formula would the user have to type in order to achieve the above stated goals?

(a) =IF (A2<100 "Within Budget", "Over Budget")
(b) =IF (A2>=100, "Over Budget", "Within Budget")
(c) =IF (A2<=100, "Over Budget", "Within Budget")
(d) =IF (A2>=100, "Over Budget", "Within Budget")

37. Find the number that must be added to the terms of the ratio 13 : 25 to make it equal to 7 : 10.

(a) 8 (b) 11
(c) 15 (d) 13

38. Given below are two statements, one is labelled as Assertion (A) and the other is labelled as Reason (R)

Assertion (A) : Large scale dams also cause greenhouse gas emissions.

Reason (R) : When submerged vegetation decays, it produces carbon dioxide, which is a green house gas

In the light of above statements, choose the most appropriate answer from the options given below:

(a) Both A and R are correct and R is the correct explanation of A
(b) Both A and R are correct but R is not correct explanation of A
(c) A is correct but R is not correct
(d) A is not correct but R is correct

39. Which of the following universities have been recognized as Institutes of Eminence?

A. Banaras Hindu University
B. Amrita Vishwa Vidya Peetham
C. Calcutta University
D. Central University of Hyderabad
E. Jawaharlal Nehru University

Choose the most appropriate answer from the options given below:

(a) A, B and E only
(b) A, B and D only
(c) C, D and E only
(d) A, B, C and D only

40. To receive e-mail, you need an e-mail provider, a connection to your provider and an e-mail application. If your Internet Service Provider (ISP) has a POP server, you have a wide choice of email applications.

What does the acronym POP stand for?

(a) Page Overlay Protocol

(b) Post Office Protocol

(c) Power Outage Protocol

(d) Postal off Protocol

41. Given below are two statements:

Statement I : The concept of cyber technology is described as a wide range of networked communication devices.

Statement II : Many sociologists are concerned with people becoming too dependent on technology

In the light of above statements, choose the most appropriate answer from the options given below:

(a) Both statement I and statement II are true

(b) Both statement I and statement II are false

(c) Statement I is true but statement II is false

(d) Statement I is false but statement II is true

42. Given below are two statements:

Statement I : Bioconcentration in humans can occur due to consumption of fish

Statement II : Bioconcentration is the tendency of hazardous substances to accumulate in human tissues.

In the light of above statements, choose the most appropriate answer from the options given below:

(a) Both statement I and statement II are true

(b) Both statement I and statement II are false

(c) Statement I is true but statement II is false

(d) Statement I is false but statement II is true

43. The Microsoft Office Power Point, there are two types of slide orientation that are supported. What are these orientation types?

(a) Portrait and Landscape

(b) Upright and Landscape

(c) Portrait and Facedown

(d) landscape and Facedown

44. In the context of curriculum, which of the following are correct?

A. Curriculum should be modified regularly

B. Curriculum should have theoretical concepts only

C. Curriculum should be derived from constitutional imperatives of the country

D. Curriculum should be made as per needs of industry and society.

E. Curriculum should be teacher-centric

Choose the most appropriate answer from the options given below:

(a) A, D and E only (b) C and D only

(c) A, C and D only (d) A, B, C and D

45. Which of the following propositions is contrary to the proposition "All women are honest"?

(a) Some women are not honest

(b) No women are honest

(c) Some women are not dishonest

(d) No women are dishonest

Read the passage and answer questions from question 46-50

There is a new movement called libertarian paternalism which is not attractive. Both words are characterized by stereotypes from popular culture and politics that make them unappealing to many.

Even worse, the concepts seem to be contradictory. If the terms are properly understood, both concepts reflect commonsense. They are far more attractive together than alone. According to libertarian strategy, people should be free to do what they like. It is also to opt out of undesirable arrangements, if they want to do so. The libertarian paternalists urge that people should be free to choose. Policies are designed to maintain or increase freedom of choice. The paternalistic aspect lies in the claim that it is legitimate for choice architects to try to influence people's behaviour. It is to make people's lives longer, healthier and better. Institutions in private sector and also the government should make conscious efforts to steer people's choices to improve their lives. A policy is paternalistic, if it tries to influence choices that make choosers better off, as judged by people themselves. It is a fact that individuals make often pretty bad decisions. These would not have been made, had they paid full attention and possessed complete information, unlimited cognitive abilities, and complete self-control. Libertarian paternalism, however, is relatively weak, soft and non-intrusive type of paternalism, because it does not force people from taking bad decisions.

46. The government and private institutions should make efforts to
(a) prevent people from taking bad decisions
(b) allow people to go their own way
(c) make people judge themselves
(d) steer people's choices for improving their lives.

47. The movement of libertarian paternalism is unattractive as it is a combination of
(a) common sense concepts
(b) dogmatic concepts
(c) contradictory concepts
(d) popular culture and politics

48. Libertarian strategy insists that people should opt for
(a) Freedom of choice
(b) Paternalistic support
(c) Even undesirable arrangements
(d) Modification of their freedom

49. Libertarian paternalists seek policies aimed to
(a) change the people's preferences
(b) preserve the people's liberty of choice
(c) burden the people with choices
(d) make the people's choice legitimate

50. The focus of the passage is on
(a) The opposition to libertarian paternalism
(b) The unlimited cognitive abilities of individuals
(c) The freedom of choices for a better society
(d) the need to ignore the defects of libertarian paternalism

Answer Key

1. (c)	**2.** (b)	**3.** (b)	**4.** (d)	**5.** (a)	**6.** (a)	**7.** (a)	**8.** (d)	**9.** (b)	**10.** (c)
11. (d)	**12.** (b)	**13.** (c)	**14.** (a)	**15.** (d)	**16.** (d)	**17.** (c)	**18.** (d)	**19.** (c)	**20.** (a)
21. (d)	**22.** (c)	**23.** (d)	**24.** (a)	**25.** (c)	**26.** (b)	**27.** (b)	**28.** (c)	**29.** (b)	**30.** (c)
31. (b)	**32.** (c)	**33.** (c)	**34.** (c)	**35.** (b)	**36.** (d)	**37.** (c)	**38.** (c)	**39.** (b)	**40.** (b)
41. (a)	**42.** (d)	**43.** (a)	**44.** (c)	**45.** (b)	**46.** (d)	**47.** (c)	**48.** (a)	**49.** (b)	**50.** (c)

Solutions

Directions (Q. 1 to 5) : Given total population = 1.5 crore i.e. 150 lakhs

City	Total Population (In Lakhs)	Literate Males (In Lakhs)	Literate Females (In Lakhs)
A	16% of 1.5 = 24	18% Of 40 = 7.2	24% of 25 = 6
B	27	4.8	4.5
C	31.5	8	3
D	22.5	6.4	4
E	30	7.6	5
F	15	6	2.5

1. Literate males in city E = 7.6 lakh
   Literate females in the city F = 2.5 lakh.
   According to question: 7.6/2.5 × 100 = 304%
2. Total population of city C = 31.5 lakh
   Total Literates = 8 + 3 = 11 lakh
   So total illiterate population of city C
   = 31.5 – 11 = 20.5 lakh
   Required difference=20.5-11=9.5 lakh
3. Literate males of city D=6.4 lakh
   Literate females of city D=4 lakh
   Required percentage
   = Difference/Literate females × 100
   = (6.4 – 4)/4 × 100 = 60%
4. Total population of city E = 30 lakh
   Literate population = 7.6 + 5 = 12.6 lakh
   Required % age = 12.6/30 × 100 = 42%
5. Total population of city A = 24 lakh
   Total literates = 7.2 + 6 = 13.2
   So total illiterate population of city A
   = 24-13.2 = 10.8 lakh
6. Kinesics is the broad field of nonverbal communication solely concerned with the interpretation of nonverbal behaviours that are associated with body movement, gestures, posture, facial expression and eye contact. Gestures reveal social status, how much a person is involved in communication and how much emotionally he or she is attached.
7. The word UNIVERSITY is encoded in the following way:

   U N I V E R S I T Y
   E I I N R S T U V Y

   In above coding scheme, letters of the word UNIVERSITY have been arranged in A-to-Z order i.e. the coded word starts from letter E which is closest to A. Then E is followed by I which is next letter to E in the word and so on. On the same pattern if the word INSTITUTION is encoded. We get IIINNOSTTTU.
10. Statement II is false as communication media does not ALWAYS provide feel good factor to its users. Here the word ALWAYS makes the statement false.
11. Here all the given categorical propositions are valid as they denote all the four categories of propositions given by Aristotle i.e All S is P is A, No S is P is E, Some S is P is I and Some S is not P is O.
12. A true zero refers to a scale where 0 indicates the absence of something. A ratio scale is a quantitative scale where there is a true zero and equal intervals between neighbouring points. Unlike on an interval scale, a zero on a ratio scale means there is a total absence of the variable one is measuring. Length, area, and population are examples of ratio scales.
13. Face-to-face and telephone conversation, video conferencing has high information richness because Receivers and Senders can see or hear beyond just the words—they can see the Sender's body language or hear the tone of their voice.
16. Semantic barrier is a barrier of words, sentences and grammar, that is why superfluousness in writing creates semantic barrier as the recipient is not able to understand the redundant message.
17. Symbol (cc) signifies Creative Commons. CC is an international non-profit organization that empowers people to grow and sustain the thriving commons of shared knowledge and culture we need to address the world's most pressing challenges and create a brighter future for all.

18. Demonstration method is a teacher centered method as teacher is all in all and students are passive participants whereas in other methods students actively participate.

19. Both qualitative and quantitative research go for transparency, answering the research questions and both explore variation.

20. Let sum of Rs. 16800 be divided as x and 16800-x
Interest = Total amount received – principal
= 19000-16800 = 2200

According to the question :

x × 6 × 2/100 + (16800 – x) × 8 × 2/100 = 2200

12x/100 + (16800 – x) × 16/100 = 2200

12x/100 + 268800 – 16x/100 = 2200

12x + 268800 – 16x/100 = 2200

268800 – 4x/100 = 2200

268800 – 4x = 220000, 48800 = 4x

X = 12200 Hence both parts are 12200 and 4600

22. 5, 9, 14, 20, 27, 35, ?
5 + 4, 9 + 5, 14 + 6, 20 + 7, 27 + 8, 35 + 9 44

24. Here both the statements are correct as triangulation is the application and combination of several research methods in the study of the same phenomenon. In triangulation researchers, while combining research, take different perspectives and get knowledge from different insights to answer research questions and promote quality research.

26. Let average weight of 30 persons be x
Average × number of persons = sum of weight
x × 30 = 30x
Let the weight of new person = w
New Average = x + 2
New Sum = 30x – 40 + w
Here number of persons remain the same
New Average × Number of persons = New Sum
(x + 2) × 30 = 30x – 40 + w
30x + 60 = 30x – 40 + w
w = 100
Hence weight of new person = 100 kg

27. In this fallacy it is clear that no one has come forward to prove that aliens did not create the crop circles, and it shows that it is fallacy of appeal to ignorance.

33. Here statement II is false as like Aristotelian syllogism, Nyaya syllogism also has three terms i.e. Sadhya, the major term, Paksha, the minor term and Linga, the middle term

34. Here R is incorrect as rote learning is practiced at memory level of teaching which caters primary education and not higher education. Moreover, rote learning is practiced without understanding the concept, so it cannot develop critical and creative thinking.

37. Ratio of numbers is 13 : 25
According to question: 13 + x/25 + x = 7/10
10(13 + x) = 7(25 + x)
130 + 10x = 175 + 7x
3x = 45 implies x =15

38. Assertion is correct as large-scale dams release Methane gas, which is a greenhouse gas. On the other hand Reason is not correct as submerged decaying vegetation releases Methane and not Carbon dioxide.

42. Statement I is false as bioconcentration does not occur in humans due to consumption of fish. This happens when a chemical is consumed or absorbed, and the body cannot catabolize or excrete it quickly enough. Mercury is a well-known chemical that will bioaccumulate in humans.

44. Curriculum should be flexible, policy inspired and learner centric. That is why answer choice no. 3 is the answer.

45. As per square of opposition, propositions of category A and E are contrary to each other. Here "All women are honest" is A category proposition and "No women are honest" is E category proposition. So answer choice no. 2 is the answer.

NTA UGC NET PAPER - 1

(Date : 04-03-2023)

The following table shows distribution of male (M) and female (F) athletes who participated in an Annual Sports Event from five different countries A-E over the years 2016 to 2021. Based on the data in the table answer the questions.

Year-wise Country-wise Distribution of Athletes

Country	A		B		C		D		E	
Year	M	F	M	F	M	F	M	F	M	F
2016	220	165	315	210	225	155	280	205	235	105
2017	330	210	420	310	345	165	420	315	390	260
2018	230	90	370	240	240	140	465	365	435	325
2019	480	245	570	420	330	210	630	470	445	290
2020	590	320	530	260	390	315	720	510	590	460
2021	410	260	320	360	540	345	780	605	680	490

1. The difference between male and female athletes from country C was the second highest in the year__________

(a) 2016 (b) 2017

(c) 2019 (d) 2021

2. The average number of female athletes who participated from country B over all the years together was__________

(a) 300 (b) 275

(c) 310 (d) 280

3. The approximate percentage decrease in the number of athletes who participated from country C in the year 2018 as compared to previous year was__________

(a) 21%

(b) 25%

(c) 30%

(d) 35%

4. The number of female athletes who participated from country E in the year 2020 was_______% of the total number of athletes who participated from country B in the year 2019.

(a) 60 (b) 56

(c) 50 (d) 46

5. In the year 2017, the total number of athletes who participated in the event was the second highest from the country__________

(a) A (b) B

(c) D (d) E

6. The quality of one's memory can be judged on the basis of his/her

(a) Power of retention

(b) Analytical ability

(c) Communication skills

(d) Mathematical numeracy

7. Given below are two statements

Statement I. Padlet is a game-based platform used in educational institutions to create quizzes, conversations and surveys

Statement II. Seesaw is an app-based platform that allows students to work together on texts, PDFs drawings and videos

In the light of above statements choose the most appropriate answer from the options given below

(a) Both statement I and statement II are correct

(b) Both statement I and statement II are incorrect

(c) Statement I is correct but statement II is incorrect

(d) Statement I is incorrect but statement II is correct

8. Given below are two statements

Statement I. Vygotsky emphasised the significant role played by adults and more abled peers in children's learning

Statement II. The zone of proximal development is the area, where the child solves a problem alone without the help of others.

In the light of above statements choose the most appropriate answer from the options given below

(a) Both statement I and statement II are correct

(b) Both statement I and statement II are incorrect

(c) Statement I is correct but statement II is incorrect

(d) Statement I is incorrect but statement II is correct

9. According to David and Johnson which of the following are the basic elements of cooperative learning groups

A. Self conceptualisation

B. Individual accountability

C. Skill development

D. Positive interdependence

E. Promotive interaction

Choose the correct answer from the options given below

(a) A, C and D only (b) A, B and E only

(c) B, D and E only (d) A, B, D and E only

10. According to Kohlberg's theory the conventional level of moral development includes the following stages

A. Obedience orientation

B. Being nice/relationships orientation

C. Social contract orientation

D. Law and order orientation

E. Universal Ethical Principles orientation

Choose the correct answer from the options given below

(a) A and E only (b) C and D only

(c) B and D only (d) B, C and E only

11. The tendency of researchers to subtly and inadvertently affect the behaviours of participants in a study, obscuring true effect of independent variable is called

(a) Placebo effect

(b) Experimental bias effect

(c) The Hawthorne effect

(d) Evaluation apprehension effect

12. Arrange the following components of a research paper written in APA style, in correct order

A. Figures B. Methods

C. Introduction D. Tables

E. Results

Choose the correct answer from the options given below

(a) C, E, B, D, A (b) C, B, E, D, A

(c) C, B, A, D,E (d) C, B, E, A, D

13. The extent to which a measure yields the same score across different times, groups of people, or versions of the instrument, is called

(a) Reliability (b) Content validity

(c) Construct validity (d) Predictive validity

14. Given below are two statements

Statement I. Snowball sampling is a type of random sampling

Statement II. Snowball sampling.is helpful when participants belong to hard-to-reach groups.

In the light of above statements choose the most appropriate answer from the options given below

(a) Both statement I and statement II are correct

(b) Both statement I and statement II are incorrect

(c) Statement I is correct but statement II is incorrect

(d) Statement I is incorrect but statement II is correct

15. In case of negatively skewed distribution

(a) Mean<Mode<Median

(b) Mean>Mode>Median

(c) Mean>Median>Mode

(d) Mean<Median<Mode

16. One of the cool media of communication is

(a) Print (b) Television

(c) Photograph (d) Radio

17. In mass communication print is considered as a/an

(a) Folk medium

(b) Electronic medium

(c) Mechanical medium

(d) Ordinary medium

18. Which of the following are characteristics of interactive communication?

A. It is decentralised

B. It is state controlled

C. It is highly centralised

D. It is a two-way communication

E. It provides universal citizenship

Choose the correct answer from the options given below

(a) A, B, C only (b) B, C, D only

(c) C, D, E only (d) A, D, E only

19. Which of the following make classroom communication interesting?

A. Many asides while speaking

B. Fruitful discussions

C3 Use of relevant transitions

D3 Finding out the correct context

E3 Pressurising the students with authoritarian commands

Choose the correct answer from the options given below

(a) A, B and C only (b) B, C and D only

(c) C, D and E only (d) A, D and E only

20. Given below are two statements

Statement I. The new technologies have brought in 'Market specification communication.'

Statement II. The second media age has made the interactive technologies of communication to change the media space.

In the light of above statements choose the most appropriate answer from the options given below

(a) Both statement I and statement II are correct

(b) Both statement I and statement II are incorrect

(c) Statement I is correct but statement II is incorrect

(d) Statement I is incorrect but statement II is correct

21. In certain coding language

A. 'odo pado fao' means 'Order packed food'

B. 'pado fao sa digo' means 'packed food is good.'

C. 'digo yao mao' means 'good young man.'

D. 'yao mao sa sito' means 'young man is strong.'

Which of the following means 'order' and 'strong' respectively in that language

(a) 'yao' and 'mao' (b) 'digo' and 'mao'

(c) 'pado' and 'sito' (d) 'odo' and 'sito'

22. In a competitive examination held in 2000, a total of 6,00000 (6 lakh) students appeared and 40% passed the examination. 40% of total students were females and the rest were males. The pass %age among males was 50%. Find the pass %age among the females.

(a) 25% (b) 30%

(c) 35% (d) 40%

23. What should replace the question mark (?) in the following series:

450, 473, 519, 588, 680, 795, ?

(a) 933 (b) 950

(c) 138 (d) 82

24. A businessman buys a house for Rs. 9.00 lakhs. He puts the house on rent and keeps 15% of each month's rent separately for repairs. After paying Rs. 2106 as annual taxes on the rent, he realizes 10% annually on investment. Find the monthly rent of the house.

(a) Rs. 10,000 (b) Rs. 9080

(c) Rs. 9030 (d) Rs. 9500

25. Sum of 3 consecutive odd numbers and 3 consecutive even numbers is 231. Also, the smallest odd number is 11 less than smallest even number. What is the sum of the largest odd number and the largest even number?

(a) 81 (b) 73

(c) 77 (d) 79

26. "First it is staying out late, then it is not calling home, then wild parties, and before you know it, your life will be completely out of control. Some day yoy will be glad that you had a lockdown." Which informal fallacy is committed in above argument?

(a) Red herring

(b) Slippery slope

(c) Strawman

(d) Appeal to authority

27. Which of the following statements are logically equivalent?

A. No philosophers are industrialists

B. No industrialists are philosophers

C. All non-industrialists are non-philosophers

D. All philosophers are non-industrialists

Choose the correct answer from the options given below

(a) A, B and C only (b) A, B and D only

(c) A, C and D only (d) B, C and D only

28. Which of the following statements are logically contradictory to each other

A. All philosophers are industrialists

B. Some philosophers are not industrialists

C. No philosophers are industrialists

D. No industrialists are philosophers

Choose the correct answer from the options given below

(a) A and B only (b) A, C and D only

(c) A and C only (d) C and D only

29. If the statement 'No philosophers are industrialists' is given as true which of the following statement can be immediately inferred from it to be true?

(a) No philosophers are rich persons

(b) All industrialists are philosophers

(c) Some philosophers are industrialists

(d) Some philosophers are not industrialists

30. According to Nyaya (classical Indian school of logic) which means of knowledge (Pramana) is used in the following argument-"The word is an effect and hence it must have an efficient cause like all objects e.g. pots, clothes etc do. That efficient cause is God."

(a) Postulation (arthapati)

(b) Inference (anumana)

(c) Comparison (upmana)

(d) Verbal Testimony (S'abda)

31. Which of the following acronyms matches incorrectly with its full form?

(a) ATM – Automatic Teller Machine

(b) SIM – Subscriber Identity Module

(c) GPS – Global Positioning Sensor

(d) GIS – Geographic Information System

32. Identify the correct order of following terms A – E to complete the paragraph given below that explains how data is sent securely over the internet using the Transport layer Security (TLS) protocol:

The browser requests the__________to identify itself by providing its_________. This is sent and a check is performed to see if it is_____. If it is the________sends a________back to the web server and data transmission begins.

A. authentic B. browser

C. certificate D. signal

E. web server

Choose the correct answer from the options given below

(a) C, B, D, A, E (b) E, C, A, B, D

(c) D, C, A, B, E (d) B, C, A, E, D

33. Given below are two statements

Statement I. AI is an artificially created environment used to give a feeling of 'being there', whereas virtual reality learns from changing circumstances

Statement II. Unlike dot matrix and inkjet printers, laser printers don't use ink when producing documents

In the light of above statements choose the most appropriate answer from the options given below

(a) Both statement I and statement II are correct

(b) Both statement I and statement II are incorrect

(c) Statement I is correct but statement II is incorrect

(d) Statement I is incorrect but statement II is correct

34. Which of the following are main benefits of networking computers and devices rather than using a number of standalone computers?

A. Devices, such as printers, can be shared, thus reducing costs

B. Licenses to run software on networks are often far cheaper than buying licences for an equivalent number of standalone computers

C. Users cannot share file and data.

D. Access to reliable data that comes from a central source, such as a file server.

Choose the correct answer from the options given below

(a) A and C only

(b) B, C and D only

(c) A, B, C and D

(d) A, B and D only

35. Match List I with List II

List I (Computer Term)	List II (Description)
A. Disc defragmenter	I. Utility that prepares a disk to allow data/files to be stored and retrieved
B. Disk formatter	II. Storage media with no moving parts
C. Device driver	III. Utility that recognizes the sectors on a hard disk so that files can be stored in contiguous data blocks
D. Solid state drive	IV. Software that communicates with OS and translates data into a format understood by the device

Choose the correct answer from the options given below

(a) A-II, B-I, C-III, D-IV

(b) A-III, B-I, C-IV, D-II

(c) A-I, B-III, C-II, D-IV

(d) A-IV, B-II, C-I, D-III

36. Which of the following is measured in Dobson units?

(a) Chloro Fluoro Carbon (CFC)

(b) Stratospheric Ozone

(c) Ultraviolet Rays

(d) Solar Radiation

37. Photo Electro Chemical (PEC) solar cells are based on

(a) Only inorganic semiconductors

(b) Only organic semiconductors

(c) Only crystal silicon semiconductor

(d) Hybrid structure of inorganic semiconductors and an electrolyte

38. Match List I with List II

List I (Summit/Protocol)	List II (Year)
A. Montreal Protocol	I. 1992
B. Rio Summit	II. 2015
C. Kyoto Protocol	III. 1987
D. Paris Agreement	IV. 1997

Choose the correct answer from the options given below

(a) A-III, B-I, C-IV, D-II

(b) A-III, B-I, C-II, D-IV

(c) A-I, B-III, C-II, D-IV

(d) A-IV, B-II, C-I, D-III

39. Thermal expansion of oceans may lead to

(a) Global warming (b) Ozone depletion

(c) Melting of glaciers (d) Sea level rise

40. Waste stabilization ponds are

A. mainly oxidation ponds

B. Used to remove pathogen and organic contents

C. Natural treatment systems

D. Extremely quick

E. Most efficient in extremely cold weather

Choose the correct answer from the options given below

(a) A, B and C only (b) B, C and D only

(c) A, B and E only (d) C, D and E only

41. Given below are two statements

Statement I. The Governor of the state is the chancellor of deemed universities

Statement II. Deemed universities can design their own syllabus and course work

In the light of above statements choose the most appropriate answer from the options given below

(a) Both statement I and statement II are correct

(b) Both statement I and statement II are incorrect

(c) Statement I is correct but statement II is incorrect

(d) Statement I is incorrect but statement II is correct

42. What is the full form of 'DIKSHA'?

(a) Digital Infrastructure for Knowledge Sharing

(b) District Institute for Knowledge Sharing

(c) Data Information and Knowledge Sharing

(d) Digital Institution for Knowledge Sharing

43. Which of the following are key ingredients of quality in-service teacher training?

A. Preparation of training material

B. Assessment of training needs

C. Development of appropriate curriculum / modules

D. Assessment of the impact and outcome of the training

Choose the correct answer from the options given below

(a) A and D only (b) B and C only

(c) A, C and D only (d) A, B, C and D

44. According to NEP 2020 more HEIs will be established and developed in underserved regions to ensure full

(a) Access, Equity and Inclusion

(b) Accountability, Equity and Integration

(c) Assessment, Equivalence and Identity

(d) Autonomy, Effectiveness and Implication

45. Which of the following recommendations were put forward by University Education Commission appointed after independence by the Indian government concerning medical education in India?

A. Medical colleges should admit a maximum of hundred students.

B. History of medicine with special reference to Indian systems should be taught in the first degree course in medicine

C. More importance should be attached to Public Health, Engineering and Nursing

D. There should be provision of ten beds per student admitted in medical college

Choose the correct answer from the options given below

(a) A and B only

(b) B and C only

(c) B, C and D only

(d) A, B, C and D

Read the following passage and answer the questions

It was in this atmosphere of intense antagonism and hostility that Gokhale introduced his Elementary Education Bill in 1910. He called it a 'small humble attempt to suggest the first steps of a journey, which is bound to prove long and tedious, but which must be performed, if the mass of our people are to emerge from their present condition'. Gokhale argued:

Free and compulsory education is first remedy of all the remedies to be applied.......without compulsion and the educational development in the last 60 years have been hopelessly slow. The only way that the world has discovered to secure universal education in a country has been by making it compulsory and free. Compulsion would operate harshly on the poorer classes of the community if it is not made free.

He suggested that only those students whose family income was Rs. 25 and above per month should pay fees; for the rest education was to be free. Out of the total expenditure required for it, two-third should be borne by the state and one-third by the local bodies. He suggested imposing additional 8 anna tax on salt on the grounds that 'my countrymen should eat less salt than that their children should continue to grow up in ignorance and darkness.'

46. According to Gokhale what %age of total expenditure on education should be borne by the state?

(a) 25% (b) 33%

(c) 66% (d) 75%

47. Given below are two statements

Statement I. Gokhale believed that education was necessary for Indian masses to be liberated from their miserable condition

Statement II. Gokhale faced little resistance in the introduction of his bill on elementary education

In the light of above statements choose the most appropriate answer from the options given below

(a) Both statement I and statement II are correct

(b) Both statement I and statement II are incorrect

(c) Statement I is correct but statement II is incorrect

(d) Statement I is incorrect but statement II is correct

48. Which can be inferred from the passage?

A. The growth of education in India was very slow prior to 1910

B. There was need to make education compulsory for all according to Gokhale

C. Gokhale believed that achieving education for all Indians was a distant dream

D. Gokhale suggested that majority of expenditure on education should be borne by local bodies.

Choose the correct answer from the options given below

(a) A, B and C only (b) B, C and D only

(c) A, B and D only (d) A, C and D only

49. Given below are two statements

Statement I. Gokhale believed that education should be made free for the poor people

Statement II. Gokhale suggested that an additional tax of 8-anna should be imposed on salt

In the light of above statements choose the most appropriate answer from the options given below

(a) Both statement I and statement II are correct

(b) Both statement I and statement II are incorrect

(c) Statement I is correct but statement II is incorrect

(d) Statement I is incorrect but statement II is correct

50. Given below are two statements. One is labelled as Assertion (A) and the other is labelled as Reason (R)

Assertion (A): Gokhale was not in favour of free education for the poor.

Reason (R): He suggested that those students whose family income was Rs. 25 per month or more, should pay education fee.

In the light of above statements choose the most appropriate answer from the options given below

(a) Both A and R are correct and R is correct explanation of A

(b) Both A and R are correct and R is NOT correct explanation of A

(c) A is correct but R is not correct

(d) A is not correct but R is correct

Answer Key

1. (b)	**2.** (a)	**3.** (c)	**4.** (d)	**5.** (b)	**6.** (a)	**7.** (d)	**8.** (c)	**9.** (c)	**10.** (c)
11. (b)	**12.** (b)	**13.** (a)	**14.** (d)	**15.** (d)	**16.** (b)	**17.** (c)	**18.** (d)	**19.** (b)	**20.** (a)
21. (d)	**22.** (a)	**23.** (a)	**24.** (c)	**25.** (a)	**26.** (b)	**27.** (b)	**28.** (a)	**29.** (d)	**30.** (b)
31. (c)	**32.** (b)	**33.** (b)	**34.** (d)	**35.** (b)	**36.** (b)	**37.** (d)	**38.** (a)	**39.** (d)	**40.** (a)
41. (d)	**42.** (a)	**43.** (d)	**44.** (a)	**45.** (d)	**46.** (c)	**47.** (c)	**48.** (a)	**49.** (a)	**50.** (d)

Solutions

1. The difference between male and female athletes from country C in different years is as follows:
2016 : 225-155 = 70,
2017 : 345-165 = 180,
2018 : 240-140 = 100,
2019 : 330-210 = 120,
2020 : 390-315 = 75,
2021 : 540-345 = 195,
So the second highest difference is in 2017.

2. The average number of female athletes who participated from country B over all the years together

$$= \frac{\text{Sum of females participated from country B over all years}}{\text{(Number of years)}}$$

$$= \frac{210+310+240+420+260+360}{6}$$

$$= \frac{1800}{6} = 300$$

3. The number of athletes who participated from country C in the year 2018, is 380
In 2017, is 510 percentage decreased

$$= \frac{\text{difference}}{\text{athelets 2017}} \times 100$$

$$= \frac{130}{510} \times 100 = 25.49\% \sim 25\%$$

4. According to Question,

$$\frac{\text{Number of female athletes who participated from country E in the year 2020}}{\text{Total number of athletes who participated from country B in the year 2016}} \times 100$$

$$= \frac{460}{990} \times 100 = 46.46\% \sim 46\%$$

5. Total number of athletes who participated in the event in the year 2017 from different countries, is as follows:
A : 540, B : 730, C : 510, D : 735, E : 650
Second highest is 730, Hence country B

7. Statement I is incorrect as Padlet is not a game-based platform, rather it works like a bulletin board. Teachers and students can organize classwork, assignments, homework & project submissions

8. Statement II is incorrect as the zone of proximal development (ZPD) is the distance between what a learner can do with help and without help.

9. According to David and Johnson cooperative Learning is a relationship among a group of students that requires five elements:
   1. positive interdependence
   2. individual accountability
   3. interpersonal skills
   4. face-to-face promotive interaction
   5. processing out

12. An APA-style paper includes the following sections: title page, abstract, introduction, method, results, discussion, and references.

14. Statement I is incorrect as snowball sampling is a type of non-probability sampling

15. In case of a negatively skewed frequency distribution, the mean is always lesser than median and the median is always lesser than the mode.

16. A distinction made by McLuhan between media such as print, photographs, radio, and movies (hot media) and media such as speech, cartoons, the telephone, and television (cool media).

21. Code for Order is 'odo' as Order is present in the first statement only, similarly odo is also present in the first statement only. Code of 'strong' is 'sito' as strong and sito are present in the last statement only.

22. Total Appeared students are 600000

Passed = 40% of 600000

$$= \frac{40 \times 600000}{100} = 240000$$

40% of total students were females, i.e.

Total females = 240000 and males = 360000

Pass percentage among males was 50%, i.e. 50% of males are pass

$$= \frac{50 \times 360000}{100} = 180000$$

Passed females = passed total – passed males

$$= 240000 - 180000 = 60000$$

Pass percentage among the females

$$= \frac{\text{Pased females}}{\text{Total females}} \times 100$$

$$= \frac{60000}{240000} \times 100 = 25\%$$

23. 450, 473, 519,588, 680, 795, ?

473 – 450 = 23 (= 23 × 1)

519 – 473 = 46 (=23 × 2)

588 – 519 = 69 (= 23 × 3)

680 – 588 = 92 (= 23 × 4)

795 – 680 = 115 (= 23 × 5)

? – 795 = 138 ~ ?= 195 + 138 = 933

24. Let the monthly rent be x

Therefore, annual amount left after repairs

$$= 12(x - 15\%x) = 12\left(\frac{17}{20x}\right) = \frac{51}{5x}\ x$$

= Also, 10% realization on investments means 10% of 9 lakhs or 90000

$$\text{Thus, } \left(\frac{51}{5}\right)x - 2106 = 90000$$

$\Rightarrow x = 9030$

25. Let the three odd numbers be x, (x + 2), (x + 4) and The three even numbers be (x + 11), (x + 13) and (x + 15)

Then,

$\Rightarrow x + (x + 2) + (x + 4) + (x + 11) + (x + 13) + (x + 15) = 231$

$\Rightarrow 6x + 45 = 231$

$\Rightarrow 6x = 186$

$\Rightarrow x = 31$

$\therefore$ Required sum :

$= (x + 4) + (x + 15)$

$= 2x + 19$

$= 2 \times 31 + 19$

$= 62 + 19$

$= 81$

26. A slippery slope fallacy occurs when someone makes a claim about a series of events that would lead to one major event, usually a bad event. In this fallacy, a person makes a claim that one event leads to another event and so on until we come to some awful conclusion. Along the way, each step or event in the faulty logic becomes more and more improbable. The present statement fully qualifies this definition.

27. Statements A, B and D are logically equivalent as 'No philosophers are industrialists' means that 'No industrialists are philosophers' because when the statement belongs to E category, reverse is also possible. Similarly No philosophers are industrialists also means that All philosophers are non-industrialists.

28. According to square of opposition statement A and B are contradictory to each other.

29. Statement 4th can be inferred to be true as there is subaltern relation of given statement with 4th statement

36. The Dobson Unit is the most common unit for measuring ozone concentration.

ALL INDIA SURVEY ON HIGHER EDUCATION-2020-21

- A total of 1,113 Universities, 43,796 Colleges and 11,296 Stand Alone Institutions were registered in AISHE 2020-21. Of them, 1,099 Universities, 41,600 colleges and 10,307 Stand Alone Institutions have filled and verified their responses.
- The number of universities has increased by 70 during 2020-21, to 1,113 in 2020-21 from 1,043 in 2019-20.
- Out of 1113 Universities, 657 are Government managed (Central Government: 235, State Government: 422), 10 are Private Deemed (aided), and 446 are Private (Unaided).
- There are 17 Universities exclusively for Women (14 State Public Universities, 2 Private Universities and One Deemed Private Aided). It was 11 in 2014-15.
- In 2020-21, there are 16 Open universities (1 Central University, 14 State Universities and 1 State Private University) and 112 Dual Mode Universities.
- Of the 1,099 Universities who responded in the Survey, there are 615 General, 188 Technical, 63 Agriculture & Allied, 71 Medical, 26 Law, 19 Sanskrit and 8 Language Universities. Remaining121 Universities were of other categories.
- The number of colleges has increased by 1453 during 2020-21, to 43,796 in 2020-21 from 42,343 in 2019-20.
- Number of colleges per lakh eligible population (population in the age-group 18-23 years) in the country is 31. It was 27 in 2014-15.
- 21.4% Colleges are Government Colleges, 13.6% are Private (Aided) and 65% are Private-unaided. o About 43% of the Universities and 61.4% Colleges are in Rural Areas.
- 10.5% Colleges (4,375) are exclusively for Female, while only 0.2% (72 Colleges) are exclusively for male.

  Uttar Pradesh, Maharashtra, Karnataka, Rajasthan, Tamil Nadu, Madhya Pradesh, Andhra Pradesh, Gujarat, Telangana and Kerala are top 10 States in terms of number of colleges.
- Among the districts, maximum number of colleges (1058) are situated in Bangalore Urban followed by Jaipur (671). About 32% of colleges are situated in 50 districts. Student Enrolment in Higher Education:
- Total enrolment in higher education has increased to nearly 4.13 crore in 2020-21 from 3.85 crore in 2019-20 (increase of 28.80 Lakh).
- The annual rate of increase in enrolment has also shown an improvement over the years. The increase in enrolment in 2020-21 over 2019-20 is 7.4%, which was 3% during 2019- 20 and 2.7% during 2018-19. Further, overall increase in enrolment since 2014-15 is 20.9%.
- A total of 2.12 crore (51.3%) male and 2.01 crore (48.7%) female students were enrolled in Higher Education. In 2019-20, number of male students enrolled was 1.96 crore and female students enrolled was 1.89 crore.
- Of the 4.13 crore students enrolled in 2020-21, 14.2% belong to Scheduled Castes, 5.8% belong to Scheduled Tribes, 35.8% are from Other Backward Classes and remaining 44.2% students are from other communities.
- The growth in enrolment of Scheduled Caste students in 2020-21 as compared to 2019-20 is 4.2%, whereas, the growth in 2019-20 over 2018-19 was 1.6%. Further, overall increase in SC Student enrolment since 2014-15 is 27.96%.
- Enrolment of Scheduled Tribes students has increased to 24.1 lakh in 2020-21 from 21.6 lakh in 2019-20. This increase (11.9%) is significantly higher than the increase recorded in previous year (4.3%). Notably, overall increase in ST Student enrolment since 2014-15 is 47%. o Enrolment of students from Other Backward Classes has increased to about 1.48 crore in 2020-21 from 1.42 crore in 2019-20. Also, overall increase in OBC Student enrolment since 2014-15 is 31.67%.
- The top 6 States in terms of Student Enrolment are Uttar Pradesh, Maharashtra, Tamil Nadu, Madhya Pradesh, Karnataka and Rajasthan. They constitute 53.17% of the total Student Enrolment.
- In the year 2020-21, Gross Enrolment Ratio (GER) in higher education for age group 18-23 years is estimated to be 27.3, as compared to 25.6 in 2019-20 as per 2011 projection, whereas, it is 27.1 in 2019-20 as per 2001 population projection. The GER in 2020-21 over 2019-20 has increased by 1.7 as per 2011 projection, which is highest ever increase in GER.

- In 2020-21, the GER for male is 26.7 and the GER for female is 27.9. o GER for Scheduled Castes Students is 23.1 and GER for Scheduled Tribes Students is 18.9. While the increase in the Scheduled Castes GER is 0.8 in the current and previous years, notably, significant increase of 1.9 is observed in the Scheduled Tribes GER in 2020-21 over 2019-20, as compared to 0.6 in 2019-20 over 2018-19.
- Notably, Government Universities constituting 59.1% of total Universities contribute 73.1% of total enrolment, Deemed Universities-Government Aided constituting 0.9% of total Universities account for 0.6% enrolment, whereas the 40% Private Universities account for only 26.3% of total enrolment.
- Further, Government Colleges despite constituting only 21.4% of total colleges based on actual response contribute 34.5% of total enrolment, Private (Aided) colleges constituting 13.6% of total colleges account for 21.1% enrolment, whereas the 65% Private Unaided Colleges account for only 44.4% of total enrolment.
- It is seen that average enrolment of Government Colleges is 1097 which is higher than that of both Private (aided) Colleges (1057) as well as Private (unaided) Colleges (465).
- About 78.09% of the students are enrolled in undergraduate level courses and remaining 11.5% are enrolled in postgraduate level courses.
- Based on actual response at undergraduate level, enrollment is highest in Arts (33.5%), followed by Science (15.5%), Commerce (13.9%) and Engineering & Technology (11.9%).
- At postgraduate level, maximum students are enrolled in Social Science stream (20.56%) followed by science (14.83%) based on actual response.
- At Ph.D. level, enrolment is highest in Engineering &Technology (27.3%) followed by Science (23.4%). o Uttar Pradesh has the highest student enrolment (16.07%) followed by Maharashtra (10.98%) and Tamil Nadu (8.06%).
- Of the total enrolment in 2020-21, the number of Student enrolment in STEM is 94,69,022 (22.89%) based on actual response. While in Science stream Female outnumbered Male, in Engineering & Technology Male outnumbered Female.
- Total number of foreign students enrolled in higher education is 48,035.
- The foreign students have come from 163 different countries.
- In 2020-21, highest share of foreign students are from Nepal (28.26%), followed by Afghanistan (8.49%), Bangladesh (5.72%), Bhutan (3.8%), Sudan (3.33%) and United States (5.12%). Top 10 countries constitute 67.48% of the total foreign students. Teaching and Non-Teaching Staff in Higher Education:
- The total number of teachers are 15,51,070 of which about 57.1% are male and 42.9% are female.
- Number of teachers has increased by 47,914 in 2020-21 over 2019-20.
- There are 75 female teachers per 100 male teachers.
- For Regular Mode Pupil Teacher Ratio (PTR) in Universities and Colleges is 24 whereas PTR for Universities and its Constituent Units, in regular mode, is 19.
- The number of non-teaching staff is 13,95,868 out of which about 65.9% are male and 34.1% are female. The average number of Female per 100 male non-teaching staff is 52. Out-Turn
- The total number of pass-out has increased to 95.4 Lakh in 2020-21 as against 94 Lakh in 2019-20.
- At the under graduate level, the highest out-turn is in Bachelor of Arts (B.A.) with 20.5 Lakh, followed by Bachelor of Science (B.Sc.) with 11.3 Lakh, Bachelor of Commerce (B.Com.) with 10.2 Lakh and 8.3 Lakh in Bachelor of Engineering (B.E.) & Bachelor of Technology (B. Tech.) combined.
- At Post-graduate level, the highest out-turn is in Master of Arts (M.A.) 5.4 Lakh, followed by Master of Science (M.Sc.) 2.9 Lakh, Master of Business Administration (MBA) 2.2 Lakh and Master of Commerce (M.Com.) 1.6 Lakh.
- In Diploma, the total number of pass-out is 8.48 Lakh.
- 25,550 students were awarded Ph.D. during 2020 with 14,422 Male and 11,128 Female. The highest number of Ph.D. was awarded in Science 6,022 followed by Engineering & Technology 4,556